Business Research Methods

EIGHTH EDITION

The McGraw-Hill/Irwin Series

Operations and Decision Sciences

Business Statistics

Business Research Methods

EIGHTH EDITION

Donald R. Cooper
Florida Atlantic University

Pamela S. Schindler
Wittenberg University

Boston   Burr Ridge, IL   Dubuque, IA   Madison, WI   New York
San Francisco   St. Louis   Bangkok   Bogotá   Caracas   Kuala Lumpur
Lisbon   London   Madrid   Mexico City   Milan   Montreal   New Delhi
Santiago   Seoul   Singapore   Sydney   Taipei   Toronto

The McGraw·Hill Companies

BUSINESS RESEARCH METHODS
International Edition 2003

10 09 08 07 06 05 04 03 02
20 09 08 07 06 05 04
CTF   BJE

ISBN 0-07-249870-6

Library of Congress Control Number: 2002108078

When ordering this title, use ISBN 0-07-123318-0

Printed in Singapore

www.mhhe.com

To my sons, Ryan and Paul Cooper, for their love; and to my dear friends in China for teaching me a new truth, da qi wan cheng.

Donald Cooper

To Bill, who in this unsettling year of family crises and terrorist attacks served again as my most reliable anchor, and to my sisters, for their humorous perspective on everything.

Pamela Schindler

Preface

In each revision we strive to make the new edition more student and faculty friendly. No matter how the instructor chooses to teach—by lecture or discussion, with written or video cases, with student projects or not—we're convinced the eighth edition of *Business Research Methods* will be just right. It's crammed full of all the elements that our reviewers—student and faculty—assure us are essential to a great learning experience in research methods. Here's how we've delivered on the primary goals for the eighth edition.

Enhance the Decision-Making Focus

Four NEW Additions to Our Process Model Series

The research process model (you'll find it on the inside cover as well as in Chapter 3, Exhibit 3–1) is the graphical representation of the key teaching tool around which the text is based. We've listened to our reviewers and simplified the model, sometimes breaking it into smaller pieces or pulling out parts, enhancing the use of color to make the phases and steps clearer, and adding new process model exhibits to several chapters. Overall, the process model series now has 22 exhibits placed throughout the chapters.

Research by Example

We've given you *even more examples* of real research decisions in this eighth edition. With more than 255 examples that cross all business disciplines, you're sure to find ones that help you learn and retain text material. Within the example group, you'll find more than two dozen examples focused on global scenarios and another two dozen examples involving the Internet. We've shared these examples in several ways:

- **Snapshot** boxes continue to offer brief but detailed research profiles. You'll find 53 of these research gems overall, including 30 NEW ones.
- **PicProfiles** are a new feature in the eighth edition. These 16 research profiles have a more narrow focus, and a distinctive visual is linked with each scenario. At first they might look like just another

photograph. But look more closely. In the extensive caption you'll find research decisions richly detailed. Many of these had their start in recent news headlines.

- **Photographs with captions** are included to make a quick point. You'll find that research companies, research sponsors, and those that serve the research industry have opened their advertising archives and shared their corporate photos throughout the eighth edition.
- **Tips** are gems of wisdom that researchers have shared with us. These will help the student of research do better research or avoid the pitfalls of less than professional research. When you see the distinctive TIP icon, read with a little more care.
- **End-of-Book Cases.** The 27 returning favorites—14 with datasets on CD and 2 with written data tables—are enriched by the addition of 2 new cases: *State Farm: Dangerous Intersections* and *The Catalyst for Women in Financial Services,* both exclusive to the eighth edition.

New Topics in Depth

With our Close-Up feature, we showcase topics that are often given inadequate attention; and we show how they are applied. In the eighth edition, we've added five new Close-Ups on proposals, child-oriented research, sampling, advanced searching of secondary sources, and the Simalto+Plus analytical technique. By boxing these topics in a Close-Up, we've made it easy for faculty to choose whether to cover the topic in the depth that is offered, at a lesser level of depth, or not at all.

A Renewed Commitment to Ethical Research

Certainly, the Enron situation has focused increasing attention on the ethical decisions in business. But we've always had a strong emphasis, devoting a chapter to the intricacies of such issues. The 8th edition goes a step farther, shining the spotlight on ethical research dilemmas in the news via additional Snapshots and PicProfiles.

Enhance the Student's Visual Memory Cues

More Than 250 Exhibits

We've explored some creative ways to make the book easier and more appealing to explore, and to ensure that the major points receive standout attention. Not just more photographs and exhibits—although you'll surely see more—but also a better use of our color palette. With more than 250 graphical exhibits, this was a daunting task and has kept the artists hopping.

- **74 exhibits have been color-enhanced** for clarity of material.
- **9 exhibits have been reconstructed** for clarity of material.
- **24 new exhibits** have been added, developed around material that reviewers said needed more attention or clarity.

We've also kept all the other learning features our student reviewers demanded:

- **Bolded key terms** make terminology easier to find and reinforce that more attention should be given to this material while reading.
- **Tip** icons hint of ways to do better quality research, especially for those students doing research projects or manager-students buying research.
- **Pull-out lists,** whether these are numbered or just have bullets, help distill a larger body of work into its essential points; a time-saver that students depend on.
- **Margin notes** help keep the reader focused on the obvious threads running through the text, from chapter to chapter, and bring material read sometimes weeks earlier back to the forefront of memory.
- **Five types of discussion questions,** each drawing upon a different level of understanding, challenge students to know the material. Each chapter has one or more new questions in this eighth edition.
  - **Terms in Review** test recall of concepts and terminology.
  - **Making Research Decisions** encourages students to test their understanding at an applied level.

- **From Concept to Practice** encourages students to put chapter exhibits to use in learning concepts.
- **Bringing Research to Life** leads students back to the opening vignette to test their ability to find concepts within these real-research-based scenarios.
- **Web Exercises** showcase the wealth of research assistance to be found on the Internet, starting with our text website (www.mhhe.com/business/cooper8).
- **Comprehensive Sources on CD and in Appendix A** have expanded with 39 new sources and dozens of updated links.
- **Glossary** has new terms and it's still located both on the student CD and on our website.
- **Summary** still ties the chapter learning objectives to the text material.
- **Examples Index** helps students locate an example they remember and want to use—now they can find it again.

Enhance Assistance for Student Projects

Besides the research process model exhibits, we retained features that students doing research projects appreciate: the sample project in the appendix, Tips, and the PowerPoint Tutorial on our website.

- We've added a **Close-Up sample proposal** as Appendix D.
- We've added a **second sample proposal** to our website.
- We've **enhanced the exhibits in Chapters 4 and 15–20,** to make it possible for the student to better visualize a report and its various parts.
- We've created a **Snapshot** that addresses **overcoming the fear of making a presentation.**

Recognize Unflagging Support

Family, both real and extended, are always the foundation of any effort this large. So we send a very special thank you to the following:

- Judith Violette, Director, Helmke Library, Indiana University–Purdue Fort Wayne, who continues to find ways to make searching secondary sources easier and more effective.

- Kelly Maguire, Student Director 2001, and Bryan Simpson, Student Director 2002, Center for Applied Management, Wittenberg University, who took on numerous duties that allowed the authors to concentrate on research and writing.

- Paul Cooper, Graphic Designer, for conceptualizing our efforts on another powerful cover.

- Jeff Stevens, for digesting and condensing the literature on Simalto+Plus, as well as writing the new section on LISREL.

We couldn't develop the wealth of examples found in the eighth edition without the gracious contributions of numerous research practitioners, especially those who worked with us on PicProfiles, Close-Ups and the two new cases. Thank you, Paulette Gerkovich, Catalyst; John Nepomuceno, State Farm; Megan Nerz, MLN Research; Tina Glover, L&E Research; Anne Hart Lamb, Bissell, Inc.; Christin Nowakowski, Informative, Inc.; Kellie Harris, Compaq; Ronna Charles, PolyVision, Inc.; and Tim Gabel, RTI International.

Our reviewers bring us insights that help clarify the changes we need and want to make in each edition. For their new perspective and the inspiration to create new solutions we thank: John Ballard, College of Mount St. Joseph; Robert Balik, Western Michigan University–Kalamazoo; Marcia Carter, University of Southern New Hampshire; David Dorsett, Florida Institute of Technology; Robert Wright, University of Illinois at Springfield; Judith McKnew, Clemson University; Cecilia Tempomi, Southwest Texas State University; Don English, Texas A&M University–Commerce, Raul Chavez, Eastern Mennonite University; Larry Banks, University of Phoenix; Caroll M. Belew, New Mexico Highlands University; Michael P. Dumler, Illinois State University; Judson Faurer, Metropolitan State College of Denver; John Hanke, Eastern Washington University; Alan G. Heffner, Silver Lake College; Burt Kaliski, New Hampshire College; Iraj Mahdavi, National University; and Randi L. Sims, Nova Southeastern University.

Like all ongoing creative projects, this book has evolved because of past contributions. We recognize J. K. Bandyioedyay, Philip Beukema, Alan D. Carey, Francis Connelly, Thomas H. Dudley, William J. Evans, Hamis Falatoon, Robert Fetter, Stewart E. Fleige, Frederick A. Grodecki, John Hanke, Claude McMillian, Ralph J. Melarango, Jay S. Mendell, Hamid Noori, Walter Nord, J. Paul Peter, Harold F. Rahmlow, Elizabeth E. Regimbal, Perri J. Stinson, Craig Swenson, Alexander Voloatta, Richard A. Wald, Eric Rusnak, Sarah Arntsen Schatz, and Carol Young.

The McGraw-Hill/Irwin team makes every revision a reality. We thank Scott Isenberg, Executive Editor; Christina Sanders, Developmental Editor; Zina Craft, Marketing Manager; Jean Lou Hess, Senior Project Manager; Keith McPherson, Design Director; Rose Hepburn, Senior Production Supervisor; Cathy Tepper, Lead Supplement Coordinator; Jeremy Cheshareck, Photo Research Coordinator; and Tony Sherman, Media Technology Producer.

We hope you find the eighth edition meets your ever-increasing expectations.

Donald Cooper
Pamela Schindler

Brief Contents

Contents

PART I

Introduction to Business Research

CHAPTER 1

Research in Business

Learning Objectives

After reading this chapter, you should understand . . .

1 **What research is and its different types.**

2 **The distinction between good research and research that falls short of professional quality.**

3 **The relationship between a manager and a research supplier.**

4 **The value of learning research process skills.**

Bringing Research to Life

"Jason Henry? I'm Myra Wines."

"Come in, Ms. Wines. We'll meet here in the conference/living room. As I told you when you called, we're just establishing our Florida office. Of course, you can see that. Watch your step around the cables."

The stylish, middle-aged woman found her way among several crates of partially unpacked computer systems to the sofa and seated herself as gracefully as she could among the heap of books, electronic gear, and unopened boxes. She snapped open a briefcase to produce a miniature cassette recorder, which she clicked on. "If this makes you nervous, I'll turn it off," she said. "I was a TV investigative reporter for 15 years. Old habits die hard . . . especially ones that have gotten you out of a dozen jams."

"Turn it off then," said the younger man, curtly. "It doesn't make me nervous, but I fail to see the need of it."

"My contact in Canada indicated you and your wife, a doctor in public health, both graduated from college in California. You moved here from Ottawa where the United Nations employed you both. You are an accountant turned business economist and consultant. You've several corporations here in Florida—to do auditing, economic analysis, epidemiological consulting, and diversified business research. What have I missed?"

"My wife, Dorrie, speaks four languages."

"I knew that. A producer in Toronto who works for United Nations TV where she taped her public service program alerted me to your move to Florida."

"Then that covers everything, doesn't it," he said with asperity, "except a birthmark above my knee."

"Your right knee," she said positively. Disbelief and irritation were evident in his expression, and quickly she added, "Just a guess. Fifty-fifty chance of being right, you know."

That broke the tension. He chuckled. "I have a gold filling in one of my teeth. Can you tell me which one?"

Now she laughed. "I never bluff against such high odds as 32-to-1."

They both smiled. Then he killed the merriment by adding, "The odds would be 31-to-1. There would be one right answer and 31 wrong. Obviously, that makes the odds 31-to-1."

Smiling through gritted teeth, Myra changed the subject. "How many computers do you have here?"

"Counting the portables, five, plus several dumb terminals. Plus three printers and one fax for incoming and one for outgoing. And a voice-mail system and a pager. I am networking all of this together, as you can see. I have six phone lines, though I need only four right now. I'm your basic unapologetic computer jockey."

Looking around at the disorder, Myra observed, "And this is your residence, too."

"We don't want the hassle of separate office space. Most of my clients in Phoenix, Butte, and Ottawa will never see the office. As far as they know, I am working out of the classiest suite in this city's best office building."

"Well, it's quite a few computers," she said doubtfully.

"I believe that you find the truth by crunching the numbers."

"I don't agree. As a reporter I learned you get the truth by staying in touch with people, watching world events, seeing the big picture, and digging for revealing details. I have four phone lines myself—one each for a fax and an answering machine, one for a computer that I use to dial into commercial online databases, and two additional phones so I can talk to two people at the same time. I have my own domestic incoming/outgoing 800 number, and if I don't run up a thousand-dollar-a-month long-distance bill for international calls, I know I'm not living right."

"Really? I find it difficult to believe that being a consumer affairs manager is so very lucrative."

"No, it isn't," she admitted with a chuckle. "After 15 years my TV station told me I needed a face-lift, and when I said no, they canned me. Just like that. I got the scariest lawyer in town—someone so vicious I had once run a week-long exposé of him—and he got me a terrific settlement. I pick up a few thousand a month by giving lectures to conventioneers. One of my best talks is 'The Angry Consumer.' I always include lots of facts that are absolutely up-to-date, because I was—and am—in daily touch with consumer advocates in every state capital, plus D.C., Ottawa, and even Tokyo and London."

"Is it all opinion and anecdote, or do you have some substantiating statistics?"

"My phone bill is astronomic."

"So it's anecdotal; that's what you're saying."

"If that's what you want to call it," she declared with a tinge of irritation. "Anyway, after one of my particularly hard-hitting talks, one member of the audience approached me, asked a lot of questions about my laptop computer, which I used to control my slide show. She was a headhunter looking for a consumer affairs manager for the company whose computer I use, MindWriter. Ultimately, after several interviews, they made me an offer I couldn't refuse."

"I know the brand. It's good equipment at a good price, but if it breaks down, you're in trouble according to the computer magazines. However, I have no firsthand evidence the magazines are accurate."

"We do have some concerns about customer satisfaction—especially in product service. The corporate higher-ups have assigned me my first task—assessing customer satisfaction, or dissatisfaction, as it may be. There is a meeting next week in Austin, Texas, to discuss the background and preliminaries. I've been told to bring my ideas and my 'number cruncher.'"

"And who would that be?" inquired Jason.

"You, I hope. I'll level with you. I am not a numbers person."

"I know that. You miscounted your telephone lines a minute ago. Fax. Answering machine. Dial-up databases. Two for personal calls. That makes five. You said four."

She flushed, counting silently to 10. This young man might know his numbers but tact escaped him. "Then you know what I'm talking about," she said a little too sharply. "I would really like to impress the folks in Texas, this being my first project, but not a soul in my office can be counted on as a number cruncher and I can't show up at the meeting without one."

"I know something about customer research, and you're right to be nervous . . ."

"Not nervous. Properly concerned."

"Concerned then. The first step will be to listen carefully and discover exactly what facts management has gathered, what they are concerned about, what the problem is from their point of view, what the problem really is at various levels of abstraction . . ."

"Listening to people. Discussing. Looking at things from different viewpoints. The kind of thing I am very good at."

"Right. And after we hear them out, we come to what I am good at: Measurement. Scaling. Survey design. Sampling the customers. Finally, we would collaborate on the report of results . . ."

"I have two tickets to Austin for next Wednesday. Can you break away from this unpacking and cabling and fly over with me?"

"Sure."

"OK. My source in Toronto says you are intelligent, prickly, and pigheaded, inclined to be overly left-brained and intolerant, but dependable, reasonably priced, and respectful of your elders. We'll work out the money details on the flight over. I think we'll get along OK."

"I am willing to proceed on that hypothesis. We'll certainly know if we can work together by the time we return from Texas."

Why Study Research?

Assume for the moment that you are the manager of your favorite full-service restaurant. (Taco Bell doesn't qualify here; think of something else.) You are experiencing significant turnover in your waiter/waitress pool, and long-time customers have been commenting that the friendly atmosphere that has historically drawn them to your door is changing. What will you do? Where will you begin in trying to solve this problem? Try another decision-making scenario: You are talking with the head of the academic department in which you are majoring. This person chairs the committee that selects the textbook for the research methodology course. How should they begin to evaluate their options?

The study of research methods provides you with the knowledge and skills you need to solve the problems and meet the challenges of a fast-paced decision-making environment. We define **business research** as a systematic inquiry whose objective is to provide information to solve managerial problems. Business research courses recognize that students preparing to manage business, not-for-profit, and public organizations—in all functional areas—need training in a disciplined process for conducting an inquiry of a **management dilemma,** the problem or opportunity that requires a management decision. Three factors stimulate an interest in a scientific approach to decision making:

1. The manager's increased need for more and better information.

2. The availability of improved techniques and tools to meet this need.

3. The resulting information overload if discipline is not employed in the process.

During the last two decades, we have witnessed dramatic changes in the business environment. Emerging from an historically economic role, the business organization

---

SNAPSHOT

Research and the Valuation of Intangibles

Since 1973, the Financial Accounting Standards Board (FASB) has assumed "responsibility for establishing standards of financial accounting and reporting." The conservative FASB recently took a mini-step toward recognizing the shift in company valuation from bricks and mortar to information. As of January 2002, companies involved in mergers will no longer have to amortize goodwill. As Neil Gross, the senior editor of *Business Week,* explained, "You don't wear out research or run out of brand power—at least most of the time. Investors need a sense of the assets' value and whether expenses to support them—such as advertising—are really productive." The FASB, encouraging "voluntary disclosures related to matters that are important to the success of the company," agreed that the "importance of voluntary disclosures is expected to increase in the future because of the fast pace of change in the business environment."

A company's stable of brands is possibly its most valuable intangible. How else can you explain the record-setting purchase of RJR Nabisco ($25.4 billion) at a significant premium over stock book value or the stockholder-welcomed investment in employee benefits by powerhouse Starbucks? The answer: Kohlberg Kravis Roberts & Co. believes some brands (Oreo cookies, Hawaiian Punch, and Winston cigarettes, among them) are very valuable and worth the price. Starbucks has learned that the experience of the customer in its stores is critical to successful expansion. So if an intangible, brand value, can drive purchase price, merger price, stock value, and employee commitment, then assessing people's willingness to pay for such things—research—is critical to understanding the present and future U.S. economy.

www.fasb.org

has evolved in response to the social and political mandates of national public policy, explosive technology growth, and continuing innovations in global communications. These changes have created new knowledge needs for the manager and new publics to consider when evaluating any decision. Other knowledge demands have arisen from problems with mergers, trade policies, protected markets, technology transfers, and macroeconomic savings-investment issues.

The trend toward complexity has increased the risk associated with business decisions, making it more important to have a sound information base. Each of the factors listed below, which characterize the complex business decision-making environment, demands that managers have more and better information on which to base decisions:

- There are more variables to consider in every decision.

- More knowledge exists in every field of management.

- Global and domestic competition is more vigorous, with many businesses downsizing to refocus on primary competencies, reduce costs, and make competitive gains.

- The quality of theories and models to explain tactical and strategic results is improving.

- Government continues to show concern with all aspects of society, becoming increasingly aggressive in protecting these various publics.

- The explosive growth of company sites on the World Wide Web, e-commerce, and company publications via desktop and electronic publishing have brought the prospect of extensive new arrays of information—but information quality is increasingly suspect.

- Workers, shareholders, customers, and the general public are demanding to be included in company decision making; they are better informed and more sensitive to their own self-interests than ever before.

- Organizations are increasingly practicing **data mining,** learning to extract meaningful knowledge from volumes of data contained within **internal databases.**

- Computer advances have allowed businesses to create the architecture for **data warehousing,** electronic storehouses where vast arrays of collected, integrated data are ready for mining.

- The power and ease of use of today's computers have given us the capability to analyze data to deal with today's complex managerial problems.

- Techniques of quantitative analysis take advantage of increasingly powerful computing capabilities.

- The number and power of the tools used to conduct research have increased, commensurate with the growing complexity of business decisions.

- Communication and measurement techniques within research have been enhanced.

To do well in such an environment, you will need to understand how to identify quality information and to recognize the solid, reliable research on which your high-risk decisions as a manager can be based. You also will need to know how to conduct such research. Developing these skills requires understanding the scientific method as it applies to the managerial decision-making environment. This book addresses your needs as an information processor.

What Is Research?

We begin with a few examples of management problems involving decision making based on information gathering. From each of these illustrations, we can abstract the essence of research. How is it carried out? What can it do? What should it not be expected to do? As you read the four cases, be thinking about the possible range of situations for conducting business research, and try answering these questions: (1) What is the decision-making dilemma facing the manager? (2) What must the researcher accomplish?

CHILDCO

You work for CHILDCO, a corporation that is considering the acquisition of a toy manufacturer. The senior vice president for development asks you to head a task force to investigate six companies that are potential candidates. You assemble a team composed of representatives from the relevant functional areas. Pertinent data are collected from public sources because of the sensitive nature of the project. You examine all of the following: company annual reports; articles in business journals, trade magazines, and newspapers; financial analysts' assessments; and company advertisements. The team members then develop summary profiles of the candidate firms based on the characteristics gleaned from the sources. The final report highlights the opportunities and problems that acquisition of the target firm would bring to all areas of the business.

NUCMED

You are the business manager for NUCMED, a large group of physicians specializing in nuclear medicine and imaging. A prominent health insurance organization has contacted you to promote a new cost containment program. The doctors' committee to whom you will make a recommendation will have a narrow enrollment window for their decision. If they choose to join, they will agree to a reduced fee schedule in exchange for easier filing procedures, quicker reimbursement, and listing on a physicians' referral network. If they decline, they will continue to deal with their patients and the insurance carrier in the current manner. You begin your investigation by mining data from patient files to learn how many are using this carrier, frequency of care visits, complexity of filings, and so on. You then consult insurance industry data to discover how many potential patients in your area use this care plan, or similar care plans with alternative insurance carriers, and the likelihood of a patient choosing or switching doctors to find one that subscribes to the proposed program. You attempt to confirm your data with information from professional and association journals. Based on this information, you develop a profile that details the number of patients, overhead, and potential revenue realized by choosing to join the plan.

ColorSplash

ColorSplash, a paint manufacturer, is having trouble maintaining profits. The owner believes inventory management is a weak area of the company's operations. In this industry, the many paint colors, types of paint, and container sizes make it easy for a firm to accumulate large inventories and still be unable to fill customer orders. The owner asks you to make recommendations. You look into the present warehousing and shipping operations and find excessive sales losses and delivery delays because of out-of-stock conditions. An informal poll of customers confirms your impression. You suspect the present inventory database and reporting system do not provide the prompt, usable information needed for appropriate production decisions.

Based on this supposition, you familiarize yourself with the latest inventory management techniques in a local college library. You ask the warehouse manager to take an accurate inventory, and you review the incoming orders for the last year. In addition, the owner shows you the production runs of the last year and his method for assessing the need for a particular color or paint type.

Modeling the last year of business using production, order, and inventory management techniques, you choose the method that provides the best theoretical profit. You run a pilot line using the new control methodology. After two months, the data show a much lower inventory and a higher order fulfillment rate. You recommend that the owner adopt the new inventory method.

York College

You work for York College's alumni association. It is eager to develop closer ties with its aging alumni, to provide strong stimuli to encourage increased donations, and to induce older, nontraditional students to return to supplement enrollment. The president's office is considering starting a retirement community geared toward university alumni and asks your association to assess the attractiveness of the proposal from an alumni viewpoint. Your director asks you to divide the study into four parts.

Phase 1. First you are to report on the number of alumni who are in the appropriate age bracket, the rate of new entries per year, and the actuarial statistics for the group. This information allows the director to assess whether the project is worth continuing.

Phase 2. Your early results reveal there are sufficient alumni to make the project feasible. The next step in the study is to describe the social and economic characteristics of the target alumni group. You review gift statistics, analyze job titles, and assess home location and values. In addition, you review files from the last five years to see how alumni responded when they were asked about their income bracket. You are able to describe the alumni group for your director when you finish.

Phase 3. It is evident that the target alumni can easily afford a retirement community as proposed. The third phase of the study is to explain the characteristics of alumni who would be interested in a university-related retirement community. For this phase, you engage the American Association of Retired Persons (AARP) and a retirement community developer. In addition, you search for information on senior citizens from the federal government. From the developer you learn what characteristics of retirement community planning and construction are most attractive to retirees. From the AARP you learn about the main services and features that potential retirees look for in a retirement community. From government publications you become familiar with existing regulations and recommendations for operating retirement communities and uncover a full range of descriptive information on the typical retirement community dweller. You make an extensive report to both the alumni director and the university president. The report covers the number of eligible alumni, their social and economic standings, and the characteristics of those who would be attracted by the retirement community.

Phase 4. The report excites the college president. She asks for one additional phase to be completed. She needs to predict the number of alumni who would be attracted to the project so she can adequately plan the size of the community. At this point, you call on the business school's research methods class for help in designing a questionnaire for the alumni. By providing telephones and funding, you arrange for the class to conduct a survey among a random sample of the eligible alumni population. In addition, you have the class devise a second questionnaire for alumni who will become eligible in the next 10 years. Using the data collected, you can predict the initial demand for the community and estimate the growth in demand over the next 10 years. You submit your final report to the director and the president.

What Is the Dilemma Facing the Manager?

The manager's predicament is fairly well defined in the four cases. Let's see how carefully you read and understood them. In CHILDCO the senior vice president for development must make a proposal to the president or possibly the board of directors about whether to acquire a toy manufacturer and, if one is to be acquired, which one of the six under consideration is the best candidate. In NUCMED the physicians in the group must decide whether to join the proposed managed health care plan of one of their primary insurers. In ColorSplash the owner of the paint manufacturer must decide whether to implement a new inventory management system. At York College, the president must propose to the board of directors whether to fund the development of a retirement community. How did you do? If you didn't come to these same conclusions, reread the cases before proceeding, to catch what you missed.

In real life, management dilemmas are not always so clearly defined. In the case of MindWriter (the "Bringing Research to Life" vignette), Myra Wines knows there is a concern about customer satisfaction, but her personal positive experience gives her no clue as to what is causing management's concern. Jason Henry has read an article in the business press that implies after-purchase service might be to blame.

In ColorSplash, rather than pinpointing the problem as one of inventory management, the paint manufacturer's owner could have faced several interactive phenomena:

1. A strike by the teamsters impacting inventory delivery to retail and wholesale customers.

2. The development of a new paint formula that offers superior coverage but requires a relatively scarce ingredient to manufacture, thereby affecting production rates.

3. A fire that destroyed the primary loading dock of the main shipping warehouse in the Midwest.

4. The simultaneous occurrence of all three events.

As the research process begins with a manager's decision-making task, accurately defining the dilemma is paramount but often difficult. We address this issue in Chapter 3.

What Must the Researcher Accomplish?

The different types of study represented by the four cases can be classified as reporting, descriptive, explanatory, or predictive.

Reporting   At the most elementary level, a **reporting study** may be made only to provide an account or summation of some data or to generate some statistics. The task may be quite simple and the data readily available. At other times, the information may be difficult to find. A reporting study calls for knowledge and skill with information sources and gatekeepers of information sources. Such a study usually requires little inference or conclusion drawing. In CHILDCO the researcher needs to know what information should be evaluated in order to value a company. In the study of management, this knowledge would be acquired primarily in courses in financial management, accounting, and marketing. Knowing the type of information needed, the researcher in CHILDCO identifies sources of information, like trade press articles and annual reports. Because of the possible effect of the toy manufacturer evaluation on the stock prices of the conglomerate instigating the study and each toy company, only public sources are used. Other reporting studies of a less sensitive nature might have the researcher interviewing source gatekeepers. In York College, for example, interviewing the director of local retirement facilities might have revealed other sources to include in the search. Such an expert is considered a gatekeeper. Early in your career, identifying gatekeepers for your firm and industry is critical to your success as a manager.

CHILDCO and the first phase of York College each illustrate a reporting study.

Purists claim that reporting studies do not qualify as research, although carefully gathered data can have great value. Others argue that at least one form, investigative reporting, has a great deal in common with widely accepted qualitative and clinical research.[1] A research design does not have to be complex and require inferences for a project to be called research. In the early part of your career, you will likely be asked to perform a number of reporting studies. Many managers consider the execution of such studies an excellent way for new employees to become familiar with their employer and its industry.

Descriptive   A **descriptive study** tries to discover answers to the questions *who, what, when, where,* and, sometimes, *how.* The researcher attempts to describe or define a subject, often by creating a profile of a group of problems, people, or events. Such studies may involve the collection of data and the creation of a distribution of the number of times the researcher observes a single event or characteristic (known as a **research variable**), or they may involve relating the interaction of two or more variables. In NUCMED, the researcher must present data that reveal who is affiliated with the insurer, who uses managed health care programs (both doctors and patients), the general trends in use of imaging technology in diagnosing illness or injury severity, and the relationship of patient characteristics, doctor referrals, and technology use patterns.

NUCMED and the second phase of York College each illustrate descriptive studies.

Descriptive studies may or may not have the potential for drawing powerful inferences. Organizations that maintain databases of their employees, customers, and suppliers already have significant data to conduct descriptive studies using internal information. Yet many firms that have such data files do not mine them regularly for the decision-making insight they might provide. In the opening vignette, Myra Wines could mine numerous company databases for insight into the nature and number of service-related problems arising after purchase and, similarly, for information about product use inquiries. A database generated by warranty registration cards could reveal significant data concerning purchaser characteristics, as well as purchase location and product use behavior. A descriptive study, however, does not explain why an event has occurred or why the variables interact the way they do.

The descriptive study is popular in business research because of its versatility across disciplines. In not-for-profit corporations and other organizations, descriptive investigations have a broad appeal to the administrator and policy analyst for planning, monitoring, and evaluating. In this context, *how* questions address issues such as quantity, cost, efficiency, effectiveness, and adequacy.[2]

ColorSplash and the third phase of York College each represent explanatory studies.

Explanatory   Academics have debated the relationship between the next two types of studies, explanatory and predictive, in terms of which precedes the other. Both types of research are grounded in theory, and theory is created to answer *why* and *how* questions. For our purposes, an **explanatory study** goes beyond description and attempts to explain the reasons for the phenomenon that the descriptive study only observed. Research that studies the relationship between two or more variables is also referred to as a *correlational study*. In an explanatory study, the researcher uses theories or at least hypotheses to account for the forces that caused a certain phenomenon to occur. In ColorSplash, believing the problem with paint stockouts is the result of inventory management, the owner asks the researcher to detail warehousing and shipping processes. This would be a descriptive study if it had stopped here. But if problems in the processes could be linked with sales losses due to an inability to make timely deliveries to retail or wholesale customers, then an explanatory study would emerge. The researcher tests this hypothesis by modeling the last year of business using the relationships between processes and results.

The final phase of York College is an example of a predictive study.

Predictive   If we can provide a plausible explanation for an event after it has occurred, it is desirable to be able to predict when and in what situations the event will occur. A **predictive study,** the fourth type, is just as rooted in theory as explanation. NATA, a national trade association for the aviation industry, may be interested in explaining the radiation risks from the sun and stars for flight crews and passengers. The variables might include altitude, proximity of air routes to the poles, time of year, and aircraft shielding. Perhaps the relations among the four variables explain the radiation risk variable. This type of study often calls for a high order of inference making. Why, for example, would a flight at a specified altitude at one time of year not produce so great a radiation risk to the airliner's occupants as the same flight in another season? The answer to such a question would be valuable in planning air routes. It also would contribute to the development of a better theory of the phenomenon. In business research, prediction is found in studies conducted to evaluate specific courses of action or to forecast current and future values.

The researcher is asked to predict for the York College president the success of the proposed retirement facility for alumni based on the number of applicants for residency the project will attract. This prediction will be based on the explanatory hypothesis that alumni frequent programs and projects sponsored by the institution because of an association they maintain between their college experience and images of youthfulness and mental and physical stimulation.

Finally, we would like to be able to control a phenomenon once we can explain and predict it. Being able to replicate a scenario and dictate a particular outcome is the objective of **control.** In York College, if we assume that the college proceeds with its retirement community and enjoys the predicted success, the president will find it attractive to be able to build a similar facility to serve another group of alumni and duplicate that success.

Control is a logical outcome of prediction. The complexity of the phenomenon and the adequacy of the prediction theory, however, largely decide success in a control study. At York College, if a control study were done of the various promotional approaches used with alumni to stimulate images of youthfulness, the promotional tactics that drew the largest number of alumni applications for residency could be identified. Once known, this knowledge could be used successfully with different groups of alumni *only if* the researcher could account for and control all other variables influencing applications.

Is Research Always Problem-Solving Based?

Applied research is used to evaluate opportunities as in CHILDCO and York College.

In the four cases, researchers were asked to respond to "problems" that managers needed to solve. **Applied research** has a practical problem-solving emphasis, although the problem solving is not always generated by a negative circumstance. Whether the "problem" is negative, like rectifying an inventory system that is resulting in lost sales (ColorSplash), or an opportunity to increase stockholder wealth through acquiring another firm (CHILDCO), problem solving is prevalent in business research.

The problem-solving nature of applied research means it is conducted to reveal answers to specific questions related to action, performance, or policy needs. In this respect, all four examples appear to qualify as applied research. Pure, or basic, research is also problem-solving based, but in a different sense. It aims to solve perplexing questions (that is, problems) of a theoretical nature that have little direct impact on action, performance, or policy decisions. **Pure research** or **basic research** in the business arena might involve a researcher for an advertising agency who is studying the results of the use of coupons versus rebates as demand stimulation tactics, but not in a specific instance or in relation to a specific client's product. In another pure research scenario, researchers might study the influence on productivity of compensation systems that pay by piece-work versus salary-plus-commission. Thus, both applied and pure research are problem-solving based, but applied research is directed much more to making immediate managerial decisions.

Some authorities equate research with basic or scientific investigations and would reject all four examples. History shows, however, that science typically has its beginnings in pragmatic problems of real life. Interest in basic research comes much later, after development of a field's knowledge. Research is too narrowly defined if it is restricted to basic or pure research.

One respected author defines scientific research as a "systematic, controlled, empirical, and critical investigation of natural phenomena guided by theory and hypotheses about the presumed relations among such phenomena."[3] The terms *systematic* and *controlled* in this definition refer to the degree to which the observations are controlled and alternative explanations of the outcome are ruled out. The terms *empirical* and *critical* point to the requirements for the researcher to test subjective beliefs against objective reality and have the findings open to further scrutiny and testing. These qualities are what this author means by "scientific." Whether all business research needs to be this stringent or should be "guided by theory and hypotheses about presumed relations" is debatable.

The classical concept of basic research does call for an hypothesis,[4] but in applied research such a narrow definition omits at least two types of investigation that are highly valued. First is the exploratory study in which the investigator knows so little about the area of study that hypotheses have not yet emerged.[5] An equally important area of study is that which purists call merely descriptive. The importance of descriptive research to business should be reinforced:

> There is no more devastating condemnation that the self-designated theorist makes of the researcher than to label his work purely descriptive. There is an implication that associates "purely descriptive" research with empty-headedness; the label also implies that as a bare minimum every healthy researcher has at least one hypothesis to test, and preferably a whole model. This is nonsense.
>
> In every discipline, but particularly in its early stages of development, purely descriptive research is indispensable. Descriptive research is the stuff out of which the mind of man, the theorist, develops the units that compose his theories. The very essence of description is to name the properties of things: You may do more, but you cannot do less and still have description. The more adequate the description, the greater is the likelihood that the units derived from the description will be useful in subsequent theory building.[6]

In answer to the question posed at the beginning of this section, "Is research always problem-solving based?" the answer is yes. Whether basic or applied, simple or complex, all research should provide an answer to some question. If managers always knew what was causing problems or offering opportunities in their realm of responsibility, there would be little need for applied research, pure research, or basic research; intuition would be all that was necessary to make quality decisions.

Any of the four types of studies—reporting, descriptive, explanatory, or predictive—can properly be called research. We also can conclude from the various examples that research is a systematic inquiry aimed at providing information to solve managerial problems. This defines the bare minimum that any effort must meet to be called research.

All four cases and the MindWriter vignette meet this definition, but they suggest different stages of scientific development. A rough measure of the development of science in any field is the degree to which explanation and prediction have replaced reporting and description as research objectives. By this standard, the development of business research is in a comparatively formative stage.

Research and the Scientific Method

The development of the scientific method in business research lags behind similar developments in the physical sciences. Physical scientists have been more rigorous in their concepts and research procedures. They are much more advanced in their theory development than are business scientists. The public domain has sponsored much physical research, some of it for hundreds of years. Governments have allocated billions of dollars to support such research, driven by the motivation to overcome disease or to improve the human condition. Nations driven by threat of war and national pride have also played a major role in the advance of physical science. Much of the findings of their research is in the public domain.

A more thorough discussion of the scientific method is included in Chapter 2.

Business research is of much more recent origin and is largely supported by business organizations that hope to achieve a competitive advantage. Research methods and findings cannot be patented, and sharing findings often results in a loss of competitive advantage. The more valuable the research result is, the greater the value in keeping it secret. Under such conditions, access to findings is obviously restricted. Even though there is a growing amount of academic business research, it receives meager support when compared to research in the physical sciences.

Business research operates in a less favorable environment in other ways, too. Physical research is normally conducted under controlled laboratory conditions; business research seldom is. Business research normally deals with topics such as human attitudes, behavior, and performance. People think they already know a lot about these topics and do not easily accept research findings that differ from their opinions.

Even with these hindrances, business researchers are making great strides in the scientific arena. New techniques are being developed, and rigorous research procedures are advancing rapidly. Computers and powerful analytical methods have contributed to this movement, but a greater understanding of the basic principles of sound research is more important.

One outcome of these trends is that research-based decision making will be more widely used in the future than it has been in the past. Managers who are not prepared for this change will be at a severe disadvantage.

What Is Good Research?

Good research generates dependable data, being derived by practices that are conducted professionally and that can be used reliably for managerial decision making. In contrast, poor research is carelessly planned and conducted, resulting in data that a manager can't use to reduce his or her decision-making risks. Good research follows the standards of the **scientific method.** We list several defining characteristics of the scientific method in Exhibit 1–1 and below, discussing the managerial dimensions of each.

1. Purpose clearly defined. The purpose of the research—the problem involved or the decision to be made—should be clearly defined and sharply delineated in terms as unambiguous as possible. Getting this in writing is valuable even in instances where the

EXHIBIT 1–1   What Actions Guarantee Good Research?

Characteristics of Research	What a Manager Should Look for in Research Done by Others or Include in Self-Directed Research	Chapter
Purpose clearly defined	• Researcher distinguishes between symptom of organization's problem, the manager's perception of the problem, and the research problem.	Chapter 3
Research process detailed	• Researcher provides complete research proposal.	Chapter 4
Research design thoroughly planned	• Exploratory procedures are outlined with constructs defined. • Sample unit is clearly described along with sampling methodology. • Data collection procedures are selected and designed.	Chapters 2, 3
High ethical standards applied	• Safeguards are in place to protect study participants, organizations, clients, and researchers. • Recommendations do not exceed the scope of the study. • The study's methodology and limitations sections reflect researcher restraint and concern for accuracy.	Chapter 5
Limitations frankly revealed	• Desired procedure is compared with actual procedure in report. • Desired sample is compared with actual sample in report. • Impact on findings and conclusions is detailed.	Chapters 6, 7, 15, 20
Adequate analysis for decision maker's needs	• Sufficiently detailed findings are tied to collection instruments.	Chapters 15–19
Findings presented unambiguously	• Findings are clearly presented in words, tables, and graphs. • Findings are logically organized to facilitate reaching a decision about the manager's problem. • Executive summary of conclusions is outlined. • Detailed table of contents is tied to the conclusions and findings presentation.	Chapters 15–20
Conclusions justified	• Decision-based conclusions are matched with detailed findings.	Chapters 15–20
Researcher's experience reflected	• Researcher provides experience/credentials with report.	Chapter 20

decision maker and researcher are the same person. The statement of the decision problem should include its scope, its limitations, and the precise meanings of all words and terms significant to the research. Failure of the researcher to do this adequately may raise legitimate doubts in the minds of research report readers as to whether the researcher has sufficient understanding of the problem to make a sound proposal attacking it. This characteristic is comparable to developing a strategic plan before developing a tactical plan or an action map for achieving an objective.

The nine criteria summarized in Exhibit 1–1 profile desirable, decision-oriented research, especially when managers perform the research themselves. These criteria create barriers to adjusting research findings to meet desired ends.

2. Research process detailed. The research procedures used should be described in sufficient detail to permit another researcher to repeat the research. Except when secrecy is imposed, research reports should reveal with candor the sources of data and the means by which they were obtained. Omission of significant procedural details makes it difficult or impossible to estimate the validity and reliability of the data and justifiably weakens the confidence of the reader in the research itself as well as any recommendations based on the research. This characteristic is comparable to developing a tactical plan.

3. Research design thoroughly planned. The procedural design of the research should be carefully planned to yield results that are as objective as possible. When a sampling of the population is involved, the report should include evidence concerning the degree of representativeness of the sample. A survey of opinions or recollections ought not to be used when more reliable evidence is available from documentary sources or by direct observation. Bibliographic searches should be as thorough and complete as possible. Experiments should have satisfactory controls. Direct observations should be recorded in writing as soon as possible after the event. Efforts should be made to minimize the influence of personal bias in selecting and recording data. This characteristic is comparable to developing detailed action plans for each tactic.

We discuss ethical research issues at length in Chapter 5.

4. High ethical standards applied. Researchers often work independently and have significant latitude in designing and executing research projects. A research design that includes safeguards against causing mental or physical harm to participants and makes data integrity a first priority should be highly valued. Ethical issues in research reflect important moral concerns about the practice of responsible behavior in society.

Consulting companies are increasingly a source for business research. In selecting a company to provide strategic direction, an organization should carefully consider the company's research skills and experience. Ernst & Young has won numerous awards for its information technology. This latest award recognizes the firm's attention to continuous learning.
www.ey.com

Researchers frequently find themselves precariously balancing the rights of their subjects against the scientific dictates of their chosen method. When this occurs, they have a responsibility to guard the welfare of the participants in the studies and also the organizations to which they belong, their clients, their colleagues, and themselves. Careful consideration must be given to those research situations in which there is a possibility for physical or psychological harm, exploitation, invasion of privacy, and/or loss of dignity. The research need must be weighed against the potential for adverse effects. Typically, you can redesign a study, but sometimes you cannot. The researcher should be prepared for this dilemma.

5. Limitations frankly revealed. The researcher should report, with complete frankness, flaws in procedural design and estimate their effect on the findings. There are very few perfect research designs. Some of the imperfections may have little effect on the validity and reliability of the data; others may invalidate them entirely. A competent researcher should be sensitive to the effects of imperfect design, and his or her experience in analyzing the data should provide a basis for estimating their influence. As a decision maker, you should question the value of research where no limitations are reported.

6. Adequate analysis for decision maker's needs. Analysis of the data should be extensive enough to reveal its significance, and the methods of analysis used should be appropriate. The extent to which this criterion is met is frequently a good measure of the competence of the researcher. Adequate analysis of the data is the most difficult phase of research for the novice. The validity and reliability of data should be checked carefully. The data should be classified in ways that assist the researcher in reaching pertinent conclusions and clearly reveal the findings that have led to those conclusions. When statistical methods are used, the probability of error should be estimated and the criteria of statistical significance applied.

7. Findings presented unambiguously. Some evidence of the competence and integrity of the researcher may be found in the report itself. For example, language that is restrained, clear, and precise; assertions that are carefully drawn and hedged with appropriate reservations; and an apparent effort to achieve maximum objectivity tend to leave a favorable impression of the researcher with the decision maker. Generalizations that outrun the evidence on which they are based, exaggerations, and unnecessary verbiage tend to leave an unfavorable impression. Such reports are not valuable to managers wading through the minefields of business decision making. Presentation of data should be comprehensive, easily understood by the decision maker, and organized so that the decision maker can readily locate critical findings.

8. Conclusions justified. Conclusions should be limited to those for which the data provide an adequate basis. Researchers are often tempted to broaden the basis of induction by including personal experiences and their interpretations—data not subject to the controls under which the research data were gathered. Equally undesirable is the all-too-frequent practice of drawing conclusions from a study of a limited population and applying them universally. Researchers also may be tempted to rely too heavily on data collected in a prior study and use it in the interpretation of a new study. Such practice sometimes occurs among research specialists who confine their work to clients in a small industry. These actions tend to decrease the objectivity of the research and weaken readers' confidence in the findings. Good researchers always specify the conditions under which their conclusions seem to be valid.

9. Researcher's experience reflected. Greater confidence in the research is warranted if the researcher is experienced, has a good reputation in research, and is a person of integrity. Were it possible for the reader of a research report to obtain sufficient

What are the consequences of faking data in research? Is it more than an ethical dilemma if you falsify the description of your methodology or if you modify your sampling plan? These are ethical and procedural issues that researchers, even famous ones, face. In its December 2001 issue, *FastCompany* asked author, consultant, and motivational speaker Tom Peters to revisit the writing of *In Search of Excellence,* the 1982 best-selling business title. In his confession #3, Peters is quoted as saying that he "faked the data" that resulted in the eight underlying principles—principles that guided American business for much of the next decade. Rather than evolving from a large study of businesses where each was selected based on its performance metrics (a probability study), he switched the research design. Instead, Peters, along with partner and coauthor Robert Waterman, asked McKinsey colleagues and other contacts to identify "cool" companies (a nonprobability, judgment sample). They conducted detailed personal interviews with contacts in those initial 62 companies, then reduced the list to 43 by a post-interview review of performance metrics. Peters, in confession #7, admits he missed some of the emerging "excellence" factors because they were "too superficial to make an impact." Some of the things his study missed: early signs of the growing influence of information technology and the importance speed would play in business. Does his confession diminish the importance of the results? www.tompeters.com, www.mckinsey.com, www.fastcompany.com

information about the researcher, this criterion perhaps would be one of the best bases for judging the degree of confidence a piece of research warrants and the value of any decision based upon it. For this reason, the research report should contain information about the qualifications of the researcher.

These nine criteria provide an excellent summary of what is desirable in decision-oriented research (see Exhibit 1–1). They are especially appropriate to guide research done by managers themselves, for they create barriers to adjusting research findings to meet desired ends rather than to reflect reality.

Criterion 2 calls for a detailed proposal specifying what will be done, but in many exploratory studies it is not possible to be that precise prior to starting the study. It is even more important, therefore, when researcher and manager are separated by organizational boundaries, to state the nature of the decision problem clearly and unambiguously (criterion 1).

The threat of bias is mentioned under criterion 3, but it should be given more emphasis. The business researcher often knows from the beginning what results the sponsor would like to have. To combat this potentially biasing influence, it may be necessary to secure an understanding between manager and researcher before stating that the objective is to uncover reality—wherever that leads.

Criterion 3 calls for complete disclosure of methods and procedures used in the research study. This also is highly desirable, because it enables others to test findings through replication. Such openness to scrutiny has a positive effect on the quality of research. However, competitive advantage often mitigates against methodology disclosure in business research. Sometimes even the acknowledgment of a study's existence is considered unwise. For example, firms like J. D. Power and Associates will not provide enough information on their methodology to repeat an automotive market study. Similarly, at the time each developed its low-cost line of desktop computers, neither Compaq nor IBM knew of the extensive research the other was doing. In the litigation by state attorneys general against cigarette companies, it proved disastrous when evidence was revealed that cigarette companies had performed studies manipulating nicotine levels to enhance the addictive power of tobacco products.

Criteria 1 through 9 should guide all research studies. Although these criteria use phraseology such as "unambiguous as possible," this only recognizes the reality of research work. The aim is always to be objective, yet we are all subjective. We also must recognize that research designs have flaws, even though calling attention to them in our work may be painful (criterion 5).

The Value of Acquiring Research Skills

CHILDCO is an example of (1), and CHILDCO, NUCMED, and ColorSplash offer examples of (2). The "Bringing Research to Life" vignette at the beginning of the chapter offers examples of (3), (4), and (5). York College is an example of (4).

You can profit by having research skills in at least five situations.

1. Manager as research-based decision maker.

2. Subordinate employee as researcher.

3. Manager as research services buyer or evaluator.

4. Manager as evaluator of secondary data sources.

5. Research specialist.

As a decision maker you'll often feel the need for more information before selecting a course of action (see the CHILDCO case). Your options are limited if there is no one to whom you can delegate this task. You must either make an intuitive judgment without gathering additional information or gather the data yourself with some reasonable level of skill. Gathering information may involve data-mining existing databases and information sources or collecting new information. At the early levels of your career in management, when your experience is limited and your intuitive judgment less reliable, it should be obvious which option is better.

In a second instance, you may be called on to do a research study for a higher level executive. Such a task, often coming early in your career, can be seen as a career-boosting opportunity; it can be your chance to make a favorable impression on that executive (see the CHILDCO, NUCMED, and ColorSplash cases).

The third scenario has you buying research services from others or evaluating proposals for research prepared by others. If you can understand the research design proposed and adequately judge the quality of the planned activities and the likelihood that such activities will assist you in making a decision, you can save your organization both time and money. Literally thousands of companies provide research services. While many specialize in a given industry or type of research, others provide a wide variety of services to meet almost any manager's needs. Some of the world's largest research firms are listed in Exhibit 1–2.

Wal-Mart Stores, Benetonville, Arkansas, is the world's largest retailer as well as one of the most profitable firms in the world. Its installed equipment provides for more than 100 terabytes of data in its data warehouse (equivalent to 16,000 bytes for every person in the world). Wal-Mart uses its customer information to negotiate some of the best prices and to more fully understand its customers and suppliers. It also uses its extensive data to reduce losses—identifying products that have high shoplifting rates and combining this data with video footage of the stores to reveal patterns of losses within the store layout. Wal-Mart recently chose not to renew its contract with Information Resources Inc., a partner of choice for consumer goods manufacturers and retailers seeking market and consumer intelligence. Wal-Mart decided it wasn't receiving enough value for sharing a very valuable asset: customer point-of-sale data. www.wal-mart.com, www.infores.com

EXHIBIT 1–2   Some of the World's Largest Research Companies

Company	Web URL	Type of Research
IMS Health	www.imshealth.com	Provides information solutions to the pharmaceutical and health care industries.
ACNielsen Corp.	www.acnielsen.com	Provides market research, information, and analysis to the consumer products and services industries.
Nielsen Media Research (division of VNU USA)	www.nielsenmedia.com	Provides television information services in the U.S. and Canada.
Information Resources Inc. (IRI)	www.infores.com	Provides UPC scanner-based business solutions to the consumer packaged goods industry.
Westat	www.westat.com	Provides research to agencies of the U.S. government, as well as businesses, foundations, and state and local governments.
Kantar Group, Ltd.	www.kantargroup.com	Provides worldwide media research and measurement for media owners, agencies, and advertisers.
Arbitron Co.	www.arbitron.com	Provides information services used to develop the local marketing strategies of the electronic media and their advertisers and agencies.
NFO Worldwide	www.nfow.com	Provides results-oriented insights so clients may develop stronger brands and market more successful products and services.
Market Facts	www.marketfacts.com	Provides global marketing research and consulting to business, government, and associations.
MMRI (Maritz Marketing Research)	www.maritz.com/mmri	Provides large-scale, custom-designed research studies that provide critical marketing information.
Taylor Nelson Sofres Intersearch (TNSIntersearch)	www.intersearch.tnsofres.com	Provides custom research, omnibus studies, attitudinal polling, and drug sample monitoring in a variety of industries.

SOURCE: Information extracted from company websites.

Because much decision making relies on using information collected during prior research projects, by having research skills you will be able to deal professionally with the fourth scenario: evaluating the applicability of prior research to assist in resolving a current management dilemma (see "Bringing Research to Life" and York College).

A fifth reason to study research methods is so that you may establish a career as a research specialist. As a specialized function, research offers attractive career opportunities, especially in financial analysis, marketing research, operations research, public relations, and human resources management. As illustrated in the chapter-opening vignette, job opportunities for research specialists exist in all fields of management and in all industries.

The Manager-Researcher Relationship

The management of the information process from gathering to reporting is an integral part of any manager's job. So it is not surprising that many managers do their own research, at least part of the time. The lower a manager is in the decision-making hierarchy, the more likely he or she is to do most of his or her own research. When managers lack either research time or talent, they may delegate the task to a staff assistant or a research specialist. This delegation of responsibility can result in greater synergy, especially if the research is decision driven and each party makes a full contribution to the joint venture. However, the separation of research user from research conductor can pose problems in data analysis, interpretation, conclusion finding, and recommendations. This is why businesses that regularly use outside research specialists often use the same firm repeatedly: Knowledge of the company, its people, and its processes is as critical as knowledge of the decision-making dilemma.

In an organizational setting, the researcher should look on the manager as a client. An effective **manager-researcher relationship** is not achieved unless both fulfill their respective obligations and several critical barriers are overcome.

Manager-Researcher Contributions

The obligations of managers are to specify their problems and provide researchers with adequate background information and access to company information gatekeepers. It is usually more effective if managers state their problems in terms of the decision choices they must make rather than specify the information they think they need. If this is done, both manager and researcher can jointly decide what information is needed.

In the opening vignette, MindWriter's customer affairs manager Myra Wines, as a staff rather than a line manager, may need assistance from managers with line responsibilities to define plausible actions that could affect postpurchase service. She has clearly been charged with the responsibility of executing the customer satisfaction study, but she does not have authority to implement conclusions affecting, for example, product engineering, product manufacture, or distributor relationships. Thus she needs to clarify with those line managers what courses of action might be taken to correct identified problems. If, however, dissatisfaction is arising because of how customers are treated when interacting with the customer affairs staff, Myra has direct line authority to determine plausible actions to correct such problems within her own domain.

Researchers also have obligations. Organizations expect them to develop a creative research design that will provide answers to important business questions. Not only should researchers provide data analyzed in terms of the problem specified, but they also should point out the implications that flow from the results. In the process, conflict may arise between what the decision maker wants and what the researcher can provide or thinks should be provided. The decision maker wants certainty and simple, explicit recommendations, while the researcher often can offer only probabilities and hedged interpretations. This conflict is inherent in their respective roles and has no simple resolution. However, a workable balance can usually be found if each person is sensitive to the demands and restrictions imposed on the other.

Manager-Researcher Conflicts

The sources of manager-researcher conflict are numerous:

- Knowledge gap between the researcher and the manager.
- Job status and internal, political coalitions to preserve status.
- Researcher's isolation from managers.

Knowledge Gap   Some conflicts between decision makers and researchers are traced to management's limited exposure to research. Managers seldom have either formal training in research methodology or research expertise gained through experience. And, due to the explosive growth of research technology in recent years, a knowledge gap has developed between managers and research specialists as model building and more sophisticated investigative techniques have come into use. Thus the research specialist removes the manager from his or her comfort zone: The manager must now put his or her faith, and sometimes his or her career, in the hands of the research specialist and hope for the best.

Job Status and Internal Coalitions   In addition, managers often see research people as threats to their personal status. Managers still view management as the domain of the "intuitive artist" who is the master in this area. They may believe a request for research assistance implies they are inadequate to the task. These fears are often justified. The researcher's function is to test old ideas as well as new ones. To the insecure manager, the researcher is a potential rival.

   The researcher will inevitably have to consider the corporate culture and political situations that develop in any organization. Members strive to maintain their niches and may seek ascendancy over their colleagues. Coalitions form and people engage in various self-serving activities, both overt and covert. As a result, research is blocked, or the findings or objectives of the research are distorted for an individual's self-serving purposes. To allow one's operations to be probed with a critical eye may be to invite trouble from others competing for promotion, resources, or other forms of organizational power.

Researcher Isolation   A third source of stress for researchers is their frequent isolation from managers. Researchers draw back into their specialty and talk among themselves. Management's lack of understanding of research techniques compounds this problem. The research department can become isolated, reducing the effectiveness of conclusions a researcher may draw from research findings.

   These problems have caused some people to advocate the use of a "research generalist." Such a person would head the research activity, help managers detail their research needs, and translate these needs into research problems. He or she also would facilitate the flow of information between manager and researcher that is so important for bringing the researcher into the decision-making process.

When Research Should Be Avoided

Not every managerial decision requires research. Business research has an inherent value only to the extent that it helps management make better decisions. Interesting information about consumers, employees, or competitors might be pleasant to have, but its value is limited if the information cannot be applied to a critical decision. If a study does not help management select more efficient, less risky, or more profitable alternatives than otherwise would be the case, its use should be questioned. Alternatively, management may have insufficient resources (time, money, or skill) to conduct an appropriate study or face a low level of risk associated with the decision at hand. In these situations, there are valid reasons to avoid business research and its associated costs in time and money. The important point is that applied research in a business environment finds its justification in the contribution it makes to the decision maker's task and to the bottom line.

   One objective of this text is to provide you with plausible solutions to potential sources of manager-researcher conflicts. In the chapters that follow, we discuss scientific research procedures and show their application to pragmatic problems of the organization manager. At a minimum, our objective is to make you a more intelligent consumer of research products prepared by others as well as enable you to perform quality research for your own decisions and those of others to whom you report.

EXHIBIT 1–3   Trends in the Research Profession and Necessary Management Safeguards

Trends in Research Profession	What Managers Should Watch For
The Positive Trends	
• Budding recognition of the importance of researcher participation in strategic planning.	• Strategic planning initiatives that have an appropriate research component.
• Emerging return to the strong, internal research group.	• Better methodologies performed by knowledgeable professionals generating significant value to management decision making.
The Negative Trends	
• Increasing pressure for rapid measurement and feedback.	• Methodologies that raise questions about the representativeness of samples.
	• Projects fielded without thoroughly understanding the management dilemma, which results in information with little value to solve the dilemma.
• Increasing pressure for research specialists to interpret research results and provide strategic recommendations.	• Research providers who may be technically competent with expertise in quantitative skills, but who are not trained or have limited training in management.
• Increasing demand for information privacy, reducing respondent willingness to cooperate.	• Research providers who are knowledgeable about extracting valuable knowledge from internal databases (data mining).
• General consulting firms moving toward functional specialization and increasingly doing their own research.	• Consultants who lack the technical skill in research methodologies creating a lack of translation from management dilemma to research protocol.
	• Consultants sharing information among specialized clients, generating a loss of intellectual capital that fosters distinctive competencies—the basis of competitive advantage.
• Continued perception of research as an expense rather than an investment in reducing uncertainty.	• Research budgets being cut during economic downturns.
• Increasingly wide range of competence among those offering services in the research industry.	• Insufficient quality of credentials among research professionals being used or considered.
	• Assignment of projects to researchers with insufficient technical background to do quality research.
• Widening cultural mindset gap between business strategists and research specialists.	• Breakdown in communication between the researcher and the manager who will use the research results, resulting in information, not knowledge.
• Consulting and industry's expectation that new hires have received scientific research training in college.	• Assuring that curricular demands placed on the new hires by their collegiate institutions have included research methodologies.
• Decrease or delay in intellectual transfer between academia and research profession.	• Assuring that firms hired as research specialists keep abreast of the newest methodologies through continuing education efforts.

SOURCE: Developed from the transcript of the American Marketing Association's Research Roundtable, September 1997.

Trends in the Research Profession and Management Safeguards

Management's demand for more, better, and quicker information is bringing many changes to the research profession. Exhibit 1–3 summarizes these changes and the safeguards needed to protect the quality of the information used in decision making. Few of these trends are positive. As a result, managers who are unfamiliar with research methodology and who rely on research information to decrease decision-making risk are all the more vulnerable. The preponderance of negative news also makes managers who are familiar with research methodology and who know what makes *good* research far more valuable to their organizations. As you are about to join this latter group, you are to be commended for your foresight.

SUMMARY

1 Research is any organized inquiry carried out to provide information for solving problems. Business research is a systematic inquiry that provides information to guide business decisions. This includes reporting, descriptive, explanatory, and predictive studies. We emphasize the last three in this book.

2 What characterizes good research? Generally, one expects good research to be purposeful, with a clearly defined focus and plausible goals, with defensible, ethical, and repeatable procedures, and with evidence of objectivity. The reporting of procedures—their strengths and weaknesses—should be complete and honest. Appropriate analytical techniques should be used; conclusions drawn should be limited to those clearly justified by the findings; and reports of findings and conclusions should be clearly presented and professional in tone, language, and appearance. Managers should always choose an investigator who has an established reputation for quality work. The research objective and its benefits should be weighed against potentially adverse effects.

3 The relationship between manager and researcher is an important one. Both share the obligation of making a project meaningful. Several factors complicate this relationship. Among these are ethical considerations and the political environment. Changes in the research industry also complicate the relationship, and the manager must safeguard against the negative changes. Among these are research being performed by individuals untrained in research protocol, pressure on research specialists to provide strategic and tactical recommendations regardless of their management experience, continuing perception of research as a nonessential expense, and as the range of necessary skills increases, the broadening range of competence possessed by individuals who call themselves research specialists.

4 The managers of tomorrow will need to know more than any managers in history. Research will be a major contributor to that knowledge. Managers will find knowledge of research methods to be of value in many situations. They may need to conduct research either for themselves or for others. As buyers of research services they will need to be able to judge research quality. Finally, they may become research specialists themselves.

KEY TERMS

applied research 12	descriptive studies 10	pure research 12
basic research 12	explanatory studies 11	reporting studies 10
business research 5	internal databases 6	research variable 10
control 12	management dilemma 5	scientific method 14
data mining 6	manager-researcher relationship 21	
data warehousing 6	predictive studies 12	

EXAMPLES

Company	Scenario	Page
Bridgestone/Firestone	Studying secondary data to understand tire tread separation.	11
CHILDCO*	Company researching the acquisition of a toy manufacturer.	7
ColorSplash*	A paint manufacturer studying inventory control options to improve profitability.	8
Ernst and Young	A conuslting services firm that does research for its clients and values the increased knowledge level of its employees.	16
Financial Accounting Standards Board	New standard for measuring "goodwill" that recognizes the value of research and brand equity.	5
Ford Motor Co.	Studying secondary data to understand Explorer rollover susceptibility.	11
MindWriter*	Laptop manufacturer hiring a research services supplier.	BRTL, throughout
NATA*	An aviation trade association study to examine radiation risks for flight crews and passengers.	12
NUCMED*	Physician specialists in nuclear medicine and imaging evaluating a health care cost containment plan.	7
Tom Peters	Research process reflected in *In Search of Excellence*.	18
York College*	A multiphase study by a university alumni association to evaluate a proposal to build a retirement community to serve alumni.	8
Wal-Mart	Maintains a mammoth data warehouse to improve profitability.	19
Webvan	How an absence of research contributed to the problems of a new business model.	7

*Due to the confidential and proprietary nature of most research, the names of some companies have been changed.

DISCUSSION QUESTIONS

Terms in Review

1. What is research? Why should there be any question about the definition of research?

2. What is the difference between applied and basic or pure research? Use a decision about how a salesperson is to be paid, by commission or salary, and describe the question that would guide applied research versus the question that would guide pure research.

Making Research Decisions

3. A human resources manager needs to have information in order to decide whether to create a custom motivation program or purchase one offered by a human resources consulting firm. What are the dilemmas the manager faces in selecting either of these alternatives?

4. You are manager of the midwestern division of a major corporation, supervising five animal-feed plants scattered over four states. Corporate headquarters asks you to conduct an investigation to determine whether any of these plants should be closed, expanded, moved, or reduced. Is there a possible conflict between your roles as researcher and manager? Explain.

5. Advise each of the following persons on a specific research study that he or she might find useful. Classify each proposed study as reporting, descriptive, explanatory, or predictive.

   a. When the management decision problem is known:

      (1) Manager of a full-service restaurant with high employee turnover.

      (2) Head of an academic department committee charged with selecting a research methods textbook.

   b. When the management decision problem has not yet been specified:

      (1) Manager of a restaurant.

      (2) Plant manager at a shoe factory.

      (3) Director of Big Brothers/Big Sisters in charge of sponsor recruiting.

      (4) Data analyst with ACNielsen research.

      (5) Human resources manager at a university.

      (6) Product manager of the Ford Explorer.

      (7) Family services officer for your county.

      (8) Office manager for a pediatrician.

6. The new president of an old, established company is facing a problem. The company is currently unprofitable and is, in the president's opinion, operating inefficiently. The company sells a wide line of equipment and supplies to the dairy industry. Some items it manufactures, and many it wholesales to dairies, creameries, and similar plants. Because the industry is changing in several ways, survival will be more difficult in the future. In particular, many equipment companies are bypassing the wholesalers and selling directly to dairies. In addition, many of the independent dairies are being taken over by large food chains. How might research help the new president make the right decisions? In answering this question, consider the areas of marketing and finance as well as the whole company.

7. You have received a research report done by a consultant for your firm, a life insurance company. The study is a survey of morale in the home office and covers the opinions of about 500 secretaries and clerks plus about 100 executives and actuaries. You are asked to comment on its quality. What will you look for?

8. As area sales manager for a company manufacturing and marketing outboard engines, you have been assigned the responsibility of conducting a research study to estimate the sales potential of your products in the domestic (U.S. or Canadian) market. Discuss key issues and concerns arising from the fact that you, the manager, are also the researcher.

**From Concept
to Practice**

9. Apply the principles in Exhibit 1–1 to the research scenario in question 8.

**Bringing
Research to Life**

10. In what type(s) of study is Myra interested (applied or basic/pure research; exploratory, predictive, or descriptive study)?

11. What evidence is presented in the vignette of data warehousing? Of data mining?

WWW Exercises

Visit our website for Internet exercises related to this chapter at
www.mhhe.com/business/cooper8.

CASES*

CALLING UP ATTENDANCE

 ### DATA DEVELOPMENT INC.*

*All cases indicating a video icon are located on the Instructor's Videotape Supplement. All nonvideo cases are in the case section of the textbook. All cases indicating a CD icon offer a data set, which is located on the accompanying CD.

REFERENCE NOTES

1. See, for example, Murray Levine, "Investigative Reporting as a Research Method: Analysis of Bernstein and Woodward's *All the President's Men," American Psychologist* 35 (1980), pp. 626–38.

2. See, for example, Elizabethann O'Sullivan and Gary R. Rassel, *Research Methods for Public Administrators* (New York: Longman, 1999).

3. Fred N. Kerlinger and Howard B. Lee, *Foundations of Behavioral Research,* 4th ed. (New York: HBJ College & School Division, 1999), p. 15.

4. An hypothesis is a statement that is advanced for the purpose of testing its truth or falsity.

5. An exploratory study describes an investigation when the final research problem has not yet been clearly fixed. Its aim is to provide the insights needed by the researcher to develop a more formal research design.

6. Reprinted with permission of Macmillan Publishing Co., Inc., from *Theory Building,* rev. ed. 1978, by Robert Dubin. Copyright © 1969 by The Free Press, a division of Macmillan Co.

REFERENCES FOR SNAPSHOTS AND CAPTIONS

Bridgestone/Firestone and Ford

Keith Bradsher, "Firestone to Stop Sales to Ford," *The New York Times on the Web,* May 22, 2001 (www.nytimes.com/2001/05/22/business/22TIRE.html).

"Bridgestone/Firestone Proudly Accepts Sixth Consecutive Supplier of the Year Award from General Motors," Bridgestone/Firestone, Inc., press release, Nashville, TN, July 30, 2001 (http://www.firestone.com/homeimgs/H010730a.htm).

"Bridgestone/Firestone, Inc. Ends Ford Tire Business in the Americas," Bridgestone/Firestone, Inc., press release, Nashville, TN, May 21, 2001 (http://www.mirror.bridgestone-firestone.com/homeimgs/H010521a.htm).

"Ford Motor Company to Replace All 13 Million Firestone Wilderness AT Tires on Its Vehicles," Bridgestone/Firestone, Inc., press release, Nashville, TN, May 22, 2001 (http://media.ford.com/newsroom/release_firestone.cfm?article_id=8361&id=92&art_ids=0&bn=1).

"GM Reaffirms Commitment to Bridgestone/Firestone Products," Bridgestone/Firestone, Inc., press release, Nashville, TN, May 24, 2001 (http://mirror.bridgestone-firestone.com/homeimgs/H010524a.htm).

"Statement by John Lampe, Chairman, CEO, and President Bridgestone/Firestone, Inc.," Bridgestone/Firestone, Inc., press release, Nashville, TN, May 22, 2001 (http://www.mirror.bridgestone-firestone.com/homeimgs/H010521a.htm).

FASB

Gerry Khermouch, "Why Advertising Matters More Than Ever," *Business Week,* August 6, 2001, pp. 56–57.

"Wielding a Mean Branding Iron," *Business Week,* August 6, 2001, pp. 52–53.

"The Best Global Brands," *Business Week,* August 6, 2001, pp. 50–57.

"FASB Issues Report on Voluntary Disclosures, Improving Business Reporting: Insights into Enhancing Voluntary Disclosures," FASB news release, January 29, 2001 (http://accounting.rutgers.edu/ raw/fasb/news/nr012901.html).

"Business Combinations and Intangible Assets—Accounting for Goodwill," Financial Accounting Series, February 14, 2001 (http://rarc.rutguers.edu/fasb/rev_ed.pdf).

Tom Peters

John Byrne, "The Real Confessions of Tom Peters," *Business Week,* December 3, 2001, p. 48.

Tom Peters and Robert Waterman, *Excellence: In Search of Excellence, Lessons from America's Best-Run Companies* (New York: Warner Books, 1982), pp. 13–24.

"Tom Peters's True Confessions," *FastCompany* 53 (December 2001), p. 78.

TomPeters! (http://www.tompeters.com/toms_world/press_kit/excellence.asp).

Wal-Mart

Dana Blankenhorn, "100 Trillion Bytes of Customer Data: How Marketers' Database Muscle Is Growing," *AdAge.com Special Report,* Summer 2001 (http://adagespecials.com/data1.shtml).

"NCR More than Doubles Warehouse for World's Leading Retailer to Over 100 Terabytes," *Dsstar: Executive Journal for Data Intensive Decision Support,* Tabor Griffin Communications (http://hpcwire.com/dsstar/99/0824/1000966.html).

Betsy Spethman, "Wal-Mart Goes Private: Retailer Control Grows as Researchers Stop Getting Scanner Data This Month," *PROMO,* July 2001, pp. 39–40.

"Wal-Mart Buys World's Largest Decision-Support System from AT&T," AT&T press release, January 9, 1995 (http://www.att.com/press/0195/950109.nca.html).

"Wal-Mart's Purchasing Data Becomes Public," *InformationWeek.com,* August 27, 2001 (http://www.informationweek.com/story/IWK20010824S0015).

Paul Westerman, *Data Warehousing: Using the Wal-Mart Model* (Morgan Kaufmann Publishers, 2001).

Webvan

Jane Black, "OnlineOnline Extra: Why Online Grocers Won't All Go Hungry," *Business Week,* May 14, 2001.

Saul Hansell, "Some Hard Lessons for Online Grocer," *New York Times on the Web,* February 19, 2001.

Saul Hansell, "Online Grocer Calls It Quits After Running Out of Money," *New York Times on the Web,* July 10, 2001.

"Online Grocer Webvan to File for Bankruptcy," *New York Times on the Web,* July 9, 2001.

CLASSIC AND CONTEMPORARY READINGS

Berry, Michael J. A., and Gordon Linhoff. *Data Mining Techniques: For Marketing, Sales, and Customer Support.* New York: John Wiley & Sons, 1997. This is a practical guide to mining business data to help business managers focus their marketing and sales strategies.

Kimball, Ralph, et al. *The Data Warehouse Lifecycle Toolkit: Expert Methods for Designing, Developing, and Deploying Data Warehouses.* New York: John Wiley & Sons, 1998. A definitive work on the business dimensional life cycle approach and data warehouse architecture.

Haas, Peter J., and J. Fred Springer. *Applied Policy Research: Concepts and Cases.* New York: Garland Reference Library of Social Science, No. 1051, 1998. Chapter 2 discusses policy research strategies and contributions.

Random, Matthew. *The Social Scientist in American Industry.* New Brunswick, NJ: Rutgers University Press, 1970. A research report of experiences of social scientists employed in industry. Chapter 7 presents a summary of findings.

Remenyi, Dan, et al. *Doing Research in Business and Management: An Introduction to Process and Method.* Thousand Oaks, CA: Sage Publishing, 1998. Chapters 1 and 2 establish the business research perspective for management students.

CHAPTER 2

Applying Scientific Thinking to Management Problems

Learning Objectives

After reading this chapter, you should understand . . .

1 **The distinctions between different approaches (styles of thinking) to problem solving.**

2 **The terminology used by professional researchers employing scientific thinking.**

3 **What is needed to formulate a solid research hypothesis.**

Bringing Research to Life

"**M**yra, have you had any experience with research suppliers?" asked Jason.

"Not like you, no. But yes, when I served in the Army Reserve," said Myra. "They never knew what to do with me, a woman, a captain, and a TV journalist. I think they feared my snoopiness would break out of control.

"So, one summer they sent me to test ammunitions and a new cannon.

"The firing range was a played-out mine, now strip-mined until it was worse than a moonscape. In its day, the site had been one of the most prosperous mining regions, where the people were known for fearlessly and proudly going out to dig and produce. The nearest town was so severely depressed that, for the pitifully few jobs we provided, the folks welcomed us in to bomb their backyard to cinders.

"The cannon we were testing was impressive. We armed it with three-inch shells, put on ear protectors and goggles and lobbed shells into the range. There would be a tremendous flash and boom, and the shells would go roaring and soaring out of sight. We would soon hear a tremendous boom coming back to us, and see dust and ash kicked up several hundred feet. We were all very happy not to be down range. When we went down range later, we'd find a huge crater and a fused puddle of iron, but nothing else but slag and molten rocks.

"There was this one problem. About every 20th shell would be a dud. It would fly off and land, and maybe kick up some dust, but explode it would not.

"On paper, this was not supposed to be a problem. The arsenal sent down an officious second lieutenant, and he showed us reports that the army had dropped such duds from hundred-foot platforms, from helicopters, had applied torches to them—everything—and had discovered them to be completely inert. The only thing he claimed would ignite one of these duds was to drop another, live bomb on it.

"Regrettably, this proved not to be the case. In the middle of the night we would hear one of these so-called duds explode. We would rush out at dawn, and sure enough, find a new crater, molten slag, molten rock, and so forth. It was quite a mystery.

"So I nosed around. I sat up one night on a hill overlooking the range, and, sure enough, I saw people with flashlights moving around in there.

"Locals were coming in at night, intending to crack open the bombs and scavenge for copper wire or anything they thought was salvageable. Except, of course, their actions ignited one of the beauties, and erased any evidence of a crime being committed by vaporizing the perpetrators on the spot.

"So I started hanging around the locals. They were involved in every kind of thrill sport. It was not unusual to see a 50-mile auto race with four ambulances on hand on the edge of the oval, to cart off the carnage to the surgical hospital in the next county. I saw men leap into cars with threadbare tires, loose wheels, malfunctioning brakes, with brake fluid and transmission fluid drooling all over the track. Nobody thought anything of this. If I asked, their answer was, 'I'll go when my number is up,' or 'It's not in my hands.'

"These good folk had lost all sense of cause and effect. They could wheel their cars out onto the track on a tire they knew was thin as tissue, and if it blew out and put them in the hospital, their reaction was 'Some days you can't win for losin'.'

"Their nonscientific attitude made sense, from a cultural-economic view. It was what let their men go down in the mines year after year. I begged the sheriff to warn them away from our range. 'What's the big problem, Captain Wines?' he asked. 'They are going to kill themselves,' I said. 'They are going to die anyway,' he said. 'We all are going to die. People die every month who never went out on the range.'

"You can't deal with such thinking by applying logic. So, we changed our procedure. We would fire the shells in the morning and spend the afternoon finding the duds, to which we attached kerosene lanterns. At dusk, a fighter-bomber would fly over the area and bomb the lanterns—and the duds—to a molecular state. It was neat and it worked."

Styles of Thinking

Research is based on reasoning. Good researchers and good managers alike practice habits of thought that reflect sound reasoning—finding correct premises, testing the connections between their facts and assumptions, making claims based on adequate evidence. Drawing supportable generalizations from limited data is the product of extending the inference process to statistical testing.

Like all specialties, research has its own terminology. To communicate our meanings with precision within a community of research users and research practitioners, who demand consistency of definitions for shared meaning, it is necessary to learn the specialized terminology of research.

At the heart of every research course is the question of perspective. Different fields of business research make different assumptions about reality and the nature of data. How one sees the world affects the kind of questions asked and what can be accepted as explanations. Reserve army captain and journalist Wines asked different questions than did the army brass. Myra asked, "What causes an inert, 'dud' bomb to explode hours after deployment?" The army asked, "What speed of impact would cause the 'dud' bomb to explode?" Of the hundreds of questions about organizations or finance or marketing that can be asked, each presupposes a "normative perspective" for that particular question. Some questions will be more productive than others for obtaining answers, especially those where the questioner correctly assumes the perspective of the respondent.

Due to selective perception and conditioning, people analyze problems differently. In this chapter, scientific inquiry, the preferred method for analyzing problems for researchers, is contrasted with other styles of thinking—induction and deduction. Both of these latter styles are necessary for reasoning throughout the research process. Also explored is the role of the scientific attitude in energizing the conduct of research. Finally, we describe how science terminology has become the specialized language of research. In that section, the building blocks for constructing theory and designing research studies are defined and explained.

Sources of Knowledge

We offer insights on evaluating external secondary data sources in Chapter 10.

Sources of knowledge range from untested opinion to highly systematic styles of thinking. As we go about our daily lives, we rarely think about how we "know" something or where this knowledge originated. From ancient times to the present, researchers have pursued the discovery of *how* we know. In the process of this discovery, researchers depend on an ability to discriminate among information sources. Researchers must, therefore, identify those sources of high quality and high value that will produce the best results for a given situation or decision facing management.

The philosophy of science provides classifications that help us with this task. Thinking styles associated with the scientific method are generally regarded as the preeminent means for securing truth, although that "truth" may not be permanent or enduring. But scientific method is not the only source of our knowledge, as this section explains.

EXHIBIT 2–1 **Styles of Thinking**

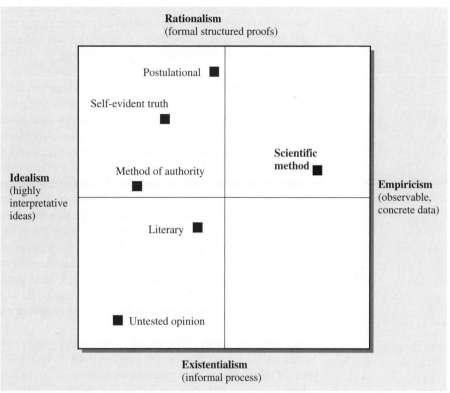

Exhibit 2–1 classifies six of the styles of thinking and locates them from the stand-point of logic.[1]

- Untested opinion
- Self-evident truth
- Method of authority
- Literary
- Scientific method
- Postulational

The axes, with end points of empiricism and rationalism, orient us. The horizontal axis ranges from a highly idealistic interpretation on one end to empiricism on the other. **Empiricism** is said "to denote observations and propositions based on sensory experience and/or derived from such experience by methods of inductive logic, including mathematics and statistics."[2] Empiricists attempt to describe, explain, and make predictions by relying on information gained through observation. This book is fundamentally concerned with empiricism—with the design of procedures to collect factual information about hypothesized relationships that can be used to decide if a particular understanding of a problem and its possible solution are correct.

In Exhibit 2–1, the vertical axis is used to represent knowledge obtained through inductive, empirical approaches or through theoretical means that are based in deductive reasoning. At one end of the vertical axis is **rationalism,** where reasoning or applying judgment is a primary source of knowledge. Rationalism differs from empiricism in that rationalists believe all knowledge can be deduced from known laws or basic truths of nature (for example, gravity). This is claimed to be possible because underlying laws structure the world logically. From the time of Sir Francis Bacon to the present, adherents of rationalism have maintained that problems are best understood and resolved through formal logic or mathematics. Such efforts, of course, operate independently of observation and data collection.

Untested Opinion   People cling to untested opinion despite contrary evidence. In the indoctrination programs of less enlightened organizations, it is not unusual for new employees to hear, "That's the way we've always done it here"—a remark that confuses entrenchment and habit with efficiency. Most families have an aging relative who holds steadfastly to a conspiracy theory for a memorable world event despite overwhelming contrary evidence. The illogical conclusions of *untested opinion* are captured by Myra's experience with the locals on the firing range. Even in the face of repeated deaths of family members or friends, the locals believed they could retrieve salvageable materials from hypothetically inert bombs. Historically, myth, superstition, and hunch have been serious competitors for scientific thinking. One writer notes that before an event occurs—an event that one is trying to predict or control—myth, superstition, and hunch offer "the reassuring feel of certainty,"[3] though seldom does that feeling of certainty persist after the event is over. Managers will find little to improve their understanding of reality from untested opinion, even though human nature indicates they should be prepared to cope with its use by contemporaries when searching for solutions to management dilemmas.

Self-Evident Truth   The sheriff in the opening vignette illustrates a way of knowing often called the method of *self-evident truth.* It was self-evident to him that people would die no matter what precautions were taken on the arsenal firing range. If citizens didn't die there, then they would die as a result of something else. Death is inevitable; it can be deduced from known laws of nature. But what about propositions that appear reasonable to one person or even to many at any one time but are not true? For example, "Everyone drives on the right side of the road." This "truth" is self-evident only to some of the world's drivers. Other propositions once considered reasonable include: "Women make inferior managers"; "Men of noble birth are natural leaders"; and "Japanese quality practices are universally applicable to U.S. productivity problems." We now dismiss these once self-evident propositions.

These young men are future aeronautical engineers with Boeing. Apply deductive and inductive reasoning to this image and develop your own conclusions concerning what will happen when they send their paper airplanes flying.

Method of Authority   Since not all propositions or assumptions are self-evident, we rely on persons of authority to improve our confidence in our knowledge. Authorities serve as important sources of knowledge but should be judged by integrity, the quality of the evidence they present, and their willingness to present an open and balanced case. Too often authority may depend on status or position rather than on true expertise. Such celebrity authorities, when acting outside their area of expertise, are often wrong. You would be wise to cautiously accept the views of such sources. Even authorities who do meet the standards of integrity, quality evidence, and balance may find their knowledge misapplied: The perennial best-seller by Stephen R. Covey, *The 7 Habits of Highly Successful People,* justly positions Covey as an "authority" on what makes some people succeed where others fail. But when the much-anticipated merger between Hyrum Smith's FranklinQuest (the time management empire) and Covey International didn't execute the assumptions underpinning the seven habits, Covey and Smith were soundly criticized for not being exceptional managers.[4] Recognizing principles of leadership and managing a merger take highly different skills. Although the merger may have Smith and Covey totally out of their comfort zone, this doesn't make the seven habits assumptions untrue or diminish the stature of these men in their respective authority arenas.

Literary Style   This problem-solving approach occupies a viewpoint toward the center of Exhibit 2–1. The literary style of thinking is used in many classic case studies in the social sciences. Case studies play a prominent role in the development of business knowledge; our nation's best graduate business programs use case studies extensively. Portions of anthropology, psychiatry, and clinical sociology also trace their roots to this origin. Abraham Maslow's theory of motivation is one example from psychology that is well known in business. The literary perspective is one where "a person, a movement, or a whole culture is interpreted, but largely in terms of the specific purposes and perspectives of the actors, rather than in terms of the abstract and general categories of the scientist's own explanatory scheme."[5] Because it is difficult to generalize from individual case studies, the literary style of thought restricts our ability to derive generally applicable knowledge or truths.

Scientific Method   Exhibit 2–1 positions the scientific method close to the empirical end of the horizontal axis. The essential tenets of science are:

- Direct observation of phenomena.
- Clearly defined variables, methods, and procedures.
- Empirically testable hypotheses.
- The ability to rule out rival hypotheses.
- Statistical rather than linguistic justification of conclusions.
- The self-correcting process.

The York College example in Chapter 1 illustrates business research that uses the scientific method.

One author notes, "Current scientific methods wed the best aspects of the logic of the rational approach with the observational aspects of the empirical orientation into a cohesive, systematic perspective."[6] The application of previously tested and verifiable procedures—the ability to detonate dud bombs with active bombs dropped from fighter planes—solved Myra's dilemma with unexploded bombs.

Postulational Style   Competing styles of thinking influence research directions in business just as they do throughout the social and behavioral sciences. The *postulational* style can be found in the upper portion of Exhibit 2–1. Studies in operations research and marketing are often postulational. For example, many firms run computer simulations of their market before a product rollout. These might examine different pricing levels or manufacturing output levels designed to optimize profitability. One goal of this perspective is to reduce the object of study to mathematical, formal terms. These terms, called *postulates,* are used to devise theorems that represent logical proofs. The objective is to deduce a mathematical model that may account for any phenomenon having similar form.

There is no single best perspective, only preferred perspectives, from which to view reality or do science. The range of available styles of thinking offers many frameworks to confront the diverse problems of business. Useful knowledge abounds; one should simply be aware of the vantage point selected to find information and the strengths and weaknesses of that position.

The Thought Process: Reasoning

Scientific inquiry has been described as a puzzle-solving activity.[7] For the researcher, puzzles are solvable problems that may be clarified or resolved through reasoning. In the opening scene of *The Sign of the Four,* Sir Arthur Conan Doyle uses a conversation between Sherlock Holmes and Dr. Watson to demonstrate the importance of precise reasoning and careful observation in the solving of puzzles and the unraveling of mysteries. Watson provides the test by handing Holmes a watch and asking him to venture an opinion on the character or habits of the late owner. Sherlock Holmes's fans are not disappointed in the outcome. After a few moments' examination, Holmes correctly infers the watch belonged to Watson's careless and untidy elder brother, a man who inherited wealth, treated his prospects foolishly, and died a drunkard. The speed of the conclusion is startling, but the trail of his reasoning process from small facts to inductions and on to conclusions, which he confirms with Watson, is a common thought process for detectives, scientists, and puzzle solvers.

Every day we reason with varying degrees of success and communicate our message, called meaning, in ordinary language or, in special cases, in symbolic, logical form. Our meanings are conveyed through one of two types of discourse: exposition or argument. *Exposition* consists of statements that describe without attempting to explain. *Argument* allows us to explain, interpret, defend, challenge, and explore meaning. Two types of argument of great importance to research are deduction and induction.

Deduction

Deduction is a form of inference that purports to be conclusive—the conclusion must necessarily follow from the reasons given. These reasons are said to *imply the conclusion* and *represent a proof.* This is a much stronger and different bond between reasons and conclusions than is found with induction. For a deduction to be correct, it must be both *true* and *valid:*

- Premises (reasons) given for the conclusion must agree with the real world (true).

- The conclusion must necessarily follow from the premises (valid).

A deduction is valid if it is impossible for the conclusion to be false if the premises are true. Logicians have established rules by which one can judge whether a deduction is valid. Conclusions are not logically justified if one or more premises are untrue or the argument form is invalid. A conclusion may still be a true statement, but for reasons other than those given. For example, consider the following simple deduction:

All regular employees can be trusted not to steal.	(Premise 1)
John is a regular employee.	(Premise 2)
John can be trusted not to steal.	(Conclusion)

If we believe that John can be trusted, we might think this is a sound deduction. But this conclusion cannot be accepted as a sound deduction unless the argument form is valid and the premises are true. In this case, the form is valid, and premise 2 can be easily confirmed. However, many may challenge the sweeping premise that "All regular employees can be trusted not to steal." While we may believe John will not steal, such a conclusion is a sound deduction only if both premises are accepted as true. If one premise fails the acceptance test, then the conclusion is not a sound deduction. This is so even if we still have great confidence in John's honesty. Our conclusion, in this case, must be based on our confidence in John as an individual rather than on a general premise that all regular employees are honest.

As researchers, we may not recognize how much we use deduction to reason out the implications of various acts and conditions. For example, in planning a survey, we might reason as follows:

Inner-city household interviewing is especially difficult and expensive.	(Premise 1)
This survey involves substantial inner-city household interviewing.	(Premise 2)
The interviewing in this survey will be especially difficult and expensive.	(Conclusion)

On reflection, it should be apparent that a conclusion that results from deduction is, in a sense, already "contained in" its premises.[8]

Induction

Inductive argument is radically different. There is no such strength of relationship between reasons and conclusions in **induction.** To induce is to draw a conclusion from one or more particular facts or pieces of evidence. The conclusion explains the facts, and the facts support the conclusion. To illustrate, suppose your firm spends $1 million on a regional promotional campaign and sales do not increase. This is a fact—sales did not increase during or after the promotional campaign. Under such circumstances, we ask, "Why didn't sales increase?"

One likely answer to this question is a conclusion that the promotional campaign was poorly executed. This conclusion is an induction because we know from experience that regional sales should go up during a promotional event. Also we know that if the promotion is poorly executed, sales will not increase. The nature of induction, however, is that the conclusion is only a hypothesis. It is one explanation, but there are others that fit the facts just as well. For example, each of the following hypotheses might explain why sales did not increase.

- Regional retailers did not have sufficient stock to fill customer requests during the promotional period.
- A strike by the employees of our trucking firm prevented stock from arriving in time for the promotion to be effective.
- A category-five hurricane closed all our retail locations in the region for the 10 days during the promotion.

In this example, we see the essential nature of inductive reasoning. The inductive conclusion is an inferential jump beyond the evidence presented—that is, although one conclusion explains the fact of no sales increase, other conclusions also can explain the fact. It may even be that none of the conclusions we advanced correctly explain the failure of sales to increase. By using induction, Myra Wines wasn't convinced that the unexploded "dud" shells were harmless. While the army's conclusion was plausible, certainly at least one other conclusion was as valid before confirmation—that the unexploded shells experienced a delay and would explode upon further handling.

For another example, let's consider the situation of Tracy Nelson, a salesperson at the Square Box Company. Tracy has one of the poorest sales records in the company. Her unsatisfactory performance prompts us to ask the question, "Why is she performing so poorly?" From our knowledge of Tracy's sales practices, the nature of box selling, and the market, we might conclude (hypothesize) that her problem is that she makes too few sales calls per day to build a good sales record. Other hypotheses might also occur to us on the basis of available evidence. Among these hypotheses are the following:

- Tracy's territory does not have the market potential of other territories.
- Tracy's sales-generating skills are so poorly developed that she is not able to close sales effectively.
- Tracy does not have authority to lower prices and her territory has been the scene of intense price-cutting by competitive manufacturers, causing her to lose many sales to competitors.
- Some people just cannot sell boxes, and Tracy is one of those people.

Each of the above hypotheses is an induction we might base on the evidence of Tracy's poor sales record, plus some assumptions or beliefs we hold about her and the selling of boxes. All of them have some chance of being true, but we would probably have more confidence in some than in others. All require further confirmation before they gain our confidence. Confirmation comes with more evidence. The task of research is largely to (1) determine the nature of the evidence needed to confirm or reject hypotheses and (2) design methods by which to discover and measure this other evidence.

Combining Induction and Deduction

Induction and deduction are used in research reasoning in a sequential manner. John Dewey describes this process as the **double movement of reflective thought.**[9] Induction occurs when we observe a fact and ask, "Why is this?" In answer to this question, we advance a tentative explanation (hypothesis). The hypothesis is plausible if it explains the event or condition (fact) that prompted the question. Deduction is the process by which we test whether the hypothesis is capable of explaining the fact. The process is illustrated in Exhibit 2–2:

1. You promote a product but sales don't increase. (Fact$_1$)
2. You ask the question, "Why didn't sales increase?" (Induction)
3. You infer a conclusion (hypothesis) to answer the question: The promotion was poorly executed. (Hypothesis)
4. You use this hypothesis to conclude (deduce) that the sales will not increase during a poorly executed promotion. You know from experience that ineffective promotion will not increase sales. (Deduction$_1$)

This example, an exercise in circular reasoning, does point out that one must be able to deduce the initiating fact from the hypothesis advanced to explain that fact. A second critical point is also illustrated in this exhibit: To test a hypothesis, one must be able to deduce from it other facts that can then be investigated. This is what classical research

EXHIBIT 2–2   Why Didn't Sales Increase?

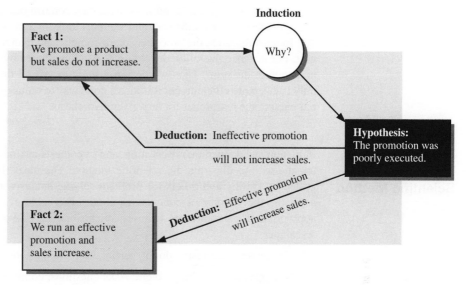

is all about. We must deduce other specific facts or events from the hypothesis and then gather information to see if the deductions are true. In this example, we deduce:

5. A well-executed promotion will result in increased sales. (Deduction$_2$)

6. We run an effective promotion and sales increase. (Fact$_2$)

How would the double movement of reflective thought work when applied to Tracy Nelson's problem? The process is illustrated in Exhibit 2–3. The initial observation (fact$_1$) leads to hypothesis$_1$ that Tracy is lazy. We deduce several other facts from the

EXHIBIT 2–3   Why Is Tracy Nelson's Performance So Poor?

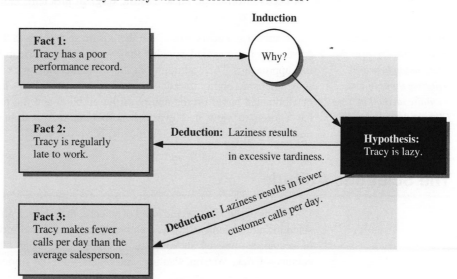

hypothesis. These are shown as fact$_2$ and fact$_3$. We use research to find out if fact$_2$ and fact$_3$ are true. If they are found to be true, they confirm our hypothesis. If they are not, our hypothesis is not confirmed, and we must look for another explanation.

In most research, the process is more complicated than these simple examples suggest. For instance, we often develop multiple hypotheses by which to explain the phenomenon in question. Then we design a study to test all the hypotheses at once. Not only is this more efficient, but it is also a good way to reduce the attachment (and potential bias) of the researcher for any given hypothesis.

Reflective Thought and the Scientific Method

Induction and deduction, observation, and hypothesis testing can be combined in a systematic way to illustrate the scientific method. The ideas that follow, originally suggested by Dewey and others for problem-solving analysis, represent one approach to assessing the validity of conclusions about observable events. They are particularly appropriate for researchers whose conclusions depend on empirical data.[10] The researcher

1. Encounters a curiosity, doubt, barrier, suspicion, or obstacle.

2. Struggles to state the problem: Asks questions, contemplates existing knowledge, gathers facts, and moves from an emotional to an intellectual confrontation with the problem.

3. Proposes hypotheses to explain the facts that are believed to be logically related to the problem.

4. Deduces outcomes or consequences of the hypotheses: Attempts to discover what happens if the results are in the opposite direction of that predicted or if the results support the expectations.

5. Formulates several rival hypotheses.

6. Devises and conducts a crucial empirical test with various possible outcomes, each of which selectively excludes one or more hypotheses.

7. Draws a conclusion, an inductive inference, based on acceptance or rejection of the hypotheses.

8. Feeds information back into the original problem, modifying it according to the strength of the evidence.

We detail the research process that explores the relationship between reflective thought and scientific method in Chapter 3.

Eminent scientists who claim there is no such thing as the scientific method, or if it exists, it is not revealed by what they write, caution researchers about using template-like approaches. Their admonitions are well taken, and we would add that the ideas presented here are highly interdependent, are not sequentially fixed, and may be expanded or eliminated based on the nature of the problem and the perspective from which one has chosen to view it. Nevertheless, beginning researchers should understand that research, when conducted scientifically, is a process.

The Scientific Attitude

If the tools of thinking are the mind of science, then the scientific attitude is the spirit. The scientific attitude unleashes the creative drive that makes discovery possible. The portraits of scientists involved in some of the most spectacular discoveries of the twentieth century—Crick, Watson, Pauling, and others—are the stories of imagination, intuition, curiosity, suspicion, anguish, the rage to know, and self-doubt. But these predispositions are not the exclusive province of the natural scientist. All researchers exercise imagination in the discovery process, in capturing the most essential aspect of the problem, or in selecting a technique that reveals a phenomenon in its most natural state.

Curiosity in its many forms characterized the persistent efforts to understand the relationship between productivity and worker satisfaction. Starting first with the Hawthorne studies, it was thought that employee satisfaction improved productivity.[11] Later research did not bear this out, and the second general conclusion was that satisfaction and productivity were not directly connected since the relationship was affected by a number of other variables. Currently, we believe that satisfaction is sought for reasons not consistently related to work, and productivity varies from simple to challenging tasks. Many contextual variables are now viewed as essential for understanding the original relationship.[12] Over 30 years elapsed while this research was being sorted out. The curiosity to ask questions compounded by the passion not to let go and a discomfort with existing answers sustained these researchers through periods of failure and self-doubt.

Thomas Kuhn, writing in *The Structure of Scientific Revolutions,* has also addressed the question of why scientists attack their problems with such passion and devotion. Scientific inquiry, he says, attracts people for a variety of motives. "Among them are the desire to be useful, the excitement of exploring new territory, the hope of finding order, and the drive to test established knowledge."[13] From applied researchers addressing a manager's need to academicians fascinated with the construction of grand theories, the attitude of science is the enabling spirit of discovery.

Understanding Theory: Components and Connections

Later in this chapter and in Part III we will use **variables** *and* **hypotheses** *to make statements and propose tests for the relationships that our research questions express.*

When we do research, we seek to know *what is* in order to understand, explain, and predict phenomena. We might want to answer the question, "What will be the employee reaction to the new flexible work schedule?" or "Why did the stock market price surge higher when all normal indicators suggested it would go down?" When dealing with such questions, we must agree on definitions. Which employees? What kind of reaction? What are the normal indicators? These questions require the use of concepts, constructs, and definitions. These components, or building blocks, of theory are reviewed in the next few sections.

Concepts

To understand and communicate information about objects and events, there must be a common ground on which to do it. Concepts serve this purpose. A **concept** is a generally accepted collection of meanings or characteristics associated with certain events, objects, conditions, situations, and behaviors. Classifying and categorizing objects or events that have common characteristics beyond any single observation create concepts. When you think of a spreadsheet or a warranty card, what comes to mind is not a single instance but collected memories of all spreadsheets and warranty cards abstracted to a set of specific and definable characteristics.

We abstract such meanings from reality and use words as labels to designate them. For example, we see a man passing and identify that he is running, walking, skipping, crawling, or hopping. These movements all represent concepts. We also have abstracted certain visual elements by which we identify that the moving object is an adult male, rather than an adult female or a truck or a horse. We use large numbers of concepts daily in our thinking, conversing, and other activities.

S N A P S H O T

ITE: Raising Questions about Danger

State Farm recently published its second list of the most dangerous intersections in the United States. The nation's largest auto insurer has been studying its proprietary accident claims data for detailed patterns since 1998. In that first year it discovered that one-third of all accidents involving State Farm–insured motorists took place in intersections. Prior studies in Michigan, Canada, and Australia indicated that low-cost changes could improve the safety of motorists in intersections—moving or improving signs or remounting traffic lights, improving light timing, and making lane markings more visible. For its study, State Farm analysts define an intersection as two roadways that intersect, excluding overpass crossings and interstate ramps. In the first study, a dangerous intersection was defined as one with the most auto crashes during the preceding year, with accident severity not a criterion. Estimated crashes were determined by weighting actual crash claims made to State Farm by a factor based upon the percentage of cars insured by State Farm in the metropolitan area where the intersection is located.

One organization, the Institute of Transportation Engineers (ITE), while complimenting the proactive stance of the auto insurer, has taken exception to the research methodology of State Farm in publishing its third annual list. In a press release, ITE has expressed its concern that "the State Farm Dangerous Intersection Initiative fails to adequately recognize ongoing efforts by the traffic engineering professionals in these jurisdictions." By selecting intersections based on its internal data of State Farm motorists and ignoring publicly available traffic volume and police accident data, ITE claims that State Farm's list is inaccurate. ITE further adds that engineers often do not have the budgets to implement the desired solutions even when they know a traffic hazard exists. How do the concepts and constructs measured here influence the intersections on the list? What is the nature of the conflicts here between researcher and information user?

www.ite.org

www.statefarm.com

Sources of Concepts   Concepts that are in frequent and general use have been developed over time through shared usage. We have acquired them through personal experience. If we lived in another society, we would hold many of the same concepts (though in a different language). Some concepts, however, are unique to a particular culture and are not readily translated into another language.

Ordinary concepts make up the bulk of communication even in research, but we often run into difficulty trying to deal with an uncommon concept or a newly advanced idea. One way to handle this problem is to borrow from other languages (for example, *gestalt*) or to borrow from other fields (for example from art, *impressionism*). The concept of gravitation is borrowed from physics and used in marketing in an attempt to explain why people shop where they do. The concept of distance is used in attitude measurement to describe degree of variability between the attitudes of two or more persons. Threshold is used effectively to describe a concept in perception studies; velocity is a term borrowed by the economist from the physicist.

Borrowing is not always practical, so we sometimes need to adopt new meanings for words (make a word cover a different concept) or develop new labels (words) for concepts. The recent broadening of the meaning of *model* is an example of the first instance; the development of concepts such as sibling and status-stress are examples of the second. When we adopt new meanings or develop new labels, we begin to develop a specialized jargon or terminology. Researchers in medicine, the physical sciences, and related fields frequently use terms that are unintelligible to outsiders. Jargon no doubt contributes to efficiency of communication among specialists, but it excludes everyone else.

Importance to Research   Concepts are basic to all thought and communication, yet in everyday use we pay little attention to the problems encountered in their use. In research, special problems grow out of the need for concept precision and inventiveness. We design hypotheses using concepts. We devise measurement concepts by which to test these hypothetical statements. We gather data using these measurement concepts. We may even invent new concepts to express ideas. The success of research hinges on (1) how clearly we conceptualize and (2) how well others understand the concepts we use. For example, when we survey people on the question of tax equity, the questions we use need to tap faithfully the attitudes of the respondents. Attitudes are abstract, yet we must attempt to measure them using carefully selected concepts.

The challenge is to develop concepts that others will clearly understand. We might, for example, ask respondents for an estimate of their family's total income. This may seem to be a simple, unambiguous concept, but we will receive varying and confusing answers unless we restrict or narrow the concept by specifying:

- Time period, such as weekly, monthly, or annually.
- Before or after income taxes.
- For head of family only or for all family members.
- For salary and wages only or also for dividends, interest, and capital gains.
- Income in kind, such as free rent, employee discounts, or food stamps.

Problems in Concept Use   The use of concepts presents difficulties that are accentuated in a research setting. First, people differ in the meanings they include under any particular label. This problem is so great in normal human communication that we often see cases where people use the same language but do not understand each other. We might all agree to the meaning of such concepts as dog, table, electric light, money, employee, and wife. We may encounter more difficulties, however, when we communicate concepts such as household, retail transaction, dwelling unit, regular user, debit, and wash sale. Still more challenging are concepts that are familiar but not well understood, such as leadership, motivation, personality, social class, and fiscal policy. For example, personality has been defined in the research literature in more than 400 ways.[14] Although this may seem extreme, writers are not able to express the complexity of the determinants of personality and its attributes (e.g., authoritarianism, risk taking, locus of control, achievement orientation, and dogmatism) in a fashion that produces agreement.

The concepts described represent progressive levels of abstraction—that is, the degree to which the concept does or does not have objective referents. Table is an objective concept in that we can point to tables and we can conjure up in our mind images of tables. An abstraction like personality is much more difficult to visualize. Such abstract concepts are often called constructs.

Constructs

As used in research in the social sciences, a **construct** is an image or idea specifically invented for a given research and/or theory-building purpose. We build constructs by combining the simpler concepts, especially when the idea or image we intend to convey is not directly subject to observation. When Jason and Myra tackle MindWriter's research study, they will struggle with the construct of a satisfied service customer.

Concepts and constructs are easily confused. Here's an example to clarify the differences involved. A human resource analyst at CadSoft, an architectural software company that employs technical writers for its product manuals, is analyzing task attributes of a

EXHIBIT 2–4   **Constructs Composed of Concepts in a Job Redesign Example**

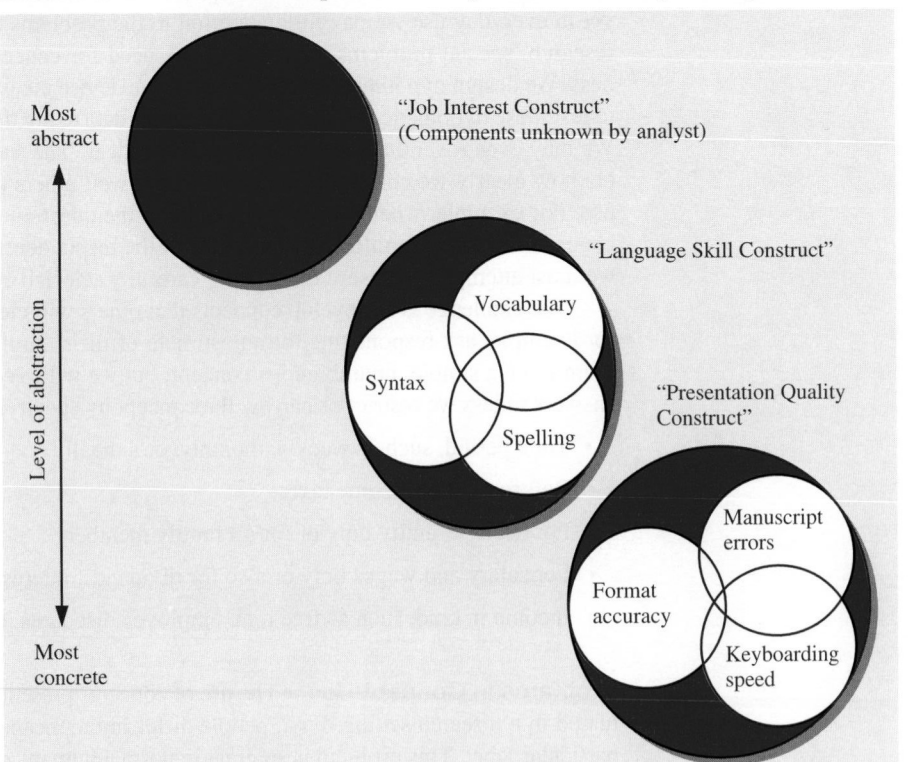

job in need of redesign. She knows the job description for a technical writer consists of three components: presentation quality, language skill, and job interest. Her job analysis reveals more specific characteristics.

Exhibit 2–4 illustrates some of the concepts and constructs she is dealing with. The concepts at the bottom of the exhibit (format accuracy, manuscript errors, and keyboarding speed) are the most concrete and easily measured. We can observe keyboarding speed, for example, and even with crude measures agree on what constitutes slow and fast keyboarders. Keyboarding speed is one concept in the group that defines a construct that the human resource analyst calls "presentation quality." Presentation quality is a nonexistent entity, a "constructed type." It is used to communicate the combination of meanings presented by the three concepts. The analyst uses it as a label for the concepts she has found empirically to be related.

Concepts in the next level in Exhibit 2–4 are vocabulary, syntax, and spelling. The analyst also finds them to be related. They form a construct that she calls "language skill." She has chosen this term because these three concepts together define the language requirement in the job description. Language skill is placed at a higher level of abstraction in the exhibit because two of the concepts that comprise it, vocabulary and syntax, are more difficult to observe and their measures are more complex.

The analyst has not yet measured the last construct, "job interest." It is the least observable and most difficult to measure. It will likely be composed of numerous concepts—many of which will be quite abstract. Researchers sometimes refer to such entities as *hypothetical constructs* because they can be inferred only from the data; thus, they are presumed to exist but must await further testing. If research ultimately shows the concepts and constructs in this example to be interrelated, and if the propositions that specify the connections can be supported, the researcher will have the beginning of a **conceptual scheme.** In graphic form it would depict the relationships among the knowledge and skill requirements necessary to clarify the job redesign effort.

Definitions

Confusion about the meaning of concepts can destroy a research study's value without the researcher or client even knowing it. If words have different meanings to the parties involved, then they are not communicating on the same wavelength. Definitions are one way to reduce this danger.

Researchers must struggle with two types of definitions: dictionary definitions and operational definitions. In the more familiar dictionary definition, a concept is defined with a synonym. For example, a customer is defined as a patron; a patron, in turn, is defined as a customer or client of an establishment; a client is defined as one who employs the services of any professional . . . , also, loosely, a patron of any shop.[15] These circular definitions may be adequate for general communication but not for research. In research, we must measure concepts and constructs, and this requires more rigorous definitions.

What operational definition did the army use for "dud" ordnance? What operational definition did Myra use?

Operational Definitions   An **operational definition** is a definition stated in terms of specific testing or measurement criteria. These terms must have empirical referents (that is, we must be able to count, measure, or in some other way gather the information through our senses). Whether the object to be defined is physical (e.g., a machine tool) or highly abstract (e.g., achievement motivation), the definition must specify characteristics and how they are to be observed. The specifications and procedures must be so clear that any competent person using them would classify the objects in the same way.

During her military service, Myra observed numerous shells that, when fired, did not explode on impact. She knew the army applied the operational definition "a shell that does not explode on impact" to the construct *dud shell.* But if asked, Myra would have applied the operational term *dud shell* only to "a shell that, once fired from a cannon, could not be made to explode by any amount of manipulation, human or mechanical." Based on her operational definition, the town's residents rarely encountered "duds" during their excursions onto the firing range.

For another example, suppose college undergraduates are to be classified by class. No one has much trouble understanding such terms as *freshman, sophomore,* and so forth. But the task may not be that simple if you must determine which students fall in each class. To do this, you need operational definitions.

Operational definitions may vary, depending on your purpose and the way you choose to measure them. Here are two different situations requiring different definitions of the same concepts.

1. You conduct a survey among students and wish to classify their answers by their class levels. You merely ask them to report their class status, and you record it. In this case, class is freshman, sophomore, junior, or senior and you accept the answer each respondent gives as correct. This is a rather casual definition process but nonetheless an operational definition. It is probably adequate in this case even though some of the respondents report inaccurately.

2. You make a tabulation of the class level of students for the university registrar's annual report. The measurement task here is more critical, so your operational definition needs to be more precise. You decide to define class levels in terms of semester hours of credit completed by the end of the spring semester and recorded in each student's record in the registrar's office:

Freshman	Fewer than 30 hours' credit
Sophomore	30 to 59 hours' credit
Junior	60 to 89 hours' credit
Senior	More than 90 hours' credit

Those examples deal with relatively concrete concepts, but operational definitions are even more critical for treating abstract ideas. Suppose one tries to measure a construct called "organizational commitment." We may intuitively understand what this means, but to attempt to measure it among workers is difficult. We would probably develop a commitment scale, or we may use a scale that has already been developed and validated by someone else. This scale then operationally defines the construct.

While operational definitions are needed in research, they also present some problems. One ever-present danger is thinking that a concept and its operational definition are the same thing. We forget that our definitions provide only limited insight into what a concept or construct really is. In fact, the operational definition may be quite narrow and not at all similar to what someone else would use when researching the same topic. When measurements by two different definitions correlate well, the correlation supports the view that each definition adequately measures the same concept.

The problem of operational definitions is particularly difficult when dealing with constructs. Constructs have few empirical referents by which to confirm that an operational definition really measures what we hope it does. The correlation between two different definition formulations strengthens the belief that we are measuring the same thing. On the other hand, if there is little or no correlation, it may mean we are tapping several different partial meanings of a construct. It may also mean one or both of the operational definitions are not true labels.

Whether you use a definitional or operational definition, its purpose in research is basically the same—to provide an understanding and measurement of concepts. We may need to provide operational definitions for only a few critical concepts, but these will almost always be the definitions used to develop the relationships found in hypotheses and theories.

Variables

Scientists operate at both theoretical and empirical levels. At the theoretical level, there is a preoccupation with identifying constructs and their relations to propositions and theory. At this level, constructs cannot, as we've said before, be observed. At the empirical level, where the propositions are converted to hypotheses and testing occurs, the scientist is likely to be dealing with variables. In practice, the term **variable** is used as a synonym for *construct* or the property being studied. In this context, a variable is a symbol to which we assign numerals or values.[16]

The numerical value assigned to a variable is based on the variable's properties. For example, some variables, said to be *dichotomous,* have only two values, reflecting the presence or absence of a property: employed-unemployed or male-female have two values, generally 0 and 1. When Myra Wines observed the cannon shells, they were exploded or unexploded. Variables also take on values representing added categories, such as the demographic variables of race or religion. All such variables that produce data that fit into categories are said to be *discrete,* since only certain values are possible. An automotive variable, for example, where "Chevrolet" is assigned a 5 and "Honda" is assigned a 6, provides no option for a 5.5.

Income, temperature, age, or a test score are examples of *continuous* variables. These variables may take on values within a given range or, in some cases, an infinite set. Your test score may range from 0 to 100, your age may be 23.5, and your present income could be $35,000.

Independent and Dependent Variables

Researchers are most interested in relationships among variables. For example, does a participative leadership style (independent variable) influence job satisfaction or performance (dependent variables) or can a superior's modeling of ethical behavior influence the behavior of the subordinate? Exhibit 2–5 lists some terms that have become synonyms for **independent variable** and **dependent variable.** It is important to remember there are no preordained variables waiting to be discovered "out there" that are automatically assigned to one category or the other. As one writer notes:

> There's nothing very tricky about the notion of independence and dependence. But there is something tricky about the fact that the relationship of independence and dependence is

EXHIBIT 2–5 Defining Independent and Dependent Variables

Independent Variable	Dependent Variable
Presumed cause	Presumed effect
Stimulus	Response
Predicted from . . .	Predicted to . . .
Antecedent	Consequence
Manipulated	Measured outcome
Predictor	Criterion

a figment of the researcher's imagination until demonstrated convincingly. Researchers **hypothesize** relationships of independence and dependence: They invent them, and then they try by reality testing to see if the relationships actually work out that way.[17]

Moderating Variables   In each relationship, there is at least one independent variable (IV) and a dependent variable (DV). It is normally hypothesized that in some way the IV "causes" the DV to occur. For simple relationships, all other variables are considered extraneous and are ignored. Myra sets out to discover why the locals are scavenging salvageable materials from the unexploded cannon shells. She hypothesizes:

> Locals' conviction that predetermined fate dictates time and place of death (IV) leads them to undertake life-threatening behaviors—scavenging on the firing range (DV).

> If locals could be warned of the danger (IV) of their actions, they would change their nocturnal behavior (DV).

The sheriff ultimately convinces Myra that only a change in army procedure will bring about the decline in shell-induced deaths caused by the nocturnal scavenging.

In a typical office, we might be interested in a study of the effect of the four-day workweek on office productivity and hypothesize the following:

> The introduction of the four-day workweek (IV) will lead to increased office productivity per worker-hour (DV).

In actual study situations, however, such a simple one-on-one relationship needs to be conditioned or revised to take other variables into account. Often one uses another type of explanatory variable of value here—the moderating variable (MV). A **moderating variable** is a second independent variable that is included because it is believed to have a significant contributory or contingent effect on the originally stated IV-DV relationship. For example, one might hypothesize that

> The introduction of the four-day workweek (IV) will lead to higher productivity (DV), especially among younger workers (MV).

In this case, there is a differential pattern of relationship between the four-day week and productivity that is the result of age differences among the workers.

Whether a given variable is treated as an independent or as a moderating variable depends on the hypothesis. If you were interested in studying the impact of length of workweek, you would make the length of week the IV. If you were focusing on the relationship of age of worker and productivity, you might use workweek length as a moderating variable. If Myra had been a reporter (rather than an army reserve captain) viewing the local death and injury statistics, she might have arrived at a different hypothesis:

> The loss of mining jobs (IV) leads to acceptance of higher-risk behaviors to earn a family-supporting income—race-car driving or nocturnal scavenging (DV)—especially due to the proximity of the firing range (MV) and the limited education (MV) of the residents.

Extraneous Variables   An almost infinite number of **extraneous variables** (EV) exists that might conceivably affect a given relationship. Some can be treated as independent or moderating variables, but most must either be assumed or excluded from the study. Fortunately, the infinite number of variables has little or no effect on a given situation. Most can be safely ignored. Others may be important, but their impact occurs in such a random fashion as to have little effect.

Using the example of the effect of the four-day workweek, one would normally think the imposition of a local sales tax, the election of a new mayor, a three-day rainy spell, and thousands of similar events and conditions would have little effect on work-week and office productivity.

However, there may be other extraneous variables to consider as possible confounding variables to our hypothesized IV-DV relationship. For example, Myra might think that level of education as it impacts job skills might have an impact on the selection of income-producing activity by the locals. This notion might lead to our introducing an extraneous variable as the **control:**

> Among residents with less than a high school education (EV-control), the loss of high-income mining jobs (IV) leads to acceptance of higher-risk behaviors to earn a family-supporting income—race-car driving or nocturnal scavenging (DV)—especially due to the proximity of the firing range (MV).

Alternatively, one might think that the *kind of work* being done would have an effect on any workweek length impact on office productivity. This might lead to our introducing a control as follows:

> In routine office work (EV-control), the introduction of a four-day workweek (IV) will lead to higher productivity (DV), especially among younger workers (MV).

In our office example, we would attempt to control for type of work by studying the effect of the four-day workweek within groups performing different types of work. In a similar way, Myra would attempt to control for employable job skills by studying the education patterns and prior employment of the scavengers who lost their lives.

Intervening Variables   The variables mentioned with regard to causal relationships are concrete and clearly measurable; they can be seen, counted, or observed in some way. Sometimes, however, one may not be completely satisfied by the explanations they give. Thus, while we may recognize that a four-day workweek results in higher productivity, we might think this is not the full explanation—that workweek length affects some intervening variable, which, in turn, results in higher productivity. An intervening variable is a conceptual mechanism through which the IV and MV might affect the DV. The **intervening variable** (IVV) may be defined as "that factor which theoretically affects the observed phenomenon but cannot be seen, measured, or manipulated; its effect must be inferred from the effects of the independent and moderator variables on the observed phenomenon."[18]

In the case of the workweek hypothesis, one might view the intervening variable (IVV) to be job satisfaction, giving a hypothesis such as:

> The introduction of a four-day workweek (IV) will lead to higher productivity (DV) by increasing job satisfaction (IVV).

Here are additional examples illustrating the relationships involving independent, moderating, controlled extraneous, and dependent variables. The management of a bank wishes to study the effect of promotion on savings. It might advance the following hypothesis:

> A promotion campaign (IV) will increase savings activity (DV), especially when free prizes are offered (MV), but chiefly among smaller savers (EV-control). The results come from enhancing the motivation to save (IVV).

Or suppose you are studying a situation involving the causes of defective parts production. You might hypothesize the following:

> Changing to worker self-inspection (IV) will reduce the number of defective parts (DV) when the part can be identified with its producer (MV) in electronic assembly work (EV-control), by stimulating the worker's sense of responsibility (IVV).

And, finally, Myra's proposal to the army hypothesizes that

> Marking "dud" shells with kerosene lanterns for same-evening detonation (IV) will reduce nocturnal scavenging (DV) among poorly educated local residents (MV) by eliminating the profit motive for such behavior (IVV).

Propositions and Hypotheses

A checklist for developing strong hypotheses is presented in Exhibit 2–6.

We define a **proposition** as a statement about concepts that may be judged as true or false if it refers to observable phenomena. When a proposition is formulated for empirical testing, we call it a **hypothesis.** As a declarative statement, a hypothesis is of a tentative and conjectural nature.

Hypotheses have also been described as statements in which we assign variables to cases. A **case** is defined in this sense as the entity or thing the hypothesis talks about. The variable is the characteristic, trait, or attribute that, in the hypothesis, is imputed to the case.[19] For example, we might form the following hypothesis:

> Executive Jones (case) has a higher-than-average achievement motivation (variable).

If our hypothesis were based on more than one case, it would be a *generalization.* For example:

> Executives in Company Z (cases) have a higher-than-average achievement motivation (variable).

Descriptive Hypotheses   Both of the above hypotheses are examples of **descriptive hypotheses.** These are propositions that typically state the existence, size, form, or distribution of some variable. For example:

- In Detroit (case), the October seasonally adjusted unemployment rate (variable) stands at 3.7 percent of the labor force.
- American cities (case) are experiencing budget difficulties (variable).

SNAPSHOT

AbioCor: A New Beat for Damaged Hearts

July 2, 2001, was a red-letter day in biomedical research when Abiomed—a developer, manufacturer, and marketer of medical products—had its AbioCor implantable replacement heart system surgically inserted in a 50-year-old man in Louisville, Kentucky. Thirty days later, the man was joking with nursing and medical staff, taking light exercise, and savoring a bite of cheesecake—even though most of his nutrition was still coming by way of a feeding tube. One member of the surgical team, Dr. Robert Dowling, said, "He was facing death 30 days ago and he knew it and now he is looking forward to life and is happy to be here." The AbioCor, which takes the space vacated by the removal of the patient's heart, is pumping seven liters of blood a minute compared with the two liters the patient's damaged heart could deliver. "Every parameter that we want to look at has gotten better," claimed Dowling. Dr. Laman Gray, Jr., also part of the research team, cau-

tioned, "It is important to remember that this is the first chapter of many volumes that we have still to learn about the use of these devices in humans."

Following a series of animal trials, the FDA granted Abiomed permission to implant up to five AbioCor systems. With only 2,000 heart transplants performed each year, there are up to 100,000 coronary heart disease patients who might be potential recipients of the AbioCor, a device designed for those with less than a 30-day life expectancy who are not eligible for a heart transplant. Assuming government permission, should Abiomed rush into production of its AbioCor system? What reasoning approaches did you use to reach this conclusion? What concepts and constructs are imbedded in this example? What hypotheses could you form from this medical trial?

www.abiomed.com

- Eighty percent of Company Z stockholders (case) favor increasing the company's cash dividend (variable).

- Seventy percent of the high school–educated males (case) scavenge in the army firing range for salvageable metals (variable).

Researchers often use a research question rather than a descriptive hypothesis. Thus, in place of the above hypotheses, we might use the following questions:

- What is the unemployment rate in Detroit?

- Are American cities experiencing budget difficulties?

- Do stockholders of Company Z favor an increased cash dividend?

- Do a majority of high school–educated male residents scavenge in the army firing range for salvageable metals?

Either format is acceptable, but the descriptive hypothesis format has several advantages:

- It encourages researchers to crystallize their thinking about the likely relationships to be found.

- It further encourages them to think about the implications of a supported or rejected finding.

- It is useful for testing statistical significance.

Relational Hypotheses   The research question format is less frequently used with a situation calling for **relational hypotheses.** These are statements that describe a relationship between two variables with respect to some case. For example, "Foreign (variable) cars are perceived by American consumers (case) to be of better quality (variable) than domestic cars." In this instance, the nature of the relationship between the two variables ("country of origin" and "perceived quality") is not specified. Is there only an implication that the variables occur in some predictable relationship, or is one variable somehow responsible for the other? The first interpretation (unspecified relationship) indicates a correlational relationship; the second (predictable relationship) indicates an explanatory, or causal, relationship.

Correlational hypotheses state merely that the variables occur together in some specified manner without implying that one causes the other. Such weak claims are often made when we believe there are more basic causal forces that affect both variables or when we have not developed enough evidence to claim a stronger linkage. Here are three sample correlational hypotheses:

- Young machinists (under 35 years of age) are less productive than those who are 35 years of age or older.

- The height of women's hemlines varies directly with the level of the business cycle.

- People in Atlanta give the president a more favorable rating than do people in St. Louis.

By labeling these as correlational hypotheses, we make no claim that one variable causes the other to change or take on different values. Other researchers, however, may view one or more of these hypotheses as reflecting cause-and-effect relationships.

With **explanatory (causal) hypotheses,** there is an implication that the existence of, or a change in, one variable causes or leads to a change in the other variable. As we noted previously, the causal variable is typically called the independent variable (IV) and the other the dependent variable (DV). *Cause* means roughly to "help make happen." So, the IV need not be the sole reason for the existence of, or change in, the DV. Here are four examples of explanatory hypotheses:

- An increase in family income (IV) leads to an increase in the percentage of income saved (DV).
- Exposure to the company's messages concerning industry problems (IV) leads to more favorable attitudes (DV) by production workers toward the company.
- Loyalty to a particular grocery store (IV) increases the probability of purchasing the private brands (DV) sponsored by that store.
- An increase in the price of salvaged copper wire (IV) leads to an increase in scavenging (DV) on the army firing range.

In proposing or interpreting causal hypotheses, the researcher must consider the direction of influence. In many cases, the direction is obvious from the nature of the variables. Thus, one would assume that family income influences savings rate rather than the reverse case. This also holds true for the army example. Sometimes our ability to identify the direction of influence depends on the research design. In the worker attitude hypothesis, if the exposure to the message clearly precedes the attitude measurement, then the direction of exposure to attitude seems clear. If information about both exposure and attitude were collected at the same time, the researcher might be justified in saying that different attitudes led to selective message perception or nonperception. Store loyalty and purchasing of store brands appear to be interdependent. Loyalty to a store may increase the probability of buying the store's private brands, but satisfaction with the store's private brand may also lead to greater store loyalty.

The Role of the Hypothesis　　In research, a hypothesis serves several important functions:

- It guides the direction of the study.
- It identifies facts that are relevant and those that are not.
- It suggests which form of research design is likely to be most appropriate.
- It provides a framework for organizing the conclusions that result.

A frequent problem in research is the proliferation of interesting information. Unless the researcher curbs the urge to include additional elements, a study can be diluted by trivial concerns that do not answer the basic questions posed by the management dilemma. The virtue of the hypothesis is that, if taken seriously, it limits what shall be studied and what shall not.

　　To consider specifically the role of the hypothesis in determining the direction of the research, suppose we use this:

　　Husbands and wives agree in their perceptions of their respective roles in purchase decisions.

The hypothesis specifies who shall be studied (married couples), in what context they shall be studied (their consumer decision making), and what shall be studied (their individual perceptions of their roles).

　　The nature of this hypothesis and the implications of the statement suggest that the best research design is a communication-based study, probably a survey or interview. We have at this time no other practical means to ascertain perceptions of people except to ask about them in one way or another. In addition, we are interested only in the roles that are assumed in the purchase or consumer decision-making situation. The study should not, therefore, involve itself in seeking information about other types of roles husbands and wives might play. Reflection upon this hypothesis might also reveal that husbands and wives disagree on their perceptions of roles but these differences may be explained in terms of additional variables, such as age, social class, background, personality differences, and other factors not associated with their difference in gender.

What Is a Good Hypothesis?   A good hypothesis should fulfill three conditions:

- Adequacy for its purpose.
- Testable.
- Better than its rivals.

For a descriptive hypothesis, *adequacy for its purpose* means it clearly states the condition, size, or distribution of some variable in terms of values meaningful to the research task. If it is an explanatory hypothesis, it must explain the facts that gave rise to the need for explanation. Using the hypothesis, plus other known and accepted generalizations, one should be able to deduce the original problem condition.

A hypothesis is *testable* if it meets the following conditions.

- It does not require techniques that are unavailable with the present state of the research art.
- It does not require an explanation that defies known physical or psychological laws.
- There are consequences or derivatives that can be deduced for testing purposes.

Generally, a hypothesis is *better than its rivals* if it

- Has a greater range than its rivals.
- Explains more facts than its rivals.
- Explains a greater variety of facts than its rivals.
- Is simple, requiring few conditions or assumptions.

MANAGEMENT

Tip

Three conditions for developing a strong hypothesis are summarized in Exhibit 2–6.

EXHIBIT 2–6   **Checklist for Developing a Strong Hypothesis**

Criteria	Interpretation
Adequacy for its purpose	❑ Does the hypothesis reveal the original problem condition?
	❑ Does the hypothesis clearly identify facts that are relevant and those that are not?
	❑ Does the hypothesis clearly state the condition, size, or distribution of some variable in terms of values meaningful to the research problem (descriptive)?
	❑ Does the hypothesis explain facts that gave rise to the need for explanation (explanatory)?
	❑ Does the hypothesis suggest which form of research design is likely to be most appropriate?
	❑ Does the hypothesis provide a framework for organizing the conclusions that result?
Testable	❑ Does the hypothesis use acceptable techniques?
	❑ Does the hypothesis require an explanation that is plausible given known physical or psychological laws?
	❑ Does the hypothesis reveal consequences or derivatives that can be deduced for testing purposes?
	❑ Is the hypothesis simple, requiring few conditions or assumptions?
Better than its rivals	❑ Does the hypothesis explain more facts than its rivals?
	❑ Does the hypothesis explain a greater variety or scope of facts than its rivals?
	❑ Is the hypothesis one that informed judges would accept as being the most likely?

Theory

Hypotheses play an important role in the development of theory. While theory development has not historically been an important aspect of business research, it is becoming more so.

A person not familiar with research uses the term *theory* to express the opposite of *fact*. In this sense, theory is viewed as being speculative or ivory tower. One hears that Professor X is too theoretical, that managers need to be less theoretical, or that some idea will not work because it is too theoretical. This is an incorrect picture of the relationship between fact and theory to the researcher.

When you are too theoretical, your basis of explanation or decision is not sufficiently attuned to specific empirical conditions. This may be so, but it does not prove that theory and fact are opposites. The truth is that fact and theory are each necessary for the other to be of value. Our ability to make rational decisions, as well as to develop scientific knowledge, is measured by the degree to which we combine fact and theory.

We all operate on the basis of theories we hold. In one sense, theories are the generalizations we make about variables and the relationships among them. We use these generalizations to make decisions and predict outcomes. For example, it is midday and you note that the outside natural light is dimming, dark clouds are moving rapidly in from the west, the breeze is freshening, and the air temperature is cooling. Would your understanding of the relationship among these variables (your weather theory) lead you to predict that something decidedly wet will probably occur in a short time?

Consider a situation where you interview two persons for possible promotion to the position of department manager. Do you have a theory about what characteristics such a person should have? Suppose you interview Ms. A and observe that she answers your questions well, openly, and apparently sincerely. She also expresses thoughtful ideas about how to improve departmental functioning and is articulate in stating her views. Ms. B, on the other hand, is guarded in her comments and reluctant to advance ideas for improvements. She answers questions by saying what "Mr. General Manager wants." She is also less articulate and seems less sincere than Ms. A. You would probably choose Ms. A, based on the way you combine the concepts, definitions, and propositions mentioned into a theory of managerial effectiveness. Your theory of managerial effectiveness, while workable, may not be a good theory because of the variables it has ignored, but it illustrates that we all use theory to guide our decisions, predictions, and explanations.

A **theory** is a set of systematically interrelated concepts, definitions, and propositions that are advanced to explain and predict phenomena (facts). In this sense, we have many theories and use them continually to explain or predict what goes on around us. To the degree that our theories are sound and fit the situation, we are successful in our explanations and predictions. Thus, while a given theory and a set of facts may not fit, they are not opposites. Our challenge is to build a better theory and to be more skillful in fitting theory and fact together.

While researchers note a difference, at times the terms theory and hypothesis are used synonymously. Doing so should not make much practical difference to your applied research.

How theory differs from hypothesis may also cause confusion. In this book, we make the general distinction that the difference between theory and hypothesis is one of *degree of complexity* and *abstraction*. In general, theories tend to be complex, abstract, and involve multiple variables. Hypotheses, on the other hand, tend to be simple, limited-variable propositions involving concrete instances.

Theory and Research   It is important for researchers to recognize the pervasiveness and value of theory. Theory serves us in many useful ways:

- Theory narrows the range of facts we need to study.

- Theory suggests which research approaches are likely to yield the greatest meaning.

- Theory suggests a system for the researcher to impose on data in order to classify them in the most meaningful way.

- Theory summarizes what is known about an object of study and states the uniformities that lie beyond immediate observation.

- Theory can be used to predict further facts that should be found.

Models

The term *model* is used throughout the various fields of business and allied disciplines with little agreement as to its definition. This may be because of the numerous functions, structures, and types of models that exist. However, most definitions agree that models represent phenomena through the use of analogy. A **model** is defined here as a representation of a system that is constructed to study some aspect of that system or the system as a whole. Models differ from theories in that a theory's role is explanation whereas a model's role is representation:

> A model is not an explanation; it is only the structure and/or function of a second object or process. A model is the result of taking the structure or function of one object or process and using that as a model for the second. When the substance, either physical or conceptual, of the second object or process has been projected onto the first, a model has been constructed.[20]

Many ideas about new product adoption, for example, can be traced to rural sociology models. These models describe how information and innovations spread throughout communities or cultures by starting with opinion leaders. The behaviors of leaders are subsequently embraced by the greater society to express homage to the leader and retain social acceptance.

Models may be used for applied or highly theoretical purposes. Almost everyone is familiar with queuing models of services. Banks, post offices, telephone voice-response units, or airport security stations feed patrons to multiple stations starting from a single line. Other models for assembly lines, transportation, and inventory also attempt to solve immediate practical needs. A model to advance a theory of quality of work life, for example, could target employee behavior under conditions of flextime, permanent part-time, job-sharing, and compressed workweek.

Description, explication, and simulation are the three major functions of modeling. Each of these functions is appropriate for applied research or theory building.

Descriptive models	Describe the behavior of elements in a system where theory is inadequate or nonexistent.
Explicative models	Extend the application of well-developed theories or improve our understanding of their key concepts.
Simulation models	Clarify the structural relations of concepts and attempt to reveal the process relations among them.[21]
• **Static**	Represent a system at one point in time.
• **Dynamic**	Represent the evolution of a system over time.

Monte Carlo simulation models are examples of static simulations. They simulate probabilistic processes using random numbers. Redistribution of market share, brand switching, and prediction of future values are examples that benefit from dynamic modeling.

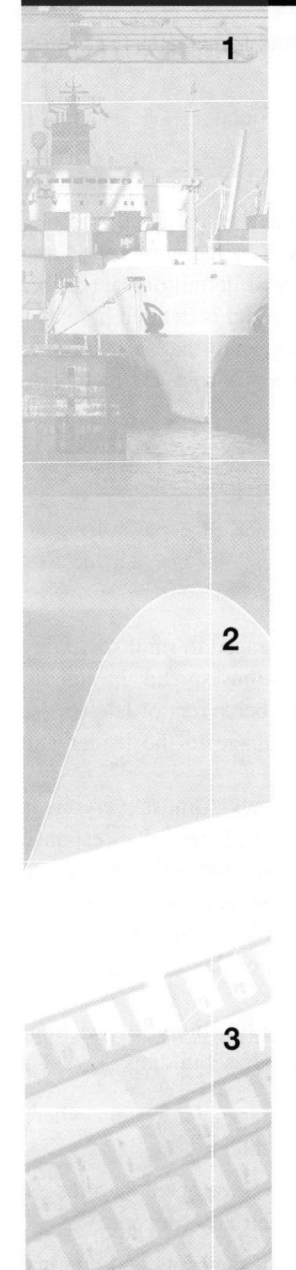

SUMMARY

1
Styles of thinking are perspectives or filters for determining how we view and understand reality. They affect what we accept as truth and specify how rigorously we test the information we receive before endorsing it. Although the scientific method is the preeminent means by which we secure empirical information, it is not the only source of truth. Other styles of thinking also have an apparent and often useful influence on business disciplines and place their imprimatur on the theory-building and problem-solving approaches of those fields.

Scientific inquiry is grounded in the inference process. This process is used for the development and testing of various propositions largely through the double movement of reflective thinking. Reflective thinking consists of sequencing induction and deduction in order to explain inductively (by hypothesis) a puzzling condition. In turn, the hypothesis is used in a deduction of further facts that can be sought to confirm or deny the truth of the hypothesis.

Researchers think of the doing of science (rather than the inspiration for discovery or the scientific attitude) as an orderly process that combines induction, deduction, observation, and hypothesis testing into a set of reflective thinking activities. Although the scientific method consists of neither sequential nor independent stages, the problem-solving process that it reveals provides insight into the way research is conducted.

2
Scientific methods and scientific thinking are based on concepts, the symbols we attach to bundles of meaning that we hold and share with others. We invent concepts to think about and communicate abstractions. We also use higher-level concepts—constructs—for specialized scientific explanatory purposes that are not directly observable. Concepts, constructs, and variables may be defined descriptively or operationally. Operational definitions, which are essential in research, must specify adequately the empirical information needed and how it will be collected. In addition, they must have the proper scope or fit for the research problem at hand.

Concepts and constructs are used at the theoretical levels; variables are used at the empirical level. Variables accept numerals or values for the purpose of testing and measurement. They may be classified as explanatory (independent, dependent, or moderating), extraneous, and intervening.

3
Propositions are of great interest in research because they may be used to assess the truth or falsity of relationships among observable phenomena. When we advance a proposition for testing, we are hypothesizing. A hypothesis describes the relationships between or among variables. A good hypothesis is one that can explain what it claims to explain, is testable, and has greater range, probability, and simplicity than its rivals.

Sets of interrelated concepts, definitions, and propositions that are advanced to explain and predict phenomena are called theories. Models differ from theories in that models are analogies or representations of some aspect of a system or of the system as a whole. Models are used for description, explication, and simulation.

KEY TERMS

case(s) 50
concept 41
conceptual scheme 45
construct 43
deduction 36
double movement of reflective
    thought 38
empiricism 33

hypothesis 50
  correlational 51
  descriptive 50
  explanatory (causal) 51
  relational 51
induction 37
model 55
operational definition 45
proposition 50

rationalism 33
theory 54
variable(s) 47
  control 49
  dependent 47
  extraneous 48
  independent 47
  intervening 49
  moderating 48

EXAMPLES

Company	Scenario	Page
Abiomed	Medical trial for the AbioCor implantable replacement heart system.	50
Army Reserve	Testing weaponry and ammunition.	BRTL, throughout
CadSoft[*]	Job description analysis for technical writers who document architectural software.	43
Institute of Traffic Engineers (ITE)	Contracting information on State Farm's Dangerous Intersection Initiative.	42
Marriott International, Inc.	An international hotel chain seeking an understanding of how hotel guests interpret the term *concierge service*.	45
State Farm Insurance	Data mining that revealed dangerous intersections.	42
York College[*]	A college alumni association studying opportunity in senior housing.	35

[*]Due to the confidential and proprietary nature of most research, the names of some companies have been changed.

DISCUSSION QUESTIONS

Terms in Review

1. Distinguish among the following sets of items, and suggest the significance of each in a research context.

   a. Concept and construct.

   b. Deduction and induction.

   c. Operational definition and dictionary definition.

   d. Concept and variable.

   e. Hypothesis and proposition.

   f. Theory and model.

   g. Scientific method and scientific attitude.

2. Describe the characteristics of the scientific method.

3. What are the differences among the research approaches (and thinking styles) that guide the predominant kinds of studies done in operations research, marketing, finance, and/or organizational behavior?

4. Here are some terms commonly found in a management setting. Are they concepts or constructs? Give two different operational definitions for each.

   a. First-line supervisor.

   b. Employee morale.

   c. Assembly line.

   d. Overdue account.

   e. Line management.

   f. Leadership.

   g. Price-earnings ratio.

   h. Union democracy.

   i. Ethical standards.

5. In your company's management development program, there was a heated discussion between some people who claimed, "Theory is impractical and thus no good," and others who claimed, "Good theory is the most practical approach to problems." What position would you take and why?

6. An automobile manufacturer observes the demand for its brand increasing as per capita income increases. Sales increases also follow low interest rates, which ease credit conditions. Buyer purchase behavior is seen to be dependent on age and gender. Other factors influencing sales appear to fluctuate almost randomly (competitor advertising, competitor dealer discounts, introductions of new competitive models).

   a. If sales and per capita income are positively related, classify all variables as dependent, independent, moderating, extraneous, or intervening.

   b. Comment on the utility of a model based on the hypothesis.

Making Research Decisions

7. You observe the following condition: "Our female sales representatives have lower customer defections than do our male sales representatives."

   a. Propose the concepts and constructs you might use to study this phenomenon.

   b. How might any of these concepts and/or constructs be related to explanatory hypotheses?

8. You are the office manager of a large firm. Your company prides itself on its high-quality customer service. Lately complaints have surfaced that an increased number of incoming calls are being misrouted or dropped. Yesterday, when passing by the main reception area, you noticed the receptionist fiddling with his hearing aid. In the process, a call came in and would have gone unanswered if not for your intervention. This particular receptionist had earned an unsatisfactory review three months earlier for tardiness. Your inclination is to urge this 20-year employee to retire or to fire him, if retirement is rejected, but you know the individual is well-liked and seen as a fixture in the company.

   a. Pose several hypotheses that might account for dropped or misrouted incoming calls.

   b. Using the double movement of reflective thought, show how you would test these hypotheses.

9. The Institute of Transportation Engineers, a nationwide trade association with thousands of members, was dissatisfied with the way that State Farm arrived at its Dangerous Intersection list.

   a. If ITE were to conduct a study of its own, what constructs and concepts would ITE define differently?

b. What hypotheses would ITE formulate to guide its version of the dangerous intersection study?

Bringing Research to Life

10. Identify and classify all the variables in the army's dud-shell research.

11. What was Myra's hypothesis for the army's dud-shell research? What was the army's hypothesis?

From Concept to Practice

12. Using Exhibits 2–2 and 2–3 as your guides, graph the inductions and deductions in the following statements. If there are gaps, supply what is needed to make them complete arguments.

a. Repeated studies indicate that economic conditions vary with—and lag 6 to 12 months behind—the changes in the national money supply. Therefore, we may conclude the money supply is the basic economic variable.

b. Research studies show that heavy smokers have a higher rate of lung cancer than do non-smokers; therefore, heavy smoking causes lung cancer.

c. Show me a person who goes to church regularly, and I will show you a reliable worker.

WWW Exercises

Visit our website for Internet exercises related to this chapter at
www.mhhe.com/business/cooper8

REFERENCE NOTES

1. The title of Exhibit 2–1 and the section "Styles of Thinking" is borrowed from Abraham Kaplan, *The Conduct of Inquiry* (San Francisco: Chandler, 1964), pp. 259–62. The axes and the positions of C. W. Churchman's inquiring systems are based on the work of I. I. Mitroff and R. O. Mason, "Business Policy and Metaphysics: Some Philosophical Considerations," *Academy of Management Review* 7 (1982), pp. 361–71. The locations of the other philosophical viewpoints in the exhibit are approximations.

2. P. McC. Miller and M. J. Wilson, eds., *A Dictionary of Social Sciences Methods* (New York: Wiley, 1983), p. 27. Also see Benjamin B. Wolman, ed., *Dictionary of Behavioral Science,* 2nd ed. (New York: Academic Press, 1989).

3. Kenneth R. Hoover, *The Elements of Social Scientific Thinking,* 5th ed. (New York: St. Martin's Press, 1991), p. 5.

4. Ronald Grover, "Gurus Who Failed Their Own Course," *Business Week,* November 8, 1999, p. 125.

5. Kaplan, *The Conduct of Inquiry.*

6. George S. Howard, *Methods in the Social Sciences* (Glenview, IL: Scott, Foresman, 1985), p. 7.

7. Thomas S. Kuhn, *The Structure of Scientific Revolutions* (Chicago: University of Chicago Press, 1970).

8. Howard Kahane, *Logic and Philosophy,* 2nd ed. (Belmont, CA: Wadsworth, 1973), p. 3.

9. John Dewey, *How We Think* (Boston: Heath, 1910), p. 79.

10. This section is based on Dewey, *How We Think,* and John R. Platt, "Strong Inference," *Science,* October 16, 1964, pp. 347–53.

11. F. J. Roethlisberger and W. J. Dickson, *Management and the Worker* (Cambridge, MA: Harvard University Press, 1939).

12. Paul R. Lawrence, "Historical Development of Organizational Behavior," in *Handbook of Organizational Behavior,* ed. Jay W. Lorsch (Englewood Cliffs, NJ: Prentice-Hall, 1987), p. 6.

13. Kuhn, *The Structure of Scientific Revolutions,* p. 37.

14. Hoover, *The Elements of Social Scientific Thinking,* p. 21.

15. *Merriam-Webster's Collegiate Dictionary,* 10th ed. (Springfield, MA: Merriam-Webster, 1999), http://www.m-w.com/cgi-bin/ dictionary.

16. Fred N. Kerlinger and Howard B. Lee, *Foundations of Behavioral Research,* 4th ed. (New York: HBJ College & School Division, 1999).

17. Hoover, *The Elements of Social Scientific Thinking,* p. 71.

18. Bruce Tuckman, *Conducting Educational Research* (New York: Harcourt Brace Jovanovich, 1972), p. 45.

19. William N. Stephens, *Hypotheses and Evidence* (New York: Thomas Y. Crowell, 1968), p. 5.

20. Leonard C. Hawes, *Pragmatics of Analoguing: Theory and Model Construction in Communication* (Reading, MA: Addison-Wesley, 1975), p. 111.

21. Ibid., pp. 116–22.

REFERENCES FOR SNAPSHOTS AND CAPTIONS

ITE / State Farm

"CBS Evening News with Dan Rather," June 30, 1999.

"Dateline NBC," June 29, 1999.

"Dateline NBC," NBC News, July 1, 1999 (http://www.dateline.msnbc.com/news/284646.asp).

"Miami Area Intersection Tops State Farm List of Most Dangerous in the United States," State Farm press release, June 27, 2001.

"State Farm's Dangerous Intersection Initiative," Institute of Transportation Engineers press release, June 25, 2001 (http://www.ite.org/ press_release.htm).

AbioCor

"Abiomed Provides Comments and Reaffirms AbioCor Clinical Trial Information Policies," Abiomed press release, July 13, 2001.

Lawrence K. Altman, "'Life Is Wonderful' for the Man with a Self-Contained Artificial Heart," *New York Times on the Web,* August 2, 2001 (http://www.nytimes.com/2001/08/02/healthy/anatomy/02hear.html).

Lawrence K. Altman, "Self-Contained Mechanical Heart Throbs for First Time in a Human," *New York Times on the Web,* July 3, 2001 (http://www.nytimes.com/learning/general/featured_articles/010705thursday.html).

"World's First AbioCor Implantable Replacement Heart Procedure Performed at Jewish Hospital by University of Louisville Surgeons," *ScienceDaily,* July 6, 2001 (http://www.sciencedaily.com/releases/2001/07/010706080839.htm).

Marriott

"About the Company," Marriott International, Inc. (http://www.marriott.com/corporateinfo/98annual/about.asp).

Brenda Roth, manager of research, Marriott International, Inc., Interview: January 2000, "Marriott History" (http://www.marriott.com/milestone.asp).

CLASSIC AND CONTEMPORARY READINGS

Beardsley, Monroe. *Practical Logic.* Englewood Cliffs, NJ: Prentice-Hall, 1969. A lucid discussion of deduction and induction as well as excellent coverage of argument analysis.

Browne, M. Neil, and Stuart M. Keeley. *Asking the Right Questions: A Guide to Critical Thinking.* Upper Saddle River, NJ: Prentice-Hall, 1997. Addresses question-asking skills and techniques necessary for evaluating different types of evidence.

Churchman, C. W. *The Design of Inquiring Systems.* New York: Basic Books, 1971. An essential work for understanding the connections between philosophy, science, and the nature of inquiry.

Hoover, Kenneth R., and Todd Donovan. *The Elements of Social Scientific Thinking.* 6th ed. New York: Worth Publishers, 1994. A brief but highly readable treatise on the elements of science and scientific thinking.

Kaplan, Abraham. *The Conduct of Inquiry.* San Francisco: Transaction Publications, 1998. A source for philosophy of science and logical reasoning.

Kerlinger, Fred N., and Howard B. Lee. *Foundations of Behavioral Research.* 4th ed. New York: HBJ College & School Division, 1999.

CHAPTER 3

The Research Process

Learning Objectives

After reading this chapter, you should understand . . .

1   **Research is decision- and dilemma-centered.**

2   **The research question is the result of careful exploration and analysis and sets the direction for the research project.**

3   **Planning research design demands an understanding of all the stages in the research process.**

4   **Reality testing at each stage of the process is critical to successful implementation of a research proposal.**

Bringing Research to Life

On the return flight from Austin, Jason and Myra were euphoric. "That went really well," he said. "Better even than I hoped for."

"Yes. Terrific," she said. "Just fine. You handled yourself very well, Jason. You were so patient. Of course, we are not home free. We have lots of work ahead before we satisfy the big bosses at Mind-Writer. But it was a good start. Definitely."

"Definitely."

They toasted each other and their visit with the MindWriter product people, especially Gracie Uhura, the product manager. They sat and sipped their drinks, enjoying a feeling of accomplishment.

"On the other hand," said Jason, by and by, "there are going to be a few problems."

"Aren't there always?"

"Gracie wants the sun, the sky, and the moon. She wants everything. Wants to know the demographic characteristics of her users . . . their job descriptions . . . their salaries . . . their ethnicities . . . their education. Wants to know their perception of your company . . . of the quality of MindWriter's specific models. Wants to know their satisfaction with the purchase channel and with the service department, too."

"What's wrong with wanting all that, if MindWriter is willing to pay?"

"I may perceive the company as hugely profitable and a bottomless source of research dollars, but you and Gracie need to keep your eye on the bottom line. You can bet there is a bean counter somewhere who will want to know how you and Gracie can justify asking all these questions. They will ask, 'What is going to be the payoff in knowing the ethnicity of customers?' And if you or Gracie can't explain the justification for needing the information, if one of you can't establish that the dollar benefit of knowing is at least as great as the dollar cost of finding out, Mr. Bean Counter is going to strike the question off the list and reduce what MindWriter is willing to pay for."

"Is there no way we can justify knowing everything Gracie wants to know? After all, this is my first project with her. It certainly wouldn't hurt my reputation within MindWriter by showing how well I can deliver what my top executives want."

"Sure there is. Or at least there may be. We can do a pilot study for her of a few hundred customers and see if the ethnic background, or the salary level, or any other nonattitudinal item that Gracie cares about, is a good indicator of satisfaction, willingness to make a repeat purchase, postpurchase service satisfaction, and so forth. If it is, maybe more extensive measurement can be justified."

"Clever!"

"Well, that's why you came to me; we do exemplary research."

"So, am I right in believing you feel we need to propose an exploratory study for that problem first, and propose a larger study later?"

"That would be standard practice. There are questions that have to be resolved before each side can commit to a major study. We want to minimize the risks to both sides. For example, Gracie wants to know the customers' perception of MindWriter's overall quality. But we have to ask ourselves, 'Are these customers really qualified to form independent opinions, or will they simply be parroting what they have read in the computer magazines or what a dealer told them?' We will have to do a pilot study of a few hundred users to determine if it is really useful to ask them their overall impression of the product."

"I follow you!"

"On the other hand, the repair problem really interests me. We can be reasonably sure that the customers know their own minds when it comes to evaluating their firsthand experience with MindWriter's service department. This business of returning a computer for service is something you experience firsthand, not something in a magazine, and it's worth studying. I had a chance last night to look over the letters you gave me."

He dug into his briefcase and extracted a sheaf of photocopies. "These are the letters the service department received about MindWriter. And here are notes on phone conversations that Gracie gave me. One person writes, 'My MindWriter was badly damaged on arrival. I could not believe its condition when I unpacked it.' And here, 'The service technicians seemed to be unable to understand my complaint, but once they understood it, they performed immediate repairs.' You and I will boil these down—and possibly dozens more like them—to

a couple of representative questions that can be pilot-tested for clarity, reliability, and validity . . . I'll explain these terms later. The point is, MindWriter has to pay for everything Gracie says she wants, what she wants that has a payoff, what she wants that has a payoff and is researchable . . . We are going to be very busy in the next few weeks."

"I understand what you are saying, believe it or not. Yes, you are starting to make good sense. I think we are going to get along."

"You know what, Myra? I'm starting to think you're right."

The Research Process

Writers usually treat the research task as a sequential process involving several clearly defined steps. No one claims that research requires completion of each step before going to the next. Recycling, circumventing, and skipping occur. Some steps are begun out of sequence, some are carried out simultaneously, and some may be omitted. Despite these variations, the idea of a sequence is useful for developing a project and for keeping the project orderly as it unfolds.

Exhibit 3–1 models the sequence of the **research process.** We refer to it often as we discuss each step in subsequent chapters. Our discussion of the questions that guide project planning and data gathering is incorporated into the model (see the elements within the pyramid in Exhibit 3–1 and compare them with Exhibit 3–2). Exhibit 3–1 also organizes this chapter and introduces the remainder of the book.

The research process begins much as the vignette suggests. A management dilemma triggers the need for a decision. For MindWriter, a growing number of complaints about postpurchase service started the process. In other situations, a controversy arises, a major commitment of resources is called for, or conditions in the environment signal the need for a decision. For MindWriter, the critical event could have been the introduction by a competitor of new technology that would revolutionize the processing speed of laptops. Such events cause managers to reconsider their purposes or objectives, define a problem for solution, or develop strategies for solutions they have identified.

In our view of the research process, the management question—its origin, selection, statement, exploration, and refinement—is the critical activity in the sequence. Throughout the chapter we emphasize problem-related steps. A familiar quotation from Albert Einstein, no less apt today than when it was written, supports this view:

> The formulation of a problem is far more often essential than its solution, which may be merely a matter of mathematical or experimental skill. To raise new questions, new possibilities, to regard old problems from a new angle requires creative imagination and marks real advance in science.[1]

Whether the researcher is involved in basic or applied research, a thorough understanding of the management question is fundamental to success in the research enterprise.

EXHIBIT 3–1   **The Research Process**

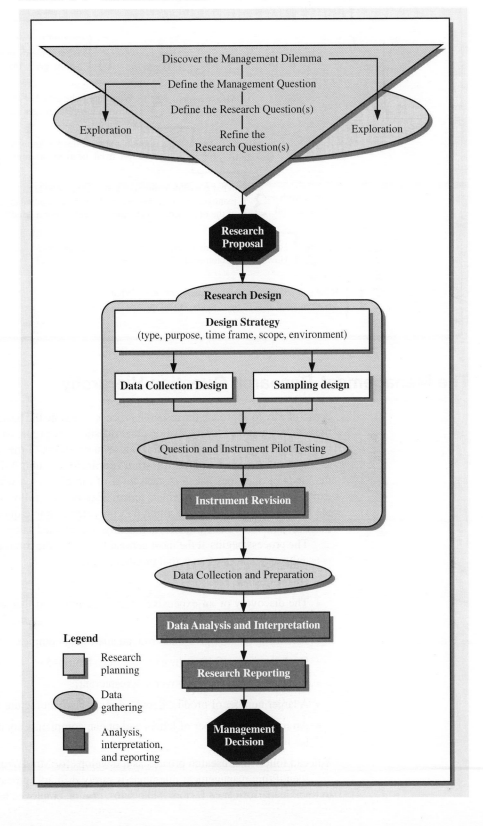

EXHIBIT 3–2 Management-Research Question Hierarchy

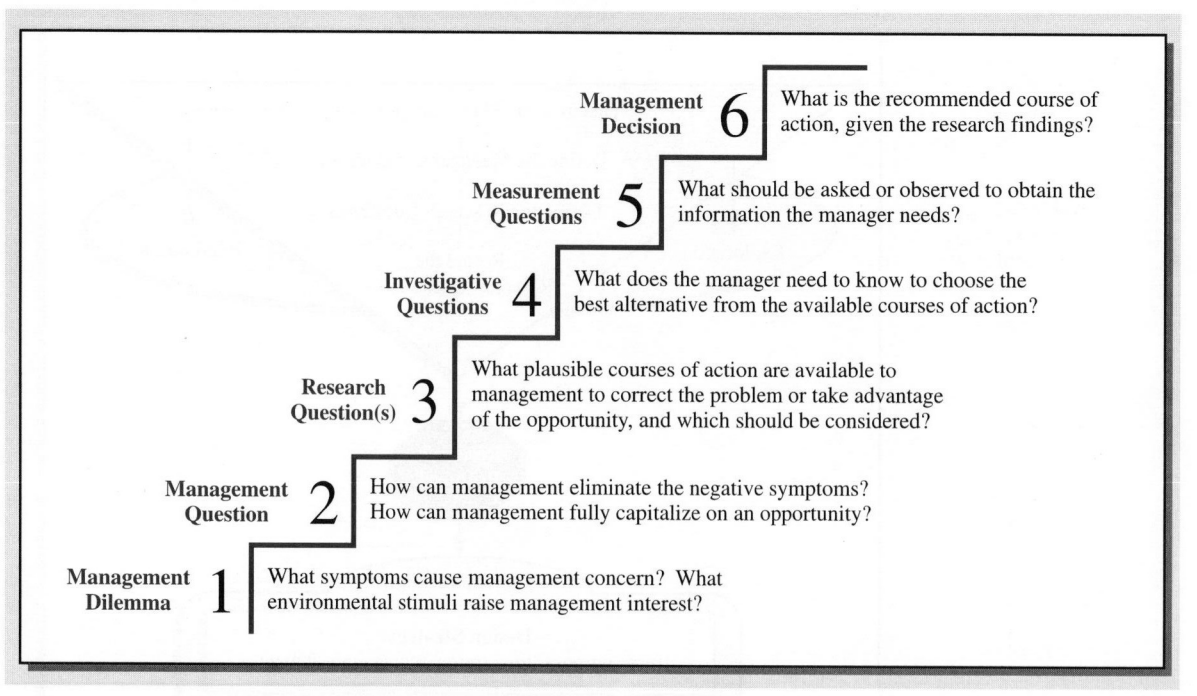

The Management-Research Question Hierarchy

A useful way to approach the research process is to state the basic dilemma that prompts the research and then try to develop other questions by progressively breaking down the original question into more specific ones. You can think of the outcome of this process as the **management-research question hierarchy.** Exhibit 3–2 provides examples of the kinds of questions asked at each level of the hierarchy, while Exhibit 3–3 further explains the process in management terms. (Exhibit 3–4 follows the MindWriter example through the process, and Exhibit 3–5 provides example questions at each stage for SalePro, a national sales organization facing unexplained sales variations by territory.)

The process begins at the most general level with the **management dilemma.** This is usually a symptom of an actual problem, such as

- Rising costs.
- The discovery of an expensive chemical compound that would increase the efficacy of a drug.
- Increasing tenant move-outs from an apartment complex.
- Declining sales (follow the example in Exhibit 3–5).
- Increasing employee turnover in a restaurant.
- A larger number of product defects during the manufacture of an automobile.
- An increasing number of letters and phone complaints about postpurchase service (as in MindWriter).

You can follow the research process as it develops for MindWriter in Exhibit 3–4.

Identifying management dilemmas is rarely difficult (unless the organization fails to track its performance factors—like sales, profits, employee turnover, manufacturing

EXHIBIT 3–3 Formulating the Research Question

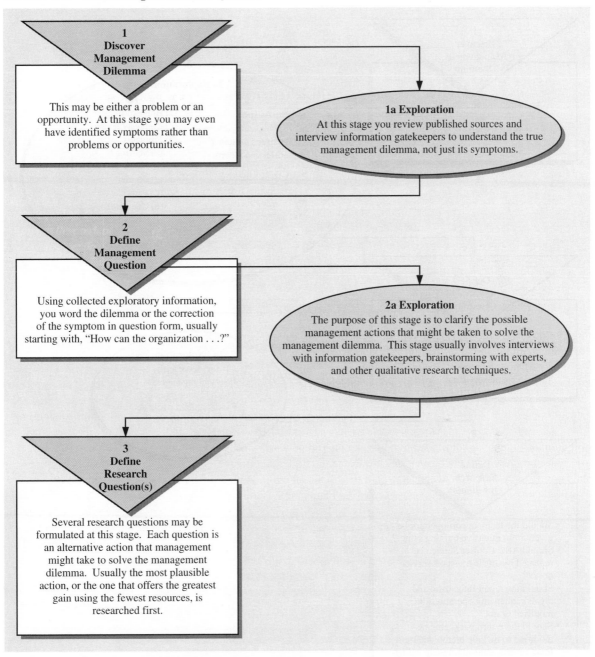

output and defects, on-time deliveries, customer satisfaction, etc.). However, choosing one dilemma on which to focus may be difficult. Choosing incorrectly will direct valuable resources (time, manpower, money, and equipment) on a path that may not provide critical decision-making information (the purpose of good research). The choice is like learning to balance a pencil on its point on your finger, a coin on its edge, or a pyramid on its pinnacle: As a manager, only practice makes you proficient. For new managers, or established managers facing new responsibilities, developing several management-research question hierarchies, each starting with a different dilemma, will assist in the

EXHIBIT 3–4   **Formulating the Research Question for MindWriter**

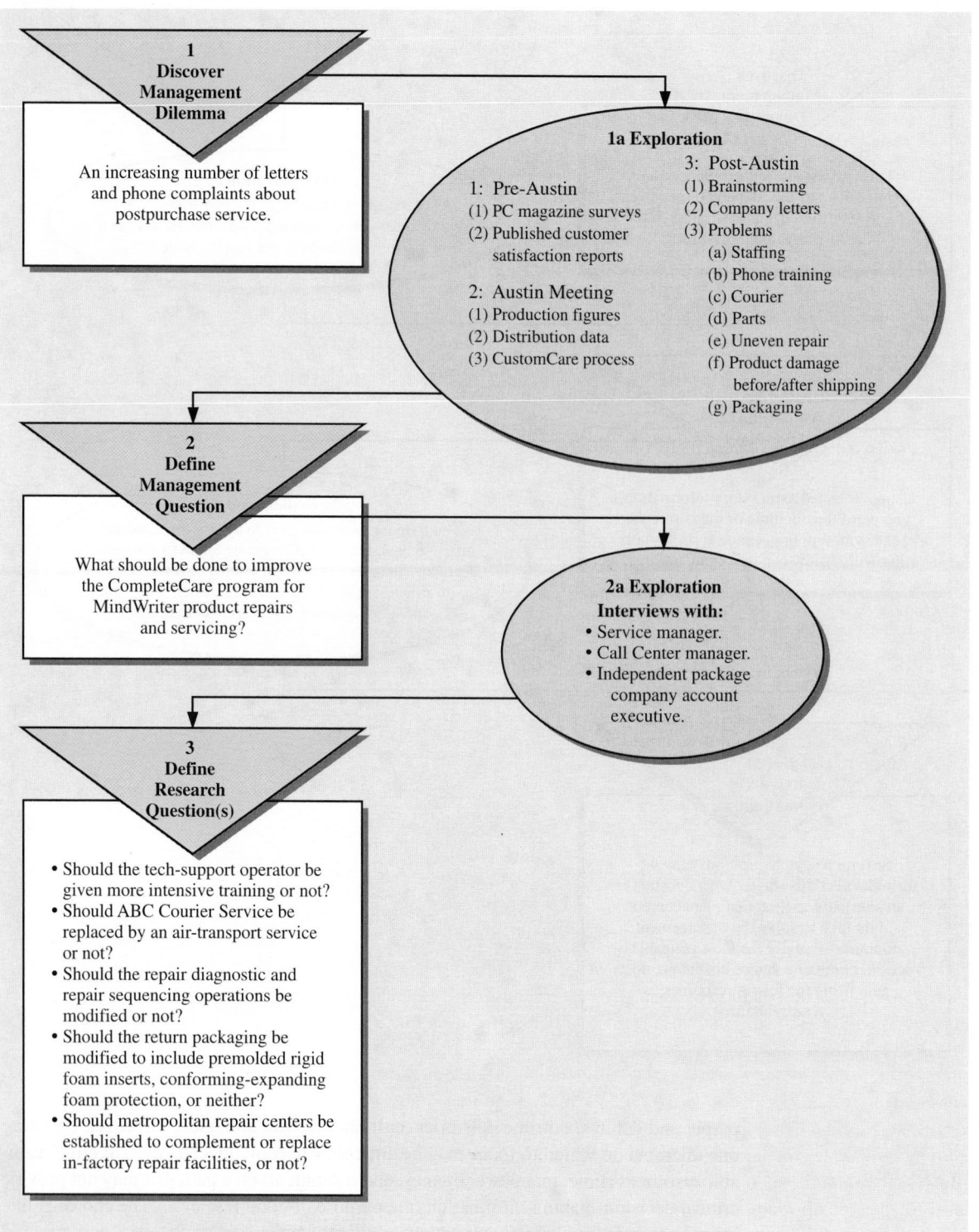

1
Discover
Management
Dilemma

An increasing number of letters
and phone complaints about
postpurchase service.

1a Exploration

1: Pre-Austin
(1) PC magazine surveys
(2) Published customer
      satisfaction reports

2: Austin Meeting
(1) Production figures
(2) Distribution data
(3) CustomCare process

3: Post-Austin
(1) Brainstorming
(2) Company letters
(3) Problems
      (a) Staffing
      (b) Phone training
      (c) Courier
      (d) Parts
      (e) Uneven repair
      (f) Product damage
           before/after shipping
      (g) Packaging

2
Define
Management
Question

What should be done to improve
the CompleteCare program for
MindWriter product repairs
and servicing?

2a Exploration
Interviews with:
• Service manager.
• Call Center manager.
• Independent package
   company account
   executive.

3
Define
Research
Question(s)

• Should the tech-support operator be
  given more intensive training or not?
• Should ABC Courier Service be
  replaced by an air-transport service
  or not?
• Should the repair diagnostic and
  repair sequencing operations be
  modified or not?
• Should the return packaging be
  modified to include premolded rigid
  foam inserts, conforming-expanding
  foam protection, or neither?
• Should metropolitan repair centers be
  established to complement or replace
  in-factory repair facilities, or not?

EXHIBIT 3–5   SalePro's Management-Research Question Hierarchy

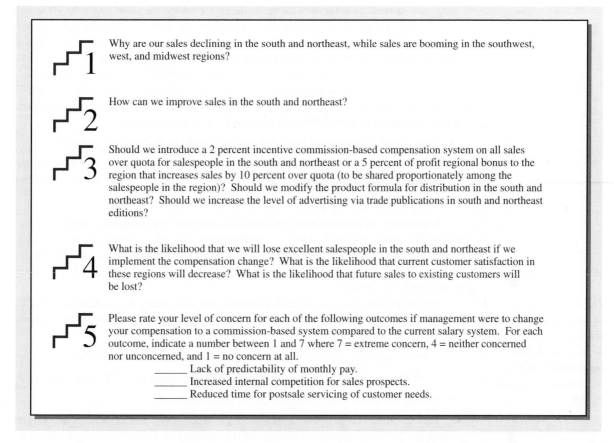

Why are our sales declining in the south and northeast, while sales are booming in the southwest, west, and midwest regions?

How can we improve sales in the south and northeast?

Should we introduce a 2 percent incentive commission-based compensation system on all sales over quota for salespeople in the south and northeast or a 5 percent of profit regional bonus to the region that increases sales by 10 percent over quota (to be shared proportionately among the salespeople in the region)? Should we modify the product formula for distribution in the south and northeast? Should we increase the level of advertising via trade publications in south and northeast editions?

What is the likelihood that we will lose excellent salespeople in the south and northeast if we implement the compensation change? What is the likelihood that current customer satisfaction in these regions will decrease? What is the likelihood that future sales to existing customers will be lost?

Please rate your level of concern for each of the following outcomes if management were to change your compensation to a commission-based system compared to the current salary system. For each outcome, indicate a number between 1 and 7 where 7 = extreme concern, 4 = neither concerned nor unconcerned, and 1 = no concern at all.
_____ Lack of predictability of monthly pay.
_____ Increased internal competition for sales prospects.
_____ Reduced time for postsale servicing of customer needs.

choice process. In all figures related to the research process model, in this and subsequent chapters, we use a pyramid to represent the management-research question hierarchy and to reinforce the precarious nature of the foundation decisions in the research process.

The Management Question

The manager must move from the management dilemma to the **management question** to proceed with the research process. The management question restates the dilemma in question form:

- What should be done to reduce employee turnover?
- What should be done to increase tenant residency and reduce move-outs?
- What should be done to reduce costs?

Management Question Categories   Management questions are too numerous to list, but we can categorize them:

- Choice of purposes or objectives.
- Generation and evaluation of solutions.
- Troubleshooting or control situation.

The first type concerns the *choice of purposes or objectives*. The general question is, "What do we want to achieve?" At the company level the question might be, "Should we at XYZ Corporation reconsider our basic corporate objectives as they concern our public image?" More narrowly, a management question on objectives might ask, "What goals should XYZ try to achieve in its next round of labor negotiations?"

A second category of management questions concerns the *generation and evaluation of solutions*. The general question is, "How can we achieve the ends we seek?" Research projects in this group usually deal with concrete problems that managers quickly recognize as useful. Projects can involve questions such as,

- "How can we achieve our five-year goal of doubled sales and net profits?"
- "What should be done to improve the CompleteCare program for MindWriter product repairs and servicing?"
- "What should be done to reduce postpurchase service complaints?"

A third class of management questions concerns the *troubleshooting or control situation*. The problem usually involves monitoring or diagnosing various ways in which an organization is failing to achieve its established goals. This group includes questions such as, "Why does our department incur the highest costs?" and "How well is our program meeting its goals?"

The definition of the management question sets the research task. So, a poorly defined management question will misdirect research efforts.

No matter how the management question is defined, many research directions can be taken. A specific question can lead to many studies. Concern for MetalWorks's company image might lead to:

- A survey among various groups to discover their attitudes toward the company.
- Secondary research into what other companies are doing to polish their images.
- A study to forecast expected changes in social attitudes.

The question concerning MetalWorks's labor negotiation objectives might prompt research into recent settlements in the industry or a survey among workers to find out how well management has met its concerns about the quality of work life. It is the joint responsibility of the researcher and the manager to choose the most productive project.

SNAPSHOT

Aquatred 3: Can It Surf to Higher Profits?

Tires certainly have taken their knocks in the new century, with fatalities caused by tread separation leading to several recalls, along with a sluggish auto market and weak tire replacement activity. Even super-performer Goodyear reported, "Sales for the first six months of 2001 were $7 billion, down from $7.3 billion in 2000. Tire volume was 108.1 million units worldwide, down 2 percent from 2000's first half."

But in the midst of all the turmoil in the tire market, Goodyear also unveiled Aquatred 3, a significantly improved version of its groundbreaking Aquatred, which launched the wet-traction segment of the market 10 years ago. In Tire Rack's latest survey, the Aquatred 3 earned customer accolades, beating all other brands in every tire characteristic, including dry traction, cornering stability, and treadwear. Not bad for a wet-traction tire carrying an unbeatable 80,000 mile warranty.

The original Aquatred took more than 10 years to develop. The research that launched the original discovered a new tire segment (the wet-traction segment), second in size only to the longer-treadlife segment. In addition, the original research studied the "*planing effect* that occurs when a conventional tire travels on wet surfaces." The discovered wedge of water "is what makes most conventional tires lose contact with the roadway."

The newly introduced third-generation tire sports two deflecting channels, rather than the one aquachannel designed into the original Aquatred. It is hoped that Aquatred 3 will catapult Goodyear to increased profitability, just as the original Aquatred made Goodyear the undisputed leader in innovation.

www.goodyear.com

The Nature of the Management Question Assume, for example, a researcher is asked to help the new management of a bank. The president is concerned about erosion of the bank's profitability (the management dilemma) and wants to turn this situation around. BankChoice is the oldest and largest of three banks in a city with a population of about 50,000. Profits have stagnated in recent years. The president and the consultant discuss the problem facing the organization and settle on this management question: "How can we improve our profit picture?"

The management question does not specify what kind of research is to be done. This question is strictly managerial in thrust. It implies that the bank's management faces the task of developing a strategy for increasing profits. The question is broad. Notice that it doesn't indicate whether management should increase profits via increased deposits, downsizing of personnel, outsourcing of the payroll function, or some other means.

To subdivide a broadly stated management question, look for the underlying causes of the management dilemma.

Further discussion between the bank president and the researcher shows there are really two questions to be answered. The problem of low deposit growth is linked to concerns of a competitive nature. While lowered deposits directly affect profits, another part of the profit weakness is associated with negative factors within the organization that are increasing costs of operation. The qualified researcher knows that the management question as stated is too broad to guide a definitive research project. As a starting point, the broadly worded question is fine, but BankChoice will want to refine its management question into these more specific subquestions:

The primary purpose of research is to reduce the level of risk of a business decision. Knowing that most new product introductions fail, this humorous ad from Greenfield Online suggests not all new product ideas are worthy of consideration and that well-executed research can save a firm from a costly mistake.

- "How can we improve deposits?"
- "How can we reduce costs?"

This separation of the management question into two subquestions may not have occurred without a discussion between the researcher and the manager.

Exploration

BankChoice has done no formal research in the past. It has little specific information about competitors or customers and has not analyzed its internal operations. To move forward in the management-research question hierarchy and define the research question, the client needs to collect some exploratory information on:

- What factors are contributing to the bank's failure to achieve a stronger growth rate in deposits?
- How well is the bank doing regarding work climate, efficiency of operations compared to industry norms, and financial condition compared to industry norms and competitors?

A small focus group is conducted among employees, and trade association data are acquired to compare financial and operating statistics from company annual reports and end-of-year division reports. From the results of these two exploratory activities, it is obvious that BankChoice's operations are not as progressive as its competitors' but it has its costs well in line. So the revised management question becomes, "What should be done to make the bank more competitive?"

The process of exploration may surface within the research process in several locations (see Exhibit 3–3). An **exploration** typically begins with a search of published data. In addition, researchers often seek out people who are well informed on the topic, especially those who have clearly stated positions on controversial aspects of the problem. Take the case of TechByte, a company interested in enhancing its position in a given technology that appears to hold potential for future growth. This interest or need might quickly elicit a number of questions:

- How fast might this technology develop?
- What are the likely applications of this technology?
- What companies now possess it, and which ones are likely to make a major effort to get it?
- How much will it take in resources?
- What are the likely payoffs?

In the above investigation of opportunities, researchers would probably begin with specific books and periodicals. They would be looking only for certain aspects in this literature, such as recent developments, predictions by informed figures about the prospects of the technology, identification of those involved in the area, and accounts of successful ventures or failures by others in the field. After becoming familiar with the literature, researchers might seek interviews with scientists, engineers, and product developers who are well known in the field. They would give special attention to those who represent the two extremes of opinion in regard to the prospects of the technology. If possible, they would talk with persons having information on particularly thorny problems in development and application. Of course, much of the information will be confidential and competitive. However, skillful investigation can uncover many useful indicators.

For MindWriter, Myra searched her local library and company archives to discover PC industry studies on service and technical support (see Exhibit 3–4), as well as published customer satisfaction comparisons among companies and products. Then in the meeting in Austin, both Myra and Jason delved deeply for Gracie's knowledge and perceptions of the CompleteCare program. They also developed a more thorough understanding of production and distribution. Shortly after returning from Austin, however, Myra and Jason have both realized from reviewing customer correspondence that they need more knowledge on product design, CompleteCare, and product handling, so they plan a second exploratory venture that will include expert interviews.

We discuss the usefulness of a literature search, experience survey, and focus groups in exploration in Chapter 6.

An unstructured exploration allows the researcher to develop and revise the management question and determine what is needed to secure answers to the proposed question.

The Research Question   Once the researcher has a clear statement of the management question, she and the manager must translate it into a research question. Consider the research question to be a fact-oriented, information-gathering question. There are many different ways to address most management dilemmas. It is at this point of formulating research questions where the insight and expertise of the manager come into play. Only reasonable alternatives should be considered. If the researcher is not part of the manager's decision-making environment, the researcher can be of minimal help in this translation. The manager's direction to the researcher is most important. If, however, the researcher is an integral part of the decision-making environment, she may assist the manager in evaluating which courses of action should and can be researched.

Focusing too early on correcting one problem versus another can misdirect the research, wasting valuable resources.

In their post-Austin brainstorming session (see Exhibit 3–4), Jason and Myra hypothesized several possible problems that could have resulted from the complaints in customer letters. Some problems are not as correctable as others (e.g., correcting parts shortages might not be within MindWriter's immediate control, but improving tech-line operator training clearly is). If MindWriter does not maintain a database of complaints, an exploratory study might have to be undertaken to determine which category of complaints is most troublesome. Incorrectly defining the research question is a fundamental weakness in the research process. Time and money can be wasted studying an alternative that won't help the manager rectify the dilemma.

The researcher's task is to assist the manager in formulating a research question that fits the need to resolve the management dilemma. A **research question** is the hypothesis of choice that best states the objective of the research study. It is a more specific management question that must be answered. It may be more than one question, or just one. A research process that answers this more specific question provides the manager with the information necessary to make the decision he or she is facing.

One of the letters Jason reads on the flight back to Florida from the MindWriter meeting in Austin describes the deplorable condition of a MindWriter laptop upon delivery to the customer. After consulting Gracie, Jason and Myra identify several credible options:

- Reinforce the shipping carton with rigid foam inserts (in place of the current plastic sling) to prevent damage to the laptop case during shipping.
- Use conforming-expanding foam insulation in the shipping carton.
- Leave the shipping carton specification as is but ship via an overnight air delivery service rather than using the current ground courier service.
- Establish authorized repair facilities in major cities, so that a customer could deliver a MindWriter for repair, eliminating shipping altogether.

These choices lead to several research questions:

- Should MindWriter change the laptop shipping specifications to include rigid foam or conforming-expanding foam or stay with the current plastic sling?
- Should MindWriter change its shipping carrier from ABC Courier Service to an air transportation service?

Managers often meet to discuss symptoms when developing the management-research question hierarchy. Whiteboard technology makes this phase of research planning easier. The managers here are using a Webster TSTM 800 Interactive Whiteboard combined with screen-projected data. This combination encourages full participant involvement in the discussion as the computerized interactive whiteboard captures detailed brainstorming notations and conclusions without the participants taking notes themselves. At the end of the discussion, all participants walk away with the same record of the event.

- Should MindWriter establish metropolitan repair centers to complement or replace its existing in-factory repair facilities?

Meanwhile at BankChoice, the president has agreed to have the research be guided by the following research question: "Should BankChoice position itself as a modern, progressive institution (with appropriate changes in services and policies) or maintain its image as the oldest, most reliable institution in town?"

Fine-Tuning the Research Question   The term *fine-tuning* might seem to be an odd usage for research, but it creates an image that most researchers come to recognize. Fine-tuning the question is precisely what a skillful practitioner must do after the exploration is complete. At this point, a clearer picture of the management and research questions begins to emerge. After a preliminary review of the literature, a brief exploratory study, or both, the project begins to crystallize in one of two ways:

1. It is apparent the question has been answered and the process is finished.

2. A question different from the one originally addressed has appeared.

The research question does not have to be materially different, but it will have evolved in some fashion. This is not cause for discouragement. The refined research question(s) will have better focus and will move the research forward with more clarity than the initially formulated question(s).

In addition to fine-tuning the original question, other research question-related activities should be addressed in this phase to enhance the direction of the project:

1. Examine the concepts and constructs to be used in the study. Are they satisfactorily defined? Have operational definitions been employed where appropriate?

MANAGEMENT
Tip

2. Review the research questions with the intent of breaking them down into specific second- and third-level questions.

3. If hypotheses are used, be certain they meet the quality tests mentioned in the preceding chapter.

4. Determine what evidence must be collected to answer the various questions and hypotheses.

5. Set the scope of the study by stating what is *not* a part of the research question. This will establish a boundary to separate contiguous problems from the primary objective.

When the characteristics or plausible causes of the problem are well defined and the research question is clearly stated, it is possible to deduce the essential subquestions that will guide the project planning at this stage of the research process. However, if the research question is somewhat or very poorly defined, the researcher will need further exploration and question revision to refine the original question and generate the material for constructing investigative questions.

Investigative Questions   Once the research question(s) has been selected, researcher thinking moves to a more specific level, that of investigative questions (see Exhibit 3–5). These questions reveal the specific pieces of information the manager feels he or she needs to know to answer the research question.

Investigative questions are questions the researcher must answer to satisfactorily arrive at a conclusion about the research question. To formulate them, the researcher takes a general research question and breaks it into more specific questions about which to gather data. This fractionating process can continue down through several levels of increasing specificity. Investigative questions should be included in the research proposal, for they guide the development of the research design. They are the foundation for creating the research data collection instrument.

The researcher working on the BankChoice project develops two major investigative questions for studying the market with several subquestions under each. The questions provide insight into the lack of deposit growth:

1. What is the public's position regarding financial services and their use?
  a. What specific financial services are used?
  b. How attractive are various services?
  c. What bank-specific and environmental factors influence a person's use of a particular service?

2. What is the bank's competitive position?
  a. What are the geographic patterns of our customers and of our competitors' customers?
  b. What demographic differences are revealed among our customers and those of our competitors?
  c. What words or phrases does the public (both customers and noncustomers) associate with BankChoice? With BankChoice's competitors?
  d. How aware is the public of the bank's promotional efforts?
  e. What opinion does the public hold of the bank and its competitors?
  f. How does growth in services compare among competing institutions?

Return again to the MindWriter situation. What does management need to know to choose among the different packaging specifications? As you develop your information needs, think broadly. In developing your list of investigative questions, include:

• Performance considerations (like the relative costs of the options, the speed of packing serviced laptops, and the condition of test laptops packaged with different materials).

- Attitudinal issues (like perceived service quality).
- Behavioral issues (like employees' ease of use in packing with the considered materials).

Measurement Questions   Measurement questions should be outlined by completion of the project-planning activities but usually await pilot testing for refinement. There are two types of measurement questions: predesigned, pretested questions, and custom-designed questions. Predesigned measurement questions are questions that have been formulated and tested by previous researchers, are recorded in the literature, and may be applied literally or be adapted for the project at hand. Some studies lend themselves to the use of these readily available measurement devices. This provides enhanced validity and can reduce the cost of the project. More often, however, the measurement questions should be custom tailored to the investigative questions. The resources for this task will be the collective insights from all the activities in the research process completed to this point, particularly insights from exploration. Later, during pilot testing of the data collection instrument(s), these custom-designed questions will be refined.

Measurement questions constitute the fifth level of the hierarchy (see Exhibit 3–2). In surveys, **measurement questions** are the questions we actually ask the respondents. They appear on the questionnaire. In an observation study, measurement questions are the observations researchers must record about each subject studied.

BankChoice conducts a survey of local residents. The questionnaire contains many measurement questions seeking information that will provide answers to the investigative questions. Two hundred residents complete questionnaires and the information collected is used to guide a reorientation of the bank's image.

MANAGEMENT
Tip

The assumptions and facts used to structure the management-research question hierarchy set the direction of the project. Using the hierarchy is a good way to think methodically about the various issues. Think of the hierarchy as six sequential levels moving from the general to the specific. While our approach suggests six discrete levels—concluding with the management decision—the hierarchy is actually more of a continuum. The investigative question stage, in particular, may involve several levels of questioning before it is possible to develop satisfactory measurement questions.

Close-Up

The next morning at 7:00 sharp, Myra appears at Jason's home office. As she presses the doorbell, she hears furniture being wrestled across the floor.

"It's open," hollers Jason.

Inside, Jason has cleared furniture and pictures from the south wall and has leaned a sheet of plywood against that wall. "There's coffee and doughnuts," he says. "But first give me a hand with this."

"This" is a roll of brown wrapping paper. The two of them work together and unroll the hard-to-handle paper left to right across the top two feet of plywood, cut it, and tack down its corners so it covers the top half of the plywood.

Then they start on the lower left side of the plywood and repeat the process until the board is fully covered.

They now have a 4- by 8-foot chartboard.

Across the top of the first sheet, Myra writes, "Satisfaction with the service department." Today they focus on the easiest task and leave the customer profile pilot study for later. Besides, Gracie is pressed for answers on how the CompleteCare repair program is being received. If she is responsive on the smaller project, they are sure they will get the OK for the more ambitious one.

They help themselves to coffee and doughnuts, pull two chairs in front of the chartboard and for five minutes stare in silence at its awful blankness.

Jason has learned a lot about MindWriter. Beginning with a visit to the Internet and an intense search through MindWriter's archives before their Austin trip, followed by the meetings in Austin, he knows the product is sold through computer superstores and independent mail-order companies. He also has learned that MindWriter ships about 5,000 portable/laptop computers per month. The product is successful yet constrained by the same supply shortages as the rest of the industry. Personal computer magazines have been consulted for their annual surveys on service, repair, and technical support. Overall customer satisfaction comparisons have been obtained from published sources.

The exploratory sessions in Austin revealed much about the CompleteCare process. Myra summarizes the information under the label "CC Process."

When customers experience a malfunction, they call an 800 number. The call center answers service, support, and ordering questions. Technical representatives are trained to:

- Take the name, phone, address, and MindWriter model number.
- Listen to the customer and ask questions to detect the nature of the problem.
- Attempt to resolve the problem if they can walk the customer through corrective steps.

If unable to resolve the problem, the representative provides a return authorization code and dispatches a package courier to pick up the unit before 5 P.M.The unit is delivered to Austin for service the next morning. The CompleteCare repair facility calls the customer if the repair information is incomplete. The unit is repaired by the end of that day and picked up by the courier. The call center then updates its database with service record information. If all goes well, the customer receives the repaired unit by 10:00 the following morning, 48 hours after MindWriter received the customer's original problem call.

When Myra finishes, Jason begins to rough out the known "problems." There are employee shortages at the call center and difficulties getting the new technical representatives trained. The courier is uneven in executing its pickup and delivery contract. MindWriter is experiencing parts availability problems for some models. And, occasionally, units are returned to the customer either not fixed or damaged in some way. Jason believes this means the service area is not doing an adequate job. But Myra asserts that problems could be in the original packing, in handling, or even from activities related to taking the boxes on and off the shipping pallets.

Because of their brainstorming, they are able to restate management's question: "What should be done to improve the CompleteCare program for MindWriter product repairs and servicing?" After exploration, Myra and Jason brainstorm the following research and investigative questions:

Research Questions

1. Should the technical representative be given more intensive training, or not?
2. Should ABC Courier Service be replaced with an overnight air transport service, or not?
3. Should the repair-diagnostic and repair-sequencing operations be modified, or not?
4. Should the return packaging be modified to include premolded rigid foam inserts, conforming-expanding foam protection, or neither?
5. Should metropolitan repair centers be established to complement or replace in-factory repair facilities, or not?

Investigative Questions

1. How well is the call center helping the customers? Is it helping the customer with instructions? What percentage of customers' technical problems is the center solving without callbacks? How long do customers wait on the phone?
2. How good is the transportation company? Does it pick up and deliver the laptop responsively? How long do customers wait for pickup? Delivery? Are the laptops damaged due to package handling? What available packaging alternatives are cost-effective?
3. How good is the repair group? What is the sequencing of the repair program, diagnostics through completion? Is the repair complete? Are customers' problems resolved? Are new repair problems emerging? Are customers' repair-time expectations being met?
4. (Do this set of questions on your own. See Discussion Question 9 at the end of this chapter.)
5. What is the overall satisfaction with CompleteCare and with the MindWriter product?

Myra now has enough information to go back to Gracie at MindWriter. In particular, Myra wants to know whether she and Jason have translated Gracie's management question in a way that will adequately fulfill Gracie's need for information. They also want to do in-depth interviews with the service manager, the call center manager, and the independent package company's account executive to determine if they are on the right track with their investigative questions. These people will be able to answer some investigative questions. The rest of the investigative questions will need to be translated into measurement questions to ask customers. If Myra and Jason are comfortable with the additional insight from their interviews (and any additional customer letters), they can then develop a questionnaire for CompleteCare customers.

Jason plans to pilot-test the questionnaire with a limited number of customers, revise the questions, set up the logistics, and then roll out the research program. Sampling will be a critical matter. If Gracie's budget is large, they can use a probability sample from the customer list that MindWriter generates every week. This will make telephone interviews possible. If a less expensive alternative is needed, however, they can propose that a questionnaire postcard survey be included with every laptop as it is returned to the customer. They also will do

random sampling from the list of customers who do not respond. Nonresponders will be interviewed on the telephone. This way Myra and Jason can be assured of a cost-effective questionnaire with correction for nonresponse bias.

Myra and Jason devise a tentative schedule before calling to arrange the follow-up interviews (see Exhibit 3–6). They want to give Gracie target dates for completion of the exploratory phase and the instrument and pilot test, as well as a deadline for the first month's results.

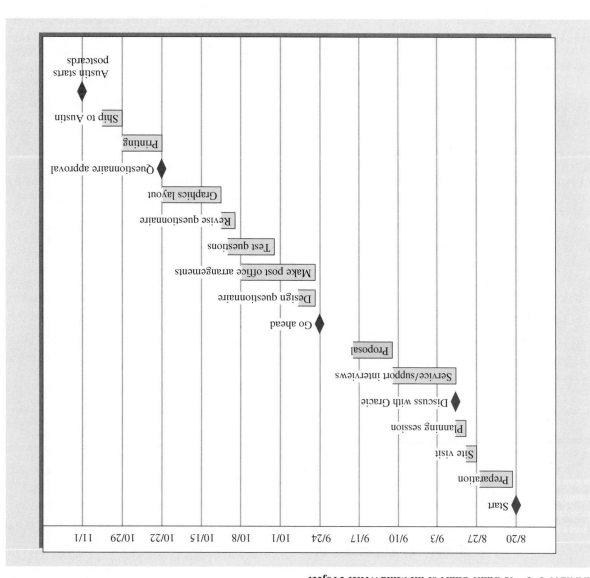

EXHIBIT 3–6   A Gantt Chart of the MindWriter Project

Research Process Problems

Although it is desirable for research to be thoroughly grounded in management decision priorities, studies can wander off target or be less effective than they should be.

The Favored Technique Syndrome

It is the role of the manager sponsoring the research to spot an inappropriate technique-driven research proposal.

We discuss research techniques and when each is appropriate in Chapters 11–14.

Some researchers are method-bound. They recast the management question so it is amenable to their favorite methodology—a survey, for example. Others might prefer to emphasize the case study, while still others wouldn't consider either approach. Not all researchers are comfortable with experimental designs. The past reluctance of most social scientists to use experimental designs is believed to have retarded the development of scientific research in the social science arena.

The availability of technique is an important factor in determining how research will be done or whether a given study can be done. Persons knowledgeable about and skilled in some techniques but not in others are too often blinded by their special competencies. Their concern for technique dominates the decisions concerning what will be studied (both investigative and measurement questions) and how (research design).

Since the advent of Total Quality Management (TQM), numerous, standardized customer satisfaction questionnaires have been developed. Jason may have done studies using these instruments for any number of his clients. Myra should be cautious. She must not let Jason steamroll her into the use of an instrument he has developed for another client, even though he might be very persuasive about its success in the past. Such a technique might not be appropriate for MindWriter's search to resolve postpurchase service dissatisfaction.

Company Database Strip-Mining

In this text, we emphasize projects that tend to be nonroutine, nonrecurring, and complex, rather than those that rely solely on database management.

The existence of a pool of information or a database can distract a manager, seemingly reducing the need for other research. As evidence of the research-as-expense-not-investment mentality mentioned in Chapter 1, managers frequently hear from superiors, "We should use the information we already have before collecting more." Modern management information systems are capable of providing massive volumes of data. This is not the same as saying modern management information systems provide substantial knowledge.

Each field in a database was originally created for a specific reason, a reason that may or may not be compatible with the management question facing the organization. The MindWriter service department's database, for example, probably contains several fields about the type of problem, the location of the problem, the remedy used to correct the problem, and so forth. Jason and Myra can accumulate facts concerning the service, and they can match each service problem with a particular MindWriter model and production sequence (from a production database), and, using yet another database (generated from warranty registration), they can match each problem to a name and address of an owner. But, having done all that, they still aren't likely to know how a particular owner uses his or her laptop or how satisfied an owner was with MindWriter's postpurchase service policies and practices.

Mining management information databases is fashionable and all types of organizations increasingly value the ability to extract meaningful information. While such data mining is often a starting point in decision-based research, rarely will such activity answer all management questions related to a particular management dilemma.

Unresearchable Questions

Not all management questions are researchable, and not all research questions are answerable. To be researchable, a question must be one for which observation or other data collection can provide the answer. Many questions cannot be answered on the basis of information alone.

Questions of value and policy often must be weighed in management decisions. In the MetalWorks study, management may be asking, "Should we hold out for a liberalization of the seniority rules in our new labor negotiations?" While information can be brought to bear on this question, such additional considerations as "fairness to the workers" or "management's right to manage" may be important to the decision. It may be possible for many of these questions of value to be transformed into questions of fact. Concerning "fairness to the workers," one might first gather information from which to estimate the extent and degree to which workers will be affected by a rule change; then one could gather opinion statements by the workers about the fairness of seniority rules. Even so, substantial value elements remain. Questions left unanswered include, "Should we argue for a policy that will adversely affect the security and well-being of older workers who are least equipped to cope with this adversity?" Even if a question can be answered by facts alone, it might not be researchable because currently accepted and tested procedures or techniques are inadequate.

Ill-Defined Management Problems

Some categories of problems are so complex, value-laden, and bound by constraints that they prove to be intractable to traditional forms of analysis. These questions have characteristics that are virtually the opposite of those of well-defined problems. One author describes the differences like this:

> To the extent that a problem situation evokes a high level of agreement over a specified community of problem solvers regarding the referents of the attributes in which it is given, the operations that are permitted, and the consequences of those operations, it may be termed unambiguous or well defined with respect to that community. On the other hand, to the extent that a problem evokes a highly variable set of responses concerning referents of attributes, permissible operations, and their consequences, it may be considered ill-defined or ambiguous with respect to that community.[2]

Another author points out that ill-defined research questions are least susceptible to attack from quantitative research methods because such problems have too many interrelated facets for measurement to handle with accuracy.[3] Yet another authority suggests there are some research questions of this type for which methods do not presently exist or, if the methods were to be invented, they still might not provide the data necessary to solve them.[4] Novice researchers should avoid ill-defined problems. Even seasoned researchers will want to conduct a thorough exploratory study before proceeding with the latest approaches.

Politically Motivated Research

It is important to remember that a manager's motivations for seeking research are not always obvious. Managers might express a genuine need for specific information on which to base a decision. This is the ideal scenario for quality research. Sometimes, however, a research study may not really be desirable but is authorized anyway, chiefly because its presence may win approval for a certain manager's pet idea. At other times, research may be authorized as a measure of personal protection for a decision maker in case he or she is criticized later. In these less-than-ideal cases, the researcher may find it more difficult to win the manager's support for an appropriate research design.

Designing the Study

Here we distinguish secondary data in exploration from secondary data collection as the principal methodology to resolve the management dilemma.

The **research design** is the blueprint for fulfilling objectives and answering questions. Selecting a design may be complicated by the availability of a large variety of methods, techniques, procedures, protocols, and sampling plans. For example, you may decide on a secondary data study, case study, survey, experiment, or simulation. If a survey is selected, should it be administered by mail, computer, telephone, the Internet, or personal interview? Should all relevant data be collected at one time or at regular intervals? What kind of structure will the questionnaire or interview guide possess? What question wording should be employed? Should the responses be scaled or open-ended? How will reliability and validity be achieved? Will characteristics of the interviewer influence responses to the measurement questions? What kind of training should the data collectors receive? Is a sample or a census to be taken? What types of sampling should be considered? These questions represent only a few of the decisions that have to be made when just one method is chosen.

We discuss identifying and classifying various research designs in Chapter 6, while in Part III we provide information on specific methodologies.

The creative researcher actually benefits from this confusing array of options. The numerous combinations spawned by the abundance of tools may be used to construct alternative perspectives on the same problem. By creating a design using diverse methodologies, researchers are able to achieve greater insight than if they followed the most frequent method encountered in the literature or suggested by a disciplinary bias. Although it must be conceded that students or managers rarely have the resources to pursue a single problem from a multimethod, multistudy strategy, the advantages of several competing designs should be considered before settling on a final one.

Jason's preference for MindWriter is to collect as much information as possible from an exploration of company records, company managers of various departments, and multiple phone surveys. Financial constraints, however, might force the substitution of a less expensive methodology: a self-administered study in the form of a postcard sent to each CompleteCare program user with his or her returned laptop, followed by phone contact with nonresponders.

S N A P S H O T

Grilled Cheese Sandwiches and the Dairy Fairy

If you were Kraft and discovered that, while sales of sliced cheese were increasing, your brand's sales were decreasing, you might turn to advertising to reverse the slide. But just what would you say—and how? Faced with this situation, Kraft sent ethnographers from Strategic Frameworking to talk with moms aged 25–64 who were fixing sandwiches in their kitchens. Focus groups then reinforced that moms feel good about giving their kids cheese because of its nutritional value. Focus groups also revealed that even though their kids preferred Kraft slices, a price difference could persuade moms to purchase a competitive brand. A subsequent phone survey by Market Facts revealed moms would buy the pricier Kraft slices due to extra calcium. Next came TV commercial tests for two spots featuring the "good-taste-plus-the-calcium-they-need" message. A spot featuring a straightforward message didn't score as high as one featuring kids scarfing down gooey grilled cheese sandwiches, but the male voice–delivered "2-out-of-5-kids-don't-get-enough-calcium" message generated guilt, not positive purchase intentions. A revised commercial featured the cheese-scarfing kids while the Dairy Fairy (an animated cow) delivered the calcium message. Subsequently, Millward Brown Group discovered through copy testing research that the dual message had finally gotten through. The TV commercial aired, delivering an 11.8 percent increase in sales and a 14.5 percent increase in base volume. Sixty-five percent of the growth in sales was attributed to the campaign.

www.kraft.com

www.strategicframeworking.com

www.marketfacts.com

www.millwardbrown.com

www.jwt.com

Sampling Design

Another step in planning the design is to identify the target population and select the sample if a census is not desired. The researcher must determine who and how many people to interview, what and how many events to observe, or what and how many records to inspect. A **sample** is a part of the target population, carefully selected to represent that population. When researchers undertake sampling studies, they are interested in estimating one or more population values and/or testing one or more statistical hypotheses.

If a study's objective is to examine the attitudes of U.S. automobile assemblers about quality improvement, the population may be defined as the entire adult population of auto assemblers employed by the auto industry in the United States. Definition of the terms *adult* and *assembler* and the relevant job descriptions included under "assembly" and "auto industry" may further limit the population under study. The investigator may also want to restrict the research to readily identifiable companies in the market, vehicle types, or assembly processes.

We describe types of samples, sample frames, and the determination of sample size in Chapter 7.

The sampling process must then give every person within the target population a known nonzero chance of selection if probability sampling is used. If there is no feasible alternative, a nonprobability approach may be used. Jason knows that his target population comprises MindWriter customers who have firsthand experience with the CompleteCare program. Given that a list of CompleteCare program users (a sample frame) is readily available each month, a probability sample is feasible.

Resource Allocation and Budgets

General notions about research budgets have a tendency to single out data collection as the most costly activity. Data collection requires substantial resources but perhaps less of the budget than clients expect. Employees must be paid, training and travel must be provided, and other expenses incurred must be paid; but this phase of the project often takes no more than one-third of the total research budget. The geographic scope and the number of observations required do affect the cost, but much of the cost is relatively independent of the size of the data-gathering effort. Thus, a guide might be that (1) project planning, (2) data gathering, and (3) analysis, interpretation, and reporting each share about equally in the budget.

Without budgetary approval, many research efforts are terminated for lack of resources (see Exhibit 3–7). A budget may require significant development and documentation as in grant and contract research, or it may require less attention as in some in-house projects or investigations funded out of the researcher's own resources. The researcher who seeks funding must be able not only to persuasively justify the costs of the project but also to identify the sources and methods of funding. One author identifies three types of budgets in organizations where research is purchased and cost containment is crucial:

- **Rule-of-thumb budgeting** involves taking a fixed percentage of some criterion. For example, a percentage of the prior year's sales revenues may be the basis for determining the marketing research budget for a manufacturer.

- **Departmental or functional area budgeting** allocates a portion of total expenditures in the unit to research activities. Government agencies, not-for-profits, and the private sector alike will frequently manage research activities out of functional budgets. Units such as human resources, marketing, or engineering then have the authority to approve their own projects.

- **Task budgeting** selects specific research projects to support on an ad hoc basis. This type is the least proactive but does permit definitive cost-benefit analysis.[5]

Valuing Research Information

There is a great deal of interplay between budgeting and value assessment in any management decision to conduct research. An appropriate research study should help managers avoid losses and increase sales or profits; otherwise, research can be wasteful. The decision maker wants a firm cost estimate for a project and an equally precise assurance that useful information will result from the study. Even if the researcher can give good cost and information estimates, the managers still must judge whether the benefits outweigh the costs.

Conceptually, the value of applied research is not difficult to determine. In a business situation, the research should produce added revenues or reduce expenses in much the same way as any other investment of resources. One source suggests that the value of research information may be judged in terms of "the difference between the result of decisions made with the information and the result that would be made without it."[6] While such a criterion is simple to state, its actual application presents difficult measurement problems.

Evaluation Methods

Ex Post Facto Evaluation   If there is any measurement of the value of research, it is usually an after-the-fact event. Twedt reports on one such effort, an evaluation of marketing research done at a major corporation.[7] He secured "an objective estimate of the contribution of each project to corporate profitability." He reports that most studies were intended to help management determine which one of two (or more) alternatives was preferable. He guesses that in 60 percent of the decision situations, the correct decision would have been made *without* the benefit of the research information. In the remaining 40 percent of the cases, the research led to the correct decision. Using these data, he estimates that the return on investment in marketing research in this company was 351 percent for the year studied. However, he acknowledges the return-on-investment figure was inflated because only the direct research costs were included.

This effort at cost-benefit analysis is commendable even though the results come too late to guide a current research decision. Such analysis may sharpen the manager's ability to make judgments about future research proposals. However, the critical problem remains, that of project evaluation *before* the study is done.

We discuss the two-stage study in Chapter 6.

Prior or Interim Evaluation   A proposal to conduct a thorough management audit of operations in a company may be a worthy one, but neither its costs nor its benefits are easily estimated in advance. Such projects are sufficiently unique that managerial experience seldom provides much aid in evaluating such a proposal. But even in these situations, managers can make some useful judgments. They may determine that a management audit is needed because the company is in dire straits and management does not understand the scope of its problems. The management information need may be so great as to ensure that the research is approved. In such cases, managers may decide to control the research expenditure risk by doing a study in stages. They can then review costs and benefits at the end of each stage and give or withhold further authorization.

Option Analysis   Some progress has been made in the development of methods for assessing the value of research when management has a choice between well-defined options. Managers can conduct a formal analysis with each alternative judged in terms of estimated costs and associated benefits and with managerial judgment playing a major role.

If the research design can be stated clearly, one can estimate an approximate cost. The critical task is to quantify the benefits from the research. At best, estimates of benefits are crude and largely reflect an orderly way to estimate outcomes under uncertain conditions. To illustrate how the contribution of research is evaluated in such a decision situation, we must digress briefly into the rudiments of decision theory.

Decision Theory   When there are alternatives from which to choose, a rational way to approach the decision is to try to assess the outcomes of each action. The case of two choices will be discussed here, although the same approach can be used with more than two choices.

Two possible actions (A_1 and A_2) may represent two different ways to organize a company, provide financing, produce a product, and so forth. The manager chooses the action that affords the best outcome—the action choice that meets or exceeds whatever criteria are established for judging alternatives. Each criterion is a combination of a **decision rule** and a **decision variable.** The decision variable might be "direct dollar savings," "contribution to overhead and profits," "time required for completion of the project," and so forth. For MindWriter, the decision variable might be number of postservice complaints or the level of postservice satisfaction. Usually the decision variable is expressed in dollars, representing sales, costs, some form of profits or contribution, or some other quantifiable measure. The decision rule may be "choose the course of action with the lowest loss possibility" or perhaps "choose the alternative that provides the greatest annual net profit." For MindWriter, the decision rule might be "choose the alternative that provides the highest level of postservice satisfaction."

You'll find an example of decision theory in Appendix B.

The alternative selected (A_1 versus A_2) depends on the decision variable chosen and the decision rule used. The evaluation of alternatives requires that (1) each alternative is explicitly stated, (2) a decision variable is defined by an outcome that may be measured, and (3) a decision rule is determined by which outcomes may be compared.

The Research Proposal

Exhibit 3–1 depicts the research proposal as an activity that incorporates decisions made during early project planning phases of the study, including the management-research question hierarchy and exploration. The proposal thus incorporates the choices the investigator makes in the preliminary steps, as depicted in Exhibit 3–7.

A written proposal is often required when a study is being suggested. It ensures that the parties concur on the project's purpose and on the proposed methods of investigation. Time and budgets are often spelled out, as are other responsibilities and obligations. Depending on the needs and desires of the manager, substantial background detail and elaboration of proposed techniques may be included.

The length and complexity of research proposals range widely. Business research proposals normally range from 1 to 10 pages. Applicants for foundation or government research grants typically file a proposal request of a few pages, often in a standardized format specified by the granting agency. A research proposal also may be

EXHIBIT 3–7   Research Proposal Process

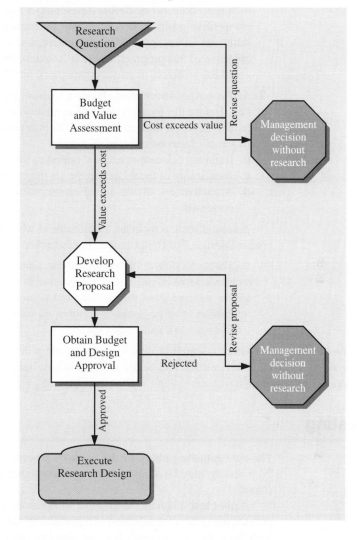

oral, where all aspects of the research are discussed but not codified in writing. This is more likely when a manager directs his or her own research or the research activities of subordinates.

Proposal Content   Every proposal, regardless of length, should include two basic sections:

- Statement of the research question.
- Brief description of research methodology.

In a brief memo-type proposal, the research question may be incorporated into a paragraph that also sets out the management dilemma, management question, and categories of investigative questions. The following statements present the management question facing the respective managers and point out the nature of the research that will be undertaken:

1. BankChoice, currently the leading bank in the city, has not been growing as fast as its major competitors. Before developing a long-range plan to enhance the bank's competitive position, it is important to determine the bank's present competitive status, its advantages and opportunities, and its major deficiencies. The primary objective of this proposed research is to develop a body of benchmark information about BankChoice, its major competitors, and the market for banking services.

2. ArtDeco Appliances must choose a location for a new plant to serve eastern markets. Before this location decision is made, a feasibility study should be conducted to determine, for each of five sites, the estimated
   a. Costs of serving existing customers.
   b. Building, relocation, tax, and operating costs.
   c. Availability of local labor in the six major crafts used in production.
   d. Attractiveness of the living environment for professional and management personnel.

A second section includes a statement of what will be done: the bare bones of the research design. For BankChoice, the researcher might propose:

> Personal interviews will be conducted with a minimum of 200 residents to determine their knowledge of, use of, and attitudes toward local banks. In addition, information will be gathered about their banking and financing practices and preferences. Other information of an economic or demographic nature also will be gathered from published sources and public agencies.

We describe more detailed research proposals in Chapter 4.

Often research proposals are much more detailed and describe specific measurement devices that will be used, time and cost budgets, sampling plans, and many other details.

Pilot Testing

The data-gathering phase of the research process typically begins with pilot testing. Pilot testing may be skipped when the researcher tries to condense the project time frame.

A **pilot test** is conducted to detect weaknesses in design and instrumentation and to provide proxy data for selection of a probability sample. It should, therefore, draw subjects from the target population and simulate the procedures and protocols that have been designated for data collection. If the study is a survey to be executed by mail, the pilot questionnaire should be mailed. If the design calls for observation by an unobtrusive researcher, this behavior should be practiced. The size of the pilot group may range from 25 to 100 subjects, depending on the method to be tested, but the respondents do not have to be statistically selected. In very small populations or special applications, pilot testing runs the risk of exhausting the supply of respondents and sensitizing them to the purpose of the study. This risk is generally overshadowed by the improvements made to the design by a trial run.

You may find it valuable to refer to Exhibit 3–1 as we overview the content sections of the research proposal.

There are a number of variations on pilot testing. Some of them are intentionally restricted to data collection activities. One form, *pretesting,* may rely on colleagues, respondent surrogates, or actual respondents to refine a measuring instrument. This important activity has saved countless survey studies from disaster by using the suggestions of the respondents to identify and change confusing, awkward, or offensive questions and techniques. One interview study was designed by a group of college professors for EducTV, an educational television consortium. In the pilot test, they discovered that the wording of nearly two-thirds of the questions was unintelligible to the target group, later found to have a median eighth-grade education. The revised instrument used the respondents' language and was successful. Pretesting may be repeated several times to refine questions, instruments, or procedures.

Data Collection

The gathering of data may range from a simple observation at one location to a grandiose survey of multinational corporations at sites in different parts of the world. The method selected will largely determine how the data are collected. Questionnaires, standardized tests, observational forms, laboratory notes, and instrument calibration logs are among the devices used to record raw data.

But what are data? One writer defines **data** as the facts presented to the researcher from the study's environment. Data may be further characterized by their abstractness, verifiability, elusiveness, and closeness to the phenomenon.[8] As *abstractions,* data are more metaphorical than real. For example, the growth in GNP cannot be observed directly; only the effects of it may be recorded. Second, data are processed by our senses—often limited in comparison to the senses of other living organisms. When sensory experiences consistently produce the same result, our data are said to be trustworthy because they may be *verified.* Third, capturing data is *elusive,* complicated by the speed at which events occur and the time-bound nature of observation. Opinions, preferences, and attitudes vary from one milieu to another and with the passage of time. For example, attitudes about spending during the late 1980s differed dramatically one decade later within the same population, due to the sustained prosperity within the final four years of the millennium. Finally, data reflect their truthfulness by *closeness to the phenomena. Secondary data* have had at least one level of interpretation inserted between the event and its recording. *Primary data* are sought for their proximity to the truth and control over error. These cautions remind us to use care in designing data collection procedures and generalizing from results.

We address data collection in detail in Part III.

Data are edited to ensure consistency across respondents and to locate omissions. In the case of survey methods, editing reduces errors in the recording, improves legibility, and clarifies unclear and inappropriate responses. Edited data are then put into a form that makes analysis possible. Because it is impractical to place raw data into a report, alphanumeric codes are used to reduce the responses to a more manageable system for storage and future processing. The codes follow various decision rules that the researcher has devised to assist with sorting, tabulating, and analyzing. Personal computers have made it possible to merge editing, coding, and data entry into fewer steps even when the final analysis may be run on a larger system.

Analysis and Interpretation

Managers need information, not raw data. Researchers generate information by analyzing data after its collection. **Data analysis** usually involves reducing accumulated data to a manageable size, developing summaries, looking for patterns, and applying statistical techniques. Scaled responses on questionnaires and experimental instruments often require the analyst to derive various functions, as well as to explore relationships among variables. Further, researchers must interpret these findings in light of the client's research question or determine if the results are consistent with their hypotheses and theories. Increasingly, managers are asking research specialists to make recommendations based on their interpretation of the data.

We address data analysis and interpretation in Chapters 15–19.

A modest example involves a market research firm that polls 2,000 people from its target population for a new generation of wallet-sized portable telephones. Each respondent will be asked four questions:

1. "Do you prefer the convenience of Pocket-Phone over existing cellular telephones?"
2. "Are there transmission problems with Pocket-Phone?"
3. "Is Pocket-Phone better suited to worldwide transmission than your existing cellular phone?"
4. "Would cost alone persuade you to purchase Pocket-Phone?"

The answers will produce 8,000 pieces of raw data. Reducing the data to a workable size will yield eight statistics: the percentage of yes and no answers to each question. When a half-dozen demographic questions about the respondents are added, the total amount of data easily triples. If the researcher scaled the four key questions rather than eliciting yes–no responses, the analysis would likely require more powerful statistical analysis than summarization.

Reporting the Results

Finally, it is necessary to prepare a report and transmit the findings and recommendations to the manager for the intended purpose of decision making. The researcher adjusts the style and organization of the report according to the target audience, the occasion, and the purpose of the research. The results of applied research may be communicated via conference call, letter, written report, oral presentation, or some combination of any or all of these methods. Reports should be developed from the manager's or information user's perspective. The sophistication of the design and sampling plan or the software used to analyze the data may help to establish the researcher's credibility, but in the end, the manager's foremost concern is solving the management dilemma. Thus, the researcher must accurately assess the manager's needs throughout the research process and incorporate this understanding into the final product, the research report.

The management decision maker occasionally shelves the research report without taking action. Inferior communication of results is a primary reason for this outcome. With this possibility in mind, a research specialist should strive for

- Insightful adaptation of the information to the client's needs.
- Careful choice of words in crafting interpretations, conclusions, and recommendations.

We cover the research report in Chapter 20.

Occasionally, organizational and environmental forces beyond the researcher's control argue against the implementation of results. Such was the case in a study conducted for the Association of American Publishers, which needed an ad campaign to encourage people to read more books. The project, costing $125,000, found that only 13 percent of Americans buy general-interest books in stores. When the time came to commit $14 million to the campaign to raise book sales, the membership's interest had faded and the project died.[9]

At a minimum, a research report should contain the following:

- An *executive summary* consisting of a synopsis of the problem, findings, and recommendations.

MANAGEMENT

- An *overview of the research*: the problem's background, literature summary, methods and procedures, and conclusions.
- A section on *implementation strategies* for the recommendations.
- A *technical appendix* with all the materials necessary to replicate the project.

SUMMARY

1 Research originates in the decision process. A manager needs specific information for setting objectives, defining tasks, finding the best strategy by which to carry out the tasks, or judging how well the strategy is being implemented.

A dilemma-centered emphasis—the problem's origin, selection, statement, exploration, and refinement—dominates the sequence of the research process. A management dilemma can originate in any aspect of an organization. A decision to do research can be inappropriately driven by the availability of coveted tools and databases. To be researchable, a problem must be subject to observation or other forms of empirical data collection.

2 How one structures the research question sets the direction for the project. A management problem or opportunity can be formulated as a hierarchical sequence of questions. At the most general level is the management dilemma. This is translated into a management question and then into a research question—the major objective of the study. In turn, the research question is further expanded into investigative questions. These questions represent the various facets of the problem to be solved, and they influence research design, including design strategy, data collection planning, and sampling. At the most specific level are measurement questions that are answered by respondents in a survey or answered about each subject in an observational study.

3 Exploration of the problem is accomplished through familiarization with the available literature, interviews with experts, focus groups, or some combination. Revision of the management or research questions is a desirable outcome of exploration and enhances the researcher's understanding of the options available for developing a successful design.

Decisions concerning the type of study, the means of data collection, measurement, and sampling plans must be made when planning the design. Most researchers undertake sampling studies because of an interest in estimating population values or testing a statistical hypothesis. Carefully constructed delimitations are essential for specifying an appropriate probability sample. Nonprobability samples are also used.

4 Budgets and value assessments determine whether most projects receive necessary funding. Their thorough documentation is an integral part of the research proposal. Proposals are required for many research projects and should, at a minimum, describe the research question and the specific task the research will undertake.

Pilot tests are conducted to detect weaknesses in the study's design, data collection instruments, and procedures. Once the researcher is satisfied that the plan is sound, data collection begins. Data are collected, edited, coded, and prepared for analysis.

Data analysis involves reduction, summarization, pattern examination, and the statistical evaluation of hypotheses. A written report describing the study's findings is used to transmit the results and recommendations to the intended decision maker. By cycling the conclusions back into the original problem, a new research iteration may begin, and findings may be applied.

KEY TERMS

data   87
data analysis   87
decision rule   84
decision variable   84
exploration   72
investigative questions   75

management dilemma   66
management question   69
management-research question
    hierarchy   66
measurement questions   76

research design   81
research process   64
research question(s)   73
pilot test   86
sample   82

EXAMPLES

Company	Scenario	Page
ArtDeco Appliances[*]	A company choosing a location for a new manufacturing plant.	86
Association of American Publishers	A trade association that conducted research to develop an ad campaign that would encourage the reading of books.	88
BankChoice[*]	A bank experiencing eroding profits and lackluster growth.	71
EducTV[*]	An educational television consortium serving a poorly educated population attempting to assess programming needs.	86
Goodyear Tire & Rubber Company	Research led to Aquatred 3, the most award-winning new product in tire industry history.	70
Kraft	Research was used to develop a new advertising strategy for Kraft Singles.	81
Market Facts, Inc.	Conducted a phone survey to discover what would make moms buy the pricier Kraft Singles.	81
Millward Brown Group	Copy testing research that revealed the "great-taste-with-more-calcium" message was correctly delivered by the Dairy Fairy as spokescharacter, not a male voice-over.	81
MetalWorks[*]	An industrial company suffering image problems approaching union negotiations.	70
MindWriter[*]	A computer company assessing customer satisfaction.	BRTL and throughout
Pocket-Phone[*]	A producer of portable, wallet-sized wireless telephones studying the data collected from a recent survey to assess the newest generation of phones.	88
SalePro[*]	A national sales organization facing unexplained sales variations by territory.	66
Strategic Frameworking	Conducted an ethnography study for Kraft to help the firm understand what moms who make lunch for their kids want.	81
TechByte[*]	A company interested in enhancing its position in a given technology that appears to hold potential for future growth.	72

[*]Due to the confidential and proprietary nature of most research, the names of some companies have been changed.

DISCUSSION QUESTIONS

Terms in Review

1. Some questions are answerable by research and others are not. Using some management problems of your choosing, distinguish between them.

2. Discuss the problems of trading off exploration and pilot testing under tight budgetary constraints. What are the immediate and long-term effects?

3. A company is experiencing a poor inventory management situation and receives alternative research proposals. Proposal 1 is to use an audit of last year's transactions as a basis for recommendations. Proposal 2 is to study and recommend changes to the procedures and systems used by the materials department. Discuss issues of evaluation in terms of

   a. Ex post facto versus prior evaluation.

   b. Evaluation using option analysis and decision theory.

Making Research Decisions

4. Confronted by low productivity, the president of Oaks International Inc. asks a research company to study job satisfaction in the corporation. What are some of the important reasons that this research project may fail to make an adequate contribution to the solution of management problems?

5. You have been approached by the editor of *Gentlemen's Magazine* to carry out a research study. The magazine has been unsuccessful in attracting shoe manufacturers as advertisers. When the sales force tried to secure advertising from shoe manufacturers, they were told men's clothing stores are a small and dying segment of their business. Since *Gentlemen's Magazine* goes chiefly to men's clothing stores, the manufacturers reasoned that it was, therefore, not a good vehicle for their advertising. The editor believes that a survey (via mail questionnaire) of men's clothing stores in the United States will probably show that these stores are important outlets for men's shoes and are not declining in importance as shoe outlets. He asks you to develop a proposal for the study and submit it to him. Develop the management-research question hierarchy that will help you to develop a specific proposal.

6. Based on an analysis of the last six months' sales, your boss notices that sales of beef products are declining in your chain's restaurants. As beef entrée sales decline, so do profits. Fearing beef sales have declined due to several newspaper stories reporting *E. coli* contamination discovered at area grocery stores, he suggests a survey of area restaurants to see if the situation is pervasive.

   a. What do you think of this research suggestion?

   b. How, if at all, could you improve on the vice president's formulation of the research question?

Bringing Research to Life

7. Take one of the possible problems causing MindWriter's management dilemma (see the "Close-Up" on page 76 and Exhibit 3–3) and develop plausible management and research questions.

8. Using the "uneven courier performance" problem or the "product damaged during repair" problem (see the "Close-Up" on page 76 and Exhibit 3–3), develop some exploration activities that would let Jason or Myra proceed to develop a more refined research question dealing with this problem.

9. Using the MindWriter postservicing packaging alternative as the research question, develop appropriate investigative questions within the management-research question hierarchy by preparing an exhibit similar to Exhibit 3–4.

**From Concept
to Practice**

10. Develop the management-research question hierarchy (Exhibits 3–2 and 3–3), citing management dilemma, management question, and research question(s) for each of the following:

    a. The production manager of a shoe factory.

    b. The president of a home health care services firm.

    c. The vice president of labor relations for an auto manufacturer.

    d. The retail advertising manager of a major metropolitan newspaper.

    e. The chief of police in a major city.

11. Develop the management-research question hierarchy for a management dilemma you face at work or with an organization to which you volunteer.

12. Develop a memo-proposal for a research study in which 300 interviews are conducted to address the management question you defined in question 11.

WWW Exercises

Visit our website for Internet exercises related to this chapter at
www.mhhe.com/business/cooper8

CASES*

CALLING UP ATTENDANCE

 GOODYEAR'S AQUATRED

INQUIRING MINDS WANT TO KNOW—NOW!

 **JOHN DEERE AND COMPANY**

KNSD, SAN DIEGO

MASTERING TEACHER LEADERSHIP

 **NCR: TEEING UP A NEW STRATEGIC
DIRECTION**

 OUTBOARD MARINE CORPORATION

**RAMADA DEMONSTRATES ITS
PERSONAL BEST**

**STATE FARM: DANGEROUS
INTERSECTIONS ON THE ROAD
TO LOSS PREVENTION**

*All cases indicating a video icon are located on the Instructor's Videotape Supplement. All nonvideo cases are in the case section of the textbook. All cases indicating a CD icon offer a data set, which is located on the accompanying CD.

REFERENCE NOTES

1. Albert Einstein and L. Infeld, *The Evolution of Physics* (New York: Simon & Schuster, 1938), p. 95.

2. Walter B. Reitman, "Heuristic Decision Procedures, Open Constraints, and the Structure of Ill-Defined Problems," in *Human Judgments and Optimality,* eds. Maynard W. Shelly II and Glenn L. Bryan (New York: Wiley, 1964), p. 285.

3. Carl M. Moore, *Group Techniques for Idea Building,* 2nd ed. (Thousand Oaks, CA: Sage Publications, 1994).

4. Fred N. Kerlinger, *Foundations of Behavioral Research,* 3rd ed. (New York: Holt, Rinehart & Winston, 1986), pp. 436–37.

5. Walter B. Wentz, *Marketing Research: Management, Method, and Cases* (New York: Harper & Row, 1979), p. 35.

6. Robert D. Buzzell, Donald F. Cox, and Rex V. Brown, *Marketing Research and Information Systems* (New York: McGraw-Hill, 1969), p. 595.

7. Dik Warren Twedt, "What Is the 'Return on Investment' in Marketing Research?" *Journal of Marketing* 30 (January 1966), pp. 62–63.

8. Paul D. Leedy, *How to Read Research and Understand It* (New York: Macmillan, 1981), pp. 67–70.

9. Roger Cohen, "For U.S. Publishers, Awash in Red Ink, the Moment of Truth Looms," *International Herald Tribune,* March 6, 1990, p. 6.

REFERENCES FOR SNAPSHOTS AND CAPTIONS

Goodyear

Mike Allen, "Goodyear's Aquatred 3" (http://www.popularmechanics.com/popmech/auto3/0008AUSTWFAM.html).

"Goodyear Aquatred 3 Tire Splashes to New Levels," Goodyear Tire and Rubber Company press release, June 20, 2001 (http://biz.yahoo.com/prnews/010621/clth006.html); (http://www.goodyear.com/cgi-bin/news/list_press.pl?key=707163050993241270357703864&country=us).

"Goodyear Reports Results for 2001's Second Quarter," Goodyear Tire and Rubber Company press release, July 23, 2001 (http://www.goodyear.com/cgi-bin/news/list_press.pl?key=46028933999589046425526379&country=us).

Scott Memmer, "Goodyear Aquatred 3: The Next Generation," Edmunds.com, April 17, 2001 (http://www.edmunds.com/news/feature/genral/43850/article.html).

McGraw-Hill Video Library.

Kraft

"Cheese, Please! Kraft Singles Talks to Moms about Kids and Calcium," *American Demographics,* March 2000, pp. s6–s7.

CLASSIC AND CONTEMPORARY READINGS

Fox, David J. *The Research Process in Education.* New York: Holt, Rinehart & Winston, 1969. Chapter 2 includes a research process model to compare with the one in this chapter.

Leedy, Paul D. *Practical Research: Planning & Design.* 6th ed. Englewood Cliffs, NJ: Prentice-Hall, 1996. Practical and readable sections guide students through the research process.

Murdick, Robert G., and Donald R. Cooper. *Business Research: Concepts and Guides.* Columbus, OH: Grid, 1982. A supplementary text with a strong emphasis on problem identification and formulation.

Selltiz, Claire; Lawrence S. Wrightsman; and Stuart M. Cook. *Research Methods in Social Relations.* 3rd ed. New York: Holt, Rinehart & Winston, 1976. Chapters 1 and 2 present a good research process example and discussion of formulating a research problem.

Tull, Donald S., and Del I. Hawkins. *Marketing Research: Meaning, Measurement, and Method.* 6th ed. New York: Macmillan, 1992. The authors provide good coverage of the valuation of research information through a Bayesian decision theory approach.

CHAPTER 4

The Research Proposal

Learning Objectives

After reading this chapter, you should understand . . .

1   The purpose of the proposal and how it is used by the researcher and management decision maker.

2   The types of proposals and the contents of each.

3   The two processes for evaluating the quality of proposals and when each is used.

Bringing Research to Life

"Come on over here and meet Robert Buffet." The president of the Economic Development Council seized Myra Wines by the elbow and propelled her across the dining room to meet a tall young man suited in navy blue pinstripes. She recognized his name: He was the local manager of a national accounting firm.

"Robert Buffet, meet Myra Wines, consumer affairs manager for MindWriter."

"Hello, Robert," she said. She studied him carefully, from his brightly shined black shoes to his razor cut hair. He was about the same age as her new consultant, Jason Henry, but something in the way he held himself suggested a self-assurance that Jason had not yet developed. This young man dressed like a banker, while Jason suggested a sincere yet somehow impatient librarian.

"And what a pleasure it is to meet you," he said in a ripe baritone voice, smiling with his lips but not his eyes, which had wandered to a prominent banker who was chatting with a competing CPA.

"Here's the situation, Myra," said the president. "The state commerce secretary has been concerned for some time about the extent to which entrepreneurial companies, which are popping up all over the state, are actually investing in job-building technology. They have contracted with Robert's firm to study the situation in five counties, assess job creation and the like, and report this back to Tallahassee."

Myra asked, "Am I right in suspecting that the governor is worried that these start-up companies are investing in robotics and computers and not creating new manufacturing jobs?"

"Basically, that is the concern, Ms. Wines," said the tall young man. "We have already cut the contract, you see, in Tallahassee, and so we have the green light to select our five sites and commence the interviewing."

"The thing is, Myra," said the president, "before their task force can come into a county and start interviewing and collecting data, they have got to have the sponsorship of a business group. In this county, it is our council that has to look over their proposal and assure the business community it is in their best interests to cooperate."

"And you want me to critically examine their proposal and let you know what I think."

"By two weeks from Friday, please," said the president, "as a favor."

"Here is a copy of our proposal," said the tall young man. "How awfully nice chatting with you." He grasped her hand, gave it one shake, patted the council president on the shoulder, and headed for the refreshment table, where a local auto dealer presented an easy target for a sales pitch.

The Purpose of the Research Proposal

A proposal is an individual's or company's offer to produce a product or render a service to a potential buyer or sponsor. The purpose of the research proposal is

1. To present the management question to be researched and relate its importance.

2. To discuss the research efforts of others who have worked on related management questions.

3. To suggest the data necessary for solving the management question and how the data will be gathered, treated, and interpreted.

In addition, a research proposal must present the researcher's plan, services, and credentials in the best possible way to encourage the proposal's selection over competitors. In contract research, the survival of companies depends on their ability to develop winning proposals.[1] A **proposal** is also known as a work plan, prospectus, outline, statement of intent, or draft plan.[2] The proposal tells us what, why, how, where, and to whom the research will be done. It must also show the benefit of doing the research.[3]

Many students and beginning researchers view the proposal as unnecessary work. In actuality, the more inexperienced a researcher is, the more important it is to have a well-planned and adequately documented proposal. The research proposal is essentially a road map, showing clearly the location from which a journey begins, the destination to be reached, and the method of getting there. Well-prepared proposals include potential problems that may be encountered along the way and methods for avoiding or working around them, much as a road map indicates alternate routes for a detour.

Sponsor Uses

All research has a sponsor in one form or another. The student researcher is responsible to the class instructor. In a corporate setting, whether the research is being done in-house by a research department or under contract to an external research firm, management sponsors the research. University-, government-, or corporate-sponsored (grant) research uses grant committees to evaluate the work.

A poorly planned, poorly written, or poorly organized proposal damages the researcher's reputation more than the decision not to submit a proposal.

A research proposal allows the sponsor to assess the sincerity of the researcher's purpose, the clarity of his or her design, the extent of his or her relevant background material, and fitness for undertaking the project. Depending on the type of research and the sponsor, various aspects of a standard proposal design are emphasized. The proposal displays the researcher's discipline, organization, and logic. It thus allows the research sponsor to assess both the researcher and the proposed design, to compare them against competing proposals on current organizational, scholastic, or scientific needs, and to make the best selection for the project.

Comparison of the research project results with the proposal is also the first step in the process of evaluating the overall research. By comparing the final product with the stated objectives, it is easy for the sponsor to decide if the research goal—a better decision on the management question—has been achieved.

Another benefit of the proposal is the discipline it brings to the sponsor. Many managers, requesting research from an in-house, departmental research project, do not adequately define the problem they are addressing. The research proposal acts as a catalyst for discussion between the person conducting the research and the manager. The researcher translates the management question, as described by the manager, into the research question and outlines the objectives of the study. Upon review, the manager

EXHIBIT 4–1   Proposal Development

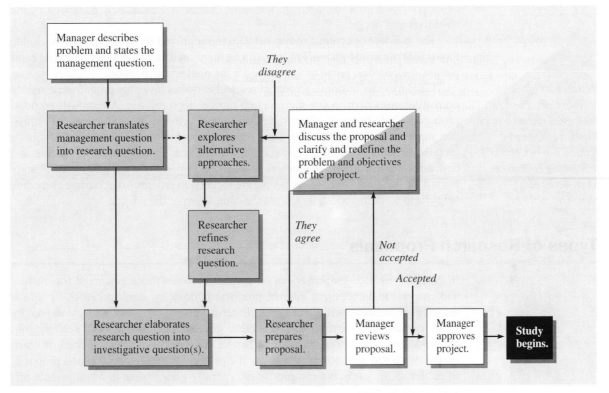

may discover that the interpretation of the problem does not encompass all the original symptoms. The proposal, then, serves as the basis for additional discussion between the manager and the researcher until all aspects of the management question are understood. Parts of the management question may not be researchable, or at least not subject to empirical study. An alternate design, such as a qualitative or policy analysis study, may need to be proposed. Upon completion of the discussions, the sponsor and researcher should agree on a carefully worded research question. As Exhibit 4–1 reveals, proposal development can work in an iterative fashion until the sponsor authorizes the research to proceed.

Appendix C provides further information on RFPs.

For an outside research contract, the process is different. Proposals are usually submitted in response to a request for bid, or **request for proposal (RFP).** The researchers may wish to convince the sponsor that his or her approach to the research question differs from that indicated by the management question specified in the initial RFP. In this way, the researcher can show superior understanding of the management dilemma compared to researchers submitting competing proposals.

Researcher Benefits

A proposal is even more beneficial for the researcher than for the sponsor. The process of writing a proposal encourages the researcher to plan and review the project's logical steps. Related management and research literature should be examined in developing the proposal. This review prompts the researcher to assess previous approaches to similar management questions and revise the research plan accordingly. Additionally, developing the proposal offers the opportunity to spot flaws in the logic, errors in assumptions, or even management questions that are not adequately addressed by the objectives and design.

The in-house or contract researcher uses the approved research proposal as a guide throughout the investigation. Progress can be monitored and milestones noted. At completion, the proposal provides an outline for the final research report.[4]

Researchers often develop Gantt charts of the logical research steps, similar to the one in Exhibit 3–6 in Chapter 3, as working documents when developing responses to RFPs.

Like any other business, a contract researcher makes his or her profit from correctly estimating costs and pricing the research project appropriately. A thorough proposal process is likely to reveal all possible cost-related activities, thus making cost estimation more accurate. As many of these cost-associated activities are related to time, a proposal benefits a researcher by forcing a time estimate for the project. These time and cost estimates encourage researchers to plan the project so work progresses steadily toward the deadline. Since many people are inclined to procrastinate, having a schedule helps them work methodically toward the completion of the project.

Types of Research Proposals

In general, research proposals can be divided between those generated for internal and external audiences. An internal proposal is done by staff specialists or by the research department within the firm. External proposals sponsored by university grant committees, government agencies, government contractors, not-for-profit organizations, or corporations can be further classified as either solicited or unsolicited. With few exceptions, the larger the project, the more complex the proposal. In public sector work, the complexity is generally greater than in a comparable private sector proposal.

There are three general levels of complexity: exploratory studies, small-scale studies, and large-scale studies. These are noted in Exhibit 4–2. The exploratory study generates the most simple research proposal. More complex and common in business is the small-scale study—either an internal study or an external contract research project. The large-scale professional study, worth up to several million dollars, is the most complex proposal we deal with here. Government agency large-scale project RFPs usually gen-

EXHIBIT 4–2   **Proposal Complexity**

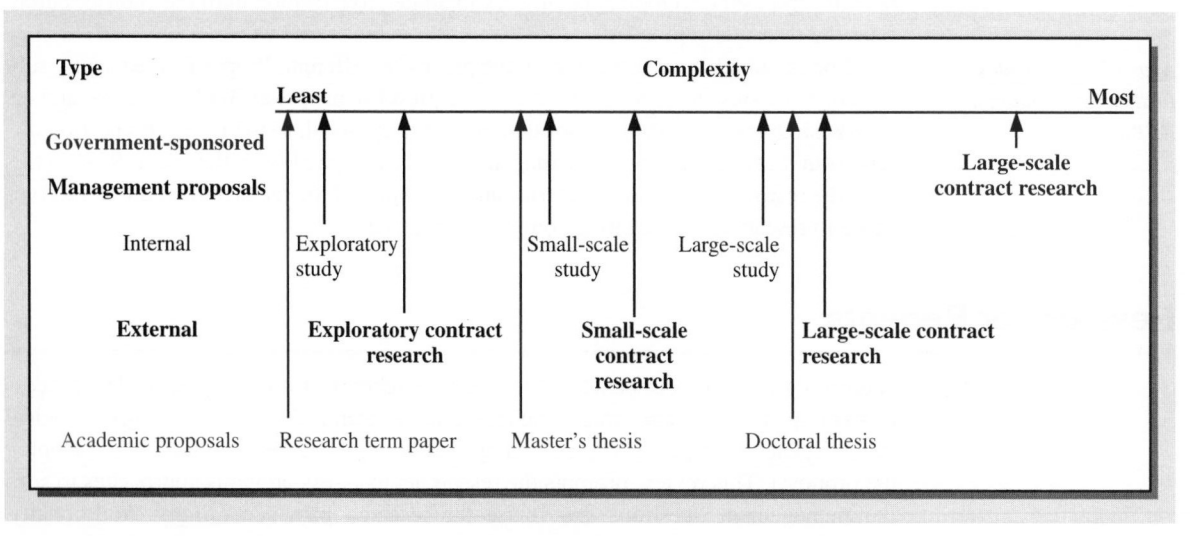

erate proposals running several hundred pages and use the same modules that we discuss next. However, each agency has unique requirements, making generalized coverage beyond the scope of this text.

Exhibit 4–3 displays a set of modules for building a proposal. Their order can represent an outline for a proposal. Based on the type of proposal you are writing you may

EXHIBIT 4–3 Modules to Include in Proposals: A Comparison of Management-Oriented Proposals and Student Proposals

Proposal Modules	Management Internal — Exploratory Study	Management Internal — Small-Scale Study	Management Internal — Large-Scale Study	Management External — Exploratory Contract	Management External — Small-Scale Contract	Management External — Large-Scale Contract	Government — Large-Scale Contract	Student — Term Paper	Student — Master's Thesis	Student — Doctoral Thesis
Executive summary		✔	✔	✔	✔	✔	✔			
Problem statement	✔	✔	✔	✔	✔	✔	✔	✔	✔	✔
Research objectives	✔	✔	✔	✔	✔	✔	✔	✔	✔	✔
Literature review			✔			✔	✔		✔	✔
Importance/ benefits of study		✔	✔	✔	✔	✔				✔
Research design	✔	✔	✔	✔	✔	✔	✔		✔	✔
Data analysis						✔	✔			✔
Nature and form of results		✔	✔		✔	✔	✔		✔	✔
Qualification of researchers				✔	✔	✔	✔			
Budget		✔	✔	✔	✔	✔	✔			
Schedule	✔	✔	✔	✔	✔	✔	✔			✔
Facilities and special resources			✔	✔	✔	✔	✔		✔	✔
Project management			✔			✔	✔			
Bibliography			✔			✔	✔	✔	✔	✔
Appendixes/ glossary of terms			✔			✔	✔		✔	✔
Measurement instrument			✔			✔	✔			✔

Take some time to review Exhibit 4–3. Compare the proposal modules suggested for each type of study. This will increase your understanding of proposals.

choose the appropriate modules for inclusion. This is a general guide, and sometimes more or less than what is shown here is appropriate for a specific purpose. For example, most small-scale studies do not require a glossary of terms. Terms are defined within the body of the proposal. However, if the proposal deals with an esoteric subject that is not familiar to management, it is appropriate to add a glossary. For a solicited study, the RFP will indicate both the content headings and their order.

Internal Proposals

Internal proposals are more succinct than external ones. At the least complex end of the continuum in Exhibit 4–2, a one- to three-page memo from the researcher to management outlining the problem statement, study objectives, research design, and schedule is enough to start an exploratory study. Privately and publicly held businesses are concerned with how to solve a particular problem, make a decision, or improve an aspect of their business. Seldom do businesses begin research studies for other reasons. Regardless of the intended audience, in the small-scale proposal, the literature review and bibliography are consequently not stressed and can often be stated briefly in the research design. Since management insists on brevity, an executive summary is mandatory for all but the most simple of proposals (projects that can be proposed in a two-page memo do not need an executive summary). Schedules and budgets are necessary for funds to be committed. For the smaller-scale projects, descriptions are not required for facilities and special resources, nor is there a need for a glossary. Since managers familiar with the problem sponsor small projects, the associated jargon, requirements, and definitions should be included directly in the text. Also, the measuring instrument and project management modules are not required. Managers will typically leave this detail for researchers.

External Proposals

An external proposal is either solicited or unsolicited. A **solicited proposal** is often in response to an RFP. The proposal is likely competing against several others for a contract or grant. An **unsolicited proposal** represents a suggestion by a contract researcher for research that might be done. An example of such a proposal might be a consulting firm proposing a research project to a client that has retained the consultancy for other purposes. Another example of an unsolicited proposal might be a research firm that proposes an omnibus study to a trade association to address problems arising from a change in the cultural or political-legal environments. The unsolicited proposal has the advantage of not competing against others but the disadvantage of having to speculate on the ramifications of a management dilemma facing the firm's management. In addition to being an outsider assessing an internal problem, the writer of an unsolicited proposal must decide to whom the document should be sent. Such proposals are often time-sensitive, so the window of opportunity might close before a redirected proposal finds its appropriate recipient.

The most important sections of the external proposal are the objectives, design, qualifications, schedule, and budget. In contract research, the results and objectives sections are the standards against which the completed project is measured. The executive summary of an external proposal may be included within the letter of transmittal. As the complexity of the project increases, more information is required about project management and the facilities and special resources. As we move toward government-sponsored research, particular attention must be paid to each specification in the RFP. To ignore or not meet any specification is to automatically disqualify your proposal as "nonresponsive."[5]

We offer a sample of an external proposal in Appendix D.

Structuring the Research Proposal

Consider again Exhibit 4–3. Using this reference, you can put together a set of modules that tailors your proposal to the intended audience. Each of the following modules is flexible, so its content and length may be adapted to specific needs.

Executive Summary

You might find it valuable to revisit the management-research question hierarchy and the research process model in Chapter 3 prior to reading this section.

The **executive summary** allows a busy manager or sponsor to understand quickly the thrust of the proposal. It is essentially an informative abstract, giving executives the chance to grasp the essentials of the proposal without having to read the details.[6] The goal of the summary is to secure a positive evaluation by the executive who will pass the proposal on to the staff for a full evaluation. As such, the executive summary should include brief statements of the management dilemma and management question, the research objectives/research question(s), and the benefits of your approach. If the proposal is unsolicited, a brief description of your qualifications is also appropriate.

Problem Statement

This section needs to convince the sponsor to continue reading the proposal. You should capture the reader's attention by stating the management dilemma, its background, its consequences, and the resulting management question. The importance of answering the management question should be emphasized here if a separate module on the importance/benefits of study is not included later in the proposal. In addition, this section should include any restrictions or areas of the management question that will not be addressed.

Problem statements too broadly defined cannot be addressed adequately in one study. It is important that the management question distinguish the primary problem from related problems clearly. Be sure your problem statement is clear without the use of idioms or clichés. After reading this section, the potential sponsor should know the management dilemma and the question, its significance, and why something should be done to change the status quo.[7]

Research Objectives

This module addresses the purpose of the investigation. It is here that you lay out exactly what is being planned by the proposed research. In a descriptive study, the objectives can be stated as the research question. Recall that the research question can be further broken down into investigative questions. If the proposal is for a causal study, then the objectives can be restated as a hypothesis.

The objectives module flows naturally from the problem statement, giving the sponsor specific, concrete, and achievable goals. It is best to list the objectives either in order of importance or in general terms first, moving to specific terms (i.e., research question followed by underlying investigative questions). The research question(s) (or hypotheses, if appropriate) should be separated from the flow of the text for quick identification.

The research objectives section is the basis for judging the remainder of the proposal and, ultimately, the final report. Verify the consistency of the proposal by checking to see that each objective is discussed in the research design, data analysis, and results sections.

Literature Review

The **literature review** section examines recent (or historically significant) research studies, company data, or industry reports that act as a basis for the proposed study.

MANAGEMENT

Tip

A literature review might reveal that the sponsor can answer the management question with a secondary data search rather than the collection of primary data. We discuss this more fully in Chapter 10.

Begin your discussion of the related literature and relevant secondary data from a comprehensive perspective, moving to more specific studies that are associated with your problem. If the problem has a historical background, begin with the earliest references.

Avoid the extraneous details of the literature; do a brief review of the information, not a comprehensive report. Always refer to the original source. If you find something of interest in a quotation, find the original publication and ensure you understand it. In this way, you will avoid any errors of interpretation or transcription. Emphasize the important results and conclusions of other studies, the relevant data and trends from previous research, and particular methods or designs that could be duplicated or should be avoided. Discuss how the literature applies to the study you are proposing; show the weaknesses or faults in the design, discussing how you would avoid similar problems. If your proposal deals solely with secondary data, discuss the relevance of the data and the bias or lack of bias inherent in it.

The literature review may also explain the need for the proposed work to appraise the shortcomings and/or informational gaps in secondary data sources. This analysis may go beyond scrutinizing the availability or conclusions of past studies and their data, to examining the accuracy of secondary sources, the credibility of these sources, and the appropriateness of earlier studies.

Close the literature review section by summarizing the important aspects of the literature and interpreting them in terms of your problem. Refine the problem as necessary in light of your findings.

Importance/ Benefits of the Study

In this section you describe explicit benefits that will accrue from your study. The importance of "doing the study now" should be emphasized. Usually, this section is not more than a few paragraphs. If you find it difficult to write, then you have probably not adequately clarified the management dilemma. Return to the analysis of the problem and ensure, through additional discussions with your sponsor or your research team or by a reexamination of the literature, that you have captured the essence of the problem.

This section also requires you to understand what is most troubling to your sponsor. If it is a potential union activity, you cannot promise that an employee survey will prevent unionization. You can, however, show the importance of this information and its implications. This benefit may allow management to respond to employee concerns and forge a linkage between those concerns and unionization.

The importance/benefits section is particularly important to the unsolicited external proposal. You must convince the sponsoring organization that your plan will meet its needs.

Research Design

In Chapter 6, we discuss design strategies.

Up to now, you have told the sponsor what the problem is, what your study goals are, and why it is important for you to do the study. The proposal has presented the study's value and benefits. The design module describes what you are going to do in technical terms. This section should include as many subsections as needed to show the phases of the project. Provide information on your proposed design for tasks such as sample selection and size, data collection method, instrumentation, procedures, and ethical requirements. When more than one way exists to approach the design, discuss the methods you have rejected and why your selected approach is superior.

Data Analysis

A brief section on the methods used for analyzing the data is appropriate for large-scale contract research projects and doctoral theses. With smaller projects, the proposed data

MANAGEMENT

*When there is no
statistical or analytical
expertise in the company,
sponsors are more likely
to hire professional help
to interpret the soundness
of this section.*

analysis would be included within the research design section. It is in this section that you describe your proposed handling of the data and the theoretical basis for using the selected techniques. The object of this section is to assure the sponsor you are following correct assumptions and using theoretically sound data analysis procedures.

This module is often an arduous section to write. You can make it easier to write, read, and understand your data analysis by using sample charts and tables featuring "dummy" data.

The data analysis section is so important to evaluating contract research proposals that the researcher should contact an expert to review the latest techniques available for use in the particular research study and compare these to the proposed techniques.

Nature and Form of Results

Upon finishing this section, the sponsor should be able to go back to the statement of the management question and research objectives and discover that each goal of the study has been covered. One should also specify the types of data to be obtained and the interpretations that will be made in the analysis. If the data are to be turned over to the sponsor for proprietary reasons, make sure this is reflected. Alternatively, if the report will go to more than one sponsor, that should be noted.

This section also contains the contractual statement telling the sponsor exactly what types of information will be received. Statistical conclusions, applied findings, recommendations, action plans, models, strategic plans, and so forth are examples of the forms of results.

Qualifications of Researchers

*Look for these elements
in a proposal when hiring
a contract researcher.*

This section should begin with the principal investigator, then provide similar information on all individuals involved with the project. Two elements are critical:

1. Professional research competence (relevant research experience, the highest academic degree held, and memberships in business and technical societies).

2. Relevant management experience.[8]

SNAPSHOT Pebble Beach: Finding the Link to Five-Star Service

Each year the Mobil Travel Guide bestows its coveted five-star rating on a very select group of restaurants and hotels. Five-star establishments stand out from four-star establishments because of "their out-of-the-ordinary attention to detail [and] the consistency with which they achieve their goals at the same high level in every aspect of their operation, from the physical environment to the cuisine and service." Pebble Beach Company is the holding company for several resorts, including The Inn at Spanish Bay, a restaurant that earned the coveted five-star award in 1999 but was unable to retain it in 2000 or 2001.

Guided by a mission stressing seven core values, Pebble Beach management believes that hiring exceptional people and keeping them fulfilled and motivated is the only

way to maintain exceptional customer service. As a result of this philosophy, Pebble Beach uses both qualitative and quantitative research to track employee concerns, performance, and attitudes. Qualitatively, Pebble Beach uses "town meetings" structured like brainstorming sessions. Quantitatively, it uses employee questionnaires, tracking responses longitudinally and matching them to shifts in critical performance measures.

If you were crafting a research proposal to determine why The Inn at Spanish Bay lost one highly valued star, what employee issues would you propose be researched? What sections would you include in your proposal?

www.pebblebeach.com

www.mobil.com

www.exxonmobiltravel.com

With so many individuals, research specialty firms, and general consultancies providing research services, the sponsor needs assurance that the researcher is professionally competent. Past research experience is the best barometer of competence, followed by the highest academic degree earned. To document relevant research experience, the researcher provides concise descriptions of similar projects. Highest degree usually follows the person's name (e.g., S. Researcher, Ph.D. in Statistics). Society memberships provide some evidence that the researcher is cognizant of the latest methodologies and techniques. These follow the relevant research experience as a string or bulleted list, with organization name followed by term of membership and any relevant leadership positions.

Researchers are increasingly in the business of providing advice, not just research services. And businesses are looking for quality advice. Comparatively, the researcher who demonstrates relevant management or industry experience will be more likely to receive a favorable nod to his or her proposal. The format of this information should follow that used for relevant research experience. The entire curriculum vitae of each researcher need not be included unless required by the RFP. However, researchers often place complete vitae information in an appendix for review by interested sponsors.

Research companies often subcontract specific research activities to firms or individuals that specialize or offer specific resources or facilities. This is especially true for studies involving qualitative research techniques such as in-depth personal interviews and focus groups. Usually brief profiles of these companies are provided in this section only if their inclusion enhances the credibility of the researcher. Otherwise, profiles of such subcontractors are included in an appendix of the final report, rather than in the proposal.

Budget

The budget should be presented in the form the sponsor requests. For example, some organizations require secretarial assistance to be individually budgeted, whereas others insist it be included in the research director's fees or the overhead of the operation. In

S N A P S H O T

Bissell: Small, Yet Powerful

When CEO Mark Bissell returned from a European business trip with a prototype appliance, a steam cleaner named Steam Gun, he challenged the marketing research director to determine the marketing for the new product within a one-month time frame. With a full-scale research project out of the question, the research director chose a small-scale ethnography study using real world observations of people's interactions with the product. He approached a local Parent Teacher Association, a ready source of female respondents, which distributed the Steam Gun to 20 volunteers. He followed up the test with in-home visits. Within 30 days, the research director knew the name must be changed and that those in the "serious cleaner" target segment would need to be convinced that steam cleaning with chemical-free water would be effective. He delivered a marketing program in the requisite time for the newly named BISSELL® Steam 'n Clean®. The primary budget item in the research was a $1,500 donation to the PTA, proving that research budgets for successful decision making come in all sizes.

www.bissell.com

EXHIBIT 4–4   **Sample Proposal Budget for a Research Program**

Budget Items	Rate	Total Days	Charge
A. Salaries			
1. Research director, Jason Henry	$200/hr	20 hours	$ 4,000
2. Associate	100/hr	10 hours	1,000
3. Research assistants (2)	20/hr	300 hours	6,000
4. Secretarial (1)	12/hr	100 hours	1,200
Subtotal			$12,200
B. Other costs			
5. Employee services and benefits			
6. Travel			$ 2,500
7. Office supplies			100
8. Telephone			800
9. Rent			
10. Other equipment			
11. Publication and storage costs			100
Subtotal			$ 3,500
C. Total of direct costs			$15,700
D. Overhead support			5,480
E. Total funding requested			$21,180

addition, limitations on travel, per diem rates, and capital equipment purchases can change the way in which you prepare a budget.

Typically, the budget should be no more than one to two pages. Exhibit 4–4 shows one format that can be used for small contract research projects. Additional information, backup details, quotes from vendors, and hourly time and payment calculations should be put into an appendix if required or kept in the researcher's file for future reference.

The budget statement in an internal research proposal is based on employee and overhead costs. The budget presented by an external research organization is not just the wages or salaries of its employees but the person-hour price that the contracting firm charges.

The detail the researcher presents may vary depending on both the sponsors' requirements and the contracting research company's policy. Some research companies, particularly in database and computerized analysis areas, quote on the basis of "man-machine hours" involved in a project. The man-machine hour is the hourly fee charged for a person with computer hardware and organizational resources. Here, rather than separating the "other costs" of Exhibit 4–4, these costs are embedded in a combined rate. One reason why external research agencies avoid giving detailed budgets is the possibility that disclosures of their costing practices will make their calculations public knowledge, reducing their negotiating flexibility. Since budget statements embody a work strategy depicted in financial terms that could be used by the recipient of the proposal to develop a replicate research plan, vendors are often doubly careful.

The budget section of an external research contractor's proposal states the total fee payable for the assignment. When it is accompanied by a proposed schedule of payment, this is frequently detailed in a purchase order. Like other large ticket-price services delivered over time in stages (e.g., building a home), payments can be paid at stages of completion. Sometimes a retainer is paid at the beginning of the contract, then a percentage at an intermediate stage, and the balance on completion of the project.

Understanding budgeting concerns is critical to a research specialist like Scientific Telephone Samples (STS), which provides random digit and business samples to those conducting telephone surveys.

MANAGEMENT
Tip

It is extremely important that you retain all information you use to generate your budget. If you use quotes from external contractors, get the quotation in writing for your file. If you estimate time for interviews, keep explicit notes on how you made the estimate. When the time comes to do the work, you should know exactly how much money is budgeted for each particular task.[9]

Some costs are more elusive than others. Do not forget to build the cost of proposal writing into your fee. Publication and delivery of final reports can be a last-minute expense that may be easily overlooked in preliminary budgets.

Schedule

Your schedule should include the major phases of the project, their timetables, and the milestones that signify completion of a phase. For example, major phases may be (1) exploratory interviews, (2) final research proposal, (3) questionnaire revision, (4) field interviews, (5) editing and coding, (6) data analysis, and (7) report generation. Each of these phases should have an estimated time schedule and people assigned to the work.

It may be helpful to you and your sponsor if you chart your schedule. You can use a Gantt chart, shown in Chapter 3, Exhibit 3–6. Alternatively, if the project is large and complex, a **critical path method (CPM)** of scheduling may be included.[10] In a CPM chart, the nodes represent major milestones, and the arrows suggest the work needed to get to the milestone. More than one arrow pointing to a node indicates all those tasks must be completed before the milestone has been met. Usually a number is placed along the arrow showing the number of days or weeks required for that task to be completed. The pathway from start to end that takes the longest time to complete is called the critical path, because any delay in an activity along that path will delay the end of the entire project. An example of a CPM chart is shown in Exhibit 4–5. Software programs designed for project management simplify scheduling and charting the schedule. Most are available for personal computers.

EXHIBIT 4–5   CPM Schedule

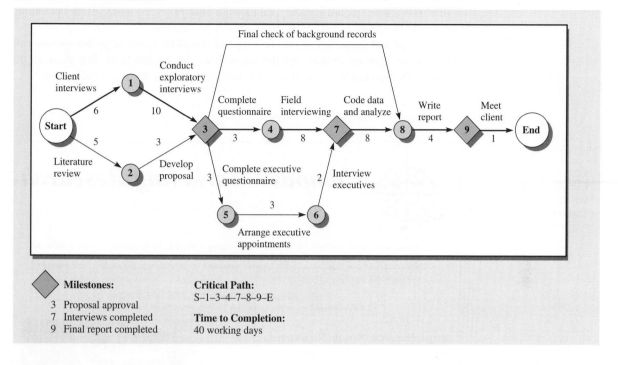

Final check of background records

Client interviews
Conduct exploratory interviews
Complete questionnaire
Field interviewing
Code data and analyze
Write report
Meet client

Start   6   ①   10
5   ②   3
Literature review
Develop proposal   3
③   3   ④   8   ⑦   8   ⑧   4   ⑨   1   **End**

Complete executive questionnaire
Interview executives
2

⑤   3   ⑥
Arrange executive appointments

Milestones:
3   Proposal approval
7   Interviews completed
9   Final report completed

Critical Path:
S–1–3–4–7–8–9–E

Time to Completion:
40 working days

Facilities and Special Resources

Often, projects will require special facilities or resources that should be described in detail. For example, a contract exploratory study may need specialized facilities for focus group sessions. Computer-assisted telephone or other interviewing facilities may be required. Alternatively, your proposed data analysis may require sophisticated computer algorithms, and therefore, you need access to an adequate system. These requirements will vary from study to study. The proposal should carefully list the relevant facilities and resources that will be used. The costs for such facility use should be detailed in your budget.

Project Management

The purpose of the **project management** section is to show the sponsor that the research team is organized in a way to do the project efficiently. A master plan is required for complex projects to show how all the phases will be brought together. The plan includes

• The research team's organization.

• Management procedures and controls for executing the research plan.

• Examples of management and technical reports.

• The research team's relationship with the sponsor.

• Financial and legal responsibility.

• Management competence.

Tables and charts are most helpful in presenting the master plan. The relationships between researchers and assistants need to be shown when several researchers are part of the team. Sponsors must know that the director is an individual capable of leading the team and acting as a useful liaison to the sponsor. In addition, procedures for information processing, record control, and expense control are critical to large operations and should be shown as part of the management procedures.

The type and frequency of progress reports should be recorded so the sponsor can expect to be kept up-to-date and the researchers can expect to be left alone to do research. The sponsor's limits on control during the process should be delineated.

Full-service research firms like Compass Marketing Research offer a wide array of facilities and services suitable for numerous proposed research designs.

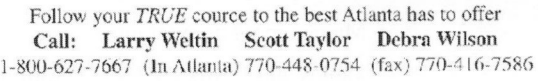

This section also discusses any details such as printing facilities, clerical help, or information-processing capabilities to be provided by the sponsor rather than the researcher. In addition, rights to the data, the results, and authority to speak for the researcher and for the sponsor are included.

Payment frequency and timing are also covered in the master plan. Finally, proof of financial responsibility and overall management competence is provided.

Bibliography

For all projects that require a literature review, a bibliography is necessary. Use the bibliographic format required by the sponsor. If none is specified, a standard style manual will provide the details necessary to prepare the bibliography.[11] Many of these sources also offer suggestions for successful proposal writing.

Appendixes

Glossary   The researcher should include a glossary of terms whenever there are many words unique to the research topic and not understood by the general management community. This is a simple section consisting of terms and definitions, similar in format to the glossary in this textbook. Also, the researcher should define any acronyms used, even if they are defined within the text (e.g., CATI for computer-assisted telephone interviewing).

Measurement Instrument   For large projects, it is appropriate to include samples of the measurement instruments if they are available when you assemble the proposal. This allows the sponsor to discuss particular changes in one or more of the instruments. If the proposal includes the development of a custom-designed measurement instrument, omit this appendix section.

Other   Any detail that reinforces the body of the proposal can be included in an appendix. This includes researcher vitae, profiles of firms or individuals to which work will be subcontracted, budget details, and lengthy descriptions of special facilities or resources.

To see how some of these elements were incorporated in the MindWriter research proposal, see Exhibit 4–6.

EXHIBIT 4–6   **Proposal for MindWriter CompleteCare Satsifaction Research**

When last we checked, Myra and Jason were preparing a proposal for Gracie Uhura, product manager at MindWriter Corporation.

Myra decided to exclude the "executive summary" for two reasons: The proposal is short and the essentials will be contained in the cover letter. The proposal follows the components discussed in this chapter. It is an appropriate adaptation for an internal, small-scale study. The module "qualification of researcher" was not needed because MindWriter's employee solicited the proposal; Myra had prejudged the researcher's qualifications.

EXHIBIT 4–6   **Continued**

Repair Process Satisfaction Proposal
Mindwriter Corporation CompleteCare Program

Problem Statement

MindWriter Corporation has recently created a service and repair program, CompleteCare, for its portable/laptop/notebook computers. This program promises to provide a rapid response to customers' service problems.

MindWriter is currently experiencing a shortage of trained technical operators in its telephone center. The package courier, contracted to pick up and deliver customers' machines to CompleteCare, has provided irregular execution. MindWriter has also experienced parts availability problems for some machine types.

Recent phone logs at the call center show complaints about CompleteCare; it is unknown how representative these complaints are and what implications they may have for satisfaction with MindWriter products.

Management desires information on the program's effectiveness and its impact on customer satisfaction to determine what should be done to improve the CompleteCare program for MindWriter product repair and servicing.

Research Objectives

The purpose of this research is to discover the level of satisfaction with the CompleteCare service program. Specifically, we intend to identify the component and overall levels of satisfaction with CompleteCare. Components of the repair process are important targets for investigation because they reveal:

(1) How customer tolerance levels for repair performance affect overall satisfaction, and

(2) Which process components should be immediately improved to elevate the overall satisfaction of those MindWriter customers experiencing product failures.

We will also discover the importance of types of product failure on customer satisfaction levels.

Importance/Benefits

High levels of user satisfaction translate into positive word-of-mouth product endorsements. These endorsements influence the purchase outcomes for (1) friends and relatives and (2) business associates.

Critical incidents, such as product failures, have the potential to either undermine existing satisfaction levels or preserve and even increase the resulting levels of product satisfaction. The outcome of the episode depends on the quality of the manufacturer's response.

An extraordinary response by the manufacturer to such incidents will preserve and enhance user satisfaction levels to the point that direct and indirect benefits derived from such programs will justify their costs.

This research has the potential for connecting to ongoing MindWriter customer satisfaction programs and measuring the long-term effects of CompleteCare (and product failure incidents) on customer satisfaction.

Research Design

Exploration: Qualitative We will augment our knowledge of CompleteCare by interviewing the service manager, the call center manager, and the independent package company's account executive. Based on a thorough inventory of CompleteCare's internal and external processes, we propose to develop a mail survey.

Questionnaire Design A self-administered questionnaire (postcard size) offers the most cost-effective method for securing feedback on the effectiveness of CompleteCare. The introduction on the postcard will be a variation of MindWriter's current advertising campaign.

Some questions for this instrument will be based on the investigative questions we presented to you previously, and others will be drawn from the executive interviews. We anticipate a maximum of 10 questions. A new five-point expectation scale, compatible with your existing customer satisfaction scales, is being designed.

Although we are not convinced that open-ended questions are appropriate for postcard questionnaires, we understand that you and Mr. Malraison like them. A comments/suggestions question will be included. In addition, we will work out a code block that captures the call center's reference number, model, and item(s) serviced.

Logistics The postal arrangements are: box rental, permit, and "business reply" privileges to be arranged in a few days. The approval for a reduced postage rate will take one to two weeks. The budget section itemizes these costs.

Pilot Test We will test the questionnaire with a small sample of customers using your tech-line operators. This will contain your costs. We will then revise the questions and forward them to our graphics designer for layout. The instrument will then be submitted to you for final approval.

Evaluation of Nonresponse Bias A random sample of 100 names will be secured from the list of customers who do not return the questionnaire. Call center records will be used for establishing the sampling frame. Nonresponders will be interviewed on the telephone and their responses compared statistically to those of the responders.

Data Analysis

We will review the postcards returned and send you a weekly report listing customers who are dissatisfied (score a "1" or "2") with any item of the questionnaire or who submit a negative comment. This will improve your timeliness in resolving customer complaints. Each month, we will provide you with a report consisting of frequencies and category percentages for each question. Visual displays of the data will be in bar chart/histogram form. We propose to include at least one question dealing with overall satisfaction (with CompleteCare and/or MindWriter). This overall question would be regressed on the individual items to determine each item's importance. A performance grid will identify items needing improvement with an evaluation of priority. Other analyses can be prepared on a time and materials basis.

EXHIBIT 4–6   Continued

> The open-ended questions will be summarized and reported by model code. If you wish, we also can provide content analysis for these questions.
>
> **Results: Deliverables**
> 1. Development and production of a postcard survey. MindWriter employees will package the questionnaire with the returned merchandise.
> 2. Weekly exception reports (transmitted electronically) listing customers who meet the dissatisfied customer criteria.
> 3. Monthly reports as described in the data analysis section.
> 4. An ASCII diskette with each month's data shipped to Austin by the fifth working day of each month.
>
> **Budget**
> **Card Layout and Printing**   Based on your card estimate, our designer will lay out and print 2,000 cards in the first run ($500). The specifications are as follows: 7-point Williamsburg offset hi-bulk with one-over-one black ink. A gray-scale layer with a MindWriter or CompleteCare logo can be positioned under the printed material at a nominal charge. The two-sided cards measure 4 1/4 by 5 1/2.
>
> This allows us to print four cards per page. The opposite side will have the business reply logo, postage paid symbol, and address.
>
> **Cost Summary**
>
> | | |
> |---|---:|
> | Interviews | $1,550.00 |
> | Travel costs | 2,500.00 |
> | Questionnaire development | 1,850.00 |
> | Equipment/supplies | 1,325.00 |
> | Graphics design | 800.00 |
> | Permit fee (annual) | 75.00 |
> | Business reply fee (annual) | 185.00 |
> | Box rental (annual) | 35.00 |
> | Printing costs | 500.00 |
> | Data entry (monthly) | 430.00 |
> | Monthly data files (each) | 50.00 |
> | Monthly reports (each) | 1,850.00 |
> | Total start-up costs | $11,150.00 |
> | Monthly run costs | $1,030.00* |
>
> *An additional fee of 0.21 per card will be assessed by the post office for business reply mail. At approximately a 30 percent return rate, we estimate the monthly cost to be less than $50.

Evaluating the Research Proposal

Proposals are subject to either formal or informal reviews. *Formal reviews* are regularly done for solicited proposals. The formal review process varies, but typically includes:

- Development of review criteria, using RFP guidelines.

- Assignment of points to each criterion, using a universal scale.

- Assignment of a weight for each criterion, based on importance of each criterion.

- Generation of a score for each proposal, representing the sum of all weighted criterion scores.

The sponsor should assign the criteria, the weights, and the scale to be used for scoring each criterion before the proposals are received. The proposal then should be evaluated with this checklist of criteria in hand. Points are recorded for each criterion reflecting the sponsor's assessment of how well the proposal meets the company's needs relative to that criterion (e.g., 1 through 10, with 10 being the largest number of points assigned to the best proposal for a particular criterion). After the review, the weighted criterion scores are added to provide a cumulative total. The proposal with the highest number of points wins the contract.

Several people, each of whom may be assigned to a particular section, typically review long and complex proposals. The formal method is most likely to be used for competitive government, university, or public sector grants and also for large-scale contracts.

Small-scale contracts are more prone to informal evaluation. In an *informal review,* the project needs, and thus the criteria, are well understood but are not usually well documented. In contrast to the formal method, a system of points is not used and the criteria are not ranked. The process is more qualitative and impressionistic. Exhibit 4–7 shows Myra Wines's informal review of the proposal discussed in the opening vignette.

In practice, many factors contribute to a proposal's acceptance and funding. Primarily, the content discussed above must be included to the level of detail required by the sponsor's RFP. Beyond the required modules, other factors can quickly eliminate a proposal from consideration or improve the sponsor's reception of the proposal, among them:

- Neatness.
- Organization, in terms of being both logical and easily understood.
- Completeness in fulfilling the RFP's specifications, including budget and schedule.
- Appropriateness of writing style.
- Submission within the RFP's timeline.

Although a proposal produced on a word processor and bound with an expensive cover will not overcome design or analysis deficiencies, a poorly presented, unclear, or disorganized proposal will not get serious attention from the reviewing sponsor. Given that multiple reviewers may be evaluating only a given section, the reviewer should be able to page through the proposal to any section of interest.

In terms of the technical writing style of the proposal, the sponsor must be able to understand the problem statement, the research design, and the methodology. The sponsor should clearly understand why the proposed research should be funded and the exact goals and concrete results that will come from the study.

The proposal also must meet specific RFP guidelines set by the sponsoring company or agency, including budgetary restrictions and schedule deadlines. A schedule that does not meet the expected deadlines will disqualify the proposal. A budget that is too high for the allocated funds will be rejected. Conversely, a low budget compared to competing proposals suggests that something is missing or there is something wrong with the researchers.

Finally, a late proposal will not be reviewed. While current project disqualification due to lateness may appear to be the worse result here, there is a possible longer-term effect created. Lateness communicates a level of disrespect for the sponsor—that the researcher's schedule is more important than the sponsor's. A late proposal also communicates a weakness in project management, which raises an issue of professional competence. This concern about competence may continue to plague the researcher during future project proposal reviews.

EXHIBIT 4–7   Informal Proposal Review

Myra Wines

200 ShellPoint Tower
Palm Beach, Florida 33480

Mr. Harry Shipley, President
Economic Development Council
1800 ShellPoint Tower
Palm Beach, Florida 33480

Dear Harry,

I have reviewed Robert Buffet's proposal for an investigation of the job creation practices of local companies and, in short, I am very much concerned with several aspects of the "proposal." It is not really a proposal at all, as it lacks sufficient detail.

First let me mention that I shared Buffet's proposal with Mr. Jason Henry, an independent research consultant working with me on a MindWriter project. Mr. Buffet and his organization may one day represent competition for Mr. Henry, and you must therefore be aware of a potential conflict of interest and perhaps discount the opinions stated here. Since I am delivering this letter to you in two days rather than the two weeks you requested, you may wish to discuss my comments with others.

What you and Mr. Buffet gave me is an abbreviated research plan for our county, but since it lacks many features found in a comprehensive proposal, I immediately saw it was not the full proposal that had been funded by the state commerce secretary. I called Tallahassee and reached a young woman who hemmed and hawed and refused to say if she was authorized to mail me the full proposal. Finally, I gave up arguing and gave her your address and told her she could mail it to you if she experienced an outbreak of belief in government-in-the-sunshine.

I then made several calls to people in Tallahassee whom I know from my days in TV. Did you know that this research idea is being floated by our senior U.S. senator, who is eager to throw a monkey wrench into the president's tax incentives plan? The senator whispered it to the governor and the governor whispered it to her commerce secretary, and here we are.

The problem statement is rather long and convoluted, but, in short, it poses the questions, "Are new high-tech companies creating jobs for residents of our county? Or are they bringing technical and manufacturing workers from outside the state and bypassing the local work force? Or are they doing research in these companies with a low level of manufacturing job creation? Or are they investing in "smart" capital equipment that does not create jobs?" If you cut through the verbiage, I think you can see the project is right dead on the mark with its questions.

The research objectives section is fairly straightforward. Buffet's people are going to identify all the companies in this county in the NAICS code groups associated with "high tech" and collect information on the number of locally hired employees in various job categories, chiefly in production, and also collect data on capital investments, debt, and other financial data, which Mr. Henry says makes good sense to collect and ought to be easy to do.

There is a section called Importance of the Study, which is full of platitudes and does not get around to mentioning the pending tax legislation. But at least the platitudes are brief.

I become nervous in the Design section. It calls for Mr. Buffet's group to go on site with a "team" and conduct in-depth interviews with the chief operating officer (COO), treasurer, and comptroller of each company and enter the data into a spreadsheet. I have double-checked this with Mr. Henry and also with a banker friend, and both of them assure me that a simple questionnaire might be mailed to the COO. There is no need whatsoever to send in a team to conduct open-ended interviews. While there might be a noncompliance problem associated with filling out a form, this might appropriately be attended to by pointing out the auspices—the state commerce secretary and your Economic Development Council—with an interview request as a last resort.

The proposal contains no budget and no specific list of researchers who will comprise the team. The firm would have carte blanche to go in with anyone on their payroll and try to induce the subjects to stray beyond the stated research objectives to talk about anything at all. Obviously such license would be a marketing tool and might allow the researchers to collect a list of researchable problems not related to the secretary's needs, as stated in the problem section.

I strongly advise you to tell Mr. Buffet to collect the information through a simple mail survey. Offer to send it out under your council's letterhead, or see if you can get the commerce office or even the governor's office to send it out. But do not subject your local business community to unstructured, free-ranging visits, which are clearly not justified by the research objectives.

Sincerely,

Myra

SUMMARY

1   A proposal is an offer to produce a research product or render a service to the potential buyer or sponsor. The research proposal presents a problem, discusses related research efforts, outlines the data needed for solving the problem, and shows the design used to gather and analyze the data.

Proposals are valuable to both the research sponsor and the researcher. The sponsor uses the proposal to evaluate a research idea. The proposal is also a useful tool to ensure that the sponsor and investigator agree on the research question. For the beginning researcher, the proposal enables learning from other researchers. In addition, the completed proposal provides a logical guide for the investigation.

2   We discuss two types of proposals: internal and external. Internal and external proposals have a problem-solving orientation. The staff of a company generates internal proposals. External proposals are prepared by an outside firm to obtain contract research. External proposals emphasize qualifications of the researcher, special facilities and resources, and project management aspects such as budgets and schedules. Within each type of proposal there are varying degrees of complexity; a proposal can vary in length from a two-page memo to more than 100 pages, from a telephone conversation to a multimedia presentation.

Proposals can be written with a set of sections or modules. The difference in type of proposal and level of project complexity determines what modules should be included.

3   Proposals can be evaluated formally or informally. The formal process uses a list of criteria and an associated point scale. The informal process is more qualitative. Important aspects beyond content include presentation style, timeliness, and credibility.

KEY TERMS

EXAMPLES

Company	Scenario	Page
Bissell, Inc.	Small-budget ethnography study to guide the development of the Steam 'n Clean marketing plan.	104
Compass Marketing Research	Providing a wide array of facilities capable of handling many research designs.	108
Economic Development Council of Palm Beach[*]	Evaluating a proposal for a study designed to ascertain job creation practices among local companies.	95
MindWriter[*]	Proposal for evaluating CompleteCare program.	BRTL, throughout

Pebble Beach Company	Research with employees to assess customer service.	103
STS (Scientific Telephone Samples)	Providing names and phone numbers for telephone studies at a low cost.	106
Mobil Travel Guide	Develops a directory of restaurants and hotels based on standards of exceptional service using a rating system developed from an observation study.	103

*Due to the confidential and proprietary nature of most research, the names of some companies have been changed.

DISCUSSION QUESTIONS

Terms in Review

1. What, if any, are the differences between solicited and unsolicited proposals?

Making Research Decisions

2. You are the new manager of market intelligence in a rapidly expanding software firm. Many product managers and corporate officers have requested market surveys from you on various products. Design a form for a research proposal that can be completed easily by your research staff and the sponsoring manager. Discuss how your form improves communication of the research objectives between the manager and the researcher.

3. Consider the new trends in desktop publishing, multimedia computer authoring and display capabilities, and inexpensive videotaping and playback possibilities. How might these be used to enhance research proposals? Give several examples of appropriate use.

4. You are the manager of a research department in a large department store chain. Develop a list of criteria for evaluating the types of research activities listed below. Include a point scale and weighting algorithm.

   a. Market research.

   b. Advertising effectiveness.

   c. Employee opinion surveys.

   d. Credit card operations.

   e. Computer service effectiveness at the individual store level.

From Concept to Practice

5. Select a research report from a management journal. Outline a proposal for the research as if it had not yet been performed. Make estimates of time and costs. Generate a CPM schedule for the project following the format in Exhibit 4–5.

6. Using Exhibit 4–3 as your guide, what modules would you suggest be included in a proposal for each of the following cases?

   a. A bank interested in evaluating the effectiveness of its community contributions in dollars and loaned executive time.

   b. A manufacturer of leather custom-designed teacher development portfolios evaluating the market potential among teachers, who are now legally required to execute a professional development plan every three years.

   c. A university studying the possible calendar change from three 11-week quarters to two 16-week semesters.

   d. A dot-com that monitors clicks on banner ads interested in developing a different pricing structure for its service.

7. Review the Seagate proposal in Appendix D on page 793. Using Exhibit 4–3 as your guide, comment on what is or what is not contained therein.

WWW Exercises   Visit our website for Internet exercises related to this chapter at
www.mhhe.com/business/cooper8

CASES*

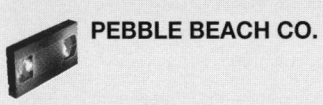 **PEBBLE BEACH CO.**

**RAMADA DEMONSTRATES ITS
PERSONAL BEST**

*All cases indicating a video icon are located on the Instructor's Videotape Supplement. All nonvideo cases are in the case
section of the textbook. All cases indicating a CD icon offer a data set, which is located on the accompanying CD.

REFERENCE NOTES

1. Charles T. Brusaw, Gerald J. Alred, and Walter E. Oliu, *Handbook of Technical Writing,* 4th ed. (New York: St. Martin's Press, 1992), p. 375.
2. Paul D. Leedy, *Practical Research: Planning and Design,* 2nd ed. (New York: Macmillan, 1980), p. 79.
3. R. Lesikar and John Pettit, *Report Writing for Business,* 9th ed. (Burr Ridge, IL: Irwin, 1995).
4. Ibid., p. 51.
5. William J. Roetzheim, *Proposal Writing for the Data Processing Consultant* (Englewood Cliffs, NJ: Prentice-Hall, 1986), p. 106.
6. Brusaw, Alred, and Oliu, *Handbook,* p. 11.
7. Philip V. Lewis and William H. Baker, *Business Report Writing* (Columbus, OH: Grid, 1978), p. 58.
8. Robert G. Murdick and Donald R. Cooper, *Business Research: Concepts and Guides* (Columbus, OH: Grid, 1982), p. 112.

9. Roetzheim, *Proposal Writing,* pp. 67–68.
10. Many texts cover project management and include details of scheduling and charting techniques such as Gantt charts and CPM charts, which are beyond the scope of this text. See, for example, Chapter 3, "Network Analysis," in Don T. Philips, A. Ravindran, and James J. Solberg, *Operations Research: Principles and Practice* (New York: Wiley, 1976); or Chapter 6, "Network Models," in K. Roscoe Davis and Patrick G. McKeon, *Quantitative Models for Management* (Boston: Kent, 1981).
11. See, for example, Kate L. Turabian, *A Manual for Writers of Term Papers, Theses, and Dissertations* (Chicago: University of Chicago Press, 1996); Joseph Gibaldi and Walter S. Achtert, *MLA Handbook for Writers of Research Papers* (New York: Modern Language Association of America, 1999); and the *Publication Manual of the American Psychological Association* (Washington, DC: APA, 1994).

REFERENCES FOR SNAPSHOTS AND CAPTIONS

Pebble Beach

"2001 Five-Star Award Winners List," *Mobil Travel Guide,* Exxon-Mobil Oil (http://www.mobil.com/mobil_consumer/travel/winners/winners_content.html).

"Inn at Spanish Bay Resort," Pebble Beach Resorts (http://www.pebblebeach.com/2b.html).

McGraw-Hill Video Library.

"Rating Criteria for Mobil Travel Guide" (http://www.maisonette.com/maisonette/fine-dining/5star.htm).

Bissell

Interview with Ann Lamb, director of communications, Bissell, Inc., August 3, 2001.

"Research on a Shoestring: How Bissell Steamrolled Its Way to the Top of Its Category," *American Demographics,* April 2001, pp. 38–39.

CLASSIC AND CONTEMPORARY READINGS

Krathwohl, David R. *How to Prepare a Research Proposal.* 3rd ed. Syracuse, NY: Syracuse University Press, 1988. A practical guide and framework for student projects.

Leedy, Paul D. *Practical Research: Planning and Design.* 6th ed. Englewood Cliffs, NJ: Prentice-Hall, 1996. Practical and readable sections guide students through the research process.

Locke, Lawrence F.; Waneen Wyrick Spiduso; and Steven J. Silverman. *Proposals That Work: A Guide to Planning Dissertations and Grant Proposals.* 4th ed. Thousand Oaks, CA: Sage Publications, 2000. An excellent guide for students and faculty advisers covering all aspects of the proposal process.

CHAPTER 5

Ethics in Business Research

Learning Objectives

After reading this chapter, you should understand . . .

1   **What issues are covered in research ethics.**

2   **The goal of "no harm" for all research activities and what constitutes "no harm" for participant, researcher, and research sponsor.**

3   **The differing ethical dilemmas and responsibilities of researchers, sponsors, and research assistants.**

4   **The role of ethical codes of conduct in professional associations.**

Bringing Research to Life

"My brother-in-law, 'Slick Billy' Henderson, has been in and out of trouble all his life," said Myra, "but hasn't spent a night in jail. He knows the difference between what is unethical and what is actually illegal."

"Have they ever prosecuted the guy?" asked Jason.

"No, but he may soon be broke. He is in computer peripherals in Silicon Valley and has taken a near-lead position in peripherals for laptop computing. Well, laptop peripherals are volatile. Do I have to tell you? They grow smaller every month and have to be sold more cheaply. According to my sister, Janet, a detailed market report was needed, which Bill could very well afford to pay for, but he decided to get it through one of his notorious fiddles. So he went to a hungry headhunter—a management placement specialist—and said he wanted to interview six candidates for senior diversification manager.

"His security chief, who Jan swears is an ex–secret police Eastern Bloc immigrant, rigged Bill's office and conference room with listening devices and recorded every interview. Bill even wore a 'wire' so he could record conversations in the men's room and over lunch. The first few interviews added greatly to Bill's understanding of the competition, but when the headhunter brought in an exec from ConToCon, the company that was Bill's number one competitor, he knew he had struck pay dirt.

"On the basis of the interview with Mr. Smithson from ConToCon, Bill decided to shut down the California production line for a certain peripheral and open production in Mexico for a smaller, faster, cheaper version. Bill summoned his vice presidents to announce his decision and provide transcripts of his interview with Smithson. Immediately, without actually reading the transcripts, Bill's chief attorney scrawled her resignation on a notepad and walked out, without even stopping to empty her office. The human resource VP caved in, however, and soon announced a layoff of their California factory employees, and the production VP flew to Mexico to ink a contract to expand a plant there."

"Did your brother actually make any of the candidates a job offer?"

"Please, Jason. He is my *brother-in-law,* not my brother, and no, he saw no need to make any offers. He told Jan that the 'tricky s.o.b.'s,' as he called them, probably never intended to work for him. He insisted that the interviewees were wasting his time and money and they only wanted job offers to extract a raise from their current employers."

"Slippery folks believe the world is populated by even slipperier folks," said Jason, philosophically.

"Well, no sooner had Bill laid off his California workers and flown to Mexico to make a down payment on a plant there, when ConToCon announced that it was expanding in California, exactly contrary to what Smithson had said. In fact, according to the trade press, Smithson was given the boot; no one ever knew why, although there was no shortage of rumors.

"So Bill has sunk his own ship and cannot bail it out now. Nevertheless, he remains unrepentant and blames the lawyer who quit, the headhunter, the interviewees, Smithson most of all, and his production VP. Bill maintains he is the victim of an innocent mistake.

"Jan filed for divorce yesterday. She has 8 by 10 glossy pictures of him frolicking on a private beach in Acapulco with a local señorita."

"And how is Bill taking this?"

"Bill is incensed, of course, and demands to know what sort of woman hires a detective to spy on her husband."

What Are Research Ethics?

As in other aspects of business, all parties in research should exhibit ethical behavior. **Ethics** are norms or standards of behavior that guide moral choices about our behavior and our relationships with others. The goal of ethics in research is to ensure that no one is harmed or suffers adverse consequences from research activities. This objective is usually achieved. However, unethical activities are pervasive and include violating nondisclosure agreements, breaking respondent confidentiality, misrepresenting results, deceiving people, invoicing irregularities, avoiding legal liability, and more.

The recognition of ethics as a problem for economic organizations was revealed in a survey where 80 percent of the responding organizations reported the adoption of an ethical code. Surprisingly, the evidence that this effort has improved ethical practices is questionable. The same study reports limited success for codes of conduct that attempt to restrain improper behavior.[1]

There is no single approach to ethics. Advocating strict adherence to a set of laws is difficult because of the unforeseen constraint put on researchers. Because of Germany's war history, for example, the government forbids many types of medical research. Consequently, the German people do not benefit from many advances in biotechnology and may have restricted access to genetically altered drugs in the future. Alternatively, relying on each individual's personal sense of morality is equally problematic. Consider the clash between those who believe death is deliverance from a life of suffering and those who value life to the point of preserving it indefinitely through mechanical means. Each value system claims superior knowledge of moral correctness.

Clearly, a middle ground between being completely code governed and ethical relativism is necessary. The foundation for that middle ground is an emerging consensus on ethical standards for researchers. Codes and regulations guide researchers and sponsors. Review boards and peer groups help researchers examine their research proposals

In April 2001, Procter & Gamble notified its competitor Unilever that more than 80 discarded documents detailing Unilever's three-year marketing plans for its hair care business had been collected by independent information agents hired by a P&G supplier. P&G voluntarily returned the documents, indicating that competitive intelligence-gathering involving documents taken from trash receptacles was a violation of its ethical standards. Unilever believes that additional information was obtained by deception, with information gatherers claiming to be market analysts. P&G and Unilever are negotiating a settlement, but Unilever believes its hair care business has been irreparably compromised.
www.pg.com
www.unilever.com

for ethical dilemmas. Many design-based ethical problems can be eliminated by careful planning and constant vigilance. In the end, responsible research anticipates ethical dilemmas and attempts to adjust the design, procedures, and protocols during the planning process rather than treating them as an afterthought. Ethical research requires personal integrity from the researcher, the project manager, and the research sponsor.

Because integrity in research is vital, we are discussing its components early in this book and emphasizing ethical behavior throughout our coverage. Our objective is to stimulate an ongoing exchange about values and practical research constraints in the chapters that follow. This chapter is organized around the theme of ethical treatment of respondents, clients, research sponsors, and other researchers. We also highlight appropriate laws and codes, resources for ethical awareness, and cases for application. Exhibit 5–1 relates each ethical issue under discussion to the research process introduced in Chapter 3.

Ethical Treatment of Participants

When ethics are discussed in research design, we often think first about protecting the rights of the participant, respondent, or subject. Whether data are gathered in an experiment, interview, observation, or survey, the respondent has many rights to be safeguarded. In general, research must be designed so a respondent does not suffer physical harm, discomfort, pain, embarrassment, or loss of privacy. To safeguard against these, the researcher should follow three guidelines:[2]

MANAGEMENT
Tip

1. Explain study benefits.

2. Explain respondent rights and protections.

3. Obtain informed consent.

Benefits

Whenever direct contact is made with a respondent, the researcher should discuss the study's benefits, being careful to neither overstate nor understate the benefits. An interviewer should begin an introduction with his or her name, the name of the research organization, and a brief description of the purpose and benefit of the research. This puts respondents at ease, lets them know to whom they are speaking, and motivates them to answer questions truthfully. In short, knowing why one is being asked questions improves cooperation through honest disclosure of purpose. Inducements to participate, financial or otherwise, should not be disproportionate to the task or presented in a fashion that results in coercion.

Sometimes the actual purpose and benefits of your study or experiment must be concealed from the respondents to avoid introducing bias. The need for concealing objectives leads directly to the problem of deception.

Deception

Deception occurs when the respondents are told only part of the truth or when the truth is fully compromised. Some believe this should never occur. Others suggest two reasons for deception: (1) to prevent biasing the respondents before the survey or experiment and (2) to protect the confidentiality of a third party (e.g., the sponsor). Deception should not be used in an attempt to improve response rates.

The benefits to be gained by deception should be balanced against the risks to the respondents. When possible, an experiment or interview should be redesigned to reduce

EXHIBIT 5–1   Ethical Issues and the Research Process

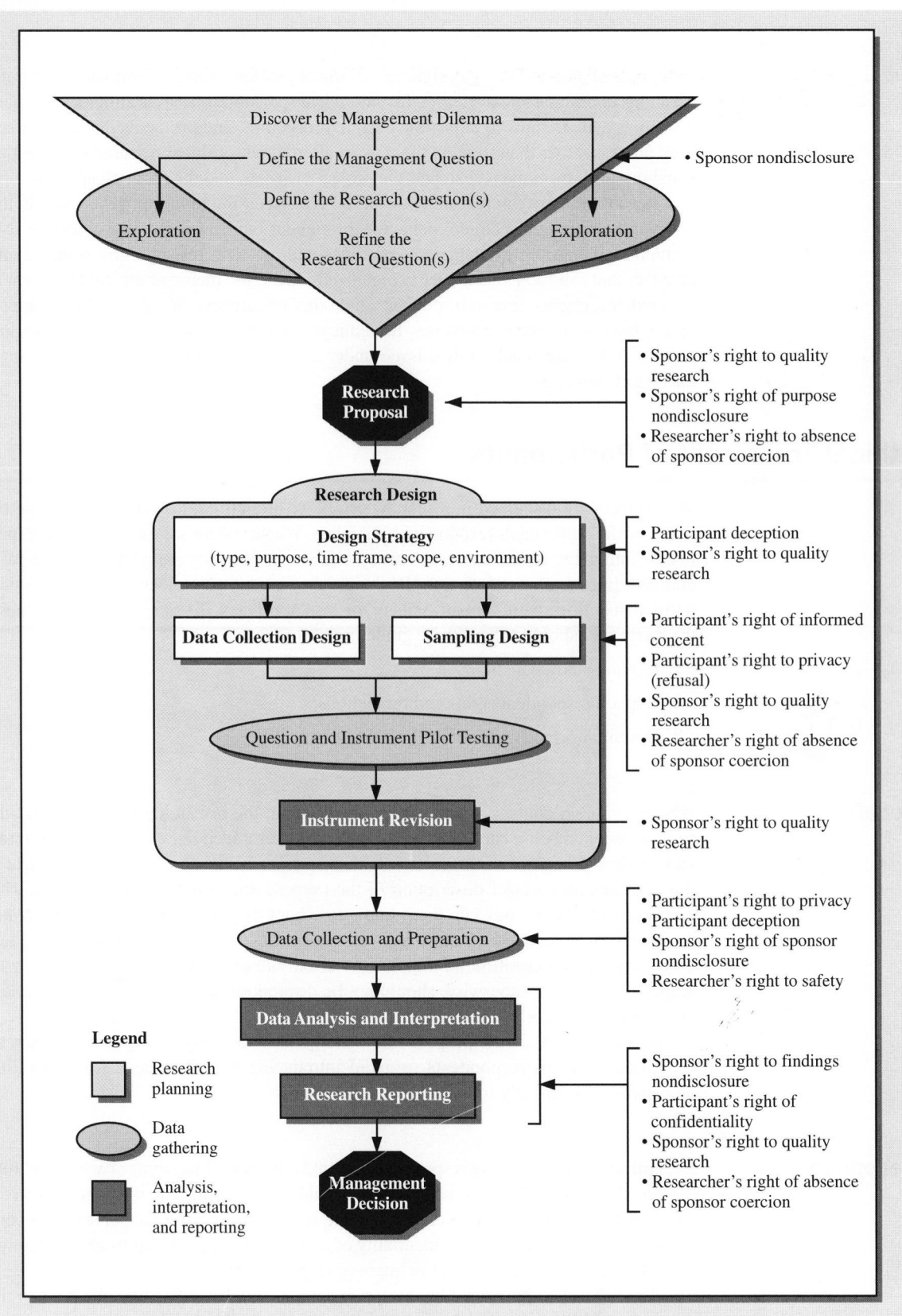

reliance on deception. In addition, the respondents' rights and well-being must be adequately protected. In instances where deception in an experiment could produce anxiety, a subject's medical condition should be checked to ensure that no adverse physical harm follows. The American Psychological Association's Ethics Code states that the use of deception is inappropriate unless deceptive techniques are justified by the study's expected scientific, educational, or applied value and equally effective alternatives that do not use deception are not feasible.[3] And finally, the respondents must have given their informed consent before participating in the research.

Informed Consent

Securing **informed consent** from respondents is a matter of fully disclosing the procedures of the proposed survey or other research design before requesting permission to proceed with the study. There are exceptions that argue for a signed consent form. When dealing with children, it is wise to have a parent or other person with legal standing sign a consent form. When doing research with medical or psychological ramifications, it is also wise to have a consent form. If there is a chance the data could harm the respondent or if the researchers offer only limited protection of confidentiality, a signed form detailing the types of limits should be obtained. For most business research, oral consent is sufficient. An example of how informed consent procedures are implemented is shown in Exhibit 5–2. In this example, a university research center demonstrates how it adheres to the highest ethical standards for survey procedures.[4]

In situations where respondents are intentionally or accidentally deceived, they should be debriefed once the research is complete.

Debriefing Participants

MANAGEMENT

Debriefing involves several activities following the collection of data:

- Explanation of any deception.
- Description of the hypothesis, goal, or purpose of the study.
- Poststudy sharing of results.
- Poststudy follow-up medical or psychological attention.

EXHIBIT 5-2   Informed Consent Procedures for Surveys

Content
Surveys conducted by the Indiana University Center for Survey Research contain the following informed consent components in their introductions:

1. Introduce ourselves—interviewer's name and Indiana University Center for Survey Research.
2. Briefly describe the survey topic (e.g., barriers to health insurance).
3. Describe the geographic area we are interviewing (e.g., people in Indiana) or target sample (e.g., aerospace engineers).
4. Tell who the sponsor is (e.g., National Endowment for the Humanities).
5. Describe the purpose(s) of the research (e.g., satisfaction with services received/provided by a local agency).
6. Give a "good-faith" estimate of the time required to complete the interview.
7. Promise anonymity and confidentiality (when appropriate).
8. Tell the respondent the participation is voluntary.
9. Tell the respondent that item-nonresponse is acceptable.
10. Ask permission to begin.

Sample Introduction
Hello, I'm [fill in NAME] from the Center for Survey Research at Indiana University. We're surveying Indianapolis area residents to ask their opinions about some health issues. This study is sponsored by the National Institutes of Health and its results will be used to research the effect of community ties on attitudes toward medical practices. The survey takes about 40 minutes. Your participation is anonymous and voluntary, and all your answers will be kept completely confidential. If there are any questions that you don't feel you can answer, please let me know and we'll move to the next one. So, if I have your permission, I'll continue.

Sample Conclusion
The respondent is given information on how to contact the principal investigator. For example: John Kennedy is the principal investigator for this study. Would you like Dr. Kennedy's address or telephone number in case you want to contact him about the study at any time?

First, the researcher shares the truth of any deception with the participants and the reasons for using deception in the context of the study's goals. In cases where severe reactions occur, follow-up medical or psychological attention should be provided to continue to ensure the participants remain unharmed by the research.

Even when research does not deceive the respondents, it is a good practice to offer them follow-up information. This retains the goodwill of the respondent, providing an incentive to participate in future research projects. For surveys and interviews, respondents can be offered a brief report of the findings. Usually, they will not request additional information. Occasionally, however, the research will be of particular interest to a respondent. A simple set of descriptive charts or data tables can be generated for such an individual.

For experiments, all participants should be debriefed in order to put the experiment into context. Debriefing usually includes a description of the hypothesis being tested and the purpose of the study. Participants who were not deceived still benefit from the debriefing session. They will be able to understand why the experiment was created. The researchers also gain important insight into what the participants thought about during and after the experiment. This may lead to modifications in future research designs. Like survey and interview respondents, participants in experiments and observational studies should be offered a report of the findings.

To what extent do debriefing and informed consent reduce the effects of deception? Research suggests that the majority of participants do not resent temporary deception and may have more positive feelings about the value of the research after debriefing than

SNAPSHOT

The Death of Consent

In 2001, research procedure at Johns Hopkins Medical School (JH) earned undesirable scrutiny. A healthy 24-year-old female volunteer, Ellen Roche, died after inhaling a drug designed to make her lungs simulate those of an asthma patient by restricting lung function. In suspending the funding of all government-funded research at Johns Hopkins, the Food and Drug Administration (FDA) cited that hexamethonium was never approved as an inhalant as it was used in the JH study. The consent form Roche signed did not disclose existing information about the dangers of the drug. JH, accepting full responsibility for Roche's death, indicated "adequate research was not available on whether hexamethonium was OK to use." The FDA also cited JH for failure to report a previous unanticipated adverse reaction when the first of the three volunteers developed a similar cough. Roche developed a cough that later led to organ failure. The government (in this case the National Institutes of Health, which funded the study) requires an ethics committee to review and approve any experiment using federal money before it is carried out on a person. A JH ethics committee approved the use of inhaled hexamethonium, but it did not seek government approval prior to conducting the experiment. Johns Hopkins controlled the largest amount of federally funded research, with a budget exceeding $300 million, prior to having all research funds suspended by this incident.

www.hopkinsmedicine.org/research/

www.fda.gov

www.nih.gov

ohrp.osophs.dhhs.gov/

those who didn't participate in the study.[5] Nevertheless, deception is an ethically thorny issue and should be addressed with sensitivity and concern for research participants.

Rights to Privacy

Privacy laws in the United States are taken seriously. All individuals have a right to privacy, and researchers must respect that right. The importance of the right to privacy is illustrated with an example.

An employee of MonsterVideo, a large video company, is also a student at the local university. For a research project, this student and his team members decide to compare the video-viewing habits of a sample of customers. Using telephone interviews, the students begin their research. After inquiring about people's viewing habits and the frequency of rentals versus purchases, the students move on to the types of films people watch. They find that most respondents answer questions about their preferences for children's shows, classics, bestsellers, mysteries, and science fiction. But the cooperation ceases when the students question the viewing frequency of pornographic movies. Without the guarantee of privacy, most people will not answer these kinds of questions truthfully, if at all. The study then loses key data.

The privacy guarantee is important not only to retain validity of the research but also to protect respondents. In the previous example, imagine the harm that could be caused by releasing information on the viewing habits of certain citizens. Clearly, the confidentiality of survey answers is an important aspect of the respondents' right to privacy.

Once the guarantee of **confidentiality** is given, protecting that confidentiality is essential. The researcher protects respondent confidentiality in several ways:

- Obtaining signed nondisclosure documents.
- Restricting access to respondent identification.

- Revealing respondent information only with written consent.
- Restricting access to data instruments where the respondent is identified.
- Nondisclosure of data subsets.

Researchers should restrict access to information that reveals names, telephone numbers, addresses, or other identifying features. Only researchers who have signed nondisclosure, confidentiality forms should be allowed access to the data. Links between the data or database and the identifying information file should be weakened. Individual interview response sheets should be inaccessible to everyone except the editors and data entry personnel. Occasionally, data collection instruments should be destroyed once the data are in a data file. Data files that make it easy to reconstruct the profiles or identification of individual respondents should be carefully controlled. For very small groups, data should not be made available because it is often easy to pinpoint a person within the group. Employee-satisfaction survey feedback in small units can be easily used to identify an individual through descriptive statistics alone. These last two protections are particularly important in human resources research.[6]

But privacy is more than confidentiality. A **right to privacy** means one has the right to refuse to be interviewed or to refuse to answer any question in an interview. Potential participants have a right to privacy in their own homes, including not admitting researchers and not answering telephones. And they have the right to engage in private behavior in private places without fear of observation. To address these rights, ethical researchers do the following:

MANAGEMENT
Tip

- Inform respondents of their right to refuse to answer any questions or participate in the study.
- Obtain permission to interview respondents.
- Schedule field and phone interviews.
- Limit the time required for participation.
- Restrict observation to public behavior only.

Data Collection in Cyberspace

Some ethicists argue that the very conduct that results in resistance from respondents—interference, invasiveness in their lives, denial of privacy rights—has encouraged researchers to investigate topics online that have long been the principal commodity of offline investigation. The novelty and convenience of communicating by computer has led researchers to cyberspace in search of abundant sources of data. Whether we call it the "wired society," "digital life," "computer-mediated communication," or "cyberculture," the growth of cyberstudies causes us to question how we gather data online, deal with participants, and present results.

In a special ethics issue of *Information Society,* scholars involved in cyberspace research concluded:

> All participants agree that research in cyberspace provides no special dispensation to ignore ethical precepts. Researchers are obligated to protect human subjects and "do right" in electronic venues as in more conventional ones. Second, each participant recognizes that cyberspace poses complex ethical issues that may lack exact analogs in other types of inquiry. The ease of covert observation, the occasional blurry distinction between public and private venues, and the difficulty of obtaining the informed consent of subjects make cyber-research particularly vulnerable to ethical breaches by even the most scrupulous scholars. Third, all recognize that because research procedures or

S N A P S H O T   Revving Information with Alliances

International company information extracted from statistical process control records might provide a company the basis for competitive advantage when controlled by a master information handler. Cummins Engines, headquartered in Columbus, Indiana, has been making customized, advanced, fuel-efficient engines for trucks, boats, and equipment for more than 80 years. In an attempt to streamline its own processes, it recruits customers to serve on its Customer Council. This panel provides ongoing information, useful not only in tracking the effectiveness of internal process performance but also in providing additional insight into industry trends. By combining its warehouse of data with customer needs and interpretations, Cummins Engines was able to develop the Signature 600 engine, a high-powered, low-vibration engine that is making heads turn—especially the competition's. In a December release, Cummins announced the Signature 600 is the power of choice for Volvo Trucks North America's two-year deal with Roush Racing to provide 770 model trucks for its NASCAR transporters.

www.cummins.com

activities may be permissible or not precluded by law or policy, it does not follow that they are necessarily ethical or allowable. Fourth, all agree that the individual researcher has the ultimate responsibility for assuring that inquiry is not only done honestly, but done with ethical integrity.[7]

Issues relating to cyberspace in research also relate to data mining. The information collection devices available today were once the tools of the spy, the science fiction protagonist, or the superhero. Smart cards, biometrics (finger printing, retinal scans, facial recognition), electronic monitoring (closed circuit television, digital camera monitoring), global surveillance, and genetic identification (DNA) are just some of the technological tools being used by today's organizations to track and understand employees, customers, and suppliers. The data mining of all this information, collected from advanced and not necessarily obvious sources, offers infinite possibilities for research abuse.

The primary ethical data-mining issues in cyberspace are privacy and consent. Smart cards, those ubiquitous credit-card-sized devices that imbed personal information on a computer chip that is then matched to purchase, employment, or other behavior data, offer the researcher implied consent to participant surveillance. But the benefits of card use may be enough to hide from an unsuspecting user the data-mining purpose of the card. For example, The Kroger Co., one of the largest grocers in the United States, offers significant discounts for enrollment in its Kroger Plus Shopper's Card program.[8] Retailers, wholesalers, medical and legal service providers, schools, government agencies, and resorts, to name a few, use smart cards or their equivalent. In most instances, participants provide, although sometimes grudgingly, the personal information requested by enrollment procedures. But in others, like when smart cards are used with those convicted of crimes and sentenced to municipal or state correction facilities or those attending specific schools, enrollment is mandatory. In some instances, mandatory sharing of information is initially for personal welfare and safety—like when you admit yourself for a medical procedure and provide detailed information about medication or prior surgery. But in others, enrollment is for less critical but potentially attractive monetary benefits—for example, free car care services when a smart card is included with the keys to a new vehicle. The bottom line is that the organization collecting the information gains a major benefit: the potential for better understanding and competitive advantage.

General privacy laws may not be sufficient to protect the unsuspecting in the cyber-space realm of data collection. The 15 European Union (EU) countries started the new century by passing the European Commission's Data Protection Directive. Under the directive, commissioners can prosecute companies and block websites that fail to live up to its strict privacy standards. Specifically, the directive prohibits the transmission of names, addresses, ethnicity, and other personal information to any country that fails to provide adequate data protection. This includes direct mail lists, hotel and travel reservations, medical and work records, and orders for products among a host of others.[9] U.S. industry and government agencies have resisted regulation of data flow. But the EU insists that it is the right of every citizen to find out what information about them is in a database and correct any mistakes. Few U.S. companies would willingly offer such access due to the high cost;[10] a perfect example of this reluctance is the difficulty individuals have correcting erroneous credit reports, even when such information is based on stolen personal identity or credit card transactions.

Yet questions remain regarding the definition of specific ethical behaviors for cyber-research, the sufficiency of existing professional guidelines, and the issue of ultimate responsibility for respondents. If researchers are responsible for the ethical conduct of their research, are they solely responsible for the burden of protecting participants from every conceivable harm?

Ethics and the Sponsor

There are also ethical considerations to keep in mind when dealing with the research client or sponsor. Whether undertaking product, market, personnel, financial, or other research, a sponsor has the right to receive ethically conducted research.

Confidentiality

Some sponsors wish to undertake research without revealing themselves. They have a right to several types of confidentiality, including sponsor nondisclosure, purpose nondisclosure, and findings nondisclosure.

Companies have a right to dissociate themselves from the sponsorship of a research project. This type of confidentiality is called **sponsor nondisclosure.** Due to the sensitive nature of the management dilemma or the research question, sponsors may hire an outside consulting or research firm to complete research projects. This is often done when a company is testing a new product idea, to avoid potential consumers from being influenced by the company's current image or industry standing. Or if a company is contemplating entering a new market, it may not wish to reveal its plans to competitors. In such cases, it is the responsibility of the researcher to respect this desire and devise a plan that safeguards the identity of the research sponsor.

Purpose nondisclosure involves protecting the purpose of the study or its details. A research sponsor may be testing a new idea that is not yet patented and may not want the competition to know of its plans. It may be investigating employee complaints and may not want to spark union activity. Or the sponsor might be contemplating a new public stock offering, where advance disclosure would spark the interest of authorities or cost the firm thousands or millions of dollars. Finally, even if a sponsor feels no need to hide its identity or the study's purpose, most sponsors want the research data and findings to be confidential, at least until the management decision is made. Thus sponsors usually demand and receive **findings nondisclosure** between themselves or their researchers and any interested but unapproved parties.

Information can make or break a business on one of the world's busiest avenues, Wall Street. That's why you need a researcher that can extract information while keeping results strictly confidential. Seaport Surveys is one such firm. It specializes in executive recruiting, as well as business to business interviewing and executive focus groups in the greater New York area. www.seaportsurveys.com

Right to Quality Research

An important ethical consideration for the researcher and the sponsor is the sponsor's **right to quality** research. This right entails:

- Providing a research design appropriate for the research question.
- Maximizing the sponsor's value for the resources expended.
- Providing data handling and reporting techniques appropriate for the data collected.

From the proposal through the design to data analysis and final reporting, the researcher guides the sponsor on the proper techniques and interpretations. Often sponsors will have heard about a sophisticated data-handling technique and will want it used even when it is inappropriate for the problem at hand. The researcher should guide the sponsor so this does not occur. The researcher should propose the design most suitable for the problem. The researcher should not propose activities designed to maximize researcher revenue or minimize researcher effort at the sponsor's expense.

As you learn about research design, sampling, statistics, and reporting techniques, you'll learn the various conditions that must be met for results to be valid.

Finally, we have all heard the remark, "You can lie with statistics." It is the researcher's responsibility to prevent that from occurring. The ethical researcher always follows the analytical rules and conditions for results to be valid. The ethical researcher reports findings in ways that minimize the drawing of false conclusions. The ethical researcher also uses charts, graphs, and tables to show the data objectively, despite the sponsor's preferred outcomes.

Sponsor's Ethics

Occasionally, research specialists may be asked by sponsors to participate in unethical behavior. Compliance by the researcher would be a breach of ethical standards. Some examples to be avoided are:

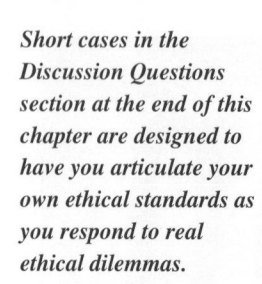

Short cases in the Discussion Questions section at the end of this chapter are designed to have you articulate your own ethical standards as you respond to real ethical dilemmas.

- Violating respondent confidentiality.
- Changing data or creating false data to meet a desired objective.
- Changing data presentations or interpretations.
- Interpreting data from a biased perspective.
- Omitting sections of data analysis and conclusions.
- Making recommendations beyond the scope of the data collected.

Let's examine the effects of complying with these types of coercion. A sponsor may offer a promotion, future contracts, or a larger payment for the existing research contract; or the sponsor may threaten to fire the researcher or tarnish the researcher's reputation. For some researchers, the request may seem trivial and the reward high. But imagine, for a moment, what will happen to the researcher who changes research results. Although there is a promise of future research, can the sponsor ever trust that researcher again? If the researcher's ethical standards are for sale, which sponsor might be the highest bidder next time? Although the promise of future contracts seems enticing, it is unlikely to be kept. Each coercive reward or punishment has an equally poor outcome. The "greater than" contracted payment is a payoff. The threats to one's professional reputation cannot be carried out effectively by a sponsor who has tried to purchase you. So the rewards for behaving unethically are illusory.

What's the ethical course? Often, it requires confronting the sponsor's demand and taking the following actions:

MANAGEMENT

Tip

- Educate the sponsor to the purpose of research.
- Explain the researcher's role in fact finding versus the sponsor's role in decision making.
- Explain how distorting the truth or breaking faith with respondents leads to future problems.
- Failing moral suasion, terminate the relationship with the sponsor.

Researchers and Team Members

Another ethical responsibility of researchers is their team's safety as well as their own. In addition, the responsibility for ethical behavior rests with the researcher who, along with assistants, is charged with protecting the anonymity of both the sponsor and the respondent.

Safety

It is the researcher's responsibility to design a project so the safety of all interviewers, surveyors, experimenters, or observers is protected. Several factors may be important to consider in ensuring a researcher's **right to safety.** Some urban areas and undeveloped rural areas may be unsafe for research assistants. If, for example, the researcher must personally interview people in a high-crime district, it is reasonable to provide a second team member to protect the researcher. Alternatively, if an assistant feels unsafe after visiting a neighborhood by car, an alternate researcher should be assigned to the destination.[11] It is unethical to require staff members to enter an environment where they feel physically threatened. Researchers who are insensitive to these concerns face both research and legal risks—the least of which involves having interviewers falsify instruments.

Ethical Behavior of Assistants

Researchers should require ethical compliance from team members just as sponsors expect ethical behavior from the researcher. Assistants are expected to carry out the sampling plan, to interview or observe respondents without bias, and to accurately record all necessary data. Unethical behavior, such as filling in an interview sheet without having asked the respondent the questions, cannot be tolerated. The behavior of the assistants is under the direct control of the responsible researcher or field supervisor. If an assistant behaves improperly in an interview or shares a respondent's interview sheet with an unauthorized person, it is the researcher's responsibility. Consequently, all assistants should be well trained and supervised.

Protection of Anonymity

As discussed previously, researchers and assistants protect the confidentiality of the sponsor's information and the anonymity of the respondents. Each researcher handling data should be required to sign a confidentiality and nondisclosure statement.

Close-Up

Do Data Warehouses Challenge Fair Play?

H. Jefferson Smith

One of the most popular concepts in information technology these days is data warehousing, which stores a company's data in a central repository. The information in the database is updated frequently and is made available to the firm's managers and employees for planning, marketing, and decision making.

Data warehouses are designed to support online analytical processing and data mining. These technologies have been described as akin to turning 100 statisticians loose on your data at the same time.

Many kinds of business questions can be answered through these technologies. You can find and track customers, analyze their behavior, segment a customer base, customize products, model past attrition behavior (thus reducing past customer defections), and refine a business strategy by massaging the warehouse data.

For example, one consumer credit company has a data warehouse that contains almost 1,000 attributes per customer. The database is so large that updates take more than 48 hours and rely on 50 different feeder files. But the payback is also large: Analysts are making more than 200 queries per day, and in-depth reports on spending patterns and demographics are available to the company's marketers. The analysts and marketers have also used the warehouse to generate targeted mailings to customers.

Nevertheless, along with the potential benefits of data warehousing come some serious considerations about fair play in the use of customer data. The various issues that arise depend on whether an organization's customers are other businesses or individual consumers.

It's Just Business

Almost every company has relationships with other firms. Some are suppliers that provide the company with products or services, while others distribute or purchase its products and services. In addition, a company has relationships with individual consumers who buy its products—either directly or through a distributor or retailer. Thus, when an enterprise warehouses data about its customers in business-to-business transactions, a corporation should think about what constitutes fair play from the perspective of several different players: the company that is its direct customer, the firms supplying that customer, and the firms or individual consumers buying that customer's products.

In general, the company with the data warehouse should follow a two-edged principle. It is fair to use the customer data to deduce ways in which the relationship with this business customer (or other potential customers of this type) could be strengthened.

It would be fair, for example, to create statistical profiles of current customers based on the warehouse data and to use those profiles to deduce which market segments might be most appropriate for future targeting. It would also be acceptable to conclude which additional products or services would be most appropriate for current customers and to focus special attention on creating and marketing those products or services to those customers.

On the other hand, it is unfair to use the customer data in any of the following three ways: First, it is unfair to do anything that might harm the customer's relationships with any of *its* suppliers or customers. Suppose, for example, that company B, after careful scrutiny of its warehoused data, realized that most of the purchases customer C made were being resold to one of C's clients, D. Obviously, both B and D could benefit if D bought its products directly from B and bypassed C. B could charge D a price that was higher than what it charged C but lower than what D paid C.

Though this scenario appears economically efficient, B's contacting D to suggest such a deal would constitute gross unfairness to C. B would be using data about its relationship with C to undercut C's position with D.

Second, it is unfair to use customer data in any way that intrudes on the customer's proprietary know-how. Suppose that its data warehouse gave company E knowledge about the specific methods and techniques that one of its customers, F, was using to design and produce its products. It would be unfair for E to reveal this information to others or to use this knowledge to take advantage of F in future negotiations.

Third, it is unfair to use customer data to change an industry structure if that change is detrimental to any of the firm's customers. Suppose, for example, that company G was a supplier to a number of firms in an industry. This industry has a value system of suppliers, manufacturers, distributors, and consumers. Several companies are involved in the manufacturing process—from raw materials to the final product—with each firm adding some value to the product.

By carefully massaging its data warehouse, G might discover a new scheme for manufacturing and distributing products that would increase the overall efficiency of the system, reduce the cost of production (leading to greater industry profits and more sales for G), and lead to greater sales and profits for *some* of the manufacturers (G's customers).

On the other hand, the scheme would hurt the sales and profits of other firms that are also G's customers. Although some people might disagree, I would argue that G had an obligation to protect the interests of *all* its customers and to take no action that would harm any of them. Since G had the data in its warehouse only because of its relationship with its customers, it would be a betrayal to use that data in a manner that would harm any of them.

Making It Personal

When a company's customers are individual consumers instead of other businesses, different rules of fairness apply because concepts of fair information use at this level are often viewed as a human rights issue. Therefore, issues related to consumer privacy—a concept quite distinct from that of corporations' right to proprietary trade knowledge—quickly come into play.

The general rules of fairness in warehousing consumer data should be the same as those that are becoming generally accepted for other applications that involve personal data:

- Consumers should be fully informed of the intended uses of data before the data are collected.

- Consumers should be allowed to opt out of any uses they find offensive.

- Data collected from consumers for one purpose should not be used for another purpose without the consumer's permission.

The rules suggest that it will be difficult to begin warehousing consumer data *unless* some up-front work has been done to ensure that the consumers were fully informed of the intended uses ahead of time and were given an opportunity to opt out.

For example, unless consumers are told in advance that transaction data will be used to assess their spending patterns and create psychographic profiles of their activities, such analysis should not be done. Fortunately, the consumer credit company discussed earlier has engaged in just such a notification program.

Assuming that the analysts have access to a set of "clean" consumer data (data gathered under the policies outlined above), they can proceed to mine the data, classifying consumers as appropriate, targeting specific customers for certain offers, and developing plans for soliciting new customers.

However, a word of warning is in order, based on experiences in the database marketing industry: The results of the mining activities should be carefully evaluated to ensure that they produce no socially negative outcomes or, at least, that the outcomes are grounded in business decisions rather than in unintended discrimination. For example, the targeting of specific residents in one urban area for special purchase offers has been called discriminatory because the offers were sent disproportionally to one racial group and excluded members of other groups.

It seems obvious that the use of data warehousing introduces new ethical challenges into both business-to-business and business-to-consumer relationships. However, the lines are not drawn clearly in all areas, and there is still room for judgment calls on many issues. Therefore, in the interest of fair play, corporate and IT executives who want to take advantage of this technology should pay serious attention to all the issues involved.

Professional Standards

Various standards of ethics exist for the professional researcher. Many corporations, professional associations, and universities have a **code of ethics.** The impetus for these policies and standards can be traced to two documents: the Belmont Report of 1979 and the *Federal Register* of 1991.[12] Society or association guidelines include ethical standards for the conduct of research. One comprehensive source contains 51 official codes of ethics issued by 45 associations in business, health, and law.[13] The business section of this source consists of ethics standards for

Accounting—American Institute of Certified Public Accountants.

Advertising—American Association of Advertising Agencies; Direct Marketing Association.

Banking—American Bankers Association.

Engineering—American Association of Engineering Societies; National Society of Professional Engineers.

Financial planning—Association for Investment Management and Research; Certified Financial Planner Board of Standards/Institute of Certified Financial Planners; International Association for Financial Planning.

Human resources—American Society for Public Administration; Society for Human Resource Management.

Insurance—American Institute for Chartered Property Casualty Underwriters; American Society of Chartered Life Underwriters and Chartered Financial Consultants.

Management—Academy of Management; The Business Roundtable.

Real estate—National Association of Realtors.

Other professional associations' codes have detailed research sections: the American Marketing Association, the American Association for Public Opinion Research, the American Psychological Association, the American Political Science Association, the American Sociological Association, and the Society of Competitive Intelligence Professionals. These associations update their codes frequently.

We commend professional societies and business organizations for developing standards. However, without enforcement, standards are ineffectual. Effective codes (1) are regulative, (2) protect the public interest and the interests of the profession served by the code, (3) are behavior-specific, and (4) are *enforceable*. A study that assessed the effects of personal and professional values on ethical consulting behavior concluded:

> The findings of this study cast some doubt on the effectiveness of professional codes of ethics and corporate policies that attempt to deal with ethical dilemmas faced by business consultants. A mere codification of ethical values of the profession or organization may not counteract ethical ambivalence created and maintained through reward systems. The results suggest that unless ethical codes and policies are consistently reinforced with a significant reward and punishment structure and truly integrated into the business culture, these mechanisms would be of limited value in actually regulating unethical conduct.[14]

Federal, state, and local governments also have laws, policies, and procedures in place to regulate research on human beings. The U.S. government began a process that covers all research having federal support. Initially implemented in 1966, the Institutional Review Boards (IRBs) engage in a risk assessment and benefit analysis review of proposed research. The Department of Health and Human Services (HHS) translated the federal regulations into policy. Most other federal and state agencies follow the HHS-developed guidelines.

Since 1981, the review requirement has been relaxed so research that is routine no longer needs to go through the complete process.[15] Each institution receiving funding from HHS or doing research for HHS is required to have its own IRB to review research proposals. Many institutions require all research, whether funded or unfunded by the government, to undergo review by the local IRB. The IRBs concentrate on two areas. First is the guarantee of obtaining complete, informed consent from participants. This can be traced to the first of 10 points in the Nuremberg Code.[16] Complete informed consent has four characteristics:

1. The respondent must be competent to give consent.
2. Consent must be voluntary, free from coercion, force, requirements, and so forth.
3. Respondents must be adequately informed to make a decision.
4. Respondents should know the possible risks or outcomes associated with the research.

The second item of interest to the IRB is the risk assessment and benefit analysis review. In the review, risks are considered when they add to the normal risk of daily life. Significantly, the only benefit considered is the immediate importance of the knowledge to be gained. Possible long-term benefits from applying the knowledge that may be gained in the research are not considered.[17]

Other federal legislation that governs or influences the ways in which research is carried out are the Right to Privacy laws. Public Law 95-38 is the Privacy Act of 1974. This was the first law guaranteeing Americans the right to privacy. Public Law 96-440, the Privacy Protection Act of 1980, carries the right to privacy further. These two laws are the basis for protecting the privacy and confidentiality of the respondents and the data.

Resources for Ethical Awareness

There is optimism for improving ethical awareness. According to the Center for Business Ethics at Bentley College, over a third of Fortune 500 companies have ethics officers, a substantial rise. Almost 90 percent of business schools have ethics programs, up from a handful several years ago.[18] Exhibit 5–3 provides a list of recommended resources for business students, researchers, and managers. The Center for Ethics and Business at Loyola Marymount University provides an online environment for discussing issues related to the necessity, difficulty, costs, and rewards of conducting business ethically. Its website offers a comprehensive list of business and research ethics links.[19]

EXHIBIT 5–3 Resources for Ethical Awareness

Journals and Magazines

Business Ethics   *Business Ethics Quarterly*   *Ethikos*   *Journal of Business Ethics*

Research, Training, and Conferences

Business ethics conferences, The Conference Board, New York, NY (212-759-0900).

Center for Professional Ethics, Manhattan College, Riverdale, NY (718-862-7442).

Center for the Study of Ethics in the Professions, Illinois Institute of Technology, Chicago, IL (312-567-3017).

Ethics Corps Training for Business Leaders, Josephson Institute of Ethics, Los Angeles, CA (310-306-1868).

Ethics Resource Center, Washington, DC (202-737-2258).

European Business Ethics Network, Breukelen, The Netherlands.

Graduate Research Ethics Education Workshop, Association of Practical and Professional Ethics, Indiana University, Bloomington, IN (812-855-6450).

Institute for Business and Professional Ethics, DePaul University, Chicago, IL (312-362-6569).

International Conference on Business Ethics, The World Center for Business Ethics/The Management Roundtable International, Inc., Denver, CO (303-759-8845).

Teaching Research Ethics, Poynter Center, Indiana University, Bloomington, IN (812-855-0261).

The Beard Center for Leadership in Ethics, A. J. Palumbo School of Business Administration, Duquesne University, Pittsburgh, PA (412-396-5475).

The Center for Business Ethics, Bentley College, Waltham, MA (617-891-2000).

The Center for Professional and Applied Ethics, University of North Carolina, Charlotte, NC (704-547-3542).

The Institute for the Study of Applied and Professional Ethics, Dartmouth College, Hanover, NH (603-646-1263).

The Program in Ethics and the Professions, Harvard University, Cambridge, MA (617-495-1336/3990).

The Wharton Ethics Program, University of Pennsylvania, Philadelphia, PA (215- 898-1166).

SUMMARY

1 Ethics are norms or standards of behavior that guide moral choices about our behavior and our relationships with others. Ethics differ from legal constraints, in which generally accepted standards have defined penalties that are universally enforced. The goal of ethics in research is to ensure that no one is harmed or suffers adverse consequences from research activities.

As research is designed, several ethical considerations must be balanced:

- Protect the rights of the *participant* or subject.
- Ensure the *sponsor* receives ethically conducted and reported research.
- Follow ethical standards when *designing research.*
- Protect the *safety* of the researcher and team.
- Ensure the *research team* follows the design.

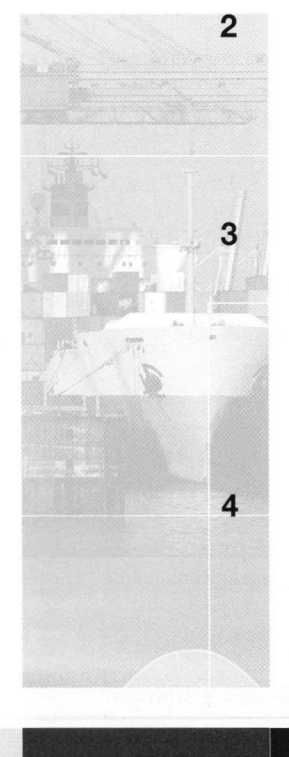

2 In general, research must be designed so a respondent does not suffer physical harm, discomfort, pain, embarrassment, or loss of privacy. Begin data collection by explaining to respondents the benefits expected from the research. Explain that their rights and well-being will be adequately protected and say how that will be done. Be certain that interviewers obtain the informed consent of the respondent. The use of deception is questionable; when it is used, debrief any respondent who has been deceived.

3 Many *sponsors* wish to undertake research without revealing themselves. Sponsors have the right to demand and receive confidentiality between themselves and the researchers. Ethical researchers provide sponsors with the research design needed to solve the managerial question. The ethical researcher shows the data objectively, despite the sponsor's preferred outcomes.

The research team's safety is the responsibility of the researcher. Researchers should require ethical compliance from team members in following the research design, just as sponsors expect ethical behavior from the researcher.

4 Many corporations and research firms have adopted a code of ethics. Several professional associations have detailed research provisions. Of interest are the American Association for Public Opinion Research, the American Marketing Association, the American Political Science Association, the American Psychological Association, and the American Sociological Association. Federal, state, and local governments have laws, policies, and procedures in place to regulate research on human beings.

KEY TERMS

EXAMPLES

National Institutes of Health	The funding agency with partial ethical oversight responsibility for Johns Hopkins's research on hexamethonium.	124
Procter & Gamble	Returned confiscated marketing documents to Unilever after discovering that contract P&G competitive intelligence agents had retrieved competitor information from trash receptacles.	120
Staples	An office supplies company using deception to collect competitive intelligence.	123
SupplyCo.*	A supplier to the automobile industry using detailed customer data to restructure industry processes.	139
U.S. Food and Drug Administration	Federal agency with oversight responsibility for Johns Hopkins's drug-performance testing for hexamethonium.	124
U.S. Department of Commerce	Complying with new European Union standards for data transmission.	128
Unilever, Inc.	Negotiating a settlement for damage to its hair care business caused by the unethical intelligence-gathering behavior of a competitor.	120

DISCUSSION QUESTIONS

Making Research Decisions

1. **A Competitive Coup in the In-Flight Magazine.** When the manager for market intelligence of AutoCorp, a major automotive manufacturer, boarded the plane in Chicago, her mind was on shrinking market share and late product announcements. As she settled back to enjoy the remains of a hectic day, she reached for the in-flight magazine. It was jammed into the seat pocket in front of her.

   Crammed into this already tiny space was a report with a competitor's logo, marked "Confidential—Restricted Circulation." It contained a description of new product announcements for the next two years. Not only was it intended for a small circle of senior executives but it also answered the questions she had recently proposed to an external research firm.

   The proposal for the solicited research could be canceled. Her research budget, already savaged, could be saved. She was home free, legally and career-wise.

   She foresaw only one problem. In the last few months, AutoCorp's newly hired ethicist had revised the firm's Business Conduct Guidelines. They now required company employees in possession of a competitor's information to return it or face dismissal. But it was still a draft and not formally approved. She had the rest of the flight to decide whether to return the document to the airline or slip it into her briefcase.

   a. What are the most prudent decisions she can make about her responsibilities to herself and others?

   b. What are the implications of those decisions even if there is no violation of law or regulation?

2. **Free Waters in Miro Beach: Boaters Inc. Versus City Government.**[20] The city commissioners of Miro Beach proposed limits on boaters who anchor offshore in waterfront areas of the St. Lucinda River adjoining the city. Residents had complained of pollution from the live-aboard boaters. The parking lot of boats created an unsightly view.

   The city based its proposed ordinance on research done by the staff. The staff did not hold graduate degrees in either public or business administration, and it was not known if staff members were competent to conduct research. The staff requested a proposal from a team of local university professors who had conducted similar work in the past. The research cost was $10,000. After receiving the proposal, the staff chose to do the work itself and not expend resources for the project. Through an unidentified source, the professors later learned their proposal contained enough information to guide the city's staff and suggested data collection areas that might provide information that could justify the boaters' claims.

Based on the staff's one-time survey of waterfront litter, "pump-out" samples, and a weekly frequency count of boats, an ordinance was drafted and a public workshop was held. Shortly after, a group of concerned boat owners formed Boaters Inc., an association to promote boating, raise funds, and lobby the commission. The group's claims were that the boaters (1) spent thousands of dollars on community goods and services, (2) did not create the litter, and (3) were being unjustly penalized because the commission's fact finding was flawed.

With the last claim in mind, the boaters flooded the city with public record requests. The clerks reported that some weeks the requests were one per day. Under continued pressure, the city attorney hired a private investigator (PI) to infiltrate Boaters Inc. to collect information. He rationalized this on the grounds that the boaters had challenged the city's grant applications in order to "blackmail the city into dropping plans to regulate the boaters."

The PI posed as a college student and worked for a time in the home of the boater organization's sponsor while helping with mailings. Despite the PI's inability to corroborate the city attorney's theory, he recommended conducting a background investigation on the organization's principal, an employee of a tabloid newspaper. (The FBI, on request of city or county police organizations, generally performs background investigations.)

The PI was not a boating enthusiast and soon drew suspicion. Simultaneously, the organization turned up the heat on the city by requesting what amounted to 5,000 pages of information—"studies and all related documents containing the word 'boat.'" Failing to get a response from Miro Beach, the boaters filed suit under the Florida Public Records Act. By this time, the city had spent $20,000.

The case stalled, went to appeal, and was settled in favor of the boaters. A year later, the organization's principal filed an invasion of privacy and slander suit against the city attorney, the PI, and the PI's firm. After six months, the suit was amended to include the city itself and sought $1 million in punitive damages.

a. What are the most prudent decisions the city can make about its responsibilities to itself and others?

b. What are the implications of those decisions even if there is no violation of law or regulation?

3. **The High Cost of Organizational Change.** It was his first year of college teaching, and there were no summer teaching assignments for new hires. But the university was kind enough to steer him to an aviation firm, Avionics Inc., which needed help creating an organizational assessment survey. The assignment was to last five weeks, but it paid about the same as teaching all summer. The work was just about as perfect as it gets for an organizational behavior specialist. Avionics Inc.'s vice president, whom he met the first day, was cordial and smooth. The researcher would report to a senior manager who was coordinating the project with the human resources and legal departments.

It was soon apparent that in the 25-year history of Avionics Inc., there had never been an employee survey. This was understandable given management's lack of concern for employee complaints. Working conditions had deteriorated without management intervention, and government inspectors counted the number of heads down at desks as an index of performance. To make matters worse, the engineers were so disgruntled that word of unionization had spread like wildfire. A serious organizing effort was planned before the VP could approve the survey.

Headquarters dispatched nervous staffers to monitor the situation and generally involve themselves with every aspect of the questionnaire. Shadowed, the young researcher began to feel apprehension turn to paranoia. He consoled himself, however, with the goodwill of 500 enthusiastic, cooperative employees who had pinned their hopes for a better working environment to the results of this project.

The data collection was textbook perfect. No one had asked to preview the findings or had shown any particular interest. In the fifth week, he boarded the corporate jet with the VP and senior manager to make a presentation at headquarters. Respondents at the headquarters location were invited to attend. Management was intent on heading off unionization by showing its confidence in the isolated nature of "a few engineers' complaints." They had also promised to engage the participants in action planning over the next few days.

An hour into the flight, the Avionics Inc. VP turned from his reading to the young researcher and said, "We have seen your results, you know. And we would like you to change two key findings. They are not all that critical to this round of fixing the 'bone orchard,' and you'll have another crack at it as a real consultant in the fall."

"But that would mean breaking faith with your employees . . . people who trusted me to present the results objectively. It's what I thought you wanted . . ."

"Yes, well, look at it this way," replied the VP. "All of your findings we can live with except these two. They're an embarrassment to senior management. Let me put it plainly. We have government contracts into the foreseeable future. You could retire early with consulting income from this place. Someone will meet us on the runway with new slides. What do you say?"

a. What are the most prudent decisions Avionics Inc. can make about its responsibilities to itself and others?

b. What are the implications of those decisions even if there is no violation of law or regulation?

4. **Data Mining Ethics and Company Growth Square Off.** SupplyCo. is a supplier to a number of firms in an industry. This industry has a structure that includes suppliers, manufacturers, distributors, and consumers. Several companies are involved in the manufacturing process—from processed parts to creation of the final product—with each firm adding some value to the product.

The scenario in the Cummins Engines video case has some of the same properties as this ethical dilemma.

By carefully mining its customer data warehouse, SupplyCo. reveals a plausible new model for manufacturing and distributing industry products that would increase the overall efficiency of the industry system, reduce costs of production (leading to greater industry profits and more sales for SupplyCo.), and result in greater sales and profits for some of the industry's manufacturers (SupplyCo.'s customers).

On the other hand, implementing the model would hurt the sales and profits of other firms that are also SupplyCo.'s customers but which are not in a position (due to manpower, plant, or equipment) to benefit from the new manufacturing/distribution model. These firms would lose sales, profits, and market share and potentially go out of business.

Does SupplyCo. have an obligation to protect the interests of *all* its customers and to take no action that would harm any of them, since SupplyCo. had the data within its warehouse only because of its relationship with its customers? (It would betray some of its customers if it were to use the data in a manner that would cause these customers harm.) Or does it have a more powerful obligation to its stockholders and employees to aggressively pursue the new model that research reveals would substantially increase its sales, profits, and market share against competitors?

a. What are the most prudent decisions SupplyCo. can make about its responsibilities to itself and others?

b. What are the implications of those decisions even if there is no violation of law or regulation?

WWW Exercises Visit our website for Internet exercises related to this chapter at
www.mhhe.com/business/cooper8

CASES*

 CUMMINS ENGINES

*All cases indicating a video icon are located on the Instructor's Videotape Supplement. All nonvideo cases are in the case section of the textbook. All cases indicating a CD icon offer a data set, which is located on the accompanying CD.

REFERENCE NOTES

1. C. S. Benson, "Codes of Ethics," *Journal of Business Ethics* (1989), pp. 305–9.
2. Elizabethann O'Sullivan and Gary R. Rassel, *Research Methods for Public Administrators* (New York: Longman, 1999).
3. American Psychological Association, *Ethical Principles of Psychologists and Code of Conduct* (Washington, DC: APA, 1997).
4. Exhibit 5–2 shows the standard procedures used for informed consent in surveys conducted by the Indiana University Center for Survey Research. Wording and protocol by CSR IU.
5. Robert A. Baron and Donn Byrne, *Social Psychology: Understanding Human Interaction* (Boston: Allyn and Bacon, 1991), p. 36.
6. Floyd J. Fowler, Jr., *Survey Research Methods,* rev. ed. (Beverly Hills, CA: Sage Publications, 1988), p. 138.
7. Jim Thomas, "Introduction: A Debate About the Ethics of Fair Practices for Collecting Social Science Data in Cyberspace," *Information Society* 12, no. 2 (1996).
8. "FAQs—Kroger Plus Shopper's Card," The Kroger Co., 2001 (http://www.kroger.com/faqs_shopperscard.htm).
9. "European Online Privacy Measures Up," *eMarketer,* October 26, 1998 (http://www.estats.com/news/102698_europri.html).
10. Robert O'Harrow, "Privacy Rules Send U.S. Firms Scrambling," *Washington Post,* October 20, 1998.
11. Fowler, *Survey Research Methods,* p. 139.
12. See Thomas, *Information Society.* The Belmont Report was produced by the National Commission for the Protection of Human Subjects of Biomedical and Behavioral Research under the title, *Ethical Principles and Guidelines for the Protection of*

Human Subjects of Research (Washington, DC: Department of Health, Education, and Welfare, 1979). The other source of ethical standards was the *Federal Register,* Part II, "Federal Policy for the Protection of Human Subjects: Notices and Rules" (Washington, DC: U.S. Government Printing Office, 1991).
13. *Codes of Professional Responsibility,* 3rd ed., ed. R. Gorlin (Washington, DC: BNA Books, 1994).
14. Jeff Allen and Duane Davis, "Assessing Some Determinant Effects of Ethical Consulting Behavior: The Case of Personal and Professional Values," *Journal of Business Ethics* (1993), p. 449.
15. Paul Davidson Reynolds, *Ethics and Social Science Research* (Englewood Cliffs, NJ: Prentice-Hall, 1982), pp. 103–8.
16. The Nuremberg Code is a set of 10 moral, ethical, and legal principles for medical experimentation on humans. It comes from the judgment of the Nuremberg Military Tribunal against doctors and scientists who committed World War II Nazi atrocities. For a full listing of the Nuremberg Code, see Jay Katz, *Experimentation with Human Beings* (New York: Russell Sage Foundation, 1972), pp. 305–6. See also Allan J. Kimmel, *Ethics and Values in Applied Social Research* (Newbury Park, CA: Sage Publications, 1988), pp. 54–56.
17. Reynolds, *Ethics and Social Science Reaearch,* pp. 103–8.
18. The Center for Business Ethics, Bentley College (Waltham, MA); http://ecampus.bentley.edu/dept/cbe/.
19. http://www.ethicsandbusiness.org/index3.htm.
20. Adapted from stories in the *Palm Beach Post* during September 1992.

REFERENCES FOR SNAPSHOTS AND CAPTIONS

Cummins Engines

McGraw-Hill Video Library.
"Medium and Heavy Trucks: Signature 600," 2001 (http://www.cummins.com/na/pages/en/products/trucks/signature600.cfm).
December 1999 (http://www.cummins.com/news/roush.html).
January 4, 2000 (http://www.cummins.com/onhigh/s600.html).

Johns Hopkins

"Funding Suspended," *ABCnews.com,* July 19, 2001 (http://more.abcnews.go.com/sections/living/dailynews/hopkins010719.html).
"Johns Hopkins Loses Federal Funding," *CBSnews.com,* July 19, 2001 (http://www.cbsnews.com/now/story/0,1597,302398-412,00.shtml).

"Johns Hopkins Takes Blame," *ABCnews.com,* July 16, 2001 (http://more.abcnews.go.com/sections/living/dailynews/hopkins010719.html).

Procter & Gamble

Julian Barnes, "Unilever Wants P&G Placed Under Monitor in Spy Case," *New York Times on the Web,* September 1, 2001 (http://www.nytimes.com/2001/09/01/business/01soap.html).
Andy Serwer, "P&G Comes Clean on Spying Operation," *Fortune.com,* August 30, 2001 (http://www.fortune.com/indexw.jhtml?channel=artcol.jhtml&doc_id=203932).

CLASSIC AND CONTEMPORARY READINGS

National Academy of Sciences. *On Being a Scientist: Responsible Conduct in Research.* 2nd ed. Washington, DC: National Academy Press, 1995. Written for beginning researchers, this source describes the ethical foundations of scientific practices, personal and professional issues, and research applications for industrial, governmental, and academic settings.

Rosnow, Ralph L., and Robert Rosenthal. *People Studying People: Artifacts and Ethics in Behavioral Research.* New York: Freeman, 1997. A potent source of analysis and advice; particularly appropriate for Chapters 13 and 14 on observation and experimentation.

Stanley, Barbara H., et al., eds. *Research Ethics: A Psychological Approach.* Lincoln: University of Nebraska Press, 1996. Addresses important issues such as the discovery and neutralization of bias, sensitivity to the interests of experimental participants, and the counterweighing factors in rules, regulations, and enforcement.

Stern, Judy E., and Deni Elliott, eds. *Research Ethics: A Reader.* Hanover, NH: University Press of New England, 1997. An insightful review of ethical issues for managers and researchers.

Weisstub, David N., ed. *Research on Human Subjects: Ethics, Law, and Social Policy.* Oxford, England: Pergamon Press, 1998. Comprehensive exploration of challenges in research ethics for policymakers and institutions, with coverage of international perspectives.

PART II

The Design
of Research

143

CHAPTER 6

Design Strategies

Learning Objectives

After reading this chapter, you should understand . . .

1   **The basic stages of research design.**

2   **The major descriptors of research design.**

3   **The major types of research designs.**

4   **The relationships that exist between variables in research design and the steps for evaluating those relationships.**

Bringing Research to Life

"**A**rghh!"

Jason Henry leaped up and tossed a paper cup full of coffee at his TV. It hit the set and bounced off, leaving coffee dripping down the screen.

"What's wrong? Are you hurt? I'M A DOCTOR!" hollered Dorrie from the bedroom. "And what time is it anyway?"

"Go back to sleep, Dorrie," replied Myra. "It's 2:30 A.M., and your husband just chose to throw his coffee at the TV, rather than drink it, because he doesn't care for the anchor on cable news."

"She's totally unscientific, you know," grumped Jason.

"She's an inexperienced kid getting her first break on the network," stated Myra, "at an hour when no sane person is watching TV anyway, let alone subjecting it to scientific criticism. So chill out, lad."

To Dorrie she shouted, "We are almost finished here, and soon you will have your husband back."

"It is terrifically unscientific," he said, "to make unsubstantiated conclusions as she did."

"I thought she did a fine job interviewing that psychiatrist—terribly amusing," said Myra. "He was a beautiful choice, with his accent and a beard that reminded me of Freud himself."

"That's not the issue, Myra, and you know it. The fact is, she should not have claimed that when the recent hurricane brushed Galveston, it caused a rash of complaints against auto dealerships."

"I thought she did a moderately good job in the interviews. That was an adorable young couple she found picketing the Mercedes dealership—the girl in a mink jacket and her husband in Gucci loafers, and both of them complaining they were powerless against big business—and you already know how effective I thought the shrink was in presenting his theory of hurricane-induced anger causing people to lash out at business."

"Not the point, again. As entertainment it was admirable. But it was rotten science. She had no before-after comparison. I want to know how many people had complaints against dealerships before the hurricane hit. Pretty clearly, she not only had no file footage of before the hurricane, but she also had no statistics. For all I know the complaint behavior has not changed."

"Do you really believe, Jason, that anyone would have the foresight to collect such information?"

"Why not? The newspapers and TV stations on the Gulf are continually hyping the threat of hurricanes. They must make a fortune selling commercial time at inflated rates during hurricane season. So, yes, they knew a hurricane was due sometime in the near future, or was at least possible, and if they were responsible they would have done baseline measurements . . ."

"Not really feasible . . ."

". . . or at least refrain from such pseudoscientific bunkum."

"Is that it? Is that your complaint?"

"That's part of it. The other part is that the hurricane brushed Galveston then skittered out into the Gulf. Forty miles away, Houston was barely touched. Did she bother to check if complaint behavior in Houston was also elevated? Because if it was, that would debunk her theory that the hurricane caused the complaint behavior. You can't blame something that occurred in one location and not in the other for causing behavior seen in both locations. Can you?"

"I guess not."

"So, what did you learn, Myra?" he asked with a touch of condescension.

She laughed heartily. "I learned not to pick a fight with you after hours of steady proposal writing. I learned that after 13 cups of coffee you become humorless, pedantic, and compulsively left-brained. I learned it is time for you to join your infinitely patient wife. See you for breakfast."

What Is Research Design?

There are many definitions of research design, but no one definition imparts the full range of important aspects. Several examples from leading authors can be cited:

> The research design constitutes the blueprint for the collection, measurement, and analysis of data. It aids the scientist in the allocation of his limited resources by posing crucial choices: Is the blueprint to include experiments, interviews, observation, the analysis of records, simulation, or some combination of these? Are the methods of data collection and the research situation to be highly structured? Is an intensive study of a small sample more effective than a less intensive study of a large sample? Should the analysis be primarily quantitative or qualitative?[1]

And:

> Research design is the plan and structure of investigation so conceived as to obtain answers to research questions. The plan is the overall scheme or program of the research. It includes an outline of what the investigator will do from writing hypotheses and their operational implications to the final analysis of data. A structure is the framework, organization, or configuration of . . . the relations among variables of a study. A research design expresses both the structure of the research problem and the plan of investigation used to obtain empirical evidence on relations of the problem.[2]

These definitions differ in detail, but together they give the essentials of **research design:**

- The design is an activity- and time-based plan.
- The design is always based on the research question.
- The design guides the selection of sources and types of information.
- The design is a framework for specifying the relationships among the study's variables.
- The design outlines procedures for every research activity.

Thus, the design provides answers for questions such as these: What techniques will be used to gather data? What kind of sampling will be used? How will time and cost constraints be dealt with?

Classification of Designs

Early in any research study, one faces the task of selecting the specific design to use. A number of different design approaches exist but, unfortunately, no simple classification system defines all the variations that must be considered. Exhibit 6–1 classifies research design using eight different descriptors.[3] A brief discussion of these descriptors illustrates their nature and contribution to research.

Degree of Research Question Crystallization   A study may be viewed as exploratory or formal. The essential distinctions between these two options are the degree of structure and the immediate objective of the study. **Exploratory studies** tend toward loose structures with the objective of discovering future research tasks. The immediate purpose of exploration is usually to develop hypotheses or questions for further research. The **formal study** begins where the exploration leaves off—it begins with a hypothesis or research question and involves precise procedures and data source specifications. The goal of a formal research design is to test the hypotheses or answer the research questions posed.

EXHIBIT 6–1   Descriptors of Research Design

Category	Options
The degree to which the research question has been crystallized	• Exploratory study • Formal study
The method of data collection	• Monitoring • Interrogation/communication
The power of the researcher to produce effects in the variables under study	• Experimental • Ex post facto
The purpose of the study	• Descriptive • Causal
The time dimension	• Cross-sectional • Longitudinal
The topical scope—breadth and depth—of the study	• Case • Statistical study
The research environment	• Field setting • Laboratory research • Simulation
The participants' perceptions of research activity	• Actual routine • Modified routine

You may find it helpful to revisit Exhibit 3–1 as we discuss these descriptors.

The exploratory-formal study dichotomy is less precise than some other classifications. All studies have elements of exploration in them, and few studies are completely uncharted. The sequence discussed in Chapter 3 (see Exhibit 3–1 and the model on the inside front cover) suggests that more formalized studies contain at least an element of exploration before the final choice of design. More detailed consideration of exploratory research is found later in this chapter.

We use the term communication to contrast with monitoring because collecting data by questioning encompasses more than the survey method.

Method of Data Collection   This classification distinguishes between **monitoring** and interrogation/communication processes. The former includes studies in which the researcher inspects the activities of a subject or the nature of some material without attempting to elicit responses from anyone. Traffic counts at an intersection, license plates recorded in a restaurant parking lot, a search of the library collection, an observation of the actions of a group of decision makers, the State Farm Dangerous Intersection Study—all are examples of monitoring. In each case the researcher notes and records the information available from observations. Monitoring for MindWriter might include "following" a computer through the repair process, documenting each activity or interaction between CompleteCare and call center employees and the damaged laptop.

In the **interrogation/communication study,** the researcher questions the subjects and collects their responses by personal or impersonal means. The collected data may result from (1) interview or telephone conversations, (2) self-administered or self-reported instruments sent through the mail, left in convenient locations, or transmitted

SNAPSHOT

The Second Global Entrepreneurship Monitor (GEM)

Researchers at the Kauffman Center for Entrepreneurial Leadership (Babson College) and the London Business School joined forces in 1997 to prove or disprove a conceptual model of cultural, economic, physical, and political factors to predict economic growth. The research design compensated for lack of control by using "a variety of nations with diversity in framework conditions, entrepreneurial sectors, business dynamics, and economic growth." The 1999 longitudinal study conducted in eight countries included various data collection methods:

- Standardized national primary data collected by each national research team.

- Two rounds of adult phone surveys of at least 1,000 adults per country (face-to-face in Japan) to measure entrepreneurial activity and attitude, completed and coordinated by an international market survey firm.

- Hour-long interviews with 4 to 39 experts (key informants) for each country.

- A detailed 12-page questionnaire completed by each key informant.

Market Facts (Arlington Heights, IL) did the first round of data collection in June 1998 (Canada, Finland, Germany, the United Kingdom, and the United States). Audience Selection, Ltd. (London), conducted the second round in March 1999 in all 10 countries. The 2000 study employed research teams from more than 21 countries, including 10 countries from the 1999 study. For the purpose of the study, entrepreneurship was defined as "any attempt to create a new business enterprise or to expand an existing business." Employing regression analysis, a weight was assigned to each factor of influence. The researchers discovered in the 1999 study that perception of opportunity (.79) and two measures of entrepreneurial potential—capacity (0.64) and motivation (0.93)—positively correlate with business start-up rates. The 2000 study created a Total Entrepreneurial Activity Index combining the nascent start-up rate (percent of adults engaged in activities related to starting a business) and the new firm rate (percent of adults reporting managing an owned-business without payroll to additional employees). This study is ongoing, but researchers thus far conclude that "support for the conceptual model is encouraging, although clearly not conclusive." Learn more about the findings in "A GEM of a Study" in the Cases section of this text.

www2.babson.edu/babson/babsoneshipp.nsf/Public/ HomePage

www.london.edu

Speed and accuracy of data collection are two factors that influence research design. Both are promised in this ad for FieldSource.

electronically or by other means, or (3) instruments presented before and/or after a treatment or stimulus condition in an *experiment*. Myra and Jason propose a communication study, using a response card inserted in the packaging of laptops returned after CompleteCare servicing.

Researcher Control of Variables   In terms of the researcher's ability to manipulate variables, we differentiate between experimental and ex post facto designs. In an **experiment,** the researcher attempts to control and/or manipulate the variables in the study. It is enough that we can cause variables to be changed or held constant in keeping with our research objectives. Experimental design is appropriate when one wishes to discover whether certain variables produce effects in other variables. Experimentation provides the most powerful support possible for a hypothesis of causation.

With an **ex post facto design,** investigators have no control over the variables in the sense of being able to manipulate them. They can only report what has happened or what is happening. It is important that the researchers using this design not influence the variables; to do so introduces bias. The researcher is limited to holding factors constant by judicious selection of subjects according to strict sampling procedures and by statistical manipulation of findings. MindWriter is planning an ex post facto design.

The Purpose of the Study   The essential difference between descriptive and causal studies lies in their objectives. If the research is concerned with finding out *who, what, where, when,* or *how much,* then the study is **descriptive.** If it is concerned with learning why—that is, how one variable produces changes in another—it is causal. Research on crime is descriptive when it measures the types of crimes committed, how often, when, where, and by whom. In a **causal study,** we try to explain relationships among variables—for instance, why the crime rate is higher in city A than in city B. At the outset, the MindWriter project is descriptive, although subsequent studies might be causal.

The Time Dimension   **Cross-sectional studies** are carried out once and represent a snapshot of one point in time. **Longitudinal studies** are repeated over an extended period. The advantage of a longitudinal study is that it can track changes over time. Jason and Myra's proposal describes a longitudinal study, with satisfaction measurements taken continuously over several months and reported monthly.

In longitudinal studies of the *panel* variety, the researcher may study the same people over time. In marketing, panels are set up to report consumption data on a variety of

S N A P S H O T   John Deere and Co.: Environmental Scanning

Like many industrial industries, agricultural and construction equipment manufacturers have their most extensive contact with the widest range of customers at trade shows. During its 160-year history, John Deere has collected both quantitative and qualitative research with its dealers at such equipment trade shows. This closeness to the customer is only part of the continuous monitoring employed by John Deere. Its success in the highly volatile industries of construction and agriculture is owed to an ability to shift its strategic and tactical actions in the face of both rapid and evolving environmental change. In the last three decades,

such changes included government actions (Carter's grain embargo of 1979), sociodemographic shifts (the move away from farming as a career), and economic downturns (the recession of the early 1990s). The research practices involved in environmental scanning are key to John Deere's ongoing success and its ability to rebound from intermittent poor performance. John Deere, with operations in more than 150 countries, had more than $239 million in income during 1999.

www.deere.com

products. These data, collected from national samples, provide a major databank on relative market share, consumer response to new products, and new promotional methods. Other longitudinal studies, such as *cohort groups,* use different subjects for each sequenced measurement. The service industry might have looked at the needs of aging baby boomers by sampling 40- to 45-year-olds in 1990 and 50- to 55-year-olds in 2000. Although each sample would be different, the population of 1945 to 1950 cohort survivors would remain the same.

Some types of information once collected cannot be collected a second time from the same person without the risk of bias. The study of public awareness of an advertising campaign over a six-month period would require different samples for each measurement.

While longitudinal research is important, the constraints of budget and time impose the need for cross-sectional analysis. Some benefits of a longitudinal study can be revealed in a cross-sectional study by adroit questioning about past attitudes, history, and future expectations. Responses to these kinds of questions should be interpreted with care, however.

The Topical Scope   The statistical study differs from the case study in several ways. **Statistical studies** are designed for breadth rather than depth. They attempt to capture a population's characteristics by making inferences from a sample's characteristics. Hypotheses are tested quantitatively. Generalizations about findings are presented based on the representativeness of the sample and the validity of the design. MindWriter plans a statistical study.

Case studies place more emphasis on a full contextual analysis of fewer events or conditions and their interrelations. Although hypotheses are often used, the reliance on qualitative data makes support or rejection more difficult. An emphasis on detail provides valuable insight for problem solving, evaluation, and strategy. This detail is secured from multiple sources of information. It allows evidence to be verified and avoids missing data. Remember the proposed monitoring study for Mind-Writer? If MindWriter tracked one or more laptops, this could serve as a case study of the CompleteCare program.

Although case studies have been maligned as "scientifically worthless" because they do not meet minimal design requirements for comparison,[4] they have a significant scientific role. It is known that "important scientific propositions have the form of universals, and a universal can be falsified by a single counterinstance."[5] Thus, a single, well-designed case study can provide a major challenge to a theory and provide a source of new hypotheses and constructs simultaneously. Discovering new hypotheses to correct postservice complaints would be the major advantage of tracking a given number of damaged MindWriter laptops through the case study design.

The Research Environment   Designs also differ as to whether they occur under actual environmental conditions (**field conditions**) or under staged or manipulated consitions (**laboratory conditions**).

To simulate is to replicate the essence of a system or process. **Simulations** are increasingly used in research, especially in operations research. The major characteristics of various conditions and relationships in actual situations are often represented in mathematical models. Role-playing and other behavioral activities may also be viewed as simulations. A simulation for MindWriter might involve an arbitrarily damaged laptop being tracked through the call center and the CompleteCare program, monitoring results at each workstation. Another popularly used simulation is the retail service study involving "mystery shoppers."

Participants' Perceptions   The usefulness of a design may be reduced when people in a disguised study perceive that research is being conducted. **Participants' perceptions** influence the outcomes of the research in subtle ways or more dramatically as we learned from the pivotal Hawthorne studies of the late 1920s. Although there is no widespread evidence of attempts by participants or respondents to please researchers through successful hypothesis guessing or evidence of the prevalence of sabotage, when participants believe that something out of the ordinary is happening, they may behave less naturally. There are three levels of perception:

1. Participants perceive no deviations from everyday routines.

2. Participants perceive deviations, but as unrelated to the researcher.

3. Participants perceive deviations as researcher-induced.[6]

The "mystery shopper" scenario is the perfect example of the final level of perception noted in the above list. If a retail sales associate knows she is being observed and evaluated—with consequences in future compensation, scheduling, or work assignment—she is likely to change her performance. In all research environments and control situations, researchers need to be vigilant to effects that may alter their conclusions. Participants' perceptions serve as a reminder to classify one's study by type, to examine validation strengths and weaknesses, and to be prepared to qualify results accordingly.

Exploratory Studies

Exploration is particularly useful when researchers lack a clear idea of the problems they will meet during the study. Through exploration researchers develop concepts more clearly, establish priorities, develop operational definitions, and improve the final research design. Exploration may also save time and money. If the problem is not as important as first thought, more formal studies can be canceled.

Exploration serves other purposes as well. The area of investigation may be so new or so vague that a researcher needs to do an exploration just to learn something about the dilemma facing the manager. Important variables may not be known or thoroughly defined. Hypotheses for the research may be needed. Also, the researcher may explore to be sure it is practical to do a formal study in the area. A federal government agency, the Office of Industry Analysis, proposed that research be done on how executives in a given industry made decisions about raw material purchases. Questions were planned asking how (and at what price spreads) one raw material was substituted for another in certain manufactured products. An exploration to discover if industry executives would divulge adequate information about their decision making on this topic was essential for the study's success.

Despite its obvious value, researchers and managers alike give exploration less attention than it deserves. There are strong pressures for quick answers. Moreover, exploration is sometimes linked to old biases about qualitative research: subjectiveness, nonrepresentativeness, and nonsystematic design. More realistically, exploration saves time and money and should not be slighted.

Qualitative Techniques

The objectives of exploration may be accomplished with different techniques. Both qualitative and quantitative techniques are applicable, although exploration relies more heavily on **qualitative techniques.** One author creates a verbal picture to differentiate the two:

Quality is the essential character or nature of something; quantity is the amount. Quality is the what; quantity the how much. Qualitative refers to the meaning, the definition or analogy or model or metaphor characterizing something, while quantitative assumes the meaning and refers to a measure of it . . . The difference lies in Steinbeck's [1941] description of the Mexican Sierra, a fish from the Sea of Cortez. One can count the spines on the dorsal fin of a pickled Sierra, 17 plus 15 plus 9. "But," says Steinbeck, "if the Sierra strikes hard on the line so that our hands are burned, if the fish sounds and nearly escapes and finally comes in over the rail, his colors pulsing and his tail beating the air, a whole new relational externality has come into being." Qualitative research would define the being of fishing, the ambiance of a city, the mood of a citizen, or the unifying tradition of a group.[7]

When we consider the scope of qualitative research, several approaches are adaptable for exploratory investigations of management questions:

MANAGEMENT
Tip

- In-depth interviewing (usually conversational rather than structured).
- Participant observation (to perceive firsthand what participants in the setting experience).
- Films, photographs, and videotape (to capture the life of the group under study).
- Projective techniques and psychological testing (such as a Thematic Apperception Test, projective measures, games, or role-playing).
- Case studies (for an in-depth contextual analysis of a few events or conditions).
- Street ethnography (to discover how a cultural subgroup describes and structures its world at the street level).
- Elite or expert interviewing (for information from influential or well-informed people in an organization or community).
- Document analysis (to evaluate historical or contemporary confidential or public records, reports, government documents, and opinions).
- Proxemics and kinesics (to study the use of space and body-motion communication, respectively).[8]

When these approaches are combined, four exploratory techniques emerge with wide applicability for the management researcher:

1. Secondary data analysis.
2. Experience surveys.
3. Focus groups.
4. Two-stage designs.

Secondary Data Analysis

The first step in an exploratory study is a search of the secondary literature. Studies made by others for their own purposes represent **secondary data.** It is inefficient to discover anew through the collection of **primary data** or original research what has already been done and reported at a level sufficient for management to make a decision.

Within secondary data exploration, a researcher should start first with an organization's own data archives. Reports of prior research studies often reveal an extensive amount of historical data or decision-making patterns. By reviewing prior studies, you can identify methodologies that proved successful and unsuccessful. Solutions that didn't receive attention in the past due to different environmental circumstances are revealed as potential subjects for further study. The researcher needs to avoid duplica-

S N A P S H O T   Smith Barney's Benchmark Job Environment Research

As part of the negotiated settlement in the landmark sexual harassment suit brought against Smith Barney by 25 current and former employees [*Martens et al. v. Smith Barney* (S.D.N.Y., 96 Civ 3779)], the financial services firm was charged with conducting research to assess underlying perceptions contributing to the illegal behavior. Catalyst, a New York firm committed to advancing women in business, conducted the multistage study ordered by Judge Constance Barker-Motley. Nine focus groups (eight single-gender, one mixed-gender) were used to help define various concepts and constructs, followed by a mail survey of 838 men and women employed in seven firms in the financial services industry. Catalyst conducted in-depth interviews with six women who left lucrative jobs in the financial services industry to start their own firms, in addition to identifying exemplary policies and programs—"best practices"—currently used in the industry. While the study revealed some similarities, it reinforced that statistically significant differences exist between men and women on key variables that define job performance and job satisfaction. To learn more about this benchmark study, see "The Catalyst for Women in Financial Services" in the Cases section of this text.

www.catalystwomen.org

www.salomonsmithbarney.com

tion in instances when prior collected data can provide sufficient information for resolving the current decision-making dilemma. While MindWriter's CompleteCare program is newly introduced, it is likely that one or more studies of the previous servicing practices and policies revealed customer attitudes on which MindWriter based the design of the current program.

We provide a detailed description of secondary data resources in Chapter 10 and Appendix A.

The second source of secondary data is published documents prepared by authors outside the sponsor organization. There are tens of thousands of periodicals and hundreds of thousands of books on all aspects of business. Data from secondary sources help us decide what needs to be done and can be a rich source of hypotheses. Special catalogs, subject guides, and electronic indexes—available in most libraries—will help in this search. In many cases you can conduct a secondary search from your home or office using a computer, an online service, or an Internet gateway. Regarding MindWriter, thousands of articles have been written on customer service, and an Internet search using the keyword *customer service* reveals tens of thousands of hits.

If one is creative, a search of secondary sources will supply excellent background information as well as many good leads. Yet, if we confine the investigation to obvious subjects in bibliographic sources, we will often miss much of the best information. Suppose the Copper Industry Association is interested in estimating the outlook for the copper industry over the next 10 years. We could search through the literature under the headings "copper production" and "copper consumption." However, a search restricted to these two topics would miss more than it finds. When a creative search of the copper industry is undertaken, useful information turns up under the following reference headings: mines and minerals; nonferrous metals; forecasting; planning; econometrics; consuming industries such as automotive and communications; countries where copper is produced, such as Chile; and companies prominent in the industry, such as Anaconda and Kennecott.

Experience Survey

While published data are a valuable resource, it is seldom that more than a fraction of the existing knowledge in a field is put into writing. A significant portion of what is known on a topic, while in writing, may be proprietary to a given organization and thus unavailable to an outside searcher. Also, internal data archives are rarely well organized, making secondary sources, even when known, difficult to locate. Thus, we will profit by seeking information from persons experienced in the area of study, tapping into their collective memories and experiences.

When we interview persons in an **experience survey,** we should seek their ideas about important issues or aspects of the subject and discover what is important across the subject's range of knowledge. The investigative format we use should be flexible enough so that we can explore various avenues that emerge during the interview.

MANAGEMENT *Tip*

- What is being done?

- What has been tried in the past without success? With success?

- How have things changed?

- What are the change-producing elements of the situation?

- Who is involved in decisions and what role does each person play?

- What problem areas and barriers can be seen?

- What are the costs of the processes under study?

- Whom can we count on to assist and/or participate in the research?

- What are the priority areas?

The product of such questioning may be a new hypothesis, the discarding of an old one, or information about the practicality of doing the study. Probing may show whether certain facilities are available, what factors need to be controlled and how, and who will cooperate in the study.

Discovery is more easily carried out if the researcher can analyze cases that provide special insight. Typical of exploration, we are less interested in getting a representative cross-section than in getting information from sources that might be insightful. Assume we study StarAuto's automobile assembly plant. It has a history of declining productivity, increasing costs, and growing numbers of quality defects. People who might provide insightful information include

- **Newcomers to the scene**—Employees or personnel who may have been recently transferred to this plant from similar plants.

- **Marginal or peripheral individuals**—Persons whose jobs place them on the margin between contending groups. First-line supervisors and lead workers are often neither management nor worker but something in between.

- **Individuals in transition**—Recently promoted employees who have been transferred to new departments.

- **Deviants and isolates**—Those in a given group who hold a different position from the majority, as well as workers who are happy with the present situation, highly productive departments and workers, and loners of one sort or another.

- **"Pure" cases** or cases that show extreme examples of the conditions under study—The most unproductive departments, the most antagonistic workers, and so forth.

- **Those who fit well and those who do not**—The workers who are well established in their organizations versus those who are not, those executives who fully reflect management views and those who do not.

- **Those who represent different positions in the system**—Unskilled workers, assemblers, superintendents, and so forth.[9]

Jason and Myra plan to interview three managers during the early phase of their research for MindWriter: (1) the service facility, (2) the call center, and (3) the contract courier service. Their emphasis should be not only on what has been done in the past but also on discovering the parameters of feasible change. They might want to expand their interviews to include long-term employees of the various departments, as their views are likely to be different from those of their managers. Because postpurchase service problems might be directly related to product design, expanding their experience survey to individuals associated with engineering and production should also be considered.

Focus Groups

Originating in sociology, focus groups became widely used in marketing research during the 1980s and are used for increasingly diverse research applications today.[10] The most common application of focus group research continues to be in the consumer arena. However, many corporations are using focus group results for diverse exploratory applications.

The topical objective of a focus group is often a new product or product concept. The output of the session is a list of ideas and behavioral observations, with recommendations by the moderator. These are often used for later quantitative testing. As a group interview tool, focus groups have applied-research potential for other functional areas of business, particularly where the generation and evaluation of ideas or the assessment of needs is indispensable. In exploratory research, the qualitative data that focus groups produce may be used for enriching all levels of research questions and hypotheses and comparing the effectiveness of design options.

A **focus group** is a panel of people, led by a trained moderator, who meet for 90 minutes to 2 hours. The facilitator or moderator uses group dynamics principles to focus or guide the group in an exchange of ideas, feelings, and experiences on a *specific topic*. Typically the focus group panel is made up of 6 to 10 respondents. Too small or too large a group results in less effective participation. The facilitator introduces the topic and encourages the group to discuss it among themselves.

Following a topical guide, the moderator will steer the discussion to ensure that all the relevant information desired by the client is considered by the group. The facilitator also keeps gregarious individuals from dominating the conversation, ensuring that each person enters the discussion. In ideal situations, the group's discussion will proceed

This focus group facility at Maritz Marketing Research, Inc., has been designed to permit the research sponsor to observe participants and confer or adjust measurement questions while the research is in progress.
www.maritz.com/mmri/

uninterrupted; however, if the discussion begins to lag, the facilitator moves it along by introducing another facet of the topic that the group has not yet considered. In some groups a questionnaire is administered to the participants before the group begins to gather additional data. Typically, one or more representatives of the client will sit behind a one-way mirror in the focus group room to observe the verbal and nonverbal interactions and responses of participants.

MindWriter could use focus groups involving employees (of the call center and service departments) to determine changes and provide an analysis of change ideas. It may want focus groups with customers (both dissatisfied and satisfied) to uncover what has occurred in their different experiences. In another application, when a large title insurance company was developing a computerized help system, it ran focus groups with its branch office administrators to discover their preferences for distributing files on the company's **intranet** (a company's proprietary network—behind a security "fire-wall" that limits access to authorized users only). In other cases, a small college used focus groups to develop a plan to attract more freshmen applications, and a blood center used a focus group to improve blood donations.[11]

Homogeneity within the Focus Group   It is often preferable, depending on the topic, to run separate focus groups for different subsets of the population. For example, a study on nutritional advice may begin with separate consumer and physician focus groups to determine the best ways to provide the advice. This type of homogeneous grouping tends to promote more intense discussion and freer interaction.[12] For consumer groups, consideration should also be given to such factors as gender, ethnicity, employment status, and education. In a recent exploratory study of discount shoppers, the attitudes about the economy and personal finances expressed by East Coast respondents and West Coast respondents were widely divergent. The client sponsor was able to use this information to build a marketing strategy tailored to each geographic area.[13]

Since most focus groups are homogeneous, locating respondents for focus groups is usually done through informal networks of colleagues, community agencies, and the target group. Sometimes researchers advertise to attract a wider range of opinions.[14]

Telephone Focus Groups   Traditional focus group participants meet face to face, usually in specialized facilities that enable respondents to interact in a comfortable setting while being observed by a sponsoring client. However, often there is a need to reach people that traditional focus groups cannot attract. With modern telephone conferencing facilities, telephone focus groups can be particularly effective in the following situations:

MANAGEMENT
Tip

- When it is difficult to recruit desired participants—members of elite groups and hard-to-find respondents such as experts, professionals, physician-specialists, high-level executives, and storeowners.

- When target group members are rare, "low incidence," or widely dispersed geographically—directors of a medical clinic, celebrities, early adopters, and rural practitioners.

- When issues are so sensitive that anonymity is needed but respondents must be from a wide geographical area—people suffering from a contagious disease, people using nonmainstream products, high-income individuals, competitors.

- When you want to conduct only a couple of focus groups but want nationwide representation.

Telephone focus groups are usually less expensive than face-to-face focus groups—by up to 40 percent. In contrast to face-to-face groups, heterogeneous telephone groups can be productive. People in traditional superior-subordinate roles can be mixed as long as they are not from the same city. A telephone focus group is less likely to be effective under the following conditions:

MANAGEMENT

- When participants need to handle a product.
- When an object of discussion cannot be sent through the mail in advance.
- When sessions will run long.
- When the participants are groups of young children.

Online Focus Groups   An emerging technique for exploratory research is to approximate group dynamics using e-mail, websites, Usenet newsgroups, or an Internet chat room. Emerging technology also makes it possible to do "live" voice-chats online, reducing or eliminating the cost associated with telephone focus groups. Posting questions to a newsgroup with an interest in the research problem can generate considerable discussion. However, online discussions are not confidential unless they take place on an intranet. Although online forum discussions are unlikely to reflect the average participants, they can be a good way of getting in touch with populations that have special interests (e.g., BMW Club members, Little League coaches, or "power computer users").

Videoconferencing Focus Groups   The third type of nonface-to-face focus group is conducted via videoconferencing. Many anticipate growth for this medium. Like telephone focus groups, videoconferencing enables significant savings. By reducing the travel time for the facilitator and the client, it means more focus groups can be accomplished in a shorter time. However, videoconferencing retains the barrier between the moderator and participants, although less so than telephone focus groups. Since large corporations and universities often have their own internal videoconferencing facilities, most videoconferencing focus groups will tend to occur within this setting.

We discuss content analysis in Chapter 15.

Recording, Analysis, and Reporting   In face-to-face settings, some moderators use large sheets of paper to record trends on the wall of the focus group room; others use a personal notepad. Facility managers produce both video- and audiotapes to enable a full analysis of the interview. The recorded conversations and moderator notes are summarized across several focus group sessions using *content analysis*. This analysis provides the research sponsor with a qualitative picture of the respondents' concerns, ideas, attitudes, and feelings.

Advantages and Disadvantages   The primary advantage of the focus group as an exploratory research tool is its ability to quickly and inexpensively grasp the core issues of a topic. Focus groups are brief, relatively inexpensive, and extremely flexible. They provide the manager, researcher, or client with a chance to observe reactions to their research questions in an open-ended group setting. Participants respond in their own words, rather than being force-fit into a formalized method. Because they can freely react to each other's responses, the unexpected often occurs.

Focus groups best enable the exploration of surprise information and new ideas. Agendas can be modified as the research team moves on to the next focus group. Even within an existing focus group, an adept facilitator can build on the ideas and insights of previous groups, getting to a greater depth of understanding. However, because they are qualitative devices, with limited sampling accuracy, results from focus groups should not be considered a replacement for quantitative analyses.

Close-Up

Qualitative Research with Children

Since the groundbreaking television perception studies of the 1970s, researchers with expertise in extracting information from children have been much in demand. One such researcher, Megan Nerz, senior partner of MLN Research (Raleigh, North Carolina), estimates that while there are numerous researchers who claim experience with children, there are only a handful of firms with true expertise. As a graduate assistant during the 1970s at the University of Hartford, Nerz participated in those early studies about the effects of television advertising on kids. She's been putting that early experience to use for more than 25 years for such clients as Kraft Foods, Nabisco, Oscar Mayer, LEGO, and the Walt Disney Company.

"Kids are wonderful to work with," claims Nerz. "They can be amusing, insightful, creative, tender, reluctant, antagonistic, withdrawn—all within the span of a few minutes. But they aren't just little adults, their cognitive skills and level of development are very specific to their age and where they are in school." Where you wouldn't worry about forming a focus group with adults of different ages, Nerz insists that in child research, focus groups should always be single-gender and members should never be further apart than one grade level or one year in age.

Qualitative research methodologies are often used with children, and while the names of some of those methods are familiar to those who conduct adult research, the procedures and techniques are different.

"When you work with adults, they have preconceived ideas and expectations of how to behave, what will happen, how they are expected to interact with the researcher and other participants. But children have no such expectations. And while you can often spend a considerable amount of time with an adult, with children your time is limited. Our children's focus groups will never be more than 1 hour and 15 minutes, so the researcher has to be extremely focused on the research objectives and on enticing the child to reveal their thoughts and impressions, their attitudes and concerns, in a very short period of time."

Recruiting: Mom as Gatekeeper

The process of screening and setting up a child research group has its own idiosyncrasies. The first rule of child research: You must deal with Mom. When trying to identify participants for a child focus group, the researcher first interviews the child's mother during the phone screening. Recruiters ask the mom about the child's ability to function in a group, ask her to describe the child's personality, to talk about how shy or outgoing the child is and whether he or she can express their opinions to others. "Often if the mom has more than one child in the target group, the recruiter will ask which of their children best matches the social characteristics we seek," explains Nerz. In the back of the researcher's mind is rule number two: You don't have time to get to know the child, so the child has to be receptive to having information "teased" from them, and be able to express how they feel. Screening continues with a phone conversation with the child. Rule number three evolves from that experience: If the child won't come to the phone, choose another child.

L&E Research (L&E), a focus group facility that MLN Research uses in Raleigh, North Carolina, recruits the participants for many of Nerz's focus groups. Adults involved in research are often recruited using purchased lists of households; in essence, the recruiting is blind. L&E takes a different approach and began building its own database of possible participants in 1990. When it needs a child of a certain gender, age, or year in school, it taps this database, which is organized by parent. Participants are recruited with periodic advertising or they can volunteer on the L&E website (see our text website for the sign-up procedure). As a result, the database is constantly updated and growing. "The turn-down rate is low," shares Tina Glover, a recruiting manager for L&E. "Parents are interested in giving their children an opportunity to participate, and to capture the $35 participation fee for their child." L&E also recruits members for child panels, whose participants are involved in up to three research-oriented activities in a single year and paid $25 each time.

The Pre-Warm-Up

While adults go through a reception procedure when arriving at a focus group facility, it takes little time and is designed to get them settled and ready to begin. "We always invite more children to the facility than we need for any given study," explains Glover, "expecting more scheduling or illness problems (with children as opposed to adults) which might cause last-minute cancellations." When they first started working with children, L&E had not expected the child's devastation when told that they wouldn't be needed that day for the research. "While adults, if dismissed, are happy to take their pay and go home, children take the release as rejection," describes Glover. When working with children, L&E now uses older, more comforting hostesses, who deliver the message to the dismissed children that they will be considered for the next group requiring children with their characteristics. "Children who are recruited for panels usually can't wait to participate again," claims Glover. "They see their involvement as their 'job.' But if we have drop-outs, those children who feel uncomfortable and don't want to participate again, we turn to our database for a match."

The Warm-Up

"With children, you have to alleviate concerns of Mom, so the warm-up is always in the presence of the parent," shared Nerz. "But we separate kids from moms as soon as possible, physically moving the parents to one end of the room. Kids need to feel comfortable with each other to be responsive. If we separate them from their parents, their natural inquisitiveness has them asking the other kids where they go to school, what they are interested in, and what video games or toys they have." The researcher has to set up expectations for the focus group with the child participant even to the point of breaking down one of Mom's rules: Don't say anything if you can't say something nice. "One job of the moderator during warm-up is to convince the child that it really is okay to tell us what they think and how they feel. They aren't going to hurt our feelings and we aren't going to get mad at them if they don't like something," claims Nerz. Some researchers believe all children are "pleasers," telling the researcher only what they believe the researcher wants to hear. Nerz disagrees. It's her experience that children can be painfully and brutally honest, creating some very uncomfortable moments for the client who is positioned behind the one-way mirror.

Adults have an image of a focus group as people sitting around a conference table talking. "Kids have tables, but they are appropriate for the child—no conference tables and no swivel chairs," shares Nerz. "If a child is roaming the room during a focus group, then the moderator has lost control." But as Nerz explains, what children are asked to do during a focus group, sometimes doesn't look like a focus group for an adult. Focus groups with young children, 6- to 8-year-olds, those with limited vocabulary because of their age and grade, often are asked to draw pictures to start the focus group. Then some time is spent with each child explaining their picture and what it tells about a trip to the grocery with Mom, or their favorite part of their house or bedroom. Older children, 11- to 12-year-olds, have better language skills. They might be provided a list of two dozen words and be asked to circle five words that describe how they feel about helping fix dinner. Older children also might be provided with images and words and be asked to create a collage. "You have to stimulate the child's creativity and cognitive skills before you can extract meaning," explains Nerz.

Children's focus groups are videotaped, as are those involving adults. And more and more, children's researchers employ FocusVision, where members of a client's management team observe the group as it takes place but via videoconferencing, often from their own offices in distant cities. "If parents won't permit videotaping, then the child is dismissed," explains Glover. "And parents can't watch the group from the observation room, either. There is too much strategy being discussed behind that one-way mirror."

Other Child-Research Techniques

A **creativity session** involves an initial phone screening, followed by a face-to-face screening with the child and a hands-on creative exercise. Usually 10 youngsters are screened to a group of four. These four are brought to an activity room, where they are encouraged to find their own special space. This may be at a table, outside on a picnic bench, on the floor in a hallway, even under a table. Child-appropriate snacks and drinks are provided, and the child is free to snack and move around during the research. The creative exercise usually takes 20–30 minutes, followed by a "building" exercise in which the four participants build on each other's ideas. This session can be an hour or more. "Children are wonderfully creative. They are unhampered by expectations. If we've done our job correctly, kids with reveal many things that adults won't," enthuses Nerz.

Observational playgroups involve observing children at play, with targeted toys or materials, usually behind one-way mirrors. **Children's panels** involve focus group activities where the same child may participate in up to three groups in a year, with each experience several months apart. "With children, something that happened in January is ancient history by June. So even if they have participated before, they have fuzzy recollections of what happened," explains Nerz. **Paired-interviews** involve two children with a moderator, either friendship-pairs or straight-pairs (children who don't know each other ahead of time). In this 45–60 minute interview, researchers track thoughts, experiences, and processes. **Depth interviews,** where researchers talk one-on-one with a child, can last an hour. One technique, **ethnographic research,** is growing in use. "I've taken pairs of preteen girls shopping for clothing and cosmetics at a mall, been to a video arcade with young boys, and done a grocery store ethnography with older girls. But 'home ethnographies' may be the most fun. You can do it with children as young as three, where shopping ethnographies are usually reserved for those nine or older. In the home you can explore how and why they decorate their rooms, what they carry in their backpacks, what foods they like to eat or cook, how they use personal or kitchen appliances, what they collect, even how they organized their closets," shares Nerz.

Strategic Decision Making

Children are involved in helping advertisers create child-involving messages by reacting to storyboards for television commercials. (Storyboards arrange the scenes of a commercial in comic strip–like panels, with dialogue and special effects noted beneath each panel.) "Unlike adults, children do better with storyboards than with the more expensive

Observational playgroups involve observing children at play, with targeted toys or materials, usually behind one-way mirrors.

videomatics or animatics (semiproduced commercials using slides or slides transitioning on video); this can save the client time and money," shares Nerz. MLN Research has also studied how children use the Internet, their reaction to visual concept boards for products (What would Mom think? Would you want this product? How would you use this product? Would your friends have one?), their reaction to packaging prototypes and changes, taste changes being considered, and insight on brand association, imagery, and brand equity.

But working with kids isn't all fun and games. Children's research has to take place after school, during school breaks, or on weekends. Some evening research

involves older children, but even those activities are usually over by 8:00 P.M. And sometimes all your best-laid plans can go awry. "Sometimes they get sick, or have a fight with their mom on the way to the research facility, or maybe they have a bad day at school. Kids can't filter out experiences, environmental stimuli, or physical symptoms of unease the way adults can." Which leads Nerz to her last rule of children's research: Be prepared for anything.

Source: This material was developed from interviews with Megan Nerz, MLN Research; Ed Eggers, L&E Research; and Tina Glover, L&E Research during September 2001.

Two-Stage Design

A useful way to design a research study is as a **two-stage design.** With this approach, exploration becomes a separate first stage with limited objectives: (1) clearly defining the research question and (2) developing the research design.

In arguing for a two-stage approach, we recognize that much about the problem is not known but should be known before effort and resources are committed. In these circumstances, one is operating in unknown areas, where it is difficult to predict the problems and costs of the study. Proposals that acknowledge the practicality of this approach are particularly useful when the research budget is inflexible. A limited exploration for a specific, modest cost carries little risk for both sponsor and researcher and often uncovers information that reduces the total research cost.

An exploratory study is finished when the researchers have achieved the following:

MANAGEMENT
Tip

- Established the major dimensions of the research task.

- Defined a set of subsidiary investigative questions that can be used as guides to a detailed research design.

- Developed several hypotheses about possible causes of a management dilemma.

- Learned that certain other hypotheses are such remote possibilities that they can be safely ignored in any subsequent study.

- Concluded additional research is not needed or is not feasible.

SNAPSHOT

Kool-Aid Regains Its Smile

What do you do when a venerable brand enjoying 100 percent awareness among moms and kids starts losing sales—even when it's still selling 500 million gallons per year? You call Sun Research Corp. (SRC) to reveal a strategy to stop the decline. SRC moderated 11 focus groups. Participants for each group were chosen to represent a market segment based on product usage. The focus groups revealed that heavy Kool-Aid users (those who use Kool-Aid at least 12 times a year) "aren't content to just add water to their Kool-Aid powder . . . [but] customize Kool-Aid by adding oranges, grapes, pineapples, fruit juice, and club soda. They also drink Kool-Aid year-round, and all family members drink it—it's not perceived as a beverage just for kids. In contrast, light/lapsed users are more likely to head out of the house for socializing."

A second round of five focus groups involving African-American households defined as heavy users and six more involving general market and light/lapsed users were conducted by MLN Research (North Carolina), Mindy Goldberg & Associates (Philadelphia), and Marketing Resources (Maryland) to test the resulting ad campaigns. The heavy-user ad campaign, sporting the tagline "How do you like your Kool-Aid?" generated a 3 percent rise in sales among African-American households. A second campaign, for general and light/lapsed users featuring Kool-Aid consumed from a portable thermos at a dog wash fund-raiser, helped generate a 2 percent sales rise in the overall market. The makers of Kool-Aid were all smiles at their 2.7 percent increase in market share during 2000.

www.kraftfoods.com/kool-aid

www.mlnresearch.com

Descriptive Studies

In contrast to exploratory studies more formalized studies are typically structured with clearly stated hypotheses or investigative questions. Formal studies serve a variety of research objectives:

1. Descriptions of phenomena or characteristics associated with a subject population (the *who, what, when, where,* and *how* of a topic).

2. Estimates of the proportions of a population that have these characteristics.

3. Discovery of associations among different variables.

The third study objective is sometimes labeled a *correlational study,* a subset of descriptive studies. A descriptive study may be simple or complex; it may be done in many settings. Whatever the form, a descriptive study can be just as demanding of research skills as the causal study, and we should insist on the same high standards for design and execution.

The BankChoice example was first introduced in Chapter 3.

The simplest descriptive study concerns a univariate question or hypothesis in which we ask about, or state something about, the size, form, distribution, or existence of a variable. In the account analysis at BankChoice, we might be interested in developing a profile of savers. We first may want to locate them in relation to the main office. The question might be, "What percentage of the savers live within a two-mile radius of the office?" Using the hypothesis format, we might predict, "60 percent or more of the savers live within a two-mile radius of the office."

We may also be interested in securing information about other variables, such as the relative size of accounts, the number of accounts for minors, the number of accounts opened within the last six months, and the amount of activity (number of deposits and withdrawals per year) in accounts. Data on each of these variables, by themselves, may have value for management decisions. Bivariate relationships between these or other variables may be of even greater interest. Cross-tabulations between the distance from the account owner's residence or employment to the branch and account activity may suggest that differential rates of activity are related to account owner location. A cross-tabulation of account size and gender of account owner may also show interrelation. Such findings do not imply a causal relationship. In fact, our task is to determine if the variables are independent (or unrelated) and if they are not, then to determine the strength or magnitude of the relationship. Neither procedure tells us which variable is the cause. For example, we might be able to conclude that gender and account size are related but not that gender is a causal factor in account size.

Descriptive studies are often much more complex than this example. One study of savers began as described and then went into much greater depth. Part of the study included an observation of account records that revealed a concentration of nearby savers. Their accounts were typically larger and more active than those whose owners lived at a distance. A sample survey of savers provided information on stages in the family life cycle, attitudes toward savings, family income levels, and other matters. Correlation of this information with known savings data showed that women owned larger accounts. Further investigation suggested that women with larger accounts were often widowed or working single women who were older than the average account holder. Information about their attitudes and savings practices led to new business strategies at the bank.

Some evidence collected led to causal questions. The correlation between nearness to the office and the probability of having an account at the office suggested the question, "Why would people who live far from the office have an account there?" In this type of question a hypothesis makes its greatest contribution by pointing out directions that the research might follow. It might be hypothesized that

1. Distant savers (operationally defined as those with addresses more than two miles from the office) have accounts at the office because they once lived near the office; they were "near" when the account decision was made.

2. Distant savers actually live near the office, but the address on the account is outside the two-mile radius; they are "near," but the records do not show this.

3. Distant savers work near the office; they are "near" by virtue of their work location.

4. Distant savers are not normally near the office but responded to a promotion that encouraged savers to bank via computer; this is another form of "nearness" in which this concept is transformed into one of "convenience."

When these hypotheses were tested, it was learned that a substantial portion of the distant savers could be accounted for by hypotheses 1 and 3. The conclusion: Location was closely related to saving at a given association. The determination of cause is not so simple, however, and these findings still fall within the definition of a descriptive study.

MindWriter could benefit from a descriptive study that profiles satisfied service customers versus dissatisfied ones. Service customer characteristics could then be matched with specific types of service problems, which could lead to identifying changes in product design or customer service policies.

Causal Studies

The correlation between location and probability of account holding at BankChoice looks like strong evidence to many, but the researcher with scientific training will argue that correlation is not causation. Who is right? The essence of the disagreement seems to lie in the concept of cause.

The Concept of Cause

One writer asserts, "There appears to be an inherent gap between the language of theory and research which can never be bridged in a completely satisfactory way. One thinks in terms of theoretical language that contains notions such as causes, forces, systems, and properties. But one's tests are made in terms of covariations, operations, and pointer readings."[15] The essential element of **causation** is that A *"produces"* B or A *"forces"* B to occur. But that is an artifact of language, not what happens. Empirically, we can never demonstrate an *A-B* causality with certainty. This is because we do not "demonstrate" such causal linkages deductively or use the form or validation of premises that deduction requires for conclusiveness. Unlike deductive syllogisms, empirical conclusions are inferences—inductive conclusions. As such, they are probabilistic statements based on what we observe and measure. But we cannot observe and measure all the processes that may account for the *A-B* relationship.

You may find it valuable to refer to Exhibit 2–2 as you read this section.

In Chapter 2 we discussed the example of sales failing to increase following a promotion. Having ruled out other causes for the flat sales, we were left with one inference that was probably *but not certainly* the cause: a poorly executed promotion.

Meeting the ideal standard of causation requires that one variable always causes another and no other variable has the same causal effect. The *method of agreement,* proposed by John Stuart Mill in the nineteenth century, states, "When two or more cases of a given phenomenon have one and only one condition in common, then that condition may be regarded as the cause (or effect) of the phenomenon."[16] Thus, if we can find Z and only Z in every case where we find *C,* and no others *(A, B, D,* or *E)* are found with Z, then we can conclude that C and Z are causally related. Exhibit 6–2 illustrates this method.

An example of the method of agreement might be the problem of occasional high absenteeism on Mondays in a factory. A study of two groups with high absenteeism (No. 1 and No. 2 in Exhibit 6–2) shows no common job, department, demographic, or personal characteristics *(A, B, D,* and *E).* However, membership in a camping club *(C)* is common across both groups. The conclusion is that club membership is associated with high absenteeism *(Z).*

The method of agreement helps rule out some variables as irrelevant. In Exhibit 6–2, *A, B, D,* and *E* are unlikely to be causes of Z. However, there is an implicit assumption that there are no variables to consider other than *A, B, C, D,* and *E.* One can never accept this supposition with certainty because the number of potential variables is infinite. In addition, while *C* may be the cause, it may instead function only in the presence of some other variable not included.

EXHIBIT 6–2 Mill's Method of Agreement

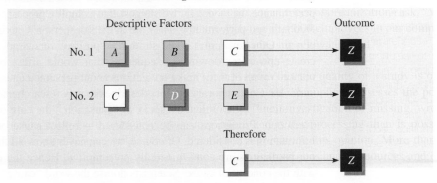

EXHIBIT 6–3   **Mill's Method of Difference**

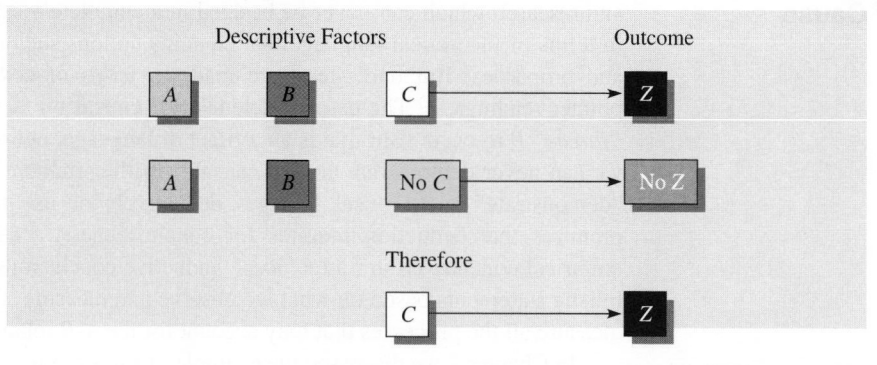

The *negative canon of agreement* states that where the absence of *C* is associated with the absence of *Z,* there is evidence of a causal relationship between *C* and *Z.* Together with the method of agreement, this forms the basis for the *method of difference:* "If there are two or more cases, and in one of them observation *Z* can be made, while in the other it cannot; and if variable *C* occurs when observation *Z* is made, and does not occur when observation *Z* is not made; then it can be asserted that there is a causal relationship between *C* and *Z.*"[17]

Using our MindWriter example, if Jason and Myra were to discover that a particular servicing problem repeatedly occurred only when a single employee was involved in the servicing of customers' laptops and never when that employee was absent, an assumption of causation might be made. The method of difference is illustrated in Exhibit 6–3. Although these methods neither ensure discovery of all relevant variables nor provide certain proof of causation, they help advance our understanding of causality by eliminating inadequate causal arguments.[18]

A more refined cause-and-effect model proposes that individual variables are not the cause of specific effects but that processes are the cause of processes.[19] Evidence for this position is illustrated in Exhibit 6–4. Here various cause-and-effect relationships between sales performance and feedback clarify the differences between simple and more complex notions of causality.[20]

In model A, we contend that feedback causes an increase in sales performance. An equally plausible explanation is shown in model B: Improvement in sales performance causes the salesperson to behave in a proactive way, seeking more feedback to apply to the next experience. Model C suggests the reinforcement history of the salesperson is the cause of both initiation of self-administered feedback and working harder to improve performance. In model D, we suggest that complex processes contribute to changes in feedback and performance. They are in the salesperson's environment and unique to the person. Other examples could show how positive versus negative reinforcement could create upward or downward sequences that would affect both feedback and performance. Yet all of them make predictions about presumed causal relationships among the variables. Contemporary authors describe the way researchers substitute "prediction" for "causation." When scientists speak of "causation," they are often referring to a kind of prediction. Predictions can be considered to reflect cause only when all the relevant information is considered. Of course, we can never know all the relevant information, so our predictions are consequentially presumptive. Hence the disillusionment in science with the concept of cause. Scientists do use the word "cause" from time to time, but do not be misled into thinking that they mean "cause" in the absolute sense.[21]

EXHIBIT 6–4   Possible Causal Models of Improved Sales Performance and Feedback

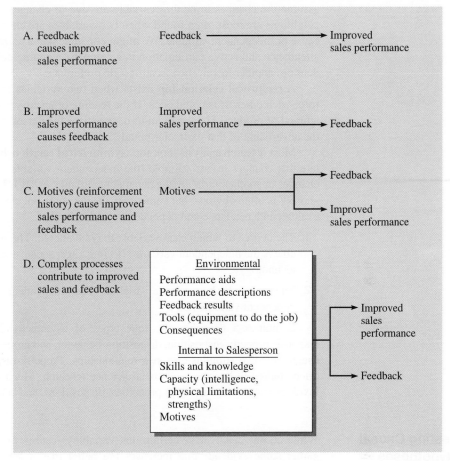

Causal inferences are going to be made. Although they are neither permanent nor universal, they allow us to build knowledge of presumed causes over time. Such empirical conclusions provide us with successive approximations to the truth. Recognizing this caveat, let's look further at the types of causal relationships of interest to business researchers.

Causal Relationships

Our concern in causal analysis is with how one variable affects, or is "responsible for," changes in another variable. The stricter interpretation of causation, found in experimentation, is that some external factor "produces" a change in the dependent variable. In business research, we often find that the cause-effect relationship is less explicit. We are more interested in understanding, explaining, predicting, and controlling relationships between variables than we are in discerning causes.

If we consider the possible relationships that can occur between two variables, we can conclude there are three possibilities:

- Symmetrical
- Reciprocal
- Asymmetrical[22]

A **symmetrical relationship** is one in which two variables fluctuate together but we assume the changes in neither variable are due to changes in the other. Symmetrical conditions are most often found when two variables are alternate indicators of another cause or independent variable. We might conclude that a correlation between low work attendance and active participation in a company camping club is the result of (dependent on) another factor, such as a lifestyle preference.

A **reciprocal relationship** exists when two variables mutually influence or reinforce each other. This could occur if the reading of an advertisement leads to the use of a brand of product. The usage, in turn, sensitizes the person to notice and read more of the advertising of that particular brand.

Most research analysts look for **asymmetrical relationships.** With these we postulate that changes in one variable (the independent variable, or *IV*) are responsible for changes in another variable (the dependent variable, or *DV*). The identification of the *IV* and *DV* is often obvious, but sometimes the choice is not clear. In these latter cases we evaluate independence and dependence on the basis of:

1. The degree to which each variable may be altered. The relatively unalterable variable is the independent variable *(IV)* (e.g., age, social status, present manufacturing technology).

2. The time order between the variables. The independent variable *(IV)* precedes the dependent variable *(DV).*

Exhibit 6–5 describes the four types of asymmetrical relationships: stimulus-response, property-disposition, disposition-behavior, and property-behavior. Experiments usually involve stimulus-response relationships. Property-disposition relationships are often studied in business and social science research. Much of ex post facto research involves relationships between properties, dispositions, and behaviors.

Testing Causal Hypotheses

MANAGEMENT
Tip

While no one can ever be certain that variable *A* causes variable *B* to occur, one can gather some evidence that increases the belief that *A* leads to *B*. In testing causal hypotheses, we seek three types of evidence:

1. Covariation between *A* and *B*.
   - Do we find that *A* and *B* occur together in the way hypothesized?
   - When *A* does not occur, is there also an absence of *B*?
   - When there is more or less of *A,* does one also find more or less of *B*?

2. Time order of events moving in the hypothesized direction.
   - Does *A* occur before *B*?

3. No other possible causes of *B*.
   - Can one determine that *C, D,* and *E* do not covary with *B* in a way that suggests possible causal connections?

Causation and Experimental Design   In addition to these three conditions, successful inference-making from experimental designs must meet two other requirements. The first is referred to as **control.** All factors, with the exception of the independent variable, must be held constant and not confounded with another variable that is not part of the study. Second, each person in the study must have an equal chance for exposure to each level of the independent variable. This is **random assignment** of subjects to groups.

Here is a demonstration of how these factors are used to detect causation. Assume you wish to conduct a survey of York College's alumni to enlist their support for a new

EXHIBIT 6–5 Four Types of Asymmetrical Causal Relationships

Relationship Type	Nature of Relationship	Examples
Stimulus-response	An event or change results in a response from some object.	• A change in work rules leads to a higher level of worker output. • A change in government economic policy restricts corporate financial decisions. • A price increase results in fewer unit sales.
Property-disposition	An existing property causes a disposition.	• Age and attitudes about saving. • Gender and attitudes toward social issues. • Social class and opinions about taxation.
Disposition-behavior	A disposition causes a specific behavior.	• Opinions about a brand and its purchase. • Job satisfaction and work output. • Moral values and tax cheating.
Property-behavior	An existing property causes a specific behavior.	• Stage of the family life cycle and purchases of furniture. • Social class and family savings patterns. • Age and sports participation.

Definitions: A *stimulus* is an event or force (e.g., drop in temperature, crash of stock market, product recall, or explosion in factory). A *response* is a decision or reaction. A *property* is an enduring characteristic of a subject that does not depend on circumstances for its activation (e.g., age, gender, family status, religious affiliation, ethnic group, or physical condition). A *disposition* is a tendency to respond in a certain way under certain circumstances (e.g., attitudes, opinions, habits, values, and drives). A *behavior* is an action (e.g., consumption practices, work performance, interpersonal acts, and other kinds of performance).

program. There are two different appeals, one largely emotional and the other much more logical in its approach. Before mailing out appeal letters to 50,000 alumni, you decide to conduct an experiment to see whether the emotional or the rational appeal will draw the greater response. You choose a sample of 300 names from the alumni list and divide them into three groups of 100 each. Two of these groups are designated as experimental groups. One gets the emotional appeal and the other gets the logical appeal. The third group is the **control group** and it receives no appeal.

Covariation in this case is expressed by the percentage of alumni who respond in relation to the appeal used. Suppose 50 percent of those who receive the emotional appeal respond, while only 35 percent of those receiving the logical appeal respond. Control group members, unaware of the experiment, respond at a 5 percent rate. We would conclude that using the emotional appeal enhances response probability.

The time sequence of events was not a problem. There could be no chance that the alumni support led to sending the letter requesting support. However, have other variables confounded the results? Could some factor other than the appeal have produced the same results? One can anticipate that certain factors are particularly likely to confound the results. One can control some of these to ensure they do not have this confounding effect. If the question studied is of concern only to alumni who attended the university as undergraduates, those who only attended graduate school are not involved. Thus, you would want to be sure the answers from the latter group did not distort the results. Control would be achieved by excluding graduate students.

A second approach to control uses **matching.** There might be reason to believe that different ratios of alumni support will come from various age groups. To control by matching, we need to be sure the age distribution of alumni is the same in all groups. In a similar way, control could be achieved by matching alumni from engineering, liberal arts, business, and other schools.

Even after using such controls, however, one cannot match or exclude other possible confounding variables. These are dealt with through random assignment.

Randomization is the basic method by which equivalence between experimental and control groups is determined. Experimental and control groups must be established so that they are equal. Matching and controlling are useful, but they do not account for all unknowns. It is best to assign subjects to either experimental or control groups at random (this is not to say haphazardly—randomness must be secured in a carefully controlled fashion according to strict rules of assignment). If the assignments are made randomly, each group should receive its fair share of different factors. The only deviation from this fair share would be that which results from random variation (luck of the draw). The possible impact of these unknown extraneous variables on the dependent variables should also vary at random. The researcher, using tests of statistical significance, can estimate the probable effect of these chance variations on the *DV* and can then compare this estimated effect of extraneous variation to the actual differences found in the *DV* in the experimental and control groups.

We emphasize that random assignment of subjects to experimental and control groups is the *basic technique* by which the two groups can be made equivalent. Matching and other control forms are supplemental ways of improving the quality of measurement. In a sense, matching and controls reduce the extraneous "noise" in the measurement system and in this way improve the sensitivity of measurement of the hypothesized relationship.

Causation and Ex Post Facto Design   Prior to the incidents following September 11, 2001, researchers at the Centers for Disease Control (CDC) in Atlanta did not have the ability to determine whether anthrax spores delivered via a letter carried by the United States Postal Service (USPS) would be capable of causing inhalation anthrax. Contraction of inhalation anthrax, a fatal disease, was considered possible only if one were exposed to a large concentration of spores. A research design involving the assignment of people to two groups—one to receive anthrax spores via letter and one to receive no exposure to anthrax spores—to test a hypothesis relating to the consequences of such exposure was unrealistic. After several deaths resulting from such suspicious mail deliveries, causation was assumed. However, the CDC could not link at least one inhalation anthrax death to the USPS handling of a suspicious letter. Does this mean that the causation conclusion of the CDC drawn from examination of the facts collected after the deaths—that one or more letters contaminated with anthrax spores caused the deaths of several individuals—cannot be supported?

Most research studies cannot be carried out experimentally by manipulating variables. Yet we still are interested in the question of causation. Instead of manipulating and/or controlling exposure to an experimental variable, we study subjects who have been exposed to the independent factor and those who have not.

Consider the situation in which several workers in a plant have developed a pattern of absenteeism on Mondays. In searching for hypotheses to explain this phenomenon,

EXHIBIT 6–6 Data on Employee Absenteeism

	Camping Club Member	
Absences	Yes	No
High	40	70
Low	10	280

we discover that some of these workers are members of a camping club formed a few months ago. Could it be that membership in the club has caused increased absenteeism? It is not practical to set up an experiment. This would require us to assign persons to join the club and then determine whether this affects their work attendance.

The better approach would be to get the list of the club's membership and review the absence record of workers, concentrating on their record of work attendance on the Mondays after a camping event. We would also take a sample of employees who are not members of the club and calculate their Monday absence rates. The results might look something like those found in Exhibit 6–6. The data suggest that membership in the camping club might be a cause of higher Monday absenteeism. Certainly the covariation evidence is consistent with this conclusion. But what other evidence will give us an even greater confidence in our conclusion?

We would like some evidence of the time order of events. It is logical to expect that if club membership causes higher absenteeism, there will be a temporal relationship. If high absenteeism were found only on the Monday immediately following a camping trip, it would be good evidence in support of our hypothesis. If absences from work occur *before* the camping trip occurs, the time order does not support our hypothesis as well.

Of course, many other factors could be causing the high absenteeism among the club members. Here again, the use of control techniques wll improve our ability to draw firm conclusions. First, in drawing a sample of nonmembers of the club, we can choose a random sample from the files of all employees. In this way, we can be more confident of a fair representation of average worker absence experiences.

More will be said about the analysis of cross-tabulation and the interpretation of relationships in Chapter 16.

We cannot use assignment of subjects in ex post facto research as we did in experimentation. However, we can gather information about potentially confounding factors and use these data to make cross-classification comparisons; in this way we can determine whether there is a relationship between club membership, absenteeism, and other factors. Assume we also gather age data on the employees under study and introduce this as a cross-classification variable; the results might look like those in Exhibit 6–7. These data suggest age is also a factor. Younger people are more likely to be among the high absentees. Part of the high absenteeism rate among club members seems to be

EXHIBIT 6–7 Cross-Tabulated Data on Employee Absenteeism

	Club Member		Nonclub Member	
Age	High Absentee	Low Absentee	High Absentee	Low Absentee
Under 30 years	36	6	30	48
30 to 45	4	4	35	117
45 and over	0	0	5	115

associated with the fact that most club members are under 30 years of age. Within age groups, it is also apparent that club members have a higher incidence of excessive absenteeism than nonmembers of the same age.

The Post Hoc Fallacy While researchers must necessarily use ex post facto research designs to address causal questions, a word of warning is in order. Club membership among persons with high absentee records is weak evidence for claiming a causal relationship. Similarly, the covariation found between variables must be interpreted carefully when the relationship is based on ex post facto analysis. The term *post hoc fallacy* has been used to describe these frequently unwarranted conclusions.

The ex post facto design is widely used in business research and often is the only approach feasible. In particular, one seeks causal explanations between variables that are impossible to manipulate. Not only can the variables not be manipulated, but the subjects usually cannot be assigned to treatment and control groups in advance. We often find that there are multiple causes rather than one. Be careful using the ex post facto design with causal reasoning. Thorough testing, validating of multiple hypotheses, and controlling for confounding variables are essential.

SUMMARY

1 If the direction of a research project is not clear, it is often wise to follow a two-step research procedure. The first stage is exploratory, aimed at formulating hypotheses and developing the specific research design. The general research process contains three major stages: (1) exploration of the situation, (2) collection of data, and (3) analysis and interpretation of results.

2 A research design is the strategy for a study and the plan by which the strategy is to be carried out. It specifies the methods and procedures for the collection, measurement, and analysis of data. Unfortunately, there is no simple classification of research designs that covers the variations found in practice. Some major descriptors of designs are

- Exploratory versus formalized.
- Observational versus interrogation/communication.
- Experimental versus ex post facto.
- Descriptive versus causal.
- Cross-sectional versus longitudinal.
- Case versus statistical.
- Field versus laboratory versus simulation.
- Subjects perceive no deviations, some deviations, or researcher-induced deviations.

3 Exploratory research is appropriate for the total study in topic areas where the developed data are limited. In most other studies, exploration is the first stage of a project and is used to orient the researcher and the study. The objective of exploration is the development of hypotheses, not testing.

Formalized studies, including descriptive and causal, are those with substantial structure, specific hypotheses to be tested, or research questions to be answered. Descriptive studies are those used to describe phenomena associated with a subject population or to estimate proportions of the population that have certain characteristics.

4

Causal studies seek to discover the effect that a variable(s) has on another (or others) or why certain outcomes are obtained. The concept of causality is grounded in the logic of hypothesis testing, which, in turn, produces inductive conclusions. Such conclusions are probabilistic and thus can never be demonstrated with certainty. Current ideas about causality as complex processes improve our understanding over Mill's canons, though we can never know all the relevant information necessary to prove causal linkages beyond a doubt.

The relationships that occur between two variables may be symmetrical, reciprocal, or asymmetrical. Of greatest interest to the research analyst are asymmetrical, relationships, which may be classified as any of the following types:

- Stimulus response
- Property-disposition
- Disposition-behavior
- Property-behavior

We test causal hypotheses by seeking to do three things. We (1) measure the covariation among variables, (2) determine the time order relationships among variables, and (3) ensure that other factors do not confound the explanatory relationships.

The problems of achieving these aims differ somewhat in experimental and ex post facto studies. Where possible, we try to achieve the ideal of the experimental design with random assignment of subjects, matching of subject characteristics, and manipulation and control of variables. Using these methods and techniques, we measure relationships as accurately and objectively as possible.

KEY TERMS

EXAMPLES

Company	Scenario	Page
Audience Selection, Ltd.	Conducted the second round of phone interview in the Global Entrepreneurship Monitor (GEM) study.	148
BankChoice[*]	A descriptive study of account owners' activity to develop new strategies for targeting large, active accounts.	161

Catalyst, Inc.	The nonprofit research organization charged with executing the court-ordered multistage research study in the Smith Barney sexual harrassment case.	153
Centers for Disease Control	Using an ex post facto design to determine causation of inhalation anthrax contamination at the USPS.	168
Copper Industry Association*	A study of the outlook of the copper industry in the next 10 years.	153
FieldSource	A program used to create a custom-selected opt-in panel used to provide quick, cost-effective samples; draws samples from 3 million participants from various demographic and lifestyle groups.	148
Global Entrepreneurship Monitor (GEM)	A longitudinal design causal study to identify government policies that foster entrepreneurship.	148
John Deere and Company	A manufacturer of construction and agriculture equipment conducting both quantitative and qualitative studies to understand its environment.	149
Kraft Foods	Used a two-stage design study to develop the sales stimulus ad campaign for Kool-Aid.	161
L&E Research	Recruits child participants for focus groups and other research studies.	158
Maritz Marketing Research, Inc.	Conducts focus groups in specially designed facilities that permit observation by the research sponsor.	155
Market Facts, Inc.	Conducted the first round of phone interviews in the Global Entrepreneurship Monitor (GEM) study.	148
Marketing Resources	Conducted ad testing in the Kool-Aid study for Kraft Foods.	161
MindWriter*	A study design for evaluation of CompleteCare satisfaction.	Throughout
Mindy Goldberg & Associates	Conducted concept testing and ad testing in the Kool-Aid study.	161
MLN Research	Conducted focus groups to test the communication elements of the Kool-Aid ad campaign. Also conducts focus groups, creative play sessions, and other research techniques involving children.	158, 161
Office of Industry Analysis*	A study to determine if executives would reveal what criteria they use when one raw material is substituted for another in manufacturing.	151
Smith Barney	The investment and financial services firm, ordered to do attitudinal research as part of the negotiated settlement of the sexual harassment suit brought by 25 current and former employees.	153
StarAuto*	An exploratory study experience survey to determine sources of declining productivity and quality.	154
Sun Research Corp.	Conducted 11 focus groups in the Kool-Aid study.	161
U.S. Postal Service	Attempting to determine the source of workers' exposure to inhalation anthrax.	168

[*]Due to the confidential and proprietary nature of most research, the names of some companies have been changed.

DISCUSSION QUESTIONS

Terms in Review

1. Distinguish between the following:

   a. Exploratory and formal studies.

   b. Experimental and ex post facto research designs.

   c. Descriptive and causal studies.

2. Establishing causality is difficult, whether conclusions have been derived inductively or deductively.

   a. Explain and elaborate on the implications of this statement.

   b. Why is ascribing causality more difficult when conclusions have been reached through induction?

   c. Correlation does not imply causation. Illustrate this point with examples from business.

3. Using yourself as the subject, give an example of each of the following asymmetrical relationships:

   a. Stimulus-response

   b. Property-disposition

   c. Disposition-behavior

   d. Property-behavior

4. Why not use more control variables rather than depend on randomization as the means of controlling extraneous variables?

5. Researchers seek causal relationships by either experimental or ex post facto research designs.

   a. In what ways are these two approaches similar?

   b. In what ways are they different?

Making Research Decisions

6. You have been asked to determine how hospitals prepare and train volunteers. Since you know relatively little about this subject, how will you find out? Be as specific as possible.

7. You are the administrative assistant for a division chief in a large holding company that owns several hotels and theme parks. You and the division chief have just come from the CEO's office, where you were informed that the guest complaints related to housekeeping and employee attitude are increasing. Your on-site managers have mentioned some tension among the workers but have not considered it unusual. The CEO and your division chief instruct you to investigate. Suggest at least three different types of research that might be appropriate in this situation.

8. Propose one or more hypotheses for each of the following variable pairs, specifying which is the *IV* and which is the *DV.* Then develop the basic hypothesis to include at least one moderating variable or intervening variable.

   a. The Index of Consumer Confidence and the business cycle.

   b. Level of worker output and closeness of worker supervision.

   c. Student GPA and level of effort in a class required by student's major.

Bringing Research to Life	**9.** Using the eight design descriptors, profile the MindWriter CompleteCare satisfaction study as described in this and preceding chapters.
From Concept to Practice	**10.** Use the eight design descriptors in Exhibit 6–1 to profile the research described in the chapter Snapshots.
WWW Exercises	Visit our website for Internet exercises related to this chapter at www.mhhe.com/business/cooper8

CASES*

A GEM OF A STUDY	 JOHN DEERE AND COMPANY
CALLING UP ATTENDANCE	RAMADA DEMONSTRATES ITS PERSONAL BEST
GOODYEAR'S AQUATRED	VOLKSWAGEN'S BEETLE
INQUIRING MINDS WANT TO KNOW—NOW!	

*All cases indicating a video icon are located on the Instructor's Videotape Supplement. All nonvideo cases are in the case section of the textbook. All cases indicating a CD icon offer a data set, which is located on the accompanying CD.

REFERENCE NOTES

1. Reprinted with permission of Macmillan Publishing from *Social Research Strategy and Tactics,* 2nd ed., by Bernard S. Phillips, p. 93. Copyright © 1971 by Bernard S. Phillips.

2. Fred N. Kerlinger, *Foundations of Behavioral Research,* 3rd ed. (New York: Holt, Rinehart & Winston, 1986), p. 279.

3. The complexity of research design tends to confuse students as well as writers. The latter respond by forcing order on the vast array of design types through the use of classification schemes or taxonomies. Generally, this is helpful, but because the world defies neat categories, this scheme, like others, may either include or exclude too much.

4. Kerlinger, *Foundations of Behavioral Research,* p. 295.

5. Abraham Kaplan, *Conduct of Inquiry* (San Francisco: Chandler, 1964), p. 37.

6. W. Charles Redding, "Research Setting: Field Studies," in *Methods of Research in Communication,* ed. Philip Emmert and William D. Brooks (Boston: Houghton Mifflin, 1970), pp. 140–42.

7. John Van Maanen, James M. Dabbs, Jr., and Robert R. Faulkner, *Varieties of Qualitative Research* (Beverly Hills, CA: Sage Publications, 1982), p. 32.

8. Catherine Marshall and Gretchen B. Rossman, *Designing Qualitative Research* (Newbury Park, CA: Sage Publications, 1989), pp. 78–108.

9. This classification is suggested in Claire Selltiz, Lawrence S. Wrightsman, and Stuart W. Cook, *Research Methods in Social Relations,* 3rd ed. (New York: Holt, Rinehart & Winston, 1976), pp. 99–101.

10. A comprehensive and detailed presentation may be found in Richard A. Krueger, *Focus Groups: A Practical Guide for Applied Research,* 2nd ed. (Thousand Oaks, CA: Sage Publications, 1994); and David L. Morgan, *Successful Focus Groups: Advancing the State of the Art* (Thousand Oaks, CA: Sage Publications, 1993). Also see Thomas L. Greenbaum, "Focus Group Spurt Predicted for the '90s," *Marketing News* 24, no. 1 (January 8, 1990), pp. 21–22.

11. "How Nonprofits Are Using Focus Groups," *Nonprofit World* 14, no. 5 (September/October 1996), p. 37.

12. P. Hawe, D. Degeling, and J. Hall, *Evaluating Health Promotion: A Health Worker's Guide* (Artarmon, N.S.W.: MacLennan & Petty, 1990).

13. "Shoppers Speak Out in Focus Groups," *Discount Store News* 36, no. 5 (March 3, 1997), pp. 23–26.

14. Hawe, Degeling, and Hall, *Evaluating Health Promotion,* p. 176.

15. Hubert M. Blalock, Jr., *Causal Inferences in Nonexperimental Research* (Chapel Hill: University of North Carolina Press, 1964), p. 5.

16. As stated in William J. Goode and Paul K. Hatt, *Methods in Social Research* (New York: McGraw-Hill, 1952), p. 75.

17. From *Methods in Social Research* by William J. Goode and Paul K. Hatt. Copyright (c) 1952, McGraw-Hill Book Company. Used with permission of McGraw-Hill Book Company.

18. Morris R. Cohen and Ernest Nagel, *An Introduction to Logic and Scientific Method* (New York: Harcourt, Brace, 1934), Chapter 13; and Blalock, *Causal Inferences,* p. 14.

19. R. Carnap, *An Introduction to the Philosophy of Science* (New York: Basic Books, 1966).

20. Content adapted from Thomas F. Gilbert, *Human Competence* (New York: McGraw-Hill, 1978). Tabular concept based on Emanuel J. Mason and William J. Bramble, *Understanding and Conducting Research,* 2nd ed. (New York: McGraw-Hill, 1989), p. 13.

21. Mason and Bramble, *Understanding and Conducting Research,* p. 14.

22. Morris Rosenberg, *The Logic of Survey Analysis* (New York: Basic Books, 1968), p. 3.

REFERENCES FOR SNAPSHOTS AND CAPTIONS

Global Entrepreneurship Monitor

"GEM: 1999 U.K. Executive Report," London Business School, ©1999.

"New Study on Entrepreneurship Reveals U.S. is Awash in Capital for New Business Start-ups: Report Indicates that Start-Up Activity Is More Prevalent than Previously Believed" (http://www.businesswire.com/cgi-bin/fheadline.cgi?day0/192090158&ticker=).

P. Reynolds, M. Hay, and S. Camp, "GEM: 1999 Executive Report," Babson College and London School of Business, ©1999.

Paul Reynolds, J. Levie, and E. Autio, "Data Collection—Analysis Strategies Operations Manual," Babson College-London Business School Global Entrepreneurship Monitor: 1999, ©1999.

Paul Reynolds, J. Levie, E. Autio, M. Hay, and W. Bygrave, "1999 Research Report: Entrepreneurship and National Economic Well-Being," ©1999 (www.babson.edu/entrep/index.html).

A. Zacharakis, W. Bygrave, and D. Shepard, "National Entrepreneurship Assessment—United States of America: 2000 Executive Report," Babson College ©2000.

A. Zacharakis, P. Reynolds, and W. Bygrave, "GEM: National Entrepreneurship Assessment—United States of America—1999 Executive Report," Babson College, ©1999.

John Deere Co.

McGraw-Hill Video Library.

Interview with Mark Rostvold, senior vice president, John Deere Co. (www.deere.com).

Kool-Aid

Joan Raymond, "All Smiles," *American Demographics,* March 2001, p. s18.

http://www.kraftfoods.com/kool-aid/ka_index.html.

Interview with Megan Nerz, MLN Research, July 2001.

Smith Barney

"Before You Ask Smith Barney to Manage Your Assets, Listen to These Sexual Harassment and Sex Discrimination Allegations," National Organization for Women (http://www.now.org/issues/wfw/smith-barney.html).

Interview with Paulette Gerkovich, project director, Catalyst, August 2001.

"NOW Issues Reaffirmation of Support for Proposed Smith Barney Settlement," National Organization for Women, April 8, 1998 (http://www.now.org/press/04-98/04-08-98.html).

"Smith Barney Bias Deal Nears OK," *Record Online* (*Times Herald Record,* a division of Ottaway Newspapers, Inc.) April 10, 1998 (http://www.th-record.com/1998/04/04-10-98/smithb.htm).

"Smith Barney's Woman Problem," *Business Week,* 1996 (http://www.businessweek.com/1996/23/b348154.htm).

"Statement of NOW President Patricia Ireland on Proposed Smith Barney Settlement," National Organization for Women, November 18, 1997 (http://www.now.org/press/11-97/11-18-97.html).

Peter Truell, "A Revised Pact Is Approved in Smith Barney Bias Case," *New York Times,* July 25, 1998.

"Women in Financial Services: The Word on the Street: Executive Summary," Catalyst, Catalyst Publication Code R47; ISBN#0-89584-219-X, ©2001.

CLASSIC AND CONTEMPORARY READINGS

Babbie, Earl R. *The Practice of Social Research.* 9th ed. Belmont, CA: Wadsworth, 2000. Contains a clear and thorough synopsis of design.

Creswell, John W. *Qualitative Inquiry and Research Design.* 5th ed. Thousand Oaks, CA: Sage Publishing, 1997. A creative and comprehensive work on qualitative research methods.

Krathwohl, David R. *Social and Behavioral Science Research: A New Framework for Conceptualizing, Implementing, and Evaluating Research Studies.* San Francisco: Jossey-Bass, 1985. Chapter 9 on causality is insightful, well reasoned, and highly recommended.

Mason, Emanuel J., and William J. Bramble. *Understanding and Conducting Research.* 2nd ed. New York: McGraw-Hill, 1989. Chapter 1 has an excellent section on causation; Chapter 2 provides an alternative classification of the types of research.

Morgan, David L., and Richard A. Kruger (eds.). *The Focus Group Kit.* Thousand Oaks, CA: Sage Publishing, 1997. A six-volume set including an overview guidebook, planning, developing questions, moderating, involving community members, and analyzing results.

Selltiz, Claire, Lawrence S. Wrightsman, and Stuart M. Cook. *Research Methods in Social Relations.* 3rd ed. New York: Holt, Rinehart & Winston, 1976. Chapters 4 and 5 discuss various types of research designs.

Strauss, Anselm, and Juliet Corbin. *Basics of Qualitative Research.* 2nd ed. Thousand Oaks, CA: Sage Publishing, 1998. A step-by-step guide with particularly useful sections on coding procedures.

CHAPTER 7

Sampling Design

Learning Objectives

After reading this chapter, you should understand . . .

1 **The two premises on which sampling theory is based.**

2 **The characteristics of accuracy and precision for measuring sample validity.**

3 **The two categories of sampling techniques and the variety of sampling techniques within each category.**

4 **The six questions that must be answered to develop a sampling plan.**

5 **The critical issues and formulas that determine the appropriate sample size.**

6 **The various sampling techniques and when each is used.**

Bringing Research to Life

From 100 feet away, Eric Burbidge—a recent hire by CityBus—saw that the approaching number 99 bus was filthy. Forty riders were docilely lined up to board—one was a letter carrier, and a collection of other blue-collar men and women comprised the rest. Some were idly thumbing through newspapers—Good! He'd learned in college that the ideal subject was thoughtful, articulate, rational, and above all, cooperative. Some were chatting, and two were ruminating slowly on hero sandwiches, which he supposed they had picked up at the tavern across the street from the bus station.

Burbidge swept past the queued passengers, taking care not to make premature eye contact, and brusquely rapped his clipboard against the bus's folding door. With a whoosh the driver snapped the door open, and Burbidge heaved himself up onto the bus. "Good evening, driver. I'm Eric Burbidge, from headquarters."

"Figures. We don't see many suits on Route 99."

"I'm here to conduct a scientific survey to determine newspaper readership, if any, of riders on this route."

"Yessir," murmured the driver, without enthusiasm.

"You must know from your employees' newsletter that the corporation is soon to announce a restructuring of the route system and schedule, pursuant to which we shall have to purchase advertising space in the leading media to reveal our new route structure, maps, and schedules."

"Won't that be a mess," muttered the driver, in the same flat tone. "And, yessir, I read your newsletter. For 15 years I have read it."

"You may have noticed that this route runs north-to-south equidistant between the twin cities . . ."

"The route runs north-south, with one city on the east and the other on the west, yessir. I caught on to that long ago, sir. Clean splits the line between East City and West City and never gets closer to one than the other. If you want to get to one city or the other, you transfer to another bus. My bus just goes straight north. Just like it shows on the route map, sir."

"As corporate research director," said Burbidge, gracefully emphasizing his point by pointing a forefinger roofward, "I take nothing for granted. I need scientific methodology to test my hypothesis that readership of newspapers on this route would be equally divided between the *East City Gazette* and the *West City Tribune.* To that very end I have prepared this survey for your riders, which with your complete cooperation I have selected to pass out along this route, on this day, at this time."

"Newspapers, you say," said the driver, showing a flicker of involvement. "I could tell you quite a lot about those newspapers . . ."

"Not required! This is a scientific survey of riders on Route 99, and anecdotal information is not appropriate. What I require of you is to let the passengers up onto the bus so I may give them these pencils and surveys, and then to refrain from swerving or unnecessarily agitating the bus while they are filling out my surveys. Do you think you can manage that?"

"I'd better turn on the inside lights, don't you think?"

"Well, of course, turn on the lights. That goes without saying."

The passengers boarded slowly, exchanging pleasantries with the driver. They were quite a little clan, Burbidge could see.

The bus rolled steadily northward, and Burbidge was pleased to see that riders hunched over his one-page survey, though he was struck by how long it took them to answer the simplest of questions. As each completed the survey, he or she shyly shuffled forward and proffered it to Burbidge without comment.

Just when he sensed everything was going as well as might be expected, two men stood up, one in the front by the driver, one in the rear, and spread their legs to straddle the aisle. A ball of newsprint was tossed into the aisle, and the passengers began whooping and batting the paper forward and back. "What is this, driver?" demanded Burbidge.

"Hockey. They are playing hockey. The idea is to knock the ball between this guy's legs or that guy's in the back."

"Aren't you going to stop them?"

"No harm done. These are a friendly bunch. Big sports fans. In fact," said the driver, whose voice had gained enthusiasm, "the East City Club plays pro hockey tonight. So, when I clean out the bus, most of the newspapers will be the *East City Gazette*." He rattled on, contributing to Burbidge's annoyance, explaining that the riders liked to study the night's pro game in advance, the better to discuss it among themselves, so newsstand sales were brisk in the terminal, but only for the newspaper that did the better job of covering the sport du jour. "Of course, tomorrow night there is pro basketball in West City, and most of the riders will pick up the *West City Tribune* at the newsstands."

"That's impossible to accept," shouted Burbidge. "Such behavior would bias my scientific survey, which asks for the paper they most recently purchased!"

"Well, you had better accept it. 'Cause I've been cleaning out this bus for five years. It's the *Gazette* before hockey, and the *Trib* before basketball. This is a hockey crowd tonight, which means extra *Gazette*s."

Burbidge was mortified and hoped he wasn't revealing his distress to the driver. But the driver added, "Course, in the mornings these folks bring the papers that the newsboys toss on their lawns, so you don't see such a situation."

"By choosing between sampling this route—morning or evening—I get a systematically different set of results," mumbled Burbidge, more to himself than to the driver. "And by choosing a hockey night or a basketball night, I further distort the results."

"Naturally," agreed the driver, with irritating enthusiasm.

The driver had now warmed to his exposition of trash-can sociological research. "Of course, by reading our company newsletter, as I do, I know that by the time you announce the new routes and schedules, we will be finished with hockey and basketball and into the baseball season." Could Burbidge detect irony in the driver's chuckle?

"If you are furnishing me information that is at all reliable, driver, then the generalizability of my survey would be contingent on whether I sample in the morning or evening, on the professional sports schedule on a particular night, and on the season of the year."

"That's part of it, yessir."

"Part of it?"

"Well, yessir . . . you see, most of these folks on the 5:15 bus are East City folks, and most of the people on the 5:45 bus are West City folks, so your outcomes would naturally depend on whether you took a survey on the 5:15 or 5:45 bus."

"How can this be?"

"Well, you see, the 5:15 bus on this route—the one you are on now—gets to Boght Corners at 5:55, and the East City folks transfer onto the eastbound bus that is waiting there for them. Most of the West City folks hang out in the bar across the street from the terminal, get on the 5:45 bus, and rendezvous at 6:25 with the westbound bus at Boght Corners."

"I see. I see." He was reconsidering the wisdom of this survey. "AND IS THERE ANYTHING ELSE you would care to share with me?"

"Only that the 5:45 boarders don't read the newspaper much at all, as they have been watching sports on the TV in the bar, are lightly soused, some of them, and can't read the small print because I don't turn on the inside lights."

"I might as well have stayed home," Burbidge muttered in despair.

The driver stopped the bus and swiveled to face Burbidge. "Wouldn't that have been a pity, sir, as I would have been deprived of this excellent lesson in scientific research."

The Nature of Sampling

Most people intuitively understand the idea of sampling. One taste from a drink tells us whether it is sweet or sour. If we select a few employment records out of a complete set, we usually assume our selection reflects the characteristics of the full set. If some of our staff favors a flexible work schedule, we infer that others will also. These examples vary in their representativeness, but each is a sample.

The basic idea of **sampling** is that by selecting some of the elements in a population, we may draw conclusions about the entire population. A **population element** is the subject on which the measurement is being taken. It is the unit of study. While an element may be a person, it can just as easily be something else. For example, each office worker questioned about a flexible work schedule is a population element, and each business account analyzed is an element of an account population. A **population** is the total collection of elements about which we wish to make some inferences. All office workers in the firm compose a population of interest; all 4,000 files define a population of interest. A **census** is a count of all the elements in a population. If 4,000 files define the population, a census would obtain information from every one of them.

In studying customer satisfaction with the service operation for MindWriter, the population of interest to Jason and Myra is all individuals who have had a laptop repaired while the CompleteCare program has been in effect. The population element is any one individual interacting with the service program.

Why Sample?

There are several compelling reasons for sampling, including: (1) lower cost, (2) greater accuracy of results, (3) greater speed of data collection, and (4) availability of population elements.

Lower Cost The economic advantages of taking a sample rather than a census are massive. Consider the cost of taking a census. In 2000, due to a Supreme Court ruling requiring a census rather than statistical sampling techniques, the U.S. Bureau of the Census increased its 2000 Decennial Census budget estimate by $1.723 billion to $4.512 billion.[1] Is it any wonder that researchers in all types of organizations ask, "Why should we spend thousands of dollars interviewing all 4,000 employees in our company if we can find out what we need to know by asking only a few hundred?"

Greater Accuracy of Results Deming argues that the quality of a study is often better with sampling than with a census. He suggests, "Sampling possesses the possibility of better interviewing (testing), more thorough investigation of missing, wrong, or suspicious information, better supervision, and better processing than is possible with complete coverage."[2] Research findings substantiate this opinion. More than 90 percent of the total survey error in one study was from nonsampling sources and only

10 percent or less was from random sampling error.[3] The U.S. Bureau of the Census shows its confidence in sampling by taking sample surveys to check the accuracy of its census. And while it is politically correct to take a census of the population, we know that segments of the population are seriously undercounted.

Greater Speed of Data Collection   Sampling's speed of execution reduces the time between the recognition of a need for information and the availability of that information. For every disgruntled customer that the MindWriter CompleteCare program generates, several prospective customers will move away from MindWriter to a competitor's laptop. So fixing the problems within the CompleteCare program will not only keep current customers coming back but will also discourage prospective customers from defecting to competitive brands due to negative word-of-mouth.

Availability of Population Elements   Some situations require sampling. When we test the breaking strength of materials, we must destroy them; a census would mean complete destruction of all materials. Sampling is also the only process possible if the population is infinite.

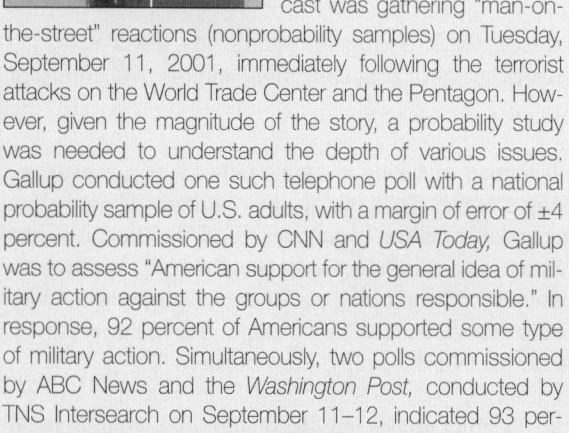

S N A P S H O T   Terrorism and the News

News organizations often conduct or commission polls to determine whether stories are potentially newsworthy or to get a sense of public opinion regarding some issue. Every network news broadcast was gathering "man-on-the-street" reactions (nonprobability samples) on Tuesday, September 11, 2001, immediately following the terrorist attacks on the World Trade Center and the Pentagon. However, given the magnitude of the story, a probability study was needed to understand the depth of various issues. Gallup conducted one such telephone poll with a national probability sample of U.S. adults, with a margin of error of ±4 percent. Commissioned by CNN and *USA Today,* Gallup was to assess "American support for the general idea of military action against the groups or nations responsible." In response, 92 percent of Americans supported some type of military action. Simultaneously, two polls commissioned by ABC News and the *Washington Post,* conducted by TNS Intersearch on September 11–12, indicated 93 percent and 94 percent support for military action.

In all of these polls, Americans also said they were willing to bide their time, finding the right time and place to retaliate. In the poll conducted by TNS Intersearch, the support was strong, even when respondents were apprised of the potential consequences of the action. An NBC News/*Wall Street Journal* poll conducted by Hart/Teeter on September

13 showed 83 percent of adults supported "forceful military action." Each of these polls surveyed between 556 and 618 adults with precision factors of ±4 to ±4.5 percent. A review of polls dating back to 1986 in the ABC News poll vault shows that early support for military action following an incident tends to hold through the duration of military action. However, the basis for such responses, going back to the retaliation in Libya, has been Americans' recollection of prompt, tactical, and decisive strikes. In a prolonged campaign, with accumulating American casualties and the likelihood of continued urban terror, support for continued engagement may wane. Only history will tell if citizen support for a military response to this historic terrorist attack will demonstrate the same resolve.

www.abcnews.com

www.msnbc.com

www.cnn.com

www.wsj.com

www.usatoday.com

www.washingtonpost.com

www.intersearch.tnsofres.com

www.hartresearch.com

www.gallup.com

Sample versus Census The advantages of sampling over census studies are less compelling when the population is small and the variability within the population is high. Two conditions are appropriate for a census study: A census is (1) *feasible* when the population is small and (2) *necessary* when the elements are quite different from each other.[4] When the population is small and variable, any sample we draw may not be representative of the population from which it is drawn. The resulting values we calculate from the sample are incorrect as estimates of the population values. Consider North American manufacturers of stereo components. Fewer than 50 companies design, develop, and manufacture amplifier and loudspeaker products at the high end of the price range. The size of this population suggests a census is feasible. The diversity of their product offerings makes it difficult to accurately sample from this group. Some companies specialize in speakers, some in amplifier technology, and others in compact disk transports. Choosing a census in this situation is appropriate.

What Is a Good Sample?

The ultimate test of a sample design is how well it represents the characteristics of the population it purports to represent. In measurement terms, the sample must be valid. Validity of a sample depends on two considerations: accuracy and precision.

Accuracy Accuracy is the degree to which bias is absent from the sample. When the sample is drawn properly, some sample elements underestimate the population values being studied and others overestimate them. Variations in these values offset each other; this counteraction results in a sample value that is generally close to the population value. For these offsetting effects to occur, however, there must be enough elements in the sample, and they must be drawn in a way to favor neither overestimation nor underestimation.

An accurate (unbiased) sample is one in which the underestimators and the overestimators are balanced among the members of the sample. There is no **systematic variance** with an accurate sample. Systematic variance has been defined as "the variation in measures due to some known or unknown influences that 'cause' the scores to lean in one direction more than another."[5] Homes on the corner of the block, for example, are often larger and more valuable than those within the block. Thus, a sample that selects corner homes only will cause us to overestimate home values in the area. Burbidge learned that in selecting Route 99 for his newspaper readership sample, the time of the day, day of the week, and season of the year of the survey dramatically reduced the accuracy and validity of his sample.

Even the large size of some samples cannot counteract systematic bias. The classic example of a sample with systematic variance was the *Literary Digest* presidential election poll in 1936, in which more than 2 million persons participated. The poll predicted Alfred Landon would defeat Franklin Roosevelt for the presidency of the United States. Your memory is correct; we've never had a president named Alfred Landon. We discovered later that the poll drew its sample from telephone owners who were in the middle and upper classes—at the time, the bastion of the Republican party—while Roosevelt appealed to the much larger working class that didn't own phones and typically voted for the Democratic party candidate.

Precision A second criterion of a good sample design is *precision of estimate.* No sample will fully represent its population in all respects. The numerical descriptors that describe samples may be expected to differ from those that describe populations because of random fluctuations inherent in the sampling process. This is called **sampling error** and reflects the influences of chance in drawing the sample members. Sampling error is what is left after all known sources of systematic variance have been accounted for. In theory, sampling error consists of random fluctuations only, although some unknown systematic variance may be included when too many or too few sample elements possess a particular characteristic. Let's say we draw a sample from an alphabetical list of MindWriter owners who are having their laptops currently serviced by the Complete-Care program. We insert a survey response card in a sample of returned laptops. Eighty percent of those surveyed had their laptops serviced by Max Jensen. And we know from our exploratory study that Max had more complaint letters about his work than any other technician. We have failed to truly randomize the sample with our alphabetical listing of possible sample elements and thus have increased our sampling error.

Precision is measured by the *standard error of estimate,* a type of standard deviation measurement; the smaller the standard error of estimate, the higher is the precision of the sample. The ideal sample design produces a small standard error of estimate. However, not all types of sample design provide estimates of precision, and samples of the same size can produce different amounts of error variance.

Types of Sample Design

The researcher makes several decisions when designing a sample. These are represented in Exhibit 7–1. The sampling decisions flow from two decisions made in the formation of the management-research question hierarchy: the nature of the management question and the specific investigative questions that evolve from the research question.

A variety of sampling techniques is available. The one the researcher should select depends on the requirements of the project, its objectives, and the funds available. In the discussion that follows, we will use three examples:

- The CityBus study introduced in the vignette at the beginning of this chapter.
- The continuing MindWriter service satisfaction study.
- A study of the feasibility of starting a dining club near the campus of Metro University.

The researchers at Metro U are exploring the feasibility of creating a dining club whose facilities would be available on a membership basis. To launch this venture, they will need to make a substantial investment. Research will allow them to reduce many risks. Thus the research question is: "Would a membership dining club be a viable enterprise?" Some investigative questions that flow from the research question include:

1. Who would patronize the club and on what basis?
2. How many would join the club under various membership and fee arrangements?
3. How much would the average member spend per month?
4. What days would be most popular?
5. What menu and service formats would be most desirable?
6. What lunch times would be most popular?
7. Given the proposed price levels, how often per month would each member have lunch or dinner?
8. What percent of the people in the population say they would join the club, based on the projected rates and services?

We use the last three investigative questions for examples and focus specifically on questions 7 and 8 for assessing the project's risks. First we will digress with other

EXHIBIT 7–1   **Sampling Design within the Research Process**

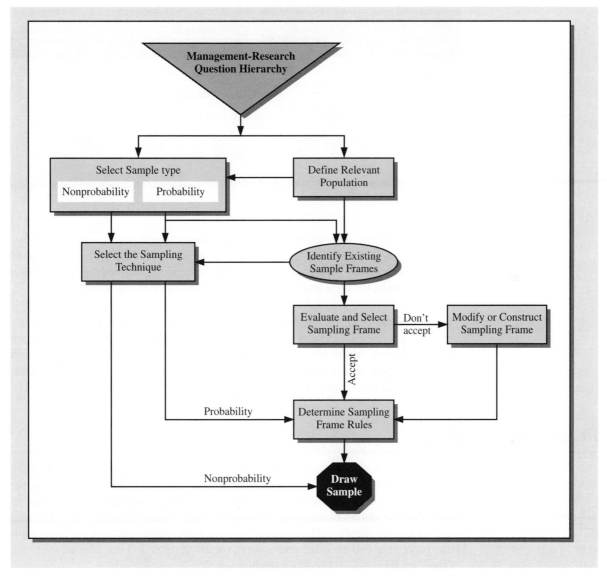

information and examples on sample design, coming back to Metro U in the next section.

In decisions of sample design, the representation basis and the element selection techniques, as shown in Exhibit 7–2, classify the different approaches.

Representation   The members of a sample are selected on a probability basis or by another means. **Probability sampling** is based on the concept of *random selection*—a controlled procedure that assures that each population element is given a known nonzero chance of selection.

In contrast, **nonprobability sampling** is arbitrary (nonrandom) and subjective. Each member does not have a known nonzero chance of being included. Allowing

EXHIBIT 7–2   Types of Sampling Designs

Element Selection	Representation Basis	
	Probability	Nonprobability
Unrestricted	Simple random	Convenience
Restricted	Complex random	Purposive
	Systematic	Judgment
	Cluster	Quota
	Stratified	Snowball
	Double	

interviewers to choose sample elements "at random" (meaning "as they wish" or "wherever they find them") is not random sampling. Only probability samples provide estimates of precision. While we are not told how Burbidge selected the riders of Bus 99 as his sample, it's clear that he did not use probability sampling techniques.

Element Selection   Whether the elements are selected individually and directly from the population—viewed as a single pool—or when additional controls are imposed, element selection may also classify samples. If each sample element is drawn individually from the population at large, it is an *unrestricted sample.* Restricted sampling covers all other forms of sampling.

Probability Sampling

The unrestricted, simple random sample is the simplest form of probability sampling. Since all probability samples must provide a known nonzero chance of selection for each population element, the **simple random sample** is considered a special case in which each population element has a *known and equal chance* of selection. In this section, we use the simple random sample to build a foundation for understanding sampling procedures and choosing probability samples. Exhibit 7–3 provides an overview of the steps involved in choosing a random sample.

Steps in Sampling Design

There are several decisions to be made in securing a sample. Each requires unique information. While the questions presented here are sequential, an answer to one question often forces a revision to an earlier one. In this section we will consider the following:

1. What is the relevant population?
2. What are the parameters of interest?
3. What is the sampling frame?
4. What is the type of sample?
5. What size sample is needed?
6. How much will it cost?

EXHIBIT 7–3   How to Choose a Random Sample

Selecting a **random sample** is accomplished with the aid of computer software, a table of random numbers, or a calculator with a random number generator. Drawing slips out of a hat or ping-pong balls from a drum serves as an alternative *if every element in the sampling frame has an equal chance of selection.* Mixing the slips (or balls) and returning them between every selection ensures that every element is just as likely to be selected as any other.

A table of random numbers (such as Appendix F, Table F–10) is a practical solution when no software program is available. Random number tables contain digits that have no systematic organization. Whether you look at rows, columns, or diagonals, you will find neither sequence nor order. Table F–10 in Appendix F is arranged into 10 columns of five-digit strings, but this is solely for readability.

Assume the researchers want a special sample from a population of 95 elements. How will the researcher begin?

1. **Assign each element within the sampling frame a unique number** from 01 to 95.

2. **Identify a random start from the random number table** (drop a pencil point-first onto the table with closed eyes. Let's say the pencil dot lands on the eighth column from the left and 10 numbers down from the top of Table F–10, marking the five digits 05067).

3. **Determine how the digits in the random number table will be assigned to the sampling frame** to choose the specified sample size (researchers agree to read the first two digits in this column downward until 10 are selected).

4. **Select the sample elements from the sampling frame** (05, 27, 69, 94, 18, 61, 36, 85, 71, and 83 using the above process. The digit 94 appeared twice and the second instance was omitted; 00 was omitted because the sampling frame started with 01).

Other approaches to selecting digits are endless; Horizontally right to left, bottom to top, diagonally across columns, and so forth. Computer selection of a simple random sample will be more efficient for larger projects.

S N A P S H O T

The Right Sample for Studying Sex Education

The Henry J. Kaiser Family Foundation (KFF), "an independent philanthropy focusing on the major health care issues facing the nation," is "primarily an operating organization that develops and runs its own research and communications programs." It recently released a study of principals, teachers, students, and their parents that challenges the "convention that Americans are reluctant to have sexual health issues taught in school; [rather] the surveys show that most parents, along with educators and students themselves, would expand sex education courses and curriculum."

How do you conduct a study on this sensitive topic? KFF chose Princeton Survey Research Associates to do several series of phone surveys. Interviews with "313 principals, 1,001 teachers of sex education classes, [and] 1,501 pairs of students and [their] parents were conducted February 2 through May 23, 1999." The principals and teachers were recruited to represent "all public, middle junior, and senior high schools enrolling grades 7 through 12 in the continental United States. They were randomly and proportionately selected from a national database of public schools by type of school." Random digit dialing was used to identify households with children between 11–19 years of age who were enrolled in public schools in grades 7 through 12. Once the student was identified, the interviewer asked to speak with the male parent or guardian (followed by the female guardian, if the male guardian was unavailable). The parent was surveyed first, followed by the student, during the same contact if possible. "At least 15 attempts were made to complete an interview at every sample school or household." At the 95 percent confidence level, the error interval was ±3 for students-parents and teachers, and ±6 percent for principals. Participation rate was 54 percent for students-parents, 72 percent for teachers, and 41 percent for principals. What do you think of the sampling done for this study? You can link to a full study report from the KFF website.

www.kff.org

www.psra.com

What Is the Relevant Population?   The definition of the population may be apparent from the management problem or the research question(s) but often it is not. Is the population for the dining club study at Metro University defined as "full-time day students on the main campus of Metro U"? Or should the population include "all persons employed at Metro U"? Or should townspeople who live in the neighborhood be included? Without knowing the target market chosen for the new venture, it is not obvious which of these is the appropriate sampling population.

There also may be confusion about whether the population consists of individuals, households, or families, or a combination of these. If a communication study needs to measure income, then the definition of the population element as individual or household can make quite a difference. In an observation study, a sample population might be nonpersonal: displays within a store or any ATM a bank owns or all single-family residential properties in a community. Good operational definitions are critical in choosing the relevant population.

Assume the Metro University Dining Club is to be solely for the students and employees on the main campus. The researchers might define the population as "all currently enrolled students and employees on the main campus of Metro U." However, this does not include family members. They may want to revise the definition to make it "current students and employees of Metro U, main campus, and their families."

In the nonprobability sample, Burbidge seems to have defined his relevant population as any rider of the CityBus system. He presumes he has an equal need to determine newspaper readership of both regular and infrequent CityBus riders, so that he might reach them with information about the new route structure, maps, and schedules. He can, however, easily reach regular riders by distributing information about the new routes via display racks on the bus for a period of time before the new routes are implemented. Infrequent riders, then, are the real population of interest of his newspaper readership study.

What Are the Parameters of Interest?   **Population parameters** are summary descriptors (e.g., incidence proportion, mean, variance) of variables of interest in the population. **Sample statistics** are descriptors of the relevant variables computed from sample data. Sample statistics are used as estimators of population parameters. The sample statistics are the basis of our inferences about the population. Depending on how measurement questions are phrased, each may collect a different type of data (see Exhibit 7–4). Each different type of data also generates different sample statistics.

We discuss data types in greater detail in Chapter 8.

Sampling from pools of special respondents, such as doctors and other professionals with time-starved occupations, often involves hiring firms that specialize in such recruiting.

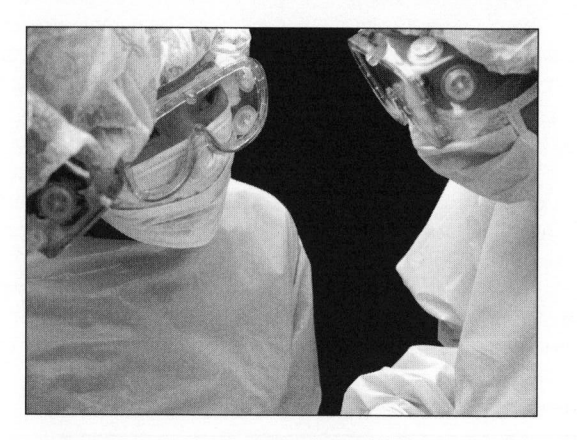

EXHIBIT 7–4 Parameter of Interest and Type of Data

Parameter of Interest	Type of Data	Example Scale
Attendance at a special event	Nominal	Participation in a promotion (yes, no)
Percent of patrons who order their steak cooked rare, regardless of health warnings	Ordinal	Doneness of meat proportion (well done, medium, rare)
Mean temperature of ideal vacation location	Interval	Temperature in degrees
Average number of store visits per month	Ratio	Actual number of store visits

When the variables of interest in the study are measured on interval or ratio scales, we use the sample mean to estimate the population mean and the sample standard deviation to estimate the population standard deviation. Asking Metro U affiliates to reveal their frequency of eating on or near campus (less than 5 times per week, greater than 5 but less than 10 times per week, or greater than 10 times per week) would provide an interval data estimator. In MindWriter, the rating of service by CompleteCare (excellent, good, fair, etc.) would be an example of an interval data estimator. Asking the CityBus riders about their number of days of ridership during the past seven days would result in ratio data.

We discuss proportion estimators in more detail later in this chapter.

When the variables of interest are measured on nominal or ordinal scales, we use the sample proportion of incidence to estimate the population proportion and the pq to estimate the population variance. The **population proportion of incidence** "is equal to the number of elements in the population belonging to the category of interest, divided by the total number of elements in the population."[6] Proportion measures are necessary for nominal data and are widely used for other measures as well. The most frequent proportion measure is the percentage. In the Metro U study, examples of nominal data are the proportion of a population that expresses interest in joining the club (for example, 30 percent; therefore p is equal to .3 and q, those not interested, equals .7) or the proportion of married students who report they now eat in restaurants at least five times a month. The CityBus study seeks to determine whether East City or West City has the most riders on Bus 99. MindWriter might want to know if men or women have experienced the most problems with laptop model 9000. These measures for CityBus and MindWriter would result in nominal data. Exhibit 7–5 indicates population parameters of interest for our three example studies.

There may also be important subgroups in the population about whom we would like to make estimates. For example, we might want to draw conclusions about the extent of dining club use that could be expected from married students versus single students, residential students versus commuter students, and so forth. Such questions have a strong impact on the nature of the sampling frame we accept, the design of the sample, and its size. Burbidge should be more interested in reaching infrequent rather than regular CityBus riders with the newspaper advertising he plans. And in the MindWriter study, Jason may be interested in comparing the responses of those who experienced poor service and those who experienced excellent service through the CompleteCare program.

EXHIBIT 7–5   Sample Population Parameters

Example	Population Parameter of Interest (type data)	Scale
CityBus	Frequency of ridership within 7 days (interval data)	More than 10 times, 6 to 10 times, 5 or fewer times
	Proportion of East City vs. West City riders (nominal data)	Actual percentage
MindWriter	Perceived quality of service (interval data)	Excellent, good, fair, poor
	Proportion of gender of Laptop 9000 customers with problems (nominal data)	Percent male, female
Metro U	Frequency of eating on or near campus within 7 days (ratio data)	Actual eating experiences
	Proportion of students/employees expressing interest (nominal data)	Actual percentage interested

What Is the Sampling Frame?   The **sampling frame** is closely related to the population. It is *the list of elements from which the sample is actually drawn.* Ideally, it is a complete and correct list of population members only. Jason should find limited problems obtaining a sampling frame of CompleteCare service users as MindWriter has maintained a database of all calls coming into the Call Center and all serial numbers of laptops serviced. As a practical matter, however, the sampling frame often differs from the theoretical population.

For the dining club study, the Metro U directory would be the logical first choice as a sampling frame. Directories are usually accurate when published in the fall, but suppose the study is being done in the spring. The directory will contain errors and omissions because some people will have withdrawn or left since the directory was published, while others will have enrolled or been hired. Usually university directories don't mention the families of students or employees. Just how much inaccuracy one can tolerate in choosing a sampling frame is a matter of judgment. You might use the directory anyway, ignoring the fact that it is not a fully accurate list. However, if the directory is a year old, the amount of error might be unacceptable. One way to make the sampling frame for the Metro U study more representative of the population would be to secure a supplemental list of the new students and employees as well as a list of the withdrawals and terminations from Metro U's registrar and human resources databases. You could then add and delete information from the original directory. Or, if their privacy policies permit, you might just request a current listing from each of these offices and use these lists as your sampling frame.

A greater distortion would be introduced if a branch campus population were included in the Metro U directory. This would be an example of a too-inclusive frame—that is, a frame that includes many elements other than the ones in which we are interested. A university directory that includes faculty and staff retirees is another example of a too-inclusive sampling frame.

We discuss screening procedures in Chapter 12.   Often you have to accept a sampling frame that includes people or cases beyond those in whom you are interested. You may have to use a telephone directory to draw a sample of business telephone numbers. Fortunately, this is easily resolved. You draw a sample from the larger population and then use a screening procedure to eliminate those who are not members of the group you wish to study.

The Metro U dining club survey is an example of a sampling frame problem that is readily solved. Often one finds this task much more of a challenge. Suppose you need to sample the members of an ethnic group, say, Asians residing in Little Rock, Arkansas. There is probably no directory of this population. While you may use the general city directory, sampling from this too-inclusive frame would be costly and inefficient as Asians represent only a small fraction of Little Rock's population. The screening task would be monumental. Since ethnic groups frequently cluster in certain neighborhoods, you might identify these areas of concentration and then use a reverse area telephone or city directory, which is organized by street address, to draw the sample. Burbidge had a definite problem as no sample frame of CityBus riders existed. While some regular riders used monthly passes, infrequent riders usually paid cash for their fares. It might have been possible for Burbidge to have anticipated this and to have developed over time a listing of customers. Bus drivers could have collected relevant contact information over a month, but the cost of contacting customers via phone or mail would have been much more expensive than the self-administered intercept approach Burbidge chose for data collection. One sampling frame available to Burbidge was a list of bus routes. This list would have allowed him to draw a probability sample using a cluster sampling technique. We discuss more complex sampling techniques later in this chapter.

What Is the Type of Sample?   The researcher faces a basic choice: a probability or nonprobability sample. With a probability sample, a researcher can make probability-based confidence estimates of various parameters that cannot be made with nonprobability samples. Choosing a probability sampling technique has several consequences. A researcher must follow appropriate procedures, so that:

- Interviewers or others cannot modify the selections made.

- Only those selected elements from the original sampling frame are included.

- Substitutions are excluded except as clearly specified and controlled according to predetermined decision rules.

Despite all due care, the actual sample achieved will not match perfectly the sample that is originally drawn. Some people will refuse to participate, and others will be difficult, if not impossible, to find. The latter represent the well-known "not-at-home" problem and require that enough callbacks be made to ensure they are adequately represented in the sample.

With personnel records available at a university and a population that is geographically concentrated, a probability sampling method is possible in the dining club study. University directories are generally available, and the costs of using a simple random sample would not be great here. Then, too, since the researchers are thinking of a major investment in the dining club, they would like to be confident they have a representative sample. The same analysis holds true for MindWriter: A sample frame is readily available, making a probability sample possible and likely.

While the probability cluster sampling technique was available to him, it is obvious that Burbidge chose nonprobability sampling, arbitrarily choosing Bus 99 as a judgment sample and attempting to survey everyone riding the bus during the arbitrary times in which he chose to ride.

What Size Sample Is Needed?   Much folklore surrounds this question. The most pervasive myths are summarized as follows:

- A sample must be large or it is not representative.

- A sample should bear some proportional relationship to the size of the population from which it is drawn.

In reality, how large a sample should be is a function of the variation in the population parameters under study and the estimating precision needed by the researcher. A sample of 400 may sometimes be appropriate, while a sample of more than 2,000 may be required in other circumstances; in another case, perhaps a sample of only 40 is needed.

Some principles that influence sample size include:

MANAGEMENT
Tip

- The greater the dispersion or variance within the population, the larger the sample must be to provide estimation precision.

- The greater the desired precision of the estimate, the larger the sample must be.

- The narrower the interval range, the larger the sample must be.

- The higher the confidence level in the estimate, the larger the sample must be.

- The greater the number of subgroups of interest within a sample, the greater the sample size must be, as each subgroup must meet minimum sample size requirements.

- If the calculated sample size exceeds 5 percent of the population, sample size may be reduced without sacrificing precision.

Since researchers can never be 100 percent certain a sample reflects its population, they must decide how much precision they need. Precision is measured by (1) the interval range in which they would expect to find the parameter estimate and (2) the degree of confidence they wish to have in that estimate.

The size of the probability sample needed can be affected by the size of the population, but only when the sample size is large compared with the population. This so-called *finite adjustment factor* enters the calculation when the calculated sample is 5 percent or more of the population. The net effect of the adjustment is to reduce the size of the sample needed to achieve a given level of precision.[7]

Other considerations often weigh heavily on the sample size decision. The conditions under which the sample is being conducted may suggest that only certain sampling techniques are feasible. One type of sample may be inappropriate because we have no list of population elements and must therefore sample geographic units. This is what happened to Burbidge in his choice of Bus 99. Since various designs have differing statistical and economic efficiencies, the choice of design will also affect the size of the sample.

The researcher also may be interested in making estimates concerning various subgroups of the population; then the sample must be large enough for each of these subgroups to meet the desired level of precision. One achieves this in simple random sampling by making the total sample large enough to ensure that each critical subgroup meets the minimum size criterion. In more complex sampling procedures, the smaller subgroups are sampled more heavily, and then the parameter estimates drawn from these subgroups are weighted. Depending on the variety of causes of MindWriter complaints about repair service, Jason and Myra's sample size might be controlled by the number of models of laptops that MindWriter services or the actual problem serviced.

How Much Will It Cost? Cost considerations influence decisions about the size and type of sample and also the data collection methods. Almost all studies have some budgetary constraint, and this may encourage a researcher to use a nonprobability sample. Probability sample surveys incur list costs for sample frames, callback costs, and a variety of other costs that are not necessary when more haphazard or arbitrary methods are used. But when the data collection method is changed, the amount and type of data that can be obtained also change. Note the effect of a $2,000 budget on sampling considerations:

Simple random sampling: $25 per interview; 80 completed interviews.

Geographic cluster sampling: $20 per interview; 100 completed interviews.

Self-administered questionnaire: $12 per respondent; 167 completed instruments.

Telephone interviews: $10 per respondent; 200 completed interviews.[8]

For CityBus the cost of sampling riders' newspaper preferences to discover where to run the route-reconfiguration announcements must be significantly less than the cost of running ads in both East City and West City dailies. Thus the nonprobability judgment sampling procedure that Burbidge used was logical from a budget standpoint. The investment required to open the dining club at Metro U also justifies the more careful probability approach taken by the students. For MindWriter, an investment in CompleteCare has already been made; Myra needs to be highly confident that her recommendations to her supervising manager to change CompleteCare procedures and policies are on target and thoroughly supported by the data collected. These considerations justify MindWriter's probability sampling approach.

Complex Probability Sampling

Simple random sampling is often impractical. Reasons include (1) it requires a population list (sampling frame) that is often not available; (2) it fails to use all the information about a population, thus resulting in a design that may be wasteful; and (3) it may be expensive to implement in both time and money. These problems have led to the development of alternative designs that are superior to the simple random design in statistical and/or economic efficiency.

A more efficient sample in a statistical sense is one that provides a given precision (standard error of the mean or proportion) with a smaller sample size. A sample that is economically more efficient is one that provides a desired precision at a lower dollar cost. We achieve this with designs that enable us to lower the costs of data collecting, usually through reduced travel expense and interviewer time.

In the discussion that follows, four alternative probability sampling approaches are considered: (1) systematic sampling, (2) stratified sampling, (3) cluster sampling, and (4) double sampling.

Systematic Sampling

A versatile form of probability sampling is **systematic sampling.** In this approach, every kth element in the population is sampled, beginning with a random start of an element in the range of 1 to k. The kth element is determined by dividing the sample size into the population size to obtain the skip pattern applied to the sampling frame. The major advantage of systematic sampling is its simplicity and flexibility. It is easier to instruct field workers to choose the dwelling unit listed on every kth line of a listing sheet than it is to use a random numbers table. With systematic sampling, there is no need to number the entries in a large personnel file before drawing a sample. To draw a systematic sample merely do the following:

MANAGEMENT

- Identify the total number of elements in the population.
- Identify the sampling ratio (k = total population size divided by size of the desired sample).
- Identify the random start.
- Draw a sample by choosing every kth entry.

Invoices or customer accounts can be sampled by using the last digit or a combination of digits of an invoice or customer account number. Time sampling is also easily accomplished. Systematic sampling would be an appropriate technique for MindWriter's CompleteCare program evaluation.

While systematic sampling has some theoretical problems, from a practical point of view it is usually treated as a simple random sample. When similar population elements are grouped within the sampling frame, systematic sampling is statistically more efficient than a simple random sample. This might occur if the listed elements are ordered chronologically, by size, by class, and so on. Under these conditions, the sample approaches a proportional stratified sample. The effect of this ordering is more pronounced on the results of cluster samples than for element samples and may call for a proportional stratified sampling formula.[9]

A concern with systematic sampling is the possible *periodicity* in the population that parallels the sampling ratio. In sampling days of the week, a 1 in 7 sampling ratio would give biased results. A less obvious case might involve a survey in an area of apartment houses where the typical pattern is eight apartments per building. Many systematic sampling fractions, such as 1 in 8, could easily oversample some types of apartments and undersample others. The only protection against this is constant vigilance by the researcher.

Another difficulty may arise when there is a *monotonic trend* in the population elements. That is, the population list varies from the smallest to the largest element or vice versa. Even a chronological list may have this effect if a measure has trended in one direction over time. Whether a systematic sample drawn under these conditions provides a biased estimate of the population mean or proportion depends on the initial random draw. Assume that a list of 2,000 commercial banks is created, arrayed from the largest to the smallest, from which a sample of 50 must be drawn for analysis. A sampling ratio of 1 to 40 (begun with a random start at 16) drawing every 40th bank would exclude the 15 largest banks and give a small-size bias to the findings. Ways to deal with this concern include:

MANAGEMENT

- Randomize the population before sampling.
- Change the random start several times in the sampling process.
- Replicate a selection of different samples.

Stratified Sampling

Most populations can be segregated into several mutually exclusive subpopulations, or strata. The process by which the sample is constrained to include elements from each of the segments is called **stratified random sampling.** University students can be divided by their class level, school or major, gender, and so forth. After a population is divided into the appropriate strata, a simple random sample can be taken within each stratum. The sampling results can then be weighted and combined into appropriate population estimates.

There are three reasons why a researcher chooses a stratified random sample: (1) to increase a sample's statistical efficiency, (2) to provide adequate data for analyzing the various subpopulations, and (3) to enable different research methods and procedures to be used in different strata.[10]

Stratification is usually more efficient statistically than simple random sampling and at worst it is equal to it. With the ideal stratification, each stratum is homogeneous internally and heterogeneous with other strata. This might occur in a sample that includes members of several distinct ethnic groups. In this instance, stratification makes a pronounced improvement in statistical efficiency.

It is also useful when the researcher wants to study the characteristics of certain population subgroups. Thus, if one wishes to draw some conclusions about activities in the different classes of a student body, stratified sampling would be used. Stratification is also called for when different methods of data collection are applied in different parts of the population. This might occur when we survey company employees at the home office with one method but must use a different approach with employees scattered over the country.

If data are available on which to base a stratification decision, how shall we go about it?[11] The ideal stratification would be based on the primary variable under study. If the major concern is to learn how often per month patrons would use the dining club, then one would like to stratify on this expected number of use occasions. The only difficulty with this idea is that if we knew this information, we would not need to conduct the study. We must, therefore, pick a variable for stratifying that we believe will correlate with the frequency of club use per month, something like work or class schedule as an indication of when a sample element might be near campus at mealtime.

Researchers often have several important variables about which they want to draw conclusions. A reasonable approach is to seek some basis for stratification that correlates well with the major variables. It might be a single variable (class level), or it might be a compound variable (class by gender). In any event, we will have done a good stratifying job if the stratification base maximizes the difference among strata means and minimizes the within-stratum variances for the variables of major concern.

SNAPSHOT

IRI's Wal-Mart Solution

2001 ushered in a new year in retailing information for U.S. consumer packaged goods (CPG) manufacturers. Prior to August 1, Information Resources, Inc. (IRI), which purchased point-of-sale data from Wal-Mart and resold it in numerous forms to manufacturers, was restricted by contract from providing a client manufacturer with specific competitors' data. When the contract expired, Wal-Mart decided it would no longer sell its point-of-sale data. So, what does a syndicated research provider do when it loses access to the data of the world's largest retailer? It changes its sampling design.

Beginning in September, IRI introduced its InfoScan® Advantage service to monitor Wal-Mart activity with consumer panel data. But IRI needed to change the design of its existing panel to better reflect Wal-Mart's customers. IRI expanded its panel almost 20 percent—to 65,000

households—added more Hispanic and African-American households, and drew more households from rural counties. While the data will not be as detailed as in the past, Ed Kuehnle, IRI's group president of IRI North American, claims "InfoScan® Advantage will provide IRI customers [CPG manufacturers like Johnson & Johnson, PepsiCo and Procter & Gamble] with the most comprehensive and in-depth information possible from the available data sources." IRI panelists record purchases with calculator-size scanners. IRI provides a view of food, drug, mass merchandise, and Wal-Mart outlets in one integrated database. "This intelligence enhances the ability of IRI clients to reduce risk in new product introductions, optimize marketing investments, and effectively execute [marketing plans] at retail."

www.infores.com

The more strata used, the closer you come to maximizing interstrata differences (differences between stratum) and minimizing intrastratum variances (differences within a given stratum). You must base the decision partially on the number of subpopulation groups about which you wish to draw separate conclusions. Costs of stratification also enter the decision. There is little to be gained in estimating population values when the number of strata exceeds six.[12]

The size of the strata samples is calculated with two pieces of information: (1) how large the total sample should be and (2) how the total sample should be allocated among strata. In deciding how to allocate a total sample among various strata, there are proportionate and disproportionate options.

Proportionate versus Disproportionate Sampling   In **proportionate stratified sampling,** each stratum is properly represented so the sample drawn from it is proportionate to the stratum's share of the total population. This approach is more popular than any of the other stratified sampling procedures. Some reasons for this include:

- It has higher statistical efficiency than will a simple random sample.

- It is much easier to carry out than other stratifying methods.

- It provides a self-weighting sample; the population mean or proportion can be estimated simply by calculating the mean or proportion of all sample cases, eliminating the weighting of responses.

On the other hand, proportionate stratified samples often gain little in statistical efficiency if the strata measures and their variances are similar for the major variables under study.

Any stratification that departs from the proportionate relationship is **disproportionate.** There are several disproportionate allocation schemes. One type is a judgmentally determined disproportion based on the idea that each stratum is large enough to secure adequate confidence levels and interval range estimates for individual strata.

A researcher makes decisions regarding disproportionate sampling, however, by considering how a sample will be allocated among strata. One author states,

> In a given stratum, take a larger sample if the stratum is larger than other strata; the stratum is more variable internally; and sampling is cheaper in the stratum.[13]

If one uses these suggestions as a guide, it is possible to develop an optimal stratification scheme. When there is no difference in intrastratum variances and when the costs of sampling among strata are equal, the optimal design is a proportionate sample.

While disproportionate sampling is theoretically superior, there is some question as to whether it has wide applicability in a practical sense. If the differences in sampling costs or variances among strata are large, then disproportionate sampling is desirable. It has been suggested that "differences of several-fold are required to make disproportionate sampling worthwhile."[14]

The process for drawing a stratified sample is:

MANAGEMENT
Tip

- Determine the variables to use for stratification.

- Determine the proportions of the stratification variables in the population.

- Select proportionate or disproportionate stratification based on project information needs and risks.

- Divide the sampling frame into separate frames for each stratum.

- Randomize the elements within each stratum's sampling frame.

- Follow random or systematic procedures to draw the sample.

Cluster Sampling

In a simple random sample, each population element is selected individually. The population can also be divided into groups of elements with some groups randomly selected for study. This is **cluster sampling.** Cluster sampling differs from stratified sampling in several ways.

Stratified Sampling	Cluster Sampling
1. We divide the population into a few subgroups, each with many elements in it. The subgroups are selected according to some criterion that is related to the variables under study.	1. We divide the population into many subgroups, each with a few elements in it. The subgroups are selected according to some criterion of ease or availability in data collection.
2. We try to secure homogeneity within subgroups and heterogeneity between subgroups.	2. We try to secure heterogeneity within subgroups and homogeneity between subgroups, but we usually get the reverse.
3. We randomly choose elements from within each subgroup.	3. We randomly choose a number of the subgroups, which we then typically study in depth.

When done properly, cluster sampling also provides an unbiased estimate of population parameters. Two conditions foster the use of cluster sampling: (1) the need for more economic efficiency than can be provided by simple random sampling and (2) the frequent unavailability of a practical sampling frame for individual elements.

Statistical efficiency for cluster samples is usually lower than for simple random samples chiefly because clusters are usually homogeneous. Families in the same block (a typical cluster) are often similar in social class, income level, ethnic origin, and so forth.

While statistical efficiency in most cluster sampling may be low, economic efficiency is often great enough to overcome this weakness. The criterion, then, is the net relative efficiency resulting from the trade-off between economic and statistical factors. It may take 690 interviews with a cluster design to give the same precision as 424 simple random interviews. But if it costs only $5 per interview in the cluster situation and $10 in the simple random case, the cluster sample is more attractive ($3,450 versus $4,240).

Area Sampling   Much research involves populations that can be identified with some geographic area. When this occurs, it is possible to use **area sampling,** the most important form of cluster sampling. This method overcomes both the problems of high sampling cost and the unavailability of a practical sampling frame for individual elements. Area sampling methods have been applied to national populations, county populations, and even smaller areas where there are well-defined political or natural boundaries.

Suppose you want to survey the adult residents of a city. You would seldom be able to secure a listing of such individuals. It would be simple, however, to get a detailed city map that shows the blocks of the city. If you take a sample of these blocks, you are also taking a sample of the adult residents of the city.

Design   In designing cluster samples, including area samples, we must answer several questions:

1. How homogeneous are the clusters?

2. Shall we seek equal or unequal clusters?

3. How large a cluster shall we take?

4. Shall we use a single-stage or multistage cluster?

5. How large a sample is needed?

1. Clusters are homogeneous. This contributes to low statistical efficiency. Sometimes one can improve this efficiency by constructing clusters to increase intracluster variance. In the dining club study, the students might have constructed clusters that included members from all classes. In area sampling, they could combine adjoining blocks that contain different income groups or social classes. Area cluster sections do not have to be contiguous, but the cost savings is lost if they are not near each other.

2. A cluster sample may be composed of clusters of equal or unequal size. The theory of clustering is that the means of sample clusters are unbiased estimates of the population mean. This is more often true when clusters are equal. It is often possible to construct artificial clusters that are approximately equal, but natural clusters, such as households in city blocks, often vary substantially. While one can deal with clusters of unequal size, it may be desirable to reduce or counteract the effects of unequal size. There are several approaches to this:

MANAGEMENT
Tip

- Combine small clusters and split large clusters until each approximates an average size.

- Stratify clusters by size and choose clusters from each stratum.

- Stratify clusters by size and then subsample, using varying sampling fractions to secure an overall sampling ratio.

In this latter case, we may seek an overall sampling fraction of 1/60 and desire that subsamples contain five elements each. One group of clusters might average about 10 elements per cluster. In the "10 elements per cluster" stratum, we might choose 1 in 30 of the clusters and then subsample each chosen cluster at a 1/2 rate to secure the overall 1/60 sampling fraction. Among clusters of 120 elements, we might select clusters at a 1/3 rate and then subsample at a 1/20 rate to secure the 1/60 sampling fraction.[15]

3. The third question concerns the size of the cluster. There is no *a priori* answer to this question. Even with single-stage clusters, say, of 5, 20, or 50, it is not clear which size is superior. Some have found that in studies using single-stage clusters, the optimal cluster size is no larger than the typical city block.[16] Comparing the efficiency of the above three cluster sizes requires that we discover the different costs for each size and estimate the different variances of the cluster means.

4. The fourth question concerns whether to use a single-stage or a multistage cluster design. For most area sampling, especially large-scale studies, the tendency is to use multistage methods.

There are four reasons that justify subsampling, in preference to the direct creation of smaller clusters and their selection in one-stage cluster sampling:

- Natural clusters may exist as convenient sampling units yet may be larger than the desired economic size.

- We can avoid the cost of creating smaller clusters in the entire population and confine it to the selected sampling units.

- The effect of clustering . . . is often less in larger clusters. For example, a compact cluster of four dwellings from a city block may bring into the sample similar dwellings, perhaps from one building; but four dwellings selected separately can be spread around the dissimilar sides of the block.

- The sampling of compact clusters may present practical difficulties. For example, independent interviewing of all members of a household may seem impractical.[17]

5. The fifth question concerns how large a sample is needed—that is, how many subjects must be interviewed or observed. The answer to this question depends heavily on the specific cluster design, and these details can be complicated. Unequal clusters and multistage samples are the chief complications, and their statistical treatment is beyond the scope of this book.[18] Here we will treat only single-stage samples with equal-size clusters (called *simple cluster sampling*). It is analogous to simple random sampling. The simple random sample is really a special case of simple cluster sampling. We can think of a population as consisting of 20,000 clusters of one student each, or 2,000 clusters of 10 students each, and so on. The only difference between a simple random sample and a simple cluster sample is the size of cluster. Since this is so, we should expect that the calculation of a probability sample size would be the same for both types.

Double Sampling

It may be more convenient or economical to collect some information by sample and then use this information as the basis for selecting a subsample for further study. This procedure is called **double sampling, sequential sampling,** or **multiphase sampling.** It is usually found with stratified and/or cluster designs. The calculation procedures are described in more advanced texts.

Double sampling can be illustrated by the dining club example. You might use a telephone survey or another inexpensive survey method to discover who would be interested in joining such a club and the degree of their interest. You might then stratify the interested respondents by degree of interest and subsample among them for intensive interviewing on expected consumption patterns, reactions to various services, and so on. Whether it is more desirable to gather such information by one-stage or two-stage sampling depends largely on the relative costs of the two methods.

Because of the wide range of sampling designs available, it is often difficult to select an approach that meets the needs of the research question and helps to contain the costs of the project. To help with these choices, Exhibit 7–6 may be used to compare the various advantages and disadvantages of probability sampling. Nonprobability sampling techniques are covered in the next section. They are used frequently and offer the researcher the benefit of low cost. However, they are not based on a theoretical framework and do not operate from statistical theory; consequently, they produce selection bias and nonrepresentative samples. Despite these weaknesses, their widespread use demands their mention here.

Nonprobability Sampling

Any discussion of the relative merits of probability versus nonprobability sampling clearly shows the technical superiority of the former. In probability sampling, researchers use a random selection of elements to reduce or eliminate sampling bias. Under such conditions, we can have substantial confidence that the sample is representative of the population from which it is drawn. In addition, with probability sample

EXHIBIT 7–6   **Comparison of Probability Sampling Designs**

Type	Description	Advantages	Disadvantages
Simple random	Each population element has an equal chance of being selected into the sample. Sample drawn using random number table/generator.	Easy to implement with automatic dialing (random digit dialing) and with computerized voice response systems.	Requires a listing of population elements. Takes more time to implement. Uses larger sample sizes. Produces larger errors. Expensive.
Systematic	Selects an element of the population at a beginning with a random start and following the sampling fraction selects every kth element.	Simple to design. Easier to use than the simple random. Easy to determine sampling distribution of mean or proportion. Less expensive than simple random.	Periodicity within the population may skew the sample and results. If the population list has a monotonic trend, a biased estimate will result based on the start point.
Stratified	Divides population into subpopulations or strata and uses simple random on each strata. Results may be weighted and combined.	Researcher controls sample size in strata. Increased statistical efficiency. Provides data to represent and analyze subgroups. Enables use of different methods in strata.	Increased error will result if subgroups are selected at different rates. Expensive. Especially expensive if strata on the population have to be created.
Cluster	Population is divided into internally heterogeneous subgroups. Some are randomly selected for further study.	Provides an unbiased estimate of population parameters if properly done. Economically more efficient than simple random. Lowest cost per sample, especially with geographic clusters. Easy to do without a population list.	Often lower statistical efficiency (more error) due to subgroups being homogeneous rather than heterogeneous.
Double (sequential or multiphase)	Process includes collecting data from a sample using a previously defined technique. Based on the information found, a subsample is selected for further study.	May reduce costs if first stage results in enough data to stratify or cluster the population.	Increased costs if indiscriminately used.

designs, we can estimate an interval range within which the population parameter is expected to fall. Thus, we can not only reduce the chance for sampling error but also estimate the range of probable sampling error present.

With a subjective approach like nonprobability sampling, the probability of selecting population elements is unknown. There are a variety of ways to choose persons or cases to include in the sample. Often we allow the choice of subjects to be made by field workers on the scene. When this occurs, there is greater opportunity for bias to enter the sample selection procedure and to distort the findings of the study. Also, we cannot estimate any range within which to expect the population parameter. Given the technical advantages of probability sampling over nonprobability sampling, why would anyone choose the latter? There are some practical reasons for using these less precise methods.

Practical Considerations

We may use nonprobability sampling procedures because they satisfactorily meet the sampling objectives. While a random sample will give us a true cross section of the population, this may not be the objective of the research. If there is no desire or need to generalize to a population parameter, then there is much less concern about whether the sample fully reflects the population. Often researchers have more limited objectives. They may be looking only for the range of conditions or for examples of dramatic variations. This is especially true in exploratory research where one may wish to contact only certain persons or cases that are clearly atypical. Burbidge would have likely wanted a probability sample if the decision resting on the data was the actual design of the new CityBus routes and schedules. However, the decision of where and when to place advertising announcing the change is a relatively low-cost one in comparison.

Additional reasons for choosing nonprobability over probability sampling are cost and time. Probability sampling clearly calls for more planning and repeated callbacks to ensure that each selected sample member is contacted. These activities are expensive. Carefully controlled nonprobability sampling often seems to give acceptable results, so the investigator may not even consider probability sampling. Burbidge's results from Bus 99 would generate questionable data, but he seemed to realize the fallacy of many of his assumptions once he spoke with Bus 99's driver—something he should have done during exploration prior to designing the sampling plan.

While probability sampling may be superior in theory, there are breakdowns in its application. Even carefully stated random sampling procedures may be subject to careless application by the people involved. Thus, the ideal probability sampling may be only partially achieved because of the human element.

It is also possible that nonprobability sampling may be the only feasible alternative. The total population may not be available for study in certain cases. At the scene of a major event, it may be infeasible to even attempt to construct a probability sample. A study of past correspondence between two companies must use an arbitrary sample because the full correspondence is normally not available.

In another sense, those who are included in a sample may select themselves. In mail surveys, those who respond may not represent a true cross section of those who receive the questionnaire. The receivers of the questionnaire decide for themselves whether they will participate. There is some of this self-selection in almost all surveys because every respondent chooses whether or not to be interviewed.

Methods

Convenience   Nonprobability samples that are unrestricted are called **convenience samples.** They are the least reliable design but normally the cheapest and easiest to conduct. Researchers or field workers have the freedom to choose whomever they find, thus the name *convenience*. Examples include informal pools of friends and neighbors, people responding to a newspaper's invitation for readers to state their positions on some public issue or a TV reporter's "man-on-the-street" intercept interviews, or using employees to evaluate the taste of a new snack food.

While a convenience sample has no controls to ensure precision, it may still be a useful procedure. Often you will take such a sample to test ideas or even to gain ideas about a subject of interest. In the early stages of exploratory research, when you are seeking guidance, you might use this approach. The results may present evidence that is so overwhelming that a more sophisticated sampling procedure is unnecessary. In an interview with students concerning some issue of campus concern, you might talk to 25 students selected sequentially. You might discover that the responses are so overwhelmingly one-sided that there is no incentive to interview further.

Purposive Sampling   A nonprobability sample that conforms to certain criteria is called *purposive sampling*. There are two major types—judgment sampling and quota sampling.

Judgment sampling occurs when a researcher selects sample members to conform to some criterion. In a study of labor problems, you may want to talk only with those who have experienced on-the-job discrimination. Another example of judgment sampling occurs when election results are predicted from only a few selected precincts that have been chosen because of their predictive record in past elections. Burbidge chose Bus 99 because the current route between East City and West City led him to believe that he could get a representation of both East City and West City riders.

When used in the early stages of an exploratory study, a judgment sample is appropriate. When one wishes to select a biased group for screening purposes, this sampling method is also a good choice. Companies often try out new product ideas on their employees. The rationale is that one would expect the firm's employees to be more favorably disposed toward a new product idea than the public. If the product does not pass this group, it does not have prospects for success in the general market.

Quota sampling is the second type of purposive sampling. We use it to improve representativeness. The logic behind quota sampling is that certain relevant characteristics describe the dimensions of the population. If a sample has the same distribution on these characteristics, then it is likely to be representative of the population regarding other variables on which we have no control. Suppose the student body of Metro U is 55 percent female and 45 percent male. The sampling quota would call for sampling students at a 55 to 45 percent ratio. This would eliminate distortions due to a nonrepresentative gender ratio. Burbidge could have improved his nonprobability sampling by considering time of day and day of week variations and choosing to distribute surveys to Bus 99 riders at various times, thus creating a quota sample.

In most quota samples, researchers specify more than one control dimension. Each should meet two tests: It should (1) have a distribution in the population that we can estimate, and (2) be pertinent to the topic studied. We may believe that responses to a question should vary, depending on the gender of the respondent. If so, we should seek proportional responses from both men and women. We may also feel that undergraduates differ from graduate students, so this would be a dimension. Other dimensions, such as the student's academic discipline, ethnic group, religious affiliation, and social group affiliation, also may be chosen. Only a few of these controls can be used. To illustrate, suppose we consider the following:

Gender: Two categories—male, female.

Class level: Two categories—graduate, undergraduate.

College: Six categories—Arts and Science, Agriculture, Architecture, Business, Engineering, other.

Religion: Four categories—Protestant, Catholic, Jewish, other.

Fraternal affiliation: Two categories—member, nonmember.

Family social-economic class: Three categories—upper, middle, lower.

In an extreme case, we might ask an interviewer to find a male undergraduate business student who is Catholic, a fraternity member, and from an upper-class home. All combinations of these six factors would call for 288 such cells to consider. This type of control is known as *precision control.* It gives greater assurance that a sample will be representative of the population. However, it is costly and too difficult to carry out with more than three variables.

When we wish to use more than three control dimensions, we should depend on *frequency control.* With this form of control, the overall percentage of those with each characteristic in the sample should match the percentage holding the same characteristic in the population. No attempt is made to find a combination of specific characteristics in a single person. In frequency control, we would probably find that the accompanying sample array is an adequate reflection of the population:

	Population	Sample
Male	65%	67%
Married	15	14
Undergraduate	70	72
Campus resident	30	28
Independent	75	73
Protestant	39	42

Quota sampling has several weaknesses. First, the idea that quotas on some variables assume a representativeness on others is argument by analogy. It gives no assurance that the sample is representative of the variables being studied. Often, the data used to provide controls may also be outdated or inaccurate. There is also a practical limit on the number of simultaneous controls that can be applied to ensure precision. Finally, the choice of subjects is left to field workers to make on a judgmental basis. They may choose only friendly looking people, people who are convenient to them, and so forth.

Despite the problems with quota sampling, it is widely used by opinion pollsters and marketing and other researchers. Probability sampling is usually much more costly and time-consuming. Advocates of quota sampling argue that while there is some danger of systematic bias, the risks are usually not that great. Where predictive validity has been checked (e.g., in election polls), quota sampling has been generally satisfactory.

Snowball This design has found a niche in recent years in applications where respondents are difficult to identify and are best located through referral networks.

In the initial stage of **snowball sampling,** individuals are discovered and may or may not be selected through probability methods. This group is then used to locate others who possess similar characteristics and who, in turn, identify others. Similar to a reverse search for bibliographic sources, the "snowball" gathers subjects as it rolls along. Various techniques are available for selecting a nonprobability snowball with provisions for error identification and statistical testing. Let's consider a brief example.

The high end of the U.S. audio market is composed of several small firms that produce ultra-expensive components used in recording and playback of live performances. A risky new technology for improving digital signal processing is being contemplated by one firm. Through its contacts with a select group of recording engineers and electronics designers, the first-stage sample may be identified for interviewing. Subsequent interviewees are likely to reveal critical information for product development and marketing.

Variations on snowball sampling have been used to study drug cultures, teenage gang activities, power elites, community relations, insider trading, and other applications where respondents are difficult to identify and contact.

Close-Up

Applying Concepts

In the Metro University Dining Club study, we explore probability sampling and the various concepts used to design the sampling process.

Exhibit 7–7 shows the Metro U Dining Club study population ($N = 20,000$) consisting of five subgroups based on their preferred lunch times. The values 1 through 5 represent the preferred lunch times of 11:00 A.M., 11:30 A.M., 12:00 noon, 12:30 P.M., and 1:00 P.M. The frequency of response (f) in the population distribution, shown beside the population subgroup, is what would be found if a census of the elements was taken. Normally, population data are unavailable or are too costly to obtain. We are pretending omniscience for the sake of the example.

Now assume we sample 10 elements from this population without knowledge of the population's characteristics. We use a sampling procedure from a statistical software program, a random number generator, or a table of random numbers. Our first sample ($n_1 = 10$) provides us with the frequencies shown below sample n_1 in Exhibit 7–7. We also calculate a mean score, $X_1 = 3.0$, for this sample. This mean would place the average preferred lunch time at 12:00 noon. The mean is a *point estimate* and our best predictor of the unknown population mean, μ (the arithmetic average of the population). Assume further that we return the first sample to the population and draw a second, third, and fourth sample by the same pro-

cedure. The frequencies, means, and standard deviations are as shown in the exhibit. As the data suggest, each sample shares some similarities with the population, but none is a perfect duplication because no sample perfectly replicates its population.

We cannot judge which estimate is the true mean (accurately reflects the population mean). However, we can estimate the interval in which the true μ will fall by using any of the samples. This is accomplished by using a formula that computes the **standard error of the mean.**

$$\sigma_{\bar{X}} = \frac{\sigma}{\sqrt{n}}$$

where

$\sigma_{\bar{X}}$ = Standard error of the mean or the standard deviation of all possible $\bar{X}$s

σ = Population standard deviation

n = Sample size

The standard error of the mean measures the standard deviation of the distribution of sample means. It varies directly with the standard deviation of the population from which it is drawn: If the standard deviation is reduced by 50 percent, the standard error will also be reduced by 50 percent. It also varies inversely with the square root of the sample size. If the square root of the sample size is doubled, the standard error is cut by one-half, provided the standard deviation remains constant.

EXHIBIT 7–7   **Random Samples of Preferred Lunch Times**

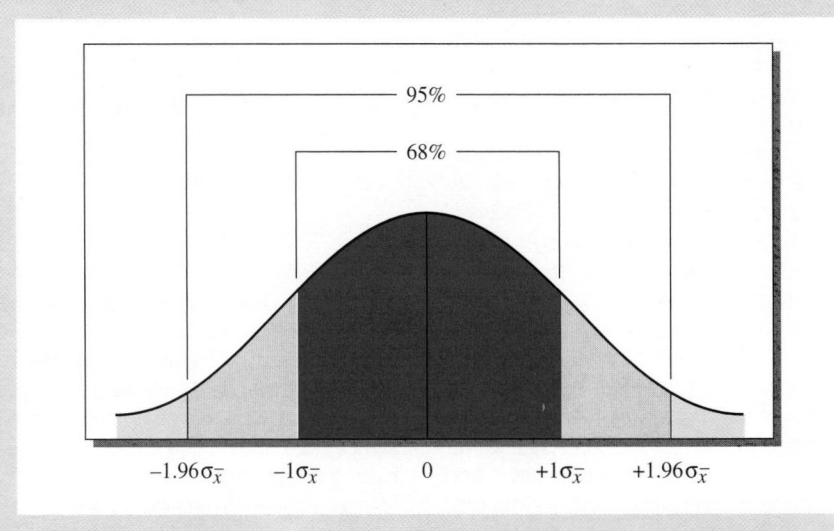

Population of preferred lunch times

	Y = Time	f
1	11:00 A.M.	2,000
2	11:30 A.M.	4,000
3	12:00 P.M.	7,000
4	12:30 P.M.	4,000
5	1:00 P.M.	3,000
		N = 20,000

μ = 3.1 or 12:01 P.M.
σ = .74 or 22.2 minutes

Samples

n_1

Y	f
1	1
2	2
3	4
4	2
5	1
n_1 =	10

$\overline{X}_1$ = 3.0
s = 1.1

n_2

Y	f
1	1
2	2
3	5
4	2
5	0
n_2 =	10

$\overline{X}_2$ = 2.8
s = 0.92

n_3

Y	f
1	0
2	1
3	5
4	1
5	3
n_3 =	10

$\overline{X}_3$ = 3.6
s = 1.07

n_4

Y	f
1	1
2	1
3	3
4	4
5	1
n_4 =	10

$\overline{X}_4$ = 3.3
s = 1.16

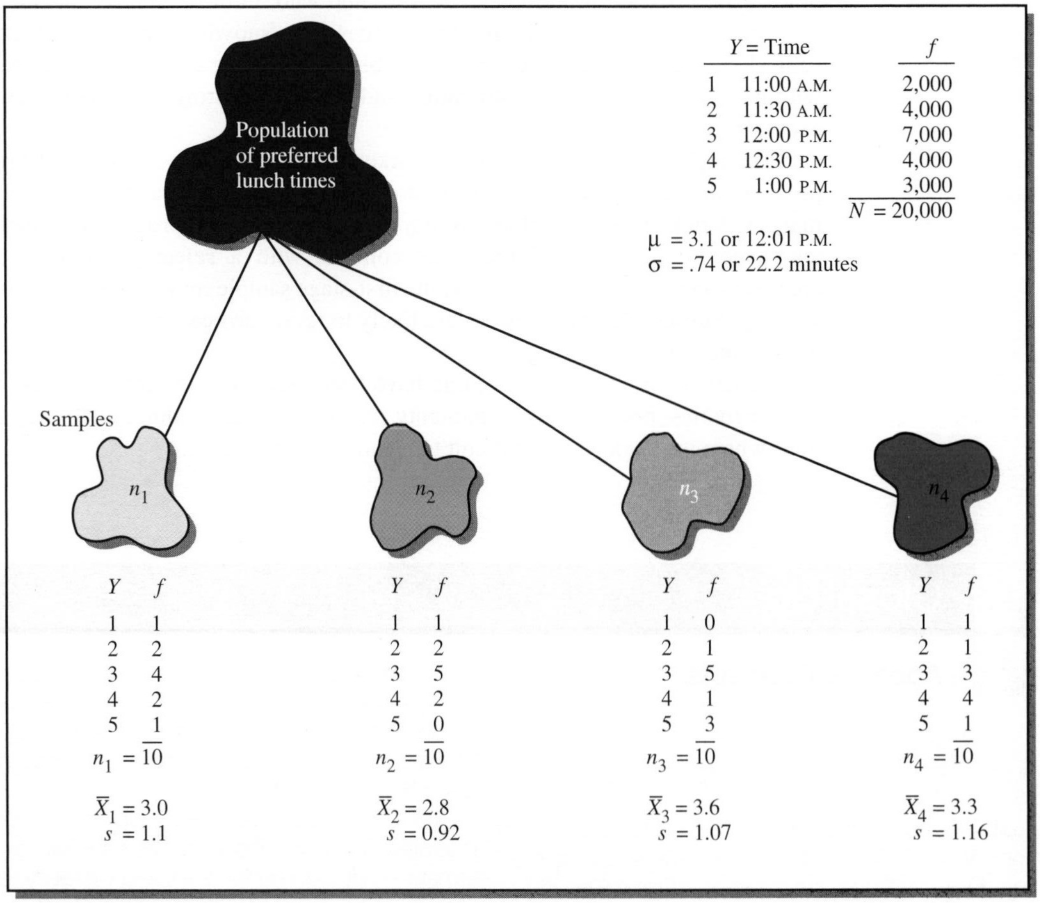

EXHIBIT 7–8   **Confidence Levels and the Normal Curve**

95%

68%

$-1.96\sigma_{\overline{x}}$ $-1\sigma_{\overline{x}}$ 0 $+1\sigma_{\overline{x}}$ $+1.96\sigma_{\overline{x}}$

Reducing the Standard Deviation	Doubling the Square Root of Sample Size
$$\sigma_{\bar{X}} = \frac{.74}{\sqrt{10}} = .234$$	$$\sigma_{\bar{X}} = \frac{.8}{\sqrt{25}} = .16$$
$$\sigma_{\bar{X}} = \frac{s}{\sqrt{n}} \qquad \sigma_{\bar{X}} = \frac{.37}{\sqrt{10}} = .117$$	$$\sigma_{\bar{X}} = \frac{.8}{\sqrt{100}} = .08$$

Let's now examine what happens when we apply sample data (n_1) from Exhibit 7–7 to the formula. The sample standard deviation will be used as an unbiased estimator of the population standard deviation.

$$\sigma_{\bar{X}} = \frac{s}{\sqrt{n}}$$

where

s = Standard deviation of the sample, n_1

$n_1 = 10$

$\bar{X}_1 = 3.0$

$s_1 = 1.15$

Substituting into the equation:

$$\sigma_{\bar{X}} = \frac{s}{\sqrt{n}} = \frac{1.15}{\sqrt{10}} = .36$$

How does this improve our prediction of μ from $\bar{X}$? The standard error creates the interval range that brackets the point estimate. In this example, μ is predicted to be 3.0 or 12:00 noon (the mean of n_1) $\pm$ .36. This range may be visualized on a continuum:

We would expect to find the true μ between 2.64 and 3.36—between 11:49 A.M. and 12:11 P.M. (If 2 = 11:30 A.M. and .64 (30 minutes) = 19.2 minutes, then 2.64 = 11:30 A.M. + 19.2 minutes, or 11:49 A.M.) Since we assume omniscience for this illustration, we know the population average value is 3.1. Further, because standard errors have characteristics like other standard scores, we have 68 percent confidence in this estimate—that is, one standard error encompasses ± 1 Z or 68 percent of the area under the normal curve (see Exhibit 7–8). Recall that the area under the curve also represents the confidence estimates that we make about our results. The combination of the interval range and the degree of confidence creates the **confidence interval.** To improve confidence to 95 percent, multiply the standard error of .36 by ± 1.96 (Z), since 1.96 Z covers 95 percent of the area under the curve (see Exhibit 7–9). Now, with 95 percent confidence, the interval in which we would find the true mean increases to $\pm .70$ (from 2.3 to 3.7 or from 11:39 A.M. to 12:21 A.M.).

Parenthetically, if we compute the standard deviation of the distribution of sample means [3.0, 2.8, 3.6, 3.3], we will discover it to be .35. Compare this to the standard error from the original calculation (.36). The result is consistent

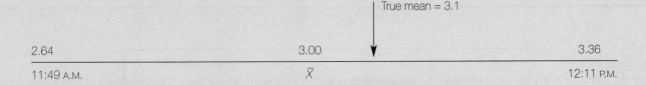

2.64	3.00	True mean = 3.1	3.36
11:49 A.M.	$\bar{X}$		12:11 P.M.

EXHIBIT 7–9 Standard Errors Associated with Areas under the Normal Curve

Standard Error (Z)	Percent of Area*	Approximate Degree of Confidence
1.00	68.27	68%
1.65	90.10	90
1.96	95.00	95
3.00	99.73	99

*Includes both tails in a normal distribution.

with the second definition of the standard error: the standard deviation of the distribution of sample means (n_1, n_2, n_3, and n_4). Now let's return to the dining club example and apply some of these concepts to the researchers' problem.

If the researchers were to interview all the students and employees in the defined population, asking them, "How many times per month would you eat at the club?" they would get a distribution something like that shown in Part A of Exhibit 7–10. The responses would range from zero to as many as 30 lunches per month with a μ and σ.

However, they cannot take a census, so μ and σ remain unknown. By sampling, the researchers find the

EXHIBIT 7–10   **A Comparison of Population Distribution, Sample Distribution, and Distribution of Sample Means of Metro U Dining Club Study**

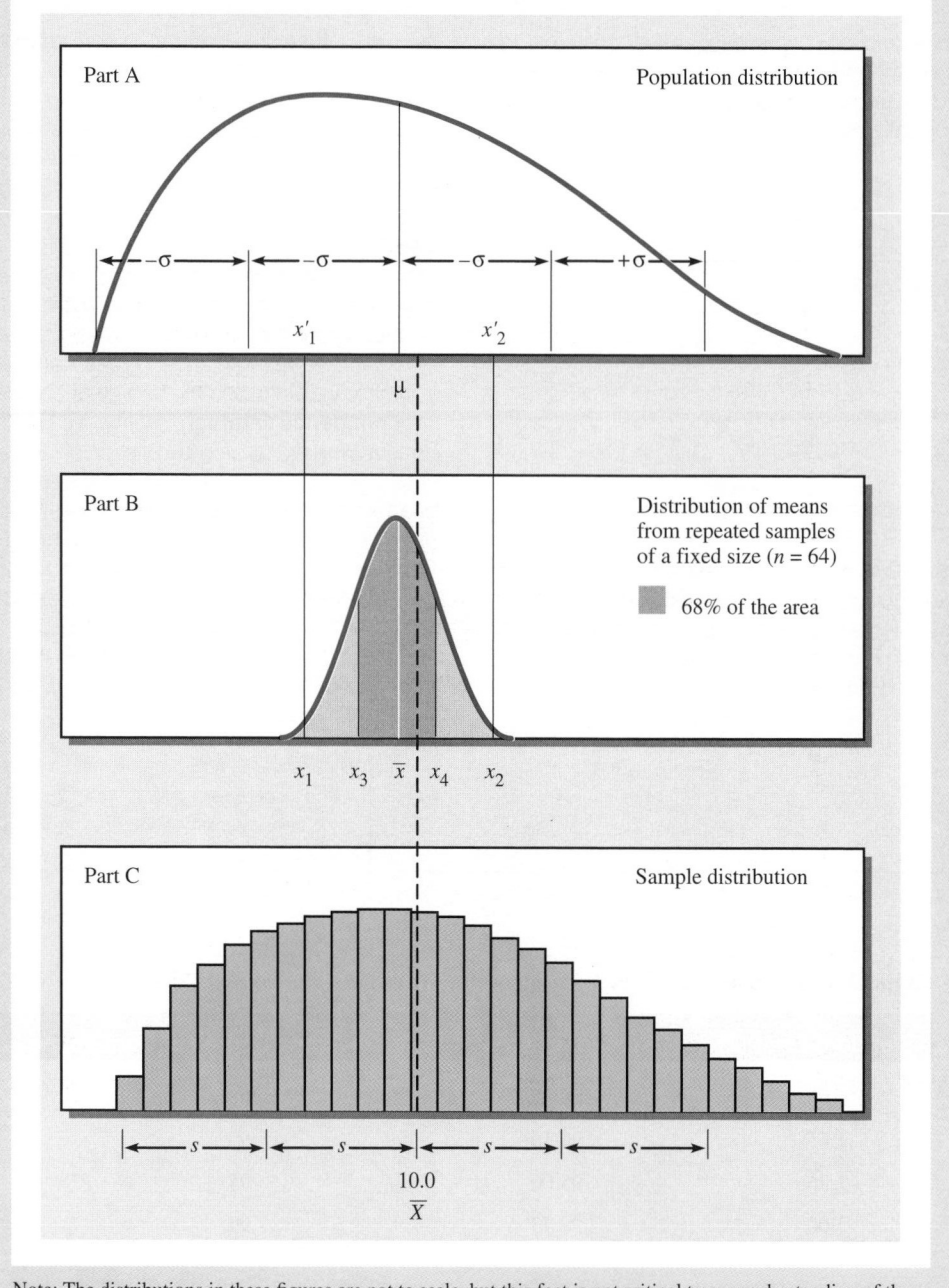

Note: The distributions in these figures are not to scale, but this fact is not critical to our understanding of the dispersion relationship depicted.

mean to be 10.0 and the standard deviation to be 4.1 eating experiences (how often they would eat at the club per month). Turning to Part C of Exhibit 7–10, three observations about this sample distribution are consistent with our earlier illustration. First, it is shown as a histogram; it represents a frequency distribution of empirical data, while the smooth curve of Part A is a theoretical distribution. Second, the sample distribution (Part C) is similar in appearance but is not a perfect duplication of the population distribution (Part A). Third, the mean of the sample differs from the mean of the population.

If the researchers could draw repeated samples as we did earlier, they could plot the mean of each sample to secure the solid line distribution found in Part B. According to the **central limit theorem,** for sufficiently large samples ($n = 30$), the sample means will be distributed around the population mean approximately in a normal distribution. Even if the population is not normally distributed, the distribution of sample means will be normal if there is a large enough set of samples.

Estimating the Interval for the Metro U Dining Club Sample Any sample mean will fall within the range of the distribution extremes shown in Part B of Exhibit 7–10. We also know that about 68 percent of the sample means in this distribution will fall between x_3 and x_4 and 95 percent will fall between x_1 and x_2.

If we project points x_1 and x_2 up to the population distribution (Part A of Exhibit 7–10) at points x'_1 and x'_2, we see the interval where any given mean of a random sample of 64 is likely to fall 95 percent of the time. Since we will not know the population mean from which to measure the standard error, we infer that there is also a 95 percent chance that the population mean is within two standard errors of the sample mean (10.0). This inference enables us to find the sample mean, mark off an interval around it, and state a confidence likelihood that the population mean is within this bracket.

Because the researchers are considering an investment in this project, they would want some assurance that the population mean is close to the figure reported in any sample they take. To find out how close the population mean is to the sample mean, they must calculate the standard error of the mean and estimate an interval range within which the population mean is likely to be.

Given a sample size of 64, they still need a value for the standard error. Almost never will one have the value for the standard deviation of the population (σ), so we must use a proxy figure. The best proxy for σ is the standard deviation of the sample (s). Here the standard deviation ($s = 4.1$) was obtained from a pilot sample:

$$\sigma_{\bar{X}} = \frac{s}{\sqrt{n}} = \frac{4.1}{\sqrt{64}} = .51$$

If one standard error of the mean is equal to 0.51 visits, then 1.96 standard errors (95 percent) are equal to 1.0 visit. The students can estimate with 95 percent confidence that the population mean of expected visits is within 10.0 ± 1.0 visit, or from 9.0 to 11.0 meal visits per month. We discuss pilot tests as part of the pretest phase in Chapter 12.

Changing Confidence Intervals The above estimate may not be satisfactory in two ways. First, it may not represent the degree of confidence the researchers want in the interval estimate, considering their financial risk. They might want a higher degree of confidence than the 95 percent level used here. By referring to a table of areas under the normal curve, they can find various other combinations of probability. Exhibit 7–11 summarizes some of those more commonly used. Thus, if the students want a greater confidence in the probability of including the population mean in the interval range, they can move to a higher standard error, say, $\bar{X} \pm 3 \sigma_X$. Now the population mean lies somewhere between $10.0 \pm 3 (0.51)$ or from 8.47 to 11.53. With 99.73 percent confidence, we can say this interval will include the population mean.

We might wish to have an estimate that will hold for a much smaller range, for example, 10.0 ± 0.2. To secure this smaller interval range, we must either (1) accept a lower level of confidence in the results or (2) take a sample large enough to provide this smaller interval with the higher desired confidence level.

If one standard error is equal to 0.51 visits, then 0.2 visits would be equal to 0.39 standard errors ($0.2/0.51 = .39$). Referring to a table of areas under the normal curve (Appendix F, Table F–1), we find that there is a 30.3 percent chance that the true population mean lies within ± 0.39 standard errors of 10.0. With a sample of 64, the sample

EXHIBIT 7–11 Estimates Associated with Various Confidence Levels in the Metro U Dining Club Study

Approximate Degree of Confidence	Interval Range of Dining Visits per Month
68%	μ is between 9.48 and 10.52 visits
90	μ is between 9.14 and 10.86 visits
95	μ is between 8.98 and 11.02 visits
99	μ is between 8.44 and 11.56 visits

mean would be subject to so much error variance that only 30 percent of the time could the researchers expect to find the population mean between 9.8 and 10.2. This is such a low level of confidence that the researchers would normally move to the second alternative; they would increase the sample size until they could secure the desired interval estimate and degree of confidence.

Calculating the Sample Based on Critical Investigative Questions   The researchers have selected two investigative question constructs as critical—"frequency of patronage" and "interest in joining"—because they believe both to be crucial to making the correct decision on the Metro U Dining Club opportunity. The first requires a point

estimate, the second a proportion. By way of review, decisions needed and decisions made by Metro U researchers are summarized in Exhibit 7–12.

With reference to precision, the 95 percent confidence level is often used, but more or less confidence may be needed in light of the risks of any given project. Similarly, the size of the interval estimate for predicting the population parameter from the sample data should be decided. When a smaller interval is selected, the researcher is saying that precision is vital, largely because inherent risks are high. For example, on a five-point measurement scale, one-tenth of a point is a very high degree of precision in comparison to a one-point interval. Given that a patron could eat up to

EXHIBIT 7–12   **Metro U Sampling Design Decisions on "Meal Frequency" and "Joining" Constructs**

Decision Issues	Metro U Decisions	
	"Meal Frequency" (interval, ratio data)	"Joining" (nominal, ordinal data)
1. The precision desired and how to quantify it:		
• The confidence researcher wants in the estimate (selected based on risk).	95% confidence ($Z = 1.96$)	95% confidence ($Z = 1.96$)
• The size of the interval estimate the researcher will accept (selected based on risk).	± .5 meals per month per person	± .10 (10 percent)
2. The expected dispersion in the population for the question used to measure precision:	0 to 30 meals	0 to 100%
• Sample mean.		
• Standard deviation.	4.1 meals	
• Sample proportion of population with the given attribute being measured.		30%
• Measure of the sample dispersion.		$pq = .30(1 - .30) = 0.21$
3. Whether a finite population adjustment should be used.	No	No
4. Estimate of standard deviation of population:		
• Standard error of mean.	.5/1.96 = 2.55	
• Standard error of the proportion.		.10/1.96 = 0.051
5. Sample size formula	Formula from page 209	Formula from page 210
6. Sample size	$n = 259^*$	$n = 96$

*Because both investigative questions were of interest, the researcher would use the larger of the two sample sizes calculated, $n = 259$, for the study.

30 meals per month at the dining club (30 days times one meal per day), anything less than one meal per day would be asking for a high degree of precision in the Metro U study. The high risk of the Metro U study warrants the 0.5 meal precision selected.

The next factor that affects the size of the sample for a given level of precision is the population dispersion. The smaller the possible dispersion, the smaller will be the sample needed to give a representative picture of population members. If the population's number of meals ranges from 18 to 25, a smaller sample will give us an accurate estimate of the population's average meal consumption. However, with a population dispersion ranging from 0 to 30 meals consumed, a larger sample is needed for the same degree of confidence in the estimates. Since the true population dispersion of estimated meals per month eaten at Metro U Dining Club is unknowable, the standard deviation of the sample is used as a proxy figure. Typically, this figure is based on any of the following:

- Previous research on the topic.
- A pilot test or pretest of the data instrument among a sample drawn from the population.
- A rule of thumb (one-sixth of the range based on six standard deviations within 99.73 percent confidence).

If the range is from 0 to 30 meals, the rule-of-thumb method produces a standard deviation of five meals. The researchers want more precision than the rule-of-thumb method provides, so they take a pilot sample of 25 and find the standard deviation to be 4.1 meals.

A final factor affecting the size of a random sample is the size of the population. When the size of the sample exceeds 5 percent of the population, the finite limits of the population constrain the sample size needed. A correction factor is available in that event.

The sample size is computed for the first construct, meal frequency, as follows:

$$\sigma_{\bar{X}} = \frac{s}{\sqrt{n}}$$

$$\sqrt{n} = \frac{s}{\sigma_{\bar{X}}}$$

$$n = \frac{s^2}{\sigma_{\bar{X}}}$$

$$n = \frac{(4.1)^2}{(.255)^2}$$

$$n = 258.5 \text{ or } 259$$

where

$$\sigma_{\bar{X}} = 0.255 \ (0.5/1.96)$$

If the researchers are willing to accept a larger interval range (± 1 meal), and thus a larger amount of risk, then they can reduce the sample size to $n = 65$.

Calculating the Sample Size for the Proportions Question The second key question concerning the dining club study was: "What percentage of the population says it would join the dining club, based on the projected rates and services?" In business, we often deal with proportion data. An example is a CNN poll that projects the percentage of people who expect to vote for or against a proposition or a candidate. This is usually reported with a margin of error of ±5 percent.

In the Metro U study, a pretest answers this question using the same general procedure as before. But instead of the arithmetic mean, with proportions, it is p (the proportion of the population that has a given attribute)[19]—in this case, interest in joining the dining club. And instead of the standard deviation, dispersion is measured in terms of $p \times q$ (in which q is the proportion of the population not having the attribute, and $q = (1 - p)$. The measure of dispersion of the sample statistic also changes from the standard error of the mean to the standard error of the proportion σ_p.

We calculate a sample size based on this data by making the same two subjective decisions—deciding on an acceptable interval estimate and the degree of confidence. Assume that from a pilot test, 30 percent of the students and employees say they will join the dining club. We decide to estimate the true proportion in the population within 10 percentage points of this figure ($p = 0.30 \pm 0.10$). Assume further that we want to be 95 percent confident that the population parameter is within ± 0.10 of the sample proportion. The calculation of the sample size proceeds as before:

$\pm\, 0.10$ = Desired interval range within which the population proportion is expected (subjective decision).

$1.96 \ \sigma_p$ = 95 percent confidence level for estimating the interval within which to expect the population proportion (subjective decision).

$\sigma_p = 0.051$ = Standard error of the proportion (0.10/1.96).

pq = Measure of sample dispersion (used here as an estimate of the population dispersion).

$$\sigma_p = \sqrt{\frac{pq}{n}}$$

$$n = \frac{pq}{\sigma_p^2}$$

$$n = \frac{.03 \times .07}{(.051)^2}$$

$$n = 81$$

The sample size of 81 persons is based on an infinite population assumption. If the sample size is less than 5 percent of the population, there is little to be gained by using a finite population adjustment. The students interpreted the data found with a sample of 81 chosen randomly from the population as: "We can be 95 percent confident that 30 percent of the respondents would say they would join the dining club with a margin of error of ±10 percent."

Previously, the researchers used pilot testing to generate the variance estimate for the calculation. Suppose this is not an option. Proportions data have a feature concerning the variance that is not found with interval or ratio data. The pq ratio can never exceed 0.25. For example, if $p = 0.5$, then $q = 0.5$, and their product is 0.25. If either p or q is greater than 0.5, then their product is smaller than 0.25 ($0.4 \times 0.6 = 0.24$, and so on). When we have no information regarding the probable p value, we can assume that $p = 0.5$ and solve for the sample size.

$$n = \frac{pq}{\sigma_p^2}$$

$$n = \frac{0.25}{(.051)^2}$$

$$n = 96$$

If we use this maximum variance estimate in the dining club example, we find the sample size needs to be 96 persons.

SUMMARY

1 Sampling is based on two premises. One is that there is enough similarity among the elements in a population that a few of these elements will adequately represent the characteristics of the total population. The second premise is that while some elements in a sample underestimate a population value, others overestimate this value. The result of these tendencies is that a sample statistic such as the arithmetic mean is generally a good estimate of a population mean.

2 A good sample has both accuracy and precision. An accurate sample is one in which there is little or no bias or systematic variance. A sample with adequate precision is one that has a sampling error that is within acceptable limits for the study's purpose.

3 A variety of sampling techniques is available. They may be classified by their representation basis and element selection techniques as shown in the accompanying table.

Probability sampling is based on random selection—a controlled procedure that ensures that each population element is given a known nonzero chance of selection. In contrast, nonprobability selection is "not random." When each sample element is drawn

	Representation Basis	
Element Selection	**Probability**	**Nonprobability**
Unrestricted	Simple random	Convenience
Restricted	Complex random	Purposive
	Systematic	Judgment
	Cluster	Quota
	Stratified	Snowball
	Double	

individually from the population at large, it is unrestricted sampling. Restricted sampling covers those forms of sampling in which the selection process follows more complex rules.

4 The simplest type of probability approach is simple random sampling. In this design, each member of the population has an equal chance of being included in a sample. In developing a probability sample, six procedural questions need to be answered:

1. What is the relevant population?
2. What are the parameters of interest?
3. What is the sampling frame?
4. What is the type of sample?
5. What size sample is needed?
6. How much will it cost?

Two kinds of estimates of a population parameter are made in probability sampling. First we make a point estimate that is the single best estimate of the population value. Then we make an interval estimate that covers the range of values within which we expect the population value to occur, with a given degree of confidence. All sample-based estimates of population parameters should be stated in terms of a confidence interval.

5 The specifications of the researcher and the nature of the population determine the size of a probability sample. These requirements are largely expressed in the following questions:

- What is the degree of confidence we want in our parameter estimate?
- How large an interval range will we accept?
- What is the degree of variance in the population?
- Is the population small enough that the sample should be adjusted for finite population?

Cost considerations are also often incorporated into the sample size decision.

6 Complex sampling is used when conditions make simple random samples impractical or uneconomical. The four major types of complex random sampling discussed in this chapter are systematic, stratified, cluster, and double sampling. Systematic sampling involves the selection of every kth element in the population, beginning with a random start between elements from 1 to k. Its simplicity in certain cases is its greatest value.

Stratified sampling is based on dividing a population into subpopulations and then randomly sampling from each of these strata. This method usually results in a smaller total sample size than would a simple random design. Stratified samples may be proportionate or disproportionate.

In cluster sampling, we divide the population into convenient groups and then randomly choose the groups to study. It is typically less efficient from a statistical viewpoint than the simple random because of the high degree of homogeneity within the clusters. Its great advantage is its savings in cost—if the population is dispersed geographically—or in time. The most widely used form of clustering is area sampling, in which geographic areas are the selection elements.

At times it may be more convenient or economical to collect some information by sample and then use it as a basis for selecting a subsample for further study. This procedure is called double sampling.

Nonprobability sampling also has some compelling practical advantages that account for its widespread use. Often probability sampling is not feasible because the population is not available. Then, too, frequent breakdowns in the application of probability sampling discount its technical advantages. You find also that a true cross section is often not the aim of the researcher. Here the goal may be the discovery of the range or extent of conditions. Finally, nonprobability sampling is usually less expensive to conduct than is probability sampling.

Convenience samples are the simplest and least reliable forms of nonprobability sampling. Their primary virtue is low cost. One purposive sample is the judgmental sample in which one is interested in studying only selected types of subjects. The other purposive sample is the quota sample. Subjects are selected to conform to certain predesignated control measures that secure a representative cross section of the population. Snowball sampling uses a referral approach to reach particularly hard-to-find respondents.

KEY TERMS

area sampling   196
census   179
central limit theorem   207
cluster sampling   196
confidence interval   205
convenience samples   200
double sampling   198
judgment sampling   201
multiphase sampling   198
nonprobability sampling   183

population   179
population element   179
population parameters   186
population proportion of
    incidence   187
probability sampling   183
quota sampling   201
sample statistics   186
sampling   179
sampling error   181

sampling frame   188
sequential sampling   198
simple random sample   184
snowball sampling   203
standard error of the mean   203
stratified random sampling   193
    disproportionate   195
    proportionate   195
systematic sampling   192
systematic variance   181

EXAMPLES

Company	Scenario	Page
ABC News	Commissioned TNS Intersearch to conduct numerous opinion polls following the September 11, 2001, attacks on the World Trade Center and the Pentagon.	180
CityBus*	A city transit authority is determining how to best promote a new route structure to current and potential riders.	BRTL and throughout
CNN	With *USA Today*, commissioned opinion polling after the September 11, 2001, attacks on the World Trade Center and the Pentagon.	180
Gallup Organization	Conducted opinion polling after the September 11, 2001, attacks on World Trade Center and the Pentagon for CNN and *USA Today*.	180
Hart/Teeter	Conducted opinion polling after the September 11, 2001, attacks on the World Trade Center and the Pentagon for NBC and *The Wall Street Journal*.	180

Henry J. Kaiser Family Foundation (KFF)	Conducted a benchmark study on U.S. public and private school sex education among teens, their parents, teachers, and principals.	185
Information Resources Inc. (IRI)	Syndicated research supplier to CPG manufacturers forced to redesign its sampling and research design when Wal-Mart chose not to renegotiate its contract to supply point-of-sale data; introduced InfoScan® Advantage.	194
Literary Digest	Published a 1936 presidential election poll that falsely predicted a Republican victory.	181
Metro University*	A study conducted to determine the feasibility of starting a membership-only dining club near campus.	182 and throughout
MindWriter*	A laptop manufacturer conducting a service program satisfaction study.	182 and throughout
NBC News	Commissioned Hart/Teeter to conduct opinion polls after the September 11, 2001, attacks on the World Trade Center and the Pentagon.	180
Princeton Survey Research Associates	The survey research organization commissioned by the Henry J. Kaiser Family Foundation for its study on sex education in America.	185
TaylorNelson Sofres (TNS) Intersearch	Conducted opinion polling after the September 11, 2001, attacks on the World Trade Center and the Pentagon for ABC News and *The Washington Post*.	180
U.S. Bureau of the Census	Substituting statistical sampling in the decennial census.	179, 191
USA Today	Commissioned Gallup to conduct opinion polling after the September 11, 2001, attacks on the World Trade Center and the Pentagon.	180
The Wall Street Journal	With NBC News, commissioned Hart/Teeter to conduct opinion polling after the September 11, 2001, attacks on the World Trade Center and the Pentagon.	180
The Washington Post	Commissioned TNS Intersearch to conduct opinion polling following the September 11, 2001, attacks on the World Trade Center and the Pentagon.	180

*Due to the confidential and proprietary nature of most research, the names of some companies have been changed.

DISCUSSION QUESTIONS

Terms in Review

1. Distinguish between

   a. Statistic and parameter.

   b. Sample frame and population.

   c. Restricted and unrestricted sampling.

   d. Standard deviation and standard error.

   e. Simple random and complex random sampling.

   f. Convenience and purposive sampling.

    g. Sample precision and sample accuracy.

    h. Systematic and error variance.

    i. Variable and attribute parameters.

    j. Point estimate and interval estimate.

    k. Proportionate and disproportionate samples.

2. Under what kind of conditions would you recommend

    a. A probability sample? A nonprobability sample?

    b. A simple random sample? A cluster sample? A stratified sample?

    c. Using the finite population adjustment factor?

    d. A disproportionate stratified probability sample?

3. You plan to conduct a survey using unrestricted sampling. What subjective decisions must you make?

4. You draw a random sample of 300 employee records from the personnel file and find that the average years of service per employee is 6.3, with a standard deviation of 3.0 years.

    a. What percentage of the workers would you expect to have more than 9.3 years of service?

    b. What percentage would you expect to have more than 5.0 years of service?

Making Research Decisions

5. Your task is to interview a representative sample of attendees for the large concert venue where you work. The new season schedule includes 200 live concerts featuring all types of musicians and musical groups. Since neither the number of attendees nor their descriptive characteristics are known in advance, you decide on nonprobability sampling. Based on past seating configurations, you can calculate the number of tickets that will be available for each of the 200 concerts. Thus, collectively, you will know the number of possible attendees for each type of music. From attendance research conducted at concerts held during the previous two years, you can obtain gender data on attendees by type of music. How would you conduct a reasonably reliable nonprobability sample?

6. A manufacturer of precision gaskets makes gaskets in two grades: military and consumer automobile. In military applications, the precise gasket thickness is far more critical than in consumer automobile applications. The production run for military applications is very small, whereas the production run for consumer applications is very large. Explain how these facts affect decisions in sample design, confidence intervals, and sample size.

7. You wish to take an unrestricted random sample of undergraduate students at Cranial University to ascertain their levels of spending per month for food purchased off campus and eaten on the premises where purchased. You ask a test sample of nine students about their food expenditures and find that on the average they report spending $20, with two-thirds of them reporting spending from $10 to $30. What size sample do you think you should take? (Assume your universe is infinite.)

8. You wish to adjust your sample calculations to reflect the fact that there are only 2,500 students in your population. How does this additional information affect your estimated sample size in question 7?

9. Your large firm is facing its first union negotiation. Your superior wants an accurate evaluation of the morale of its large number of computer technicians. What size sample would you draw if it was to be an unrestricted sample?

Bringing Research to Life

10. Design an alternative nonprobability sample that will be more representative of infrequent and potential riders for the CityBus project.

11. How would you draw a cluster sample for the CityBus project?

**From Concept
to Practice**

12. Using Exhibit 7–6 as your guide, for each sampling technique describe the sampling frame for a study of employers' skill needs in new hires using the industry in which you are currently working or wish to work.

WWW Exercises

Visit our website for Internet exercises related to this chapter at
www.mhhe.com/business/cooper8

CASES*

A GEM OF A STUDY

 NCR: TEEING UP A NEW STRATEGIC DIRECTION

 GOODYEAR'S AQUATRED

 OUTBOARD MARINE CORPORATION

CALLING UP ATTENDANCE

PEBBLE BEACH COMPANY

CAN THIS STUDY BE SAVED?

STATE FARM: DANGEROUS INTERSECTIONS

INQUIRING MINDS WANT TO KNOW—NOW!

THE CATALYST FOR WOMEN IN FINANCIAL SERVICES

 KNSD SAN DIEGO

 VOLKSWAGEN'S BEETLE

MATCH WITS WITH JASON

*All cases indicating a video icon are located on the Instructor's Videotape Supplement. All nonvideo cases are in the case section of the textbook. All cases indicating a CD icon offer a data set, which is located on the accompanying CD.

REFERENCE NOTES

1. United States Department of Commerce, Press Release CB99-CN.22, June 2, 1999. http://www.census.gov/Press-Release/www/1999/cb99.html.
2. W. E. Deming, *Sample Design in Business Research* (New York: Wiley, 1960), p. 26.
3. Henry Assael and John Keon, "Nonsampling versus Sampling Errors in Survey Research," *Journal of Marketing Research* (Spring 1982), pp. 114–23.
4. A. Parasuraman, *Marketing Research,* 2nd ed. (Reading, MA: Addison-Wesley, 1991), p. 477.
5. Fred N. Kerlinger, *Foundations of Behavioral Research,* 3rd ed. (New York: Holt, Rinehart & Winston, 1986), p. 72.
6. Amir D. Aczel, *Complete Business Statistics* (Burr Ridge, IL: Irwin, 1996), p. 180.
7. The correction for a finite population is shown in the example below:
   If a finite population of 20,000 is considered, the sample size is 256 for an interval of ± .5 meals and 95 percent confidence.

$$\sigma_{\bar{X}} = \frac{s}{\sqrt{n-1}} = \sqrt{\frac{N-n}{N-1}} = 0.255 = \frac{4.1}{\sqrt{n-1}} \times \sqrt{\frac{20{,}000-n}{20{,}000-1}}$$

or

$$n = \frac{s^2 N + \sigma_{\bar{X}}^2 (N-1)}{s^2 + \sigma_{\bar{s}}^2 (N-1)}$$

$$n = 256$$

where
N = Size of the population
n = Size of the sample

8. All estimates of costs are hypothetical.
9. Leslie Kish, *Survey Sampling* (New York: Wiley, 1965), p. 188.
10. Ibid., pp. 76–77.
11. Typically, stratification is carried out before the actual sampling, but when this is not possible, it is still possible to stratify after the fact. Ibid., p. 90.
12. W. G. Cochran, *Sampling Techniques,* 2nd ed. (New York: Wiley, 1963), p. 134.

13. Ibid., p. 96.

14. Kish, *Survey Sampling,* p. 94.

15. For detailed treatment of these and other cluster sampling methods and problems, see Kish, *Survey Sampling,* pp. 148–247.

16. J. H. Lorie and H. V. Roberts, *Basic Methods of Marketing Research* (New York: McGraw-Hill, 1951), p. 120.

17. Kish, *Survey Sampling,* p. 156.

18. For specifics on these problems and how to solve them, the reader is referred to the many good sampling texts. Two that have been mentioned already are Kish, *Survey Sampling,* chapters 5, 6, and 7; and Cochran, *Sampling Techniques,* chapters 9, 10, and 11.

19. A proportion is the mean of a dichotomous variable when members of a class receive the value of 1, and nonmembers receive a value of 0.

REFERENCES FOR SNAPSHOTS AND CAPTIONS

Terrorism

"Poll: 83 Percent Back Military Action," MSNBC, September 13, 2001 (http://www.msnbc.com/news/628177.asp).

Jeff Jones, "The Impact of the Attacks on America," Gallup Poll News Service, Gallup Organization, September 14, 2001 (http://www.gallup.com/poll/releases/pr010914c.asp).

Gary Langer, "Gauging Support: History Suggests Steady Support for Military Action," ABCNews.com, September 18, 2001 (http://more.abcnews.go.com/sections/politics/dailynews/wtc_poll010918.html).

Gary Langer, "Prayers for Victims, Support for Reprisals: Poll: Public Responds to Terror Attacks," ABCNews.com, September 11, 2001 (http://more.abcnews.go.com/sections/us/dailynews/wtc_abcpoll010911.html).

Gary Langer, "Standing United: American Public Closes Ranks Behind Bush and Anti-Terror Measures," ABCNews.com, September 15, 2001 (http://abcnews.go.com/scetions/DailyNews/wtc_poll010914.html).

Gary Langer, "Support for Bush: 2-1 Backing for War on Terrorism; Inaction Seen as the Greater Peril," ABCNews.com, September 21, 2001 (http://abcnews.go.com/sections/politics/DailyNews/wtc_poll010921.html).

Frank Newport, "Retaliation," Gallup News Service, Gallup Organization, September 14, 2001 (http://www.gallup.com/poll/releases/pr010914b.asp).

The Henry J. Kaiser Family Foundation

"About The Henry J. Kaiser Family Foundation" (http://www.kff.org/about/).

"Sex Education in America: A View from Inside the Nation's Classrooms," Reproductive and Sexual Health: The Henry J. Kaiser Family Foundation (http://www.kff.org/sections.cgi?section=repro&sub_section=re-sexed&disp=10).

"Summary of Findings: Sex Education in America: A Series of National Surveys of Students, Parents, Teachers, and Principals," The Henry J. Kaiser Family Foundation, September 2000 (http://www.kkf.org/content/2000/3048/sexED.pdf).

Diana Jean Schemo, "Survey Finds Parents Favor More Detailed Sex Education," *New York Times on the Web,* October 4, 2000 (http://www.nytimes.com/2000/10/04/national/04SEX.html).

U.S. Census

2000 Census Questionnaire, U.S. Census Bureau, United States Department of Commerce.

John Fetto, "Lust for Statistics," *American Demographics,* March 2001, pp. 68–70.

James Heckman, "Polls Debate, Researchers Wait, Time's Short," *Marketing News,* March 29, 1999.

Joan Raymond, "The Multicultural Report," *American Demographics,* November 2001, p. s6.

The Census, U.S. Census Bureau, United States Department of Commerce (http://www.census.gov/census/).

IRI

Christopher T. Heun, "Information Resources Redesigns Its Market Research Data," Informationweek.com, CPM United Business Media, August 21, 2001.

"IRI Launches Proprietary InfoScan Advantage to Track Wal-Mart Sales Information," press release, Information Resources, Inc. August 21, 2001 (http://www.infores.com/public/global/news/glo_new_082101.htm).

CLASSIC AND CONTEMPORARY READINGS

Deming, W. Edwards. *Sample Design in Business Research.* New York: Wiley, 1990. A classic by the late author, an authority on sampling.

Kalton, Graham. *Introduction to Survey Sampling.* Beverly Hills, CA: Sage Publications, 1983. An overview with particular attention to survey applications.

Kish, Leslie. *Survey Sampling.* New York: Wiley, 1995. A widely read reference on survey sampling, recently updated.

Namias, Jean. *Handbook of Selected Sample Surveys in the Federal Government.* New York: St. John's University Press, 1969. A unique collection of illustrative uses of sampling for surveys carried out by various federal agencies. Of interest both for the sampling designs presented and for the information on the methodology used to develop various government statistical data.

Yates, F. *Sampling Methods for Censuses and Surveys.* 4th ed. New York: Oxford University Press, 1987. A readable text with emphasis on sampling practices.

CHAPTER 8

Measurement

Learning Objectives

After reading this chapter, you should understand . . .

1   **The distinction between measuring objects, properties, and indicants of properties.**

2   **The similarities and differences between the four scale types used in measurement and when each is used.**

3   **The four major sources of measurement error.**

4   **The criteria for evaluating the soundness of a measurement approach.**

Bringing Research to Life

The executive director of White Ice Compound gestured broadly at the still snow-capped Canadian Rockies that enveloped the complex and discouraged casual visitation for most of the year. "It has been three very happy years for me here, though not easy on my ego since I let corporate North America intrude on our idyllic existence. Not that I blame them for my shortcomings."

"You mean the MindWriter people?" prompted Jason. "The ones who flew me up here? My clients?"

The executive director propelled Jason straight across a manicured lawn toward the refreshment tent, where her faculty and paying guests were basking in postconcert euphoria, following a stirring performance of Beethoven by the White Ice Summer Festival Orchestra.

"Please, don't misunderstand," said the executive director. "They have been fine tenants . . . good corporate citizens . . . generous contributors to our little community. When I rented them a part of our compound for use in corporate education, they quite generously insisted that I avail myself of some of their training for midlevel managers. And I have to admit, now, that their managerial style makes me feel like an inadequate cellist with a stiff wrist, not an executive director evolving toward competence."

"Well, if we are going to help you," ventured Jason, "you had better tell me quickly what you do here. I have a 4 P.M. flight out."

"Surely. We in White Ice have a simple, never-varying rhythm of activity. By the middle of September, the paying guests, the visiting artists, the musicians, and the tourists have left White Ice and I bring in artisans for two weeks of intensive repairs and renovations. Then I prepare financial and artistic reports for the three foundations that have endowed us and also draw up an agenda for capital improvements and special events, which becomes the basis for frantic proposal writing during the weeks preceding Christmas. From January to April, I am on the phone to travel agents from Mexico City to Juneau to arrange a tight reservation and scheduling process, so that we maximize the use of the facilities during our season. I have developed the ability to keep track of the cash flow, which is not easy, with Canadian and U.S. dollars mingled.

"During the winter my artistic directors, Frances Braun and Igor Starvinsky—they have been Mr. and Mrs. Braun-Starvinsky for 30 years—prepare the program and hire the musicians, coordinating closely with me on the budget. This is quite complicated, as most of the performing artists spend only two weeks with us, so that fully 600 artists are part of this orchestra over the course of a summer.

"Then in the early spring I hear from the colleges in British Columbia, who send me their music scholarship students for summer employment as dishwashers, waiters, cleaners, and the like."

"Sounds as if you are right on top of the finances," said Jason, "and I suppose in your seminars with the MindWriter people they told you cash flow is one of three things that must be watched most carefully."

"Oh, yes indeed," the executive director laughed. "Gauging cash flow is not the problem. I descend from a line of genteel poverty. Measuring customer satisfaction—the second of the critical three factors for the MindWriter folks—now that was a problem for me—at first. The care and frequency with which they measure customer satisfaction in the MindWriter seminars dumbfounded me. Throughout a seminar, morning, afternoon, or evening, everyone breaks for coffee and is required to fill out a critique of the speaker. The results are tabulated by the time the last coffee cup has been picked up, and the seminar leader has been given feedback. Is he or she presenting material too slowly or too quickly? Are there too many jokes or not enough? Are concrete examples being used often enough? Do the participants want a hard copy of the slides? They measure attitudinal data six times a day and even query you about the meals, including taste, appearance, cleanliness and speed, friendliness, and accuracy of service.

"My problem is employee commitment, specifically commitment of the orchestral performers to the White Ice Festival. None of the other directors in my North American association of artistic and executive directors has nearly the rapid turnover of performers we have here, so they are not much help."

"Quoting the MindWriter standard line, 'Employee satisfaction is the third leg of the three- legged stool on which performance is based,'" said Jason. "The Braun-Starvinskys have the most contact with performers; they could be your eyes and ears. Ask them to listen carefully."

The executive director laughed ironically. "Jason," she said, "look over my shoulder. Directly behind me is a couple in their mid-sixties. Please describe as exactly as you can the behavior you observe."

"You mean the fellow in the sweatshirt and the woman with her hair in a bun?" whispered Jason. "He is sleeping. And the woman is nevertheless talking to him nonstop. Ah! Now she's shaking him awake. But he appears to fall right back to sleep. Does she ever stop talking?"

"There you have them, Jason—the Braun-Starvinskys, my artistic directors. He stays up all night composing, and all day, when he is not conducting, he snoozes. And she never stops expressing her opinions, be they lifelong prejudices or vagrant musings. Therefore she never listens well enough to later give a coherent report of anything she has heard or been told. If I have to rely on them for feedback,

everything would be filtered and distorted beyond recognition."

"It is just as well. Untrained observers can be highly unreliable and inaccurate in measuring and reporting behavior," said Jason. "Have you tried a suggestion box?"

"No, but I do send a letter to each visiting performer soliciting bouquets and brickbats. Do you want to know what some of the performers have written?"

"Shoot," said Jason. "But, quickly, please. I don't want to fly through these mountains at night in a small plane."

"Here is just a sample: 'Starvinsky never listens to our ideas.' 'A day under Braun feels like a week on a Los Angeles freeway.' 'We are all highly trained college teachers of music, but we are treated like children.'

"Clearly our performers aren't our only concern. The restaurant employees, the hospitality staff, the stage carpenters, the . . . "

"Hold on," said Jason, scribbling furiously on a napkin. "I can see you have a problem. I'm making a note to send you some research indexes on work innovation and job motivation. In fact, I believe one identifies and measures five different dimensions of worker attitudes. You'll find it interesting and maybe it is something you can use. Meanwhile, will you send me your customer satisfaction instrument for concert goers?"

"Of course, Jason. And be sure I shall act quickly on your suggestions. The *Vancouver Sun* has commented on our inability to sustain a steady tempo and tonation. When a businessperson fouls up, the mistake may not be evident for days or weeks. But when our orchestra strikes a sour note, 600 audience members receive the message at the speed of sound."

The Nature of Measurement

In everyday usage, measurement occurs when an established yardstick verifies the height, weight, or another feature of a physical object. How well you like a song, a painting, or the personality of a friend is also a measurement. In a dictionary sense, to measure is to discover the extent, dimensions, quantity, or capacity of something, especially by comparison with a standard. We measure casually in daily life, but in research the requirements for measurement are rigorous.

Measurement in research consists of assigning numbers to empirical events in compliance with a set of rules. This definition implies that measurement is a three-part process:

1. Selecting observable empirical events.

2. Developing a set of **mapping rules:** a scheme for assigning numbers or symbols to represent aspects of the event being measured.

3. Applying the mapping rule(s) to each observation of that event.[1]

Assume you are studying people who attend an auto show where all of the year's new models are on display. You are interested in learning the male-to-female ratio among attendees. You observe those who enter the show area. If a person is female, you record an F; if male, an M. Any other symbols such as 0 and 1 or # and % also may be used if you know what group the symbol identifies. Exhibit 8–1 uses this example to illustrate the above components.

Researchers might also want to measure the desirability of the styling of the new Espace van. They interview a sample of visitors and assign, with a different mapping rule, their opinions to the following scale:

What is your opinion of the styling of the Espace van?

Very desirable ⌊——————⌊——————⌊——————⌊——————⌋ Very undesirable
              5   4   3   2   1

EXHIBIT 8–1   Characteristics of Measurement

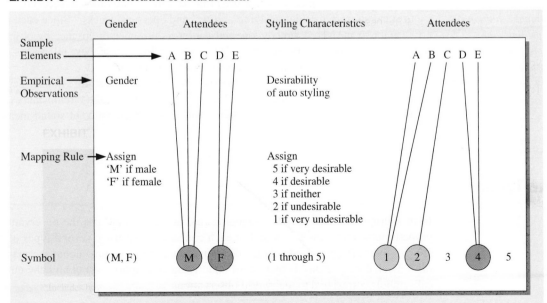

All measurement theorists would call the opinion rating scale on page 221 a form of measurement, but some would challenge the male-female classification. Their argument is that measurement must involve quantification—that is, "the assignment of numbers to objects to represent amounts or degrees of a property possessed by all of the objects."[2] Our discussion endorses the more general view that numbers as symbols within a mapping rule can reflect both qualitative and quantitative concepts.

The goal of measurement—indeed the goal of "assigning numbers to empirical events in compliance with a set of rules"—is to provide the highest quality, lowest error data for testing hypotheses. Researchers deduce from a hypothesis that certain conditions should exist. Then they measure for these conditions in the real world. If found, the data lend support to the hypothesis; if not, researchers conclude the hypothesis is faulty. An important question at this point is, "Just what does one measure?"

What Is Measured?

Variables being studied in research may be classified as objects or as properties. **Objects** include the things of ordinary experience, such as tables, people, books, and automobiles. Objects also include things that are not as concrete, such as genes, attitudes, neutrons, and peer-group pressures. **Properties** are the characteristics of the objects. A person's physical properties may be stated in terms of weight, height, and posture. Psychological properties include attitudes and intelligence. Social properties include leadership ability, class affiliation, or status. These and many other properties of an individual can be measured in a research study.

In a literal sense, researchers do not measure either objects or properties. They measure indicants of the properties or indicants of the properties of objects. It is easy to observe that *A* is taller than *B* and that *C* participates more than *D* in a group process. Or suppose you are analyzing members of a sales force of several hundred people to learn what personal properties contribute to sales success. The properties are age, years of experience, and number of calls made per week. The indicants in these cases are so accepted that one considers the properties to be observed directly.

Earlier we discussed operational definitions for constructs and concepts. You might find it helpful to revisit Exhibit 2–4 in Chapter 2.

In contrast, it is not easy to measure properties like "motivation to succeed," "ability to stand stress," "problem-solving ability," and "persuasiveness." Since each property cannot be measured directly, one must infer its presence or absence by observing some indicant or pointer measurement. When you begin to make these inferences, there is often disagreement about how to operationalize the indicants.

Not only is it a challenge to measure such constructs, but a study's quality depends on what measures are selected or developed and how they fit the circumstances. The nature of measurement scales, sources of error, and characteristics of sound measurement are considered next.

Data Types

In measuring, one devises some mapping rule and then translates the observation of property indicants using this rule. For each concept or construct, several types of data are possible; the appropriate choice depends on what you assume about the mapping rules. Each data type has its own set of underlying assumptions about how the numerical symbols correspond to real-world observations.

EXHIBIT 8–2   **Types of Data and Their Measurement Characteristics**

Type of Data	Characteristics of Data	Basic Empirical Operation	Example
Nominal	Classification but no order, distance, or origin	Determination of equality	Gender (male, female)
Ordinal	Classification and order but no distance or unique origin	Determination of greater or lesser value	Doneness of meat (well, medium well, medium rare, rare)
Interval	Classification, order, and distance but no unique origin	Determination of equality of intervals or differences	Temperature in degrees
Ratio	Classification, order, distance, and unique origin	Determination of equality of ratios	Age in years

Mapping rules have four characteristics:

1. **Classification:** Numbers are used to group or sort responses. No order exists.

2. **Order:** Numbers are ordered. One number is greater than, less than, or equal to another number.

3. **Distance:** Differences between numbers are ordered. The difference between any pair of numbers is greater than, less than, or equal to the difference between any other pair of numbers.

4. **Origin:** The number series has a unique origin indicated by the number zero.

Combinations of these characteristics of classification, order, distance, and origin provide four widely used classification of measurement scales: (1) nominal, (2) ordinal, (3) interval, and (4) ratio.

The characteristics of these measurement scales are summarized in Exhibit 8–2. Deciding which data type is appropriate for your research needs should be seen as a process (see Exhibit 8–3).

Nominal Data

In business and social science research, nominal data are probably more widely collected than any other. With **nominal data,** you are collecting information on a variable that naturally or by design can be grouped into two or more categories that are mutually exclusive and collectively exhaustive. If data were collected from the performing artists at the White Ice Compound, each artist could be classified by whether he or she stayed the summer or departed early. Every performer would fit into one of the two groups within the variable *duration of employment.*

MANAGEMENT

The counting of members in each group is the only possible arithmetic operation when a nominal scale is employed. If we use numerical symbols within our mapping rule to identify categories, these numbers are recognized as labels only and have no quantitative value. Nominal classifications may consist of any number of separate groups if the groups are mutually exclusive and collectively exhaustive. Thus, one might classify the residents of a city according to their expressed religious preferences. Mapping Rule A given in the table on page 225 is not a sound nominal scale because it is not collectively exhaustive. Mapping Rule B meets the minimum requirements, although this classification may be more useful for some research purposes than others.

EXHIBIT 8–3 Moving from Investigative to Measurement Questions

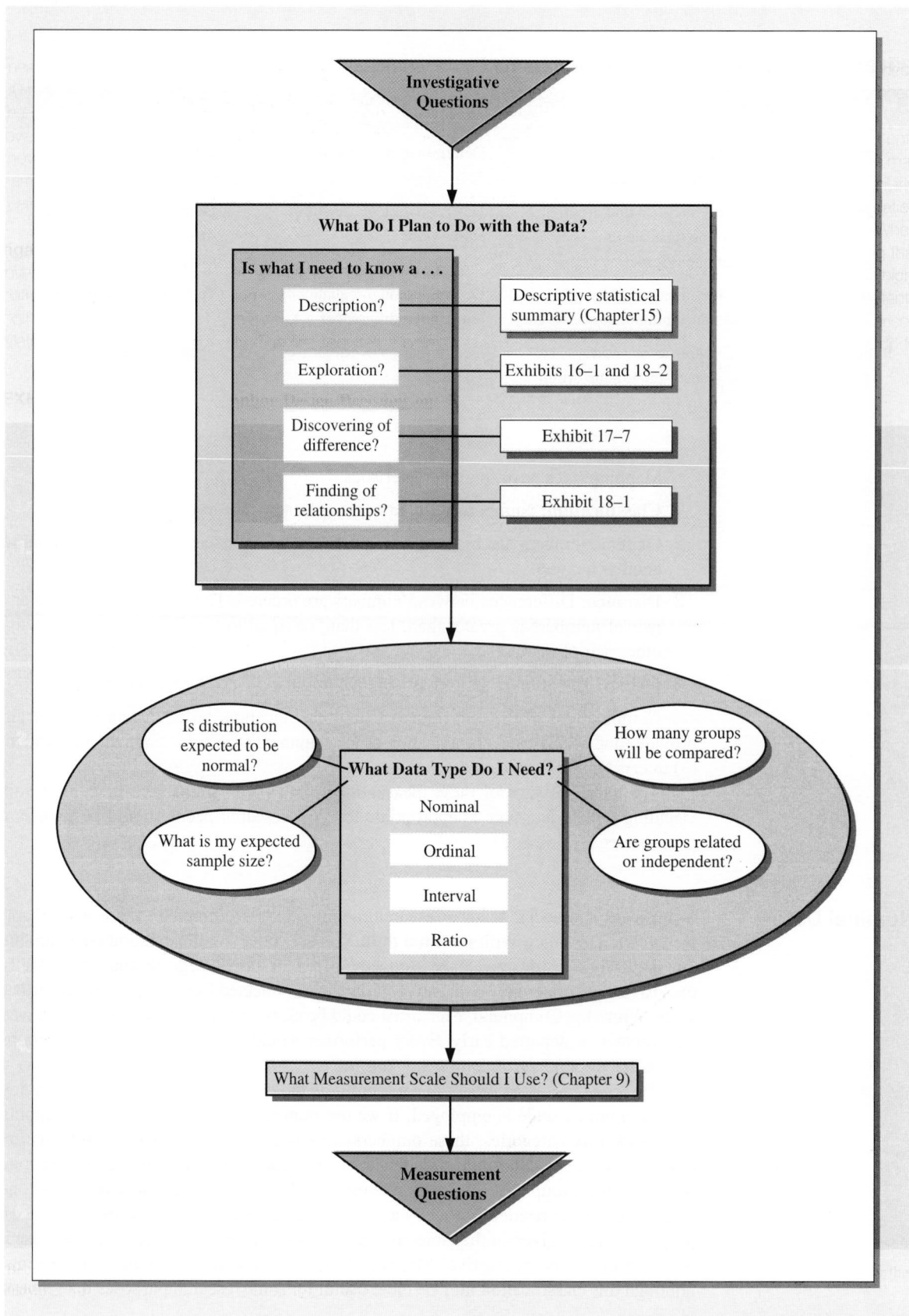

Religious Preferences	
Mapping Rule A	**Mapping Rule B**
1 = Baptist	1 = Protestant
2 = Catholic	2 = Catholic
3 = Jewish	3 = Jewish
4 = Lutheran	4 = Other
5 = Methodist	
6 = Presbyterian	
7 = Protestant	

Nominal scales are the least powerful of the four data types. They suggest no order or distance relationship and have no arithmetic origin. The scale wastes any information a sample element might share about varying degrees of the property being measured.

Since the only quantification is the number count of cases in each category (the frequency distribution), the researcher is restricted to the use of the mode as the measure of central tendency.[3] You can conclude which category has the most members, but that is all. There is no generally used measure of dispersion for nominal scales. Several tests for statistical significance may be utilized; the most common is the chi-square test. For measures of association, phi, lambda, or other measures may be appropriate.

While nominal data are weak, they are still useful. If no other scale can be used, one can almost always classify one set of properties into a set of equivalent classes. Nominal measures are especially valuable in exploratory work where the objective is to uncover relationships rather than secure precise measurements. This data type is also widely used in survey and other ex post facto research when data are classified by major subgroups of the population. Classifications such as respondents' marital status, gender, political persuasion, and exposure to a certain experience abound. Cross-tabulations of these and other variables provide insight into important data patterns.

Jason visited White Ice because of MindWriter's extensive research into customer satisfaction related to White Ice's manager training. His visit revealed White Ice's need for some exploratory nominal data on employee satisfaction. Orchestra performers could be divided into groups based on their appreciation of the Braun-Starvinskys (favorable, unfavorable), on their attitude toward facilities (suitable, not suitable), or on their perception of how performers were treated (as adults, as children).

MANAGEMENT

Tip

We discuss significance tests and measures of association in Chapters 17 and 18.

Ordinal Data

Ordinal data include the characteristics of the nominal scale plus an indicator of order. Ordinal data are possible if the transitivity postulate is fulfilled. This postulate states: If *a* is greater than *b* and *b* is greater than *c*, then *a* is greater than *c*.[4] The use of an ordinal scale implies a statement of "greater than" or "less than" (an equality statement is also acceptable) without stating how much greater or less. While ordinal measurement speaks of "greater than" and "less than" measurements, other descriptors may be used—"superior to," "happier than," "poorer than," or "above." Like a rubber yardstick, it can stretch varying amounts at different places along its length. Thus, the real difference between ranks 1 and 2 on a happiness scale may be more or less than the difference between ranks 2 and 3.

An ordinal concept can be generalized beyond the three cases used in the simple illustration of $a > b > c$. Any number of cases can be ranked.

A third extension of the ordinal concept occurs when more than one property is of interest. We may ask a taster to rank varieties of carbonated soft drinks by flavor, color, carbonation, and a combination of these characteristics. We can secure the combined ranking either by asking the respondent to base his or her ranking on the combination of properties or by constructing a combination ranking of the individual rankings on each property. To develop this overall index, the researcher typically adds and averages ranks for each of the three properties. This procedure is technically incorrect for ordinal data and, especially for a given respondent, may yield misleading results. When the number of respondents is large, however, these errors average out. A more sophisticated way to combine a number of dimensions into a total index is to use a multidimensional scale (see Chapter 19).

The researcher faces another difficulty when combining the rankings of several respondents. Here again, it is not uncommon to use weighted sums of rank values for a combined index. If there are many observations, this approach will probably give adequate results, though it is not theoretically correct. A better way is to convert ordinal data into interval data, the values of which can then be added and averaged. One well-known example is *Thurstone's Law of Comparative Judgment*.[5] In its simplest form, Thurstone's procedure says the distance between scale positions of two objects, *A* and *B*, depends on the percentage of judgments in which *A* is preferred to *B*.

MANAGEMENT

Tip

Examples of ordinal data include opinion and preference scales. Because the numbers of such scales have only a rank meaning, the appropriate measure of central tendency is the median. A percentile or quartile measure reveals the dispersion. Correlation is restricted to various rank-order methods. Measures of statistical significance are technically confined to that body of methods known as *nonparametric methods*.[6]

Researchers in the behavioral sciences differ about whether more powerful parametric significance tests are appropriate with ordinal measures. One position is that this use of parametric tests is incorrect on both theoretical and practical grounds:

> If the measurement is weaker than that of an interval scale, by using parametric methods tests the researcher would "add information" and thereby create distortions.[7]

At the other extreme, some behavioral scientists argue that parametric tests are usually acceptable for ordinal data:

> The differences between parametric and rank-order tests were not great insofar as significance level and power were concerned.[8]

A view between these extremes recognizes that there are risks in using parametric procedures on ordinal data, but these risks are usually not great:

> The best procedure would seem to be to treat ordinal measurements as though they were interval measurements but to be constantly alert to the possibility of gross inequality of intervals.[9]

Because nonparametric tests are abundant, simple to calculate, have good power efficiencies, and do not force the researcher to accept the assumptions of parametric testing, we advise their use with nominal and ordinal data. It is understandable, however, that because parametric tests (such as the *t*-test or analysis of variance) are so versatile, accepted, and understood, they will continue to be used with ordinal data when those data approach interval data characteristics.

Jason believed White Ice could potentially benefit by using professionally developed, well-tested work evaluation and job motivation indexes (see the opening vignette). Because of the constructs measured (work innovation, job motivation), we know after applying the test that one employee is more motivated than another, that one employee generates more ideas than another. By applying numerical scores to the variation in motivation, we can assume the collection of interval data.

Interval Data

Interval data have the power of nominal and ordinal data plus one additional strength: They incorporate the concept of equality of interval (the distance between 1 and 2 equals the distance between 2 and 3). Calendar time is such a scale. For example, the

Burke wants companies to think about monitoring customer service before a problem occurs through careful development of measurement and management processes. www.burke.com

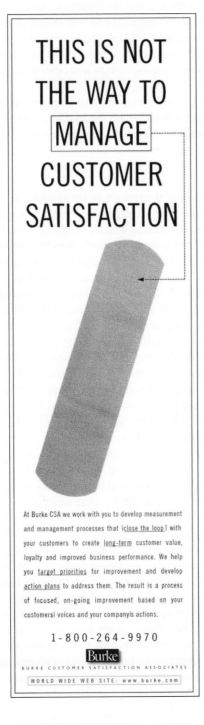

elapsed time between 3 and 6 A.M. equals the time between 4 and 7 A.M. One cannot say, however, 6 A.M. is twice as late as 3 A.M. because "zero time" is an arbitrary origin. Centigrade and Fahrenheit temperature scales are other examples of classical interval scales. Both have an arbitrarily determined zero point. Many attitude scales are presumed to be interval. Thurstone's differential scale was an early effort to develop such a scale.[10] Users also treat intelligence scores, semantic differential scales, and many other multipoint graphical scales as interval.

When a scale is interval, you use the arithmetic mean as the measure of central tendency. You can compute the average time of first arrival of trucks at a warehouse or the average attitude value for union workers versus nonunion workers on an election. The standard deviation is the measure of dispersion for arrival times or worker opinions. Product moment correlation, *t*-tests, *F*-tests, and other parametric tests are the statistical procedures of choice.[11]

When the distribution of scores computed from interval data lean in one direction or the other (skewed right or left) we use the median as the measure of central tendency and the interquartile range as the measure of dispersion. The reasons for this are discussed in Chapter 15.

Ratio Data

Ratio data incorporate all of the powers of the previous data types plus the provision for absolute zero or origin. Ratio data represent the actual amounts of a variable. Measures of physical dimensions such as weight, height, distance, and area are examples. In the behavioral sciences, few situations satisfy the requirements of the ratio scale—the area of psychophysics offering some exceptions. In business research, we find ratio scales in many areas. There are money values, population counts, distances, return rates, productivity rates, and amounts of time in a time-period sense.

Swatch's BeatTime—a proposed standard global time introduced at the 2000 Olympics and that may gain favor as more of us participate in cross-time-zone chats (Internet or otherwise)—is a ratio scale. It offers a standard time with its origin at 0 beats (12 midnight in Biel, Switzerland, at the new Biel Meridian timeline). A day is comprised of 1,000 beats, with a "beat" worth 1 minute, 26.4 seconds.[12]

With the White Ice project, Jason could measure the relationship of job satisfaction with a performer's age, the number of years he or she has played professionally, and the number of times he or she has participated in the White Ice summer festival. Each of these examples represents ratio data. For practical purposes, however, the analyst would make the same choice of statistical technique as with interval data.

All statistical techniques mentioned up to this point are usable with ratio scales. Other manipulations carried out with real numbers may be done with ratio-scale values. Thus, multiplication and division can be used with this scale but not with the others mentioned. Geometric and harmonic means are measures of central tendency, and coefficients of variation may also be calculated.

Researchers often encounter the problem of evaluating variables that have been measured at different data levels. The possession of a CPA by an accountant is a nominal, dichotomous variable, and salary is a ratio variable. Certain statistical techniques require the measurement levels to be the same. Since the nominal variable does not have the characteristics of order, distance, or point of origin, we cannot create them artificially after the fact. The ratio-based salary variable, on the other hand, can be reduced. Rescaling salary downward into high-low, high-medium-low, or another set of categories simplifies the comparison of nominal data. This example may be generalized to other measurement situations—that is, converting or rescaling a variable involves reducing the measure from the more powerful and robust level to a lesser one.[13] The loss of measurement power accompanying this decision is sometimes costly in that only nonparametric statistics can then be used in data analysis. Thus, the design of the measurement questions should anticipate such problems and avoid them when possible.

Sources of Measurement Differences

The ideal study should be designed and controlled for precise and unambiguous measurement of the variables. Since 100 percent control is unattainable, error does occur. Much potential error is systematic (results from a bias) while the remainder is random (occurs erratically). One authority has pointed out several sources from which measured differences can come.[14]

The Prince Corporation image study starts here and is used throughout this chapter.

Assume you are conducting an ex post facto study of the residents of a major city. The study concerns the Prince Corporation, a large manufacturer with its headquarters and several major plants located in the city. The objective of the study is to discover the public's opinions about the company and the origin of any generally held adverse opinions.

Ideally, any variation of scores among the respondents would reflect true differences in their opinions about the company. Attitudes toward the firm as an employer, as an ecologically sensitive organization, or as a progressive corporate citizen would be accurately expressed. However, four major error sources may contaminate the results: (1) the respondent, (2) the situation, (3) the measurer, and (4) the data collection instrument.

Error Sources

The Respondent   Opinion differences that affect measurement come from relatively stable characteristics of the respondent. Typical of these are employee status, ethnic group membership, social class, and nearness to plants. The skilled researcher will anticipate many of these dimensions, adjusting the design to eliminate, neutralize, or otherwise deal with them. However, even the skilled researcher may not be as aware of less obvious dimensions. The latter variety might be a traumatic experience a given respondent had with the Prince Corporation or its personnel. Respondents may be reluctant to express strong negative (or positive) feelings, express opinions which they perceive as different from those of others, or they may have little knowledge about Prince but be reluctant to admit ignorance. This reluctance can lead to an interview of "guesses."

Respondents may also suffer from temporary factors like fatigue, boredom, anxiety, or other distractions; these limit the ability to respond accurately and fully. Hunger, impatience, or general variations in mood may also have an impact.

The portable compact disk player, in combination with CD-burning technology, has made the custom CD not only desirable but also feasible. Measuring attitudes about copyright and its protection is important for publishers, entertainers, and distributors as they search for new business models to accommodate rapidly advancing technology.

S N A P S H O T

Measuring Attitudes about Copyright Infringement

In the midst of the Napster file-swapping controversy, and in connection with an issue centering on privacy issues, the editors of *American Demographics* hired TNS Intersearch to conduct a study of adults regarding their behavior and attitudes relating to copyright infringement. The survey instrument for the telephone study asked 1,051 adult respondents several questions about activities that might or might not be considered copyright infringement. The lead question asked about specific copyright-related activities:

Do you know someone who has done or tried to do any of the following?

1. Copying software not licensed for personal use.

2. Copying a prerecorded videocassette such as a rental or purchased video.

3. Copying a prerecorded audiocassette or compact disk.

4. Downloading music free of charge from the Internet.

5. Photcopying pages from a book or maga-zine.

A subsequent question asked respondents, "In the future, do you think that the amount of *(ACTIVITY)* will increase, decrease, or stay the same?" Also each respondent was asked to select a phrase from a list of four phrases "that best describes how you feel about *(ACTIVITY)*," and to select a phrase from a list of four phrases that "best describes what you think may happen as a result of *(ACTIVITY)*." The last content question asked the degree to which respondents would feel favorably toward a company which provided "some type of media content for free": more favorable, less favorable, or "it wouldn't impact your impression of the company." As you might expect, younger adults had different behaviors and attitudes compared to older adults on some indicants. What measurement issues were involved in this study?

www.americandemographics.com

www.intersearch.tnsofres.com

Situational Factors   These potential problem areas are legion. Any condition that places a strain on the interview or measurement session can have serious effects on the interviewer-respondent rapport. If another person is present, that person can distort responses by joining in, by distracting, or by merely being present. If the respondents believe anonymity is not ensured, they may be reluctant to express certain feelings. Curbside or intercept interviews are unlikely to elicit elaborate responses, while in-home interviews more often do.

The Measurer   The interviewer can distort responses by rewording, paraphrasing, or reordering questions. Stereotypes in appearance and action introduce bias. Inflections of voice and conscious or unconscious prompting with smiles, nods, and so forth may encourage or discourage certain replies. Careless mechanical processing—checking of the wrong response or failure to record full replies—will obviously distort findings. In the data analysis stage, incorrect coding, careless tabulation, and faulty statistical calculation may introduce further errors.

The Instrument   A defective instrument can cause distortion in two major ways. First, it can be too confusing and ambiguous. The use of complex words and syntax beyond respondent comprehension is typical. Leading questions, ambiguous meanings, mechanical defects (inadequate space for replies, response choice omissions, and poor printing), and multiple questions suggest the range of problems.

A more elusive type of instrument deficiency is poor selection from the universe of content items. Seldom does the instrument explore all the potentially important issues. The Prince Corporation study might treat company image in areas of employment and ecology but omit the company management's civic leadership, its support of local education programs, or its position on minority issues. Even if the general issues are studied, the questions may not cover enough aspects of each area of concern. While we might study the Prince Corporation's image as an employer in terms of salary and wage scales, promotion opportunities, and work stability, perhaps such topics as working conditions, company management relations with organized labor, and retirement and other benefit programs should also be included.

The Characteristics of Sound Measurement

What are the characteristics of a good measurement tool? An intuitive answer to this question is that the tool should be an accurate counter or indicator of what we are interested in measuring. In addition, it should be easy and efficient to use. There are three major criteria for evaluating a measurement tool: validity, reliability, and practicality.

- *Validity* refers to the extent to which a test measures what we actually wish to measure.
- *Reliability* has to do with the accuracy and precision of a measurement procedure.
- *Practicality* is concerned with a wide range of factors of economy, convenience, and interpretability.[15]

In the following sections, we discuss the nature of these qualities and how researchers can achieve them in their measurement procedures.

Validity

Many forms of validity are mentioned in the research literature, and the number grows as we expand the concern for more scientific measurement. This text features two major forms: external and internal validity.[16] The external validity of research findings refers to the data's ability to be generalized across persons, settings, and times; we discussed this in reference to sampling in Chapter 7, and more will be said about this in Chapter 14.[17] In this chapter, we discuss only internal validity. Internal validity is further limited in this discussion to the ability of a research instrument to measure what it is purported to measure. Does the instrument really measure what its designer claims it does?

Validity in this context is the extent to which differences found with a measuring tool reflect true differences among respondents being tested. We want the measurement tool to be sensitive to all the nuances of meaning in the variable and to changes in nuances of meaning over time. The difficulty in meeting the test of validity is that usually one does not know what the true differences are. Without direct knowledge of the dimension being studied, you must face the question, "How can one discover validity without directly confirming knowledge?" A quick answer is to seek other relevant evidence that confirms the answers found with the measurement device, but this leads to a second question, "What constitutes relevant evidence?" There is no quick answer this time. What is relevant depends on the nature of the research problem and the researcher's judgment. One way to approach this question is to organize the answer according to measure-relevant types. One widely accepted classification consists of three major forms of validity: (1) content validity, (2) criterion-related validity, and (3) construct validity (see Exhibit 8–4).[18]

Content Validity The **content validity** of a measuring instrument (the composite of measurement scales) is the extent to which it provides adequate coverage of the

EXHIBIT 8–4   **Summary of Validity Estimates**

Type	What Is Measured	Methods
Content	Degree to which the content of the items adequately represents the universe of all relevant items under study.	Judgmental or panel evaluation with content validity ratio
Criterion-related	Degree to which the predictor is adequate in capturing the relevant aspects of the criterion.	Correlation
Concurrent	Description of the present; criterion data are available at same time as predictor scores.	
Predictive	Prediction of the future; criterion data are measured after the passage of time.	
Construct	Answers the question, "What accounts for the variance in the measure?" Attempts to identify the underlying construct(s) being measured and determine how well the test represents it (them).	Judgmental Correlation of proposed test with established one Convergent-discriminant techniques Factor analysis Multitrait-multimethod analysis

The management-research question hierarchy discussed in Chapter 3 helps to reduce research questions into specific investigative and measurement questions that have content validity.

investigative questions guiding the study. If the instrument contains a representative sample of the universe of subject matter of interest, then content validity is good. To evaluate the content validity of an instrument, one must first agree on what elements constitute adequate coverage. In the Prince Corporation study, one must decide what knowledge, attitudes, and opinions are relevant to the measurement of corporate public image and then decide which forms of these opinions are relevant positions on these topics. In the White Ice study, Jason must first determine what factors are influencing employee satisfaction before determining if published indexes can be of value. If the data collection instrument adequately covers the topics that have been defined as the relevant dimensions, we conclude the instrument has good content validity.

Determination of content validity is judgmental and can be approached in several ways. First, the designer may determine it through a careful definition of the topic of concern, the items to be scaled, and the scales to be used. This logical process is often intuitive and unique to each research designer.

A second way to determine content validity is to use a panel of persons to judge how well the instrument meets the standards. A panel independently assesses the test items for a performance test. It judges each item to be essential, useful but not essential, or not necessary in assessing performance of a relevant behavior. The "essential" responses on each item from each panelist are evaluated by a content validity ratio, and those meeting a statistical significance value are retained. In both informal judgments and in this systematic process, "content validity is primarily concerned with inferences about test *construction* rather than inferences about test *scores*."[19]

It is important not to define *content* too narrowly. If you were to secure only superficial expressions of opinion in the Prince Corporation public opinion survey, it would probably not have adequate content coverage. The research should delve into the processes by which these opinions came about. How did the respondents come to feel as they do, and what is the intensity of feeling? The same would be true of Mind-

The picket line of strikers, like those seen here for the United Mine Workers of America, is a sight commonly associated with union membership. Peter D. Hart Research Associates, conducting a Society for Human Resource Management (SHRM) worker motivation study for the AFL-CIO, measured via an ordinal measurement scale that younger workers' interest in forming unions was growing not in numbers but in strength of conviction. Comparing a 1999 study with two previous studies conducted in 1997 and 1996, 7 percent more participants selected "would definitely/probably vote for union representation." What would you look for in assessing the soundness of this measurement?

Writer's evaluation of service quality and satisfaction. It is not enough to know a customer is dissatisfied. The manager charged with enhancing or correcting the program needs to know what processes, employees, parts, and time sequences within the CompleteCare program have led to that dissatisfaction.

Criterion-Related Validity   **Criterion-related validity** reflects the success of measures used for prediction or estimation. You may want to predict an outcome or estimate the existence of a current behavior or condition. These are *predictive* and *concurrent* validity, respectively. They differ only in a time perspective. An opinion questionnaire that correctly forecasts the outcome of a union election has predictive validity. An observational method that correctly categorizes families by current income class has concurrent validity. While these examples appear to have simple and unambiguous validity criteria, there are difficulties in estimating validity. Consider the problem of estimating family income. There clearly is a knowable true income for every family. However, we may find it difficult to secure this figure. Thus, while the criterion is conceptually clear, it may be unavailable.

In other cases, there may be several criteria, none of which is completely satisfactory. Consider again the problem of judging success among the sales force at SalesPro. A researcher may want to develop a pre-employment test that will predict sales success. There may be several possible criteria, none of which individually tells the full story. Total sales per salesperson may not adequately reflect territory market potential, competitive conditions, or the different profitability rates of various products. One might rely on the sales manager's overall evaluation, but how unbiased and accurate are those impressions? The researcher must ensure that the validity criterion used is itself "valid." One source suggests that any criterion measure must be judged in terms of four qualities: (1) relevance, (2) freedom from bias, (3) reliability, and (4) availability.[20]

A criterion is *relevant* if it is defined and scored in the terms we judge to be the proper measures of salesperson success. If you believe sales success is adequately measured by dollar sales volume achieved per year, then it is the relevant criterion. If you believe success should include a high level of penetration of large accounts, then sales volume alone is not fully relevant. In making this decision, you must rely on your judgment in deciding what partial criteria are appropriate indicants of salesperson success.

Freedom from bias is attained when the criterion gives each salesperson an equal opportunity to score well. The sales criterion would be biased if it did not show adjustments for differences in territory potential and competitive conditions.

A *reliable* criterion is stable or reproducible. An erratic criterion (using monthly sales, which are highly variable from month to month) can hardly be considered a reliable standard by which to judge performance on a sales employment test. Yet if an unreliable criterion is the only one available, it is often chosen for the study's purpose. In such a case, it is possible to use a *correction for attenuation* formula that lets you see what the correlation between the test and the criterion would be if they were made perfectly reliable.[21]

Finally, the information specified by the criterion must be *available.* If it is not available, how much will it cost and how difficult will it be to secure? The amount of money and effort that should be spent on development of a criterion depends on the importance of the problem for which the test is used.

Chapter 18 describes statistical techniques used to find correlation between variables.

Once there are test and criterion scores, they must be compared in some way. The usual approach is to correlate them. For example, you might correlate test scores of 40 new salespeople with first-year sales achievements adjusted to reflect differences in territorial selling conditions.

Construct Validity   One may also wish to measure or infer the presence of abstract characteristics for which no empirical validation seems possible. Attitude scales and aptitude and personality tests generally concern concepts that fall in this category. Although this situation is much more difficult, some assurance is still needed that the measurement has an acceptable degree of validity.

In attempting to evaluate **construct validity,** we consider both the theory and the measuring instrument being used. If we were interested in measuring the effect of ceremony on organizational culture, the way in which "ceremony" was operationally defined would have to correspond to an empirically grounded theory. Once assured that the construct was meaningful in a theoretical sense, we would next investigate the adequacy of the instrument. If a known measure of ceremony in organizational culture was available, we might correlate the results obtained using this measure with those derived from our new instrument. Such an approach would provide us with preliminary indications of *convergent* validity. If Jason were to develop a work innovation index for artistic personnel at White Ice and, when compared, the results revealed the same indications as a predeveloped, established index, Jason's instrument would have convergent validity. Similarly, if Jason and Myra developed an instrument to measure satisfaction with the CompleteCare program and the derived measure could be confirmed with a standardized customer satisfaction measure, convergent validity would exist.

An example of factor analysis is described in Chapter 19.

Returning to our example above, another method of validating the ceremony construct would be to separate it from other constructs in the theory or related theories. To the extent that ceremony could be separated from stories or symbols, we would have completed the first steps toward *discriminant* validity. Established statistical tools such as factor analysis and multitrait-multimethod analysis help determine the construct adequacy of a measuring device.[22]

In the Prince Corporation study, you may be interested in securing a judgment of "how good a citizen" the corporation is. Variations in respondent ratings may be drastically affected if substantial differences exist among the respondents regarding what constitutes proper corporate citizenship. One respondent may believe that any company is an economic organization designed to make profits for its stockholders. She sees relatively little role for corporations in the wide-ranging social issues of the day. At the other end of the continuum, another respondent views the corporation as a leader in solving social problems, even at the cost of profits.

Both of these respondents might understand Prince's role in the community but judge it quite differently in light of their differing views about what its role should be. If these different views were held, you would theorize that other information about these respondents would be logically compatible with their judgments. You might expect the first respondent to oppose high corporate taxes, to be critical of increased involvement of government in family affairs, and to believe that a corporation's major responsibility is to its stockholders. The second respondent would be more likely to favor high corporate income taxes, to opt for more governmental involvement in daily life, and to believe that a corporation's major responsibility is a social one.

Respondents may not be consistent on all questions because the measurements may be crude and the "theory" may be deficient. When hypothesized tests do not confirm the measurement scale, you are faced with a two-sided question: Is your measurement instrument invalid, or is your theory invalid? These answers require more information or the exercise of judgment.

We discuss the three forms of validity separately, but they are interrelated, both theoretically and operationally. Predictive validity is important for a test designed to predict employee success. In developing such a test, you would probably first postulate the factors (constructs) that provide the basis for useful prediction. For example, you would advance a theory about the variable in employee success—an area for construct validity. Finally, in developing the specific items for inclusion in the success prediction test, you would be concerned with how well the specific items sample the full range of each construct (a matter of content validity).

In the corporate image study for the Prince Corporation, both content and construct validity considerations have been discussed, but what about criterion-related validity? The criteria are less obvious than in the employee success prediction, but judgments will be made of the quality of evidence about the company's image. The criteria used may be both subjective—Does the evidence agree with what we believe?—and objective—Does the evidence agree with other research findings?

Looking at Exhibit 8–5, we can approach the concepts of validity and reliability by using an archer's bow and target as an analogy. High reliability means that repeated arrows shot from the same bow would hit the target in essentially the same place— although not necessarily the intended place (first row of the graphic). If we had a bow

EXHIBIT 8–5
Understanding Validity and Reliability

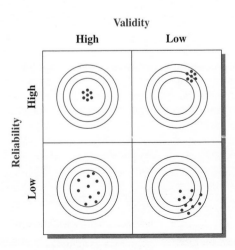

with high validity as well, then every arrow would hit the bull's-eye (upper left panel). If reliability is low or decreases for some reason, arrows would be more scattered (lacking similarity or closeness like those shown in the second row).

High validity means that the bow would shoot true every time. It would not pull to the right or send an arrow careening into the woods. Arrows shot from a high validity bow will be clustered around a central point (the bull's-eye), even when they are dispersed by reduced reliability (first column of the graphic). We wouldn't hit the bull's-eye we were aiming at because the low validity bow—like the flawed data collection instrument— would not perform as planned. When low validity is compounded by low reliability, the pattern of arrows is not only off bull's-eye but is also dispersed (lower right panel).

Reliability

Reliability means many things to many people, but in most contexts the notion of consistency emerges. A measure is reliable to the degree that it supplies consistent results. **Reliability** is a necessary contributor to validity but is not a sufficient condition for validity. The relationship between reliability and validity can be simply illustrated with the use of a bathroom scale. If the scale measures your weight correctly (using a concurrent criterion such as a scale known to be accurate), then it is both reliable and valid. If it consistently overweighs you by six pounds, then the scale is reliable but not valid. If the scale measures erratically from time to time, then it is not reliable and therefore cannot be valid. So if a measurement is not valid, it hardly matters if it is reliable—because it does not measure what the designer needs to measure in order to solve the research problem. In this context, reliability is not as valuable as validity, but it is much easier to assess.

Reliability is concerned with estimates of the degree to which a measurement is free of random or unstable error. Reliable instruments can be used with confidence that transient and situational factors are not interfering. Reliable instruments are robust; they work well at different times under different conditions. This distinction of time and condition is the basis for frequently used perspectives on reliability—stability, equivalence, and internal consistency (see Exhibit 8–6).

SNAPSHOT

Surfing for the Perfect Measurement

When Web banner ads, and the newer superstitial ads or interactive marketing units (IMUs)—larger ads with voice and motion in pop-up windows similar to TV commercials—were first aired, they were heralded as the first truly measurable advertising medium. With a measurement called the *click-through rate,* advertisers could track the number of potential customers who saw an ad, clicked on the ad, arrived at the advertiser's website, and then bought a product online. But while Web advertising has grown faster than any other medium, to an estimated $5.4 billion, advertisers are no longer sure whether the click-through rate measures anything meaningful. "Click-through rates are a misleading statistic—they aren't indicative of raised awareness or of consumer interest," says Scot McLernon, who is executive vice president for ad sales at MarketWatch.com. While advertisers can compute cost measures (cost per click or cost per conversion to purchase from ad click), Web advertising has substantiated rather than disproved a well-known adage: Response to advertising is often delayed and certainly not direct. Some firms, like MarketWatch.com, aren't counting click-through rates at all, hoping to persuade "the advertising industry to view online ads as tools for branding rather than direct marketing." Others, like Interactive Advertising Bureau (IAB), demonstrate that advertisers are resorting to tried-and-true, but far less exacting, ad effectiveness measures: conducting online surveys among those who recall having seen ads and measuring brand awareness, product association with message, purchase intent, and brand favorability. In its latest study by "Dynamic Logic, [IAB] found that the new larger ad units (IMUs) are 25 percent more effective in lifting key brand metrics such as brand awareness and message association—even at one exposure." What type of data and what measurement scales have firms involved with Web advertising been using to measure effectiveness? What should advertisers use?

www.cbs.marketwatch.com

www.dynamiclogic.com

www.iab.net

EXHIBIT 8–6 Summary of Reliability Estimates

Type	Coefficient	What Is Measured	Methods
Test-retest	Stability	Reliability of a test or instrument inferred from examinee scores. Same test is administered twice to same subjects over an interval of less than six months.	Correlation
Parallel forms	Equivalence	Degree to which alternative forms of the same measure produce same or similar results. Administered simultaneously or with a delay. Interrater estimates of the similarity of judges' observations or scores.	Correlation
Split-half KR20 Cronbach's alpha	Internal consistency	Degree to which instrument items are homogeneous and reflect the same underlying construct(s).	Specialized correlational formulas

Maritz recognizes that understanding customers, employees, and other stakeholders starts with solid measurement even when the delivery is automated. www.maritz.com/mmri

Stability   A measure is said to possess **stability** if you can secure consistent results with repeated measurements of the same person with the same instrument. An observational procedure is stable if it gives the same reading on a particular person when repeated one or more times. It is often possible to repeat observations on a subject and to compare them for consistency. When there is much time between measurements, there is a chance for situational factors to change, thereby affecting the observations. The change would appear incorrectly as a drop in the reliability of the measurement process.

Stability measurement in survey situations is more difficult and less easily executed than in observational studies. While you can observe a certain action repeatedly, you usually can resurvey only once. This leads to a test-retest arrangement—with comparisons between the two tests to learn how reliable they are. Some of the difficulties that can occur in the test-retest methodology and cause a downward bias in stability include:

MANAGEMENT
Tip

- **Time-delays between measurements**—leads to situational factor changes (also a problem in observation studies).

- **Insufficient time between measurements**—permits the respondent to remember previous answers and repeat them, resulting in biased reliability indicators.

- **Respondent's discernment of a disguised purpose**—may introduce bias if the respondent holds opinions related to the purpose but not assessed with current measurement questions.

- **Topic sensitivity**—occurs when the respondent seeks to learn more about the topic or form new and different opinions before the retest.

- **Introduction of extraneous moderating variables between measurements**—may result in a change in the respondent's opinions from factors unrelated to the research.

A suggested remedy is to extend the interval between test and retest (from two weeks to a month). While this may help, the researcher must be alert to the chance an outside factor will contaminate the measurement and distort the stability score. Consequently, stability measurement through the test-retest approach has limited applications. More interest has centered on equivalence.

Equivalence   A second perspective on reliability considers how much error may be introduced by different investigators (in observation) or different samples of items being studied (in questioning or scales). Thus, while stability is concerned with personal and situational fluctuations from one time to another, **equivalence** is concerned with variations at one point in time among observers and samples of items. A good way to test for the equivalence of measurements by different observers is to compare their scoring of the same event. An example of this is the scoring of Olympic figure skaters by a panel of judges.

In studies where a consensus among experts or observers is required, the similarity of the judges' perceptions is sometimes questioned. How does a panel of supervisors render a judgment on merit raises, a new product's packaging, or future business trends? *Interrater reliability* may be used in these cases to correlate the observations or scores of the judges and render an index of how consistent their ratings are. In Olympic figure skating, a judge's relative positioning of skaters (by establishing a rank order for each judge and comparing each judge's ordering for all skaters) is a means of measuring equivalence.

The major interest with equivalence is typically not how respondents differ from item to item but how well a given set of items will categorize individuals. There may be many differences in response between two samples of items, but if a person is classified the same way by each test, then the tests have good equivalence.

One tests for item sample equivalence by using alternative or parallel forms of the same test administered to the same persons simultaneously. The results of the two tests are then correlated. Under this condition, the length of the testing process is likely to affect the subjects' responses through fatigue, and the inferred reliability of the parallel form will be reduced accordingly. Some measurement theorists recommend an interval between the two tests to compensate for this problem. This approach, called *delayed equivalent forms,* is a composite of test-retest and the equivalence method. As in test-retest, one would administer form X followed by form Y to half the examinees and form Y followed by form X to the other half to prevent "order-of-presentation" effects.[23]

MANAGEMENT
Tip

The researcher can include only a limited number of measurement questions in an instrument. This limitation implies that a sample of measurement questions from a content domain has been chosen and another sample producing a similar number will need to be drawn for the second instrument. It is frequently difficult to create this second set. Yet if the pool is initially large enough, the items may be randomly selected for each instrument. Even with more sophisticated procedures used by publishers of standardized tests, it is rare to find fully equivalent and interchangeable questions.[24]

Internal Consistency   A third approach to reliability uses only one administration of an instrument or test to assess the **internal consistency** or homogeneity among the items. The *split-half* technique can be used when the measuring tool has many similar questions or statements to which the subject can respond. The instrument is administered and the results are separated by item into even and odd numbers or into randomly selected halves. When the two halves are correlated, if the results of the correlation are high, the instrument is said to have high reliability in an internal consistency sense. The high correlation tells us there is similarity (or homogeneity) among the items. The potential for incorrect inferences about high internal consistency exists when the test contains many items—which inflates the correlation index.

The Spearman-Brown correction formula is used to adjust for the effect of test length and to estimate reliability of the whole test. A problem with this approach is that the way the test is split may influence the internal consistency coefficient. To remedy this, other indexes are used to secure reliability estimates without splitting the test's items. The *Kuder-Richardson Formula 20 (KR20)* and *Cronbach's coefficient alpha* are two frequently used examples. Cronbach's alpha has the most utility for multi-item scales at the interval level of measurement. The KR20 is the method from which alpha was generalized and is used to estimate reliability for dichotomous items (see Exhibit 8–6).

Improving Reliability   The researcher can improve reliability by choosing among the following:

MANAGEMENT
Tip

- Minimize external sources of variation.

- Standardize conditions under which measurement occurs.

- Improve investigator consistency by using only well-trained, supervised, and motivated persons to conduct the research.

- Broaden the sample of measurement questions used by adding similar questions to the data collection instrument or adding more observers or occasions to an observational study.

- Improve internal consistency of an instrument by excluding data from analysis drawn from measurement questions eliciting extreme responses. This approach requires the assumption that a high total score reflects high performance and a low total score, low performance. One selects the extreme scorers—say, the top 20 percent and bottom 20 percent—for individual analysis. By this process, you can distinguish those items that differentiate high and low scorers. Items that have little discriminatory power can then be dropped from the test.

Practicality

The scientific requirements of a project call for the measurement process to be reliable and valid, while the operational requirements call for it to be practical. **Practicality** has been defined as *economy, convenience,* and *interpretability.*[25] While this definition refers to the development of educational and psychological tests, it is meaningful for business measurements as well.

Economy   Some trade-off usually occurs between the ideal research project and the budget. Instrument length is one area where economic pressures dominate. More items give more reliability, but in the interest of limiting the interview or observation time (and therefore costs), we hold down the number of measurement questions. The choice of data collection method is also often dictated by economic factors. The rising cost of personal interviewing first led to an increased use of long-distance telephone surveys and subsequently to the current rise in online surveys. In standardized tests, the cost of test materials alone can be such a significant expense that it encourages multiple reuse. Add to this the need for fast and economical scoring, and we see why computer scoring and scanning are attractive.

MANAGEMENT Tip

Convenience   A measuring device passes the convenience test if it is easy to administer. A questionnaire with a set of detailed but clear instructions, with examples, is easier to complete correctly than one that lacks these features. In a well-prepared study, it is not uncommon for the interviewer instructions to be several times longer than the interview questions. Naturally, the more complex the concepts, the greater is the need for clear and complete instructions. We can also make the instrument easier to administer by giving close attention to its design and layout. Crowding of material, poor reproductions of illustrations, and the carryover of items from one page to the next make completion of the instrument more difficult.

Interpretability   This aspect of practicality is relevant when persons other than the test designers must interpret the results. It is usually but not exclusively an issue with standardized tests. In such cases, the designer of the data collection instrument provides several key pieces of information to make interpretation possible:

- A statement of the functions the test was designed to measure and the procedures by which it was developed.
- Detailed instructions for administration.
- Scoring keys and instructions.
- Norms for appropriate reference groups.
- Evidence about reliability.
- Evidence regarding the intercorrelations of subscores.
- Evidence regarding the relationship of the test to other measures.
- Guides for test use.

Close-Up

Earlier, Jason Henry agreed to send the executive director at White Ice some useful tools for measuring job satisfaction and motivation. In reviewing his files, he found a piece of research conducted at five geographically separate units of the Tennessee Valley Authority, three divisions of an electronics company, and five departments of an appliance manufacturing company. The procedure for developing the measures was first to hold a number of informal interviews with supervisory and nonsupervisory employees. From the knowledge acquired, the researchers constructed the questions. These were then pretested and revised twice on separate groups of TVA employees. Out of this process came the six-item questionnaire on interest in work innovation shown in Exhibit 8–7. This instrument and the others were completed by employees of the three companies. The reliability of the Interest in

Work Innovation Index was measured by a test-retest of individual questions. The retest was done one month after the first test. Correlating the test-retest scores question by question gave the following results (see the Pearson correlation coefficient in Chapter 18 for more information on how these correlation coefficients were computed):

Question	r
Q1	.72
Q2	.72
Q3	.64
Q4	.67
Q5	.54
Q6	.85

EXHIBIT 8–7   Interest in Work Innovation Index[*]

1. In your kind of work, if a person tries to change his usual way of doing things, how does it generally turn out?

   (1) _____ Usually turns out worse; the tried and true methods work best in my work.

   (3) _____ Usually doesn't make much difference.

   (5) _____ Usually turns out better; our methods need improvement.

2. Some people prefer doing a job in pretty much the same way because this way they can count on always doing a good job. Others like to go out of their way in order to think up new ways of doing things. How is it with you on your job?

   (1) _____ I always prefer doing things pretty much in the same way.

   (2) _____ I mostly prefer doing things pretty much in the same way.

   (4) _____ I mostly prefer doing things in new and different ways.

   (5) _____ I always prefer doing things in new and different ways.

3. How often do you try out, on your own, a better or faster way of doing something on the job?

   (5) _____ Once a week or more often.

   (4) _____ Two or three times a month.

   (3) _____ About once a month.

   (2) _____ Every few months.

   (1) _____ Rarely or never.

4. How often do you get chances to try out your own ideas on the job, either before or after checking with your supervisor?

   (5) _____ Several times a week or more.

   (4) _____ About once a week.

   (3) _____ Several times a month.

   (2) _____ About once a month.

   (1) _____ Less than once a month.

EXHIBIT 8–7   Concluded

5. In my kind of job, it's usually better to let my supervisor worry about new or better ways of doing things.

  (1) _____ Strongly agree.

  (2) _____ Mostly agree.

  (4) _____ Mostly disagree.

  (5) _____ Strongly disagree.

6. How many times in the past year have you suggested to your supervisor a different or better way of doing something on the job?

  (1) _____ Never had occasion to do this during the past year.

  (2) _____ Once or twice.

  (3) _____ About three times.

  (4) _____ About five times.

  (5) _____ Six to ten times.

  (6) _____ More than ten times had occasion to do this during the past year.

*Numbers in parentheses preceding each response category indicate the score assigned to each response.

Source: Martin Patchen, *Some Questionnaire Measures of Employee Motivation and Morale,* Monograph No. 41 (Ann Arbor: Institute for Social Research, The University of Michigan, 1965), pp. 15–16.

The researchers measured criterion-based validity by comparing worker scores on the six questions to ratings of the same workers by their supervisors. Supervisors were asked to "think of specific instances where employees in their units had suggested new or better ways of doing the job. They then ranked employees they personally knew on 'looking out for new ideas.'"[26] The median correlation between the index scores and the supervisor ratings was about .35. At TVA, where there was an active suggestion system in operation, they also found that the index scores of those making suggestions were significantly higher than those not making suggestions.

Construct validity was evaluated by comparing scores on the Interest in Work Innovation Index to other job-related variables. Mean scores on the index were computed for 90 work groups at TVA. These means were then correlated with group scores on other variables that were hypothesized to relate to interest in innovation. The results are shown in Exhibit 8–8.

The researchers concluded, "The Index of Interest in Work Innovation, while a rough one, shows adequate relia-bility and sufficient evidence of validity to warrant its use in making rough distinctions among groups of people (or among units)."[27] In addition, they tested a short version of the index (items 1, 5, and 6) and found its validity to be almost equal to that of the longer form.

Having reviewed this research study with its derived indexes, Jason forwarded what he found to the symphony director. She would decide if it was adaptable or if she should develop her own instrument. Managers and researchers frequently assume they need a device tailored to their unique situation. This decision can be costly and time-consuming. Reliability testing may be ignored and validity assessments may be confined to impressions about content. Typically, there is no comparable evidence from other studies by which to calibrate the findings.

If Jason's recommendation proves to be inadequate, a further search of existing measures will reveal many established ones that might fit the director's needs. Most are copyrighted but available from commercial sources.

EXHIBIT 8–8 Relation of Scores on Interest in Work Innovation Index[*] to Scores on Other Job-Related Variables[†] for 90 Work Groups at TVA (Pearson product-moment correlation coefficient, *r*)

Correlation	Variable Name	Correlation	Variable Name
.44[‡]	Job difficulty	−.05	Pressure from peers to do a good job
.39[‡]	Identification with own occupation	.36[‡]	General job motivation
.29[‡]	Control over work methods	.36[‡]	Willingness to disagree with supervisors
.28[‡]	Perceived opportunity for achievement	.12	Acceptance of changes in work situation
.19	Feedback on performance	.00	Identification with TVA
.13	Control over goals in work	.21[‖]	Overall satisfaction (with pay, promotion, supervisors, and peers)
.06	Need for achievement[§]		

[*]The shorter three-item Index B was used for these correlations.
[†]Variables listed are all indexes; each index is composed of several specific questions.
[‡]$p < .01$, 2-tailed *t*-test.
[§]This is the Achievement Risk Preference Scale developed by P. O'Connor and J. W. Atkinson (1960).
[‖]$p < .05$, 2-tailed t-test.
Source: Martin Patchen, *Some Questionnaire Measures of Employee Motivation and Morale*, Monograph No. 41 (Ann Arbor: Institute for Social Research, The University of Michigan, 1965), p. 24.

SUMMARY

1 While people measure things casually in daily life, research measurement is more precise and controlled. In measurement, one settles for measuring properties of the objects rather than the objects themselves. An event is measured in terms of its duration. What happened during it, who was involved, where it occurred, and so forth, are all properties of the event. To be more precise, what are measured are indicants of the properties. Thus, for duration, one measures the number of hours and minutes recorded. For what happened, one uses some system to classify types of activities that occurred. Measurement typically uses some sort of scale to classify or quantify the data collected.

2 There are four scale types. In increasing order of power, they are nominal, ordinal, interval, and ratio. Nominal scales classify without indicating order, distance, or unique origin. Ordinal data show magnitude relationships of more than and less than but have no distance or unique origin. Interval scales have both order and distance but no unique origin. Ratio scales possess all of these features.

3 Instruments may yield incorrect readings of an indicant for many reasons. These may be classified according to error sources: (1) the respondent or subject, (2) situational factors, (3) the measurer, and (4) the instrument.

4 Sound measurement must meet the tests of validity, reliability, and practicality. Validity reveals the degree to which an instrument measures what it is supposed to measure to assist the researcher in solving the research problem. Three forms of validity are used to evaluate measurement scales. Content validity exists to the degree that a measure provides an adequate reflection of the topic under study. Its determination is primarily judgmental and intuitive. Criterion-related validity relates to our ability to predict some outcome or estimate the existence of some current condition. Construct validity is the

most complex and abstract. A measure has construct validity to the degree that it conforms to predicted correlations of other theoretical propositions.

A measure is reliable if it provides consistent results. Reliability is a partial contributor to validity, but a measurement tool may be reliable without being valid. Three forms of reliability are stability, equivalence, and internal consistency. A measure has practical value for the research if it is economical, convenient, and interpretable.

KEY TERMS

EXAMPLES

Company	Scenario	Page
American Demographics	Sponsored a study on the attitudes toward copyright infringement.	230
Burke CSA	A research company using measurement scales to provide companies with customer feedback.	227
Dynamic Logic	Research firm that studied ad effectiveness measures being used to evaluate Internet advertising.	236
Espace Van*	Measuring attendees' reactions at an auto show.	221
Interactive Advertising Bureau	A trade association's research reveals what ad sellers are using to measure ad effectiveness.	236
MarketWatch.com	An ad seller trying to determine the best way to evaluate ad effectiveness.	236
Peter D. Hart Research Associates, AFL-CIO	A study to determine motivating factors for retaining and recruiting workers in a tight job market; further analysis regarding young workers' interest in unions.	233
Prince Corporation*	A study to discover the public's opinions about the company and the origin of any generally held adverse opinions.	229
SalesPro*	A study to evaluate sales performance.	233
Society for Human Resource Management (SHRM)	A study to determine motivating factors for retaining and recruiting workers in a tight job market; further analysis regarding young workers' interest in unions.	233
Swatch Co.	The use of BeatTime as a ratio scale.	228
TaylorNelson Sofres (TNS) Intersearch	A study for *American Demographics* about adult attitudes related to copyright infringement, included in its special issue on privacy.	230
Tennessee Valley Authority	Instrument development; reliability and validity emphasis.	241

| White Ice Summer Festival Orchestra[*] | A study of conditions influencing the rapid turnover of performers. | BRTL, Close-Up, throughout |

[*]Due to the confidential and proprietary nature of most research, the names of some companies have been changed.

DISCUSSION QUESTIONS

Terms in Review

1. What can we measure about the four objects listed below? Be as specific as possible.

   a. Laundry detergent

   b. Employees

   c. Factory output

   d. Job satisfaction

2. What are the essential differences among nominal, ordinal, interval, and ratio scales? How do these differences affect the statistical analysis techniques we can use?

3. What are the four major sources of measurement error? Illustrate by example how each of these might affect measurement results in a face-to-face interview situation.

4. Do you agree or disagree with the following statements? Explain.

   a. Validity is more critical to measurement than reliability.

   b. Content validity is the most difficult type of validity to determine.

   c. A valid measurement is reliable, but a reliable measurement may not be valid.

   d. Stability and equivalence are essentially the same thing.

Making Research Decisions

5. You have data from a corporation on the annual salary of each of its 200 employees.

   a. Illustrate how the data can be presented as ratio, interval, ordinal, and nominal data.

   b. Describe the successive loss of information as the presentation changes from ratio to nominal.

6. Below are listed some objects of varying degrees of abstraction. Suggest properties of each of these objects that can be measured by each of the four basic types of scales.

   a. Store customers.

   b. Voter attitudes.

   c. Hardness of steel alloys.

   d. Preference for a particular common stock.

   e. Profitability of various divisions in a company.

7. You have been asked by the head of marketing to design an instrument by which your private, for-profit school can evaluate the quality and value of its various curricula and courses. How might you try to ensure that your instrument has

   a. Stability?

   b. Equivalence?

   c. Internal consistency?

   d. Content validity?

   e. Predictive validity?

   f. Construct validity?

8. A new hire at Mobil Oil, you are asked to assume the management of the Mobil Restaurant Guide. Each restaurant striving to be included in the guide needs to be evaluated. Only a select few restaurants may earn the five-star status. What dimensions would you choose to measure to apply the one to five stars in the Mobil Restaurant Guide?

9. You have been asked to develop an index of student morale at your school.

   a. What constructs or concepts might you employ?

   b. Choose several of the major concepts and specify their dimensions.

   c. Select observable indicators that you might use to measure these dimensions.

   d. How would you compile these various dimensions into a single index?

   e. How would you judge the reliability and/or validity of these measurements?

From Concept to Practice

10. Using Exhibits 8–7 and 8–2, match each question to its appropriate data type. For each data type not represented, develop a measurement question that would obtain that type of data.

WWW Exercises

Visit our website for Internet exercises related to this chapter at www.mhhe.com/business/cooper8

CASES*

A GEM OF A STUDY

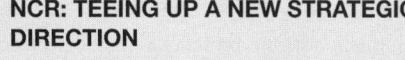 **PEBBLE BEACH CO.**

CALLING UP ATTENDANCE

RAMADA DEMONSTRATES ITS PERSONAL BEST

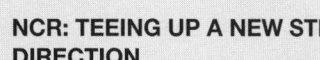 **DATA DEVELOPMENT, INC.**

STATE FARM: DANGEROUS INTERSECTIONS

 NCR: TEEING UP A NEW STRATEGIC DIRECTION

THE CATALYST FOR WOMEN IN FINANCIAL SERVICES

*All cases indicating a video icon are located on the Instructor's Videotape Supplement. All nonvideo cases are in the case section of the textbook. All cases indicating a CD icon offer a data set, which is located on the accompanying CD.

REFERENCE NOTES

1. Fred N. Kerlinger, *Foundations of Behavioral Research*, 3rd ed. (New York: Holt, Rinehart & Winston, 1986), p. 396; and S. Stevens, "Measurement, Statistics, and the Schemapiric View," *Science* (August 1968), p. 384.

2. W. S. Torgerson, *Theory and Method of Scaling* (New York: Wiley, 1958), p. 19.

3. We assume the reader has had an introductory statistics course in which measures of central tendency such as arithmetic mean, median, and mode have been treated. Similarly, we assume familiarity with measures of dispersion such as the standard deviation, range, and interquartile range. For a brief review of these concepts, refer to the Descriptive Statistics section in Chapter 15 or see an introductory statistics text.

4. While this might intuitively seem to be the case, consider that one might prefer *a* over *b*, *b* over *c*, yet *c* over *a*. These results

cannot be scaled as ordinal data because there is apparently more than one dimension involved.

5. L. L. Thurstone, *The Measurement of Values* (Chicago: University of Chicago Press, 1959).

6. Parametric tests are appropriate when the measurement is interval or ratio and when we can accept certain assumptions about the underlying distributions of the data with which we are working. Nonparametric tests usually involve much weaker assumptions about measurement scales (nominal and ordinal), and the assumptions about the underlying distribution of the population are fewer and less restrictive. More on these tests is found in Chapters 17–19 and Appendix E.

7. Sidney Siegel, *Nonparametric Statistics for the Behavioral Sciences* (New York: McGraw-Hill, 1956), p. 32.

8. Norman A. Anderson, "Scales and Statistics: Parametric and Nonparametric," *Psychological Bulletin* 58, no. 4, pp. 315–16.

9. Kerlinger, *Foundations,* p. 403.

10. See Chapter 9 for a discussion of the differential scale.

11. See Chapters 17 and 18 for a discussion of these procedures.

12. To learn more about Swatch's BeatTime, visit: http://www.swatch.com/internettime/internettime.php3.

13. The exception involves the creation of a dummy variable for use in a regression or discriminant equation. A nonmetric variable is transformed into a metric variable through the assignment of a 0 or 1 and used in a predictive equation.

14. Claire Selltiz, Lawrence S. Wrightsman, and Stuart W. Cook, *Research Methods in Social Relations,* 3rd ed. (New York: Holt, Rinehart & Winston, 1976), pp. 164–69.

15. Robert L. Thorndike and Elizabeth Hagen, *Measurement and Evaluation in Psychology and Education,* 3rd ed. (New York: Wiley, 1969), p. 5.

16. Examples of other conceptualizations of validity are factorial validity, job-analytic validity, synthetic validity, rational validity, and statistical conclusion validity.

17. Thomas D. Cook and Donald T. Campbell, "The Design and Conduct of Quasi Experiments and True Experiments in Field Settings," in *Handbook of Industrial and Organizational Psychology,* ed. Marvin D. Dunnette (Chicago: Rand McNally, 1976), p. 223.

18. *Standards for Educational and Psychological Tests and Manuals* (Washington, DC: American Psychological Association, 1974), p. 26.

19. Wayne F. Cascio, *Applied Psychology in Personnel Management* (Reston, VA: Reston Publishing, 1982), p. 149.

20. Thorndike and Hagen, *Measurement and Evaluation,* p. 168.

21. See, for example, Cascio, *Applied Psychology,* pp. 146–47; and Edward G. Carmines and Richard A. Zeller, *Reliability and Validity Assessment* (Beverly Hills, CA: Sage Publications, 1979), pp. 48–50.

22. Emanuel J. Mason and William J. Bramble, *Understanding and Conducting Research* (New York: McGraw-Hill, 1989), pp. 260–63.

23. Cascio, *Applied Psychology,* pp. 135–36.

24. Mason and Bramble, *Understanding and Conducting Research,* p. 268.

25. Thorndike and Hagen, *Measurement and Evaluation,* p. 199.

26. Martin Patchen, *Some Questionnaire Measures of Employee Motivation and Morale,* Monograph No. 41 (Ann Arbor: Institute for Social Research, The University of Michigan, 1965), p. 17.

27. Ibid., p. 25.

REFERENCES FOR SNAPSHOTS AND CAPTIONS

Internet Advertising

"Interactive Advertising Bureau (IAB), DoubleClick, MSN, and CNET Networks Release Groundbreaking Online Brand Research Findings," IAB press release, July 18, 2001 (http://www.iab.net/news/content/brand_research.html).

Christopher Saunders, "Industry Players Seek to Distance Themselves from Click-Throughs," *InternetNews,* July 9, 2001 (http://www.internetnews.com/IAR/article/0,,12_797851,00.html).

Rob Walker, "System for Measuring Clicks Is Under Assault," *The New York Times on the Web,* August 27, 2001 (http://www.nytimes/2001/08/027/technology/27NECO.html?ex=1000139238&ei=1&en=c315615dca93ee07).

Interest in Unions

"Education, Collective Action and New Rules Can Make Things Better," Peter D. Hart Research Associates (AFL-CIO) to SHRM, May 1999 (http://www.aflcio.org/articles/high_hopes/4.htm).

Copyright Infringement

John Fetto, "Americans Voice Their Opinions on Intellectual Property Rights Violations," *American Demographics,* September 2000, p. 8.

Measurement instrument prepared by TaylorNelson Sofres Intersearch.

Data tabulation generated by TaylorNelson Sofres Intersearch

CLASSIC AND CONTEMPORARY READINGS

Cascio, Wayne F. *Applied Psychology in Personnel Management.* 4th ed. Englewood Cliffs, NJ: Prentice-Hall, 1990.

Cook, Thomas D., and Donald T. Campbell. "The Design and Conduct of Quasi Experiments and True Experiments in Field Settings." In *Handbook of Industrial and Organizational Psychology,* ed. Marvin D. Dunnette. Chicago: Rand McNally, 1976, Chapter 7.

Embretson, Susan E., and Scott L. Hershberger. *The New Rules of Measurement.* Mahwah, NJ: Lawrence Erlbaum Associates, 1999. Bridges the gap between theoretical and practical measurement.

Guilford, J. P. *Psychometric Methods.* 2nd ed. New York: McGraw-Hill, 1954.

Kelley, D. Lynn. *Measurement Made Accessible: A Research Approach Using Qualitative, Quantitative, and TQM Methods.* Thousand Oaks, CA: Sage Publications 1999. Sections on bias, reliability, and validity are appropriate for this chapter.

Kerlinger, Fred N., and Howard B. Lee. *Foundations of Behavioral Research.* 4th ed. New York: HBJ College & School Division, 1999.

Newmark, Charles S. *Major Psychological Assessment Instruments.* 2nd ed. Boston: Allyn and Bacon, 1996.

Nunnally, J. C., and Ira Bernstein. *Psychometric Theory.* 3rd ed. New York: McGraw-Hill, 1994.

Thorndike, Robert M. *Measurement and Evaluation in Psychology and Education.* 6th ed. Upper Saddle River, NJ: Prentice-Hall, 1996.

CHAPTER 9

Measurement Scales

Learning Objectives

After reading this chapter, you should understand . . .

1   The six critical decisions involved in selecting an appropriate measurement scale.

2   The various scale formats for measurement and how to construct each.

3   The five ways that measurement scales are constructed.

Bringing Research to Life

They boarded the sleek corporate jet in Palm Beach and were taken aft to meet with the general manager of MindWriter, who was seated at a conference table that austerely held one sheaf of papers and a white telephone.

"I'm Jean-Claude Malraison," the general manager said. "Myra, please sit here . . . and you must be Jason Henry. On the flight up from Caracas I read your proposal for the CompleteCare project. I intend to sign your contract if you answer one question to my satisfaction about the schedule.

"I took marketing research in college and didn't like it, so you talk fast, straight, and plainly unless we both decide we need to get technical. If the phone rings, ignore it and keep talking. When you answer my one question I'll put you off the plane in the first Florida city that has a commercial flight back to . . . to . . . "

"This is Palm Beach, Jean-Claude," said the steward.

"What I don't like is that you are going to hold everything up so you can develop a scale for the questionnaire. Scaling is what I didn't like in marketing research. It is complicated and it takes too much time. Why can't you use some of the scales our marketing people have been using? Why do you have to reinvent the wheel?" The manager jabbed a finger toward Myra.

"Our research staff agrees with us that it would be inappropriate to adapt surveys developed for use in our consumer products line," said Myra smoothly.

"OK. Computers are not the same as toaster ovens and VCRs. Gotcha. Jason, what is going to be different about the scales you intend to develop?"

"When we held focus groups with your customers, they continually referred to the need for your product service to 'meet expectations' or 'exceed expectations.' The hundredth time we heard this we realized . . . "

"It's our company credo, 'Under-promise and exceed expectations.'"

"Well, virtually none of the scales developed for customer satisfaction deal with expectations. We want a scale that ranges in five steps from 'Met few expectations' to 'Exceeded expectations,' but we don't know what to name the in-between intervals so that the psychological spacing is equal between increments. We think 'Met many expectations' and 'Met most expectations' and 'Fully met expectations' will be OK, but we want to be sure."

"You are not being fussy here, are you, Jason?"

"No. Because of the way you are running your service operation, we want great precision and reliability."

"Justify that, please, Myra."

"Well, Jean-Claude, besides setting up our own repair force, we have contracted with an outside organization to provide repairs in certain areas, with the intention after six months of comparing the performance of the inside and outside repair organizations and giving the future work to whoever performs better. We feel that such an important decision, which involves the job security of MindWriter employees, must have full credibility."

"I can accept that. Good." The manager scribbled his signature on the contract. "You'll receive this contract in three days, after it has wended its way past the paper pushers. Meantime, we'll settle for a handshake. Nice job, so far, Myra. You seem to have gotten a quick start with MindWriter. Congratulations, Jason."

"We can put them down in Orlando," said the steward.

"No," said Jean-Claude. "We are only five minutes out. Turn the plane around and put these folks out where they got on. They can start working this afternoon . . . Gosh, is that the beach out there? It looks great. I've got to get some sun one of these days."

"You do look pale," said Myra, sympathetically.

"*Fais gaffe, tu m'fais mal!*" he muttered under his breath.

The Nature of Measurement Scales

When you develop measurement questions for your research study, you often may choose between standardized scales and custom-designed ones. When what you measure is concrete (for example the length of an assembly line), we usually choose a standardized measure (like measuring the assembly line with an electronic range finder or tape measure). When what we want to measure is a more abstract and complex construct (like customer attitudes about a product service program), standardized measures may neither exist nor provide a close enough fit to a particular manager's scenario. In these situations, developing a customized scale to measure the construct is the only option. Otherwise, we are left measuring a construct with a tool designed for something else. This would be like measuring the length of the assembly line with our forearm instead of visible laser beam technology.

This chapter covers procedures that will help you understand measurement scales so that you might select or construct measures that are appropriate for your research. We concentrate here on the problems of measuring more complex constructs, like attitudes and opinions.

Scaling Defined

Scaling is a "procedure for the assignment of numbers (or other symbols) to a property of objects in order to impart some of the characteristics of numbers to the properties in question."[1]

What Is Scaled?   Procedurally, we assign numbers to indicants of the properties of objects. Thus, one assigns a number scale to the various levels of heat and cold and calls it a thermometer. If you want to measure the temperature of the air, you know that a property of temperature is that its variation leads to an expansion or contraction of mercury. A glass tube with mercury provides an indicant of temperature change by the rise or fall of the mercury in the tube.

In another context, you might devise a scale to measure the durability (property) of paint. You secure a machine with an attached scrub brush that applies a predetermined amount of pressure as it scrubs. You then count the number of brush strokes that it takes to wear through a 10-mil thickness of paint. The scrub count is the indicant of the paint's durability. Or you may judge a person's supervisory capacity (property) by asking a peer group to rate that person on various questions (indicants) that you create.

Scale Selection

Scaling may be reviewed in several ways, but here we cover those approaches that are of greatest value for management research.[2] Selection or construction of a measurement scale requires decisions in six key areas:

MANAGEMENT
Tip

- Study objective
- Response form
- Degree of preference
- Data properties
- Number of dimensions
- Scale construction

Study Objective   Researchers face two general study objectives:

- To measure certain characteristics of the respondents who complete the study.

- To use respondents as judges of the objects or indicants presented to them.

Assume you've been contracted by the city of Miro Beach to conduct a study supposedly of voters' approval or disapproval of one or more regulatory programs. In the first type of study, your scale would measure the voters' political orientation as conservative or liberal. You might combine each person's answers to form an indicator of that person's political orientation. The emphasis in this first study objective is on measuring attitudinal differences among people. With the second study objective, you might use the same data but in this case you are truly interested in how satisfied people are with different governmental programs. In this study objective, your true interest is in the differences in the acceptance level of one or more regulatory programs.

Response Form   Measurement scales are of three types: *rating, ranking,* and *categorization.* A **rating scale** is used when respondents score an object or indicant without making a direct comparison to another object or attitude. For example, they may be asked to evaluate the styling of a new automobile on a five-point rating scale. **Ranking scales** constrain the study participant to make comparisons among two or more indicants or objects. Respondents may be asked to choose which one of a pair of cars has more attractive styling. They could also be asked to order the importance of comfort, ergonomics, performance, and price for the target vehicle. **Categorization** asks respondents to put themselves or property indicants in groups or categories. Asking auto show respondents to identify their gender or ethnic background or to indicate whether a particular prototype car design would attract a youthful or mature clientele would require a categorization response strategy.

Degree of Preference   Measurement scales may involve *preference* measurement or *nonpreference* evaluation. In the former, each respondent is asked to choose the object he or she favors or the solution he or she would prefer. In the latter, respondents are asked to judge which object has more of some characteristic or which solution takes the most resources, without reflecting any personal preference toward objects or solutions.

Data Properties   Measurement scales also may be viewed in terms of the data properties generated by each scale. Chapter 8 indicated that data are classified as nominal, ordinal, interval, or ratio. The assumptions underlying each data type determine how a particular measurement scale's data can be handled statistically.

Number of Dimensions   Measurement scales are either *unidimensional* or *multidimensional.* With a **unidimensional scale,** one seeks to measure only one attribute of the respondent or object. One measure of employee potential is promotability. It is a single dimension. Several items may be used to measure this dimension and, by combining them into a single measure, a manager may place employees along a linear continuum of promotability. **Multidimensional scaling** recognizes that an object might be better described in an attribute space of *n* dimensions rather than on a unidimensional continuum. The employee promotability variable might be better expressed by three distinct dimensions—managerial performance, technical performance, and teamwork.

Scale Construction   We can classify measurement scales by the methods used to build them. Five construction approaches are used in research practice:

- **Arbitrary:** A scale is custom-designed to measure a property or indicant.
- **Consensus:** Judges evaluate the items to be included.
- **Item analysis:** Measurement scales are tested with a sample of respondents.
- **Cumulative:** Scales are chosen for their conformity to a ranking of items with ascending and descending discriminating power.
- **Factoring:** Scales are constructed from intercorrelations of items from other studies.[3]

Arbitrary scales may measure the concepts for which they have been designed, but the researcher has no advance evidence of a particular scale's validity and reliability. Nevertheless, researchers commonly choose this construction approach. *Consensus scales* are developed by a panel of judges who evaluate the items to be included based on topical relevance and lack of ambiguity.

In *item analysis,* after administering the test, a total score is calculated for each scale. Individual items (a scale or part of a scale) are then analyzed to determine which best discriminate between persons or objects with high total scores and low total scores.

In the *cumulative* approach, the endorsement of an item that represents an extreme position results in the endorsement of all items of less extreme positions.

Finally, in *factoring* common factors account for the relationships. The relationships are measured statistically through factor analysis or cluster analysis.

The business researcher studies both the type of measurement scale and the scale's construction when selecting an appropriate scale. These topics form the basis for the remainder of the chapter.

Response Methods

In Chapter 8, we said that questioning is a widely used stimulus for measuring concepts and constructs. A manager may be asked his or her views concerning an employee. The response is, " a good machinist," "a troublemaker," "a union activist," "reliable," or "a fast worker with a poor record of attendance." These answers, because they represent such different frames of reference for evaluating the worker and thus lack comparability, would be of limited value to the researcher.

MANAGEMENT

Two approaches improve the usefulness of such replies. First, various properties may be separated and the respondent asked to judge each specific facet. Here, the researcher would substitute several distinct questions for a single one. Second, the researcher can replace the free-response reply with structuring devices. To quantify dimensions that are essentially qualitative, rating or ranking scales are used.

Rating Scales

One uses rating scales to judge properties of objects without reference to other similar objects. These ratings may be in such forms as "like-dislike," "approve-indifferent-disapprove," or other classifications using even more categories.

Number of Scale Points   There is little conclusive support for choosing a three-point scale over scales with five or more points. Some researchers think that more points on a rating scale provide an opportunity for greater sensitivity of measurement and extraction of variance. The most widely used scales range from three to seven points, but it does not seem to make much difference which number is used—with two exceptions.[4] First, a larger number of scale points is needed to produce accuracy when using single-dimension versus multiple-dimension scales. Second, in cross-cultural measurement, the culture may condition respondents to a standard metric—a 10-point scale in Italy, for example.

Alternative Scales   Examples of rating scales are shown in Exhibit 9–1. This exhibit amplifies the overview presented in this section.[5] Later in the chapter, construction techniques for some commonly used rating scales are presented.

The **simple category scale** (also called a *dichotomous scale*) offers two mutually exclusive response choices. In Exhibit 9–1 they are yes and no but they could just as easily be important and unimportant, agree and disagree, or another set of discrete categories had the question been different. This response strategy is particularly useful for demographic questions or where a dichotomous response is adequate.

When there are multiple options for the rater but only one answer is sought, the **multiple choice, single-response scale** is appropriate. Our example has five options. The primary alternatives should encompass 90 percent of the range with the "other" category completing the respondent's list. When there is no possibility for "other" or exhaustiveness of categories is not critical, the "other" response may be omitted. Both the multiple choice, single-response and the simple category scale produce nominal data.

A variation, the **multiple choice, multiple-response scale** (also called a *checklist*) allows the rater to select one or several alternatives. In this example we are measuring seven items with one question, and it is possible that all seven sources for home design were consulted. The cumulative feature of this scale can be beneficial when a complete picture of the respondent's choices is desired, but it may also present a problem for reporting when research sponsors expect the responses to sum to 100 percent. This scale generates nominal data.

The **Likert scale** is the most frequently used variation of the *summated rating scale*. Summated scales consist of statements that express either a favorable or unfavorable attitude toward the object of interest. The respondent is asked to agree or disagree with each statement. Each response is given a numerical score to reflect its degree of attitudinal favorableness, and the scores may be totaled to measure the respondent's attitude. In our example, the respondent chooses one of five levels of agreement. The numbers indicate the value to be assigned to each possible answer with 1 the least favorable impression of Internet superiority and 5 the most favorable. These values are normally not printed on the instrument but are shown in Exhibit 9–1 to indicate the scoring system. Between 20 and 25 properly constructed questions about an attitude object would be required for a reliable Likert scale.

Likert scales help us compare one person's score with a distribution of scores from a well-defined sample group. This measurement scale is useful for a manager when the organization plans to conduct an experiment or undertake a program of change or improvement. The researcher can measure attitudes before and after the experiment or change, or judge whether the organization's efforts have had the desired effects. This scale produces interval data.

The **semantic differential scale** measures the psychological meanings of an attitude object. Managers use this scale for brand image and other marketing studies of institutional images, political issues and personalities, and organizational studies. It is based on the proposition that an object can have several dimensions of connotative meaning. The meanings are located in multidimensional property space, called *semantic space*. The method consists of a set of bipolar rating scales, usually with seven

EXHIBIT 9–1   Sample Rating Scales

Simple Category Scale (dichotomous) data: nominal	"I plan to purchase a MindWriter laptop in the next 12 months." ☐ Yes ☐ No
Multiple Choice Single-Response Scale data: nominal	"What newspaper do you read most often for financial news?" ☐ *East City Gazette* ☐ *West City Tribune* ☐ Regional newspaper ☐ National newspaper ☐ Other (specify: _____)
Multiple Choice Multiple-Response Scale (checklist) data: nominal	"Check *any* of the sources you consulted when designing your new home:" ☐ Online planning services ☐ Magazines ☐ Independent contractor/builder ☐ Developer's models/plans ☐ Designer ☐ Architect ☐ Other (specify: _____)

Likert Scale Summated Rating
data: interval

"The Internet is superior to traditional libraries for comprehensive searches."

STRONGLY AGREE (5)	AGREE (4)	NEITHER AGREE NOR DISAGREE (3)	DISAGREE (2)	STRONGLY DISAGREE (1)

Semantic Differential Scale
data: interval

Lands' End Catalog

FAST ___ : ___ : ___ : ___ : ___ : ___ : ___ : SLOW
HIGH QUALITY ___ : ___ : ___ : ___ : ___ : ___ : ___ : LOW QUALITY

Numerical Scale
data: ordinal or*
interval

EXTREMELY FAVORABLE	5	4	3	2	1	EXTREMELY UNFAVORABLE

Employee's cooperation in teams ___
Employee's knowledge of task ___
Employee's planning effectiveness ___

Continued

points, by which one or more respondents rate one or more concepts on each scale item. In the example in Exhibit 9–1, two sets of bipolar pairs are shown, one from the traditional source and one adapted to the research purpose. Based on the construction requirements discussed later, we might choose 10 scale items to score the "Lands' End Catalog."

EXHIBIT 9–1 Concluded

Multiple Rating List Scale
data: interval

"Please indicate how important or unimportant each service characteristic is:"

	IMPORTANT						UNIMPORTANT
Fast reliable repair	7	6	5	4	3	2	1
Service at my location	7	6	5	4	3	2	1
Maintenance by manufacturer	7	6	5	4	3	2	1
Knowledgeable technicians	7	6	5	4	3	2	1
Notification of upgrades	7	6	5	4	3	2	1
Service contract after warranty	7	6	5	4	3	2	1

Fixed Sum Scale
data: ratio

"Taking all the supplier characteristics we've just discussed and now considering *cost*, what is their relative importance to you (dividing 100 units between):"

Being one of the lowest cost suppliers	
All other aspects of supplier performance	
Sum	100

Stapel Scale
data: ordinal or*
interval

(Company Name)

+5	+5	+5
+4	+4	+4
+3	+3	+3
+2	+2	+2
+1	+1	+1
Technology Leader	Exciting Products	World-Class Reputation
−1	−1	−1
−2	−2	−2
−3	−3	−3
−4	−4	−4
−5	−5	−5

Graphic Rating Scale
data: ordinal or*
interval or ratio

"How likely are you to recommend CompleteCare to others?" (place an X at the position along the line that best reflects your judgment)

VERY LIKELY ⊢——————————————⊣ VERY UNLIKELY

(alternative with graphic)

* In chapter 8 we noted that researchers differ in the ways they treat data from certain scales. If you are unable to establish the linearity of the measured variables or you cannot be confident that you have equal intervals, it is proper to treat data from these scales as ordinal.

The semantic differential has several advantages. It produces interval data. It is an efficient and easy way to secure attitudes from a large sample. These attitudes may be measured in both direction and intensity. The total set of responses provides a comprehensive picture of the meaning of an object and a measure of the subject doing the rating. It is a standardized technique that is easily repeated but escapes many problems of response distortion found with more direct methods.

Numerical scales have equal intervals that separate their numeric scale points. The verbal anchors serve as the labels for the extreme points. Numerical scales are often 5-point scales, as shown in the exhibit, but may have 7 or 10 points. The respondent writes a number from the scale next to each item. If numerous questions about employee performance were included in the example, the scale would provide both an absolute measure of importance and a relative measure (ranking) of the various items rated. The scale's linearity, simplicity, and production of ordinal or interval data make it popular for managers and researchers.

The **multiple rating list scale** is similar to the numerical scale but differs in two ways: (1) It accepts a circled response from the rater, and (2) the layout allows visualization of the results. The advantage is that a mental map of the respondent's evaluations is evident to both the rater and the researcher. This scale produces interval data.

A scale that helps the researcher discover proportions is the **fixed sum scale.** In the example, two categories are presented that must sum to 100. Up to 10 categories may be used, but both respondent precision and patience suffer when too many stimuli are proportioned and summed. A respondent's ability to add is also taxed in some situations; thus this is not a response strategy that can be effectively used with children or the uneducated. The advantage of the scale is its compatibility with percent (100 percent) and the fact that continuous data (versus discrete categories) can be compared for the alternatives. The scale is used to record attitudes, behavior, and behavioral intent. It produces interval data.

The **stapel scale** is used as an alternative to the semantic differential, especially when it is difficult to find bipolar adjectives that match the investigative question. In the example in Exhibit 9–1 there are three attributes of corporate image. The scale is composed of the word (or phrase) identifying the image dimension and a set of 10 response categories for each of the three attributes. Fewer response categories are sometimes used. Respondents select a plus number for the characteristic that describes the named company. The more accurate the description, the larger is the positive number. Similarly, the less accurate the description, the larger is the negative number chosen. Ratings range from +5 to –5, very accurate to very inaccurate. Like the semantic differential, stapel scales usually produce interval data.

The **graphic rating scale** was created to enable researchers to discern fine differences. Theoretically, an infinite number of ratings is possible if the respondent is sophisticated enough to differentiate and record them. The respondent checks his or her response at any point along a continuum. Usually, the score is a measure of length (millimeters) from either end point. The results are usually treated as interval data. The difficulty is in coding and analysis. This response strategy requires more time than scales with predetermined categories. Other graphic rating scales use pictures, icons, or other visuals to communicate with the rater and represent a variety of data types. Graphic scales are often used with children, whose more limited vocabulary prevents the use of scales anchored with words.

Errors to Avoid with Rating Scales   The value of rating scales for measurement purposes depends on the assumption that a person can and will make good judgments. Before accepting respondents' ratings, we should consider their tendencies to make errors of three types:[6] (1) leniency, (2) central tendency, and (3) halo effect.

Leniency.   The error of **leniency** occurs when a respondent is either an "easy rater" or a "hard rater." The latter is an error of *negative leniency.* Raters are inclined to score people higher whom they know well and with whom they are ego involved. There is also the opposite—where acquaintances are rated lower because one is aware of the tendency toward positive leniency and attempts to counteract it. A way to deal with *positive leniency* is to design the rating scale to anticipate it. An example might be an asymmetrical scale that has only one unfavorable descriptive term and four favorable terms (poor—fair—good—very good—excellent). The scale designer expects that the mean ratings will be near "good" and that there will be a symmetrical distribution about that point.

Central Tendency.   Raters are reluctant to give extreme judgments, and this fact accounts for the error of **central tendency.** This is most often seen when the rater does not know the object or property being rated. To counteract this type of error try the following:

MANAGEMENT

- Adjust the strength of descriptive adjectives.

- Space the intermediate descriptive phrases farther apart.

- Provide smaller differences in meaning between the steps near the ends of the scale than between the steps near the center.

- Use more points in the scale.

Halo.   The **halo effect** is the systematic bias that the rater introduces by carrying over a generalized impression of the subject from one rating to another. You expect the student who does well on the first question of an examination to do well on the second. You conclude a report is good because you like its form, or you believe someone is intelligent because you agree with him or her. Halo is a pervasive error. It is especially difficult to avoid when the property being studied is not clearly defined, not easily observed, not frequently discussed, involves reactions with others, or is a trait of high moral importance.[7] One way to counteract the halo effect is to rate one trait at a time for all subjects or to have one trait per page.

Rating scales are widely used in management research and generally deserve their popularity. The results obtained with careful use compare favorably with other methods.

Ranking Scales

In ranking scales, the subject directly compares two or more objects and makes choices among them. Frequently, the respondent is asked to select one as the "best" or the "most preferred." When there are only two choices, this approach is satisfactory, but it often results in "ties" when more than two choices are found. For example, assume respondents are asked to select the most preferred among three or more models of a product. In response, 40 percent choose model A, 30 percent choose model B, and 30 percent choose model C. Which is the preferred model? The analyst would be taking a risk to suggest that A is most preferred. Perhaps that interpretation is correct, but 60 percent of the respondents chose some model other than A. Perhaps all B and C voters would place A last, preferring either B or C to it. This ambiguity can be avoided by using some of the techniques described in this section.

MANAGEMENT

Using the **paired-comparison scale,** the respondent can express attitudes unambiguously by choosing between two objects. Typical of paired comparisons would be the sports car preference example in Exhibit 9–2. The number of judgments required in a paired comparison is $[(n)(n-1)/2]$, where n is the number of stimuli or objects to be judged. When four cars are evaluated, the respondent evaluates six paired comparisons $[(4)(3)/2 = 6]$.

EXHIBIT 9–2   **Ranking Scales**

Paired-Comparison Scale
data: ordinal

"For each pair of two-seat sports cars listed, place a check beside the one you would most prefer if you had to choose between the two."

___ BMW Z3   ___ Chevrolet Corvette
___ Porsche Boxster   ___ Porsche Boxster

___ Chevrolet Corvette   ___ Porsche Boxster
___ BMW Z3   ___ Dodge Viper

___ Chevrolet Corvette   ___ Dodge Viper
___ Dodge Viper   ___ BMW Z3

Forced Ranking Scale
data: ordinal

"Rank the radar detection features in your order of preference. Place the number 1 next to the most preferred, 2 by the second choice, and so forth."

___ User programming
___ Cordless capability
___ Small size
___ Long-range warning
___ Minimal false alarms

Comparative Scale
data: ordinal

"Compared to your previous mutual fund's performance, the new one is:"

SUPERIOR		ABOUT THE SAME		INFERIOR
1	2	3	4	5

S N A P S H O T

Mastering Leadership in Education

In an attempt to respond to the less-than-stellar performance of their students on standardized tests, many states are mandating new educational standards for teachers. Ohio is one such state. Starting with year 2002 graduates of education programs, all teachers of kindergarten through high school will need to earn a master's degree within five to seven years of licensure in order to maintain their teaching certification. Wittenberg University, a nationally ranked, private liberal arts institution in Ohio, has been training teachers for 150 years through a bachelor of arts in education. The faculty in its education department recently mailed a survey to more than 2,000 teachers in its five-county market area to determine the attractiveness of Wittenberg as a source for the required master's degree. This mail survey generated nearly 800 responses and indicated the market is receptive to attending Wittenberg for the required master's degree in education. Respondents' enthusiasm was tempered only by concerns about price. Looking at the instrument provided with the case "Mastering Teacher Leadership" in the Cases section of the text, did the survey designers scale the items to be measured correctly?

www.wittenberg.edu

EXHIBIT 9–3   **Response Patterns of 200 Union Members' Paired Comparisons on Five Suggestions for Bargaining Proposal Priorities**

Paired-comparison data may be treated in several ways. If there is substantial consistency, we will find that if *A* is preferred to *B*, and *B* to *C*, then *A* will be consistently preferred to *C*. This condition of transitivity need not always be true but should occur most of the time. When it does, take the total number of preferences among the comparisons as the score for that stimulus. Assume a union bargaining committee is considering five major demand proposals. The committee would like to know how the union membership ranks these proposals. One option would be to ask a sample of the members to pair-compare the personnel suggestions. With a rough comparison of the total preferences for each option, it is apparent that *B* is the most popular.

	Suggestion				
	A	**B**	**C**	**D**	**E**
A	—	164*	138	50	70
B	36	—	54	14	30
C	62	146	—	32	50
D	150	186	168	—	118
E	130	170	150	82	—
Total	378	666	510	178	268
Rank order	3	1	2	5	4
M_p	0.478	0.766	0.610	0.278	0.368
Z_j	−0.060	0.730	0.280	−0.590	−0.340
R_j	0.530	1.320	0.870	0.000	0.250

*Interpret this cell, 164 members preferred suggestion *B* (column) to suggestion *A* (row).

In another example we might compare two bargaining proposals available to union negotiators (see Exhibit 9–3). Generally, there are more than two stimuli to judge, resulting in a potentially tedious task for respondents. If 15 suggestions for bargaining proposals are available, 105 paired comparisons would be made.

Reducing the number of comparisons per respondent without reducing the number of objects can lighten this burden. You can present each respondent with only a sample of the stimuli. In this way, each pair of objects must be compared an equal number of times. Another procedure is to choose a few objects that are believed to cover the range of attractiveness at equal intervals. All other stimuli are then compared to these few standard objects. If 36 automobiles are to be judged, four may be selected as standards and the others divided into four groups of eight each. Within each group, the eight are compared to each other. Then the 32 are individually compared to each of the four standard automobiles. This reduces the number of comparisons from 630 to 240.

Paired comparisons run the risk that respondents will tire to the point that they give ill-considered answers or refuse to continue. Opinions differ about the upper limit, but five or six stimuli are not unreasonable when the respondent has other questions to

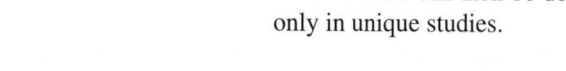

answer. If the data collection consists only of paired comparisons, as many as 10 stimuli are reasonable.

While a paired comparison provides ordinal data, there are methods for converting it to interval data. The Law of Comparative Judgment involves converting the frequencies of preferences (such as in Exhibit 9–3) into a table of proportions that are then transformed into a Z matrix by referring to the table of areas under the normal curve.[8] Guilford's *composite-standard* method is another alternative.[9]

The **forced ranking scale** shown in Exhibit 9–2 lists attributes that are ranked relative to each other. This method is faster than paired comparisons and is usually easier and more motivating to the respondent. With five items, it takes 10 paired comparisons to complete the task, and the simple forced ranking of five is easier. Also, ranking has no transitivity problem where *A* is preferred to *B*, and *B* to *C*, but *C* is preferred to *A*.

A drawback to forced ranking is the number of stimuli that can be handled by this method. Five objects can be ranked easily, but respondents may grow careless in ranking 10 or more items. In addition, rank ordering produces ordinal data since the distance between preferences is unknown.

Often the manager or researcher is interested in benchmarking. This calls for a standard by which other programs, processes, brands, points of sale, or people can be compared. The **comparative scale** is ideal for such comparisons if the respondents are familiar with the standard. In the Exhibit 9–2 example, the standard is the respondent's previous mutual fund. The new fund is being assessed relative to it. The provision to compare yet other funds to the standard is not shown in the example but is nonetheless available to the researcher.

Some researchers treat the data produced by comparative scales as interval data since the scoring reflects an interval between the standard and what is being compared. We would treat the rank or position of the item as ordinal data unless the linearity of the variables in question could be supported.

None of the ranking methods covered is particularly useful when there are many items. The method of **successive intervals** is sometimes used to sort the items (usually one per card) into piles or groups representing a succession of values. From the sort, an interval scale can then be developed.[10] This procedure is not used frequently and then only in unique studies.

Measurement Scale Construction

Earlier, we discussed scales by the techniques used to construct them. Of the five techniques, three are used frequently: the *arbitrary* approach, *item analysis,* and *factoring.* They are emphasized in this section along with a preview of *multivariate* scales (described in more detail in Chapter 19). *Consensus* and *cumulative* methods receive less attention because they are time-consuming to construct or have fewer management applications. They are briefly mentioned because of their influence on current methods.

Arbitrary Scaling

We design **arbitrary scales** by collecting several items that we believe are unambiguous and appropriate to a given topic. Some are chosen for inclusion in the instrument. To illustrate, consider a company image study. We choose a sample of items that we believe are the components of company image:

How do you regard (Company X's) reputation?

1. As a place to work?   Bad _____ _____ _____ _____ _____ Good

2. As a sponsor of civic projects?   Bad _____ _____ _____ _____ _____ Good

3. For ecological concern?   Bad _____ _____ _____ _____ _____ Good

4. As an employer of minorities?   Bad _____ _____ _____ _____ _____ Good

We might score each of these from 1 to 5, depending on the degree of favorableness reported. The results may be studied in several ways. Totals may be made by individual items, by company, by companies as places to work, for ecological concern, and so on. Totals for each company or for individuals may be calculated to determine how they compare to others. Based on a total for these four items, each company would receive from 4 to 20 points from each respondent. These data may also be analyzed from a respondent-centered point of view. Thus, we might use the attitude scores of each individual to study differences among individuals.

Arbitrary scales are easy to develop, inexpensive, and can be designed to be highly specific. They provide useful information and are adequate if developed skillfully. There are also weaknesses. The design approach is subjective. The researcher's insight and ability offer the only assurance that the items chosen are a representative sample of the universe of content (the totality of what constitutes "company image"). We have no evidence that respondents will view all items with the same frame of reference.

While arbitrary scales are often used, there has been a great effort to develop construction techniques that overcome some of their deficiencies. An early attempt was consensus scaling.

Consensus Scaling

Consensus scaling requires items to be selected by a panel of judges and then evaluated on (1) relevance to the topic area, (2) potential for ambiguity, and (3) the level of attitude they represent. A widely known form of this approach is the Thurstone **equal-appearing interval scale.** Also known as the *Thurstone scale,* this approach resulted in an interval rating scale for attitude measurement. Often 50 or more judges evaluate a large number of statements expressing different degrees of favorableness toward an

Assume you are asked by Galaxy Department Stores to study the shopping habits and preferences of teen girls. Galaxy is seeking a way to compete with specialty stores that are far more successful in serving this market segment. Galaxy is considering the construction of an intrastore boutique catering to these teens. What measurement issues would determine your construction of measurement scales?

object. There is one statement per card. The judges sort each card into 1 of 11 piles representing their evaluation of the degree of favorableness that the statement expresses. The judge's agreement or disagreement with the statement is not involved. Of the 11 piles, 3 are identified to the judges by labels of "favorable" and "unfavorable" at the extremes and "neutral" at the midpoint. The eight intermediate piles are unlabeled to create the impression of equal-appearing intervals between the three labeled positions.

This method of scale construction is rarely used in applied management research these days. Its cost, time, and staff requirements make it impractical. The importance of this historic method, however, is its influence on the Likert and semantic differential scales.

Item Analysis Scaling

Item analysis scaling is a procedure for evaluating an item based on how well it discriminates between those persons whose total score is high and those whose total score is low. The most popular scale using this approach is the summated or Likert scale.

Item analysis involves calculating the mean scores for each scale item among the low scorers and high scorers. The item means between the high-score group and the low-score group are then tested for significance by calculating t values. Finally, the 20 to 25 items that have the greatest t values (significant differences between means) are selected for inclusion in the final scale.[11]

Likert-type scales are relatively easy to construct compared to the equal-appearing interval scale.[12] The first step is to collect a large number of statements that meet two criteria: (1) Each statement is believed to be relevant to the attitude being studied. (2) Each is believed to reflect a favorable or unfavorable position on that attitude. People similar to those who are going to be studied are asked to read each statement and to state the level of their agreement with it, using a five-point scale. A scale value of 1 might indicate a strongly unfavorable attitude; 5, a strongly favorable attitude (see Exhibit 9–1).

Each person's responses are then added to secure a total score. The next step is to array these total scores and select some portion representing the highest and lowest *total scores,* say, the top 25 percent and the bottom 25 percent. These two extreme groups represent people with the most favorable and least favorable attitudes toward the topic being studied. The extremes are the two criterion groups by which we evaluate individual statements. Through a comparative analysis of response patterns to each statement by members of these two groups, we learn which statements consistently correlate with low favorability and which correlate with high favorability attitudes.

This procedure is illustrated in Exhibit 9–4. In evaluating response patterns of the high and low groups to the statement "I consider my job exciting," we secure the results shown. After finding the t values for each statement, we rank-order them and select those statements with the highest t values. As an approximate indicator of a statement's discrimination power, Edwards suggests using only those statements whose t value is 1.75 or greater, provided there are 25 or more subjects in each group.[13] To safeguard against response-set bias, we should word approximately one-half of the statements to be favorable and word the other half to be unfavorable.

The Likert scale has many advantages that account for its popularity. It is easy and quick to construct. Each item that is included has met an empirical test for discriminating ability. Since respondents answer each item, it is probably more reliable and it provides a greater volume of data than many other scales.

EXHIBIT 9–4 **Evaluating a Scale Statement by Item Analysis**

Response Categories	Low Total Score Group				High Total Score Group			
	X	f	fX	fX^2	X	f	fX	fX^2
Strongly agree	5	3	15	75	5	22	110	550
Agree	4	4	16	64	4	30	120	480
Undecided	3	29	87	261	3	15	45	135
Disagree	2	22	44	88	2	4	8	16
Strongly disagree	1	15	15	15	1	2	2	2
Total		73	177	503		73	285	1,183
		n_L	ΣX_L	ΣX_L^2		n_H	ΣX_H	ΣX_H^2

Steps:

1. For the statement "I consider my job exciting," we select the data from the bottom 25 percent of the distribution (low total score group) and the top 25 percent (high total score group). There are 73 people in each group. The remaining 50 percent in the middle of the distribution is not considered for this analysis. For each of the response categories, the scale's value (X) is multiplied by the frequency or number of respondents (f) who chose that value. These values produce the product (fX). This number is then multiplied by X (fX^2). For example, there are 3 respondents in the low score group who scored a 5 (strongly agreed with the statement): (fX) = 5 × 3 = 15; (fX^2) = 15 × 5 = 75.

2. The frequencies, products, and squares are summed.

3. A mean score for each group is computed.

4. Deviation scores are computed, squared, and summed as required by the formula.

5. The data are tested in a modified t-test that compares the high and low scoring groups for the item. Notice the mean scores in the numerator of the formula.

6. The calculated value is compared with a criterion, 1.75. If the calculated value (in this case, 8.92) is equal to or exceeds the criterion, the statement is said to be a good discriminator of the measured attitude. (If it is less than the criterion, we would consider it a poor discriminator of the target attitude and delete it from the measuring instrument.) We then select the next item and repeat the process.

Cumulative Scaling

Total scores on **cumulative scales** have the same meaning. Given a person's total score, it is possible to estimate which items were answered positively and negatively. A pioneering scale of this type was the **scalogram**. Scalogram analysis is a procedure for determining whether a set of items forms a unidimensional scale.[14] A scale is unidimensional if the responses fall into a pattern in which endorsement of the item reflecting the extreme position results also in endorsing all items that are less extreme.

Assume we are surveying opinions regarding a new style of running shoe. We have developed a preference scale of four items:

1. The *Airsole* is good looking.

2. I will insist on *Airsole* next time because it is great looking.

3. The appearance of *Airsole* is acceptable to me.

4. I prefer the *Airsole* style to other styles.

Respondents indicate whether they agree or disagree. If these items form a unidimensional scale, the response patterns will approach the ideal configuration shown in Exhibit 9–5.

A score of 4 indicates all statements are agreed upon and represents the most favorable attitude. Persons with a score of 3 should disagree with item 2 but agree with all

EXHIBIT 9–5 Ideal Scalogram Response Pattern

Item				
2	**4**	**1**	**3**	**Respondent Score**
X	X	X	X	4
—	X	X	X	3
—	—	X	X	2
—	—	—	X	1
—	—	—	—	0

X = Agree

— = Disagree

others, and so on. According to scalogram theory, this pattern confirms that the universe of content (attitude toward the appearance of this running shoe) is scalable.

The scalogram and similar procedures for discovering underlying structure are useful for assessing behaviors that are highly structured, such as social distance, organizational hierarchies, and evolutionary product stages.[15] Although used less often today, the scalogram retains potential for managerial applications.

Factor Scaling

Factor scales include a variety of techniques that have been developed to address two problems: (1) how to deal with the universe of content that is multidimensional and (2) how to uncover underlying (latent) dimensions that have not been identified by exploratory research.

SNAPSHOT — A Survey of Controversy: RU486

The Food and Drug Administration's approval of the sale of mifepristone (RU486), "the first dedicated medical abortion pill regimen," on September 28, 2000, heralded a period of some concern in medical practices as well as private and public health facilities. Fearing a "dramatic transformation of the abortion landscape," many physicians claimed they would stay on the sidelines. One year later, a landmark study by the Henry J. Kaiser Family Foundation (KFF) reveals whether those fears were realized.

KFF hired Princeton Survey Research Associates (PSRA) to conduct a phone survey of 790 health care providers, including 595 gynecologists and 195 family practitioners, internists, and general practitioners between May and August 2000. PSRA randomly drew the sample of physicians from the American Medical Association's master file. Doctors were asked to reveal the degree to which they had performed surgical abortion in the previous five years or their reasons for not providing this service (personal convictions, hospital policy, etc.). Each interview also included questions to measure physician familiarity with medical abortion regimen, as well as its perceived safety and effectiveness. Finally, interviewers asked physicians whether they had prescribed mifepristone since its FDA approval, whether they had previously participated in clinical trials of the drug during its FDA-approval process, their reasons for prescribing or not prescribing mifepristone, and their future intentions for prescribing mifepristone plus their reasons for acting as they predicted.

Given the controversial nature of the subject and physicians' expressed concerns, what measurement issues should have been considered and which scales would have been appropriate for this first-year benchmark study? To see the measurement questions used, see the KFF website.

www.kff.org

www.psra.com

These techniques are designed to intercorrelate items so their degree of interdependence may be detected. There are many approaches that the advanced student will want to explore, such as latent structure analysis (of which the scalogram is a special case), factor analysis, cluster analysis, and metric and nonmetric multidimensional scaling. We limit the discussion in this section to the semantic differential (SD), which is based on factor analysis.[16]

We provide an illustration of factor analysis and multidimensional scaling in Chapter 19.

Osgood and his associates developed the *semantic differential method* to measure the psychological meanings of an object to an individual.[17] They produced a long list of adjective pairs useful for attitude research. Searching *Roget's Thesaurus* for such adjectives, they located 289 pairs. These were reduced to 76 pairs that were formed into rating scales. They chose 20 concepts that evoked the psychological meanings they wished to probe. The concepts from this historical study illustrate the wide applicability of the technique to persons, abstract concepts (such as leadership), events, institutions, and physical objects.[18]

By factor analyzing the data, they concluded that semantic space is multidimensional rather than unidimensional. Three factors contributed most to meaningful judgments by respondents: (1) evaluation, (2) potency, and (3) activity. The evaluation dimension usually accounts for one-half to three-fourths of the extractable variance. (The evaluation dimension is the only dimension possessed by Likert scales.) Potency and activity are about equal and together account for a little over one-fourth of the extractable variance. Occasionally, the potency and activity dimensions combine to form "dynamism." Results of the *Thesaurus* study are shown in Exhibit 9–6.

The SD scale should be adapted to each research problem. SD construction involves the following steps.

MANAGEMENT

1. Select the concepts. The concepts are nouns, noun phrases, or nonverbal stimuli such as visual sketches. Concepts are chosen by judgment and reflect the nature of the investigative question. In the MindWriter study, one concept might be "Call Center accessibility." Or in a study to evaluate multiple candidates for an executive position in an industry association, the concept might be a candidate, "Darnell Williams."

2. Select the original bipolar word pairs or pairs you adapt to your needs. If the traditional Osgood items are used, several criteria guide your selection. The first is the factor(s) composition.

- You need at least three bipolar pairs for each factor to use evaluation, potency, and activity. Scores on these individual items should be averaged, by factor, to improve their test reliability.

- The scale must be relevant to the concepts being judged. Choose adjectives that allow connotative perceptions to be expressed. Irrelevant concept-scale pairings yield neutral midpoint values that convey little information.

- Scales should be stable across subjects and concepts. A pair such as "large–small" may be interpreted by some to be denotative when judging a physical object such as an "automobile" but may be used connotatively in judging abstract concepts such as "quality management."

- Scales should be linear between polar opposites and pass through the origin. A pair that fails this test is "rugged–delicate," which is nonlinear on the evaluation dimension. When used separately, both adjectives have favorable meanings.[19]

In Exhibit 9–7 we see the scale being used by a panel of corporate leaders to rate candidates for an industry leadership position. The selection of concepts in this case is simple; there are three candidates, plus a fourth—the ideal candidate.

EXHIBIT 9–6　**Results of the Thesaurus Study**

Evaluation (E)	Potency (P)	Activity (A)
Good–bad	Hard–soft	Active–passive
Positive–negative	Strong–weak	Fast–slow
Optimistic–pessimistic	Heavy–light	Hot–cold
Complete–incomplete	Masculine–feminine	Excitable–calm
Timely–untimely	Severe–lenient	
	Tenacious–yielding	

Subcategories of Evaluation			
Meek Goodness	**Dynamic Goodness**	**Dependable Goodness**	**Hedonistic Goodness**
Clean–dirty	Successful–unsuccessful	True–false	Pleasurable–painful
Kind–cruel	High–low	Reputable–disreputable	Beautiful–ugly
Sociable–unsociable	Meaningful–meaningless	Believing–skeptical	Sociable–unsociable
Light–dark	Important–unimportant	Wise–foolish	Meaningful–meaningless
Altruistic–egotistical	Progressive–regressive	Healthy–sick	
Grateful–ungrateful		Clean–dirty	
Beautiful–ugly			
Harmonious–dissonant			

SOURCE: Adapted from Charles E. Osgood, G. J. Suci, and P. H. Tannenbaum, *The Measurement of Meaning* (Urbana, IL: University of Illinois Press, 1957), Table 5, pp. 52–61.

EXHIBIT 9–7　**SD Scale for Analyzing Candidates for an Industry Leadership Position**

Analyze (candidate) for current position:

(E)	Sociable	(7): ____: ____: ____: ____: ____: ____: ____:	(1) Unsociable
(P)	Weak	(1): ____: ____: ____: ____: ____: ____: ____:	(7) Strong
(A)	Active	(7): ____: ____: ____: ____: ____: ____: ____:	(1) Passive
(E)	Progressive	(7): ____: ____: ____: ____: ____: ____: ____:	(1) Regressive
(P)	Yielding	(1): ____: ____: ____: ____: ____: ____: ____:	(7) Tenacious
(A)	Slow	(1): ____: ____: ____: ____: ____: ____: ____:	(7) Fast
(E)	True	(7): ____: ____: ____: ____: ____: ____: ____:	(1) False
(P)	Heavy	(7): ____: ____: ____: ____: ____: ____: ____:	(1) Light
(A)	Hot	(7): ____: ____: ____: ____: ____: ____: ____:	(1) Cold
(E)	Unsuccessful	(1): ____: ____: ____: ____: ____: ____: ____:	(7) Successful

EXHIBIT 9–8   **Graphic Representation of SD Analysis**

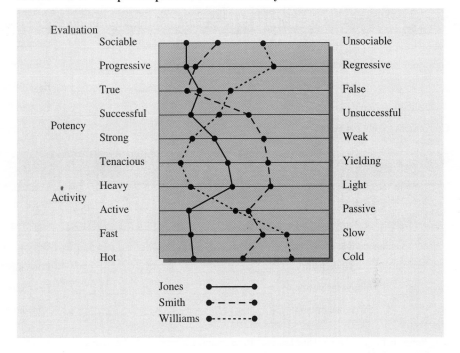

The nature of the problem determines the selection of dimensions and bipolar pairs. Since the person who wins this position must influence business leaders, we decide to use all three factors. The candidate must deal with many people, often in a social setting; must have high integrity; and must take a leadership role in encouraging more progressive policies in the industry. The position will also involve a high degree of personal activity. Based on these requirements, we choose 10 scales to score the candidates from 7 to 1. The negative signs in the original scoring procedure (−3, −2, −1, 0, +1, +2, +3) were found to produce coding errors. Exhibit 9–7 illustrates the scale used for the research. The letters along the left side, which show the relevant factor, would be omitted from the actual scale, as would the numerical values shown. Note also that the evaluation, potency, and activity scales are mixed, and about half are reversed to minimize the halo effect. To analyze the results, the set of evaluation (E) values is averaged, as are those for the potency (P) and activity (A) dimensions.

The data are plotted in Exhibit 9–8. Here the adjective pairs are reordered so evaluation, potency, and activity descriptors are grouped together with the ideal factor reflected by the left side of the scale. Profiles of the three candidates may be compared to each other and to the ideal.

Adapting SD Scales to the Management Question   One study explored a retail store image using 35 pairs of words or phrases classified into eight groups. These word pairs were especially created for the study. Excerpts from this scale are presented in Exhibit 9–9. Other categories of scale items were "general characteristics of the company," "physical characteristics of the store," "prices charged by the store," "store personnel," "advertising by the store," and "your friends and the store." Since the scale pairs are closely associated with the characteristics of the store and its use, one could develop image profiles of various stores.

EXHIBIT 9–9   Adapting SD Scales for Retail Store Image Study

Convenience of Reaching the Store from Your Location		
Nearby	___: ___: ___: ___: ___: ___: ___:	Distant
Short time required to reach store	___: ___: ___: ___: ___: ___: ___:	Long time required to reach store
Difficult drive	___: ___: ___: ___: ___: ___: ___:	Easy drive
Difficult to find parking place	___: ___: ___: ___: ___: ___: ___:	Easy to find parking place
Convenient to other stores I shop	___: ___: ___: ___: ___: ___: ___:	Inconvenient to other stores I shop

Products Offered		
Wide selection of different kinds of products	___: ___: ___: ___: ___: ___: ___:	Limited selection of different kinds of products
Fully stocked	___: ___: ___: ___: ___: ___: ___:	Understocked
Undependable products	___: ___: ___: ___: ___: ___: ___:	Dependable products
High quality	___: ___: ___: ___: ___: ___: ___:	Low quality
Numerous brands	___: ___: ___: ___: ___: ___: ___:	Few brands
Unknown brands	___: ___: ___: ___: ___: ___: ___:	Well-known brands

SOURCE: Robert F. Kelly and Ronald Stephenson, "The Semantic Differential: An Information Source for Designing Retail Patronage Appeals," *Journal of Marketing* 31 (October 1967), p. 45.

Advanced Scaling Techniques

New construction approaches have removed many of the deficiencies of traditional scales. Some have evolved to handle specific management research applications. Most techniques mentioned in this section rely on complex computer algorithms and require an understanding of multivariate statistics. Students interested in further information on these topics should refer to the statistical examples in Chapter 19 and the references.

Multidimensional scaling (MDS) describes a collection of techniques that deal with property space in a more general manner than the semantic differential. With MDS, one can scale objects, people, or both in ways that provide a visual impression of the relationships among variables. The data-handling characteristics of MDS provide several options: ordinal input (with interval output), and fully metric (interval) and non-metric modes. The various techniques use proximities as input data. A **proximity** is an index of perceived similarity or dissimilarity between objects. The objects might be 20 nations (or 10 primary exports) that respondents are asked to judge in pairs of possible combinations as to their similarity. By means of a computer program, the ranked or rated relationships are then represented as points on a map in multidimensional space.[20]

We may think of three types of attribute space, each representing a multidimensional map. First, in *objective* space a product can be positioned in terms of, say, its price, taste, and brand image. Second, a person's perceptions also may be positioned in *subjective* space using similar dimensions. These maps do not always coincide, but they do provide information about perceptual disparities. Since the subjective maps vary over time, they also provide important trend data. Third, we can describe our preferences for the object's *ideal* attributes. All objects close to the ideal are more preferred than those farther away. These various configurations are said to reflect the "hidden structure" of the

EXHIBIT 9–10   **Multidimensional Map of Beer Preferences**

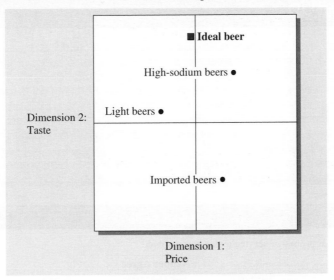

data and make complicated problems much easier to understand. In Exhibit 9–10 two dimensions are plotted: price and taste. The high-sodium beers are closest to the ideal beer on the price dimension while the imported beers are farthest away.

Another approach, representing a collection of techniques, is **conjoint analysis.** Conjoint analysis is used to measure complex decision making that requires multiattribute judgments. Its primary focus has been the explanation of consumer behavior with numerous applications in product development and marketing.[21]

When discovering and learning about products, consumers define a set of attributes or characteristics they use to compare competing brands or models in a product class. Using these attributes, they evaluate the product range and eliminate some brands. Then a final set of alternatives (including a nonpurchase or delayed purchase decision) is developed. These evaluations can change if there is new information about additional competitors, corrections to attribute knowledge, or further thoughts about the attribute. Algebraic theory can be used to model these cognitive processes and develop statistical approximations that reveal the rules the consumer follows in decision making.[22]

For example, a consumer might be considering the purchase of a personal computer. MindWriter has a fast processing speed and a high price. Brand X has a low price and a slower processor. The consumer's choice will be evidence of the utility of the processing-speed attribute. Simultaneously, other attributes are being evaluated—such as memory, portability, graphics support, and user friendliness.

Conjoint analysis can produce a scaled value for each attribute as well as a utility value for attributes that have levels (e.g., memory may have a range of 128 to more than 512 megabytes). Both ranking and rating inputs may be used to evaluate product attributes. Conjoint analysis is not restricted to marketing applications, nor should it be considered a single generalized technique (see Chapter 19).

Finally, advanced students who are interested in the above techniques may also wish to investigate *magnitude estimation scaling.*[23] Magnitude scales provide access to ratio measurement and open new alternatives to management problems previously addressed through ordinal scales alone. *Rasch models* also offer alternative approaches to a range of traditional measures from dichotomous responses to Likert-type response formats.[24]

Close-Up

Myra and Jason had been working on scaling for the CompleteCare project for a week when the call came to Myra to report her progress to MindWriter's general manager, Jean-Claude. They had narrowed the choice to three scales: a Likert scale, a conventional rating scale with two verbal anchors, and their hybrid expectation scale. All were five-point scales that were presumed to measure at the interval level.

They needed a statement that could accompany the scale for preliminary evaluation. Returning to their list of

investigative questions, they found a question that seemed to capture the essence of the repair process: "Are customers' problems resolved?" Translated into an assertion for the scale, the statement became, "Resolution of problems that prompted service/repair." They continued to labor over the wording of the verbal anchors after their meeting with Jean-Claude. It was important for the distance between the numbers to resemble the psychological distance implied by the words. Appropriate versions of the investigative question were constructed and then the scales were added:

Likert Scale

The problem that prompted service/repair was resolved.

Strongly Disagree	Disagree	Neither Agree nor Disagree	Agree	Strongly Agree
1	2	3	4	5

Conventional Likert Rating Scale (MindWriter's favorite)

To what extent are you satisfied that the problem that prompted service/repair was resolved?

Very Dissatisfied				Very Satisfied
1	2	3	4	5

Hybrid Expectation Scale

Resolution of the problem that prompted service/repair.

Met few expectations	Met some expectations	Met most expectations	Met all expectations	Exceeded expectations
1	2	3	4	5

EXHIBIT 9–11   **Plot of MindWriter Scale Evaluation**

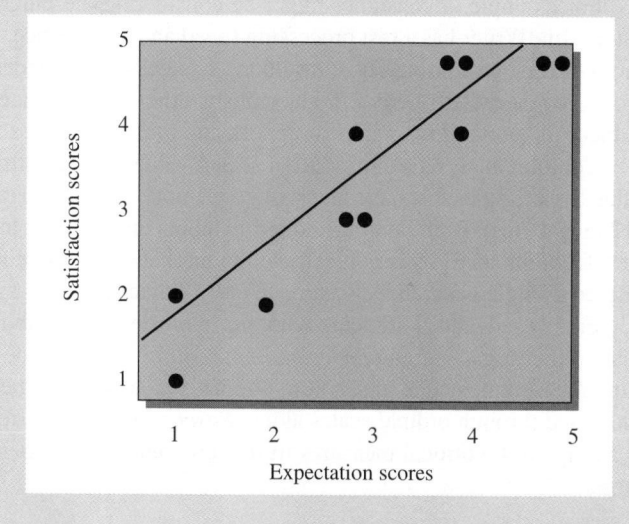

After consulting with MindWriter's research staff, Myra and Jason discussed the advantages of their scale. Myra suggested it was unlikely that CompleteCare would meet none of the customers' expectations. And, with errors of positive leniency, *none* should be replaced by the term *few* so the low end of the scale would be more relevant. Jason had read a *Marketing News* article that said Likert scales and scales similar to MindWriter's frequently produced a heavy concentration of 4s and 5s—a common problem in customer satisfaction research.

They also considered a seven-point scale to remedy this but in the end thought the term *exceeded* on the expectation scale could compensate for scores that clustered on the positive end, making the end point less susceptible to leniency.

They were ready for a pilot test. They decided to compare their hybrid expectation scale with MindWriter's conventional Likert rating scale. The Likert scale required that they create more potential items than they had room for on the postcard. Using the CompleteCare database, names,

addresses, and phone numbers were selected. Thirty customers were selected at random from those who had recent service. They chose the delayed equivalent forms method for reliability testing (see Chapter 8). Myra administered the expectation scale followed by the satisfaction scale to half of the respondents and the satisfaction scale followed by the expectation scale to the other half. Each half sample experienced a time delay. No "order-of-presentation" effects were found. Subsequently, they correlated the satisfaction scores with the expectation scores and plotted the results, shown in Exhibit 9–11.

Satisfaction and expectation were positively correlated for "problem resolution" ($r = .90$); reliability based on equivalence was supported. An assessment of test-retest reliability ($r = .93$) showed that the expectation scale had a higher degree of stability over the one-week interval than did the satisfaction scale ($r = .75$). Their scale also produced linear results (as evidenced by the plot).

The decision was made. Myra and Jason would use the new hybrid expectation scale for the CompleteCare project.

SUMMARY

1 Scaling describes the procedures by which we assign numbers to measurements of opinions, attitudes, and other concepts. Selection of a measurement scale to best meet our needs involves six decisions:

- **Study objective:** Do we measure the characteristics of the respondent or the stimulus object?
- **Response form:** Do we measure with a rating scale or a ranking scale?
- **Degree of preference:** Do we measure our preferences or make nonpreference judgments?
- **Data properties:** Do we measure with nominal, ordinal, interval, or ratio data?
- **Number of dimensions:** Do we measure using a unidimensional or multidimensional scale?
- **Scale construction:** Do we develop scales by arbitrary decision, consensus, item analysis, cumulative scaling, or factor analysis?

In this chapter, two classifications—the response form and scale construction techniques—were emphasized.

2 When using rating scales, one judges an object in absolute terms against certain specified criteria. Several scales were proposed: simple category; multiple choice, single-response; multiple choice, multiple-response; Likert scales; semantic differential; numerical scales; multiple rating lists; fixed sum scales; stapel scales; and graphic rating scales. When you use ranking methods, you make relative comparisons against other similar objects. Three well-known methods are the paired-comparison, forced ranking, and the comparative scale.

3   Scaled measurement strategies are classified by the techniques used to construct them. Of the five techniques, three are used frequently: the arbitrary approach, item analysis, and factoring. Consensus and cumulative methods receive less attention because they are time-consuming or have fewer business applications. Arbitrary scales are designed by the researcher's own subjective selection of items. These scales are simple to construct and have content validity only.

In the consensus method, a panel is used to judge the relevance, ambiguity, and attitude level of scale items. Those items that are judged best are then included in the final instrument. The Thurstone method of equal-appearing intervals is a historic consensus method that has given impetus for many current scales.

With the item analysis approach, one develops many items believed to express either a favorable or an unfavorable attitude toward some general object. These items are then pretested to decide which ones discriminate between persons with high total scores and those with low total scores on the test. Those items that meet this discrimination test are included in the final instrument. The most successful Likert scales are developed using this approach.

With the cumulative approach scales, it is possible to estimate how a respondent has answered individual items by knowing the total score. The items are related to each other on a particular attitude dimension, so that if one agrees with a more extreme item, one will also agree with items representing less extreme views. The scalogram is the classic example.

Factoring develops measurement questions through factor analysis or similar correlation techniques. It is particularly useful in uncovering latent attitude dimensions, and it approaches scaling through the concept of multidimensional attribute space. The semantic differential scale is an example.

Other developments in scaling include multidimensional scaling and conjoint analysis. Each represents a family of related techniques with a variety of applications for handling complex judgments. Magnitude estimation and Rasch models provide an avenue for reconceptualizing traditional scaling techniques for greater efficiency and freedom from error.

KEY TERMS

EXAMPLES

Company	Scenario	Page
Airsole*	Constructing agreement items for a scale.	263
Galaxy Department Stores*	Seeking to assess teen shopping preferences prior to constructing intrastore teen boutiques.	261
Henry J. Kaiser Family Foundation (KFF)	One-year tracking study to assess physicians' knowledge and attitudes regarding mifepristone (RU486).	264
MindWriter*	Evaluating the CompleteCare program for servicing laptops.	BRTL, Close-Up, 269
Miro Beach City Government*	Evaluating voters' approval or disapproval of a regulatory program.	251
Princeton Survey Research Associates	Conducted the phone survey of physicians in KFF's one-year tracking study of physicians' knowledge and attitudes regarding mifepristone (RU486).	264
Wittenberg University Department of Education	Determining demand for a new program.	258

*Due to the confidential and proprietary nature of most research, the names of some companies have been changed.

DISCUSSION QUESTIONS

Terms in Review

1. Discuss the relative merits of and problems with:

   a. Rating and ranking scales.

   b. Likert and differential scales.

   c. Unidimensional and multidimensional scales.

Making Research Decisions

2. Suppose your firm had planned a major research study for November 2001. Given the incidents of September 11, your superior decides to add a question to the study. The question must measure consumers' confidence that the U.S. economic system will be able to rebound following the terrorist attacks of September and the subsequent effects of those incidents (increased layoffs, higher unemployment, numerous firms failing to meet their sales and profit projections, lower holiday retail sales, war on terrorism). Draft a scale of each of the following types to measure that confidence level.

   a. Fixed sum scale.

   b. Likert-type summated scale.

   c. Semantic differential scale.

   d. Stapel scale.

   e. Forced ranking scale.

3. An investigative question in your employee satisfaction study seeks to assess employee "job involvement." Create a measurement question that uses the following scales:

   a. A graphic rating scale.

   b. A multiple rating list.

   c. Which do you recommend and why?

4. You receive the results of a paired-comparison preference test of four soft drinks from a sample of 200 persons. The results are as follows:

	Koak	Zip	Pabze	Mr. Peepers
Koak	—	50*	115	35
Zip	150	—	160	70
Pabze	85	40	—	45
Mr. Peepers	165	130	155	—

*Read as 50 persons preferred Zip to Koak.

  a. How do these brands rank in overall preference in this sample?

  b. Develop an interval scale for these four brands.

5. One of the problems in developing rating scales is the choice of response terms to use. Below are samples of some widely used scaling codes. Do you see any problems with them?

  a. Yes _____ Depends _____ No _____

  b. Excellent _____ Good _____ Fair _____ Poor _____

  c. Excellent _____ Good _____ Average _____ Fair _____ Poor _____

  d. Strongly Approve _____ Approve _____ Uncertain _____ Disapprove _____ Strongly Disapprove _____

6. You are working on a consumer perception study of four brands of bicycles. You will need to develop measurement questions and scales to accomplish the following tasks. Also be sure to explain which data levels (nominal, ordinal, interval, ratio) are appropriate and which quantitative techniques you will use.

  a. Prepare an overall assessment of all the brands.

  b. Provide a comparison of the brands for each of the following dimensions:
     (1) Styling
     (2) Durability
     (3) Gear quality
     (4) Brand image

7. Below is a Likert-type scale that might be used to evaluate your opinion of the educational program you are in. There are five response categories: Strongly Agree through Neither Agree nor Disagree to Strongly Disagree. If 5 represents the most positive attitude, how would the different items be valued?

  a. This program is not very challenging.
     SA A N D SD

  b. The general level of teaching is good.
     SA A N D SD

  c. I really think I am learning a lot from this program.
     SA A N D SD

  d. Students' suggestions are given little attention here.
     SA A N D SD

  e. This program does a good job of preparing one for a career.
     SA A N D SD

  f. This program is below my expectations.
     SA A N D SD

Record your answers to the above items. In what two different ways could such responses be used? What would be the purpose of each?

**Bringing
Research to Life**

8. What is the basis of Jason and Myra's argument for the need of an arbitrary scale to address customer expectations?

**From Concept
to Practice**

9. Using the response strategies within Exhibit 9–1 or 9–2, which would be appropriate and add insight to understanding the various indicants of student demand for the academic program in which they are enrolled?

WWW Exercises

Visit our website for Internet exercises related to this chapter at
www.mhhe.com/business/cooper8

CASES*

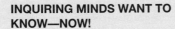

A GEM OF A STUDY

NCR: TEEING UP A NEW STRATEGIC DIRECTION

BBQ PRODUCT CROSSES OVER THE LINES OF VARIED TASTES

PEBBLE BEACH CO.

CALLING UP ATTENDANCE

RAMADA DEMONSTRATES ITS PERSONAL BEST

CUMMINS ENGINES

THE CATALYST FOR WOMEN IN FINANCIAL SERVICES

INQUIRING MINDS WANT TO KNOW—NOW!

VOLKSWAGEN'S BEETLE

MASTERING TEACHER LEADERSHIP

*All cases indicating a video icon are located on the Instructor's Videotape Supplement. All nonvideo cases are in the case section of the textbook. All cases indicating a CD icon offer a data set, which is located on the accompanying CD.

REFERENCE NOTES

1. Bernard S. Phillips, *Social Research Strategy and Tactics,* 2nd ed. (New York: Macmillan, 1971), p. 205.

2. For a discussion of various scale classifications, see W. S. Torgerson, *Theory and Methods of Scaling* (New York: Wiley, 1958), Chapter 3.

3. E. A. Suchman and R. G. Francis, "Scaling Techniques in Social Research," in *An Introduction to Social Research,* ed. J. T. Doby (Harrisburg, PA: Stackpole, 1954), pp. 126–29.

4. A study of the historic research literature found that more than three-fourths of the attitude scales used were of the five-point type. An examination of more recent literature suggests that the five-point scale is still common but there is a growing use of longer scales. For the historic study, see Daniel D. Day, "Methods in Attitude Research," *American Sociological Review* 5 (1940), pp. 395–410. Single versus multiple-item scaling requirements are discussed in Jum C. Nunnally, *Psychometric Theory* (New York: McGraw-Hill, 1967), Chapter 14.

5. This section is adapted from Pamela L. Alreck and Robert B. Settle, *The Survey Research Handbook* (Burr Ridge, IL: Irwin, 1995), Chapter 5.

6. J. P. Guilford, *Psychometric Methods* (New York: McGraw-Hill, 1954), pp. 278–79.

7. P. M. Synonds, "Notes on Rating," *Journal of Applied Psychology* 9 (1925), pp. 188–95.

8. See L. L. Thurstone, "A Law of Comparative Judgment," *Psychological Review* 34 (1927), pp. 273–86.

9. Guilford, *Psychometric Methods.*

10. See Milton A. Saffir, "A Comparative Study of Scales Constructed by Three Psychophysical Methods," *Psychometrica* 11, no. 3 (September 1937), pp. 179–98.

11. Allen L. Edwards, *Techniques of Attitude Scale Construction* (New York: Appleton-Century-Crofts, 1957), pp. 152–54.

12. One study reported that the construction of a Likert scale took only half the time required to construct a Thurstone scale. See

L. L. Thurstone and K. K. Kenney, "A Comparison of the Thurstone and Likert Techniques of Attitude Scale Construction," *Journal of Applied Psychology* 30 (1946), pp. 72–83.

13. Edwards, *Techniques,* p. 153.

14. Louis Guttman, "A Basis for Scaling Qualitative Data," *American Sociological Review* 9 (1944), pp. 139–50.

15. John P. Robinson, "Toward a More Appropriate Use of Guttman Scaling," *Public Opinion Quarterly* 37 (Summer 1973), pp. 260–67.

16. For more on the process of factor analysis, see Chapter 19.

17. Charles E. Osgood, G. J. Suci, and P. H. Tannenbaum, *The Measurement of Meaning* (Urbana, IL: University of Illinois Press, 1957).

18. Ibid., p. 49. See also James G. Snider and Charles E. Osgood, eds., *Semantic Differential Technique* (Chicago: Aldine, 1969).

19. Ibid., p. 79.

20. See, for example, Joseph B. Kruskal and Myron Wish, *Multidimensional Scaling* (Beverly Hills, CA: Sage Publications, 1978); Paul Green and V. R. Rao, *Applied Multidimensional Scaling: A Comparison of Approaches and Algorithms* (New York: Holt, Rinehart & Winston, 1972); and Paul E. Green and F. J. Carmone, *Multidimensional Scaling in Marketing Analysis* (Boston: Allyn & Bacon, 1970).

21. See P. Cattin and D. R. Wittink, "Commercial Use of Conjoint Analysis: A Survey," *Journal of Marketing* 46 (1982), pp. 44–53; and Cattin and Wittink, "Commercial Use of Conjoint Analysis: An Update" (paper presented at the ORSA/TIMS Marketing Science Meetings, Richardson, TX, March 12–15, 1986).

22. Jordan J. Louviere, *Analyzing Decision Making: Metric Conjoint Analysis* (Beverly Hills, CA: Sage Publications, 1988), pp. 9–11.

23. See, for example, Milton Lodge, *Magnitude Scaling: Quantitative Measurement of Opinions* (Beverly Hills, CA: Sage Publications, 1981); and Donald R. Cooper and Donald A. Clare, "A Magnitude Estimation Scale for Human Values," *Psychological Reports* 49 (1981).

24. David Andrich, *Rasch Models for Measurement* (Beverly Hills, CA: Sage Publications, 1988).

REFERENCES FOR SNAPSHOTS AND CAPTIONS

RU486

"One Year Later: Medical Abortion After FDA Approval," The Henry J. Kaiser Family Foundation, September 24, 2001 (http://www.kff.org/content/2001/3170/).

"National Survey of Women's Health Care Providers on Reproductive Health: Medical Abortion Results: Selected Findings from the Kaiser/Harvard Health News Index (August 2001): Public Knowledge and Awareness of Mifepristone," The Henry J. Kaiser Family Foundation, September 24, 2001 (http://www.kff.org/content/2001/3170/SurveyToplinesNew.pdf).

Wittenberg Unversity

Interview with Dr. Robert Welker, project director, Master of Education, Wittenberg University, December 16, 1999.

Survey instrument used in Master of Education market test.

CLASSIC AND CONTEMPORARY READINGS

Edwards, Allen L. *Techniques of Attitude Scale Construction.* New York: Irvington, 1979. Thorough discussion of basic unidimensional scaling techniques.

Kerlinger, Fred N., and Howard B. Lee. *Foundations of Behavioral Research.* 4th ed. New York: HBJ College & School Division, 1999.

Krebs, Dagmar, and Peter Schmidt, ed. *New Directions in Attitude Measurement.* Chicago: Walter De Gruyter, 1993.

Miller, Delbert C. *Handbook of Research Design and Social Measurement.* 5th ed. Thousand Oaks, CA: Sage Publications, 1991. Presents a large number of existing sociometric scales and indexes as well as information on their characteristics, validity, and sources.

Osgood, Charles E., George J. Suci, and Percy H. Tannenbaum. *The Measurement of Meaning.* Urbana, IL: University of Illinois Press, 1957. The basic reference on SD scaling.

PART III

The Sources and Collection of Data

CHAPTER 10

Exploring Secondary Data

Learning Objectives

After reading this chapter, you should understand . . .

1 **The purpose and process of exploratory research.**

2 **Two types and three levels of management decision-related secondary sources.**

3 **The five types of external information and the five critical factors for evaluating the value of a source and its content.**

4 **The process for conducting a productive literature search of external sources, including print and electronic sources.**

5 **The process for conducting a productive literature search with Web-based sources.**

6 **What is involved in internal data mining and how internal data mining techniques differ from literature searches.**

Bringing Research to Life

"Tell me what you know about big banks, Jason," Myra asked.

"Well, for my master's thesis I wrote an econometric model of the Federal Reserve System."

"Swell," she said, impatiently. She dropped into a chair and locked her eyes onto his, a gesture that convinced him she was reading his thoughts before his mouth could say them. "Academic economic research, yes. Very impressive, I'm sure." This acerbic remark she sweetened with a wry smile and then prodded: "The political climate for banks. What do you know, Jason?"

"Well, Myra, it's never good for banks when liberals are running Congress and the White House. Is it?"

"The big banks can feel the eyes of Uncle Sam on them, morning, noon, and night. Which brings us to this." She produced his appointment planner from the top of his desk. "I stopped by today to drop off the draft of my final report for the economic council, the one you said you'd review and give me some feedback on. Thought I'd pencil myself into your planner for Wednesday. I could not help noticing you have an appointment this very noon with a Mr. Armand Croyand of Denver. Do you know who he is?"

"No, not really. He identified himself as the principal of Croyand Associates and wanted a few minutes of my time over lunch, as he was swinging through town. I was free, and I said OK."

"Saying yes to a meeting was a smart move," claimed Myra. "Leaving for the meeting without discovering in advance who Croyand is . . . well, that would be dumb.

"Since your modem never sleeps, nor does the online database of the *Rocky Mountain News,* a few minutes ago I dialed in. Want to know what a few dollars of computer time discovered? Mr. Croyand and his associates are the long-time research organization working for InterMountBanc, headquartered in Colorado, and he has a reputation for doing fine, deep, imaginative real estate research.

"Further rummaging in the *News*'s database reveals that several of the directors recently resigned rather than face scrutiny of their private dealings, and that the new CEO of InterMountBanc and the new directors are all Mr. Clean types who have publicly pledged to stand by the highest ethical standards.

"Now, the plot thickens, doesn't it? I dipped next into the online database of the *Miami Herald,* AND WHAT DO I FIND? I find that InterMountBanc is heavily invested in that new Westridge development in West County, the one that Ed Byldor is throwing up, the one that is now stopped dead in its tracks while the county commission, in all its wisdom, awaits recommendations from the county planners."

"You are telling me, then, that Mr. Armand Croyand is in town on business and I must treat this as a serious business lunch."

"I am telling you to go to lunch loaded for bear, because this could lead to a very big contract. How are you going to handle Mr. Croyand?"

"Well, first," considered Jason, "I will go into the *Herald*'s online database and see if the planning commission has taken a public position on Westridge." Myra nodded. "I have to swing by the Chamber of Commerce in an hour to drop off a final report of the aviation study, and that will give me a chance to discover what they have picked up off the record about Westridge, the planning council, and the county commission. If they are sensitive to public opinion, that works in my favor, since I have a political polling background. If they are worried about real estate values, that is harder, but I suppose I can call the library and find out the address of some trade association that can give me a jump start.

"And since the county government center is within walking distance, I'll check the minutes of the county commission for any reports it has received from the planning council."

"Good. What else will you do while you are in the governmental center?"

"Something else?"

"Think."

He thought. "I'll check the bulletin board in the lobby and see when the planning council is due to hold its next public meeting, and I'll see if Westridge is on the agenda of the county commission meeting for this coming Tuesday."

"OK, so far. And suppose you run into one of the commissioners. What will you do?"

"Ask about his take on the Westridge project?"

"Now you're talking," smiled Myra. "When you meet Croyand, concentrate on what he is telling you, and let him discover almost by accident that you are on top of the real estate situation in West County. Make him believe his prowess as a researcher directed him to you, and that he found exactly the right person to help him here in Florida. Let your secondary research scream quietly of your competence."

The Exploratory Phase Search Strategy

As the exploration process modeled with the management-research question hierarchy suggests (see Exhibit 10–1), exploration of secondary sources may be useful at any stage of the hierarchy. But most researchers find a review of secondary sources critical to moving from management question to research question. In moving from management question to research question, the researcher uses both internal and external secondary sources. We address external sources first. Our discussion of data mining of internal sources completes the chapter.

EXHIBIT 10–1   Integration of Secondary Data into the Research Process

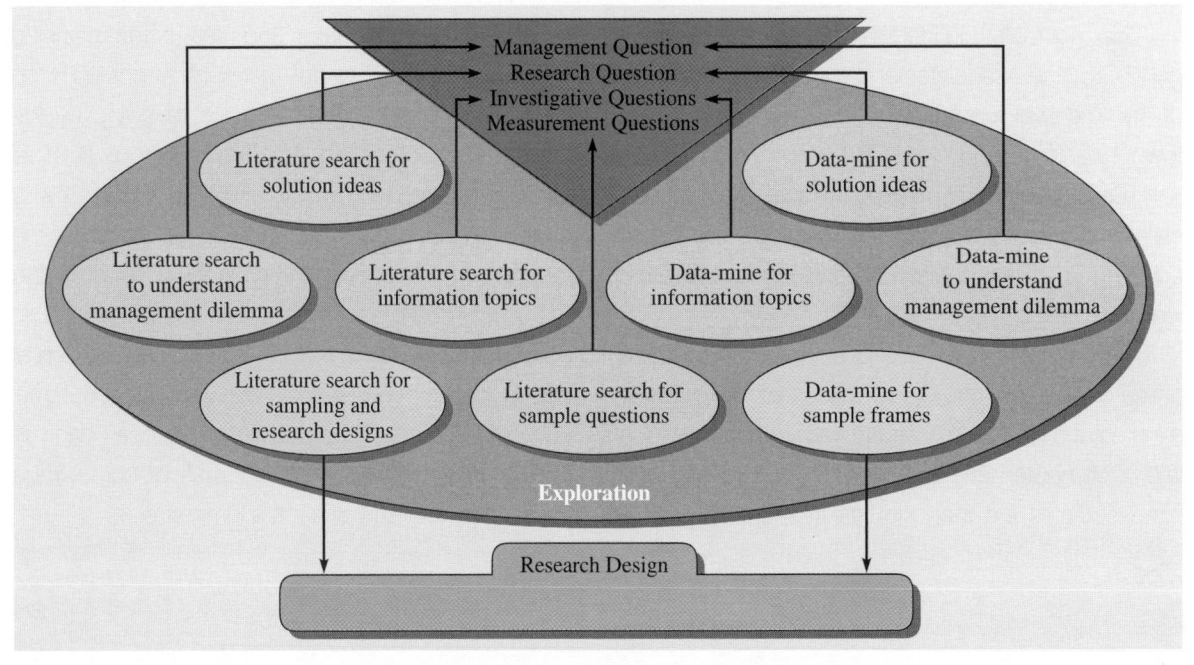

In this **exploratory research** phase of your project, your objective is to accomplish the following:

- Expand your understanding of the management dilemma.
- Look for ways others have addressed and/or solved problems similar to your management dilemma or management question.
- Gather background information on your topic to refine the research question.
- Identify information that should be gathered to formulate investigative questions.
- Identify sources for and actual questions that might be used as measurement questions.
- Identify sources for and actual sample frames that might be used in sample design.

In most cases the exploration phase will begin with a literature search—a review of books as well as articles in journals or professional literature that relate to your management dilemma. A literature search requires the use of the library's online catalog and one or more bibliographic databases or indexes. For some topics, it may be useful to consult a handbook or specialized encyclopedia first to establish a list of key terms, people, or events that have influenced your topic and also to determine what the major publications are and who the foremost authors are. Other reference materials will be incorporated into your search strategy as needed. In general, this **literature search** has five steps:

1. Define your management dilemma or management question.
2. Consult encyclopedias, dictionaries, handbooks, and textbooks to identify key terms, people, or events relevant to your management dilemma or management question.
3. Apply these key terms, people, or events in searching indexes, bibliographies, and the Web to identify specific secondary sources.
4. Locate and review specific secondary sources for relevance.
5. Evaluate the value of each source and its content.

The result of your literature search may be a solution to the management dilemma. In such a case, no further research is necessary. Often, however, the management question remains unresolved, so the decision to proceed generates a research proposal (see Chapter 4). The resulting proposal covers at minimum a statement of the research question and a brief description of proposed research methodology (see Chapter 4). The proposal summarizes the findings of the exploratory phase of the research, usually with a bibliography of secondary sources that have led to the decision to propose a formal research study.

In this chapter we will concentrate on the exploration phase of the project and focus on finding, selecting, and evaluating information in both printed and electronic formats. As you learned in Chapter 6, the first step in an exploratory study is a search of the secondary literature. We defined secondary literature as "studies made by others for their own purposes." These studies, representing primary research to their authors, actually represent only a subset of all the information sources available.

Levels of Information

As you explore your problem or topic, you may consider many different types of information sources, some much more valuable than others. Information sources are generally categorized into three levels: (1) primary sources, (2) secondary sources, and (3) tertiary sources.

Primary sources are original works of research or raw data without interpretation or pronouncements that represent an official opinion or position. Included among the primary sources are memos, letters, complete interviews or speeches (in audio, video, or written transcript formats), laws, regulations, court decisions or standards, and most government data, including census, economic, and labor data. Primary sources are always the most authoritative because the information has not been filtered or interpreted by a second party. Information from all of the above will become your secondary literature supporting *your* original research. Internal sources of primary data would include inventory records, personnel records, purchasing requisition forms, statistical process control charts, and similar data.

Secondary sources are interpretations of primary data. Encyclopedias, textbooks, handbooks, magazine and newspaper articles, and most newscasts are considered secondary information sources. Indeed, nearly all reference materials fall into this category. Internally, sales analysis summaries and investor annual reports would be examples of secondary sources as they are compiled from a variety of primary sources. To an outsider, however, the annual report is viewed as a primary source, as it represents the official position of the corporation. A firm searching for secondary sources can search either internally or externally, as Exhibit 10–2 depicts.

Tertiary sources may be an interpretation of a secondary source but generally are represented by indexes, bibliographies, and other finding aids (e.g., Internet search engines).

From the beginning, it is important to remember that all information is not of equal value. As the source levels indicate, primary sources have more value than secondary

EXHIBIT 10–2   **Secondary Sources for Developing the Management-Research Question Hierarchy**

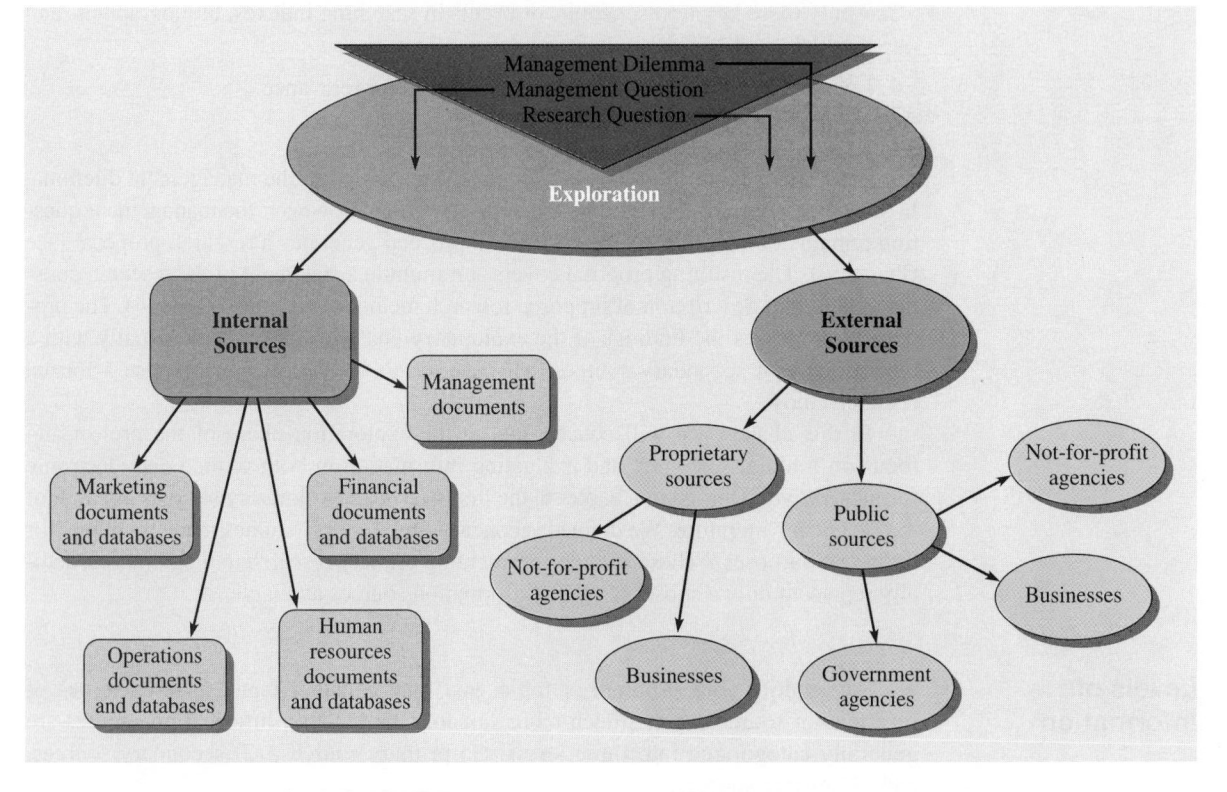

sources, and secondary sources have more value than tertiary sources. In the opening vignette, Myra reads a *Rocky Mountain News* account (a secondary source) but suggests that Jason check the county council minutes (a primary source). While the *Rocky Mountain News* may have excellent staff writers who verify every detail in every story with two or more corroborating sources, Myra doesn't know this for sure. Since Jason's acceptance by a new potential client is likely to hinge on his appearing knowledgeable about the Westridge development, verifying the account is important. *If the information is essential to solving the management dilemma, it is wise to verify it in a primary source.*

Types of Information Sources

We provide a list of key business resources in Appendix A and on your CD.

There are dozens of types of information sources, each with a special function. In this section we describe five of the information types used most by business researchers. Later in this chapter we will provide a more in-depth examination of three information types: bibliographic databases, government information, and the World Wide Web.

Indexes and Bibliographies   **Indexes** and **bibliographies** are the mainstay of any library because they help you identify and locate a single book or journal article from among the millions published. The single most important bibliography in any library is its online catalog. As with all other information types, there are many specialized indexes and bibliographies unique to business topics. These can be very useful in a literature search to find authors and titles of prior works on the topic of interest.

Dictionaries   **Dictionaries** are so ubiquitous they probably need no explanation. We all use them to verify spelling or grammar usage or to define terms. In business, as in every field, there are many specialized dictionaries that define words, terms, or jargon unique to a discipline. Most of these specialized dictionaries include in their word lists information on people, events, or organizations that shape the discipline. They are also an excellent place to find acronyms. A growing number of dictionaries and glossaries (terms in a specialized field, area, or topic plus their definitions) are now available on the Web. One of these is the Federal Reserve Bank of Chicago's *Glossaries of Financial Terms* (www.chicagofed.org/publications/glossary/index.cfm). An example of a printed business dictionary is the *Dictionary of Business and Management.* Information from dictionaries and glossaries may be used to identify key terms for a search of an online or printed database.

Encyclopedias   Use an **encyclopedia** to find background or historical information on a topic or to find names or terms that can enhance your search results in other sources. For example, you might use an encyclopedia to find when Microsoft introduced Windows, then use that date to draw more information from an index to the time period. Encyclopedias are also helpful in identifying the experts in a field and the key writings on any topic. The *Encyclopedia of Company Histories* and the *New Palgrave Dictionary of Economics and the Law* are two examples of specialized multivolume encyclopedias.

Handbooks   A **handbook** is a collection of facts unique to a topic. Handbooks often include statistics, directory information, a glossary of terms, and other data such as laws and regulations essential to a field. *The best handbooks include source references for the facts they present.* The *Statistical Abstract of the United States* is probably the most valuable and frequently used handbook available. It contains an extensive variety of facts, an excellent and detailed index, and a gateway to even more in-depth data for every table included.

Directories   **Directories** are used for finding names and addresses as well as other data. While many are available and useful in printed format, directories in digitized format that can be searched by certain characteristics or sorted and then downloaded are far more useful. Many are available free through the Web, but the most comprehensive directories are proprietary (that is, must be purchased). An especially useful directory available in most libraries either in print or electronic format is the *Encyclopedia of Associations* (called *Associations Unlimited* on the Web), which provides a list of public and professional organizations plus their locations and contact numbers.

Evaluating Information Sources

As you begin to collect information about your topic, one thing you will certainly want to do is conduct a **source evaluation.** Librarians evaluate and select information sources based on five factors that can be applied to any type of source, whether printed or electronic. These are

- Purpose
- Scope
- Authority
- Audience
- Format

Exhibit 10–3 summarizes the critical questions a researcher asks when applying these factors to the evaluation of Web sources.

Purpose   The **purpose** of the source is what the author (or in the case of many Internet sites, the collective authors in an institution) is trying to accomplish. In general, the purpose may be to enlighten or to entertain. Among purposes in the enlighten subset, authors may be attempting to establish credibility, broaden knowledge within a field or discipline, establish a company image, and, for websites, even manage inventory or sell merchandise. Often, for proprietary sources, the purpose is to make the search process easier for those who buy. For instance, the purpose of a source may be to consolidate Web advertising sources and make these available to students (www.advertising.utexas.edu/world/). Or the purpose may be to define basic computer terms so nontechnical managers can communicate with technical staff. Once you determine the purpose of the source, you will also want to determine whether or how it provides a bias to the information presented. Bias is the absence of a balanced presentation of information. Most researchers expect company websites to be biased in favor of the company. However, we expect sources offered by independent organizations to be more balanced, presenting both positive and negative information about relevant organizations without favoring one or the other.

Scope   Tied closely to the purpose of the source is its **scope.** What is the date of publication? What time period does this source cover? How much of the topic is covered and to what depth? Is the material covered local, regional, national, or international? If the source is bibliographic, how comprehensive is it? If it is a biographical source or a directory or a bibliography, what are the criteria for inclusion? *If you do not know the scope of your information sources, you may miss essential information by relying on an incomplete source.*

This single factor led to tragic results in a university clinical research project in 2001. The medical researcher combed the literature online, found no problems, and proceeded to offer a drug to a health volunteer who then died of complications. The

EXHIBIT 10–3 Evaluating Websites as Information Sources

Evaluation Factor	Questions to Answer
Purpose	• Why does the site exist? • How evident is the purpose it is trying to convey? • Does it achieve its purpose? • How does its purpose affect the type and bias of information presented?
Authority	• What are the credentials of the author or institution or organization sponsoring the site? • Does the site give you a means of contacting anyone for further information? • Who links to this site? • If facts are supplied, where do they come from?
Scope	• How old is the information? • How often is it updated? • How much information is available? • Is it selective or comprehensive? • What are the criteria for inclusion? • If applicable, what geographic area or time period or language does it cover? • How does the information presented compare with similar sites? • Is it a series of links only (a metasite), or is there added value? • What is the nature of the added value? • What information did you expect to find that was missing? • Is the site self-contained or does it link to other websites?
Audience	• Whom does the site cater to? • What level of knowledge or experience is assumed? • How does this intended audience affect the type and bias of the information?
Format	• How quickly can you find needed information? • How easy is the site to use? Is it intuitive? • Does it load quickly? • Is the design appealing? • Are there navigation buttons? • Is there a site map or search button? • Is there an easily identifiable help button? • Is Help helpful? • Are pages in ASCII or graphic format? • Is the information downloadable into a spreadsheet or word-processing program, if desired?

salient reports on the ill effects of the drug had been published in the early 1960s and were too old to be included in the online database used by the researcher.[1]

Authority   Of major concern to any information user is the **authority** of the source. We have already noted that primary sources are the most authoritative. In any source, both the author and the publisher are indicators of the authority. The author and the author's credentials should be given both in printed and electronic sources. Footnotes should be provided when appropriate. If credentials are not given, then it is best to check a biographical source. Credentials may include the author's educational background, his/her position, or his/her other published and reviewed work.

Authority also applies to Web resources where anyone can post anything. In this environment it is always important to check the credentials of the site. For instance, data and statements about cancer are much more likely to be authoritative if they come from the National Cancer Institute or the American Cancer Society than from a personal page with no information about the author or producer. Any personal page on the Web is suspect unless the author's, or in some cases the institution's, credentials can be verified. Credentials alone are not always enough. Most scholarly articles are validated by a system called *peer review* in which colleagues from other institutions are asked to comment anonymously on the research presented. In several recent cases authors with very good credentials have bypassed the peer review process and published directly on the Web. In at least one instance the research was seriously flawed. Even the best scholars can make mistakes, so imagine what nonexperts might publish on the Web.

Audience   **Audience** is also an important factor in evaluating an information source and it, too, is tied to the purpose of the source. The audience for this textbook is college students. More specifically, its audience is college students who are studying or majoring in business or public administration, some of whom are practicing managers. While others, for example educators, may benefit from the information, the authors take great care to select examples and to write in terms that management students will easily relate to.

It is often difficult to determine the intended audience for some Web resources, as many websites are designed to serve multiple audiences. The Web is available to all, so Web designers need to be especially creative both in capturing their audience(s) and in moving them to the appropriate section(s) of their website. While an organization may have several different print publications geared to different users, all the users on the Web go through one home page or portal. Universities, for example, have a very difficult time. Should they target their site to alumni or donors whom they count on for support? Or to prospective students? Or to current students? Or to faculty and staff? Luckily, technology is helping solve this problem, by helping the Web server to first identify characteristics of the user (through cookies) and then select the appropriate home page to deliver.

Brokerage firm Charles Schwab has no confusion on purpose or audience. In a recent ad, Charles Schwab is quoted as follows: "I see the Internet as the single most empowering force for the individual investor."[2] The Schwab.com website is designed to empower every single Charles Schwab customer, with rapid market summary updates and research on companies and funds. The numerous awards Schwab has won for its website indicate it is doing well at achieving its aims. It also uses an intranet to provide key information to its employees.[3]

When you are evaluating the plausible audience of a source, look for key indicators including vocabulary, types of information, and questions or directions that guide the search. CNNfn (www.cnnfn.com) clearly has a well-educated audience composed of people who are serious investors and people who are more than mildly interested in—

or who rely on information about—the global economy. Indicators of this are not only the site's coverage in general, but also the great detail offered and the emphasis on up-to-the-minute business news stories and data on U.S. and world markets. The site focuses on services that will facilitate investing. In addition, the site provides information about CNN-sponsored television programs, currency, and travel information—all of which relate to the U.S. and global economy.

Format   **Format** factors may vary from source to source but in general relate to how the information is presented and how easy it is to find a specific piece of information. In a printed source, the arrangement of the information—alphabetical? hierarchical? chronological?—nearly always has an impact on the retrieval of information. Indexes are usually essential. Do cross-references link one term to related terms? How are acronyms handled? Is the reference to an item? Table number? Page? How do type fonts or color help you find information?

The format of an electronic source or website is generally related to design. Web designers contend with a variety of Internet browsers, individual computer "preferences," and a wide variety of modem or Internet access speeds. On the one hand, the designer wants the page to look great and have the coolest bells and whistles. On the other hand, the designer has to plan for users who are not very patient. People with visual impairments, using text only or specialized software that "reads" the page, must be taken into consideration, too. A page that takes even 30 seconds to load may be abandoned while the user goes on to something else. Users can't flip through pages on the Web nearly so quickly or effectively as they can with a reference book. Navigation becomes an issue. If you are holding a book, you know how to get back to the title page. If you are using a website, you want to be able to go forward one screen, backward one screen, return to home page, search the site from any page and quickly find the home page. On every page within a site, you should be able to see the name of the site owner and the last time the page was updated and, preferably, you should be able to contact the author or site manager.[4]

Searching a Bibliographic Database

In a **bibliographic database,** each record is a bibliographic citation to a book or a journal article. In your university library, the online catalog is an example of a bibliographic database.

There are several bibliographic databases available to business researchers. (See Appendix A and your CD.) Some of the more popular and comprehensive business bibliographic databases are:

MANAGEMENT
Tip

- ABI/Inform (from Proquest Information and Learning).
- Business and Industry (from Gale Group).
- Business Source (from EBSCO).
- Dow Jones Interactive.
- Lexis-Nexis Universe (from a division of Reed Elsevier).

Most of the above databases offer numerous purchase options both in the amount and type of coverage. Some include abstracts, short summaries of the articles cited. Nearly all of the above databases include the contents of around two-thirds of the indexed journals in full text, although the amount and the specific titles may vary widely from database to database. Full-text options vary from an exact image of the page to ASCII-text-only or text-plus-graphics. Search options also vary considerably from database to database. It is for these reasons that most libraries supporting business programs offer more than one business periodical database.

MANAGEMENT

Tip

The process of searching bibliographic databases and retrieving results is basic to all databases.

1. Select a database appropriate to your topic.

2. Construct a **search query** (also called a *search statement*).

   • Review and evaluate search results.

   • Modify the search query, if necessary.

3. Save those valuable results of your search.

4. Retrieve articles not available in the database.

5. Supplement your results with information from Web sources.

Select a Database   Most of us select the most convenient database without regard to its scope; but considering the database contents and its limitations and criteria for inclusion at the beginning of your search will probably save you time in the long run. Remember that a library's online catalog is a bibliographic database that will help identify books and perhaps other media on a topic. While journal or periodical *titles* are listed in a library's online catalog, periodical or journal *articles* are rarely included. Use books for older, more comprehensive information. Use periodical articles for more current information or for information on very specific topics. A librarian can suggest one or more appropriate databases for the topic you are researching.

The Close-Up provides direction for advanced database searches, including how initial searches are modified to obtain more relevant results.

Close-Up

Advanced Searching

In advanced searches, you use your knowledge of the database to make the search more productive.

Construct the Search Query

Use the keywords from your management question to prepare a query for the database. Bibliographic databases, including the library's online catalog, all have similar search options, such as a basic keyword search, an advanced search, and a way to choose a subject from a browse list. Like all databases, bibliographic databases consist of several standard fields.

In most bibliographic databases, all searches are keyword searches, but it is possible to search for a specific author or title or series (a known-item search) by limiting your results to a specific field of the bibliographic record. This is especially important if you are researching a prolific author such as Peter Drucker, who may have many works both by and about him. If you do not limit or narrow your search to a specific field, then you will conduct a general keyword search of all the records in the database. Because of the size of most databases, single word searches generally yield results that are not very useful

unless the single word is very unique. Instead, examine your management question for all relevant keywords and variations and establish a more precise search query using the connectors described on the next page.

The most important thing to remember about search engines for the Web or for databases is that they do not all work alike. In fact, they have widely varying search protocols. What you do not know can act against you. So, if finding good information is important to you, take a couple of minutes to determine what special features and search options are used. For instance, if you enter a multiword term, what happens? Does the database search your term as a phrase? Or does it insert a connector such as *and* or *or* between each word? How does it handle stopwords (the, in, and other similar small words)? The results will vary considerably in these three scenarios.

Standard Search Fields for Monographs	
Author	Publisher
Title	Series
Subject headings	

Limiters in Book Catalogs	
Language	Type of publication
Date of publication	Format (book, video, etc.)

Standard Search Fields for Periodical Databases	
Author	Abstract
Title of article	Company name
Subject headings	NAICS/SIC code
Periodical title	

Limiters in Periodical Databases	
Date	Periodical title
Full text	Peer review (scholarly journals)

Search Strategy Options

Basic Searching If you have a unique term, try a basic search using that term. Most bibliographic databases will present the results list in reverse data order; that is, the most recently published items will appear first. Review the list of items your search has retrieved. Are there too many?

Not enough? Are they very relevant or not very relevant? If they meet the Goldilocks test of "just right," then you can move on to the next step (saving results).

Advanced Searching If you have retrieved too few or no relevant items, or if you have retrieved hundreds of items, you should consider modifying your search query. Start with the most relevant items in the results list. Then do one of the following:

- Search for the cited works (the bibliography) of the full-text articles.
- Search for other works by the author or authors of the relevant citations.
- Check the subject headings assigned to the articles. Are there any more precise terms or synonyms that would improve your search results? More importantly, are there pairs of terms that appear in all of the most relevant items? Is there a thesaurus with the database that defines or expands the terminology used in the subject headings?

As a result of your examination of the relevant citations and any background preparation you have done in other sources such as encyclopedias, you should now have one or more keywords and synonyms for each concept. You can now use Boolean operators or connectors (see Exhibit 10– 4)

EXHIBIT 10–4 **Review of Advanced Search Options**

Expanding Your Search	Narrowing Your Search	
OR	**AND**	**Phrases**
Use **OR** to search for plurals, synonyms, or spelling variations. Either or both terms will be present in results. • woman **OR** women • business **OR** corporation • international **OR** foreign	Use **AND** to require that all terms you specify be present in the results. • child **AND** advertising	Use a term consisting of two or more words. Some phrases require double quotes to enclose the phrase, while others do not. • human resource management • "human resource management"
Truncation	**NOT**	**ADJ**
Symbols (**?, *, !**) that replace one or more characters or letters in a word or at the end of a word. • electr* (retrieves electricity, electric, electrical) • child? (retrieves children, childish, child's)	Use **NOT** to eliminate terms from your search. But use **NOT** with care. It is easy to eliminate the good with the unwanted. • medicine **NOT** nursing • Caribbean **NOT** Cuba	ADJ requires the first term specified to immediately precede the last term specified. • six **ADJ** sigma
	Limiters	
	Conditions (**date, publication type, language**) for limiting your search. Most databases also offer *field limiting*, limiting the occurrences of your search to a specific database field, such as the author field, title, etc. Some bibliographic databases offer the convenience of limiting the search results to peer-reviewed articles or to articles only available in full text. Use the latter with care as some significant articles may be overlooked even though they are available in the library.	

EXHIBIT 10–5 Advanced Searching Process

Step 1: Build a list of synonyms for each concept in the management question.				
Concept A	**Operator**	**Concept B**	**Operator**	**Concept C**
training	**AND**	**sex* harassment**	**AND**	**lawsuit***
awareness behavior professional development		wom*n female gender men		law courts legal
Step 2: Create and search with a concept group by combining each term in a column with OR. Put each concept group in parentheses. Then combine each concept group with AND.				
(training OR awareness OR behavior OR professional development) AND (sex* harassment OR wom*n OR men OR female OR gender) AND (lawsuit OR legal OR law OR courts)				

to combine terms or sets of terms to expand or narrow your search. There are four basic Boolean operators or connectors: OR, AND, NOT, and ADJ.

Think of your management question as a series of keywords. For example, your management question might be, "How can I design an appropriate training or awareness program to prevent sexual harassment lawsuits in my company?" In this example, concept A would be training; concept B would be harassment; concept C would be lawsuits. In the most basic of keyword searches, you

could use a keyword search with the operator AND to combine them:

training AND harassment AND lawsuits

If your search results are inadequate, you might need to expand your search statement with synonyms connected with the operator OR. For our sample management question, your search would look like Exhibit 10–5. If your search results are too numerous, you will need to limit your search.

Save Results of Search While the temptation to print may be overwhelming, remember that if you download your results, you can cut and paste quotations, tables, and other information into your proposal without rekeying. In either case, make sure you keep the bibliographic information for your footnotes and bibliography. Most databases offer the choice of marking the records and printing or downloading them all at once or printing them one by one.

Retrieve Articles For articles not available in full text online, retrieval will normally require the additional step of searching the library's online catalog (unless there is a link from the database to the catalog) to determine if the desired issue is available and where it is located. Many libraries offer a document delivery service for articles not available. Some current articles may be available on the Web or via a fee-based service.

Searching the World Wide Web for Information

The World Wide Web is a vast information, business, and entertainment resource that would be difficult, if not foolish, to overlook. Millions of pages of data are publicly available, and the size of the Web doubles every few months.[5] But searching and retrieving reliable information on the Web is a great deal more problematic than searching a bibliographic database. There are no standard database fields, no carefully defined subject hierarchies (called *controlled vocabulary*), no cross-references, no synonyms, no selection criteria, and, in general, no rules. There are dozens of search engines and they all work differently, but how they work is not always easy to determine. Nonetheless, the convenience of the Web and the extraordinary amount of information to be found on it are compelling reasons for using it as an information source.

As you can see in Exhibit 10–6, the basic steps to searching the Web are similar to those outlined for searching a bibliographic database. As you approach the Web, you start at the same point: focusing on your management question. Are you looking for a known item (for example, IBM's website or that of the American Marketing Association)? Are you looking for information on a specific topic? If you are looking for a specific topic, what are its parameters? For example, if your topic is managed health care, are you hoping to find statistics, marketing ideas, public policy issues, accounting standards, or evidence of its impact on small business?

There are perfectly legitimate reasons to browse for information, and with its hypertext linking system, the Web is the ultimate resource for browsing. The trick is to browse and still stay focused on the topic at hand. In the browse mode you do not have any particular target. You follow hypertext links from site to site for the sheer joy of discovery. This is somewhat analogous to window shopping at the mall or browsing the bookshelves in the library. It may or may not be fruitful. And browsing is not likely to be efficient. Researchers often work on tight deadlines, as managers often cannot delay critical decisions. Therefore, researchers rarely have the luxury of undirected browsing.

Below we detail those steps in the Web search process that pose altered behavior for Web searches.

Select a Search Engine or Directory   A search for specific information or for a specific site that will help you solve your management question requires a great deal more skill and knowledge than browsing. Start by selecting one or more Internet search engines. Web search engines vary considerably in the following ways:

- The types of Internet sources they cover (http, telnet, Usenet, ftp, etc.).
- The way they search Web pages (every word? titles or headers only?).
- The number of pages they include in their indexes.

EXHIBIT 10–6   **Web Search Process Compared to Bibliographic Search Process**

Bibliographic Search Process	Web Search Process
1. Select a database appropriate to your topic.	**1.** Select a search engine or directory.*
	2. Determine your search options.*
2. Construct a search query.	**3.** Construct a search query.*
• Review and evaluate search results.	• Review and evaluate search results.
• Modify the search query, if necessary.	• Modify the search query, if necessary.
3. Save those valuable results of your search.	**4.** Save those valuable results of your search.*
4. Retrieve articles not available in the database.	
5. Supplement your results with information from Web sources.	**5.** Supplement your results with information from non-Web sources.*

*Denotes a variation.

- The search and presentation options they offer.
- The frequency with which they are updated.

Furthermore, some information publicly indexable via the Web is not retrievable at all using current Web search engines. Among the material open to the public, but not indexed by search engines, is the following: [6]

MANAGEMENT

Tip

- Pages that are proprietary (that is, fee-based) and/or password-protected, including the contents of bibliographic and other databases. Some password-protected databases, such as the Thomas Register, are actually free and available to the public after initial registration.

- Pages accessible only through a search form (databases), including such highly popular Web resources as library catalogs, e-commerce catalogs (such as Lands'End®, Amazon.com®, and similar offerings), and the Security and Exchange Commission's EDGAR catalog of SEC filings. If you want to find the price of a book at Amazon.com, you first will have to find the Amazon.com page, then search the database for the title.

- Poorly designed framed pages.

- Some non-HTML or nonplain-text pages, especially PDF graphics files, for which no text alternative is offered. These pages cannot be retrieved using any current search engine.

- Pages excluded by the Robots Exclusion Standard (usually implemented with a robots.txt file). This standard is used by Web administrators to tell indexing robots that certain pages are off-limits. An outstanding example of this is the U.S. government's extensive information resource called GPO Access (described below).

The search engine, portal, or directory you select may well be determined by how comprehensive you want your results to be.[7] If you want to use some major sites only, then start with a directory such as Yahoo!®. If, however, you are interested in gathering comments and opinions that are the focus of usenet groups, then use a more inclusive search engine such as Northern Light®. At least within the publicly indexable pages, one approach emphasizes selectivity, and the other, comprehensiveness. *If you are interested in comprehensiveness, use more than one search engine.* You are likely to yield very different and perhaps better results using additional search engines.

What is the difference between a search engine, a portal, and a directory? Directories rely on human intervention to select, index, and categorize Web contents. Subject directories build an index based on Web pages or websites, but not on words within a page. Presenting a series of subject categories that are then further subdivided, Yahoo!® (http://www.yahoo.com/) was the first Web subject directory and is still one of the most popular choices for finding information on the Web. This is because most users are satisfied with a few good sites rather than a long list of possibilities.

A search engine's different software components allow it to search and retrieve Web pages. These include:

- Software that automatically sends robots, sometimes called spiders, out to comb the Web going from server to server to build an index of the words, pages, and files that are publicly indexable.

- Algorithms that determine how those pages will be selected and prioritized for display.

- User interface software that determines the search options available to the user.

Robots may be sent to roam the Web on a daily basis or on a six-week basis, so it is possible that some newer pages may not be included in the index developed by a particular search engine. Most search engines try for at least a monthly update of their indexes. Some robots may only search the upper-level pages and totally ignore valuable pages buried within the site.

The algorithm used by the search engine can have an enormous impact on the type and quantity of information retrieved. Search algorithms determine whether every word is to be included or only the top 50 or so words; whether more weight will be given to words in metadata or titles or in words used frequently. The possibilities are limitless and are the major reason that results from one search may vary considerably from those of another search.

A **portal** is, as the name suggests, a gateway to the Web. A portal often includes a directory, a search engine, and other user features such as news and weather. Most Internet service providers (ISP) are portals to the Web. The AOL® homepage is an example. This portal uses information based on past user search behavior to determine what to offer on the opening screen. Therefore, some valuable search engines, indexes, directories, and more may be relegated to an "other search aids" category. If as a researcher your behavior differs from the majority pattern, you have to be more knowledgeable about search strategies to bypass those front-line strategies offered by the portal. Several ISP portals now offer subscribers the option of customizing the portal with the user-chosen search engines and secondary sources. Most of the major search engines are now actually portals to the Web that include their search engine. Specialized portals are increasingly popular. An industry portal, one type of specialized portal, lists many different resources about a specific industry. Competia Express, the competitive intelligence site (http://www.competia.com/express/index.html), offers industry portals for many different industries.

Determine Your Search Options   Nearly all search services have a Help button that will lead you to information about the search protocols and options of that particular search engine. How does the search engine work? Can you combine terms using Boolean operators (AND, OR, NOT) or other connectors? How do you enter phrases? Truncate terms? Determine output display? Limit by date or other characteristic? Some search engines provide a basic and an advanced search option. How do they differ?

Construct a Search Query and Enter Your Search Term(s)   The Web is not a database nor does it have a controlled vocabulary. Therefore, you must be as specific as possible, using the keywords in your management question and any variations you can think of. It is up to you to determine synonyms, variant spellings, and broader or narrower terms that will help you retrieve the information you need. This may involve some trial and error. For instance, a general term (such as *business*) would be useless in a search engine that purports to index every word in every document.

Save Results of Your Search   If you have found good information, you will want to keep it for future reference so that you can cite it in your proposal or refer to it later in the development of your investigative questions. If you do not keep documents, you may have to reconstruct your search. At a future time, given that some portion of the Web is revised and updated daily, those same documents may no longer be available.

Supplement Your Results with Information from Non-Web Sources   There is still a great deal of information in books, journals, and other print sources that is not available on the Web. While many novice researchers start and end here, the more sophisticated researcher knows a Web search is just one of many important options.

**Searching
for Specific Types
of Information
on the Web**

MANAGEMENT
Tip

Once you have defined your topic and established your search terms, you need to determine whether you are looking for a specific site (known-item) or an address of a person or institution (who), a geographic place name and location (where), or a topic (what).

***Known-Item* Searches**   In the same way that search protocols for the library's online catalog vary between a known-item (author or exact title), and a more general keyword search, the way you query the Web for an exact item also varies from a more general query. A general trend among search engines is to establish algorithms that will yield more precise results. One of the first to follow this trend was the search engine Google® (http://www.google.com/), which debuted in 1998. Google® and others like it help you retrieve the most precise results from known-item searches by creating an algorithm that interprets a link to a site as a vote for that site. The sites that receive the most votes (links) rise to the top of the results list in a known-item search. The Google® system also emphasizes the importance of the linking page in its algorithm.

***Who* Searches**   In the "who" searches, you are looking for an e-mail address, a phone number, a street address, or a Web address of a person or institution. For this type of information you will first need to identify a database containing the information you need and then search that database according to its search protocols. At this writing, almost all Web search engines and portal sites partner with infoUSA® (http://www.infoUSA.com/) to supply the phone number databases for their white and yellow page services.[8] See "Finding People on the Net" (http://alabanza.com/kabacoff/Inter-Links/phone.html) for a site listing many "who" options.

***Where* Searches**   A "where" option comprises the mapping services that help you locate an address on a map or discover the route from one place to another. Mapping services are databases tied to geographical information systems (GIS). Popular sites are Lycos® Roadmaps (http://www.lycos.com/roadmap.html) and MapQuest® (http://www.mapquest.com).

Today's sophisticated databases include more than numbers representing data. Many contain detailed geographic images, like the one here provided by Space Imaging, a leading supplier of visual information products, geographic information products, and related services. Space Imaging collects and/or distributes earth imagery from the Indian Remote Sensing satellites, the U.S. Landsat satellites, and radar imaging systems from Canada, Japan, and Europe. The company also delivers high-resolution aerial imagery collected by its own Digital Airborne Imaging System. Among a long list of activities, these digital information databases are used in insurance and risk management, mapping, telecommunications and utilities planning, and real estate planning and development, as well as security enhancement. This image of Sidney was used in planning the last Summer Olympics. Visit Space Imaging's Internet gallery to see a different perspective of news events.
www.spaceimaging.com

***What* Searches**   As we have already noted, search engines vary considerably in the way they work and in their size. If you are searching for a very unusual term, select one of the more comprehensive search engines, such as Northern Light® (http://www. northern-light.com/) or AltaVista® (http://altavista.digital.com/). Generally, it is more efficient to start with a directory such as Yahoo!® or one of the more specialized directories on the Web. Some especially good specialized sites are the Argus Clearinghouse (http://www. clearinghouse.net/), featuring subject guides on dozens of topics prepared by librarians and other specialists, and INFOMINE® Scholarly Internet Resource Collections from the University of California housed at University of California-Riverside (http://infomine. ucr.edu/). See Exhibit 10–7 or Appendix A for a selection of business-related websites.

Since the Web was introduced to the world in 1992, Web technology has been seeking ways to make the contents more accessible. The dynamic nature of the Web, its lightning growth rate, the ephemeral nature of some Web pages, the different skill levels and interests of users, and the lack of standards make this an enormous challenge. Trends indicate that the Web will continue to grow and that we will continue to apply new technologies to tapping the information available on this vast and unique resource.[9] Already some search engines are better able to identify key resources. Efforts are under way to adopt standardized metatags included in the coding to describe the contents of Web pages. Some search engines are using expert systems to learn more about the information requestor. This is already being used extensively to target advertisements and is being used more frequently to "select" from among several options the information source that will be delivered to the requestor. More efforts are being made to index a larger portion of the Web content but, at the same time, efforts are also under way to improve the relevancy of the results delivered for any one search.

Government Information

Government publications, especially those of the U.S. government, are mandatory resources for many business research projects. The agencies of the U.S. government, considered as a whole, are the largest publishing body in the world. The government

The U.S. government is the world's largest source of data and information used by managers in all types of organizations.

MANAGEMENT

EXHIBIT 10–7 Selected Websites for General Business Research

Site ID	Site URL	Sponsor
Advertising World	http://advertising.utexas.edu/world/	Department of Advertising, University of Texas, Austin
Annual Reports Online	http://www.zpub.com/sf/arl/aarl-www.html	Annual Reports Library, San Francisco
BizLink, Your On-line Business Resource	http://www.bizlink.org/	Public Library of Charlotte and Mecklenburg County
Business and Economics Resources Online	http://lcweb.loc.gov/rr/business/beonline/beonline.html	Library of Congress
CNNfn-the Financial Network	http://cnnfn.com	CNN America, Inc.
Electronic Commerce	http://ecommerce.about.com	About.com Inc.
ENTERWeb (Enterprise Development Website)	http://www.enterweb.org/	ENTERWeb
Guide to Labor-Oriented Internet Resources	http://www.lib.berkeley.edu/IIRL/iirlnet.html	Institute of Industrial Relations Library, University of California, Berkeley
Hoover's Online	http://www.hoovers.com	Hoover's, Inc.
Industry Research Desk	http://www.virtualpet.com/industry/rdindex2.htm	Polsen Enterprises Research Services
MSU-CIBER International Business Resources on the WWW	http://ciber.bus.msu.edu/busres.htm	Michigan State University Center for International Business Education and Research
Rutgers Accounting Web	http://accounting.rutgers.edu/	Accounting Research Center, Rutgers University
Tax and Accounting Sites Directory	http://www.taxsites.com/	Schmidt Enterprises
Thomas Register of American Manufacturers	http://www.thomasregister.com/ index.html	Thomas Publishing Co.
VIBES: Virtual International Business and Economics Resources	http://libweb.uncc.edu/ref-bus/vibehome.htm	J. Murrey Atkins Library, University of North Carolina, Charlotte
WorkIndex ("gateway to human resource solutions")	http://workindex.com	*Human Resource Executive Magazine,* in cooperation with the Cornell School of Industrial Relations

collects and provides access to a wide variety of social, economic, and demographic data. In addition, government laws and regulations, court decisions, policy papers, and studies all have a potential impact on business. Additionally, the government provides directories, maps, and other information sources. Specialists are available throughout the government to provide individual assistance.

Searching for government information is a complicated task that usually requires some knowledge of how government functions. In recent years, the U.S. government has been working aggressively to make its information available, not only through the Depository Library Program, but also through the development of electronic resources. As a result, information that used to be tucked into the farthest corners of the library is now readily available and searchable on the Web. In many libraries, the entire government documents collection is included in the library's catalog with links to Internet resources. In this section of the chapter, we examine three of the most useful government information types. A list of selected government resources on the Web is included in Exhibit 10–8.

Government Organization   Two of the most useful resources regarding government organization are:

- *U.S. Government Manual* (published annually); http://www.access.gpo.gov/nara/nara001.html (updated annually).

- *Congressional Directory* (published annually); http://www.access.gpo.gov/congress/cong016.html (updated regularly).

EXHIBIT 10–8   **A List of Selected Government Sources**

Source	Internet
CBDNet (Commerce Business Daily) (a listing of government procurement, sales, and contract awards)	http://cbdnet.access.gpo.gov
Economic Indicators	http://www.access.gpo.gov/congress/cong002.html
Economic Statistics Briefing Room (current economic statistics)	http://www.whitehouse.gov/fsbr/esbr.html
EDGAR Database of Corporate Information (SEC filings)	http://www.sec.gov/edgar.shtml
Federal Bulletin Board	http://fedbbs.access.gpo.gov
FedStats	http://www.fedstats.gov
FirstGov: Business	http://www.firstgov.gov/topics/business.html
GPO Access	http://www.access.gpo.gov/su_docs/
Stat-USA (includes National Trade Data Bank)	http://www.stat-usa.gov/
Thomas (U.S. Congress on the Internet)	http://thomas.loc.gov
U.S. Bureau of Economic Analysis	http://www.bea.doc.gov/
U.S. Bureau of Labor Statistics	http://stats.bls.gov/
U.S. Bureau of the Census	http://www.census.gov/
U.S. Department of Commerce	http://www.doc.gov/
U.S. Department of Labor	http://www.dol.gov/
U.S. Patent and Trademark Office	http://www.uspto.gov/
U.S. Small Business Administration	http://www.sbaonline.sba.gov/

The *U.S. Government Manual* describes the functions of every government agency and is particularly useful for identifying key personnel and agency contacts, including those at the local and regional levels. Generally very knowledgeable and helpful, these people are invaluable in any research project for their ability to cut through red tape and to answer questions pertinent to their agencies.

The *Congressional Directory* lists members of Congress and Congressional committees, as well as key personnel throughout the U.S. government.

Laws, Regulations, and Court Decisions   Government information regarding these key areas and other legal information can be obtained by consulting GPO Access (http://www.access.gpo.gov/su_docs/). GPO Access is the government's official and real-time site for finding government information. Included at this site is the complete *Monthly Catalog of U.S. Government Publications.* Use it to identify the full range of government publications, printed and electronic, issued in or after 1994.

Especially valuable on GPO Access are the databases covering laws, regulations, and congressional debates and publications. The key databases for laws and regulations are:

- **Congressional Bills.** Provides texts of varying versions of bills. Only a small portion of this collection ever becomes law, but the topics can reveal trends of interest to business researchers.

- **Public Laws.** Provides the texts of laws as they are passed; covers 1994 to the present. The printed version of this source is called the *U.S. Statutes at Large.*

- **U.S. Code.** A codification of laws currently in effect and as revised over time. Also available in libraries as a printed document.

- **Federal Register.** "The official daily publication for rules, proposed rules, and notices of federal agencies and organizations, as well as executive orders and other presidential documents;"[10] covers 1995 to the present. Also available in libraries as a printed or microfiche document.

- **Code of Federal Regulations (CFR).** "A codification of the general and permanent rules originally published in the Federal Register by the executive departments and agencies of the federal government."[11] A printed version is available in libraries.

GPO Access includes other valuable databases, including the Supreme Court decisions from 1937 to the present, the *Economic Report of the President,* the *U.S. Budget, Commerce Business Daily* (CBDNet), and GAO reports. New databases are added regularly.

Many libraries have created local gateways to GPO Access that help speed information retrieval (http://www.access.gpo.gov/congress/cong002.html). GPO Access offers dozens of fields to search and these can be searched independently or together. Searching each database independently provides more flexibility and more precise searching options because there are some fields that are unique to a particular database. In general, search options are similar to other databases. Use the search hints for each file for more details and special search possibilities.

Government Statistics   Information regarding government statistics may be obtained by consulting the following sources:

- *Statistical Abstract of the United States* (http://www.census.gov/prod/www/statistical-abstract-us.html).

- FedStats (http://www.fedstats.gov).

- U.S. Bureau of the Census (http://www.census.gov/).

MANAGEMENT

The government collects statistics on just about every topic imaginable—from crimes to hospital beds, from teachers to tax revenue, from steel production to flower imports. For any statistical inquiry, start with the *Statistical Abstract of the United States.* This annual compendium compiles statistics issued by nearly every government agency as well as additional data from selected nongovernment organizations. Many are time series tables covering several years, or even decades. All tables indicate the source of the statistics. These sources can then be consulted if desired for even more comprehensive data. Check the library's catalog or ask the librarian to find these more specialized resources. Some may be available via FedStats.

FedStats is an online compilation of statistics provided by more than 70 U.S. agencies, including the Census Bureau, the Bureau of Labor Statistics, and the Federal Bureau of Investigation. Use the search option or the directory option to find the needed statistical tables. An especially useful feature of FedStats is the state and regional statistical data option.

No discussion of government statistical information would be complete without an examination of the U.S. Bureau of the Census. The Census Bureau is probably most well known for the Decennial Census of Population and Housing. The first such census was taken in 1790 to meet the Constitutional mandate for apportioning seats in Congress. It has been taken in every year ending in zero since that date. Now it is used not only to apportion seats in the House of Representatives, but also for allocation of federal aid to states and for a myriad of other purposes. The decennial census asks a certain core of questions of everyone. These are known as the *100%-questions.* While these may vary slightly from census to census, age, race, gender, relationship, and Hispanic origin are fairly constantly collected. A longer questionnaire is sent to a sample of the population. These additional questions used in conjunction with the data from 100%-questions are used by government agencies at all levels, local planners, business and industry, schools, and social service agencies among others for planning, grant writing, economic development, and many other purposes.

To make census information easier to understand, the Census Bureau, in cooperation with local planning agencies, has created a multilevel mapping system. The entire country is mapped into small units called blocks. Data from 100%-questions is available for all blocks, but sample data is not. Both 100%-question data and sample data are available for census tracts (groups of blocks) and for larger mapped units such as cities, metropolitan statistical areas, counties, and states. Tracts are especially valuable to local level researchers because their boundaries remain mostly constant from census to census, thus allowing comparison. In cases where there is population growth, tracts may be split from one census to another and therefore may need to be added together to achieve comparable statistics. Metropolitan statistical areas, defined by the Office of Management and Budget, consist of a large population nucleus, together with adjacent communities having a high degree of social and economic integration with that core. Metropolitan statistical areas comprise one or more entire counties, except in New England, where cities and towns are the basic geographic units.

In addition to the decennial census, the Census Bureau conducts the economic census in years ending in two and seven, covering all areas of the economy from the national to the local level. Both the decennial census and the economic census are supplemented by numerous survey reports, including the new American Community Survey, initiated to provide more up-to-date information on American communities. In fact, the Census Bureau has proposed using the American Community Survey—instead of the long (sample) questionnaire used through 2000—in the next decennial census. For an overview of the many report topics available, see the Subjects A–Z listing on the Census Bureau website (http://www. census.gov/).

Mining Internal Sources

An organization's own internal historical data is often an underutilized source of information in the exploratory phase. Due to employee turnover, the researcher may lack knowledge that such historical data exist or, based on time or budget constraints and the lack of an organized archive, the researcher may choose to ignore such data. While digging through data archives can be as simplistic as sorting through a file containing past patient records or inventory shipping manifests, or rereading company reports and management-authored memos that have grown dusty with age, we will concentrate the remainder of our discussion on more sophisticated structures and techniques.

A **data warehouse** is an electronic repository for databases that organizes large volumes of data into categories to facilitate retrieval, interpretation, and sorting by end-users. The data warehouse provides an accessible archive to support dynamic organizational intelligence applications. The key words here are dynamically accessible. Data warehouses that offer archaic methods for data retrieval are seldom used. Data in a data warehouse must be continually updated to ensure that managers have access to data appropriate for real-time decisions. In a data warehouse, the contents of departmental computers are duplicated in a central repository where standard architecture and consistent data definitions are applied. These data are available to departments or cross-functional teams for direct analysis, or through intermediate storage facilities or **data marts** that compile locally required information. The entire system must be constructed for integration and compatibility among the different data marts.

SNAPSHOT   Will XP Release a Hailstorm of Abuse with Passport?

The Windows XP operating system is bundled with two software programs that the Electronic Privacy Information Center (EPIC), an advocacy group concerned with protecting personal privacy, feels oversteps a business's need to know. Passport is Microsoft's authentication technology that stores and reveals passwords as Web users access different sites. "Hailstorm will enable a person to store [personal information in a] vast database at Microsoft. [Hailstorm shares] personal information according to a user's instructions and [automates] making doctor's appointments, buying music online, booking airline tickets and handling other tasks." According to Microsoft, Hailstorm services "are oriented around people. They give users control of their own data and information, protecting personal information and requiring the consent of the individual with respect to who can access the information, what they can do with it, and how long they have that permission to do so." The executive director of EPIC, Marc Rotenberg, in his intention to file a complaint with the Federal Trade Commission, expressed concern that Microsoft "has not established itself as the Fort Knox of Internet privacy." Microsoft indicates the changes in Windows XP are heralded by expectations that the desktop PC will less and less be the device chosen for accessing the Web as hand-held devices and cell phones become more commonplace. EPIC fears Windows XP's marriage with Passport and Hailstorm is bad news for those of us who want to protect our privacy. According to Bob Muglia, Microsoft group vice president of the .NET Services Group, "Hailstorm turns the industry debate over online privacy on its head. It starts with the fundamental assumption that the user owns and controls their personal information and is empowered to decide who gets to decide with whom they share any of their information and under what terms." Given that most large corporations and many smaller ones are developing extensive customer databases, what are the possible abuses that should concern researchers?

www.epic.org

www.microsoft.com

www.ftc.gov

The term **data mining** describes the process of discovering knowledge from databases stored in data marts or data warehouses. The purpose of data mining is to identify valid, novel, useful, and ultimately understandable patterns in data.[12] Similar to traditional mining, where we search beneath the surface for valuable ore, data mining searches large databases for indispensable information for managing an organization. Both require sifting a large amount of material to discover a profitable vein. Data mining is a useful tool, an approach that combines exploration and discovery with confirmatory analysis.

The more accessible the databases that comprise the data warehouse, the more likely a researcher will use such databases to reveal patterns. Thus researchers are more likely to mine electronic databases than paper ones. It will be useful to remember that data in a data warehouse were once primary data, collected for a specific purpose. When researchers data-mine a company's data warehouse, all the data contained within that database have become secondary data. The patterns revealed will be used for purposes other than those originally intended. For example, in an archive of sales invoices, we have a wealth of data about what was sold, how much of each item or service, at what price level, to whom, and where and when and how the products were shipped. Initially the company generated the sales invoice to facilitate the process of getting paid for the items shipped. When a researcher mines that sales invoice archive, the search is for patterns of sales, by product, category, region of the country or world, price level, shipping methods, etc. Therefore, data mining forms a bridge between primary and secondary data.

Traditional database queries are unidimensional and historical—for example, "How much beer was sold during December 1999 in the Sacramento area?" In contrast, data mining attempts to discover patterns and trends in the data and to infer rules from these patterns. For example, an analysis of retail sales by Sacramento FastShop identified products that are often purchased together—like beer and diapers—although they may appear to be unrelated. With the rules discovered from the data mining, a manager is able to support, review, and/or examine alternative courses of action for solving a management dilemma, alternatives which may later be studied further in the collection of new primary data.

Evolution of Data Mining

The complex algorithms used in data mining have existed for more than two decades. The U.S. government has employed customized data-mining software using neural networks, fuzzy logic, and pattern recognition to spot tax fraud, eavesdrop on foreign

Numerous companies build large consumer purchase behavior databases by collecting purchases made via store-owned credit programs or frequent purchase cards not linked directly with payment plans. Studying such data can reveal the likely success of a new product introduction or the sales lift effect of a coupon drop.

EXHIBIT 10–9   The Evolution of Data Mining

Evolutionary Step	Investigative Question	Enabling Technologies	Characteristics
Data collection (1960s)	"What was my average total revenue over the last five years?"	Computers, tapes, disks	Retrospective, static data delivery
Data access (1980s)	"What were unit sales in California last December?"	Relational databases (RDBMS), structured query language (SQL), ODBC	Retrospective, dynamic data delivery at record level
Data navigation (1990s)	"What were unit sales in California last December? Drill down to Sacramento."	Online analytic processing (OLAP), multidimensional databases, data warehouses	Retrospective, dynamic data delivery at multiple levels
Data mining (2000)	"What's likely to happen to Sacramento unit sales next month? Why?"	Advanced algorithms, multiprocessor computers, massive databases	Prospective, proactive information delivery

communications, and process satellite imagery.[13] Until recently, these tools have been available only to very large corporations or agencies due to their high costs. However, this is rapidly changing.

In the evolution from *business data* to *information,* each new step has built on previous ones. For example, large database storage is crucial to the success of data mining. The four stages listed in Exhibit 10–9 were revolutionary because each allowed new management questions to be answered accurately and quickly.[14]

The process of extracting information from data has been done in some industries for years. Insurance companies often compete by finding small market segments where the premiums paid greatly outweigh the risks. They then issue specially priced policies to a particular segment with profitable results. However, two problems have limited the effectiveness of this process: Getting the data has been both difficult and expensive, and processing it into information has taken time—making it historical rather than predictive. Now, instead of incurring high data collection costs to resolve management questions, secondary data are available to assist the manager's decision making. It was State Farm Insurance's ability to mine its extensive nationwide database of accident locations and conditions at intersections that allowed it to identify high risk intersections and then plan a primary data study to determine alternatives to modify such intersections.

Functional areas of management and select industries are currently driving datamining projects: marketing, customer service, administrative/financial analysis, sales, manual distribution, insurance, fraud detection, and network management (see Exhibit 10–10).[15] Data-mining technology provides two unique capabilities to the researcher or manager: pattern discovery and prediction.

Pattern Discovery   Data-mining tools can be programmed to sweep regularly through databases and identify previously hidden patterns. An example of pattern discovery is the detection of stolen credit cards based on analysis of credit card transaction

See the **State Farm: Dangerous Intersections** *case in the case section of this text.*

EXHIBIT 10–10   Data Mining in Business

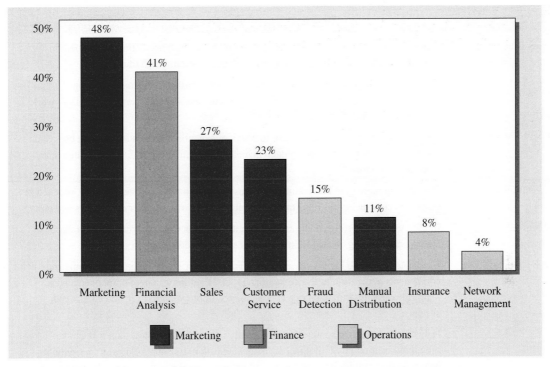

records. MasterCard processes 12 million transactions daily and uses data mining to detect fraud.[16] Other uses include finding retail purchase patterns (used for inventory management), identifying call center volume fluctuations (used for staffing), and locating anomalous data that could represent data entry errors (used to evaluate the need for training, employee evaluation, or security).

Predicting Trends and Behaviors   A typical example of a predictive problem is targeted marketing. Using data from past promotional mailings to identify the targets most likely to maximize return on investment, future mailings can be more effective. Bank of America and Mellon Bank both use data-mining software to pinpoint marketing programs that attract high-margin, low-risk customers. Bank of America focuses on credit lines and retail lending; Mellon Bank has used data mining to optimize its home equity line of credit marketing to existing customers.[17] Other predictive problems include forecasting bankruptcy and loan default and finding population segments with similar responses to a given stimulus. Data-mining tools also can be used to build risk models for a specific market, such as discovering the top 10 most significant buying trends each week (see Exhibit 10–11).

Data-Mining Techniques[18]

An understanding of statistics is essential to the data-mining process. Data-mining tools perform exploratory and confirmatory statistical analysis to discover and validate relationships. Data-mining tools even extend confirmatory statistical approaches by allowing the automated examination of large numbers of hypotheses. Suppose there are 12 variables in the MindWriter survey and we have a process whose outcome can be predicted when three variables are in a particular range. But we are unfamiliar with the repair process and don't know which variables are relevant. With this small problem

EXHIBIT 10–11   Sample Data-Mining Applications

Company	Use of Data Mining
Blue Cross Blue Shield	Mines data on member and provider questions about insurance claims and patient history, as well as inquiry/call history to improve call center staffing and training.[1]
BMW	Uses data mining in the execution of its "stochastic crash-simulation technology," enabling "design improvements to the crashworthiness and safety of automobiles" while reducing product design cycle time. [5]
Coca-Cola FEMSA	This Mexican bottler and distributor to Mexico, Argentina, and Latin America uses data mining to decrease stock-outs, reduce inventory, minimize variability in operations, and manage promotions.[2]
Colgate-Palmolive Company	Operating in more than 200 countries, it uses data mining to improve forecasts, production plans, and customer order fulfillment, as well as reduce overall order cycle times and costs.[2]
Dow Chemical	Its data warehouse stores news articles about clients, as well as a complete purchase history; data mining is used to improve sales visit effectiveness.[1]
Hewlett-Packard	Used data mining to identify every World Trade Center customer and its systems and components at the time of the September 11, 2001, collapse. These components were matched with on-hand inventory in warehouses, in preparation to replace destroyed systems.[1]
IBM	Helps biologists make sense of the drastically increased amount of data that can be brought to bear on any biological or medical question. Its *GeneMine* was "designed to help scientists rapidly infer, validate, and propose experimental tests for the likely functions of unknown genes."[4]
Meineke Discount Muffler Shops	This 900-plus franchised nationwide retail service provider adds more than 5,000 customer and service records each week to an extensive data warehouse it then mines using MapInfo's MapMarker to make more effective advertising decisions and identify new franchise locations.[7]
The Gillette Company	Partnered with PricewaterhouseCoopers, it uses data mining to plan on-location promotional store displays for its German retailers.[3]
Wal-Mart Stores	Uses data mining to design and modify store layouts to reduce shoplifting and theft.[6]

[1]Extracted from "Software to Track Customers' Needs Helped Firms React," *New York Times* on the Web, October 1, 2001 (http://www.nytimes.com/2001/10/01/technology/01CRM.html).

[2]Extracted from supply-chain management special advertising section, *Business Week,* October 8, 2001.

[3]Extracted from SAP Customer Success Stories (http://www.mysap.com/solutions/crm/customersuccesses.asp/Gillette_50050088.pdf).

[4]Extracted from "The GeneMine System for Genome/Proteome Annotation and Collaborative Data Mining," *IBM Systems Journal* 40, no. 2, 2001 (http://www.research.ibm.com/journal/sj/402/lee.html).

[5]"BMW Pioneers Stochastic Crash Simulation for Improved Vehicle Safety," Silicon Graphics Inc. (http://www.sgi.com/manufacturing/success/bmw.html).

[6]"NCR More than Doubles Data Warehouse for World's Leading Retailer to Over 100 Terabytes" (http://hpcwire.com/dsstart/99/0824/100966.html).

[7]S. Reese, "Bad Mufflers Make Good Data," *American Demographics,* November 1998, pp. 42–44.

there are $12 \times 11 \times 10 = 1,320$ combinations. If you spent a minute examining a plot of each pair of variables, you could easily spend 22 hours on the problem.

You may want to review data-mining software and download the demo for SPSS (http://www.spss. com/clementine/newshow/ sld003.htm) or explore the SAS Enterprise Miner (http://www.sas. com/service/consult/ usconsult/miningcompaq. html). Also visit Compaq's Advanced Data Mining Center (http://www. compaq.com, keyword search: data mining, or http://www.sas.com/ partners/directory/ compaq/index.html).

Numerous techniques are used in data mining; often they are used together. The type of data available and the nature of information sought determine the technique used. Here we explore the first five techniques listed below and mention several others (to be covered in later chapters):

- Data visualization
- Clustering
- Neural networks
- Tree models
- Classification
- Estimation
- Association
- Market-basket analysis
- Sequence-based analysis
- Fuzzy logic
- Genetic algorithms
- Fractal-based transformation

Data Visualization By viewing aggregated data on multiple dimensions (e.g., product, brand, date of sale, and region), both the analyst and the end-user gain a deeper, more intuitive understanding of the data in picture form. A multidimensional database typically contains three axes: (1) *dimensions,* like the fields in a table; (2) *measurements,* aggregate computations to be viewed; and (3) *hierarchies,* which impose structure on the dimensions. The set {month, quarter, year} is a time-based hierarchy.[19] Using this approach, the researcher views the data at various levels ("drill down/drill up"). Starting with a total of sales of breakfast cereal by region, the researcher observes that one region is more profitable than others. Next, she drills down to sales by store and discovers that one store is outperforming all others. Looking deeper yet reveals that this store spends the most on training warehousing personnel.

Data visualization uses two types of interactive queries. The first type is usually available to the end-user via a query language. The second, for complex queries that go beyond traditional two-dimensional row and column data analysis, uses online analytical processing (OLAP) tools. Multidimensional analysis, another phrase for OLAP, provides fast, flexible data summarization, analyses, and reporting capabilities with the ability to view trends over time. So, complex queries such as, "How much coffee did we sell last month in Sacramento, compared to the same month last year?" can be answered quickly.

We discuss cluster analysis in more detail in Chapter 19.

Clustering **Clustering** enables the researcher to segment a population. This approach assigns each data record to a group or segment. The assignment process is performed automatically by clustering algorithms that identify the similar characteristics in the data set and then partition them into groups often referred to as the "nearest neighbors."

Clustering is often used as the first step in data mining. For example, clustering may be used to segment a customer database for further analysis of customers' buying habits to decide which segments to target for a new sales campaign.

Neural Networks   **Neural networks,** or *artificial neural networks (ANN),* are collections of simple processing nodes that are connected. Each node operates only on its local data and on the inputs it receives via the connections. The result is a nonlinear predictive model that resembles biological neural networks and learns through training.

The neural model has to train its network on a training data set. One drawback is that no explanation of the results is available. Neural networks are best used where a predictive model is more useful than an explanatory model. For database marketing, a neural network can be constructed that predicts whether a specific person is likely to purchase a particular product. This enables the marketing organization to be very specific in its target marketing, reducing costs and dramatically improving sales "hits."

Tree Models   This technique segregates data by using a hierarchy of if-then statements based on the values of the variables and creates a tree-shaped structure that represents the segregation decisions. **Decision tree models** are faster and easier to understand than neural networks, but the data must be interval or categorical. Specific decision tree methods include classification and regression trees (CART) and chi-square automatic interaction detection (CHAID), a type of Automatic Interaction Detection model (see Chapter 16, Exhibit 16–20).

Classification   **Classification** uses a set of preclassified examples to develop a model that can classify the population of records at large. Fraud detection and risk assessments of credit applications are particularly well suited to this type of analysis. Classification frequently employs decision trees or neural network-based classification algorithms (see descriptions, below).

Classification begins with training the software with a set of preclassified sample transactions. For a fraud detection application, this would include complete records of both fraudulent and valid activities. The algorithm uses these cases as criteria to set the parameters for proper discrimination. Once developed, the model can correctly classify new records into the same predefined classes. For example, a model capable of classifying loan applicants may generate a rule stating, "If applicant earns $45,000, is between 35 and 45 years old, and lives in a specific zip code, then the applicant is a good credit risk." **Estimation** is a variation of classification. Instead of using a binary classifier (e.g., a loan applicant is a good risk or a bad risk), estimation generates a score (e.g., of creditworthiness), based on a prescored training set.

Other Mining Techniques   **Association** is the process used to recognize and understand patterns in the data. The goal is to find, across large numbers of small transactions, trends that can be used to understand and exploit natural buying patterns.

The most common form of association is **market-basket analysis.** A classic example of market-basket analysis was the discovery that beer and diapers are often purchased during the evening in the same transaction. Presumably this is not because babies like beer before bed, but because the baby's father buys the diapers and chooses to purchase beer at the same time. Information from market-basket analysis can lead stores to change their layout, adjust their inventories, or introduce a targeted promotional campaign. In the financial sector, association can be used to analyze customers' accounts. The patterns identified may be used to create a "bundle" of service offerings.

Results from association analyses are often expressed in terms of confidence, such as, "Seventy-five percent of all transactions in which soft drinks were purchased also included potato chips." The results of the association analysis often trigger additional analysis to help the manager understand why the association exists.

A variant of traditional market-basket analysis, **sequence-based analysis** ties together a series of activities or purchases (for example, using an account number, a credit card, or a frequent-flyer number). The association algorithm takes into account not only the combination of items but also the order of the items. Rules derived from these relationships can be used to predict a specific purchase based on previous purchases. In health care, such methods can be used to predict the course of a disease and order preventive care.

Fuzzy logic, genetic algorithms, and fractal transforms are used in more complex mining operations. **Fuzzy logic,** an extension of conventional (Boolean) logic, handles the concept of partial truth—truth values between "completely true" and "completely false." **Genetic algorithms** are optimization techniques that use processes analogous to mutation, natural selection, and genetics for search and identification of meaningful relationships. Fractal geometry was originally applied to the compression of topographic images. It is a mathematical means of compressing data with no data. Models using **fractal-based transformation** can work on many gigabytes of data, offering the possibility of identifying tiny subsets of data that have common characteristics. For example, fractal-based transformations would enable a researcher to discover the 5 customers out of 5 million who responded to a Neiman Marcus catalog offering.

Data-Mining Process

Data mining, as depicted in Exhibit 10–12, involves a five-step process:[20]

- **Sample:** Decide between census and sample data.
- **Explore:** Identify relationships within the data.
- **Modify:** Modify or transform data.
- **Model:** Develop a model that explains the data relationships.
- **Assess:** Test the model's accuracy.

To better visualize the connections between the techniques just described and the process steps listed in this section, you may want to download a demonstration version of data-mining software from the Internet.

For an appropriate sampling technique, choose from among those described in Chapter 7.

Sample   Exhibit 10–12 suggests that the researcher must decide whether to use the entire data set or a sample of the data.[21] If the data set in question is not large, if the processing power is high, or if it is important to understand patterns for every record in the database, sampling should not be done. However, if the data warehouse is very large (terabytes of data), the processing power is limited, or speed is more important than complete analysis, it is wise to draw a sample. In some instances, researchers may use a data mart for their sample—with local data that are appropriate for their geography. Alternatively, the researcher may select an appropriate sampling technique. Since fast turnaround for decisions is often more important than absolute accuracy, sampling is appropriate.

We explore EDA techniques in Chapter 16.

If general patterns exist in the data as a whole, these patterns will be found in the sample. If a niche is so tiny that it is not represented in a sample yet is so important that it influences the big picture, it will be found using exploratory data analysis (EDA).

Explore   After the data are sampled, the next step is to explore them visually or numerically for trends or groups. Both visual and statistical exploration (data visualization) can be used to identify trends. The researcher also looks for outliers to see if the data need to be cleaned, cases need to be dropped, or a larger sample needs to be drawn.

EXHIBIT 10–12   Data-Mining Process

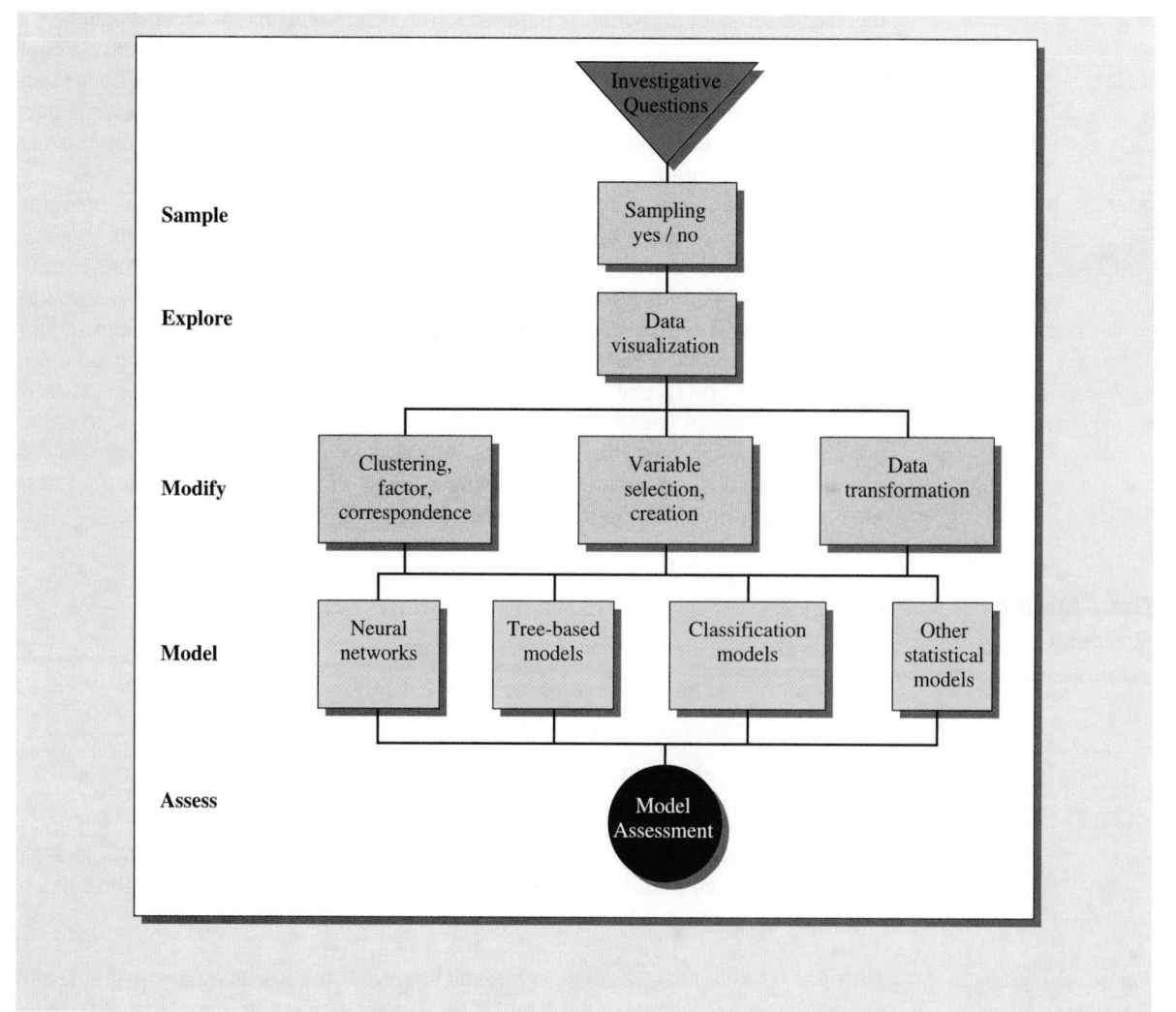

Modify   Based on the discoveries in the exploration phase, the data may require modification. Clustering, fractal-based transformation, and the application of fuzzy logic are completed during this phase as appropriate. A data reduction program, such as factor analysis, correspondence analysis, or clustering, may be used (see Chapter 19). If important constructs are discovered, new factors may be introduced to categorize the data into these groups. In addition, variables based on combinations of existing variables may be added, recoded, transformed, or dropped.

At times, descriptive segmentation of the data is all that is required to answer the investigative question. However, if a complex predictive model is needed, the researcher will move to the next step of the process.

Model   Once the data are prepared, construction of a model begins. Modeling techniques in data mining include neural networks as well as decision tree, sequence-based, classification and estimation, and genetic-based models.

Assess   The final step in data mining is to assess the model to estimate how well it performs. A common method of assessment involves applying a portion of data that was not used during the sampling stage. If the model is valid, it will work for this "holdout" sample. Another way to test a model is to run the model against known data. For example, if you know which customers in a file have high loyalty and your model predicts loyalty, you can check to see whether the model has selected these customers accurately.

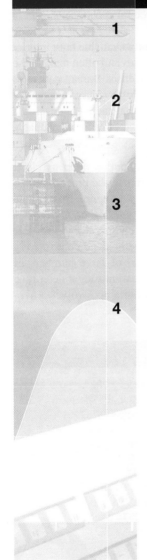

SUMMARY

1   The exploratory phase of the research process uses secondary data to expand understanding of the management dilemma, look for ways others have addressed and/or solved problems similar to the management dilemma or management question, and gather background information on the topic to refine the research question.

2   Researching secondary sources is complex and challenging. There are two categories of sources available (external and internal) and three types of sources (primary, secondary, and tertiary). Primary sources are original works of research or raw data without interpretation. Secondary sources are interpretations of primary data. Tertiary sources may be interpretations of secondary sources or, more commonly, finding aids such as indexes, bibliographies, and Internet search engines.

3   There are generally five types of information sources used in most literature searches, including indexes and bibliographies, dictionaries, encyclopedias, handbooks, and directories. Each is useful to a literature search in a variety of ways. One of the harder tasks associated with using secondary sources is evaluating the quality of the information. Five factors to consider when evaluating the quality of the source are purpose, scope, authority, audience, and format.

4   The process for searching bibliographic databases applies to both print and online sources.

   1. Select a database appropriate to your topic.

   2. Construct a search query (or search statement).

      • Review and evaluate search results.

      • Modify the search query, if necessary.

   3. Save those valuable results of your search.

   4. Retrieve articles not available in the database.

   5. Supplement your results with information from Web sources.

      Many online and Web-based sources use Boolean logic for constructing search queries, but protocols do differ. One purpose for reviewing the results of your original search is to modify it with newly discovered information. The researcher should check the bibliographies of cited works, check the subject headings assigned to the extracted articles, and search for works by referenced authors.

5   The basic steps for searching Web-based sources include a critical last step that novice researchers often skip.

   1. Select a search engine or directory.

   2. Determine your search options.

3. Construct a search query and enter your search term(s).

- Review and evaluate search results.

- Modify your search query, if necessary.

4. Save those valuable results of your search.

5. Supplement your results with information from non-Web sources.

When doing a Web-based search, several options are available: known-item searches, "who" searches, "where" searches, and "what" searches. Due to the special characteristics of each type of search, each starts with a different search strategy. Several special sites have evolved to offer the researcher assistance for each type of search. These can be found in Appendix A.

U.S. government data are exceptionally detailed and readily available both in print and on the Web. All government agencies provide detailed studies and often make these results available in full text or in summary tables. The U.S. Census Bureau generates the most complete databases on the U.S. population, being most well known for the decennial census. The Census Bureau has partnered with local agencies to develop a multilevel mapping system for its data, making the bureau an even more valuable source of data.

6   Managers faced with current decisions requiring immediate attention often overlook internal data in a company's data warehouse. Data mining refers to the process of discovering knowledge from databases. Data-mining technology provides two unique capabilities to the researcher or manager: pattern discovery and the prediction of trends and behaviors. Data-mining tools perform exploratory and confirmatory statistical analyses to discover and validate relationships. These tools even extend confirmatory statistical approaches by allowing the automated examination of large numbers of hypotheses. The type of data available and the nature of information sought determine which of the numerous data-mining techniques to select. Data mining involves a five-step process: sample, explore, modify, model, and assess.

KEY TERMS

EXAMPLES

Company	Scenario	Page
Advertising World (University of Texas)	Developing a portal to advertising websites of interest to students and practitioners.	296
Bank of America	Using data-mining software to pinpoint marketing programs that attract high-margin, low-risk customers.	303
Blue Cross Blue Shield	Using data mining to staff and train customer service call centers.	304
BMW	Using data mining to design improvements to the crashworthiness and safety of automobiles.	304
Charles Schwab	Describes the Internet's importance to investor research.	286
CNNfn	Design of a website for a special-interest audience.	286
Coca-Cola FEMSA	Using data mining for inventory, production, and promotion management in Mexico, Argentina, and Latin America.	304
Colgate-Palmolive Company	Using data mining to improve forecasting, production, and customer order fulfillment.	304
Croy and Associates[*]	Conducting secondary research to prepare for an interview with a potential research client.	BRTL
Dow Chemical	Using data mining to increase sales call effectiveness.	304
Hewlett-Packard	Using data mining to respond to the September 11, 2001, World Trade Center collapse.	304
IBM	Using its *GeneMine* technology to help biologists develop better cures and treatments for disease.	304
MasterCard	Detection of stolen credit cards based on data mining of credit card transactions.	303
Meineke Discount Muffler Shops	Using data mining to plan more effective advertising, as well as select new locations.	304
Mellon Bank	Using data mining to optimize home equity line of credit marketing to existing customers.	303
MindWriter[*]	Finding variables of association to predict repair success.	303
Neiman Marcus	Fractal-based transformations to discover likely customers for catalog merchandise.	307
Sacramento FastShop	Unidimensional and historical query in data mining; finding and explaining combination purchases.	301
Space Imaging	Using multiple sources of geospatial data to create map-accurate and information-rich products for government and industry.	294
State Farm Insurance	Using data mining to reveal the most accident-prone intersections within the United States and Canada.	302
The Gillette Company (with Pricewaterhouse-Coopers LLP)	Using data mining to plan on-location promotional store displays for German retailers.	304

| U.S. government | Using data mining to detect tax fraud, eavesdrop on foreign communications, and process satellite imagery. | 295 |
| Wal-Mart Stores | Using data mining to design and modify store layouts to reduce shoplifting and theft. | 304 |

*Due to the confidential and proprietary nature of most research, the names of some companies have been changed.

DISCUSSION QUESTIONS

Terms in Review

1. Explain how each of the five evaluation factors for a secondary source influences its management decision-making value.

   a. Purpose

   b. Scope

   c. Authority

   d. Audience

   e. Format

2. Define the distinctions between primary, secondary, and tertiary sources in a secondary search.

3. What is data mining?

4. Explain how internal data-mining techniques differ from a literature search.

5. Some researchers find that their sole sources are secondary data. Why might this be? Name some management questions for which secondary data sources are probably the only ones feasible.

Making Research Decisions

6. Assume you are asked to investigate the use of mathematical programming in accounting applications. You decide to depend on secondary data sources. What search tools might you use? Which do you think would be the most fruitful? Sketch a flow diagram of your search sequence.

7. What problems of secondary data quality must researchers face? How can they deal with them?

8. Below are a number of requests that a staff assistant might receive. What specific tools or services would you expect to use to find the requisite information? (Hint: Use Appendix A and the CD that accompanies this text.)

   a. The president wants a list of six of the best references on executive compensation that have appeared during the last year.

   b. Has the FTC published any recent statements (within the last year) concerning its position on quality stabilization?

   c. I need a list of the major companies located in Greensboro, North Carolina.

   d. Please get me a list of the directors of General Motors, Microsoft, and Morgan Stanley & Co.

   e. Is there a trade magazine that specializes in the flooring industry?

   f. I would like to track down a study of small-scale service franchising that was recently published by a bureau of business research at one of the southern universities. Can you help me?

Bringing Research to Life

9. Using Exhibits 10–4, 10–5, and 10–6, state the research question and then the search plan that Jason should have conducted before his meeting with Armand Croyand.

10. What government sources should be included in Jason's search?

From Concept to Practice

11. Using Exhibits 10–4, 10–5, and 10–6, state a research question and then plan a bibliographic and Web search.

WWW Exercises

Visit our website for Internet exercises related to this chapter at www.mhhe.com/business/cooper8

CASES*

A GEM OF A STUDY

 KNSD SAN DIEGO

MCDONALD'S TESTS CATFISH SANDWICH

 OUTBOARD MARINE CORPORATION

 PEBBLE BEACH CO.

RAMADA DEMONSTRATES ITS PERSONAL BEST

STATE FARM: DANGEROUS INTERSECTIONS

THE CATALYST FOR WOMEN IN FINANCIAL SERVICES

*All cases indicating a video icon are located on the Instructor's Videotape Supplement. All nonvideo cases are in the case section of the textbook. All cases indicating a CD icon offer a data set, which is located on the accompanying CD.

REFERENCE NOTES

1. Faith McLellan, "1966 and All That—When Is a Literature Search Done?" *The Lancet* 358 (August 25, 2001), p. 646.
2. Ad in *Business Week,* June 28, 1999, p. 3.
3. "Lots of online brokers say they are number one. Here's what some of the industry sources have to say," Schwab.com, January 1, 2001 (http://www.schwab.com/SchwabNOW/SNLibrary/SNLib132/SN132mainAwardsAndRatingsHome/).
4. For general information on evaluating reference sources, see William A. Katz, *Introduction to Reference Work,* 7th ed., McGraw-Hill, 1997. For more information about evaluating Web resources, see "Checklist for a Business/Marketing Web Page" (Widener University, Wolfgram Memorial Library. Compiled by Jan Alexander and Marsh Tate, 1999; http://www2.widener.edu/Wolfgram-Memorial-Library/busmark.htm); "Evaluating World Wide Web Resources" (Indiana University Libraries, 1999; http://www.indiana.edu/~libinstr/worksheets/evaluating_web.html); and the metasite "Evaluating Information Sources" (Alastair Smith, 2000; http://www.vuw.ac.nx/-agsmith/evaln/evaln.htm).
5. Good sources for Web size estimates are the studies by Steve R. Lawrence and C. Lee Giles, "Searching the World Wide Web," *Science* 280 (April 1998), pp. 98–100, and "Accessibility of Information on the Web," *Nature* 400 (July 8, 1999), pp. 107–9, with updated summary data at http://www.wwwmetrics.com.
6. Michael Dahm, "Counting Angels on a Pinhead: Critically Interpreting Web Size Estimates," *Online* 24 (January/February 2000), pp. 35–44. This article further interprets the pioneering research by authors Steve R. Lawrence and C. Lee Giles (op. cit.).
7. The May/June 1999 issue of *Online* focuses on search engine technology. See, for example, Danny Sullivan, "Crawling under the Hood: An Update on Search Engine Technology," *Online* 23 (May/June 1999), pp. 30–38. See also Danny Sullivan's "Search Engine Watch" (http://searchenginewatch.com/) and Greg Notess's "Search Engine Showdown" (http://www.notess.com/search/) for current information about search engines and their features.
8. Greg R. Notess, "Duplicative Databases: Yellow Pages from infoUSA," *Database* 22 (February/March 1999), pp. 73–76.
9. See, for example, the June 22, 1999, issue of *PC Magazine* for a special report detailing "Ten Trends That Are Defining the Future" (Introduction, p. 100).
10. "Federal Register Online Via GPO Access" (http://www.access.gpo.gov/su_docs/aces/aces140.html).
11. "About the Code of Federal Regulations" (http://www.access.gpo.gov/nara/about-ctr.html#page1).
12. R. Srikant and R. Agrawal, "Mining Sequential Patterns: Generalizations and Performance Improvements," *Proceedings,* 5th International Conference on Extending Database Technology, Paris, France, March 1996.
13. B. DePompe, "There's Gold in Databases," *CMP Publications,* January 8, 1996; website: http://techweb.cmp.com/iwk.
14. Table adapted from DIG White Paper 95/01, "An Overview of Data Mining at Dun & Bradstreet," Data Intelligence Group, Pilot Software, Cambridge, MA (September 1995).
15. "Data Mining: Plumbing the Depths of Corporate Databases," *Computerworld Customer Publication,* insert to *Computerworld,* April 21, 1997, p. 12.
16. DePompe, *CMP Publications;* website: http://techweb.cmp.com/iwk.
17. "Data Mining: Plumbing the Depths of Corporate Databases," *ComputerWorld,* pp. 6, 18.
18. The section on data-mining techniques was adapted from Bruce Moxon, "Defining Data Mining," DBMS Data Warehouse Supplement, *DBMS Online* (August 1996), http://www.dbmsmag. com; Mark Kantrowitz, Erik Horstkotte, and Cliff Joslyn, "Fuzzy Logic FAQ," http://comp.ai.fuzzynewsgroup; DIG White Paper 95/01; and Michael Bell, "A Data Mining FAQ," Quintillion Corporation, Web page: http://www.qwhy.com/dmfaq.htm.
19. Information Discovery Inc.; website: http://www.idi.com.
20. SAS Institute Inc., "Data Mining," website: http://www.sas.com.
21. Exhibit 10–12 was adapted from SAS Institute Inc., "Data Mining," website: http://www.sas.com.

REFERENCES FOR SNAPSHOTS AND CAPTIONS

Microsoft

"Microsoft Announces Hailstorm, a New Set of XML Web Services Designed to Give Users Greater Control," Microsoft press release, March 19, 2001 (http://www.microsoft.com/press-pass/features/2001/mar01/03-19hailstorm.asp).

Steve Lohr, "Privacy Group Is Taking Issue with Microsoft," *The NewYork Times on the Web,* July 25, 2001 (http://www. nytimes.com/2001/07/25/technology/ebusiness/25COMP. html?todaysheadlines).

Space Imaging

"The Company," Spaceimaging.com (January 1, 2002) (http://www. spaceimaging.com/newsroom/press_kits/factsheet.htm).

CLASSIC AND CONTEMPORARY READINGS

Berry, Michael J. A., and Gordon Linoff. *Mastering Data Mining: The Art and Science of Customer Relationship Management.* New York: John Wiley & Sons, 1999.

Fayyad, U. M., and G. Piatesky-Shapiro. *Advances in Knowledge Discovery and Data Mining.* Cambridge, MA: AAAI Press-MIT Press, 1996. An excellent text that provides an overview of knowledge discovery and data mining using statistical methods.

Katz, William A. *Introduction to Reference Work.* 7th ed. New York: McGraw-Hill, 1997.

Woy, James (ed.). *Encyclopedia of Business Information Sources,* 14th ed. Gale Group, 2000.

CHAPTER 11

Survey Methods: Communicating with Participants

Learning Objectives

After reading this chapter, you should understand . . .

1   The process for selecting the appropriate and optimal communication approach.

2   What factors affect participation in communication studies.

3   The major sources of error in communication studies and how to minimize them.

4   The major advantages and disadvantages of the three communication approaches.

5   Why an organization might outsource a communication study.

Bringing Research to Life

"**J**ason, you'll enjoy this," Myra called as she arrived for her meeting on the economic council research proposal. She was waving a letter above her head and smiling widely.

"You remember me telling you about my Aunt Edna, the not-so-retired attorney in Albany? Well, she sent this for my—our—amusement."

Edna Koogan, P. A., Attorney at Law
P. O. Box 8219-2767
Albany, New York 12212-2767

Dr. Edith Coblenz, M.D.
3456 Barshoot Building
Albany, New York 12212

Dear Edith,

I want you to have my side of this morning's incident at the Albany Outpatient Laser Clinic Inc. I am sure you have by now heard from the business manager and the admissions director and possibly the anesthetist. You are a stockholder in the center, I know, and as your former lawyer and current patient, I thought I owed you a warning and explanation.

You told me to report to the center at 7 A.M. for a workup in preparation for eye surgery tomorrow. I caught a cab and was there at 6:55 promptly and was then obliged to stand outside in lightly drifting snow until the doors opened. They were late opening the admissions department.

I identified myself as your patient, and at once the receptionist called someone from the back room and said, "Ms. Koogan's personal physician is Dr. Coblenz," which is, of course, not true, as you are my eye doctor, and my personal physician is Dr. Burke in Troy. But I was too cold to argue and there were people lined up behind me.

A fellow who had scooted in from the back insisted on taking my glasses and medications with him "for a workup," as he said. As soon as he had disappeared with my glasses the first admissions clerk disappeared and a second one appeared and handed me a "questionnaire" to fill out. It appeared to be a photocopy of a photocopy of a photocopy and was very faintly printed in small gray type on a light gray sheet. When I pointed out that I was about to be admitted for treatment of glaucoma, a leading cause of blindness, she told me, "Do the best you can." When I objected emphatically, she seemed taken aback. I suppose most of her 80-year-old patients are more compliant, but I guess I am an intractable old attorney.

Was I wrong to object to the questionnaire being too faint and the type too small? Am I the first glaucoma patient who has ever been treated at the Laser Center? One would think they would understand you can't ask someone blind in one eye to fill out such a questionnaire, especially without her glasses. She finally, grudgingly, asked me to sit by her side, so she could help me.

There were several questions about my name, address, age, and occupation. Then she wanted to know the name of the admitting physician and then the phone number (but not the name) of the physician who was most familiar with my health. I said the admitting physician was an eye doctor and the physician most familiar with my health was a GP, and asked, which did she want the phone number for, the eye doctor or the GP? She became very angry then and admonished me to try and "get over that bad attitude." Then she told me to go over and sit somewhere and fill out the form as best I could.

A very nice patient (hemorrhoids, no vision problems) heard our conversation and offered to help me. She began reading the questionnaire and came to the item "Past Medical History: Yes or No." She didn't think this made any sense, and neither did I, because everyone has a past medical history, and no one would answer no; but after a while we decided that it meant I should answer yes or no to all of the questions underneath, such as: Did I have diabetes? Did I have heart disease? When we came to "Have you ever had or been treated for a recent cold or the flu?" we could not decide if it meant, have I ever had the flu? Or have I had flu recently (I had flu six months ago, but is that "recent"?) so we asked the receptionist, and she became almost speechless and said she would get me some help.

After a while the "help" appeared—a nurse who wanted to measure my blood pressure and induce me to take a blue pill, which she said would be good for my "nerves." I refused and pointed out rather curtly that this was not a gulag but an admissions department, a place of business, for crying out loud, where they ought to be able to handle a little criticism from someone trained to elicit accurate information.

By then several nice people had pitched in to help me with the questionnaire. But this made it even harder to decide on the answers, because we understood so many of the questions differently and couldn't agree. When we came to "Are all your teeth intact?" One man thought it meant, "Do you have false teeth?" And another thought it meant, "Do you have any broken dentures?" But a woman who assured me her son is a dentist said it meant, "Do you have any loose teeth?" We decided to settle that by eeny-meany-miney-moe.

Then there was the question "Do you have limited motion of your neck?" and by then everyone was enjoying the incongruity of these questions. Of course I have limited motion of the neck. Doesn't everyone? We decided to save that question for later clarification.

After all of the yes-no questions there came various other stumpers, such as "Please list your current medications." The problem is, of course, that I have purple eye drops and yellow eye drops, but the young man had taken them away from me "for a workup," so I had no way of accurately answering the questions. I was pretty sure one of them was glucagon, so I guessed and put that down, but then I had second thoughts and scratched it out. (When I got home, I checked and it was betagan, not glucagon.)

There were four of us working on the questionnaire by then, and we were laughing and crowing and having a high time and discharging our anxieties, which got the admissions clerk very flustered and annoyed. So she called the anesthetist, a stuck-up young fellow who said he had written the questionnaire himself and had never had any problems with it. That is when I told him, if he had not had any problems with this questionnaire, this proved it was better to be lucky than smart.

He said he was going to overlook my "attitude" because he knew I was old and anxious about the coming operation, and I told him I was going to take my business somewhere else because of the bilaterality problem. "What is that?" he asked. I said, I have two eyes, and if anyone as dumb as him went after me with a knife, he would probably take the wrong eye.

I caught a cab and sent my neighbor back for my glasses. As your lawyer, I urge you not to further involve yourself with such fools.

Lovingly,

Edna

Characteristics of the Communication Approach

The researcher determines the data collection approach largely by identifying the types of information needed—investigative questions the researcher must answer—and the desired data type (nominal, ordinal, interval, or ratio) for each of these questions. The characteristics of the sample unit—specifically, whether a participant can articulate his or her ideas, thoughts, and experiences—also play a role in the decision. Part A of Exhibit 11–1 shows the relationship of these decisions to the research process detailed in Chapter 3. Part B indicates how the researcher's choice of a communication (versus an observation) approach affects the following:

- The creation and selection of the measurement questions.

- Sampling issues (previously explored in Chapter 7), which drive contact and call-back procedures.

- Instrument design (to be discussed in Chapter 12), which incorporates attempts to reduce error and create respondent-screening procedures.

- Data collection processes, which create the need for follow-up procedures (when self-administered instruments are used) and possible interviewer training (when personal or telephone interviewing methods are used).

Research designs can be classified by the *approach* used to gather primary data. There are really only two alternatives. We can *observe* conditions, behavior, events, people, or processes. Or we can *communicate* with people about various topics, including participants' attitudes, motivations, intentions, and expectations. In this chapter we focus on the choices the researcher must make once the communication approach has been chosen (Exhibit 11–2), by discussing the characteristics and applications of the various communication approaches as well as their individual strengths and weaknesses (summarized in Exhibit 11–4).

The communication approach differs significantly from the observation approach discussed in Chapter 13.

The **communication approach** involves surveying people and recording their responses for analysis. The great strength of the **survey** as a primary data collecting approach is its versatility. It does not require that there be a visual or other objective perception of the information sought by the researcher. Abstract information of all types can be gathered by questioning others. We seldom learn much about opinions and attitudes except by surveying. This is also true of intentions and expectations. Information about past events is often available only through surveying people who remember the events. Thus, the choice of a communication versus an observation approach may seem an obvious one, given the directions in which investigative questions may lead, as shown in Exhibit 11–2.

However, sometimes the investigative questions leave the option of choosing either approach. Surveying is more efficient and economical than observation. A few well-chosen questions can yield information that would take much more time and effort to gather by observation. A survey that uses the telephone, mail, or the Internet as the medium of communication can expand geographic coverage at a fraction of the cost and time required by observation.

The most appropriate applications for surveying are those where participants are uniquely qualified to provide the desired information. We expect such facts as age, income, and immediate family situation to be appropriate survey topics.

EXHIBIT 11–1 Data Collection Approach: Impact on the Research Process

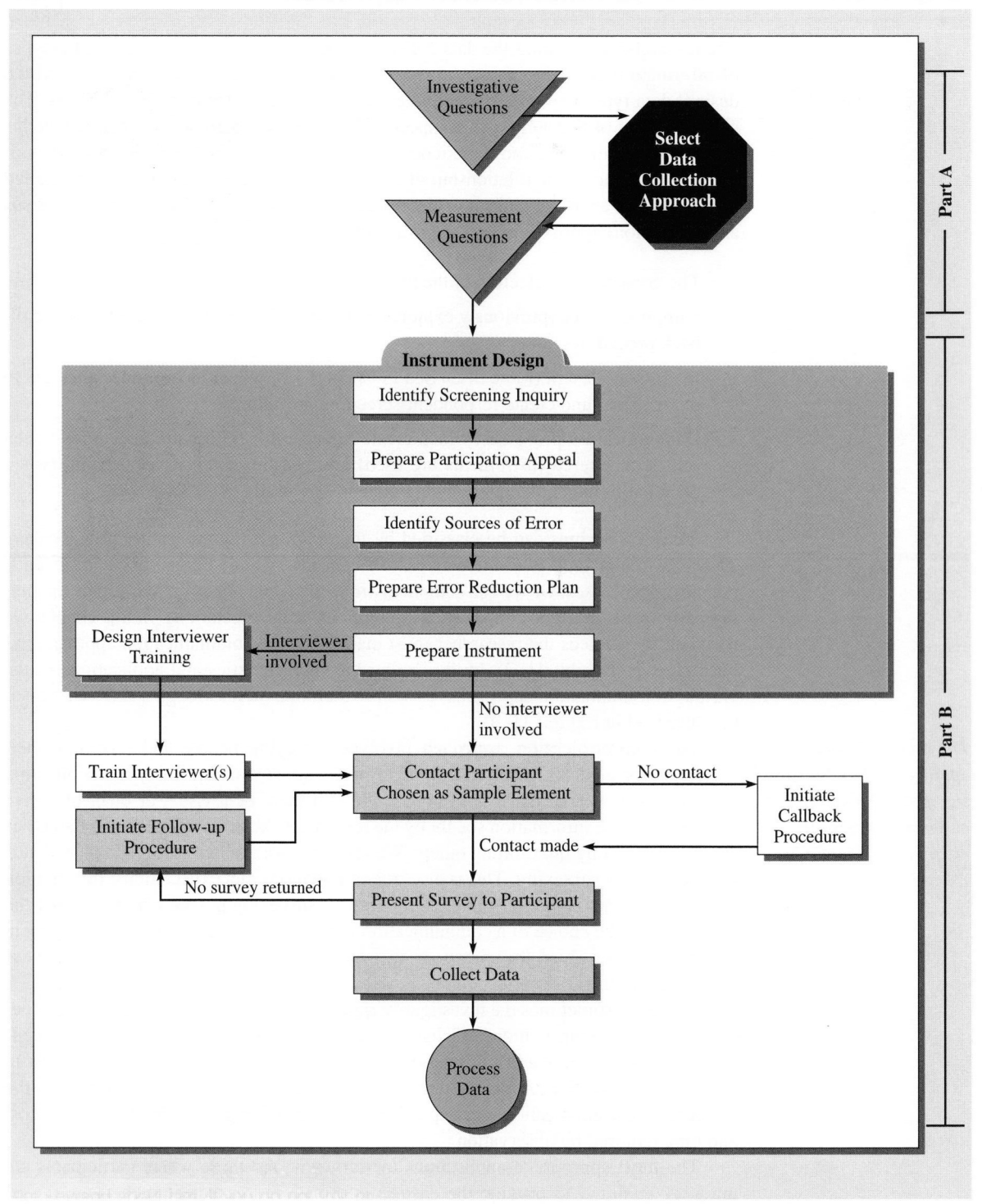

EXHIBIT 11–2 Selecting a Communication Data Collection Method

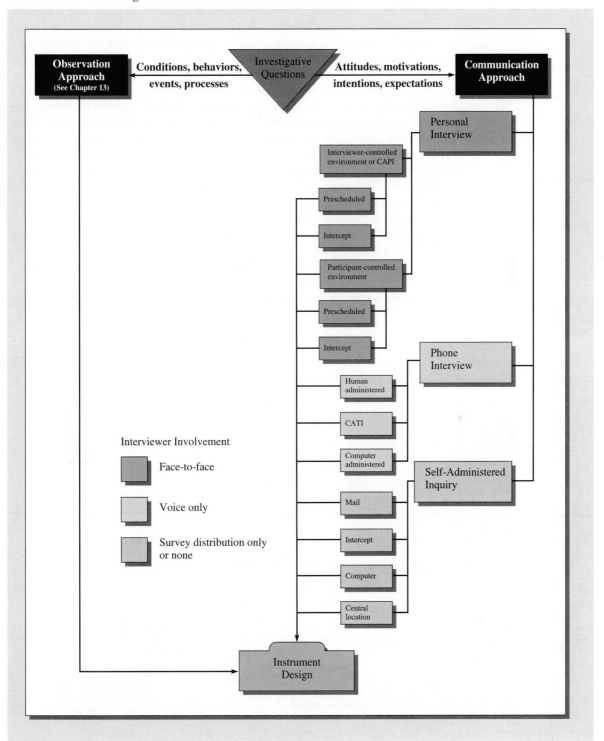

Questions can be used to inquire about subjects that are exclusively internal to the participant. We include here items such as attitudes, opinions, expectations, and intentions. Such information can be made available to the researcher if the right questions are asked of participants. It becomes, finally, a matter of whether to ask direct or indirect questions in order to collect the most meaningful data.

The communication approach has its shortcomings, however. Its major weakness, depicted in Exhibit 11–3, is that the quality and quantity of information secured depends heavily on the ability and willingness of participants to cooperate. Often, people refuse an interview or fail to reply to a mail- or computer-delivered survey. There may be many reasons for this unwillingness to cooperate. Certain people at certain times fail to see any value in participation; they may be suspicious of or fear the interview experience for some reason; or they may view the topic as too sensitive and thus the interview as potentially embarrassing or intrusive. Previous encounters with marketers who have attempted to disguise their sales pitch as a research survey can also erode participants' willingness to cooperate.

Even if individuals agree to participate, they may not possess the knowledge being sought. If we ask participants to report on events that they have not personally experienced, we need to assess the replies carefully. If our purpose is to learn what the participant *understands* to be the case, it is legitimate to accept the answers given. But if our intent is to learn what the event or situation *actually was,* we must recognize that the

EXHIBIT 11–3   **Factors Influencing Participant Motivation**

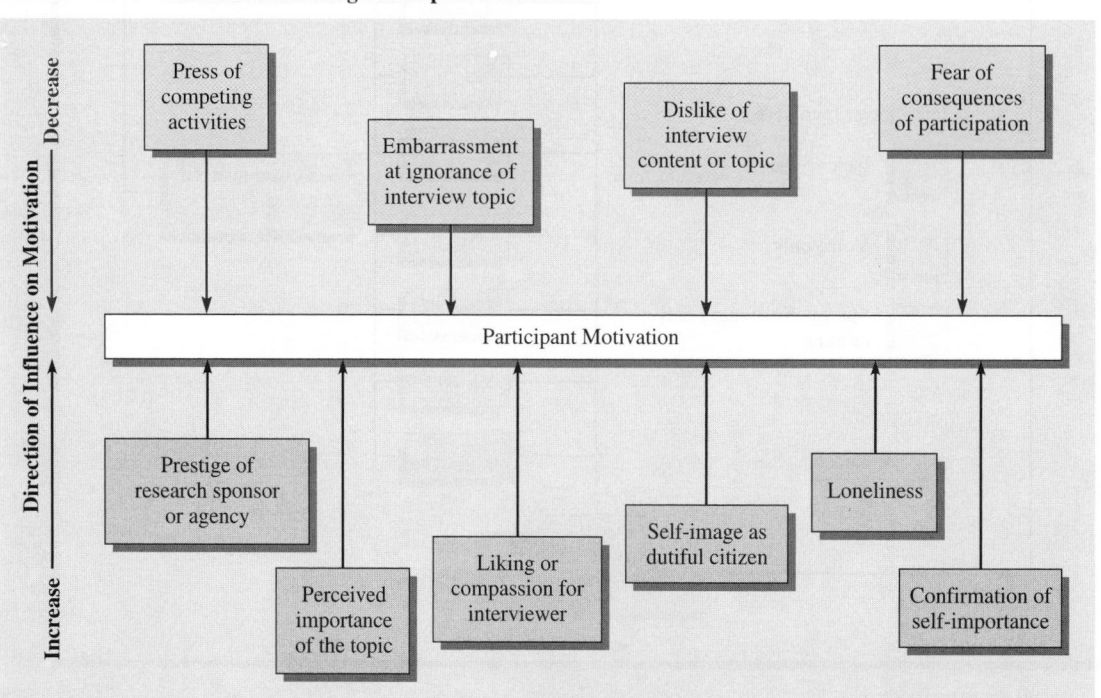

SOURCE: Influenced by Robert L. Kahn and Charles F. Cannell, "Interviewing," in David L. Sills, ed., International Encyclopedia of the Social Sciences, 8, p. 153. Copyright © 1968 by Crowell Collier and Macmillan, Inc.

participant is reporting secondhand data and the accuracy of the information declines. We should not depend on these secondhand sources if a more direct source can be found. A family or group member should be asked about another member's experience only when there is no other way to get the information directly.

In the MindWriter study, only those individuals who have experienced difficulty with their laptops and gone through the CompleteCare program have direct knowledge of the service process. Although some associates and family members are likely to have some secondhand knowledge of their experience, no one but the actual laptop owners are likely to give Jason or Myra as clear a picture of what works and what doesn't with CompleteCare. Aunt Edna, on the other hand, had a totally different experience when she went in for laser surgery to correct her vision problem. Answers to many of the questions on the patient survey might have been known by a caregiver, especially since Edna was over 80 years old and experiencing eye problems serious enough to warrant surgery. And the clinic's admissions department could have been confident that such information was as accurate as if given by Edna herself.

Sometimes a participant may not have an opinion on the topic of concern. Under these circumstances, their proper response should be "don't know" or "have no opinion." Too often, participants feel obliged to express some opinion even if they do not have one. In those cases, it is difficult for researchers to know how true or reliable the answers are.

Participants may also interpret a question or concept differently from what was intended by the researcher. This occurs when the individual answers a question that is different from the one being asked. Also, a participant may intentionally mislead the researcher by giving false information. It is difficult for a researcher to identify these occasions. Thus, survey responses should be accepted for what they are—statements by individuals that reflect varying degrees of truth. Despite these weaknesses, communicating with research participants is a principal method of management research.

Choosing a Communication Method

Once the researcher has determined that surveying is the appropriate data collection approach, various means may be used to secure information from individuals. A researcher can conduct a survey by personal interview, telephone, mail, computer, or a combination of these. As noted in Exhibit 11–4, while there are commonalities among these approaches, several considerations are unique to each.

Personal Interviewing

A **personal interview** (i.e., face-to-face communication) is a two-way conversation initiated by an interviewer to obtain information from a participant. The differences in the roles of interviewer and participant are pronounced. They are typically strangers, and the interviewer generally controls the topics and patterns of discussion. The consequences of the event are usually insignificant for the participant. The participant is asked to provide information and has little hope of receiving any immediate or direct benefit from this cooperation. With her poor eyesight and the problems of question clarity that Edna experienced at the Albany Outpatient Laser Clinic, a personal interview, rather than the intercept/self-administered questionnaire, might have been a preferable communication method.

EXHIBIT 11-4   Comparison of Communication Approaches

	Personal Interviews	Telephone Interviews	Self-Administered Surveys
Description	People selected to be part of the sample are interviewed in person by a trained interviewer.	People selected to be part of the sample are interviewed on the telephone by a trained interviewer.	Questionnaires are: (a) Mailed, faxed, or couriered to be self-administered—with return mechanism generally included; (b) Computer-delivered via intranet, Internet, and online services—computer stores/ forwards completed instruments automatically; (c) People intercepted/studied via paper or computerized instrument in central location—without interviewer assistance.

Advantages

Personal Interviews:
- Good cooperation from respondents.
- Interviewer can answer questions about survey, probe for answers, use follow-up questions, and gather information by observation.
- Special visual aids and scoring devices can be used.
- Illiterate and functionally illiterate respondents can be reached.
- Interviewer can prescreen respondent to ensure he/she fits the population profile.
- CAPI—computer-assisted personal interviewing: Responses can be entered into a portable microcomputer to reduce error and cost.

Telephone Interviews:
- Lower costs than personal interview.
- Expanded geographic coverage without dramatic increase in costs.
- Uses fewer, more highly skilled interviewers.
- Reduced interviewer bias.
- Fastest completion time.
- Better access to hard-to-reach respondents through repeated callbacks.
- Can use computerized random-digit dialing.
- CATI—computer-assisted telephone interviewing: Responses can be entered directly into a computer file to reduce error and cost.

Self-Administered Surveys:
- Allows contact with otherwise inaccessible respondents (e.g., CEOs).
- Incentives may be used to increase response rate.
- Often lowest-cost option.
- Expanded geographic coverage without increase in costs (a).
- Requires minimal staff (a).
- Perceived as more anonymous (a).
- Allows respondents time to think about questions (a).
- More complex instruments can be used (b).
- Fast access to the computer-literate (b).
- Rapid data collection (b,c).
- Respondent who cannot be reached by phone (voice) may be accessible (b,c).
- Sample frame lists viable locations rather than prospective respondents (b,c).
- Visuals may be used (b,c).

Disadvantages

Personal Interviews:
- High costs.
- Need for highly trained interviewers.
- Longer period needed in the field collecting data.
- May be wide geographic dispersion.
- Follow-up is labor intensive.
- Not all respondents are available or accessible.
- Some respondents are unwilling to talk to strangers in their homes.
- Some neighborhoods are difficult to visit.
- Questions may be altered or respondent coached by interviewers.

Telephone Interviews:
- Response rate is lower than for personal interview.
- Higher costs if interviewing geographically dispersed sample.
- Interview length must be limited.
- Many phone numbers are unlisted or not working, making directory listings unreliable.
- Some target groups are not available by phone.
- Responses may be less complete.
- Illustrations cannot be used.

Self-Administered Surveys:
- Low response rate in some modes.
- No interviewer intervention available for probing or explanation (a).
- Cannot be long or complex (a).
- Accurate mailing lists needed (a).
- Often respondents returning survey represent extremes of the population—skewed responses (a).
- Anxiety among some respondents (b).
- Directions/software instruction needed for progression through the instrument (b).
- Computer security (b).
- Need for low-distraction environment for survey completion (c).

A harbormaster in Finland hired Rubinstein Consulting to help with a human resource problem. When a shift ended, workers deserted their posts, abandoning tools and expensive machinery wherever they stood. Rubinstein chose in-depth personal interviews among current and potential workers to understand the problem and identify a plausible new recruiting plan. The research revealed that older workers had an entitlement mentality: A job was their right. Rubinstein's research also discovered that younger workers, especially those exiting mandatory military service, would be enticed by the salaries but also would want to prove themselves. These workers would be far more dedicated to both company and job—expecting no job to be for a lifetime and anxious to perform. The new recruiting plan that Rubinstein devised for targeting younger workers promised potentially higher worker turnover but delivered much higher productivity and lower costs in the area of damaged equipment. www.rubinsteinconsulting.fi

Evaluation of the Personal Interview

There are real advantages as well as clear limitations to personal interviewing. The greatest value lies in the depth of information and detail that can be secured. It far exceeds the information secured from telephone and self-administered studies via intercepts (e.g., in malls or, as with Edna, in a doctor's office), mail surveys, or computer (both intranet and Internet). The interviewer can also do more things to improve the quality of the information received than with another method.

The absence of assistance in interpreting questions in the Albany clinic study was a clear weakness that would have been improved by the presence of an interviewer. Interviewers can note conditions of the interview, probe with additional questions, and gather supplemental information through observation. Edna was obviously in good spirits and very relaxed after she and her fellow patients had critiqued the questionnaire. This attitude would have been observed and noted by an interviewer. Of course, we're hopeful that the interviewer would correctly interpret laughter as a sign of humor and not as a negative attitude, as did the admissions clerk.

Interviewers also have more control than with other kinds of interrogation. They can prescreen to ensure the correct participant is replying, and they can set up and control interviewing conditions. They can use special scoring devices and visual materials, as is done with **computer-assisted personal interviewing (CAPI).** Interviewers also can adjust the language of the interview as they observe the problems and effects the interview is having on the participant.

With such advantages, why would anyone want to use any other survey method? Probably the greatest reason is that personal interviewing is costly, in terms of both money and time. A personal interview may cost anywhere from a few dollars to several hundred dollars for an interview with a hard-to-reach person. Costs are particularly high if the study covers a wide geographic area or has stringent sampling requirements. An exception to this is the **intercept interview** that targets participants in centralized locations such as shoppers in retail malls. Intercept interviews reduce costs associated with the need for several interviewers, training, and travel. Product and service demonstrations also can be coordinated, further reducing costs. Their cost-effectiveness, however, is offset when representative sampling is crucial to the study's outcome. Exhibit 11–5 offers some helpful tips when intercept interviews are an appropriate research design. The intercept interview would have been a possibility in the Albany clinic study, although more admissions clerks would likely have been needed if volunteers were not available to perform this task.

Costs have risen rapidly in recent years for most communication methods because changes in the social climate have made personal interviewing more difficult. Many people today are reluctant to talk with strangers or to permit visits in their homes. Interviewers are reluctant to visit unfamiliar neighborhoods alone, especially for evening interviewing. Finally, results of personal interviews can be affected adversely by interviewers who alter the questions asked or in other ways bias the results. As Edna and her friends discussed the Albany clinic survey, they each applied their own operational definitions to the concepts and constructs being asked. This confusion created a bias that might have been eliminated by a well-trained interviewer. Interviewer bias is discussed in more depth later in this chapter. If we are to overcome these deficiencies, we must appreciate the conditions necessary for interview success.

Requirements for Success   Three broad conditions must be met in order to have a successful personal interview:

MANAGEMENT

Tip

- The participant must possess the information being targeted by the investigative questions.
- The participant must understand his or her role in the interview as the provider of accurate information.
- The participant must perceive adequate motivation to cooperate.

The interviewer can do little about the participant's information level. Screening questions can qualify participants when there is doubt about their ability to answer. This is the study designer's responsibility.

Increasing Participation[1]

Interviewers can influence respondents in many ways. An interviewer can explain what kind of answer is sought, how complete it should be, and in what terms it should be

EXHIBIT 11–5   Tips on Intercept Survey Design

MANAGEMENT

Tip

1. When screening for multiple studies at the same time, make your questionnaire distinctive:
   - Use colored paper.
   - Use paper with a distinctive color or pattern edge.

2. Make surveys clipboard-friendly:
   - Never print questions on both sides of the paper.
   - Keep font style and point size legible in inconsistent and dim light.
   - Confine your questionnaire to four pages or less.

3. Write the "respondent approach" section to include answers to the following often-asked questions:
   - What's the study about?
   - What's in it for me if I participate?
   - How long will it take?

4. Limit the number of screening questions to avoid participant termination:
   - Keep screening question(s) to the point: Ask only for critical data.
   - Build screening questions on facts, not assumptions or generalities.
   - If you need to speak with the primary purchaser, don't specify gender, family status, or age in the screeners.

5. Keep screening question(s) safe from respondents' eyes:
   - Choose normal, not bold, type style.
   - Put in parentheses or use another separation device.

6. Don't overuse skip patterns: The more cumbersome the patterns, the more likely they won't be followed consistently or effectively.

7. Don't force the interviewer to remember responses to questions on previous pages in order to ask questions on the current page.

8. Tally where respondents terminate the screening process or survey:
   - Include a horizontal string of question numbers at the bottom of each page so the interviewer can circle the number of the next question after termination.

SOURCE: www.quirks.com/CGI-BIN/SM40i.exe?docid=3000:58911&%70assArticleId=52; E. B. Feltser, "Pain-Free Mall Intercepts," *Quirk's Marketing Research Review,* November 1996.

expressed. Interviewers can even do some coaching in the interview, although this can be a biasing factor.

Participant motivation is a responsibility of the interviewer. Studies of reactions to many surveys show that participants can be motivated to participate in personal interviews and, in fact, can even enjoy the experience. In one study, more than 90 percent of participants said the interview experience was interesting, and three-fourths reported they were willing to be interviewed again.[2] In intercept/self-administered studies, the interviewer's primary role is to encourage participation as the participant completes the survey on his or her own. Taking away Edna's glasses, along with the natural anxiety associated with eye surgery, would not have encouraged Edna's participation. However, the "required" nature of the information (we assume surgery would not commence without prior completion of the questionnaire) guaranteed Edna's participation, no matter how grudgingly given.

Increasing Participants' Receptiveness   As depicted in Exhibit 11–4, a variety of forces affect participant motivation in an interview. Many of these involve the interviewer. At first, it may seem easy to question another person about various topics, but research interviewing is not so simple. What we do or say as interviewers can make or break a study. Participants often react more to their feelings about the interviewer than to the content of the questions. It is also important for the interviewer to ask the questions properly, record the responses accurately, and probe meaningfully. To achieve these aims, the interviewer must be trained to carry out those procedures that foster a good interviewing relationship.

The first goal in an interview is to establish a friendly relationship with the participant. Three factors will help with participant receptiveness.

- The participant must believe that the experience will be pleasant and satisfying.
- The participant must believe that answering the survey is an important and worthwhile use of his or her time.
- The participant must dismiss any mental reservations that he or she might have about participation.

Whether the experience will be pleasant and satisfying depends heavily on the interviewer. Typically, participants will cooperate with an interviewer whose behavior reveals confidence and who engages people on a personal level. Effective interviewers are differentiated not by demographic characteristics but by these interpersonal skills. By confidence, we mean that most participants are immediately convinced they will want to participate in the study and cooperate fully with the interviewer. An engaging personal style is one where the interviewer instantly establishes credibility by adapting to the individual needs of the participant.

For the participant to think that answering the survey is important and worthwhile, some explanation of the study's purpose is necessary, although the amount will vary. It is the interviewer's responsibility to discover what explanation is needed and to supply it. Usually, the interviewer should state the purpose of the study, tell how the information will be used, and suggest what is expected of the participant. Participants should feel that their cooperation would be meaningful to themselves and to the survey results. When this is achieved, more participants will express their views willingly.

Participants often have reservations about being interviewed that must be overcome. They may suspect the interviewer is a disguised salesperson, or has an illegitimate purpose. In addition, they may also feel inadequate or fear the questioning will embarrass them. Techniques for the successful interviewing of participants in environments they control—particularly their homes—follow.

The Introduction   The participant's first reaction to the request for an interview is at best a guarded one. Interviewer appearance and action are critical in forming a good first impression. Interviewers should immediately identify themselves by name and organization and provide any special identification. Introductory letters or other information confirms the study's legitimacy. In this brief but critical period, the interviewer must display friendly intentions and stimulate the participant's interest.

The interviewer's introductory explanations should be no more detailed than necessary. Too much information can introduce a bias. However, some participants will demand more detail. For them, the interviewer might explain the objective of the study, its background, how the participant was selected, the confidential nature of the interview (if it is), and the benefits of the research findings. Researchers must be prepared to deal with questions such as: "How did you happen to pick me?"; "Who gave you my name?"; "I don't know enough about this"; "Why don't you go next door?"; and "Why are you doing this study?"[3]

The home interview typically involves two stages. The first occurs at the door when the introductory remarks are made, but this is not a satisfactory location for many interviews. In trying to secure entrance, the interviewer will find it more effective to suggest the desired action rather than to ask permission. "May I come in?" can be easily countered with a participant's "No." "I would like to come in and talk with you about X" is likely to be more successful.

If the Participant Is Busy or Away   If it is obvious that the participant is busy, it may be a good idea to give a general introduction and try to stimulate enough interest to arrange an interview at another time. If the designated participant is not at home, the interviewer should briefly explain the proposed visit to the person who is contacted. It is desirable to establish good relations with intermediaries since their attitudes can help in contacting the proper participant. Interviewers contacting participants door to door often leave calling or business cards with their affiliation and a number where they can be reached to reschedule the interview.

Establishing a Good Relationship   The successful interview is based on rapport—meaning a relationship of confidence and understanding between interviewer and participant. Interview situations are often new to participants, and they need help in defining

---

S N A P S H O T

Personal Interviews Provide Relief

Bayer Consumer Care inherited Aleve, a long-duration over-the-counter painkiller, from Procter & Gamble in 1996. Since its launch in 1994, P&G hadn't been able to move Aleve beyond a 6 percent market share. Bayer chose CLT Research Associates to identify potential Aleve users. CLT conducted in-home interviews with a random sample of 800 men and women aged 18–75 who had used a non-prescription pain reliever in the past year. The research revealed that 24 percent of those interviewed could be defined as *pain-busters* (heavy users of analgesics who were likely to try new products to gain relief). More than one-third of those identified as pain-busters had tried Aleve. Bayer's task was to use the research to identify a strategy to get pain-busters to choose Aleve when they faced their analgesic-stocked medicine cabinet.

First, Moskowitz Jacobs, Inc., had 249 respondents rate various statements about Aleve. Statements that promised "control over pain" or "freedom to do the things you want" were discovered as important emotional triggers for consumers interested in minimizing the number of pills they took

to relieve pain—Aleve's differential advantage. Next Bayer managers analyzed syndicated data from Medioscope, Nielsen Panel Data, MRI, and Simmons and conducted a series of focus groups moderated by Viewpoints Consulting, Inc., to flesh out findings. The sum of this research revealed Aleve users were more likely to suffer from arthritis and back pain than the average analgesic user. This helped Bayer define the benefit of Aleve as "liberation from tough pain, making a dramatic difference in the quality of life." The resulting "Dramatic Difference" ad campaign boosted the subsequent year's sales by 16 percent, with a rise in market share to 7 percent, its highest ever.

www.aleve.com

www.cltresearch.com

www.smrb.com

http://acnielsen.com

their roles. The interviewer can help by conveying that the interview is confidential (if it is) and important and that the participant can discuss the topics with freedom from censure, coercion, or pressure. Under these conditions, the participant can obtain much satisfaction in "opening up" without pressure being exerted.

Gathering the Data   To this point, the communication aspects of the interviewing process have been stressed. Having completed the introduction and established initial rapport, the interviewer turns to the technical task of gathering information. The interview centers on a prearranged question sequence. The technical task is well defined in studies with a structured survey procedure (in contrast to an exploratory interview situation). The interviewer should follow the exact wording of the questions, ask them in the order presented, and ask every question that is specified. When questions are misunderstood or misinterpreted, they should be repeated.

A difficult task in interviewing is to make certain the answers adequately satisfy the question's objectives. To do this, the interviewer must learn the objectives of each question from a study of the survey instructions or by asking the research project director. It is important to have this information well in mind because many first responses are inadequate even in the best-planned studies.

The technique of stimulating participants to answer more fully and relevantly is termed **probing.** Since it presents a great potential for bias, a probe should be neutral and appear as a natural part of the conversation. Appropriate probes (those that when used will elicit the desired information while injecting a limited amount of bias) should be specified by the designer of the data collection instrument. There are several different probing styles:

MANAGEMENT

- **A brief assertion of understanding and interest.** With comments such as "I see" or "yes" or "uh-huh," the interviewer can tell the participant that the interviewer is listening and is interested in more.

- **An expectant pause.** The simplest way to suggest to the participant to say more is a pause along with an expectant look or a nod of the head. This approach must be used with caution. Some participants have nothing more to say, and frequent pausing could create some embarrassing silences and make them uncomfortable, reducing their willingness to participate further.

- **Repeating the question.** This is particularly useful when the participant appears not to understand the question or has strayed from the subject.

- **Repeating the participant's reply.** The interviewer can do this while writing it down. Such repetition often serves as a good probe. Hearing thoughts restated often promotes revisions or further comments.

- **A neutral question or comment.** Such comments make a direct bid for more information. Examples are: "How do you mean?" "Can you tell me more about your thinking on that?" "Why do you think that is so?" "Anything else?"[4]

- **Question clarification.** When the answer is unclear or is inconsistent with something already said, the interviewer may suggest the participant failed to understand fully. Typical of such probes is, "I'm not *quite* sure I know what you mean by that—could you tell me a little more?" or "I'm sorry, but I'm not sure I understand. Did you say previously that . . . ?" It is important that the interviewer take the blame for failure to understand so as not to appear to be cross-examining the participant.

A specific type of response that requires persistent probing is the "I don't know" answer. This is a satisfactory response if the participant really does not know. But too often "I don't know" means the participant does not understand, wants time to think, or is trying to evade the question. The interviewer can best probe this type of reply by using the expectant pause or by making some reassuring remark such as, "We are interested in your ideas about this."[5]

Recording the Interview   While the methods used in recording will vary, the interviewer usually writes down the answers of the participant. Some guidelines can make this task more efficient. First, record responses as they occur. If you wait until later, you lose much of what is said. If there is a time constraint, the interviewer should use some shorthand system that will preserve the essence of the participant's replies without converting them into the interviewer's paraphrases. Abbreviating words, leaving out articles and prepositions, and using only keywords are good ways to do this.

Another technique is for the interviewer to repeat the response while writing it down. This helps to hold the participant's interest during the writing and checks the interviewer's understanding of what the participant said. Normally the interviewer should start the writing when the participant begins to reply. The interviewer also should record all probes and other comments on the questionnaire in parentheses to set them off from responses.

Study designers sometimes create a special interview instrument for recording participant answers. This may be integrated with the interview questions or may be a separate document. In such instances the likely answers are anticipated, allowing the interviewer to check participant answers or to record ranks or ratings. However, all interview instruments must permit the entry of unexpected responses.

Selection and Training   The job requirements for interviewers include some college experience, good communication skills, flexible schedules, willingness to tolerate intermittent work hours, and mobility. These requirements result in an interviewer profile that is largely composed of college-educated white females who have few childcare responsibilities.[6] Little research evidence suggests that other profiles would increase performance or reduce error except in studies where the question directly involves ethnicity or religion or where volunteer interviewers are used. The former would imply that matching for race or religion should be considered, and the latter cautions against the use of volunteers because of attrition, recording error, and training-related problems.

Field interviewers receive varying degrees of training, ranging from brief written instructions to extensive sessions. Commercial research firms often provide lower levels of training, while governmental, educational, and similar research organizations provide more extensive training. Evidence supports the value of training. In one widely cited study, intensive training produced significant improvements in interviewer performance. The training effect was so great that performance of individual interviewers before training was a poor predictor of post-training performance.[7]

Written instructions should be provided in all studies. Instructions should cover at least the general objectives of the study and mention something about the problems encountered in tests of the interview procedure and how they were solved. In addition, most questions should be discussed separately, giving the interviewer some insight into the purpose of the question, examples of adequate and inadequate responses, and other suggestions such as how to probe for more information. Definitions of concepts or constructs should be included so interviewers can explain and interpret in a standardized manner.

Several sources suggest an interview training program should accomplish the following:

MANAGEMENT

Tip

- Provide new interviewers with the principles of measurement; give them an intellectual grasp of the data collection function and a basis for evaluating interviewing behavior.
- Provide practice in introductions and introductory materials.
- Teach the techniques of interviewing.
- Teach wording and "skip" instructions to help with a smooth and consistent flow of questions.
- Teach how to probe.
- Provide experience in recording answers of different types and on different scales.
- Provide the opportunity for practice and evaluation by conducting interviews under controlled conditions.
- Offer careful evaluation of interviews, especially at the beginning of actual data collection. Such evaluation should include a review of interview protocols.[8]

Interview Problems

In personal interviewing, the researcher must deal with bias and cost. While each is discussed separately, they are interrelated. Biased results grow out of three types of error: sampling error, nonresponse error, and response error.

Nonresponse Error   In communication studies, **nonresponse error** occurs when the responses of participants differ in some systematic way from the responses of nonparticipants. This occurs when the researcher (1) cannot locate the person (the predesignated sample element) to be studied or (2) is unsuccessful in encouraging that person to participate. This is an especially difficult problem when you are using a probability sample of subjects. If the researcher must interview predesignated persons, the task is to find them. Failure to locate a predesignated participant can be due to inaccessibility. In central cities, getting access to the participant can be a problem, as apartment security and locations that produce safety problems for nighttime follow-up may complicate household access.[9] In suburban areas, gated developments prohibit free access to interviewees. One study of nonresponse found that only 31 percent of all first calls (and 20 percent of all first calls in major metropolitan areas) were completed.

Solutions to reduce errors of nonresponse include:

MANAGEMENT

Tip

- Establishing and implementing callback procedures.
- Creating a nonresponse sample and weighting results from this sample.
- Substituting another individual for the missing nonparticipant.

Callbacks.   The most reliable solution to nonresponse problems is to make **callbacks.** If enough attempts are made, it is usually possible to contact most target participants, although unlimited callbacks are expensive.[10] An original contact plus three callbacks should usually secure about 85 percent of the target participants. Yet in one study, 36 percent of central city residents still were not contacted after three callbacks.[11] One way to improve the productivity of callbacks is to vary them by time of day and day of the week. Sometimes neighbors can suggest the best time to call.

Weighting.   Another approach that has been used successfully is to treat all remaining nonparticipants as a new subpopulation after a few callbacks. A random sample is then drawn from this group, and every effort is made to complete this sample with a 100 percent response rate. Findings from this nonparticipant sample can then be weighted into the total population estimate.[12] In a survey in which central city residents are underrepresented, we can weight the results of interviews that are completed with such residents to give them full representation in the results. The weakness of this approach is that weighted returns often differ from those that would be secured if successful callbacks were made. Thus, an unknown but possibly substantial bias is introduced. Weighting for nonresponse after only one contact attempt will probably not overcome nonresponse bias, but participant characteristics converge on their population values after two to three callbacks.[13]

Substitution.   A third way to deal with the nonresponse problem is to substitute someone else for the missing participant, but this is dangerous. "At home" participants are likely to differ from "not at home" persons in systematic ways. One study suggested that "not at home" persons are younger, better educated, more urban, and have a higher income than the average.[14]

If one must substitute, it is better for the interviewer to ask others in the household about the designated participant. This approach has worked well "when questions are objective, when informants have a high degree of observability with respect to participants, when the population is homogeneous, and when the setting of the interview provides no clear-cut motivation to distort responses in one direction or another."[15]

Response Error   When the data reported differ from the actual data, **response error** occurs. Response error can occur during the interview (created by either the interviewer or participant) or during preparation of data for analysis.

Participant-initiated error occurs when the participant fails to answer fully and accurately—either by choice or because of inaccurate or incomplete knowledge. One study found that participants typically underestimated cash and other liquid assets by as much as 25 to 50 percent. Other data, such as income and purchases of consumer durables, are more accurately reported. Participants also have difficulty in reporting fully and accurately on topics that are sensitive or involve ego matters. Consistent control or elimination of this bias is a problem that has yet to be solved. The best advice is to use trained interviewers who are knowledgeable about such problems.

Interviewer error is also a major source of response bias. From the introduction to the conclusion of the interview, there are many points where the interviewer's control of the process can affect the quality of the data. Study designers should strive to eliminate several different kinds of error evolving from the interview techniques just discussed.

MANAGEMENT
Tip

- **Failure to secure full participant cooperation.** The sample loses credibility and is likely to be biased if interviewers do not do a good job of enlisting participant cooperation. Certainly there is a question about the quality of the data collected from Edna during the Albany clinic study. Toward the end of the communication, there is some doubt about the seriousness with which questions were answered. Stressing the importance of the information to the upcoming surgery and having a receptionist trained to serve as question interpreter/prober could reduce this type of error.

- **Failure to consistently execute interview procedures.** The precision of survey estimates will be reduced and there will be more error around estimates to the extent that interviewers are inconsistent in ways that influence the data. In the Albany clinic study, providing differing concept or construct definitions to different clinic patients would have created bias.

- **Failure to establish appropriate interview environment.** Answers may be systematically inaccurate or biased when interviewers fail to appropriately train and motivate participants or fail to establish a suitable interpersonal setting.[16] Since the Albany clinic study asked for factual rather than attitudinal data, interviewer-injected bias would have been limited. If the clinic had required the admissions clerk (who insulted Edna by referring to her negative attitude) to also conduct a postsurgery study of patient satisfaction, the results of the latter study may have been influenced by interviewer bias.

- **Falsification of individual answers or whole interviews.** Perhaps the most insidious form of interviewer error is cheating. Surveying is difficult work, often done by part-time employees, usually with only limited training and under little direct supervision. At times, falsification of an answer to an overlooked question is perceived as an easy solution to counterbalance the incomplete data. This easy, seemingly harmless first step can be followed by more pervasive forgery. It is not known how much of this occurs, but it should be of constant concern to research directors as they develop their data collection design and those organizations that outsource survey projects.

- **Inappropriate influencing behavior.** It is also obvious that an interviewer can distort the results of any survey by inappropriate suggestions, word emphasis, tone of voice, body language, and question rephrasing. These activities, whether premeditated or merely due to carelessness, are widespread. This problem was investigated using a simple structured questionnaire and planted participants who then reported on the interviewers. The conclusion was "the high frequency of deviations from instructed behavior is alarming."[17]

- **Failure to record answers accurately and completely.** Error may result from an interview recording procedure that forces the interviewer to summarize or interpret participant answers or that provides insufficient space to record answers as provided by the participant.

- **Physical presence bias.** Interviewers can influence participants in unperceived ways. Older interviewers are often seen as authority figures by young participants, who modify their responses accordingly. Some research indicates that perceived social distance between interviewer and participant has a distorting effect, although the studies do not fully agree on just what this relationship is.[18]

In light of the numerous studies on the various aspects of interview bias, the safest course for researchers is to recognize that there is a constant potential for response error.

Costs   While professional interviewers' wage scales are typically not high, interviewing is costly, and these costs continue to rise. Much of the cost results from the substantial interviewer time taken up with administrative and travel tasks. Participants are often geographically scattered, and this adds to the cost. Repeated contacts (recommended at six to nine per household) are expensive. In recent years, some professional research organizations have attempted to gain control of these spiraling costs. Interviewers have typically been paid an hourly rate, but this method rewards inefficient interviewers and often results in field costs exceeding budgets.[19] The U.S. Bureau of the Census and the National Opinion Research Center have experimented with production standards and a formula pay system that provide an incentive for efficient interviewers. This approach has cut field costs about 10 percent and has improved the accuracy of the forecasts of fieldwork costs.

A second approach for reducing field costs has been to preschedule personal interviews. Telephone calls to set up appointments for interviews are reported to reduce personal calls by 25 percent without reducing cooperation rates.[20] Telephone screening is also valuable when a study is concerned with a rare population. In one such case, where blind persons were sought, it was found that telephone screening of households was one-third the cost of screening on a face-to-face basis.[21]

A third means of reducing high field costs is to use self-administered questionnaires. In one study, a personal interview was conducted in the household with a self-administered questionnaire left for one or more other members of the household to complete. In this study, the cost per completed case was reduced by half when compared to conducting individual personal interviews. A comparison between a personal interview and a self-administered questionnaire seeking the same data showed that there was generally sufficient similarity of answers to enable them to be combined.[22]

Telephone Interviewing

The telephone can be helpful in arranging personal interviews and screening large populations for unusual types of participants. Studies have also shown that making prior notification calls can improve the response rates of mail surveys. However, the **telephone interview** makes its greatest contribution in survey work as a unique mode of communication to collect information from participants.

Evaluation of the Telephone Interview

Of the advantages that telephone interviewing offers, probably none ranks higher than its moderate cost. One study reports that sampling and data collection costs for telephone surveys can run from 45 to 64 percent lower than comparable personal interviews.[23] Much of the savings comes from cuts in travel costs and administrative savings from training and supervision. When calls are made from a single location, the researcher may use fewer yet more skilled interviewers. Telephones are especially economical when callbacks to maintain probability sampling are involved and participants are widely scattered. Long-distance service options make it possible to interview nationally at a reasonable cost.

With the widespread use of computers, telephone interviewing can be combined with immediate entry of the responses into a data file by means of terminals, personal computers, or voice data entry. This brings added savings in time and money. **Computer-assisted telephone interviewing (CATI)** is used in research organizations throughout the world. A CATI facility consists of acoustically isolated interviewing carrels organized around supervisory stations. The telephone interviewer in each carrel has a personal computer or terminal that is networked to the phone system and to the central data-processing unit. A software program that prompts the interviewers with introductory statements, qualifying questions, and precoded questionnaire items drives surveying. These materials appear on the interviewers' monitors. CATI works with a telephone number management system to select numbers, dial the sample, and enter responses. One facility, the Survey Research Center at the University of Michigan, consists of 60 carrels with 100 interviewers working in shifts from 8 A.M. to midnight (EST) to call nationwide. When fully staffed, it produces more than 10,000 interview hours per month.[24]

Another means of securing immediate response data is the **computer-administered telephone survey.** Unlike CATI, there is no interviewer. A computer calls the phone number, conducts the interview, places data into a file for later tabulation, and terminates the contact. The questions are voice-synthesized, and the participant's answer and computer timing trigger continuation or disconnect. This mode is often compared to the self-administered questionnaire (discussed later in the chapter) and offers the advantage

RTI International Call Center Services employs over 400 interviewers, institutional contactors, quality control monitors, team leaders and supervisors in its two state-of-the-art call centers located in Greenville and Raleigh, North Carolina. The call centers typically conduct between 10 and 30 different data collection efforts concurrently, with staff members completing over 100,000 telephone interviews annually. Call center staff come from all walks of life—many are students or others who work as interviewers part-time in the evenings and on weekends. RTI International conducts rigorous training with all telephone staff on standardized interviewing techniques, strategies for gaining participant cooperation, and the use of its computer-assisted telephone interviewing system.
www.rti.org

of participant privacy. One study showed that the *noncontact* rate for the electronic survey mode is similar to other telephone interviews when a random phone list is used. It also found that rejection of this mode of data collection affects the *refusal* rate (and thus nonresponse bias) because people hang up more easily on a computer than on a human.[25] The **noncontact rate** is a ratio of potential but unreached contacts (no answer, busy, answering machine, and disconnects but not refusals) to all potential contacts. The **refusal rate** refers to the ratio of participants who decline the interview to all potential contacts.

When compared to either personal interviews or mail surveys, the use of telephones brings a faster completion of a study, sometimes taking only a day or so for the fieldwork. When compared to personal interviewing, it is also likely that interviewer bias, especially bias caused by the physical appearance, body language, and actions of the interviewer, is reduced by using telephones.

Almost 94 percent of U.S. households have telephone service.[26] Access to participants through low-cost, efficient means has made telephone interviewing a very attractive alternative for marketing, public opinion, and academic researchers.

Finally, behavioral norms work to the advantage of telephone interviewing. If someone is present, a ringing phone is usually answered, and it is the caller who decides the purpose, length, and termination of the call.[27] New technology, notably caller identification systems where the receiver can decide whether a call is answered based on caller identity, is expected to increase the noncontact rate associated with telephone surveys.

There are also disadvantages to using the telephone for research. A skilled researcher will evaluate the use of a telephone survey to minimize the effect of these disadvantages.

MANAGEMENT
Tip

- Inaccessible households (no telephone service).
- Inaccurate or nonfunctioning numbers.
- Limitation on interview length (fewer measurement questions).
- Limitations on use of visual or complex questions.
- Ease of interview termination.
- Less participant involvement.
- Distracting physical environment.

Inaccessible Households Even given the passage of the Telecommunications Act of 1996, meant to ensure that all Americans would possess telephone service, 18.4 percent of households with incomes below the poverty line are still without telephone service.[28] Usage rates are not as high in households composed of single adults, less educated and poorer minorities, and individuals employed as nonprofessional, nonmanagerial workers.[29] Additionally, 20 percent of American households move each year, generating many obsolete numbers and new households for which numbers have not yet been published. Also, it is estimated that about 22 percent of all household phone numbers are unlisted.[30] Meanwhile, the number of inaccessible individuals continues to increase as cellular and wireless phone use increases, as many of these numbers are unlisted. These variations in participant availability by phone can be a source of bias.

Inaccurate or Nonfunctioning Numbers Another source says the highest incidence of nonlisting is in the West, in large metropolitan areas, among nonwhites, and for persons between 18 and 34 years of age.[31] Several methods have been developed to overcome the deficiencies of directories; among them are techniques for choosing phone numbers by using random-digit dialing or combinations of directories and random-digit dialing.[32] **Random dialing procedures** normally require choosing phone exchanges or exchange blocks and then generating random numbers within these blocks for calling.[33] However, increasing demand for multiple phone lines by both households and individuals has generated new phone area codes and local exchanges. This too increases the inaccuracy rate.

Limitation on Interview Length A limit on interview length is another disadvantage of the telephone, but the degree of this limitation depends on the participant's interest in the topic. Ten minutes has generally been thought of as ideal, but interviews of 20 minutes or more are not uncommon. Interviews ran for one and a half hours in one long-distance survey.[34]

Limitations on Use of Visual or Complex Questions In telephone interviewing, it is difficult to use maps, illustrations, visual aids, complex scales, or measurement techniques (however, in some instances, these might be supplied via fax or e-mail prior to the prescheduled interview). The medium also limits the complexity of the survey and the use of visualization techniques possible with personal interviewing. For example, in personal interviews, participants are sometimes asked to sort or rank an array of cards containing different responses to a question. For participants who cannot visualize a scale or other measurement device that the interview is attempting to describe, one solution has been to employ a nine-point scaling approach and to ask the respondent to visualize it by using the telephone dial or keypad.[35]

Ease of Interview Termination   Some studies suggest that the response rate in telephone studies is lower than for comparable face-to-face interviews. One reason is that participants find it easier to terminate a phone interview. Telemarketing practices may also contribute. Public reaction to investigative reports of wrongdoing and unethical behavior within telemarketing activities places an added burden on the researcher, who must try to convince a participant that the phone interview is not a pretext for soliciting contributions or selling products.

Less Participant Involvement   Telephone surveys can result in less thorough responses, and those interviewed by phone find the experience to be less rewarding than a personal interview. Participants report less rapport with telephone interviewers than with personal interviewers. Given the growing costs and difficulties of personal interviews, it is likely that an even higher share of surveys will be by telephone in the future. Thus, it behooves management researchers using telephone surveys to attempt to improve the enjoyment of the interview. One authority suggests:

> We need to experiment with techniques to improve the enjoyment of the interview by the participant, maximize the overall completion rate, and minimize response error on specific measures. This work might fruitfully begin with efforts at translating into verbal messages the visual cues that fill the interaction in a face-to-face interview: the smiles, frowns, raising of eyebrows, eye contact, etc. All of these cues have informational content and are important parts of the personal interview setting. We can perhaps purposefully choose those cues that are most important to data quality and participant trust and discard the many that are extraneous to the survey interaction.[36]

Distracting Physical Environment   Speculation has also surfaced in regard to the increasing practice of substituting one's home or office phone with cellular and wireless phones. In regard to telephone surveys, this raises concerns about the changing environment in which such surveys might be conducted, the resulting quality of data collected under possibly distracting circumstances, and the possible increase in refusal rates.

Telephone Interview Trends

Future trends in telephone interviewing bear watching. Answering machines and multiline households will affect sampling. So will the variations among the 60 telephone companies' services and the degree of cooperation that will be extended to researchers. There is also concern for the ways in which random-digit dialing can be made to deal with nonworking and ineligible numbers.[37]

Answering machines could pose potentially complex response-rate problems since they are estimated to have substantial penetration in American households. Previous research discovered that most answering-machine households are accessible; the subsequent contact rate was greater in answering-machine households than in no-machine households and about equal with busy-signal households. Other findings suggested that (1) individuals with answering machines were more likely to participate, (2) machine use was more prevalent on weekends than on weekday evenings, and (3) machines were more commonplace in urban than in rural areas.

Voice-mail options offered by local phone service providers have less market penetration but are gaining increasing acceptance. Questions about the sociodemographics

SNAPSHOT
A Zap-Attack on Telephone Surveys

Privacy concerns have been fueling a decline in telephone survey participation for the last decade, but a product introduced late in 2001 may have even further-reaching ramifications for this type of research. The TeleZapper, by Privacy Technologies, Inc., uses technology to detect predictive-dialer computers' in-coming calls, disconnects the call before contact is made between the caller and the potential participant, and then sends a signal to the dialer that the phone number is disconnected. When the predictive dialer hears the signal tone, it disconnects and removes the number from the call list. While the device was intended to "zap" unwanted calls from telemarketers, Privacy Technologies claims that calls from other organizations that use predictive-dialer computers (charitable organizations, opinion and political pollsters, as well as marketing researchers) also will be zapped.

One saving grace for researchers is the $49.95 price. To many, the price may outweigh the inconvenience of the disruptive call. But to others, the price may seem a small investment in protection against marketing "scams." Another bright spot for researchers is that not all use predictive dialers—manually dialed calls to a potential research participant cannot be zapped.

www.privacytechnologies.com

of users and nonusers and the relationship of answering-machine/voice-mail technology to the rapid changes in the wireless market remain to be answered.[38] Caller identification technology, the assignment of facsimile machines or computer modems to dedicated phone lines, and technology that identifies computer-automated dialers and sends a disconnect signal in response are all expected to have an impact on the noncontact rate of phone interviews.

Self-Administered Surveys

The **self-administered questionnaire** has become ubiquitous in modern living. Service evaluations of hotels, restaurants, car dealerships, and transportation providers furnish ready examples. Often a short questionnaire is left to be completed by the participant in a convenient location or is packaged with a product. User registrations, product information requests in magazines, warranty cards, the MindWriter repair study, and the Albany clinic study are self-administered. Self-administered **mail surveys** are delivered not only by the U.S. Postal Service, but also via fax and courier service. Other delivery modalities include *computer-delivered* and *intercept* studies.

Computer-delivered self-administered questionnaires use organizational intranets, the Internet, or online services to reach their participants. Participants may be targeted (as when BizRate, an online e-business rating service, sends an e-mail to a registered e-purchaser to participate in a survey) or self-selecting (as when a computer screen pop-up window offers a survey to an individual who clicks on a particular website or when a potential participant responds to a postcard inquiry looking for participants). A 2001 Gartner Research Dataquest® survey found that 61 percent of U.S. households are actively online and, once connected, 91 percent are likely to continue their Internet subscription.[39] Is it any wonder, then, why computer-delivered self-administered surveys have caught the fancy of business? See Exhibit 11–6.

Intercept studies may use a traditional paper questionnaire or a computer-delivered survey. The respondent participates without interviewer assistance usually in a predetermined environment such as a shopping mall. All modes have special problems and unique advantages (see Exhibit 11–4).

EXHIBIT 11–6   The Web as a Research Venue[40]

Web Attractions	Example
Short turnaround of results; results are tallied as respondents complete surveys.	A soft drink manufacturer got results from a Web survey in just five days.
Ability to use visual stimuli.	Florida's tourism office used eye movement tracking to enhance its website and improve its billboard and print ads.
Ability to do numerous surveys over time.	A printer manufacturer did seven surveys in six months during the development of one of its latest products.
Ability to attract participants who wouldn't participate in another research project, including international respondents.	An agricultural equipment manufacturer did a study using two-way pagers provided free to farmers to query users about its equipment—respondents usually unavailable by phone or PC.
Respondents feel anonymous.	Anonymity was the necessary ingredient for a study on impotence conducted by a drug manufacturer.
Shortened turnaround from survey draft to execution of survey.	A Hewlett-Packard survey using Greenfield Online's *QuickTake* took two weeks to write, launch, and field—not the standard three months using non-Web venues.
Experiences unavailable by other means.	• One major advertising agency is conducting Web research using virtual supermarket aisles that respondents wander through, reacting to client products and promotions. • LiveWorld has developed a packaging study showing more than 75 images of labels and bottle designs.
Web Drawbacks	
Recruiting the right sample is costly and time-consuming; unlike phone and mail sample frames, no lists exist.	TalkCity, working for Whitton Associates and Fusion5, set up a panel of 3,700 teens for a survey to test new packaging for a soft drink using phone calls, referrals, e-mail lists, banner ads, and website visits. It drew a sample of 600 for the research. It cost more than $50,000 to set up the list.
Converting surveys to the Web can be expensive.	LiveWorld's teen study cost $50,000–$100,000 to set up, with additional fees with each focus group or survey. The total price tag was several hundred thousand dollars.
It takes technical as well as research skill to field a Web survey.	A 10–15 minute survey can take up to five days of technical expertise to field and test.
While research is more compatible with numerous browsers, the technology isn't perfect.	A well-known business magazine did a study among a recruited sample only to have the survey abort on question 20 of a larger study.

Much of what researchers know about self-administered surveys has been learned from experiments conducted with mail surveys and personal experience. So as we explore the strengths and weaknesses of the various self-administered methods, we will start with this body of knowledge.

Costs

Self-administered surveys of all types typically cost less than personal interviews. This is true of mail surveys, as well as of computer-delivered and intercept studies, too. Telephone and mail costs are in the same general range, although in specific cases either may be lower. The more geographically dispersed the sample, the more likely it is that self-administered surveys via computer or mail will be the low-cost method. A mail or computer-delivered study can cost less because it is often a one-person job. And computer-delivered studies (including CAPI and CATI studies) eliminate the cost of printing surveys, a significant cost of both mail studies and personal interviewing.

Sample Accessibility

Another asset to using mail is that researchers can contact participants who might otherwise be inaccessible. Some people, such as major corporate executives and physicians, are difficult to reach in person or by phone, as gatekeepers (secretaries, office managers, and assistants) limit access. But researchers can often access these special participants by mail or computer. When the researcher has no specific person to contact—say, in a study of corporations—the mail or computer-delivered survey may be routed to the appropriate participant.

Careful Consideration

While intercept studies still pressure participants for a relatively quick turnaround, in a mail survey the participant can take more time to collect facts, talk with others, or consider replies at length than is possible in a telephone or personal interview. Computer-delivered studies, especially those accessed via e-mail links to the Internet, usually have time limitations on both access and completion once started. And once started, computer-delivered studies cannot be easily interrupted by the participant to seek information not immediately known.

Anonymity

Mail surveys are typically perceived as more impersonal, providing more anonymity than the other communication modes, including other methods for distributing self-administered questionnaires.

Topic Coverage

A major limitation of self-administered surveys concerns the type and amount of information that can be secured. Researchers normally do not expect to obtain large amounts of information and cannot probe deeply into topics. Participants will generally refuse to cooperate with a long and/or complex mail, computer-delivered, or intercept questionnaire unless they perceive a personal benefit. Returned mail questionnaires with many questions left unanswered testify to this problem, but there are also many exceptions. One general rule of thumb is that the participant should be able to answer the questionnaire in no more than 10 minutes—similar to the guidelines proposed for telephone studies. On the other hand, one study of the general population found more than a 70 percent response to a questionnaire calling for 158 answers.[41]

Nonresponse Error

Another major weakness of the self-administered study is nonresponse error. Many studies have shown that better-educated participants and those more interested in the topic answer mail surveys. A high percentage of those who reply to a given survey have usually replied to others, while a large share of those who do not respond are habitual nonparticipants.[42] Mail surveys with a return of about 30 percent are often considered "satisfactory," but there are instances of response rates that exceed 70 percent.[43] In either case, there are many nonresponders, and we usually know nothing about how those who answer differ from those who do not answer.

Reducing Nonresponse Error

The research literature is filled with ways to improve mail survey returns and much of this knowledge may be applied to other modes of delivering self-administered surveys. Seemingly every possible variable has been studied. Over 200 methodological articles have been published on efforts to improve mail response rates. Two review articles concluded that few variables consistently showed positive response rates.[44] Several practical suggestions emerge from the conclusions.[45]

Follow-Ups   Follow-ups, or reminders, are very successful in increasing response rates. Since each successive follow-up produces more returns, the very persistent (and well-financed) researcher can potentially achieve an extremely high total response rate. However, the value of additional information thus obtained must be weighed against the costs required for successive contacts.

Preliminary Notification   There is evidence that advance notification, particularly by telephone, is effective in increasing response rates; it also serves to accelerate the rate of return. However, follow-ups are a better investment than preliminary notification.

Concurrent Techniques

1. *Questionnaire Length.* Although common sense suggests that short questionnaires should obtain higher response rates than longer questionnaires, research evidence does not support this view.

2. *Survey Sponsorship.* There is little experimental evidence concerning the influence of survey sponsorship on response rates; however, the sparse evidence that does exist suggests that official or "respected" sponsorship increases response rates.

3. *Return Envelopes.* The inclusion of a stamped, return envelope encourages response because it simplifies questionnaire return.

4. *Postage.* Many tests regarding postage are reported in the literature, but few studies have tested the same variables. The existing evidence shows that expedited delivery is very effective in increasing response rates. Findings do not show a significant advantage for first class over third class, for commemorative stamps over ordinary postage, for stamped mail over metered mail, or for multiple small denomination stamps over single larger denomination stamps.

5. *Personalization.* Personalization of the mailing has no clear-cut advantage in terms of improved response rates. Neither personal inside addresses nor individually signed cover letters significantly increased response rates; personally typed cover letters proved to be somewhat effective in most but not all cases cited. The one study that tested the use of a titled signature versus one without a title did show a significant advantage in favor of the title.

6. *Cover Letters.* The influence of the cover letter on response rates has received almost no experimental attention, although the cover letter is considered an inte-

gral part of the mail survey package. It is the most logical vehicle for persuading individuals to respond, yet the few studies that are reported offer no insights as to its formulation.

7. *Anonymity.* Experimental evidence shows that the promise of anonymity to participants, either explicit or implied, has no significant effect on response rates.

8. *Size, Reproduction, and Color.* The few studies that examined the effects of questionnaire size, method of reproduction, and color found no significant difference in response rates.

9. *Money Incentives.* A monetary incentive sent with the questionnaire is very effective in increasing response rates. Larger sums bring in added response, but at a cost that may exceed the value of the added information.

10. *Deadline Dates.* The few studies that tested the impact of deadline dates found that they did not increase the response rate; however, they did serve to accelerate the rate of questionnaire return.

Researchers are equivocal about these suggestions and conclusions because "the manipulation of one or two techniques independently of all others may do little to stimulate response."[46] The computer-delivered survey, however, has made the collective execution of many of these suggestions more attractive. Once the computer-delivered survey is crafted, the cost of redelivery via computer—thereby decreasing nonresponse error—is very low. Preliminary notification via e-mail is also accomplished in a more timely and less costly way than by phone or mail. The return mechanism for the computer-delivered study is usually the click of a mouse or a single keystroke. Personalization of the survey cover letter—the e-mail that links the respondent to the survey— is easily accomplished. The computer also makes the use of color within a survey, even color photographs, a viable option—one not often considered with paper surveys due to cost. And video clips—never an option with a mail survey—are possible with a computer-delivered survey. Even the delivery of monetary and other incentives has been simplified with the use of e-currencies. However, employing all the stimulants for participation that have been researched cannot overcome a participant's inability to complete an Internet survey due to technology snafus. These glitches are likely to continue to plague participation as long as researchers and participants use different computer platforms, operating systems, and software.

Efforts should be directed toward the more important question of maximizing the overall probability of response. The Total Design Method (TDM), consisting of two parts, is proposed to meet this need.[47] First, the researcher must identify the aspects of the survey process that affect the response rate, either qualitatively or quantitatively. Each aspect must be shaped to obtain the best response. Second, the researcher must organize the survey effort so the design intentions are carried out in detail. The results achieved in 48 surveys using TDM showed response rates of 50 to 94 percent, with a median response rate of 74 percent.[48] TDM procedures suggest minimizing the burden on participants by designing surveys that:

MANAGEMENT
Tip

- Are easy to read.
- Offer clear response directions.
- Include personalized communication.
- Provide information about the survey in a cover letter (or via advance notification).
- Are followed by researcher contacts to encourage response.[49]

Maximizing the Mail Survey

MANAGEMENT

To maximize the overall probability of response, attention must be given to each point of the survey process where the response may break down.[50] For example:

- The wrong address and wrong postage can result in nondelivery or nonreturn.
- The envelope or fax cover sheet may look like junk mail and be discarded without being opened.
- Lack of proper instructions for completion may lead to nonresponse.
- The wrong person may open the envelope or receive the fax and fail to call it to the attention of the right person.
- A participant may find no convincing explanation for completing the survey and thus discard it.
- A participant may temporarily set the questionnaire aside and fail to complete it.
- The return address may be lost so the questionnaire cannot be returned.

Efforts to overcome these problems will vary according to the circumstances, but some general suggestions can be made for mail surveys and, by extension, for self-administered questionnaires using different delivery modes. With a questionnaire, a cover letter and return mechanism should be sent. Incentives, such as dollar bills, coins, or gift coupons, often are attached to the letter in commercial studies. Follow-ups are usually needed to get the maximum response. Opinions differ about the number and timing of follow-ups; in general, the timing of follow-ups should be adapted for different delivery modes. TDM uses the follow-ups described below:

1. **One week later**—A preprinted postcard is sent to all recipients thanking them for returns and reminding others to complete and mail the questionnaire.

2. **Three weeks after the original mailing**—A new questionnaire is sent, along with a letter telling nonparticipants that the questionnaire has not been received and repeating the basic appeal of the original letter.

3. **Seven weeks after the original mailing**—A third cover letter and questionnaire are sent by certified mail to the remaining nonparticipants.

An appeal for cooperation is essential and may be altruistic or more expedient. The former is often found when the questionnaire is short, easy to complete, and does not require much effort from a participant. Anonymity may or may not be mentioned. A brief letter emphasizes the "Would you do me a favor?" approach. Often a token is sent to symbolize the researcher's appreciation. Sometimes this is not powerful enough. Then an appeal must stress how important the problem is to a group with which the participant identifies.

The cover letter should also convey that the participant's help is needed to solve a problem. Researchers are portrayed as reasonable people making a reasonable appeal for help. They are intermediaries between the person asked for help and an important issue. The total effect must be personalized to convey to participants that they are important to the study. The standard is to make the appeal comparable in appearance and content to what one would expect in a business or professional letter.

Finally, a mixed model can be used to improve response. One study compared the use of "drop-off" delivery of a self-administered questionnaire to a mail survey.[51] Under the drop-off system, a lightly trained survey taker personally delivered the questionnaires to target households and returned in a couple of days for the completed instrument. Response rates for the drop-off system were typically above 70 percent—much higher than for comparable mail surveys. In addition, the cost per completed questionnaire was from 18 to 40 percent lower than for mail surveys.

Beyond a higher response rate and lower cost per response, the drop-off delivery gives greater control over sample design, permits thorough identification of the participants' geographic location, and allows the researcher to eliminate those who fall outside a predefined sample frame (persons of the wrong age, income, or other characteristics). Additional information also can be gathered by observation on the visits. However, the cost advantage is probably restricted to studies where participants can be reached with little travel.

Drop-off delivery has much in common with intercept studies that employ self-administered completion of a questionnaire. The researcher can encourage the selected participant to complete the questionnaire, stressing the importance of his or her participation and the ease of completion, and then indicate the procedure for returning it. These activities are likely to increase response rates and reduce nonresponse error.

Self-Administered Survey Trends

Computer surveying is surfacing at trade shows, where participants complete surveys while making a visit to a company's booth. Continuous tabulation of results provides a stimulus for attendees to visit a particular exhibit as well as giving the exhibitor detailed information for evaluating the productivity of the show. This same technology easily transfers to other situations where large groups of people congregate.

Companies are now using intranet capabilities to evaluate employee policies and behavior. Ease of access to electronic mail systems makes it possible for both large and small organizations to use computer questioning with both internal and external participant groups. Many techniques of traditional mail surveys can be easily adapted to computer-delivered questionnaires (e.g., follow-ups to nonparticipants are more easily executed and are less expensive).

It is not unusual to find registration procedures and full-scale surveying being done on World Wide Web sites. University sites are asking prospective students about their interests, and university departments are evaluating current students' use of online materials. A short voyage on the Internet reveals organizations using their sites to evaluate customer service processes, build sales-lead lists, evaluate planned promotions and product changes, determine supplier and customer needs, discover interest in job openings, evaluate employee attitudes, and more. Advanced and easier-to-use software for designing Web surveys is here.

If you understand HTML standards and Web-survey programming, you will find a very useful Web-Survey Tutorial at http://www.researchinfo.com.

The **Web-based questionnaire** has the power of CATI systems, but without the expense of network administrators, specialized software, or additional hardware. As a solution for Internet or intranet websites, you need only a personal computer and Web access. Most products are browser-driven with design features that allow custom survey creation and modification.

Two primary options are proprietary solutions offered through research firms and off-the-shelf software designed for researchers who possess the knowledge and skills we describe here and in Chapter 12. With fee-based services, you are guided (often online) through problem formulation, questionnaire design, question content, response strategy, and wording and sequence of questions. Their staff generates the questionnaire HTML code, hosts the survey at their server, and provides data consolidation and reports. Off-the-shelf software is a strong alternative. At this writing, *PC Magazine* has reviewed six packages containing well-designed user interfaces and advanced data preparation features.[52] The advantages of these software programs are:

- Questionnaire design in a word processing environment.

- Ability to import questionnaire forms from text files.

- A coaching device to guide you through question and response formatting.

- Question and scale libraries.
- Automated publishing to a Web server.
- Real-time viewing of incoming data.
- Ability to edit data in a spreadsheet-type environment.
- Rapid transmission of results.
- Flexible analysis and reporting mechanisms.

Ease of use is not the only influence pushing the popularity of Web-based instruments. Cost is a major factor. It is much less expensive than conventional survey research. Although fees are based on the number of completions, a sample of 100 might cost one-sixth of a conventional telephone interview. Bulk mailing and e-mail data collection have also become more cost-effective because any instrument may be configured as an e-mail questionnaire.

Selecting an Optimal Method

The choice of a communication method is not as complicated as it might first appear. By comparing your research objectives with the strengths and weaknesses of each method, you will be able to choose one that is suited to your needs. The summary of advantages and disadvantages of personal interviews, telephone interviews, and self-administered questionnaires presented in Exhibit 11–4 should be useful in making such a comparison.

When your investigative questions call for information from hard-to-reach or inaccessible participants, the telephone interview, mail- or computer-delivered survey should be considered. However, if data must be collected very quickly, the mail survey would likely be ruled out because of lack of control over the returns. Alternatively, you may decide your objective requires extensive questioning and probing; then the personal interview should be considered.

If none of the choices turns out to be a particularly good fit, it is possible to combine the best characteristics of two or more alternatives into a *mixed mode*. Although this decision will incur the costs of the combined modes, the flexibility of tailoring a method to your unique needs is often an acceptable trade-off.

In the MindWriter study, Jason plans to insert a postcard questionnaire (a self-administered study delivered via courier) in each laptop returned by the CompleteCare repair service. Not all customers will return their questionnaires, creating nonresponse bias. The postcard format doesn't permit much space for encouraging customer response. Alerting customers to the importance of returning the response card by phone (to announce impending courier delivery of a repaired laptop) might improve the research design. Participants would not be in the best frame of mind if they received a damaged laptop; dissatisfaction could lead to a decreased response rate and an increase in call center contacts. Combining the study with standard procedures for verifying delivery by the courier might also be needed.

Jason and Myra's proposal contains a follow-up procedure—telephoning nonparticipants to obtain their answers when response cards are not returned. This will likely decrease nonresponse error. Where most of the study participants are answering measurement questions without assistance, telephone interviewing creates the possibility of interviewer bias at an unknown level for at least part of the data.

In the Albany clinic study, the researcher could have taken several actions to improve the quality of the data. Distributing the questionnaire to the patient's eye doctor or to the patient (by mail) prior to arrival would have increased the accuracy of identifying medications, diagnoses, hospitalizations, and so forth. The patient's eye doctor was in the best position to encourage compliance with the collection process but was not consulted. Having the patient bring the completed questionnaire to the admissions procedure, where the admissions clerk could review the completed instrument for accuracy and completeness, would have given the researcher the opportunity to clarify any confusion with the questions, concepts, and constructs. Finally, pretesting the instrument with a sample of patients would have revealed difficulties with the process and operational definitions. Edna's concerns could have been eliminated before they surfaced.

Ultimately, all researchers are confronted by the practical realities of cost and deadlines. As Exhibit 11–4 suggests, on the average, personal interviews are the most expensive communication method and take the most field time unless a large field team is used. Telephone interviews are moderate in cost and offer the quickest option, especially when CATI is used. Questionnaires administered by mail are the least expensive, although these traditionally require a longer data collection period. When your desired sample is available via the Internet, emerging Internet surveying may prove to be the least expensive communication method with the most rapid (simultaneous) data availability. The use of the computer to select participants and reduce coding and processing time will continue to improve the cost-to-performance profiles of these methods in the future.

Most of the time, an optimal method will be apparent. However, managers' needs for information often exceed their internal resources. Such factors as specialized expertise, a large field team, unique facilities, or a rapid turnaround prompt managers to seek assistance from research vendors of survey-related services.

Outsourcing Survey Services

Commercial suppliers of research services vary from full-service operations to specialty consultants. When confidentiality is likely to affect competitive advantage, the manager or staff will sometimes prefer to bid only a phase of the project. Alternatively, the organization's staff members may possess such unique knowledge of a product or service that they must fulfill a part of the study themselves. Regardless, the exploratory work, design, sampling, data collection, or processing and analysis may be contracted separately or as a whole. Most organizations use a *request for proposal (RFP)* to describe their requirements and seek competitive bids (see Appendix C).

Research firms also offer special advantages that their clients do not typically maintain in-house. Centralized-location interviewing, focus group facilities, or computer-assisted telephone facilities may be particularly desirable for certain research needs. A professionally trained staff with considerable experience in similar management problems is another benefit. Data-processing and statistical analysis capabilities are especially important for some projects. Other vendors have specially designed software for interviewing and data tabulation.[53] Panel suppliers provide another type of research service with emphasis on longitudinal survey work.[54] By using the same participants over time, **panels** can track trends in attitudes toward issues or products, product adoption or consumption behavior, and a myriad of other research interests. Suppliers of panel data can secure information from personal and telephone interviewing techniques as well as from the mail and mixed modes. Diaries are a common means of chronicling events of research interest by the panel members. These are mailed back to the research organization. Point-of-sale terminals and scanners aid electronic data collection for panel-type participant groups. And mechanical devices placed in the homes of panel members may be used to evaluate media usage.

SUMMARY

1 The communication approach involves questioning or surveying people and recording their responses for analysis. Communication is accomplished via personal interviews, telephone interviews, or self-administered surveys, with each method having its specific strengths and weaknesses. The optimal communication method is the one that is instrumental for answering your research question and dealing with the constraints imposed by time, budget, and human resources. The opportunity to combine several survey methodologies makes the use of the mixed mode desirable in many projects.

2 Successful communication requires that we seek information the participant can provide and that the participant understand his or her role and motivated to play that role. Motivation, in particular, is a task for the interviewer. Good rapport with the participant should be established quickly, and then the technical process of collecting data should begin. The latter often calls for skillful probing to supplement the answers volunteered by the participant. Simplicity of directions and instrument appearance are additional factors to consider in encouraging response in self-administered communication studies.

3 Two factors can cause bias in interviewing. One is nonresponse. It is a concern with all types of surveys. Some studies show that first calls often secure less than 20 percent of the designated participants. Various methods are useful for increasing this representation, the most effective being making callbacks until an adequate number of completed interviews has been secured. The second factor is response error, which occurs when the participant fails to give a correct or complete answer. The interviewer also can contribute to response error. The interviewer can provide the main solution for both of these two types of errors.

4 The major advantages of personal interviewing are the ability to explore topics in great depth, achieve a high degree of interviewer control, and provide maximum interviewer flexibility for meeting unique situations. However, this method is costly and time-consuming, and its flexibility can result in excessive interviewer bias.

   Telephone interviewing has become much more popular in recent years because of the diffusion of telephone service in American households and the low cost of this method compared with personal interviewing. Long-distance telephone interviewing has grown. There are also disadvantages to telephone interviewing. Many phone numbers are unlisted, and directory listings become obsolete quickly. There is also a limit on the length and depth of interviews conducted using the telephone.

   The self-administered questionnaire can be delivered by the U.S. Postal Service, facsimile, a courier service, a computer, or intercept. Computer-delivered self-administered questionnaires use organizational intranets, the Internet, or online services to reach their participants. Participants may be targeted or self-selecting. Intercept studies may use a traditional questionnaire or a computerized instrument in environments where interviewer assistance is minimal.

5 Outsourcing survey services offers special advantages to managers. A professionally trained research staff, centralized-location interviewing, focus group facilities, and computer-assisted facilities are among them. Specialty firms offer software and computer-based assistance for telephone and personal interviewing as well as for mail and mixed modes. Panel suppliers produce data for longitudinal studies of all varieties.

KEY TERMS

EXAMPLES

Company	Scenario	Page
Albany Outpatient Laser Clinic Inc.*	A preprocedure self-administered study of patient issues and attitudes.	BRTL and throughout
Bayer Consumer Care	Used personal interviews, phone interviews, and syndicated data to reposition Aleve; resulting ad campaign increased market share by 7 percent, a major feat in the highly competitive analgesic category.	329
BizRate	An independent company that uses purchaser panels (computer-delivered self-administered surveys) to evaluate e-business customer service.	339
CLT Research Associates	Conducted more than 800 in-home personal interviews in the Aleve respositioning research.	329
Gartner Research	A full-service research firm whose Dataquest service provides global market intelligence for the IT and telecom industries.	339
Greenfield Online	A provider of computer-delivered surveying for Hewlett-Packard's study of printer performance.	340
Hewlett-Packard	Used Greenfield Online's QuickTake Web survey to shorten the turnaround time for data collection.	340
LiveWorld	Prepared a 10–15 minute computer-delivered packaging survey employing 75 images of bottle shapes and label designs as visualization techniques.	340
MindWriter*	A descriptive study of customer satisfaction with the CompleteCare servicing center for laptops.	322
Moskowitz Jacobs, Inc.	Conducted phone surveys to help Bayer identify emotional triggers for the new ad campaign to reposition Aleve.	329
Privacy Technologies, Inc.	Introduced an electronic device that rejects in-coming calls from predictive dialers used by telephone researchers.	339
RTI International	Annually fields 100,000 telephone interviews in its two state-of-the-art CATI facilities.	336
Rubinstein Consulting	Used personal interviews to determine an alternative recruiting program for a harbormaster in Finland.	325

| TalkCity | Developed an online teen panel using phone solicitation, referrals, purchased e-mail lists, banner ads, and website visits from which it drew a sample of 600 teens for a soft drink packaging study. | 340 |
| Viewpoints Consulting, Inc. | Used focus groups to identify that Aleve users represented a distinct segment of the pain-relief market. | 329 |

*Due to the confidential and proprietary nature of most research, the names of some companies have been changed.

DISCUSSION QUESTIONS

Terms in Review

1. Distinguish among response error, interviewer error, and nonresponse error.

2. How do environmental factors affect response rates in personal interviews? How can we overcome these environmental problems?

Making Research Decisions

3. Assume you are planning to interview shoppers in a shopping mall about their views on increased food prices and what the federal government should do about them. In what different ways might you try to motivate shoppers to cooperate in your survey?

4. In recent years, in-home personal interviews have grown more costly and more difficult to complete. Suppose, however, you have a project in which you need to talk with people in their homes. What might you do to hold down costs and increase the response rate?

5. In the following situations, decide whether you would use a personal interview, telephone survey, or self-administered questionnaire. Give your reasons.

   a. A survey of the residents of a new subdivision on why they happened to select that area in which to live. You also wish to secure some information about what they like and do not like about life in the subdivision.

   b. A poll of students at Metro University on their preferences among three candidates who are running for presidency of the student government.

   c. A survey of 58 wholesale grocery companies, scattered over the eastern United States, on their personnel management policies for warehouse personnel.

   d. A survey of financial officers of the Fortune 500 corporations to learn their predictions for the economic outlook in their industries in the next year.

   e. A study of applicant requirements, job tasks, and performance expectations as part of a job analysis of student work-study jobs on a college campus of 2,000 students, where 1,500 are involved in the work-study program.

6. You decide to take a telephone survey of 40 families in the 721-exchange area. You want an excellent representation of all subscribers in the exchange area. Explain how you will carry out this study.

7. You plan to conduct a mail survey of the traffic managers of 1,000 major manufacturing companies across the country. The study concerns their company policies regarding the payment of moving expenses for employees who are transferred. What might you do to improve the response rate of such a survey?

8. A major corporation agrees to sponsor an internal study on sexual harassment in the workplace. This is in response to concerns expressed by its female employees. How would you handle the following issues:

   a. Sample selection.

   b. The communication approach (self-administered, telephone, personal interview, and/or mixed).

c. The purpose: Fact finding, awareness, relationship building, and/or change.

d. Minimization of response and nonresponse error.

Bringing Research to Life

9. Define the appropriate communication study for Albany Outpatient Laser Clinic.

From Concept to Practice

10. Using Exhibit 11–1 as your guide, graph the communication study you designed in question 9.

WWW Exercises

Visit our website for Internet exercises related to this chapter at www.mhhe.com/business/cooper8

CASES*

 CUMMINS ENGINES

 DATA DEVELOPMENT, INC.

INQUIRING MINDS WANT TO KNOW—NOW!

 MASTERING TEACHER LEADERSHIP

 NCR: TEEING UP A NEW STRATEGIC DIRECTION

RAMADA DEMONSTRATES ITS PERSONAL BEST

STURGEL DIVISION

THE CATALYST FOR WOMEN IN FINANCIAL SERVICES

*All cases indicating a video icon are located on the Instructor's Videotape Supplement. All nonvideo cases are in the case section of the textbook. All cases indicating a CD icon offer a data set, which is located on the accompanying CD.

REFERENCE NOTES

1. One of the top research organizations in the world is the Survey Research Center of the University of Michigan. The material in this section draws heavily on the *Interviewer's Manual,* rev. ed. (Ann Arbor, Survey Research Center, University of Michigan, 1976); and Floyd J. Fowler, Jr., *Survey Research Methods* (Beverly Hills, CA: Sage Publications, 1988), Chapter 7.

2. Robert L. Kahn and Charles F. Cannell, *The Dynamics of Interviewing* (New York: Wiley, 1957), pp. 45–51.

3. Survey Research Center, *Interviewer's Manual,* p. 8.

4. Ibid., pp. 15–16.

5. Ibid., p. 17.

6. Fowler, *Survey Research Methods,* p. 112.

7. S. A. Richardson, B. S. Dohrenwend, and D. Klein, *Interviewing: Its Forms and Functions* (New York: Basic Books, 1965), pp. 328–58.

8. Reprinted by special permission from Charles F. Cannell and Robert L. Kahn, "Interviewing," in *The Handbook of Social Psychology,* 2nd ed., vol. 2, eds. G. Lindzey and E. Aronson (Reading, MA: Addison-Wesley, 1968). See also, Fowler, *Survey Research Methods,* p. 115; and P. J. Guenzel, T. R. Berk-

mans, and Charles F. Cannell, *General Interviewing Techniques* (Ann Arbor: Institute for Social Research, University of Michigan, 1983).

9. In one study, 5.5 percent of white participants and 11 percent of nonwhite respondents were still not contacted after six calls. See W. C. Dunkleberg and G. S. Day, "Nonresponse Bias and Callbacks in Sample Surveys," *Journal of Marketing Research,* May 1974, Table 3.

10. Ibid.

11. Fowler, *Survey Research Methods,* p. 50.

12. C. H. Fuller, "Weighting to Adjust for Survey Nonresponse," *Public Opinion Quarterly,* Summer 1974, pp. 239–46.

13. Dunkleberg and Day, "Nonresponse Bias," Table 3.

14. Ibid., pp. 160–68.

15. Eleanore Singer, "Agreement between Inaccessible Respondents and Informants," *Public Opinion Quarterly,* Winter 1972–73, pp. 603–11.

16. Fowler, Survey Research Methods, p. 111.

17. B. W. Schyberger, "A Study of Interviewer Behavior," *Journal of Marketing Research,* February 1967, p. 35.

18. B. S. Dohrenwend, J. A. Williams, Jr., and C. H. Weiss, "Interviewer Biasing Effects: Toward a Reconciliation of Findings," *Public Opinion Quarterly,* Spring 1969, pp. 121–29.

19. Seymour Sudman, *Reducing the Costs of Surveys* (Chicago: Aldine, 1967), p. 67.

20. Ibid., p. 59.

21. Ibid., p. 63.

22. Ibid., p. 53.

23. Robert M. Groves and Robert L. Kahn, *Surveys by Telephone* (New York: Academic Press, 1979), p. 223.

24. Institute for Social Research, *ISR Newsletter* (Ann Arbor: University of Michigan, 1991–92), p. 3.

25. Michael J. Havice, "Measuring Nonresponse and Refusals to an Electronic Telephone Survey," *Journalism Quarterly,* Fall 1990, pp. 521–30.

26. Mark Cooper, "Ensuring Telephone Access in the Digital Age: A Report by the Center for Media Education," Center for Media Education, February 25, 1998 (http://www.cme.org/telephoneaccess.html).

27. See, for example, J. H. Frey, Jr., *Survey Research by Telephone* (Beverly Hills, CA: Sage Publications, 1983).

28. Cooper, ibid. (http://www.cme.org/telephoneaccess.html).

29. See, for example, Groves and Kahn, *Surveys by Telephone.*

30. R. W. Graves, "An Empirical Comparison of Two Telephone Sample Designs," *Journal of Marketing Research,* November 1978, p. 622.

31. G. J. Glasser and G. D. Metzger, "National Estimates of Nonlisted Telephone Households and Their Characteristics," *Journal of Marketing Research,* August 1975, p. 360.

32. G. J. Glasser and G. D. Metzger, "Random Digit Dialing as a Method of Telephone Sampling," *Journal of Marketing Research,* February 1972, pp. 59–64; and Seymour Sudman, "The Uses of Telephone Directories for Survey Sampling," *Journal of Marketing Research,* May 1973, pp. 204–7.

33. A block is defined as an exchange group composed of the first four or more digits of a seven-digit number, such as 721-0, 721-1, and so forth.

34. Sudman, *Reducing the Costs of Surveys,* p. 65.

35. J. J. Wheatley, "Self-Administered Written Questionnaires or Telephone Interviews," *Journal of Marketing Research,* February 1973, pp. 94–95.

36. Groves and Kahn, *Surveys by Telephone,* p. 223.

37. Paul J. Lavrakas, *Telephone Survey Methods: Sampling, Selection, and Supervision,* 2nd ed. (Thousand Oaks, CA: Sage Publications, 1993), p. 16.

38. Peter S. Tuckel and Barry M. Feinberg, "The Answering Machine Poses Many Questions for Telephone Survey Researchers," *Public Opinion Quarterly,* Summer 1991, pp. 200–217.

39. "Gartner Dataquest Survey Shows 61 Percent of U.S. Households Actively Using the Internet," Gartner Inc., press release, August 30, 2001 (http://www4.gartner.com/5_about/press_releases/2001/pr20010829b.html).

40. These examples are drawn from the personal experience of the authors, as well as from Noah Shachtman, "Why the Web Works as a Market Research Tool," *AdAge.com,* Summer 2001 (http://adage.com/tools2001).

41. Don A. Dillman, *Mail and Telephone Surveys* (New York: Wiley, 1978), p. 6.

42. D. Wallace, "A Case for and against Mail Questionnaires," *Public Opinion Quarterly,* Spring 1954, pp. 40–52.

43. Don A. Dillman, "Increasing Mail Questionnaire Response in Large Samples of the General Public," *Public Opinion Quarterly,* Summer 1972, pp. 254–57.

44. Leslie Kanuk and Conrad Berenson, "Mail Surveys and Response Rates: A Literature Review," Journal of Marketing Research, November 1975, pp. 440–53; and Arnold S. Linsky, "Stimulating Responses to Mailed Questionnaires: A Review," *Public Opinion Quarterly* 39 (1975), pp. 82–101.

45. Kanuk and Berenson, "Mail Surveys," p. 450. Reprinted from the *Journal of Marketing Research,* published by the American Marketing Association.

46. Dillman, *Mail and Telephone Surveys,* p. 8.

47. Ibid., p. 12.

48. Ibid., pp. 22–24.

49. Total Design Method (http://survey.sesrc.wsu.edu/tdm.htm), February 4, 2000. Don Dillman is Professor of Sociology and Rural Sociology and Deputy Director of Research and Development of the Social and Economic Sciences Research Center at Washington State University.

50. Dillman, *Mail and Telephone Surveys,* pp. 160–61.

51. C. H. Lovelock, Ronald Still, David Cullwick, and Ira M. Kaufman, "An Evaluation of the Effectiveness of Drop-Off Questionnaire Delivery," *Journal of Marketing Research,* November 1976, pp. 358–64.

52. Nelson King, "[Web-based Surveys] How They Work," *PC Magazine,* January 18, 2000 (http://www.pcmag.com).

53. There are a number of sources for research services, some of which are annotated. For current listings, consult the latest edition of the *Marketing Services Guide & The American Marketing Association Membership Directory* (Chicago: American Marketing Association); *Consultants and Consulting Organizations Directory* (Detroit: Gale Research Corporation); or the research section of *Marketing News.*

54. A list of panel vendors is provided by Duane Davis, *Business Research for Decision Making,* 4th ed. (Belmont, CA: Wadsworth, 1996), p. 283.

REFERENCES FOR SNAPSHOTS AND CAPTIONS

Aleve

Sara Eckel, "Road to Recovery," *American Demographics,* March 2001, p. s8.

Privacy Technologies

"Frequently Asked Questions," Privacy Technologies, Inc., January 3, 2001 (http://www.telezapper.com/faq.htm#3).

"Product Literature," Privacy Technologies, Inc., January 3, 2001 (http://www.privacytechnologies.com/product.asp).

RTI International

Interview with Tim Gabel, director of computing, RTI International, December 17, 2001.

Rubinstein Consulting

Interview with Amil Rubinstein, project manager, Rubinstein Consulting, December 5, 1999.

CLASSIC AND CONTEMPORARY READINGS

Arksey, Hilary, and Peter T. Knight. *Interviewing for Social Scientists: An Introductory Resource with Examples.* Thousand Oaks, CA: Sage Publications, 1999.Covers design, improvization, success rates, specialized contexts, and transforming findings into results.

Dexter, Louis A. *Elite and Specialized Interviewing.* Evanston, IL: Northwestern University Press, 1970. Discusses the techniques and problems of interviewing "people in important or exposed positions."

Dillman, Don A. *Mail and Telephone Surveys.* New York: Wiley, 1978. A classic on mail and telephone surveys.

Dillman, Don A. *Mail and Internet Surveys: The Tailored Design Method.* New York: Wiley, 1999. The Tailored Design Method, which expands on the Total Design Concept of Dillman's classic work, takes advantage of computers, electronic mail, and the Internet to better our understanding of survey requirements.

Fowler, Floyd J., Jr. *Survey Research Methods.* 2nd ed. Thousand Oaks, CA: Sage Publications, 1993. An excellent overview of all aspects of the survey process.

Groves, R. M., et al. *Telephone Survey Methodology.* New York: Wiley, 1989. An important reference on telephone data-collection techniques.

Lavrakas, Paul J. *Telephone Survey Methods: Sampling, Selection, and Supervision.* 2nd ed. Thousand Oaks, CA: Sage Publications, 1993. This specialized work takes an applied perspective of interest to students and managers. Chapters 3, 5, and 6 on supervision are particularly useful.

Nesbary, Dale, K. *Survey Research and the World Wide Web.* Needham Heights, MA: Allyn & Bacon, 2000. Screen shots from Windows and FrontPage, e-mail survey construction, and Internet orientation for survey research.

CHAPTER 12

Instruments for Participant Communication

Learning Objectives

After reading this chapter, you should understand . . .

1   The link forged by the management-research question hierarchy between the management dilemma and the communication instrument.

2   The influence of communication method on instrument design.

3   The three general classes of information and what each contributes to the instrument.

4   The influence of question content, question wording, response strategy, and preliminary analysis planning on question construction.

5   Each of the numerous question design issues influencing instrument quality, reliability, and validity.

6   Sources for measurement questions.

7   The importance of pretesting questions and instruments.

Bringing Research to Life

"While visiting my hometown," shared Jason, "I was invited to a dinner meeting—at the country club, no less—to plan our Palm Grove High School reunion."

"So, you overcame your deeply ingrained *reverse* snobbery, and went?" asked Myra.

"Let's say that I was curious. It started poorly. I arrived during cocktail hour, feeling altogether out of place among the crowd. The old resentments returned. Then Stanton shambles over to me. I'd been the outcast with no leadership skills, no musical skills, no sports skills, no car. Stanton was the class scoundrel, whose dad owned the bank. As repulsive as he was, he had the right car, the right clothes, and the right address. He's become fleshy and dissipated, but he still dresses beautifully. When he clapped his meaty paw heartily on my shoulder, I felt an electrical thrill of . . . acceptance. Nina, the beautiful Nina, who after 10 years is still ensconced on a pedestal, whose father had been mayor for as long as anyone remembers and publisher of the newspaper, smiled at me, the whole bunch of them turned ever so slightly toward me, and suddenly—I belonged."

"Remarkable, Jason," said Myra. "You are so gullible!"

"Stanton—Stan to his friends—is a vice president, Nina is an associate publisher, and the others own auto dealerships, radio stations, majority shares in airlines, sports franchises. Stanton said he had been *following my career closely,* and that by all accounts I was doing *brilliantly* in economics research for *major corporations* and *federal agencies,* even consulting with CEOs *person-to-person* on matters of *top policy.*"

"Stanton was buttering you up."

"And I believed every hyperbole as if they were describing my actual life. Stanton wanted to know if I collected information about people's incomes, their banking, their 'love lives' . . . Nina, too, asked about *that* topic, though also about whether I polled people's reading habits and TV watching.

"As to the reunion, the fundamentals were easy enough to plan. But we came inevitably to the question of publicity: What, who, and how? And that was when Stanton said, 'We all know that Jason here is a hotshot pollster with a gold-plated reputation, and I am sure we can count on him to do something special.'

"Before I knew it, Stanton and Nina had maneuvered me into taking a mail poll of our entire class, which would become the basis of a citywide barrage of newspaper publicity. We would ask in my mail poll about graduates' lives and livelihoods to place a story on the business page and ask about their families and avocations for the lifestyle section, and we would no doubt find some angle by which to grub for space in other sections. I was to draft a dozen questions and forward them to Stanton for duplication and mailing. The surveys would be mailed back to Stanton and coded by his secretary. Then a data file would be e-mailed to me for analysis."

"Well," said Myra, "it was simple and straightforward, and you have done this several times for church groups and nonprofits, though I recollect that in each instance you grumbled about entrusting such sensitive work to 'amateurs.' What did Stan do to turn this into a disaster?"

"On the Monday following our dinner, the program committee wrote a letter to all our graduates, in which they laid out their plans in a general sort of way and also trumpeted that one of their own alumni—who was an important consultant to the nation's 50 top companies—would be conducting a scientific and authoritative mail survey, toward having ready for the reunion a picture of where the class had traveled and how high it had risen since graduation. Again they flattered me, and they urged every member of the class to respond fully and openly. The hoopla must have been extensive, because my mother

355

called to tell me that she had encountered some of my classmates and their parents in the supermarket, and all had expressed considerable excitement. I've got to admit that I began to believe my own press clippings. I was the scientific wunderkind of our graduating class. As to the questions, when I wrote them they turned out to be fairly innocuous items from the University of Michigan's general social survey from the previous year, not original with me, but used by permission. I sent the survey to Stanton.

"Four weeks passed. I chafed with eagerness to receive the data diskettes but did not even receive my own questionnaire to fill out and return. This was strange, I thought; I had heard nothing. Stanton and Nina failed to return my calls.

"Then my mother phoned and said she'd seen Lucia in the supermarket, and Lucia said she thought I was a pig. Now Lucia's brother was my best pal, and I'd taken Lucia to the senior dance and had been a perfect gentleman. She teaches kindergarten now, and she called me a pig. And later another fellow—a semithug who had played football—told Mother I had better not come back to town, because there was a bunch who planned to 'set me straight' if they saw me. And one day the principal saw Mom coming down the street and ran into the men's room of a service station—to avoid her."

"What was going on?"

"After asking a few of the right people, Mom extracted a copy of the survey Stanton mailed."

He reached into his desk and passed Myra a sheet that had been angrily torn, then taped together.

"It appears that, without asking me, Stanton and Nina added a few questions to satisfy their own prurient curiosities."

The type was very small for a mail survey. She ran her finger down the sheet, at first reading each item approvingly. Suddenly her finger paused over one question, then advanced slowly over several others. Her mouth opened in astonishment, and she slowly blushed, turning progressively more florid, from brow to shoulders. She dropped the survey sheet and covered her mouth, but was unable to stifle first a gasp, then a guffaw.

"Why they most certainly were naughty, Jason, weren't they? I would never ask anyone such questions—I would not even admit that people in a small town had even heard of these things." She removed her eyeglasses and studied his unhappy face. "And you say this went out over your name?"

"Yes. I've made a mess of things, Myra. To save the cost of printing and mailing the survey and coding the data, I allowed Stanton to take control and insert his creepy questions. My reputation is ruined in the town where I grew up, people will be looking strangely at Mom for years, and we have lost the opportunity to learn about the fortunes of my classmates. The worst part is, of course, that I let my emotions cloud my good scientific judgment. I am going to write a letter of apology and hope that Nina allows it to run in her father's newspaper. I'll make up a cock-and-bull story about a mistake at the printer's."

"Too bad nobody will ever believe that story," commiserated Myra.

Developing the Instrument Design Strategy

New researchers often want to draft questions immediately. They are reluctant to go through the preliminaries that make for successful surveys. Exhibit 12–1 is a suggested flowchart for instrument design. The procedures followed in developing an instrument vary from study to study, but the flowchart suggests three phases. Each phase is discussed in this chapter, starting with a review of the management-research question hierarchy and its application to the MindWriter customer satisfaction study. We conclude the chapter with a discussion of procedures for pretesting the completed instrument.

EXHIBIT 12–1   Flowchart for Instrument Design

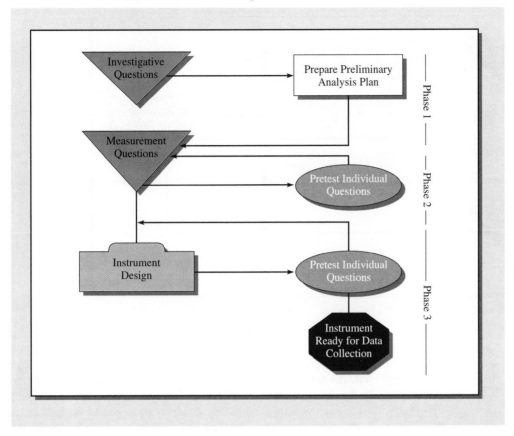

Management-Research Question Hierarchy Revisited: Phase 1

We discussed how to refine a management dilemma and take it through the research process in Chapter 3 and depicted the process in Exhibit 3–1.

The management-research question hierarchy is the foundation of successful instrument development (see Exhibit 12–2). The process of moving from the general management dilemma to specific measurement questions goes through four question levels:

1. **Management question**—The dilemma, stated in question form, that the manager needs resolved.

2. **Research question(s)**—The fact-based translation of the question the researcher must answer to contribute to the solution of the management question.

3. **Investigative questions**—Specific questions the researcher must answer to provide sufficient detail and coverage of the research question. Within this level, there may be several questions as the researcher moves from the general to the specific.

4. **Measurement questions**—Questions participants must answer if the researcher is to gather the needed information and resolve the management question.

Addressing the *management-research question hierarchy* is the first step in planning for the collection of data. Investigative questions are the core of the researcher's information needs. In many studies, an exploratory investigation helps the researcher understand all dimensions of the subject. In the Prince Corporation image study (see Chapter 8), many exploratory interviews were needed to ensure all investigative topics were

EXHIBIT 12–2   Flowchart for Instrument Design: Phase 1

```
┌────────────────────────────────────────────────────────────────────────┐
│                                                                          │
│   ▼ Investigative        Select Data Type                                │
│     Questions            (nominal, ordinal, interval, ratio)             │
│                                                                          │
│                          Select Communication         Prepare Preliminary│
│                          Approach                      Analysis Plan     │
│                          (personal, phone, electronic, mail)             │
│                                                                          │
│                          Select Process Structure                        │
│                          (structured vs. unstructured vs.                │
│                          combination; disguised vs. undisguised)         │
│                                                                          │
│   ▼ Measurement                                                          │
│     Questions                                                            │
│                                                                          │
└────────────────────────────────────────────────────────────────────────┘
```

covered. In the Albany Outpatient Laser Clinic study (see Chapter 11), the eye surgeon would know from experience the types of medical complications that could result in poor recovery. Thus, the list of information needs (investigative questions) would be specific and easily developed without extensive exploration studies. The cochairs of Jason's high school reunion planning committee obviously had a hidden agenda. Jason had one list of investigative questions, and they had a distinctly different list. In the MindWriter project, exploration was limited to several interviews and an in-depth study of company service records because the concepts were not complicated and the researchers had experience in the industry.

The MindWriter "Close-Up" in this section reveals the thinking that leads to the final questionnaire and shows you the direction of this chapter. Normally, once the researcher understands the connection between the investigative questions and the potential measurement questions, a strategy for the survey is the next logical step. This proceeds to getting down to the particulars of instrument design. The following are prominent among the strategic concerns.

MANAGEMENT

1. What type of data is needed to answer the management question?

2. What communication approach will be used?

3. Should the questions be structured, unstructured, or some combination?

4. Should the questioning be undisguised or disguised? If the latter, to what degree?

Close-Up

Instrument Design for MindWriter

Replacing an imprecise management question with specific measurement questions is an exercise in analytical reasoning. We described that process incrementally in the MindWriter "Close-Up" features in Chapters 3, 4, and 9. In Chapter 3, Myra and Jason's fact finding at MindWriter resulted in their ability to state the management dilemma in terms of management, research, and investigative questions. Adding context to the questions allowed them to construct the proposal described in Chapter 4. In Chapter 9, they returned to the list of investigative questions and selected one question to use in testing their scaling approach. Here is a brief review of the steps Jason and Myra have taken so far and the measurement questions that have resulted.

Synopsis of the Problem

MindWriter Corporation's new service and repair program for laptop computers, CompleteCare, was designed to provide a rapid response to customers' service problems. Management has received several complaints, however. Management needs information on the program's effectiveness and its impact on customer satisfaction. There is also a shortage of trained technical operators in the company's telephone center. The package courier is uneven in executing its pickup and delivery contract. Parts availability problems exist for some machine types. Occasionally, customers receive units that are either not fixed or damaged in some way.

Management Question: What should be done to improve the CompleteCare program for MindWriter laptop repairs and servicing to enhance customer satisfaction?

Research Questions

1. Should the technical representatives be given more intensive training, or not?

2. Should ABC Courier Service be replaced by an overnight air transport, or not?

3. Should the repair diagnostic and repair sequencing operations be modified, or not?

4. Should the return packaging be modified to include premolded rigid foam inserts, conforming-expanding foam protection, or neither?

5. Should metropolitan repair centers be established to complement or replace in-factory repair facilities, or not?

Investigative Questions

a. Are customers' expectations being met in terms of the time it takes to repair the systems? What is the customers' overall satisfaction with the CompleteCare service program and the MindWriter product?

b. How well is the call center helping customers? Is it helping them with instructions? What percentage of customers' technical problems is it solving without callbacks or subsequent repairs? How long must customers wait on the phone?

c. How good is the transportation company? Does it pick up and deliver the system responsively? How long must customers wait for pickup and delivery? Are the laptops damaged due to package handling?

d. How good is the repair group? What problems are most common? What repair processes are involved in fixing these problems? For what percentage of laptops is the repair completed within the promised time limit? Are customers' problems fully resolved? Are there new problems with the newer models? How quickly are these problems diagnosed?

e. How are repaired laptops packaged for return shipping? What is the cost of alternative rigid foam inserts and expandable-foam packaging? Would new equipment be required if the packaging were changed? Would certain shipping-related complaints be eliminated with new packaging materials?

The extensive scope of the research questions and resulting measurement questions forced MindWriter to reassess the scope of the desired initial research study, to determine where to concentrate its enhancement efforts. Management chose a descriptive rather than a prescriptive scope.

Measurement Questions

The measurement questions used for the self-administered package insert instrument are shown in Exhibit 12–3.[1] Of the investigative questions in *(b)*, the first two are addressed as "responsiveness" and "technical competence" with telephone assistance in the questionnaire. The second two investigative questions in *(b)* may be answered by accessing the company's service database. The questionnaire's three-part question on courier service parallels investigative question *(c)*. Specific service deficiencies will be recorded in the "Comments/Suggestions" section. Investigative questions under *(d)* and *(e)* are covered with questionnaire items 3, 4, and 5. Since deficiencies in item 5 may be attributed to both the repair facility and the courier, the reasons will be cross-checked during analysis. Questionnaire item 6 uses the same language as the last investigative question in *(a)*. Questionnaire item 7 is an extension of item 6 but attempts to secure an impression of behavioral intent to use CompleteCare again. Finally, the last item will make known the extent to which change is needed in CompleteCare by revealing repurchase intention as linked to product and service experience.

EXHIBIT 12–3   Measurement Questions for the MindWriter Study

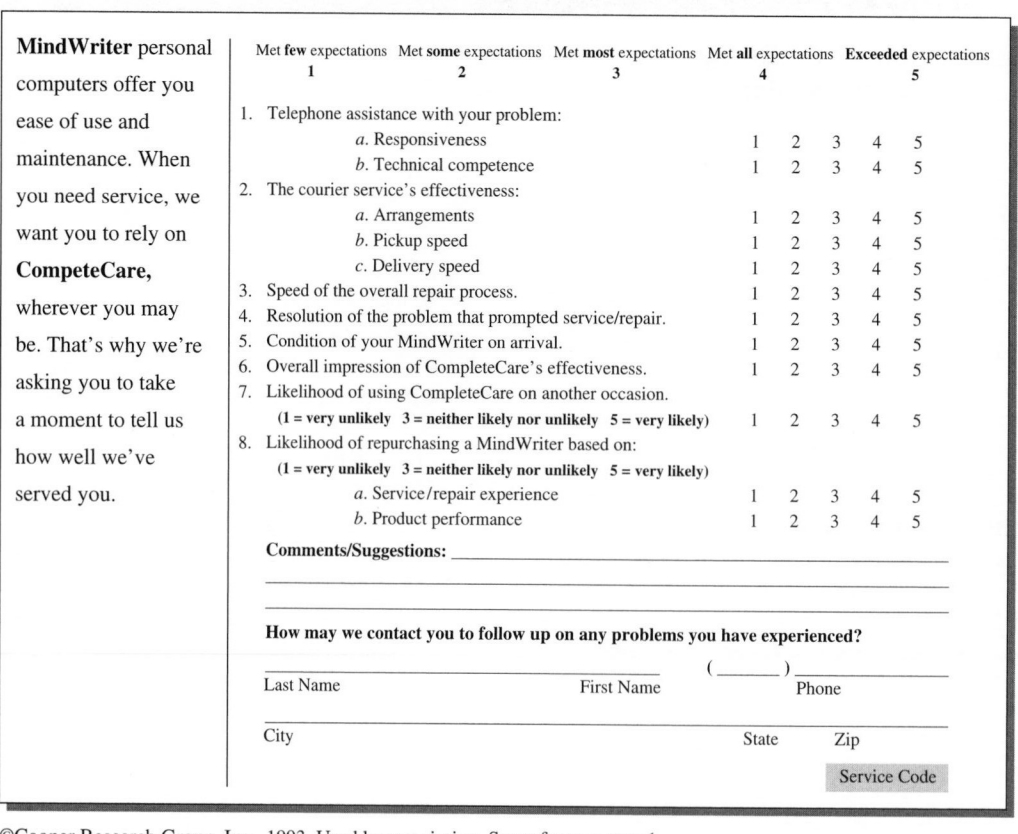

MindWriter personal computers offer you ease of use and maintenance. When you need service, we want you to rely on **CompeteCare,** wherever you may be. That's why we're asking you to take a moment to tell us how well we've served you.

	Met **few** expectations	Met **some** expectations	Met **most** expectations	Met **all** expectations	**Exceeded** expectations
	1	2	3	4	5

1. Telephone assistance with your problem:
    a. Responsiveness   1 2 3 4 5
    b. Technical competence   1 2 3 4 5
2. The courier service's effectiveness:
    a. Arrangements   1 2 3 4 5
    b. Pickup speed   1 2 3 4 5
    c. Delivery speed   1 2 3 4 5
3. Speed of the overall repair process.   1 2 3 4 5
4. Resolution of the problem that prompted service/repair.   1 2 3 4 5
5. Condition of your MindWriter on arrival.   1 2 3 4 5
6. Overall impression of CompleteCare's effectiveness.   1 2 3 4 5
7. Likelihood of using CompleteCare on another occasion.
    (1 = very unlikely   3 = neither likely nor unlikely   5 = very likely)   1 2 3 4 5
8. Likelihood of repurchasing a MindWriter based on:
    (1 = very unlikely   3 = neither likely nor unlikely   5 = very likely)
    a. Service/repair experience   1 2 3 4 5
    b. Product performance   1 2 3 4 5

Comments/Suggestions: _____

How may we contact you to follow up on any problems you have experienced?

Last Name _____ First Name _____ (_____) _____ Phone

City _____ State _____ Zip _____

Service Code

©Cooper Research Group, Inc., 1993. Used by permission. See reference note 1.

Type of Data

Data type determines the analytical procedures that are possible during data analysis. Chapter 8 discussed nominal, ordinal, interval, and ratio data and how the characteristics of each type influence the analysis (statistical choices and hypothesis testing). We demonstrate how to code and extract the data from the instrument, select appropriate descriptive measures or tests, and analyze the results in Chapters 15–19.

Communication Approach

As discussed in Chapter 11, communication-based research may be conducted by personal interview, telephone, mail, computer, or some combination of these. Decisions regarding which method to use as well as where to interact with the participant (at home, at a neutral site, at the sponsor's place of business, etc.) will affect the design of the instrument. In personal interviewing and computer questioning, it is possible to use graphics and other questioning tools more easily than when questioning is done by mail or phone. The differing delivery mechanisms result in different introductions, instructions, instrument layout, and conclusions.

In the MindWriter example, these decisions were easy. The dispersion of participants, the necessity of a service experience, and budget limitations all dictated a mail

SNAPSHOT

Express Data at $750 per Question

During the controversy surrounding Napster and the music industry in 2000–2002, *American Demographics* wanted to run a story on intellectual property right violations. It turned to TaylorNelsonSofres (TNS) Intersearch and its *Express* omnibus study to determine current attitudes on copyright violations. Each week, Wednesday through Sunday, the *Express* study reaches 1,000 carefully chosen males and females by phone. *Express* is not a panel; different participants are selected each week. *American Demographics* editor Rebecca Gardyn discussed with Intersearch the topic and the information it wanted to know. "One question they had was whether respondents had appropriated copyrighted material without paying for it," shared Brenda Edwards, vice president of marketing communications for Intersearch.

Express follows a general rule-of-thumb that a particular client's questions not exceed two minutes of phone time on the omnibus. This translates to approximately six simple, standard questions (not complex multipart, multiscale, or branching questions). "A client receives the data pertaining to

their questions from *Express* on Monday afternoon by 3:00 P.M.," explains Edwards. The data thus gathered provided substantiation for the *American Demographics* article published in September 2000. Eight percent of those responding "knew someone" who had copied computer software; 14 percent knew someone who had copied a prerecorded videocassette; 28 percent knew someone who had copied a prerecorded audio cassette or disk; 20 percent knew someone who had downloaded music free of charge from the Internet; and 46 percent knew someone who had photocopied pages from a book or magazine. You can see the actual study questions and the cross-tabulated data as they were delivered to *American Demographics* on this text's website.

www.intersearch.tnsofres.com

www.americandemographics.com

survey where the participant received the instrument either at home or at work. The danger in using a telephone survey as a follow-up to nonparticipants is that memory decay might alter participants' answers due to the passage of time between return of the laptop and MindWriter contact with the participant by telephone.

Some of the same issues dictated a mail survey in Jason's reunion study; we could add to the previous list the sensitivity of the prurient questions added by Stanton and Nina and the desire of most participants to maintain anonymity in the face of such questions. In the Prince Corporation study, there was a desire to use telephone interviews because of cost savings. However, the study objectives called for data that could not be collected easily by telephone. Edna probably would have preferred a personal interview to the self-administered study provided by the Albany clinic.

Question Structure

The degree of question and response structure also must be decided upon. Response strategy decisions (the type of question used) depend on the content and objectives of specific questions. Question wording is affected largely by the communication mode chosen and attempts to control bias. Questionnaires and **interview schedules** (*interview schedule* is an alternative term for the questionnaire used in an interview) can range from those that have a great deal of structure to those that are essentially unstructured. Both questionnaires and interview schedules contain three types of measurement questions.

MANAGEMENT
Tip

- Administrative questions.

- Classification questions.

- Target questions (structured or unstructured).

Administrative questions identify the participant, interviewer, interview location, and conditions. These questions are rarely asked of the participant but are necessary to study patterns within the data and identify possible error sources. **Classification questions** are usually sociological-demographic variables that allow participants' answers to be grouped so patterns are revealed and can be studied. **Target questions** address the investigative questions of a specific study. Target questions may be **structured** (they present the participants with a fixed set of choices, often called *closed questions*) or **unstructured** (they do not limit responses but do provide a frame of reference for participants' answers, sometimes referred to as *open-ended questions*).

In the MindWriter self-administered mail questionnaire, it was necessary to use structured questions to get the most information possible from the limited space on the form. In the exploratory stages of the Prince Corporation study, both questions and responses were unstructured, but in the final project both were largely structured. At the Albany clinic, Edna faced a series of open-ended questions, because anticipating medications and health history for a wide variety of individuals would be a gargantuan task for a researcher and would take up far too much space. Jason's reunion study was limited to 12 questions from the University of Michigan's lifestyle index, all of which are structured questions to facilitate analysis of data from large numbers of participants on a repeat basis.

The type of interview also affects question structure. In extremely unstructured interviews, the interviewer's task is to encourage the participant to talk in-depth about a set of topics. The **in-depth interview** encourages participants to share as much information as possible in an unconstrained environment. The interviewer uses a minimum of prompts and guiding questions.

Many of the Snapshot features developed for this text involved in-depth interviews with unstructured questions.

With more focused in-depth interviews, the researcher provides additional guidance by using a set of questions to promote discussion and elaboration by the participant. In these interviews, the researcher guides the topical direction and coverage. Whether the interview is focused or more in-depth, the aim is to provide a relaxed environment in which the participant will be open to fully discuss topics. This kind of questioning is often used in exploratory research or where the investigator is dealing with complex topics that do not lend themselves to structured interviewing. If we were doing case research among various participants in a major event, a substantial portion of the questioning would be unique to each participant and would benefit from an unstructured approach.

Interviews with participants in **focus groups** are widely used in exploratory research. As we noted in Chapter 6, the interviewer-moderator generally has a list of specific points he or she would like to see discussed, and these are used to prompt the group members. When the discussion stays within these bounds, the interviewer lets group members continue their interaction.

Disguising Objectives and Sponsors

Another consideration in communication instrument design is whether the purpose of the study should be disguised. Some degree of disguise is often present in survey questions, especially to shield the study's sponsor. A **disguised question** is designed to conceal the question's true purpose. We disguise the sponsor and the objective of a study if the researcher believes that participants will respond differently than they would if both or either were known.

The accepted wisdom is that often we must disguise the study's objective or sponsor or abandon the research. The decision about when to use disguised questioning may be made easier by identifying four situations where disguising the study objective is or is not an issue:

- Willingly shared, conscious-level information.
- Reluctantly shared, conscious-level information.

- Knowable, limitedly-conscious-level information.
- Subconscious-level information.

Willingly Shared, Conscious-Level Information   When requesting this type of information, either disguised or undisguised questions may be used, but the situation rarely requires disguised techniques. Example: "Have you attended the showing of a foreign language film in the last six months?" In the MindWriter study, the questions revealed in Exhibit 12–3 ask for information that the participant should know and be willing to provide.

Reluctantly Shared, Conscious-Level Information   When we ask for an opinion on some topic on which participants may hold a socially unacceptable view, we often use projective techniques (a disguised questioning method) because participants may not give their true feelings or may give stereotyped answers. The researcher can encourage more accurate answers by phrasing the questions in a hypothetical way or by asking how "people around here feel about this topic." The assumption is that responses to these questions will indirectly reveal the participant's opinions. In Jason's high school reunion study, the objective for collecting information on classmates' love lives was not disclosed—in part that is why most people did not return the study. As the researcher, Jason surely wishes that his identity were not disclosed.

Knowable, Limitedly-Conscious-Level Information   Asking about individual attitudes when participants know they hold the attitude but have not explored why they hold the attitude may encourage the use of disguised questions. A classic example is a study of government bond buying during World War II.[2] A survey sought reasons why, among people with equal ability to buy, some bought more war bonds than others. Frequent buyers had been personally solicited to buy bonds while most infrequent buyers had not received personal solicitation. No direct *why* question to participants could have provided the answer to this question because participants did not know they were receiving differing solicitation approaches. Example: "What is it about air travel during stormy weather that attracts you?"

Subconscious-Level Information   Seeking insight into the basic motivations underlying attitudes or consumption practices may or may not require disguised techniques. **Projective techniques** (such as sentence completion tests, cartoon or balloon tests, and word association tests) thoroughly disguise the study objective, but they are

Information gathered by Census 2000, the most comprehensive survey in the United States, is used for allocating funds at the federal, state, and local levels, as well as for numerous marketing and human resource purposes.

We revisit the CityBus (Chapter 7), Prince Corporation (8), Albany Laser Clinic (11), and Metro University (7) studies throughout this chapter.

often difficult to interpret. Example: Interview probes—"Would you say, then, that the attitude you just expressed indicates you oppose or favor requiring adult drivers to declare their position on being an organ donor at the time of license renewal?"

In the MindWriter study, the questions were direct, and the specific information sought was undisguised. Customers knew they were evaluating their experience with the service and repair program at MindWriter; thus the purpose of the study and its sponsorship were also undisguised. While the sponsorship of the study that Burbidge conducted for CityBus was revealed, the objective of the study (where and when advertising should be run to announce changes in the bus route and schedule) was not revealed. In the Prince Corporation study, the questions concerned only a few companies, giving the sponsor only a limited disguise. Many questions sought direct answers, but sometimes indirect questioning was used to seek answers on sensitive topics or to reduce stereotypical answers. While the sponsor of the Albany clinic study was obvious, multiple interpretations from several questions suggest that the study's objective was not apparent.

Preliminary Analysis Plan

You might find it useful to review Exhibit 11–1, "Data Collection Approach," in Chapter 11.

Researchers are concerned with adequate coverage of the topic and with securing the information in its most usable form. A good way to test how well the study plan meets those needs is to develop "dummy" tables that display the data one expects to secure. This serves as a check on whether the planned measurement questions meet the data needs of the research question. It also helps the researcher determine the type of data needed for each question—a preliminary step to developing measurement questions for investigative questions.

Constructing and Refining the Measurement Questions: Phase 2

Drafting the questions begins once you develop a complete list of investigative questions and decide on the collection processes to be used. In Phase 2 (see Exhibit 12–4) you draft specific measurement questions considering subject content, the wording of each question (influenced by the degree of disguise and the need to provide operational definitions for constructs and concepts), and response strategy (each producing a different level of data as needed for your preliminary analysis plan). In Phase 3 you must address topic and question sequencing. We discuss these topics sequentially, although in practice the process is not orderly. For this discussion, we assume the questions are structured. The order, type, and wording of the measurement questions, the introduction, the instructions, the transitions, and the closure in a quality communication instrument should accomplish the following:

- Encourage each participant to provide accurate responses.
- Encourage each participant to provide an adequate amount of information.
- Discourage each participant from refusing to answer specific questions.
- Discourage each participant from early discontinuation of participation.
- Leave the participant with a positive attitude about survey participation.

Question Content

Four questions, covering numerous issues, guide the instrument designer in selecting appropriate question content:

EXHIBIT 12–4   Flowchart for Instrument Design: Phase 2

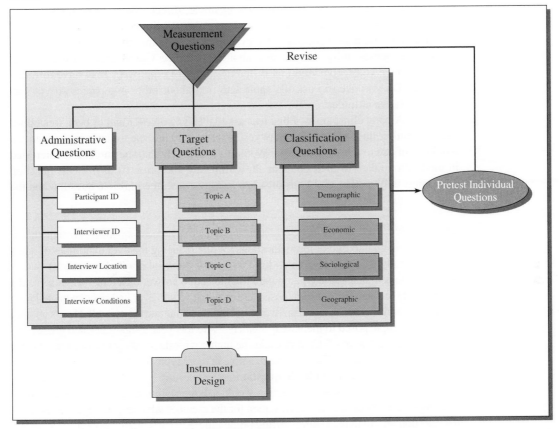

MANAGEMENT
Tip

- Should this question be asked?
- Is the question of proper scope and coverage?
- Can the participant adequately answer this question, as asked?
- Will the participant willingly answer this question, as asked?

Should This Question Be Asked?
Issue 1: Purposeful versus Interesting.   Questions that merely produce "interesting information" cannot be justified on either economic or research grounds. Challenge each question's function. Does it contribute significant information toward answering the research question? Will its omission limit or prevent the thorough analysis of other data? Can we infer the answer from another question? A good question designer knows the value of learning more from fewer questions.

Is the Question of Proper Scope and Coverage?
Issue 2: Incomplete or Unfocused.   We can test this content issue by asking, "Will this question reveal all we need to know?" We sometimes ask participants to reveal their motivations for particular behaviors or attitudes by asking them, "Why?"

This simple question is inadequate to probe the range of most causal relationships. When studying product use behavior, for example, direct two or three questions on product use to the heavy-use consumer and only one question to the light user.

Questions are also inadequate if they do not provide the information you need to interpret responses fully. If you ask about the Prince Corporation's image as an employer, have you recognized that different groups of employees may have different reactions? Do you need to ask the same question about other companies so you can evaluate relative attitudes?

In the Albany clinic study, Edna was asked, "Have you ever had or been treated for a recent cold or flu?" If Edna answers yes, what exactly has she told the researcher that would be of use to her eye surgeon? Wouldn't it be likely that the surgeon is interested in medication taken to treat colds or flu within, say, the prior 10 days? This question also points to two other problems of scope and coverage: the multiple question and the imprecise question.

Issue 3: Multiple Questions.   Does the question request so much content that it should be broken into two or more questions? While reducing the overall number of questions in a study is highly desirable, don't try to ask **double-barreled questions:** two or more questions in one that the participant might need to answer differently to preserve the accuracy of the data. The question posed to Edna ("Have you ever had or been treated for a recent cold or flu?") fires more than two barrels. It asks four questions in all. Here's another common example posed to menswear retailers: "Are this year's shoe sales and gross profits higher than last year's?" Couldn't sales be higher with stagnant profits, or profits higher with level or lower sales? This second example is more typical of the problem of multiple questions. A less obvious **multiple question** is the question we ask to identify a family's TV station preference. A better question would ask the station preference of each family member separately or, alternatively, screen for the member who most often controls channel selection on Monday evenings during prime time. Also, it's highly probable that no one station would serve as an individual's preferred station when we cover a wide range of time (8–11 P.M.). This reveals another problem, the imprecise question.

Issue 4: Precision.   To test a question for precision ask, "Does the question ask precisely what we want and need to know?" We sometimes ask for a participant's income when we really want to know the family's total annual income before taxes in the past calendar year. We ask what a participant purchased "last week" when we really want to know what he or she purchased in a "typical 7-day period during the past 90 days." Edna was asked her cold and flu history during the time frame "ever." It is hard to imagine an 80-year-old woman who has never experienced a cold or flu and equally hard to assume Edna hasn't been treated for one or both at some time in her life.

A second precision issue deals with common vocabulary between researcher and participant. To test your question for this problem, ask, "Do I need to offer operational definitions of concepts and constructs used in the question?"

Can the Participant Answer Adequately?

Issue 5: Time for Thought.   Although the question may address the topic, is it asked in such a way that the participant will be able to frame an answer, or is it reasonable to assume that the participant can determine the answer? This is also a question that drives sample design, but once the ideal sample unit is determined, researchers often assume that participants who fit the sample profile have all the answers, preferably on the tips of their tongues. To frame a response to some questions takes time and thought; such questions are best left to self-administered questionnaires.

Issue 6: Participation at the Expense of Accuracy. Participants typically want to cooperate in interviews; thus they assume giving any answer is more helpful than denying knowledge of a topic. Their desire to impress the interviewer may encourage them to give answers based on no information. A classic illustration of this problem occurred with the following question:[3] "Which of the following statements most closely coincides with your opinion of the Metallic Metals Act?" The response pattern shows that 70 percent of those interviewed had a fairly clear opinion of the Metallic Metals Act; however, *there is no such act.* The participants apparently assumed that if a question was asked, they should provide an answer. Given reasonable-sounding choices, they selected one even though they knew nothing about the topic.

To counteract this tendency to respond at any cost, **filter questions** are used to qualify a participant's knowledge. If the MindWriter service questionnaire is distributed via mail to all recent purchasers of MindWriter products, we might ask, "Have you required service for your machine since its purchase?" Only those for whom service was provided could provide the detail and scope of the responses indicated in the investigative question list. If such a question is asked in a phone interview, we would call the question a **screen,** because it is being used to determine whether the person on the other end of the phone line is a qualified sample unit.

Assuming that participants have prior knowledge or understanding may be risky. The risk is getting many answers that have little basis in fact. The Metallic Metals Act illustration may be challenged as unusual, but in another case, a Gallup report revealed that 45 percent of the persons surveyed did not know what a "lobbyist in Washington" was, and 88 percent could not give a correct description of "jurisdictional strike."[4] This points to the need for operational definitions as part of question wording.

Issue 7: Presumed Knowledge. The question designer should consider the participants' information level when determining the content and appropriateness of a question. In some studies, the degree of participant expertise can be substantial, and simplified explanations are inappropriate and discourage participation. In asking the public about gross margins in menswear stores, we would want to be sure the "general public" participant understands the nature of "gross margin." If our sample unit were a merchant, explanations might not be needed. A high level of knowledge among our sample units, however, may not eliminate the need for operational definitions. Among merchants, gross margin per unit in dollars is commonly accepted as the difference between cost and selling price; but when offered as a percentage rather than a dollar figure, it can be calculated as a percentage of unit selling price or as a percentage of unit cost. A participant answering from the "cost" frame of reference would calculate gross margin at 100 percent; another participant, using the same dollars and the "selling price" frame of reference, would calculate gross margin at 50 percent. If a construct is involved and differing interpretations of a concept are feasible, operational definitions may still be needed.

Issue 8: Recall and Memory Decay. The adequacy problem also occurs when you ask questions that overtax participants' recall ability. People cannot recall much that has happened in their past, unless it was dramatic. Your mother may remember everything about your arrival if you were her first child: the weather, time of day, even what she ate prior to your birth. If you have several siblings, her memory of subsequent births may be less complete. If the events surveyed are of incidental interest to participants, they will probably be unable to recall them correctly even a short time later. An unaided recall question, "What radio programs did you listen to last night?" might identify as few as 10 percent of those individuals who actually listened to a program.[5]

Issue 9: Balance (General versus Specific). Answering adequacy also depends on the proper balance between generality and specificity. We often ask questions in terms too general and detached from participants' experiences. Asking for average annual consumption of a product may make an unrealistic demand for generalization on people who do not think in these terms. Why not ask how often the product was used last week or last month? Too often participants are asked to recall individual use experiences over an extended time and to average them for us. This is asking participants to do the researcher's work and encourages substantial response errors. It may also contribute to a higher refusal rate and higher discontinuation rate.

There is a danger in being too narrow in the time frame applied to behavior questions. We may ask about movie attendance for the last seven days, although this is too short a time span on which to base attendance estimates. It may be better to ask about attendance, say, for the last 30 days. There are no firm rules about this generality-specificity problem. Developing the right level of generality depends on the subject, industry, setting, and experience of the question designer.

Issue 10: Objectivity. The ability of participants to answer adequately is also often distorted by questions whose content is biased by what is included or omitted. The question may explicitly mention only the positive or negative aspects of the topic or make unwarranted assumptions about the participant's position. Consider an experiment in which the following two forms of a question were asked:

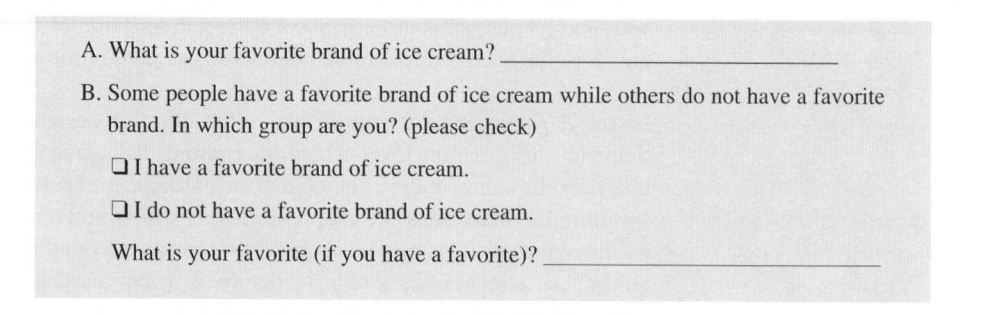

A. What is your favorite brand of ice cream? _____

B. Some people have a favorite brand of ice cream while others do not have a favorite brand. In which group are you? (please check)

❏ I have a favorite brand of ice cream.

❏ I do not have a favorite brand of ice cream.

What is your favorite (if you have a favorite)? _____

Fifty-seven randomly chosen graduate business students answered version A, and 56 answered version B. Their responses are shown in the accompanying table.

Response	Version A	Version B
Named a favorite brand	77%[*]	39%[*]
Named a favorite flavor rather than a brand	19	18
Had no favorite brand	4	43
Total	100%	100%
	n = 57	n = 56

[*]Significant difference at the 0.001 level.

The probable cause of the difference in brand preference is that A is a **leading question.** It assumes and suggests that everyone has a favorite brand of ice cream and will report it. Version B indicates the participant need not have a favorite.

A deficiency in both versions is that about one participant in five misinterpreted the meaning of the term *brand*. This misinterpretation cannot be attributed to low education, low intelligence, lack of exposure to the topic, or quick or lazy reading of the question. The subjects were students who had taken at least one course in marketing in which branding was prominently treated. (Word confusion difficulties are discussed in greater detail later in this chapter.)

Will the Participants Answer Willingly?

Issue 11: Sensitive Information.   Even if participants have the information, they may be unwilling to give it. Some topics are considered too sensitive to discuss with strangers. These vary from person to person, but one study suggests the most sensitive topics concern money matters and family life.[6] More than one-fourth of those interviewed mentioned these as the topics about which they would be "least willing to answer questions." Participants of lower socioeconomic status also included political matters in this "least willing" list.

Participants also may be unwilling to give correct answers for ego reasons. Many exaggerate their incomes, the number of cars they own, their social status, and the amount of high-prestige literature they read. They also minimize their ages and the amount of low-prestige literature they read. Many participants are reluctant to try to give an adequate response. Often this will occur when they see the topic as irrelevant to their own interests or to their perception of the survey's purpose. They participate half-heartedly, often answer with "don't know," give negative replies, refuse to be interviewed, or give stereotypical responses. The lack of response to Jason's high school reunion survey was attributed to the inclusion of questions about classmates' lascivious activities. This information was far too sensitive to risk being mentioned in a potentially embarrassing article in the hometown paper.

Question Wording

It is frustrating when people misunderstand a question that has been painstakingly written. This problem is partially due to the lack of a shared vocabulary. The difficulty of understanding long and complex sentences or involved phraseology aggravates the problem further. Our dilemma arises from the requirements of question design (the need to be explicit, to present alternatives, and to explain meanings). All contribute to longer and more involved sentences.[7]

The difficulties caused by question wording exceed most other sources of distortion in surveys. They have led one social scientist to conclude:

> To many who worked in the Research Branch it soon became evident that error or bias attributable to sampling and to methods of questionnaire administration were relatively small as compared with other types of variations—especially variation attributable to different ways of wording questions.[8]

While it is impossible to say which wording of a question is best, we can point out several areas that cause participant confusion and measurement error. The diligent question designer will put a given question through many revisions before it satisfies these criteria.[9]

MANAGEMENT

- Is the question stated in terms of a shared vocabulary?
- Does the question contain vocabulary with a single meaning?
- Does the question contain unsupported or misleading assumptions?
- Does the question contain biased wording?

- Is the question correctly personalized?
- Are adequate alternatives presented within the question?

The Albany clinic study illustrated several of these problems. The multiple question about Edna's "referring physician" and "physician most knowledgeable about her health" was further distorted by a request for a phone number. Edna didn't know which doctor's phone number was being requested. By offering space for only one number, the data collection instrument implied that both parts of the question might refer to the same doctor. The questions about past medical history did not offer clear directions. Questions (about having the flu) either did not include time frames or had unrealistic time frames (the term "ever"). The question about "intact teeth" generated several plausible interpretations. Another question about neck movement assumed every participant had the same operational definition for "limited motion of your neck." A talented researcher did not design the clinic's study questionnaire.

The MindWriter study (see Exhibit 12–3) simplified the process by using the same response strategy for each factor the participant was asked to evaluate. The study basically asks, "How did our CompleteCare service program work for you when you consider each of the following factors?" It accomplishes this as it sets up the questioning with, "Take a moment to tell us how well we've served you." Because the sample includes CompleteCare users only, the underlying assumption that participants have used the service is acceptable. The language is appropriate for the participant's likely level of education. And the open-ended question used for "comments" adds flexibility to capture any unusual circumstances not covered by the structured factor list.

Issue 12: Shared Vocabulary. Because surveying is an exchange of ideas between interviewer and participant, each must understand what the other says, and this is possible only if the vocabulary used is common to both parties.[10] Two problems arise. First, the words must be simple enough to allow adequate communication with persons of limited education. This is dealt with by reducing the level of word difficulty to simple English words and phrases (more is said about this in the section on word clarity).

In the Marriott concierge study introduced in Chapter 2, researchers anticipated a potential problem by arranging for bilingual interviewers.

Technical language is the second issue. Even highly educated participants cannot answer questions stated in unfamiliar technical terms. Technical language also poses difficulties for interviewers. In one study of how corporation executives handled various financial problems, interviewers had to be conversant with technical financial terms. This necessity presented the researcher with two alternatives—hiring people knowledgeable in finance and teaching them interviewing skills or teaching financial concepts to experienced interviewers.[11] This vocabulary problem also exists where similar or identical studies are conducted in different countries and multiple languages.

A great obstacle to effective question wording is the choice of words. Questions to be asked of the public should be restricted to the 2,000 most common words in the English language.[12] Even the use of simple words is not enough. Many words have vague references or meanings that must be gleaned from their context. In a repair study, technicians were asked, "How many radio sets did you repair last month?" This question may seem unambiguous, but participants interpreted it in two ways. Some viewed it as a question of them alone; others interpreted "you" more inclusively, as referring to the total output of the shop. There is also the possibility of misinterpreting "last month," depending on the timing of the questioning. Using "during the last 30 days" would be much more precise and unambiguous. Typical of the many problem words are *any, could, would, should, fair, near, often, average,* and *regular.* One author recommends that after stating a question as precisely as possible, we should test each word against this checklist:

MANAGEMENT

- Does the word chosen mean what we intend?

- Does the word have multiple meanings? If so, does the context make the intended meaning clear?

- Does the word chosen have more than one pronunciation? Is there any word with similar pronunciation with which the chosen word might be confused?

- Is a simpler word or phrase suggested or possible?[13]

In the Prince Corporation study, what percentage of the population would understand the terms *conglomerate* or *multinational company?* We cause other problems when we use abstract concepts that have many overtones or emotional qualifications.[14] Without concrete referents, meanings are too vague for the researcher's needs. Examples of such words are *business, government,* and *society.* Suppose that in the Prince Corporation study we asked the question, "How involved is business in the affairs of our society?" What is meant by "involved"? What parts of "society"? Is there such a thing as "business" per se?

Shared vocabulary issues are addressed by using the following:

MANAGEMENT

- Simple rather than complex words.

- Interviewers with content knowledge.

- Commonly known, unambiguous words.

- Precise words.

Issue 13: Unsupported Assumptions.

Unwarranted assumptions contribute to many problems of question wording. A metropolitan newspaper, *Midwest Daily,* conducted a study in an attempt to discover what readers would like in its redesigned lifestyle section. One notable question asked readers: "Who selects your clothes? You or the man in your life?" In this age of educated, working, independent women, the question managed to offend a significant portion of the female readership. In addition, *Midwest Daily* discovered that many of its female readers were younger than researchers originally assumed and the only man in their lives was their father, not the spousal or romantic relationship alluded to by the questions that followed. Once men reached this question, they assumed that the paper was interested in serving only the needs of female readers. The unwarranted assumptions built into the questionnaire caused a significantly smaller response rate than expected and caused several of the answers to be uninterpretable.

Issue 14: Frame of Reference.

Inherent in word meaning problems is also the matter of a frame of reference. Each of us understands concepts, words, and expressions in light of our own experience. The U.S. Bureau of the Census wanted to know how many people were in the labor market. To learn whether a person was employed, it asked, "Did you do any work for pay or profit last week?" The researchers erroneously assumed there would be a common frame of reference between the interviewer and participants on the meaning of *work.* Unfortunately, many persons viewed themselves primarily or foremost as homemakers or students. They failed to report that they also worked at a job during the week. This difference in frame of reference resulted in a consistent underestimation of the number of people working in the United States.

In a subsequent version of the study, this question was replaced by two questions, the first of which sought a statement on the participant's major activity during the week. If the participant gave a nonwork classification, a second question was asked to determine if he or she had done any work for pay besides this major activity. This revision increased the estimate of total employment by more than 1 million people, half of them working 35 hours or more per week.[15]

The frame of reference can be controlled in two ways. First, the interviewer may seek to learn the frame of reference used by the participant. When asking participants to evaluate their reasons for judging a labor contract offer, the interviewer must learn the frames of reference they use. Is the contract offer being evaluated in terms of the specific offer, the failure of management to respond to other demands, the personalities involved, or the personal economic pressures that have resulted from a long strike?

Second, it is useful to specify the frame of reference for the participant. In asking for an opinion about the new labor contract offer, the interviewer might specify that the question should be answered based on the participant's opinion of the size of the offer, the sincerity of management, or another frame of reference of interest.

Issue 15: Biased Wording.

Bias is the distortion of responses in one direction. It can result from many of the problems already discussed, but word choice is often the major source. Obviously such words or phrases as *politically correct* or *fundamentalist* must be used with great care. Strong adjectives can be particularly distorting. One alleged opinion survey concerned with the subject of preparation for death included the following question: "Do you think that decent, low-cost funerals are sensible?" Who could be against anything that is decent or sensible? There is a question about whether this was a legitimate survey or a burial service sales campaign, but it shows how suggestive an adjective can be.

Congressional representatives have been known to use surveys as a means of communicating with their constituencies. "Would you have me vote for a balanced budget if it means higher costs for supplemental Social Security benefits which you have already earned?" Questions are often worded, however, to imply the issue stance that the representative favors.

We can also strongly bias the participant by using prestigious names in a question. In a historic survey on whether the war and navy departments should be combined into a single defense department, one survey said, "General Eisenhower says the army and navy should be combined," while the other version omitted his name. Given the first version (name included), 49 percent of the participants approved of having one department; given the second version, only 29 percent favored one department.[16]

We also can bias response through the use of superlatives, slang expressions, and fad words. These are best excluded unless they are critical to the objective of the question. Ethnic references should also be stated with care.

Issue 16: Personalization.

How personalized should a question be? Should we ask, "What would *you* do about . . .?" Or should we ask, "What would *people with whom you work* do about . . .?" The effect of personalization is shown in a classic example reported by Cantril.[17] A split test was made of a question concerning attitudes about the expansion of U.S. armed forces in 1940:

Should the United States do any of the following at this time?

A. Increase our armed forces further, even if it means more taxes.

B. Increase our armed forces further, even if you have to pay a special tax.

Eighty-eight percent of those answering question A thought the armed forces should be increased, while only 79 percent of those answering question B favored increasing the armed forces.

These and other examples show that personalizing questions changes responses, but it is not clear whether this change is for better or for worse. We often cannot tell which method is superior. Perhaps the best that can be said is that when either form is acceptable, we should choose that which appears to present the issues more realistically. If there are doubts, then split survey versions should be used.

Issue 17: Adequate Alternatives. Have we adequately expressed the alternatives with respect to the point of the question? It is usually wise to express each alternative explicitly to avoid bias. This is illustrated well with a pair of questions that were asked of matched samples of participants.[18] These forms were used:

A. Do you think most manufacturing companies that lay off workers during slack periods could arrange things to avoid layoffs and give steady work right through the year?

B. Do you think most manufacturing companies that lay off workers in slack periods could avoid layoffs and provide steady work right through the year, or do you think layoffs are unavoidable?

	A	B
Company could avoid layoffs	63%	35%
Could not avoid layoffs	22	41
No opinion	15	24

Often the above issues are simultaneously present in a single question. Exhibit 12–5 reveals several questions drawn from actual mail surveys. We've identified the problem issues and suggest one solution for improvement. While the suggested improvement might not be the only possible solution, it does correct the issues identified. What other solutions could be applied to correct the problems identified?

Response Strategy

A third major decision area in question design is the degree and form of structure imposed on the participant. The various response strategies offer options that include **unstructured response** (or *open-ended response,* the free choice of words) and **structured response** (or *closed response,* specified alternatives provided). Free responses, in turn, range from those in which the participants express themselves extensively to those in which participants' latitude is restricted by space, layout, or instructions to choose one word or phrase, as in a "fill-in" question. Closed responses typically are categorized as dichotomous, multiple-choice, checklist, rating, or ranking response strategies.

Situational Determinants of Response Strategy Choice Several situational factors affect the decision of whether to use open-ended or closed questions.[19] The decision is also affected by the degree to which these factors are known to the interviewer. The factors are:

MANAGEMENT
Tip

- Objectives of the study.
- Participant's level of information about the topic.
- Degree to which participant has thought through the topic.
- Ease with which participant communicates.
- Participant's motivation level to share information.

EXHIBIT 12–5   Reconstructing Questions

	Poor Measurement Question	Improved Measurement Question

Problems: Checklist appears to offer options that are neither exhaustive nor mutually exclusive. Also, it doesn't fully address the content needs of understanding why people choose a hotel when they travel for personal reasons versus business reasons.

Solution: Organize the alternatives. Create subsets within choices; use color or shading to highlight subsets. For coding ease, expand the alternatives so the participant does not frequently choose "Other."

Poor Measurement Question

If your purpose for THIS hotel stay included personal pleasure, for what ONE purpose specifically?

☐ Visit friend/relative   ☐ Sightseeing
☐ Weekend escape   ☐ Family event
☐ Sporting event   ☐ Vacation
☐ Other: _____

Improved Measurement Question

Which reason BEST explains your purpose for THIS personal pleasure hotel stay?

☐ Dining
☐ Shopping
☐ Entertainment
    . . . was this for a . . .   ☐ Sport-related event?
                                       ☐ Theater, musical, or other
                                          performance?
                                       ☐ Museum or exhibit?
☐ Visit friend/relative
    . . . was this for a special event?   ☐ YES   ☐ NO
☐ Vacation
    . . . was this primarily for . . .   ☐ Sightseeing?
                                            ☐ Weekend escape?
☐ Other: _____

Problems: Double-barreled question; no time frame for the behavior. "Frequently" is an undefined construct for eating behavior, depending on the study's purpose, "order" is not as powerful a concept for measurement as others (e.g., purchase, consume, or eat).

Solution: Split the questions; expand the response alternatives; clearly define the construct you want to measure.

Poor Measurement Question

When you eat out, do you frequently order appetizers and dessert?

☐ YES   ☐ NO

Improved Measurement Question

Considering your personal eating experiences away from home in the last 30 days, did you purchase an appetizer or dessert more than half the time?

	More Than Half the Time	Less Than Half the Time
Purchased an appetizer	☐	☐
Purchased a dessert	☐	☐
Purchased neither appetizers nor desserts.	☐	☐

Problems: Nonspecific time frame; likely to experience memory decay; nonspecific screen (not asking what you really need to know to qualify a participant).

Solution: Replace "ever" with a more appropriate time frame; screen for the desired behavior.

Poor Measurement Question

Have you ever attended a college basketball game?

☐ YES   ☐ NO

Improved Measurement Question

In the last six months, have you been a spectator at a basketball game played by college teams on a college campus?

☐ YES   ☐ NO

Problems: Question faces serious memory decay as a coat may not be purchased each year; aren't asking if the coat was a personal purchase or for someone else; nor do you know the type of coat purchased; nor do you know whether the coat was purchased for full price or at a discount.

Poor Measurement Question

How much did you pay for the last coat you purchased?

Improved Measurement Question

Did you purchase a dress coat for your personal use in the last 60 days?

☐ YES   ☐ NO

Thinking of this dress coat, how much did you pay? (to the nearest dollar) $ _____ .00

Was this coat purchase made at a discounted price?

☐ YES   ☐ NO

Issue 18: Objective of the Study. If the objective of the question is only to classify the participant on some stated point of view, then the closed question will serve well. Assume you are interested only in whether a participant approves or disapproves of a certain corporate policy. A closed question will provide this answer. This response strategy ignores the full scope of the participant's opinion and its antecedents. If the objective is to explore a wider territory, then an open-ended question (free-response strategy) is preferable.

Open-ended questions are appropriate when the objective is to discover opinions and degrees of knowledge. They are also appropriate when the interviewer seeks sources of information, dates of events, and suggestions, or when probes are used to secure more information. When the topic of a question is outside the participant's experience, the open-ended question may offer the better way to learn his or her level of information. Open-ended questions also help to uncover certainty of feelings and expressions of intensity, although well-designed closed questions can do the same.

Finally, it may be better to use open-ended questions when the interviewer does not have a clear idea of the participant's frame of reference or level of information. Such conditions are likely to occur in exploratory research or in pilot testing. Closed questions are better when there is a clear frame of reference, the participant's level of information is predictable, and the researcher believes the participant understands the topic.

Issue 19: Thoroughness of Prior Thought. If a participant has developed a clear opinion on the topic, a closed question does well. If an answer has not been thought out, an open-ended question may give the participant a chance to ponder a reply, then elaborate on and revise it.

Issue 20: Communication Skill. Open-ended questions require a stronger grasp of vocabulary and a greater ability to frame responses than do closed questions.

Issue 21: Participant Motivation. Experience has shown that closed questions typically require less motivation and answering them is less threatening to participants. But the response alternatives sometimes suggest which answer is appropriate; for this reason, closed questions may be biased.

While the open-ended question offers many advantages, closed questions are generally preferable in large surveys. They reduce the variability of response, make fewer demands on interviewer skills, are less costly to administer, and are much easier to code and analyze. After adequate exploration and testing, we can often develop closed questions that will perform as effectively as open-ended questions in many situations. Experimental studies suggest that closed questions are equal or superior to open-ended questions in many more applications than is commonly believed.[20]

Response Strategies Illustrated

The characteristics of participants, the nature of the topic(s) being studied, the type of data needed, and your analysis plan dictate the response strategy. Examples of the strategies described in this section are found in Exhibit 12–6.

Free-Response Strategy **Free-response questions,** also known as *open-ended questions,* ask the participant a question while the interviewer pauses for the answer (which is unaided), or the participant records his or her ideas in his or her own words in the space provided on a questionnaire.

EXHIBIT 12–6 **Alternative Response Strategies**

Free response	What factors influenced your enrollment in Metro U?
Dichotomous selection	Did you attend either of the "A Day at College" programs at Metro U? ❑ YES ❑ NO
(Paired-comparison dichotomous selection)	In your decision to attend Metro U, which was more influential: the semester calendar or the many friends attending from your hometown? ❑ Semester calendar. ❑ Many friends attending from hometown.
Multiple choice	Which one of the following factors was most influential in your decision to attend Metro U? ❑ Good academic reputation. ❑ Specific program of study desired. ❑ Enjoyable campus life. ❑ Many friends from home attend. ❑ High quality of the faculty.
Checklist	Which of the following factors encouraged you to apply to Metro U? (Check all that apply.) ❑ Tuition cost. ❑ Specific program of study desired. ❑ Parents' preferences. ❑ Opinion of brother or sister. ❑ Many friends from home attend. ❑ High school counselor's recommendation. ❑ High quality of the faculty. ❑ Good academic reputation. ❑ Enjoyable campus life. ❑ Closeness to home.
Rating	Each of the following factors has been shown to have some influence on a student's choice in applying to Metro U. Using your own experience, for each factor please tell us whether the factor was "strongly influential," "somewhat influential," or "not at all influential."

	Strongly Influential	Somewhat Influential	Not at All Influential
Good academic reputation	❑	❑	❑
Enjoyable campus life	❑	❑	❑
Many friends from home attend	❑	❑	❑
High quality of the faculty	❑	❑	❑
Semester calendar	❑	❑	❑

Ranking	Please rank-order your top three factors from the following list based on their influence in encouraging you to apply to Metro U. Use 1 to indicate the most encouraging factor, 2 the next most encouraging factor, etc. _____ Closeness to home. _____ Enjoyable campus life. _____ Good academic reputation. _____ High quality of the faculty. _____ High school counselor's recommendation. _____ Many friends from home attend. _____ Opinion of brother or sister. _____ Parents' preferences. _____ Specific program of study desired. _____ Tuition cost.

Dichotomous Response Strategy   A topic may present clearly *dichotomous* choices: Something is a fact or it is not; a participant can either recall or not recall information; a participant attended or didn't attend an event. **Dichotomous questions** suggest opposing responses, but this is not always the case. One response may be so unlikely that it would be better to adopt the middle-ground alternative as one of the two choices. For example, if we ask participants whether they are underpaid or overpaid, we are not likely to get many selections of the latter choice. The better alternatives to present to the participant might be "underpaid" and "fairly paid."

In many two-way questions, there are potential alternatives beyond the stated two alternatives. If the participant cannot accept either alternative in a dichotomous question, he or she may convert the question to a multiple-choice or rating question by writing in his or her desired alternative. For example, the participant may prefer an alternative such as "don't know" to a yes-no question, or "no opinion" when faced with a favor-oppose option. In other cases, when there are two opposing or complementary choices, the participant may prefer a qualified choice ("yes, if X doesn't occur," or "sometimes yes and sometimes no," or "about the same"). Thus, two-way questions may become multiple-choice or rating questions and these additional responses should be reflected in your revised analysis plan. Dichotomous questions generate nominal data.

Multiple-Choice Response Strategy   **Multiple-choice questions** are appropriate where there are more than two alternatives or where we seek gradations of preference, interest, or agreement; the latter situation also calls for rating questions. While such questions offer more than one alternative answer, they request the participant to make a single choice. Multiple-choice questions can be efficient, but they also present unique design problems.

Assume we ask whether mine safety rules should be determined by the (1) mine companies, (2) miners, (3) federal government, or (4) state government. One type of problem occurs when one or more responses have not been anticipated. For example, the union has not been mentioned in the alternatives on mine safety rules. Many participants might combine this alternative with "miners," but others will view "unions" as a distinct alternative. Exploration prior to drafting the measurement question attempts to identify the most likely choices.

A second problem occurs when the list of choices is not exhaustive. Participants may want to give an answer that is not offered as an alternative. This may occur when the desired response is one that combines two or more of the listed individual alternatives. Many people may believe the federal government and the miners acting jointly should set mine safety rules, but the question does not include this response. When the researcher tries to provide for all possible options, the list of alternatives can become exhausting. We guard against this by discovering the major choices through exploration and *pretesting* (discussed in detail below). We may also add the category "other (please specify)" as a safeguard to provide the participant an acceptable alternative for all other options. In our analysis of a self-administered questionnaire we may create a combination alternative.

Yet another problem occurs when the participant divides the question of mine safety into several questions, each with different alternatives. Some participants may believe rules dealing with air quality should be set by a federal agency, while those dealing with length of workday or number of workers per square foot should be set by mine company and union representatives. Still others want local management-worker committees to make rules. To address this problem, the instrument designer would need to divide the question. Pretesting should reveal if a multiple-choice question is really a multiple question.

Another challenge in alternative selection occurs when the choices are not mutually exclusive (the participant thinks two or more responses overlap). In a multiple-choice question that asks students, "Which one of the following factors was most influential in your decision to attend Metro U?" these response alternatives might be listed:

1. Good academic reputation.

2. Specific program of study desired.

3. Enjoyable campus life.

4. Many friends from home attend.

5. High quality of the faculty.

Some participants might view items 1 and 5 as overlapping, and some may see items 3 and 4 in the same way.

It is also important to seek a fair balance in choices. One study showed that an off-balance presentation of alternatives biases the results in favor of the more heavily offered side.[21] If four gradations of alternatives are on one side of an issue and two are offered reflecting the other side, responses will tend to be biased toward the better-represented side.

It is necessary in multiple-choice questions to present reasonable alternatives—particularly when the choices are numbers or identifications. If we ask, "Which of the following numbers is closest to the number of students enrolled in American colleges and universities today?" the following choices might be presented:

1. 75,000

2. 750,000

3. 7,500,000

4. 25,000,000

5. 75,000,000

It should be obvious to most participants that at least three of these choices are not reasonable, given general knowledge about the population of the United States.

The order in which choices are given can also be a problem. Numbers are normally presented in order of magnitude. This practice introduces a bias. The participant assumes that if there is a list of five numbers, the correct answer will lie somewhere in the middle of the group. Researchers are assumed to add a couple of incorrect numbers on each side of the correct one. To counteract this tendency to choose the central position, put the correct number at an extreme position more often when you design a multiple-choice question.

Order bias with non-numeric alternatives often leads the participant to choose the first alternative (*primacy effect*) or the last alternative (*recency effect*) over the middle ones. Using the *split-ballot technique* can counteract this bias. To implement this strategy in face-to-face interviews, list the alternatives on a card to be handed to the participant when the question is asked. Cards with different choice orders can be alternated to ensure positional balance. Leave the choices unnumbered on the card so participants reply by giving the choice itself rather than its identifying number. It is a good practice to use cards like this any time there are four or more choice alternatives. This saves the interviewer's reading time and ensures a more valid answer by keeping the full range of choices in front of the participant.

In most multiple-choice questions, there is also a problem of ensuring that the choices represent a unidimensional scale—that is, the alternatives to a given question should represent different aspects of the same *conceptual dimension.* In the college selection example, the list included features associated with a college that might be attractive to a student. This list, while not exhaustive, illustrated aspects of the concept "college attractiveness factors within the control of the college." The list did not mention other factors that might affect a school attendance decision. Parents and peer advice, local alumni efforts, and one's high school adviser may influence the decision, but these represent a different conceptual dimension of "college attractiveness factors"—those not within the control of the college.

Multiple-choice questions usually generate nominal data. When the choices are numbers, this response structure will produce at least interval and sometimes ratio data. When the choices represent ordered numerical ranges (for example, a question on family income) or a verbal rating scale (for example, a question on how you prefer your steak prepared: well done, medium well, medium rare, or rare), the multiple-choice question generates ordinal data.

Checklist Response Strategy   When you want a participant to give multiple responses to a single question, you will ask the question in one of three ways. If relative order is not important, the **checklist** is the logical choice. Questions like "Which of the following factors encouraged you to apply to Metro U? (Check all that apply)" force the participant to exercise a dichotomous response (yes, encouraged; no, didn't encourage) to each factor presented. Of course you could have asked for the same information as a series of dichotomous selection questions, one for each individual factor, but that would have been time- and space-consuming. Checklists are more efficient. Checklists generate nominal data.

Rating Response Strategy   **Rating questions** ask the participant to position each factor on a companion scale, either verbal, numeric, or graphic. "Each of the following factors has been shown to have some influence on a student's choice to apply to Metro U. Using your own experience, for each factor please tell us whether the factor was 'strongly influential,' 'somewhat influential,' or 'not at all influential.'" Generally, rating-scale structures generate ordinal data; some carefully crafted scales generate interval data.

Ranking Strategy   When relative order of the alternatives is important, the **ranking question** is ideal. "Please rank-order your top three factors from the following list based on their influence in encouraging you to apply to Metro U. Use 1 to indicate the most encouraging factor, 2 the next most encouraging factor, etc." The checklist strategy would provide the three factors of influence, but we would have no way of knowing the importance the participant places on each factor. Even in a personal interview, the order in which the factors are mentioned is not a guarantee of influence. Ranking as a response strategy solves this problem.

One concern surfaces with ranking activities. How many presented factors should be ranked? If you listed the 15 brands of potato chips sold in a given market, would you have the participant rank all 15 in order of preference? In most instances it is helpful to remind yourself that while participants may have been selected for a given study due to their experience or likelihood of having desired information, this does not mean that they have knowledge of all conceivable aspects of an issue, only with some. It is always better to have participants rank only those elements with which they are familiar. If you want motivation to remain strong, avoid asking a participant to rank more than seven items even if your list is longer. Ranking generates ordinal data.

All types of response strategies have their advantages and disadvantages. Several different strategies are often found in the same questionnaire, and the situational factors mentioned earlier are the major guides in this matter. There is a tendency, however, to use closed questions instead of the more flexible open-ended type. Exhibit 12–7 summarizes some important considerations in choosing between the various response strategies.

Sources of Existing Questions

The tools of data collection should be adapted to the problem, not the reverse. Thus, the focus of this chapter has been on crafting an instrument to answer specific investigative questions. But inventing and refining questions demands considerable time and effort. For some topics, a careful review of the related literature and an examination of existing instrument sourcebooks can shorten this process.

A review of literature will reveal instruments used in similar studies that may be obtained by writing the researchers or, if copyrighted, purchased through a clearinghouse. Many instruments are available through compilations and sourcebooks. While these tend to be oriented to social science applications, they are a rich source of ideas for tailoring questions to meet a manager's needs. Several compilations are recommended; we have suggested them in Exhibit 12–8.[22]

Borrowing items from existing sources is not without risk. It is quite difficult to generalize the reliability and validity of selected items or portions of a questionnaire that have been taken out of the original context. Pretesting is also warranted if it is necessary to report the reliability and validity of the instrument being constructed. Time and situation-specific fluctuations should be scrutinized. Remember that the original estimates are only as good as the sampling and testing procedures, and many researchers you borrow from may not have reported that information.

EXHIBIT 12–7 Characteristics of Response Strategies

Characteristics	Dichotomous	Multiple Choice	Checklist	Rating	Rank Ordering	Free Response
Type of data	Nominal	Nominal, ordinal, or ratio	Nominal	Ordinal or interval	Ordinal	Nominal or ratio
Usual number of answer alternatives provided	2	3 to 10	10 or fewer	3 to 7	10 or fewer	None
Desired number of participant answers	1	1	10 or fewer	7 or fewer	7 or fewer	1
Used to provide . . .	Classification	Classification, order, or specific numerical estimate	Classification	Order or distance	Order	Classification (of idea), order, or specific numerical estimate

EXHIBIT 12–8 Sources of Questions

Author(s)	Title	Source
Philip E. Converse, Jean D. Dotson, Wendy J. Hoag, and William H. McGee III, eds.	*American Social Attitudes Data Sourcebook, 1947–1978*	Cambridge, MA: Harvard University Press, 1980
Alec Gallup and George H. Gallup, ed.	*The Gallup Poll Cumulative Index: Public Opinion, 1935–1997*	Wilmington, DE: Scholarly Resources, Inc., 1999
George H. Gallup, Jr., ed.	*The Gallup Poll: Public Opinion 1998*	Wilmington, DE: Scholarly Resources, Inc., 1999
Elizabeth H. Hastings and Philip K. Hastings, eds.	*Index to International Public Opinion 1986–1987*	Westport, CT: Greenwood Press, 1988
Philip K. Hastings and Jessie C. Southwick, eds.	*Survey Data for Trend Analysis: An Index to Repeated Questions in the U.S. National Surveys Held by the Roper Public Opinion Research Center*	Storrs, CT: Roper Center for Public Opinion Research, Inc., 1974
Elizabeth Martin, Diana McDuffee, and Stanley Presser	*Sourcebook of Harris National Surveys: Repeated Questions 1963–1976*	Chapel Hill: Institute for Research in Social Science, University of North Carolina Press, 1981
National Opinion Research Center	*General Social Surveys 1972–1985: Cumulative Code Book*	Chicago: NORC, 1985
John P. Robinson, Robert Athanasiou, and Kendra B. Head	*Measures of Occupational Attitudes and Occupational Characteristics*	Ann Arbor: Institute for Social Research, University of Michigan, 1968
John P. Robinson, Philip R. Shaver, and Lawrence S. Wrightsman	*Measures of Personality and Social-Psychological Attitudes*	San Diego, CA: Academic Press, 1991

Language, phrasing, and idioms can also pose problems. Questions tend to age and may not appear (or sound) as relevant to the participant as freshly worded ones would. Integrating existing and newly constructed questions is problematic. When adjacent questions are relied on to carry context in one questionnaire and then are not selected for the customized application, the newly selected question is left without necessary meaning.[23] Whether an instrument is constructed from scratch or adapted from the ideas of others, pretesting is recommended.

Drafting and Refining the Instrument: Phase 3

MANAGEMENT
Tip

As depicted in Exhibit 12–9, Phase 3 of instrument design—drafting and refinement—is a multistep process.

1. Develop the participant-screening process (personal or phone interview), along with the introduction.

2. Arrange the measurement question sequence:
   a. Identify topic groups.
   b. Establish a logical sequence for the question groups and questions within groups.
   c. Develop transitions between these groups.

EXHIBIT 12–9   Flowchart for Instrument Design: Phase 3

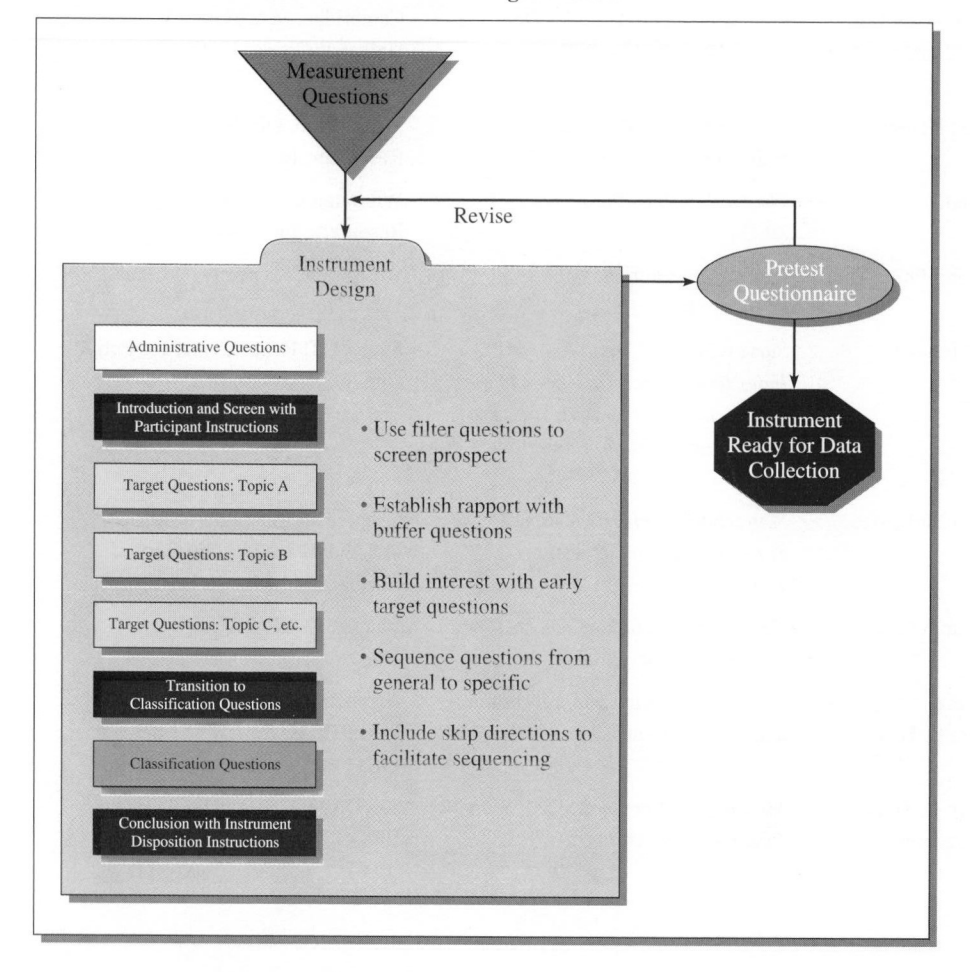

3. Prepare and insert instructions—for the interviewer or participant—including termination, skip directions, and probes.

4. Create and insert a conclusion, including a survey disposition statement.

5. Pretest specific questions and the instrument as a whole.

Introduction and Participant Screening

The introduction must supply the sample unit with the motivation to participate in the study. It must reveal enough about the forthcoming questions, usually by revealing some or all of the topics to be covered, for participants to judge their interest level and their ability to provide the desired information. In any communication study, the introduction also reveals the amount of time participation is likely to take. In a personal or phone interview, the introduction usually contains a filter or screen question to determine if the potential participant has the knowledge or experience necessary to participate in the study. The introduction also reveals the research organization or sponsor (unless the study is disguised) and possibly the objective of the study. At a minimum, a phone or personal interviewer will introduce himself or herself to help establish critical rapport with the potential participant. Exhibit 12–10 provides a sample introduction and other components of a telephone study of nonparticipants to a self-administered mail survey.

EXHIBIT 12–10   Sample Components of Communication Instruments

Introduction	Good evening. May I please speak with (name of participant)? Mr. (participant's last name), I'm (your name), calling on behalf of MindWriter Corporation. You recently had your MindWriter laptop serviced at our CompleteCare Center. Could you take five minutes to tell us what you thought of the service provided by the center?
Transition	The next set of questions asks about your family and how you enjoy spending your nonworking or personal time.
Instructions for . . . *a.* Terminating (following filter or screen question)	I'm sorry, today we are only talking with individuals who eat cereal at least three days per week, but thank you for speaking with me. (Pause for participant reply.) Good-bye.
b. Participant discontinue	Would there be a time I could call back to complete the interview? (Pause; record time.) We'll call you back then at (repeat day, time). Thank you for talking with me this evening. Or: I appreciate your spending some time talking with me. Thank you.
c. Skip directions (between questions or groups of questions)	3. Did you purchase boxed cereal in the last 7 days? ❑ Yes ❑ No (skip to question 7)
d. Disposition instructions	A postage-paid envelope was included with your survey. Please refold your completed survey and mail it to us in the postage-paid envelope.
Conclusion *a.* Phone or personal interview	That's my last question. Your insights and the ideas of other valuable customers will help us to make the CompleteCare program the best it can be. Thank you for talking with us this evening. (Pause for participant reply). Good evening.
b. Self-administered (usually precedes the disposition instructions)	Thank you for sharing your ideas about the CompleteCare program. Your insights will help us serve you better.

Measurement Question Sequencing

Often the content of one question (called a **branched question**) assumes other questions have been asked and answered. The psychological order of the questions is also important; question sequence can encourage or discourage commitment and promote or hinder the development of researcher-participant rapport.

The design of survey questions is influenced by the need to relate each question to the others in the instrument. The basic principle used to guide sequence decisions is: *The nature and needs of the participant must determine the sequence of questions and the organization of the interview schedule.* Four guidelines are suggested to implement this principle:

1. The question process must quickly awaken interest and motivate the participant to participate in the interview. Put the more interesting topical target questions early.

2. The participant should not be confronted by early requests for information that might be considered personal or ego threatening. Put questions that might influence the participant to discontinue or terminate the questioning process near the end.

3. The questioning process should begin with simple items and move to the more complex, and move from general items to the more specific. Put taxing and challenging questions later in the questioning process.

4. Changes in the frame of reference should be small and should be clearly pointed out. Use transition statements between different topics of the target question set.

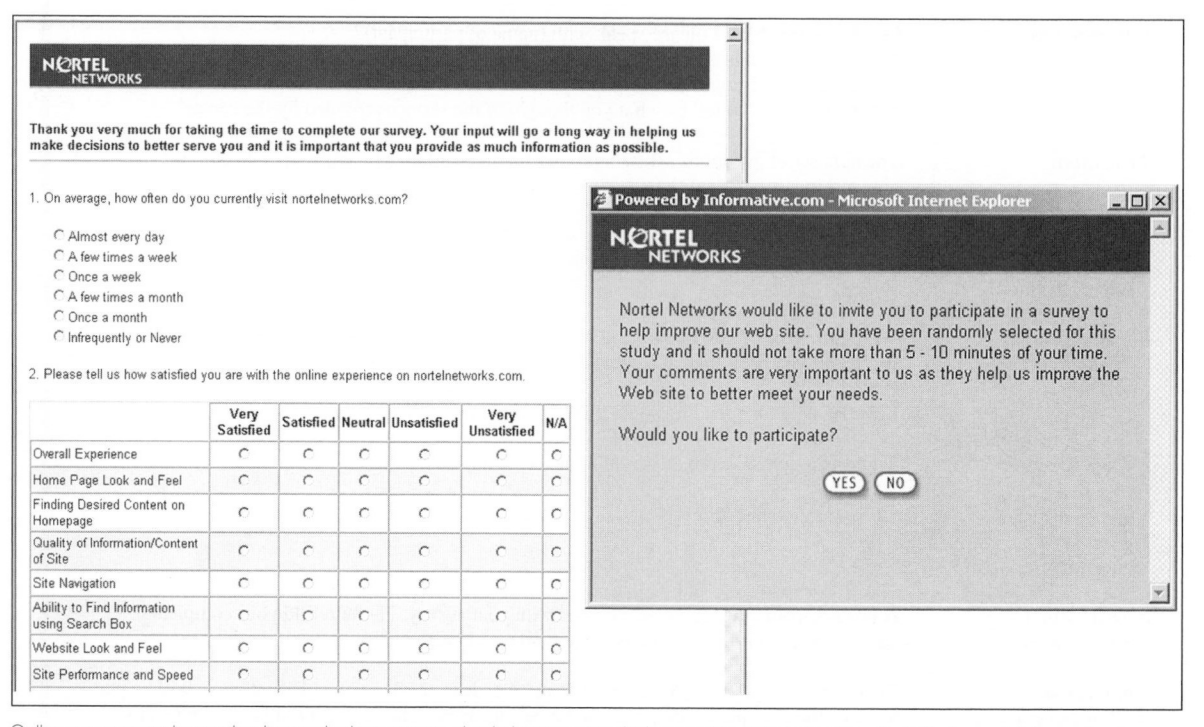

Online surveys are becoming increasingly common, due in large part to their speed in data collection, flexibility in containing not only verbal but graphical elements, access to difficult-to-contact or inaccessible participants, and their lower cost of large-sample completion. Each mouse click by a participant on one of the response buttons generates an entry in a detailed statistical database. Designers often put only one or two questions to a screen so that the participant must submit data frequently—thus eliminating total data loss caused by early participant discontinuation. Many Web surveys comprise an invitation to participate followed by a detailed survey incorporating a variety of response strategies. This online survey conducted by Informative, Inc., is designed to evaluate Nortel Networks' website. The image shows the original invitation plus the first screen of the survey containing two response strategies, a multiple-choice/single response, and a multi-item rating scale.

Awaken Interest and Motivation We awaken interest and stimulate motivation to participate by choosing or designing questions that are attention getting and not controversial. If the questions have human-interest value, so much the better. It is possible that the early questions will contribute hard data to the major study objective, but their major task is to overcome the motivational barrier.

Sensitive and Ego-Involving Information Regarding the introduction of sensitive information too early in the process, two forms of this error are common. Most studies need to ask for personal classification information about participants. Participants normally will provide these data, but the request should be made toward the end. If made immediately, it often causes participants to feel threatened, dampening their interest and motivation to continue. It is also dangerous to ask any question at the start that is too personal. For example, participants in one survey were asked whether they suffered from insomnia. When the question was asked immediately after the interviewer's introductory remarks, about 12 percent of those interviewed admitted to having insomnia. When a matched sample was asked the same question after two **buffer questions** (neutral questions designed chiefly to establish rapport with the participant), 23 percent admitted suffering from insomnia.[24]

Complex to Simplistic Deferring complex questions or simple questions that require much thought can help reduce the number of "don't know" responses that are so prevalent early in interviews.

General to Specific The procedure of moving from general to more specific questions is sometimes called the **funnel approach.** The objectives of this procedure are to learn the participant's frame of reference and to extract the full range of desired information while limiting the distortion effect of earlier questions on later ones. This process may be illustrated with the following series of questions:

1. How do you think this country is getting along in its relations with other countries?
2. How do you think we are doing in our relations with Iran?
3. Do you think we ought to be dealing with Iran differently than we are now?
4. (*If yes*) What should we be doing differently?
5. Some people say we should get tougher with Iran and others think we are too tough as it is; how do you feel about it?[25]

The first question introduces the general subject and provides some insight into the participant's frame of reference. The second question narrows the concern to a single country, while the third and fourth seek views on how the United States should deal with Iran. The fifth question illustrates a specific opinion area and would be asked only if this point of toughness had not been covered in earlier responses. Question 4 is an example of a branched question; the response to the previous question determines whether or not question 4 is asked of the participant.

There is also a risk of interaction whenever two or more questions are related. Question-order influence is especially problematic with self-administered questionnaires, because the participant is at liberty to refer back to questions previously answered. In an attempt to "correctly align" two responses, accurate opinions and attitudes may be sacrificed. The two questions shown in the following table were asked in a national survey at the start of World War II:[26]

	Percent Answering Yes	
Question	**A. Asked First**	**B. Asked First**
A. Should the United States permit its citizens to join the French and British armies?	45%	40%
B. Should the United States permit its citizens to join the German army?	31	22

Apparently, some participants who first endorsed enlistment with the Allies felt obliged to extend this privilege to joining the German army. Where the decision was first made against joining the German army, a percentage of the participants felt constrained from approving the option to join the Allies.

Question Groups and Transitions   The last question-sequencing guideline suggests arranging questions to minimize shifting in subject matter and frame of reference. Participants often interpret questions in the light of earlier questions and miss shifts of perspective or subject unless they are clearly stated. Participants fail to listen carefully and frequently jump to conclusions about the import of a given question before it is completely stated. Their answers are strongly influenced by their frame of reference. Any change in subject by the interviewer may not register with them unless it is made strong and obvious. Most questionnaires that cover a range of topics are divided into sections with clearly defined transitions between sections to alert the participant to the change in frame of reference. Exhibit 12–10 provides a sample of a transition in the CompleteCare study when measurement questions changed from service-related questions to personal and family-related questions.

Instructions

MANAGEMENT
Tip

Instructions to the interviewer or participant attempt to ensure that all participants are treated equally, thus avoiding building error into the results. Two principles form the foundation for good instructions: clarity and courtesy. Instruction language needs to be unfailingly simple and polite.

Instruction topics include:

- **Termination of an unqualified participant**—How to terminate an interview when the participant does not correctly answer the screen or filter questions.

- **Termination of a discontinued interview**—How to conclude an interview when the participant decides to discontinue.

- **Skip directions**—Instructions for moving between topic sections of an instrument when movement is dependent on the answer to specific questions or when branched questions are used.

- **Disposition instructions**—Telling the respondent to a self-administered instrument about the disposition of the completed questionnaire.

In a self-administered questionnaire, instructions must be contained within the survey instrument. Personal interviewer instructions sometimes are in a document separate from the questionnaire (a document thoroughly discussed during interviewer training) or are distinctly and clearly marked (highlighted, printed in colored ink, or boxed on the computer screen) on the data collection instrument itself. Sample instructions are presented in Exhibit 12–10.

Conclusion

The role of the conclusion is to leave the participant with the impression that his or her involvement has been valuable. Subsequent researchers may need this individual to participate in new studies. If every interviewer or instrument expresses appreciation for participation, cooperation in subsequent studies is more likely. A sample conclusion is shown in Exhibit 12–10.

Overcoming Instrument Problems

MANAGEMENT
Tip

There is no substitute for a thorough understanding of question wording, question content, and sequencing issues. However, the researcher can do several things to help improve survey results, among them:

- Build rapport with the participant.
- Redesign the questioning process.
- Explore alternative response strategies.
- Use methods other than surveying to secure the data.
- Pretest all the survey elements.

Build Rapport with the Participant   Most information can be secured by direct undisguised questioning if rapport has been developed. Rapport is particularly useful in building participant interest in the project, and the more interest participants have, the more cooperation they will give. One can also overcome participant unwillingness by providing some material compensation for cooperation. This approach has been especially successful in mail surveys.

The assurance of confidentiality also can increase participants' motivation. One approach is to give discrete assurances, both by question wording and interviewer comments and actions, that all types of behavior, attitudes, and positions on controversial or sensitive subjects are acceptable and normal. Where you can say so truthfully, *guarantee* that participants' answers will be used only in combined statistical totals. If participants are convinced that their replies contribute to some important purpose, they are more likely to be candid, even about taboo topics.

Redesign the Questioning Process   You can redesign the questioning process to improve the quality of answers by modifying the administrative process and the response strategy. We might show that confidentiality is indispensable to the administration of the

Managers may sometimes need information quickly to resolve a problem or take advantage of a brief window of opportunity. RTI International, an industry leader in the development and use of state-of-the-art software systems to improve the quality of survey data, formed a strategic alliance with Knowledge Networks to use its probability-based panel of U.S. households to conduct fast-turnaround studies. The Web-enabled panel offers clients access to a statistically valid random sample of households (not just Internet users) who participate in studies via the Internet from their homes. "It's proved a great way for researchers to get very quick access to many (or just a few) sample members," claims Tim Gabel, RTI's director of research computing.
www.rti.org
www.knowledgenetworks.com

survey by using a group administration of questionnaires, accompanied by a ballot-box collection procedure. Even in face-to-face interviews, the participant may fill in the part of the questionnaire containing sensitive information and then seal the entire instrument in an envelope. While this does not guarantee confidentiality, it does suggest it.

We can also develop appropriate questioning sequences that will gradually lead a participant from "safe" questions to those that are more sensitive. As already noted in our discussion of disguised questions, indirect questioning (using projective techniques) is a widely used approach for securing opinions on sensitive topics. The participants are asked how "other people" or "people around here" feel about a topic. It is assumed the participants will reply in terms of their own attitudes and experiences, but this outcome is hardly certain. Indirect questioning may give a good measure of the majority opinion on a topic but fail to reflect the views either of the participant or of minority segments.

With certain topics, it is possible to secure answers by using a proxy code. When we seek family income classes, we can hand the participant a card with income brackets like these:

A. Under $25,000 per year.   C. $50,000 to $74,999 per year.

B. $25,000 to $49,999 per year.   D. $75,000 and over per year.

The participant is then asked to report the appropriate bracket as either A, B, C, or D. For some reason, participants are more willing to provide such an obvious proxy measure than to verbalize actual dollar values.

Explore Alternative Response Strategies   At the original question drafting, try developing positive, negative, and neutral versions of each type of question. This practice dramatizes the problems of bias, helping you to select question wording that minimizes such problems. Sometimes use an extreme version of a question rather than the expected one.

Minimize nonresponses to particular questions by recognizing the sensitivity of certain topics. In a self-administered instrument, for example, asking a multiple-choice question about income or age, where incomes and ages are offered in ranges, is usually more successful than using a free-response question (such as, What is your age, please? _____).

We discuss the use of similar unobtrusive measures in Chapter 13.

Use Methods Other Than Surveying   Sometimes surveying will not secure the information needed. A classic example concerns a survey conducted to discover magazines read by participants. An unusually high rate was reported for prestigious magazines, and an unusually low rate was reported for tabloid magazines. The study was revised so that the subjects, instead of being interviewed, were asked to contribute their old magazines to a charity drive. The collection gave a more realistic estimate of readership of both types of magazines.[27] Another study on the use of similar unobtrusive measures cites many other types of research situations where unique techniques have been used to secure more valid information than was possible from a survey.[28]

The Value of Pretesting

The final step toward improving survey results is pretesting (see Exhibits 12–4 and 12–10). There are abundant reasons for pretesting individual questions, questionnaires, and interview schedules. In this section we discuss several and raise questions to help you plan an effective test of your instrument. Most of what we know about pretesting is prescriptive. According to contemporary authors,

> There are no general principles of good pretesting, no systematization of practice, no consensus about expectations, and we rarely leave records for each other. How a pretest was conducted, what investigators learned from it, how they redesigned their questionnaire on the basis of it—these matters are reported only sketchily in research reports, if at all.[29]

Nevertheless, conventional wisdom suggests that **pretesting** not only is an established practice for discovering errors but also is useful for training the research team. Ironically, professionals who have participated in scores of studies are more likely to pretest an instrument than is a beginning researcher hurrying to complete a project. Revising questions five or more times is not unusual. Yet inexperienced researchers often underestimate the need to follow the design-test-revise process.

Participant Interest An important purpose of pretesting is to discover participants' reactions to the questions. If participants do not find the experience stimulating when an interviewer is physically present, how will they react on the phone or in the self-administered mode? Pretesting should help to discover where repetitiveness or redundancy is bothersome or what topics were not covered that the participant expected. An alert interviewer will look for questions or even sections that the participant perceives to be sensitive or threatening or topics about which the participant knows nothing.

Meaning Questions that we borrow or adapt from the work of others carry an authoritativeness that may prompt us to avoid pretesting them, but they are often most in need of examination. Are they still timely? Is the language relevant? Do they need context from adjacent questions? Newly constructed questions should be similarly checked for meaningfulness to the participant. Does the question evoke the same meaning as that intended by the researcher? How different is the researcher's frame of reference from that of the average participant? Words and phrases that trigger a "what do you mean?" response from the participant need to be singled out for further refinement.

Question Transformation Participants do not necessarily process every word in the question. They also may not share the same definitions for the terms they hear. When this happens, participants modify the question to make it fit their own frame of reference or simply change it so it makes sense to them. Probing is necessary to discover how participants have transformed the question when this is suspected.[30]

Continuity and Flow In self-administered questionnaires, questions should read effortlessly and flow from one to another and from one section to another. In personal and telephone interviews, the sound of the question and its transition must be fluid as well. A long set of questions with nine-point scales that worked well in a mail instrument would not be effective on the telephone unless you were to ask participants to visualize the scale as the touch keys on their phone. Moreover, transitions that may appear redundant in a self-administered questionnaire may be exactly what needs to be heard in personal or telephone interviewing.

Question Sequence Question arrangement can play a significant role in the success of the instrument. Many authorities recommend starting with stimulating questions and placing sensitive questions last. Since questions concerning income and family life are most likely to be refused, this is often good advice for building trust before getting into a refusal situation. However, interest-building questions need to be tested first to be sure they are stimulating. And when background questions are asked earlier in the interview, some demographic information will be salvaged if the interview stops unexpectedly. Pretesting with a large enough group permits some experimentation with question sequence.

Skip Instructions   In interviews and questionnaires, skip patterns and their contingency sequences may not work as envisioned on paper. **Skip patterns** are designed to route or sequence the response to another question contingent on the answer to the previous question (branched questions). Pretesting in the field helps to identify problems with box-and-arrow schematics that the designers may not have thought of. By correcting them in the revision stage, we also avoid problems with flow and continuity.

Variability   With a small group of participants, pretesting cannot provide definitive quantitative conclusions but will deliver an early warning about items that may not discriminate among participants or places where meaningful subgrouping may occur in the final sample. With 25 to 100 participants in the pretest group, statistical data on the proportion of participants answering yes or no or marking "strongly agree" to "strongly disagree" can supplement the qualitative information noted by the interviewers. This information is useful for sample size calculations and for getting preliminary indications of reliability problems with scaled questions.

Length and Timing   Most draft questionnaires or interview schedules suffer from lengthiness. By timing each question and section, the researcher is in a better position to make decisions about modifying or cutting material. In personal and telephone interviews, labor is a project expense. Thus, if the budget influences the final length of the questionnaire, an accurate estimate of elapsed time is essential. Videotaped or audiotaped pretests may also be used for this purpose. Their function in reducing errors in data recording is widely accepted.

Pretesting Options

There are various ways that pretesting can be used to refine an instrument. They range from informal reviews by colleagues to creating conditions similar to those of the final study.

Researcher Pretesting   Designers typically test informally in the initial stages and build more structure into the tests along the way. Fellow instrument designers can do the first-level pretest. Their many differences of opinion are likely to create numerous suggestions for improvement. Usually at least two or three drafts can be effectively developed by bringing research colleagues into the process.

Participant Pretesting   Participant pretests require that the questionnaire be field-tested by sample participants or participant surrogates (individuals with characteristics and backgrounds similar to the desired participants).

Field pretests also involve distributing the test instrument exactly as the actual instrument will be distributed. Most studies use two or more pretests. National projects may use one trial to examine local reaction and another to check for regional differences. Although many researchers try to keep pretest conditions and times close to what they expect for the actual study, personal interview and telephone limitations make it desirable to test in the evenings or on weekends in order to interview people who are not available for contact at other times.

Test mailings are useful, but it is often faster to use a substitute procedure. In the MindWriter example, the managers who were interviewed in the exploratory study were later asked to review the pilot questionnaire. The interviewers left them alone and returned later. Upon their return, they went over the questions with each manager. They explained that they wanted the manager's reactions to question clarity and ease of answering. After several such interviews, the instrument was revised and the testing process was repeated with customers. With minor revision, the questionnaire was reproduced and prepared for inserting into the computer packing material.

Collaborative Pretests.   Different approaches taken by interviewers and the participants' awareness of those approaches affect the pretest. If the researcher alerts participants to their involvement in a preliminary test of the questionnaire, the participants are essentially being enlisted as collaborators in the refinement process. Under these conditions, detailed probing of the parts of the question, including phrases and words, is appropriate. Because of the time required for probing and discussion, it is likely that only the most critical questions will be reviewed. The participant group may therefore need to be conscripted from colleagues and friends to secure the additional time and motivation needed to cover an entire questionnaire. If friends or associates are used, experience suggests that they introduce more bias than strangers, argue more about wording, and generally make it more difficult to accomplish other goals of pretesting such as timing the length of questions or sections.[31]

Occasionally, a highly experienced researcher may improvise questions during a pretest. When this occurs, it is essential to record the interview or take detailed notes so the questionnaire may be reconstructed later. Ultimately, a team of interviewers would be required to follow the interview schedule's prearranged sequence of questions. Only experienced investigators should be free to depart from the interview schedule during a pretest and explore participants' answers by adding probes.

Noncollaborative Pretests.   When the researcher does not inform the participant that the activity is a pretest, it is still possible to probe for reactions but without the cooperation and commitment of time provided by collaborators. The comprehensiveness of the effort also suffers because of flagging cooperation. The virtue of this approach is that the questionnaire can be tested under conditions approaching those of the final study. This realism is similarly useful for training interviewers.

SUMMARY

1 The instrument design process starts with a comprehensive list of investigative questions drawn from the management-research question hierarchy. Instrument design is a three-phase process with numerous issues within each phase: (1) developing the instrument design strategy, (2) constructing and refining the measurement questions, and (3) drafting and refining the instrument.

2 Several choices must be made in designing a communication study instrument. Surveying can be a face-to-face interview, or it can be much less personal, using indirect media and self-administered questionnaires. The questioning process can be unstructured, as in in-depth interviewing, or the questions can be clearly structured. Responses may be unstructured and open-ended or structured with the participant choosing from a list of possibilities. The degree to which the objectives and intent of the questions should be disguised must also be decided.

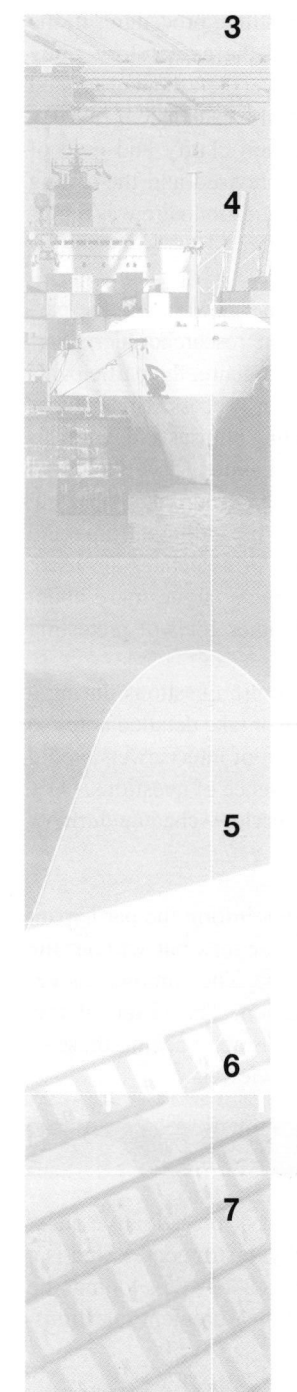

3 Instruments obtain three general classes of information. Target questions address the investigative questions and are the most important. Classification questions concern participant characteristics and allow participants' answers to be grouped for analysis. Administrative questions identify the participant, interviewer, and interview location and conditions.

4 Question construction involves three critical decision areas. They are (1) question content, (2) question wording, and (3) response strategy. Question content should pass the following tests: Should the question be asked? Is it of proper scope? Can and will the participant answer adequately?

Question wording difficulties exceed most other sources of distortion in surveys. Retention of a question should be confirmed by answering: Is the question stated in terms of a shared vocabulary? Does the vocabulary have a single meaning? Does the question contain misleading assumptions? Is the wording biased? Is it correctly personalized? Are adequate alternatives presented?

The study's objective and participant factors affect the decision of whether to use open-ended or closed questions. Each response strategy generates a specific level of data, with available statistical procedures for each data type influencing the desired response strategy. Participant factors include level of information about the topic, degree to which the topic has been thought through, ease of communication, and motivation to share information. The decision is also affected by the interviewer's perception of participant factors.

Both dichotomous response and multiple-choice questions are valuable, but on balance, the latter are preferred if only because few questions have only two possible answers. Checklist, rating, and ranking strategies are also common.

5 Question sequence can drastically affect participant willingness to cooperate and the quality of responses. Generally, the sequence should begin with efforts to awaken the participant's interest in continuing the interview. Early questions should be simple rather than complex, easy rather than difficult, nonthreatening, and obviously germane to the announced objective of the study. Frame-of-reference changes should be minimal, and questions should be sequenced so early questions do not distort replies to later ones.

6 Sources of questions for the construction of questionnaires include the literature on related research and sourcebooks of scales and questionnaires. Borrowing items has attendant risks, such as time and situation-specific problems, or reliability and validity. Incompatibility of language and idiom also needs to be considered.

7 Pretesting the instrument is recommended to identify problems before the actual collection of data begins. Insights and ideas for refining instruments result from thoroughness in pretesting. Effective revision is the result of determining participant interest, discovering if the questions have meaning for the participant, checking for participant modification of a question's intent, examining question continuity and flow, experimenting with question-sequencing patterns, evaluating skip instructions for the interviewers, collecting early warning data on item variability, and fixing the length and timing of the instrument.

KEY TERMS

administrative question   361
branched question   384
buffer question   385
checklist   379
classification question   361
dichotomous question   377
disguised question   362
double-barreled question   366
filter question   367
focus group   362

free-response question   375
funnel approach   385
in-depth interview   362
interview schedule   361
leading question   368
multiple-choice question   377
multiple question   366
pretesting   389
projective techniques   363

ranking question   379
rating question   379
screen question   367
skip pattern   390
structured question   362
structured response   373
target question   362
unstructured question   362
unstructured response   373

EXAMPLES

Company	Scenario	Page
Albany Outpatient Laser Clinic	A survey of patients awaiting eye surgery.	Throughout
American Demographics	Used TaylorNelsonSofres Intersearch to measure attitudes on copyright for a special issue on privacy.	361
Census 2000	The largest survey in the United States; provides data for a variety of purposes.	363
Gallup	Participants provide answers to questions they don't understand.	367
Informative, Inc.	A provider of real-time customer feedback to Nortel Networks through the deployment of an Internet survey.	384
Knowledge Networks	A provider of probability-sampled Web-based surveys, working with RTI International on Internet surveys.	387
KNSD	A San Diego TV station that undertook a segmentation study—KNowSanDiego—of its viewing audience.	380
Metro University*	Conducted a study of student interest in a membership-dining club.	Throughout
*Midwest Daily**	Conducted a study of readership in designing a new lifestyle section.	371
MindWriter*	Customer satisfaction survey included with repaired laptops after servicing by the CompleteCare Center.	Throughout
National Opinion Research Center	A source of questions for measuring U.S. trends.	381
Nortel Networks Corporation	A company with a portfolio of products, services, and solutions, working with Informative, Inc., to evaluate the quality of its website via an Internet survey.	384
Palm Grove High School*	The 10-year reunion planning committee is planning to assess the success of its graduates via a questionnaire.	BRTL, Throughout
Prince Corporation*	A study of corporate image and character among stakeholders.	357
Roper Starch Worldwide	A source of questions for measuring U.S. trends.	381

RTI International	A research company with extensive CATI and CAPI capabilities working with Knowledge Networks on a Web-based panel.	387
SRI (Stanford Research Institute)	The creator of the VALS survey, used by numerous product and service marketers to gain an understanding of the influences of values and lifestyles on purchase behavior.	380
TaylorNelsonSofres (TNS) Intersearch	Provider of *Express,* a weekly omnibus study used by *American Demographics* to measure attitudes about copyright issues.	361
U.S. Census Bureau	Designed a confusing question regarding participants' employment.	371
University of Michigan	The source of lifestyle index questions used in MindWriter's CompleteCare study.	362

*Due to the confidential and proprietary nature of most research, the names of some companies have been changed.

DISCUSSION QUESTIONS

Terms in Review

1. Distinguish between:
   a. Direct and indirect questions.
   b. Open-ended and closed questions.
   c. Research, investigative, and measurement questions.
   d. Alternative response strategies.

2. Why is the survey technique so popular? When is it not appropriate?

3. What special problems do open-ended questions have? How can these be minimized? In what situations are open-ended questions most useful?

4. Why might a researcher wish to disguise the objective of a study?

5. One of the major reasons why survey research may not be effective is that the survey instruments are less useful than they should be. What would you say are the four possible major faults of the survey instrument design?

6. Why is it desirable to pretest survey instruments? What information can you secure from such a pretest? How can you find the best wording for a question on a questionnaire?

7. One design problem in the development of survey instruments concerns the sequence of questions. What suggestions would you give to researchers designing their first questionnaire?

8. One of the major problems facing the designer of a survey instrument concerns the assumptions made. What are the major "problem assumptions"?

Making Research Decisions

9. Below are six questions that might be found on questionnaires. Comment on each as to whether or not it is a good question. If it is not, explain why. (Assume that no lead-in or screening questions are required. Judge each question on its own merits.)
   a. Do you read *National Geographic* magazine regularly?
   b. What percentage of your time is spent asking for information from others in your organization?
   c. When did you first start chewing gum?
   d. How much discretionary buying power do you have each year?
   e. Why did you decide to attend Big State University?
   f. Do you think the president is doing a good job now?

10. In a class project, students developed a brief self-administered questionnaire by which they might quickly evaluate a professor. One student submitted the following instrument. Evaluate the questions asked and the format of the instrument.

Professor Evaluation Form

1. Overall, how would you rate this professor? _____ Good _____ Fair _____ Poor

2. Does this professor

   a. Have good class delivery? _____

   b. Know the subject? _____

   c. Have a positive attitude toward the subject? _____

   d. Grade fairly? _____

   e. Have a sense of humor? _____

   f. Use audiovisuals, case examples, or other classroom aids? _____

   g. Return exams promptly? _____

3. What is the professor's strongest point? _____

4. What is the professor's weakest point? _____

5. What kind of class does the professor teach? _____

6. Is this course required? _____

7. Would you take another course from this professor? _____

11. Below is a copy of a cover letter and mail questionnaire received by a professor who is a member of the American Society of Training Directors. Please evaluate the usefulness and tone of the letter and the questions and format of the instrument.

Dear ASTD Member:

In partial fulfillment of master's degree work, I have chosen to do a descriptive study of the industrial trainer in our area. Using the roster of the ASTD as a mailing list, your name came to me. I am enclosing a short questionnaire and a return envelope. I hope you will take a few minutes and fill out the questionnaire as soon as possible, as the sooner the information is returned to me, the better.

Sincerely,
Professor XYZ

Questionnaire

Directions: Please answer as briefly as possible.

1. With what company did you enter the field of training? _____

2. How long have you been in the field of training? _____

3. How long have you been in the training department of the company with which you are presently employed? _____

4. How long has the training department in your company been in existence?

   _____

5. Is the training department a subset of another department? If so, what department?

   _____

6. For what functions (other than training) is your department responsible?

   _____

7. How many people, including yourself, are in the training department of your company (Local plant or establishment) _____

8. What degrees do you hold and from what institutions? _____
   Major _____   Minor _____

9. Why were you chosen for training? What special qualifications prompted your entry into training? _____

_____

_____

10. What experience would you consider necessary for an individual to enter into the field of training with your company? Include both educational requirements and actual experience. _____

Bringing Research to Life

12. Design the letter that might accompany Jason's high school reunion study to encourage participant rapport and involvement.

13. What questions should have been asked on Jason's high school reunion study to obtain the necessary data to develop the ostensibly desired newspaper article?

From Concept to Practice

14. Using Exhibits 12–1, 12–2, 12–4, and 12–9, develop the flowchart for the high school reunion study in Question 13.

WWW Exercises

Visit our website for Internet exercises related to this chapter at
www.mhhe.com/business/cooper8

CASES*

INQUIRING MINDS WANT TO KNOW—NOW!

 KNSD SAN DIEGO

 **MASTERING TEACHER LEADERSHIP**

 NCR: TEEING UP A NEW STRATEGIC DIRECTION

 PEBBLE BEACH CO.

THE CATALYST FOR WOMEN IN FINANCIAL SERVICES

 **T-SHIRT DESIGNS**

VIOLENCE ON TV

 **VOLKSWAGEN'S BEETLE**

*All cases indicating a video icon are located on the Instructor's Videotape Supplement. All nonvideo cases are in the case section of the textbook. All cases indicating a CD icon offer a data set, which is located on the accompanying CD.

REFERENCE NOTES

1. The MindWriter questionnaire used in this example is based on a pilot instrument by Cooper Research Group, Inc., 1993, for an unidentified client who shares the intellectual property rights. No part of the format, question wording, sequence, scale, or references to MindWriter © 2000 may be produced or transmitted in any form or by any means, electronic or mechanical, including photocopy, recording, or any information storage and retrieval system, without permission in writing from Cooper Research Group, Inc. Reprinted with permission.

2. Dorwin Cartwright, "Some Principles of Mass Persuasion," *Human Relations* 2 (1948), p. 266.

3. Sam Gill, "How Do You Stand on Sin?" *Tide,* March 14, 1947, p. 72.

4. Stanley L. Payne, *The Art of Asking Questions* (Princeton, NJ: Princeton University Press, 1951), p. 18.

5. *Unaided recall* gives respondents no clues as to possible answers. *Aided recall* gives them a list of radio programs that played last night and then asks them which ones they heard. See Harper W. Boyd, Jr., and Ralph Westfall, *Marketing Research,* 3rd ed. (Homewood, IL: Irwin, 1972), p. 293.

6. Gideon Sjoberg, "A Questionnaire on Questionnaires," *Public Opinion Quarterly* 18 (Winter 1954), p. 425.

7. More will be said on the problems of readability in Chapter 20, "Presenting Results: Written and Oral Reports."

8. S. A. Stouffer et al., *Measurement and Prediction: Studies in Social Psychology in World War II,* vol. 4 (Princeton, NJ: Princeton University Press, 1950), p. 709.

9. An excellent example of the question revision process is presented in Payne, *The Art of Asking Questions,* pp. 214–25. This example illustrates that a relatively simple question can go

through as many as 41 different versions before being judged satisfactory.

10. Robert L. Kahn and Charles F. Cannell, *The Dynamics of Interviewing* (New York: Wiley, 1957), p. 108.
11. Ibid., p. 110.
12. Payne, *The Art of Asking Questions,* p. 140.
13. Ibid., p. 141.
14. Ibid., p. 149.
15. Gertrude Bancroft and Emmett H. Welch, "Recent Experiences with Problems of Labor Force Measurement," *Journal of the American Statistical Association* 41 (1946), pp. 303–12.
16. National Opinion Research Center, *Proceedings of the Central City Conference on Public Opinion Research* (Denver, CO: University of Denver, 1946), p. 73.
17. Hadley Cantril, ed., *Gauging Public Opinion* (Princeton, NJ: Princeton University Press, 1944), p. 48.
18. Payne, *The Art of Asking Questions,* pp. 7–8.
19. Kahn and Cannell, *The Dynamics of Interviewing,* p. 132.
20. Barbara Snell Dohrenwend, "Some Effects of Open and Closed Questions on Respondents' Answers," *Human Organization* 24 (Summer 1965), pp. 175–84.
21. Cantril, *Gauging Public Opinion,* p. 31.
22. Jean M. Converse and Stanley Presser, *Survey Questions: Handcrafting the Standardized Questionnaire* (Beverly Hills, CA: Sage Publications, 1986), pp. 50–51.

23. Ibid., p. 51.
24. Frederick J. Thumin, "Watch for These Unseen Variables," *Journal of Marketing* 26 (July 1962), pp. 58–60.
25. F. Cannell and Robert L. Kahn, "The Collection of Data by Interviewing," in *Research Methods in the Behavioral Sciences,* eds. Leon Festinger and Daniel Katz (New York: Holt, Rinehart & Winston, 1953), p. 349.
26. Cantril, *Gauging Public Opinion,* p. 28.
27. Perceival White, *Market Analysis* (New York: McGraw-Hill, 1921).
28. Eugene J. Webb, Donald T. Campbell, Richard D. Schwartz, and Lee Sechrest, *Unobtrusive Measures: Nonreactive Research in the Social Sciences* (Chicago: Rand McNally, 1966).
29. Converse and Presser, *Survey Questions,* p. 52.
30. W. R. Belson, *The Design and Understanding of Survey Questions* (Aldershot, England: Gower, 1981), pp. 76–86.
31. The sections on methods and purposes of pretesting have been largely adapted from Converse and Presser, *Survey Questions,* pp. 51–64; and Survey Research Center, *Interviewer's Manual,* rev. ed. (Ann Arbor: Institute for Social Research, University of Michigan, 1976), pp. 133–34. For an extended discussion of the phases of pretesting, see Converse and Presser, *Survey Questions,* pp. 65–75.

REFERENCES FOR SNAPSHOTS AND CAPTIONS

Express

Interview with Brenda Edwards, vice president marketing communications, TNS Intersearch, July 2001.

Informative, Inc.

Interview with Christin Nowakowski, senior manager of marketing communications, Informative, Inc., August 20, 2001.

KNSD

McGraw-Hill Video Library.
"About VALS: The Proven Segmentation System," SRI Consulting Business Intelligence (http://future.sri.com/VALS/about.shtml).

"The VALS Segment Profiles," SRI Consulting Business Intelligence (http://future.sri.com/VALS/types.shtml).
"About Us," KNSD (NBC739) (www.knsd.com); (http://publish.nbc739.com/tvsd/email/index.shtml); (http://publish.nbc739.com/tvsd/about/.backup.history.shtml); (http://publish.nbc739.com/tvsd/about/.backup.marketing.shtml).

RTI International, Inc.

Interview with Tim Gabel, director of research computing, RTI International, Inc., December 14, 2001.

CLASSIC AND CONTEMPORARY READINGS

Converse, Jean M., and Stanley Presser. *Survey Questions: Handcrafting the Standardized Questionnaire.* Beverly Hills, CA: Sage Publications, 1986. A worthy successor to Stanley Payne's classic. Advice on how to write survey questions based on professional experience and the experimental literature.

Dillman, Don A. *Mail and Internet Surveys: The Tailored Design Method.* New York: Wiley, 1999. A contemporary treatment of Dillman's classic work.

Fink, Arlene, and Jaqueline Kosecoff. *How to Conduct Surveys: A Step-by-Step Guide.* Thousand Oaks, CA: Sage Publications, 1998. Emphasis on computer-assisted and interactive surveys and a good section on creating questions.

Kahn, Robert L., and Charles F. Cannell. *The Dynamics of Interviewing.* New York: Wiley, 1957. Chapters 5 and 6 cover questionnaire design.

Payne, Stanley L. *The Art of Asking Questions.* Princeton, NJ: Princeton University Press, 1951. An enjoyable book on the many problems encountered in developing useful survey questions. A classic resource.

Sudman, Seymour, and Norman N. Bradburn. *Asking Questions: A Practical Guide to Questionnaire Design.* San Francisco: Jossey-Bass, 1982. This book covers the major issues in writing individual questions and constructing scales. The emphasis is on structured questions and interview schedules.

CHAPTER 13

Observational Studies

Learning Objectives

After reading this chapter, you should understand . . .

1   When observation studies are most useful.

2   The distinctions between monitoring nonbehavioral and behavioral activities.

3   The strengths of the observation approach in research design.

4   The weaknesses of the observation approach in research design.

5   The three perspectives from which the observer-participant relationship may be viewed in observation studies.

6   The various designs of observation studies.

Bringing Research to Life

Myra had just finished telling Jason about a hair-raising few weeks in the Middle East during her days as a foreign correspondent when Dorrie arrived laden with mugs of coffee and cookies. "I come bearing coffee and other late-night stimulants, against my own best advice," shared Dorrie. "But I see you're already on a break."

"Just sharing scary experiences," smiled Myra.

"For scariness, nothing matches Jason's experience with Otto Darnell," claimed Dorrie.

"You mean *the* Otto Darnell, the infamous 'O Darn,' who dropped the winning pass in the Rose Bowl?" asked Myra.

"That Otto, yes," said Jason. "He dropped the pass with 20 seconds to go—and in the end zone—and all he could say was, 'Oh, darn,' hence his nickname. On paper he looked like an All-American wide receiver. But he was always dropping things, and if he were here I would not offer him a cup of coffee over Dorrie's white carpet.

"Otto's uncle owns an electronics assembly plant (ProSec) that makes miniature TV cameras for industrial and bank security and such. Right after the Rose Bowl, he asked us up, to maybe take Otto's mind off his football foul-up and also to brainstorm a production problem. Around 5 o'clock every afternoon, the quality of assembled cameras deteriorated. Uncle Fred had six women assembling the cameras—good, loyal, hard workers—and he could not pinpoint the quality problem. If he sat and watched them, they were on their best behavior and followed standard operating procedures, and their quality stayed up. Likewise, if they knew he was spying on them with one of his cameras. But if they suspected that he'd stopped watching, bugs began to creep into quality, and always around 5 P.M.

"Otto and I questioned the women. They denied deviating from the standards, and, of course, they were not going to 'rat out' anybody in their group. But Otto was watching carefully and told me later that five of the women took covert glances at a sixth, Bertha, who looked fidgety. She was a huge, good-natured, serious woman, ferociously devoted to an honest day's work, to my uncle, and to the company; but she looked nervous. And she would not look Otto in the eyes.

"Otto gets the idea of filming the six women from outside, without much likelihood that they would see us, so long as we didn't attract their attention to the window.

"The problem was, this was a fifth-story window. So we decided to lower a camera, attached by cable to a TV-video monitor-recorder, by a pole from a sixth-floor window. I was supposed to watch the monitor and tell Otto, 'pan left,' 'pan right,' until we had rolled enough tape to see where the problem was.

"No sooner had Otto opened the window than I heard, 'Oh, darn.' He had dropped the camera, and I could see it swinging below the window by its thread of optical cable. So I leaned way out the window to snare it, knowing that if Otto were to set his hands on it, he would surely make matters worse. Not that they weren't bad enough—as time was flying.

"I felt Otto grab me by the ankles and amid my frantic protests he lowered me out the window. In a stage whisper he said, 'Grab it, and hold it, and pan it left and right, very slowly.'

"So there I was upside down and trying not to look down at the five-and-a-half-story drop into a snowbank.

"I could see the six women at work, and every now and then Bertha would dip her hand into her left smock pocket and bring her hand up to her mouth and then reach down to pick up a chip and press the chip into the circuit board. This was not standard operation.

"The camera happened to be pointed toward Bertha when I carelessly let it rap against the window. Bertha glances up, stops the assembly line and warily strolls over to the window and cranks it open. All of this was against standard procedures, of course—stopping the line, leaving the workstation, opening the window, and I had a very bad feeling about what was going to happen next. And I was dizzy, and nauseous, and cold.

"She sees me, and with the camera pointing straight in her face. She reaches back into her hair and withdraws a hat pin which is holding her bandanna in place. Then she thrusts the hatpin past the camera and sticks the huge pin in Otto's big ham of a hand, and that was when he yelped, 'Oh, darn,' and let go of my left ankle.

"Now the video goes black, as I let go of the camera and it breaks loose from its cable. There I am, swinging around, first looking in the window, looking at the moon, looking at the parking lot, looking down at the snowbank maybe 40 feet below, all at the same time, it seemed.

"I must have grabbed Bertha, because I remember that Otto was pulling up and Bertha was pulling back, and Bertha won, thank goodness! Bertha falls backward, pulling me through the window on top of her.

"Everyone calmed down when they recognized me. And we had the good wits to check the contents of Bertha's pocket. It was full of greasy, salted peanuts. The poor gal was not able to wait until her 6 P.M. dinner break and was feeding herself secretly and quietly. Then with greasy fingers she would pick up a chip and press the greasy pins into the circuit board.

"Uncle Fred advanced the supper hour to 4:45 and the problem disappeared."

"Quite a triumph of observation," said Myra.

"It was craziness," said Jason. "I was a lunatic to trust Otto to lean out the window and not drop the camera. It took us half an hour the next morning to dig the camera out of a snowbank, and I could not stop thinking, this might be me, buried head down in the snow. Overall, it was no great coup of observation. I mean, ask yourself, why hadn't the people in quality control noticed grease on the circuit boards?"

The Uses of Observation

Much of what we know comes from observation. We notice coworkers' reactions to political intrigue, the sounds of the assembly area, the smell of perfume, the taste of office coffee, the smoothness of the vice president's marble desk, and a host of other stimuli. While such observation may be a basis for knowledge, the collection processes are often haphazard.

Observation qualifies as scientific inquiry when it is conducted specifically to answer a research question, is systematically planned and executed, uses proper controls, and provides a reliable and valid account of what happened. The versatility of observation makes it an indispensable primary source method and a supplement for other methods. Many academics have a limited view of observation, relegating it to a minor technique of field data collection. This ignores its potential for forging business decisions and denies its historic stature as a creative means of obtaining primary data. Exhibit 13–1 depicts the use of observation in the research process.

EXHIBIT 13–1 **Observation and the Research Process**

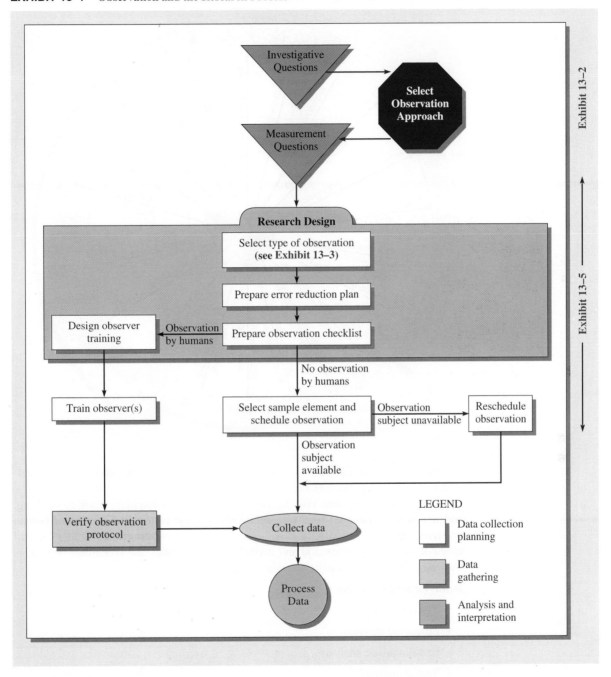

In Chapter 11, we said that research designs are classified by the *approach* used to gather primary data: We can *observe*, or we can *communicate*. Exhibit 13–2 describes the conditions under which observation is an appropriate method for data collection. It also contrasts those conditions with ones we are familiar with from the communication

EXHIBIT 13–2   Selecting the Data Collection Method

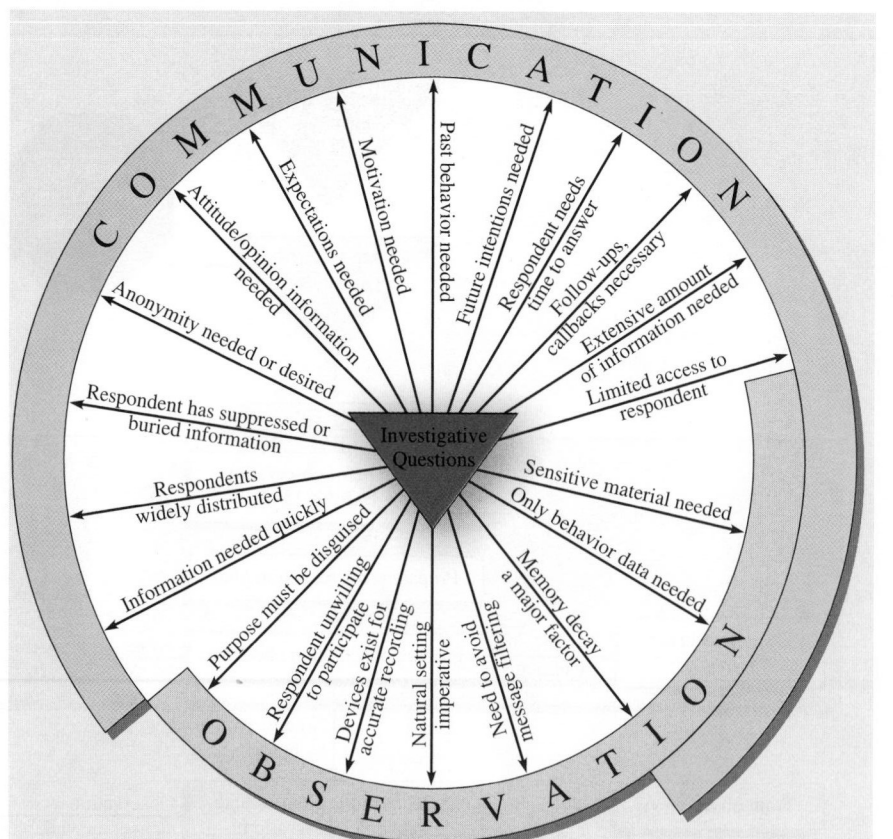

modes discussed in Chapter 11—personal interview, telephone interview, and self-administered survey (see Exhibit 11–2).

Besides collecting data visually, observation involves listening, reading, smelling, and touching. Behavioral scientists define observation in terms of animal or human behavior, but this too is limiting. As used in this text, **observation** includes the full range of monitoring behavioral and nonbehavioral activities and conditions, which, as shown in Exhibit 13-3, can be classified roughly as follows:

Behavioral observation

- Nonverbal analysis
- Linguistic analysis
- Extralinguistic analysis
- Spatial analysis

Nonbehavioral observation

- Record analysis
- Physical condition analysis
- Physical process analysis

EXHIBIT 13–3   **Selecting an Observation Approach**

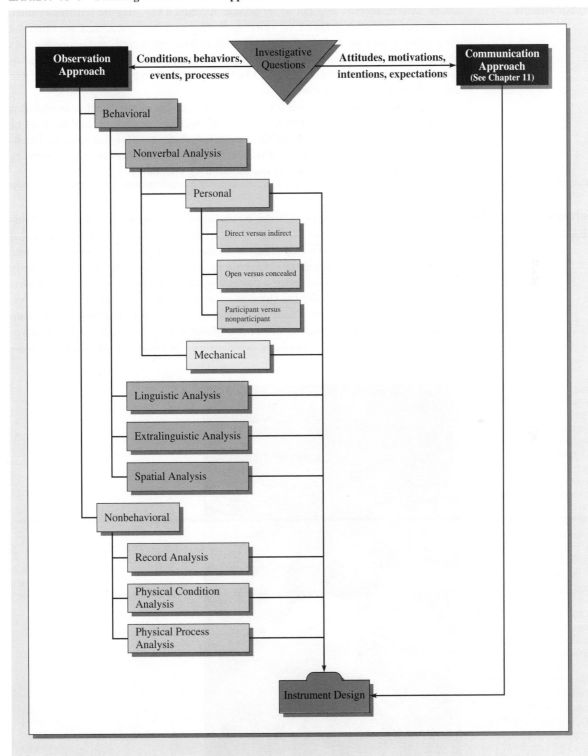

Nonbehavioral Observation

A prevalent form of observation research is **record analysis.** This may involve histori-cal or current records and public or private records. They may be written, printed, sound-recorded, photographed, or videotaped. Historical statistical data are often the only sources used for a study. Analysis of current financial records and economic data also provides a major data source for studies. Other examples of this type of observa-tion are the *content analysis* (described in Chapter 15) of competitive advertising and the analysis of personnel records.

Physical condition analysis is typified by store audits of merchandise availability, studies of plant safety compliance, analysis of inventory conditions, and analysis of financial statements. **Process** or **activity analysis** includes time/motion studies of man-ufacturing processes and analysis of traffic flows in a distribution system, paperwork flows in an office, and financial flows in the banking system.

Behavioral Observation

The observational study of persons can be classified into four major categories.[1] **Non-verbal behavior** is the most prevalent of these and includes body movement, motor expressions, and even exchanged glances. At the level of gross body movement, one might study how a salesperson travels a territory. At a fine level, one can study the body movements of a worker assembling a product or time-sample the activity of a depart-ment's work force to discover the share of time each worker spends in various ways. More abstractly, one can study body movement as an indicator of interest or boredom, anger or pleasure in a certain environment. Motor expressions such as facial move-ments can be observed as a sign of emotional states. Eye blink rates are studied as indi-

Space and organization consultants use observation to learn how individuals work, organize, and store material needed for productive work and generally use work space. Both nonverbal behaviors (movement of piles, movement around obstacles, repeated sorting, frantic searching, phone and computer use patterns, etc.) and linguistic behaviors (frustrated utterances, etc.) can be observed via human or mechanical means to aid the consultant in finding solutions. After years of observation, reorganizing guru and author Julie Morgenstern claims everyone can organize his or her space for more efficient and satisfying work. Based on the evidence of clutter and seeming disorganization in this office, we can only hope that not only her research but also her solutions are up to the task. www.juliemorgenstern.com

cators of interest in advertising messages. Exchanged glances are of interest in studies of interpersonal behavior.

Linguistic behavior is a second frequently used form of behavior observation. One simple type familiar to most students is the tally of "ahs" or other annoying sounds or words a professor makes or uses during a class. More serious applications are the study of a sales presentation's content or the study of what, how, and how much information is conveyed in a training situation. A third form of linguistic behavior involves interaction processes that occur between two people or in small groups. Bales has proposed one widely used system for classifying such linguistic interactions.[2]

Behavior also may be analyzed on an extralinguistic level. Sometimes **extralinguistic behavior** is as important a means of communication as linguistic behavior. One author has suggested there are four dimensions of extralinguistic activity.[3] They are (1) *vocal,* including pitch, loudness, and timbre; (2) *temporal,* including the rate of speaking, duration of utterance, and rhythm; (3) *interaction,* including the tendencies to interrupt, dominate, or inhibit; and (4) *verbal stylistic,* including vocabulary and pronunciation peculiarities, dialect, and characteristic expressions. These dimensions could add substantial insight to the linguistic content of the interactions between supervisors and subordinates or salespeople and customers.

A fourth type of behavior study involves **spatial relationships,** especially how a person relates physically to others. One form of this study, *proxemics,* concerns how people organize the territory about them and how they maintain discrete distances between themselves and others. A study of how salespeople physically approach customers and a study of the effects of crowding in a workplace are examples of this type of observation.

Often in a study, the researcher will be interested in two or more of these types of information and will require more than one observer. In these forms of behavior study, it is also important to consider the relationship between observers and participants.

Evaluation of the Observational Method

Observation is the only method available to gather certain types of information. The study of records, mechanical processes, and young children, as well as other inarticulate participants, falls into this category. Another value of observation is that we can collect the original data at the time they occur. We need not depend on reports by others. Every respondent filters information no matter how well intentioned he or she is. Forgetting occurs, and there are reasons why the respondent may not want to report fully and fairly. Observation overcomes many of these deficiencies of questioning.

A third strength is that we can secure information that most participants would ignore either because it is so common and expected or because it is not seen as relevant. For example, if you are observing buying activity in a store, there may be conditions important to the research study that the shopper does not notice or consider important, such as: What is the weather? What is the day of the week or the time of the day? How heavy is customer traffic? What is the level of promotional activity in competing stores? We can expect to learn only a few of the answers to these questions from most participants.

The fourth advantage of observation is that it alone can capture the whole event as it occurs in its natural environment. Whereas the environment of an experiment may seem contrived to participants, and the number and types of questions limit the range of responses gathered from respondents, observation is less restrictive than most primary collection methods. Also, the limitations on the length of data collection activities imposed by surveys or experiments are relaxed for observation. You may be interested in all the conditions surrounding a confrontation at a bargaining session between union and management representatives. These sessions may extend over time, and any effort to study the unfolding of the negotiation is facilitated by observation. Questioning could seldom provide the insight of observation for many aspects of the negotiation process.

Finally, participants seem to accept an observational intrusion better than they respond to questioning. Observation is less demanding of them and normally has a less biasing effect on their behavior than does questioning. In addition, it is also possible to conduct disguised and unobtrusive observation studies much more easily than disguised questioning.

The observational method has some research limitations. The observer normally must be at the scene of the event when it takes place, yet it is often impossible to predict where and when the event will occur. One way to guard against missing an event is to observe for prolonged periods until it does occur, but this strategy brings up a second disadvantage. Observation is a slow and expensive process that requires either human observers or costly surveillance equipment.

A third limitation of observation is that its most reliable results are restricted to information that can be learned by overt action or surface indicators. To go below the surface, the observer must make inferences. Two observers will probably agree on the nature of various surface events, but the inferences they draw from such data are much more variable.

Fourth, the research environment is more likely suited to subjective assessment and recording of data than to controls and quantification of events. When control is exercised through active intervention by the researchers, their participation may threaten the validity of what is being assessed. Even when sample sizes are small, the observation records can be disproportionately large and difficult to analyze.

Fifth, observation is limited as a way to learn about the past. It is similarly limited as a method by which to learn what is going on in the present at some distant place. It is also difficult to gather information on such topics as intentions, attitudes, opinions, or preferences. Nevertheless, any consideration of the merits of observation confirms its value when used with care and understanding.

The Observer-Participant Relationship

Interrogation presents a clear opportunity for interviewer bias. The problem is less pronounced with observation but is still real. The relationship between observer and participant may be viewed from three perspectives:

- Whether the observation is direct or indirect.
- Whether the observer's presence is known or unknown to the participant.
- What role the observer plays.

Directness of Observation

Direct observation occurs when the observer is physically present and personally monitors what takes place. This approach is very flexible because it allows the observer to react to and report subtle aspects of events and behaviors as they occur. He or she is also free to shift places, change the focus of the observation, or concentrate on unexpected events if they occur. A weakness of this approach is that observers' perception

Television networks and stations measure audience viewing patterns to assist in making numerous decisions, among them program continuation or discontinuation, program location on the schedule, and advertising rates. They share this viewer data with advertisers, who then use the data to make network, station, and program selections. Nielsen Media Research partially collects its television viewer data for both broadcast and cable with electronic devices labeled "people meters." The people meter measures three things: the tuning station of the TV set (on, off, time); what channel/station is being tuned; and who is watching (via assigned code buttons). Additionally, households in the 53 largest markets have set-tuning meters that measure and transmit set-tuning data on a daily basis. There are 5,000 households in the national sample and more than 20,000 households in various local samples used to represent more than 102 million TV households in the United States. To supplement the people meter data, more than 1.6 million households provide written viewership diaries during four measurement periods known as "sweeps." Sweeps, usually two weeks long, occur in November, February, May, and July of each year. Which part of Nielsen's research design employs observation techniques?
www.nielsenmedia.com

circuits may become overloaded as events move quickly, and observers must later try to reconstruct what they were not able to record. Also, observer fatigue, boredom, and distracting events can reduce the accuracy and completeness of observation.

Indirect observation occurs when the recording is done by mechanical, photographic, or electronic means. For example, a special camera that takes one frame every second may be mounted in a department of a large store to study customer and employee movement. Indirect observation is less flexible than direct observation but is also much less biasing and may be less erratic in accuracy. Another advantage of indirect observation is that the permanent record can be reanalyzed to include many different aspects of an event. Electronic recording devices, which have improved in quality and declined in cost, are being used more frequently in observation research.

Concealment

A second factor affecting the observer-participant relationship concerns whether the participant should know of the observer's presence. When the observer is known, there is a risk of atypical activity by the participant. This is why Otto dangled Jason out the

The Point of Purchase Advertising Institute estimates that manufacturers provide retailers with more than $9 billion of display materials each year. Manufacturers then hire researchers to evaluate whether these displays have been used, and used as intended.

sixth-floor window. The initial entry of an observer into a situation often upsets the activity patterns of the participants, but this influence usually dissipates quickly, especially when participants are engaged in some absorbing activity or the presence of observers offers no potential threat to the participants' self-interest. The potential bias from participant awareness of observers is always a matter of concern, however.

Observers use **concealment** to shield themselves from the object of their observation. Often, technical means such as one-way mirrors, hidden cameras, or microphones are used. These methods reduce the risk of observer bias but bring up a question of ethics. Hidden observation is a form of spying, and the propriety of this action must be reviewed carefully.

A modified approach involves partial concealment. The presence of the observer is not concealed, but the objectives and participant of interest are. A study of selling methods may be conducted by sending an observer with a salesperson who is making calls on customers. However, the observer's real purpose may be hidden from both the salesperson and the customer (e.g., she may pretend she is analyzing the display and layout characteristics of the stores they are visiting).

SNAPSHOT

Progressive Wants Your Autograph™

Progressive Insurance, Inc., started near Cleveland in 1937 by two lawyers, has been shaking up the insurance industry for decades. But its maverick attitude has become increasingly evident during the last 10 years. Its impressive string of firsts includes: 24-hour service, insurance over the Web, Immediate Response© (which settles claims within minutes rather than weeks using specialized technology-equipped sports utility vehicles), and its free rate comparison service. Recently, some Texas drivers have been experiencing lower insurance rates due to a patented information transfer process being tested called Autograph™. Most drivers' insurance rates are determined based on a company's past realized losses with a class of automobile and a class of driver. Autograph™ provides Progressive with detailed data about when, where, and how much the insured vehicle has been driven. The data are reported periodically and automatically using cellular communication technology. Thus automobile insurance rates are based on current, not historic, driving patterns—if you drive less, you pay less—similar to the way phone, electric, and gas utilities price their services. The Autograph™ collection device is about the size of a videocassette. And this rate-reducer also packs some special safety features: for an additional monthly fee, Progressive can track your vehicle if it's stolen, remotely unlock your doors, offer roadside and directional assistance, and even detect when your battery is low.

www.progressive.com

Structured, human, participant observation within the retail environment is used to judge customer service, as done here by a male mystery shopper evaluating the product knowledge and selling skills of a female sales associate.

Participation

The third observer-participant issue is whether the observer should participate in the situation while observing. A more involved arrangement, **participant observation,** exists when the observer enters the social setting and acts as both an observer and a participant. Sometimes he or she is known as an observer to some or all of the participants; at other times the true role is concealed. While reducing the potential for bias, this again raises an ethical issue. Often participants will not have given their consent and will not have knowledge of or access to the findings. After being deceived and having their privacy invaded, what further damage could come to the participants if the results became public? This issue needs to be addressed when concealment and covert participation are used.

Participant observation makes a dual demand on the observer. Recording can interfere with participation, and participation can interfere with observation. The observer's role may influence the way others act. Because of these problems, participant observation is used less in business research than, say, in anthropology or sociology. It is typically restricted to cases where nonparticipant observation is not practical—for example, a study of the functioning of a traveling auditing team.

Conducting an Observational Study

The Type of Study

Observation is found in almost all research studies, at least at the exploratory stage. Such data collection is known as **simple observation.** Its practice is not standardized, as one would expect, because of the discovery nature of exploratory research. The decision to use observation as the major data collection method may be made as early as the moment the researcher moves from research questions to investigative questions. The latter specify the outcomes of the study—the specific questions the researcher must answer with collected data. If the study is to be something other than exploratory, **systematic observation** employs standardized procedures, trained observers, schedules for recording, and other devices for the observer that mirror the scientific procedures of other primary data methods. Systematic studies vary in the emphasis placed on recording and encoding observational information:

> At one end of the continuum are methods that are unstructured and open-ended. The observer tries to provide as complete and nonselective a description as possible. On the other end of the continuum are more structured and predefined methods that itemize, count, and categorize behavior. Here the investigator decides beforehand which behavior will be recorded and how frequently observations will be made. The investigator using structured observation is much more discriminating in choosing which behavior will be recorded and precisely how [it is] to be coded.[4]

One author classifies observational studies by the degree of structure in the environmental setting and the amount of structure imposed on the environment by the researcher,[5] as reflected in Exhibit 13–4. The researcher conducting a class 1, completely unstructured, study would be in a natural or field setting endeavoring to adapt to the culture. A typical example would be an ethnographic study in which the researcher, as a participant-observer, becomes a part of the culture and describes in great detail everything surrounding the event or activity of interest. Donald Roy, in the widely used case in organizational behavior, "Banana Time," took a punch press job in a factory to describe the rituals that a small work group relied on to make their highly repetitive, monotonous work bearable.[6] With other purposes in mind, business researchers may use this type of study for hypothesis generation.

Class 4 studies—completely structured research—are at the opposite end of the continuum from completely unstructured field investigations. The research purpose of class 4 studies is to test hypotheses; therefore, a definitive plan for observing specific, operationalized behavior is known in advance. This requires a measuring instrument, called an **observational checklist,** which is analogous to a questionnaire. Exhibit 13–5 shows the parallels between survey design and checklist development. Checklists should possess a high degree of precision in defining relevant behavior or acts and have mutually exclusive and exhaustive categories. The coding is frequently closed, thereby simplifying data analysis. The participant groups being observed must be comparable and the laboratory conditions identical. The classic example of a class 4 study was Bales's investigation into group interaction.[7] Many team-building, decision-making, and assessment center studies follow this structural pattern.

The two middle classes of observation studies emphasize the best characteristics of either researcher-imposed controls or the natural setting. In class 2, the researcher uses the facilities of a laboratory—videotape recording, two-way mirrors, props, and stage sets—to introduce more control into the environment while simultaneously reducing the time needed for observation. In contrast, a class 3 study takes advantage of a structured observational instrument in a natural setting.

EXHIBIT 13–4   **Classification of Observation Studies**

Research Class	Environment	Purpose	Research Tool
1. Completely unstructured	Natural setting	Generate Hypotheses	
2. Unstructured	Laboratory		
3. Structured	Natural setting		Observation Checklist
4. Completely structured	Laboratory	Test Hypotheses	Observation Checklist

EXHIBIT 13–5   Flowchart for Observation Checklist Design

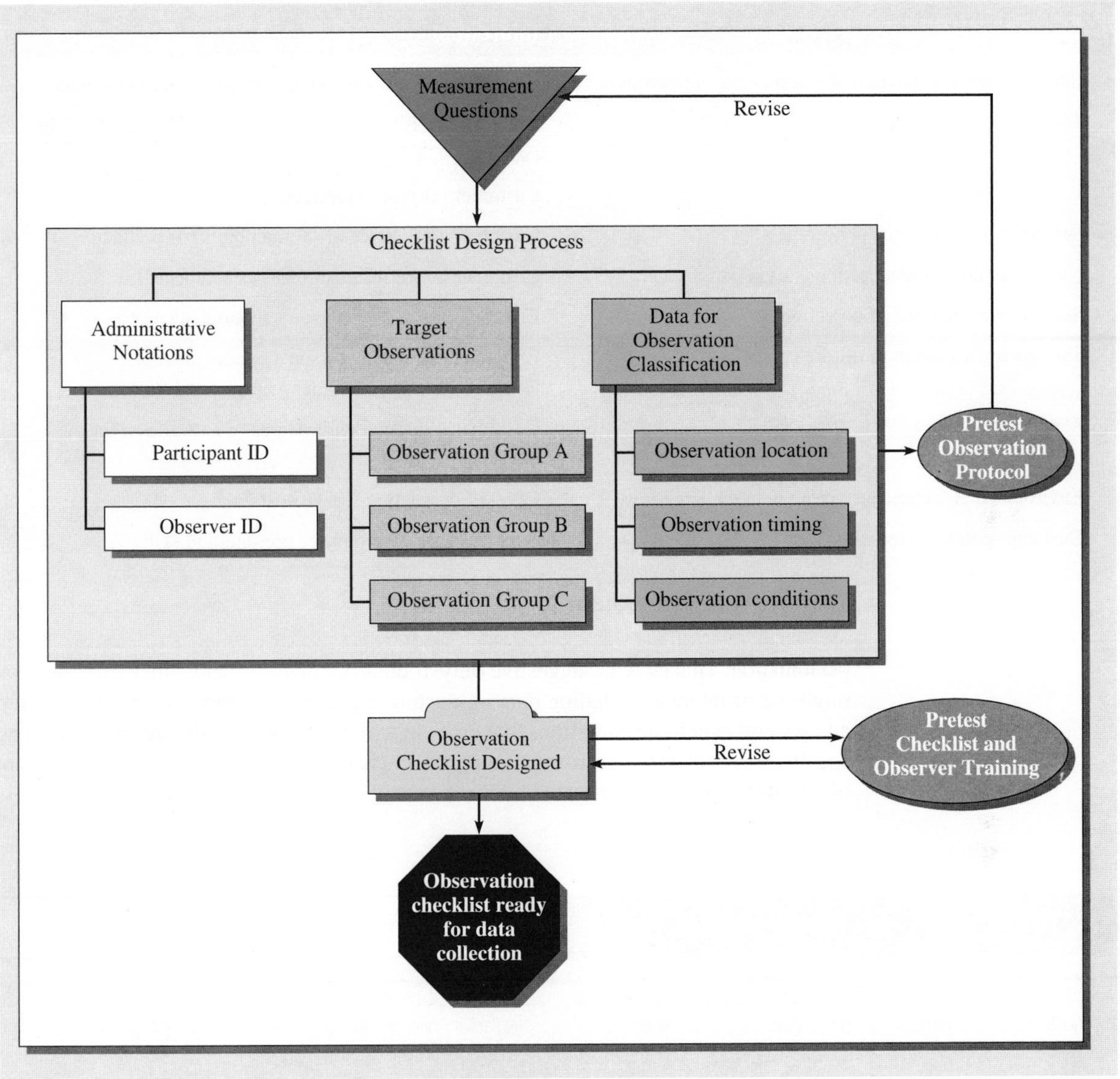

Content Specification

Specific conditions, events, or activities that we want to observe determine the observational reporting system (and correspond to measurement questions). To specify the observation content, we should include both the major variables of interest and any other variables that may affect them. From this cataloging, we then select those items we plan to observe. For each variable chosen, we must provide an operational definition if there is any question of concept ambiguity or special meanings. Even if the concept is a common one, we must make certain that all observers agree on the measurement terms by which to record results. For example, we may agree that variable W will be reported by count, while variable Y will be counted and the effectiveness of its use judged qualitatively.

Observation may be at either a *factual* or an *inferential* level. Exhibit 13–6 shows how we could separate the factual and inferential components of a salesperson's

EXHIBIT 13–6   Content of Observation: Factual Versus Inferential

Factual	Inferential
Introduction/identification of salesperson and customer.	Credibility of salesperson. Qualified status of customer.
Time and day of week.	Convenience for the customer. Welcoming attitude of the customer.
Product presented.	Customer interest in product.
Selling points presented per product.	Customer acceptance of selling points per product.
Number of customer objections raised per product.	Customer concerns about features and benefits.
Salesperson's rebuttal of objection.	Effectiveness of salesperson's rebuttal attempts.
Salesperson's attempt to restore controls.	Effectiveness of salesperson's control attempt. Consequences for customer who prefers interaction.
Length of interview.	Customer's/salesperson's degree of enthusiasm for the interview.
Environmental factors interfering with the interview.	Level of distraction for the customer.
Customer purchase decision.	General evaluation of sales presentation skill.

presentation. This table is suggestive only. It does not include many other variables that might be of interest, including data on customer purchase history; company, industry, and general economic conditions; the order in which sales arguments are presented; and specific words used to describe certain product characteristics. The particular content of observation will also be affected by the nature of the observation setting.

S N A P S H O T

Pervasive Commerce: Science Fiction or Our Future?

A consortium of 36 consumer packaged goods (CPG) manufacturers, research companies, and universities is working to change the way consumers generate and deliver purchase and consumption information, as well as how this information is integrated with detailed supply chain management information. If the Auto ID Center gets its way, all future CPGs will contain radio frequency identification (RFID) smart labels that will send signals to Internet databases and track a specific product unit through manufacturing, warehousing, retailing, consumer storage and consumption, and the recycling center. The RFID embedded label could continuously transmit information ranging from a unique electronic product code, to consumption status, to environmental conditions like temperature and moisture content, which influence product freshness.

This research methodology would still require consumer compliance, similar to the way consumers agree to be part of ACNielsen's Homescan panel today. An agree-able consumer would permit an "interrogator" to be placed in his or her car, home, office, or some combination. The interrogator, through its antenna, transceiver, and decoder, would receive information from the RFID tag and transmit information to a host computer. While the RFID industry has been growing aggressively, it still has too little production capacity to make enough tags for this vision to be a reality. And our refrigerators and microwaves would need to be equipped to read and transmit data, too. But according to John Stermer, ACNielsen's senior vice president for e-business market development, "There is no debate that pervasive commerce, intelligently deployed, will redefine the competitive landscape for the CPG industry."

www.autoidcenter.org
www.acnielsen.com
http://trolleyscan.com.za

Observer Training

There are a few general guidelines for the qualification and selection of observers:

- **Concentration:** Ability to function in a setting full of distractions.
- **Detail-oriented:** Ability to remember details of an experience.
- **Unobtrusive:** Ability to blend with the setting and not be distinctive.
- **Experience level:** Ability to extract the most from an observation study.

An obviously attractive observer may be a distraction in some settings but ideal in others. The same can be said for the characteristics of age or ethnic background.

If observation is at the surface level and involves a simple checklist or coding system, then experience is less important. Inexperience may even be an advantage if there is a risk that experienced observers may have preset convictions about the topic. Regardless, most observers are subject to fatigue, halo effects, and **observer drift,** which refers to a decay in reliability or validity over time that affects the coding of categories.[8] Only intensive videotaped training relieves these problems.

The observers should be thoroughly versed in the requirements of the specific study. Each observer should be informed of the outcomes sought and the precise content elements to be studied. Observer trials with the instrument and sample videotapes should be used until a high degree of reliability is apparent in their observations. When there are interpretative differences between observers, they should be reconciled.

Data Collection

The data collection plan specifies the details of the task. In essence it answers the questions *who, what, when, how,* and *where.*

Who? What qualifies a participant to be observed? Must each participant meet a given criterion—those who initiate a specific action? Who are the contacts to gain entry (in an ethnographic study), the intermediary to help with introductions, the contacts to reach if conditions change or trouble develops? Who has responsibility for the various aspects of the study? Who fulfills the ethical responsibilities to the participants?

What? The characteristics of the observation must be set as sampling elements and units of analysis. This is achieved when event-time dimension and "act" terms are defined. In **event sampling,** the researcher records selected behavior that answers the investigative questions. In **time sampling,** the researcher must choose among a time-point sample, continuous real-time measurement, or a time-interval sample. For a time-point sample, recording occurs at fixed points for a specified length. With continuous measurement, behavior or the elapsed time of the behavior is recorded. Like continuous measurement, time-interval sampling records every behavior in real time but counts the behavior only once during the interval.[9]

Assume the observer is instructed to observe a quality control inspection for 10 minutes out of each hour (a duration of two minutes each for five times). Over a prolonged period, if the samples are drawn randomly, time sampling can give a good estimate of the pattern of activities. In a time-interval sampling of workers in a department, the outcome may be a judgment of how well the department is being supervised. In a study of sales presentations using continuous real-time sampling, the research outcome may be an assessment of a given salesperson's effectiveness or the effectiveness of different types of persuasive messages.

Other important dimensions are defined by acts. What constitutes an *act* is established by the needs of the study. It is the basic unit of observation. Any of the following could be defined as an act for an observation study:

- A single expressed thought.
- A physical movement.
- A facial expression.
- A motor skill.

Although acts may be well defined, they often present difficulties for the observer. A single statement from a sales presentation may include several thoughts about product advantages, a rebuttal to an objection about a feature, or some remark about a competitor. The observer is hard-pressed to sort out each thought, decide whether it represents a separate unit of observation, and then record it quickly enough to follow continued statements.

When?　Is the time of the study important, or can any time be used? In a study of out-of-stock conditions in a supermarket, the exact times of observation may be important. Inventory is shipped to the store on certain days only, and buying peaks occur on other days. The likelihood of a given product being out of stock is a function of both time-related activities.

How?　Will the data be directly observed? If there are two or more observers, how will they divide the task? How will the results be recorded for later analysis? How will the observers deal with various situations that may occur—when expected actions do not take place or when someone challenges the observer in the setting?

Where?　Within a spatial confine, where does the act take place? In a retail traffic pattern study, the proximity of a customer's pause space to a display or directional sign might be recorded. Must the observation take place in a particular location within a larger venue? The location of the observation, such as a sales approach observation within a chain of retail stores, can significantly influence the acts recorded.

Observers face unlimited variations in conditions. Fortunately, most problems do not occur simultaneously. When the plans are thorough and the observers well trained, observational research is quite successful.

SNAPSHOT

Envirosell: Studies Reveal Left-Hand Retail

World retailers collect and subscribe to numerous data sources, but they need knowledge from that data to craft their merchandising, staffing, and promotion strategies, as well as their store designs. Retail giants (e.g., GAP, Limited, Starbucks, Radio Shack, McDonald's) turn to consultant Paco Underhill when they want to know how consumers buy what they do and what barriers prevent or discourage buying. Underhill describes himself as a "commercial researcher, which means I am part scientist, part artist, and part entrepreneur." His company, Envirosell, has offices in the United States, Milan, Sidney, and Sao Paulo. Envirosell concentrates on the third segment of retail information,

drawn from observation (segment 1 is register data and segment 2 is communication studies). In a recent ABC News live e-chat, Underhill said, "the principal differences in 1st world shopping patterns are governed more by education and income than by ethnicity . . . but the Brits and Aussies [do] tend to walk as they drive. This sets up some very peculiar retail [shopping] patterns, because their walking patterns set up a left-hand dominance, whereas in the U.S. and much of the rest of the world, our walking patterns set up a right-hand dominance."

www.envirosell.com

Unobtrusive Measures

Up to this point, our discussion has focused on direct observation as a traditional approach to data collection. Like surveys and experiments, some observational studies—particularly participant observation—require the observer to be physically present in the research situation. This contributes to a **reactivity response,** a phenomenon where participants alter their behavior in response to the researcher. (You are familiar with the historic research at Western Electric and the so-called Hawthorne effect—introduced in Chapter 6—and the reactions interviewers produce in participants that bias the findings of a study.)

Close-Up

Designing the Observational Study

The design of an observational study follows the same pattern as other research. Once the researcher has specified the investigative questions, it is often apparent that the best way to conduct the study is through observation. Guidance for conducting an observation and translating the investigative question(s) into an observational checklist is the subject of this section. We first review the procedural steps and then explain how to create a checklist.

Most studies that use the observational method follow a general sequence of steps that parallel the research process. Here we adapt those steps to the terminology of the observational method:

- Define the content of the study.

- Develop a data collection plan that identifies the observational targets, sampling strategy, and acts (operationalized as a checklist or coding scheme).

- Secure and train observers.

- Collect the data.

- Analyze the data.

In this chapter's "Bringing Research to Life," we recounted a humorous incident in a quality control situation that used observation. Assume our concerns are more serious. We have limited resources, so the study will be small. ProSec Electronics' management is concerned about a deterioration of quality in its assembled product—security cameras—toward the end of each day. The management question is, "Why are products failing quality assurance in the afternoon?" The research question might be stated, "What factors affect the quality of assembled cameras?" Although we presume that management is correct about the time, we will allow the data to confirm this. The investigative questions could then include: "What is the variability due to changes in parts vendors? Inventory? Does the manufacturing procedure change during the day?

Is it shift-dependent? To what extent is the failure rate contingent on time of day? What is the role of workplace conditions? Is it linked to assembler performance?"

Further assume that, through interviewing, we isolate the *content of the study* to assembler behavior in the natural environment. The major variables of interest will be operationalized from the assembler's job description and the environmental conditions of the assembly area.

The *observational targets* will be the assemblers and their acts (physical behavior consistent with the job description). We have chosen to sample during the late afternoon, initially, and we will use *time sampling* on a *continuous* basis. This allows us to record all relevant behavior and complete an environmental checklist. The observation will be *direct,* and we will operate from *concealment* using the one-way mirror on the door to the assembly area.

A tour of the assembly area reveals a rectangular room with east- and west-facing windows. The workstations run the length of the rectangle, splitting the room in half and facing north. Comfortable chairs are present, and parts bins are to the right of each workstation, requiring the assembler to turn westward to select parts. The windows have shades, and there is both general and task lighting.

The variables to be measured (measurement questions) were derived from the investigative questions on workplace conditions and assembler performance. Notes taken on the tour improved our understanding of contextual variables. By examining the workplace first, we can assess and begin to rule out environmental variables (lighting, temperature, noise, and other variables controlled by the production facility) before moving on to behavioral characteristics. Both checklists will be revised after pretesting. The *observational checklist* for the assembly environment features a range of measures from graphic rating scales to category scales. It is shown in Exhibit 13–7.

The assemblers are subject to periodic and unscheduled supervisory visits and normal workplace rules for a drug-free environment. Nevertheless, the foremost ethical concern is restricting the observations to assembly activities.

EXHIBIT 13–7   Environmental Observation Checklist

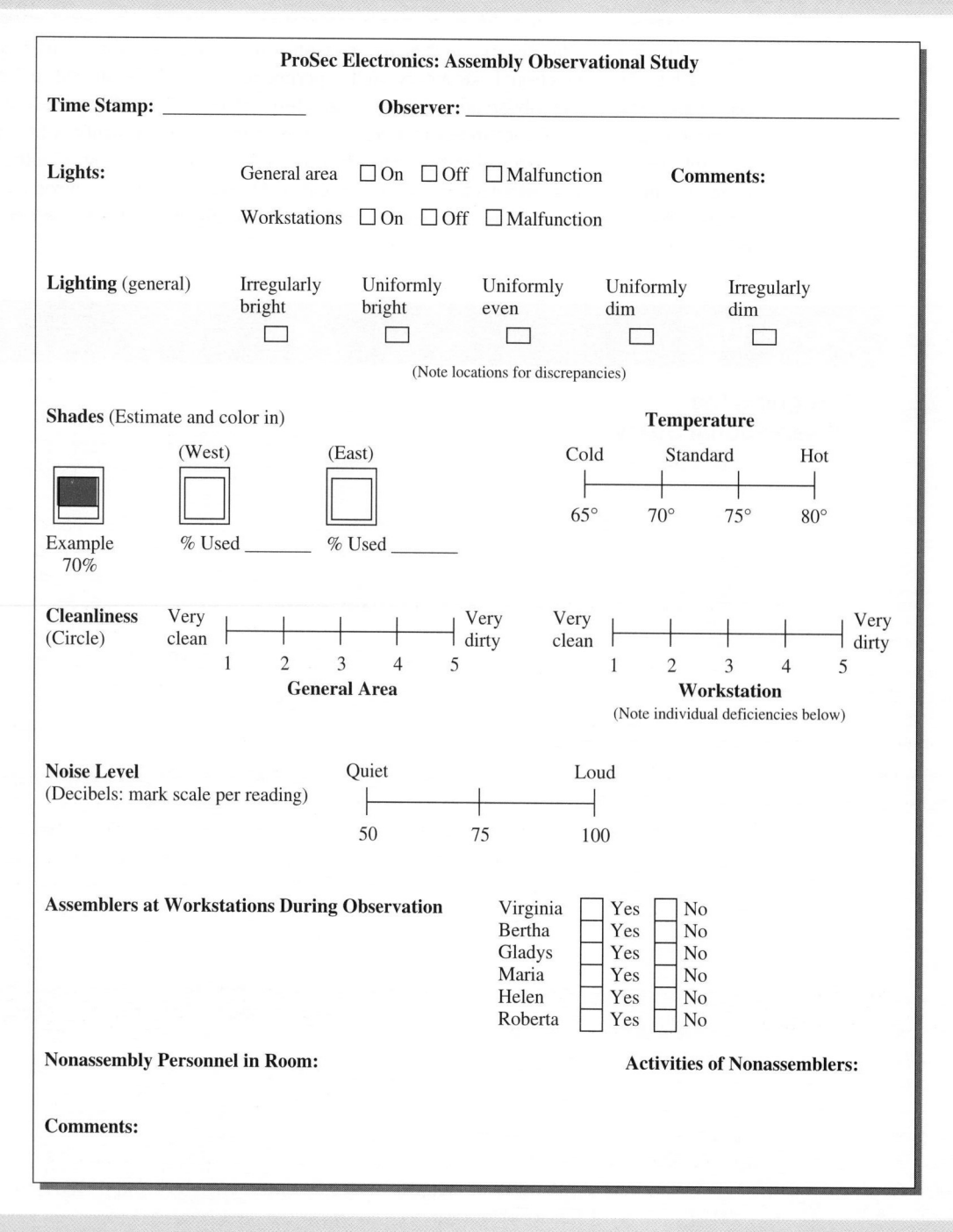

Using the company's cameras, we will run one on wide angle for context and the other zoomed-in to capture individual assembler behavior on a *time-interval* sampling. The observation will be videotaped so a consistent stimulus may be used to train observers, pretest and refine the checklists, and obtain a benchmark for later comparison. The behavioral checklist will be devised after studying the job descriptions and viewing the preliminary videotape.

Webb and his colleagues have given us an insight into some very innovative observational procedures that can be both nonreactive and inconspicuously applied. Called **unobtrusive measures,** these approaches encourage creative and imaginative forms of indirect observation, archival searches, and variations on simple and contrived observation.[10] Of particular interest are measures involving indirect observation based on **physical traces** that include *erosion* (measures of wear) and *accretion* (measures of deposit).

Natural erosion measures are illustrated by the frequency of replacement of vinyl floor tile in front of museum exhibits as an indicator of exhibit popularity. The study of wear and tear on book pages is a measure of library book use. Counting the remaining brochures in a car dealer's display rack after a favorable magazine review suggests consumer interest.

Physical traces also include natural accretion such as discovering the listenership of radio stations by observing car radio settings as autos are brought in for service. Another type of unobtrusive study involves estimating liquor and magazine consumption by collecting and analyzing family trash. An interesting application compared beer consumption reports acquired through interviews with the findings of sampled trash. If the interview data were valid, the consumption figures for the area were at 15 percent. However, the validity was questioned when the beer can count from trash supported a 77 percent consumption rate.[11]

William Rathje is a professor of archaeology at the University of Arizona and founder of the Garbage Project in Tucson. His study of trash, refuse, rubbish, and litter resulted in the subdiscipline that the *Oxford English Dictionary* has termed *garbology*. By excavating landfills, he has gained insight into human behavior and cultural patterns—sometimes sorting the contents of up to 150 coded categories. His previous studies have shown that "people will describe their behavior to satisfy cultural expectations, like the mothers in Tucson who unanimously claimed they made their baby food from scratch, but whose garbage told a very different tale."[12]

Physical trace methods present a strong argument for use based on their ability to provide low-cost access to frequency, attendance, and incidence data without contamination from other methods or reactivity from participants. They are excellent "triangulation" devices for cross-validation. Thus, they work well as supplements to other methods. Designing an unobtrusive study can test a researcher's creativity, and one must be especially careful about inferences made from the findings. Erosion results may have occurred because of wear factors not considered, and accretion material may be the result of selective deposit or survival.

SUMMARY

1 Observation is one of the few options available for studying records, mechanical processes, lower animals, small children, and complex interactive processes. We can gather data as the event occurs and can come closer to capturing the whole event than with interrogation. On the other hand, we have to be present to catch the event or have some recording device on the scene to do the job.

2 Observation includes a variety of monitoring situations that cover nonbehavioral and behavioral activities.

3 The strengths of observation as a data collection method include:

- Securing information about people or activities that cannot be derived from experiments or surveys.

- Avoiding participant filtering and forgetting.
- Securing environmental context information.
- Optimizing the naturalness of the research setting.
- Reducing obtrusiveness.

4 Observation may be limited by

- The difficulty of waiting for long periods to capture the relevant phenomena.
- The expense of observer costs and equipment.
- The reliability of inferences from surface indicators.
- The problems of quantification and disproportionately large records.
- The limitation on presenting activities and inferences about cognitive processes.

5 We can classify observation in terms of the observer-participant relationship. This relationship may be viewed from three perspectives: (1) Is the observation direct or indirect? (2) Is the observer's presence known or unknown? (3) Is the observer a participant or nonparticipant?

6 The design of an observational study follows the same general pattern as other research. Observational studies fall into four general types based on the degree of structure and the nature of the observational environment. The researcher must define the content of the study; develop a data collection plan that identifies participants, sampling strategy, and "acts" (often operationalized as a checklist or coding scheme); secure and train observers; and launch the study.

Unobtrusive measures offer an unusual and creative approach to reducing reactivity in observational research by indirect observation and other methods. Measures of erosion and accretion serve as ways to confirm the findings from other methods or operate as singular data sources.

KEY TERMS

concealment 408	observational checklist 410	reactivity response 415
direct observation 406	observation 402	record analysis 404
event sampling 413	observer drift 413	simple observation 409
extralinguistic behavior 405	participant observation 409	spatial relationships 405
indirect observation 406	physical condition analysis 404	systematic observation 409
linguistic behavior 405	physical traces 417	time sampling 413
nonverbal behavior 404	process (activity) analysis 404	unobtrusive measures 417

EXAMPLES

Company	Scenario	Page
CPG industry	Testing the use of RFID technology for tracking exchanges, as well as product use, storage, and speed of comsumption.	412
Envirosell	A comparison of store traffic behavior in the United States, Great Britain, and Australia.	414

Point of Purchase Advertising Institute	A trade association that determines the value of retail display materials.	408
Progressive Insurance, Inc.	Tracking actual driver behavior with a "black box" device for cars.	408
ProSec Electronics*	An observational study to discover process or equipment errors contributing to defective merchandise.	BRTL, Throughout
TaskMasters (Julie Morgenstern)	The use of observation by professional organizers to reveal space use and storage behavior.	404
TrolleyScan	Provider of RFID tags for the CPG industry, marking a new phase of direct observation for the future.	412

*Due to the confidential and proprietary nature of most research, the names of some companies have been changed.

DISCUSSION QUESTIONS

Terms in Review

1. Compare the advantages and disadvantages of the survey to those of observation. Under which circumstances could you make a case for using observation?

2. What ethical risks are involved in observation? In the use of unobtrusive measures?

3. Based on present or past work experience, suggest problems that could be resolved by using observation-based data.

4. Distinguish between the following:

   a. The relative value of communication and observation.

   b. Nonverbal, linguistic, and extralinguistic analysis.

   c. Factual and inferential observation.

Making Research Decisions

5. The observer-participant relationship is an important consideration in the design of observational studies. What kind of relationship would you recommend in each of the following cases?

   a. Observations of professional conduct in the classroom by the student author of a course evaluation guide.

   b. Observation of retail shoppers by a researcher who is interested in determining customer purchase time by type of goods purchased.

   c. Observation of a focus group interview by a client.

   d. Effectiveness of individual farmworker organizers in their efforts to organize employees of grape growers.

6. Assume you are the manufacturer of modular office systems and furniture as well as office organization elements (desktop and wall organizers, filing systems, etc.). Your company has been asked to propose an observational study to examine the use of office space by white-collar and managerial workers for a large insurance company. This study will be part of a project to improve office efficiency and paperwork flow. It is expected to involve the redesign of office space and the purchase of new office furniture and organization elements.

   a. What are the varieties of information that might be observed?

   b. Select a limited number of content areas for study, and operationally define the observation acts that should be measured.

7. Develop a checklist to be used by observers in the previous study.

   a. Determine how many observers you need and assign two or three to a specific observation task.

   b. Compare the results of your group members' checklists for stability of recorded perceptions.

8. You wish to analyze the pedestrian traffic that passes a given store in a major shopping center. You are interested in determining how many shoppers pass by this store, and you would like to classify these shoppers on various relevant dimensions. Any information you secure should be obtainable from observation alone.

   a. What other information might you find useful to observe?

   b. How would you decide what information to collect?

   c. Devise the operational definitions you would need.

   d. What would you say in your instructions to the observers you plan to use?

   e. How might you sample this shopper traffic?

Bringing Research to Life

9. Develop the investigative questions that should have guided Jason and Otto's mechanical observation study of production processes at Otto's uncle's company.

From Concept to Practice

10. Using Exhibit 13–3, identify the type of study described in each of the Snapshots featured in this chapter.

CASES*

ENVIROSELL

*All cases indicating a video icon are located on the Instructor's Videotape Supplement. All nonvideo cases are in the case section of the textbook. All cases indicating a CD icon offer a data set, which is on the accompanying CD.

REFERENCE NOTES

1. K. E. Weick, "Systematic Observational Methods," in *The Handbook of Social Psychology,* vol. 2, eds. G. Lindzey and E. Aronson (Reading, MA: Addison-Wesley, 1968), p. 360.
2. R. Bales, *Interaction Process Analysis* (Reading, MA: Addison-Wesley, 1950).
3. Weick, "Systematic Observational Methods," p. 381.
4. Louise H. Kidder and Charles M. Judd, *Research Methods in Social Relations,* 5th ed. (New York: Holt, Rinehart & Winston, 1986), p. 292.
5. Kenneth D. Bailey, *Methods of Social Science,* 2nd ed. (New York: Free Press, 1982), pp. 252–54.
6. Donald F. Roy, "'Banana Time,' Job Satisfaction, and Informal Interaction," *Human Organization* 18, no. 4 (Winter 1959–60), pp. 151–68.
7. Robert F. Bales, *Personality and Interpersonal Behavior* (New York: Holt, Rinehart & Winston, 1970).
8. Kidder and Judd, *Research Methods in Social Relations,* pp. 298–99.
9. Ibid., p. 291.
10. E. J. Webb, D. T. Campbell, R. D. Schwartz, L. Sechrest, and J. B. Grove, *Nonreactive Measures in the Social Sciences,* 2nd ed. (Boston: Houghton Mifflin, 1981).
11. W. L. Rathje and W. W. Hughes, "The Garbage Project as a Nonreactive Approach: Garbage In . . . Garbage Out?" In *Perspectives on Attitude Assessment: Surveys and Their Alternatives,* eds. H. W. Sinaiko and L. A. Broedling (Washington, DC: Smithsonian Institution, 1975).
12. William Grimes, "If It's Scientific, It's 'Garbology,'" *International Herald Tribune,* August 15–16, 1992, p. 17.

REFERENCES FOR SNAPSHOTS AND CAPTIONS

Envirosell

Live e-chat with Paco Underhill, July 8, 1999 (http://www.abcnews.go.com/sections/politics/DailyNews/chat_990511underhill.html). McGraw-Hill Video Library.

Nielsen Media Research

"Nielsen Families," "Our Research & Products," and "Universe Estimates," Nielsen Media Research (http://www.nielsenmedia.com/FAQ).

Professional Organizers

"About NAPO," National Association of Professional Organizers, February 11, 2002 (http://www.napo.net/goweek/gwk.html#aboutnapo).

Julie Morgenstern. *Organizing from the Inside Out* (New York: Henry Holt and Company, ©1998).

Julie Morgenstern, TaskMasters, February 11, 2002 (http://juliemorgenstern.com/task_masters.html).

Progressive

Chuck Salter, "Progressive Makes Big Claims," *FastCompany,* November 1998.

Progressive Press Kit, Progressive, December 1998.

RFID

"Press Releases," Trolley Scan (Pty) Ltd. (http://www.trolleyscan.com/pressrel.html).

"Radio Frequency ID: A New Era for Marketers?" *Consumer Insight,* ACNielsen, 2001 (http://acnielsen.com/pubs/ci/2001/q4/features/radio.htm).

Vivek Agarwal, "Assessing the Benefits of Auto-ID Technology in the Consumer Goods Industry," Auto ID Center, 2001 (http://www.autoidcenter.org/research/CAM-WH-003.pdf).

CLASSIC AND CONTEMPORARY READINGS

Bailey, Kenneth D. *Methods of Social Research.* 4th ed. New York: Free Press, 1994. Includes a thorough discussion of observational strategies.

Bales, Robert F. *Personality and Interpersonal Behavior.* New York: Holt, Rinehart & Winston, 1970. From a pioneer in interaction process analysis, a model for structured observation, checklists, and coding schemes.

Denzin, Norman K., and Yvonna S. Lincoln. *Handbook of Qualitative Research.* 2nd ed. Thousand Oaks, CA: Sage Inc., 2000. Of particular interest is Part 3 on strategies of inquiry and Part 4 on methods of collecting and analyzing empirical materials.

Hoyle, Rick H., Monica J. Harris, and Charles M. Judd. *Research Methods in Social Relations.* 7th ed. Belmont, CA: Wadsworth Publishing, 2001. Good overview of observational types and sampling plans.

Webb, Eugene J., Donald T. Campbell, Richard D. Swartz, and Lee B. Sechrest. *Unobtrusive Measures.* Thousand Oaks, CA: Sage Inc., 1999. The revised edition of the classic source of information on all aspects of unobtrusive measures. Excellent examples and ideas for project planning.

CHAPTER 14

Experimentation

Learning Objectives

After reading this chapter, you should understand . . .

1   **The uses for experimentation.**

2   **The advantages and disadvantages of the experimental method.**

3   **The seven steps of a well-planned experiment.**

4   **Internal and external validity with experimental research designs.**

5   **The three types of experimental designs and the variations of each.**

Bringing Research to Life

"Oh, did I wake you?" Jason asks innocently, as he rubs his hand on his very pregnant wife's abdomen.

Coming groggily awake, Dorrie mumbles, "It's not time. Go back to sleep."

"Dorrie, hon'—I've been thinking . . . we shouldn't wait. We should give them names . . . now."

"Names? Now?"

"We'll call them Terry and Robin. Whether boys or girls, either way the names will fit."

They lay side by side in the darkness, in silence. Silence maybe meant he was thinking and would rouse her again. No use fighting to regain sleep. Hear him out. "Why the hurry, Jason?"

"I want you to talk to them. I want you to say, 'Robin, dearest, this is your mommy,' and 'Terry, your mommy and daddy love you terrifically much.'"

"Sweet. May I go back to sleep now?"

"This has possibilities, you know . . ."

"Please, no *possibilities!*" groans Dorrie. "No twilight zone ideas, grasped at in the gray area between conscious and unconscious, wakefulness and sleep, and proposed with utter seriousness."

"Say you read poetry to Robin. You say, 'Robin, this is for you, and it is by a very famous poet, William Blake . . .'"

"'Tyger, tyger, burning bright . . .'"

"That's the idea. Say you read poetry to Robin and maybe sing to Terry. Well, maybe it is not so good an idea letting you sing to little Terry, because you do not sing nearly as well as you read poetry. We would want the differential treatments to be delivered with more or less equal efficacy, wouldn't we? So, maybe you should read Shakespeare to Terry and Blake to Robin, and then, in puberty, we will see if one has a preference for Shakespeare over Blake."

She rolled over on an elbow. "I see. You are suggesting that as the twins share the same genetic makeup they will differentially emphasize contrasting environmental stimuli administered during the earliest development of their central nervous systems."

"Yes."

"You woke me for this?"

"Yes, whatever treatment . . . stimuli . . . remarks . . . you direct to them through internal dialogue, such as poetry by Blake and Shakespeare, will fall on almost identically genetically endowed organisms . . . Of course, I would have to trust you to adhere to the experimental protocols we devise."

"Following your ridiculous line of thought, perhaps Blake and Shakespeare would not be good alternative treatments, since they wrote in different styles and were not contemporaries . . . assuming we take all of this seriously . . . which I don't."

"I am not sure I have heard you express equal enthusiasm for Blake and Shakespeare, so you will surely bias the administration of the treatment in favor of Blake, your favorite."

"Let me understand this, sweetheart." Dorrie was fully awake now and irritated. "I might not stick to the protocols, and you do not trust me to avoid bias in administering the 'treatments' with equal enthusiasm."

"Well, at the conscious level, I have to trust you, because you are a doctor . . .

". . . and my wife and life's companion . . . and the mother of our children . . .

". . . and you understand the importance of nice clean experimentation. But, yes, biases might be present at the subconscious level and remain difficult to control."

She sat up. "Wanting to call the babies by name is a sentimental impulse. My heart says it is sweet of you to want me to talk to them, but my brain says this is a cruel experiment. Nevertheless, let's talk about 'nice clean experimentation,' as you call it.

"Jason, we are talking about our children here, not genetically created identical twin embryos. First, you cannot differentially direct treatment to one or the other. Never—no, not in my wildest dreams—should I believe one of my unborn babies knows he is Robin or Terry. Second, when they reach an age when they attend nursery school, we will totally lose our ability to differentially apply stimuli . . ."

"Would you consider home schooling?"

"I'm a public health doctor, Jason. Doctors don't work at home! That's why we have hospitals!"

"OK, OK. No need to get huffy."

"Jason, I am experiencing the joys and pains of a multiple pregnancy. There are certain hormonal changes . . . which I have heard you indelicately call 'gland things,' but I am a professional person and am well aware of my responsibilities—to the public, to you, to my unborn children, and to myself—to maintain my emotional equilibrium. So lay off, Jason!"

"I'm sorry I woke you. OK?"

"Waking me is only part of the problem. It's what you woke me for—this lame idea that just popped into your head, this notion to manipulate your own offspring, which you forced on me without any critical thinking in advance."

"Well, I was curious, that's all. I was brainstorming."

"If you were doing research in the university or hospital, you would not float such a lame idea. A human subjects committee would roast you for such an ethically questionable idea, starting with . . . I don't know . . . starting with whether unborn children are able to give informed consent, whether I am able to give consent on their behalf, and ending up, maybe, by asking what right you have to try to alter the artistic sensibilities of anyone's offspring. You don't get away with crazy ideas like this in business research, do you?"

A long silence followed. "Swell," he said. "Can we get back to sleep, then?"

"Let's hope so." She pulled his face close, so that by the light shining in from a street lamp he could see how rigid her lips were. "This year I am part of a program to administer treatments to 150 mortally ill subjects. They know that 75 of them are receiving an experimental treatment and 75 receiving colored saline solution. It's a double-blind experiment, so I have no idea who is receiving the placebo.

"Do you have any idea what it means to know you are withholding the promise of life from 75 human beings? Do you grasp what it means to look into their eyes and have them look back and maybe cry, so an unspoken message passes—'Don't let me die'—?

"When I became a doctor, I expected to do my best to save every life. But my fellow doctors are counting on me for proof, Jason, so they may justify the treatment and request funding. I am not playing games with people, Jason. I am letting people die so others may live.

"Experimentation is about needing to know something so badly that you cannot live without an answer, because others cannot live without an answer. What experimentation is *not* about is having a brainstorm or scratching a mental itch. Experimentation is responsibility."

What Is Experimentation?

Why do events occur under some conditions and not under others? Research methods that answer such questions are called *causal* methods. (Recall the discussion of causality in Chapter 6.) Ex post facto research designs, where a researcher interviews respondents or observes what is or what has been, also have the potential for discovering causality. The distinction between these methods and experimentation is that the researcher is required to accept the world as it is found, whereas an experiment allows the researcher to alter systematically the variables of interest and observe what changes follow.

In this chapter we define experimentation and discuss its advantages and disadvantages. An outline for the conduct of an experiment is presented as a vehicle to introduce important concepts. The questions of internal and external validity are also examined: Does the experimental treatment determine the observed difference, or was some extraneous variable responsible? And, how can one generalize the results of the study across times, settings, and persons? The chapter concludes with a review of the most widely accepted designs and a "Close-Up" example.

You may wish to revisit our discussion of causality in Chapter 6.

Experiments are studies involving intervention by the researcher beyond that required for measurement. The usual intervention is to manipulate some variable in a setting and observe how it affects the subjects being studied (e.g., people or physical entities). The researcher manipulates the independent or explanatory variable and then observes whether the hypothesized dependent variable is affected by the intervention.

An example of such an intervention is the study of bystanders and thieves.[1] In this experiment, students were asked to come to an office where they had an opportunity to see a fellow student steal some money from a receptionist's desk. A confederate of the experimenter, of course, did the stealing. The major hypothesis concerned whether people observing a theft would be more likely to report it (1) if they observed the crime alone or (2) if they were in the company of someone else.

There is at least one **independent variable (IV)** and one **dependent variable (DV)** in a causal relationship. We hypothesize that in some way the IV "causes" the DV to occur. The independent or explanatory variable in our example was the state of either being alone when observing the theft or being in the company of another person. The dependent variable was whether the subjects reported observing the crime. The results suggested that bystanders were more likely to report the theft if they observed it alone rather than in another person's company.

On what grounds did the researchers conclude that people who were alone were more likely to report crimes observed than people in the company of others? Three types of evidence form the basis for this conclusion. First, there must be an agreement between independent and dependent variables. The presence or absence of one is associated with the presence or absence of the other. Thus, more reports of the theft (DV) came from lone observers (IV_1) than from paired observers (IV_2).

Second, beyond the correlation of independent and dependent variables, the time order of the occurrence of the variables must be considered. The dependent variable should not precede the independent variable. They may occur almost simultaneously, or the independent variable should occur before the dependent variable. This requirement is of little concern since it is unlikely that people could report a theft before observing it.

The third important support for the conclusion comes when researchers are confident that other extraneous variables did not influence the dependent variable. To ensure that these other variables are not the source of influence, researchers control their ability to confound the planned comparison. Under laboratory conditions, standardized conditions for control can be arranged. The crime observation experiment was carried out in a laboratory set up as an office. The entire event was staged without the observers' knowledge. The receptionist whose money was to be stolen was instructed to speak and act in a specific way. Only the receptionist, the observers, and the "criminal" were in the office. The same process was repeated with each trial of the experiment.

While such controls are important, further precautions are needed so that the results achieved reflect only the influence of the independent variable on the dependent variable.

An Evaluation of Experiments

Advantages

When we elaborated on the concept of cause in Chapter 6, we said causality could not be proved with certainty but the probability of one variable being linked to another could be established convincingly. The experiment comes closer than any primary data collection method to accomplishing this goal. The foremost advantage is the researcher's ability to manipulate the independent variable. Consequently, the probability that changes in the dependent variable are a function of that manipulation increases. Also, a control group serves as a comparison to assess the existence and potency of the manipulation.

The second advantage of the experiment is that contamination from extraneous variables can be controlled more effectively than in other designs. This helps the researcher

Experimental research frequently requires special expertise and facilities that can accommodate multistage designs, like the facilities offered by the Canadian firm Research House Inc.
www.research-house.ca

isolate experimental variables and evaluate their impact over time. Third, the convenience and cost of experimentation are superior to other methods. These benefits allow the experimenter opportunistic scheduling of data collection and the flexibility to adjust variables and conditions that evoke extremes not observed under routine circumstances. In addition, the experimenter can assemble combinations of variables for testing rather than having to search for their fortuitous appearance in the study environment.

Fourth, **replication**—repeating an experiment with different subject groups and conditions—leads to the discovery of an average effect of the independent variable across people, situations, and times. Fifth, researchers can use naturally occurring events and, to some extent, field experiments to reduce subjects' perceptions of the researcher as a source of intervention or deviation in their everyday lives.

Disadvantages

The artificiality of the laboratory is arguably the primary disadvantage of the experimental method. However, many subjects' perceptions of a contrived environment can be improved by investment in the facility. Second, generalization from nonprobability samples can pose problems despite random assignment. The extent to which a study can be generalized from college students to managers or executives is open to question. And when an experiment is unsuccessfully disguised, volunteer subjects are often those with the most interest in the topic. Third, despite the low costs of experimentation, many applications of experimentation far outrun the budgets for other primary data collection methods. Fourth, experimentation is most effectively targeted at problems of the present or immediate future. Experimental studies of the past are not feasible, and studies about intentions or predictions are difficult. Finally, management research is often concerned with the study of people. There are limits to the types of manipulation and controls that are ethical.

Conducting an Experiment[2]

In a well-executed experiment, researchers must complete a series of activities to carry out their craft successfully. Although the experiment is the premier scientific methodology for establishing causation, the resourcefulness and creativeness of the researcher are needed to make the experiment live up to its potential. In this section, we discuss seven activities the researcher must accomplish to make the endeavor successful:

MANAGEMENT

1. Select relevant variables.

2. Specify the level(s) of the treatment.

3. Control the experimental environment.

4. Choose the experimental design.

5. Select and assign the subjects.

6. Pilot-test, revise, and test.

7. Analyze the data.

Selecting Relevant Variables

Throughout the book we have discussed the idea that a research problem can be conceptualized as a hierarchy of questions starting with a management problem. The researcher's task is to translate an amorphous problem into the question or hypothesis that best states the objectives of the research. Depending on the complexity of the problem, investigative questions and additional hypotheses can be created to address specific facets of the study or data that need to be gathered. Further, we have mentioned that a **hypothesis** is a relational statement because it describes a relationship between two or more variables. It must also be **operationalized,** a term we used earlier in discussing how concepts are transformed into variables to make them measurable and subject to testing.

Consider the following research question as we work through the seven points listed above:

> Does a sales presentation that describes product benefits in the introduction of the message lead to improved retention of product knowledge?

Since a hypothesis is a tentative statement—a speculation—about the outcome of the study, it might take this form:

> Sales presentations in which the benefits module is placed in the introduction of a 12-minute message produce better retention of product knowledge than those where the benefits module is placed in the conclusion.

The researchers' challenges at this step are to

MANAGEMENT

Tip

1. Select variables that are the best operational representations of the original concepts.
2. Determine how many variables to test.
3. Select or design appropriate measures for them.

The researchers would need to select variables that best operationalize the concepts *sales presentation, product benefits, retention,* and *product knowledge.* The product's classification and the nature of the intended audience should also be defined. In addition, the term *better* could be operationalized statistically by means of a significance test.

The number of variables in an experiment is constrained by the project budget, the time allocated, the availability of appropriate controls, and the number of subjects being tested. For statistical reasons, there must be more subjects than variables.[3]

The selection of measures for testing requires a thorough review of the available literature and instruments. In addition, measures must be adapted to the unique needs of the research situation without compromising their intended purpose or original meaning.

Specifying the Levels of Treatment

The **treatment levels** of the independent variable are the distinctions the researcher makes between different aspects of the treatment condition. For example, if salary is hypothesized to have an effect on employees exercising stock purchase options, it might be divided into high, middle, and low ranges to represent three levels of the independent variable.

The levels assigned to an independent variable should be based on simplicity and common sense. In the sales presentation example, the experimenter should not select 8 minutes and 10 minutes as the starting points to represent the two treatment levels if the average message about the product is 12 minutes long. Similarly, if the benefits module is placed in the first and second minutes of the presentation, observable differences may not occur because the levels are too close together. Thus, in the first trial, the researcher is likely to position the midpoint of the benefits module the same interval from the end of the introduction as from the end of the conclusion (see Exhibit 14–1).

Under an entirely different hypothesis, several levels of the independent variable may be needed to test order-of-presentation effects. Here we use only two. Alternatively, a **control group** could provide a base level for comparison. The control group is composed of subjects who are not exposed to the independent variable(s), in contrast to those who receive the **experimental treatment** (manipulation of the independent variable[s]).

EXHIBIT 14–1 Benefits Module Effectiveness Based on Timing of Inclusion

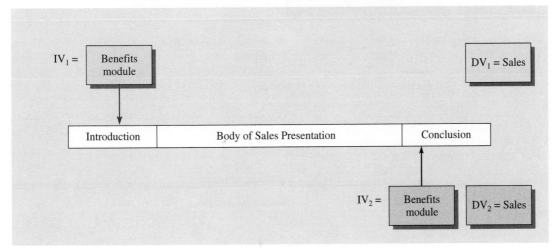

Controlling the Experimental Environment

Chapter 2 discussed the nature of extraneous variables and the need for their control.

Dorrie described a double-blind study in the opening vignette.

In our sales presentation experiment, extraneous variables can appear as differences in age, gender, race, dress, communications competence, and many other characteristics of the presenter, the message, or the situation. These have the potential for distorting the effect of the treatment on the dependent variable and must be controlled or eliminated. However, at this stage, we are principally concerned with **environmental control,** holding constant the physical environment of the experiment. The introduction of the experiment to the subjects and the instructions would likely be videotaped for consistency. The arrangement of the room, the time of administration, the experimenter's contact with the subjects, and so forth, must all be consistent across each administration of the experiment.

Other forms of control involve subjects and experimenters. When subjects do not know if they are receiving the experimental treatment, they are said to be **blind.** When the experimenters do not know if they are giving the treatment to the experimental group or to the control group, the experiment is said to be **double blind.** Both approaches control unwanted complications such as subjects' reactions to expected conditions or experimenter influence.

Choosing the Experimental Design

Many of the experimental designs are diagrammed and described later in this chapter.

Unlike the general descriptors of research design that were discussed in Chapter 6, experimental designs are unique to the experimental method. They serve as positional and statistical plans to designate relationships between experimental treatments and the experimenter's observations or measurement points in the temporal scheme of the study. In the conduct of the experiment, the researchers apply their knowledge to select one design that is best suited to the goals of the research. Judicious selection of the design improves the probability that the observed change in the dependent variable was caused by the manipulation of the independent variable and not by another factor. It simultaneously strengthens the generalizability of results beyond the experimental setting.

Selecting and Assigning Subjects

The subjects selected for the experiment should be representative of the population to which the researcher wishes to generalize the study's results. This may seem self-evident, but we have witnessed several decades of experimentation with college sophomores that contradict that assumption. In the sales presentation example, corporate

SNAPSHOT

Effect of Magazine Advertising on Sales

For the first time, the Magazine Publishers of America (MPA) has a definitive study demonstrating that magazine advertising does positively affect not only the incidence of sales but also the dollar value and quantity of sales. ACNielsen sent 50,000 households in its ACNielsen Household Scanner Panel™ a four-color questionnaire featuring the covers of April, May, and June issues of 14 magazines. Panelists scanned the bar codes of the covers of the magazines they had read. The scanned information was uploaded to ACNielsen, where demographically matched panels of 4,000 households each were constructed. Half of each panel had been exposed to magazine ads for 1 of the 10 brands being tracked, while the other half had not. Actual sales data drawn from records of scanned purchases were compared. Households exposed to magazine ads were more likely to purchase those brands, and dollar sales also increased among 8 of the 10 brands studied. You can link to the complete MPA study report from our text website or learn more about the ACNielsen Household Scanner Panel™.

www.magazine.org

www.acnielsen.com

buyers, purchasing managers, or others in a decision-making capacity would provide better generalizing power than undergraduate college students *if* the product in question was targeted for industrial use rather than to the consumer.

We discussed random sampling in Chapter 7.

The procedure for random sampling of experimental subjects is similar in principle to the selection of respondents for a survey. The researcher first prepares a sampling frame and then assigns the subjects for the experiment to groups using a randomization technique. Systematic sampling may be used if the sampling frame is free from any form of periodicity that parallels the sampling ratio. Since the sampling frame is often small, experimental subjects are recruited; thus they are a self-selecting sample. However, if randomization is used, those assigned to the experimental group are likely to be similar to those assigned to the control group. **Random assignment** to the groups is required to make the groups as comparable as possible with respect to the dependent variable. Randomization does not guarantee that if a pretest of the groups was conducted before the treatment condition, the groups would be pronounced identical; but it is an assurance that those differences remaining are randomly distributed. In our example, we would need three randomly assigned groups—one for each of the two treatments and one for the control group.

When it is not possible to randomly assign subjects to groups, **matching** may be used. Matching employs a nonprobability quota sampling approach. The object of matching is to have each experimental and control subject matched on every characteristic used in the research. This becomes more cumbersome as the number of variables and groups in the study increases. Since the characteristics of concern are only those that are correlated with the treatment condition or the dependent variable, they are easier to identify, control, and match.[4] In the sales presentation experiment, if a large part of the sample was composed of businesswomen who had recently completed communications training, we would not want the characteristics of gender, business experience, and communication training to be disproportionately assigned to one group.

Some authorities suggest a **quota matrix** as the most efficient means of visualizing the matching process.[5] In Exhibit 14–2, one-third of the subjects from each cell of the matrix would be assigned to each of the three groups. If matching does not alleviate the assignment problem, a combination of matching, randomization, and increasing the sample size would be used.

EXHIBIT 14–2 Quota Matrix Example

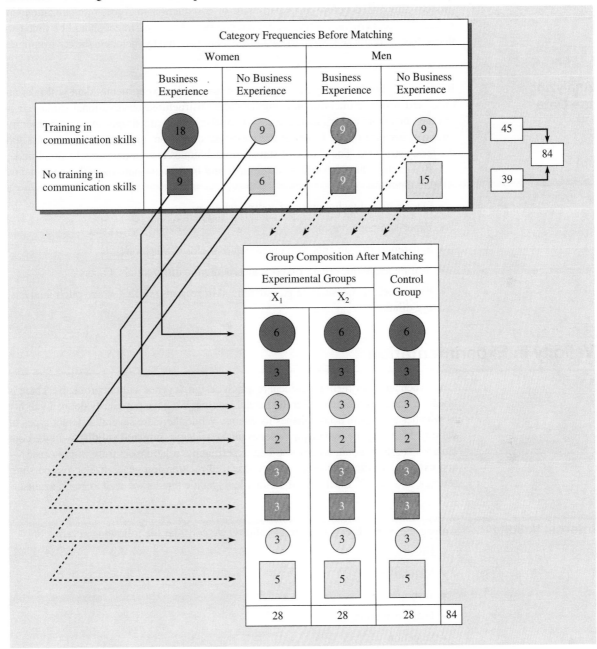

Pilot-Testing, Revising, and Testing

The procedures for this stage are similar to those for other forms of primary data collection. Pilot testing is intended to reveal errors in the design and improper control of extraneous or environmental conditions. Pretesting the instruments permits refinement before the final test. This is the researcher's best opportunity to revise scripts, look for control problems with laboratory conditions, and scan the environment for factors that might confound the results. In field experiments, researchers are sometimes caught off guard by events that have a dramatic effect on subjects: the test marketing of a competitor's product announced before an experiment, or a reduction in force, reorganization, or merger before a crucial organizational intervention. The experiment should be timed so that subjects are not sensitized to the independent variable by factors in the environment.

Analyzing the Data

If adequate planning and pretesting have occurred, the experimental data will take an order and structure uncommon to surveys and unstructured observational studies. It is not that data from experiments are easy to analyze; they are simply more conveniently arranged because of the levels of the treatment condition, pretests and post-tests, and the group structure. The choice of statistical techniques is commensurately simplified.

Researchers have several measurement and instrument options with experiments. Among them are

- Observational techniques and coding schemes.
- Paper-and-pencil tests.
- Self-report instruments with open-ended or closed questions.
- Scaling techniques (e.g., Likert scales, semantic differentials, Q-sort).
- Physiological measures (e.g., galvanic skin response, EKG, voice pitch analysis, eye dilation).

Validity in Experimentation

Even when an experiment is the ideal research design, it is not without problems. There is always a question about whether the results are true. We have previously defined validity as whether a measure accomplishes its claims. While there are several different types of validity, here only the two major varieties are considered: **internal validity**—do the conclusions we draw about a demonstrated experimental relationship truly imply cause?—and **external validity**—does an observed causal relationship generalize across persons, settings, and times?[6] Each type of validity has specific threats we need to guard against.

Internal Validity

Among the many threats to internal validity, we consider the following seven:

- History
- Maturation
- Testing
- Instrumentation
- Selection
- Statistical regression
- Experimental mortality

History   During the time that an experiment is taking place, some events may occur that confuse the relationship being studied. In many experimental designs, we take a control measurement (O_1) of the dependent variable before introducing the manipulation (X). After the manipulation, we take an after-measurement (O_2) of the dependent variable. Then the difference between O_1 and O_2 is the change that the manipulation has caused.

A company's management may wish to find the best way to educate its workers about the financial condition of the company before this year's labor negotiations. To assess the value of such an effort, managers give employees a test on their knowledge of the company's finances (O_1). Then they present the educational campaign (X) to these employees, after which they again measure their knowledge level (O_2). This design, known as a pre-experiment because it is not a very strong design, can be diagrammed as follows:

$$O_1 \qquad\qquad X \qquad\qquad O_2$$

Pretest   Manipulation   Post-test

Between O_1 and O_2, however, many events could occur to confound the effects of the education effort. A newspaper article might appear about companies with financial problems, a union meeting might be held at which this topic is discussed, or another occurrence could distort the effects of the company's education test.

Maturation   Changes also may occur within the subject that are a function of the passage of time and are not specific to any particular event. These are of special concern when the study covers a long time, but they may also be factors in tests that are as short as an hour or two. A subject can become hungry, bored, or tired in a short time, and this condition can affect response results.

Testing   The process of taking a test can affect the scores of a second test. The mere experience of taking the first test can have a learning effect that influences the results of the second test.

Instrumentation   This threat to internal validity results from changes between observations in either the measuring instrument or the observer. Using different questions at each measurement is an obvious source of potential trouble, but using different observers or interviewers also threatens validity. There can even be an instrumentation problem if the same observer is used for all measurements. Observer experience, boredom, fatigue, and anticipation of results can all distort the results of separate observations.

Selection   An important threat to internal validity is the differential selection of subjects for experimental and control groups. Validity considerations require that the groups be equivalent in every respect. If subjects are randomly assigned to experimental and control groups, this selection problem can be largely overcome. Additionally, matching the members of the groups on key factors can enhance the equivalence of the groups.

Statistical Regression   This factor operates especially when groups have been selected by their extreme scores. Suppose we measure the output of all workers in a department for a few days before an experiment and then conduct the experiment with only those workers whose productivity scores are in the top 25 percent and bottom 25 percent. No matter what is done between O_1 and O_2, there is a strong tendency for the average of the high scores at O_1 to decline at O_2 and for the low scores at O_1 to increase. This tendency results from imperfect measurement that, in effect, records some persons abnormally high and abnormally low at O_1. In the second measurement, members of both groups score more closely to their long-run mean scores.

Experiment Mortality   This occurs when the composition of the study groups changes during the test. Attrition is especially likely in the experimental group and with each dropout, the group changes. Because members of the control group are not affected by the testing situation, they are less likely to withdraw. In a compensation incentive study, some employees might not like the change in compensation method and may withdraw from the test group; this action could distort the comparison with the control group that has continued working under the established system, perhaps without knowing a test is under way.

All the threats mentioned to this point are generally, but not always, dealt with adequately in experiments by random assignment. However, five additional threats to internal validity are independent of whether or not one randomizes.[7] The first three have the effect of equalizing experimental and control groups.

1. **Diffusion or imitation of treatment.** If people in the experimental and control groups talk, then those in the control group may learn of the treatment, eliminating the difference between the groups.

2. **Compensatory equalization.** Where the experimental treatment is much more desirable, there may be an administrative reluctance to deprive the control group members. Compensatory actions for the control groups may confound the experiment.

3. **Compensatory rivalry.** This may occur when members of the control group know they are in the control group. This may generate competitive pressures, causing the control group members to try harder.

4. **Resentful demoralization of the disadvantaged.** When the treatment is desirable and the experiment is obtrusive, control group members may become resentful of their deprivation and lower their cooperation and output.

5. **Local history.** The regular history effect already mentioned impacts both experimental and control groups alike. However, when one assigns all experimental persons to one group session and all control people to another, there is a chance for some idiosyncratic event to confound results. This problem can be handled by administering treatments to individuals or small groups that are randomly assigned to experimental or control sessions.

External Validity

Internal validity factors cause confusion about whether the experimental treatment (X) or extraneous factors are the source of observation differences. In contrast, external validity is concerned with the interaction of the experimental treatment with other factors and the resulting impact on the ability to generalize to (and across) times, settings, or persons. Among the major threats to external validity are the following interactive possibilities.

The Reactivity of Testing on X   The reactive effect refers to sensitizing subjects via a pretest so they respond to the experimental stimulus (X) in a different way. A before-measurement of a subject's knowledge about the ecology programs of a company will often sensitize the subject to various experimental communication efforts that might be made about the company. This before-measurement effect can be particularly significant in experiments where the IV is a change in attitude.

Interaction of Selection and X   The process by which test subjects are selected for an experiment may be a threat to external validity. The population from which one selects subjects may not be the same as the population to which one wishes to generalize results. Suppose you use a selected group of workers in one department for a test of the piecework incentive system. The question may remain as to whether you can extrapolate those results to all production workers. Or consider a study in which you ask a cross-section of a population to participate in an experiment, but a substantial number refuses. If you conduct the experiment only with those who agree to participate (self-selection), can the results be generalized to the total population?

Other Reactive Factors   The experimental settings themselves may have a biasing effect on a subject's response to *X*. An artificial setting can obviously produce results that are not representative of larger populations. Suppose the workers who are given the incentive pay are moved to a different work area to separate them from the control group. These new conditions alone could create a strong reactive condition.

If subjects know they are participating in an experiment, there may be a tendency to role-play in a way that distorts the effects of *X*. Another reactive effect is the possible interaction between *X* and subject characteristics. An incentive pay proposal may be more effective with persons in one type of job, with a certain skill level, or with a certain personality trait.

Problems of internal validity can be solved by the careful design of experiments, but this is less true for problems of external validity. External validity is largely a matter of generalization, which, in a logical sense, is an inductive process of extrapolating beyond the data collected. In generalizing, we estimate the factors that can be ignored and that will interact with the experimental variable. Assume that the closer two events are in time, space, and measurement, the more likely they are to follow the same laws. As a rule of thumb, first seek internal validity. Try to secure as much external validity as is compatible with the internal validity requirements by making experimental conditions as similar as possible to conditions under which the results will apply.

Experimental Research Designs

The many experimental designs vary widely in their power to control contamination of the relationship between independent and dependent variables. The most widely accepted designs are based on this characteristic of control: (1) pre-experiments, (2) true experiments, and (3) field experiments (see Exhibit 14–3).

Pre-Experimental Designs

All three pre-experimental designs are weak in their scientific measurement power—that is, they fail to control adequately the various threats to internal validity. This is especially true of the one-shot case study.

One-Shot Case Study   This may be diagrammed as follows:

X	O	
Treatment or manipulation of independent variable	Observation or measurement of dependent variable	**(1)**

An example is an employee education campaign about the company's financial condition without a prior measurement of employee knowledge. Results would reveal only how much the employees know after the education campaign, but there is no way to judge the effectiveness of the campaign. How well do you think this design would meet the various threats to internal validity? The lack of a pretest and control group makes this design inadequate for establishing causality.

EXHIBIT 14–3   Key to Design Symbols

X	An X represents the introduction of an experimental stimulus to a group. The effects of this independent variable(s) are of major interest.
O	An O identifies a measurement or observation activity.
R	An R indicates that the group members have been randomly assigned to a group.

The X's and O's in the diagram are read from left to right in temporal order.

$$O\ X\ O\ O$$
Time

X's and O's vertical to each other indicate that the stimulus and/or observation take place simultaneously.

$X\ O$
O
Time
q

Parallel rows that are not separated by dashed lines indicate that comparison groups have been equalized by the randomization process.

$X\ O$
O

Those separated with a dashed line have not been so equalized.

$O\ X\ O$

O

One-Group Pretest–Post-Test Design   This is the design used earlier in the educational example. It meets the various threats to internal validity better than the one-shot case study, but it is still a weak design. How well does it control for history? Maturation? Testing effect? The others?

$$\begin{array}{ccc} O & X & O \\ \text{Pretest} & \text{Manipulation} & \text{Post-test} \end{array} \qquad \textbf{(2)}$$

Static Group Comparison   This design provides for two groups, one of which receives the experimental stimulus while the other serves as a control. In a field setting, imagine this scenario. A forest fire or other natural disaster is the experimental treatment, and psychological trauma (or property loss) suffered by the residents is the measured outcome. A pretest before the forest fire would be possible, but not on a large scale (as in the California fires). Moreover, timing of the pretest would be problematic. The control group, receiving the post-test, would consist of residents whose property was spared.

$$X \qquad\qquad O_1$$
$$\text{-------} \qquad \text{------} \qquad\qquad \textbf{(3)}$$
$$O_2$$

The addition of a comparison group creates a substantial improvement over the other two designs. Its chief weakness is that there is no way to be certain that the two groups are equivalent.

True Experimental Designs

The major deficiency of the pre-experimental designs is that they fail to provide comparison groups that are truly equivalent. The way to achieve equivalence is through matching and random assignment. With randomly assigned groups, we can employ tests of statistical significance of the observed differences.

It is common to show an X for the test stimulus and a blank for the existence of a control situation. This is an oversimplification of what really occurs. More precisely, there is an X_1 and an X_2, and sometimes more. The X_1 identifies one specific independent variable while X_2 is another independent variable that has been chosen, often arbitrarily,

---

S N A P S H O T

Vanguard Experiments with Philips Electronics' 401k Savings Rates

Vanguard, a major provider of retirement benefit programs, is conducting an experiment within Philips Electronics North America to determine whether employees can be encouraged to increase the amount they save in their 401k retirement plans. When asked if they could increase their savings, most employees indicated that they live "paycheck to paycheck" and therefore cannot save more. Yet financial planners know that most people can save 1 percent, 3 percent, or even 5 percent more of their income over time and not notice a difference in their standard of living. The Vanguard/Philips experiment attempts to overcome this "painful to save" barrier by having workers agree to save more in the *future*—not today. In the experiment, which began in February 2002, about 800 workers in two geographically separate and distinct divisions of Philips (D_1 and D_2) have been invited to join the SmartSave program. Under the program, they have the choice of increasing their 401k savings rate by 1, 2, or 3 percent drawn from a future pay increase. The rate change will occur on April 1 of each year, at the time of future merit increases. Whatever rate they choose, that increase will occur each April during the life of the experiment, unless they decide to discontinue or increase their savings rate.

SmartSave is being introduced with lots of fanfare, including a newsletter, two teaser postcards, SmartSave posters in the workplace, a required-attendance meeting on company time in which the program will be explained,

and company raffles for participants. Additionally, workers in D_2 are being offered one-on-one meetings with a local financial planner. Vanguard and Philips will analyze several pre- and post-metrics:

- Number of people enrolled in the Philips 401k plan.
- Distribution of SmartSave participants at the 1 percent, 2 percent, and 3 percent levels.
- The average 401k savings rate.
- The SmartSave participation rate.
- The number of SmartSave participants who in April choose to abandon, continue, or increase their rate increase.

The experiment involves fewer than 10 percent of Philips employees, but SmartSave will be expanded if savings and participation rates increase. If successful, Vanguard will have a tool to boost the assets it manages in retirement plans, while helping thousands of Americans enjoy a more secure retirement—a win-win situation from any perspective. Can you diagram the Vanguard/Phillips experiment?

www.philips.com

www.vanguard.com

as the control case. Different levels of the same independent variable may also be used, with one level serving as the control.

Pretest–Post-Test Control Group Design   This design consists of adding a control group to the one-group pretest–post-test design and assigning the subjects to either of the groups by a random procedure (R). The diagram is:

$$R \quad O_1 \quad X \quad O_2$$
$$R \quad O_3 \qquad O_4$$

(4)

The effect of the experimental variable is

$$E = (O_2 - O_1) - (O_4 - O_3)$$

In this design, the seven major internal validity problems are dealt with fairly well, although there are still some difficulties. Local history may occur in one group and not the other. Also, if communication exists between people in test and control groups, there can be rivalry and other internal validity problems.

Maturation, testing, and regression are handled well because one would expect them to be felt equally in experimental and control groups. Mortality, however, can be a problem if there are different dropout rates in the study groups. Selection is adequately dealt with by random assignment.

The record of this design is not as good on external validity, however. There is a chance for a reactive effect from testing. This might be a substantial influence in attitude change studies where pretests introduce unusual topics and content. Nor does this design ensure against reaction between selection and the experimental variable. Even random selection may be defeated by a high decline rate by subjects. This would result in using a disproportionate share of people who are essentially volunteers and who may not be typical of the population. If this occurs, we will need to replicate the experiment several times with other groups under other conditions before we can be confident of external validity.

Post-Test-Only Control Group Design   In this design, the pretest measurements are omitted. Pretests are well established in classical research design but are not really necessary when it is possible to randomize. The design is:

$$R \quad X \quad O_1$$
$$R \qquad O_2$$

(5)

The experimental effect is measured by the difference between O_1 and O_2. The simplicity of this design makes it more attractive than the pretest–post-test control group design. Internal validity threats from history, maturation, selection, and statistical regression are adequately controlled by random assignment. Since the subjects are measured only once, the threats of testing and instrumentation are reduced, but different mortality rates between experimental and control groups continue to be a potential problem. The design reduces the external validity problem of testing interaction effect, although other problems remain.

Extensions of True Experimental Designs

True experimental designs have been discussed in their classical forms, but researchers normally use an operational extension of the basic design. These extensions differ from the classical design forms in (1) the number of different experimental stimuli that are considered simultaneously by the experimenter and (2) the extent to which assignment procedures are used to increase precision.

Researchers know that as many as 60 percent of purchase decisions are made in the store. Thus marketers aggressively seek in-store space to place temporary displays, shelf-talkers, and instant coupons, as well as ceiling signs and banners. Even the floor is contested real estate. So the ability to demonstrate the effectiveness of promotional materials is critical. FLOORgraphics, Inc., uses a longitudinal design, tracking sales of products in matched groups of stores (test and control groups). After test stores receive the FLOORad, relative sales in both groups are again compared to pre-ad performance and to each other. Research shows the FLOORad effect (the percentage sales increase directly due to the FLOORad) can lift sales 20–40 percent depending on the product category. www.floorgraphics.com

Check this website for examples of industrial experiments: http://www.statsoft.com/textbook/stathome.html.

Before we consider the types of extensions, some terms that are commonly used in the literature of applied experimentation must be introduced. **Factor** is widely used to denote an independent variable. Factors are divided into treatment levels, which represent various subgroups. A factor may have two or more levels, such as (1) male and female; (2) large, medium, and small; or (3) no training, brief training, and extended training. These levels should be operationally defined.

Factors also may be classified by whether the experimenter can manipulate the levels associated with the subject. **Active factors** are those the experimenter can manipulate by causing a subject to receive one level or another. Treatment is used to denote the different levels of active factors. With the second type, the **blocking factor,** the experimenter can only identify and classify the subject on an existing level. Gender, age group, customer status, and organizational rank are examples of blocking factors, because the subject comes to the experiment with a pre-existing level of each.

Up to this point, the assumption is that experimental subjects are people, but this is often not so. A better term for subject is **test unit;** it can refer equally well to an individual, organization, geographic market, animal, machine type, mix of materials, and innumerable other entities.

Completely Randomized Design The basic form of the true experiment is a completely randomized design. To illustrate its use, and that of more complex designs, consider a decision now facing the pricing manager at the Top Cannery. He would like to know what the ideal difference in price is between the Top's private brand of canned vegetables and national brands such as Del Monte and Stokely's.

Ever wonder how consumer product companies test the effectiveness of their creations? At Hill Top Research, Inc., founded in 1947 and the largest consumer product testing firm in the world, they use a variety of devices—including the human nose. In one deodorant study subjects were brought to a test site that contained a *hot room*. Researchers applied the product being tested to each subject's armpit, followed by the insertion of a cotton pad under each arm which subjects retained by pressing their arms to their sides. Researchers then led subjects to the *hot room*—where temperatures are warm enough to make anyone sweat. When the subjects exit the room after the defined period of time,

the cotton pad is removed for analysis, then the odor detective does his or her job. A cup with a small hole in the bottom is placed against the subject's armpit (to assure uniform distance between nose and pit), and then the detective positions her nose near the hole and inhales. With a successful formulation, the odor detective does not detect a strong or offensive odor. What are some of the variables a researcher would need to control in this study? What sources of error must be controlled?

www.hill-top.com

It is possible to set up an experiment on price differentials for canned green beans. Eighteen company stores and three price spreads (treatment levels) of 7 cents, 12 cents, and 17 cents between the company brand and national brands are used for the study. Six of the stores are assigned randomly to each of the treatment groups. The price differentials are maintained for a period, and then a tally is made of the sales volumes and gross profits of the canned green beans for each group of stores.

This design can be diagrammed as follows:

$$R \quad O_1 \quad X_1 \quad O_2$$
$$R \quad O_3 \quad X_3 \quad O_4 \qquad \qquad \textbf{(6)}$$
$$R \quad O_5 \quad X_5 \quad O_6$$

Here, O_1, O_3, and O_5 represent the total gross profits for canned green beans in the treatment stores for the month before the test. X_1, X_3, and X_5 represent 7-cent, 12-cent, and 17-cent treatments, while O_2, O_4, and O_6 are the gross profits for the month after the test started.

It is assumed that the randomization of stores to the three treatment groups was sufficient to make the three store groups equivalent. Where there is reason to believe this is not so, we must use a more complex design.

Randomized Block Design   When there is a single major extraneous variable, the randomized block design is used. Random assignment is still the basic way to produce equivalence among treatment groups, but something more may be needed for two reasons. The more critical reason is that the sample being studied may be so small that it is risky to depend on random assignment alone to guarantee equivalence. Small samples, such as the 18 company stores, are typical in field experiments because of high costs or because few test units are available. Another reason for blocking is to learn whether treatments bring different results among various groups of subjects.

Consider again the canned green beans pricing experiment. Assume there is reason to believe that lower-income families are more sensitive to price differentials than are higher-income families. This factor could seriously distort our results unless we stratify the stores by customer income. Therefore, each of the 18 stores is assigned to one of three income blocks and randomly assigned, within blocks, to the price difference treatments. The design is shown in the accompanying table.

In this design, one can measure both main effects and interaction effects. The **main effect** is the average direct influence that a particular treatment has independent of other factors. The **interaction effect** is the influence of one factor on the effect of another. The main effect of each price differential is secured by calculating the impact of each of the three treatments averaged over the different blocks. Interaction effects occur if you find that different customer income levels have a pronounced influence on customer reactions to the price differentials. (See Chapter 17, "Hypothesis Testing.")

		Blocking Factor—Customer Income		
Active Factor—Price Difference		**High**	**Medium**	**Low**
7 cents	R	X_1	X_1	X_1
12 cents	R	X_2	X_2	X_2
17 cents	R	X_3	X_3	X_3

(7)

Note: The O's have been omitted. The horizontal rows no longer indicate a time sequence, but various levels of the blocking factor. However, before-and-after measurements are associated with each of the treatments.

Whether the randomized block design improves the precision of the experimental measurement depends on how successfully the design minimizes the variance within blocks and maximizes the variance between blocks. If the response patterns are about the same in each block, there is little value to the more complex design. Blocking may be counterproductive.

Latin Square Design   The Latin square design may be used when there are two major extraneous factors. To continue with the pricing example, assume we decide to block on the size of store and on customer income. It is convenient to consider these two blocking factors as forming the rows and columns of a table. Each factor is divided into three levels to provide nine groups of stores, each representing a unique combination of the two blocking variables. Treatments are then randomly assigned to these cells so that a given treatment appears only once in each row and column. Because of this restriction, a Latin square must have the same number of rows, columns, and treatments. The design looks like the table below.

	Customer Income		
Store Size	**High**	**Medium**	**Low**
Large	X_3	X_1	X_2
Medium	X_2	X_3	X_1
Small	X_1	X_2	X_3

(8)

Treatments can be assigned by using a table of random numbers to set the order of treatment in the first row. For example, the pattern may be 3, 1, 2 as shown above. Following this, the other two cells of the first column are filled similarly, and the remaining treatments are assigned to meet the restriction that there can be no more than one treatment type in each row and column.

The experiment is carried out, sales results are gathered, and the average treatment effect is calculated. From this, we can determine the main effect of the various price spreads on the sales of company and national brands. With cost information, we can discover which price differential produces the greatest margin.

A limitation of the Latin square is that we must assume there is no interaction between treatments and blocking factors. Therefore, we cannot determine the interrelationships among store size, customer income, and price spreads. This limitation exists because there is not an exposure of all combinations of treatments, store sizes, and customer income groups. To do so would take a table of 27 cells, while this one has only 9. This can be accomplished by repeating the experiment twice to furnish the number needed to provide for every combination of store size, customer income, and treatment. If one is not especially interested in interaction, the Latin square is much more economical.

Factorial Design   One commonly held misconception about experiments is that the researcher can manipulate only one variable at a time. This is not true; with factorial designs, you can deal with more than one treatment simultaneously. Consider again the pricing experiment. The president of the chain might also be interested in finding the effect of posting unit prices on the shelf to aid shopper decision making. The accompanying table can be used to design an experiment that includes both the price differentials and the unit pricing.

Unit Price Information?	Price Spread		
	7 Cents	12 Cents	17 Cents
Yes	X_1Y_1	X_1Y_2	X_1Y_3
No	X_2Y_1	X_2Y_2	X_2Y_3

(9)

This is known as a 2×3 factorial design in which we use two factors: one with two levels and one with three levels of intensity. The version shown here is completely randomized, with the stores being randomly assigned to one of six treatment combinations. With such a design, it is possible to estimate the main effects of each of the two independent variables and the interactions between them. The results can help to answer the following questions:

1. What are the sales effects of the different price spreads between company and national brands?
2. What are the sales effects of using unit-price marking on the shelves?
3. What are the sales-effect interrelations between price spread and the presence of unit-price information?

We discuss the statistical aspects of covariance analysis when we present analysis of variance (ANOVA) in Chapter 17.

Covariance Analysis   We have discussed direct control of extraneous variables through blocking. It is also possible to apply some degree of indirect statistical control on one or more variables through analysis of covariance. Even with randomization, one may find that the before-measurement shows an average knowledge level difference between experimental and control groups. With covariance analysis, one can adjust statistically for this before-difference. Another application might occur if the canned green beans pricing experiment were carried out with a completely randomized design, only to reveal a contamination effect from differences in average customer income levels. With covariance analysis, one can still do some statistical blocking on average customer income even after the experiment has been run.

SNAPSHOT
Business Experiments on the Web?

We all know the Internet is useful for data collection. But experiments? Web samples are usually not representative of the populations we want to make inferences about. There are other concerns: Web access, uninvited participants, multiple trials by the same individual, "team" responses, distracting environments, and the lack of a probability sample for statistical inference. All of these issues currently stir debate. However, for some business studies, there are advantages to using a Web experiment.

Eric DeRosia, a marketing PhD student at the University of Michigan, has devised the "e-Experiment." According to DeRosia, "The software's purpose is to facilitate primary research over the Web in fields such as psychology and consumer behavior." He claims advantages and disadvantages over traditional laboratory experiments. In a pilot study of 125 marketing students who were randomly assigned to a supervised group lab and an outside lab on the Web, responses to stimuli from attitude and brand honesty scales revealed strikingly similar reliability coefficients. In some ways, DeRosia notes, Web experiments provide more control over stimulus timing, response code verification (out-of-range responses), and participants who peek ahead or change previous answers. By randomly assigning participants to experimental treatments and by controlling which questions are presented and their order, many objections to Web experiments are tackled. For e-Experiment to work properly, it needs a small CGI program on a Web server. Such programs pose security risks for universities and businesses, thus requiring a third-party vendor to host the research. Future programming will make this unnecessary.

In the meantime, other software is being released that continues the promise of e-Experiment: rapid data collection, graphical interface, open- and closed-question programming, randomization, estimation of participant loss rates, response time calculation, and authentication of participation (for rewards or incentives).

www-personal.umich.edu/~ederosia/e-exp/

Field Experiments: Quasi- or Semi-Experiments[8]

Under field conditions, we often cannot control enough of the extraneous variables or the experimental treatment to use a true experimental design. Because the stimulus condition occurs in a natural environment, a **field experiment** is required.

A modern version of the bystander and thief field experiment, mentioned at the beginning of the chapter, involves the use of electronic article surveillance to prevent shrinkage due to shoplifting. In a proprietary study, a shopper came to the optical counter of an upscale mall store and asked the salesperson to see special designer frames. The salesperson, a confederate of the experimenter, replied that she would get them from a case in the adjoining department and disappeared. The "thief" selected two pairs of sunglasses from an open display, deactivated the security tags at the counter, and walked out of the store.

Thirty-five percent of the subjects (store customers) reported the theft upon the return of the salesperson. Sixty-three percent reported it when the salesperson asked about the shopper. Unlike previous studies, the presence of a second customer did not reduce the willingness to report a theft.

This study was not possible with a control group, a pretest, or randomization of customers, but the information gained was essential and justified a compromise of true experimental designs. We use the pre-experimental designs previously discussed or quasi-experiments to deal with such conditions. In a quasi-experiment, we often cannot know when or to whom to expose the experimental treatment. Usually, however, we can decide when and whom to measure. A quasi-experiment is inferior to a true experimental design but is usually superior to pre-experimental designs. In this section, we consider a few common quasi-experiments.

Nonequivalent Control Group Design This is a strong and widely used quasi-experimental design. It differs from the pretest–post-test control group design, because the test and control groups are not randomly assigned. The design is diagrammed as follows:

$$
\begin{array}{ccc}
O_1 & X & O_2 \\
\text{------} & \text{------} & \text{------} \\
O_3 & & O_4
\end{array}
\tag{10}
$$

There are two varieties. One is the *intact equivalent design,* in which the membership of the experimental and control groups is naturally assembled. For example, we may use different classes in a school, membership in similar clubs, or customers from similar stores. Ideally, the two groups are as alike as possible. This design is especially useful when any type of individual selection process would be reactive.

The second variation, the *self-selected experimental group design,* is weaker because volunteers are recruited to form the experimental group, while nonvolunteer subjects are used for control. Such a design is likely when subjects believe it would be in their interest to be a subject in an experiment—say, an experimental training program.

Comparison of pretest results $(O_1 - O_3)$ is one indicator of the degree of equivalence between test and control groups. If the pretest results are significantly different, there is a real question about the groups' comparability. On the other hand, if pretest observations are similar between groups, there is more reason to believe internal validity of the experiment is good.

Separate Sample Pretest-Post-Test Design   This design is most applicable when we cannot know when and to whom to introduce the treatment but we can decide when and whom to measure. The basic design is:

$$
\begin{array}{cccc}
R & O_1 & (X) & \\
R & & X & O_2
\end{array}
\tag{11}
$$

The bracketed treatment (X) is irrelevant to the purpose of the study but is shown to suggest that the experimenter cannot control the treatment.

This is not a strong design because several threats to internal validity are not handled adequately. History can confound the results but can be overcome by repeating the study at other times in other settings. In contrast, it is considered superior to true experiments in external validity. Its strength results from its being a field experiment in which the samples are usually drawn from the population to which we wish to generalize our findings.

We would find this design more appropriate if the population were large, if a before-measurement were reactive, or if there were no way to restrict the application of the treatment. Assume a company is planning an intense campaign to change its employees' attitudes toward energy conservation. It might draw two random samples of employees, one of which is interviewed about energy use attitudes before the information campaign. After the campaign the other group is interviewed.

Group Time Series Design   A time series design introduces repeated observations before and after the treatment and allows subjects to act as their own controls. The single treatment group design has before-after measurements as the only controls. There is also a multiple design with two or more comparison groups as well as the repeated measurements in each treatment group.

The time series format is especially useful where regularly kept records are a natural part of the environment and are unlikely to be reactive. The time series approach is also a good way to study unplanned events in an ex post facto manner. If the federal government would suddenly begin price controls, we could still study the effects of this action later if we had regularly collected records for the period before and after the advent of price control.

The internal validity problem for this design is history. To reduce this risk, we keep a record of possible extraneous factors during the experiment and attempt to adjust the results to reflect their influence.

Close-Up

A Job Enrichment Quasi-Experiment[9]

One theory of job attitudes holds that "hygiene" factors, which include working conditions, pay, security, status, interpersonal relationships, and company policy, can be a major source of dissatisfaction among workers but have little positive motivational power. This theory says that the positive motivator factors are intrinsic to the job; they include achievement, recognition for achievement, the work itself, responsibility, and growth or advancement.[10]

A study of the value of job enrichment as a builder of job satisfaction was carried out with laboratory technicians, or "experimental officers" (EOs), at British Chemical. The project was a multiple group time series quasi-experiment. The project is diagrammed at the end of this "Close-Up."

Two sections of the department acted as experimental groups and two sections acted as control groups. It is not clear how these groups were chosen, but there was no mention of random assignment. One of the experimental groups and one of the control groups worked closely together, while the other two groups were separated geographically and were engaged in different research. Hygiene factors were held constant during the research, and the studies were kept confidential to avoid the tendency of participants to act in artificial ways.

A before-measurement was made using a job reaction survey instrument. This indicated the EOs typically had low morale, and many wrote of their frustrations. All EOs were asked to write monthly progress reports, and these were used to assess the quality of their work. The assessment was made against eight specifically defined criteria by a panel of three managers who were not members of the department. These assessors were never told which laboratory technicians were in the experimental group and which were in the control group.

The study extended over a year, with the treatments introduced in the experimental groups at the start of the 12-month study period. Changes were made to give experimental group EOs important chances for achievement; these changes also made the work more challenging. Recognition of achievement was given, authority over certain aspects was increased, new managerial responsibilities were assigned to the senior EOs, added advancements were given to others, and the opportunity for self-initiated work was provided. After about six months, these same changes were instituted with one of the control groups, while the remaining group continued for the entire period as a control. Several months of EO progress reports were available as a prior base line for evaluation. The results of this project are shown in Exhibit 14–4.

$$O\ O\ O\ X\ O\ O\ O\ O\ O\ O\ O\ O\ O\ O\ O$$

$$O\ O\ O\ O\ O\ O\ O\ O\ X\ O\ O\ O\ O\ O\ O$$

$$O\ O\ O\ O\ O\ O\ O\ O\ O\ O\ O\ O\ O\ O\ O$$

EXHIBIT 4–4 **Assessment of EOs' Monthly Reports**

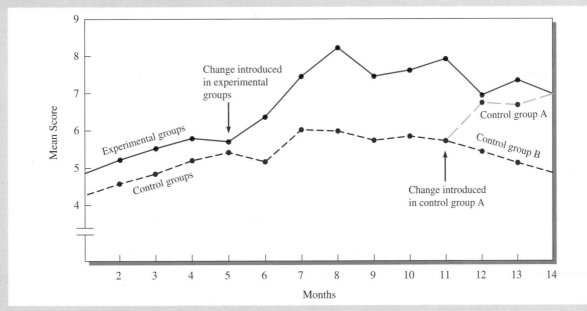

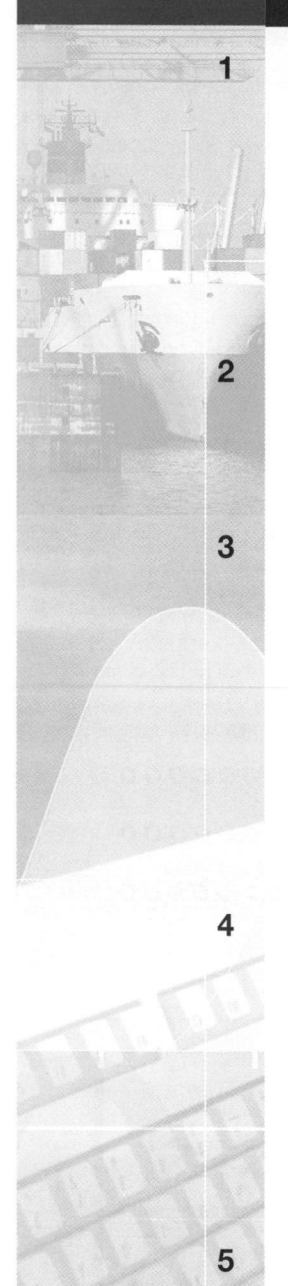

SUMMARY

1   Experiments are studies involving intervention by the researcher beyond that required for measurement. The usual intervention is to manipulate a variable (the independent variable) and observe how it affects the subjects being studied (the dependent variable).

An evaluation of the experimental method reveals several advantages: (1) the ability to uncover causal relationships, (2) provisions for controlling extraneous and environmental variables, (3) convenience and low cost of creating test situations rather than searching for their appearance in business situations, (4) the ability to replicate findings and thus rule out idiosyncratic or isolated results, and (5) the ability to exploit naturally occurring events.

2   Some advantages of other methods that are liabilities for the experiment include: (1) the artificial setting of the laboratory, (2) generalizability from nonprobability samples, (3) disproportionate costs in select business situations, (4) a focus restricted to the present and immediate future, and (5) ethical issues related to the manipulation and control of human subjects.

3   Consideration of the following activities is essential for the execution of a well-planned experiment:

1. Select relevant variables for testing.

2. Specify the levels of treatment.

3. Control the environmental and extraneous factors.

4. Choose an experimental design suited to the hypothesis.

5. Select and assign subjects to groups.

6. Pilot-test, revise, and conduct the final test.

7. Analyze the data.

4   We judge various types of experimental research designs by how well they meet the tests of internal and external validity. An experiment has high internal validity if one has confidence that the experimental treatment has been the source of change in the dependent variable. More specifically, a design's internal validity is judged by how well it meets seven threats. These are history, maturation, testing, instrumentation, selection, statistical regression, and experiment mortality.

External validity is high when the results of an experiment are judged to apply to some larger population. Such an experiment is said to have high external validity regarding that population. Three potential threats to external validity are testing reactivity, selection interaction, and other reactive factors.

5   Experimental research designs include (1) pre-experiments, (2) true experiments, and (3) quasi-experiments. The main distinction among these types is the degree of control that the researcher can exercise over validity problems.

Three pre-experimental designs were presented in the chapter. These designs represent the crudest form of experimentation and are undertaken only when nothing stronger is possible. Their weakness is the lack of an equivalent comparison group; as a result, they fail to meet many internal validity criteria. They are the (1) one-shot control study, (2) one-group pretest–post-test design, and (3) static group comparison.

Two forms of the true experiment were also presented. Their central characteristic is that they provide a means by which we can assure equivalence between experimental

and control groups through random assignment to the groups. These designs are (1) pretest–post-test control group and (2) post-test-only control group.

The classical two-group experiment can be extended to multigroup designs in which different levels of the test variable are used as controls rather than the classical nontest control. In addition, the true experimental design is extended into more sophisticated forms that use blocking. Two such forms, the randomized block and the Latin square, were discussed. Finally, the factorial design was discussed in which two or more independent variables can be accommodated.

Between the extremes of pre-experiments, with little or no control, and true experiments, with random assignment, there is a gray area in which we find quasi-experiments. These are useful designs when some variables can be controlled, but equivalent experimental and control groups usually cannot be established by random assignment. There are many quasi-experimental designs, but only three were covered in this chapter: (1) nonequivalent control group design, (2) separate sample pretest–post-test design, and (3) group time series design.

KEY TERMS

active factors   439
blind   429
blocking factors   439
control group   428
dependent variable (DV)   425
double blind   429
environmental control   429
experimental treatment   428

experiments   425
external validity   432
factor   439
field experiment   443
hypothesis   428
independent variable (IV)   425
interaction effect   441
internal validity   432

main effect   441
matching   430
operationalized   428
quota matrix   430
random assignment   430
replication   427
test unit   439
treatment levels   428

EXAMPLES

Company	Scenario	Page
ACNielsen	Ad recall survey and purchasing behavior data drawn from its Household Scanner Panel™ served as the test and control groups for the Magazine Publishers of America study on ad effectiveness.	430
British Chemical[*]	A study of the value of job enrichment as a builder of job satisfaction.	445
FLOORgraphics, Inc.	Using test and control groups to determine the effectiveness of FLOORads.	439
Hill Top Research, Inc.	Human odor detectives employed to test the effectiveness of underarm deodorants.	440
Magazine Publishers of America (MPA)	Conducted a study to prove the sales lift following magazine advertising using the purchasing behavior of a panel.	430
Philips Electronics North America	Sponsoring a research study to encourage employees to increase their 401k savings rate.	437
Research House Inc.	A Canadian firm offering a variety of facilities for different types of studies.	426

| Top Cannery[*] | An experiment to determine the ideal price difference between private and national brands. | 439 |
| Vanguard | Conducting a study to determine whether employees will save more in 401k savings if their savings increase comes from future raises rather than current earnings. | 437 |

[*]Due to the confidential and proprietary nature of most research, the names of some companies have been changed.

DISCUSSION QUESTIONS

Terms in Review

1. Distinguish between the following:

   a. Internal validity and external validity.

   b. Pre-experimental design and quasi-experimental design.

   c. History and maturation.

   d. Random sampling, randomization, and matching.

   e. Active factors and blocking factors.

   f. Environmental variables and extraneous variables.

2. Compare the advantages of experiments with the advantages of survey and observational methods.

3. Why would a noted business researcher say, "It is essential that we always keep in mind the model of the controlled experiment, even if in practice we have to deviate from an ideal model"?

4. What ethical problems do you see in conducting experiments with human subjects?

5. What essential characteristics distinguish a true experiment from other research designs?

Making Research Decisions

6. A lighting company seeks to study the percentage of defective glass shells being manufactured. Theoretically, the percentage of defectives is dependent on temperature, humidity, and the level of artisan expertise. Complete historical data are available for the following variables on a daily basis for a year:

   a. Temperature (high, normal, low).

   b. Humidity (high, normal, low).

   c. Artisan expertise level (expert, average, mediocre).

   Some experts feel that defectives also depend on production supervisors. However, data on supervisors in charge are available for only 242 of the 365 days. How should this study be conducted?

7. Describe how you would operationalize variables for experimental testing in the following research question: What are the performance differences between 10 microcomputers connected in a local-area network (LAN) and one minicomputer with 10 terminals?

8. A pharmaceuticals manufacturer is testing a drug developed to treat cancer. During the final stages of development the drug's effectiveness is being tested on individuals for different (1) dosage conditions and (2) age groups. One of the problems is patient mortality during experimentation. Justify your design recommendations through a comparison of alternatives and in terms of external and internal validity.

   a. Recommend the appropriate design for the experiment.

   b. Explain the use of control groups, blinds, and double blinds if you recommend them.

9. You are asked to develop an experiment for a study of the effect that compensation has on the response rates secured from personal interview subjects. This study will involve 300

people who will be assigned to one of the following conditions: (1) no compensation, (2) $1 compensation, and (3) $3 compensation. A number of sensitive issues will be explored concerning various social problems, and the 300 people will be drawn from the adult population. Describe how your design would be set up if it were (a) a completely randomized design, (b) a randomized block design, (c) a Latin square, and (d) a factorial design (suggest another active variable to use). Which would you use? Why?

10. What type of experimental design would you recommend in each of the following cases? Suggest in some detail how you would design each study:

   a. A test of three methods of compensation of factory workers. The methods are hourly wage, incentive pay, and weekly salary. The dependent variable is direct labor cost per unit of output.

   b. A study of the effects of various levels of advertising effort and price reduction on the sale of specific branded grocery products by a retail grocery chain.

   c. A study to determine whether it is true that the use of fast-paced music played over a store's public address system will speed the shopping rate of customers without an adverse effect on the amount spent per customer.

Bringing Research to Life

11. Identify an experiment done with subjects who are twins that would meet the criteria that Dorrie feels must be met for experimentation.

From Concept to Practice

12. Using Exhibit 14–3, diagram an experiment described in one of the Snapshots featured in this chapter using research design symbols.

13. For experiments and surveys on the Web, visit http://www.psych.upenn.edu/links.html#webexpts and participate in an online experiment. Prepare a short paper describing your experience and make suggestions for improving the experimental design.

WWW Exercises   Visit our website for Internet exercises related to this chapter at www.mhhe.com/business/cooper8

CASES*

 ENVIROSELL, INC.   **RETAILERS UNHAPPY WITH DISPLAYS FROM MANUFACTURERS**

 GOODYEAR'S AQUATRED

*All cases indicating a video icon are located on the Instructor's Videotape Supplement. All nonvideo cases are in the case section of the textbook. All cases indicating a CD icon offer a data set, which is located on the accompanying CD.

REFERENCE NOTES

1. Bibb Latane and J. M. Darley, *The Unresponsive Bystander: Why Doesn't He Help?* (New York: Appleton-Century-Crofts, 1970), pp. 69–77. Research into the responses of bystanders who witness crimes was stimulated by an incident in New York City where Kitty Genovese was attacked and killed in the presence of 38 witnesses who refused to come to her aid or summon authorities.

2. This section is largely adapted from Julian L. Simon and Paul Burstein, *Basic Research Methods in Social Science,* 3rd ed. (New York: Random House, 1985), pp. 128–33.

3. For a thorough explanation of this topic, see Helena C. Kraemer and Sue Thiemann, *How Many Subjects? Statistical Power Analysis in Research* (Beverly Hills, CA: Sage Publications, 1987).

4. Kenneth D. Bailey, *Methods of Social Research,* 2nd ed. (New York: Free Press, 1982), pp. 230–33.

5. The concept of a quota matrix and the tabular form for Exhibit 14–2 were adapted from Earl R. Babbie, *The Practice of Social Research,* 5th ed. (Belmont, CA: Wadsworth, 1989), pp. 218–19.

6. Donald T. Campbell and Julian C. Stanley, *Experimental and Quasi-Experimental Designs for Research* (Chicago: Rand McNally, 1963), p. 5.

7. Thomas D. Cook and Donald T. Campbell, "The Design and Conduct of Quasi-Experiments and True Experiments in Field Settings," in *Handbook of Industrial and Organizational Psychology*, ed. Marvin D. Dunnette (Chicago: Rand McNally, 1976), p. 223.

8. For an in-depth discussion of many quasi-experiment designs and their internal validity, see ibid., pp. 246–98.

9. William J. Paul, Jr., Keith B. Robertson, and Frederick Herzberg, "Job Enrichment Pays Off," *Harvard Business Review* (March–April 1969), pp. 61–78.

10. Frederick J. Herzberg, "One More Time: How Do You Motivate Employees?" *Harvard Business Review* (January–February 1968), pp. 53–62.

REFERENCES FOR SNAPSHOTS AND CAPTIONS

e-Experiments

Eric DeRosia, "True Experiments on the Web," Working Paper 99-021 (Ann Arbor, MI: University of Michigan Business School) (http://www-personal.umich.edu/~ederosia/e-exp).

FLOORad

Antonia DeMatto, FLOORgraphics, Inc.
"Raising the Roof with Floor Ads," *Business Week*, September 16, 1999 (http://www.businessweek.com:/smallbiz/news/coladvice/reallife/r1990916.htm?scriptFramed).
"Floor Show: Savvy Ideas to Boost Sales," *Entrepreneur* (http://www.entrepreneur.com/Magazines/MA_SegArticle/0,1539,227019----2-,00.html).

Hill Top Research

"Good Morning America," ABC News, March 3, 2000 (www.hilltop.com/consumer.html).

Vanguard/Philips

Richard H. Thaler and Shlomo Benartzi, "Save More Tomorrow: Using Behavioral Economics to Increase Employee Saving," Working Paper, August 2001.
Louis Uchitelle, "Economic View: Why It Takes Psychology to Make People Save," *The New York Times*, January 13, 2002, p. 4, sec. 3.
Steve Utkus, Vanguard, interview on February 4, 2002.

MPA

Lorraine Calvacca, "Making a Case for the Glossies," *American Demographics*, July 1999, pp. 36–37 (http://www.magazine.org/resources/downloads/Sales_Scan_Highlights.pdf).

CLASSIC AND CONTEMPORARY READING

Campbell, Donald T., and M. Jean Russo. *Social Experimentation.* Thousand Oaks, CA: Sage Publishing, 1998. The evolution of the late Professor Campbell's thinking on validity control in experimental design.

Campbell, Donald T., and Julian C. Stanley. *Experimental and Quasi-Experimental Designs for Research.* Chicago: Rand McNally, 1963. A universally quoted discussion of experimental designs in the social sciences.

Cook, Thomas D., and Donald T. Campbell. "The Design and Conduct of Quasi-Experiments and True Experiments in Field Settings." In *Handbook of Industrial and Organizational Psychology.* 2nd ed., edited by Marvin D. Dunnette and Leaetta M. Hough. Palo Alto, CA: Consulting Psychologists Press, 1990. *Quasi-Experimentation: Design and Analysis Issues for Field Settings.* Chicago: Rand McNally, 1979. Major authoritative works on both true and quasi-experiments and their design. Already classic references.

Edwards, Allen. *Experimental Design in Psychological Research.* 4th ed. New York: Holt, Rinehart & Winston, 1972. A complete treatment of experimental design with helpful illustrative examples.

Green, Paul E., Donald S. Tull, and Gerald Albaum. *Research for Marketing Decisions.* 5th ed. Englewood Cliffs, NJ: Prentice-Hall, 1988. A definitive text with sections on the application of experimentation to marketing research.

Kirk, Roger E. *Experimental Design: Procedures for the Behavioral Sciences.* 3rd ed. Belmont, CA: Brooks/Cole, 1994. An advanced text on the statistical aspects of experimental design.

Krathwohl, David R. *Social and Behavioral Science Research: A New Framework for Conceptualizing, Implementing, and Evaluating Research Studies.* San Francisco: Jossey-Bass, 1985. Chapters 3, 4, and 5 present a convincing argument for reformulating internal and external validity into broader concepts. A conceptually refreshing approach.

PART IV

Analysis and Presentation of Data

CHAPTER 15

Data Preparation and Description

Learning Objectives

After reading this chapter, you should understand . . .

1 **The importance of editing the collected raw data to detect errors and omissions.**

2 **How coding is used to assign numbers and other symbols to answers in order to classify responses.**

3 **The use of content analysis to interpret and summarize open questions.**

4 **Problems and solutions for "don't know" responses.**

5 **The options for data entry and manipulation.**

6 **How to select descriptive statistics to summarize the collected data and check for errors.**

Bringing Research to Life

Dorrie Henry arrived for lunch, joining Jason and Myra, who were wrapping up a Mind-Writer meeting. The conversation naturally turned to one of Jason's early research projects.

"As a public health doctor," said Dorrie, "I work with statistics—life-threatening ones. I understand Jason's perfectionism and why he carries it to such extremes. You know how 'difficult' he can be when he is under stress."

Myra responded by arching her eyebrows and laughing mirthlessly.

"I can see this turning into a bashing Jason story," Jason groaned.

"Has Jason told you about our near blowup over the bus line survey? No? Before we moved down here and he connected with you, Jason was retained by a bus line up north to assist in a sample survey of 2,000 passengers. The line had just dismissed its research director, a horrible chap named Burbidge, who could not relate to the blue-collar riders.

"Jason had a 20-question survey of 2,000 randomly selected riders, a total of 40,000 items to be coded, some of them multiple choice, some of them numerical entry, some free response. He estimated this would take 15 seconds an item, on the average, a total of 10,000 minutes, which he rounded up to 12,000 minutes. Call it 200 person-hours, then. He decided to hire 25 temporary personnel for one eight-hour data entry shift."

"That sounds reasonable," said Myra.

"Well, of course it was quite reasonable. What wasn't 'reasonable' was Jason. Since CityBus received a county subsidy, the bus line had to follow county purchasing procedures and put the data entry out for competitive bidding.

"As board member of a nonprofit organization that provides temporary employment for former mental patients, I insisted on bidding for the data entry work, over Jason's strongest objections. He had never expressed any objections to my finding work for these people before, but when I wanted them involved in his own work, he became prickly, hostile, self-pitying, irritable, and hypercritical."

"I've seen that side of Jason," grinned Myra.

"Would you like me to leave so you can shred me without compunction?" replied Jason.

"I'm certain you have," said Dorrie, ignoring Jason, "and certainly you know what motivated it— the most intense desire for accuracy and reliability."

"Which, as his client, I not only appreciate but demand," supported Myra. "See, Jason, Dorrie's not really telling tales."

"Thanks to his association with you, Myra, he has learned to moderate the acting-out of his anxieties, for which I thank you. But on the inside he ceaselessly worries about threats to validity.

"I won the CityBus contract, and Jason had no choice. The contract had me bringing my crew in at 5 P.M. on a Friday evening to bus line HQ, putting each worker in a separate office, using 25 networked computers in employee offices. Each member of the crew, sitting in a separate office, was given 80 surveys to encode, 10 an hour, for eight hours.

"Jason procured a data entry program, which we ran off the system server. The program very cleverly contrived to prevent errors of data entry, so far as possible. For instance, if a survey item—a question—called for choosing between 'Ride the bus less than twice a week,' 'Ride the bus at least twice but less than 8 times,' or 'Ride the bus 8 or more times,' the data clerk would put a cursor over the correct answer and press ENTER. Making a mistake would be difficult, because the screen would closely resemble the printed page. If the item called for "Enter your age," and the clerk entered a three-digit number, the computer would beep loudly, to indicate that ages less than 10 and greater than 99 were considered suspect.

"Jason continued to face the prospect of DEN—data entry night—with thinly disguised opposition. He grumbled that my crew would ruin the results of his carefully crafted research. I reminded him that these people were not visually impaired and had no intellectual deficits. They were just folks who were not yet ready to reenter the workplace or were ready but suffered unreasonable discrimination, of exactly the sort Jason was showing.

"Anyway, while it was prudent to warn the HQ staff to secure their offices, Jason went overboard and infected the office staff with his nervousness and negativity about my crew coming in to use their computers. At 4:45 P.M., our bus arrived with me, my crew, and a supervisory social worker, to find office workers departing carrying out their potted plants. Did they think my crew were herbivores? It was a flagrant insult, and I felt awful."

"You are going to tell the part where I redeem myself, aren't you?" asked Jason plaintively.

"Jason, concerned with human error, double-checked the data entry. A 26th crew member ran up and down the halls all night retrieving randomly sampled surveys, which Jason compared with the already entered data in the server. He warned me that if he found more than a certain error rate he intended to stop the operation and send everyone home. He was working himself into a lather, looking for trouble he was not going to find.

"As he was pulling the forms generated by 25 workers, he had to work at least as fast as any one of them to keep up, slightly faster in fact, and very frankly I had serious doubts that he would not make more errors than my crew and blame the errors on them. He skipped supper at 8 P.M. and worked steadily and crankily and drank too much black coffee. No bathroom breaks or stretch breaks for super sleuth. But at 10 P.M., five hours into our eight-hour shift, he threw down his surveys, smiled broadly, murmured 'darn good,' strolled off to the bathroom, returned, ate two peanut butter and jelly sandwiches and made a few dumb jokes.

"It seems," continued Dorrie, "the discrepancy rate between his coding and my crew was less than 1 percent for the first five hours. He spent the next two hours humming 'Strangers in the Night,' over and over again and running preliminary frequency distributions and cross-tabulations."

"In the end, Jason was 'big' enough to express considerable satisfaction with your crew, right?" inquired Myra.

"Of course. After all, when HQ office workers came back Monday, toting their philodendrons, they found their offices clean, orderly, and mysteriously mint-scented. Each of my crew had cleaned the keyboards and monitor screens with little sanitized towelettes. And Jason had error-free data in the bargain."

Introduction

Once the data begin to flow in, attention turns to data analysis. If the project has been done correctly, the analysis planning is already done. Back in the research design stage or at least by completion of the proposal or the pilot test, decisions should have been made about how to analyze the data. Unfortunately, many researchers wait until the analysis stage to decide what to do. This results in the late discovery that some data will not be collected, will be collected in the wrong form, or will exhibit unanticipated characteristics.

This chapter addresses two topics. The first is *data preparation,* which includes editing, coding, and data entry. These activities ensure the accuracy of the data and their conversion from raw form to reduced and classified forms that are more appropriate for analysis. Second, preparing a descriptive statistical summary is the preliminary step leading to an understanding of the collected data. If your research objective is reporting or basic description, this section is particularly valuable. We discuss the definitions and applications of descriptive statistics, specifically the characteristics of location, spread, and shape that give us insight into the distributions of respondent observations.

Before concluding this introduction, we must comment briefly on our assumption for this part of the book. The book was developed for and with graduate students. It may be used successfully with undergraduates if an elementary statistics course was a prerequisite. Without that grounding, some of the ideas presented may require remedial study.

Editing

MANAGEMENT

The customary first step in analysis is to edit the raw data. **Editing** detects errors and omissions, corrects them when possible, and certifies that minimum data quality standards have been achieved. The editor's purpose is to guarantee that data are:

- Accurate.
- Consistent with intent of the question and other information in the survey.
- Uniformly entered.
- Complete.
- Arranged to simplify coding and tabulation.

In the following question asked of military officers, one respondent checked two categories, indicating that he was in the reserves and currently serving on active duty.

> Please indicate your current military status:
> ☑ Active duty officer
> ❑ National Guard officer
> ☑ Reserve officer
> ❑ Separated officer
> ❑ Retired officer

The editor's responsibility is to decide which of the responses is both consistent with the intent of the question or other information in the survey and most accurate for this individual respondent.

Field Editing

In large projects, field editing review is a responsibility of the field supervisor. It, too, should be done soon after the data have been gathered. During the stress of data collection, the researcher often uses ad hoc abbreviations and special symbols. Soon after the interview, experiment, or observation, the investigator should review the reporting forms. It is difficult to complete what was abbreviated or written in shorthand or noted illegibly if the entry is not caught that day. When entry gaps are present from interviews, a callback should be made rather than guessing what the respondent "probably would have said." Self-interviewing has no place in quality research.

A second important control function of the field supervisor is to validate the field results. This normally means he or she will reinterview some percentage of the respondents, at least on some questions. Many commercial research firms will recontact about 10 percent of the respondents.

Central Editing

At this point, the data should get a thorough editing. For a small study, the use of a single editor produces maximum consistency. In large studies, the tasks may be broken down so that each editor can deal with one entire section. This approach will not identify inconsistencies between answers in different sections. However, this problem can be handled by identifying points of possible inconsistency and having one editor check specifically for them.

Sometimes it is obvious that an entry is incorrect, is entered in the wrong place, or states time in months when it was requested in weeks. When replies clearly are inappropriate or missing, the editor can sometimes detect the proper answer by reviewing the other information in the schedule. This practice, however, should be limited to those few cases where it is obvious what the correct answer is. It may be better to contact the respondent for correct information, if time and budget allow. Another alternative is for the editor to strike out the answer if it is clearly inappropriate. Here an editing entry of "no answer" or "unknown" is called for.

Another editing problem concerns faking an interview that never took place. This armchair interviewing is difficult to spot, but the editor is in the best position to do so. One approach is to check responses to open-ended questions. These are most difficult to fake. Distinctive response patterns in other questions will often emerge if faking is occurring. To uncover this, the editor must analyze the instruments used by each interviewer.

Here are some useful rules to guide editors in their work:

MANAGEMENT
Tip

- Be familiar with instructions given to interviewers and coders.

- Do not destroy, erase, or make illegible the original entry by the interviewer; original entries should be crossed out with a single line to remain legible.

- Make all entries on an instrument in some distinctive color and in a standardized form.

- Initial all answers changed or supplied.

- Place initials and date of editing on each instrument completed.

Coding

Coding involves assigning numbers or other symbols to answers so the responses can be grouped into a limited number of classes or categories. The classifying of data into limited categories sacrifices some data detail but is necessary for efficient analysis. Instead of requesting the word *male* or *female* in response to a question that asks for the identification of one's gender, we could use the codes "M" or "F." Normally this variable would be coded 1 for male and 2 for female or 0 and 1. If we use M and F, or other letters, in combination with numbers and symbols, the code is *alphanumeric.* When numbers are used exclusively, the code is *numeric.*

Coding helps the researcher to reduce several thousand replies to a few categories containing the critical information needed for analysis. In coding, *categories* are the partitioning of a set; and *categorization* is the process of using rules to partition a body of data.

Coding Rules

Four rules guide the establishment of category sets. The categories should be:

- Appropriate to the research problem and purpose.

- Exhaustive.

- Mutually exclusive.
- Derived from one classification principle.

Appropriateness   Categories must provide the best partitioning of data for testing hypotheses and showing relationships. Year-by-year age differences may be important to the question being researched. If so, wider age classifications hamper the analysis. If specific income, attitude, or reason categories are critical to the testing relationship, then we must choose the best groupings. In particular, choose class boundaries that match those being used for comparisons. It is disheartening, late in a study, to discover that age, income, or other frequency classes do not precisely match those of the data with which we wish to make comparisons.

Exhaustiveness   A large number of "other" responses suggests our classification set may be too limited. In such cases, we may not be tapping the full range of information in the data. Failure to present an adequate list of alternatives is especially damaging when multiple-choice questions are used. Any answer that is not specified in the set will surely be underrepresented in the tally.

While the exhaustiveness requirement in a single category set may be obvious, a second aspect is less apparent. Does the one set of categories fully capture all the information in the data? For example, responses to an open-ended question about family economic prospects for the next year may originally be classified only in terms of being optimistic or pessimistic. It may also be enlightening to classify responses in terms of other concepts such as the precise focus of these expectations (income or jobs) and variations in responses between family heads and others in the family.

Mutual Exclusivity   Another important rule is that category components should be mutually exclusive. This standard is met when a specific answer can be placed in one and only one cell in a category set. For example, in an occupation survey, the classifications may be (1) professional, (2) managerial, (3) sales, (4) clerical, (5) crafts, (6) operatives, and (7) unemployed. Some respondents will think of themselves as being in more than one of these groups. The person who views selling as a profession and spends time supervising others may fit in three of these categories. A function of operational definitions is to provide categories that are composed of mutually exclusive elements. Here, operational definitions of the occupations to be classified in "professional," "managerial," and "sales" should clarify the situation. The problem of how to handle an unemployed salesperson brings up a fourth rule of category design.

Single Dimension   The need for a category set to follow a single classificatory principle means every class in the category set is defined in terms of one concept. Returning to the occupation survey example, the person in the study might be both a salesperson and unemployed. The "salesperson" label expresses the concept *occupation type;* the response "unemployed" is another dimension concerned with *current employment status* without regard to the respondent's normal occupation. When a category set uses more than one dimension, it will normally not be mutually exclusive unless the cells in the set combine the dimensions (employed manager, unemployed manager, and so on).

**Codebook
Construction**

A **codebook,** or *coding scheme,* contains each variable in the study and specifies the application of coding rules to the variable. It is used by the researcher or research staff as a guide to make data entry less prone to error and more efficient. It is also the definitive source for locating the positions of variables in the data file during analysis. In many statistical programs, the coding scheme is integral to the data file. Most codebooks—computerized or not—contain the question number, variable name, location of the variable's code on the input medium, descriptors for the response options, and whether the variable is alpha or numeric. An example of a paper-based codebook is shown in Exhibit 15–1. When pilot testing has been conducted, there should be sufficient infor-

EXHIBIT 15–1   **Sample Codebook of Questionnaire Items**

Question	Variable Number	Code Description	Variable Name
_____	1	Record number	RECNUM
_____	2	Respondent number	RESID
1	3	5 digit zip code 99999 = Missing	ZIP
2	4	2 digit birth year 99 = Missing	BIRTH
3	5	Gender 1 = Male 2 = Female 9 = Missing	GENDER
4	6	Marital status 1 = Married 2 = Widow(er) 3 = Divorced 4 = Separated 5 = Never married 9 = Missing	MARITAL
5	7	Own–Rent 1 = Own 2 = Rent 3 = Provided 9 = Missing	HOUSING
6		Reason for purchase 1 = Mentioned 0 = Not mentioned	
	8	Bought home	HOME
	9	Birth of child	BIRTHCHD
	10	Death of relative or friend	DEATH
	11	Promoted	PROMO
	12	Changed job/career	CHGJOB
	13	Paid college expenses	COLLEXP
	14	Acquired assets	ASSETS
	15	Retired	RETIRED
	16	Changed marital status	CHGMAR
	17	Started business	STARTBUS
	18	Expanded business	EXPBUS
	19	Parent's influence	PARENT
	20	Contacted by agent	AGENT
	21	Other	OTHER

mation about the variables to prepare a codebook. A preliminary codebook used with pilot data may reveal coding problems that will need to be corrected before the data for the final study are collected and processed.

Coding Closed Questions

The responses to closed questions include scaled items and others for which answers can be anticipated. When codes are established early in the research process, it is possible to precode the questionnaire. **Precoding** is particularly helpful for data entry because it makes the intermediate step of completing a coding sheet unnecessary. The data are accessible directly from the questionnaire. A respondent, interviewer, field supervisor, or researcher (depending on the data collection method) is able to assign an appropriate numerical response on the instrument by checking, circling, or printing it in the proper coding location.

Exhibit 15–2 shows questions in the sample codebook. When precoding is used, editing may precede data processing. Note question 4, where the respondent may

EXHIBIT 15–2 Sample Questionnaire Items

1. What is the zip code of your residence? _ _ _ _ _

2. What is the year of your birth? 19_ _

3. Gender (1) Male
       (2) Female

   Indicate
   your choice ———▶ _
   by number

4. What is your marital status?
       (1) Married
       (2) Widow(er)
       (3) Divorced
       (4) Separated
       (5) Never married

   Indicate
   your choice ———▶ _
   by number

5. Do you own or rent your primary residence?
       (1) Own
       (2) Rent
       (3) Living quarters provided

   Indicate
   your choice ———▶ _
   by number

6. What prompted you to purchase your most recent life insurance policy?

   _____

   _____

   _____

   _____

   _____

   _____

choose between five characteristics of marital status and enter the number of the item best representing present status in the coding portion of the questionnaire. This code is later transferred to an input medium for analysis.

Coding Open-Ended Questions

Closed questions are favored by researchers over open-ended questions for their efficiency and specificity. They are easier to measure, record, code, and analyze. But there are situations where insufficient information or lack of a hypothesis prohibits preparing response categories in advance. Other reasons for using open-ended responses include the need to measure sensitive or disapproved behavior, discover salience, or encourage natural modes of expression.[1] However, analyzing enormous volumes of open-ended questions has always been a nightmare for researchers. The varieties of answers one may encounter is staggering. In Exhibit 15–2, question 6 illustrates the use of an open-ended question for which advance knowledge of response options was not available. The answer to "What prompted you to purchase your most recent life insurance policy?" was to be filled in by the respondent as a short-answer essay. After preliminary evaluation, response categories (shown in the codebook, Exhibit 15–1) were created for that item. Although most responses could be accounted for by the derived categories, an "other" category was established to meet the coding rule of exhaustiveness.

Using Content Analysis for Open Questions

Content analysis measures the semantic content or the *what* aspect of a message. Its breadth makes it a flexible and wide-ranging tool that may be used as a methodology or as a problem-specific technique. Trend-watching organizations like the BrainReserve, the Naisbitt Group, SRI International, and Inferential Focus use variations on content analysis for selected projects, often spotting changes from newspapers or magazine articles before they can be confirmed statistically. The Naisbitt Group's content analysis of 2 million local newspaper articles compiled over a 12-year period resulted in the publication of *Megatrends*. After a brief review of the characteristics of content analysis, we will consider one of its many problem-specific applications: handling open questions.

Content analysis has been described as "a research technique for the objective, systematic, and quantitative description of the manifest content of a communication."[2] Because this definition is sometimes confused with simply counting obvious message aspects such as words or attributes, more recent interpretations have broadened the definition to include latent as well as manifest content, the symbolic meaning of messages, and qualitative analysis. One author states:

> In any single written message, one can count letters, words, or sentences. One can categorize phrases, describe the logical structure of expressions, ascertain associations, connotations, denotations, elocutionary forces, and one can also offer psychiatric, sociological, or political interpretations. All of these may be simultaneously valid. In short, a message may convey a multitude of contents even to a single receiver.[3]

Content analysis follows a systematic process, starting with the selection of a unitization scheme. The units may be syntactical, referential, propositional, or thematic.

- *Syntactical* units are illustrated by words, which are the smallest and most reliable units.

- *Referential* units may be objects, events, persons, and so forth, to which an expression refers. An advertiser may refer to a product as a "classic," a "power performer," or "ranked first in safety"—each denoting the same object.

- *Propositional* units use several frameworks. One might show the relationships among the actor, the mode of acting, and the object—for example, "subscribers [actor] to this periodical save [mode of acting] $15 [object of the action] over the single issue rate."

- *Thematic* units are higher-level abstractions inferred from their connection to a unique structure or pattern in the content. A response to a question about working conditions may reflect a temporal theme: the past ("how good things used to be here"), the present ("the need to talk with management now before production gets worse"), or the future ("employee expectations to be involved in planning and goal setting").

Other aspects of the content analysis methodology include:

- Selection of a sampling plan.
- Development of recording and coding instructions.
- Data reduction.
- Inferences about the context.
- Statistical analysis.

Content analysis guards against selective perception of the content, provides for the rigorous application of reliability and validity criteria, and is amenable to computerization.

The data to be content-analyzed include materials of interest to management researchers: books, chapters, historical documents, speeches, interviews, advertisements, promotional brochures, group interactions, paragraphs, and words. Any recorded activity with its own syntax and semantics is subject to measurement and analysis. Thus, content analysis may be used to analyze written, audio, or video data from experiments, observations, surveys, and secondary data studies.

Let's look at an informal application of content analysis to a problematic open question. In this example, which we are processing without linguistics software technology, suppose employees in the assembly operation of a unionized manufacturing firm are asked, "How can management-employee relations be improved?" A sample of the responses yields the following:

- Management should treat the worker with more respect.
- Managers should stop trying to speed up the assembly line.

- Working conditions in the shop are terrible. Managers should correct them.
- The foreman should be fired. He is unfair in his treatment of workers.
- Managers should form management-worker councils in the department to iron out problems and improve relations.
- Management should stop trying to undermine union leadership.
- Management should accept the union's latest proposals on new work rules.

The first step in analysis requires that the units developed reflect the objectives for which the data were collected. The research question is concerned with learning what the assemblers think is the locus of responsibility for improving company-employee relations. The categories selected are keywords and referential units. The first pass through the data produces a few general categories, shown in Exhibit 15–3. These categories are mutually exclusive and contain only one concept dimension. The use of "other" makes the category set exhaustive. If the sample suggested that many respondents identified the need for action by the public, government, or regulatory bodies, then including all of them in "other" would ignore much of the richness of the data.

Since responses to this type of question often suggest specific actions, the second evaluation of the data uses propositional units. This identifies action objects and the actors previously discovered. If we used only the set of categories in Exhibit 15–3, the analysis would omit a considerable amount of information. The second analysis produces categories for action planning:

- Human relations.
- Production processes.
- Working conditions.
- Other action areas.
- No action area identified.

How can we categorize a response suggesting a combined management-production process? Exhibit 15–4 illustrates a combination of alternatives. By taking the categories of the first list with the action areas, it is possible to get an accurate frequency count of the joint classification possibilities for this question.

Using available software, the researcher can spend much less time coding open-ended responses and capturing categories. Software also eliminates the high cost of

EXHIBIT 15–3   Open Question Coding Example (before revision)
Question: "How can management-employee relations be improved?"

Locus of Responsibility	Mentioned	Not Mentioned
A. Management	_____	_____
B. Union	_____	_____
C. Worker (other than union)	_____	_____
D. Joint management-union	_____	_____
E. Joint management-workers	_____	_____
F. Other	_____	_____

EXHIBIT 15–4   Open Question Coding (after revision)
Question: "How can management-employee relations be improved?"

Locus of Responsibility	Frequency (*n* = 100)
A. Management	
1. Human relations	15
2. Production processes	45
3. Working conditions	25
4. Other action areas	10
5. No action area identified	5
B. Union	
1. Human relations	10
2. Production processes	10
3. Working conditions	65
4. Other action areas	15
5. No action area identified	0
C. Worker (other than union)	
D.	
E.	
F. Other	

sending responses to outside coding firms. What would take a coding staff several days may now be done in a few hours.

By applying statistical algorithms to create categories from open-ended survey responses, various programs allow you to import responses in a tab-delimited (ASCII) file format and then automatically penetrate the chaos of diverse answers by stemming, aliasing, and excluding words that obscure important terms which are necessary to define meaningful categories.

- *Stemming* uses powerful linguistics technology to comb through responses, search for derivations of common root words, and combine terms to create stemmed aliases (search, searching, searches).

- *Aliasing* combines synonyms (smart, wise, intelligent) into automatic aliases.

- *Exclusion* filters for trivial words (be, is, the, of), to create a list of included terms valuable for constructing meaningful categories.[4]

When using menu-driven programs, an autocategorization option creates manageable categories by clustering terms that occur together throughout the data set. Then, with a few keystrokes, you can modify categorization parameters and refine your results. Once your categories are consistent with the research and investigative questions, you select what you want to export to a data file or in tab-delimited format. The output, in the form of tables and plots, serves as modules for your final report. Exhibit 15–5 shows a plot produced by a content analysis of MindWriter complaints data. The distances between pairs of terms reveal how likely the pair occurs together and the colors represent categories.

EXHIBIT 15–5   **Proximity Plot of MindWriter Customer Complaints**

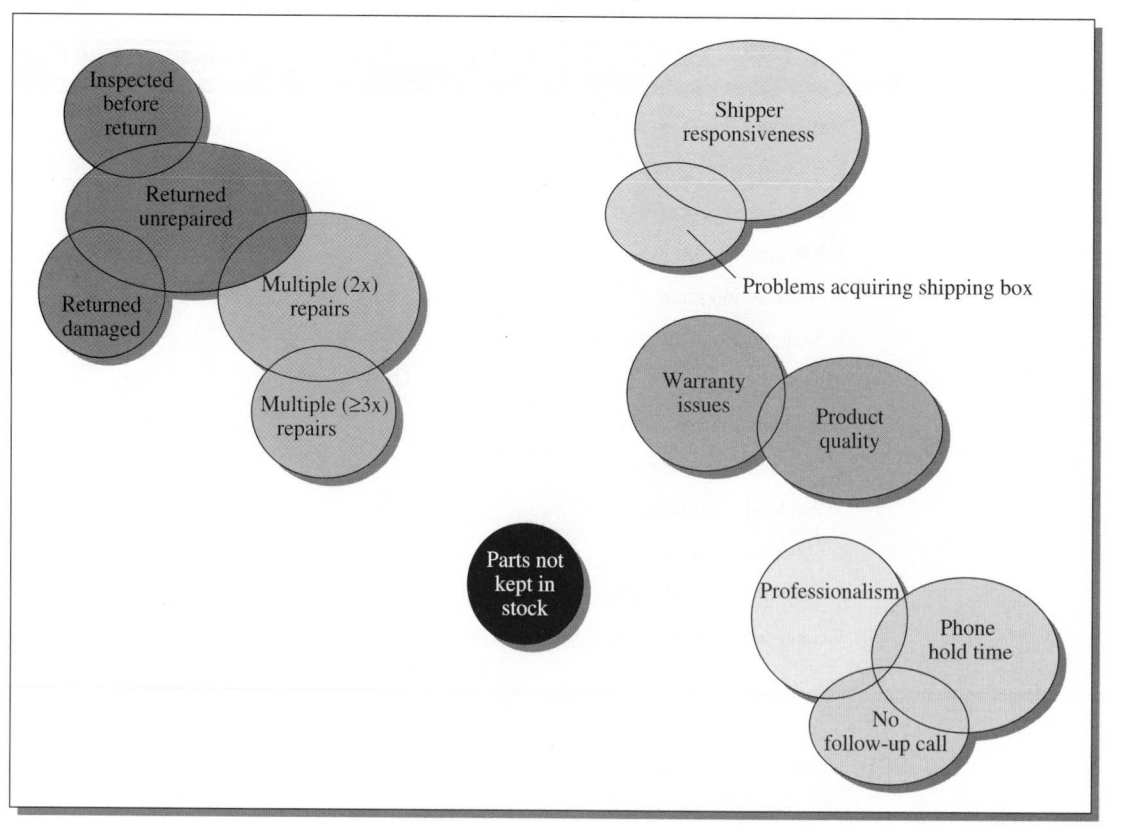

"Don't Know" Responses

The **"don't know" (DK) response** presents special problems for data preparation. When the DK response group is small, it is not troublesome. But there are times when it is of major concern, and it may even be the most frequent response received. Does this mean the question that elicited this response is useless? The answer is, "It all depends." Most DK answers fall into two categories.[5] First, there is the legitimate DK response when the respondent does not know the answer. This response meets our research objectives; we expect DK responses and consider them to be useful.

In the second situation, a DK reply illustrates the researcher's failure to get the appropriate information. Consider the following illustrative questions:

1. Who developed the Managerial Grid concept?

2. Do you believe the new president's fiscal policy is sound?

3. Do you like your present job?

4. Which of the various brands of chewing gum do you believe has the best quality?

5. How often each year do you go to the movies?

It is reasonable to expect that some legitimate DK responses will be made to each of these questions. In the first question, the respondents are asked for a level of information that they often will not have. There seems to be little reason to withhold a correct answer if known. Thus, most DK answers to this question should be considered as legitimate. A DK response to the second question presents a different problem. It is not immediately clear whether the respondent is ignorant of the president's fiscal policy or knows the policy but has not made a judgment about it. The researchers should have asked two questions: In the first, they would have determined the respondent's level of awareness of fiscal policy. If the interviewee passed the awareness test, then a second question would have secured judgment on fiscal policy.

In the remaining three questions, DK responses are more likely to be a failure of the questioning process, although some will surely be legitimate. The respondent may be reluctant to give the information. A DK response to question 3 may be a way of saying, "I do not want to answer that question." Question 4 might also elicit a DK response in which the reply translates to, "This is too unimportant to talk about." In question 5, the respondents are being asked to do some calculation about a topic to which they may attach little importance. Now the DK may mean, "I do not want to do that work for something of so little consequence."

Dealing with Undesired DK Responses   The best way to deal with undesired DK answers is to design better questions at the beginning. Researchers should identify the questions for which a DK response is unsatisfactory and design around it. Interviewers, however, often inherit this problem and must deal with it in the field. Several actions are then possible. First, good interviewer-respondent rapport will motivate respondents to provide more usable answers. When interviewers recognize an evasive DK response, they can repeat the question or probe for a more definite answer. The interviewer may also record verbatim any elaboration by the respondent and buck the problem on to the editor.

If the editor finds many undesired responses, little can be done unless the verbatim comments can be interpreted. Understanding the real meaning relies on clues from the respondent's answers to other questions. One way to do this is to estimate the allocation of DK answers from other data in the questionnaire. The pattern of responses may parallel income, education, or experience levels. Suppose a question concerning whether employees like their present jobs elicits the answers in Exhibit 15–6. The correlation between years of service and the "don't know" answers and the "no" answers suggests that most of the "don't knows" are disguised "no" answers.

There are several ways to handle "don't know" responses in the tabulations. If there are only a few, it does not make much difference how they are handled, but they will probably be kept as a separate category. If the DK response is legitimate, it should remain as a separate reply category. When we are not sure how to treat it, we should keep it as a separate reporting category and let the reader make the decision.

EXHIBIT 15–6   **Handling "Don't Know" Responses**

Years of Service	Do You Like Your Present Job?		
	Yes	No	Don't Know
Less than 1 year	10%	40%	38%
1–3 years	30	30	32
4 years or more	60	30	30
Total	100%	100%	100%
n =	650	150	200

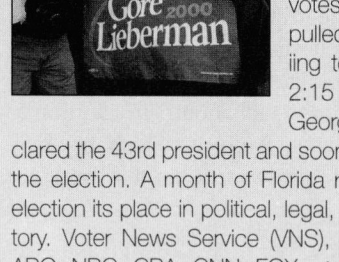

S N A P S H O T   VNS: A Black Eye for Research

A little before 8:00 P.M. on November 7, 2000, major news sources declared Al Gore the winner of Florida's electoral votes. Two hours later they pulled their prediction, reverting to "too close to call." At 2:15 A.M. on November 8, George W. Bush was declared the 43rd president and soon after Al Gore conceded the election. A month of Florida recounts gave the 2000 election its place in political, legal, news, and research history. Voter News Service (VNS), run by a consortium of ABC, NBC, CBA, CNN, FOX, and the Associated Press, was responsible for the exit polls. Exit polls, regarded as reliable indicators of voting results, conduct intercept interviews with voters as they leave voting booths. Voters provide who they voted for, why, and extensive demographic and psychographic information. How could an established polling organization and world-recognized news organizations' research fail so miserably? The answer can be traced to the following factors: (1) the use of a biased sample, with too many surveys completed in heavily Democratic precincts; (2) miscounted or misentered data in Duvall County (home of Jacksonville); and (3) a rush to judgment for the news value of an early "call" when statistically the margin between candidates was truly too close to decide. Antitrust advocates claim that collusion versus competition resulted in poor methodology and seek to break up VNS before another "campaign fiasco" occurs.

November 2000 Presidential Election: Timeline for Poll-Based Actions

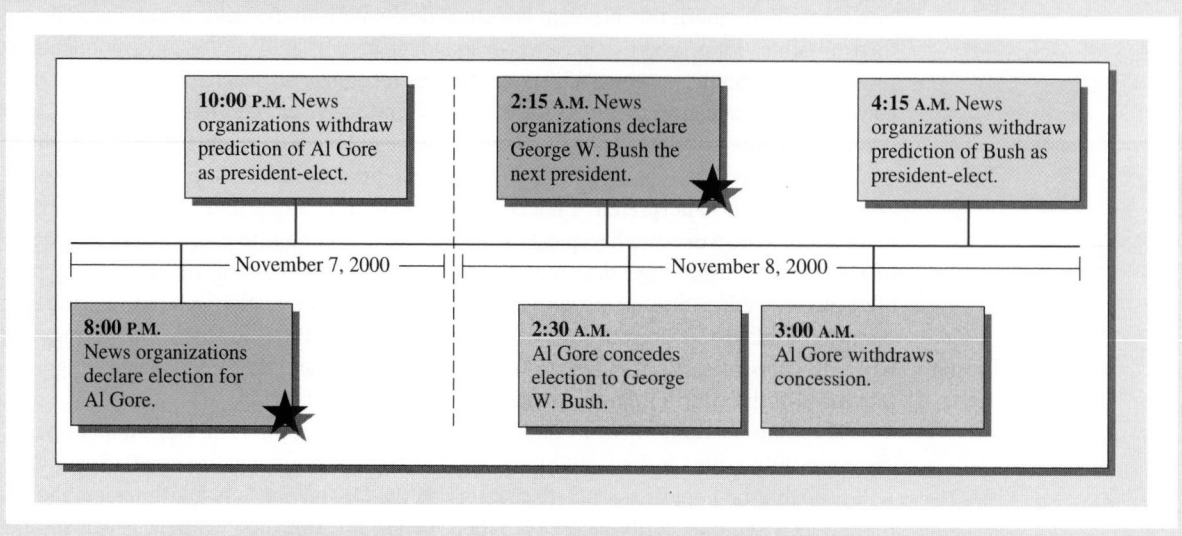

Another way to treat DK responses is to assume they occur almost randomly. Using this approach, we distribute them among the other answers in the same ratio that the other answers occur. This assumes that those who reply "don't know" are proportionally distributed among all of the groups studied. This can be achieved either by prorating the DK responses or by excluding all DK replies from the tabulation. The latter approach is better since it does not inflate the actual number of other responses.

Data Entry

Researchers have profited from new and more efficient ways of speeding up the research process (see Exhibit 15–7). **Data entry** converts information gathered by secondary or primary methods to a medium for viewing and manipulation. Keyboarding remains a mainstay for researchers who need to create a data file immediately and store it in a minimal space on a variety of media.

EXHIBIT 15–7 · **Methods of Data Entry**

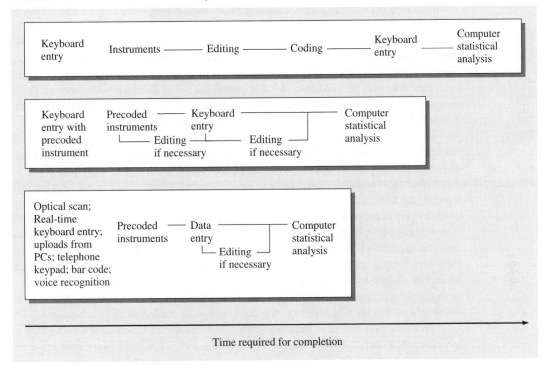

Time required for completion

If you use a PC image scanner, you probably are familiar with **optical character recognition** programs that transfer printed text into computer files in order to edit and use it without retyping. There are other, related applications. **Optical scanning** instruments—the choice of testing services—âre efficient for researchers. Examinees darken small circles, ellipses, or sets of parallel lines to choose a test answer. Optical scanners process the marked-sensed questionnaires and store the answers in a file. Depending on the scanner model (we are referring to dedicated units like NCS, Scantron, etc.), readers can process up to 8,000 forms per hour. This method, most often associated with standardized and preprinted forms, has been adopted by designers for data entry and preprocessing. It reduces the number of times data are handled, thereby reducing the number of errors that are introduced.

In a far more flexible format, **optical mark recognition (OMR)** uses a spreadsheet style interface to read and process user-created forms. The primary advantages are:

- **Speed:** About 10 times faster than manual keying.
- **Accuracy:** Error reduction from keying or stray marks.
- **Cost:** Savings on data entry, form design, and reproduction.
- **Convenience:** Makes viewing the data easy and provides charts and reports.

The researcher creates OMR forms with a word processor, page layout program, or survey design package and includes bubbles, fill-in marks, checkboxes, bar codes, and image fields. Data collected from questionnaires, reader reply cards, tests, interviews, observation forms, or checklists—virtually any paper-based medium—can be processed this way. A photocopier, laser printer, or local print shop then duplicates the forms. Special papers, drop-out inks, or the pencils associated with traditional OMR are not needed since the respondent may use markers, pens, pencils, or even crayons with the plain paper forms.

Most OMR products have "trainable" software, so your questionnaire need not conform to a particular design. Training involves creating a template by scanning in your form, displaying the image, and then, with a mouse, dragging boxes around the marking areas to define how each mark should be translated.[6] Once the template is created, a flatbed scanner can be used to read the data. For projects with hundreds or thousands of pages, a high-speed, sheet-fed scanner is essential. Scanned images of the collected data may be edited, saved, and processed with tabulation tools internal to the software. Many researchers export the results in multiple formats to statistical, database, and spreadsheet applications for more sophisticated analysis.

In addition to reading prescanned forms and questionnaire faxes, one program allows you to convert your paper-based OMR surveys into online surveys for the Internet or an intranet and then merge the results.[7]

Other techniques include direct response entry, of which voting procedures used in several states are an example. With a specially prepared punch card, citizens cast their votes by pressing a pen-shaped instrument against the card next to the preferred candidate. This opens a small hole in a specific column and row of the card. The cards are collected and placed directly into a card reader. This method also removes the coding and entry steps. Another governmental application is the 1040EZ form used by the Internal Revenue Service. It is designed for computerized number and character recognition. Similar character recognition techniques are employed for many forms of data collection. Again, both approaches move the response from the question to data analysis with little handling.

The declining cost of technology has allowed most researchers access to desktop or portable computers or networks to larger computers. This technology enables computer-assisted telephone or personal interviews to be completed with answers entered directly for processing, eliminating intermediate steps and errors.

The increase in computerized random-digit dialing has encouraged other data collection innovations. **Voice recognition** and response systems, while still far from mature, are providing some interesting alternatives for the telephone interviewer. Such systems can be used with software that is programmed to call specific three-digit pre-

By 2004 Princess Cruises will have 15 ships and 30,000 berths sailing 7 to 72 days to more than six continents on more than 150 itineraries. Princess carries more than 700,000 passengers each year and processes 245,000 customer satisfaction surveys each year—distributed to each cabin on the last day of each cruise. Princess uses scannable surveys rather than human data-entry for one reason: in the one-week to 10-day analysis lag created by human data-entry, 10 cruises could be completed with another 10 under way. For a business that prides itself on customer service, not knowing about a problem could be enormously damaging. Princess has found that scannable surveys generate more accurate data entry, while reducing processing and decision-response time—critical time in the cruise industry. www.princess.com

fixes and randomly generated four-digit numbers, reaching a random sample within a set geographical area. Upon getting a voice response, the computer branches into a questionnaire routine. Currently, the systems are programmed to record the verbal answers, but voice recognition is improving quickly enough so that these systems will soon translate voice responses into data files. Telephone keypad response is another capability made possible by computers linked to telephone lines. Using the telephone keypad (touch tone), the respondent answers questions by pressing the appropriate number. The computer captures the data by "listening," decoding the tone's electrical signal, and storing the numeric or alphabetic answer in a data file.

Field interviewers can use portable computers or electronic notebooks instead of clipboards and pencils. With a built-in communications modem or cellular link, their files can be sent directly to another computer in the field or to a remote site. This lets supervisors inspect data immediately or simplifies processing at a central facility.

From a crude bull's-eye code in 1948 to the adoption of the Universal Product Code (UPC) in 1973, the **bar code** developed from a technological curiosity to a business mainstay. The concept, originally modifying movie soundtrack technology and Morse code for bar elements and optical character recognition for scanning, was initially tested by the railroads on their gravel cars. The first actual bar code systems went into a General Motors plant to monitor the production and distribution of automobile axles and to the General Trading Company for directing shipments to the proper loading bays. After a 1970s study by McKinsey & Company that predicted unprecedented savings in the grocery industry, the Kroger grocery chain pilot-tested a production system and bar codes became ubiquitous in that industry.[8]

The bar code is split into two halves of six digits each. It is used in numerous applications: point-of-sale terminals, hospital patient ID bracelets, inventory control, product and brand tracking, promotional technique evaluation, shipping cartons, marathon runners, at rental car locations to speed the return of cars and generate invoices, and to track insects' mating habits. The military uses two-foot-long bar codes to label boats in storage. The codes appear on business documents, truck parts, and timber in lumberyards. Federal Express shipping labels use a code called Codabar. Improvements to the basic UPC include the European Article Numbering system, which has an extra pair of digits and may become the world's most widely used system. Other codes, containing letters as well as numbers, have potential for researchers.

Bar code technology is used to simplify the interviewer's role as a data recorder. Instead of writing (or typing) information about the respondents and their answers by hand, the interviewer can pass a bar code wand over the appropriate codes. The data are recorded in a small, lightweight unit for translation later. In the large-scale processing project Census 2000, the Census Data Capture Center used bar codes to identify residents.

Even with these time reductions between data collection and analysis, continuing innovations in multimedia technology are being developed by the personal computer business. The capability to integrate visual images, streaming video, audio, and data may soon replace video equipment as the preferred method for recording an experiment,

Data capture for Census 2000 used a bar code to connect the census question data with the responding household's address.

39023-0002392-45-110-411-69

*****************AUTOCR**R-001

SNAPSHOT

Intelligence in Real Time

Historically, when Hewlett-Packard (HP) needed information about product performance, it waited for the product to hit the market in volume. Then, according to Beth Olson, market research manager for HP's product support division, HP would conduct time-consuming, expensive, traditional, one-on-one interviews. Recently, HP teamed with Decisive Technology, a firm that designs and implements Internet-based customer intelligence solutions for real-time customer feedback. Its product, MarketView, publishes the results immediately and continuously on a secure website.

"With [Decisive's] MarketView, we were able to communicate very effectively with our 'wired' customers, obtaining information phenomenally fast, and in a format that allowed people throughout HP to access and act on the information," shared Olson.

www.hp.com

www.decisive.com

interview, or focus group. A copy of the response data could be extracted for data analysis, but the audio and visual images would remain intact for later evaluation.

Other techniques on the horizon will continue to improve research efficiency and effectiveness. Although technology will never replace researcher judgment, it can reduce data-handling errors, decrease time between data collection and analysis, and help provide more usable information.

Data Entry Formats

A full-screen editor, where an entire data file can be edited or browsed, is a viable means of data entry for statistical packages like SPSS or SAS. The same software makes accessing data from databases, spreadsheets, data warehouses, or data marts effortless.

For large projects, database programs serve as valuable data entry devices. A **database** is a collection of data organized for computerized retrieval. Programs allow users to define data fields and link files so that storage, retrieval, and updating are simplified. The relationship between data fields, records, files, and databases is illustrated in Exhibit 15–8. A company's personnel records serve as an example of a database. Employee information may be kept in several files: salary and position, education, benefits, and home and family. The data are separated so that authorized people can see only those parts pertinent to their needs. However, the files may be linked so that when, say, a woman changes her name, the change is entered once and all the files are updated.

Researchers consider database entry when they have large amounts of potentially linked data that will be retrieved and tabulated in different ways over time. Another application of a database program is as a "front-end" entry mechanism. A telephone interviewer may ask the question "How many children live in your home?" The computer's software has been programmed to accept any answer between 0 and 20. If a "P" is accidentally struck, the program will not accept the answer and will return the interviewer to the question. With a precoded online instrument, much of the editing needed previously is done by the program. In addition, the program can be set for automatic conditional branching. In the example, an answer of 1 or greater causes the program to prompt the questioner to ask the ages of the children. A 0 causes the age question to be automatically skipped. Although this option is available whenever interactive computing is used, front-end processing is typically done within the database design. The database will then store the data into a set of linked files that allow the data to be easily sorted. Descriptive statistics and tables are readily generated from within the database.

EXHIBIT 15–8 Data Fields, Records, Files, and Databases

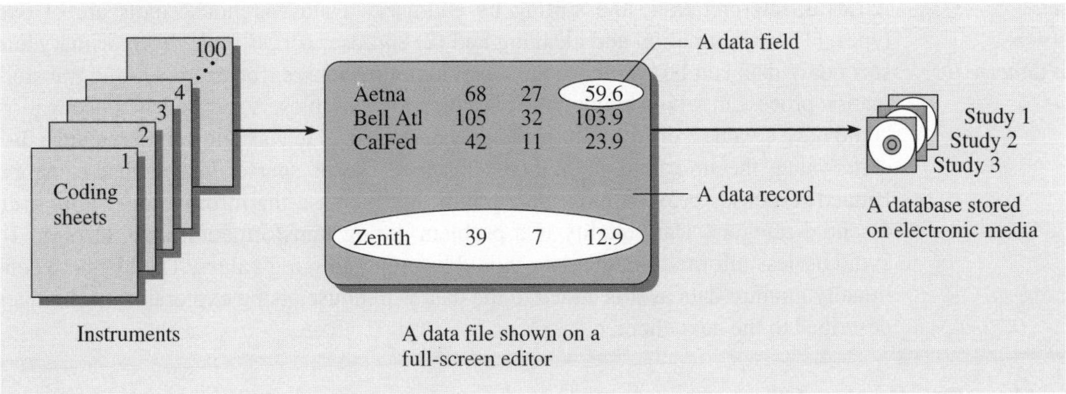

Data fields represent single elements of information (e.g., an answer to a question, a description, a number, a statement, etc.). Data fields can contain numeric, alphabetic, or symbolic information. A **record** is a set of data fields that are related. Records are the rows of a data file or spreadsheet program worksheet. **Data files** are sets of records that are grouped together for storage on diskettes, disks, tapes, CD-ROM, or optical disks. **Databases** are made up of one or more data fields that are interrelated.

SOURCES: Company data; public domain.

Spreadsheets are a specialized type of database. For data that need organizing, tabulating, and simple statistics, spreadsheets provide an easy-to-learn mechanism. They also offer some database management, graphics, and presentation capabilities. Data entry on a **spreadsheet** uses numbered rows and letter columns with a matrix of thousands of cells into which an entry may be placed. Spreadsheets allow you to type numbers, formulas, and text into appropriate cells. Many statistics programs for personal computers and also charting and graphics applications have data editors similar to the Excel™ spreadsheet format shown in Exhibit 15–9. This is a convenient and flexible means for entering and viewing the data.

EXHIBIT 15–9 Data Entry Using Spreadsheets

	A	B	C	D	E	F
1	100 Best Rank2001	Employ_US	Job Grow%	Trng_hr/yr	Ent_Sal_Prof	Revenues (Mil)
2	Edward Jones	25324	15	132	61690	2200
3	Container Store	1677	12	162	37400	225
4	SAS Institute	4309	14	32	49375	1120
5	TDIndustries	1368	7	32	45000	205
6	Synovus Financial	10995	4	52	41400	1395
7	Xilinx	2047	14	90	60000	1659
8	Plante & Moran	1240	1	60	40000	151
9	Qualcomm	5931	0	21	65000	2680
10	Alston & Bird	1338	18	40	100000	223
11	Baptist Health Care	4068	6	55	34798	647
12	Frank Russell	1068	9		51957	500
13	Hypertherm	566	5	30	45000	
14	CDW	2781	14	41	69500	3842
15	Fenwick & West	626	0	70	125000	146
16	Cisco Systems	26872	4		62000	22293

SOURCE: "The Best of 100 Companies to Work For," *Fortune,* February 4, 2002, pp. 72–80.

End-user tools for accessing data warehouses were discussed in Chapter 10.

A **data warehouse** organizes large volumes of data into categories to facilitate retrieval, interpretation, and sorting by end-users. Data warehouse tools are of two types: (1) transformation and cleaning and (2) end-user access tools. Both primary and secondary data can be warehoused. With survey responses, for example, one transformation process involves *binning* the classification variables. A respondent's occupation could have a value from 1 to 20. If each occupational code was allowed to remain a discrete value, the information might be lost because of sparse data in that category. Binned responses provide more data points and increase the information within each essential category. Data quality is a problem during transformation and cleaning. To avoid useless information, the data should have few missing values. The key is to continually monitor data as it is added to the data warehouse, using exploratory techniques described in the next chapter.

Descriptive Statistical Summaries

Describing Distributions

In the first part of the chapter, we discussed how responses are coded and entered. Creating numerical summaries of this process provides valuable insights into its effectiveness. For example, **missing data,** information that is missing about a respondent or case

EXHIBIT 15–10   Characteristics of Distributions

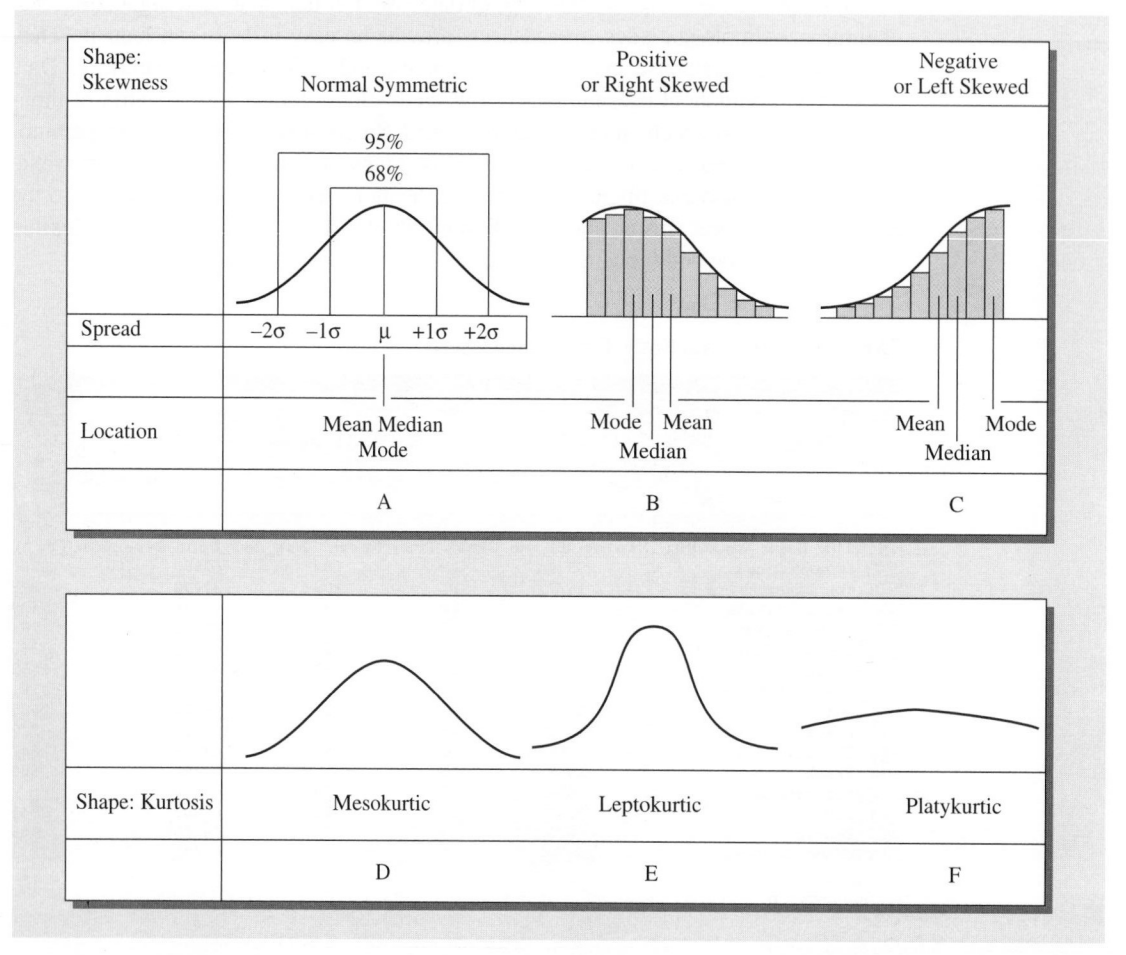

for which other information is present, may be detected. Miscoded, out-of-range data, extreme values, and other problems also may be rectified after a preliminary look at the data set.[9] To understand each variable's characteristics, first consider the type of scale on which it was measured. With nominal measurements (e.g., company classifications like high-tech, financial, and retailing), each category is represented by a numerical code that refers back to a verbal description of the category. With ordinal data, the item's rank, reflecting a position in the range from the lowest to the highest, is entered. The same is true with interval-ratio scores. When these data are tabulated, they may be arrayed from the lowest to the highest scores on their scales. Together with the frequency of occurrence, the observations form a **distribution** of values.

Many variables of interest have distributions that approximate a **standard normal distribution.** This distribution, shown in Part A of Exhibit 15–10, is the most significant theoretical distribution in statistics. It is a standard of comparison for describing distributions of sample data and is used with inferential statistics that assume normally distributed variables.

Examine the sample distribution of variables from the MindWriter dataset shown in Exhibit 15–11. These data were collected on a five-point interval scale. There are no missing data in variable 1A, although it is apparent that a range of 6 and a maximum

EXHBIT 15–11   MindWriter Dataset: Missing and Out-of-Range Data

Case	1A	1B	2A	2B	2C
1	5.0	5.0	5.0	5.0	9.0
2	7.0	3.0		4.0	9.0
3	5.0	5.0	5.0	5.0	5.0
4	5.0	5.0	4.0		
5	1.0			2.0	
6	5.0	5.0	5.0	5.0	9.0
7	5.0	5.0	5.0	5.0	5.0
8	4.0	3.0	3.0	3.0	3.0
9	4.0	4.0	5.0	5.0	5.0
10	4.0	5.0		4.0	5.0
11	2.0	5.0	4.0	4.0	5.0
12	6.0	4.0	3.0	3.0	4.0
13	5.0	5.0		3.0	5.0
14	5.0	5.0	5.0	5.0	5.0
15	5.0	4.0	5.0	5.0	4.0
Valid	15	14	11	14	13
Missing	0	1	4	1	2
Mean	4.53	4.50	4.45	4.14	5.61
Range	6	2	2	3	6
Minimum	1	3	3	2	3
Maximum	7	5	5	5	9

value of 7 invalidate the calculated mean or average score. Variables 1B and 2B have one case missing but values that are within range. Variable 2A is missing four cases, or 27 percent of its data points. The last variable, 2C, has a range of 6, two missing values, and three values coded as "9." A "9" is often used as a DK or missing value code when the scale has a range less than nine points. In this case both blanks and 9s are present—a coding concern. Notice that the fifth respondent answered only two of the five questions and the second respondent had two miscoded answers and one missing value. Finally, using descriptive indexes of shape, discussed later in this section, you can find three variables that depart from the symmetry of the normal distribution. They are skewed (or pulled) to the left by a disproportionately small number of 1s and 2s. And, one variable's distribution is peaked beyond normal dimensions. We have just used the minimum and maximum values, the range, and mean and have already discovered errors in coding, problems with respondent answer patterns, and missing cases.

Now let's look at some other descriptive tools for this purpose. The characteristics of location, spread, and shape are helpful initial tools for cleaning the data, discovering problems, and summarizing distributions. Their definitions, applications, and formulas fall under the heading of **descriptive statistics.** Although the definitions will be familiar to most readers, we take the following perspective on the characteristics of distributions:

We illustrate techniques for visualizing data patterns in Chapter 16.

- A distribution's shape is just as consequential as its location and spread.

- The choice of summary statistics to describe a singe variable is contingent on the appropriateness of those statistics for the shape of the distribution.

- Visual representations are ultimately superior to numerical ones for discovering a distribution's shape and should be used before selecting remedies to correct anomalies in the data.[10]

Measures of Location

Refer to Exhibit 15–9 for the values of the variables in these examples.

Summarizing the information from our collected data often requires the description of "typical" values. The data in Exhibit 15–9 are a subset of the 2002 *Fortune* magazine article "The 100 Best Companies to Work For." Suppose we want to know the typical score for companies' job growth (%). We might define *typical* as the average response (mean); the middle value, when the distribution is sorted from lowest to highest (median); or the most frequently occurring value (mode). The common **measures of location,** often called **central tendency** or *center,* include the mean, median, and mode.

$$\bar{X} = \sum_{i=1}^{n} \frac{X_i}{n}$$

For the job growth variable in Exhibit 15–9, the distribution of responses is: 15, 12, 14, 7, 4, 14, 1, 0, 18, 6, 9, 5, 14, 0, 4. The arithmetic average, or **mean,** of the 15 values is: $15 + 12 + 14 + 7 + 4 + 14 + 1 + 0 + 18 + 6 + 9 + 5 + 14 + 0 + 4 / 15 = 8.2$ (or, an average of 8.2% job growth). Note that 2 of the top 15 companies had zero job growth.

The **median** is the midpoint of the distribution. Half of the observations in the distribution fall above and the other half fall below the median. When the distribution has an even number of observations, the median is the average of the two middle scores. The median is the most appropriate locator of center for ordinal data and has resistance to extreme scores, thereby making it a preferred measure for interval-ratio data when their distributions are not normal. The median is sometimes symbolized by M or *mdn.*

From the sample distribution for the U.S. employees variable, the median of the 15 values is 2047. The distribution is ordered: 566, 626, 1068, 1240, 1338, 1368, 1677,

2047, 2781, 4068, 4309, 5931, 10995, 25324, and 26872; since the total number of values is 15, the midpoint is the middle value of this distribution. If the distribution had 16 values, the median would be the average of the values for the 7th and 8th cases.

The **mode** is the most frequently occurring value. When there is more than one score that has the highest yet equal frequency, the distribution is bimodal or multimodal. When every score has an equal number of observations, there is no mode. The mode is the location measure for nominal data and a point of reference along with the median and mean for examining spread and shape. In our example, the most frequently occurring value for the training hours/year variable is 32.

Measures of Spread

The common **measures of spread,** alternatively referred to as *dispersion* or **variability,** are the variance, standard deviation, range, interquartile range, and quartile deviation. They describe how scores cluster or scatter in a distribution.

The **variance** is the average of the squared deviation scores from the distribution's mean. It is a measure of score dispersion about the mean. If all the scores are identical, the variance is 0. The greater the dispersion of scores, the greater the variance. Both the variance and the standard deviation are used with interval-ratio data. The symbol for the sample variance is s^2, and the population variance is the Greek letter sigma, squared (σ^2). The variance is computed by summing the squared distance from the mean for all cases and dividing the sum by the total number of cases minus one.

$$s^2 = \sum_{i=1}^{n} \frac{(X_1 - \bar{X})^2}{n-1}$$

For the percent of job growth variable, we would compute the variance as:

$$s^2 = (15 - 8.2)^2 + (12 - 8.2)^2 + \ldots + (4 - 8.2)^2/14 = 5.96$$

The **standard deviation** summarizes how far away from the average the data values typically are. It is perhaps the most frequently used measure of spread because it improves interpretability by removing the variance's square and expressing deviations in their original units (e.g., revenues in dollars, not dollars squared). It is also an important concept for descriptive statistics because it reveals the amount of variability of individuals within the dataset. Like the mean, the standard deviation is affected by extreme scores. The symbol for the sample standard deviation is *s,* and a population standard deviation is σ. Alternatively, it is labeled *std. dev.*

$$s = \sqrt{s^2}$$

The standard deviation for the percent of job growth variable in our example is 5.96.

The **range** is the difference between the largest and smallest score in the distribution. The revenues (millions) variable has a range of 22147 (22293 – 146). Unlike the standard deviation, it is computed from only the minimum and maximum scores; thus, it is a very rough measure of spread. With the range as a point of comparison, it is possible to get an idea of the homogeneity (small std. dev.) or heterogeneity (large std. dev.) of the distribution. For homogeneous distribution, the ratio of the range to the standard deviation should be between 2 and 6. In the revenues example, the ratio is 22147 / 5759.7 = 3.84. A number above 6 would indicate a high degree of heterogeneity. The range provides useful but limited information for all data. It is mandatory for ordinal data.

Quartiles are used to build boxplots of the data. Their construction is described in Chapter 16.

The **interquartile range (IQR)** is the difference between the first and third quartiles of the distribution. It is also called the *midspread.* Ordinal or ranked data use this measure in conjunction with the median. It is also used with interval-ratio data when asymmetrical distributions are suspected or for exploratory analysis. Recall the following relationships. The minimum value of the distribution is the 0th percentile; the maximum, the 100th percentile. The first quartile (Q_1) is the 25th percentile; the median, or Q_2, is the 50th percentile. The third quartile (Q_3) is the 75th percentile.

The **quartile deviation,** or semi-interquartile range, is expressed as

$$Q = \frac{Q_1 - Q_3}{2}$$

The quartile deviation is always used with the median for ordinal data. It is helpful for interval-ratio data of a skewed nature. In a normal distribution, the median plus one quartile deviation (Q) on either side encompasses 50 percent of the observations. Eight Qs cover approximately the range. Q's relationship with the standard deviation is constant ($Q = .6745s$) when scores are normally distributed. For the percent of job growth variable, Q is: $14 - 4 / 7 = 1.43$.

Measures of Shape

The **measures of shape,** *skewness* and *kurtosis,* describe departures from the symmetry of a distribution and its relative flatness (or peakedness), respectively. They are related to statistics known as *moments,* which use deviation scores ($X - \bar{X}$). The variance, for example, is a second power moment. The measures of shape use third and fourth power deviations for their computations and are often difficult to interpret when extreme scores are in the distribution. Generally, shape is best communicated through visual displays. From a practical standpoint, the calculation of skewness and kurtosis is best with spreadsheet or statistics software.

Skewness is a measure of a distribution's deviation from symmetry. In a symmetrical distribution, the mean, median, and mode are in the same location. A distribution that has cases stretching toward one tail or the other is called *skewed.* As shown in Exhibit 15–10, when the tail stretches to the left, to smaller values, it is negatively skewed. Scores stretching toward the right, toward larger values, skew the distribution positively. Note the relationship between the mean, median, and mode in asymmetrical distributions. The mean and standard deviation are called *dimensional* measures. That is, they are expressed in the same units as the measured quantities. In contrast, skewness is considered a nondimensional measure because it is an index which only characterizes the shape of the distribution. The symbol for skewness is *sk.*

$$sk = \frac{n}{(n-1)(n-2)} \sum \left(\frac{x_i - \bar{X}}{s} \right)^3$$

where s is the sample standard deviation (the unbiased estimate of sigma).

When a distribution approaches symmetry, *sk* is approximately 0. With a positive skew, *sk* will be a positive number; with negative skew, *sk* will be a negative number. The calculation of skewness for our sample revenue data produces an index of 3.5 and reveals a positive skew (see Exhibit 15–12).

As illustrated in the lower portion of Exhibit 15–10, **kurtosis** is a measure of a distribution's peakedness (or flatness). It is also a nondimensional index. Distributions that have scores which cluster heavily or pile up in the center (along with more observations than normal in the extreme tails) are peaked or *leptokurtic.* Flat distributions, with scores more evenly distributed and tails fatter than a normal distribution, are called *platykurtic.* Intermediate or *mesokurtic* distributions are neither too peaked nor too flat. The symbol for kurtosis is *ku.*

EXHIBIT 15–12 Shape Characteristics in Spreadsheet Variable Revenue

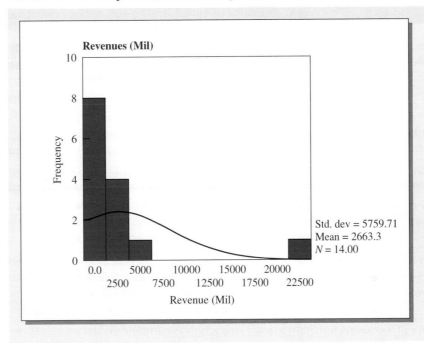

$$ku = \left\{ \frac{n(n + 1)}{(n - 1)(n - 2)(n - 3)} \sum \left(\frac{x_i - \bar{x}}{s} \right)^4 \right\} - \frac{3(n - 1)^2}{(n - 2)(n - 3)}$$

where s is the sample standard deviation (the unbiased estimate of sigma).

The value of ku for a normal or mesokurtic distribution is close to 0. A leptokurtic distribution will have a positive value, and the platykurtic distribution will be negative. As with skewness, the larger the absolute value of the index, the more extreme is the characteristic. In the revenues example, the kurtosis is calculated as +12.7, which suggests a strong deviation from a normally shaped curve with peaking contributed by greater frequency of values in the range of 146 to 647 million (see Exhibit 15–12).

SUMMARY

1 The first step in data preparation is to edit the collected raw data to detect errors and omissions that would compromise quality standards. The editor is responsible for making sure the data are accurate, consistent with other data, uniformly entered, and ready for coding. In survey work, it is common to use both field and central editing.

2 Coding is the process of assigning numbers and other symbols to answers so we can classify the responses into categories. Categories should be appropriate to the research problem, exhaustive of the data, mutually exclusive, and unidimensional. The reduction of information through coding requires the researcher to design category sets carefully, using as much of the data as possible. Codebooks are guides to reduce data entry error and serve as a compendium of variable locations and other information for the analysis stage.

3   Closed questions include scaled items and other items for which answers are anticipated. Precoding of closed items avoids tedious completion of coding sheets for each response. Open questions are more difficult to code since answers are not prepared in advance, but they do encourage disclosure of complete information. A systematic method for analyzing open questions is called content analysis. It uses preselected sampling units to produce frequency counts and other insights into data patterns.

4   "Don't know" replies are evaluated in light of the question's nature and the respondent. While many DKs are legitimate, some result from questions that are ambiguous or from an interviewing situation that is not motivating. It is better to report DKs as a separate category unless there are compelling reasons to treat them otherwise.

5   Data entry is accomplished by keyboard entry from precoded instruments, optical scanning, real-time keyboarding, telephone pad data entry, bar codes, voice recognition, OMR, and data transfers from electronic notebooks and laptop computers. Database programs, spreadsheets, and editors in statistical software programs offer flexibility for entering, manipulating, and transferring data for analysis, warehousing, and mining.

6   The objective of descriptive statistical analysis is to develop sufficient knowledge to describe a body of data. This is accomplished by understanding the data levels for the measurements we choose, their distributions, and characteristics of location, spread, and shape. The discovery of miscoded values, missing data, and other problems in the dataset is enhanced with descriptive statistics.

KEY TERMS

EXAMPLES

Company	Scenario	Page
BrainReserve	A trend-spotting organization that uses content analysis.	460
Campbell Soup Company	Content analysis is used to structure the promotional message for V-8.	460
CityBus	Using competitive bidding to acquire data-entry personnel.	453
Decisive Technology	Developed MarketView software that allows Hewlett-Packard to quickly and less expensively evaluate new products online.	470

Federal Express	Use of bar codes (called Codabar) on shipping labels.	469
Fortune	Evaluates the 100 best companies to work for in a tough year; what makes a great workplace.	474
General Motors	Development of bar coding for inventory analysis.	469
General Trading Company	Use of bar coding to direct shipments to appropriate loading bays.	469
Hewlett-Packard	How online software from Decisive Technology provides quicker, less costly evaluation of new products.	470
Inferential Focus	A trend-spotting organization that uses content analysis.	460
Kroger	Pioneering use of bar code data in the grocery industry.	469
MindWriter[*]	Content analysis of customer complaints; evaluation of missing data with statistics.	463
Naisbitt Group	A trend-spotting organization that uses content analysis.	460
PhaseOne Communications	Conducted content analysis of V-8 ads for Campbell Soup, resulting in a more effective promotional campaign.	460
Princess Cruises P&O Princess Cruises plc	Quick turnaround for a customer satisfaction study using optical scanning for data entry.	468
SAS	A statistical package for data entry and analysis.	470
SPSS, Inc.	A statistical package for data entry and analysis.	470
Stanford Research Institute (SRI) International	A research organization that uses content analysis.	460
U.S. Census Bureau	Using bar-coding to provide tracking of participation and faster data analysis.	469
U.S. Internal Revenue Service	Use of computerized number and character recognition to process 1040EZ forms.	468
Voter News Service (VNS)	The election polling consortium of ABC, NBC, CBA, CNN, FOX, and the Associated Press, responsible for the early mispredictions in the 2000 presidential election.	466

[*]Due to the confidential and proprietary nature of most research, the names of some companies have been changed.

DISCUSSION QUESTIONS

Terms in Review

1. Define or explain:

   a. Coding rules.

   b. Spreadsheet data entry.

   c. Bar codes.

   d. Precoded instruments.

   e. Measures of shape.

   f. Content analysis.

   g. Missing values.

    h. Optical mark recognition.

    i. Measures of spread.

2. How should the researcher handle "don't know" responses?

3. Why is the standard deviation a more useful statistic than the variance?

Making Research Decisions

4. A problem facing shoe store managers is that many shoes eventually must be sold at markdown prices. This prompts us to conduct a mail survey of shoe store managers in which we ask, "What methods have you found most successful for reducing the problem of high markdowns?" We are interested in extracting as much information as possible from these answers to better understand the full range of strategies that store managers use. Establish what you think are category sets to code 500 responses similar to the 14 given below. Try to develop an integrated set of categories that reflects your theory of markdown management. After developing the set, use it to code the 14 responses.

    a. Have not found the answer. As long as we buy style shoes, we will have markdowns. We use PMs on slow merchandise, but it does not eliminate markdowns. (PM stands for "push-money"—special item bonuses for selling a particular style of shoe.)

    b. Using PMs before too old. Also reducing price during season. Holding meetings with salespeople indicating which shoes to push.

    c. By putting PMs on any slow-selling items and promoting same. More careful check of shoes purchased.

    d. Keep a close watch on your stock, and mark down when you have to—that is, rather than wait, take a small markdown on a shoe that is not moving at the time.

    e. Using the PM method.

    f. Less advance buying—more dependence on in-stock shoes.

    g. Sales—catch bad guys before it's too late and close out.

    h. Buy as much good merchandise as you can at special prices to help make up some markdowns.

    i. Reducing opening buys and depending on fill-in service. PMs for salespeople.

    j. Buy more frequently, better buying, PMs on slow-moving merchandise.

    k. Careful buying at lowest prices. Cash on the buying line. Buying closeouts, FDs, overstock, "cancellations." (FD stands for "factory-discontinued" style.)

    l. By buying less "chanceable" shoes. Buy only what you need, watch sizes, don't go overboard on new fads.

    m. Buying more staple merchandise. Buying more from fewer lines. Sticking with better nationally advertised merchandise.

    n. No successful method with the current style situation. Manufacturers are experimenting, the retailer takes the markdowns—cuts gross profit by about 3 percent—keep your stock at lowest level without losing sales.

5. Define a small sample of class members, work associates, or friends and ask them to answer the following in a paragraph or two: "What are your career aspirations for the next five years?" Use one of the four basic units of content analysis to analyze their responses. Describe your findings as frequencies for the unit of analysis selected.

6. What is the median of the distribution 123, 154, 160, 187?

7. What happens to the mean and median in a set of five scores when the largest one is increased by several points? Set A: 12, 13, 23, 32, 43; Set A altered: 12, 13, 23, 32, 143.

From Concept to Practice

8. Select the variables in Exhibit 15–9 and enter their values into a spreadsheet.

   a. Compute their means, medians, and modes. Which variables have similar means and medians?

   b. Compute the standard deviations. Can you find any variables with proportionately larger standard deviations? What can you infer about the distributions' shapes?

   c. Now compute skewness and kurtosis. Which variables have the least skewness? The most kurtosis?

WWW Exercises

Visit our website for Internet exercises related to this chapter at www.mhhe.com/business/cooper8

CASES*

 AGRICOMP

AIDS RATES FOR FEMALES

 HEALTHY LIFESTYLES

INQUIRING MINDS WANT TO KNOW—NOW!

 MASTERING TEACHER LEADERSHIP

 NCR: TEEING UP A NEW STRATEGIC DIRECTION

 XEROX ABUSES

*All cases indicating a video icon are located on the Instructor's Videotape Supplement. All nonvideo cases are in the case section of the textbook. All cases indicating a CD icon offer a data set, which is located on the accompanying CD.

REFERENCE NOTES

1. Jean M. Converse and Stanley Presser, *Survey Questions: Handcrafting the Standardized Questionnaire* (Beverly Hills, CA: Sage Publications, 1986), pp. 34–35.
2. B. Berelson, *Content Analysis in Communication Research* (New York: Free Press, 1952), p. 18.
3. Klaus Krippendorff, *Content Analysis: An Introduction to Its Methodology* (Beverly Hills, CA: Sage Publications, 1980), p. 22.
4. Based on the operation of the SPSS, Inc., product TextSmart.
5. Hans Zeisel, *Say It with Figures,* 6th ed. (New York: Harper & Row, 1985), pp. 48–49.
6. See the description of Remark Office OMR® found at: http://www.principiaproducts.com.
7. Remark Web Survey® is a product of Principia Products, Inc., 16 Industrial Blvd., Suite 102, Paoli, PA, 19301.
8. Adapted from a history of bar code development: http://www.lascofittings.com/BarCode-EDI/bc-history.htm.
9. For a thorough discussion of missing data analysis and remedies in multivariate data, see Joseph F. Hair, Jr., et al., *Multivariate Data Analysis,* 5th ed. (Upper Saddle River, NJ: Prentice Hall, 1998), pp. 46–64.
10. Frederick Hartwig, with Brian E. Dearing, *Exploratory Data Analysis* (Beverly Hills, CA: Sage Publications, 1979), p. 15.

REFERENCES FOR SNAPSHOTS AND CAPTIONS

Decisive/Hewlett-Packard

"Hewlett-Packard Uses Decisive Technology's MarketView℠ to Analyze and Enhance Customers' After-Purchase Experiences," press release, Decisive Technology, April 6, 1999 (http://www.decisive.com/html/news/hp.htm).

Princess Cruises

"About Princess," P&O Princess Cruises plc, 02/09/2002 (http://www.princess.com/about).

J. Rydholm, "Scanning the Seas," *Quirk's Market Research Review,* May 1993 (http://www.quirks.com/articles/article_print.asp?arg_articleid=207).

V-8

"Good-Bye Guesswork," The Advertising Education Foundation, 1995 (http://www.campbellsoup.com/OurBrands/v8juice.cfm).

VNS

"A Bad Day at the Exit Polls," Savanna Morning News, November 9, 2000 (http://www.savannamorningnews.com/sma/stories/110900/locsurvey.shtml).

"Antitrust Group Urges U.S. to Break Up Voter News Service," Anti-Trust Institute, November 27, 2000 (http://www.antitrustinstitute.org/recent/90.cfm).

"Internet Exit Poll Leaks Election Day," ABC News, November 7, 2000 (http://www.abcnews.go...News/ELECTION_exitpolls001107.html).

Poll results at (www.cnn.com/election/2000/epolls/us/p000.html) or (www.abcnews.go.com/sections...2000vote/general/exitpoll_hub.html).

CLASSIC AND CONTEMPORARY READINGS

Aczel, Amir D., and Jayauel Sounderpandian. *Complete Business Statistics.* 5th ed. Chicago: Irwin/McGraw-Hill, 2001. See Chapter 1 on descriptive statistics and Chapter 4 on the normal distribution.

Bux, William E., and Kenneth L. Gorman. *DataEntry Activities for Windows.* Cincinnati, OH: Thomson Learning, 2000. Fundamentals of data entry in a self-paced learning package suitable for novice computer users.

Foster, Jeremy. *Data Analysis Using SPSS® for Windows® Version 8 to 10: A Beginner's Guide.* Thousand Oaks, CA: Sage Publishing, 2001. The first 15 chapters deal with data management: merging, sorting, coding, grouping; and fundamentals of descriptive analysis.

Strauss, Anselm, and Juliet Corbin. *Basics of Qualitative Research: Techniques and Procedures for Developing Grounded Theory.* Thousand Oaks, CA: Sage Publishing, 1998. Part II (10 chapters) illustrates several approaches to coding procedures for qualitative data.

Zeisel, Hans. *Say It with Figures.* 6th ed. New York: Harper & Row, 1985. The entire book is worth reading for its excellent discussion of numerical presentation.

CHAPTER 16

Exploring, Displaying, and Examining Data

Learning Objectives

After reading this chapter, you should understand . . .

1   **That exploratory data analysis techniques provide better diagnostics than traditional summary statistics by emphasizing visual representations of the data.**

2   **How statistical process control charts offer understandable and reliable displays for evaluating point values, trends, and special causes of variation in a process.**

3   **The uses of Geographic Information Systems for mapping, detecting patterns in the data, and discovering relationships between different sets of spatially referenced information.**

4   **How cross-tabulation is used to evaluate relationships involving categorical variables, serves as a framework for later statistical testing, and makes table-based analysis using one or more control variables an efficient tool for decision making.**

Bringing Research to Life

"Is my being early for our meeting a problem?" asked Myra, as she slid past a pile of computer printouts stacked precariously high just inside the door to Jason's office. "Might the industrious team in your outer office be studying my MindWriter Project 2 data?"

"Give me just a second," mumbled Jason, as he quickly wrote a note on a Post-it and slapped it on a pencil sketch of a graph and jotted another to a histogram. "Sammye, you want to come get these?" Jason called to one of the team members in the outer office.

Meanwhile, Myra chose an available chair and used the time to review her notes. She was here to convince Jason to take on yet another project for MindWriter. This one had a short turnaround.

Turning his attention on Myra, Jason extracted a folder lying on the credenza behind him. "Actually those worker-bees are new members of my staff, graduate students from the university. They're assigned to the City Center for Performing Arts project," shared Jason. "It's because of your recommendation that I got the job. I thought you knew."

"Of course I knew. I've been serving on CCPA's board for two years. Will you be presenting the preliminary analysis at the next meeting, this Friday?"

"Of course not! The preliminary analysis is strictly for us. While we may develop presentation charts that might be presented to the center, it is just as likely that none of the material you see stacked here will end up in the report as-is. Didn't you learn the general timetable for such projects on the first MindWriter project? We are nowhere near ready to write the client report. We just finished cleaning the data file yesterday. This morning I ran a full set of frequencies. Jill, David, and Sammye started their preliminary analysis . . . uh, 90 minutes ago."

"Anything interesting on the initial cross-tabs?"

"Well, well. You did learn something," observed Jason with a smile.

Myra smiled in return as she raised an expressive eyebrow and waited for Jason to respond.

"Just before you got here, three of the early cross-tabs appeared to show some support for the board's assumptions about the alcohol issue—on whether current patrons endorse the selling of beer and wine during intermissions. But we're not far enough into the data to say which of your board's assumptions are fully correct and which might have to be modified based on the patterns emerging within subgroups of the sample. We'll probably have to do some recoding of the age and race variables for the patterns to emerge clearly. The team is also interested in the differences between ethnic groups in future performance preferences. We've also finished coding each patron's address with its GIS (Geographic Information Systems) code. The preliminary mapping begins tomorrow; I hired a master's candidate in geography to provide the mapping. I've scheduled a conference call for . . . (Jason flips his desk calendar pages to the following week) . . . Friday of next week to talk with Jackson Murray and other members of the CCPA project team."

"When the board approved your proposed analysis plan," shared Myra, "I don't remember seeing any reference to those cute, box-like diagrams with tails I see on that graph you just handed to Sammye."

"Most of what we'll be doing the next three days involves more graphical displays than statistical ones. Right now we're just getting a sense of what the data are telling us. We'll decide what, if any, new analyses to add to the proposed plan by this Friday. It's this early work that lays the groundwork for the more sophisticated analyses that follow. There isn't anything glamorous about it, but without it we might miss some crucial findings."

Jason paused for effect, then said, "By the way, that 'cute little diagram' is called a boxplot. I actually did several during the preliminary analysis phase for MindWriter's CompleteCare study. I didn't give them to you because I would have had to explain how to interpret them and . . ."

". . . and anything you have to explain isn't clear enough," finished Myra. "I learned Jason's Rule #1 on reporting to clients very well on MindWriter-1."

Myra modified her position in the chair, leaning slightly toward Jason. Just before she spoke, Jason observed, "Oh, no! You're changing into your 'It's time to get down to business' posture. So what's the new project you want to discuss . . . and the impossible deadline you need me to meet?"

"Just hear me out, Jason. MindWriter's LT3000 product group has decided it needs to use 'superiority in custom-designed systems' as its claim in a new ad campaign, but legal says we don't have enough data to support the claim. The ad agency we have chosen has a short window of opportunity. We need supporting data within 10 days." Myra held up her hand to stop the objection she anticipated from Jason. "We know you don't have time to collect new primary data and analyze it in 10 days . . . so I brought the next best thing. I've got three boxes of miscellaneous records in my trunk . . ."

Jason groaned. "Let's go see what you brought me. Then we'll see if this project is even feasible."

Introduction

The convenience of data entry via spreadsheet, optimal mark recognition (OMR), or with the data editor of a statistical program makes it tempting to move directly to statistical analysis. Why waste time finding out if the data confirm the hypothesis that motivated the study? Why not obtain descriptive statistical summaries (based on our discussion in Chapter 15) and then test hypotheses?

In Chapter 2, we said research conducted scientifically is a puzzle-solving activity. We also noted that an attitude of curiosity, suspicion, and imagination was essential to the discovery process. It is natural, then, that exploration of the data would be an integral part of our perspective. When the study's purpose is not the production of causal inferences, confirmatory data analysis is not required. When it is, we advocate discovering as much as possible about the data before selecting the appropriate means of confirmation. Exhibit 16–1 reminds you of the importance of data visualization as an integral element in the data analysis process and as a necessary step prior to hypothesis testing.

Depending on the type of management question, we can discover a great deal about our data through exploratory data analysis, statistical process control charting, geographical information system mapping, and cross-tabulation.

Exploratory Data Analysis

Exploratory data analysis (EDA) is both a data analysis perspective and a set of techniques.[1] In exploratory data analysis, the data guide the choice of analysis—or a revision of the planned analysis—rather than the analysis presuming to overlay its structure on the data without the benefit of the analyst's scrutiny. This is comparable to our position that research should be problem-oriented rather than tool-driven. The flexibility to respond to the patterns revealed by successive iterations in the discovery process is an

EXHIBIT 16–1   Data Analysis in the Research Process

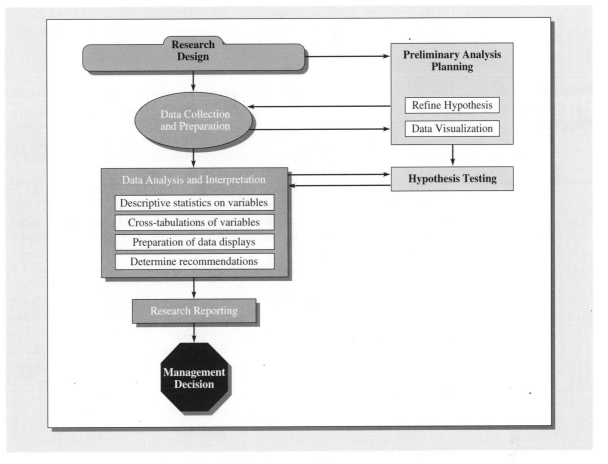

important attribute of this approach. By comparison, **confirmatory data analysis** occupies a position closer to classical statistical inference in its use of significance and confidence. But confirmatory analysis may also differ from traditional practices by using information from a closely related data set or by validating findings through the gathering and analyzing of new data.[2]

One authority has compared exploratory data analysis to the role of police detectives and other investigators and confirmatory analysis to that of judges and the judicial system. The former are involved in the search for clues and evidence; the latter are preoccupied with evaluating the strength of what is found. Exploratory data analysis is the first step in the search for evidence, without which confirmatory analysis has nothing to evaluate.[3] Consistent with that analogy, EDA shares a commonality with exploratory designs, not formalized ones. Because it doesn't follow a rigid structure, it is free to take many paths in unraveling the mysteries in the data—to sift the unpredictable from the predictable.

A major contribution of the exploratory approach lies in the emphasis on visual representations and graphical techniques over summary statistics. Summary statistics, as you will see momentarily, may obscure, conceal, or even misrepresent the underlying structure of the data. When numerical summaries are used exclusively and accepted without visual inspection, the selection of confirmatory models may be precipitous, and based on flawed assumptions. Consequently, it may produce erroneous conclusions.[4] For these reasons, data analysis should begin with visual inspection. After that, it is not only possible but also desirable to cycle between exploratory and confirmatory approaches.

Frequency Tables, Bar Charts, and Pie Charts[5]

Several useful techniques for displaying data are not new to EDA. They are essential to any examination of the data. For example, a **frequency table** is a simple device for arraying data. An example is presented in Exhibit 16–2. It arrays data by assigned numerical value, with columns for percent, percent adjusted for missing values, and cumulative percent. Sector, the nominal variable that describes the business classifications or markets of the sampled corporations, provides the observations for this table. Although there are 100 observations, the small number of categories makes the variable easily tabled. The same data are presented in Exhibit 16–3 using a bar chart and a pie chart. The values and percentages are more readily understood in this graphic format, and visualization of the sector categories and their relative sizes is improved.

When the variable of interest is measured on an interval-ratio scale and is one with many potential values, these techniques are not particularly informative. Exhibit 16–4 is a condensed frequency table of the highest total return to investors measured in percentages of the top 48 companies in this category taken from the Fortune 500.[6] Only two values, 59.9 and 66, have a frequency greater than 1. Thus, the primary contribution of this table is an ordered list of values. If the table were converted to a bar chart, it would have 48 bars of equal length and two bars with two occurrences. And bar charts do not reserve spaces for values where no observations occur within the range. Constructing a pie chart for this variable would also be pointless.

EXHIBIT 16–2   A Frequency Table of Market Sector (Forbes Industry List)

Value Label	Value	Frequency	Percent	Valid Percent	Cumulative Percent
Chemicals and materials	1	10	10.0	10.0	10.0
Consumer products	2	8	8.0	8.0	18.0
Durables/capital equipment	3	7	7.0	7.0	25.0
Energy	4	13	13.0	13.0	38.0
Financial	5	24	24.0	24.0	62.0
Health	6	4	4.0	4.0	66.0
High-tech	7	11	11.0	11.0	77.0
Insurance	8	6	6.0	6.0	83.0
Retailing	9	7	7.0	7.0	90.0
Other	10	10	10.0	10.0	100.0
Total		100	100.0	100.0	

Valid cases 100   Missing cases 0

EXHIBIT 16–3   Nominal Variable Displays (Forbes Industry List)

Sector	%
Chemicals and materials	10
Consumer products	8
Durables/capital equipment	7
Energy	13
Financial	24
Health	4
High-tech	11
Insurance	6
Retailing	7
Other	10
	100

Histograms

The histogram is a conventional solution for the display of interval-ratio data. **Histograms** are used when it is possible to group the variable's values into intervals. Histograms are constructed with bars (or asterisks that represent data values) where each value occupies an equal amount of area within the enclosed area. Data analysts find histograms useful for (1) displaying all intervals in a distribution, even those without observed values, and (2) examining the shape of the distribution for skewness, kurtosis, and the modal pattern. When looking at a histogram, one might ask: Is there a single hump (a mode)? Are subgroups identifiable when multiple modes are present? Are straggling data values detached from the central concentration?[7]

EXHIBIT 16–4   **Return to Investors of the Top 48 in the Fortune 500**

	Value	Frequency	Percent	Cum. Percent		Value	Frequency	Percent	Cum. Percent
1	54.9	1	2	2	25	75.6	1	2	54
2	55.4	1	2	4	26	76.4	1	2	56
3	55.6	1	2	6	27	77.5	1	2	58
4	56.4	1	2	8	28	78.9	1	2	60
5	56.8	1	2	10	29	80.9	1	2	62
6	56.9	1	2	12	30	82.2	1	2	64
7	57.8	1	2	14	31	82.5	1	2	66
8	58.1	1	2	16	32	86.4	1	2	68
9	58.2	1	2	18	33	88.3	1	2	70
10	58.3	1	2	20	34	102.5	1	2	72
11	58.5	1	2	22	35	104.1	1	2	74
12	59.9	2	4	26	36	110.4	1	2	76
13	61.5	1	2	28	37	111.9	1	2	78
14	62.6	1	2	30	38	118.6	1	2	80
15	64.8	1	2	32	39	123.8	1	2	82
16	66.0	2	4	36	40	131.2	1	2	84
17	66.3	1	2	38	41	140.9	1	2	86
18	67.6	1	2	40	42	146.2	1	2	88
19	69.1	1	2	42	43	153.2	1	2	90
20	69.2	1	2	44	44	163.2	1	2	92
21	70.5	1	2	46	45	166.7	1	2	94
22	72.7	1	2	48	46	183.2	1	2	96
23	72.9	1	2	50	47	206.9	1	2	98
24	73.5	1	2	52	48	218.2	1	2	100

The values for the return to investors variable presented in Exhibit 16–4 were measured on a ratio scale and are easily grouped. Other variables possessing an underlying order are similarly appropriate for histograms. A histogram would not be used for a nominal variable like sector (Exhibit 16–3) that has no order to its categories.

A histogram of the return to investors variable taken from the Fortune 500 ranked by performance listing is shown in Exhibit 16–5. The midpoint for each interval for the variable of interest, return to investors, is shown on the horizontal axis, the frequency or number of observations in each interval on the vertical axis. We erect a vertical bar above the midpoint of each interval on the horizontal scale. The height of the bar corresponds with the frequency of observations in the interval above which it is erected. This histogram was constructed with intervals 20 increments wide, and the last interval con-

EXHIBIT 16–5   Histogram of Fortune 500 Data

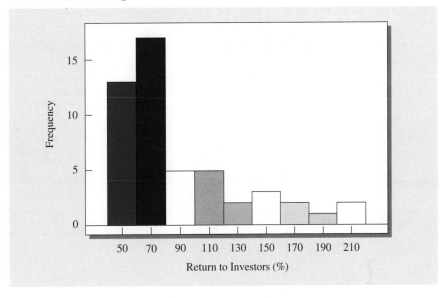

tains only two observations, 206.9 and 218.2. These values are found in the Fortune 500 frequency table (Exhibit 16–4). Intervals with 0 counts show gaps in the data and alert the analyst to look for problems with spread. When the upper tail of the distribution is compared with the frequency table, we find three extreme values (183.2, 206.9, and 218.2). Along with the peaked midpoint and reduced number of observations in the upper tail, this histogram warns us of irregularities in the data.

Stem-and-Leaf Displays[8]

The **stem-and-leaf display** is an EDA technique that is closely related to the histogram. It shares some of its features but offers several unique advantages. It is easy to construct by hand for small samples or may be produced by computer programs.

In contrast to histograms, which lose information by grouping data values into intervals, the stem-and-leaf presents actual data values that can be inspected directly without the use of enclosed bars or asterisks as the representation medium. This feature reveals the distribution of values within the interval and preserves their rank order for finding the median, quartiles, and other summary statistics. It also eases linking a specific observation back to the data file and to the subject that produced it.

Visualization is the second advantage of stem-and-leaf displays. The range of values is apparent at a glance, and both shape and spread impressions are immediate. Patterns in the data—such as gaps where no values exist, areas where values are clustered, or outlying values that differ from the main body of the data—are easily observed.

In order to develop a stem-and-leaf display for the data in Exhibit 16–4, the first digits of each data item are arranged to the left of a vertical line. Next, we pass through the return to investor percentages in the order they were recorded and place the last digit for each item (the unit position, 1.0) to the right of the vertical line. Note that the digit to the right of the decimal point is ignored. The last digit for each item is placed on the horizontal row corresponding to its first digit(s). Now it is a simple matter to rank-order the digits in each row, creating the stem-and-leaf display shown in Exhibit 16–6.

EXHIBIT 16–6   A Stem-and-Leaf Display of Fortune 500 Data

5	4 5 5 6 6 6 7 8 8 8 8 9
6	1 2 4 6 6 7 9 9
7	0 2 2 3 5 6 7 8
8	0 2 2 6 8
9	
10	2 4
11	0 1 8
12	3
13	1
14	0 6
15	3
16	3 6
17	
18	3
19	
20	6
21	8

Each line or row in this display is referred to as a *stem,* and each piece of information on the stem is called a *leaf.* The first line or row is

5 | 4 5 5 6 6 6 7 8 8 8 8 9

The meaning attached to this line or row is that there are 12 items in the data set whose first digit is five: 54, 55, 55, 56, 56, 56, 57, 58, 58, 58, 58, and 59. The second line,

6 | 1 2 4 6 6 7 9 9

shows that there are eight return to investors percentage values whose first digit is six: 61, 62, 64, 66, 66, 67, 69, and 69. The stem is the digit(s) to the left of the vertical line (6 for this example), and the leaf is the digit(s) to the right of the vertical line (1, 2, 4, 6, 6, 7, 9, 9).

When the stem-and-leaf display shown in Exhibit 16–6 is turned upright (rotated 90 degrees to the left), the shape is the same as that of the histogram shown in Exhibit 16–5.

Boxplots[9]

The **boxplot,** or *box-and-whisker plot,* is another technique used frequently in exploratory data analysis.[10] A boxplot reduces the detail of the stem-and-leaf display and provides a different visual image of the distribution's location, spread, shape, tail length, and outliers. Boxplots are extensions of the **five-number summary** of a distribution. This summary consists of the median, upper and lower quartiles, and the largest and smallest observations. The median and quartiles are used because they are particularly **resistant statistics.** *Resistance* is a characteristic that "provides insensitivity to localized misbehavior in data."[11] Resistant statistics are unaffected by outliers and change only slightly in response to the replacement of small portions of the data set.

Recall the previous discussion of the mean and standard deviation in Chapter 15. Now assume we take the data set [5,6,6,7,7,7,8,8,9]. The mean of the set is 7, the standard deviation 1.23. If the 9 is replaced with 90, the mean becomes 16 and the standard deviation increases to 27.78. The mean is now two times larger than most of the numbers in the distribution, and the standard deviation is more than 22 times its original size. Changing only one of nine values has disturbed the location and spread summaries to the point where they no longer represent the other eight values. Both the mean and the standard deviation are considered **nonresistant statistics;** they are susceptible to the effects of extreme values in the tails of the distribution and do not represent typical values well under conditions of asymmetry. The standard deviation is particularly problematic because it is computed from the squared deviations from the mean.[12] In contrast, the median and quartiles are highly resistant to change. When we changed the 9 to 90, the median remained at 7 and the lower and upper quartiles stayed at 6 and 8, respectively. Because of the nature of quartiles, up to 25 percent of the data can be made extreme without perturbing the median, the rectangular composition of the plot, or the quartiles themselves. These characteristics of resistance are incorporated into the construction of boxplots.

Boxplots may be constructed easily by hand or by computer programs. The basic ingredients of the plot are the (1) rectangular plot that encompasses 50 percent of the data values, (2) a center line (or other notation) marking the median and going through the width of the box, (3) the edges of the box, called hinges, and (4) the whiskers that extend from the right and left hinges to the largest and smallest values.[13] These values may be found within 1.5 times the **interquartile range (IQR)** from either edge of the box. These components and their relationships are shown in Exhibit 16–7.

EXHIBIT 16–7 **Boxplot Components**

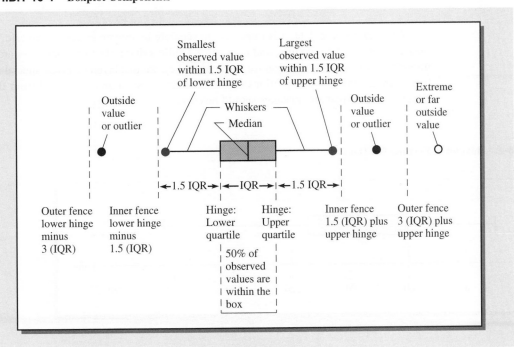

We can create a boxplot of the return to investors variable from the information provided in Exhibit 16–4. With the five-number summary, we have the basis for a skeletal plot.

Minimum	Lower Hinge	Median	Upper Hinge	Maximum
54.90	59.90	73.20	110.78	218.20

The plot shown in Exhibit 16–8 started with these data and the following calculations. You may construct your own boxplot with the data in Exhibit 16–4 and the SPSS Explore procedure. Beginning with the box, the ends are drawn using the lower and upper quartile (hinge) data. The median is drawn in at 73.2. Then the IQR is calculated $(110.78 - 59.9 = 50.88)$. From this we can locate the lower and upper fences. The fences are −25.44 and 187.1. Next, the smallest and largest data values from the distribution within the fences are used to determine the whisker length. These values are 54.90 and 183.20. We are now able to see the outliers in relation to the "main body" of the data. **Outliers** are data points that exceed +1.5 IQRs of a boxplot's hinges. Data values for the outliers are added, and identifiers may be provided for interesting values. The completed boxplot is shown in Exhibit 16–8.

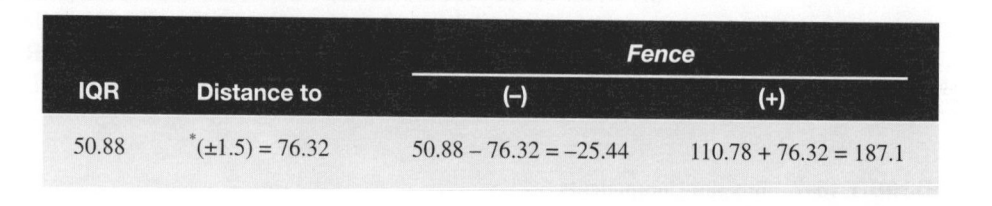

		Fence	
IQR	Distance to	(−)	(+)
50.88	$^{*}(\pm 1.5) = 76.32$	$50.88 - 76.32 = -25.44$	$110.78 + 76.32 = 187.1$

When examining data, it is important to separate legitimate outliers from errors in measurement, editing, coding, and data entry. Outliers that reflect unusual cases are an important source of information for the study. They are displayed or given special statistical treatment, or other portions of the data set are sometimes shielded from their effects. Outliers that are mistakes should be corrected or removed.

EXHIBIT 16–8   Boxplot of Fortune 500 Data

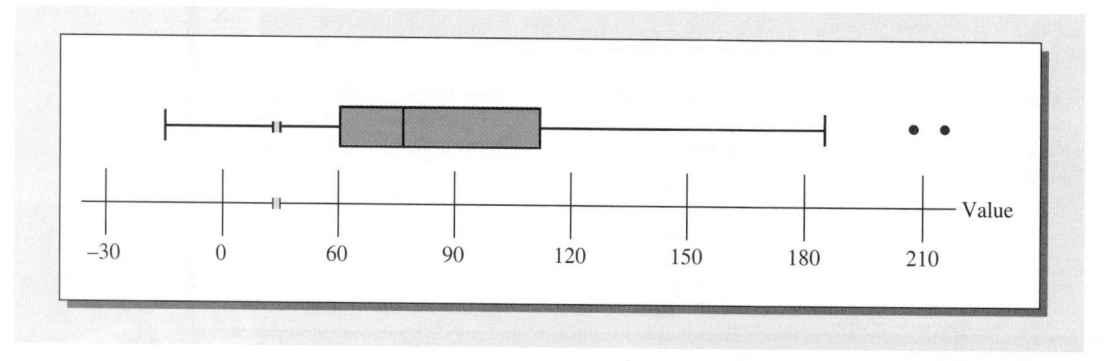

EXHIBIT 16–9 **Diagnostics with Boxplots**

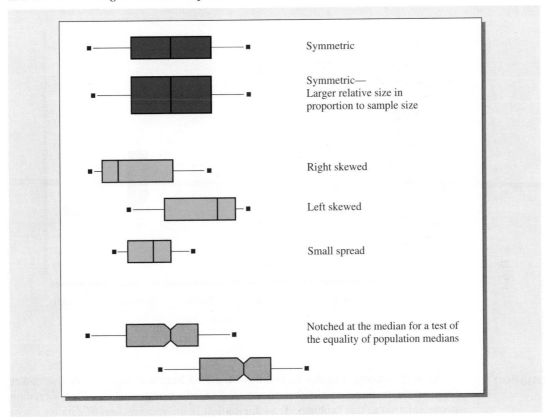

Exhibit 16–9 summarizes several comparisons that are of help to the analyst. Box-plots are an excellent diagnostic tool, especially when graphed on the same scale. The upper two plots in the exhibit are both symmetric, but one is larger than the other. Larger box widths are sometimes used when the second variable, from the same measurement scale, comes from a larger sample size. The box widths should be proportional to the square root of the sample size, but not all plotting programs account for this.[14] Right- and left-skewed distributions and those with reduced spread are also presented clearly in the plot comparison. Finally, groups may be compared by means of multiple plots. One variation, in which a notch at the median marks off a confidence interval to test the equality of group medians, takes us a step closer to hypothesis testing.[15] Here the sides of the box return to full width at the upper and lower confidence intervals. When the intervals do not overlap, we can be confident, at a specified confidence level, that the medians of the two populations are different.

In Exhibit 16–10, multiple boxplots compare five sectors on the return to investors variable. The overall impression is one of potential problems for the analyst: unequal variances, skewness, and extreme outliers. Note the similarities of the profiles of finance and retailing in contrast to the high-tech and insurance sectors. If hypothesis tests are planned, further examination of this plot for each sector would require a stem-and-leaf display and a five-number summary. From this, we could make decisions on test selection and whether the data should be transformed or reexpressed before further analysis.

EXHIBIT 16–10   Boxplot Comparison of Sectors

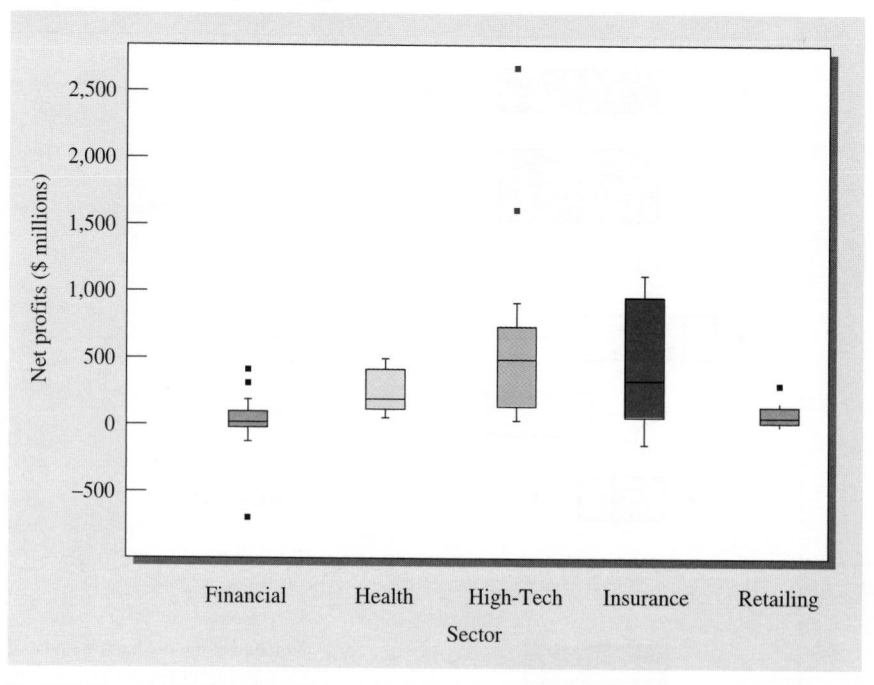

Transformation[16]

Some of the examples in this section have departed from normality. While this makes for good illustrations, such data pose special problems in data analysis. Transformation is one solution to this problem. **Transformation** is the reexpression of data on a new scale using a single mathematical function for each data point. Although nominal and ordinal data may be transformed, the procedures are beyond the scope of this book. We will consider only interval-ratio scale transformations here.

The fact that data collected on one scale are found to depart from the assumptions of normality and constant variance does not preclude reexpressing them on another scale. What is discovered, of course, must be linked to the original data.

We transform data for several reasons: (1) to improve interpretation and compatibility with other data sets, (2) to enhance symmetry and stabilize spread, and (3) to improve linear relationships between and among variables. We improve interpretation when we find alternate ways to understand the data and discover patterns or relationships that may not have been revealed on the original scales. A **standard score,** or *Z score,* may be calculated to improve compatibility among variables that come from different scales and require comparison. Z scores convey distance in standard deviation units with a mean of 0 and a standard deviation of 1. This is accomplished by converting the raw score, X_i, to

$$Z = \frac{X_i - \bar{X}}{s}$$

Z scores improve interpretation through their reference to the normal curve and our understanding of the areas under it.

Conversion of centimeters to inches, stones to pounds, liters to gallons, or Celsius to Fahrenheit are examples of linear conversions that change the scale but do not change symmetry or spread. Many statisticians consider these data as manipulations rather than transformations.

Nonlinear transformations are often needed to satisfy the other two reasons for reexpressing data. Normality and constancy of variance are important assumptions for many parametric statistical techniques. A transformation to reduce skewness and stabilize variance makes it possible to use various confirmatory techniques without violating their assumptions. Analysis of the relationship between variables also benefits from transformation. Improved predictions and better diagnostics of fit and residuals (as in regression analysis) are frequent payoffs.

Transformations are defined with power, p, as the reexpression of x with x^{p}.[17] Exhibit 16–11 shows the most frequently used power transformations.

We use *spread-and-level* plots to guide our choice of a power transformation. By plotting the log of the median against the log of the interquartile range, we can find the slope of the plot: where p, the power we are seeking, is equal to $1 - slope$. Although 1/4 and 1/3 powers often result—and are sometimes preferred—many computer programs require rounding the transformation to the nearest half power.

The return to investors variable is used to illustrate this concept. The data distribution shows a right skew. The five-number summary (data in millions of dollars) reveals an extreme score as the maximum data point:

Minimum	Lower Hinge	Median	Upper Hinge	Maximum
54.9	59.9	73.2	110.78	218.2

The largest observation, 218.2, is only approximately 0.5 IQRs beyond the main body of data, and there is only one other value beyond the fence.

A quick calculation of the ratio of the largest observation to the smallest (218.2/54.9 = 3.97) serves as the final confirmation that transformation might not be worthwhile. It is desirable for this informal index to be greater than 20; with ratios less than 2, transformation is not practical.[18] From this information, we might conclude that the return to investors variable is not a good candidate for transformation.

When researchers communicate their findings to management, the advantages of reexpression must be balanced against pragmatism: Some transformed scales have no

EXHIBIT 16–11   **Frequently Used Power Transformations**

Power	Transformation
3	Cube
2	Square
1	No change: existing data
1/2	Square root
0	Logarithm (usually Lg_{10})
−1/2	Reciprocal root
−1	Reciprocal
−2	Reciprocal square
−3	Reciprocal cube

As this Booth Research Services ad suggests, the researcher's purpose is to make sense of numerous data displays and thus assist the research sponsor in making an appropriate management decision. www.boothresearch.com

familiar analogies. Logarithmic dollars can be explained, but how about reciprocal root dollars? Attitude and preference scales might be better understood transformed, but the question of interpretation remains.

Throughout this section we have exploited the visual techniques of exploratory data analysis to look beyond numerical summaries and gain insight into the behavior of the data. Few of the approaches have stressed the need for advanced mathematics, and all have an intuitive appeal for the analyst. When the more common ways of summarizing location, spread, and shape have conveyed an inadequate picture of the data, we have used more resistant statistics to protect us from the effects of extreme scores and occasional errors. We have also emphasized the value of transforming the original scale of the data during preliminary analysis rather than at the point of hypothesis testing.

Improvement and Control Analysis

Statistical process control (SPC) uses statistical tools to analyze, monitor, and improve process performance. A process is any business system that transforms inputs to outputs. Assembling automobiles, manufacturing plastic pipe, preparing restaurant meals, and service and administrative business activities are all made up of processes. Processes that operate within control limits are stable, predictable, and responsive to improvement. Walter Shewhart at Bell Laboratories defined this concept for production processes during the 1920s; it was later expanded by W. Edwards Deming to become an integral part of **Total Quality Management (TQM).**

The element of the process control system that pertains to displaying data is its charting system. SPC charts provide easily understood and reliable visuals for evaluating point values and trends and can graphically depict variation. Control charts help

EXHIBIT 16–12   **Control Chart Characteristics**

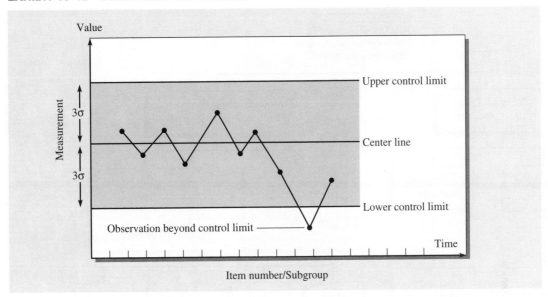

managers focus on special causes of variation in a process by revealing whether a system is under control (as an early warning of change) and substantiate results from improvements (confirming results).

A **control chart** displays sequential measurements of a process together with a center line and control limits. Limit lines provide guides for evaluating performance. These lines show the dispersion of data within a statistical boundary (generally three standard deviations above and below the average or center line). If an observation falls beyond the area marked by the **upper control limit (UCL)** or the **lower control limit (LCL),** there is evidence that the process is out of control or special causes are adversely affecting it. However, even if all data points are within the boundaries, the time plot (the sequence of points along the X-axis) can reveal that the process has sudden jumps, drifts, cycles, or the beginning of a trend. The elements that make up a control chart are shown in Exhibit 16–12.

Types of Control Charts

The selection of a control chart depends on the level of data you are measuring. Exhibit 16–13 provides a diagram for selecting an appropriate chart. In this exhibit, *variables data* refer to ratio or interval measurements (such as the diameter of a bearing, units/hour, the thickness of a plastic film, temperature, or blood pressure). Variables data are typically presented in X-bar charts and R-charts and X-bar charts and s-charts. Attributes data are nominal or categorical data that can be counted. Examples include the number of defects/part, abnormals/1,000 processed, and scratches per item. Attributes data are usually nonconforming units shown in control charts called *c-, u-, p-,* and *np-charts.* Variables data have the advantage because they reveal how close we are to a specification—just as interval data provide more information on attitudes than do nominal data.

X-bar charts and R-charts are often displayed together, as illustrated in Exhibit 16–15. The measurements describe an outboard motor manufacturer whose motors for small fishing boats require control to deliver a constant 10 horsepower. The process characteristics are reported in Exhibit 16–14 showing small subgroups of three observations per subgroup. (This type of control chart usually has constant size samples of

EXHIBIT 16–13   **Control Chart Selection**

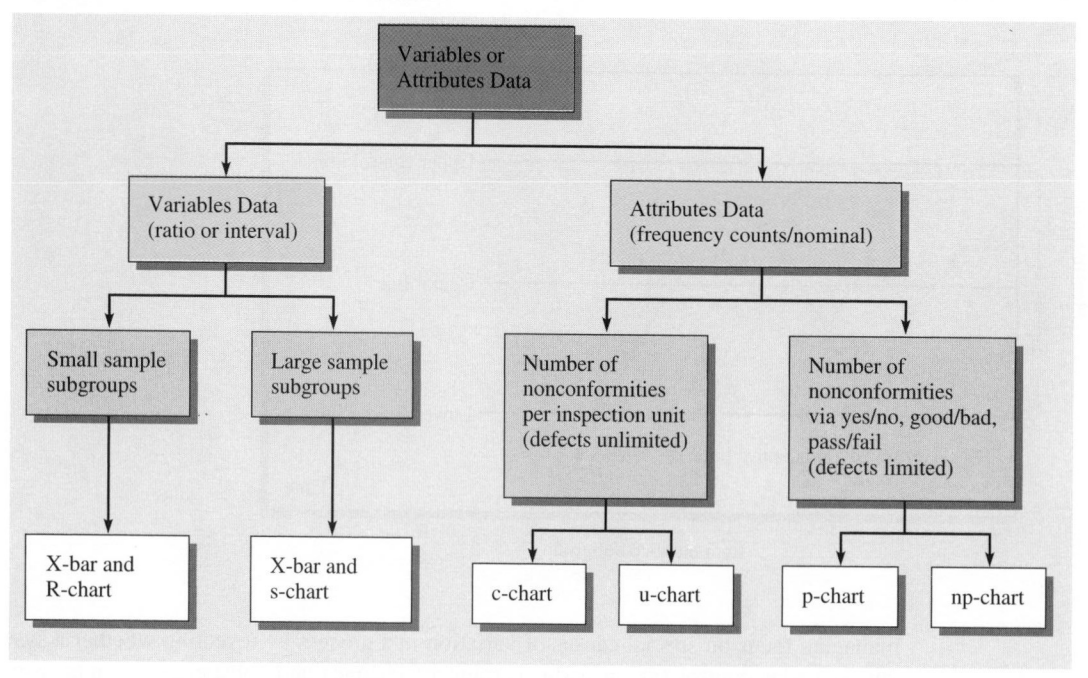

EXHIBIT 16–14   **MerK Outboard Motor Data**

Subgroup	Horsepower Output		
1	10.22	10.31	9.79
2	10.25	10.33	10.12
3	10.37	9.92	10.80
4	10.46	9.94	10.26
5	10.06	9.39	10.31
6	10.59	10.15	10.23
7	10.82	10.85	10.20
8	10.52	10.14	10.07
9	10.13	10.69	10.15
10	9.88	10.32	10.31

two to five measurements per subgroup.) We first evaluate the variance, as represented by the range, since it is important to keep the variability of the process low. Although the R-chart in Exhibit 16–15 suggests the process is technically in control, we can see fluctuations throughout the range.

There are no assignable causes for these discrepancies, so we proceed to analyze the X-bar chart in Exhibit 16–15. Here it is apparent that subgroups 5 and 7 under- and overproduce, respectively. One inference is that we should monitor production and secure further samples.

EXHIBIT 16–15   R-Chart and X-Bar Chart for MerK Outboard Motor Data

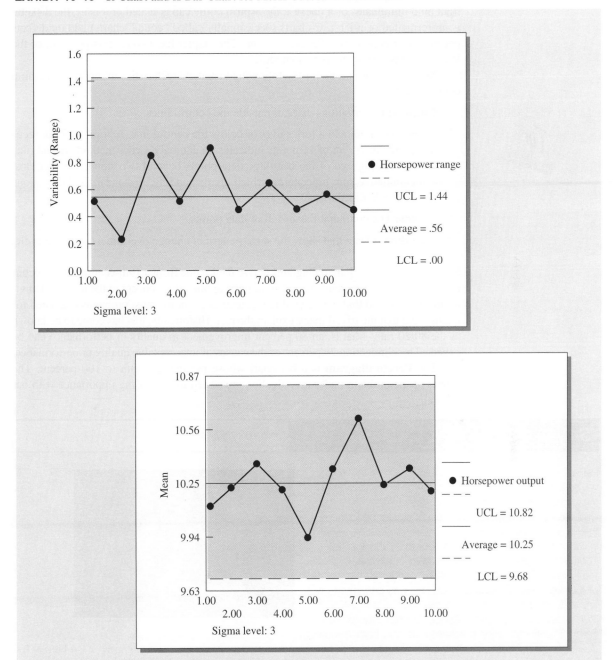

X-bar charts and s-charts (sample standard deviation) are also used jointly. The sample standard deviation is a more efficient indicator of process variability, especially with larger sample sizes. However, it is less sensitive in detecting special causes of variation when a single value in a subgroup is found to be unusual.

Other varieties of control charts have a layout similar to the charts in Exhibit 16–15 but differ as to purpose. The c-chart and p-chart are used primarily for attributes data.

P-charts ("proportion" charts) show the percentage of production that is defective. The light bulb illuminates or it doesn't; the aspirin bottle cap is sealed or it isn't; the diskette is preformatted or it isn't. C-charts (occasionally called "count" charts) add up defects per unit over consecutive periods of time: The stapler has two defects per unit, or the television has one defect per submodule.

Managers should look for the following visual characteristics in reports containing control charts:

MANAGEMENT
Tip

1. **Outliers:** Observations that fall outside the control lines.

2. **Runs:** Data points in a series over or below the central line. A "run" of 7 consecutive points or 10 out of 11 points indicates an anomaly. Other methods reveal runs such as finding two of the last three data points beyond two standard deviations, and cumulative sum procedures, which involve adding up standardized deviations from the calculated mean.

3. **Trends:** The continual rise or fall of data points.

4. **Periodicity:** Data that show the same pattern of change over time, creating a cycle.

Pareto Diagram   Pareto diagrams derive their name from a 19th-century Italian economist. In quality management, J. M. Juran first applied this concept to the industrial environment. He noted that only a vital few defects account for most problems evaluated for quality, and that the trivial many explain the rest. Historically, this has come to be known as the 80/20 rule—that is, an 80 percent improvement in quality or performance can be expected by eliminating 20 percent of the causes of unacceptable quality or performance.

The **Pareto diagram** is a bar chart whose percentages sum to 100 percent. The causes of the problem under investigation are sorted in decreasing importance with bar

---

S N A P S H O T   Does a Dummy Ever Lie?

Recently Ford Motor Co. has been much in the safety news, first with roll-overs of its Explorer SUV, not to mention the dissolution of its century-old alliance with Firestone. Until recently, Ford Motor Co. thought its star performer—the Ford F-150 truck—was not only popular but also safe. In laboratory offset crash tests, however, the Insurance Institute for Highway Safety concluded otherwise. It gave the Ford F-150 a "poor" rating after it performed the worst of four vehicles tested. The crash test was performed on one extended-cab vehicle of similar weight from each of four manufacturers (GM, Toyota, DaimlerChrysler, and Ford). The trucks were purchased directly from a local dealer. The crash test simulated a 40-mile-per-hour head-on collision, with each truck slamming into a stationary barrier with the left half of the front bumper. Only in the Toyota Motor Company's full-size Tundra truck did the safety cage maintain its integrity, protecting the driver "dummy" from all but minor injuries. In the Ford, the driver dummy flew uncontrolled within the cab before ending in a position beneath the steering column. Even the dummy couldn't survive the head trauma inflicted by the twisted metal carnage that had been the Ford F-150's occupant compartment. Ford said that the crash test was just one of many

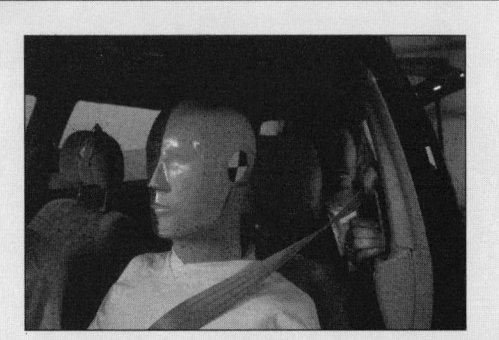

conducted on its vehicles and that, overall, the Ford F-150 was safe. For example, it showed little damage in one such test where the Ford F-150 slammed full-bumper into a stationary barrier. How would you assess the quality of the institute's experiment and its resulting evaluation of Ford?

www.hwysafety.org

www.toyota.com

www.ford.com

EXHIBIT 16–16   Pareto Diagram of MindWriter Repair Complaints

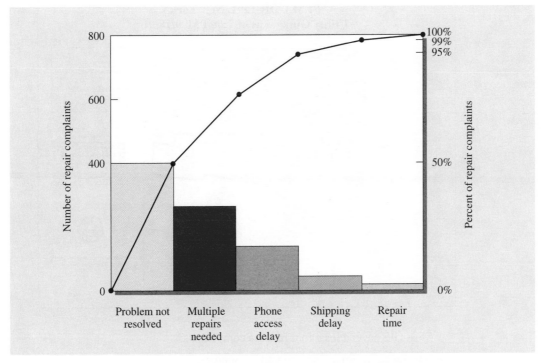

height descending from left to right. The pictorial array that results reveals the highest concentration of quality improvement potential in the fewest number of remedies. An analysis of MindWriter customer complaints is depicted as a Pareto diagram in Exhibit 16–16. The cumulative frequency line in this exhibit shows that the top two problems (the repair did not resolve the customers' problem, and the product was returned multiple times for repair) accounted for 80 percent of the perceptions of inadequate repair service.

Geographic Information Systems

See an example of a GIS display in Chapter 20.

Geographic Information Systems (GIS) refers to systems of hardware and software and procedures that capture, store, manipulate, integrate, and display spatially referenced data for solving complex planning and management problems.[19]

GIS works by stacking different data sets on top of each other so that the data points from variables of interest align on a common geographical referent, allowing the user to drill through the layers and visualize the relationships among different sets of information. Its software does more, however, than draw maps on top of each other. The database system and computational buffers have specific capabilities for dealing with spatially referenced information as well as the algorithms necessary to analyze simultaneously the many layers of data.

There are numerous management applications for GIS mapping and analysis. A market analyst might seek information on sales targeting, health care or hospital network placement, real estate site selection, or customer locations. Public managers use GIS to answer questions about incorporation boundaries, emergency service delivery, school districts, redevelopment plans, natural resource preservation, and the service requirements of growing populations.

The Federal Emergency Management Agency (FEMA) uses its Mapping and Analysis Center to provide national level GIS support for the agency's mission in responding to disasters. Here we see power outages in the vicinity of New York's World Trade Center on September 18, 2001. www.gismaps.fema.gov

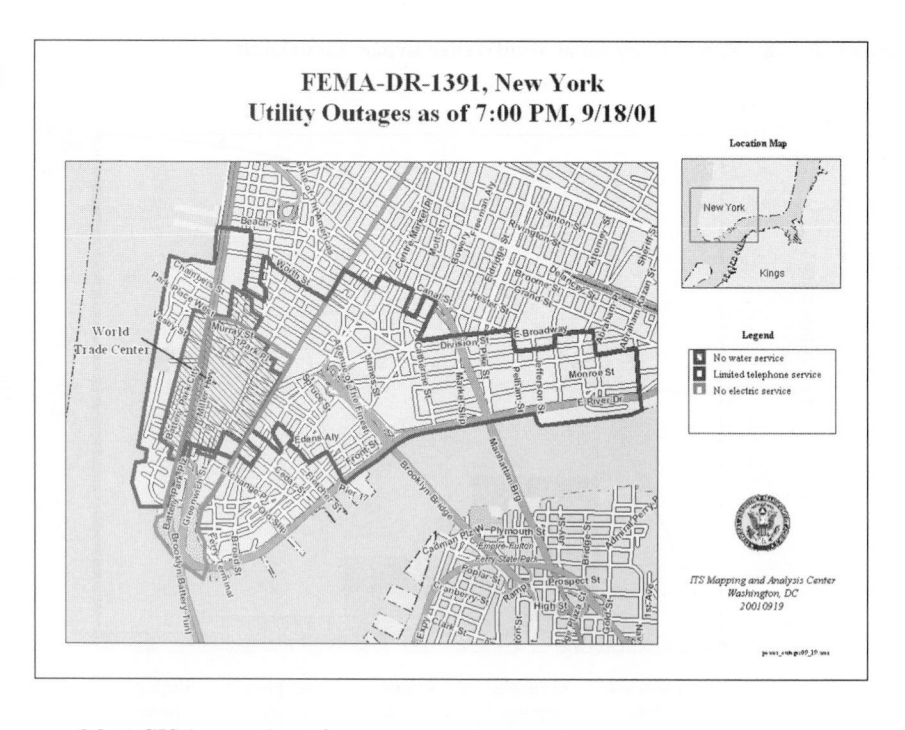

Most GIS have at least four process components:

- Integrating information from various sources.
- Capturing data.
- Projection and restructuring.
- Modeling.

Integrating Information

The primary requirement for GIS data is that a variable's location is known. A location may be a zip code, census boundary, survey marker, highway marker, or coordinates of longitude, latitude, and elevation. Data appropriate for GIS analysis are those that can be located spatially. By integrating variables from different sources, combinations of mapped variables may be created to simulate and analyze new ones. For example, a GIS mapping program and water company billing information could be used to simulate the impact of discharge from neighborhood septic systems on an environmentally sensitive wetland downstream.[20]

With existing information, census or zip code tabular data can be mapped to form layers of thematic information. In health care, we may want to know if the services provided match the needs of a defined geographical population. The resulting map could answer questions like: Where are certain services in higher demand? What is the best location for a new facility? Is public transportation adequate for patient access?[21]

Capturing Data

The most labor-intensive component of GIS is data capture and editing. All map objects must be specified and their spatial relationships entered. Variables related to each object are indexed. In Chapter 15 we said that editing detects errors and omissions, correcting them when possible, so quality standards may be achieved. Scanners record map imperfections as precisely as correct features. Contour lines that should not be connected or boundaries that do not exist produce false information in the spatial analysis that mislead the analyst during drill-down through the layers.

S N A P S H O T Saving Lives with Research

Emergency services are the lifeline for millions of people every day. So when Ohio's Springfield Fire Department (SFD) noted a disturbing trend in 1997 response-time data, it needed a potentially life-saving solution. Target response time for SFD is less than eight minutes for fire emergencies and less than six minutes for medical emergencies in this community of 79,000 people. Among several options, SFD wanted to identify the possible location for a new fire station. So it turned to Dr. Olga Medvedkov, a GIS expert.

Medvedkov applied *MapInfo* and *ArcView* software to the fire department's extensive database of 911 calls. "Residents generate between 16,000 and 17,000 calls per year to our emergency system," shared Medvedkov. "Approximately 90 percent of these calls are for medical emergencies, with the remaining 10 percent for fire." Medvedkov's team geo-coded each 911 call, applying a geographic tag that described its U.S. Census block location. Then each call was plotted to a Census-block map of the city. "With its sparser population, high number of nursing homes, and older population, response times were often lengthier in the northern part of the city," explained Medvedkov. "The department was considering a new station in that location." But after seeing the spatial data display, SFD determined the sectors served by Station 8, an older and poorer part of the city, generated a more significant concentration of calls with unacceptable response times. This area was really the better location choice to reduce the largest number of calls to within the target response time."

Projection

Projection is a mathematical process for converting a three-dimensional curved surface to a two-dimensional medium such as paper or a computer screen. Since different types of maps are used, a computer program must restructure information collected from sources with different projections to a common one. Satellite images, for example, are often used for rural land use or agricultural planning but since digital data of the earth's surface are collected and stored differently, the data sources must be made compatible for mapping.

Modeling

A significant benefit of GIS is modeling. Therefore, the possible uses of the data exceed maplike outputs (roads, buildings, contours). The researcher might select two locations and ask the program to calculate the best route between them. Then factors like adjacency (what is next to what), proximity (how close one thing is to another), and containment (what is enclosed by what) come into play. Our "best route" question now extracts traffic density, construction, known bottlenecks, and hazardous intersections from different data sets to provide the best response time for an emergency vehicle.

Cross-Tabulation

Cross-tabulation is a technique for comparing two classification variables, such as gender and selection by one's company for an overseas assignment. The technique uses tables having rows and columns that correspond to the levels or values of each variable's categories. Exhibit 16–17 is an example of a computer-generated cross-tabulation. This table has two rows for gender and two columns for assignment selection. The combination of the variables with their values produces four **cells.** Each cell contains a count of the cases of the joint classification and also the row, column, and total percentages. The number of row cells and column cells is often used to designate the size of the table, as in this 2 × 2 table. The cells are individually identified by their row and column numbers, as illustrated. Row and column totals, called **marginals,**

EXHIBIT 16–17   **SPSS Cross-Tabulation of Gender by Overseas Assignment Opportunity**

Cell content ——

Cell 2, 1
(row 2, column 1)

Marginals

```
                          OVERSEAS ASSIGNMENT

        Count
        Row Pct     Yes        No
        Col Pct                          Row
        Tot Pct      1          2        Total

GENDER                22         40         62
Male      1         35.5       64.5       62.0
                    78.6       55.6
                    22.0       40.0

                       6         32         38
Female    2         15.8       84.2       38.0
                    21.4       44.4
                     6.0       32.0

        Column        28         72        100
        Total       28.0       72.0      100.0
```

appear at the bottom and right "margins" of the table. They show the counts and percentages of the separate rows and columns.

When tables are constructed for statistical testing, we call them **contingency tables,** and the test determines if the classification variables are independent. Of course, tables may be larger than 2×2.

The Use of Percentages

Percentages serve two purposes in data presentation. First, they simplify the data by reducing all numbers to a range from 0 to 100. Second, they translate the data into standard form, with a base of 100, for relative comparisons. In a sampling situation, the number of cases that fall into a category is meaningless unless it is related to some base. A count of 28 overseas assignees has little meaning unless we know it is from a sample of 100. Using the latter as a base, we conclude that 28 percent of this study's sample has an overseas assignment.

While the above is useful, it is even more useful when the research problem calls for a comparison of several distributions of data. Assume the previously reported data were collected five years ago and the present study had a sample of 1,500, of which 360 were selected for overseas assignments. By using percentages, we can see the relative relationships and shifts in the data (see Exhibit 16–18).

With two-dimension tables, the selection of a row or column will accentuate a particular distribution or comparison. This raises the question about which direction the percentages should be calculated. Most computer programs offer options for presenting percentages in both directions and interchanging the rows and columns of the table. But in situations when one variable is hypothesized to be the presumed cause, is thought to affect or predict a response, or is simply antecedent to the other variable, we label it the *independent* variable. Percentages should then be computed in the direction of this variable. Thus, if the independent variable is placed on the row, select row percentages; if it is on the column, select column percentages. In which direction should the percentages run in the previous example? If only the column percentages are

EXHIBIT 16–18   Comparison of Percentages in Cross-Tabulation Studies of Gender by Overseas Assignment

		Study 1 OVERSEAS ASSIGNMENT					Study 2 OVERSEAS ASSIGNMENT		
	Count Row Pct Col Pct Tot Pct	Yes 1	No 2	Row Total		Count Row Pct Col Pct Tot Pct	Yes 1	No 2	Row Total
GENDER Male 1		22 35.5 78.6 22.0	40 64.5 55.6 40.0	62 62.0	GENDER Male 1		225 25.0 62.5 15.0	675 75.0 59.2 45.0	900 60.0
Female 2		6 15.8 21.4 6.0	32 84.2 44.4 32.0	38 38.0	Female 2		135 22.5 37.5 9.0	465 77.5 40.8 31.0	600 40.0
Column Total		28 28.0	72 72.0	100 100.0	Column Total		360 24.0	1140 76.0	1500 100.0

reported, we imply that assignment status has some effect on gender. This is implausible. When percentages are reported by rows, the implication is that gender influences selection for overseas assignments.

Care should be taken in interpreting percentages from tables. Consider again the data in Exhibit 16–18. From the first to the second study, it is apparent that the percentage of females selected for overseas assignment rose from 6 to 9 percent of their respective samples. This is not to be confused with the percentage of women in the samples who happen to be assignees. Among all *women eligible* for selection in the first study, 15.8 percent were assigned and 84.2 percent were not. Among all *overseas selectees* in the first study, 21.4 percent were women. Similar comparisons can be made for the other categories.

Percentages are used by virtually everyone dealing with numbers—and often incorrectly. The following guidelines, if used during analysis, will help to prevent errors in reporting.[22]

MANAGEMENT
Tip

- **Averaging percentages.** Percentages cannot be averaged unless each is weighted by the size of the group from which it is derived. Thus, a simple average will not suffice; it is necessary to use a weighted average.

- **Use of too large percentages.** This often defeats the purpose of percentages—which is to simplify. A large percentage is difficult to understand and is confusing. If a 1,000 percent increase is experienced, it is better to describe this as a tenfold increase.

- **Using too small a base.** Percentages hide the base from which they have been computed. A figure of 60 percent when contrasted with 30 percent would appear to suggest a sizable difference. Yet if there are only three cases in the one category and six in the other, the differences would not be as significant as they have been made to appear with percentages.

- **Percentage decreases can never exceed 100 percent.** This is obvious, but this type of mistake occurs frequently. The higher figure should always be used as the base. For example, if a price was reduced from $1 to $.25, the decrease would be 75 percent (75/100).

LIMRA International is a trade association for the financial services industry. It believed that one high-growth segment of its market was small businesses, as these potential customers had been growing as a segment and had the resources to afford financial services. To assist its membership in capitalizing on this potential, LIMRA undertook a massive study of the U.S. small business sector, involving telephone interviews with financial decision makers in 1,622 businesses having fewer than 100 employees. Government agencies or units were excluded, as were businesses in financial services (financial, insurance, and real estate) and nonprofit organizations. Each interviewee who agreed to participate further was mailed a follow-up questionnaire; 533 respondents returned completed surveys.

The study was designed to (1) provide a broad profile of this market segment, including a profile of the small busi-

ness principal; (2) assess the potential of group life, health care and retirement plans; and (3) recommend actions for taking advantage of the market opportunities identified. The last time LIMRA had done a similar study was in 1994. The 2000 study found a significant number of new small businesses, many of which provided some group benefit (70 percent, compared to 64 percent), and sponsored retirement or pension plans (43 percent, compared to 26 percent). Most change was motivated by a tight job market, "declines in the cost of benefits relative to gains in wages/salaries, changes in tax laws, and passage of the Small Business Job Protection Act of 1996." What would you want to consider before analyzing the results of this study?

www.limra.org

EXHIBIT 16–19   SPSS Cross-Tabulation with Control and Nested Variables

	Control Variable					
	Category 1			Category 2		
	Nested Variable			Nested Variable		
	cat 1	cat 2	cat 3	cat 1	cat 2	cat 3
Stub...	Cells...					

	SEX OF EMPLOYEE			
	MALES		FEMALES	
	MINORITY CLASSIFICATION		MINORITY CLASSIFICATION	
	WHITE	NONWHITE	WHITE	NONWHITE
EMPLOYMENT CATEGORY				
CLERICAL	16%	7%	18%	7%
OFFICE TRAINEE	7%	3%	17%	2%
SECURITY OFFICER	3%	3%		
COLLEGE TRAINEE	7%	0%	1%	
EXEMPT EMPLOYEE	6%	0%	0%	
MBA TRAINEE	1%	0%	0%	
TECHNICAL	1%			

Other Table-Based Analysis

The recognition of a meaningful relationship between variables generally signals a need for further investigation. Even if one finds a statistically significant relationship, the questions of why and under what conditions remain. The introduction of a **control variable** to interpret the relationship is often necessary. Cross-tabulation tables serve as the framework.

Statistical packages like Minitab, SAS, and SPSS have among their modules many options for the construction of *n*-way tables with provision for multiple control variables. Suppose you are interested in creating a cross-tabulation of two variables with one control. Whatever the number of values in the primary variables, the control variable with five values determines the number of tables. For some applications, it is appropriate to have five separate tables; for others, it might be preferable to have adjoining tables or have the values of all the variables in one. Management reports are of the latter variety. Exhibit 16–19 presents an example in which all three variables are handled under the same banner. Programs such as this one can handle far more complex tables and statistical information.[23]

An advanced variation on *n*-way tables is **automatic interaction detection (AID).** AID is a sequential partitioning procedure that begins with a dependent variable and a set of predictors. It searches among up to 300 variables for the best single division according to each predictor variable, chooses one, and splits the sample using chi-square tests to create multiway splits. These subgroups then become separate samples for further analysis. The search procedure is repeated to find the variable that, when split into parts, makes the next largest contribution to the reduction of unexplained variation in each subsample, and so on.

Exhibit 16–20 shows the tree diagram that resulted from an AID study of Mind-Writer's CompleteCare repair service. The initial dependent variable is the overall

EXHIBIT 16–20 Automatic Interaction Detection Example (MindWriter's Repair Satisfaction)

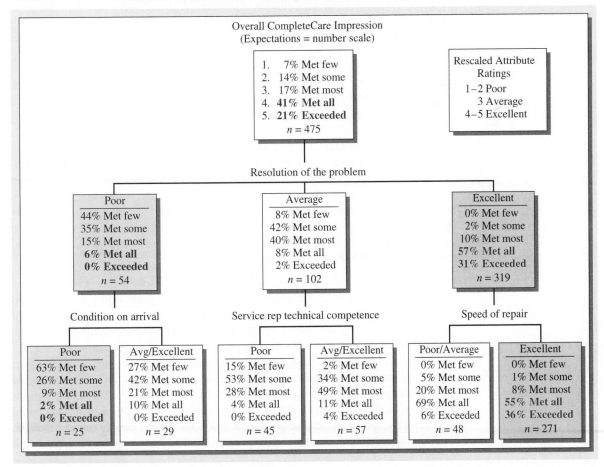

impression of the repair service. This variable was measured on an interval scale. The variables that contribute to perceptions of repair effectiveness were also measured on the same scale but were rescaled to nominal data for this example (1–2 = poor, 3 = average, and 4–5 = excellent). The top box shows that 62 percent of the respondents rated the repair service as excellent (41% + 21%). The best predictor of effectiveness is "resolution of the problem." On the left side of the tree, customers who rated "resolution of the problem" as poor have fewer expectations being met or exceeded than the average (6% versus 62%). A poor rating on "condition on arrival" exacerbates this, reducing the total satisfied group to 2 percent.

On the right side of the tree, for those customers who rated "resolution of the problem" as excellent, the repair met or exceeded the average respondent's expectations (88% versus 62%). Excellent scores on "speed of repair" further improved this rating, taking the total satisfaction up to 91 percent. This analysis alerts decision makers at MindWriter to the best- and worst-case scenarios for the service, how to recover during a problematic month, and which "key drivers" of the process should receive corrective resources.

SUMMARY

1

The objective of exploratory data analysis is to learn as much as possible about the data. Exploratory data analysis (EDA) simplifies this goal by providing a perspective and set of tools to search for clues and patterns. EDA augments rather than supplants traditional statistics. In addition to numerical summaries of location, spread, and shape, EDA uses visual displays to provide a complete and accurate impression of distributions and variable relationships.

Frequency tables array data from highest to lowest values with counts and percentages. They are most useful for inspecting the range of responses and their repeated occurrence. Bar charts and pie charts are appropriate for relative comparisons of nominal data. Histograms are optimally used with continuous variables where intervals group the responses.

Stem-and-leaf displays and boxplots are EDA techniques that provide visual representations of distributions. The former present actual data values using a histogram-type device that allows inspection of spread and shape. Boxplots use the five-number summary to convey a detailed picture of a distribution's main body, tails, and outliers. Both stem-and-leaf displays and boxplots rely on resistant statistics to overcome the limitations of descriptive measures that are subject to extreme scores. Transformation may be necessary to reexpress metric data so as to reduce or remove problems of asymmetry, inequality of variance, or other abnormalities.

2

The feature of statistical process control that pertains to displaying data is its charting system. SPC charts provide reliable visuals for evaluating point values and trends and graphically depicting variation. Control charts help managers focus on special causes of variation by revealing whether a system is under control (as an early warning of change) and substantiating results from improvements (confirming results).

A control chart displays sequential measurements of a process together with a center line and control limits. The selection of a control chart depends on the level of data (data type) you are measuring. Managers should look for the following visual characteristics in reports containing control charts: (1) outliers: observations falling outside the control lines; (2) runs: data points in a series over or below the central line; (3) trends: the continual rise or fall of data points; and (4) periodicity: data that show the same pattern of change over time, creating a cycle.

The Pareto diagram is a bar chart whose percentages sum to 100 percent. The causes of the problem under investigation are sorted in decreasing importance with bar height descending from left to right. Its pictorial array reveals the highest concentration of quality improvement potential in the fewest number of remedies.

3 Geographic Information Systems (GIS) refers to systems of hardware and software and procedures that capture, store, manipulate, integrate, and display spatially referenced data. GIS stacks different data sets on top of each other, so that the data points from variables of interest align on a common geographical referent, allowing the user to drill down and visualize the relationships. A GIS locator may be a zip code, census boundary, or coordinates of longitude, latitude, and elevation.

Most GIS have at least four process components: (1) integrating information from various sources, (2) capturing data, (3) projection and restructuring, and (4) modeling. By integrating variables from different sources, combinations of mapped variables may be created to simulate and analyze new ones. Data capture and editing is the most labor-intensive component of GIS because of the numerous variables and map objects. Projection converts a three-dimensional curved surface to a two-dimensional medium such as paper or a computer screen. Data collected and stored in different formats must be restructured for mapping. GIS modeling answers "what if" questions for such diverse applications as sales targeting, natural resource preservation, emergency service delivery, and service requirements of growing populations.

4 The evaluation of relationships involving categorical variables employs cross-tabulation. The tables used for this purpose consist of cells and marginals. The cells contain combinations of count, row, column, and total percentages. The tabular structure is the framework for later statistical testing.

Computer software for cross-classification analysis makes table-based analysis with one or more control variables an efficient tool for decision making. An advanced variation on *n*-way tables is automatic interaction detection (AID).

KEY TERMS

EXAMPLES

Company	Scenario	Page
Booth Research Services	Digesting reams of data to assist research sponsors in making management decisions.	498
City Center for Performing Arts	Preliminary data analysis described.	BRTL

Federal Emergency Management Agency (FEMA)	Using GIS to provide national-level support in responding to disasters.	504
Forbes Industry List	Industries, business classifications, and market sectors displayed to illustrate frequency tables and pie and bar charts.	488
Ford Motor Co.	Challenged the Insurance Institute for Highway Safety's crash tests results and conclusions.	502
Fortune 500	Database used to demonstrate the construction of histograms, stem-and-leaf displays, and boxplot techniques.	488
Insurance Institute for Highway Safety	Conducted safety experiment involving frontal offset crash tests of competitive, full-sized trucks, including those manufactured by Ford, GM, DaimlerChrysler, and Toyota.	502
LIMRA International	Conducted a large-scale telephone survey of 1,622 small businesses for the financial services industry.	508
MerK Outboard[*]	Manufacturer of outboard motors for small fishing boats whose manufacturing process uses control charts to assure production quality at design specifications.	500
MindWriter[*]	(1) A content analysis of MindWriter customer complaints depicted as a Pareto diagram.	503
	(2) An AID tree diagram of MindWriter's CompleteCare repair service; factors driving overall customer satisfaction.	509
Springfield Fire Department	Using GIS analysis to determine the ideal location for a new fire station.	505

[*]Due to the confidential and proprietary nature of most research, the names of some companies have been changed.

DISCUSSION QUESTIONS

Terms in Review

1. Define or explain:
   a. Marginals.
   b. Pareto diagram.
   c. Standard scores (Z scores).
   d. Control chart.
   e. Nonresistant statistics.
   f. Lower control limit.
   g. The five-number summary.
   h. Geographic Information Systems.
   i. Spread-and-level plots.

Making Research Decisions

2. How should the researcher handle "don't know" responses?
3. How do the following detect errors in the data?
   a. Histogram.
   b. Stem-and-leaf display.
   c. Boxplot.
   d. Cross-tabulation.

EXHIBIT 16–21   Data Table for Discussion Questions 5–6

	Market Value	Sales	Sector		Market Value	Sales	Sector
1	24983.00	8966.00	2	26	9009.00	17533.00	4
2	31307.00	126932.00	3	27	7842.00	11113.00	2
3	57193.00	54574.00	7	28	5431.00	19671.00	8
4	57676.00	86656.00	4	29	5811.00	11389.00	5
5	60345.00	62710.00	7	30	16257.00	15242.00	2
6	22190.00	96146.00	3	31	16247.00	10211.00	7
7	36566.00	39011.00	2	32	18548.00	9593.00	7
8	44646.00	36112.00	7	33	13620.00	9691.00	7
9	25022.00	50220.00	4	34	10750.00	12844.00	3
10	26043.00	25099.00	1	35	12450.00	18398.00	2
11	13152.00	53794.00	2	36	16729.00	20276.00	7
12	11234.00	25047.00	5	37	16532.00	8730.00	7
13	26666.00	23966.00	4	38	5111.00	17635.00	10
14	20747.00	17424.00	7	39	9116.00	8588.00	4
15	25826.00	13996.00	7	40	26325.00	25922.00	2
16	15423.00	32416.00	4	41	8249.00	16103.00	2
17	15263.00	14150.00	8	42	8407.00	14083.00	3
18	18146.00	17600.00	1	43	18537.00	11990.00	10
19	18739.00	15351.00	4	44	23866.00	29443.00	4
20	7875.00	22605.00	2	45	6872.00	19532.00	7
21	8122.00	37970.00	5	46	4319.00	10018.00	5
22	18072.00	11557.00	5	47	9505.00	12937.00	7
23	6404.00	11449.00	7	48	3891.00	15654.00	8
24	16056.00	20054.00	8	49	8090.00	7492.00	4
25	16056.00	13211.00	7	50	11119.00	12345.00	7

From Concept to Practice

4. Use the data in Exhibit 16–4 to construct a stem-and-leaf display.

   a. Where do you find the main body of the distribution?

   b. How many values reside outside the inner fence(s)?

5. Select the sales variable from Exhibit 16–21.

   a. Create a five-number summary.

   b. Construct a boxplot.

   c. Interpret the distribution and results with summary measures and descriptive statistics.

   d. Transform the variable into Z scores.

   e. Identify and comment on outliers, if any.

6. Select the market value variable from Exhibit 16–21 and construct a histogram with available software.

    a. What is the gain in information with 5,000-, 2,000-, or 1,000-unit intervals?

    b. Which would be the best interval to convey results to management?

    c. Why would these data need reexpression?

    d. What is the optimal power transformation for these data?

7. Suppose you were preparing two-way tables of percentages for the following pairs of variables. How would you run the percentages?

    a. Age and consumption of breakfast cereal.

    b. Family income and confidence about the family's future.

    c. Marital status and sports participation.

    d. Crime rate and unemployment rate.

8. You study the attrition between students who enter college as freshmen and those who stay to graduate. You find the following relationships between attrition, aid, and distance of home from school. What is your interpretation? Consider all variables and relationships.

	Aid		*Home Near Aid*		*Home Far Aid*	
	Yes	**No**	**Yes**	**No**	**Yes**	**No**
Drop out	25%	20%	5%	15%	30%	40%
Stay	75	80	95	85	70	60

9. A local health agency is experimenting with two appeal letters, A and B, with which to raise funds. It sends out 400 of the A appeal and 400 of the B appeal (divided equally among working-class and middle-class neighborhoods). The agency secures the results shown in the table below.

    a. Which appeal is the best?

    b. Which class responded better?

    c. Is appeal or social class a more powerful independent variable?

	Appeal A		*Appeal B*	
	Middle Class	**Working Class**	**Middle Class**	**Working Class**
Contribution	20%	40%	15%	30%
No contribution	80	60	85	70
	100%	100%	100%	100%

10. Assume you have collected data on employees of a large organization in a major metropolitan area. You analyze the data by type of work classification, education level, and whether the workers were raised in a rural or urban setting. The results are shown below. How would you interpret them?

Annual Employee Turnover per 100 Employees

| | Part A | | Part B | | | |
| | | | High Education | | Low Education | |
	Salaried	Wage	Salaried	Wage	Salaried	Wage
Rural	8	16	6	14	18	18
Urban	12	16	10	12	19	20

11. Analyze the MerK Outboard Motor data as shown and produce R- and X-bar charts. Compare your results to Exhibit 16–15. What has occurred in the manufacturing process?

Subgroup Sample	Horsepower Output		
1	10.22	10.31	8.43
2	11.25	10.33	10.12
3	10.37	9.92	11.80
4	7.53	9.94	9.94
5	10.06	9.39	10.31
6	12.01	10.15	10.23
7	7.95	8.25	8.55
8	10.13	10.69	10.16
9	10.82	11.25	11.13
10	9.88	8.95	9.25

WWW Exercises

Visit our website for Internet exercises related to this chapter at www.mhhe.com/business/Cooper8

CASES*

AGRICOMP

HEALTHY LIFESTYLES

INQUIRING MINDS WANT TO KNOW—NOW!

 KNSD SAN DIEGO

MASTERING TEACHER LEADERSHIP

NCR: TEEING UP A NEW STRATEGIC DIRECTION

XEROX ABUSES

*All cases indicating a video icon are located on the Instructor's Videotape Supplement. All nonvideo cases are in the case section of the textbook. All cases indicating a CD icon offer a data set, which is located on the accompanying CD.

REFERENCE NOTES

1. John W. Tukey, *Exploratory Data Analysis* (Reading, MA: Addison-Wesley, 1977).
2. David C. Hoaglin, Frederick Mosteller, and John W. Tukey, eds., *Understanding Robust and Exploratory Data Analysis* (New York: John Wiley & Sons, 1983), p. 2.
3. Tukey, *Exploratory Data Analysis,* pp. 2–3.
4. Frederick Hartwig with Brian E. Dearing, *Exploratory Data Analysis* (Beverly Hills, CA: Sage Publications, 1979), pp. 9–12.
5. The exhibits in this section were created with statistical and graphic programs particularly suited to exploratory data analysis. The authors acknowledge the following vendors for evaluation and use of their products: SPSS, Inc., 233 S. Wacker Dr., Chicago, IL, 60606; and Data Description, P.O. Box 4555, Ithaca, NY, 14852.
6. "Fortune 500 Ranked by Performance," *The Fortune 500,* April 28, 1997, p. F-30.
7. Paul F. Velleman and David C. Hoaglin, *Applications, Basics, and Computing of Exploratory Data Analysis* (Boston: Duxbury Press, 1981), p. 13.
8. John Hanke, Eastern Washington University, contributed this section. For further references to stem-and-leaf displays, see John D. Emerson and David C. Hoaglin, "Stem-and-Leaf Displays," in *Understanding Robust and Exploratory Data Analysis,* pp. 7–31; and Velleman and Hoaglin, *Applications,* pp. 1–13.
9. This section is adapted from the following excellent discussions of boxplots: Velleman and Hoaglin, *Applications,* pp. 65–76; Hartwig, *Exploratory Data Analysis,* pp. 19–25; John D. Emerson and Judith Strenio, "Boxplots and Batch Comparison," in *Understanding Robust and Exploratory Data Analysis,* pp. 59–93; and Amir D. Aczel, *Complete Business Statistics* (Homewood, IL: Irwin, 1989), pp. 723–28.
10. Tukey, *Exploratory Data Analysis,* pp. 27–55.
11. Hoaglin et al., *Understanding Robust and Exploratory Data Analysis,* p. 2.
12. Several robust estimators that are suitable replacements for the mean and standard deviation we do not discuss here—for example, the trimmed mean, trimean, the M-estimators (such as Huber's, Tukey's, Hampel's, and Andrew's estimators), and the median absolute deviation (MAD). See Hoaglin et al., *Understanding Robust and Exploratory Data Analysis,* Chapter 10; and SPSS, Inc., *SPSS Base 9.0 User's Guide* (Chicago: SPSS, Inc., 1999), Chapter 13.
13. The difference between the definition of a hinge and a quartile is based on variations in their calculation. We use Q_1, 25th percentile, and *lower hinge* synonymously; and Q_3, 75th percentile, and *upper hinge,* similarly. There are technical differences, although they are not significant in this context.
14. R. McGill, J. W. Tukey, and W. A. Larsen, "Variations of Box Plots," *The American Statistician* 32 (1978), pp. 12–16.
15. See J. Chambers, W. Cleveland, B. Kleiner, and John W. Tukey, *Graphical Methods for Data Analysis* (Boston: Duxbury Press, 1983).
16. This section is based on the discussion of transformation in John D. Emerson and Michael A. Stoto, "Transforming Data," in *Understanding Robust and Exploratory Data Analysis,* pp. 97–127; and Velleman and Hoaglin, *Applications,* pp. 48–53.
17. Hoaglin et al., *Understanding Robust and Exploratory Data Analysis,* p. 77.
18. Ibid., p. 125.
19. Tor Bernhardsen, *Geographic Information Systems: An Introduction* (New York: John Wiley & Sons, 1999).
20. Example from the U.S. Geological Survey FAQ for GIS: http://www.usgs.gov (March 4, 2000).
21. See examples in "Geographical Mapping and Analysis in Health Care," SPSS White Paper, 1998, p. 3, http://www.spss.com (March 15, 2000).
22. Harper W. Boyd, Jr., and Ralph Westfall, *Marketing Research,* 3rd ed. (Homewood, IL: Irwin, 1972), p. 540.
23. SPSS, Inc., *SPSS Tables 8.0* (Chicago: SPSS, Inc., 1998), with its system file: Bank Data.

REFERENCES FOR SNAPSHOTS AND CAPTIONS

Ford F-150

"What Is Offset Crash Testing?" Insurance Institute for Highway Safety (http://www.hwysafety.org/vehicle_ratings/ce/offset.htm#).

"Crashworthiness," Insurance Institute for Highway Safety, June 4, 2001 (http://www.hwysafety.org/vehicle_ratings/ce/pdfs/large_pickups.pdf).

"New Crash Test Results: Ratings of Four Large Pickups Range from Good for Toyota Tundra to Poor for Ford F-150, Dodge Ram," Insurance Institute for Highway Safety, June 4, 2001.

LIMRA

"U.S. Small Businesses in 2000: A Dynamic Market," © 2001, LIMRA International, Inc.

New York Power Outages (September 2001)

FEMA-DR-1391, New York Utility Outages as of 7:00 P.M., 9/18/01. The Federal Emergency Management Agency's Mapping and Analysis Center (MAC) provides national-level Geographic Information System (GIS) support and coordination to the agency. GIS mapping products are available for the New York City World Trade Center Attack, the attack on the Pentagon, and the latest disasters, along with the current year and an archive of prior-year disasters (http://www.gismaps.fema.gov/2001pages/DR1391.shtml).

Springfield Fire Department

"Hot Spots in Springfield," Olga Medvedkov, 2000.

Olga Medvedkov, project supervisor, Springfield SFD-GIS study, interview, June 2000.

CLASSIC AND CONTEMPORARY READINGS

DeMers, Michael. *Fundamentals of Geographic Information Systems.* New York: John Wiley & Sons, 2000. Methodical coverage of basic input requirements, data management, reporting concepts, and ample depth in explaining spatial analysis issues. Highly regarded for its readability by students.

Evans, James R., and William M. Lindsay. *Management and the Control of Quality.* Mason, OH: South-Western Publishing, 2002. Technically detailed coverage of quality improvement techniques.

Hoaglin, David C., Frederick Mosteller, and John W. Tukey, eds. *Understanding Robust and Exploratory Data Analysis.* New York: John Wiley & Sons, 2000. A complete and advanced treatment by influential writers in this field. Especially well-organized topical coverage.

Velleman, Paul F., and David C. Hoaglin. *Applications, Basics, and Computing of Exploratory Data Analysis.* Boston: Duxbury Press, 1981. The basics of EDA are presented in a straightforward style with helpful examples and excellent connections to computer applications.

CHAPTER 17

Hypothesis Testing

Learning Objectives

After reading this chapter, you should understand . . .

1   **The distinction between the two approaches to hypothesis testing.**

2   **The distinction between a statistically significant difference and one that is of practical importance for a manager.**

3   **The six-step hypothesis testing procedure.**

4   **The differences between parametric and nonparametric tests and when to use each.**

5   **The factors that influence the selection of an appropriate test of statistical significance.**

6   **How to interpret the various test statistics.**

Bringing Research to Life

"**A**re you and Dorrie entertaining ghosts and goblins tonight?" Myra asked as she and Jason wrapped up their meeting.

"Absolutely. Our new neighborhood has a tradition of elaborate celebrations. I've been assigned the task of telling scary stories near the cider and donut table."

"You're too much the scientist to believe in things that go bump in the night. What story will you tell to the diminutive apparitions toting trick-or-treat bags?"

"Well back in my grad student days, a fellow student, Don Ticker, was a constant annoyance. No matter how often I explained to him, he never caught on to the idea of statistical post hoc analysis . . ."

"You're sure to be a hit with diminutive mermaids and aspiring Barneys," drawled Myra sarcastically. "What does this have to do with Halloween?"

Ignoring her interruption, Jason continued. "Don would take a set of data with 100 interval variables, say, and calculate the Pearson correlation coefficients among all the variables, which leaves you with 4,950 actual computations for the statistics program to print out—100 variables times 99 then divide by two (because the correlation of X with Y is the same as Y with X). The program will give you 4,950 Pearson correlation coefficients, therefore 4,950 statistical tests of significance to interpret."

"If you say so, Jason."

He saw her interest was flagging. "Do you follow me so far? Whether a relationship is statistically significant is a very big issue."

"No doubt it is . . . to a statistician. Your point is what, Jason? Something to do with a Halloween story, remember?"

"My point is, if you instruct your statistics program to flag all the results that appear to be significant at the level of $p = .05$, on average 250 of the calculations will be flagged as significant, though they may signify nothing more than sampling error."

"By now you've surely lost your 3- to 5-year-old audience. Get on with the Halloween story, would you?"

"In a moment. Choosing .05 as the probability level of statistical significance means you have consciously decided to risk that .05 or 1/20 of the results flagged as significant may actually be spurious. But you would have no way of telling which of the flagged results were spurious and which were due to real effects.

"Ticker would take his Day-Glo™ yellow marker and circle all the ostensibly significant results, and whip himself into a frenzy. He would grab his printout and run down the hallway with the printout streaming along behind, whooping and wanting to show his results around. But, of course, if he had preplanned his analysis, based on logical hypotheses, he would have saved countless hours and reams of computer paper."

"How all this relates to a scary Halloween story, I fail to see."

"It was on the afternoon before Halloween that I was about to break through to a solution on my own research when I was jolted by one of Don's dashes down the hall, breaking my attention. I reviewed all of my favorite writers of the bizarre, Edgar Allan Poe, H. P. Lovecraft, Stephen King, all masters of the macabre, but found no suitable punishment for the untimely interruption.

"That afternoon, late, the sky was dark, Myra, and there was a chill. Later, there was a moon but it had hid itself behind leaden clouds, and when it appeared, it threw shadows of the most bizarre shapes that I would only reveal to a counselor. No matter how you try, on that one night of the year, you had to wonder if retributive justice were not available. For it was Halloween."

"The truth is," Myra said, "it was just a little bit of fun for a graduate student with not much of a life, it was just a bit of a tingle to believe that on this night powerful things were loose in the world, and that the Don Tickers of the world, with their post hoc analyses and spurious results, might encounter one of them . . . "

"Quite right. On arriving home, I tumbled onto the sofa, intending to catch a few winks. Yet I descended into one of those oppressively lucid dreams in which one knows one is dreaming but cannot gain control or float upward to consciousness. I was back in Burley Hall confronting a specter dressed in a black shroud, his face covered by a black veil. He was tall, at least seven feet, and he held a shepherd's crook, which he wielded effortlessly despite its length and thickness.

"Down the hall came Donald Ticker. His printout trailed behind him, by 25 or 30 feet. The specter thrust his shepherd's crook between Ticker's knees and hooked the near knee. Ticker became fully airborne six feet off the floor.

"At this point, I snapped awake. It was 6 A.M. I was cold, but sweating. I was filled with trepidation, not reassured by rationality, so I sped off to Burley Hall.

"Even at 6:15 Burley Hall is a busy place, what with students who have stayed up all night in the computer lab and the assistant professors eager to arrive before the senior faculty. The premonition was awful but the guilt was worse. Surely post hoc data analysis was a practice to be discouraged but a venial sin at worst.

"A knot of students and junior faculty were gathered outside my cubbyhole. To one side leaned the crook as I remembered it, long and sturdy."

"Was it Ticker's mangled corpse?"

"No, but there in the carpet, outside my office, exactly where the dream took place . . . right there . . . as clearly as could be, we could see embossed in the carpet the face—the nose and eyebrows, the lips, even—and two handprints—all 10 digits showing distinctly—of Don Ticker, imprinted in the carpet of Burley Hall! And from that day to this, Ticker has not reappeared."

Myra's pupils had dilated, revealing only a narrow rim of blue iris.

Jason chuckled. "Got ya, didn't I?" he asked. "What do you think of my story, Myra?"

"You are a lying little sadist, Jason, and a prevaricating sociopath. But a word of advice: You may have captured my attention toward the end, but resurrect a Stephen King tale and save the little ones from boredom!"

Introduction

Induction and deduction were discussed in Chapter 2.

In Chapters 15 and 16, we discussed the procedures for data preparation and preliminary analysis. The next step for many studies is hypothesis testing.

Just as your understanding of scientific reasoning was an important foundation in the last two chapters, recollection of the specific differences between induction and deduction is fundamental to hypothesis testing. *Inductive reasoning* moves from specific facts to general but tentative conclusions. We can never be absolutely sure that inductive conclusions are flawless. With the aid of probability estimates, we can qualify our results and state the degree of confidence we have in them. Statistical inference is an application of inductive reasoning. It allows us to reason from evidence found in the sample to conclusions we wish to make about the population.

Inferential statistics is the second of two major categories of statistical procedures, the other being descriptive statistics. We used descriptive statistics in Chapter 15 when describing distributions. Under the heading **inferential statistics,** two topics are discussed in this book. The first, estimation of population values, was used with sampling in Chapter 7, but we will return to it here briefly. The second, testing statistical hypotheses, is the primary subject of this chapter.

In the next few sections, we will refresh your memory of hypothesis testing and look at selected statistical tests. Many are basic, but they illustrate the diverse types of data and situations a researcher may encounter. A section on nonparametric techniques in Appendix E provides further study for readers with a special interest in nominal and ordinal variables.

Hypothesis Testing

Having detailed your hypotheses in your preliminary analysis planning, the purpose of hypothesis testing is to determine the accuracy of your hypotheses due to the fact that you have collected a sample of data, not a census. Exhibit 17–1 reminds you of the relationships among your design strategy, data collection activities, preliminary analysis, and hypothesis testing.

We evaluate the accuracy of hypotheses by determining the statistical likelihood that the data reveal true differences—not random sampling error. We evaluate the importance of a statistically significant difference by weighing the practical significance of any change that we measure.

Testing Approaches

There are two approaches to hypothesis testing. The more established is the classical or sampling-theory approach; the second is known as the Bayesian approach. **Classical statistics** are found in all of the major statistics books and are widely used in research applications. This approach represents an objective view of probability in which the decision making rests totally on an analysis of available sampling data. A hypothesis is established; it is rejected or fails to be rejected, based on the sample data collected.

Bayesian statistics are an extension of the classical approach. They also use sampling data for making decisions, but they go beyond them to consider all other available information. This additional information consists of subjective probability estimates stated in terms of degrees of belief. These subjective estimates are based on general experience rather than on specific collected data. They are expressed as a prior distribution that can be revised after sample information is gathered. The revised estimate, known as a *posterior distribution,* may be further revised by additional information, and so on. Various decision rules are established, cost and other estimates can be introduced, and the expected outcomes of combinations of these elements are used to judge decision alternatives. The Bayesian approach, based on the centuries-old Bayes theorem, has emerged as an alternative hypothesis-testing procedure since the mid-1950s.

An example of Bayesian decision making is presented in Appendix B on the topic of valuing research information. The reader interested in learning more about Bayesian statistics is referred to the suggested readings at the end of this chapter.

Statistical Significance

Following the sampling-theory approach, we accept or reject a hypothesis on the basis of sampling information alone. Since any sample will almost surely vary somewhat from its population, we must judge whether these differences are statistically significant or insignificant. A difference has **statistical significance** if there is good reason to believe the difference does not represent random sampling fluctuations only. For example, the controller of e-WEAR, an e-commerce division of a large retail chain, may be concerned about a possible slowdown in payments by the company's customers. She measures the rate of payment in terms of the average age of receivables outstanding. Generally, the company has maintained an average of about 50 days with a standard deviation of 10 days. Suppose the controller has all of the customer accounts analyzed and finds the average is now 51 days. Is this difference statistically significant from 50?

EXHIBIT 17–1   Hypothesis Testing and the Research Process

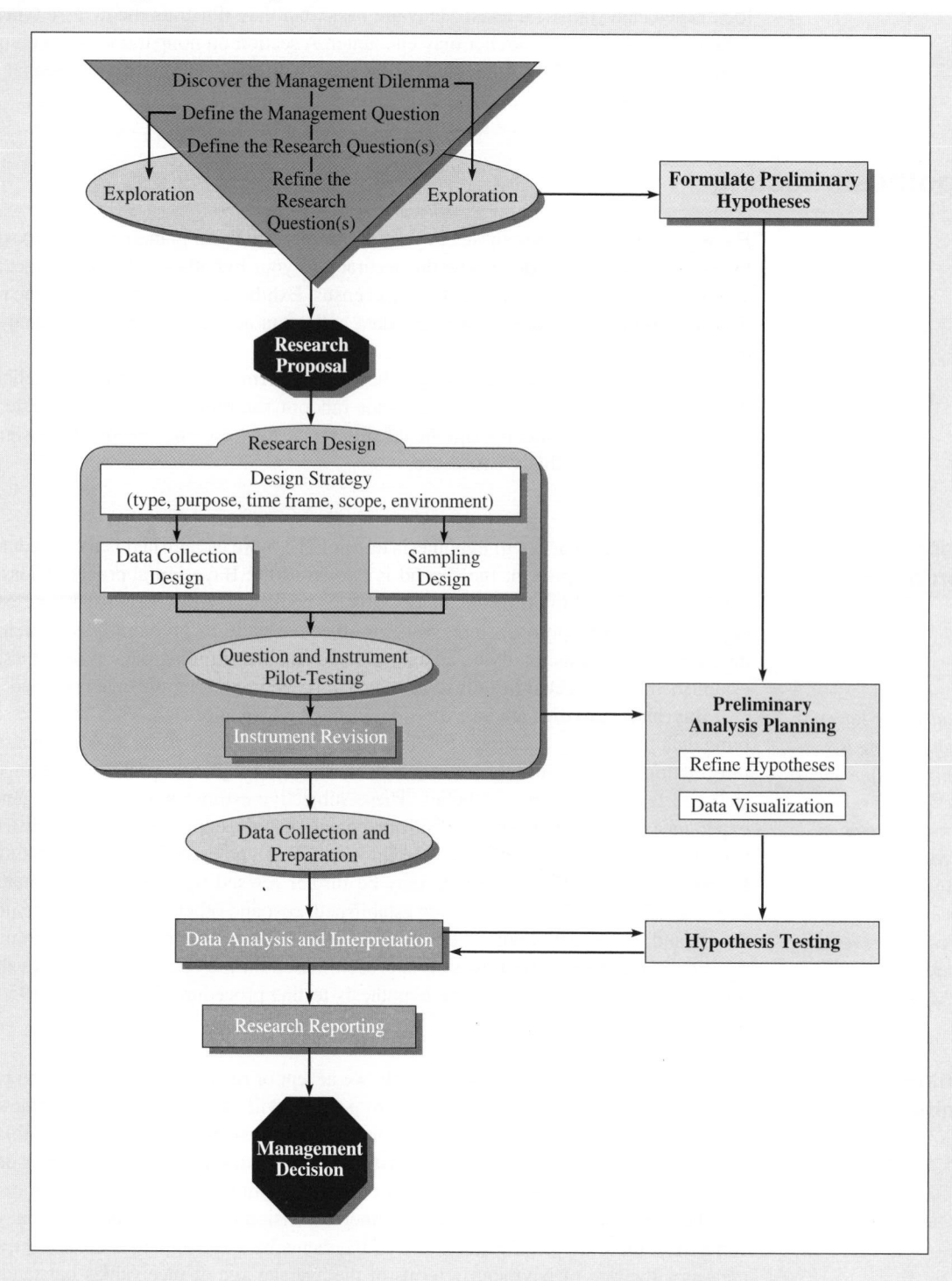

Of course it is, because the difference is based on a census of the accounts and there is no sampling involved. It is a fact that the population average has moved from 50 to 51 days. While it is of statistical significance, whether it is of **practical significance** is another question. If the controller judges that this variation has no real importance, then it is of little practical significance.

Since it would be too expensive to analyze all of e-WEAR's receivables frequently, we normally resort to sampling. Assume a sample of 25 accounts is randomly selected and the average number of days outstanding is calculated to be 54. Is this statistically significant? The answer is not obvious. It is significant if there is good reason to believe the average age of the total group of receivables has moved up from 50. Since the evidence consists of only a sample, consider the second possibility, that this is only a random sampling error and thus is not significant. The task is to judge whether such a result from this sample is or is not statistically significant. To answer this question, one needs to consider further the logic of hypothesis testing.

The Logic of Hypothesis Testing

In classical tests of significance, two kinds of hypotheses are used. The **null hypothesis** is used for testing. It is a statement that no difference exists between the parameter (a measure taken by a census of the population or a prior measurement of a sample of the population) and the statistic being compared to it (a measure from a recently drawn sample of the population). Analysts usually test to determine whether there has been no change in the population of interest or whether a real difference exists. Why not state the hypothesis in a positive form? Why not state that any difference between the sample statistic and the population parameter is due to some reason? Unfortunately, this type of hypothesis cannot be tested definitively. Evidence that is consistent with a hypothesis stated in a positive form can almost never be taken as conclusive grounds for accepting the hypothesis. A finding that is consistent with this type of hypothesis might be consistent with other hypotheses too, and thus does not demonstrate the truth of the given hypothesis.

For example, suppose a coin is suspected of being biased in favor of heads. The coin is flipped 100 times and the outcome is 52 heads. It would not be correct to jump to the conclusion that the coin is biased simply because more than the expected number of 50 heads resulted. The reason is that 52 heads is consistent with the hypothesis that the coin is fair. It would not be surprising to flip a fair coin 100 times and observe 52 heads. On the other hand, flipping 85 or 90 heads in 100 flips would seem to contradict the hypothesis of a fair coin. In this case there would be a strong case for a biased coin.

In the e-WEAR example, the null hypothesis states that the population parameter of 50 days has not changed. A second, **alternative hypothesis** holds that there has been a change in average days outstanding (i.e., the sample statistic of 54 indicates the population value probably is no longer 50). The alternative hypothesis is the logical opposite of the null hypothesis.

The e-WEAR example can be explored further to show how these concepts are used to test for significance.

MANAGEMENT

- The null hypothesis (H_0) is: There has been no change from the 50 days average age of accounts outstanding.

The alternative hypothesis (H_A) may take several forms, depending on the objective of the researchers. The H_A may be of the "not the same" or the "greater than" or "less than" form:

- The average age of accounts has changed from 50 days.

- The average age of receivables has increased (decreased) from 50 days.

These types of alternative hypotheses correspond with two-tailed and one-tailed tests. A **two-tailed test,** or *nondirectional test,* considers two possibilities: The average could be more than 50 days, or it could be less than 50 days. To test this hypothesis, the regions of rejection are divided into two tails of the distribution. A **one-tailed test,** or *directional test,* places the entire probability of an unlikely outcome into the tail specified by the alternative hypothesis. In Exhibit 17–2, the first diagram represents a nondirectional hypothesis, and the second is a directional hypothesis of the "greater than" variety. Hypotheses for the example may be expressed in the following form:

Null	$H_0:\mu$	$=$	50 days
Alternative	$H_A:\mu$	$\neq$	50 days (not the same case)
or	$H_A:\mu$	$>$	50 days (greater than case)
or	$H_A:\mu$	$<$	50 days (less than case)

MANAGEMENT
Tip

In testing these hypotheses, adopt this decision rule: Take no corrective action if the analysis shows that one cannot reject the null hypothesis. Note "not to reject" rather than "accept" the null hypothesis. It is argued that a null hypothesis can never be proved and therefore cannot be "accepted." Here, again, we see the influence of inductive reasoning. Unlike deduction, where the connections between premises and conclusions provide a legitimate claim of "conclusive proof," inductive conclusions do not possess that advantage. Statistical testing gives only a chance to (1) disprove (reject) or (2) fail to reject the hypothesis. Despite this terminology, it is common to hear "accept the null" rather than the clumsy "fail to reject the null." In this discussion, the less formal "accept" means "fail to reject" the null hypothesis.

If we reject a null hypothesis (finding a statistically significant difference), then we are accepting the alternative hypothesis. In either accepting or rejecting a null hypothesis, we can make incorrect decisions. A null hypothesis can be accepted when it should have been rejected or rejected when it should have been accepted.

These problems are illustrated with an analogy to the American legal system.[1] In our system of justice, the innocence of an indicted person is presumed until proof of guilt beyond a reasonable doubt can be established. In hypothesis testing, this is the null hypothesis; there should be no difference between the presumption and the outcome unless contrary evidence is furnished. Once evidence establishes beyond reasonable doubt that innocence can no longer be maintained, a just conviction is required. This is

EXHIBIT 17–2   **One- and Two-Tailed Tests at the 5% Level of Significance**

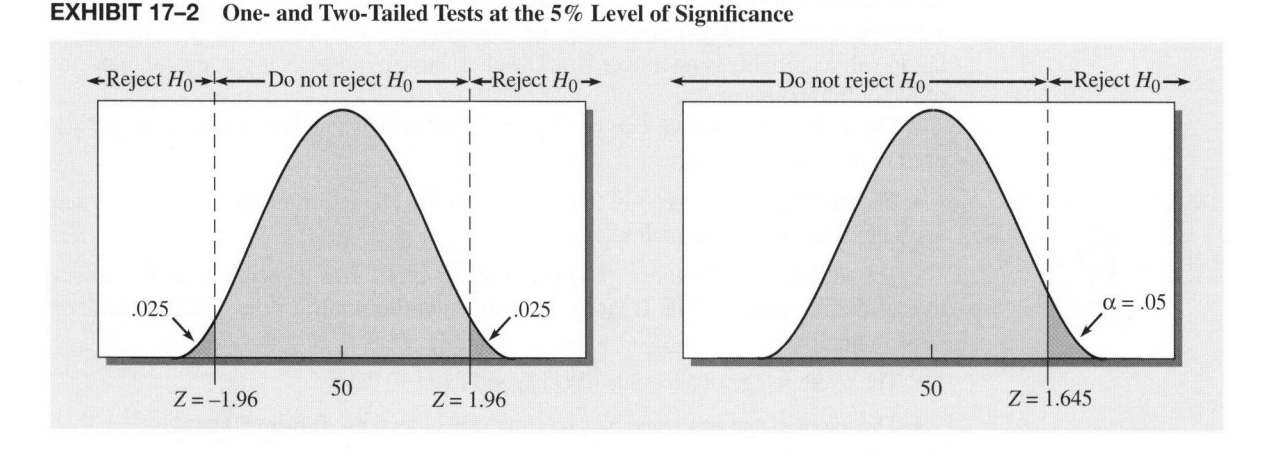

EXHIBIT 17–3   **Comparison of Statistical Decisions to Legal Analogy**

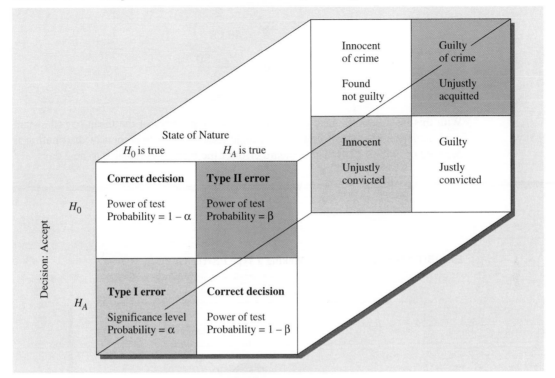

equivalent to rejecting the null hypothesis and accepting the alternative hypothesis. Incorrect decisions or errors are the other two possible outcomes. We can unjustly convict an innocent person, or we can acquit a guilty person.

Exhibit 17–3 compares the statistical situation to the legal one. One of two conditions exists in nature—either the null hypothesis is true or the alternative hypothesis is true. An indicted person is innocent or guilty. Two decisions can be made about these conditions: One may accept the null hypothesis or reject it (thereby accepting the alternative). Two of these situations result in correct decisions; the other two lead to decision errors.

When a **Type I error** (α) is committed, a true null hypothesis is rejected; the innocent person is unjustly convicted. The α value is called the level of significance and is the probability of rejecting the true null. With a **Type II error** (β), one fails to reject a false null hypothesis; the result is an unjust acquittal with the guilty person going free. In our system of justice, it is more important to reduce the probability of convicting the innocent than acquitting the guilty. Similarly, hypothesis testing places a greater emphasis on Type I errors than on Type II errors. Next we shall examine each of these errors in more detail.

Type I Error   Assume the e-WEAR controller's problem is deciding whether the average age of accounts receivable has changed. Assume the population mean is 50 days, the standard deviation of the population is 10 days, and the size of the sample is 25 accounts.

$$Z = \frac{\bar{X} - \mu}{\sigma_{\bar{X}}}$$

$$-1.96 = \frac{\bar{X}_c - 50}{2}$$

$$\bar{X}_c = 46.08$$

$$1.96 = \frac{\bar{X}_c - 50}{2}$$

$$\bar{X}_c = 53.92$$

With this information, one can calculate the standard error of the mean ($\sigma_{\bar{X}}$ (the standard deviation of the distribution of sample means). This hypothetical distribution is pictured in Exhibit 17–4. The standard error of the mean is calculated to be 2 days.

$$\sigma_{\bar{X}} = \frac{\sigma}{\sqrt{n}} = \frac{10}{\sqrt{25}} = 2$$

EXHIBIT 17–4   **Probability of Making a Type I Error Given H_0 Is True**

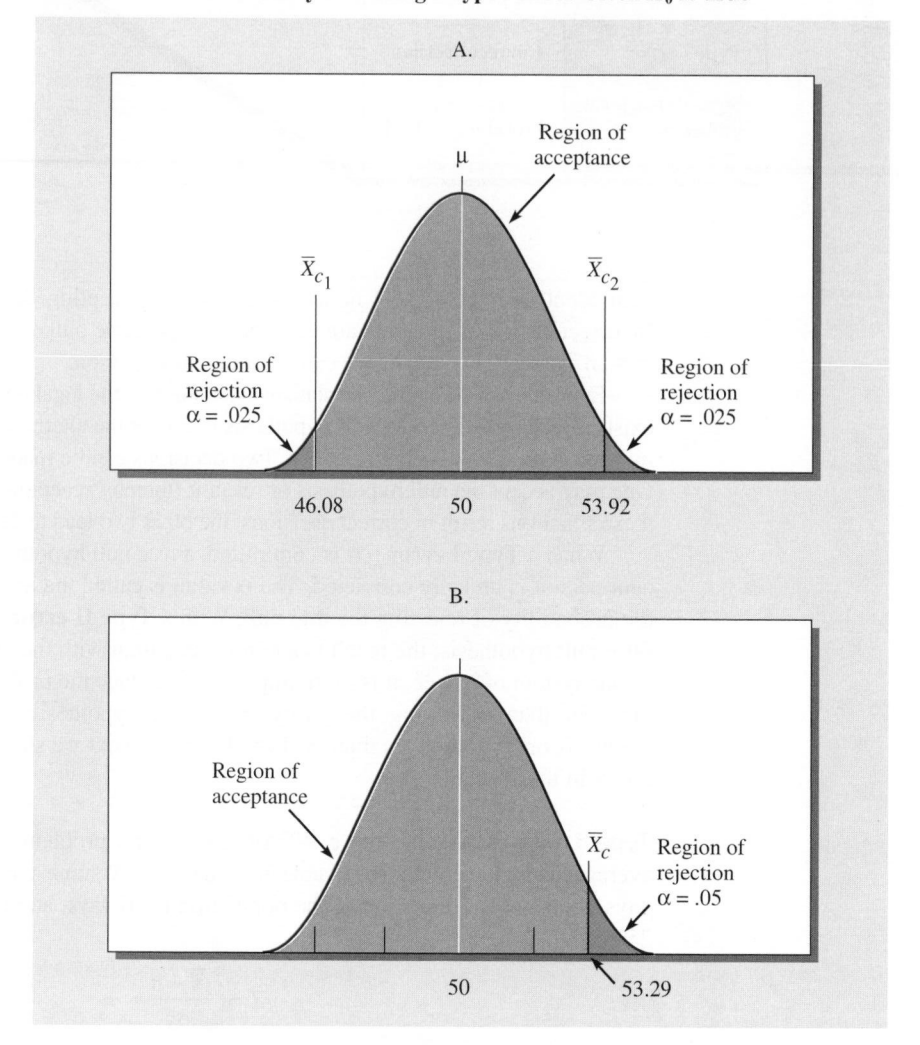

If the decision is to reject H_0 with a 95 percent confidence interval ($\alpha = .05$), a Type I error of .025 in each tail is accepted (assumes a two-tailed test). In Part A of Exhibit 17–4, see the **regions of rejection** indicated by the shaded areas. The area between these two regions is known as the **region of acceptance.** The dividing points between rejection and acceptance areas are called **critical values.** Since the distribution of sample means is normal, the critical values can be computed in terms of the standardized random variable,[2] where

$Z = 1.96$ (significance level = .05)

$\bar{X}_c$ = The critical value of the sample mean

μ = The population value stated in $H_0 = 50$

$\sigma_{\bar{X}}$ = The standard error of a distribution of means of samples of 25

The probability of a Type I error is

$$\alpha = .05, \text{ or } 5\%$$

The probability of a correct decision if the null hypothesis is true is 95 percent. By changing the probability of a Type I error, you move critical values either closer to or farther away from the assumed parameter of 50. This can be done if a smaller or larger α error is desired and critical values are moved to reflect this. You can also change the Type 1 error and the regions of acceptance by changing the size of the sample. For example, if you take a sample of 100, the critical values that provide a Type I error of .05 are 48.04 and 51.96.

The alternative hypothesis concerned a change in either direction from 50, but the controller may be interested only in increases in the age of receivables. For this, one uses a one-tailed (greater than) H_A and places the entire region of rejection in the upper tail of the distribution. One can accept a 5 percent α risk and compute a new critical value (X_c). (See Appendix Table F-1 to find the Z value of 1.645 for the area of .05 under the curve.) Substitute this in the Z equation and solve for $\bar{X}_c$.

$$Z = 1.645 = \frac{\bar{X}_c - 50}{2}$$

$$\bar{X}_c = 53.29$$

This new critical value, the boundary between the regions of acceptance and rejection, is pictured in Part B of Exhibit 17–4.

Type II Error   The controller would commit a Type II error (β) by accepting the null hypothesis ($\mu = 50$) when in truth it had changed. This kind of error is difficult to detect. The probability of committing a β error depends on five factors: (1) the true value of the parameter, (2) the α level we have selected, (3) whether a one- or two-tailed test was used to evaluate the hypothesis, (4) the sample standard deviation, and (5) the size of the sample. We secure a different β error if the new β moves from 50 to 54 than if it moves only to 52. We must compute separate β error estimates for each of a number of assumed new population parameters and $\bar{X}_c$ values.

To illustrate, assume μ has actually moved to 54 from 50. Under these conditions, what is the probability of our making a Type II error if the critical value is set at 53.29? This may be expressed in the following fashion:

$P(A_2|S_1) = \alpha = .05$ (assume a one-tailed alternative hypothesis)

$P(A_1|S_2) = \beta = ?$

If the new μ is 54, then

$$\sigma_{\bar{X}} = \frac{\sigma}{\sqrt{n}} = \frac{10}{\sqrt{25}} = 2$$

$$Z = \frac{\bar{X} - \mu}{\sigma_{\bar{X}}} = \frac{53.29 - 54}{2} = -.355$$

Using Table F–1 in Appendix F, we interpolate between .35 and .36 Z scores to find the .355 Z score. The area between the mean and Z is .1387. β is the tail area, or the area below the Z, and is calculated as

$$\beta = .50 - .1387 = .36$$

This condition is shown in Exhibit 17–5. With an α of .05 and a sample of 25, there is a 36 percent probability of a Type II (β) error if the μ is 54. We also speak of the **power of the test**—that is $(1 - \beta)$. For this example, the power of the test equals 64 percent $(1 - .36)$—that is, we will correctly reject the false null hypothesis with a 64 percent probability. A power of 64 percent is less than the 80 percent minimum percentage usually needed.

There are several ways to reduce a Type II error. We can shift the critical value closer to the original μ of 50; but to do this, we must accept a bigger α. Whether to take this action depends on the evaluation of the relative α and β risks. It might be desirable to enlarge the acceptable α risk because a worsening of the receivables situation would probably call for increased efforts to stimulate collections. Committing a Type I error would mean only that we engaged in efforts to stimulate collections when the situation had not worsened. This act probably would not have many adverse effects even if the days of credit outstanding had not increased.

A second way to reduce Type II error is to increase sample size. For example, if the sample were increased to 100, the power of the test would be much stronger.

EXHIBIT 17–5   Probability of Making a Type II Error

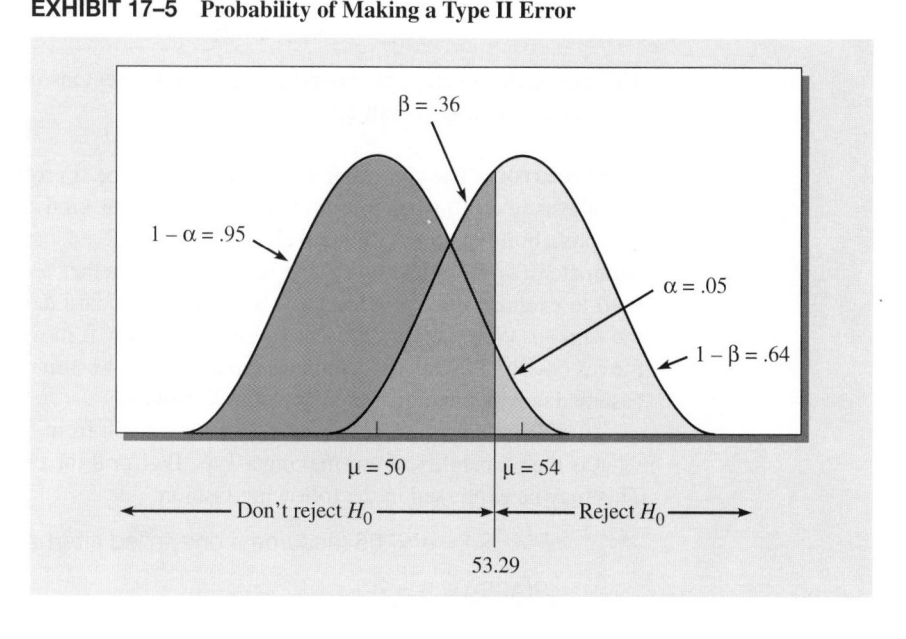

$$\sigma_{\bar{X}} = \frac{\sigma}{\sqrt{n}} = \frac{10}{\sqrt{100}} = 1$$

$$Z = \frac{\bar{X} - \mu}{\sigma_{\bar{X}}} = \frac{53.29 - 54}{1} = -.71$$

$$\beta = .50 - .2612 = .24$$

This would reduce the Type II error to 24 percent and increase the power of the test to 76 percent.

A third method seeks to improve both α and β errors simultaneously and is difficult to accomplish. We know that measuring instruments, observations, and recording produce error. By using a better measuring device, tightening the observation and recording processes, or devising a more efficient sample, we can reduce the variability of observations. This diminishes the standard error of estimate and in turn reduces the sampling distributions' spread. The net effect is that there is less tail area in the error regions.

Statistical Testing Procedures

Testing for statistical significance follows a relatively well-defined pattern, although authors differ in the number and sequence of steps. One six-stage sequence is as follows:

1. **State the null hypothesis.** While the researcher is usually interested in testing a hypothesis of change or differences, the null hypothesis is always used for statistical testing purposes.

MANAGEMENT

2. **Choose the statistical test.** To test a hypothesis, one must choose an appropriate statistical test. There are many tests from which to choose, and there are at least four criteria that can be used in choosing a test. One is the power efficiency of the test. A more powerful test provides the same level of significance with a smaller sample than a less powerful test. In addition, in choosing a test, one can consider how the sample is drawn, the nature of the population, and the type of measurement scale used. For instance, some tests are useful only when the sequence of scores is known or when observations are paired. Other tests are appropriate only if the population has certain characteristics; still other tests are useful only if the measurement scale is interval or ratio. More attention is given to test selection later in the chapter.

3. **Select the desired level of significance.** The choice of the **level of significance** should be made before we collect the data. The most common level is .05, although .01 is also widely used. Other α levels such as .10, .025, or .001 are sometimes chosen. The exact level to choose is largely determined by how much α risk one is willing to accept and the effect that this choice has on β risk. The larger the α, the lower is the β.

4. **Compute the calculated difference value.** After the data are collected, use the formula for the appropriate significance test to obtain the calculated value.

5. **Obtain the critical test value.** After we compute the calculated t, χ^2, or other measure, we must look up the critical value in the appropriate table for that distribution. The critical value is the criterion that defines the region of rejection from the region of acceptance of the null hypothesis.

6. **Interpret the test.** For most tests if the calculated value is larger than the critical value, we reject the null hypothesis and conclude that the alternative hypothesis is supported (although it is by no means proved). If the critical value is larger, we conclude we have failed to reject the null.[3]

Probability Values (*p* Values)

According to the "interpret the test" step of the statistical test procedure, the conclusion is stated in terms of rejecting or not rejecting the null hypothesis based on a reject region selected before the test is conducted. A second method of presenting the results of a statistical test reports the extent to which the test statistic disagrees with the null hypothesis. This method has become popular because analysts want to know what percentage of the sampling distribution lies beyond the sample statistic on the curve, and most statistical computer programs report the results of statistical tests as probability values (*p* values). The *p* value is the probability of observing a sample value as extreme as, or more extreme than, the value actually observed, given that the null hypothesis is true. This area represents the probability of a Type I error that must be assumed if the null hypothesis is rejected. The *p* value is compared to the significance level (α), and on this basis the null hypothesis is either rejected or not rejected. If the *p* value is less than the significance level, the null hypothesis is rejected (if *p* value $< \alpha$, reject null). If *p* is greater than or equal to the significance level, the null hypothesis is not rejected (if *p* value $> \alpha$, don't reject null).

Statistical data analysis programs commonly compute the *p* value during the execution of a hypothesis test. The following example will help illustrate the correct way to interpret a *p* value.

In Part B of Exhibit 17–4 the critical value was shown for the situation where the controller was interested in determining whether the average age of accounts receivable had increased. The critical value of 53.29 was computed based on a standard deviation of 10, sample size of 25, and the contoller's willingness to accept a 5 percent α risk. Suppose that the sample mean equaled 55. Is there enough evidence to reject the null hypothesis? If the *p* value is less than .05, the null hypothesis will be rejected. The *p* value is computed as follows.

The standard deviation of the distribution of sample means is 2. The appropriate *Z* value is

$$Z = \frac{\bar{X} - \mu}{\sigma_{\bar{X}}}$$

$$Z = \frac{55 - 50}{2}$$

$$Z = 2.5$$

The *p* value is determined using the standard normal table. The area between the mean and a *Z* value of 2.5 is .4938. The *p* value is the area above the *Z* value (shown in Part B of Exhibit 17–4). The probability of observing a *Z* value at least as large as 2.5 is only .0062 (.5000 − .4932 = .0062) if the null hypothesis is true.

This small *p* value represents the risk of rejecting the null hypothesis. It is the probability of a Type I error if the null hypothesis is rejected. Since the *p* value (*p* = .0062) is smaller than α = .05, the null hypothesis is rejected. The controller can conclude that the average age of the accounts receivable has increased. The probability that this conclusion is wrong is .0062.

Tests of Significance

This section provides an overview of statistical tests that are representative of the vast array available to the researcher. After a review of the general types of tests and their assumptions, the procedures for selecting an appropriate test are discussed. The remainder of the section contains examples of parametric and nonparametric tests for one-

S N A P S H O T

Content Analysis Unreels Drug Use in Movies

Are American teens exposed to unrealistic drug usage, or to unrealistic consequences from such use? Mediascope, a nonprofit organization concerned with responsible depictions of social and health issues in the media, recently completed for the Office of National Drug Control Policy a content analysis of the top 200 rental movies to determine their depiction of substance use. The researchers used the Video Software Dealers Association's most popular (top 100) home video titles based on rental income during two sequential years. Movies were categorized as follows: action adventure, comedy, or drama. Data were also collected on each title's Motion Picture Association of America (MPAA) rating (G, PG, PG-13, or R). Although technically teens should have been excluded from R-rated titles (which made up 48 percent of the overall sample), the study included all 20 of the most popular teen movies as identified in a prior independent study.

Trained coders watched all 200 movies, paying particular attention to alcohol, tobacco, illicit drugs, over-the-counter medicines, prescription medicines, inhalants, and unidentified pills. Coders ignored substances administered by medical personnel in a hospital or health-related scenario. *Substance use* included explicit portrayals of consumption. *Substance appearance* was noted when evidence of materials or paraphernalia was noted without any indication of use. Coders identified *dominant messages* about substance use, and the *consequences* of use. Coders also noted

scenes depicting illicit drug use or those depicting use by characters known to be under 18. *Prevalence of use* was determined by counting the characters in each movie and determining not only the percentage of characters using drugs but also whether the character had a major or minor role. Coders profiled characters by age, gender, and ethnicity, as well as other characteristics. *Frequency of substance abuse* was determined for each five-minute interval of each movie, with the presence or absence of various substances noted, starting with the completion of the title credits and ending when the final credits began. How would the last movie you watched have fared under this scrutiny?

www.mediacampaign.org

www.americacares.org

www.vsda.org

sample, two-sample, and *k*-sample cases. Readers needing a comprehensive treatment of significance tests are referred to the suggested readings at the end of this chapter.

Types of Tests

There are two general classes of significance tests: parametric and nonparametric. **Parametric tests** are more powerful because their data are derived from interval and ratio measurements. **Nonparametric tests** are used to test hypotheses with nominal and ordinal data. Parametric techniques are the tests of choice if their assumptions are met. Assumptions for parametric tests include the following:

MANAGEMENT

- The observations must be independent—that is, the selection of any one case should not affect the chances for any other case to be included in the sample.

- The observations should be drawn from normally distributed populations.

- These populations should have equal variances.

- The measurement scales should be at least interval so that arithmetic operations can be used with them.

The researcher is responsible for reviewing the assumptions pertinent to the chosen test. Performing diagnostic checks on the data allows the researcher to select the most appropriate technique. The normality of a distribution may be checked in several ways.

We have previously discussed the measures of location, shape, and spread for preliminary analysis and considered graphic techniques for exploring data patterns and examining distributions. Another diagnostic tool is the **normal probability plot.** This plot compares the observed values with those expected from a normal distribution.[4] If the data display the characteristics of normality, the points will fall within a narrow band along a straight line. An example is shown in the upper left panel of Exhibit 17–6.

An alternative way to look at this is to plot the deviations from the straight line. These are shown in a "detrended" plot in the upper right panel of the figure. Here we would expect the points to cluster without pattern around a straight line passing horizontally through 0. In the bottom two panels of Exhibit 17–6, there is neither a straight line in the normal probability plot nor a random distribution of points about 0 in the detrended plot. Visually, the bottom two plots tell us the variable is not normally distributed. In addition, two separate tests of the hypothesis that the data come from normal distributions are rejected at a significance level of less than .01.[5]

If we wished to check another assumption—say, one of equal variance—a spread-and-level plot would be appropriate. Statistical software programs often provide diagnostic tools for checking assumptions. These may be nested within a specific statistical procedure, such as analysis of variance or regression, or provided as a general set of tools for examining assumptions.

Parametric tests place different emphasis on the importance of assumptions. Some tests are quite robust and hold up well despite violations. For others, a departure from linearity or equality of variance may threaten the validity of the results.

Nonparametric tests have fewer and less stringent assumptions. They do not specify normally distributed populations or homogeneity of variance. Some tests require independence of cases; others are expressly designed for situations with related cases. Nonparametric tests are the only ones usable with nominal data; they are the only technically correct tests to use with ordinal data, although parametric tests are sometimes employed in this case. Nonparametric tests may also be used for interval and ratio data, although they waste some of the information available. Nonparametric tests are also easy to understand and use. Parametric tests have greater efficiency when their use is appropriate, but even in such cases nonparametric tests often achieve an efficiency as high as 95 percent. This means the nonparametric test with a sample of 100 will provide the same statistical testing power as a parametric test with a sample of 95.

How to Select a Test

MANAGEMENT

In attempting to choose a particular significance test, the researcher should consider at least three questions:

- Does the test involve one sample, two samples, or k samples?

- If two samples or k samples are involved, are the individual cases independent or related?

- Is the measurement scale nominal, ordinal, interval, or ratio?

Additional questions may arise once answers to these are known: What is the sample size? If there are several samples, are they of equal size? Have the data been weighted? Have the data been transformed? Often such questions are unique to the selected technique. The answers can complicate the selection, but once a tentative choice is made, most standard statistics textbooks will provide further details.

Decision trees provide a more systematic means of selecting techniques. One widely used guide from the Institute for Social Research starts with questions about the

EXHIBIT 17–6   Probability Plots and Tests of Normality

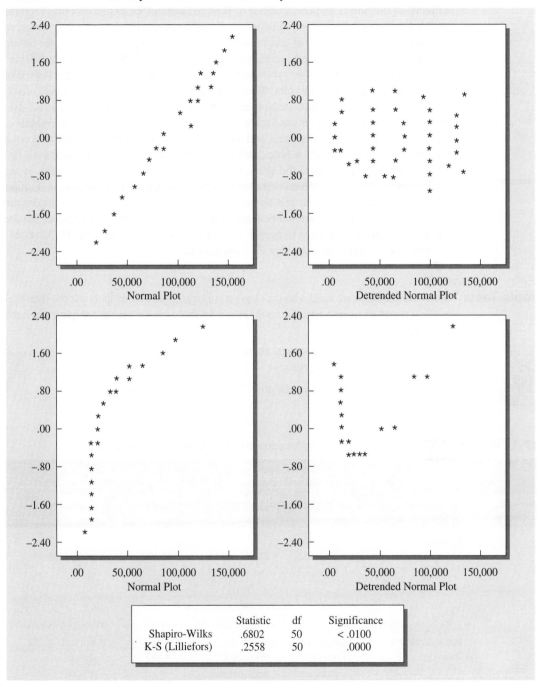

	Statistic	df	Significance
Shapiro-Wilks	.6802	50	< .0100
K-S (Lilliefors)	.2558	50	.0000

number of variables, nature of the variables (continuous, discrete, dichotomous, independent, dependent, and so forth), and level of measurement. It goes through a tree structure asking detailed questions about the nature of the relationships being searched, compared, or tested. Over 130 solutions to data analysis problems are paired with commonly asked questions.[6]

An expert system offers another approach to choosing appropriate statistics. Capitalizing on the power and convenience of personal computers, expert system programs provide a comprehensive search of the statistical terrain just as a computer search of secondary sources does. Most programs ask about your research objectives, the nature of your data, and the intended audience for your final report. When you are not 100 percent confident of your answers, you can bracket them with an estimate of the degree of your certainty. One such program, Statistical Navigator, covers eight categories of statistics from exploratory data analysis through reliability testing and multivariate data analysis. In response to your answers, a report is printed containing recommendations, rationale for selections, references, and the statistical packages that offer the suggested procedure.[7] SPSS and SAS include coaching and help modules with their software.

In this chapter, we used the above three criteria to develop a classification of the major parametric and nonparametric tests and measures. This is shown in Exhibit 17–7.[8] For example, if your testing situation involves two samples, the samples are independent, and the data are interval, the figure suggests the *t*-test of differences as the appropriate choice. The most frequently used of the tests listed in Exhibit 17–7 are covered next. For additional examples see Appendix E.

One-Sample Tests

One-sample tests are used when we have a single sample and wish to test the hypothesis that it comes from a specified population. In this case we encounter questions such as these:

MANAGEMENT

- Is there a difference between observed frequencies and the frequencies we would expect, based on some theory?
- Is there a difference between observed and expected proportions?

EXHIBIT 17–7   Recommended Statistical Techniques by Measurement Level and Testing Situation

Measurement Level	One-Sample Case	Two-Samples Case Related Samples	Two-Samples Case Independent Samples	k-Samples Case Related Samples	k-Samples Case Independent Samples
Nominal	• Binomial • χ^2 One-sample	• McNemar	• Fisher exact test • χ^2 Two-samples test	• Cochran Q	• χ^2 for *k* samples
Ordinal	• Kolmogorov-Smirnov one-sample test • Runs test	• Sign test • Wilcoxon matched-pairs test	• Median test • Mann-Whitney U • Kolmogorov-Smirnov • Wald-Wolfowitz	• Friedman two-way ANOVA	• Median extension • Kruskal-Wallis one-way ANOVA
Interval and ratio	• *t*-test • *Z* test	• *t*-test for paired samples	• *t*-test • *Z* test	• Repeated-measures ANOVA	• One-way ANOVA • *n*-way ANOVA

- Is it reasonable to conclude that a sample is drawn from a population with some specified distribution (normal, Poisson, and so forth)?
- Is there a significant difference between some measures of central tendency ($\overline{X}$) and its population parameter (μ)?

A number of tests may be appropriate in this situation. The parametric test is discussed first.

Parametric Tests The Z or t-test is used to determine the statistical significance between a sample distribution mean and a parameter.

The **Z distribution** and **t distribution** differ. The t has more tail area than that found in the normal distribution. This is a compensation for the lack of information about the population standard deviation. Although the sample standard deviation is used as a proxy figure, the imprecision makes it necessary to go farther away from 0 to include the percentage of values in the t distribution necessarily found in the standard normal.

When sample sizes approach 120, the sample standard deviation becomes a very good estimate of σ; beyond 120, the t and Z distributions are virtually identical.

Some typical real-world applications of the one-sample test are:

- Finding the average monthly balance of credit card holders compared to the average monthly balance five years ago.
- Comparing the failure rate of computers in a 20-hour test of quality specifications.
- Discovering the proportion of people who would shop in a new district compared to the assumed population proportion.
- Comparing the average income taxes collected this year to last year's income tax revenues.

Example. To illustrate the application of the t-test to the one-sample case, consider again the controller's problem mentioned earlier. With a sample of 100 accounts, she finds that the mean age of outstanding receivables is 52.5 days, with a standard deviation of 14. Do these results indicate the population mean might still be 50 days?

In this problem, we have only the sample standard deviation (s). This must be used in place of the population standard deviation (σ). When we substitute s for σ, we use the t distribution, especially if the sample size is less than 30. We define t as

$$t = \frac{\overline{X} - \mu}{s/\sqrt{n}}$$

This significance test is conducted by following the six-step procedure recommended earlier.

1. **Null hypothesis.** H_0: = 50 days.
   $\qquad\qquad\qquad H_A$: > 50 days (one-tailed test).

2. **Statistical test.** Choose the t-test because the data are ratio measurements. Assume the underlying population is normal and we have randomly selected the sample from the population of customer accounts.

3. **Significance level.** Let $\alpha = .05$, with $n = 100$.

4. **Calculated value.**

$$t = \frac{52.5 - 50}{14/\sqrt{100}} \quad \frac{2.5}{1.4} = 1.786; \qquad \text{d.f.} = n - 1 = 99$$

5. Critical test value. We obtain this by entering the table of critical values of t (see Appendix Table F–2 at back of book), with 99 degrees of freedom (d.f.) and a level of significance value of .05. We secure a critical value of about 1.66 (interpolated between d.f. = 60 and d.f. = 120 in Table F–2).

6. Interpret. In this case, the calculated value is greater than the critical value (1.786 > 1.66), so we reject the null hypothesis and conclude that the average accounts receivable outstanding has increased.

Nonparametric Tests   A variety of nonparametric tests may be used in a one-sample situation, depending on the measurement scale used and other conditions. If the measurement scale is nominal (classificatory only), it is possible to use either the binomial test or the chi-square (χ^2) one-sample test. The binomial test is appropriate when the population is viewed as only two classes, such as male and female, buyer and nonbuyer, and successful and unsuccessful, and all observations fall into one or the other of these categories. The binomial test is particularly useful when the size of sample is so small that the χ^2 test cannot be used.

Chi-Square Test   Probably the most widely used nonparametric test of significance is the **chi-square (χ^2) test.** It is particularly useful in tests involving nominal data but can be used for higher scales. Typical are cases where persons, events, or objects are grouped in two or more nominal categories such as "yes-no," "favor-undecided-against," or class "A, B, C, or D."

Using this technique, we test for significant differences between the *observed* distribution of data among categories and the *expected* distribution based on the null hypothesis. Chi-square is useful in cases of one-sample analysis, two independent samples, or k independent samples. It must be calculated with actual counts rather than percentages.

In the one-sample case, we establish a null hypothesis based on the expected frequency of objects in each category. Then the deviations of the actual frequencies in each category are compared with the hypothesized frequencies. The greater the difference between them, the less is the probability that these differences can be attributed to chance. The value of χ^2 is the measure that expresses the extent of this difference. The larger the divergence, the larger is the χ^2 value.

The formula by which the χ^2 test is calculated is

$$\chi^2 = \sum_{i=1}^{k} \frac{(O_i - E_i)^2}{E_i}$$

in which

O_i = Observed number of cases categorized in the ith category.

E_i = Expected number of cases in the ith category under H_0.

k = The number of categories.

There is a different distribution for χ^2 for each number of degrees of freedom (d.f.), defined as $(k - 1)$ or the number of categories in the classification minus 1.

$$\text{d.f.} = k - 1$$

With chi-square contingency tables of the two-sample or k-sample variety, we have both rows and columns in the cross-classification table. In that instance, d.f. is defined as rows minus 1 $(r - 1)$ times columns minus 1 $(c - 1)$.

$$\text{d.f.} = (r - 1)(c - 1)$$

In a 2×2 table there is 1 d.f., and in a 3×2 table there are 2 d.f. Depending on the number of degrees of freedom, we must be certain the numbers in each cell are large enough to make the χ^2 test appropriate. When d.f. = 1, each expected frequency should be at least 5 in size. If d.f. > 1, then the χ^2 test should not be used if more than 20 percent of the expected frequencies are smaller than 5, or when any expected frequency is less than 1. Expected frequencies can often be increased by combining adjacent categories. Four categories of freshmen, sophomores, juniors, and seniors might be classified into upper class and lower class. If there are only two categories and still there are too few in a given class, it is better to use the binomial test.

Assume a survey of student interest in the Metro University dining club discussed in Chapter 7 is taken. We have interviewed 200 students and learned of their intentions to join such a club. We would like to analyze the results by living arrangement (type and location of student housing and eating arrangements). The 200 responses are classified into the four categories shown in the accompanying table. Do these variations indicate there is a significant difference among these students, or are these sampling variations only? Proceed as follows:

Living Arrangement	Intend to Join	Number Interviewed	Percent (No. Interviewed/200)	Expected Frequencies (Percent × 60)
Dorm/fraternity	16	90	45	27
Apartment/rooming house, nearby	13	40	20	12
Apartment/rooming house, distant	16	40	20	12
Live at home	15	30	15	9
Total	60	200	100	60

1. **Null hypothesis.** H_0: $O_i = E_i$. The proportion in the population who intend to join the club is independent of living arrangement. In H_A: $O_i \neq E_i$, the proportion in the population who intend to join the club is dependent on living arrangement.

2. **Statistical test.** Use the one-sample χ^2 to compare the observed distribution to a hypothesized distribution. The χ^2 test is used because the responses are classified into nominal categories and there are sufficient observations.

3. **Significance level.** Let $\alpha = .05$.

4. **Calculated value.**

$$\chi^2 = \sum_{i=1}^{k} \frac{(O_i - E_i)^2}{E_i}$$

Calculate the expected distribution by determining what proportion of the 200 students interviewed were in each group. Then apply these proportions to the number who intend to join the club. Then calculate the following:

$$\chi^2 = \frac{(16-27)^2}{27} + \frac{(13-12)^2}{12} + \frac{(16-12)^2}{12} + \frac{(15-9)^2}{9}$$

$$= 4.48 + 0.08 + 1.33 + 4.0$$

$$= 9.89$$

$$\text{d.f.} = (4-1)(2-1) = 3$$

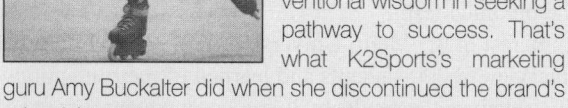

If you were trying to compete with RollerBlade, a brand synonymous with the in-line skating phenomenon, you'd be tempted to challenge conventional wisdom in seeking a pathway to success. That's what K2Sports's marketing guru Amy Buckalter did when she discontinued the brand's advertising program.

In-line skates are traditionally sold in sporting goods stores, an environment characterized by high employee turnover. K2Sports developed a national ambassador program, designed to demonstrate skate sales techniques to young, part-time salespeople. The teach-by-example ambassador program started by sending young skating enthusiasts to sporting goods retailers in southern California. These ambassadors essentially serve as part-time employees for a relatively short period of time in any one store. On days when an ambassador is in the store, a retailer's sales of in-line skates triple, with no less than 70 percent of skates sold being the K2Sports brand. As the ambassador program rolls nationwide, the impressive sales results continue.

Is the repeated sales success of the ambassador program an experiment that proves a causal relationship between K2Sports's ambassador program and retailers' sales increase?

www.k2sports.com

5. **Critical test value.** Enter the table of critical values of χ^2 (see Appendix Table F–3), with 3 d.f., and secure a value of 7.82 for $\alpha = .05$.

6. **Interpret.** The calculated value is greater than the critical value, so the null hypothesis is rejected.

Two Independent Samples Tests

The need to use **two independent samples tests** is often encountered in business research. We might compare the purchasing predispositions of a sample of subscribers from two magazines to discover if they are from the same population. Similarly, a test of output methods from two production lines or the price movements of common stock from two samples could be compared. A study of worker productivity from two groups or different samples from a public opinion poll would also use this method.

Parametric Tests   The Z and t-tests are frequently used parametric tests for independent samples, although the F test also can be used.

The **Z test** is used with large sample sizes (exceeding 30 for both independent samples) or with smaller samples when the data are normally distributed and population variances are known. The formula for the Z test is

$$Z = \frac{(\bar{X}_1 - \bar{X}_2) - (\mu_1 - \mu_2)0}{\sqrt{\dfrac{S_1^2}{n_1} + \dfrac{S_2^2}{n_2}}}$$

With small sample sizes, normally distributed populations, and assuming equal population variances, the t-test is appropriate:

$$t = \frac{(\bar{X}_1 - \bar{X}_2) - (\mu_1 - \mu_2)0}{\sqrt{S_p^2 \left(\dfrac{1}{n_1} + \dfrac{1}{n_2} \right)}}$$

where

$(\mu_1 - \mu_2)$ is the difference between the two population means

S_p^2 is associated with the pooled variance estimate:

$$S_p^2 = \frac{(n_1 - 1)\, S_1^2 + (n_2 - 1)\, S_2^2}{n_1 + n_2 - 2}$$

To illustrate this application, consider a problem that might face a manager at Dean Merrill Brokerage who wishes to test the effectiveness of two methods for training new account executives. The company selects 22 trainees who are randomly divided into two experimental groups. One receives type A and the other type B training. The trainees are then assigned and managed without regard to the training they have received. At the year's end, the manager reviews the performances of employees in these groups and finds the following results:

	A Group	B Group
Average hourly sales	$\bar{X}_1 = \$1{,}500$	$\bar{X}_2 = \$1{,}300$
Standard deviation	$s_1 = 225$	$s_2 = 251$

Following the standard testing procedure, we will determine whether one training method is superior to the other.

1. **Null hypothesis.** H_0: There is no difference in sales results produced by the two training methods.

   H_A: Training method A produces sales results superior to those of method B.

2. **Statistical test.** The t-test is chosen because the data are at least interval and the samples are independent.

3. **Significance level.** $\alpha = .05$ (one-tailed test).

4. **Calculated value.**

$$t = \frac{(1,500 - 1,300) - 0}{\sqrt{\dfrac{(10)(225)^2 + (10)(251)^2}{20}\left(\dfrac{1}{11} + \dfrac{1}{11}\right)}}$$

$$= \frac{200}{101.63} = 1.97, \qquad \text{d.f.} = 20$$

There are $n - 1$ degrees of freedom in each sample, so total d.f. is:

$$\text{d.f.} = (11 - 1) + (11 - 1) = 20$$

5. **Critical test value.** Enter Appendix Table F–2 with d.f. = 20, one-tailed test, $\alpha = .05$. The critical value is 1.725.

6. **Interpret.** Since the calculated value is larger than the critical value (1.97 > 1.725), reject the null hypothesis and conclude that training method A is superior.

Nonparametric Tests   The chi-square (χ^2) test is appropriate for situations in which a test for differences between samples is required. It is especially valuable for nominal data but can be used with ordinal measurements. When parametric data have been reduced to categories, they are frequently treated with χ^2 although this results in a loss of information. Preparing to solve this problem is the same as presented earlier although the formula differs slightly:

$$\chi^2 = \sum_i \sum_j \frac{(O_{ij} - E_{ij})^2}{E_{ij}}$$

in which

O_{ij} = Observed number of cases categorized in the ijth cell.

E_{ij} = Expected number of cases under H_0 to be categorized in the ijth cell.

Suppose Containers Inc. is implementing a smoke-free workplace policy and is interested in whether smoking affects worker accidents. Since the company has complete reports of on-the-job accidents, a sample of names of workers were drawn who were involved in accidents during the last year. A similar sample from among workers who had no reported accidents in the last year is drawn. Members of both groups are interviewed to determine if they are smokers or not. The results appear in the table at the top of the next page.

The expected values have been calculated and are shown. The testing procedure is:

1. **Null hypothesis.** H_0: There is no difference in on-the-job accident occurrences between smokers and nonsmokers.

   H_A: There is a difference in on-the-job accident occurrences between smokers and nonsmokers.

Smoker	Count Expected values	On-the-Job Accident		Row Total
		Yes	No	
	Heavy	12 8.24	4 7.75	16
	Moderate	9 7.73	6 7.27	15
	Nonsmoker	13 18.03	22 16.97	35
	Column Total	34	32	66

2. **Statistical test.** χ^2 is appropriate but it may waste some of the data because the measurement appears to be ordinal.

3. **Significance level.** $\alpha = .05$, with d.f. $= (3 - 1)(2 - 1) = 2$.

4. **Calculated value.** The expected distribution is provided by the marginal totals of the table. If there is no relationship between accidents and smoking, there will be the same proportion of smokers in both accident and nonaccident classes. The numbers of expected observations in each cell are calculated by multiplying the two marginal totals common to a particular cell and dividing this product by n. For example,

$$\frac{34 \times 16}{66} = 8.24, \text{ the expected value in cell (1,1)}$$

$$\chi^2 = \frac{(12 - 8.24)^2}{8.24} + \frac{(4 - 7.75)^2}{7.75} + \frac{(9 - 7.73)^2}{7.73} + \frac{(6 - 7.72)^2}{7.772}$$

$$+ \frac{(13 - 18.03)^2}{18.03} + \frac{(22 - 16.97)^2}{16.97}$$

$$= 6.86$$

5. **Critical test value.** Enter Appendix Table F–3 and find the critical value 5.99 with $\alpha = .05$ and d.f. $= 2$.

6. **Interpret.** Since the calculated value is greater than the critical value, the null hypothesis is rejected.

For chi-square to operate properly, data must come from random samples of multinomial distributions, and the expected frequencies should not be too small. We previously noted the traditional caution that expected frequencies below 5 should not compose more than 20 percent of the cells, and no cell should have an E_i of less than 1. Some research has argued that these restrictions are too severe.[9]

In another type of χ^2, the 2×2 table, a correction known as *Yates' correction for continuity* is often applied when sample sizes are greater than 40 or when the sample is between 20 and 40 and the values of E_i are 5 or more. The formula for this correction is

$$\chi^2 = \frac{n\left(|AD - BC| - \dfrac{n}{2}\right)^2}{(A + B)(C + D)(A + C)(B + D)}$$

where the letters represent the cells designated as

A	B
C	D

When the continuity correction is applied to the data shown in Exhibit 17–8, a χ^2 value of 5.25 is obtained. The observed level of significance for this value is .02192. If the level of significance had been set at .01, we would accept the null hypothesis. However, had we calculated χ^2 without correction, the value would have been 6.25, which has an observed level of significance of .01242. Some researchers may be tempted to reject the null at this level. (But note that the critical value of χ^2 at .01 with 1 d.f. is 6.64. See Appendix Table F–3.) The literature is in conflict regarding the merits of Yates' correction, but this example suggests one should take care when interpreting 2×2 tables.[10] To err on the conservative side would be in keeping with our prior discussion of Type I errors.

The Mantel-Haenszel test and the likelihood ratio also appear in Exhibit 17–8. The former is used with ordinal data, so it does not apply; the latter, based on maximum likelihood theory, produces results similar to Pearson's chi-square.

Two Related Samples Test

The **two related samples tests** concern those situations in which persons, objects, or events are closely matched or the phenomena are measured twice. One might compare the output of specific workers before and after vacations, the performance of the same stocks at two intervals, or the effects of an experimental stimulus when persons were

EXHIBIT 17–8 **Comparison of Corrected and Noncorrected Chi-Square Results Using SPSS Procedure Crosstab**

```
                      INCOME BY POSSESSION OF CPA

                              CPA
                  Count
                           Yes      No
                                                Row
                            1        2         Total
          INCOME      ─────────────────────
                  High 1     30       30         60
                                                60.0

                  Low 2      10       30         40
                                                40.0

                  Column     40       60        100
                  Total     40.0     60.0      100.0

Chi-Square                          Value     D.F.     Significance

Pearson                            6.25000      1         .01242
Continuity Correction              5.25174      1         .02192
Likelihood Ratio                   6.43786      1         .01117
Mantel-Haenszel                    6.18750      1         .01287
Minimum Expected Frequency: 16.000
```

Star signs are religiously followed by some and are a source of amusement to others. In a lighthearted study conducted by the Sydney-based insurance company Suncorp Metway, the number of car accident claims over a three-year period were compared with star signs. More than 14,500 drivers born between May 21 and June 21 (Geminis) had crashed their cars. Warren Duke, national manager of personal insurance, said, ". . . it was interesting that Geminis, typically described as restless, easily bored, and frustrated by things moving slowly, had more car accidents than any other sign." Those with the fewest were Capricorns, said to be patient and careful. Women also had more claims than men in 2001, according to the study. Duke added, "Women make significantly fewer claims than men until their late twenties, but after that women, aged 29 and over, edge ahead of men, making slightly more claims." Suncorp Metway has no intention of using astrology as a rating factor in determining a customer's motor insurance premium. But it had fun looking for trends. How might you construct a chi-square test of star sign by gender? What variables would you use as controls?

Most likely to file an accident claim by star sign

1. Gemini (May 21–June 21)
2. Taurus (April 20–May 20)
3. Pisces (February 19–March 20)
4. Virgo (August 23–September 22)
5. Cancer (June 22–July 22)
6. Aquarius (January 20–February 18)
7. Aries (March 21–April 19)
8. Leo (July 23–August 22)
9. Libra (September 23–October 22)
10. Sagittarius (November 22–December 21)
11. Scorpio (October 23–November 21)
12. Capricorn (December 22–January 19)

www.suncorpmetway.com.au

randomly assigned to groups and given pretests and post-tests. Both parametric and nonparametric tests are applicable under these conditions.

Parametric Tests The t-test for independent samples would normally be inappropriate for this situation because one of its assumptions is that observations are independent. This problem is solved by a formula where the difference is found between each matched pair of observations, thereby reducing the two samples to the equivalent of a one-sample case—that is, there are now several differences, each independent of the other, for which one can compute various statistics.

In the following formula, the average difference, $\bar{D}$, corresponds to the normal distribution when the α difference is known and the sample size is sufficient. The statistic t with $(n - 1)$ degrees of freedom is defined as

$$t = \frac{\bar{D}}{S_D/\sqrt{n}}$$

where

$$\bar{D} = \frac{\Sigma D}{n}$$

$$S_D = \sqrt{\frac{\Sigma D^2 - \frac{(\Sigma D)^2}{n}}{n - 1}}$$

To illustrate this application, we use two years of *Forbes* sales data (in millions of dollars) from 10 companies found in Exhibit 17–9.

1. **Null hypothesis.** H_0: $\mu = 0$; there is no difference between the two years' sales records. H_A: $\neq 0$; there is a difference between sales for Year 1 and Year 2.

2. **Statistical test.** The matched- or paired-samples *t*-test is chosen because there are repeated measures on each company, the data are not independent, and the measurement is ratio.

3. **Significance level.** Let $\alpha = .01$, with $n = 10$ and d.f. $= n - 1$.

4. **Calculated value.**

$$t = \frac{\bar{D}}{S_D/\sqrt{n}} = \frac{3,578.10}{570.98} = 6.28; \quad \text{d.f.} = 9$$

5. **Critical test value.** Enter Appendix Table F–2, with d.f. = 9, two-tailed test, $\alpha = .01$. The critical value is 3.25.

6. **Interpret.** Since the calculated value is greater than the critical value (6.28 > 3.25), reject the null hypothesis and conclude there is a statistically significant difference between the two years of sales.

A computer solution to the problem is illustrated in Exhibit 17–10. Notice that an *observed significance level* is printed for the calculated *t* value. With SPSS, this is often rounded and would be interpreted as significant at the .0005 level. The correlation coefficient, to the left of the *t* value, is a measure of the relationship between the two pairs of scores. In situations where matching has occurred (such as husbands' and wives' scores), it reveals the degree to which the matching has been effective in reducing the variability of the mean difference.

Nonparametric Tests The *McNemar test* may be used with either nominal or ordinal data and is especially useful with before-after measurement of the same subjects.

EXHIBIT 17–9   Sales Data for Paired-Samples *t*-Test (dollars in millions)

Company	Sales Year 2	Sales Year 1	Difference D	D^2
GM	126932	123505	3427	11744329
GE	54574	49662	4912	24127744
Exxon	86656	78944	7712	59474944
IBM	62710	59512	3192	10227204
Ford	96146	92300	3846	14791716
AT&T	36112	35173	939	881721
Mobil	50220	48111	2109	4447881
DuPont	35099	32427	2632	6927424
Sears	53794	49975	3819	14584761
Amoco	23966	20779	3187	10156969
Totals			$\Sigma D = 35781$	$\Sigma D^2 = 157364693$

EXHIBIT 17–10 **SPSS Output for Paired-Samples *t*-Test**

	---*t*-tests for paired samples---			
Variable	Number of Cases	Mean	Standard Deviation	Standard Error
Year 2 Sales	10	62620.9	31777.649	10048.975
Year 1 Sales	10	59038.8	31072.871	9836.104

(Difference Mean)	Standard Deviation	Standard Error	Corr.	2-tail Prob.	t Value	Degrees of Freedom	2-tail Prob.
3582.1000	1803.159	570.209	.999	.000	6.28	9	.000

Test the significance of any observed change by setting up a fourfold table of frequencies to represent the first and second set of responses:

	After	
Before	**Do Not Favor**	**Favor**
Favor	*A*	*B*
Do not favor	*C*	*D*

Since $A + D$ represents the total number of people who changed (B and C are no-change responses), the expectation under a null hypothesis is that $1/2\ (A + D)$ cases change in one direction and the same proportion in the other direction. The McNemar test uses the following transformation of the χ^2 test:

$$\chi^2 = \frac{(|A - D| - 1)^2}{A + D} \quad \text{with d.f.} = 1$$

The "minus 1" in the equation is a correction for continuity since the χ^2 is a continuous distribution and the observed frequencies represent a discrete distribution.

To illustrate this test's application, we use survey data from SteelShelf Corporation, whose management decided to tell employees of the "values of teamwork" in an internal education campaign. Managers took a random sample of their employees before the campaign, asking them to complete a questionnaire on their attitudes on this topic. On the basis of their responses, the workers were divided into equal groups reflecting their favorable or unfavorable views of teamwork. After the campaign, the same 200 employees were asked again to complete the questionnaire. They were again classified as to favorable or unfavorable attitudes. The testing process is:

1. Null hypothesis. H_0: $P(A) = P(D)$.
H_A: $P(A) \neq P(D)$.

2. Statistical test. The McNemar test is chosen because nominal data are used and the study involves before-after measurements of two related samples.

3. **Significance level.** Let $\alpha = .05$, with $n = 200$.

4. **Calculated value.**

$$\chi^2 = \frac{(|10 - 40| - 1)^2}{10 + 40} = \frac{29^2}{50} = 16.82; \text{ d.f.} = 1$$

Before	After Unfavorable	Favorable
Favorable	$A = 10$	$B = 90$
Unfavorable	$C = 60$	$D = 40$

5. **Critical test value.** Enter Appendix Table F–3, and find the critical value to be 3.84 with $\alpha = .05$ and d.f. = 1.

6. **Interpret.** The calculated value is greater than the critical value (16.82 > 3.84), indicating one should reject the null hypothesis. In fact, χ^2 is so large that it would have surpassed an α of .001.

k Independent Samples Tests

In management and economic research, we often use *k* **independent samples tests** when three or more samples are involved. Under this condition, we are interested in learning whether the samples might have come from the same or identical populations. When the data are measured on an interval-ratio scale and we can meet the necessary assumptions, analysis of variance and the *F* test are used. If preliminary analysis shows the assumptions cannot be met or if the data were measured on an ordinal or nominal scale, a nonparametric test should be selected.

As with the two-samples case, the samples are assumed to be independent. This is the condition of a completely randomized experiment when subjects are randomly assigned to various treatment groups. It is also common for an ex post facto study to require comparison of more than two independent sample means.

Parametric Tests   The statistical method for testing the null hypothesis that the means of several populations are equal is **analysis of variance (ANOVA).** *One-way analysis of variance* is described in this section. It uses a single-factor, fixed-effects model to compare the effects of one factor (brands of coffee, varieties of residential housing, types of retail stores) on a continuous dependent variable. In a fixed-effects model, the levels of the factor are established in advance, and the results are not generizable to other levels of treatment. For example, if coffee were Jamaican grown, Colombian grown, and Honduran grown, we could not extend our inferences to coffee grown in Guatemala or Mexico.

To use ANOVA, certain conditions must be met. The samples must be randomly selected from normal populations, and the populations should have equal variances. In addition, the distance from one value to its group's mean should be independent of the distances of other values to that mean (independence of error). ANOVA is reasonably robust, and minor variations from normality and equal variance are tolerable. Nevertheless, the analyst should check the assumptions with the diagnostic techniques previously described.

Analysis of variance, as the name implies, breaks down or partitions total variability into component parts. Unlike the *t*-test, which uses sample standard deviations,

ANOVA uses squared deviations of the variance so computation of distances of the individual data points from their own mean or from the grand mean can be summed (recall that standard deviations sum to zero).

In an ANOVA model, each group has its own mean and values that deviate from that mean. Similarly, all the data points from all of the groups produce an overall *grand mean.* The total deviation is the sum of the squared differences between each data point and the overall grand mean.

The total deviation of any particular data point may be partitioned into *between-groups variance* and *within-groups variance.* The between-groups variance represents the effect of the **treatment,** or factor. The differences of between-group means imply that each group was treated differently, and the treatment will appear as deviations of the sample means from the grand mean. Even if this were not so, there would still be some natural variability among subjects and some variability attributable to sampling. The within-groups variance describes the deviations of the data points within each group from the sample mean. This results from variability among subjects and from random variation. It is often called *error.*

Intuitively, we might conclude that when the variability attributable to the treatment exceeds the variability arising from error and random fluctuations, the viability of the null hypothesis begins to diminish. And this is exactly the way the test statistic for analysis of variance works.

The test statistic for ANOVA is the *F* **ratio.** It compares the variance from the last two sources:

$$F = \frac{\text{Between-groups variance}}{\text{Within-groups variance}} = \frac{\text{Mean square}_{between}}{\text{Mean square}_{within}}$$

where

$$\text{Mean square}_{between} = \frac{\text{Sum of squares}_{between}}{\text{Degrees of freedom}_{between}}$$

$$\text{Mean square}_{within} = \frac{\text{Sum of squares}_{within}}{\text{Degrees of freedom}_{within}}$$

To compute the *F* ratio, the sum of the squared deviations for the numerator and denominator are divided by their respective degrees of freedom. By dividing, we are computing the variance as an average or mean, thus the term *mean square.* The degrees of freedom for the numerator, the mean square between groups, is one less than the number of groups ($k - 1$). The degrees of freedom for the denominator, the mean square within groups, is the total number of observations minus the number of groups ($n - k$).

If the null hypothesis is true, there should be no difference between the populations, and the ratio should be close to 1. If the population means are not equal, the numerator should manifest this difference, and the *F* ratio should be greater than 1. The *F* distribution determines the size of ratio necessary to reject the null hypothesis for a particular sample size and level of significance.

To illustrate one-way ANOVA, consider Travel Industry Magazine's reports from international travelers about the quality of in-flight service on various carriers from the United States to Europe. Before writing a feature story coinciding with a peak travel period, the magazine decided to retain a researcher to secure a more balanced perspective on the reactions of travelers. The researcher selected passengers who had current impressions of the meal service, comfort, and friendliness of a major carrier. Three airlines were chosen and 20 passengers were randomly selected for each airline. The data, found in Exhibit 17–11,[11] are used for this and the next two examples. For the one-way

EXHIBIT 17–11   Data Table: Analysis of Variance Examples

	Flight Service					Flight Service			
	Rating 1	Rating 2	Airline	Seat Selection		Rating 1	Rating 2	Airline	Seat Selection
1	40	36	1	1	32	70	80	2	2
2	28	28	1	1	33	73	79	2	2
3	36	30	1	1	34	72	88	2	2
4	32	28	1	1	35	73	89	2	2
5	60	40	1	1	36	71	72	2	2
6	12	14	1	1	37	55	58	2	2
7	32	26	1	1	38	68	67	2	2
8	36	30	1	1	39	81	85	2	2
9	44	38	1	1	40	78	80	2	2
10	36	35	1	1	41	92	95	3	1
11	40	42	1	2	42	56	60	3	1
12	68	49	1	2	43	64	70	3	1
13	20	24	1	2	44	72	78	3	1
14	33	35	1	2	45	48	65	3	1
15	65	40	1	2	46	52	70	3	1
16	40	36	1	2	47	64	79	3	1
17	51	29	1	2	48	68	81	3	1
18	25	24	1	2	49	76	69	3	1
19	37	23	1	2	50	56	78	3	1
20	44	41	1	2	51	88	92	3	2
21	56	67	2	1	52	79	85	3	2
22	48	58	2	1	53	92	94	3	2
23	64	78	2	1	54	88	93	3	2
24	56	68	2	1	55	73	90	3	2
25	28	69	2	1	56	68	67	3	2
26	32	74	2	1	57	81	85	3	2
27	42	55	2	1	58	95	95	3	2
28	40	55	2	1	59	68	67	3	2
29	61	80	2	1	60	78	83	3	2
30	58	78	2	1					
31	52	65	2	2					

Airline: 1 = Delta; 2 = Lufthansa; 3 = KLM.

Seat Selection: 1 = Economy; 2 = Business.

All data are hypothetical.

analysis of variance problem, we are concerned only with the columns labeled "Flight Service Rating 1" and "Airline." The factor, airline, is the grouping variable for three carriers.

Again, we follow the procedure:

1. **Null hypothesis.** H_0: $\mu_{A1} = \mu_{A2} = \mu_{A3}$.
   H_A: The means are not equal.

2. **Statistical test.** The F test is chosen because we have k independent samples, accept the assumptions of analysis of variance, and have interval data.

3. **Significance level.** Let $\alpha = .05$, and d.f. = [numerator $(k - 1) = (3 - 1) = 2$], [denominator $(n - k) = (60 - 3) = 57$] = (2, 57).

4. **Calculated value.**

$$F = \frac{MS_b}{MS_W} = \frac{5822.017}{205.695} = 28.304, \text{ d.f. } (2, 57)$$

See summary in Exhibit 17–12.

5. **Critical test value.** Enter Appendix Table F–9, with d.f. (2, 57), $\alpha = .05$. The critical value is 3.16.

6. **Interpret.** Since the calculated value is greater than the critical value (28.3 > 3.16), we reject the null hypothesis and conclude there are statistically significant differences between two or more pairs of means. Note in Exhibit 17–12 that the p value equals .0001. Since the p value (.0001) is less than the significance level (.05), we have a second method for rejecting the null hypothesis.

The ANOVA model summary in Exhibit 17–12 is a standard way of summarizing the results of analysis of variance. It contains the sources of variation, degrees of freedom, sum of squares, mean squares, and calculated F value. The probability of rejecting the null hypothesis is computed up to 100 percent α—that is, the probability value column reports the exact significance for the F ratio being tested.

A Priori Contrasts. When we compute a t-test, it is not difficult to discover the reasons why the null is rejected. But with one-way ANOVA, how do we determine which pairs are not equal? We could calculate a series of t-tests, but they would not be independent of each other and the resulting Type I error would increase substantially. Obviously, this is not recommended. If we decided in advance that a comparison of specific populations was important, a special class of tests known as ***a priori*** **contrasts** could be used after the null was rejected with the F test (*a priori* because the decision was made before the test).[12]

A modification of the F test provides one approach for computing contrasts:

$$F = \frac{MS_{CON}}{MS_W}$$

The denominator, the within-groups mean square, is the same as the error term of the one-way's F ratio (recorded in the summary table, Exhibit 17–12). We have previously referred to the denominator of the F ratio as the error variance estimator. The numerator of the contrast test is defined as

$$MS_{CON} = SS_{CON} = \frac{\left(\sum_j c_j \bar{x}_j\right)^2}{\sum_j \dfrac{c_j^2}{n}}$$

EXHIBIT 17–12   **Summary Tables for One-Way ANOVA Example**

Model Summary						
Source		d.f.	Sum of Squares	Mean Square	*F* Value	*p* Value
Model	Airline	2	11644.033	5822.017	28.304	.0001
Residual	Error	57	11724.550	205.694		
Total		59	23368.583			

Factor: Airline.

Dependent: Flight Service Rating 1.

Means Table				
	Count	Mean	Std. Dev.	Std. Error
Delta	20	38.950	14.006	3.132
Lufthansa	20	58.900	15.089	3.374
KLM	20	72.900	13.902	3.108

Scheffé's S Multiple Comparison Procedure					
	Vs.	Diff.	Crit. Diff.	*p* Value	
Delta	Lufthansa	19.950	11.400	.0002	S
	KLM	33.950	11.400	.0001	S
Lufthansa	KLM	14.000	11.400	.0122	S

S = Significantly different at the .05 level.

Significance level: .05.

All data are hypothetical.

where

C_j = the contrast coefficient for the group j

n_j = the number of observations recorded for group j

A contrast is useful for experimental and quasi-experimental designs when the researcher is interested in answering specific questions about a subset of the factor. For example, in a comparison of coffee products, we have a factor with six levels. The levels, blends of coffee, are meaningfully ordered. Assume we are particularly interested in two Central American grown blends and one Colombian blend. Rather than looking at all possible combinations, we can channel the power of the test into fewer degrees of freedom by stating the comparisons of interest. This increases our likelihood of detecting differences if they really exist.

Multiple Comparison Tests.   For the probabilities associated with the contrast test to be properly used in the report of our findings, it is important that the contrast strategy be devised ahead of the testing. In the airline study, we had no theoretical reason for an

EXHIBIT 17–13 Selection of Multiple Comparison Procedures

Test	Pairwise Comparisons	Complex Comparisons	Equal *n*'s Only	Unequal *n*'s	Equal Variances Assumed	Unequal Variances Not Assumed
Fisher LSD	X			X	X	
Bonferroni	X		X	X		
Tukey HSD	X		X		X	
Tukey-Kramer	X			X	X	
Games-Howell	X			X		X
Tamhane T2	X			X		X
Scheffé S		X		X	X	
Brown-Forsythe		X		X		X
Newman-Keuls	X		X		X	
Duncan	X		X		X	
Dunnett's T3						X
Dunnett's C						X

a priori contrast. However, examining the means table (Exhibit 17–12) revealed that the airline means were quite disparate. Comparisons after the results are compared require post hoc tests or pairwise **multiple comparison procedures** to determine which means differ. Range tests find homogeneous subsets of means that are not different from each other. Multiple comparisons test the difference between each pair of means and indicate significantly different group means at an α level of .05, or another level that you specify. Multiple comparison tests use group means and incorporate the MS_{error} term of the F ratio. Together they produce confidence intervals for the population means and a criterion score. Differences between the mean values may be compared.

There are more than a dozen such tests with different optimization goals: maximum number of comparisons, unequal cell size compensation, cell homogeneity, Type I or Type II error reduction, and so forth. The merits of various tests have produced considerable debate among statisticians, leaving the researcher without much guidance for the selection of a test. In Exhibit 17–13, we provide a general guide. For the example in Exhibit 17–12, we chose Scheffé's S. It is a conservative test that is robust to violations of assumptions.[13] The computer calculated the critical difference criterion as 11.4; all the differences between the pairs of means exceed this. The null hypothesis for the Scheffé was tested at the .05 level. Therefore, we can conclude that all combinations of flight service mean scores differ from each other.

While the table in Exhibit 17–12 provides information for understanding the rejection of the one-way null hypothesis and the Scheffé null, in Exhibit 17–14 we use plots for the comparisons. The means plot shows relative differences among the three levels of the factor. The means by standard deviations plot reveals lower variability in the opinions recorded by the hypothetical Delta and KLM passengers. Nevertheless, these two groups are sharply divided on the quality of in-flight service, and that is apparent in the upper plot.

EXHIBIT 17–14   One-Way Analysis of Variance Plots

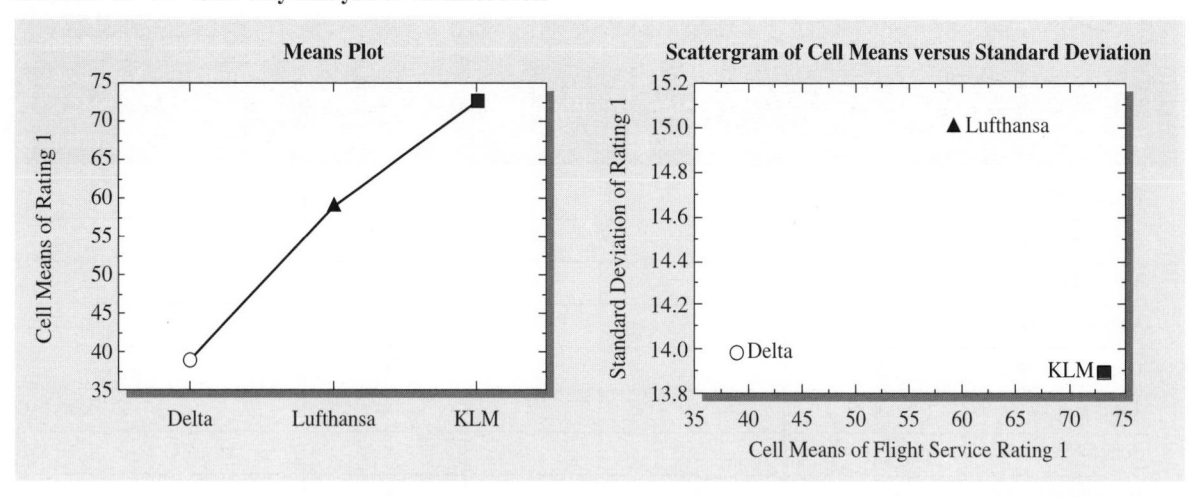

Exploring the Findings with Two-Way ANOVA   Is the airline on which the passengers traveled the only factor influencing perceptions of in-flight service? By extending the one-way ANOVA, we can learn more about the service ratings. There are many possible explanations. We have chosen to look at the seat selection of the travelers in the interest of brevity.

Recall that in Exhibit 17–11, data were entered for the variable seat selection: economy and business-class travelers. Adding this factor to the model, we have a *two-way* analysis of variance. Now three questions may be considered with one model:

- Are differences in flight service ratings attributable to airlines?
- Are differences in flight service ratings attributable to seat selection?
- Do the airline and the seat selection interact with respect to flight service ratings?

The third question reveals a distinct advantage of the two-way model. A separate one-way model on airlines averages out the effects of seat selection. Similarly, a single factor test of seat selection averages out the effects of the airline. But an interaction test of airline by seat selection considers them *jointly.*

Exhibit 17–15 reports a test of the hypotheses for these three questions. The significance level was established at the .01 level. We first inspect the interaction effect, airline by seat selection, since the individual *main effects* cannot be considered separately if factors operate jointly. The interaction was not significant at the .01 level, and the null is accepted. Now the separate main effects, airline and seat selection, can be verified. As with the one-way ANOVA, the null for the airline factor was rejected, and seat selection was also found significant at .0001.

Means and standard deviations listed in the table are plotted in Exhibit 17–16. We note a band of similar deviations for economy-class travelers and a band of lower variability for business class—with the exception of one carrier. The plot of cell means confirms visually what we already know from the summary table: There is no interaction between airline and seat selection ($p = .185$). If an interaction had occurred, the lines connecting the cell means would have crossed rather than displaying a parallel pattern.

Analysis of variance is an extremely versatile and powerful method that may be adapted to a wide range of testing applications. Discussions of further extensions in *n*-way and experimental designs may be found in the list of suggested readings.

EXHIBIT 17–15   **Summary Table for Two-Way ANOVA Example**

Model Summary					
Source	d.f.	Sum of Squares	Mean Square	F Value	p Value
Airline	2	11644.033	5822.017	39.178	.0001
Seat selection	1	3182.817	3182.817	21.418	.0001
Airline by seat selection	2	517.033	258.517	1.740	.1853
Residual	54	8024.700	148.606		

Dependent: Flight Service Rating 1.

Means Table Effect: Airline by Seat Selection				
	Count	Mean	Std. Dev.	Std. Error
Delta economy	10	35.600	12.140	3.839
Delta business	10	42.300	15.550	4.917
Lufthansa economy	10	48.500	12.501	3.953
Lufthansa business	10	69.300	9.166	2.898
KLM economy	10	64.800	13.037	4.123
KLM business	10	81.000	9.603	3.037

All data are hypothetical.

EXHIBIT 17–16   **Two-Way Analysis of Variance Plots**

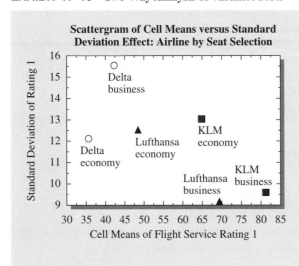

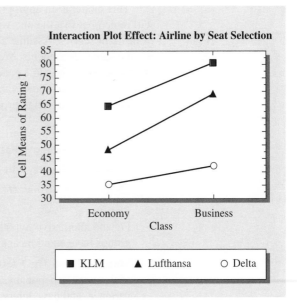

Nonparametric Tests   When there are k independent samples for which nominal data have been collected, the chi-square test is appropriate. It can also be used to classify data at higher measurement levels, but metric information is lost when reduced. The k-sample χ^2 test is an extension of the two independent samples cases treated earlier. It is calculated and interpreted in the same way.

The Kruskal-Wallis test is appropriate for data that are collected on an ordinal scale or for interval data that do not meet F-test assumptions, that cannot be transformed, or that for another reason prove to be unsuitable for a parametric test. Kruskal-Wallis is a one-way analysis of variance by ranks. It assumes random selection and independence of samples and an underlying continuous distribution.

Data are prepared by converting ratings or scores to ranks for each observation being evaluated. The ranks range from the highest to the lowest of all data points in the aggregated samples. The ranks are then tested to decide if they are samples from the same population. An application of this technique is provided in Appendix E.

k Related Samples Case

Parametric Tests   A **k related samples test** is required for situations where (1) the grouping factor has more than two levels, (2) observations or subjects are matched or the same subject is measured more than once, and (3) the data are at least interval. In experimental or ex post facto designs with k samples, it is often necessary to measure subjects several times. These repeated measurements are called **trials.** For example, multiple measurements are taken in studies of stock prices, products evaluated by quality assurance, inventory, sales, and measures of human performance. Hypotheses for these situations may be tested with a univariate or multivariate general linear model. The latter is beyond the scope of this discussion.

The repeated-measures ANOVA is a special type of n-way analysis of variance. In this design, the repeated measures of each subject are related just as they are in the related t-test when only two measures are present. In this sense, each subject serves as its own control requiring a within-subjects variance effect to be assessed differently than the between-groups variance in a factor like airline or seat selection. The effects of the correlated measures are removed before calculation of the F ratio.

This model is an appropriate solution for the data presented in Exhibit 17–11. You will remember that the one-way and two-way examples considered only the first rating of in-flight service. Assume a second rating was obtained after a week by reinterviewing the same respondents. We now have two trials for the dependent variable, and we are interested in the same general question as with the one-way ANOVA, with the addition of how the passage of time affects perceptions of in-flight service.

Following the testing procedure, we state:

1. **Null hypotheses.**

   (1) Airline: H_0: $\mu_{A1} = \mu_{A2} = \mu_{A3}$

   (2) Ratings: H_0: $\mu_{R1} = \mu_{R2}$

   (3) Ratings $\times$ Airline: H_0: $(\mu_{R2A1} - \mu_{R2A2} - \mu_{R2A3})$
   $$= (\mu_{R1A1} - \mu_{R1A2} - \mu_{R1A3})$$

   For the alternative hypotheses, we will generalize to the statement that not all the groups have equal means for each of the three hypotheses.

2. **Statistical test.** The F test for repeated measures is chosen because we have related trials on the dependent variable for k samples, accept the assumptions of analysis of variance, and have interval data.

3. Significance level. Let $\alpha = .05$ and d.f. = [airline (2, 57), ratings (1, 57), ratings by airline (2, 57)].

4. Calculated values. See summary in Exhibit 17–17.

5. Critical test value. Enter Appendix Table F–9, with d.f. (2, 57), $\alpha = .05$ and (1, 57), $\alpha = .05$. The critical values are 3.16 (2, 57) and 4.01 (1, 57).

6. Interpret. The statistical results are grounds for rejecting all three null hypotheses and concluding there are statistically significant differences between means in all three instances. We conclude the perceptions of in-flight service were significantly affected by the different airlines, the interval between the two measures had a significant effect on the ratings, and the measures' time interval and the airlines interacted to a significant degree.

The ANOVA summary table in Exhibit 17–17 records the results of the tests. A means table provides the means and standard deviations for all combinations of ratings

EXHIBIT 17–17 Summary Tables for Repeated-Measures ANOVA

Model Summary					
Source	d.f.	Sum of Squares	Mean Square	F Value	p Value
Airline	2	35527.550	17763.775	67.199	.0001
Subject (group)	57	15067.650	264.345		
Ratings	1	625.633	625.633	14.318	.0004
Ratings by air. . . .	2	2061.717	1030.858	23.592	.0001
Ratings by subj. . . .	57	2490.650	43.696		

Dependent: Flight service ratings 1 and 2.

Means Table Ratings by Airline				
	Count	Mean	Std. Dev.	Std. Error
Rating 1, Delta	20	38.950	14.006	3.132
Rating 1, Lufthansa	20	58.900	15.089	3.374
Rating 1, KLM	20	72.900	13.902	3.108
Rating 2, Delta	20	32.400	8.268	1.849
Rating 2, Lufthansa	20	72.250	10.572	2.364
Rating 2, KLM	20	79.800	11.265	2.519

Means Table Effect: Ratings				
	Count	Mean	Std. Dev.	Std. Error
Rating 1	60	56.917	19.902	2.569
Rating 2	60	61.483	23.208	2.996

All data are hypothetical.

EXHIBIT 17–18   Repeated-Measures ANOVA Plot

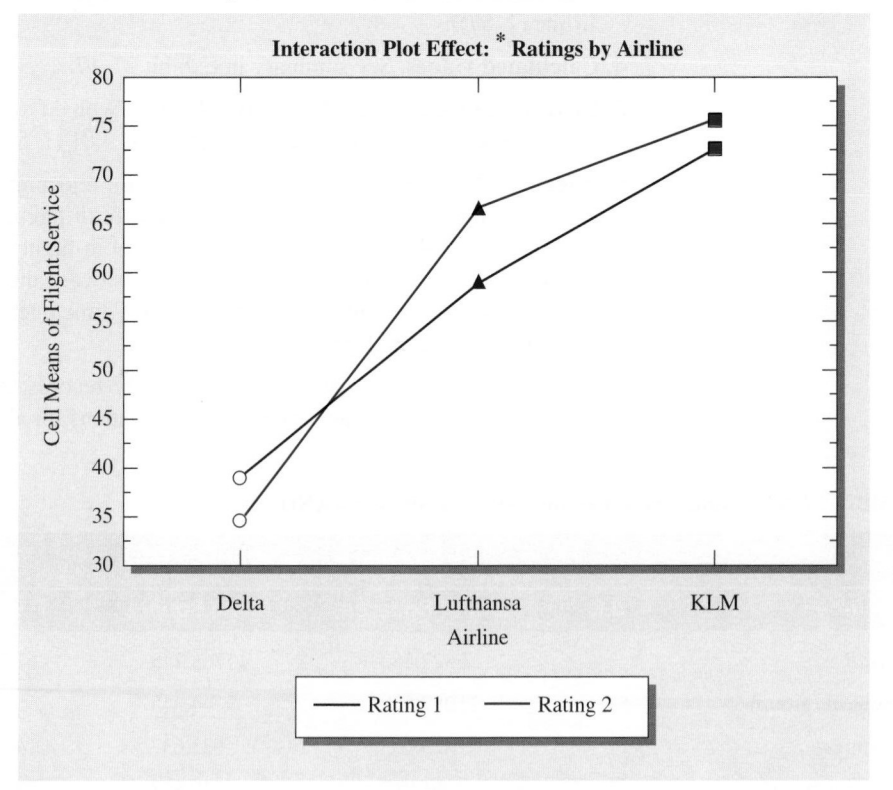

All data are hypothetical.

by airline. A second table of means reports the differences between flight service ratings 1 and 2. In Exhibit 17–18, there is an interaction plot for these data. Note that the second in-flight service rating was improved in two of the three groups after one week, and for the third carrier, there was a decrease in favorable response. The intersecting lines in the interaction plot reflect this finding.

Nonparametric Tests   When the k related samples have been measured on a nominal scale, the Cochran Q test is a good choice.[14] This test extends the McNemar test, discussed earlier, for studies having more than two samples. It tests the hypothesis that the proportion of cases in a category is equal for several related categories.

When the data are at least ordinal, the Friedman two-way analysis of variance is appropriate. It tests matched samples, ranking each case and calculating the mean rank for each variable across all cases. It uses these ranks to compute a test statistic. The product is a two-way table where the rows represent subjects and the columns represent the treatment conditions.[15]

SUMMARY

1

There are two approaches to hypothesis testing—classical or sampling theory statistics and the Bayesian approach. With classical statistics, we make inferences about a population based on evidence gathered from a sample. Although we cannot state unequivo-

cally what is true about the entire population, representative samples allow us to make statements about what is probably true and how much error is likely to be encountered in arriving at a decision. The Bayesian approach also employs sampling statistics but has an additional element of prior information to improve the decision maker's judgment. With prudent use of prior probabilities, the Bayesian approach will also provide good results.

2 A difference between two or more sets of data is statistically significant if it actually occurs in a population. To have a statistically significant finding based on sampling evidence, we must be able to calculate the probability that some observed difference is large enough that there is little chance it could result from random sampling. Probability is the foundation for deciding on the acceptability of the null hypothesis, and sampling statistics facilitate acquiring the estimates.

3 Hypothesis testing can be viewed as a six-step procedure:

1. Establish a null hypothesis as well as the alternative hypothesis. It is a one-tailed test of significance if the alternative hypothesis states the direction of difference. If no direction of difference is given, it is a two-tailed test.

2. Choose the statistical test on the basis of the assumption about the population distribution and measurement level. The form of the data can also be a factor. In light of these considerations, one typically chooses the test that has the greatest power efficiency or ability to reduce decision errors.

3. Select the desired level of confidence. While $\alpha = .05$ is the most frequently used level, many others are also used. The α is the significance level that we desire and is typically set in advance of the study. Alpha or Type I error is the risk of rejecting a true null hypothesis and represents a decision error. The β or Type II error is the decision error that results from accepting a false null hypothesis. Usually, one determines a level of acceptable α error and then seeks to reduce the β error by increasing the sample size, shifting from a two-tailed to a one-tailed significance test, or both.

4. Compute the actual test value of the data.

5. Obtain the critical test value, usually by referring to a table for the appropriate type of distribution.

6. Interpret the result by comparing the actual test value with the critical test value.

4 Parametric and nonparametric tests are applicable under the various conditions described in the chapter. They were also summarized in Exhibit 17–6. Parametric tests operate with interval and ratio data and are preferred when their assumptions can be met. Diagnostic tools examine the data for violations of those assumptions. Nonparametric tests do not require stringent assumptions about population distributions and are useful with less powerful nominal and ordinal measures.

5 In selecting a significance test, one needs to know, at a minimum, the number of samples, their independence or relatedness, and the measurement level of the data. Statistical tests emphasized in the chapter were the Z and t-tests, analysis of variance, and chi-square. The Z and t-tests may be used to test for the difference between two means. The t-test is chosen when the sample size is small. Variations on the t-test are used for both independent and related samples.

One-way analysis of variance compares the means of several groups. It has a single grouping variable, called a factor, and a continuous dependent variable. Analysis of variance (ANOVA) partitions the total variation among scores into between-groups

(treatment) and within-groups (error) variance. The F ratio, the test statistic, determines if the differences are large enough to reject the null hypothesis. ANOVA may be extended to two-way, n-way, repeated measures, and multivariate applications.

Chi-square is a nonparametric statistic that is used frequently for cross-tabulation or contingency tables. Its applications include testing for differences between proportions in populations and testing for independence. Corrections for chi-square were discussed.

KEY TERMS

EXAMPLES

Company	Scenario	Page
American legal system	Correct and incorrect decisions about hypothesis testing are compared to the U.S. legal system's presumption of innocence until guilt is proven.	524
Colgate-Palmolive Co.	Study of toothbrushing ergonomics revealed that some users change their grip more than 100 times during brushing and that thicker-handled brushes promote longer brushing.	539
Containers Inc.	Implementing a smoke-free workplace policy by evaluating the relationship between accidents and smoking.	540
Dean Merrill Brokerage[*]	Testing the effectiveness of two sales training methods for account executive trainees.	539
e-WEAR[*]	Controller of e-commerce division of large retail chain evaluates receivables.	521
Forbes sales data	Testing for significances between two years of sales in 10 companies.	544
The Gillette Co.	Its fatter Oral-B toothbrush for "power grippers" earned complaints from users, as it wouldn't fit in toothbrush holders; further research revealed this was a problem in less than 19 percent of households with built-in holders.	539
K2Sports	A study reveals the effectiveness of a retailers sales associate training program for an in-line skates manufacturer.	538

[*]Due to the confidential and proprietary nature of most research, the names of some companies have been changed.

DISCUSSION QUESTIONS

Terms in Review

1. Distinguish between the following:

   a. Parametric tests and nonparametric tests.

   b. Type I error and Type II error.

   c. Null hypothesis and alternative hypothesis.

   d. Acceptance region and rejection region.

   e. One-tailed tests and two-tailed tests.

   f. Type II error and the power of the test.

2. Summarize the steps of hypothesis testing. What is the virtue of this procedure?

3. In analysis of variance, what is the purpose of the mean square between and the mean square within? If the null hypothesis is accepted, what do these quantities look like?

4. Describe the assumptions for ANOVA, and explain how they may be diagnosed.

Making Research Decisions

5. Suggest situations where the researcher should be more concerned with Type II error than with Type I error.

   a. How can the probability of a Type I error be reduced? A Type II error?

   b. How does practical significance differ from statistical significance?

   c. Suppose you interview all the members of the freshman and senior classes and find that 65 percent of the freshmen and 62 percent of the seniors favor a certain ecological proposal. Is this difference significant?

6. What hypothesis-testing procedure would you use in the following situations?

   a. A test classifies applicants as accepted or rejected. On the basis of data on 200 applicants, we test the hypothesis that success is not related to gender.

b. A production batch of 26 gaskets must be evaluated on thickness specifications: A 3-mm thickness is specified by the quality control department.

c. A company manufactures automobiles at two different facilities. We want to know if the gas mileage is the same for vehicles from both facilities. There are samples of 45 units from each facility.

d. A company has three categories of managers: (1) with professional qualifications but without work experience; (2) with professional qualifications and with work experience; and (3) without professional qualifications but with work experience. A study exists that measures each manager's motivation level (classified as high, normal, and low). A hypothesis of no relation between manager category and motivation is to be tested.

e. A company has 24 salespersons. The test must evaluate whether their sales performance is unchanged or has improved after a training program.

f. A company has to evaluate whether it should attribute increased sales to product quality, advertising, or an interaction of product quality and advertising.

7. You conduct a survey of a sample of 25 members of this year's graduating class and find that the average GPA is 3.2. The standard deviation of the sample is 0.4. Over the last 10 years, the average GPA has been 3.0. Is the GPA of this year's class significantly different from the long-run average? At what alpha level would it be significant?

8. You are curious about whether the professors and students at your school are of different political persuasions. So you take a sample of 20 professors and 20 students drawn randomly from each population. You find that 10 professors say they are conservative and six students say they are conservative. Is this a statistically significant difference?

9. You contact a random sample of 36 graduates of Western University and learn that their starting salaries were $28,000 last year. You then contact a random sample of 40 graduates from Eastern University and find that their average starting salary was $28,800. In each case, the standard deviation of the sample was $1,000.

a. Test the null hypothesis that there is no difference between average salaries received by the graduates of the two schools.

b. What assumptions are necessary for this test?

10. A random sample of students is interviewed to determine if there is an association between class and attitudes toward corporations. With the following results, test the hypothesis that there is no difference among students on this attitude.

	Favorable	Neutral	Unfavorable
Freshmen	100	50	70
Sophomores	80	60	70
Juniors	50	50	80
Seniors	40	60	90

11. You do a survey of business school students and liberal arts school students to find out how many times a week they read a daily newspaper. In each case, you interview 100 students. You find the following:

$X_b = 4.5$ times per week

$s_b = 1.5$

$X_{la} = 5.6$ times per week

$s_{la} = 2.0$

Test the hypothesis that there is no significant difference between these two samples.

12. One-Koat Paint Company has developed a new type of porch paint that it hopes will be the most durable on the market. The R&D group tests the new product against the two leading competing products by using a machine that scrubs until it wears through the coating. One-Koat runs five trials with each product and secures the following results (in thousands of scrubs):

Trial	One-Koat	Competitor A	Competitor B
1	37	34	24
2	30	19	25
3	34	22	23
4	28	31	20
5	29	27	20

Test the hypothesis that there are no differences between the means of these products ($\alpha = .05$).

13. A computer manufacturer is introducing a new product specifically targeted at the home market and wishes to compare the effectiveness of three sales strategies: computer stores, home electronics stores, and department stores. Numbers of sales by 15 salespeople are recorded below:

Electronics store: 5, 4, 3, 3, 3

Department store: 9, 7, 8, 6, 5

Computer store: 7, 4, 8, 4, 3

a. Test the hypothesis that there is no difference between the means of the retailers ($\alpha = .05$).

b. Select a post hoc test, if necessary, to determine which groups differ in mean sales ($\alpha = .05$).

14. A financial analyst is interested in whether there was a significant change in profits for utilities from one period to another. A random sample of 11 companies from the Forbes 500 contributed the following data:

Company	Profits Year 1	Profits Year 2
Ohio Edison	218.9	361.0
Kentucky Utilities	79.4	82.3
PSI Holdings	99.1	125.2
Idaho Power	49.0	84.7
NY State E & G	171.5	157.8
Northeast Utilities	224.8	203.2
Southwestern Public Service	105.0	124.9
Pacific Corp.	446.8	465.6
Scana	120.7	122.6
Puget Sound Power & Light	128.2	117.7
Public Service Colorado	124.9	148.8

a. Should a test of independent or related samples be used?

b. Is there a difference in profits between the two years?

15. The *Fortune* magazine annual list of the 40 richest self-made Americans under the age of 40 (*Fortune,* September 17, 2001), revealed some interesting changes. With the collapse of the dot-coms, the new super-rich from sports and entertainment joined the list.

    a. Devise a grouping variable to classify the companies in the accompanying table (e.g., Internet, computers, celebrities).

    b. Using one-way analysis of variance, test the hypothesis that there is no difference in net worth among the groups.

Rank	Name	Company	Net Worth ($ in millions)
1	Michael Dell	Dell Computer	16,300
2	Pierre Omidyar	eBay	4,390
3	Jeff Skoll	eBay	2,630
4	Ted Waitt	Gateway, Inc.	1,870
5	Jeff Bezos	Amazon.Com, Inc.	1,230
6	Vinny Smith	Quest Software	780
7	David Filo	Yahoo	730
8	Jerry Yang	Yahoo	721
9	Rob Glaser	RealNetworks	635
10	Dan Snyder	Washington Redskins	604
11	Greg Reyes	Brocade Communications Systems	518
12	Jen-Hsun Huang	Nvidia	507
13	Michael Jordan	Washington Wizards	398
14	Joe Liemandt	Trilogy Software	390
15	Jeanette Symons	Zhone Technologies	374
16	Pantas Sutardja	Marvell Technology	363
17	John Schnatter	Papa John's International	293
18	Sanjay Kumar	Computer Associates International, Inc.	270
19	Tom Cruise	Cruise/Wagner Productions	251
20	Percy Miller (Master P)	No Limit	249
21	James T. Demetriades	SeeBeyond Technology	239
22	Sean Combs (P. Diddy)	Bad Boy Entertainment	231
23	Jerry Greenberg	Sapient	225
24	J. Stuart Moore	Sapient	224
25	Sudhakar Ravi	SonicWALL	219
26	Sreekanth Ravi	SonicWALL	219

Rank	Name	Company	Net Worth ($ in millions)
27	David Hitz	Network Appliance	202
28	John L. MacFarlane	Openwave Systems Inc.	198
29	Jeffrey Citron	Vonage	194
30	Raul Fernandez	Dimension Data North America	188
31	Eric Greenberg	Innovation Investments	187
32	Chris Klaus	Internet Security Systems	187
33	Anousheh Ansari	Sonus	180
34	Halsey Minor	12 Entrepreneuring	180
35	Michael Saylor	Microstrategy	180
36	Jim Carrey	Pit Bull Productions	171
37	Jonathan M. Rothberg	CuraGen	168
38	Marc Andreessen	Loudcloud	166
39	Nav Sooch	Silicon Laboratories	162
40	Tiger Woods	ETW	160

16. A consumer testing firm is interested in testing two competing antivirus products for personal computers. It wants to know how many strains of virus will be removed. The data are:

	Removed by Q-Cure?	
Removed by Anti-V?	**Yes**	**No**
Yes	45	33
No	58	20

Are Anti-V and Q-Cure equally effective ($\alpha = .05$)?

17. A researcher for an auto manufacturer is examining preferences for styling features on larger sedans. Buyers were classified as "first-time" and "repeat," resulting in the following table.

	Preference	
	European Styling	**Japanese Styling**
Repeat	40	20
First-time	8	32

a. Test the hypothesis that buying characteristic is independent of styling preference ($\alpha = .05$).

b. Should the statistic be adjusted?

**From Concept
to Practice**

18. Using the data in Exhibit 17–11 for the variables Flight Service Rating 2 and Airline (2, 3), test the hypothesis of no difference between means.

WWW Exercises

Visit our website for Internet exercises related to this chapter at
www.mhhe.com/business/cooper8

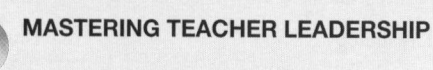
CASES*

HITECH ENGINEERING

**INQUIRING MINDS WANT
TO KNOW—NOW!**

MASTERING TEACHER LEADERSHIP

PERFORMANCE EVALUATIONS

RUBBERGATE

VIOLENCE ON TV

WASTE PAPER

*All cases indicating a video icon are located on the Instructor's Videotape Supplement. All nonvideo cases are in the case section of the textbook. All cases indicating a CD icon offer a data set, which is located on the accompanying CD.

REFERENCE NOTES

1. A more detailed example is found in Amir D. Aczel and Jayauel Sounderpandian, *Complete Business Statistics,* 5th ed. (Chicago: Irwin/McGraw-Hill, 2001).

2. The standardized random variable, denoted by Z, is a deviation from expectancy and is expressed in terms of standard deviation units. The mean of the distribution of a standardized random variable is 0, and the standard deviation is 1. With this distribution, the deviation from the mean by any value of X can be expressed in standard deviation units.

3. Procedures for hypothesis testing are reasonably similar across authors. This outline was influenced by Sidney Siegel, *Nonparametric Statistics for the Behavioral Sciences* (New York: McGraw-Hill, 1956), Chapter 2.

4. Marija J. Norusis/SPSS, Inc., *SPSS for Windows Base System User's Guide, Release 6.0* (Chicago: SPSS, Inc., 1993), pp. 601–06.

5. For further information on these tests, see ibid., pp. 187–88.

6. F. M. Andrews, L. Klem, T. N. Davidson, P. M. O'Malley, and W. L. Rodgers, *A Guide for Selecting Statistical Techniques for Analyzing Social Science Data* (Ann Arbor: Institute for Social Research, University of Michigan, 1976).

7. Statistical Navigator is a product from The Idea Works, Inc.

8. Exhibit 17–7 is partially adapted from Siegel, *Nonparametric Statistics,* flyleaf.

9. See B. S. Everitt, *The Analysis of Contingency Tables* (London: Chapman and Hall, 1977).

10. The critiques are represented by W. J. Conover, "Some Reasons for Not Using the Yates' Continuity Correction on 2×2 Contingency Tables," *Journal of the American Statistical Association* 69 (1974), pp. 374–76; and N. Mantel, "Comment and a Suggestion on the Yates' Continuity Correction," *Journal of the American Statistical Association* 69 (1974), pp. 378–80.

11. This data table and the analysis of variance tables and plots in this section were prepared with SuperANOVA™.

12. See, for example, Roger E. Kirk, *Experimental Design: Procedures for the Behavioral Sciences* (Belmont, CA: Brooks/Cole, 1982), pp. 115–33. An exceptionally clear presentation for step-by-step hand computation is found in James L. Bruning and B. L. Kintz, *Computational Handbook of Statistics,* 2nd ed. (Glenview, IL: Scott, Foresman, 1977), pp. 143–68. Also, when you use a computer program, the reference manual typically provides helpful advice in addition to the set-up instructions.

13. Kirk, *Experimental Design,* pp. 90–115. Alternatively, see Bruning and Kintz, *Computational Handbook of Statistics,* pp. 113–32.

14. For a discussion and example of the Cochran Q test, see Sidney Siegel and N. J. Castellan, Jr., *Nonparametric Statistics for the Behavioral Sciences,* 2nd ed. (New York: McGraw-Hill, 1988).

15. For further details, see Siegel and Castellan, Jr., *Nonparametric Statistics.*

REFERENCES FOR SNAPSHOTS AND CAPTIONS

K2Sports

Michele Marchetti, "Extreme Selling," *Sales and Marketing Management,* October 1, 1999, p. 108.

Amy Buckalter, K2Sports.

http://www.k2sports.com

Mediascope

"New Study Looks at Drugs in Movies and Songs," America Cares, Inc., April 1999 (http://www.americacares.org/drugs_in_movies.htm).

"Substance Use in Popular Movies and Music," Office of National Drug Control Policy, April 1999 (http://www.mediacampaign.org/publications/movies/movie_partIV.html).

Star Signs

"Forget Defensive Driving, Its in the Stars," news release, Suncorp Metway, February 10 2002. For more information contact Warren Duke, national manager, personal insurance, or Catherine Hughes, public affairs (http://corporate.suncorpnetway.com.au/news/news_articles.asp).

Toothbrushes

Mark Maremont, "There's One Cavity New Toothbrushes Just Can't Handle," *The Wall Street Journal,* March 24, 2000, p. 1.

CLASSIC AND CONTEMPORARY READINGS

Aczel, Amir D., and J. Sounderpandian. *Complete Business Statistics.* 5th ed. Chicago: Irwin/McGraw-Hill, 2001. This excellent text is characterized by highly lucid explanations and numerous examples.

Cohen, Jacob. *Statistical Power Analysis for the Behavioral Sciences.* Mahwah, NJ: Lawrence Erlbaum Associates, 1990. A key reference on conducting power analysis.

DeFinetti, Bruno. *Probability, Induction, and Statistics.* New York: Wiley, 1972. A highly readable work on subjective probability and the Bayesian approach.

Kanji, Gopal K. *100 Statistical Tests.* Thousand Oaks, CA: Sage Publications, 1999. Coverage of the most commonly used statistics that students will encounter.

Kirk, Roger E. *Experimental Design: Procedures for the Behavioral Sciences.* 3rd ed. Belmont, CA: Brooks/Cole, 1995. An advanced text on the statistical aspects of experimental design.

Levine, David M., Timothy C. Krehbiel, and Mark L. Berenson. *Business Statistics: A First Course.* Upper Saddle River, NJ: Prentice-Hall, 1999. For students or managers without recent statistical coursework, this text provides an excellent review.

Siegel, Sidney, and N. J. Castellan, Jr. *Nonparametric Statistics for the Behavioral Sciences.* 2nd ed. New York: McGraw-Hill, 1988. The classic book on nonparametric statistics.

Winer, B. J .*Statistical Principles in Experimental Design.* 2nd ed. New York: McGraw-Hill, 1971. Another classic source. Thorough coverage of analysis of variance and experimental design.

CHAPTER 18

Measures of Association

Learning Objectives

After reading this chapter, you should understand . . .

1   How correlation analysis may be applied to study relationships between two or more variables.

2   The uses, requirements, and interpretation of the product moment correlation coefficient.

3   How predictions are made with regression analysis using the method of least squares to minimize errors in drawing a line of best fit.

4   How to test regression models for linearity and whether the equation is effective in fitting the data.

5   The nonparametric measures of association and the alternatives they offer when key assumptions and requirements for parametric techniques cannot be met.

Bringing Research to Life

Myra arrived for an analysis meeting with Jason and found a round, bald little man sitting at Jason's desk, studying the screen of a laptop computer, stroking his gray beard and smiling broadly.

"Myra," said Jason, "meet my Uncle Jack."

"Really? At last I meet the famous—or should I say infamous—uncle? I feared you were imaginary."

"Reports of my being imaginary are greatly exaggerated, if I may paraphrase Mark Twain."

It seemed to her he should have been taller. The ex-biggest painting contractor on Long Island ought to be more ample, she felt. Maybe he had shrunk upon retiring to Florida. Uncle Jack was the kind of unassuming diminutive old fellow who often proved to have money, or power, or both, though no one would have guessed.

Uncle Jack began to rub his laptop computer and grin even more broadly. "I wanted Jason to see that I am taking *good care* of this MindWriter." Myra thought it was a great "box," but what made this one so special?

"This little computer," said Uncle Jack, "has made me the political kingpin of the Boca Beach Condominium Association, Phases One *and* Two. Not to mention all the widows who want to meet with me. Which I had better not mention, as I have only been widowed for a short while and don't want this getting back to my boys on Long Island. I gave the painting business to my three boys and—hey, I'm 75 and deserve some fun—I moved to Boca Raton. For three months I played golf in the morning and sat by the pool and played cards in the afternoon. For three months, seven days, I did this. Do I have to tell you? I was going crazy.

"Then my next-door neighbor Marty 'headed south,' and his wife gave me his MindWriter."

Myra tried to imagine what was south of Florida and why Marty would go there without his wife. Uncle Jack saw the confusion and explained, "She 'planted him,' is what I mean. Do you follow me? He died, he met his 'necessary end,' if I may quote from Julius Caesar. And what was a widow going to do with this computer?

"So now I had a laptop, and what was I going to do with it? Jason came through Boca Raton and copied me a program from his computer, but it was a statistical program, free from the Internet. That's all he had that he could give me without breaking the copyright law, a statistical program from the Internet. And me the guy who had to take statistics three times at Brooklyn College in 1948, to get a lousy C+.

"Something developed pretty soon. We had a dirty guy, Sandy Plover, who had come down from being a big electrical contractor in Jersey and got himself into condo politics. Sandy had not become successful up North without developing a sense of who holds power, what their weaknesses are, and how the politicians agitate the electorate. Being a natural-born troublemaker, he waited for his chance to agitate. Well, the sheriff had launched a statistics-reporting program, and the statistical results had started to come in. Now, it happens there is a creek that divides our condominium into two halves of roughly equal population, Oceanside and Gladeside, the former being slightly tonier. And it further happens that the incidence of arrests resulting from police calls to Oceanside, where he lives, is higher than in Gladeside."

Uncle Jack wrote the following:

H_1: Gladeside residents get special treatment when it comes to solving crimes and thus live in a safer environment due to their higher incomes and greater political power.

H_0: Gladeside and Oceanside receive the same attention from the police.

In Gladeside:

Police calls without arrest	46	
Police calls resulting in arrests	4	50

In Oceanside:

Police calls without arrest	40	
Police calls resulting in arrests	10	50

"I doubt that Sandy would have paid attention, except that in both sides of the condo association the total number of police calls happened to be 50, which made it easy for him to see that in Oceanside the rate of arrests was twice that in Gladeside."

"Actually," said Myra, "I'm surprised there would be any police calls in such a tony condo community."

"We are old," said Uncle Jack, "but not dead.

"In any case, Sandy's finely honed political instincts told him he was going to go nowhere by trying to turn the condo against the sheriff. It would be much, much better, he saw, to try and turn voters of Oceanside against those in Gladeside. And so he decided to complain about the disparate impact of arrests, though being self-educated, he had never heard that expression, 'disparate.' All he knew is that here was an opportunity to make trouble and thereby make a name, because in Oceanside were mostly folks moved down from Brooklyn, and in Gladeside folks from the Bronx, and there was an undercurrent, if you know what I mean."

"But the ethics . . ."

". . . meant nothing to Sandy. He told me, 'I think I am gonna kick some butt and make a name for myself down here.'

"Right away, you can see his strategy. Sandy thought he would make more mileage by whipping our side of the association against the other. This had something to do with his wanting to run in a jurisdiction where elections were not done at large but on a single-district basis, and something to do with his rabble-rousing instincts, which had always been impeccable."

Jason interrupted with a minilecture on the politics of statistics. "The trouble with the police calls as an issue is that sheriffs' offices nowadays are well staffed with statistically educated analysts who know very well how to rebut oddball claims."

"Personally, I miss the old days, when if you worked for the cops, you busted bad guys' heads and never mind statistics. But I understand nowadays you don't mess with crime statistics without one of the pencil-heads rebutting you. So I punched the numbers into this MindWriter here to double-check the stats. I did the obvious first, just what I supposed a police analyst would have done. I ran a cross-tabulation and a chi-square test of the hypothesis that the arrests in Oceanside were disproportionate to those in Gladeside."

"But," said Myra, "you only have to look at the numbers to see they are."

"Yes, but what you have there is the 'eyeball' fallacy, as my dear old professor called it almost 50 years ago. As I explained to Sandy, 100 police encounters resulting in a few arrests is nothing, nada, not a large enough sample to trust a quick peek and a leap to a conclusion. You run it through the computer, and, sure enough, although the ratios seem to be out of whack, they are not statistically significant. You cannot support disparate impact. No way."

Jason said, "Granting that 10 arrests per 50 is bigger than 4 per 50, Uncle Jack saw that a statistician would say that it is not significantly bigger, would say that it is not disproportionate enough to convince a *scientist* that the police were acting differently in the two sides of town. A statistician would say, wait and see, let the story unfold, collect a bigger sample."

"How did Sandy accept your explanation, Jack?"

"Like the mad dog he was. To quote my favorite poet, 'There are chords in the hearts of the most reckless which cannot be touched without emotion.'"

"Emerson?" asked Myra.

"Poe," said Uncle Jack. "Underrated as a poet, overrated as a mystery writer. Well, as for Sandy, he was ready to shoot the messenger, very much bothered, at first, that I would not support his political strategy, and he grumbled that I did not understand such things, that you had to do bad to do good, which I am not sure I agree with, and that I was maybe too much overeducated to ever understand the need just to get on with investigating issues. Me, overeducated, an English major!

"But I was not interested in right and wrong, I said, and he could be pretty sure the sheriff would come roaring back with a statistical analysis to throw cold water over Sandy."

"Did you bring him around?"

"That jerk, come around? Never. He ran to the papers, they splashed his numbers all over the third page of the local section on Monday, and Tuesday the sheriff came back with his experts and made Sandy look like a fool . . . except that it was a slow news day on Tuesday and the paper gave the story plenty of ink, on page one, if you can believe it. So Sandy was washed up, and I am now the resident genius. What I do is look at the opponents' polling results and deny their validity for the newspapers and TV. If the opposing party is ahead by a few poll points, I scoff at the thinness of the margin. If their lead is wide, I belittle the size of the sample and intimate that any statistician would see through them."

Jason provided the scholarly footnote. "Uncle Jack is colorful, amusing, and good-natured in debunking his opponents' polls, and the newspaper writers, who understand less statistics than anyone, have never challenged him to substantiate his claims. What he learned from me is that statistics is so complicated, and scares so many people, that you can claim or deny anything. And he is usually right to debunk the polls, since for a preelection political poll to be taken seriously there has to be a large enough sample to produce significant results. And there has to be a big enough spread between winners and losers to protect against a last-minute shift in voter sentiment. In the small, closely contested voting precincts of condominium politics, hardly any poll can meet two such stringent criteria."

"Right, Jason. I sit in the clubhouse and people come over and want to know what I think about the Middle East, campaign reform, everything. When you have a computer, to paraphrase Tevya, 'they think you really know.'"

Introduction

You might want to review our discussion of relational hypotheses in Chapter 2.

In the previous chapter, we emphasized testing hypotheses of *difference*. However, management questions in business frequently revolve around the study of relationships between two or more variables. Then, a *relational hypothesis* is necessary. In the research question "Are U.S. kitchen appliances perceived by American consumers to be of better quality than foreign kitchen appliances?" the nature of the relationship between the two variables ("country of origin" and "perceived quality") is not specified. The implication, nonetheless, is that one variable is responsible for the other. A correct relational hypothesis for this question would state that the variables occur together in some specified manner without implying that one causes the other.

Various objectives are served with correlation analysis. The strength, direction, shape, and other features of the relationship may be discovered. Or tactical and strategic questions may be answered by predicting the values of one variable from those of another. Let's look at some typical management questions:

- In the mail-order business, excessive catalog costs quickly squeeze margins. Many mailings fail to reach receptive or active buyers. What is the relationship between various categories of mailings that delete inactive customers and the improvement in profit margins?

- Medium-sized companies often have difficulty attracting the cream of the MBA crop, and when they are successful, they have trouble retaining them. What is the relationship between the ranking of candidates based on executive interviews and the ranking obtained from testing and assessment?

- Retained cash flow, undistributed profits plus depreciation, is a critical source of funding for equipment investment. During a period of decline, capital spending suffers. What is the relationship between retained cash flow and equipment investment over the last year? Between cash flow and dividend growth?

- Aggressive U.S. high-tech companies have invested heavily in the European chip market, and their sales have grown 20 percent over the three largest European firms. Can we predict next year's sales based on present investment?

All these questions may be evaluated by means of measures of association. And all call for different techniques based on the level at which the variables were measured or the intent of the question. The first three use nominal, ordinal, and interval data, respectively. The last one is answered through simple bivariate regression.

With correlation, one calculates an index to measure the nature of the relationship between variables. With regression, an equation is developed to predict the values of a dependent variable. Both are affected by the assumptions of measurement level and the distributions that underlie the data.

Exhibit 18–1 lists some common measures and their uses. The chapter follows the progression of the exhibit, first covering bivariate linear correlation, then simple regression, and concluding with nonparametric measures of association. Exploration of data through visual inspection and diagnostic evaluation of assumptions continues to be emphasized.

Bivariate Correlation Analysis

Bivariate correlation analysis differs from nonparametric measures of association and regression analysis in two important ways. First, parametric correlation requires two continuous variables measured on an interval or ratio scale. Second, the coefficient does not distinguish between independent and dependent variables. It treats the variables symmetrically since the coefficient r_{xy} has the same interpretation as r_{yx}.

Pearson's Product Moment Coefficient r

The **Pearson** (product moment) **correlation coefficient** varies over a range of +1 through 0 to –1. The designation r symbolizes the coefficient's estimate of linear association based on sampling data. The coefficient ρ represents the population correlation.

Correlation coefficients reveal the magnitude and direction of relationships. The *magnitude* is the degree to which variables move in unison or opposition. The size of a correlation of +.40 is the same as one of –.40. The sign says nothing about size. The degree of correlation is modest. The coefficient's sign signifies the *direction* of the relationship. Direction tells us whether large values on one variable are associated with large values on the other (and small values with small values). When the values correspond in this way, the two variables have a positive relationship: As one increases, the other also increases. Family income, for example, is positively related to household

EXHIBIT 18–1   Commonly Used Measures of Association

Measurement	Coefficient	Comments and Uses
Interval and Ratio	**Pearson (product moment) correlation coefficient**	For continuous linearly related variables.
	Correlation ratio (eta)	For nonlinear data or relating a main effect to a continuous dependent variable.
	Biserial	One continuous and one dichotomous variable with an underlying normal distribution.
	Partial correlation	Three variables; relating two with the third's effect taken out.
	Multiple correlation	Three variables; relating one variable with two others.
	Bivariate linear regression	Predicting one variable from another's scores.
Ordinal	**Gamma**	Based on concordant-discordant pairs: $(P - Q)$; proportional reduction in error (PRE) interpretation.
	Kendall's tau b	$P - Q$ based; adjustment for tied ranks.
	Kendall's tau c	$P - Q$ based; adjustment for table dimensions.
	Somers's d	$P - Q$ based; asymmetrical extension of gamma.
	Spearman's rho	Product moment correlation for ranked data.
Nominal	**Phi**	Chi-square (CS) based for 2×2 tables.
	Cramer's V	CS based; adjustment when one table dimension > 2.
	Contingency coefficient C	CS based; flexible data and distribution assumptions.
	Lambda	PRE-based interpretation.
	Goodman & Kruskal's tau	PRE-based with table marginals emphasis.
	Uncertainty coefficient	Useful for multidimensional tables.
	Kappa	Agreement measure.

food expenditures. As income increases, food expenditures increase. Other variables are inversely related. Large values on the first variable are associated with small values on the second (and vice versa). The prices of products and services are inversely related to their scarcity. In general, as products decrease in available quantity, their prices rise. The absence of a relationship is expressed by a coefficient of approximately zero.

Scatterplots for Exploring Relationships

Scatterplots are essential for understanding the relationships between variables. They provide a means for visual inspection of data that a list of values for two variables cannot. Both the direction and the shape of a relationship are conveyed in a plot. With a little practice, the magnitude of the relationship can be seen.

EXHIBIT 18–2   **Scatterplots of Correlations between Two Variables**

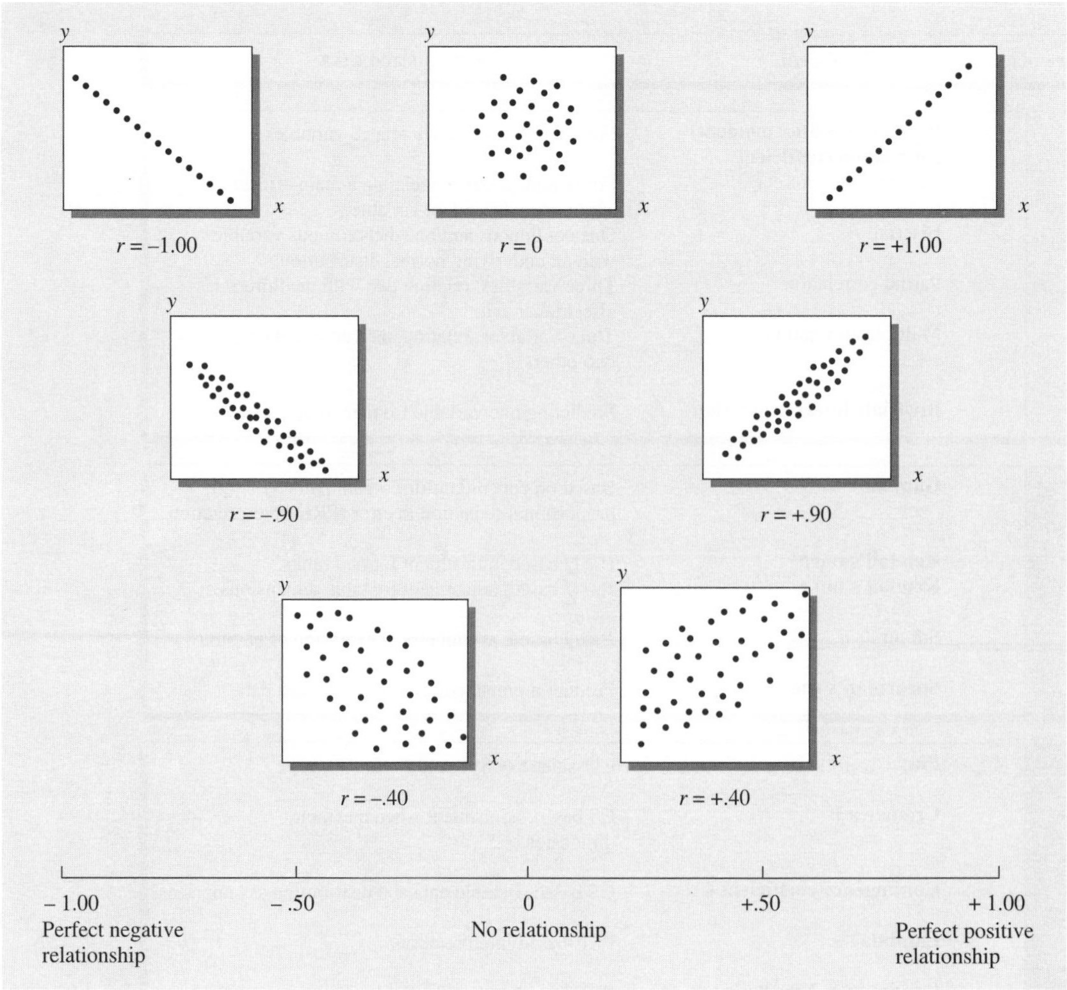

MANAGEMENT
Tip

Exhibit 18–2 contains a series of scatterplots that depict some relationships across the range *r*. The three plots on the left side of the figure have their points sloping from the upper left to the lower right of each *x–y* plot.[1] They represent different magnitudes of negative relationships. On the right side of the figure, three plots have opposite patterns and show positive relationships.

When stronger relationships are apparent (for example, the ±.90 correlations), the points cluster close to an imaginary straight line passing through the data. The weaker relationships (±.40) depict a more diffuse data cloud with points spread farther from the line.

The shape of linear relationships is characterized by a straight line, whereas nonlinear relationships have curvilinear, parabolic, and compound curves representing their shapes. Pearson's *r* measures relationships in variables that are linearly related. It cannot distinguish linear from nonlinear data. Summary statistics alone do not reveal the appropriateness of the data for the model, as the following example illustrates.

One author constructed four small data sets possessing identical summary statistics but displaying strikingly different patterns.[2] Exhibit 18–3 contains these data and Exhibit 18–4 plots them. In Plot 1 of the figure, the variables are positively related.

EXHIBIT 18–3 Four Data Sets with the Same Summary Statistics

S_s	X_1	Y_1	X_2	Y_2	X_3	Y_3	X_4	Y_4
1	10	8.04	10	9.14	10	7.46	8	6.58
2	8	6.95	8	8.14	8	6.77	8	5.76
3	13	7.58	13	8.74	13	12.74	8	7.71
4	9	8.81	9	8.77	9	7.11	8	8.84
5	11	8.33	11	9.26	11	7.81	8	8.47
6	14	9.96	14	8.10	14	8.84	8	7.04
7	6	7.24	6	6.13	6	6.08	8	5.25
8	4	4.26	4	3.10	4	5.39	19	12.50
9	12	10.84	12	9.13	12	8.15	8	5.56
10	7	4.82	7	7.26	7	6.42	8	7.91
11	5	5.68	5	4.74	5	5.73	8	6.89
Pearson's r	.81642		.81624		.81629		.81652	
r^2	.66654		.66624		.66632		.66671	
Adjusted r^2	.62949		.62916		.62925		.62967	
Standard error	1.23660		1.23721		1.23631		1.23570	

EXHIBIT 18–4 Different Scatterplots for the Same Summary Statistics

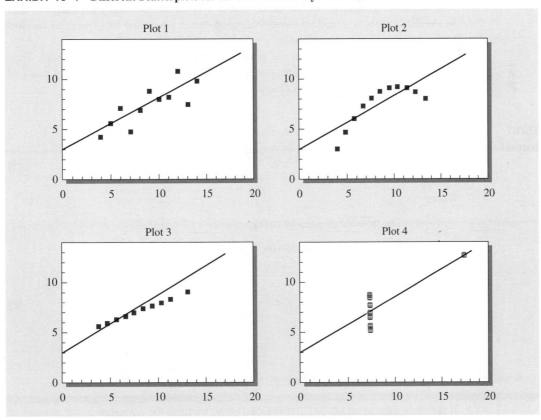

Their points follow a superimposed straight line through the data. This example is well suited to correlation analysis. In Plot 2, the data are curvilinear in relation to the line, and r is an inappropriate measure of their relationship. Plot 3 shows the presence of an influential point that changed a coefficient that would have otherwise been a perfect +1.0. The last plot displays constant values of x (similar to what you might find in an animal or quality-control experiment). One leverage point establishes the fitted line for these data.

We will return to these concepts and the process of drawing the line when we discuss regression. For now, comparing Plots 2 through 4 with Plot 1 suggests the importance of visually inspecting correlation data for underlying patterns. Careful analysts make scatterplots an integral part of the inspection and exploration of their data. Although small samples may be plotted by hand, statistical software packages save time and offer a variety of plotting procedures.

The Assumptions of r

Like other parametric techniques, correlation analysis makes certain assumptions about the data. Many of these assumptions are necessary to test hypotheses about the coefficient.

The first requirement for r is **linearity.** All of the examples in Exhibit 18–2 with the exception of $r = 0$ illustrate a relationship between variables that can be described by a straight line passing through the data cloud. When $r = 0$, no pattern is evident that could be described with a single line. Parenthetically, it is also possible to find coefficients of 0 where the variables are highly related but in a nonlinear form. As we have seen, plots make such findings evident.

The second assumption for correlation is a **bivariate normal distribution**—that is, the data are from a random sample of a population where the two variables are normally distributed in a joint manner.

Often these assumptions or the required measurement level cannot be met. Then the analyst should select a nonlinear or nonparametric measure of association, many of which are described later in this chapter.

Computation and Testing of r

The formula for calculating Pearson's r is

$$r = \frac{\Sigma(X - \bar{X})(Y - \bar{Y})}{(N - 1)s_x s_y} \tag{1}$$

where

N = The number of pairs of cases.

s_x, s_y = The standard deviations for X and Y.

Alternatively,

$$r = \frac{\Sigma xy}{\sqrt{(\Sigma x^2)(\Sigma y^2)}} \tag{2}$$

since

$$s_x = \sqrt{\frac{\Sigma x^2}{N}} \quad s_y = \sqrt{\frac{\Sigma y^2}{N}}$$

If the numerator of equation (2) is divided by N, we have the *covariance,* the amount of deviation that the X and Y distributions have in common. With a positive covariance, the

EXHIBIT 18–5   Computation of Pearson's Product Moment Correlation

Corporation	Net Profits ($ mil.) X	Cash Flow ($ mil.) Y	Deviations from Means				
			$(X - \bar{X})x$	$(Y - \bar{Y})y$	xy	x^2	y^2
1	82.6	126.5	–93.84	–178.64	16763.58	8805.95	31912.25
2	89.0	191.2	–87.44	–113.94	9962.91	7645.75	12982.32
3	176.0	267.0	–0.44	–38.14	16.78	0.19	1454.66
4	82.3	137.1	–94.14	–168.04	15819.29	8862.34	28237.44
5	413.5	806.8	237.06	501.66	118923.52	56197.44	251602.56
6	18.1	35.2	158.34	–269.94	42742.30	25071.56	72867.60
7	337.3	425.5	160.86	120.36	19361.11	25875.94	14486.53
8	145.8	380.0	–30.64	74.86	–2293.71	938.81	5604.02
9	172.6	326.6	–3.84	21.36	–82.02	14.75	456.25
10	247.2	355.5	70.76	50.36	3563.47	5006.98	2536.13
	$\bar{X} = 176.44$	$\bar{Y} = 305.14$			$\Sigma xy = 224777.23$		
	$s_x = 216.59$	$s_y = 124.01$				$\Sigma x^2 = 138419.71$	
							$\Sigma y^2 = 422139.76$

variables move in unison; with a negative one, they move in opposition. When the covariance is 0, there is no relationship. The denominator for equation (2) represents the maximum potential variation that the two distributions share. Thus, correlation may be thought of as a ratio.

Exhibit 18–5 contains a random subsample of 10 firms of the Forbes 500 sample. The variables chosen to illustrate the computation of r are cash flow and net profits. Beneath each variable is its mean and standard deviation. In columns 4 and 5 we obtain the deviations of the X and Y values from their means, and in column 6 we find the product. Columns 7 and 8 are the squared deviation scores.

Substituting into the formula, we get

$$r = \frac{224777.23}{\sqrt{138419.71} * \sqrt{422139.76}} = .9298$$

In this subsample, net profits and cash flow are positively related and have a very high coefficient. As net profits increase, cash flow increases; the opposite is also true. Linearity of the variables may be examined with a scatterplot such as the one shown in Exhibit 18–6. The data points fall along a straight line.

Common Variance as an Explanation   The amount of common variance in X (net profits) and Y (cash flow) may be summarized by r^2, the **coefficient of determination.** As Exhibit 18–7 shows, the overlap between the two variables is the proportion of their common or shared variance.

EXHIBIT 18–6   Plot of Forbes 500 Net Profits with Cash Flow

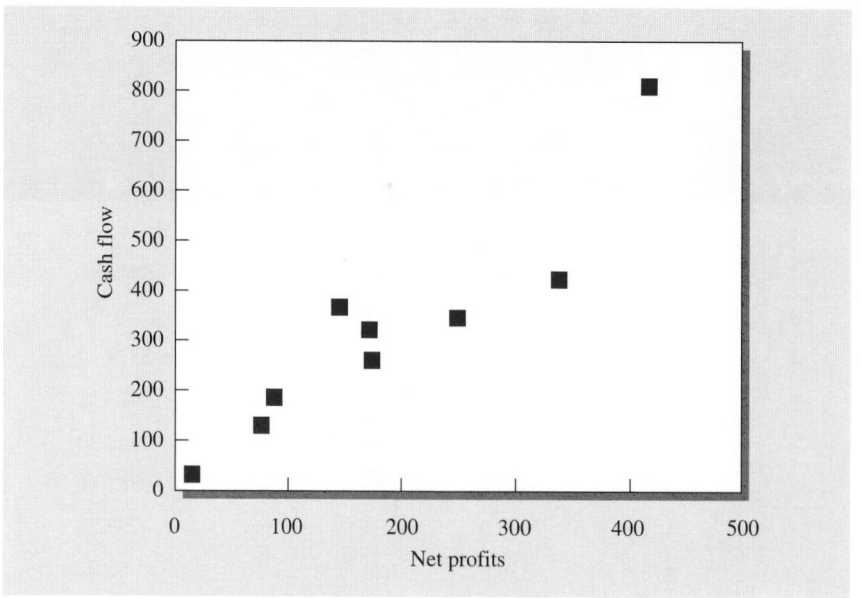

EXHIBIT 18–7   Diagram of Common Variance

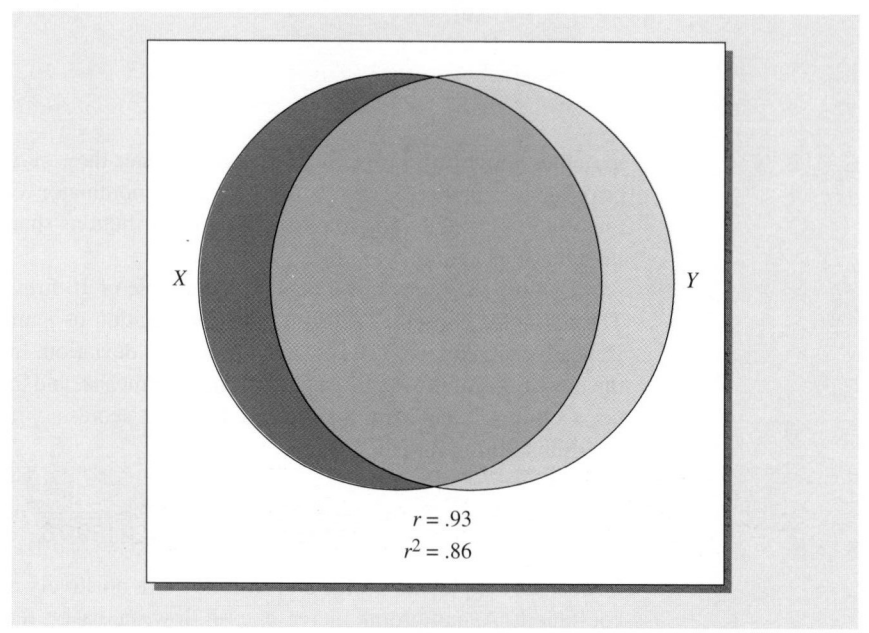

$r = .93$
$r^2 = .86$

The area of overlap represents the percentage of the total relationship accounted for by one variable or the other. So 86 percent of the variance in X is explained by Y, and vice versa.

Testing the Significance of r Is the coefficient representing the relationship between net profits and cash flow real, or does it occur by chance? This question tries to discover whether our r is a chance deviation from a population p of zero. In other situations, the researcher may wish to know if significant differences exist between two or more rs. In either case, r's significance should be checked before r is used in other calculations or comparisons. For this test, we must have independent random samples from a bivariate normal distribution. Then the Z or t-test may be used for the null hypothesis, $p = 0$.

The formula for small samples is

$$t = \frac{r}{\sqrt{\dfrac{1 - r^2}{n - 2}}}$$

where

$r = .93$

$n = 10$

Substituting into the equation, we calculate t:

$$t = \frac{.93}{\sqrt{\dfrac{1 - .86}{8}}} = 7.03$$

With $n - 2$ degrees of freedom, the statistical program calculates the value of t (7.03) at a probability less than .005 for the one-tailed alternative, $H_A: \rho > 0$. We reject the hypothesis that there is no linear relationship between net profits and cash flow in the population. The above statistic is appropriate when the null hypothesis states a correlation of 0. It should be used only for a one-tailed test.[3] However, it is often difficult to know in advance whether the variables are positively or negatively related, particularly when a computer removes our contact with the raw data. Software programs produce two-tailed tests for this eventuality. The observed significance level for a one-tailed test is half of the printed two-tailed version in most programs.

Correlation Matrix A **correlation matrix** is a table used to display coefficients for more than two variables. Exhibit 18–8 shows the intercorrelations among six variables for the full Forbes 500 data set.[4]

EXHIBIT 18–8 **Correlation Matrix for Forbes 500 Sample**

	Assets ($ mil.)	Cash Flow ($ mil.)	Number Employed (thousands)	Market Value ($ mil.)	Net Profits ($ mil.)	Sales ($ mil.)
Assets	1.0000					
Cash flow	.3426	1.0000				
Employed	.3898	.8161	1.0000			
Market value	.3642	.9353	.8106	1.0000		
Net profits	.2747	.9537	.7467	.9101	1.0000	
Sales	.5921	.7990	.8831	.7485	.7261	1.0000

Notes: All coefficients are statistically significant, $p < .01$.

$n = 100$.

It is conventional for a symmetrical matrix to report findings in the triangle below the diagonal. The diagonal contains coefficients of 1.00 that signify the relationship of each variable with itself. Journal articles and management reports often show matrices with coefficients at different probability levels. A symbol beside the coefficient keys the description of differences to a legend. The practice of reporting tests of the null hypothesis, $r = 0$, was followed in Exhibit 18–8.

Correlation matrices have utility beyond bivariate correlation studies. Interdependence among variables is a common characteristic of most multivariate techniques. Matrices form the basis for computation and understanding of the nature of relationships in multiple regression, discriminant analysis, factor analysis, and many others. Such applications call for variations on the standard matrix. Pooled within-groups covariance matrices average the separate covariances for several groups and array the results as coefficients. Total or overall correlation matrices treat coefficients as if they came from a single sample.

Interpretation of Correlations

You might want to review the nature of causation in Chapter 6.

A correlation coefficient of any magnitude or sign, whatever its statistical significance, does not imply causation. Increased net profits may cause an increase in market value, or improved satisfaction may cause improved performance in certain situations, but correlation provides no evidence of cause and effect. Several alternate explanations may be provided for correlation results:

- *X* causes *Y.*
- *Y* causes *X.*
- *X* and *Y* are activated by one or more other variables.
- *X* and *Y* influence each other reciprocally.

Ex post facto studies seldom possess sufficiently powerful designs to demonstrate which of these conditions could be true. By controlling variables under an experimental design, we may obtain more rigorous evidence of causality.

MANAGEMENT
Tip

Take care to avoid so-called **artifact correlations,** where distinct groups combine to give the impression of one. The upper panel of Exhibit 18–9 shows data from two business sectors. If all the data points for the *X* and *Y* variables are aggregated and a correlation is computed for a single group, a positive correlation results. Separate calculations for each sector (note that points for Sector A form a circle, as do points for Sector B) reveal *no* relationship between the *X* and *Y* variables. A second example shown in the lower panel contains a plot of data on assets and sales. We have enclosed and highlighted the data for the financial sector. This is shown as a narrow band enclosed by an ellipse. These companies score high on assets and low in sales—all are banks. When the data for banks are removed and treated separately, the correlation is nearly perfect (.99). When banks are returned to the sample and the correlation is recalculated, the overall relationship drops to the mid-.80s. In short, data hidden or nested within an aggregated set may present a radically different picture.

Another issue affecting interpretation of coefficients concerns practical significance. Even when a coefficient is statistically significant, it must be practically meaningful. In many relationships, other factors combine to make the coefficient's meaning misleading. For example, in nature we expect rainfall and the height of reservoirs to be positively correlated. But in states where water management and flood control mechanisms are complex, an apparently simple relationship may not hold. Techniques like partial and multiple correlation or multiple regression are helpful in sorting out confounding effects.

EXHIBIT 18–9   **Artifact Correlations**

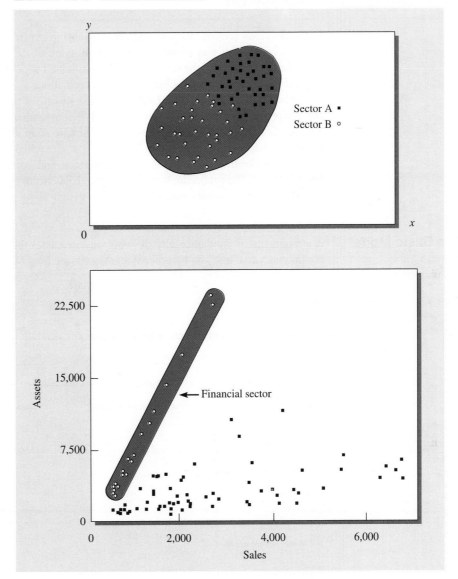

With large samples, even exceedingly low coefficients can be statistically significant. This "significance" only reflects the likelihood of a linear relationship in the population. Should magnitudes less than .30 be reported when they are significant? It all
depends. We might consider the correlations between variables such as cash flow, sales,
market value, or net profits to be interesting revelations of a particular phenomenon
whether they were high, moderate, or low. The nature of the study, the characteristics of
the sample, or other reasons will be determining factors. But a coefficient is not remarkable simply because it is statistically significant.

By probing the evidence of direction, magnitude, statistical significance, and common variance together with the study's objectives and limitations, we reduce the
chances of reporting trivial findings. Simultaneously, the communication of practical
implications to the reader will be improved.

Bivariate Linear Regression[5]

In the previous section, we focused on relationships between variables. The product moment correlation was found to represent an index of the magnitude of the relationship, the sign governed the direction, and r^2 explained the common variance. Relationships also serve as a basis for estimation and prediction.

When we take the observed values of X to estimate or predict corresponding Y values, the process is called *simple prediction.*[6] When more than one X variable is used, the outcome is a function of multiple predictors. Simple and multiple predictions are made with a technique called **regression analysis.**

The similarities and differences of regression and correlation are summarized in Exhibit 18–10. Their relatedness would suggest that beneath many correlation problems is a regression analysis that could provide further insight about the relationship of Y with X.

The Basic Model

A straight line is fundamentally the best way to model the relationship between two continuous variables. The bivariate linear regression may be expressed as

$$Y = \beta_0 + \beta_1 X_i$$

EXHIBIT 18–10   Comparison of Bivariate Linear Correlation and Regression

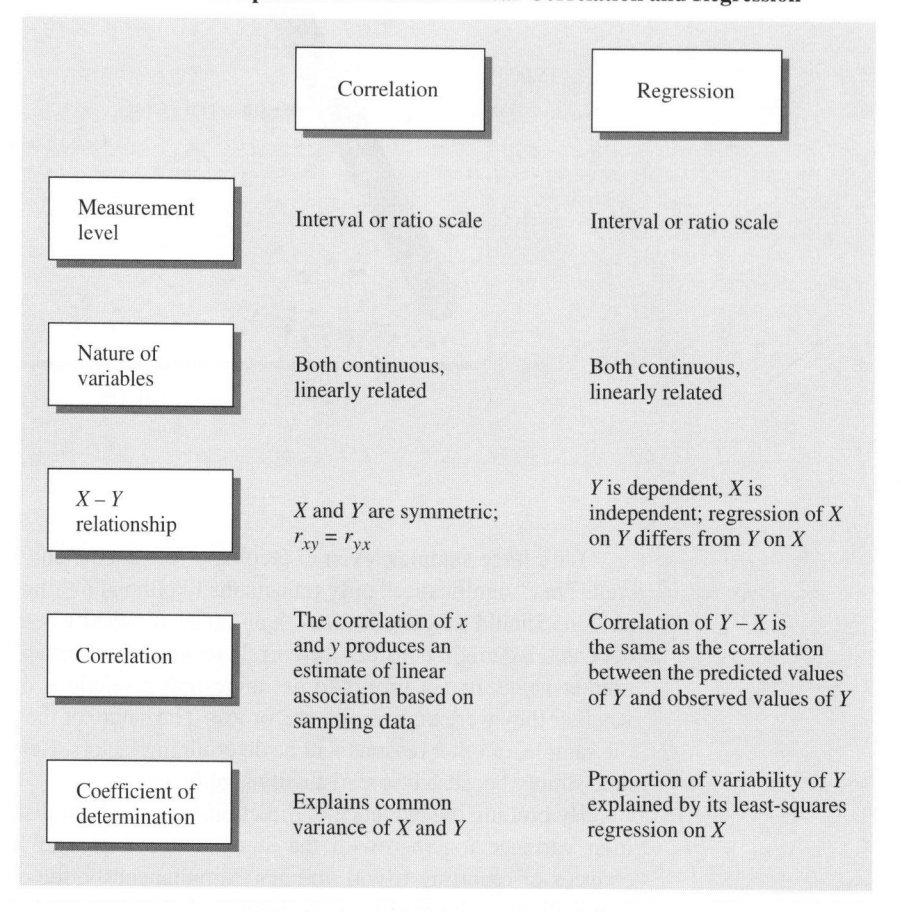

	Correlation	Regression
Measurement level	Interval or ratio scale	Interval or ratio scale
Nature of variables	Both continuous, linearly related	Both continuous, linearly related
$X - Y$ relationship	X and Y are symmetric; $r_{xy} = r_{yx}$	Y is dependent, X is independent; regression of X on Y differs from Y on X
Correlation	The correlation of x and y produces an estimate of linear association based on sampling data	Correlation of $Y - X$ is the same as the correlation between the predicted values of Y and observed values of Y
Coefficient of determination	Explains common variance of X and Y	Proportion of variability of Y explained by its least-squares regression on X

where the value of the dependent variable Y is a linear function of the corresponding value of the independent variable X_i in the ith observation. The slope, β_1, and the Y intercept, β_0, are known as **regression coefficients.** The **slope,** β_1, is the change in Y for a one-unit change in X. It is sometimes called the "rise over run." This is defined by the formula

$$\beta_1 = \frac{\Delta Y}{\Delta X}$$

This is the ratio of change (Δ) in the rise of the line relative to the run or travel along the X axis. Exhibit 18–11 shows a few of the many possible slopes you may encounter.

The **intercept,** β_0, is the value for the linear function when it crosses the Y axis; it is the estimate of Y when $X = 0$. A formula for the intercept based on the mean scores of the X and Y variables is

$$\beta_0 = \bar{Y} - \beta_1 \bar{X}$$

Concept Application

The price of investment-grade red wine is influenced in several ways, not the least of which is tasting. Tasting from the barrel is a major determinant of market *en primeur* or futures contracts, which represent about 60 percent of the harvest. After the wine rests for 18 to 24 months in oak casks, further tasting occurs, and the remaining stock is released.

Weather is widely regarded as responsible for pronouncements about wine quality. A Princeton economist has elaborated on that notion. He suggested that just a few facts about local weather conditions may be better predictors of vintage French red wines than the most refined palates and noses.[7] The regression model developed predicts an auction price index for about 80 wines from winter and harvest rainfall amounts and average growing-season temperatures. Interestingly, the calculations suggested that the 1989 Bordeaux would be one of the best since 1893. The "guardians of tradition" reacted hysterically to these methods yet agreed with the conclusion.

EXHIBIT 18–11 Examples of Different Slopes

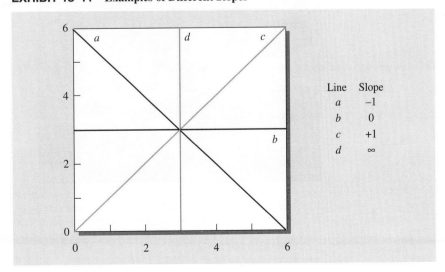

Line	Slope
a	−1
b	0
c	+1
d	∞

Our first example will use one predictor with highly simplified data. Let X represent the average growing-season temperature in degrees Celsius and Y the price of a 12-bottle case in French francs. The data appear below.

X Average Temperature Celsius	Y Price per Case (FF)
12	2000
16	3000
20	4000
24	5000
$\bar{X} = 18$	$\bar{Y} = 3500$

The plotted data in Exhibit 18–12 show a linear relationship between the pairs of points and a perfect positive correlation, $r_{yx} = 1.0$. The slope of the line is calculated:

$$\beta_1 = \frac{Y_i - Y_j}{X_i - X_j} = \frac{4000 - 3000}{20 - 16} = \frac{1000}{4} = 250$$

where the X_iY_i values are the data points (20, 4000) and X_jY_j are points (16, 3000). The intercept β_0 is –1000, the point at which $X = 0$ in this plot. This area is off the graph and appears in an insert on the figure.

$$\beta_0 = \bar{Y} - \beta_1\bar{X} = 3500 - 250\,(18) = -1000$$

Substituting into the formula, we have the simple regression equation

$$Y = -1000 + 250\,X_i$$

France's Bordeaux Business School offers a master of business administration in the wine sector. Surprised? Business schools throughout Europe are increasingly tailoring their programs with innovative degrees that respond to the changing environment of business. In addition to wine, MBA specializations focus on the music industry, luxury brands, sports management, agribusiness, e-business, consulting, and public-sector specialities.
www.iht.com

EXHIBIT 18–12 **Plot of Wine Price by Average Growing Temperature**

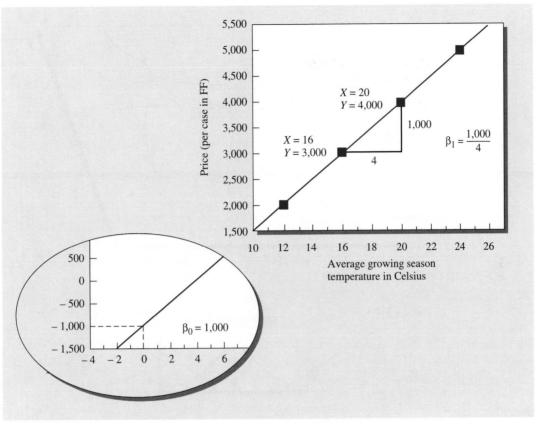

We could now predict that a warm growing season with 25.5°C temperature would bring a case price of 5375 French francs. $\hat{Y}$ (called Y-hat) is the predicted value of Y.

$$\hat{Y} = -1000 + 250(25.5) = 5375$$

Unfortunately, one rarely comes across a data set composed of four paired values, a perfect correlation, and an easily drawn line. A model based on such data is *deterministic* in that for any value of X, there is only one possible corresponding value of Y. It is more likely that we will collect data where the values of Y vary for each X value. Considering Exhibit 18–13, we should expect a distribution of price values for the temperature X = 16, another for X = 20, and another for *each* value of X. The means of these Y distributions will also vary in some systematic way with X. These variabilities lead us to construct a *probabilistic* model that also uses a linear function.[8] This function is written

$$Y_i = \beta_0 + \beta_1 X_i + \varepsilon_1$$

where ε symbolizes the deviation of the ith observation from the mean, $\beta_0 + \beta_1 X_i$.

As shown in Exhibit 18–13, the actual values of Y may be found above or below the regression line represented by the mean value of Y ($\beta_0 + \beta_1 X_i$) for a particular value of X. These deviations are the error in fitting the line and are often called the **error term.**

EXHIBIT 18–13   Distribution of Y for Observations of X

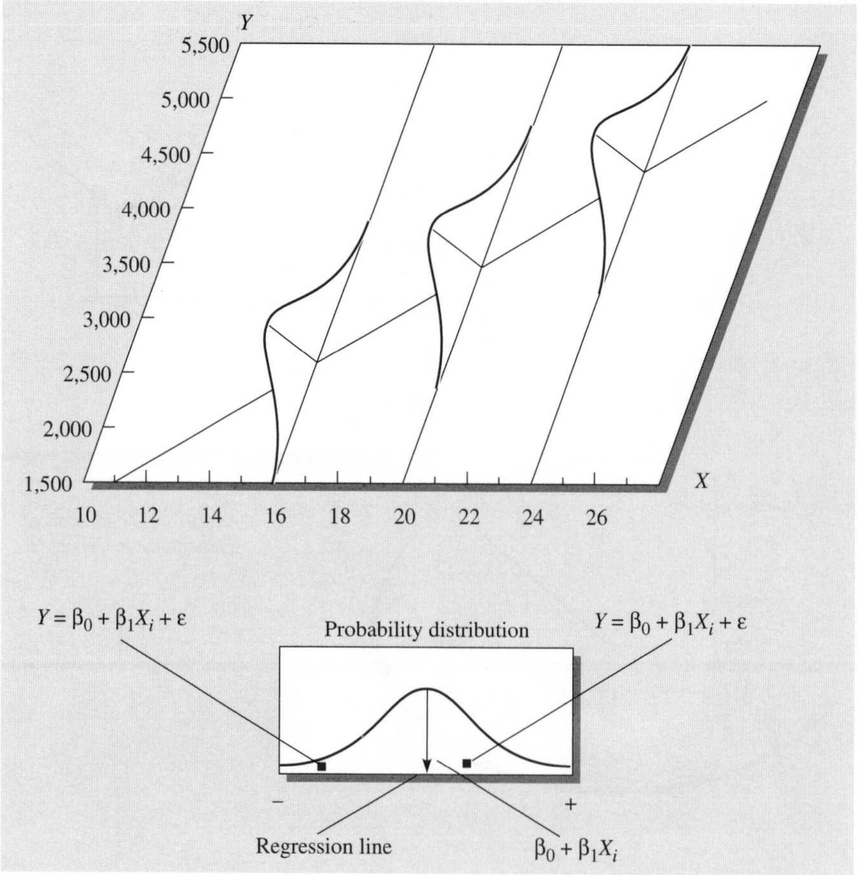

Method of Least Squares

Exhibit 18–14 contains a new data set for the wine price example. Our prediction of Y from X must now account for the fact that the X and Y pairs do not fall neatly along the line. Actually, the relationship could be summarized by several lines. Exhibit 18–15 suggests a few alternatives based on visual inspection—all of which produce errors, or vertical distances from the observed values to the line. The **method of least squares** allows us to find a regression line, or line of best fit, which will keep these errors to a minimum. It uses the criterion of minimizing the total squared errors of estimate. When we predict values of Y for each X_i, the difference between the actual Y_i and the predicted $\hat{Y}$ is the error. This error is squared and then summed. The line of best fit is the one that minimizes the total squared errors of prediction.[9]

$$\sum_{i=1}^{n} e_i^2 \text{ minimized}$$

Regression coefficients β_0 and β_1 are used to find the least-squares solution. They are computed as follows:

$$\beta_1 = \frac{\Sigma XY - \dfrac{(\Sigma X)(\Sigma Y)}{n}}{\Sigma X^2 - \dfrac{(\Sigma X)^2}{n}}$$

$$\hat{\beta}_0 = \bar{Y} - \hat{\beta}_1 \bar{X}$$

Substituting data from Exhibit 18–14 into both formulas, we get

$$\beta_1 = \frac{748633.5 - \dfrac{(196.1)(35988)}{10}}{4043.77 - \dfrac{(196.1)^2}{10}} = 216.439$$

$$\hat{\beta}_0 = 3598.8 - (216.439)(19.61) = -645.569$$

The predictive equation is now $\hat{Y} = -645.57 + 216.44 \, X_i$.

Drawing the Regression Line   Before drawing the regression line, we select two values of X to compute. Using values 13 and 24 for X_i, the points are

$$\hat{Y} = -645.57 + 216.44(13) = 2168.15$$

$$\hat{Y} = 645.57 + 216.44(24) = 4548.99$$

Comparing the line drawn in Exhibit 18–16 to the trial lines in Exhibit 18–15, one can readily see the success of the least-squares method in minimizing the error of prediction.

Residuals   We now turn our attention to the plot of standardized residuals in Exhibit 18–17. A **residual** is what remains after the line is fit or $(Y_i - \hat{Y}_i)$. When standardized, residuals are comparable to Z scores with a mean of 0 and a standard deviation of 1. In this plot, the standardized residuals should fall between 2 and –2, be randomly distributed about zero, and show no discernible pattern. All these conditions say the model is applied correctly.

EXHIBIT 18–14   **Data for Wine Price Study**

	Y Price (FF)	X Temperature (C°)	XY	Y²	X²
1	1813.00	11.80	21393.40	3286969.00	139.24
2	2558.00	15.70	40160.60	6543364.00	246.49
3	2628.00	14.00	36792.00	6906384.00	196.00
4	3217.00	22.90	73669.30	10349089.00	524.41
5	3228.00	20.00	64560.00	10419984.00	400.00
6	3629.00	20.10	72942.90	13169641.00	404.01
7	3886.00	17.90	69559.40	15100996.00	320.41
8	4897.00	23.40	114589.80	23980609.00	547.56
9	4933.00	24.60	121351.80	24334489.00	605.16
10	5199.00	25.70	133614.30	27029601.00	660.49
Σ	35988.00	196.10	748633.50	141121126.00	4043.77
Mean	3598.80	19.61			
s	1135.66	4.69			
Sum of squares (SS)	11607511.59	198.25	42908.82		

EXHIBIT 18–15   **Scatterplot and Possible Regression Lines Based on Visual Inspection: Wine Price Study**

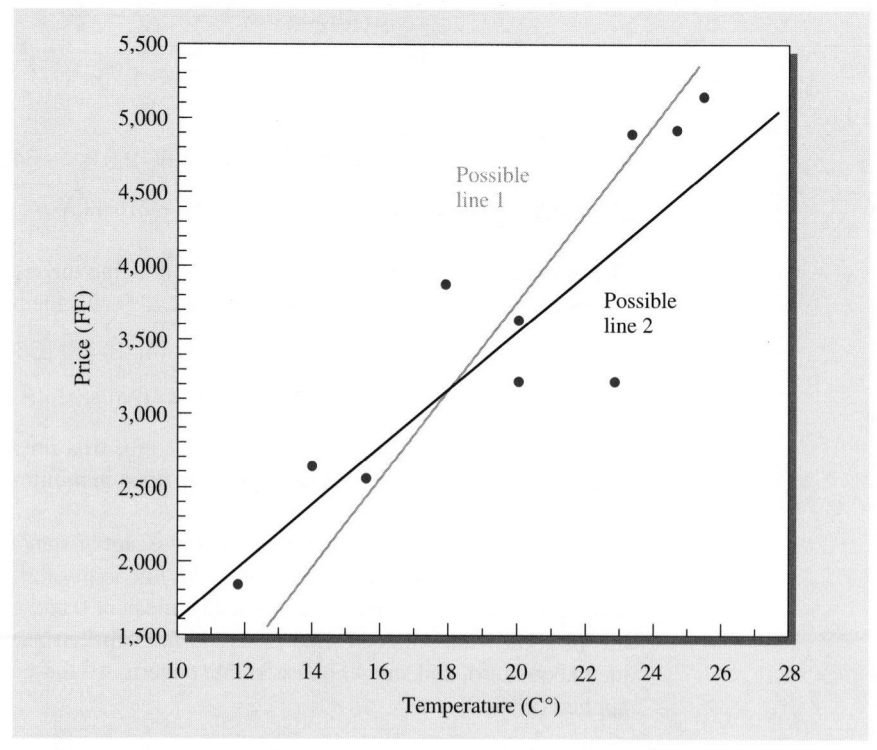

EXHIBIT 18–16   **Drawing the Least-Squares Line: Wine Price Study**

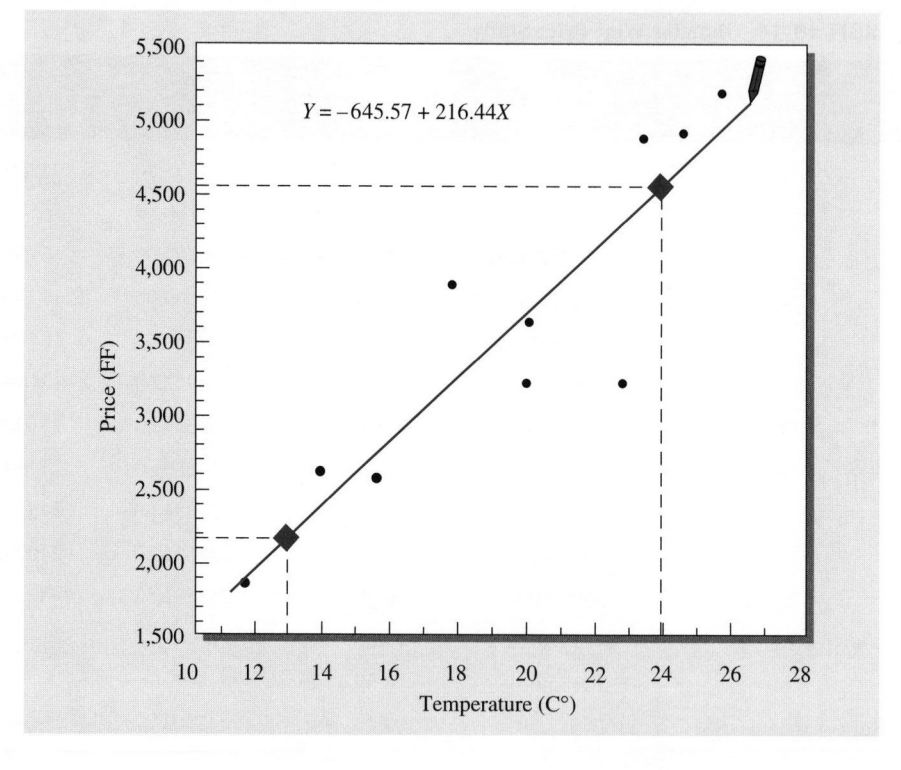

What do Harvard, Yale, UCLA, Columbia, the Kellogg School of Management at Northwestern, Pennsylvania's Wharton Business School, and Berkeley's Hass School of Business have in common? They are among a growing number of B-schools where wine clubs have flourished. Some have even added wine education to the business curriculum.

While medical research has shown moderate drinking to reduce the risk of heart disease, that's not the appeal for students who believe that it can be an effective tool for shaping positive business relationships. Brian Scanlon of Harvard's Wine & Cuisine Society summed it up this way: "Wine knowledge is an indispensable skill in today's business environment. If you're at a crucial business dinner and you want to pick the perfect wine to create the right atmosphere, you need to know the vintages, the regions and the best winemakers."

Vineyard owners couldn't be more supportive. Jack Cakebread of Cakebread Cellars, on a promotional tour at business schools around the country, reported the relationship between age and visitation frequency at their tasting room. Almost 70 percent of visitors are in their 20s and 30s. Although wine industry research forecasts a drop in wine enthusiasm for "Generation X," the future corporate executives represent a radically different segment.

David Mogridge is on a student team at Berkeley that brings in lecturers on a wide range of topics like growing, shipping, legal issues, branding, and strategy. In an interview with Eric Zelko of *Wine Spectator,* Mogridge said playfully, "When I think about it, everything I learned in business school, I learned in wine class."

www.winespectator.com

EXHIBIT 18–17   Plot of Standardized Residuals: Wine Price Study

Case	−3.0	0.0	3.0	Y Price	Predicted Price	Residual
1		*.		1,813	1,908.4112	−95.4112
2		*.		2,558	2,752.5234	−194.5234
3		· *		2,628	2,384.5771	243.4229
4	*	·		3,217	4,310.8844	−1,093.8844
5	*	·		3,228	3,683.2112	−455.2112
6		*		3,629	3,704.8551	−75.8551
7		· *		3,886	3,228.6893	657.3107
8		· *		4,897	4,419.1039	477.8961
9		· *		4,933	4,678.8307	254.1693
10		· *		5,199	4,916.9137	282.0863

In our example, we have one residual at −2.2, a random distribution about zero, and few indications of a sequential pattern. It is important to apply other diagnostics to verify that the regression assumptions are met. Various software programs provide plots and other checks of normality, linearity, equality of variance, and independence of error.[10]

Predictions

If we wanted to predict the price of a case of investment-grade red wine for a growing season that averages 21°C, our prediction would be

$$\hat{Y} = -645.57 + 216.44(21) = 3899.67$$

This is a *point prediction* of Y and should be corrected for greater precision. As with other confidence estimates, we establish the degree of confidence desired and substitute into the formula

$$\hat{Y} \pm t_{\alpha/2}s\sqrt{1 + \frac{1}{10} + \frac{(X - \bar{X})^2}{SS_x}}$$

where

$t_{\alpha/2}$ = The two-tailed critical value for t at the desired level (95 percent in this example).

s = The standard error of estimate (also the square root of the mean square error from the analysis of variance of the regression model) (see Exhibit 18–20).

SS_x = The sum of squares for X (Exhibit 18–14).

$$3899.67 \pm (2.306)(538.559)\sqrt{1 + \frac{1}{10} + \frac{(21 - 19.61)^2}{198.25}}$$
$$3899.67 \pm 1308.29$$

We are 95 percent confident of our prediction that a case of investment-quality French red wine grown in a particular year at 21°C average temperatures will be initially priced at 3899.67 ± 1308.29, or from approximately 2591 to 5208 FF. The comparatively large band width results from the amount of error in the model (reflected by r^2), some peculiarities in the Y values, and the use of a single predictor.

It is more likely that we would want to predict the average price of *all* cases grown at 21°C. This prediction would use the same basic formula omitting the first digit (the 1) under the radical. A narrower *confidence* band is the result since the average of all Y values is being predicted from a given X. In our example, the confidence interval for 95 percent is 3899.67 ± 411.42, or from 3488 to 4311 FF.

The predictor we selected, 21°C, was close to the mean of X (19.61). Because the **prediction and confidence bands** are shaped like a bow tie, predictors farther from the mean have larger band widths. For example, X values of 15, 20, and 25 produce confidence bands of ±565, ±397, and ±617, respectively. This is illustrated in Exhibit 18–18. The farther one's selected predictor is from X, the wider is the prediction interval.

Testing the Goodness of Fit

With the regression line plotted and a few illustrative predictions, we should now gather some evidence of **goodness of fit**—how well the model fits the data. The most important test in bivariate linear regression is whether the slope, β_1, is equal to zero.[11] We have already observed a slope of zero in Exhibit 18–11, line *b*. Zero slopes result from various conditions:

- Y is completely unrelated to X, and no systematic pattern is evident.
- There are constant values of Y for every value of X.
- The data are related but represented by a nonlinear function.

The *t*-Test   To test whether $\beta_1 = 0$, we use a two-tailed test (since the actual relationship is positive, negative, or zero). The test follows the t distribution for $n - 2$ degrees of freedom.

$$t = \frac{b_1}{s(b_1)} = \frac{216.439}{34.249} = 5.659$$

EXHIBIT 18–18   Prediction and Confidence Bands Based on Proximity to X

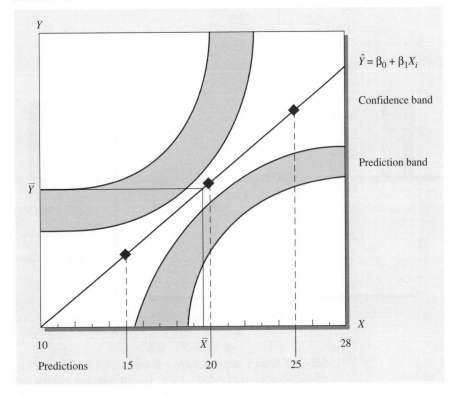

where

> b_1 was previously defined as the slope β_1.

> $s(b_1)$ is the standard error of β_1.[12]

We reject the null, $\beta_1 = 0$, because the calculated t is greater than any t value for 8 degrees of freedom and $\alpha = .01$.

The *F* Test   Computer printouts generally contain an analysis of variance (ANOVA) table with an F test of the regression model. In bivariate regression, t and F tests produce the same results since t^2 is equal to F. In multiple regression, the F test has an overall role for the model, and each of the independent variables is evaluated with a separate t-test. From the last chapter, recall that ANOVA partitions variance into component parts. For regression, it comprises explained deviations, $\hat{Y} - \bar{Y}$, and unexplained deviations, $Y - \hat{Y}$. Together they constitute the total deviation, $Y - \bar{Y}$. This is shown graphically in Exhibit 18–19. These sources of deviation are squared for all observations and summed across the data points.

In Exhibit 18–20, we develop this concept sequentially concluding with the F test of the regression model for the wine data. Based on the results presented in that table, we find statistical evidence of a linear relationship between variables. The alternative hypothesis, $r^2 \neq 0$, is accepted with $F = 32.02$, d.f., $(1,8)$, $p < .005$. The null hypothesis for the F test had the same effect as $\beta_1 = 0$ since we could select either test.

Coefficient of Determination   In predicting the values of Y without any knowledge of X, our best estimate would be $\bar{Y}$, its mean. Each predicted value that does not

EXHIBIT 18–19   **Components of Variation**

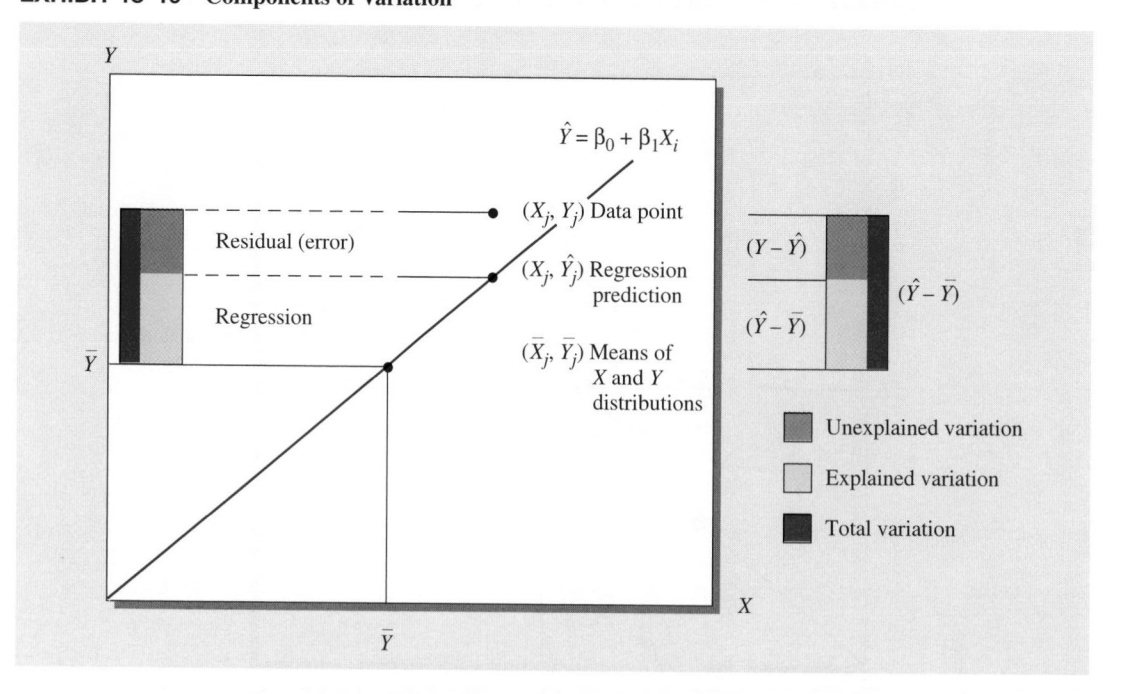

fall on Y contributes to an error of estimate, $(Y - \bar{Y})$. The total squared error for several predictions would be $\Sigma(Y_i - \bar{Y})^2$. By introducing known values of X into a regression equation, we attempt to reduce this error even further. Naturally, this is an improvement over using $\bar{Y}$, and the result is $(\hat{Y} - \bar{Y})$. The total improvement based on several estimates is $\Sigma(\hat{Y}_i - \bar{Y})^2$, the amount of variation explained by the relationship between X and Y in the regression. Based on the formula, the *coefficient of determination* is the ratio of the line of best fit's error over that incurred by using Y. One purpose of testing, then, is to discover whether the regression equation is a more effective predictive device than the mean of the dependent variable.

As in correlation, the coefficient of determination is symbolized by r^2.[13] It has several purposes. As an index of fit, it is interpreted as the total proportion of variance in Y explained by X. As a measure of linear relationship, it tells us how well the regression line fits the data. It is also an important indicator of the predictive accuracy of the equation. Typically, we would like to have an r^2 that explains 80 percent or more of the variation. Lower than that, predictive accuracy begins to fall off. The coefficient of determination, r^2, is calculated like this:

$$r^2 = \frac{\sum_{i=1}^{n} (\hat{Y} - \bar{Y})^2}{\sum_{i=1}^{n} (Y - \bar{Y})^2} = \frac{SS_r}{SS_e} = 1 - \frac{SS_e}{SS_t}$$

For the wine price study, r^2 was found by using the data from the bottom of Exhibit 18–20.

$$r^2 = 1 - \frac{2320368.49}{11607511.60} = .80$$

Eighty percent of the variance in price may be explained by growing-season temperatures. With actual data and multiple predictors, our results would improve.

EXHIBIT 18–20 **Progressive Application of Partitioned Variance Concept**

General Concept

$(\hat{Y} - \bar{Y})$	+	$(Y - \hat{Y})$	=	$(Y - \bar{Y})$
Explained Variation (the regression relationship between X and Y)		Unexplained Variation (cannot be explained by the regression relationship)		Total Variation

ANOVA Application

$\displaystyle\sum_{i=1}^{n}(\hat{Y}-\bar{Y})^2$	$\displaystyle\sum_{i=1}^{n}(Y-\hat{Y})^2$	$\displaystyle\sum_{i=1}^{n}(Y-\bar{Y})^2$
SS_r Sum of Squares Regression	SS_e Sum of Squares Error	SS_t Sum of Squares Total

Contents of Summary Table				
Source	**Degrees of Freedom**	**Sum of Squares**	**Mean Square**	***F* Ratio**
Regression	1	SS_r	$MS_r = \dfrac{SS_r}{1}$	MS_r
Error	$n-2$	SS_e	$MS_e = \dfrac{SS_e}{n-2}$	$\overline{MS_e}$
Total		SS_t		

ANOVA Summary Table: Test of Regression Model				
Source	**Degrees of Freedom**	**Sum of Squares**	**Mean Square**	***F* Ratio**
Regression	1	9,287,143.11	9,287,143.11	32.02
Residual (error)	8	2,320368.49	290,046.06	
Total		11,607,511.60		
			Significance of $F = .0005$	

Nonparametric Measures of Association[14]

Measures for Nominal Data

Nominal measures are used to assess the strength of relationships in cross-classification tables. They are often used with chi-square or may be used separately. In this section, we provide examples of three statistics based on chi-square and two that follow the proportional reduction in error approach.

There is no fully satisfactory all-purpose measure for categorical data. Some are adversely affected by table shape and number of cells; others are sensitive to sample size or marginals. It is perturbing to find similar statistics reporting different coefficients for the same data. This occurs because of a statistic's particular sensitivity or the way it was devised.

Technically, we would like to find two characteristics with nominal measures:

- When there is no relationship at all, the coefficient should be 0.
- When there is a complete dependency, the coefficient should display unity or 1.

This does not always happen. In addition to the sensitivity problem, analysts should be alerted to the need for careful selection of tests.

You may wish to review our discussion of chi-square in Chapter 17.

Chi-Square-Based Measures   Exhibit 18–21 reports a 2 × 2 variation of the Containers Inc. shipping study on smoking and job-related accidents introduced in Chapter 17. In this example, the observed significance level is less than the testing level ($\alpha =$

EXHIBIT 18–21   Chi-Square-Based Measures of Association

		On-the-Job Accident			
	Count	Yes	No	Row Total
Smoker Yes		21	10	31
No		13	22	35
	Column Total	34	32	66

Chi-Square	Value	d.f.	Significance
Pearson	6.16257	1	.01305
Community correction	4.99836	1	.02537

Minimal expected frequency 15.030

Statistic	Value	Approximate Significance
Phi	.30557	.01305*
Cramer's V	.30557	.01305*
Contingency coefficient C	.29223	.01305*

*Pearson chi-square probability.

.05), and the null hypothesis is rejected. A correction to chi-square is provided. We now turn to measures of association to detect the strength of the relationship. Notice that the exhibit also provides an approximate significance of the coefficient based on the chi-square distribution. This is a test of the null hypothesis that no relationship exists between the variables of accidents and smoking.

The first **chi-square-based measure** is applied to smoking and on-the-job accidents. It is called **phi (ϕ).** Phi ranges from 0 to +1.0 and attempts to correct χ^2 proportionately to N. Phi is best employed with 2×2 tables like this one since its coefficient can exceed +1.0 when applied to larger tables. Phi is calculated:

$$\phi = \sqrt{\frac{\chi^2}{N}} = \sqrt{\frac{6.616257}{66}} = .3056$$

Phi's coefficient shows a moderate relationship between smoking and job-related accidents. There is no suggestion in this interpretation that one variable causes the other, nor is there an indication of the direction of the relationship.

Cramer's V is a modification of phi for larger tables and has a range up to 1.0 for tables of any shape. It is calculated like this:

$$V = \sqrt{\frac{\chi^2}{N(k-1)}} = \sqrt{\frac{6.616257}{66(1)}} = .3056$$

where

k = the lesser number of rows or columns.

In Exhibit 18–21, the coefficient is the same as phi.

The **contingency coefficient C** is reported last. It is not comparable to other measures and has a different upper limit for various table sizes. The upper limits are determined as

$$\sqrt{\frac{k-1}{k}}$$

where

k = the number of columns.

For a 2×2 table, the upper limit is .71; for a 3×3, .82; and for a 4×4, .87. Although this statistic operates well with tables having the same number of rows as columns, its upper-limit restriction is not consistent with a criterion of good association measurement. C is calculated as

$$C = \sqrt{\frac{\chi^2}{\chi^2 + N}} = \sqrt{\frac{6.616257}{6.61625} + 66} = .2922$$

The chief advantage of C is its ability to accommodate data in almost every form: skewed or normal, discrete or continuous, and nominal or ordinal.

Proportional Reduction in Error **Proportional reduction in error (PRE)** statistics are the second type used with contingency tables. Lambda and tau are the examples discussed here. The coefficient **lambda (λ)** is based on how well the frequencies of one nominal variable offer predictive evidence about the frequencies of another. Lambda is asymmetrical—allowing calculation for the direction of prediction—and symmetrical, predicting row and column variables equally.

EXHIBIT 18–22 Proportional Reduction in Error Measures

What is your opinion about capping executives' salaries?

	Count Row Pct.	Favor	Do not Favor	Row Total
	Managerial	90 82.0	20 18.0	110
Occupational Class	White collar	60 43.0	80 57.0	140
	Blue collar	30 20.0	120 80.0	150
	Column Total	180 45.0%	220 55.0%	400 100.0%

Chi-Square	Value	d.f.	Significance
Pearson	98.38646	2	.00000
Likelihood ratio	104.96542	2	.00000

Minimum expected frequency 49.500

Statistic	Value	ASEI	T Value	Approximate Significance
Lambda:				
symmetric	.30233	.03955	6.77902	
with occupation dependent	.24000	.03820	5.69495	
with opinion dependent	.38889	.04555	7.08010	
Goodman & Kruskal tau:				
with occupation dependent	.11669	.02076		.00000*
with opinion dependent	.24597	.03979		.00000*

*Based on chi-square approximation.

The computation of lambda is straightforward. In Exhibit 18–22, we have results from an opinion survey with a sample of 400 shareholders. Only 180 out of 400 (45 percent) favor capping executives' salaries; 220 (55 percent) do not favor it. With this information alone, if asked to predict the opinions of an individual in the sample, we would achieve the best prediction record by always choosing the modal category. Here it is "do not favor." By doing so, however, we would be wrong 180 out of 400 times. The probability estimate for an incorrect classification is .45, $P(1) = (1 - .55)$.

Now suppose we have prior information about the respondents' occupational status and are asked to predict opinion. Would it improve predictive ability? Yes, we would make the predictions by summing the probabilities of all cells that are not the modal value for their rows (for example, cell [2, 1] is 20/400 or .05):

$$P(2) = \text{cell } (1, 2) \ .05 + \text{cell } (2, 1) \ .15 + \text{cell } (3, 1) \ .075 = .275$$

Lambda is then calculated:

$$\lambda = \frac{P(1) - P(2)}{P(1)} = \frac{.45 - .275}{45} = .3889$$

Note that the asymmetric lambda in Exhibit 18–22, where opinion is the dependent variable, reflects this computation. As a result of knowing the respondents' occupational classification, we improve our prediction by 39 percent. If we wish to predict occupational classification from opinion instead of the opposite, a λ of .24 would be secured. This means that 24 percent of the error in predicting occupational class is eliminated by knowledge of opinion on the executives' salary question. Lambda varies between 0 and 1, corresponding with no ability to eliminate errors to elimination of all errors of prediction.

Goodman and Kruskal's **tau** (τ) uses table marginals to reduce prediction errors. In predicting opinion on executives' salaries without any knowledge of occupational class, we would expect a 50.5 percent correct classification and a 49.5 percent probability of error. These are based on the column marginal percentages in Exhibit 18–22.

Column Marginal		Column Percent	°	Correct Cases
180	*	45	=	81
220	*	55	=	121
Total correct classification				202

Correct classification of the opinion variable = .505 = $\dfrac{202}{400}$

Probability of error, $P(1) = (1 - .505) = .495$

When additional knowledge of occupational class is used, information for correct classification of the opinion variable is improved to 62.7 percent with a 37.3 percent probability of error. This is obtained by using the cell counts and marginals for occupational class (refer to Exhibit 18–22), as shown below:

Row 1	$\left(\dfrac{90}{110}\right)90 + \left(\dfrac{20}{110}\right)20$	=	73.6364 + 3.6364	=	77.2727
Row 2	$\left(\dfrac{60}{140}\right)60 + \left(\dfrac{80}{140}\right)80$	=	25.7143 + 45.7142	=	71.4286
Row 3	$\left(\dfrac{30}{150}\right)30 + \left(\dfrac{120}{150}\right)120$	=	6.0 + 96.0	=	102.0000

Total correct classification (with additional information on occupational class) 250.7013

Correct classification of opinion variable = .627 = $\dfrac{250.7}{400}$

Probability of error, $P(2) = (1 - .627) = .373$

Tau is then computed like this:

$$\tau \frac{P(1) - P(2)}{P(1)} = \frac{.495 - .373}{.495} = .246$$

Exhibit 18–22 shows that the information about occupational class has reduced error in predicting opinion to approximately 25 percent. The table also contains information on the test of the null hypothesis that tau = 0 with an approximate observed significance level and asymptotic error (for developing confidence intervals). Based on the small observed significance level, we would conclude that tau is significantly different from a coefficient of 0 and that there is an association between opinion on executives' salaries and occupational class in the population from which the sample was selected. We can also establish the confidence level for the coefficient at the 95 percent level as approximately .25 ± .04.

Measures for Ordinal Data

When data require **ordinal measures,** there are several statistical alternatives. In this section we will illustrate:

- Gamma.
- Kendall's tau *b* and tau *c.*
- Somers's *d.*
- Spearman's rho.

All but Spearman's rank-order correlation are based on the concept of concordant and discordant pairs. None of these statistics require the assumption of a bivariate normal distribution, yet by incorporating order, most produce a range from –1.0 (a perfect negative relationship) to +1.0 (a perfect positive one). Within this range, a coefficient with a larger magnitude (absolute value of the measure) is interpreted as having a stronger relationship. These characteristics allow the analyst to interpret both the direction and the strength of the relationship.

Exhibit 18–23 presents data for 70 managerial employees of KeyDesign, a large industrial design firm. All 70 employees have been evaluated for coronary risk by the firm's health insurer. The management levels are ranked, as are the fitness assessments by the physicians. If we were to use a nominal measure of association with this data (such as Cramer's *V*), the computed value of the statistic would be positive since order is not present in nominal data. But using ordinal measures of association reveals the actual nature of the relationship. In this example, all coefficients have negative signs.

The information in the exhibit has been arranged so the number of concordant and discordant pairs of individual observations may be calculated. When a subject that

EXHIBIT 18–23   **Tabled Ranks for Management and Fitness Levels at Key Design**

		Management Level			
	Count	Lower	Middle	Upper	
	High	14	4	2	20
Fitness	Moderate	18	6	2	26
	Low	2	6	16	24
		34	16	20	70

Statistic	Value*
Gamma	–.70242
Kendall's tau b	–.51279
Kendall's tau c	–.49714
Somers's d	
Symmetric	–.51263
With fitness dependent	–.52591
With management-level dependent	–.50000

*The t value for each coefficient is –5.86451.

ranks higher on one variable also ranks higher on the other variable, the pairs of observations are said to be **concordant.** If a higher ranking on one variable is accompanied by a lower ranking on the other variable, the pairs of observations are **discordant.** Let P stand for concordant pairs and Q stand for discordant. When concordant pairs exceed discordant pairs in a $P - Q$ relationship, the statistic reports a positive association between the variables under study. As discordant pairs increase over concordant pairs, the association becomes negative. A balance indicates no relationship between the variables. Exhibit 18–24 summarizes the procedure for calculating the summary terms needed in all the statistics we are about to discuss.[15]

Goodman and Kruskal's **gamma** (γ) is a statistic that compares concordant and discordant pairs and then standardizes the outcome by maximizing the value of the denominator. It has a proportional reduction in error (PRE) interpretation that connects nicely with what we already know about PRE nominal measures. Gamma is defined as

$$\gamma = \frac{P - Q}{P + Q} = \frac{172 - 984}{172 + 984} = \frac{-812}{1156} = -.7024$$

For the fitness data, we conclude that as management level increases, fitness decreases. This is immediately apparent from the larger number of discordant pairs. A more precise explanation for gamma takes its absolute value (ignoring the sign) and relates it to PRE. Hypothetically, if one was trying to predict whether the pairs were concordant or discordant, one might flip a coin and classify the outcome. A better way is to make the prediction based on the preponderance of concordance or discordance;

EXHIBIT 18–24   **Calculation of Concordant (P), Discordant (Q), Tied (T_x, T_y), and Total Paired Observations: KeyDesign Example**

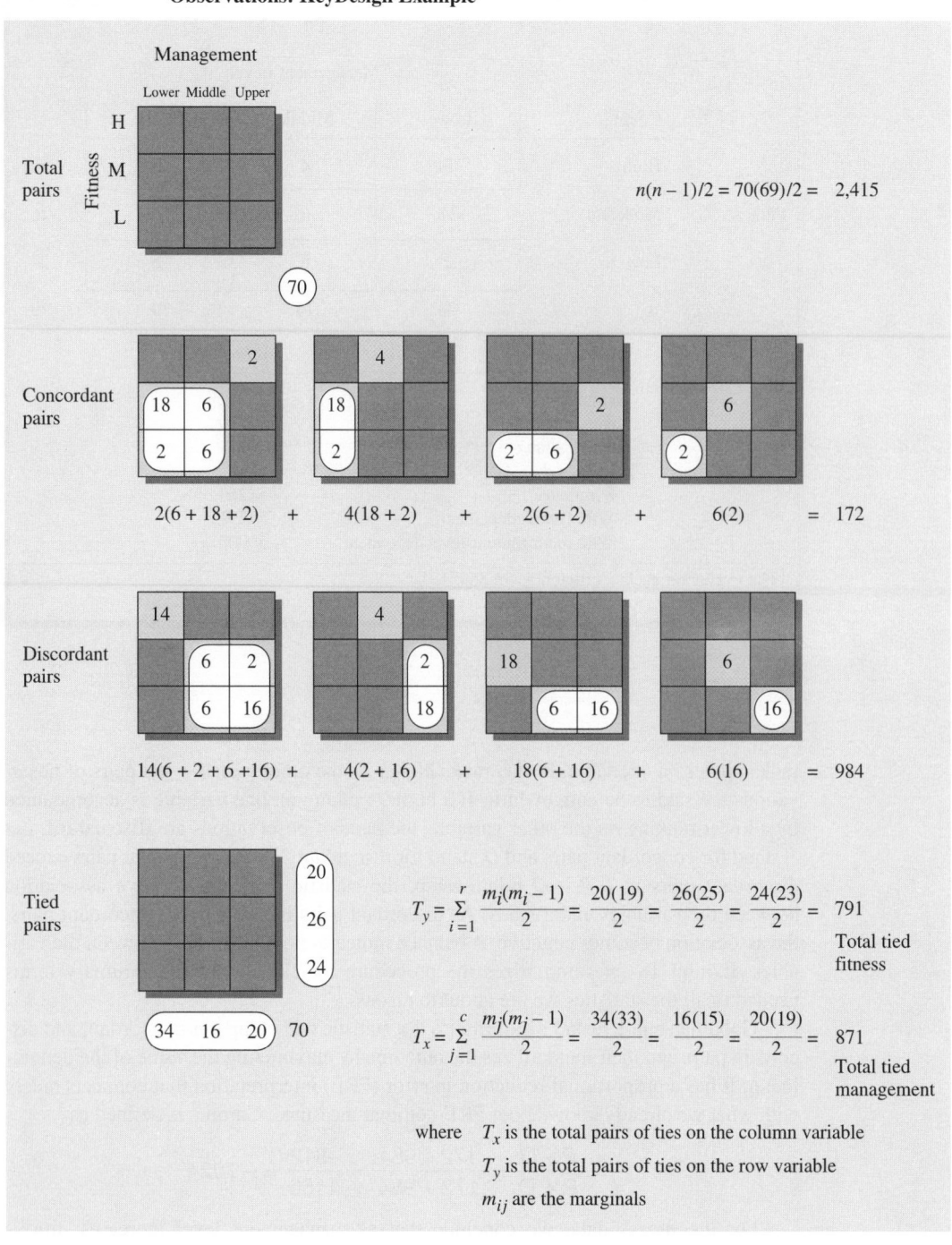

$n(n-1)/2 = 70(69)/2 = 2,415$

Concordant pairs

$2(6+18+2) \quad + \quad 4(18+2) \quad + \quad 2(6+2) \quad + \quad 6(2) \quad = 172$

Discordant pairs

$14(6+2+6+16) + \quad 4(2+16) \quad + \quad 18(6+16) \quad + \quad 6(16) \quad = 984$

Tied pairs

$$T_y = \sum_{i=1}^{r} \frac{m_i(m_i-1)}{2} = \frac{20(19)}{2} = \frac{26(25)}{2} = \frac{24(23)}{2} = 791$$
Total tied fitness

$$T_x = \sum_{j=1}^{c} \frac{m_j(m_j-1)}{2} = \frac{34(33)}{2} = \frac{16(15)}{2} = \frac{20(19)}{2} = 871$$
Total tied management

where T_x is the total pairs of ties on the column variable

T_y is the total pairs of ties on the row variable

m_{ij} are the marginals

the absolute value of gamma is the proportional reduction in error when prediction is done the second way. For example, you would get a 50 percent hit ratio using the coin. A PRE of .70 improves your hit ratio to 85 percent ($.50 \times 70$) + (.50) = .85.

With a γ of $-.70$, 85 percent of the pairs are discordant and .15 percent are concordant.[16] There are almost six times as many discordant pairs as concordant pairs. In situations where the data call for a 2×2 table, the appropriate modification of gamma is Yule's Q.[17]

Kendall's **tau *b*** (τ_b) is a refinement of gamma that considers tied pairs. A tied pair occurs when subjects have the same value on the X variable, on the Y variable, or on both. For a given sample size, there are $n(n-1)/2$ pairs of observations.[18] After concordant pairs and discordant pairs are removed, the remainder are tied. Tau b does not have a PRE interpretation but does provide a range of -1.0 to $+1.0$ for square tables. Its compensation for ties uses the information found in Exhibit 18–24. It may be calculated as

$$\tau_b = \frac{P - Q}{\sqrt{\left(\frac{n(n-1)}{2} - T_x\right)\left(\frac{n(n-1)}{2} - T_y\right)}}$$

$$= \frac{172 - 984}{\sqrt{(2415 - 871)(2415 - 791)}} = -.5128$$

Kendall's **tau *c*** (τ_c) is another adjustment to the basic $P - Q$ relationship of gamma. This approach to ordinal association is suitable for tables of any size. Although we illustrate tau c, we would select tau b since the cross-classification table for the fitness data is square. The adjustment for table shape is seen in the formula

$$\tau_c = \frac{2m(P - Q)}{N^2(m - 1)} = \frac{2(3)(172 - 984)}{(70)^2(3 - 1)} - .4971$$

where m is the smaller number of rows or columns.

Somers's *d* rounds out our coverage of statistics employing the concept of concordant-discordant pairs. This statistic's utility comes from its ability to compensate for tied ranks and adjust for the direction of the dependent variable. Again, we refer to the preliminary calculations provided in Exhibit 18–24 to compute the symmetric and asymmetric ds. As before, the symmetric coefficient (equation 3) takes the row and column variables into account equally. The second and third calculations show fitness as the dependent and management level as the dependent, respectively.

$$d_{sym} = \frac{(P - Q)}{n(n - 1) - T_x T_y/2} = \frac{-812}{1584} = -.5126 \tag{3}$$

$$d_{y-x} = \frac{(P - Q)}{\frac{n(n - 1)}{2} - T_x} = \frac{-812}{2415 - 871} = -.5259 \tag{4}$$

$$d_{x-y} = \frac{(P - Q)}{\frac{n(n - 1)}{2} - T_y} = \frac{-812}{2415 - 791} = -.5000 \tag{5}$$

The **Spearman's rho** (ρ) correlation is a popular ordinal measure. Along with Kendall's tau, it is among the most widely used of ordinal techniques. Rho correlates ranks between two ordered variables. Occasionally, researchers find continuous variables with too many abnormalities to correct. Then scores may be reduced to ranks and calculated with Spearman's rho.

As a special form of Pearson's product moment correlation, rho's strengths outweigh its weaknesses. When data are transformed by logs or squaring, rho remains unaffected. Second, outliers or extreme scores that were troublesome before ranking no longer pose a threat since the largest number in the distribution is equal to the sample size. Third, it is an easy statistic to compute. The major deficiency is its sensitivity to tied ranks. Too many ties distort the coefficient's size. However, there are rarely too many ties to justify the correction formulas available.

To illustrate the use of rho, consider a situation where Dean Merrill, a brokerage firm, is recruiting account executive trainees. Assume the field has been narrowed to 10 applicants for final evaluation. They arrive at the company headquarters, go through a battery of tests, and are interviewed by a panel of three executives. The test results are evaluated by an industrial psychologist who then ranks the 10 candidates. The executives produce a composite ranking based on the interviews. Your task is to decide how well these two sets of ranking agree. Exhibit 18–25 contains the data and preliminary calculations. Substituting into the equation, we get

$$r_s = 1 - \frac{6\Sigma d^2}{n^3 - n} = \frac{6(57)}{(10)^3 - 10} = .654$$

where n is the number of subjects being ranked.

The relationship between the panel's and the psychologist's ranking is moderately high, suggesting agreement between the two measures. The test of the null hypothesis that there is no relationship between the measures ($r_s = 0$) is rejected at the .05 level with $n - 2$ degrees of freedom.

$$t = r_s \sqrt{\frac{n - 2}{1 - r_s^2}} = \sqrt{\frac{8}{1 - .4277}} = 2.45$$

EXHIBIT 18–25   **Dean Merrill Data for Spearman's rho**

Applicant	Rank by Panel x	Rank by Psychologist y	d	d^2
1	3.5	6	−2.5	6.25
2	10	5	5	25.00
3	6.5	8	−1.5	2.25
4	2	1.5	0.5	0.25
5	1	3	−2	4.00
6	9	7	2	4.00
7	3.5	1.5	2	4.00
8	6.5	9	−2.5	6.25
9	8	10	−2	4.00
10	5	4	1	1.00
				57.00

Note: Tied ranks were assigned the average (of ranks) as if no ties had occurred.

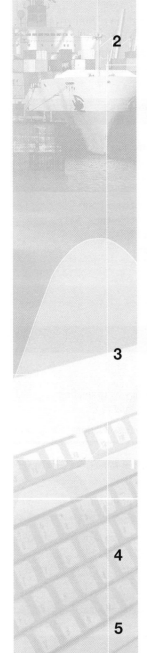

SUMMARY

1   Management questions frequently involve relationships between two or more variables. Correlation analysis may be applied to study such relationships. A correct correlational hypothesis states that the variables occur together in some specified manner *without* implying that one causes the other.

2   Parametric correlation requires two continuous variables measured on an interval or ratio scale. The product moment correlation coefficient represents an index of the magnitude of the relationship: Its sign governs the direction and its square explains the common variance. Bivariate correlation treats X and Y variables symmetrically and is intended for use with variables that are linearly related.

Scatterplots allow the researcher to visually inspect relationship data for appropriateness of the selected statistic. The direction, magnitude, and shape of a relationship are conveyed in a plot. The shape of linear relationships is characterized by a straight line, whereas nonlinear relationships are curvilinear or parabolic or have other curvature. The assumptions of linearity and bivariate normal distribution may be checked through plots and diagnostic tests.

A correlation matrix is a table used to display coefficients for more than two variables. Matrices form the basis for computation and understanding of the nature of relationships in multiple regression, discriminant analysis, factor analysis, and many multivariate techniques.

A correlation coefficient of any magnitude or sign, regardless of statistical significance, does not imply causation. Similarly, a coefficient is not remarkable simply because it is statistically significant. Practical significance should be considered in interpreting and reporting findings.

3   Regression analysis is used to further our insight into the relationship of Y with X. When we take the observed values of X to estimate or predict corresponding Y values, the process is called simple prediction. When more than one X variable is used, the outcome is a function of multiple predictors. Simple and multiple predictions are made with regression analysis.

A straight line is fundamentally the best way to model the relationship between two continuous variables. The method of least squares allows us to find a regression line, or line of best fit, that minimizes errors in drawing the line. It uses the criterion of minimizing the total squared errors of estimate. Point predictions made from well-fitted data are subject to error. Prediction and confidence bands may be used to find a range of probable values for Y based on the chosen predictor. The bands are shaped in such a way that predictors farther from the mean have larger band widths.

4   We test regression models for linearity and to discover whether the equation is effective in fitting the data. An important test in bivariate linear regression is whether the slope is equal to zero. In bivariate regression, t-tests and F tests of the regression produce the same result since t^2 is equal to F.

5   Often the assumptions or the required measurement level for parametric techniques cannot be met. Nonparametric measures of association offer alternatives. Nominal measures of association are used to assess the strength of relationships in cross-classification tables. They are often used in conjunction with chi-square or may be based on the proportional reduction in error (PRE) approach.

Phi ranges from 0 to +1.0 and attempts to correct chi-square proportionately to N. Phi is best employed with 2×2 tables. Cramer's V is a modification of phi for larger tables and has a range up to 1.0 for tables of any configuration. Lambda, a PRE statistic, is based on how well the frequencies of one nominal variable offer predictive evidence about the frequencies of another. Goodman and Kruskal's tau uses table marginals to reduce prediction errors.

Measures for ordinal data include gamma, Kendall's tau b and tau c, Somers's d, and Spearman's rho. All but Spearman's rank-order correlation are based on the concept of concordant and discordant pairs. None of these statistics require the assumption of a bivariate normal distribution, yet by incorporating order, most produce a range from -1 to $+1$.

KEY TERMS

EXAMPLES

Company	Scenario	Page
Containers Inc.*	Implementing a smoke-free workplace policy by evaluating the relationship between accidents and smoking.	592
Dean Merrill*	A brokerage firm uses an ordinal measure of association in recruiting account executive trainees.	600
European MBA programs	Specialty programs in business administration reflect emerging market niches.	582
Forbes 500 data	The relationship between cash flow and net profits in 10 companies.	575
KeyDesign*	Managerial employees at a large industrial design firm are evaluated for coronary risk.	596
McDonald's	Evaluating the effectiveness of a cashless payment system.	596
Mobil Oil Corp. (Speedpass)	Originator of the Speedpass system now being tested by select McDonald's restaurants in the Chicagoland area.	596
UCLA, U of PA, UC-Berkeley, Columbia, Harvard, Yale, and Northwestern universities	Business schools with wine clubs.	587

*Due to the confidential and proprietary nature of most research, the names of some companies have been changed.

DISCUSSION QUESTIONS

Terms in Review

1. Distinguish between the following:

    a. Regression coefficient and correlation coefficient.

    b. $r = 0$ and $\rho = 0$.

    c. The test of the true slope, the test of the intercept, and $r^2 = 0$.

    d. r^2 and r.

    e. A slope of 0.

    f. F and t^2.

2. Describe the relationship between the two variables in the four plots.

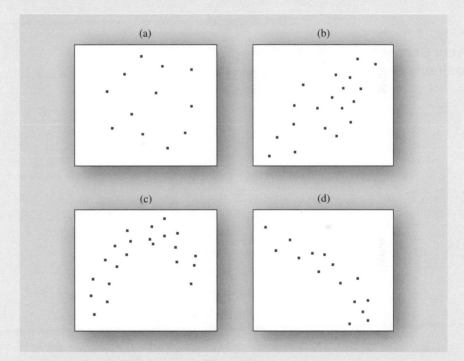

Making Research Decisions

3. A tax on the market value of stock and bond transactions has been proposed as one remedy for the budget deficit. The following data were collected on a sample of 60 registered voters by a polling organization.

	Education		
Opinion About Market Tax	**H.S.**	**College Grad.**	**MBA**
Favorable	15	5	0
Undecided	10	8	2
Unfavorable	0	2	18

    a. Compute gamma for the table.

    b. Compute tau *b* or tau *c* for the same data.

  c. What accounts for the differences?

  d. Decide which is more suitable for this data.

4. Using the table data in question 3, compute Somers's *d* symmetric and then use opinion as the dependent variable. Decide which approach is best for reporting the decision.

5. A research team conducted a study of voting preferences among 130 registered Democrats and 130 registered Republicans before an election on a specific tax proposal. They secured the following results:

	Favor	Against
Democrats	50	80
Republicans	90	40

 Calculate an appropriate measure of association and decide how to present your results.

From Concept to Practice

6. Using this data,

X	Y
3	6
6	10
9	15
12	24
15	21
18	20

  a. Create a scatterplot.

  b. Find the least-squares line.

  c. Plot the line on the diagram.

  d. Predict: Y if X is 10.
     Y if X is 17.

7. A home pregnancy test claims to be 97 percent accurate when consumers obtain a positive result. To what extent are the variables of "actual clinical condition" and "test readings" related?

  a. Compute phi, Cramer's *V*, and the contingency coefficient for the table below. What can you say about the strength of the relationship between the two variables?

  b. Compute lambda for this data. What does this statistic tell you?

*Actual Clinical Condition * Test Readings of In-Vitro Diagnostic Cross-Tabulaion*				
		Test Readings of In-Vitro Diagnostic		
Count		**Positive**	**Negative**	**Total**
Actual clinical condition	Pregnant	451 accurate	36 innacurate	487
	Not pregnant	15 innacurate	183 accurate	198
Total		466	219	685

8. Fill in the missing blocks for the ANOVA summary table on net profits and market value used with regression analysis.

ANOVA Summary Table				
	d.f.	**Sum of Squares**	**Mean Square**	**F**
Regression	1	11116995.47	☐	☐
Error	☐	☐	116104.63	
Total	9	12045832.50		

a. What does the *F* tell you? ($\alpha = .05$).

b. What is the *t* value? Explain its meaning.

9. Using a computer program, produce a correlation matrix for the following data:

Forbes 500 Random Subsample (dollars in millions)					
Assets	**Sales**	**Market Value**	**Net Profit**	**Cash Flow**	**Number of Employees (thousands)**
1034.00	1510.00	697.00	82.60	126.50	16.60
956.00	785.00	1271.00	89.00	191.20	5.00
1890.00	2533.00	1783.00	176.00	267.00	44.00
1133.00	532.00	752.00	82.30	137.10	2.10
11682.00	3790.00	4149.00	413.50	806.80	11.90
6080.00	635.00	291.00	18.10	35.20	3.70
31044.00	3296.00	2705.00	337.30	425.50	20.10
5878.00	3204.00	2100.00	145.80	380.00	10.80
1721.00	981.00	1573.00	172.60	326.60	1.90
2135.00	2268.00	2634.00	247.20	355.50	21.20

10. Secure Spearman rank-order correlations for the largest Pearson coefficient in the matrix from question 9. Explain the differences between the two findings.

11. Using the matrix data in question 9, select a pair of variables and run a simple regression. Then investigate the appropriateness of the model for the data using diagnostic tools for evaluating assumptions.

12. For the data below,

X	Y	X	Y
25	5	9	25
19	7	8	26
17	12	7	28
14	23	3	20
12	20		

a. Calculate the correlation between X and Y.

b. Interpret the sign of the correlation.

c. Interpret the square of the correlation.

d. Plot the least-squares line.

e. Test for a linear relationship:

(1) $\beta_1 = 0$.

(2) $r = 0$.

(3) An F test.

WWW Exercises   Visit our website for Internet exercises related to this chapter at
www.mhhe.com/business/cooper8

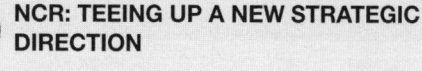

CASES*

 MASTERING TEACHER LEADERSHIP

 PERFORMANCE EVALUATIONS

NCR: TEEING UP A NEW STRATEGIC DIRECTION

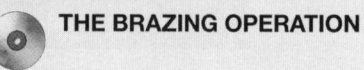 **THE BRAZING OPERATION**

 OVERDUE BILLS

WORKLOAD RATINGS

*All cases indicating a video icon are located on the Instructor's Videotape Supplement. All nonvideo cases are in the case section of the textbook. All cases indicating a CD icon offer a data set, which is located on the accompanying CD.

REFERENCE NOTES

1. Typically, we plot the x (independent) variable on the horizontal axis and the y (dependent) variable on the vertical axis. Although correlation does not distinguish between independent and dependent variables, the convention is useful for consistency in plotting and will be used later with regression.

2. F. J. Anscombe, "Graphs in Statistical Analysis," *American Statistician* 27 (1973), pp. 17–21. Cited in Samprit Chatterjee and Bertram Price, *Regression Analysis by Example* (New York: Wiley, 1977), pp. 7–9.

3. Amir D. Aczel, *Complete Business Statistics,* 2nd ed. (Homewood, IL: Irwin, 1993), p. 433.

4. The coefficient for net profits and cash flow in the example calculation used a subsample ($n = 10$) and was found to be .93. The matrix shows the coefficient as .95. The matrix calculation was based on the larger sample ($n = 100$).

5. This section is partially based on the concepts developed by Emanuel J. Mason and William J. Bramble, *Understanding and Conducting Research* (New York: McGraw-Hill, 1989), pp. 172–82; and elaborated in greater detail by Aczel, *Complete Business Statistics,* pp. 414–29.

6. Technically, estimation uses a concurrent criterion variable where prediction uses a future criterion. The statistical procedure is the same in either case.

7. Peter Passell, "Can Math Predict a Wine? An Economist Takes a Swipe at Some Noses," *International Herald Tribune,* March 5, 1990, p. 1; Jacques Neher, "Top Quality Bordeaux Cellar Is an Excellent Buy," *International Herald Tribune,* July 9, 1990, p. 8.

8. See Alan Agresti and Barbara Finlay, *Statistical Methods for the Social Sciences* (San Francisco: Dellen Publishing, 1986), pp. 248–49. Also see the discussion of basic regression models in John Neter, William Wasserman, and Michael H. Kutner, *Applied Linear Statistical Models* (Homewood, IL: Irwin, 1990), pp. 23–49.

9. We distinguish between the error terms $\varepsilon_1 = Y_i - E[Y_i]$ and the residual $e_i = (Y_i - \hat{Y}_i)$. The first is based on the vertical deviation of Y_i from the true regression line. It is unknown and estimated. The second is the vertical deviation of Y_i from the fitted $\hat{Y}$ on the estimated line. See Neter et al., *Applied Linear Statistical Models,* p. 47.

10. For further information on software-generated regression diagnostics, see the most current release of software manuals for SPSS, MINITAB, BMDP, and SAS.

11. Aczel, *Complete Business Statistics,* p. 434.

12. This calculation is normally listed as the standard error of the slope (SE B) on computer printouts. For these data it is further defined as:

$$s(b_1) + \frac{8}{\sqrt{SS_x}} = \frac{538.559}{\sqrt{198.249}} = 38.249$$

where

s = The standard error of estimate (and the square root of the mean square error of the regression)

SS_x = The sum of squares for the X variable

13. Computer printouts use uppercase (R^2) because most procedures are written to accept multiple and bivariate regression.

14. The table output for this section has been modified from SPSS and is described in Norusis/SPSS, Inc., *SPSS Base System User's Guide.* For further discussion and examples of nonparametric measures of association, see S. Siegel and N. J. Castellan, Jr., *Nonparametric Statistics for the Behavioral Sciences,* 2nd ed. (New York: McGraw-Hill, 1988).

15. Calculation of concordant and discordant pairs is adapted from Agresti and Finlay, *Statistical Methods for the Social Sciences,* pp. 221–23.

16. We know that the percentage of concordant plus the percentage of discordant pairs sums to 1.0. We also know their difference is –.70. The only numbers satisfying these two conditions are .85 and .15 (.85 + .15 = 1.0, .15 – .85 = –.70).

17. G. U. Yule and M. G. Kendall, *An Introduction to the Theory of Statistics* (New York: Hafner, 1950).

18. M. G. Kendall, *Rank Correlation Methods,* 4th ed. (London: Charles W. Griffin, 1970).

REFERENCES FOR SNAPSHOTS AND CAPTIONS

Business School Wine Clubs

E. Zelko, "Graduates of Wine," *Wine Spectator* 24, no. 15 (January 2000), pp. 88–90.

Specialized MBAs

M. Rowe, "Learning the Business of Wine, Sports, and Music," *International Herald Tribune,* (May 14, 2001), p. 18.

Speedpass

"McDonald's Accepts Speedpass for Fast Stomach Fill Up," press release (http://www.cardfrum.com/html/news/090800_1.htm).

"McDonald's Expands Cashless Test," *PROMO XTRA!,* June 4, 2001.

"Speedpass Expands to More than 400 McDonald's Restaurants in Chicagoland Area," press release (http://biz.yahoo.com/bw/010531/0270.html).

CLASSIC AND CONTEMPORARY READINGS

Aczel, Amir D., and Jayauel Sounderpandian. *Complete Business Statistics.* 5th ed. Chicago: Irwin/McGraw-Hill, 2001. The chapter on simple regression/ correlation has impeccable exposition and examples and is highly recommended.

Agresti, Alan, and Barbara Finlay. *Statistical Methods for the Social Sciences.* 3rd ed. Upper Saddle River, NJ: Prentice-Hall, 1997. Very clear coverage of nonparametric measures of association.

Chatterjee, Samprit, and Bertram Price. *Regression Analysis by Example.* 3rd ed. New York: Wiley, 1999. Updated version of widely used examples textbook.

Cohen, Jacob, and Patricia Cohen. *Applied Multiple Regression/ Correlation Analysis for the Behavioral Sciences.* 2nd ed. Mahwah, NJ: Lawrence Erlbaum Associates, 1983. A classic reference work.

Neter, John, Michael H. Kutner, Christopher J. Nachtsheim, and William Wasserman. *Applied Linear Statistical Models.* 4th ed. Burr Ridge, IL: Irwin, 1996. Chapters 1 through 10 and 15 provide an excellent introduction to regression and correlation analysis.

Siegel, S., and N. J. Castellan, Jr. *Nonparametric Statistics for the Behavioral Sciences.* 2nd ed. New York: McGraw-Hill, 1988.

CHAPTER 19

Multivariate Analysis: An Overview

Learning Objectives

After reading this chapter, you should understand . . .

1 How to classify and select multivariate techniques.

2 That multiple regression explains or predicts a metric dependent variable from a set of metric independent variables.

3 That discriminant analysis classifies people or objects into (categorical) groups using several metric predictors.

4 How multivariate analysis of variance assesses the relationship between two or more metric dependent variables and independent classificatory variables.

5 How structural equation modeling explains causality among constructs that cannot be directly measured—specifying causal relationships, connections, and unexplained variance among the constructs.

6 The ways conjoint analysis assists researchers to discover the importance of product or service attributes and the levels of features that are most desirable.

7 How principal components analysis extracts uncorrelated factors from an initial set of variables and factor analysis reduces the number of variables to discover the underlying constructs.

8 The use of cluster analysis techniques for grouping similar objects or people.

9 How perceptions of products or services are revealed numerically and geometrically by multidimensional scaling.

Bringing Research to Life

Dorrie Henry would have tolerated Henry Parker's habit of dropping in unexpectedly if he were not a bore, and a grabbing bore at that, one who had to seize you by the lapel or grasp your elbow while he shared his every vagrant thought. He was displaying his annoying habits at this very moment.

"I was driving by and saw two cars in your driveway and said, 'Henry, if Cousin Dorrie and her Jason are home on a Wednesday, then you had better stop in for a lemonade and a chat.'" This was supposed to be the day she caught up on her medical record keeping and Jason did tax reports for both of them. But here she was with Henry's arm draped on her shoulder and him waving his iced lemonade wildly to and fro.

She extricated herself by leveling with him. "Henry, I am not at all comfortable with you holding me so tightly." When she saw she had hurt his feelings, she softened her assertiveness with a little lie. "There is a strain of flu running around the clinic, you know, and though I am certainly immune, I would hate to pass it to you."

"Oh, sure, no problem, *doctor.* Anyway, *doctor,* I mostly want to fill your husband in on some late-breaking developments." In a single smooth motion he spun loose from his grip on Dorrie and surprised Jason with a lock on Jason's left forearm. Dorrie saw Jason's pupils first dilate and then contract, in a sure sign of annoyance, and she feared he would deal with Henry not as diplomatically as she had.

Jason had a name for Henry, "Ceteribus Parker," an allusion to *ceteribus paribus,* the Latin words for "all things being equal." It was Henry's annoying practice, while holding you in his firm grip (if you let him do so), to make amazingly improbable comparisons between people, groups, institutions, products, services, practices—anything and everything—by declaring the likes of "All things being equal, Mercury would seem to be a more congenial planet on which

life might emerge than Earth." Meaning, if you allowed for its atmosphere being nonexistent, and its temperature being 1,380 degrees Fahrenheit, there was presumably *something* about its gravitational fields or length of day that fitted Henry's preferred cosmology. *"Ceteribus paribus,"* he once said, "my electric bill would be cheaper if I lived in Antarctica than in Death Valley." You cannot argue against that kind of pseudoscientific blather.

Now Henry was lecturing Jason about an appointment he had taken as the business's representative to the governing board of the public housing authority. "The best tenants are the Pantamarians," he declared. "All things being equal, they are the most law-abiding and hard-working tenants."

"You mean Panamanians," Jason stated indifferently. It wasn't even a question, just a flat accusation of error.

"No, no, not Panamanians. These folks are *Pantamarians.* They are English-speakers from little islands in the Caribbean. Never heard of Pantamarie before I was put on the Authority, but, I tell you, they are the most law-abiding tenants . . ."

". . . *ceteribus paribus,"* echoed Jason ironically, as the very same words slipped from Henry's mouth. Dorrie saw signs of Jason's increasing impatience, as the color flushed his neck and he struggled to free himself from her cousin's grip.

"Do be more specific," urged Jason. "Are you telling me that the Pantamarians—have I got that right? Pantamarians?—have the lowest crime rate in the Authority? You must have data—you take federal funds, don't you? So you must have data."

"Well," said Henry, evasively, "you have got to allow for these Pantamarians having very large families. And they did not get much schooling, back home."

"So what is not equal is their family size and education. Right? What else? What else is not equal?"

Jason had leaned forward into Henry's grip and was now staring icily into Dorrie's cousin's eyes. Henry let loose his grip, set down his beverage, and reached for a handful of cocktail napkins, which he began to dab at his brow, mouth, and neck.

"Oh, well, you know. They are young. And there are other things. You know. Other things." Henry's voice had trailed off to a mere whisper as Jason bore in conversationally.

"No, I don't know. But I have good news for you, Henry. You can be sure that the Authority staff has been keeping really good records. We can go down there right now—wonderful of you to drop in on a working day—and ask the staff to roll out its records. Family size, education, age, everything. You can bet you have all that and more in your computers down there at the Authority. The Federal Housing and Urban Development people won't give you a penny without it."

Henry stumbled into a chair. He was trembling.

"Be right back," said Jason. He reappeared almost at once, carrying his laptop. "Good news, Henry. There are statistical techniques called *multivariate analysis* that in fact make all other things equal. Look here: This is a data cable. Let's hop in the car and run down to the Authority. You flash your identification, and I suck the data out of its computer. We set crime rate as the dependent variable—you know what that means, don't you?—and country of origin as the independent variable. Then we apply a technique called *analysis of covariance,* correcting for the effects of education, age, household size, whatever.

"Or maybe we do a *factor analysis* with Caribbean country of origin, the population count for 2000, GDP per capita, teacher ratios, female life expectancy, births and deaths, and the infant mortality rate per 1,000 of the population, radios and phones per 100 people, hospital beds, age, and family size. Then we'd know which variables are worth studying.

"Better yet, Henry, we could take the results of our *factor analysis* and run a *multiple regression* with crime rate as the dependent variable and the new factors which we output from the factor analysis as our predictors.

"Wait, this is the best one yet," Jason said excitedly. "We take your famous Pantamarians and the same data for their neighboring country and see if we can correctly classify them with a *discriminant analysis.*"

"And *voilà!!!* Your Pantamarians are the most law-abiding tenants, or they aren't. *Ceteribus paribus!!!!*"

Henry grabbed at his chest. "In my pocket," he croaked. "My pill box." Dorrie moved fast and had placed a nitro pill under Henry's tongue before Jason realized what was happening.

After she'd stabilized Henry and called for Cousin Anita to take him to his family doctor, Jason remained remorse-free. "That's the beautiful part of understanding multivariate analysis," he asserted. "In 10 minutes I would have shown Henry up for the old blowhard he is."

Following this inexcusable thrust, Jason slept for three nights on the sofa.

Introduction

In recent years, multivariate statistical tools have been applied with increasing frequency to research problems. This recognizes that many problems we encounter are more complex than the problems bivariate models can explain. Simultaneously, computer programs have taken advantage of the complex mathematics needed to manage multiple variable relationships. Today, computers with fast processing speeds and versatile software bring these powerful techniques to researchers.

Throughout the functional areas of management, more and more problems are being addressed by considering multiple independent and/or multiple dependent variables. Sales managers base forecasts on various product history variables; marketers consider the complex set of buyer preferences and preferred product options; financial analysts classify levels of credit risk based on a set of predictors; and human resource managers devise future wage and salary compensation plans with multivariate techniques.

Many of the examples presented in this text could be considered multivariate problems. The revenue improvements for a physicians' group that decided to join a different insurance program were based on multiple factors. In another example, the aviation industry was attempting to control radiation risks for passengers and crew by altering the proximity of air routes to the poles, aircraft shielding, altitude, and other variables. The price of investment-grade wine was forecast based on spring and harvest rainfall and growing-season temperatures.

One author defines **multivariate analysis** as "those statistical techniques which focus upon, and bring out in bold relief, the structure of simultaneous relationships among three or more phenomena."[1] Our overview of multivariate analysis seeks to illustrate the meaning of this definition while building on your understanding of bivariate statistics from the last few chapters. Several common multivariate techniques and examples will be discussed.

Because a complete treatment of this subject would require a thorough consideration of the mathematics, assumptions, and diagnostic tools appropriate for each technique, our coverage is necessarily limited. Readers needing greater detail are referred to the suggested readings at the end of the chapter.

Selecting a Multivariate Technique

Multivariate techniques may be classified as **dependency** and **interdependency techniques.** Selecting an appropriate technique starts with an understanding of this distinction. If criterion and predictor variables exist in the research question, then we will have an assumption of dependence. Multiple regression, multivariate analysis of variance (MANOVA), and discriminant analysis are techniques where criterion or dependent variables and predictor or independent variables are present. Alternatively, if the variables are interrelated without designating some dependent and others independent, then interdependence of the variables is assumed. Factor analysis, cluster analysis, and multidimensional scaling are examples of interdependency techniques.

Exhibit 19–1 provides a diagram to guide in the selection of techniques. Let's take an example to show how you might make a decision. Every other year since 1978, the Roper organization has tracked public opinion toward business by providing a list of items that are said to be the responsibility of business. The respondents are asked whether business fulfills these responsibilities "fully, fairly well, not too well, or not at all well." The following issues make up the list:[2]

- Developing new products and services.

- Producing good-quality products and services.

- Making products that are safe to use.

- Hiring minorities.

- Providing jobs for people.

- Being good citizens of the communities in which they operate.

EXHIBIT 19-1 Selecting from the Most Common Multivariate Techniques

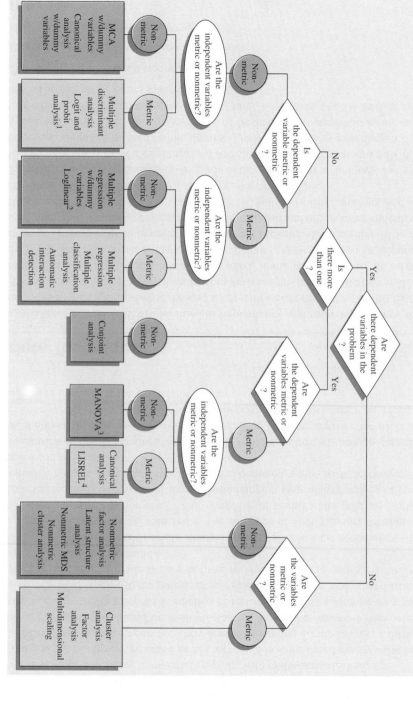

Notes:

[1]The independent variable is metric only in the sense that a transformed proportion is used.

[2]The independent variable is metric only when we consider that the number of cases in the cross-tabulation cell are used to calculate the logs.

[3]Factors may be considered nonmetric independent variables in that they organize the data into groups. We do not classify MANOVA and other multivariate analysis of variance models.

[4]LISREL refers to a linear structural equations model for latent variables. It is a family of models appropriate for confirmatory factor analysis, path analysis, time series analysis, recursive and nonrecursive models, and covariance structure models. Because it may handle dependence and interdependence, metric and nonmetric, it is arbitrarily placed in this diagram.

SOURCE: Partially adapted from T. C. Kinnear and J. R. Taylor, "Multivariate Methods in Marketing: A Further Attempt at Classification," *Journal of Marketing*, October 1971, p. 57; and J. F. Hair, Jr., Rolph E. Anderson, Ronald L. Tatham, and Bernie J. Grablowsky, *Multivariate Data Analysis* (Tulsa, OK: Petroleum Publishing Co., 1979), pp. 10–14.

- Paying good salaries and benefits to employees.
- Charging reasonable prices for goods and services.
- Keeping profits at reasonable levels.
- Advertising honestly.
- Paying their fair share.
- Cleaning up their own air and water pollution.

You have access to data on these items and wish to know if they could be reduced to a smaller set of variables that would account for most of the variation among respondents. In response to the first question in Exhibit 19–1, you correctly determine there are no dependent variables in the data set. You then check to see if the variables are **metric** or **nonmetric measures.** In the figure, *metric* refers to ratio and interval measurements, and *nonmetric* refers to data that are nominal and ordinal. Based on the measurement scale, which appears to have equal intervals, and preliminary findings that show a linear relationship between several variables, you decide the data are metric. This decision leads you to three options: multidimensional scaling, cluster analysis, or factor analysis. *Multidimensional scaling* develops a geometric picture or map of the locations of some objects relative to others. This map specifies how the objects differ. *Cluster analysis* identifies homogeneous subgroups or clusters. *Factor analysis* looks for patterns among the variables to discover if an underlying combination of the original variables (a factor) can summarize the original set. Based on your research objective, you select factor analysis.

Suppose you are interested in predicting family food expenditures from family income, family size, and whether the family's location is rural or urban. Returning to Exhibit 19–1, you conclude there is a singular dependent variable, family food expenditures. You decide this variable is metric since dollars are measured on a ratio scale. The independent variables, income and family size, also meet the criteria for metric data. However, you are not sure about the location variable since it appears to be a dichotomous nominal variable. According to the figure, your choices are automatic interaction detection (AID), multiple classification analysis (MCA), and multiple regression. You recall from Chapter 16 that AID was designed to locate the most important interaction effects and typically uses numerous independent variables in its sequential partitioning procedure. MCA handles weak predictors (including nominal variables), correlated predictors, and nonlinear relationships. Multiple regression is the extension of bivariate regression. You believe that your data exceed the assumptions for the first two techniques and that by treating the nominal variable's values as 0 or 1, you could use it as an independent variable in a multiple regression model. You prefer this to losing information from the other two variables—a certainty if you reduce them to nonmetric data.

In the next two sections, we will extend this discussion as we illustrate dependency and interdependency techniques.

Dependency Techniques

Multiple Regression

Multiple regression is used as a descriptive tool in three types of situations. First, it is often used to develop a self-weighting estimating equation by which to predict values for a criterion variable (DV) from the values for several predictor variables (IVs). Thus, we might try to predict company sales on the basis of new housing starts, new marriage rates, annual disposable income, and a time factor. Another prediction study might be one in which we estimate a student's academic performance in college from the variables of rank in high school class, SAT verbal scores, SAT quantitative scores, and a rating scale reflecting impressions from an interview.

Second, a descriptive application of multiple regression calls for controlling for confounding variables to better evaluate the contribution of other variables. For example, one might wish to control the brand of a product and the store in which it is bought to study the effects of price as an indicator of product quality.[3] A third use of multiple regression is to test and explain causal theories. In this approach, often referred to as **path analysis,** regression is used to describe an entire structure of linkages that have been advanced from a causal theory.[4] In addition to being a descriptive tool, multiple regression is also used as an inference tool to test hypotheses and to estimate population values.

Method   Multiple regression is an extension of the bivariate linear regression presented in Chapter 18. The terms defined in that chapter will not be repeated here. Although **dummy variables** (nominal variables coded 0, 1) may be used, all other variables must be interval or ratio. The generalized equation is

$$Y = \beta_0 + \beta_1 X_1 + \beta_2 X_2 + \ldots + \beta_n X_n + \varepsilon$$

where

β_0 = A constant, the value of Y when all X values are zero.

β_i = The slope of the regression surface or the response surface. The β represents the regression coefficient associated with each X_i.

ε = An error term, normally distributed about a mean of 0. For purposes of computation, the ε is assumed to be 0.

The regression coefficients are stated either in raw score units (the actual X values) or as **standardized coefficients** (X values restated in terms of their standard deviations). In either case, the value of the regression coefficient states the amount that Y varies with each unit change of the associated X variable when the effects of all other X variables are being held constant. When the regression coefficients are standardized, they are called **beta weights** (β), and their values indicate the relative importance of the associated X values, particularly when the predictors are unrelated. For example, in an equation where $\beta_1 = .60$ and $\beta_2 = .20$, one concludes that X_1 has three times the influence on Y as does X_2.

Example   In a Snapshot later in this chapter, we describe an e-business that uses multivariate approaches to understand its target market in the global "hybrid mail" business. SuperLetter's basic service enables users to create a document on any PC and send it in a secure encrypted mode over the Internet to a distant international terminal near the addressee, where it will be printed, processed, and delivered via the local postal service. Spread like a "fish net" over the world's major commercial markets, the network connects corresponding parties, linking the world's "wired" with its "non-wired."

We use multiple regression in this example to evaluate the key drivers of customer usage for hybrid mail. Among the explanatory variables are customer perceptions of: (1) cost/speed valuation, (2) security (limits on changing, editing, or forwarding a document and document privacy), (3) reliability, (4) receiver technology (hard copy for receivers with no e-mail or fax access), and (5) impact/emotional value (reducing e-mail spam clutter and official/important appearance). We have chosen the first three variables, all measured on 5-point scales, for this equation:

Y = customer usage

X_1 = cost/speed valuation

X_2 = security

X_3 = reliability

SPSS computed the model and the regression coefficients. Most statistical packages provide various methods for selecting variables for the equation. The equation can be built with all variables or specific combinations or you can select a method that sequentially adds or removes variables (forward selection, backward elimination, and stepwise selection). **Forward selection** starts with the constant and adds variables that result in the largest R^2 increase. **Backward elimination** begins with a model containing all independent variables and removes the variable that changes R^2 the least. **Stepwise selection,** the most popular method, combines forward and backward sequential approaches. The independent variable that contributes the most to explaining the dependent variable is added first. Subsequent variables are included based on their incremental contribution over the first variable and whether they meet the criterion for entering the equation (e.g., a significance level of .01). Variables may be removed at each step if they meet the removal criterion, which is a larger significance level than for entry.

The standard elements of a stepwise output are shown in Exhibit 19–2. In the upper portion of the exhibit there are three models. In Model 1, cost/speed is the first variable to enter the equation. This model consists of the constant and the variable cost/speed. Model 2 adds the security variable to cost/speed. Model 3 consists of all three independent variables. In the summary statistics for Model 1, you see that cost/speed explains 77 percent of customer usage (see the R^2 column). This is increased by 8 percent in Model 2 when security is added (see R^2 Change column). When reliability is added in Model 3, accounting for only 2 percent, 87 percent of customer usage is explained.

The other reported statistics have the following interpretations.

1. Adjusted R square for Model 3 = .871. R^2 is adjusted to reflect the model's goodness of fit for the population. The net effect of this adjustment is to reduce the R^2 from .873 to .871, thereby making it comparable to other R^2s from equations with a different number of independent variables.

2. Standard error of Model 3 = .4937. This is the standard deviation of actual values of Y about the regression line of estimated Y values.

3. Analysis of variance measures whether or not the equation represents a set of regression coefficients that, in total, are statistically significant from zero. The critical value for F is found in Appendix Table G–9, with degrees of freedom for the numerator equaling k, the number of independent variables, and for the denominator, $n - k - 1$, where n for Model 3 is 183 observations. Thus, d.f. = (3, 179). The equation is statistically significant at less than the .05 level of significance (see the column labeled "Significant F Change").

4. Regression coefficients for all three models are shown in the lower table of Exhibit 19–2. The column headed "B" shows the unstandardized regression coefficients for the equation. The equation may now be constructed as:

$$Y = -.093 + .448X_1 + .315X_2 + 254X_3$$

EXHIBIT 19–2   **Multiple Regression Analysis of Hybrid Mail Customer Usage, Cost/Speed Valuation, Security, and Reliability**

Model Summary

Model	R	R^2	Adjusted R^2	Std. Error of the Estimate	R^2 Change	F Change	d.f.1	d.f.2	Sig. F Change
					Change Statistics				
1	.879	.772	.771	.6589	.772	612.696	1	181	.000
2	.925	.855	.854	.5263	.083	103.677	2	180	.000
3	.935	.873	.871	.4937	.018	25.597	3	179	.000

1 Predictors: (constant), cost/speed.
2 Predictors: (constant), cost/speed, security.
3 Predictors: (constant), cost/speed, security, reliability.

Coefficients

Model		Unstandardized Coefficients B	Std. Error	Standardized Coefficients Beta	t	Sig.	Collinearity Statistics VIF
1	(Constant)	.579	.151		3.834	.000	
	Cost/Speed	.857	.035	.879	24.753	.000	1.000
2	(Constant)	9.501E-02	.130		.733	.464	
	Cost/Speed	.537	.042	.551	12.842	.000	2.289
	Security	.428	.042	.437	10.182	.000	2.289
3	(Constant)	−9.326E-02	.127		−.734	.464	
	Cost/Speed	.448	.043	.460	10.428	.000	2.748
	Security	.315	.045	.321	6.948	.000	3.025
	Reliability	.254	.050	.236	5.059	.000	3.067

Dependent variable: Customer usage.

5. The column headed "Beta" gives the regression coefficients expressed in standardized form. When these are used, the regression Y intercept is zero. Standardized coefficients are useful when the variables are measured on different scales. The beta coefficients also show the relative contribution of the three independent variables to the explanatory power of this equation. The cost/speed valuation variable explains more than either of the other two variables.

6. Standard error is a measure of the sampling variability of each regression coefficient.

7. The column headed "t" measures the statistical significance of each of the regression coefficients.

Again compare these to the table of t values in Appendix Table G–9, using degrees of freedom for one independent variable. All three regression coefficients are judged to be significantly different from zero. Therefore, the regression equation shows the relationship between the dependent variable, customer usage of hybrid mail, and three independent variables: cost/speed, security, and reliability. The regression coefficients are both individually and jointly statistically significant. The independent variable cost/speed influences customer usage the most, followed by security and then reliability.

Collinearity—or **multicollinearity,** the situation where two or more of the independent variables are highly correlated—can have damaging effects on multiple regression. When this condition exists, the estimated regression coefficients can fluctuate widely from sample to sample, making it risky to interpret the coefficients as an indicator of the relative importance of predictor variables. Just how high can acceptable correlations be between independent variables? There is no definitive answer, but correlations at a .80 or greater level should be dealt with in one of two ways: (1) Choose one of the variables and delete the other, or (2) create a new variable that is a composite of the highly intercorrelated variables and use this new variable in place of its components. Making this decision with a correlation matrix alone is not always advisable. In the example just presented, Exhibit 19–2 contains a column labeled "Collinearity Statistics" that shows a variable inflation factor (VIF) index. This is a measure of the effect of the other independent variables on a regression coefficient. Large values, usually 10.0 or more, suggest collinearity or multicollinearity. With the three predictors in the hybrid mail example, multicollinearity is not a problem.

We discuss the correlation matrix, which displays multiple combinations of two variable relationships, in Chapter 18.

Another difficulty with regression occurs when researchers fail to evaluate the equation with data beyond those used originally to calculate it. A practical solution is to set aside a portion of the data (from a fourth to a third) and use only the remainder to compute the estimating equation. This is called a **holdout sample.** One then uses the equation on the holdout data to calculate an R^2. This can then be compared to the original R^2 to determine how well the equation predicts beyond its database.

SNAPSHOT Teeing Up a New Strategic Direction

NCR Country Club (NCRCC) has undergone a dramatic transformation within the last three years with the construction of a multimillion-dollar clubhouse and dining facility, but the changes have been built on the long-standing tradition of fine golf and dining. Started in 1954 as an employee benefit of the National Cash Register Co. but now an open-membership club, this country club located near Dayton (OH) hosts two 18-hole golf courses. The NCRCC South course, a par 71 championship course of 6,824 yards of heavily wooded rolling countryside, has played host to the PGA Championship (1996), the U.S. Open (1986), and the U.S. Mid-Amateur (1998) and is consistently ranked by *Golf Digest* as one of the top 100 courses in the U.S.

When its aging membership started to decrease and a one-year membership referral drive didn't dramatically reverse the trend, NCRCC turned to the McMahon Group, a research and strategic golf-course management specialist, for insight and direction. Through an extensive two-stage research design employing six focus groups of 10–15 people each, followed by 886 membership surveys, McMahon's research helped NCRCC design a new strategic direction. Sophisticated modeling and analysis led to new facilities for swimming and fitness that turned this proud golf and dining organization into a full-service club for 2,000 with amenities to serve its new target member (the under-46, golf-oriented household, with one or more children under 21 still living at home).

www.mcmahongroup.com

www.ncr.com

Discriminant Analysis

Researchers often wish to classify people or objects into two or more groups. One might need to classify persons as either buyers or nonbuyers, good or bad credit risks, or superior, average, or poor performers in some activity. The objective is to establish a procedure to find the predictors that best classify subjects.

Method   **Discriminant analysis** joins a nominally scaled criterion or dependent variable with one or more independent variables that are interval or ratio scaled. Once the discriminant equation is found, it can be used to predict the classification of a new observation. This is done by calculating a linear function of the form

$$D_i = d_0 + d_1X_1 + d_2X_2 + \ldots + d_pX_p$$

where

D_i is the score on discriminant function i.

The d_is are weighting coefficients; d_0 is a constant.

The Xs are the values of the discriminating variables used in the analysis.

A single discriminant equation is required if the categorization calls for two groups. If three groups are involved in the classification, it requires two discriminant equations. If more categories are called for in the dependent variable, it is necessary to calculate a separate discriminant function for each pair of classifications in the criterion group.

While the most common use for discriminant analysis is to classify persons or objects into various groups, it can also be used to analyze known groups to determine the relative influence of specific factors for deciding into which group various cases fall. Assume we have supervisory ratings that enable us to classify administrators as successful or unsuccessful on administrative performance. We might also be able to secure test results on three measures: ability to work with others (X_1), motivation for administrative work (X_2), and general professional skill (X_3). Suppose the discriminant equation is:

$$D = .06X_1 + .45X_2 + .30X_3$$

Since discriminant analysis uses standardized values for the discriminant variables, we conclude from the coefficients that ability to work with others is less important than the other two in classifying administrators.[5]

Example   An illustration of the method takes us back to the problem in the last chapter where Dean Merrill, a brokerage firm, is hiring MBAs for its account executives program. Over the years the firm has had indifferent success with the selection process. You are asked to develop a procedure to improve this. It appears that discriminant analysis is a perfect technique. You begin by gathering data on 30 MBAs who have been hired in recent years. Fifteen of these have been successful employees while the other 15 have been unsatisfactory. The personnel files provide the following information that can be used to conduct the analysis:

X_1 = Years of prior work experience.

X_2 = GPA in graduate program.

X_3 = Employment test scores.

An algorithm determines how well these three independent variables will correctly classify those who are judged successful from those judged unsuccessful. The classifi-

EXHIBIT 19–3 Discriminant Analysis Classification Results of MBA Hires at Dean Merrill

Actual Group		Number of Cases	Predicted Group Membership	
			0	1
Unsuccessful	0	15	13	2
			86.7%	13.3%
Successful	1	15	3	12
			20.0%	80.0%

Note: Percent of "grouped" cases correctly classified: 83.33%.

cation results are shown in Exhibit 19–3. This indicates that 25 of the 30 ($30 - 3 - 2 = 25$) cases have been correctly classified using these three variables.

The standardized and unstandardized discriminant function coefficients are as follows:

	Unstandardized	Standardized
X_1	.36084	.65927
X_2	2.61192	.57958
X_3	.53028	.97505
(constant)	12.89685	

These results indicate that X_3 (the employment test) has the greatest discriminating power. Several significance tests are also computed. One, Wilk's lambda, has a chi-square transformation for testing the significance of the discriminant function. It indicates the equation is statistically significant at the $\alpha = .0004$ level. Using the discriminant equation,

$$D = .659X_1 + .580X_2 + .975X_3$$

you can now predict whether future candidates are likely to be successful account executives.

MANOVA

Multivariate analysis of variance, or **MANOVA,** is a commonly used multivariate technique. MANOVA assesses the relationship between two or more dependent variables and classificatory variables or factors. In business research, MANOVA can be used to test differences among samples of employees, customers, manufactured items, production parts, and so forth.

Method MANOVA is similar to the univariate ANOVA described earlier, with the added ability to handle several dependent variables. If ANOVA is applied consecutively to a set of interrelated dependent variables, erroneous conclusions may result. MANOVA can correct this by simultaneously testing all the variables and their interrelationships. MANOVA employs sums-of-squares and cross-products (SSCP) matrices to test for differences among groups. The variance between groups is determined by

EXHIBIT 19–4   **MANOVA Techniques Show These Three Centroids to Be Unequal in the CalAudio Study**

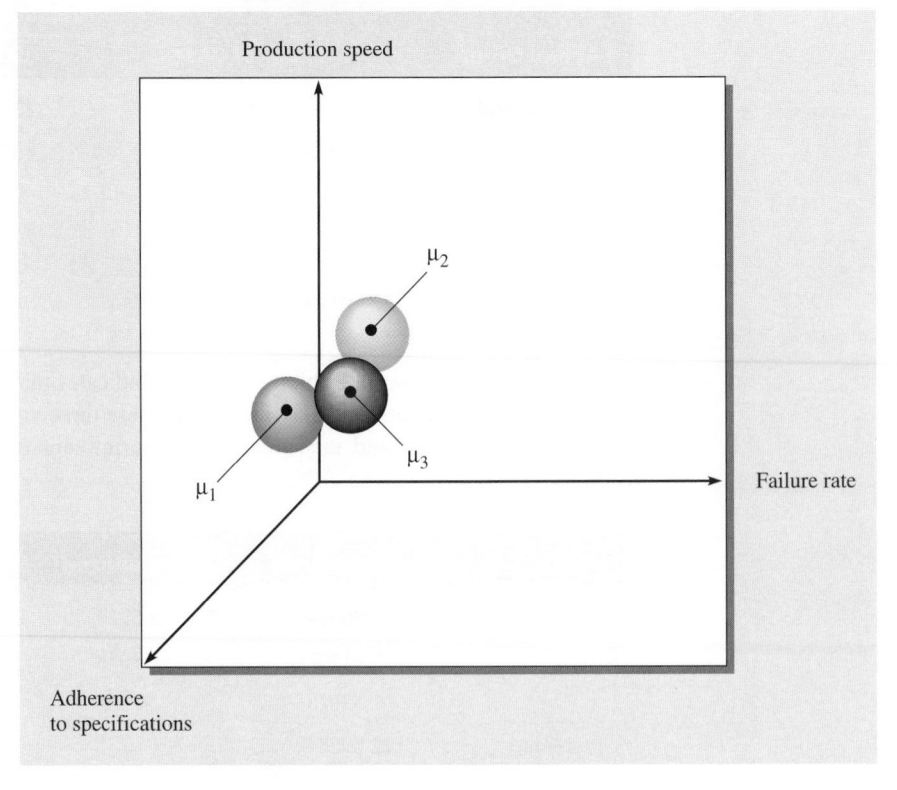

partitioning the total SSCP matrix and testing for significance. The F ratio, generalized to a ratio of the within-group variance and total-group variance matrices, tests for equality among treatment groups.

MANOVA examines similarities and differences among the multivariate mean scores of several populations. The null hypothesis for MANOVA is that all of the **centroids** (multivariate means) are equal, H_0: $\mu_1 = \mu_2 = \mu_3 = \ldots \mu_n$. The alternative hypothesis is that the vectors of centroids are unequal, H_A: $\mu_1 \neq \mu_2 \neq \mu_3 \neq \ldots \mu_n$. Exhibit 19–4 shows graphically three populations whose centroids are unequal, allowing the researcher to reject the null hypothesis. When the null hypothesis is rejected, additional tests are done to better understand the data. Several alternatives may be considered:

1. Univariate F tests can be run on the dependent variables.

2. Simultaneous confidence intervals can be produced for each variable.

3. Stepdown analysis, like stepwise regression, can be run by computing F values successively. Each value is computed after the effects of the previous dependent variable are eliminated.

4. Multiple discriminant analysis can be used on the SSCP matrices. This aids in the discovery of which variables contribute to the MANOVA's significance.[6]

Example   To illustrate, let's look at CalAudio, a firm that manufactures compact disk (CD) players. The plant manager is concerned about the quality of CD players coming off the manufacturing line. Two measures are used to assess quality in this example: adherence to product specifications and time before failure. Measured on a 0–100 scale

EXHIBIT 19–5 MANOVA Cell Means and Standard Deviations in CalAudio Study

VARIABLE	FACTOR	LEVEL	MEAN	STD. DEV.
FAILURE				
	METHOD	1	158.867	4.998
	METHOD	2	181.067	5.994
	For entire sample		169.967	12.524
SPECIFICATIONS				
	METHOD	1	89.800	2.077
	METHOD	2	94.800	2.178
	For entire sample		92.300	3.292
SPEED				
	METHOD	1	2.126	.061
	METHOD	2	2.599	.068
	For entire sample		2.362	.249

with 100 meeting all product specifications, the specification variable is averaging approximately 90. The mean time before failure is calculated in weeks; it is approximately 159 weeks, or three years.

The plant manager asks the industrial engineering department to devise a modified manufacturing procedure that will improve the quality measures but not change the production rate significantly. A new method is designed that includes more efficient parts handling and "burn-in" time where CD players are powered up and run at high temperatures.

Engineering takes a sample of 15 CD players made with the old manufacturing method and 15 made with the new method. The players are measured for their adherence to product specifications and are stress-tested to determine their time before failure. The stress test uses accelerated running conditions and adverse environmental conditions to simulate years of use in a short time.

Exhibit 19–5 shows the mean and standard deviation of the dependent variables (failure, specifications, and manufacturing speed) for each level of method.[7] Method 1 represents the current manufacturing process, and method 2 is the new process. The new method extended the time before failure to 181 weeks, compared to 159 weeks for the existing method. The adherence to specifications is also improved, up to 95 from 90. But the manufacturing speed is slower by approximately 30 minutes (.473 hour).

We have used diagnostics to check the assumptions of MANOVA except for equality of variance. Both levels of the manufacturing method variable produce a matrix, and the equality of these two matrices must be determined. Exhibit 19–6 contains homogeneity of variance tests for separate dependent variables and a multivariate test. The former are known as univariate tests. The multivariate test is a comparable version that tests the variables simultaneously to determine whether MANOVA should proceed.

The significance levels of Cochran's C and Bartlett-Box F do not allow us to reject any of the tests for the dependent variables considered separately. This means the two methods have equal variances in each dependent variable. This fulfills the univariate assumptions for homogeneity of variance. We then consider the variances and covariances simultaneously with Box's M, also found in Exhibit 19–6. Again, we are unable to reject the homogeneity of variance assumption regarding the matrices. This satisfies the multivariate assumptions.

EXHIBIT 19–6   MANOVA Homogeneity of Variance Tests in the CalAudio Study

```
VARIABLE            TEST                        RESULTS

FAILURE

        Cochran's C (14,2) =          .58954, P = .506 (approx.)
        Bartlett-Box F (1,2352) =     .44347, P = .506

SPECIFICATIONS

        Cochran's C (14,2) =          .52366, P = .862 (approx.)
        Bartlett-Box F (1,2352) =     .03029, P = .862

SPEED

        Cochran's C (14,2) =          .55526, P = .684 (approx.)
        Bartlett-Box F (1,2352) =     .16608, P = .684

    Multivariate Test for Homogeneity of Dispersion Matrices

        Box's M =                     6.07877
        F with (6,5680) DF =          .89446, P = .498 (approx.)
        Chi-Square with 6 DF =        5.37320, P = .497 (approx.)
```

EXHIBIT 19–7   Bartlett's Test of Sphericity in the CalAudio Study

```
Statistics for WITHIN CELLS correlations

Log (Determinant) =              -3.92663
Bartlett's test of sphericity =  102.74687 with 3 D.F.
Significance =                    .000

F(max) criterion =               7354.80161 with (3,28) D.F.
```

When MANOVA is applied properly, the dependent variables are correlated. If the dependent variables are unrelated, there would be no necessity for a multivariate test, and we could use separate F tests for failure, specifications, and speed much like the ANOVAs in Chapter 17. Bartlett's test of sphericity helps us decide if we should continue analyzing MANOVA results or return to separate univariate tests. In Exhibit 19–7, we will look for a determinant value that is close to 0. This implies that one or more dependent variables is a linear function of another. The determinant has a chi-square transformation that simplifies testing for statistical significance. Since the observed significance is below that set for the model ($\alpha = .05$), we are able to reject the null hypothesis and conclude there are dependencies among the failure, specifications, and speed variables.

We now move to the test of equality of means that considers the three dependent variables for the two levels of manufacturing method. This test is analogous to a t-test or an F test for multivariate data. The sums-of-squares and cross-products (SSCP) matrices are used. Exhibit 19–8 shows three tests, including the Hotelling T^2. All the tests provided are compared to the F distribution for interpretation. Since the observed

EXHIBIT 19–8 Multivariate Tests of Significance in the CalAudio Study

```
Multivariate Tests of Significance (S = 1, M = 1/2, N = 12)

Test Name       Value       Exact F   Hypoth. DF   Error DF   Sig. of F

Hotelling      51.33492    444.90268      3.00        26.00       .000
Pillai           .98089    444.90268      3.00        26.00       .000
Wilks            .01911    444.90268      3.00        26.00       .000
```

Note: *F* statistics are exact.

EXHIBIT 19–9 Univariate Tests of Significance in the CalAudio Study

```
Univariate F-Tests with (1,28) D.F.

Variable   Hypoth. SS   Error SS   Hypoth. MS   Error MS          F   Sig. of F

FAILURE    3696.30000   852.66667  3696.30000    30.45238  121.37967     .000
SPECS       187.50000   126.80000   187.50000     4.52857   41.40379     .000
SPEED         1.67560      .11593     1.67560      .00414  404.68856     .000
```

Note: *F* statistics are exact.

significance level is less than $\alpha = .05$ for the T^2 test, we reject the null hypothesis that said methods 1 and 2 provide equal results with respect to failure, specifications, and speed. Similar results are obtained from the Pillai trace and Wilks' statistic.

Finally, to detect where the differences lie, we can examine the results of univariate *F* tests in Exhibit 19–9. Since there are only two methods, the *F* is equivalent to t^2 for a two-sample *t*-test. The significance levels for these tests do not reflect that several comparisons are being made, and we should use them principally for diagnostic purposes. This is similar to problems that require the use of multiple comparison tests in univariate analysis of variance. Note, however, that there are statistically significant differences in all three dependent variables resulting from the new manufacturing method. Techniques for further analysis of MANOVA results were listed at the beginning of this section.

See Chapter 17's discussion of multiple comparison procedures.

LISREL[8]

First developed by Karl Jöreskog in 1973, **LISREL** (an acronym for *linear structural relationships*) is still a commonly accepted term for referring to both the software program and the general statistical method for modeling the analysis of covariance structures. While several other programs have been written since, with EQS and AMOS ranking among the most popular, LISREL is still the most widely referenced package for estimation of the covariance structure model, also frequently referred to as structural equation modeling (SEM). LISREL is a powerful alternative to other multivariate techniques, such as multiple regression, MANOVA, and canonical analysis—which are limited to representing only a single relationship between the dependent and independent variables. The major advantages of LISREL are that it can estimate multiple and interrelated dependence relationships, and that it can represent unobserved concepts, or *latent variables,* in those relationships and account for measurement error in the estimation process.

LISREL is a technique that allows for separate relationships for each of a set of dependent variables. In its most basic sense, LISREL provides an efficient estimation technique for a series of multiple regression equations projected simultaneously. The general LISREL model consists of two submodels: a measurement model and a structural model. The *measurement model* allows the researcher to use several observed variables as factors of a single unobserved independent or dependent variable. This provides the link between observed scores on measurement instruments and the underlying constructs they are designed to measure. Using confirmatory factor analysis (CFA), the researcher can evaluate the contribution of each manifest variable as well as incorporate how well the overall instrument measures the concept into the estimation of the relationships between dependent and independent variables.

The *structural model* is the "path" model that defines relationships among the unobserved variables. It specifies which latent variables cause changes in the values of other latent variables in the model. The development of the structural model requires the incorporation of theory, previous experience, or other guidelines to help the researcher discern which independent variables predict each dependent variable.

LISREL is usually viewed as a confirmatory rather than an exploratory procedure; however, its flexibility provides the researcher with a versatile modeling program that can be applied to a variety of research objectives. Three distinct strategies appropriate for LISREL include:

- The strictly confirmatory strategy.
- The competing models approach.
- The model development strategy.

In the *strictly confirmatory approach*, the researcher specifies a single model, which is tested using LISREL's goodness-of-fit tests to assess its statistical significance. This allows the researcher to discern whether the pattern of variances and covariances in the data is consistent with the specified structural model. However, research has shown this approach is subject to *confirmation bias* and tends to confirm that the model fits the data. Accordingly, other unexamined models may fit the data as well or better, and an accepted model is confirmed as being only one of several possible acceptable models.

Using the *competing models strategy*, the researcher may test several causal models against each other to determine which has the best fit. By examining models with different hypothetical structural relationships, the researcher comes much closer to comparing competing "theories." This is a much stronger test than a comparison of slight modifications of a single theory. An example is a comparison of equivalent models—alternatives that differ in proposed relationships but that have the same number of parameters and the same level of model fit.

The *model development strategy* differs from the strictly confirmatory and competing models approaches in that the researcher seeks to improve the model by modifying the structural and measurement models. In practice, much of the research combines confirmatory and exploratory purposes, especially in cases where theory provides only the framework for a model, which must then be empirically tested. The tested model is often found to be deficient in some way, and an alternative model is then tested based on changes suggested by the LISREL modification indexes. This is perhaps the most common approach found in the literature. However, this approach may be problematic if the post hoc models that are confirmed do not fit new data. One way to possibly avoid this problem is for researchers to use a *cross-validation* approach that uses a calibration data sample to develop the model and an independent validation sample for confirmation.

Method LISREL is a several-step process that begins with the development of a theoretical model based on causal relationships. In order to assume causality, the researcher must satisfy four general requirements:

1. There must be sufficient association between the two variables being considered.

2. The assumed cause must occur prior to the observed effect.

3. There must be a lack of viable alternative causal variables.

4. There must be a theoretical basis for the relationship.

Researchers must be careful to consider all key predictive variables in order to avoid **specification error,** a bias that overestimates the importance of the variables included in the model.

The second step is to construct a **path diagram** that allows the researcher to present the predictive and associative relationships among the constructs and indicators in the model. The path diagram includes various shapes, lines, and notation, and researchers using LISREL must understand how the geometric symbolism depicted in the schematic models relates to the regression or matrix equations. In path diagrams, three types of arrows are used to depict all of the relationships in the model. Straight arrows denote causal relationships from one variable to another; a curved arrow or line indicates a covariance between constructs; and a straight arrow with two heads shows a reciprocal relationship between constructs. Exhibit 19–10 illustrates some other key symbols frequently used in path diagrams.

The matrices used in LISREL equations are represented using Greek notation. A *matrix* is a collection of numbers written in rows and columns, and the numbers within the matrix are its *elements*. These elements represent the parameters in the model. A matrix with only one column but multiple rows is called a **vector.** Matrices are most commonly represented by uppercase Greek letters, and the elements of a matrix are denoted using lowercase Greek letters. The observed measures are indicated using Roman letters—independent variables are labeled *X-variables,* and dependent variables are labeled *Y-variables.* At the most, eight matrices and four vectors define a general LISREL model, although the actual number of matrices required will depend on the particular model specified.

EXHIBIT 19–10   Symbols Frequently Used in Path Diagrams

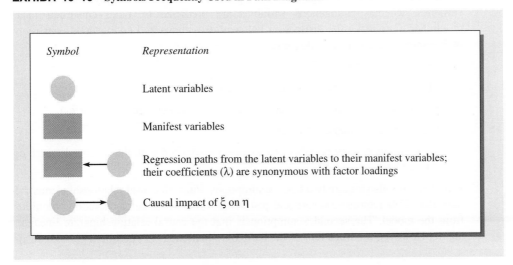

Symbol	Representation
	Latent variables
	Manifest variables
	Regression paths from the latent variables to their manifest variables; their coefficients (λ) are synonymous with factor loadings
	Causal impact of ξ on η

EXHIBIT 19–11 A Summary of Matrix and Greek Notation[9]

Greek Letter	Full Matrix	Matrix Elements	Type
Measurement Model			
Lambda-X	Λ_X	λ_X	Regression
Lambda-Y	Λ_Y	λ_Y	Regression
Theta delta	Θ_δ	θ_δ	Var/cov
Theta epsilon	Θ_ε	θ_ε	Var/cov
Nu	—	ν	Vector
Structural Model			
Gamma	Γ	γ	Regression
Beta	B	β	Regression
Phi	Φ	φ	Var/cov
Psi	Ψ	ψ	Var/cov
Xi	—	ξ	Vector
Eta	—	η	Vector
Zeta	—	ζ	Vector

For the general LISREL model, the measurement model is composed of two regression matrices, two variance-covariance matrices among errors of measurement, and one vector representing the endogenous factor. The structural model comprises two variance-covariance matrices (one among the exogenous factors and one among the residual errors associated with the endogenous factors) and three vectors representing the exogenous variables, endogenous variables, and errors associated with the endogenous variables, respectively. A summary of these matrices and vectors is presented in Exhibit 19–11.

In the path diagram, each of the constructs is specified as being exogenous (independent) or endogenous (dependent). Exogenous variables are not predicted by other variables, whereas endogenous variables are predicted by other constructs. The researcher must make the distinction between exogenous and endogenous constructs with respect to each of the following:

1. The number of factors (ξ or η).

2. The number of observed variables (X or Y).

3. Relationships between the observed variables and latent factors (λ_X or λ_Y).

4. Factor variances and covariances (φ).

5. Error variances (and possibly covariances) associated with the observed variables (Θ_δ or Θ_ε).

Path diagrams also require two basic assumptions. First, all causal relationships must be indicated. This requires a theoretical justification for including or excluding variables from the model. The second assumption is that the causal relationships are linear in nature. However, modifications of the LISREL equation, as in multiple regression, usu-

EXHIBIT 19–12 Path Analysis of X and Y Constructs[10]

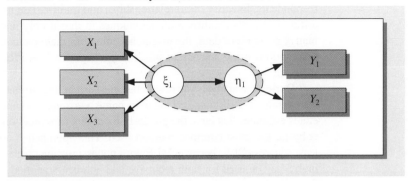

EXHIBIT 19–13 The LISREL CFA Model Relative to the LISREL Full Model[11]

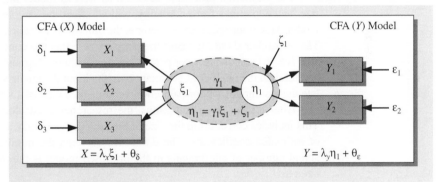

ally allow for the model to remain robust against this assumption. An example of a simple path analysis is shown in Exhibit 19–12.

After the path diagram is hypothesized, the third stage in LISREL is to convert the path diagram into a more formal set of structural and measurement models. This is accomplished through a set of equations that define (1) the structural equations linking the constructs; (2) the measurement model specifying exogenous and endogenous variables; and (3) a set of matrices indicating any hypothetical covariances among the constructs or variables. The goal for this stage is to develop a connection between the operational definitions of the constructs and the theory for the proper test.

The measurement model, commonly referred to as a **confirmatory factor analysis (CFA)** model, is achieved similar to exploratory factor analysis (EFA) and details on its methodology are provided in that section of the chapter. The main difference between EFA and CFA is that in EFA there are no constraints on variable loading; accordingly, each variable has a loading on each factor. In CFA, the researcher specifies which variables, or *indicators,* define each construct. To develop the structural model, each endogenous construct becomes a dependent variable in a separate equation. Exhibit 19–13 illustrates that *relative to the structural model* there are two CFA models with a theoretical causal relationship, γ_1, between ξ_1 and η_1. δ and ε represent the measurement error associated with the observed variables, and ζ_1 is the residual error in the prediction of η_1 from ξ_1.

Next, the researcher must select the input matrix type and estimate the proposed model. At this point the researcher must test whether the data seriously violate any of

LISREL's four basic assumptions: independent observations, random sampling of respondents, linearity of all relationships, and multivariate normality. Because LISREL differs from other multivariate techniques in that it only uses the variance-covariance matrix as its input data, the researcher must run diagnostic tests for violations of these assumptions using a separate statistics package, such as PRELIS, SPSS, SAS, or other software.

During the analysis the researcher must select the estimation procedure used to yield the overall LISREL model. True to its name, *maximum likelihood estimation (MLE)* generates estimates that have the greatest probability of reproducing the observed data. MLE is by far the most common method used. This approach is advantageous over ordinary least squares (OLS) because MLE does not assume uncorrelated error terms and, accordingly, may be used for both recursive and nonrecursive models. Other estimation procedures, such as bootstrapping, simulation, and jackknifing—all of which generate samples for comparing models—are also appropriate in special circumstances.

The estimation procedure selected, as well as model misspecification error, model size, and departures from normality, will all affect the sample size required for a robust model. Model misspecification error is the omission of important constructs or indicators. The researcher should increase the sample size if this is a concern. An appropriate model size is 5–10 respondents per parameter; an absolute minimum sample size is one that is greater than the number of covariances in the input data matrix. However, if the data violate the assumption of normality, we recommend a ratio of 15 respondents per parameter.

After testing the assumptions, the researcher must identify the structural model. This includes considering the size of the covariance matrix in proportion to the number of estimated coefficients. The difference between the number of covariances and the actual number of coefficients in the proposed model is the *degrees of freedom,* calculated as:

$$\text{d.f.} = \tfrac{1}{2}[(p + q)(p + q + 1)] - t$$

where:

p = The number of endogenous indicators.

q = The number of exogenous indicators.

t = The number of estimated coefficients in the proposed model.

The *order condition* states that the model must be just-identified or over-identified, meaning the d.f. of the model must be equal to or greater than zero. The goal of the researcher is to achieve an acceptable fit with the largest number d.f. obtainable, which causes the model to be in its most generalizable state. In addition to meeting the order condition, the model also must meet the *rank condition.* That is, the researcher must algebraically determine if each parameter is uniquely estimated. A set of heuristics is available so that the researcher will not have to complete this task in its entirety.

Next, the researcher must evaluate the goodness-of-fit criteria. *Goodness-of-fit tests* are used to determine whether the model should or should not be rejected. If the model is not rejected, the researcher will continue the analysis and interpret the path coefficients in the model. LISREL currently provides at least 15 different goodness-of-fit measures, each of which can be categorized as one of three types of measures: (1) an absolute fit measure, (2) an incremental fit measure, or (3) a parsimonious fit measure. The type of fit index to report will be specific to the researcher's situation.

After the model is fit, the measurement model is reassessed with each construct evaluated for unidimensionality and composite reliability. Unidimensionality is an assumption for calculating reliability. Reliability measures, such as *Cronbach's alpha,* do not ensure unidimensionality, but they do detect whether the indicators of a construct have an acceptable fit on a single factor model. A test for construct reliability—to verify that indicators are consistent in their measurement—is not available on LISREL but can be calculated easily with the equation:

Construct reliability = Σ(standardized loading)^2/Σ(standardized loading)^2 + Σ_{ej}

In addition to the estimated coefficients, the researcher also considers the standard errors and *t* values for each coefficient. Because of the sensitivity of MLE with smaller sample sizes, the critical values should be conservative (a significance of either .025 or .01). And similar to multiple regression analysis, the overall R^2 is a comparative measure of fit for each LISREL equation.

As we said earlier in the section, the model can be compared with competing or nested models to find the best fit among a set of models and, if necessary, respecified to produce a model with better fit. However, at this point the researcher should be careful to evaluate only the empirical relationships—those which are not essential to the model's underlying theory. Relationships between constructs and indicators essential to the model's underlying theory should not be modified. This allows the researcher to compare several competing models with the same theoretical foundation. The researcher also can look for possible improvements by examining the residuals of the predicted covariance matrix. Residual values ±2.58 are considered statistically significant at the .05 level. Additionally, other tools, such as the *modification index* and the *unexpected change parameter,* can be used to assess goodness of overall model fit. However, each time modifications are made, the researcher must reevaluate the modified model.

Example Assume we wish to develop a model for employee performance. In conceptualizing our measurement model, we first consider a hypothetical two-factor model for employee performance with the two factors being *training* and *motivation.* These will be designated as exogenous constructs, since training and motivation are believed to have a causal effect on performance. For this example, training consists of two indicators: *formal education* and *on-the-job training.* Motivation is measured by three indicators: motivation test 1, motivation test 2, and the empirical observation of behavior as measured on a scale. A diagrammatic representation of the exogenous model is shown in Exhibit 19–14. Here, the two-factor CFA model consists of training and motivation, with each factor measured by two and three indicators, respectively. The curved two-headed arrow denotes that training and motivation are correlated.

Performance is considered to be an endogenous factor, in that it is believed to be caused by motivation and training. This variable is measured by *manager's observation* and by the *measurement of work output.* The schematic representation of this CFA model is presented in Exhibit 19–15.

The full measurement model consists of a pair of CFA models identical to those developed individually. LISREL allows the researcher to test and interpret the parameters of the measurement model in exactly the same way as the parameters of the individual CFA models were tested and interpreted. The full measurement model is expressed diagrammatically in Exhibit 19–16.

The structural model component would then causally relate performance to training and motivation, as well as training and motivation to their respective indicators using a system of linear structural equations. Remember that the researcher must make the distinction between the exogenous and endogenous variables, and there is no specification of causal relationships among latent variables in CFA modeling. Accordingly, the residual error (ζ) associated with the prediction of performance from motivation and training in the measurement model will be zero.

EXHIBIT 19–14 Path Diagram for Employee Performance (Exogenous Variable Model)

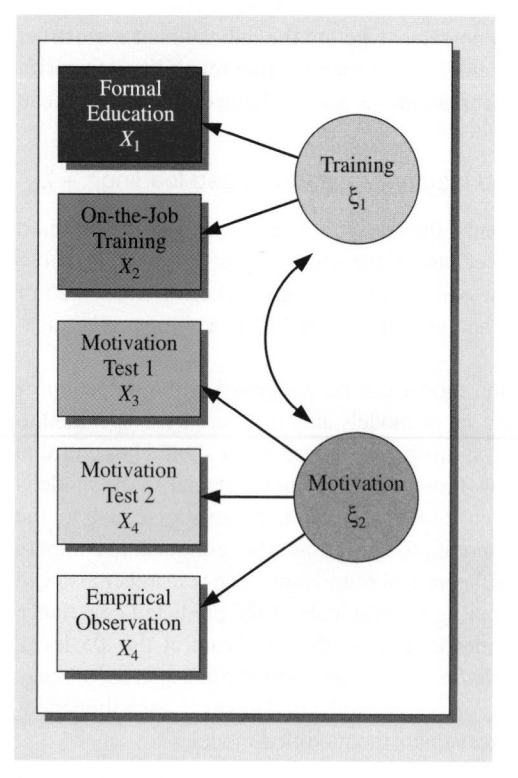

EXHIBIT 19–15 Path Diagram for Employee Performance (Endogenous Variable Model)

EXHIBIT 19–16 Path Diagram for Employee Performance (Full Measurement Model)

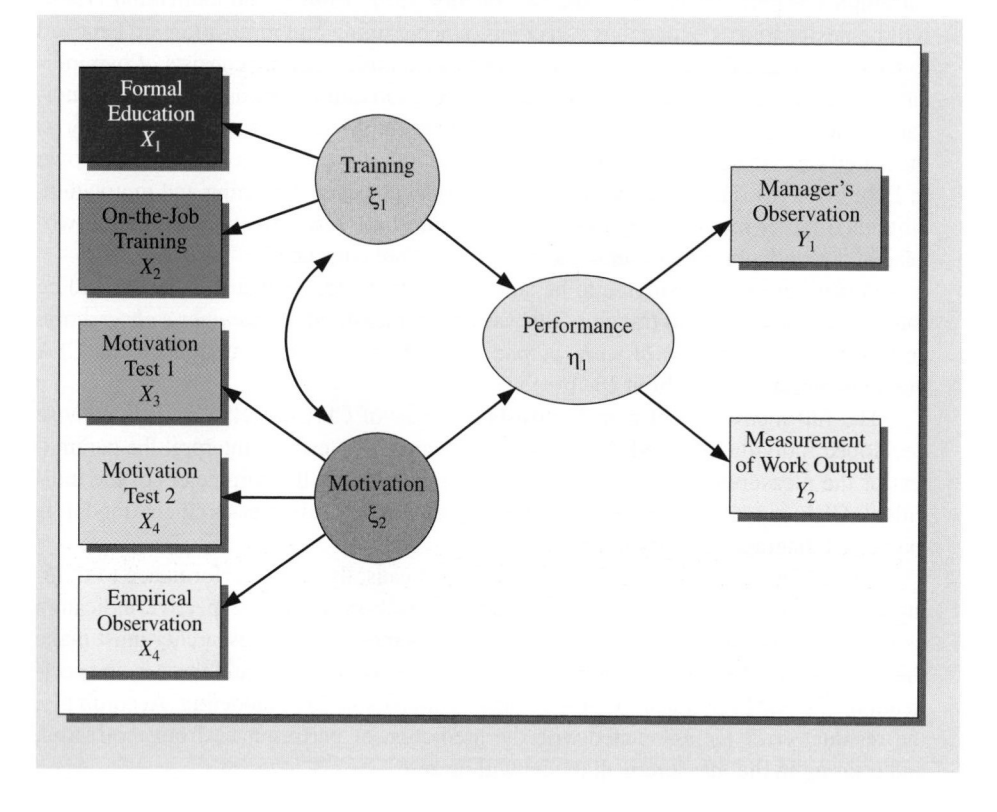

Conjoint Analysis

In management research, the most common applications for conjoint analysis are market research and product development. Consumers buying a MindWriter computer, for example, may evaluate a set of attributes to choose the product that best meets their needs. They may consider brand, speed, price, educational values, games, or capacity for work-related tasks. The attributes and their features require the buyer to make trade-offs in the final decision making.

Method **Conjoint analysis** typically uses input from nonmetric independent variables. Normally, we would use cross-classification tables to handle such data, but even multiway tables become quickly overwhelmed by the complexity. If there were three prices, three brands, three speeds, two levels of educational values, two categories for games, and two categories for work assistance, the model would have 216 decision levels ($3 \times 3 \times 3 \times 2 \times 2 \times 2$). A choice structure this size poses enormous difficulties for respondents and analysts. Conjoint analysis solves this problem with various optimal scaling approaches, often with loglinear models, to provide researchers with reliable answers that could not be obtained otherwise.

The objective of conjoint analysis is to secure *part-worths,* or **utility scores,** that represent the importance of each aspect of a product or service in the subjects' overall preference ratings. Utility scores are computed from the subjects' rankings or ratings of a set of cards. Each card in the deck describes one possible configuration of combined product attributes.

The first step in a conjoint study is to select the attributes most pertinent to the purchase decision. This may require an exploratory study such as a focus group, or it could be done by an expert with thorough market knowledge. The attributes selected are the independent variables, which are called *factors.* The possible values for an attribute are called *factor levels.* In the MindWriter example, the speed factor may have levels of 800 megahertz (MHz), 1 gigahertz, and 1.5 gigahertz. Speed, like price, approaches linear measurement characteristics since consumers typically choose higher speeds and lower prices. Other factors like brand are measured as discrete variables.

After selecting the factors and their levels, a computer program determines the number of product descriptions necessary to estimate the utilities. SPSS procedures ORTHOPLAN, PLANCARDS, and CONJOINT build a file structure for all possible combinations, generate the subset required for testing, produce the card descriptions, and analyze results. The command structure within these procedures provides for holdout sampling, simulations, and other requirements frequently used in commercial applications.[12]

Example Watersport enthusiasts know the dangers of ultraviolet (UV) light. It fades paint and clothing; yellows surfboards, skis, and sailboards; and destroys sails. More important, UV damages the eye's retina and cornea. At the beginning of the 1990s, Americans were spending $1.3 billion on 189 million pairs of sunglasses, most of which failed to provide adequate UV protection. Manufacturers of sunglasses for specialty markets have improved their products to such a degree that all of the companies in our example advertised 100 percent UV protection. Many other features influence trends in this market. For this example, we chose four factors from information contained in a review of sun protection products.[13]

Brand		Style	Flotation	Price
Bolle	A	Multiple color choices for frames, lenses, and temples	Yes	$100
Hobbies	B	Multiple color choices for frames, lenses, and straps	No	72
Oakley		(no hard temples)		60
Ski Optiks	C	Limited colors for frames, lenses, and temples		40

EXHIBIT 19–17   **Concept Cards for Conjoint Sunglasses Study**

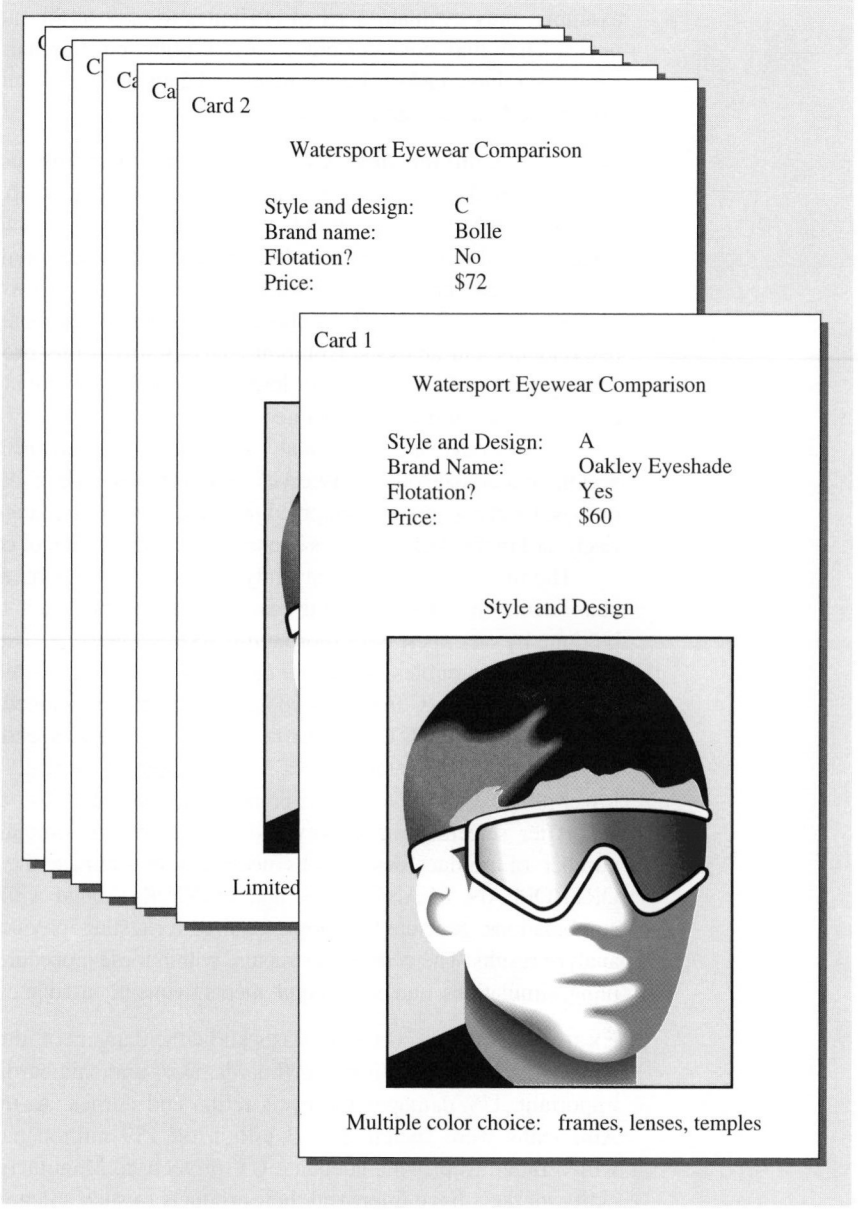

This is a $4 \times 4 \times 3 \times 2$ design, or a 96-option full-concept study. The algorithm selected 16 cards to estimate the utilities for the full concept. Combinations of interest that were not selected can be estimated later from the utilities. In addition, four holdout cards were administered to subjects but evaluated separately. The cards shown in Exhibit 19–17 were administered to a small sample ($n = 10$). Subjects were asked to order their cards from most to least desirable. The data produced the results presented in Exhibits 19–18 and 19–19.

Exhibit 19–18 contains the results of the eighth subject's preferences. This individual was an avid boardsailor, and flotation was the most important attribute for her, followed by style and price and then brand. From her preferences, we can compute her total utility score:

EXHIBIT 19–18   Conjoint Results for Subject 8, Sunglasses Study

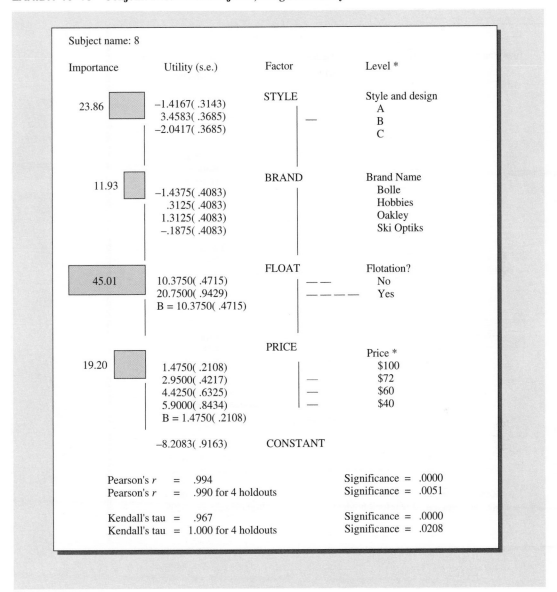

Subject name: 8

| Importance | Utility (s.e.) | Factor | Level * |

STYLE — Style and design
- 23.86 — −1.4167(.3143) — A
- 3.4583(.3685) — B
- −2.0417(.3685) — C

BRAND — Brand Name
- 11.93 — −1.4375(.4083) — Bolle
- .3125(.4083) — Hobbies
- 1.3125(.4083) — Oakley
- −.1875(.4083) — Ski Optiks

FLOAT — Flotation?
- 45.01 — 10.3750(.4715) — No
- 20.7500(.9429) — Yes
- B = 10.3750(.4715)

PRICE — Price *
- 19.20 — 1.4750(.2108) — $100
- 2.9500(.4217) — $72
- 4.4250(.6325) — $60
- 5.9000(.8434) — $40
- B = 1.4750(.2108)

−8.2083(.9163)   CONSTANT

Pearson's r = .994   Significance = .0000
Pearson's r = .990 for 4 holdouts   Significance = .0051

Kendall's tau = .967   Significance = .0000
Kendall's tau = 1.000 for 4 holdouts   Significance = .0208

*Subject reversed decision once.

(Style B) 3.46 + (Oakley brand) 1.31 + (flotation) 20.75

+ (price @ $40) 5.90 + (constant) − 8.21 = 23.21

If brand and price remain unchanged, a design that uses a hard temple with limited color choices (Style C) and no flotation would produce a considerably lower total utility score for this respondent. For example:

(Style C) − 2.04 + (Oakley brand) 1.31 + (no float) 10.38

+ (price @ $40) 5.90 + (constant) − 8.21 = 7.34

EXHIBIT 19–19   Conjoint Results for Sunglasses Study Sample ($n = 10$)

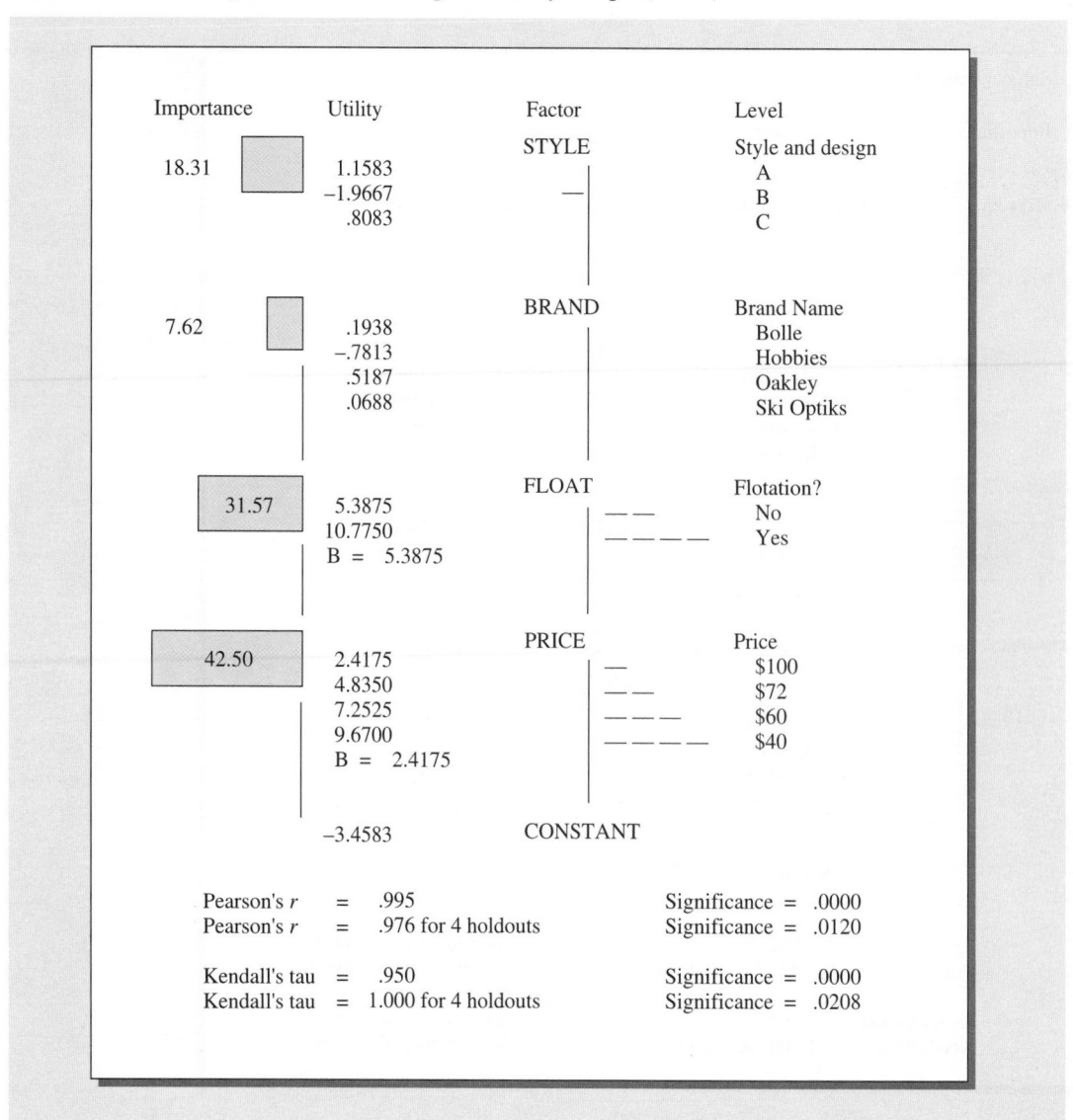

We could also calculate other combinations that would reveal the range of this individual's preferences. Our prediction that respondents would prefer less expensive prices did not hold for the eighth respondent as revealed by one asterisk next to the price factor in Exhibit 19–18. She reversed herself once on price to get flotation. Other subjects also reversed once on price to trade off for other factors.

The results for the sample are presented in Exhibit 19–19. In contrast to individuals, the sample placed price first in importance, followed by flotation, style, and brand. Group utilities may be calculated just as we did for the individual. At the bottom of the printout we find Pearson's r and Kendall's tau. Each was discussed in Chapter 18. In this application, they measure the relationship between observed and estimated preferences. Since holdout samples (in conjoint, regression, discriminant, and other methods) are not used to construct the estimating equation, the coefficients for the holdouts are often a more realistic index of the model's fit.

Conjoint analysis is an effective tool used by researchers to match preferences to known characteristics of market segments and design or target a product accordingly.

Interdependency Techniques

Factor Analysis   **Factor analysis** is a general term for several specific computational techniques. All have the objective of reducing to a manageable number many variables that belong together and have overlapping measurement characteristics. The predictor-criterion relationship that was found in the dependence situation is replaced by a matrix of inter-correlations among several variables, none of which is viewed as being dependent on another. For example, one may have data on 100 employees with scores on six attitude scale items.

Method   Factor analysis begins with the construction of a new set of variables based on the relationships in the correlation matrix. While this can be done in a number of ways, the most frequently used approach is **principal components analysis.** This method transforms a set of variables into a new set of composite variables or principal components that are not correlated with each other. These linear combinations of variables, called **factors,** account for the variance in the data as a whole. The best combination makes up the first principal component and is the first factor. The second principal component is defined as the best linear combination of variables for explaining the variance *not* accounted for by the first factor. In turn, there may be a third, fourth, and kth component, each being the best linear combination of variables not accounted for by the previous factors.

The process continues until all the variance is accounted for, but as a practical matter it is usually stopped after a small number of factors has been extracted. The output of a principal components analysis might look like the hypothetical data shown in Exhibit 19–20.

Numerical results from a factor study are shown in Exhibit 19–21. The values in this table are correlation coefficients between the factor and the variables (.70 is the r

EXHIBIT 19–20 **Principal Components Analysis from a Three-Variable Data Set**

Extracted Components	% of Variance Accounted for	Cumulative Variance
Component no. 1	63%	63%
Component no. 2	29	92
Component no. 3	8	100

Component 2
Component 1
Component 3

EXHIBIT 19–21 **Factor Matrices**

	A Unrotated Factors			B Rotated Factors	
Variable	I	II	h^2	I	II
A	.70	−.40	.65	.79	.15
B	.60	−.50	.61	.75	.03
C	.60	−.35	.48	.68	.10
D	.50	.50	.50	.06	.70
E	.60	.50	.61	.13	.77
F	.60	.60	.72	.07	.85
Eigenvalue	2.18	1.39			
Percent of variance	36.30	23.20			
Cumulative percent	36.30	59.50			

between variable A and factor I). These correlation coefficients are called **loadings.** Two other elements in Exhibit 19–21 need explanation. *Eigenvalues* are the sum of the variances of the factor values (for factor I the eigenvalue is $.70^2 + .60^2 + .50^2 + .60^2 + .60^2$). When divided by the number of variables, an eigenvalue yields an estimate of the amount of total variance explained by the factor. For example, factor I accounts for 36 percent of the total variance. The column headed h^2 gives the **communalities,** or estimates of the variance in each variable that is explained by the two factors. With variable A, for example, the communality is $.70^2 + (−.40)^2 = .65$, indicating that 65 percent of the variance in variable A is statistically explained in terms of factors I and II.

In this case, the unrotated factor loadings are not enlightening. What one would like to find is some pattern in which factor I would be heavily loaded (have a high *r*) on some variables and factor II on others. Such a condition would suggest rather "pure" constructs underlying each factor. You attempt to secure this less ambiguous condition

EXHIBIT 19–22 **Orthogonal Factor Rotations**

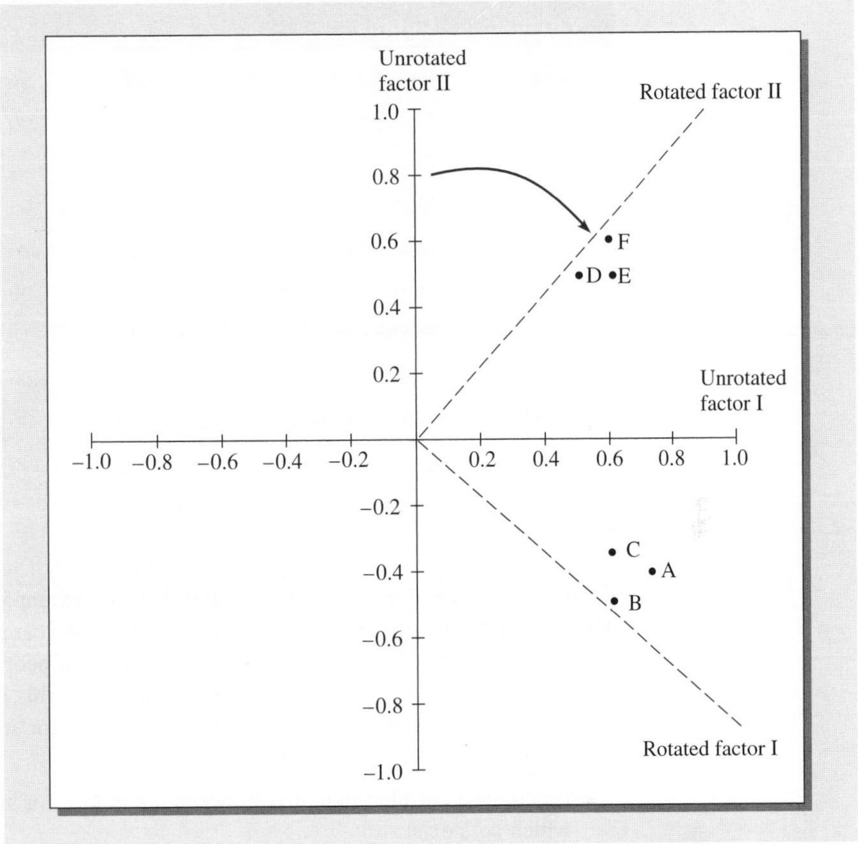

between factors and variables by **rotation.** This procedure can be carried out by either orthogonal or oblique methods, but only the former will be illustrated here.

To understand the rotation concept, consider that you are dealing only with simple two-dimensional rather than multidimensional space. The variables in Exhibit 19–21 can be plotted in two-dimensional space as shown in Exhibit 19–22. Two axes divide this space, and the points are positioned relative to these axes. The location of these axes is arbitrary, and they represent only one of an infinite number of reference frames that could be used to reproduce the matrix. As long as you do not change the intersection points and keep the axes at right angles, when an orthogonal method is used you can rotate the axes to find a better solution or position for the reference axes. "Better" in this case means a matrix that makes the factors as pure as possible (each variable loads onto as few factors as possible). From the rotation shown in Exhibit 19–22, it can be seen that the solution is improved substantially. Using the rotated solution suggests that the measurements from six scales may be summarized by two underlying factors (see the rotated factors section of Exhibit 19–21).

The interpretation of factor loadings is largely subjective. There is no way to calculate the meanings of factors; they are what one sees in them. For this reason, factor analysis is largely used for exploration. One can detect patterns in latent variables, discover new concepts, and reduce data. Factor analysis is also applied to test hypotheses with confirmatory models using LISREL.

EXHIBIT 19–23   **Correlation Coefficients, Metro U MBA Study**

Variable	Course	V1	V2	V3	V10
V1	Financial Accounting	1.00	.56	.17	−.01
V2	Managerial Accounting	.56	1.00	−.22	.06
V3	Finance	.17	−.22	1.00	.42
V4	Marketing	−.14	.05	−.48	−.10
V5	Human Behavior	−.19	−.26	−.05	−.23
V6	Organization Design	−.21	−.00	−.56	−.05
V7	Production	−.44	−.11	−.04	−.08
V8	Probability	.30	.06	.07	−.10
V9	Statistical Inference	−.05	.06	−.32	.06
V10	Quantitative Analysis	−.01	.06	.42	1.00

Example   Student grades make for an interesting example. The director of Metro U's MBA program has been reviewing grades for the first-year students and is struck by the patterns in the data. His hunch is that distinct types of people are involved in the study of management, and he decides to gather evidence for this idea.

Suppose a sample of 21 grade reports is chosen for students in the middle of the GPA range. Three steps are followed:

1. Calculate a correlation matrix between the grades for all pairs of the 10 courses for which data exist.

2. Factor-analyze the matrix by the principal components method.

3. Select a rotation procedure to clarify the factors and aid in interpretation.

Exhibit 19–23 shows a portion of the correlation matrix. These data represent correlation coefficients between the 10 courses. For example, grades secured in V1 (Financial Accounting) correlated rather well (0.56) with grades received in course V2 (Managerial Accounting). The next best correlation with V1 grades is an inverse correlation (−.44) with grades in V7 (Production).

After the correlation matrix, the extraction of components is shown in Exhibit 19–24. While the program will produce a table with as many as 10 factors, you choose, in this case, to stop the process after three factors have been extracted. Several features in this table are worth noting. Recall that the communalities indicate the amount of variance in each variable that is being "explained" by the factors. Thus, these three factors account for about 73 percent of the variance in grades in the financial accounting course. It should be apparent from these communality figures that some of the courses are not explained well by the factors selected.

The eigenvalue row in Exhibit 19–24 is a measure of the explanatory power of each factor. For example, the eigenvalue for factor 1 is 1.83 and is computed as follows:

$$1.83 = (.41)^2 + (.01)^2 + \ldots + (.25)^2$$

The percent of variance accounted for by each factor in Exhibit 19–24 is computed by dividing eigenvalues by the number of variables. When this is done, one sees that the three factors account for about 43 percent of the total variance in course grades.

EXHIBIT 19–24   Factor Matrix Using Principal Factor with Iterations, Metro U MBA Study

Variable	Course	Factor 1	Factor 2	Factor 3	Communality
V1	Financial Accounting	.41	.71	.23	.73
V2	Managerial Accounting	.01	.53	−.16	.31
V3	Finance	.89	−.17	.37	.95
V4	Marketing	−.60	.21	.30	.49
V5	Human Behavior	.02	−.24	−.22	.11
V6	Organization Design	−.43	−.09	−.36	.32
V7	Production	−.11	−.58	−.03	.35
V8	Probability	.25	.25	−.31	.22
V9	Statistical Inference	−.43	.43	.50	.62
V10	Quantitative Analysis	.25	.04	.35	.19
Eigenvalue		1.83	1.52	.95	
Percent of variance		18.30	15.20	9.50	
Cumulative percent		18.30	33.50	43.00	

EXHIBIT 19–25   Varimax Rotated Factor Matrix, Metro U MBA Study

Variable	Course	Factor 1	Factor 2	Factor 3
V1	Financial Accounting	.84	.16	−.06
V2	Managerial Accounting	.53	−.10	.14
V3	Finance	−.01	.90	−.37
V4	Marketing	−.11	−.24	.65
V5	Human Behavior	−.13	−.14	−.27
V6	Organization Design	−.08	−.56	−.02
V7	Production	−.54	−.11	−.22
V8	Probability	.41	−.02	−.24
V9	Statistical Inference	.07	.02	.79
V10	Quantitative Analysis	−.02	.42	.09

In an effort to further clarify the factors, a varimax (orthogonal) rotation is used to secure the matrix shown in Exhibit 19–25. The heavy factor loadings for the three factors are as follows:

Factor 1		Factor 2		Factor 3	
Financial Accounting	.84	Finance	.90	Marketing	.65
Managerial Accounting	.53	Organization Design	−.56	Statistical Inference	.79
Production	−.54				

Interpretation   The varimax rotation appears to clarify the relationship among course grades, but as pointed out earlier, the interpretation of the results is largely subjective. We might interpret the above results as showing three kinds of students, classified as the accounting, finance, and marketing types. Other interpretations could be made as well.

A number of problems affect the interpretation of these results. Among the major ones are these:

1. The sample is small and any attempt at replication might produce a different pattern of factor loadings.

2. From the same data, another number of factors rather than three can result in different patterns.

3. Even if the findings are replicated, the differences may be due to the varying influence of professors or the way they teach the courses rather than to the subject content.

4. The labels may not truly reflect the latent construct that underlies any factors we extract.

This suggests that factor analysis can be a demanding tool to use. It is powerful, but the results must be interpreted with great care.

Cluster Analysis   Unlike techniques for analyzing the relationships between variables, **cluster analysis** is a set of techniques for grouping similar objects or people. Originally developed as a classification device for taxonomy, its use has spread because of classification work in medicine, biology, and other sciences. Its visibility in those fields and the availability of high-speed computers to carry out the extensive calculations have sped its adoption in engineering, economics, marketing, and a host of other areas.

Cluster analysis shares some similarities with factor analysis, especially when factor analysis is applied to people (*Q*-analysis) instead of to variables. It differs from discriminant analysis in that discriminant analysis begins with a well-defined group composed of two or more distinct sets of characteristics in search of a set of variables to separate them. Cluster analysis starts with an undifferentiated group of people, events, or objects and attempts to reorganize them into homogeneous subgroups.

Method Five steps are basic to the application of most cluster studies:

1. Selection of the sample to be clustered (e.g., buyers, medical patients, inventory, products, employees).

2. Definition of the variables on which to measure the objects, events, or people (e.g., financial status, political affiliation, market segment characteristics, symptom classes, product competition definitions, productivity attributes).

3. Computation of similarities among the entities through correlation, Euclidean distances, and other techniques.

4. Selection of mutually exclusive clusters (maximization of within-cluster similarity and between-cluster differences) or hierarchically arranged clusters.

5. Cluster comparison and validation.

Different clustering methods can and do produce different solutions. It is important to have enough information about the data to know when the derived groups are real and not merely imposed on the data by the method.

The example shown in Exhibit 19–26 shows a cluster analysis of individuals based on three dimensions: age, income, and family size. Cluster analysis could be used to segment the car-buying population into distinct markets. For example, cluster A might be targeted as potential minivan or sport-utility vehicle buyers. The market segment represented by cluster B might be a sports and performance car segment. Clusters C and D could both be targeted as buyers of sedans, but the C cluster might be the luxury buyer. This form of clustering or a hierarchical arrangement of the clusters may be used to plan marketing campaigns and develop strategies.

EXHIBIT 19–26   Cluster Analysis on Three Dimensions

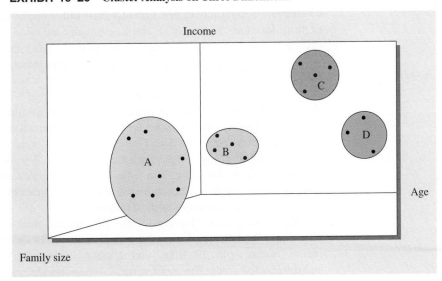

EXHIBIT 19–27   Film, Country, Genre, and Cluster Membership

Film	Country	Genre	Case	Number of Clusters			
				5	4	3	2
Cyrano de Bergerac	France	DramaCom	1	1	1	1	1
Il y a des Jours	France	DramaCom	4	1	1	1	1
Nikita	France	DramaCom	5	1	1	1	1
Les Noces de Papier	Canada	DramaCom	6	1	1	1	1
Leningrad Cowboys . . .	Finland	Comedy	19	2	2	2	2
Storia de Ragazzi . . .	Italy	Comedy	13	2	2	2	2
Conte de Printemps	France	Comedy	2	2	2	2	2
Tatie Danielle	France	Comedy	3	2	2	2	2
Crimes and Misdem . . .	USA	DramaCom	7	3	3	3	2
Driving Miss Daisy	USA	DramaCom	9	3	3	3	2
La Voce della Luna	Italy	DramaCom	12	3	3	3	2
Che Hora E	Italy	DramaCom	14	3	3	3	2
Attache-Moi	Spain	DramaCom	15	3	3	3	2
White Hunter Black . . .	USA	PsyDrama	10	4	4	3	2
Music Box	USA	PsyDrama	8	4	4	3	2
Dead Poets Society	USA	PsyDrama	11	4	4	3	2
La Fille aux All . . .	Finland	PsyDrama	18	4	4	3	2
Alexandrie, Encore . . .	Egypt	DramaCom	16	5	3	3	2
Dreams	Japan	DramaCom	17	5	3	3	2

Example   Serious movie fans find that Paris offers one of the world's best selections of films. Residents of New York and Los Angeles are often surprised to discover their cities are eclipsed by Paris's average of 300 films per week shown in over 100 locations.

We selected ratings from 12 cinema reviewers using sources ranging from *Le Monde* to international publications sold in Paris. The reviews reputedly influence box-office receipts, and the entertainment business takes them seriously.

The object of this cluster example was to classify 19 films into homogeneous subgroups. The production companies were American, Canadian, French, Italian, Spanish, Finnish, Egyptian, and Japanese. Three genres of film were represented: comedy, dramatic comedy, and psychological drama. Exhibit 19–27 shows the data by film name, country of origin, and genre. The table also lists the clusters for each film using the *average linkage method.* This approach considers distances between all possible pairs rather than just the nearest or farthest neighbor.

The sequential development of the clusters and their relative distances are displayed in a diagram called a *dendogram.* Exhibit 19–28 shows that the clustering procedure begins with 19 films and continues until all the films are again an undifferentiated group. The solid vertical line shows the point at which the clustering

EXHIBIT 19–28   **Dendogram of Film Study Using Average Linkage Method**

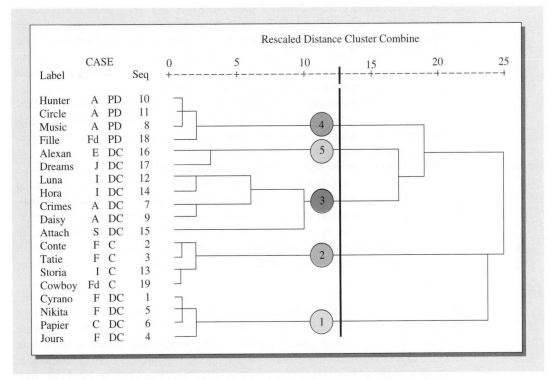

solution best represents the data. This determination was guided by coefficients provided by the SPSS program for each stage of the procedure. Five clusters explain this
data set.

The first cluster shown in Exhibit 19–28 has three French-language films and one
Canadian film, all of which are dramatic comedies. Cluster two consists of comedy
films. Two French and two other European films joined at the first stage, and then these
two groups came together at the second stage. Cluster three, composed of dramatic
comedies, is otherwise diverse. It is made up of two American films with two Italian
films adding to the group at the fourth stage. Late in the clustering process, cluster three
is completed when a Spanish film is appended. In cluster four, we find three American
psychological dramas combined with a Finnish film at the second stage. In cluster five,
two very different dramatic comedies are joined in the third stage.

Cluster analysis classified these productions based on reviewers' ratings. The similarities and distances are influenced by film genre and culture (as defined by the translated language).

**Multidimensional
Scaling**

Multidimensional scaling (MDS) creates a special description of a respondent's perception about a product, service, or other object of interest. This often helps the business researcher to understand difficult-to-measure constructs such as product quality or
desirability. In contrast to variables that can be measured directly, many constructs are
perceived and cognitively mapped in different ways by individuals. With MDS, items
that are perceived to be similar will fall close together in multidimensional space, and
items that are perceived to be dissimilar will be farther apart.

Method   We may think of three types of attribute space, each representing a multidimensional map. First, there is *objective space,* in which an object can be positioned in terms of its measurable attributes: its flavor, weight, and nutritional value. Second, there is *subjective space,* where perceptions of the object's flavor, weight, and nutritional value may be positioned. Objective and subjective attribute assessments may coincide, but often they do not. A comparison of the two allows us to judge how accurately an object is being perceived. Individuals may hold different perceptions of an object simultaneously, and these may be averaged to present a summary measure of perceptions. In addition, a person's perceptions may vary over time and in different circumstances; such measurements are valuable to gauge the impact of various perception-affecting actions, such as advertising programs.

With a third map we can describe respondents' preferences using the object's attributes. This represents their ideal; all objects close to this ideal point are interpreted as preferred by respondents to those that are more distant. Ideal points from many people can be positioned in this preference space to reveal the pattern and size of preference clusters. These can be compared to the subjective space to assess how well the preferences correspond to perception clusters. In this way, cluster analysis and MDS can be combined to map market segments and then examine products designed for those segments.

Example   We illustrate multidimensional scaling with a study of 16 companies from *Business Week*'s "Executive Compensation Scoreboard."[14] The companies chosen are from the natural resources (fuel) segment of the scoreboard. *Business Week* data included executive total compensation (salary, bonus, and long-term compensation for two years), shareholders' return (the year-end value based on $100 invested in corporate stock for two prior years), and the company's return on common equity (ROE) for a three-year period. We created a metric algorithm measuring the similarities among the 16 companies based on total executive compensation and the ROE. The matrix of similarities is shown in Exhibit 19–29. Higher numbers reflect the items that are more dissimilar.

EXHIBIT 19–29   **Similarities Matrix of 16 Companies, Executive Compensation**

	1	2	3	4	5	6	7	8	9	10	11	12	13	14	15	16
1	0															
2	3.9	0														
3	4.7	6.7	0													
4	4.4	2.8	4.7	0												
5	14.0	12.4	18.5	15.2	0											
6	4.9	6.9	0.2	4.9	18.7	0										
7	0.8	3.7	4.1	3.7	14.5	4.3	0									
8	6.0	2.1	8.5	4.0	11.8	8.7	5.8	0								
9	4.3	6.9	1.1	5.3	18.3	1.2	3.8	8.9	0							
10	8.2	4.9	8.5	4.1	15.3	8.6	7.6	3.9	9.3	0						
11	8.6	8.7	4.7	5.9	21.1	4.5	7.8	9.7	5.7	7.7	0					
12	2.2	3.7	6.9	5.5	11.8	7.1	2.8	5.5	6.5	8.5	10.5	0				
13	8.4	9.8	3.7	7.2	22.0	3.5	7.8	11.2	4.5	10.0	2.9	10.6	0			
14	12.8	13.4	8.2	10.6	25.8	8.1	12.1	14.4	9.1	12.0	4.7	14.9	4.6	0		
15	19.1	18.2	23.8	21.0	6.2	24.0	19.7	17.8	23.4	21.5	26.9	16.9	27.4	31.5	0	
16	2.6	5.2	2.1	4.0	16.5	2.3	2.0	7.2	1.9	8.0	6.3	4.8	5.8	10.3	21.7	0

SOURCE: Similiarities matrix based on data from "Executive Compensation Scoreboard," *International Business Week,* May 7, 1990, pp. 74–75.

If we were using respondents and producing a matrix of similarities among the perception of objects, we might obtain ordinal data. Then the matrix would contain ranks with 1 representing the most similar pair and n indicating the most dissimilar pair.

A computer program is used to analyze the data matrix and generate a spatial map.[15] The objective is to find a multidimensional spatial pattern that best reproduces the original order of the data. For example, the most similar pair (companies 3, 6) must be located in this multidimensional space closer together than any other pair. The least similar pair (companies 14, 15) must be the farthest apart. The computer program presents these relationships as a geometric configuration so all distances between pairs of points closely correspond to the original matrix.

Determining how many dimensions to use is complex. The more dimensions of space we use, the more likely the results will closely match the input data. Any set of n points can be satisfied by a configuration of $n - 1$ dimensions. Our aim, however, is to secure a structure that provides a good fit for the data and has the fewest dimensions. MDS is best understood using two or at most three dimensions.

Most algorithms include the calculation of a **stress index** (S-stress or Kruskal's stress) that ranges from the worst fit (1) to the perfect fit (0). This study, for example, had a stress of .001. Another index, R^2, is interpreted as the proportion of variance of transformed data accounted for by distances in the model. A result close to 1.0 is desirable.

In the executive compensation example, we conclude that two dimensions represent an acceptable geometric configuration, as shown in Exhibit 19–30. The distance

EXHIBIT 19–30 Multidimensional Scaling Plot of Natural Resource Companies' Return on Equity and Executive Compensation

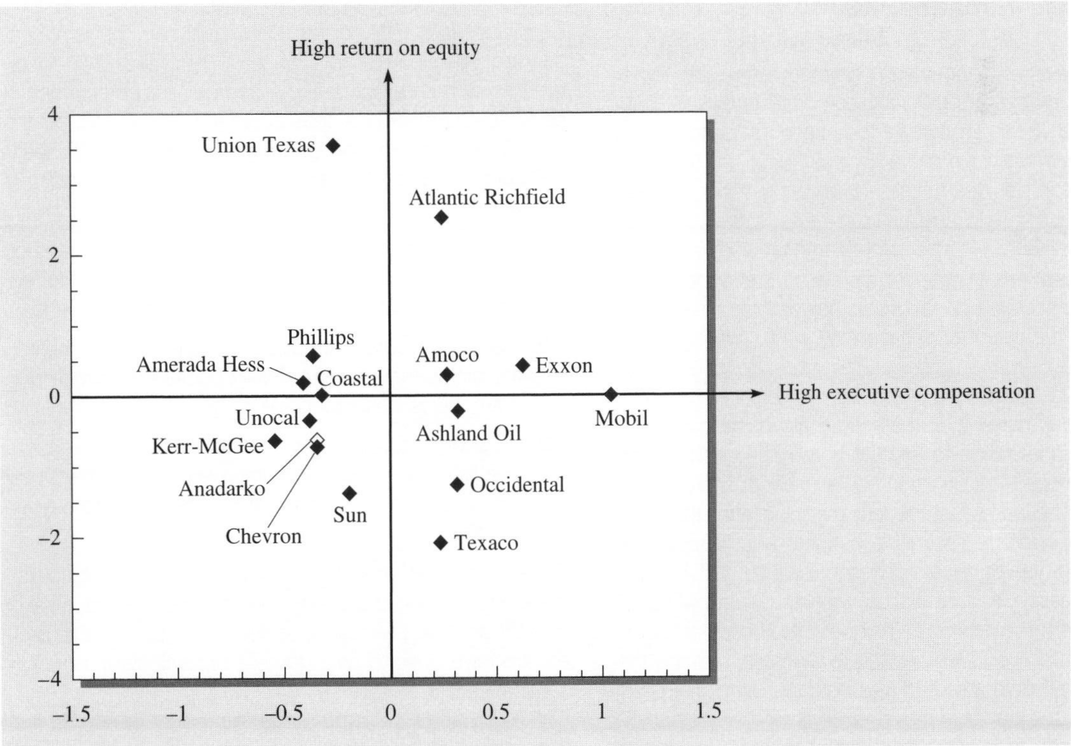

SOURCE: Input data from *International Business Week,* May 7, 1990, pp. 74–75.

between Anadarko and Chevron (3, 6) is the shortest, while that between Texaco and Union Texas Petro Holdings (14, 15) is the longest. As with factor analysis, there is no statistical solution to the definition of the dimensions represented by the X and Y axes. The labeling is judgmental and depends on the insight of the researcher, analysis of information collected from respondents, or another basis. Respondents sometimes are asked to state the criteria they used for judging the similarities, or they are asked to judge a specific set of criteria. In this example, the horizontal dimension approximates the total executive compensation while the vertical dimension represents return on equity.

Consistent with raw data, Union Texas and Atlantic Richfield have high ROE but compensate their executives close to the sample mean. In contrast, Exxon and Mobil generated an ROE close to the sample's average while providing higher compensation for their executives. We could hypothesize that the latter two companies may be more difficult to run—are larger and more complex—but that would need to be confirmed with another study. The clustering of companies in attribute space shows that they are perceived to be similar along the dimensions measured.

MDS is most often used to assess perceived similarities and differences among objects. Using MDS allows the researcher to understand constructs that are not directly measurable. The process provides a spatial map that shows similarities in terms of relative distances. It is best understood when limited to two or three dimensions that can be graphically displayed.

Close-Up

Simalto+Plus™[16]

As part of MindWriter's CompleteCare project, Jason needs to assess customer satisfaction among MindWriter's corporate computer buyers. To identify and prioritize the areas of performance where investment in improvement will have the greatest pay-off, Jason decides to use a trade-off technique called Simalto+Plus™ (Simultaneous Multi-Level Trade-Off).[17]

Simalto+Plus™ is a conjoint-related technique used to predict consumers' purchasing behavior. It recognizes that since resources are limited, buyers seldom can have all the features of a product or service they want, and satisfying one set of needs is often at the expense of another. Simalto+Plus™ is distinguished from other conjoint techniques in that, rather than mathematically deriving correlation coefficients, Simalto+Plus™ is a rule-based expert system that operates similar to neural network analyses.

Neural networks use nodes, modeled after the neurons in the brain, to recognize patterns and linkages by summarizing values in a nonlinear manner, with values being expressed as connection weights. Simalto+Plus™ uses a pattern-recognition technique called *notice and prefer* which inductively identifies the relationships among the variables. Grid data are used as input, and Simalto+Plus™ learns from the patterns provided on an individual participant basis and then infers their relevance into a rule base. The approach is similar to that used in optical character reading when a document is scanned.

Instead of relying on a single algorithm, Simalto+Plus™ customizes its own rule set. This is necessary because participants will have provided only a relatively small number of patterns compared to the billions of possible combinations that could be developed on the grid. The underlying premise for the Simalto+Plus™ rules is that choice is most likely to occur for the specifications that cause the most individual satisfaction. For example:

1. If two service programs differ by only one feature, then the buyer will select the service program with the features that most closely match the buyer's preferences.

2. If service program specifications are of equal merit to the buyer, then the buyer will choose the service program that is less expensive.

3. If a designed service program becomes more expensive than the buyer's available budget, then the buyer will have lower probability of purchasing from a given vendor.

While these rules are simple, they, and other rules, form a system for making inferences and applying them as a set of "if . . . then" type predictions stated as the percentage preference for a specific arrangement of particular product or service features.

Because of the large range of product or service feature combinations that can be modeled, Simalto+Plus™ follows an analytic process to determine the product or service feature combinations that best meet consumers' preferences. This process occurs in three phases. Phase 1 involves identifying key driving features and levels above the base product. This phase includes three steps: (1) current product profiling; (2) identifying the most important features; and (3) identifying unacceptable features. Phase 2 entails identifying winning potential products. This requires (1) reprioritizing the existing products' features; and (2) identifying bonused improvements. Phase 3 involves testing the relative brand value of the product or service (using a questionnaire) and determining the brand image using a Brand Image/Equity grid. The Simalto+Plus™ analytic process is summarized in Exhibit 19–31.

The core of Jason's research is a series of grid exercises (Exhibit 19–32) that deconstruct the MindWriter

CompleteCare services into 30 separate attributes, each with between three and eight different levels of performance. For example, repair speed after receiving the computer at the CompleteCare facility might have four levels of performance: shipped next day, shipped by third day, shipped within five days, and shipped within seven days. For Jason's scales, the descriptions are provided in words, rather than numerically. Jason had previously validated the descriptions through focus groups and interviews with both consumers and MindWriter employees involved in different areas of MindWriter product design, service, and support.

Jason conducts the interviews with upper-level managers at the client-companies by telephone. The Simalto+Plus™ grid is faxed to participants prior to the interview with

EXHIBIT 19–31   Simalto+Plus™ Analytic Procedure

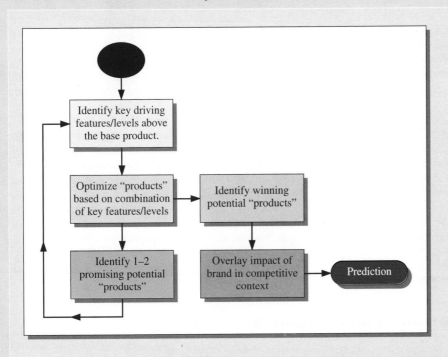

EXHIBIT 19–32   Simalto+Plus™ Grid Exercises

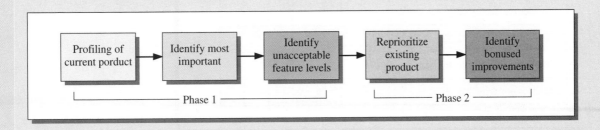

a brief description of how it will be used. The participants are asked to complete the grid as the questions are asked, while Jason also completes a copy on his end.

The first step (Phase I) in Jason's MindWriter Simalto+ Plus™ research is to establish a benchmark measure of satisfaction among large corporations, MindWriter's high-end clients. During the interview, participants are asked to first identify, for each of the 30 attributes in the grid, the performance level that best represents the service they expect to receive from a quality business computer manufacturer. Next, participants are asked to identify, for each of the 30 attributes, the current level of service they obtained both from MindWriter and from the best other business computer vendor with whom they also do business. Using the profile of delivered service provided by MindWriter as a "benchmark" or starting point, participants are then asked to make a maximum of 10 improvements—shifts from the current service performance to a higher level of performance—based on any selection of product or service attributes and level changes. However, each attribute level is weighted by the approximate investment cost of implementation. Participants are allowed to make more than one improvement for a given product or service attribute, but they are limited to spending a preset number of improvement "points." Participants selecting more expensive service improvements can make fewer improvements in other areas. This "trade-off" procedure allows MindWriter to identify, through improvement "votes," each participant's individual priorities.

Phase 3 of the Simalto+Plus™ process focuses on the importance of brand value and brand image in consumers' purchasing decisions. Instead of treating the brand as a product or service feature, Simalto+Plus™ looks at brand separately to provide a more comprehensive assessment of both relative brand value and brand image.

Relative brand value is determined through questions that ask how much more or less than the currently owned brand is the participant willing to pay to purchase a product of another brand. Brand image and equity are evaluated using an exercise similar to the Simalto+Plus™ grids used in phases one and two. The brand image/equity grid includes 15–20 brand image/equity traits, with brands being evaluated on each characteristic using a nonmetric "poor-to-excellent" scale (see Exhibit 19–33). The last stage is a *brand improvement* exercise in which participants award points to brand improvements to make a particular brand more acceptable. This is typically a two-part process used to generate first- and second-level improvements.

Following the phone interviews, Jason feeds the data from the Simalto+Plus™ grids into a PC-based expert system, a software program specially designed to translate the raw data into a predictive model. This model quantifies the overall impact of making single or multiple box improvements in any service feature area. In this process, each participant is a separate unit for the purposes of preference allocation. The predictive model involves no averaging. And, using the pattern of responses for the expected and current performance levels, Jason is able to demonstrate graphically where MindWriter is falling short of expectation in its current level of service and how MindWriter compares with its competition, the best other business computer vendors.

Through its "notice and prefer" process, Simalto+Plus™ allows Jason to build the predictive model to propose specific actions or performance improvements in a rank order of impact for individual improvements, while also demonstrating the closeness/distance between ranked improvements. However, it is important to note that this is not simply a matter of choosing the top-ranked individual improvements, as the selection of these may be closely correlated and would not add dramatically to overall perceptual gain. This is due to the way individual participants are treated as whole units in preference allocation. The optimum combination could well include an improvement outside the individual top 10.

EXHIBIT 19–33   Example Simalto+Plus™ Brand Image/Equity Grid

	Poor Couldn't be worse				Excellent Couldn't be better		
Treats you like a valued customer							
Provides top quality customer service							
Offers good value							
Offers durable, reliable products							
Resolves problems quickly							

With Simalto+Plus™, Jason is able to identify combinations of several improvements that collectively would achieve the greatest impact. Simalto+Plus™ also illustrates how comparable satisfaction gains can be made with several different combinations of improvements. This is where the weighting points become especially effective in identifying the combination of improvements that will yield the best balance between satisfaction gain and investment cost.

Subsequently, Jason uses Simalto+Plus™ in association with clustering techniques to compare the optimal improvements appropriate for different groups of consumers, with clusters developed on the basis of distinctive differences in needs, current perceptions, and improvement priorities.

In sum, the Simalto+Plus™ analysis allows Jason to (1) provide MindWriter with clear guidance on what actions are needed and valued, (2) relate satisfaction to the match between expectation and delivered performance, and (3) demonstrate clearly whether MindWriter is doing better or worse than the best other business computer vendors. Simalto+Plus™ can be used for researching trade-offs for a variety of products and services. It also can be used to evaluate job design and compensation programs, as well as social service and government programs. In the bonused improvement exercise, dollar budgets can be used as an alternative to bonus "points."

Jason's next research assignment has him using Simalto+Plus™ to assist in the design of the ideal MindWriter laptop. Exhibits 19–34 and 19–35 are drafts of the grids he will use in this next multivariate exercise.

EXHIBIT 19–34 Example Simalto+Plus™ Grid with Features and Levels

PC Features	Levels for Each Feature								
Processor Speed	400 MHz	600 MHz	800 MHz	1.0 GHz	1.2 GHz	1.4 GHz	1.6 GHz	1.8 GHz	2.0 GHz
Hard Drive Capacity	8 GB	10 GB	15 GB	20 GB	30 GB	40 GB	60 GB	80 GB	100 GB
Memory—RAM	64 MB	128 MB	192 MB	256 MB	320 MB	384 MB	448 MB	512 MB	
CD-ROM Drive	None $0 **current**	48x Max CD—ROM Drive add $50	8x/4x/32x CD—RW Drive add $80	16x/10x/40x CD—CD-RW Drive add $100	24x/10x/40x CD—CD-RW Drive add $140	CD-RW and DVD Combination Drive add $250 **reprioritized**			

EXHIBIT 19–35 Example Simalto+Plus™ Grid with Features and Levels: Bonused Improvements

PC Features	Levels for Each Feature								
Processor Speed	433 MHz $0 **current**	600 MHz add $25	800 MHz add $40	1.0 GHz add $55 **reprioritized**	1.2 GHz add $75	1.4 GHz add $90	1.6 GHz add $125	1.8 GHz add $165	2.0 GHz add $210
Hard Drive Capacity	8 GB $0 **current**	10 GB add $20 **reprioritized**	15 GB add $40	20 GB add $50	30 GB add $65	40 GB add $80	60 GB add $100	80 GB add $140	100 GB add $180
Memory—RAM	64 GB $0 **current**	128 MB add $20	192 MB add $40	256 MB add $80 **reprioritized**	320 MB add $120	384 MB add $160	448 MB add $200	512 MB add $240	
CD-ROM Drive	None $0 **current**	48x Max CD—ROM Drive add $50	8x/4x/32x CD—RW Drive add $80	16x/10x/40x CD—CD-RW Drive add $100	24x/10x/40x CD—CD-RW Drive add $140	CD-RW and DVD Combination Drive add $250 **reprioritized**			

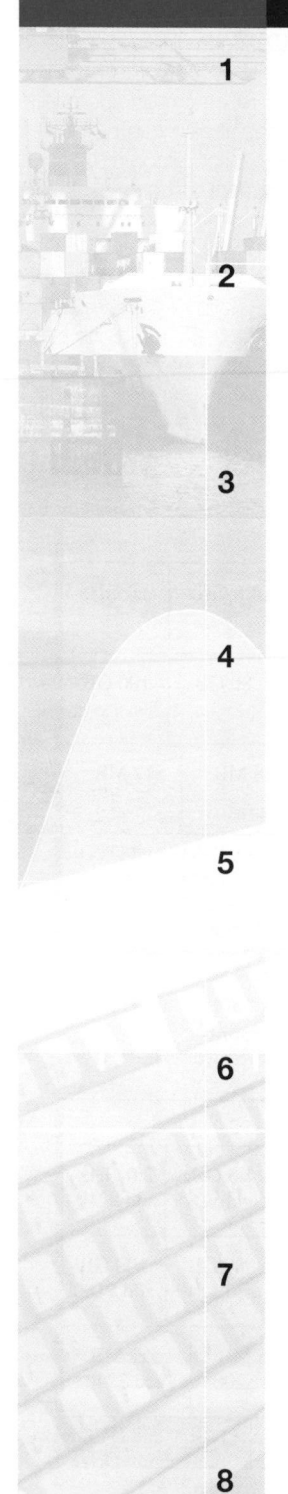

SUMMARY

1   Multivariate techniques are classified into two categories: dependency and interdependency. When a problem reveals the presence of criterion and predictor variables, we have an assumption of dependence. If the variables are interrelated without designating some dependent and others independent, then interdependence of the variables is assumed. The choice of techniques is guided by the number of dependent and independent variables involved and whether they are measured on metric or nonmetric scales.

2   Multiple regression is an extension of bivariate linear regression. When a researcher is interested in explaining or predicting a metric dependent variable from a set of metric independent variables (although dummy variables may also be used), multiple regression is often selected. Regression results provide information on the statistical significance of the independent variables, the strength of association between one or more of the predictors and the criterion, and a predictive equation for future use.

3   Discriminant analysis is used to classify people or objects into groups based on several predictor variables. The groups are defined by a categorical variable with two or more values, whereas the predictors are metric. The effectiveness of the discriminant equation is based not only on its statistical significance but also on its success in correctly classifying cases to groups.

4   Multivariate analysis of variance, or MANOVA, is one of the more adaptive techniques for multivariate data. MANOVA assesses the relationship between two or more metric dependent variables and classificatory variables or factors. MANOVA is most commonly used to test differences among samples of people or objects. In contrast to ANOVA, MANOVA handles multiple dependent variables, thereby simultaneously testing all the variables and their interrelationships.

5   The LISREL technique is extremely useful in explaining causality among constructs that cannot be directly measured. LISREL has two parts, a measurement model and a structural equation model. The measurement model is used to relate the observed, recorded, or measured variables to the latent variables (constructs). The structural equation model specifies causal relationships, causal effects, and unexplained variance among the constructs.

6   Conjoint analysis is a technique that typically handles nonmetric independent variables. Conjoint analysis allows the researcher to determine the importance of product or service attributes and the levels or features that are most desirable. Respondents provide preference data by ranking or rating cards that describe products. These data become utility weights of product characteristics by means of optimal scaling and loglinear algorithms.

7   Principal components analysis extracts uncorrelated factors that account for the largest portion of variance from an initial set of variables. Factor analysis also attempts to reduce the number of variables and discover the underlying constructs that explain the variance. A correlation matrix is used to derive a factor matrix from which the best linear combination of variables may be extracted. In many applications, the factor matrix will be rotated to simplify the factor structure.

8   Unlike techniques for analyzing the relationships between variables, cluster analysis is a set of techniques for grouping similar objects or people. The cluster procedure starts with an undifferentiated group of people, events, or objects and attempts to reorganize them into homogeneous subgroups.

9 Multidimensional scaling (MDS) is often used in conjunction with cluster analysis or conjoint analysis. It allows a respondent's perception about a product, service, or other object of attitude to be described in a spatial manner. MDS helps the business researcher to understand difficult-to-measure constructs such as product quality or desirability, which are perceived and cognitively mapped in different ways by different individuals. Items judged to be similar will fall close together in multidimensional space and are revealed numerically and geometrically by spatial maps.

KEY TERMS

EXAMPLES

PricewaterhouseCoopers	A widely respected consulting firm enters a strategic alliance with EntryPoint to provide instant information and website click-throughs.	635
Sunglasses manufacturers	Comparison of the desirability of four manufacturers' products using "full concept" conjoint analysis.	631
SuperLetter.com	A hybrid mail e-business uses diverse multivariate techniques to understand its customer base.	614, 640

*Due to the confidential and proprietary nature of most research, the names of some companies have been changed.

DISCUSSION QUESTIONS

Terms in Review

1. Distinguish among multidimensional scaling, cluster analysis, and factor analysis.

2. Describe the differences between dependency techniques and interdependency techniques. When would you choose a dependency technique?

Making Research Decisions

3. How could discriminant analysis be used to provide insight into MANOVA results where the MANOVA has one independent variable (a factor with two levels)?

4. Describe how you would create a conjoint analysis study of off-road vehicles. Restrict your brands to three, and suggest possible factors and levels. The full-concept description should not exceed 256 decision options.

5. What type of multivariate method do you recommend in each of the following cases and why?

   a. You want to develop an estimating equation that will be used to predict which applicants will come to your university as students.

   b. You would like to predict family income using such variables as education and stage in family life cycle.

   c. You wish to estimate standard labor costs for manufacturing a new dress design.

   d. You have been studying a group of successful salespeople. You have given them a number of psychological tests. You want to bring meaning out of these test results.

6. Sales of a product are influenced by the salesperson's level of education and gender, as well as consumer income, ethnicity, and wealth.

   a. Formulate this statement as a multiple regression model (form only, without parameter estimation).

   b. Specify dummy variables.

   c. If the effects of consumer income and wealth are not additive alone, and an interaction is expected, specify a new variable to test for the interaction.

7. What multivariate technique would you use to analyze each of the following problems? Explain your choice.

   a. Employee job satisfaction (high, normal, low) and employee success (0–2 promotions, 3–5 promotions, 5+ promotions) are to be studied in three different departments of a company.

   b. Consumers making a brand choice decision between three brands of coffee are influenced by their own income levels and the extent of advertising of the brands.

   c. Consumer choice of color in fabrics is largely dependent on ethnicity, income levels, and the temperature of the geographical area. There is detailed areawide demographic data on income levels, ethnicity, and population, as well as the weather bureau's historical data on temperature. How would you identify geographical areas for selling dark-colored fabric? You have sample data for 200 randomly selected consumers: their fabric color choice, income, ethnicity, and the average temperature of the area where they live.

From Concept to Practice

8. An analyst sought to predict the annual sales for a home-furnishing manufacturer using the following predictor variables:

   X_1 = Marriages during the year.

   X_2 = Housing starts during the year.

   X_3 = Annual disposable personal income.

   X_4 = Time trend (first year = 1, second year = 2, and so forth).

   Using data for 24 years, the analyst calculated the following estimating equation:

   $$Y = 49.85 - .068X_1 + .036X_2 + 1.22X_3 - 19.54X_4$$

   The analyst also calculated an $R^2 = .92$ and a standard error of estimate of 11.9. Interpret the above equation and statistics.

9. A researcher was given the assignment of predicting which of three actions would be taken by the 280 employees in the Desota plant that was going to be sold to its employees. The alternatives were to:

   a. Take severance pay and leave the company.

   b. Stay with the new company and give up severance pay.

   c. Take a transfer to the plant in Chicago.

   The researcher gathered data on employee opinions, inspected personnel files and the like, and then did a discriminant analysis. Later, when the results were in, she found the results listed below. How successful was the researcher's analysis?

Actual Decision	Predicted Decision		
	A	B	C
A	80	5	12
B	14	60	14
C	10	15	70

10. You are working with a consulting group that has a new project for the Palm Grove School System. The school system of this large county has individuals with purchasing, service, and maintenance responsibilities. They were asked to evaluate the vendor/distribution channels of products that the county purchases.

   The evaluations were on a 10-point metric scale for the following variables:

   Delivery speed—Amount of time for delivery once the order has been confirmed.
   Price level—Level of price charged by the product suppliers.
   Price flexibility—Perceived willingness to negotiate on price.
   Manufacturer's image—Manufacturer or supplier's image.
   Overall service—Level of service necessary to preserve a satisfactory relationship between buyer and supplier.
   Sales force—Overall image of the manufacturer's sales representatives.
   Product quality—Perceived quality of a particular product.

   The data are found at www.mhhe.com/business/cooper8.

Your task is to complete an exploratory factor analysis on the survey data. The purpose for the consulting group is twofold: (1) to identify the underlying dimensions of these data; and (2) to create a new set of variables for inclusion into subsequent assessments of the vendor/distribution channels.

Issues to consider in your analysis:

a. Methodology: (a) desirability of principal components versus principal axis factoring, (b) decisions on criteria for number of factors to extract, (c) rotation of the factors, (d) factor loading significance, and (e) interpretation of the rotated matrix.

b. Prepare a report summarizing your findings and interpreting your results.

WWW Exercises

Vist our website for Internet exercises related to this chapter at www.mhhe.com/business/cooper8

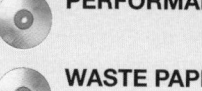

CASES*

MASTERING TEACHER LEADERSHIP

MEDICAL LABORATORIES

NCR: TEEING UP A NEW STRATEGIC DIRECTION

PERFORMANCE EVALUATIONS

WASTE PAPER

*All cases indicating a video icon are located on the Instructor's Videotape Supplement. All nonvideo cases are in the case section of the textbook. All cases indicating a CD icon offer a data set, which is located on the accompanying CD.

REFERENCE NOTES

1. Jagdish N. Sheth, ed., *Multivariate Methods for Market and Survey Research* (Chicago: American Marketing Association, 1977), p. 3.
2. William Schneider, "Opinion Outlook," *National Journal* (July 1985).
3. Benson Shapiro, "Price Reliance: Existence and Sources," *Journal of Marketing Research,* August 1973, pp. 286–89.
4. For a discussion of path analysis, see Elazar J. Pedhazur, *Regression in Behavioral Research: Explanation and Prediction,* 2nd ed. (New York: Holt, Rinehart & Winston, 1982), chap. 15.
5. Fred Kerlinger, *Foundations of Behavioral Research,* 3rd ed. (New York: Holt, Rinehart & Winston, 1986), p. 562.
6. Joseph F. Hair, Jr., Rolph E. Anderson, Ronald L. Tatham, and William C. Black, *Multivariate Data Analysis with Readings* (New York: Macmillan, 1992), pp. 153–81.
7. This section is based on the SPSS procedure MANOVA, described in Marija J. Norusis/SPSS, Inc., *SPSS Advanced Statistics Users Guide* (Chicago: SPSS, Inc., 1990), pp. 71–104.
8. This section was prepared by Jeff Stevens, School of Public Administration, Florida Atlantic University. It is based on J. Hair, R. Anderson, R. Tatham, and W. Black, *Multivariate Data Analysis with Readings,* 5th ed. (Upper Saddle River, NJ: Prentice-Hall, 1998); J. Scott Long, *Covariance Structure*

Models: An Introduction to LISREL (Thousand Oaks, CA: Sage Publishing, 1984); J. Scott Long, *Confirmatory Factor Analysis: A Preface to LISREL* (Thousand Oaks, CA: Sage Publishing, 1983); and Barbara M. Byrne, *A Primer of LISREL: Basic Applications and Programming for Confirmatory Factor Analytic Models* (NY: Springer-Verlag, 1989).
9. From B. M. Byrne, *A Primer of LISREL: Basic Applications and Programming for Confirmatory Factor Analytic Models* (NY: Springer-Verlag, 1989), p. 8.
10. Ibid., p. 9.
11. Ibid., p. 9.
12. SPSS, Inc., *SPSS Categories* (Chicago: SPSS, Inc., 1990).
13. Product specifications adapted from Lewis Rothlein, "A Guide to Sun Protection Essentials," *Wind Rider* (June 1990), pp. 95–103.
14. "Executive Compensation Scoreboard," *International Business Week,* May 7, 1990, pp. 74–75.
15. See the ALSCAL procedure in Marija J. Norusis/SPSS, Inc., *SPSS Base System User's Guide* (Chicago: SPSS, Inc., 1990), pp. 397–416.
16. The Close-Up in this chapter was created by Jeff Stevens, School of Public Administration, Florida Atlantic University, and adapted to the MindWriter vignette by the authors. It is based on Sue Coyne, *Optimizing Customer Retention and Loy-*

alty Strategies Through More Effective Research, CLT Research Associates, paper presented April 29, 1998, Distributech Utilities Conference, Tampa, FL. For information on the technique, see J. L. Green, E. Goldsmith, and C. Parish, *The Simalto+Plus™ Approach to Optimal Product Specification,*

paper presented at 1991 AMA Research Conference, Denver, CO.

17. J. L. Green, E. Goldsmith, and C. Parish, *The Simalto+Plus™ Approach to Optimal Product Specification* (1991). A paper presented at 1991 AMA Research Conference, Denver, CO.

REFERENCES FOR SNAPSHOTS AND CAPTIONS

NCR Country Club

"NCR Country Club McMahon Group Study Report, 1999," McMahon Group.

"NCR Country Club Membership Brochure, 1999," NCR Country Club Association.

Frank Vain, president of McMahon Group, interview, July 2000.

PricewaterhouseCoopers LLP

B. Jordheim, "Building a Smarter Brand," *Sales and Marketing Management,* October 1999, p. 105.

Marla Sawasky, product manager for TelecomInsider, interview, July 2000.

SuperLetter.com

Christopher Schultheiss, founder and CEO, SuperLetter.com, interview, July 2000.

CLASSIC AND CONTEMPORARY READINGS

Hair, Joseph F., Jr., Rolph E. Anderson, Ronald L. Tatham, and William C. Black. *Multivariate Data Analysis with Readings.* 5th ed. Upper Saddle River, NJ: Prentice-Hall, 1998. A very readable book covering most multivariate statistics.

Sage Series in Quantitative Applications in the Social Sciences. Thousand Oaks, CA: Sage Publishing. This monograph series includes papers on most multivariate methods.

Schumaker, Randall A., and Richard G. Lomax. *A Beginner's Guide to Structural Equation Modeling.* Mahwah, NJ: Lawrence Erlbaum Associates, 1996. An introduction to structural models.

Stevens, James P. *Applied Multivariate Statistics for the Social Sciences.* 3rd ed. Mahwah, NJ: Lawrence Erlbaum Associates, 1999. Comprehensive coverage with computer examples.

CHAPTER 20

Presenting Results: Written and Oral Reports

Learning Objectives

After reading this chapter, you should understand . . .

1   **That a quality presentation of research findings can have an inordinate effect on a reader's or a listener's perceptions of a study's quality.**

2   **The contents, types, lengths, and technical specifications of research reports.**

3   **That the writer of a research report should be guided by questions of purpose, readership, circumstances/limitations, and use.**

4   **That while some statistical data may be incorporated in the text, most statistics should be placed in tables, charts, or graphs.**

5   **That oral presentations of research findings should be developed with concern for organization, visual aids, and delivery in unique communication settings. Presentation quality can enhance or detract from what might otherwise be excellent research.**

Bringing Research to Life

"**H**as it occurred to you that your draft of the MindWriter report has not been touched in the last two days? The stack of marked-up pages is right there on your desk, and you have been working all around it."

Jason frowned and momentarily flicked his eyes to the papers and immediately glanced away at his shoe tops.

But Myra plunged ahead with her complaint. "It's no big deal, you know. You promised to chop out three pages of methodology that nobody will care about but your fellow statistics jocks . . ." Jason shot her an aggrieved look. ". . . And to remove your recommendations and provide them in a separate, informal letter so that Gracie or I can distribute them under our name and claim credit for your 'brilliance.'"

"I think I have writer's block."

"No. Writer's block is when you can't write. You have already written. You can't *un*write; that's the problem. You have *un*writer's block."

"Well, it isn't funny, Myra. That report might as well be a 15,000-volt power line. I know that if I touch it, I'll never be able to let go."

"OK, Jason. You are right. It isn't funny to have an emotional block against writing . . . or unwriting, but you do not want to see me, as your client, fretting over your delay."

"It's not an emotional problem, Myra."

"Well, of course it is. It always is. Your brain has not deteriorated, has it? In the last week?

"Some people do great research and then panic when they have to decide what goes in the report and what doesn't. Or they can't take all the great ideas running around in their heads and express their abstractions in words. Or they don't believe they are smart enough to communicate with their clients, or vice versa. So they freeze up. There is some sort of emotional problem around this MindWriter report, Jason, and you have got to face it."

"But I love the MindWriter project."

"Ah, *there's* the problem," she said.

"What? That I love it? Loving it is a problem?"

"Jason, I have heard you say that you hated projects for other clients, and I have heard you say that you *liked* projects. But this is the first time I have heard you say you *loved* a project."

"I still don't see the problem."

"Then let me tell you a story. My son-in-law has been assigned to a submarine tender in Iceland. My daughter wants to bring the kids and move in with me. I think I am going to have to tell her no, and the decision is killing me."

"The decision."

"She is my only child. After Harry was gone I raised her alone. I would have been a network anchor, Jason, if I hadn't made it my number one priority to raise Janice. I had to be her father and mother. The week she married I stayed awake for three days and nights, just crying. Not because she married a bad person, but because I had to let go. There comes a time when, after you have nurtured something, you have to let go. Then it isn't yours. It is someone else's, or it is its own thing, but it is not yours.

"When something is not yours anymore . . . when someone is their own person . . . or some work is passed to someone else . . . you don't own it. You do not get to go back and change it. It is out of your hands."

She paused. "Take Janice. She is a delight. I love to have her and the kids for a visit. But she can't come back. I have my life. She has hers. I don't own her anymore. She is not mine the way she was, and it is very important that I accept that unconditionally."

"I think I know what you mean. This MindWriter project was my baby—well, yours and mine. If I chop five pages out of the report, it is finished. Then it belongs to you—and, I guess, Gracie. I don't own it anymore. I can't fix it. I can't change anything. I can't have second thoughts."

"Fix it, then. Send us an invoice. Write a proposal for follow-up work. Do *something,* Jason. Find another project you love just as much. Finish it. Let go and move on."

The Written Research Report

It may seem unscientific and even unfair, but a poor final report or presentation can destroy a study. Research technicians may appreciate the brilliance of badly reported content, but most readers will be influenced by the quality of the reporting. This fact should prompt researchers to make special efforts to communicate clearly and fully.

The research report contains findings, analyses of findings, interpretations, conclusions, and sometimes recommendations. The researcher is the expert on the topic and knows the specifics in a way no one else can. Because a research report is an authoritative one-way communication, it imposes a special obligation for maintaining objectivity. Even if your findings seem to point to an action, you should demonstrate restraint and caution when proposing that course.

Reports may be defined by their degree of formality and design. The formal report follows a well-delineated and relatively long format. This is in contrast to the informal or short report.

Short Reports

Short reports are appropriate when the problem is well defined, is of limited scope, and has a simple and straightforward methodology. Most informational, progress, and interim reports are of this kind: a report of cost-of-living changes for upcoming labor negotiations or an exploration of filing "dumping" charges against a foreign competitor.

Short reports are about five pages. If used on a website, they may be even shorter. At the beginning, there should be a brief statement about the authorization for the study, the problem examined, and its breadth and depth. Next come the conclusions and recommendations, followed by the findings that support them. Section headings should be used.

A letter of transmittal is a vehicle to convey short reports. A five-page report may be produced to track sales on a quarterly basis. The report should be direct, make ample use of graphics to show trends, and refer the reader to the research department for further information. Detailed information on the research method would be omitted, although an overview could appear in an appendix. The purpose of this type of report is to distribute information quickly in an easy-to-use format. Short reports are also produced for clients with small, relatively inexpensive research projects.

The letter is a form of a short report. Its tone should be informal. The format follows that of any good business letter and should not exceed a few pages. A letter report is often written in personal style (*we, you*), although this depends on the situation.

Memorandum reports are another variety and follow the *To, From, Subject* format. These suggestions may be helpful for writing short reports:

MANAGEMENT
Tip

- Tell the reader why you are writing (it may be in response to a request).

- If the memo is in response to a request for information, remind the reader of the exact point raised, answer it, and follow with any necessary details.

- Write in an expository style with brevity and directness.

Medical Radar International (MRI), a Swedish research company, works exclusively in the pharmaceutical field. It conducts its syndicated study—Radar Dynamics—on the use of pharmaceuticals by doctors across several European countries, by interviewing 150 to 300 physicians (depending on the size of the country) twice each year.

Using a variety of SPSS software products, including *In2quest's In2data* for database development, *Quantum* for fast data tabulation, and *SmartViewer,* MRI can report results quickly. With *SmartViewer* Web server software, a

pharmaceutical company participating in the syndicated study can view password-protected results from Medical Radar's own website, even customizing the data in tables that specifically suit its needs, while the underlying data are tamper-protected. Staffan Hallstram, systems manager at MRI, reports Web distribution is the "ideal method" for distributing its syndicated research reports.

www.medical-radar.com

www.spss.com

- If time permits, write the report today and leave it for review tomorrow before sending it.
- Attach detailed materials as appendixes when needed.

Long Reports

Long reports are of two types, the technical or base report and the management report. The choice depends on the audience and the researcher's objectives.

Many projects will require both types of reports: a **technical report,** written for an audience of researchers, and a **management report,** written for the nontechnically oriented manager or client. While some researchers try to write a single report that satisfies both needs, this complicates the task and is seldom satisfactory. The two types of audiences have different technical training, interests, and goals.

The Technical Report This report should include full documentation and detail. It will normally survive all working papers and original data files and so will become the major source document. It is the report that other researchers will want to see because it has the full story of what was done and how it was done.

While completeness is a goal, you must guard against including nonessential material. A good guide is that sufficient procedural information should be included to enable others to replicate the study. This includes sources of data, research procedures, sampling design, data-gathering instruments, index construction, and data analysis methods. Most information should be attached in an appendix.

A technical report should also include a full presentation and analysis of significant data. Conclusions and recommendations should be clearly related to specific findings. Technical jargon should be minimized but defined when used. There can be brief references to other research, theories, and techniques. While you expect the reader to be familiar with these references, it is useful to include some short explanations, perhaps as footnotes or endnotes.

The Management Report Sometimes the client has no research background and is interested in results rather than in methodology. The major communication medium in this case is the management report. It is still helpful to have a technical report if the client later wishes to have a technical appraisal of the study.

Because the management report is designed for a nontechnical audience, the researcher faces some special problems. Readers are less concerned with methodological details but more interested in learning quickly the major findings and conclusions. They want help in making decisions. Often the report is developed for a single person and needs to be written with that person's characteristics and needs in mind.

The style of the report should encourage rapid reading and quick comprehension of major findings, and it should prompt understanding of the implications and conclusions. The report tone is journalistic and must be accurate. Headlines and underlining for emphasis are helpful; pictures and graphs often replace tables. Sentences and paragraphs should be short and direct. Consider liberal use of white space and wide margins. It may be desirable to put a single finding on each page. It also helps to have a theme running through the report and even graphic or animated characters designed to vary the presentation.

Research Report Components

Research reports, long and short, have a set of identifiable components. Usually headings and subheadings divide the sections. Each report is individual; sections may be dropped or added, condensed or expanded to meet the needs of the audience. Exhibit 20–1 lists four types of reports, the sections that are typically included, and the general order of presentation. Each of these formats can be modified to meet the needs of the audience.

The technical report follows the flow of the research. The prefatory materials, such as a letter of authorization and a table of contents, are first. An introduction covers the purpose of the study and is followed by a section on methodology. The findings are presented next, including tables and other graphics. The conclusions section includes recommendations. Finally, the appendixes contain technical information, instruments, glossaries, and references.

In contrast to the technical report, the management report is for the nontechnical client. The reader has little time to absorb details and needs a prompt exposure to the most critical findings; thus the report's sections are in an inverted order. After the prefatory and introductory sections, the conclusions with accompanying recommendations are presented. Individual findings are presented next, supporting the conclusions already made. The appendixes present any required methodological details. The order of the management report allows clients to grasp the conclusions and recommendations quickly, without much reading. Then, if they wish to go further, they may read on into the findings. The management report should make liberal use of visual displays.

The short technical report covers the same items as the long technical report but in an abbreviated form. The methodology is included as part of the introduction and takes no more than a few paragraphs. Most of the emphasis is placed on the findings and conclusions. A memo or letter format covers only the minimum: what the problem is and what the research conclusions are.

Prefatory Items

Prefatory materials do not have direct bearing on the research itself. Instead, they assist the reader in using the research report.

Letter of Transmittal   When the relationship between the researcher and the client is formal, a **letter of transmittal** should be included. This is appropriate when a report is for a specific client (e.g., the company president) and when it is generated for an out-

EXHIBIT 20–1 Research Report Sections and Their Order of Inclusion

Report Modules	Short Report		Long Report	
	Memo or Letter	Short Technical	Management	Technical
Prefatory information		1	1	1
Letter of transmittal		√	√	√
Title page		√	√	√
Authorization statement		√	√	√
Executive summary		√	√	√
Table of contents			√	√
Introduction	1	2	2	2
Problem statement	√	√	√	√
Research objectives	√	√	√	√
Background	√	√	√	√
Methodology		√ (briefly)	√ (briefly)	3
Sampling design				√
Research design				√
Data collection				√
Data analysis				√
Limitations		√	√	√
Findings		3	4	4
Conclusions	2	4	3	5
Summary and conclusions	√	√	√	√
Recommendations	√	√	√	√
Appendixes		5	5	6
Bibliography				7

side organization. The letter should refer to the authorization for the project and any specific instructions or limitations placed on the study. It should also state the purpose and the scope of the study. For many internal projects, it is not necessary to include a letter of transmittal.

Title Page   The title page should include four items: the title of the report, the date, and for whom and by whom it was prepared. The title should be brief but include the following three elements: (1) the variables included in the study, (2) the type of relationship among the variables, and (3) the population to which the results may be applied.[1] Redundancies such as "A Report of" and "A Discussion of" add length to the title but little else. Single-word titles are also of little value. Here are three acceptable ways to word report titles:

> *Descriptive study:*   *The Five-Year Demand Outlook for Plastic Pipe in the United States*
>
> *Correlation study:*   *The Relationship between the Value of the Dollar in World Markets and Relative National Inflation Rates*
>
> *Causal study:*   *The Effect of Various Motivation Methods on Worker Attitudes among Textile Workers*

Authorization Letter   When the report is sent to a public organization, it is common to include a letter of authorization showing the authority for undertaking the research. This is especially true for reports to federal and state governments and nonprofit organizations. The letter not only shows who sponsored the research but also delineates the original request.

Executive Summary   An **executive summary** can serve two purposes. It may be a report in miniature—covering all the aspects in the body of the report, but in abbreviated form. Or it may be a concise summary of the major findings and conclusions, including recommendations. Two pages are generally sufficient for executive summaries. Write this section after the rest of the report is finished. It should not include new information but may require graphics to present a particular conclusion. Expect the summary to contain a high density of significant terms since it is repeating the highlights of the report.

Table of Contents   As a rough guide, any report of several sections that totals more than 6 to 10 pages should have a table of contents. If there are many tables, charts, or other exhibits, they should also be listed after the table of contents in a separate table of illustrations.

Introduction

The introduction prepares the reader for the report by describing the parts of the project: the problem statement, research objectives, and background material.[2] In most projects, the introduction can be taken from the research proposal with minor editing.

Problem Statement   The problem statement contains the need for the research project. The problem is usually represented by a management question. It is followed by a more detailed set of objectives.

Research Objectives   The research objectives address the purpose of the project. These objectives may be research questions and associated investigative questions. In correlational or causal studies, the hypothesis statements are included. As we discussed in Chapter 2, hypotheses are declarative statements describing the relationship between two or more variables. They state clearly the variables of concern, the relationships among them, and the target group being studied. Operational definitions of critical variables should be included.

Background   Background material may be of two types. It may be the preliminary results of exploration from an experience survey, focus group, or another source. Alternatively, it could be secondary data from the literature review. A traditional organizational scheme is to think of the concentric circles of a target. Starting with the outside ring, the writer works toward the center. The bull's eye contains the material directly related to the problem. Sources and means for securing this information are presented in Chapter 10 and in Appendix A.

Previous research, theory, or situations that led to the management question are also discussed in this section. The literature should be organized, integrated, and presented in a way that connects it logically to the problem. The background includes definitions, qualifications, and assumptions. It gives the reader the information needed to understand the remainder of the research report.[3]

Background material may be placed before the problem statement or after the research objectives. If it is composed primarily of literature review and related research, it should follow the objectives. If it contains information pertinent to the management problem or the situation that led to the study, it can be placed before the problem statement (where it is found in many applied studies).

Methodology

In short reports and management reports, the methodology should not have a separate section; it should be mentioned in the introduction, and details should be placed in an appendix. However, for a technical report, the methodology is an important section, containing at least five parts.

Sampling Design   The researcher explicitly defines the target population being studied and the sampling methods used. For example, was this a probability or nonprobability sample? If probability, was it simple random or complex random? How were the elements selected? How was the size determined? How much confidence do we have, and how much error was allowed?

Explanations of the sampling methods, uniqueness of the chosen parameters, or other points that need explanation should be covered with brevity. Calculations should be placed in an appendix instead of in the body of the report.

Research Design   The coverage of the design must be adapted to the purpose. In an experimental study, the materials, tests, equipment, control conditions, and other devices should be described. In descriptive or ex post facto designs, it may be sufficient to cover the rationale for using one design instead of competing alternatives. Even with a sophisticated design, the strengths and weaknesses should be identified and the instrumentation and materials discussed. Copies of materials are placed in an appendix.

Data Collection   This part of the report describes the specifics of gathering the data. Its contents depend on the selected design. Survey work generally uses a team with field and central supervision. How many were involved? What was their training? How were they managed? When were the data collected? How much time did it take? What were the conditions in the field? How were irregularities handled? In an experiment, we would want to know about subject assignment to groups, the use of standardized procedures and protocols, the administration of tests or observational forms, manipulation of the variables, and so forth.

Typically, you would include a discussion on the relevance of secondary data that guided these decisions. Again, detailed materials such as field instructions should be included in an appendix.

Data Analysis   This section summarizes the methods used to analyze the data. Describe data handling, preliminary analysis, statistical tests, computer programs, and other technical information. The rationale for the choice of analysis approaches should be clear. A brief commentary on assumptions and appropriateness of use should be presented.

Limitations   This topic is often handled with ambivalence. Some people wish to ignore the matter, feeling that mentioning limitations detracts from the impact of the study. This attitude is unprofessional and possibly unethical. Others seem to adopt a masochistic approach of detailing everything. The section should be a thoughtful presentation of significant methodology or implementation problems. An evenhanded approach is one of the hallmarks of an honest and competent investigator. All research studies have their limitations, and the sincere investigator recognizes that readers need aid in judging the study's validity.

Findings

This is generally the longest section of the report. The objective is to explain the data rather than draw interpretations or conclusions. When quantitative data can be presented, this should be done as simply as possible with charts, graphics, and tables.

The data need not include everything you have collected. The criterion for inclusion is, "Is this material important to the reader's understanding of the problem and the findings?" However, make sure to show findings unfavorable to your hypotheses as well as those that support them.

It is useful to present findings in numbered paragraphs or to present one finding per page with the quantitative data supporting the findings presented in a small table or chart on the same page (see Exhibit 20–2). While this arrangement adds to the bulk of the report, it is convenient for the reader.

EXHIBIT 20–2 **Example of a Findings Page in Central City Bank Market Study**

Findings:

1. In this city, *commercial banks are not the preferred savings medium.* Banks are in a weak third place behind money market accounts.

2. Customers of the Central City Bank have a *somewhat more favorable attitude toward bank savings* and less of a preference for government bonds.

Question:

Suppose that you have just received an extra $1,000 and have decided to save it. Which of the savings methods listed would be your preferred way to save it?

❏ Government bonds
❏ Savings and loan
❏ Bank savings
❏ Credit union
❏ Stock
❏ Other

Savings Method	Total Replies	Central City Bank Customers	Other Bank Customers
Government bonds	24%	20%	29%
Savings and loan	43	45	42
Bank	13	18	8
Credit union	9	7	11
Stock	7	8	5
Other	4	2	5
Total	100%	100%	100%
	$n = 216$	$n = 105$	$n = 111$

Conclusions

Summary and Conclusions   The summary is a brief statement of the essential findings. Sectional summaries may be used if there are many specific findings. These may be combined into an overall summary. In simple descriptive research, a summary may complete the report, because conclusions and recommendations may not be required.

Findings state facts; conclusions represent inferences drawn from the findings. A writer is sometimes reluctant to make conclusions and leaves the task to the reader. Avoid this temptation when possible. As the researcher, you are the one best informed on the factors that critically influence the findings and conclusions.

Conclusions may be presented in a tabular form for easy reading and reference. Summary findings may be subordinated under the related conclusion statement. These may be numbered to refer the reader to pages or tables in the findings sections.

Recommendations   There are usually a few ideas about corrective actions. In academic research, the recommendations are often further study suggestions that broaden or test understanding of the subject area. In applied research the recommendations will usually be for managerial action rather than research action. The writer may offer several alternatives with justifications.

Appendixes

The appendixes are the place for complex tables, statistical tests, supporting documents, copies of forms and questionnaires, detailed descriptions of the methodology, instructions to field workers, and other evidence important for later support. The reader who wishes to learn about the technical aspects of the study and to look at statistical breakdowns will want a complete appendix.

Bibliography

The use of secondary data requires a bibliography. Proper citation, style, and formats are unique to the purpose of the report. The instructor, program, institution, or client often specifies style requirements. The uniqueness of varying requirements makes detailed examples in this chapter impractical although the endnotes and references in this book provide an example. As cited in Chapter 4, on the research proposal, we recommend the *Publication Manual of the American Psychological Association;* Kate L. Turabian, *A Manual for Writers of Term Papers, Theses, and Dissertations;* and Joseph Gibaldi and Walter S. Achtert, *MLA Handbook for Writers of Research Papers.*

Writing the Report

Students often give inadequate attention to reporting their findings and conclusions. This is unfortunate. A well-presented study will often impress the reader more than a study with greater scientific quality but a weaker presentation. Report-writing skills are especially valuable to the junior executive or management trainee who aspires to rise in an organization. A well-written study frequently enhances career prospects.

Prewriting Concerns

Before writing, one should ask again, "What is the purpose of this report?" Responding to this question is one way to crystallize the problem.

The second prewriting question is, "Who will read the report?" Thought should be given to the needs, temperament, and biases of the audience. You should not distort facts to meet these needs and biases but should consider them while developing the presentation. Knowing who will read the report may suggest its appropriate length. Generally, the higher the report goes in an organization, the shorter it should be.

Another consideration is technical background—the gap in subject knowledge between the reader and the writer. The greater the gap, the more difficult it is to convey the full findings meaningfully and concisely.

The third prewriting question is, "What are the circumstances and limitations under which you are writing?" Is the nature of the subject highly technical? Do you need statistics? Charts? What is the importance of the topic? A crucial subject justifies more effort than a minor one. What should be the scope of the report? How much time is available? Deadlines often impose limitations on the report.

Finally, "How will the report be used?" Try to visualize the reader using the report. How can the information be made more convenient? How much effort must be given to getting the attention and interest of the reader? Will the report be read by more than one person? If so, how many copies should be made? What will be the distribution of the report?

The Outline   Once the researcher has made the first analysis of the data, drawn tentative conclusions, and completed statistical significance tests, it is time to develop an outline. A useful system employs the following organization structure:

I. Major Topic Heading
　　A. Major subtopic heading
　　　　1. Subtopic
　　　　　　a. Minor subtopic
　　　　　　　　(1) Further detail
　　　　　　　　　　(a) Even further detail

Software for developing outlines and visually connecting ideas simplifies this once-onerous task. Two styles of outlining are widely used—the **topic outline** and the **sentence outline.** In the topic outline, a key word or two is used. The assumption is that the writer knows its significance and will later remember the nature of the argument represented by that word or phrase or, alternatively, the outliner knows that a point should be made but is not yet sure how to make it.

The sentence outline expresses the essential thoughts associated with the specific topic. This approach leaves less development work for later writing, other than elaboration and explanation to improve readability. It has the obvious advantages of pushing the writer to make decisions on what to include and how to say it. It is probably the best outlining style for the inexperienced researcher because it divides the writing job into its two major components—what to say and how to say it.

Here is an example of the type of detail found with each of these outlining formats:

Topic Outline	Sentence Outline

I. Demand
   A. How measured
      1. Voluntary error
      2. Shipping error
         a. Monthly variance
	I. Demand for refrigerators.
	   A. Measured in terms of factory shipments as reported to the U.S. Department of Commerce.
	      1. Error is introduced into year-to-year comparisons because reporting is voluntary.
	      2. A second factor is variations from month to month because of shipping and invoicing patterns.
	         a. Variations up to 30 percent this year depending on whether shipments were measured by actual shipment date or invoice date.

The Bibliography   Long reports, particularly technical ones, require a bibliography. A bibliography documents the sources used by the writer. Although bibliographies may contain work used as background or for further study, it is preferable to include only sources used for preparing the report.

Bibliographic retrieval software allows researchers to locate and save references from online services and translate them into database records. Entries can be further searched, sorted, indexed, and formatted into bibliographies of any style. Many retrieval programs are network compatible and connect to popular word processors. Chapter 10 also mentions a recording system for converting source notes to footnotes and bibliographies.

Style manuals provide guidelines on form, section and alphabetical arrangement, and annotation. Projects using many electronic sources may benefit from the comparison of APA and MLA citations in Exhibit 20–3.

Writing the Draft

Once the outline is complete, decisions can be made on the placement of graphics, tables, and charts. Each should be matched to a particular section in the outline. It is helpful to make these decisions before your first draft. While graphics might be added later or tables changed into charts, it is helpful to make a first approximation of the graphics before beginning to write. Choices for reporting statistics will be reviewed later in this chapter.

Each writer uses different mechanisms for getting thoughts into written form. Some will write in longhand, relying on someone else to transcribe their prose into word-processed format. Others are happiest in front of a word processor, able to add, delete, and move sections at will. Whichever works for you is the best approach to use.

Computer software packages check for spelling errors and provide a thesaurus for looking up alternative ways of expressing a thought. A CD-ROM can call up the 20-volume *Oxford English Dictionary,* believed to be the greatest dictionary in any language. Common word confusion (*there* for *their, to* for *too,* or *effect* for *affect*) will

EXHIBIT 20–3   **Citing Electronic Sources**

Type	APA	MLA
Full-text sources from library resources (online and CD-ROM)	Last name of author, first initial. (Year, month day). Title. *Journal* [Type of medium], volume (issue), paging if given or other indicator of length. Available: supplier/database name and number/identifier number, item, or accession number [access date].	Last name of author, first initial. "Title." *Journal* [Type of medium] volume.issue (year): paging if given or other indicator of length. Available: supplier/database name and number/identifier number, item or accession number [access date].*
	Crow, P. (1994). GATT shows progress in Congress. *The Oil and Gas Journal* [Online], 92(49), 32 (1p.). Available: Information Access/ Expanded Academic Index ASAP/ A15955498 [1996, March 13].	Crow, P. "GATT Shows Progress in Congress." *The Oil and Gas Journal* [Online] 92.49 (1994): 32–33. Online. Available: Information Access Company. *Expanded Academic Index ASAP.* 13 Mar. 1996.
WWW sites: Individual works with print equivalent	Last name of author/editor, first initial. (Year, month day). *Title* (Edition). [Type of medium]. Producer. Available: address or source/path/file [access date].	Last name of author/editor, first name. *Title of Print Version of Work.* Edition statement. Place of publication: publisher, date. *Title of Electronic Work.* Medium [Online]. Information supplier. Available protocol: http://www.address.goes.here. Access date [dy mo yr].
	Bartlett, J. (1995, March). *Familiar quotations: Passages, phrases & proverbs traced to their sources* (9th ed.). [Online]. Columbia University. Available: http//www. columbia.edu/acis/bartleby/bartlett/ [1996, March 19].	Bartlett, J. *Familiar Quotations: Passages, Phrases & Proverbs Traced to Their Sources in Ancient & Modern Literature.* 9th ed. Boston: Little, Brown & Co., 1901. *Familiar Quotations: Passages, Phrases & Proverbs Traced to Their Sources.* Online. Columbia University. Available HTTP: http://www.columbia.edu/acis/ bartleby/bartlett. 19 Mar. 1996.

not be found by standard spelling checkers. Advanced programs will scrutinize your report for grammar, punctuation, capitalization, doubled words, transposed letters, homonyms, style problems, and readability level. The style checker will reveal misused words and indicate awkward phrasing. Exhibit 20–4 shows sample output from a commercial package used on one of this text's vignettes. The program shown writes comments to a text file, prepares a backup copy of the original, and generates a statistics report. The statistics summarize the program's evaluation of readability, grade level, and sentence structure. Comparisons to "reference" documents, or documents that you submit for comparison, may be made. The software cannot guarantee an error-free report but will greatly reduce your time in proofreading and enhance the style of the completed product.[4]

EXHIBIT 20–3   Concluded

Type	APA	MLA
WWW sites: Parts of works	Last name of author/editor, first initial. (Year, month day). Title of article or document. In Title of Source (edition), [Online], volume (issue), paging or indicator of length. Available: address or source/path/file [access date].	Last name of author, first name. "Title of Article or Document." *Title of Journal, Newsletter, or Conference* volume.issue number (year) or date of publication: number of pages or pars. Medium [online]. Available protocol: http://www.address.goes. here. Access date [dy mo yr].
	Steinfield, C., Kraut, R., & Plummer, A. (1995). The impact of interorganizational networks on buyer-seller relationships. *Journal of Computer-Mediated Communication* [Online], 1(3), 56 paragraphs. Available: http://shum.juji.ac.il/jcmc/vol1/issue3/steinfld.html [1996, April 22].	Steinfield, C., Kraut, R., & Plummer, A. "The Impact of Interorganizational Networks on Buyer-Seller Relationships." *Journal of Computer-Mediated Communication* 1.3 (1995): 56 pars. Online. Available HTTP: http://shum.juji.ac.il/jcmc/vol1/issue3/steinfld.html. 22 Apr. 1996.
WWW sites: E-mail, listserv, and discussion list messages	Last name of author, first initial (if known). (Year, month day). Subject of message. Discussion List [Online]. Available e-mail: LISTSERV@e-mail address [Access date].	Last name of author, first name (if known). "Subject line from posting." Date. Medium [online]. Discussion List. Available e-mail: LISTSERV @e-mail address. Access date.
	Wagner, K. (1996, February 6). Re: Citing/evaluating web resources. NETLIBS [Online]. Available e-mail netlibs@qut.edu.au [1996, February 7].	Wagner, Kurt W. "Re: Citing/ evaluating web resources." Online. NETLIBS. Available e-mail: netlibs @qut.edu.au 7 Feb. 1996.
WWW sites: Home pages	Last name of author/editor, first initial (if known). (Last update or copyright date). Home Page Title [Home page of . . .]. Available: http//www.address. goes.here [Access date].	
	House, P. (1997, March 26—last update). The Smithsonian: America's treasure house for learning [Home Page of the Smithsonian Institution]. [Online]. Available: http://www.si.edu/newstart.htm [1997, March 27].	

*Access date not needed if CD-ROM.

SOURCE: Adapted from *APA Guides for Citing Electronic Sources and Guidelines for Citing Electronic Sources—MLA,* Cedarville College Centennial Library, Cedarville, OH, 45314.

EXHIBIT 20–4   Grammar and Style Proofreader Results

Statistics

Statistics for: Chapter 3 Vignette   Problems marked/detected: 8/8

Readability Statistics

Flesch Reading Ease: 66	Flesch-Kincaid Grade Level: 8
Gunning s Fog Index: 11	

Paragraph Statistics

Number of paragraphs: 25   Average length: 2.2 sentences

Sentence Statistics

Number of sentences: 55		Passive voice:	4
Average length:	13.8 words	Short (< 12 words) :	39
End with ? :	2	Long (> 28 words) :	7
End with ! :	0		

Word Statistics

Number of words: 759   Average length: 4.58 letters

Document Summary for: Chapter 3 Vignette   Problems detected: 8

Readability Statistics	Interpretation
Grade level:	Preferred level for most readers.
8 (Flesch-Kincaid)	
Reading ease score:	This represents 6 to 10 years
66 (Flesch)	of schooling.
Passive voice:	Writing may be difficult to read or
331	ambiguous for this writing style.
Average sentence length:	Most readers could easily understand
13.8 words	sentences of this length.
Average word length:	Vocabulary used in this document
1.50 syl.	is understandable for most readers.
Average paragraph length:	Most readers could easily follow
2.2 sentences	paragraphs of this length.

Comparisons

Readability Comparison Chart

Flesch Reading Ease Score

Chapter 3 Vignette — 66
Gettysburg Address — 64
Hemingway short story — 86
Life insurance policy — 45

Flesch-Kincaid Grade Level

Chapter 3 Vignette — 8
Gettysburg Address — 11
Hemingway short story — 5
Life insurance policy — 13

Sentence Statistics Comparison Chart

Average Sentence per Paragraph

Chapter 3 Vignette — 2.2
Gettysburg Address — 4.1
Hemingway short story — 2.8
Life insurance policy — 3.2

Average Words per Sentence

Chapter 3 Vignette — 13.8
Gettysburg Address — 26.8
Hemingway short story — 13.5
Life insurance policy — 23.9

Word Statistics Comparison Chart

Average Letters per Word

Chapter 3 Vignette — 4.5
Gettysburg Address — 4.2
Hemingway short story — 4.0
Life insurance policy — 4.7

Readability   Sensitive writers consider the reading ability of their audience to achieve high readership. You can obtain high readership more easily if the topic interests the readers and is in their field of expertise. In addition, you can show the usefulness of the report by pointing out how it will help the readers. Finally, you can write at a level that is appropriate to the readers' reading abilities. To test writing for difficulty level, there are standard **readability indexes.** The Flesch Reading Ease Score gives a score between 0 and 100. The lower the score, the harder the material is to read. The Flesch-Kincaid Grade Level and Gunning's Fog Index both provide a score that corresponds with the grade level needed to easily read and understand the document. Although it is possible to calculate these indexes by hand, some software packages will do it automatically. The most sophisticated packages allow you to specify the preferred reading level. Words that are above that level are highlighted to allow you to choose an alternative.

Advocates of readability measurement do not claim that all written material should be at the simplest level possible. They argue only that the level should be appropriate for the audience. They point out that comic books score about 6 on the Gunning scale (that is, a person with a sixth-grade education should be able to read that material). *Time* usually scores about 10, while *The Atlantic* is reported to have a score of 11 or 12. Material that scores much above 12 becomes difficult for the public to read comfortably. Such measures obviously give only a rough idea of the true readability of a report. Good writing calls for a variety of other skills to enhance reading comprehension.

Comprehensibility   Good writing varies with the writing objective. Research writing is designed to convey information of a precise nature. Avoid ambiguity, multiple meanings, and allusions. Take care to choose the right words—words that convey thoughts accurately, clearly, and efficiently. When concepts and constructs are used, they must be defined, either operationally or descriptively.

Words and sentences should be carefully organized and edited. Misplaced modifiers run rampant in carelessly written reports. Subordinate ideas mixed with major ideas make the report confusing to readers, forcing them to sort out what is important and what is secondary when this should have been done for them.

Finally, there is the matter of pace. **Pace** is defined as

> *The rate at which the printed page presents information to the reader . . . The proper pace in technical writing is one that enables the reader to keep his mind working just a fraction of a second behind his eye as he reads along. It logically would be slow when the information is complex or difficult to understand; fast when the information is straightforward and familiar. If the reader's mind lags behind his eye, the pace is too rapid; if his mind wanders ahead of his eye (or wants to) the pace is too slow.[5]*

If the text is overcrowded with concepts, there is too much information per sentence. By contrast, sparse writing has too few significant ideas per sentence. Writers use a variety of methods to adjust the pace of their writing:

MANAGEMENT
Tip

- Use ample white space and wide margins to create a positive psychological effect on the reader.

- Break large units of text into smaller units with headings to show organization of the topics.

- Relieve difficult text with visual aids when possible.

- Emphasize important material and deemphasize secondary material through sentence construction and judicious use of italicizing, underlining, capitalization, and parentheses.

- Choose words carefully, opting for the known and short rather than the unknown and long. Graduate students, in particular, seem to revel in using jargon, pompous constructions, and long or arcane words. Naturally, there are times when technical terms are appropriate. Scientists communicate efficiently with jargon, but the audiences for most applied research are not scientifically trained and need more help than many writers supply.

- Repeat and summarize critical and difficult ideas so readers have time to absorb them.

- Make strategic use of service words. These are words that "do not represent objects or ideas, but show relationship. Transitional words, such as the conjunctions, are service words. So are phrases such as 'on the other hand,' 'in summary,' and 'in contrast.'"[6]

Tone   Review the writing to ensure the tone is appropriate. The reader can, and should, be referred to, but researchers should avoid referring to themselves. One author notes that the "application of the 'you' attitude . . . makes the message sound like it is written to the reader, not sent by the author. A message prepared for the reader conveys sincerity, personalization, warmth, and involvement on the part of the author."[7] To accomplish this, remove negative phrasing and rewrite the thought positively. Do not change your recommendations or your findings to make them positive. Instead, review the phrasing. Which of the following sounds better?

> End users do not want the Information Systems Department telling them what software to buy.
>
> End users want more autonomy over their computer software choices.

The messages convey the same information, but the positive tone of the second message does not put readers from the Information Systems Department on the defensive.

Final Proof   It is helpful to put the draft away for a day before doing the final editing. Go to the beach, ride a bicycle in the park, or see a movie—do anything that is unrelated to the research project. Then return to the report and read it with a critical eye. Does the writing flow smoothly? Are there transitions where they are needed? Is the organization apparent to the reader? Do the findings and conclusions adequately meet the problem statement and the research objectives? Are the tables and graphics displaying the proper information in an easy-to-read format? After assuring yourself that the draft is complete, write the executive summary.

Presentation Considerations

The final consideration in the report-writing process is production. Reports can be typed; printed on an ink-jet, laser, color, or other printer; or sent out for typesetting. Most student and small research reports are typed or produced on a computer printer. The presentation of the report conveys to the readers the professional approach used throughout the project. Care should be taken to use compatible fonts throughout the entire report. The printer should produce consistent, easy-to-read letters on quality paper. When reports are photocopied for more than one reader, make sure the copies are clean and have no black streaks or gray areas.

Overcrowding of text creates an appearance problem. Readers need the visual relief provided by ample white space. We define "ample" as one inch of white space at the top, bottom, and right-hand margins. On the left side, the margin should be at least one and one-fourth inches to provide room for binding or punched holes. Even greater margins will often improve report appearance and help to highlight key points or sections. Overcrowding also occurs when the report contains page after page of large blocks of unbroken text. This produces an unpleasant psychological effect on readers because of its formidable appearance. Overcrowded text, however, may be avoided in the following ways.

MANAGEMENT
Tip

- Use shorter paragraphs. As a rough guide, any paragraph longer than half a page is suspect. Remember that each paragraph should represent a distinct thought.

- Indent parts of text that represent listings, long quotations, or examples.

- Use headings and subheadings to divide the report and its major sections into homogeneous topical parts.

- Use vertical listings of points (such as this list).

Inadequate labeling creates another physical problem. Each graph or table should contain enough information to be self-explanatory. Text headings and subheadings also help with labeling. They function as signs for the audience, describing the organization of the report and indicating the progress of discussion. They also help readers to skim the material and to return easily to particular sections of the report.

Close-Up: MindWriter Written Report

A written report is the culmination of the MindWriter project, which has illustrated the research process throughout the book. Jason's contract for the CompleteCare project requires a report about the size of a student term project. Although repetitive portions have been omitted to conserve space, it should give the reader some idea of how an applied project of this size is summarized. Descriptive statistics and simple graphics are used to analyze and present most of the data. References to chapters where specific details may be reviewed are shown in the marginal comments.

The presentation of findings follows the content specifications of Exhibit 20–1 for short reports. It falls between a memo/letter and a short technical report. The objective was to make it available quickly for feedback to the Complete-Care team. It was therefore set up as a facsimile document.

The fax cover sheet acts as a temporary transmittal letter until the plain paper copies are sent.

It provides all necessary identification and contact information. The writer's and recipient's relationship makes using first names appropriate.

Authorization for the study. Scope of findings (month). Specific instructions for process issues.

Request for follow-up by the client to reduce the study's limitations.

Progress update and feedback on improvements.

FAX Transmittal Memo

To:	Ms. Gracie Uhura	**From:**	Jason Henry
Company:	MindWriter Corp.	**Company:**	Henry Associates
Location:	Austin, TX Bldg 5	**Location:**	Palm Beach, FL
Telephone:	512.555.1234	**Telephone:**	407.555.4321
Fax:	512.555.1250	**Fax:**	407.555.4357

Total number of pages including this one: 10

January 5, 2003

Dear Gracie,

This fax contains the CompleteCare December report requested by Mr. Malraison through Myra Wines. You may expect the plain paper copies tomorrow morning for distribution.

We hope that the Call Center will complete the nonrespondent surveys so that we can discover the extent to which these results represent all CompleteCare customers.

This month's findings show improvements in the areas we discussed last week by telephone. The response rate is also up. You will be delighted to know that our preliminary analysis shows improvements in the courier's ratings.

Best regards,

Jason

Title contains reference to a known survey and program. Descriptions of variables, relationships, and population are unnecessary.

The recipient of the report, corporation, and date appear next.

The report's preparer, location, and telephone number facilitate contact for additional information.

The information level identifies this as a restricted circulation document for in-house use only.

CompleteCare Customer Survey Results for December

**Prepared for Ms. Gracie Uhura
MindWriter Corporation
January 2003**

**Henry Associates
Research Services
200 ShellPoint Tower
Palm Beach, Florida 33480**

407.555.4321

MindWriter CONFIDENTIAL

Title repeated.

Section headings are used.

Introduction contains period of coverage for report, management question, and secondary research objective.

An overview of the report's contents allows readers to turn to specific sections of interest.

The executive summary provides a synopsis of essential findings. It is the report in miniature—six paragraphs.

Both positive and negative results are capsulized.

Criteria for indexes are provided as reminders.

MindWriter CompleteCare December Results

Introduction

This report is based on the December data collected from the MindWriter Complete-Care Survey. The survey asks customers about their satisfaction with the Complete-Care repair and service system. Its secondary purpose is to identify monthly improvement targets for management.

The findings are organized into the following sections: (1) an executive summary, (2) the methods used, (3) the Service Improvement Grid, (4) detailed findings for each question, and (5) patterns in the open-ended questions.

Executive Summary

The highest degrees of satisfaction with CompleteCare were found in the categories of "delivery speed" and "pickup speed." Average scores on these items were between 4.2 and 4.4 on a 5-point scale. "Speed of repair," "condition on arrival," and "overall impression of CompleteCare's effectiveness" also scored relatively well. They were above the *met all expectations* level (see appropriate charts).

Several questions were below the *met all expectations* level. From the lowest, "Call Center's responsiveness," to "Call Center's technical competence," and "courier service's arrangements," the average scores ranged from 2.0 to 3.9. In general, ratings have improved since November with the exception of "condition on arrival."

The three items generating the most negative comments are (1) problems with the courier's arrangements, (2) long telephone waits, and (3) transfer among many people at the Call Center. These same comments carry over for the last two months.

CompleteCare's criteria for Dissatisfied Customers consist of negative comments in the Comments/Suggestions section or ratings of less than three (3.0) on questions one through eight. Forty-three percent of the sample met these criteria, down from 56 percent last month. By counting only customers' comments (positive/negative or +/–), the percentage of Dissatisfied Customers would be 32 percent.

The ratio of negative to positive comments was 1.7 to 1, an improvement over November's ratio (2.3 to 1).

The methodology, reported in brief, reminds the reader of the data collection method, nature and format of the questionnaire, scales used, and target measurement issues.

The sample, a self-selecting nonprobability sample, and the response rate are shown. With respondents' data from the postcards and the Call Center's files on nonrespondents, a future study on nonresponse bias is planned.

This section begins the Findings section. Findings consist of the action planning grid and detailed results sections. The headings were specified by the client.

The method for creating the planning grid and the grid's contents are highlighted.

When the expectation-based satisfaction scores are adjusted for perceived importance, "Call Center responsiveness," "Call Center technical competence," and "courier arrangements" are identified as action items. "Repair speed" and "problem resolution" maintained high importance scores and are also rated above average.

Methodology

The data collection instrument is a postage-paid postcard that is packed with the repaired product at the time the unit is shipped back to the customer.

The survey consists of 12 satisfaction questions measured on five-point scales. The questions record the degree to which the components of the CompleteCare process (arrangements for receiving the customer's computer through return of the repaired product) meet customers' *expectations*. A final categorical question asks whether customers will use CompleteCare again. Space for suggestions is provided.

Sample

The sample consisted of 175 customers who provided impressions of Complete-Care's effectiveness. For the four-week period, the response rate was 35 percent with no incentive given. Nothing is yet known about the differences between respondents and nonrespondents.

Service Improvement Grid

The grid on page three compares the degree to which expectations were met along with the *derived importance* of those expectations. The average scores for both axes determine the dividing lines for the four quadrants. The quadrants are labeled to identify actionable items and to highlight those that bear watching for improvement or deterioration.

The **Concentrate Efforts** quadrant is the area where customers are marginally satisfied with service but consider service issues important. Question 1a, "Call Center's responsiveness," Question 1b, "Call Center's technical competence," and Question 2a, "courier arrangements," are found here. "Technical competence" was similarly rated last month. Its perceived importance was rated higher in previous months. "Courier arrangements" has increased in perceived importance over previous reports.

The statistical technique for producing the grid is correlation. A modification of scatterplots was used to create a plot with reference lines (see Chapter 18).

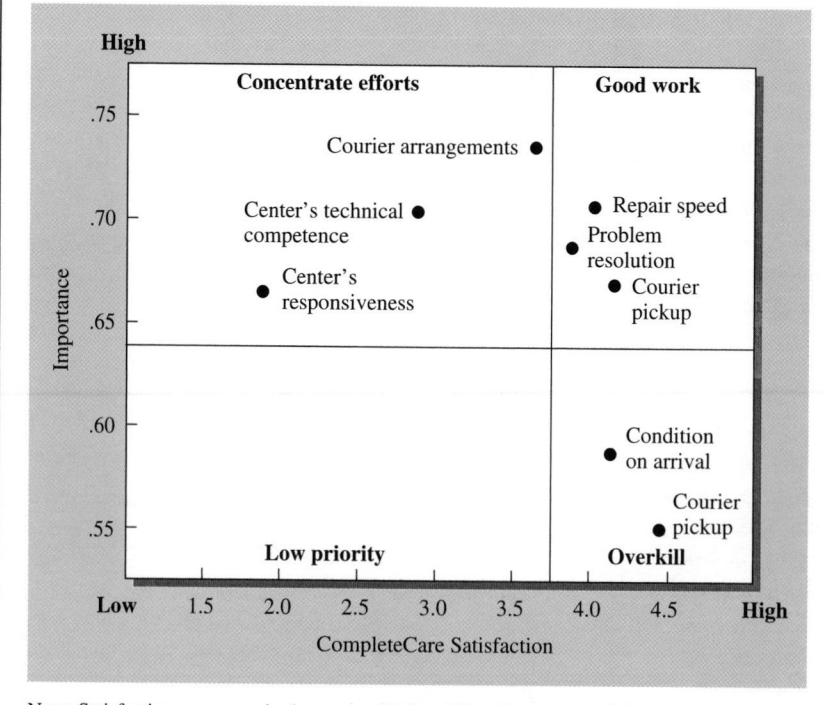

Note: Satisfaction scores are in the range of 1.0 to 5.0 and importance is in the range of 0 to 1.0.

The contents of each quadrant are described. Comparisons and connections to the next section are previewed.

In the **Good Work** quadrant, CompleteCare has, on average, *met all expectations* with the "repair speed" and "courier pickup" questions. Their mean scores are greater than 4.0 and considered important by respondents. "Problem resolution" has improved but remains a borderline concern.

There are no items in the **Low Priority** quadrant.

Overkill, the last quadrant, contains two questions. Question 5, "condition on arrival," has improved its ratings over last month but has dropped slightly on the importance scale because the average of importance scores (horizontal line) moved upward. Question 2c, "courier delivery speed," has a high satisfaction rating, but respondents considered this item to have lower importance than most issues in CompleteCare.

Detailed findings show the results of individual questions. This section announces the two-part content and presents, briefly and in a direct style, the most pertinent outcomes.

Detailed Findings

The figures that follow provide (1) a comparison of the mean scores for each of the questions for the last three months and (2) individual question results. The latter contains frequencies for the scale values, percentages for each category, mean scores, standard deviations, and valid cases for each question. (See Appendix for question wording and placement.)

The three-month comparison (October, November, December) shows results for all scaled questions. December data bars (in black) reveal improvements on all average scores (vertical axis) except Question 5, "condition on arrival." Most aspects of the service/repair process have shown improvement over the three-month period.

This graphic gives the reader a three-month view of all the questions at a glance. Vertical bars are the simplest and easiest to read for the amount of space allocated. Horizontal grid lines guide the eye from the bar tops to the closest value on the mean score axis.

Charts similar to these may be produced by the same spreadsheet that handles data entry. Charting programs offer other options and will import the data from spreadsheets.

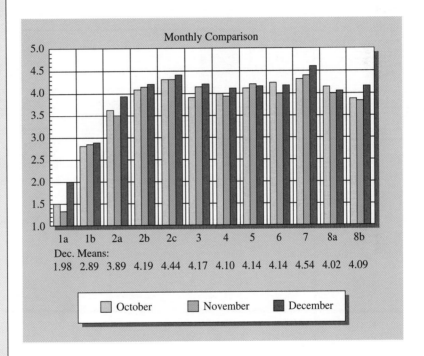

Monthly Comparison

Dec. Means:
1.98 2.89 3.89 4.19 4.44 4.17 4.10 4.14 4.14 4.54 4.02 4.09

The first individual item is reported with mean scores, percentages, and recommendations for improvement.

This chart conveys the message of low responsiveness rather well but does not have a label for the vertical axis. It is easy to confuse percentages with the number of respondents (which it is supposed to represent).

Similar reporting formats are skipped.

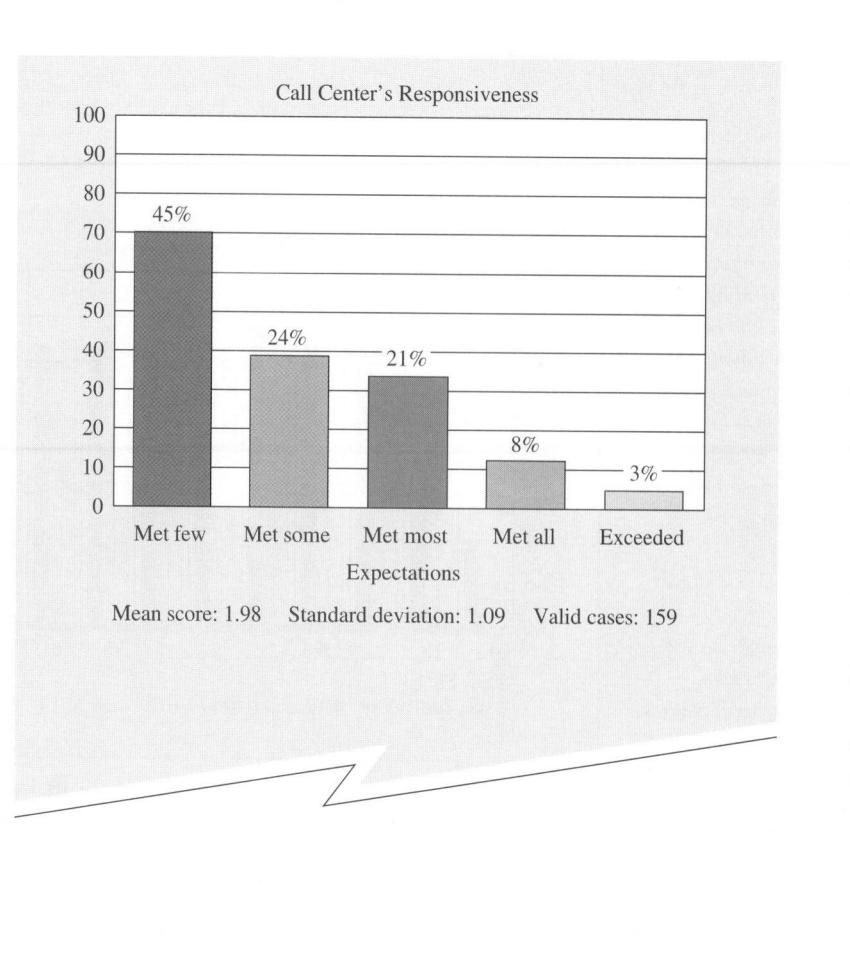

Question 1a. Call Center's Responsiveness.   This question has the lowest mean score of the survey. Using a top-box method of reporting (combining the top two categories), 11 percent of the respondents felt that the Call Center met or exceeded their expectations for service responsiveness. This has improved only marginally since November and has significant implications for program targets. Based on our visit and recent results, we recommend that you begin immediately the contingency programs we discussed: additional training for Call Center operators and implementation of the proposed staffing plan.

Call Center's Responsiveness

Met few 45%
Met some 24%
Met most 21%
Met all 8%
Exceeded 3%

Expectations

Mean score: 1.98   Standard deviation: 1.09   Valid cases: 159

Question 6 shows the respondents' overall impression of CompleteCare. It would be an ideal dependent variable for a regression study in which questions 1 through 5 were the independent variables (see Chapters 17 and 18).

Question 6. Overall Impression of CompleteCare's Effectiveness. CompleteCare has increased the number of truly satisfied respondents with 46 percent (versus 43 percent in November) in the *exceeded expectations* category. The top-box score has increased to 75 percent of respondents (against 70 percent in November).

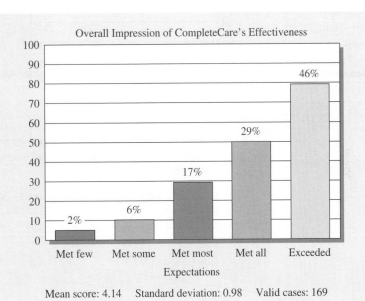

Overall Impression of CompleteCare's Effectiveness

Mean score: 4.14   Standard deviation: 0.98   Valid cases: 169

Question 8a is another question for more detailed research. It allows the researcher to connect the variables that describe the service/repair experience with repurchase intentions.

Question 8a. Likelihood of Repurchasing MindWriter Based on Service/Repair Experience. Respondents' average scores (4.02) for this likelihood scale are the highest this month since measurement began. Improvement of the courier service's arrangements with customers and the resolution of the problem that prompted service appear to be the best predictors of repurchase at this time.

Using regression, it was possible to identify two key influences for this question.

Question 8b (not shown) is similar, asking about the relation of product performance to repurchase intention.

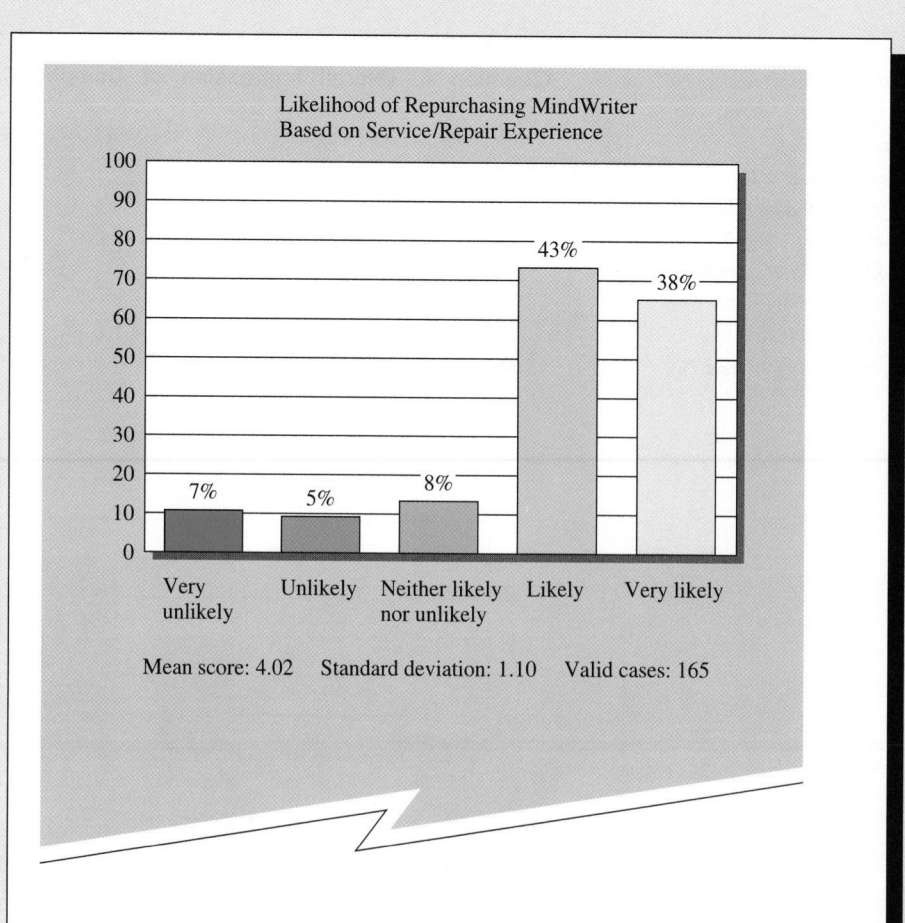

The questionnaire has one open-ended question that encourages respondents to make comments or suggestions.

Content analysis is used to distill the reponses (see Chapter 15).

Patterns in the Open-Ended Questions

The following categories were found when the comments and suggestions were ana-lyzed. The ratio of negative to positive comments was 1.7 to 1. Pickup problems con-tinue to be "courier only" problems and coordination between MindWriter's telephone support and the courier. Customers complain of holding on the phone for long periods and being transferred between support people. Problems with service are split between large problems that have not been fixed and small, nuisance problems that customers are prepared to live with. Positive comments commend turnaround and service and also praise specific technical operators.

Although content analysis produces more than frequency counts of recurring themes, it is a labor-intensive process. The project's restrictive budget and the needs of the audience made this section of the report adequate for its purpose.

Negative Comments	Count
Shipping	19
Pickup problems (15)	
Delivery problems (2)	
Box damage (1)	
The courier charged customer (1)	
Call Center	19
Too long on hold (9)	
Transferred call too frequently/confusion (8)	
Untrained/hard to understand (2)	
Service	13
Problem continues (5)	
Small things not fixed/damaged (6)	
Took too long (2–7 weeks) (2)	
Product	6
Multiple repairs needed (3)	
Paint wears off (2)	
General dislike of product (1)	
Positive Comments	
General positive comment about the process	13
Quick response	12
Great service	7
Helpful phone personnel	6
Other Comments	
MindWriter shouldn't need to be repaired	4
Provide more information on what was done	2
Offer extended warranty	1
Won't use MindWriter Call Center again	1

Appendix Contents
Sample Questionnaire

MindWriter personal computers offer you ease of use and maintenance. When you need service, we want you to rely on *CompleteCare,* wherever you may be. That's why we're asking you to take a moment to tell us how well we've served you.

Met **few** expectations	Met **some** expectations	Met **most** expectations	Met **all** expectations	**Exceeded** expectations
1	2	3	4	5

1. Telephone assistance with your problem: 1   2   3   4   5
    a. Responsiveness   1   2   3   4   5
    b. Technical competence   1   2   3   4   5
2. The courier service's effectiveness:
    a. Arrangements   1   2   3   4   5
    b. Pickup speed   1   2   3   4   5
    c. Delivery speed   1   2   3   4   5
3. Speed of the overall repair process.   1   2   3   4   5
4. Resolution of the problem that prompted service/repair.   1   2   3   4   5
5. Condition of your MindWriter on arrival.   1   2   3   4   5
6. Overall impression of CompleteCare's effectiveness.   1   2   3   4   5
7. Likelihood of using CompleteCare on another occasion.
    (1 = very unlikely   3 = neither likely nor unlikely   5 = very likely)   1   2   3   4   5
8. Likelihood of repurchasing a MindWriter based on:
    (1 = very unlikely   3 = neither likely nor unlikely   5 = very likely)
    a. Service/repair experience   1   2   3   4   5
    b. Product performance   1   2   3   4   5

Comments/Suggestions: _____
_____
_____

How may we contact you to follow up on any problems you have experienced?

_____   (_____) _____
Last Name   First Name   Phone

_____
    City   State   Zip

        Service Code

The report's appendix contains a copy of the questionnaire (see Chapter 12).

Presentation of Statistics[8]

The presentation of statistics in research reports is a special challenge for writers. Four basic ways to present such data are in (1) a text paragraph, (2) semitabular form, (3) tables, or (4) graphics.

Text Presentation

This is probably the most common method of presentation when there are only a few statistics. The writer can direct the reader's attention to certain numbers or comparisons and emphasize specific points. The drawback is that the statistics are submerged in the text, requiring the reader to scan the entire paragraph to extract the meaning. The following material has a few simple comparisons but becomes more complicated when text and statistics are combined.

A comparison of the three aerospace and defense companies from the high-tech stratum of the Forbes 500 sample shows that Sundstrand had the best sales growth record over the years 1988–1989. Its growth was 8.0 percent—with sales significantly lower than the other two firms in the sample. This compares to sales growth for Rockwell International of 3.3 percent, and Allied-Signal was third at only 0.8 percent sales increase. Rockwell International generated the most profits in 1989 among the three companies. Rockwell's net profits were $720.7 million as compared to $528 million for Allied-Signal and $120.8 million for Sundstrand.

Semitabular Presentation

When there are just a few figures, they may be taken from the text and listed. Lists of quantitative comparisons are much easier to read and understand than embedded statistics. An example of a semitabular presentation is shown below.

A comparison of the three aerospace-defense companies in the Forbes 500 sample shows that Sundstrand showed the best sales growth over a one-year period. Rockwell International generated the highest net profits for the year.

	Annual Sales Growth	1989 Net Profits ($ millions)
Sundstrand	8.0%	$120.8
Rockwell	3.3	720.7
Allied-Signal	0.8	528.0

Tabular Presentation

Tables are generally superior to text for presenting statistics, although they should be accompanied by comments directing the reader's attention to important figures. Tables facilitate quantitative comparisons and provide a concise, efficient way to present numerical data.

Tables are either general or summary in nature. General tables tend to be large, complex, and detailed. They serve as the repository for the statistical findings of the study and are usually in the appendix of a research report.

Summary tables contain only a few key pieces of data closely related to a specific finding. To make them inviting to the reader (who often skips them), the table designer should omit unimportant details and collapse multiple classifications into composite measures that may be substituted for the original data.

EXHIBIT 20–5   Sample Tabular Findings

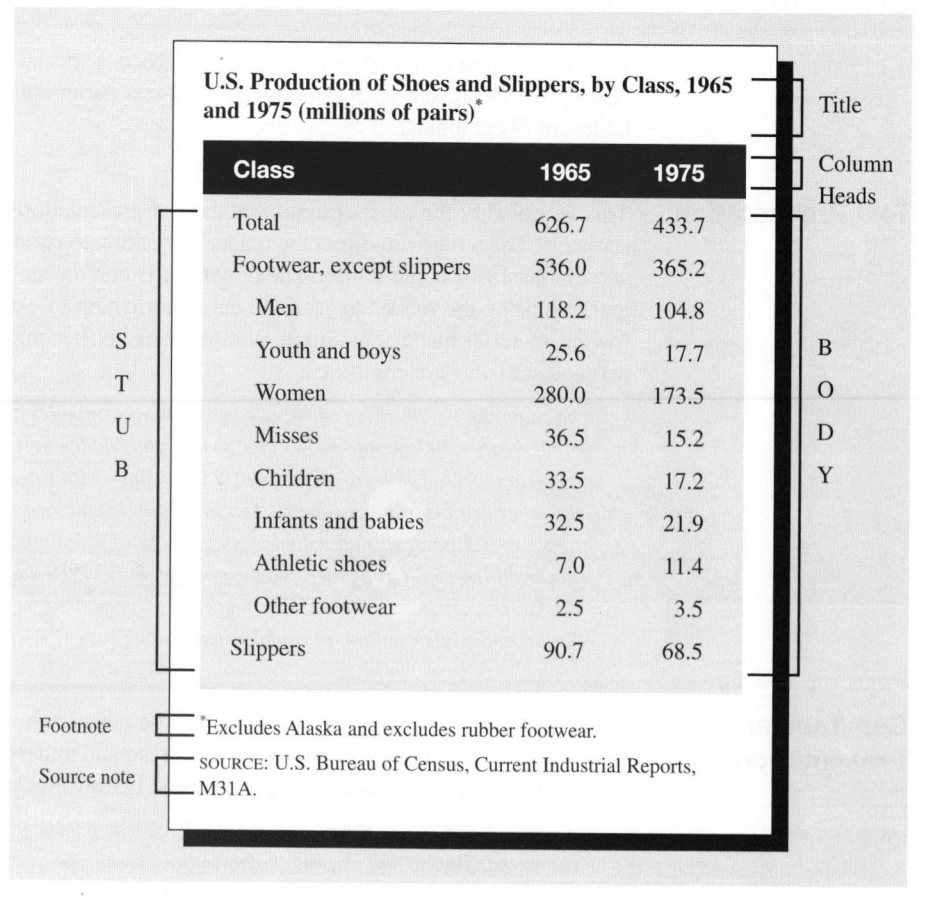

Class	1965	1975
Total	626.7	433.7
Footwear, except slippers	536.0	365.2
Men	118.2	104.8
Youth and boys	25.6	17.7
Women	280.0	173.5
Misses	36.5	15.2
Children	33.5	17.2
Infants and babies	32.5	21.9
Athletic shoes	7.0	11.4
Other footwear	2.5	3.5
Slippers	90.7	68.5

U.S. Production of Shoes and Slippers, by Class, 1965 and 1975 (millions of pairs)[*]

*Excludes Alaska and excludes rubber footwear.

SOURCE: U.S. Bureau of Census, Current Industrial Reports, M31A.

Any table should contain enough information for the reader to understand its contents. The title should explain the subject of the table, how the data are classified, the time period, or other related matters. A subtitle is sometimes included under the title to explain something about the table; most often this is a statement of the measurement units in which the data are expressed. The contents of the columns should be clearly identified by the column heads, and the contents of the stub should do the same for the rows. The body of the table contains the data, while the footnotes contain any needed explanations. Footnotes should be identified by letters or symbols such as asterisks, rather than by numbers, to avoid confusion with data values. Finally, there should be a source note if the data do not come from your original research. Exhibit 20–5 illustrates the various parts of a table.

Graphics

Compared with tables, graphs show less information and often only approximate values. However, they are more often read and remembered than tables. Their great advantage is that they convey quantitative values and comparisons more readily than tables. With personal computer charting programs, you can easily turn a set of numbers into a chart or graph.

There are many different graphic forms. Exhibit 20–6 shows the most common ones and how they should be used. Statistical explanation charts such as boxplots,

EXHIBIT 20–6 Guide to Graphs

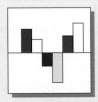

Column Compares sizes and amounts of categories usually for the same time. Places categories on *X* axis and values on *Y* axis.

Bar Same as the column but positions categories on *Y* axis and values on *X* axis. Deviations, when used, distinguish positive from negative values.

Stacked Bar In either bar or column, shows how components contribute to the total of the category.

Pie Shows relationship of parts to the whole. Wedges are row values of data.

Stacked Pie Same as pie but displays two or more data series.

Multiple Pie Uses same data as stacked pie but plots separate pies for each column of data without stacking.

Line Compares values over time to show changes in trends.

Filled Line Similar to line chart, but uses fill to highlight series.

Area (surface) Like line chart, compares changing values but emphasizes relative value of each series.

Step Compares discrete points on the value axis with vertical lines showing difference between points. Not for showing a trend.

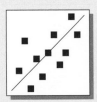

Scatter Shows if relationship between variables follows a pattern. May be used with one variable at different times.

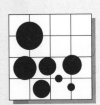

Bubble Used to introduce third variable (dots of different sizes). Axes could be sales, profits; bubbles are assets.

Spider (and Radar) Radiating lines are categories; values are distances from center (shows multiple variables e.g., performance, ratings, progress).

Polar Shows relationship between a variable and angle measured in degrees (cyclical trends, pollution source vs. wind direction, etc.).

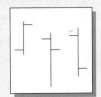

Open Hi Lo Close Shows fluctuating values in a given period (hour, day). Often used for investments.

Boxplots Displays distribution(s) and compares characteristics of shape (Chapter 16).

Pictographic Special chart that uses pictures or graphic elements in lieu of bars.

stem-and-leaf displays, and histograms were discussed in Chapter 16. Line graphs, area, pie, and bar charts, and pictographs and 3-D graphics receive additional attention here.

Line Graphs   Line graphs are used chiefly for time series and frequency distribution. There are several guidelines for designing a **line graph:**

- Put the time units or the independent variable on the horizontal axis.
- When showing more than one line, use different line types (solid, dashed, dotted, dash-dot) to enable the reader to easily distinguish among them.
- Try not to put more than four lines on one chart.
- Use a solid line for the primary data.

It is important to be aware of perceptual problems with line diagrams. The first is the use of a zero baseline. Since the length of the bar or distance above the baseline indicates the statistic, it is important that graphs give accurate visual impressions of values. A good way to achieve this is to include a zero baseline on the scale on which the curves are plotted. To set the base at some other value is to introduce a visual bias. This can be seen by comparing the visual impressions in Parts A and B of Exhibit 20–7. Both are accurate plots of the gross national product of the United States from 1972 through 1977. In Part A, however, using the baseline of zero places the curve well up on the chart and gives a better perception of the relation between the absolute size of GNP and the changes from year to year. The graph in Part B, with a baseline at $1,000 billion, can easily give the impression that the growth was at a more rapid rate. When space or other reasons dictate using shortened scales, the zero base point should still be used but with

EXHIBIT 20–7   U.S. Gross National Product, 1972–1977 (dollars in billions)

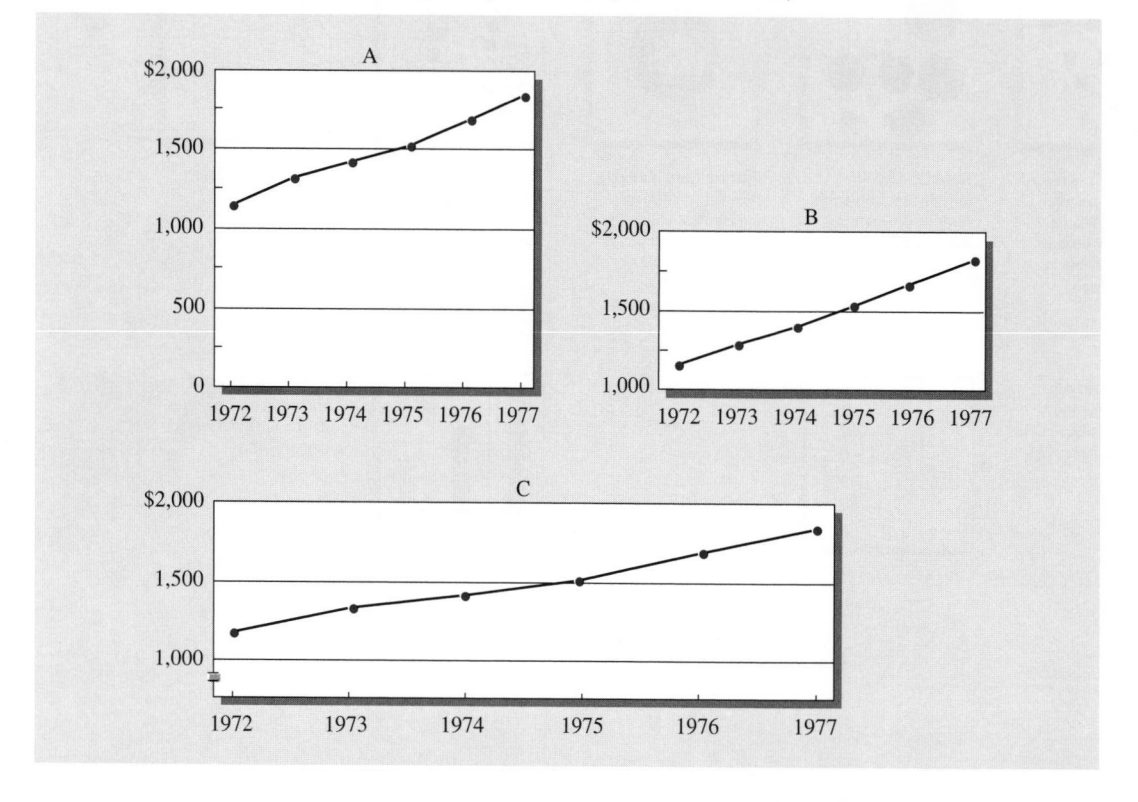

a break in the scale as shown in Part C of Exhibit 20–7. This will warn the reader that the scale has been reduced.

The balance of size between vertical and horizontal scales also affects the reader's impression of the data. There is no single solution to this problem, but the results can be seen by comparing Parts B and C in Exhibit 20–7. In Part C, the horizontal scale is twice that in Part B. This changes the slope of curve, creating a different perception of growth rate.

A third distortion with line diagrams occurs when relative and absolute changes among two or more sets of data are shown. In most charts, we use arithmetic scales where each space unit has identical value. This shows the absolute differences between variables, as in Part A of Exhibit 20–8, which presents the total U.S. population and that of the three Pacific states. This is an arithmetically correct way to present these data; but if we are interested in rates of growth, the visual impressions from a semilogarithmic scale are more accurate. A comparison of the line diagrams in Parts A and B of Exhibit 20–8 shows how much difference a semilogarithmic scale makes. Each is valuable and each can be misleading. In Part A, notice that both areas have been growing in population and that the population of the Pacific states is only a small portion of total U.S. population. One can even estimate what this proportion is. Part B gives insight into growth rates that are not clear from the arithmetic scale. Part B shows that the Pacific states' population has grown at a much faster rate than the U.S. population as a whole.

Area (Stratum or Surface) Charts   An **area chart** is also used for a time series. Consisting of a line that has been divided into component parts, it is best used to show changes in patterns over time. The same rules apply to stratum charts as to line charts (see Exhibit 20–6).

EXHIBIT 20–8   **Population of the United States and Pacific States Area, 1920–1970 (millions)**

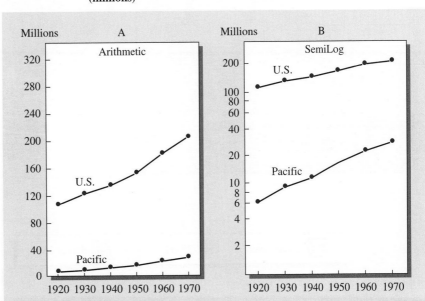

SOURCE: U.S. Department of Commerce.

Pie Charts   **Pie charts** are another form of area chart. They are often used with business data. However, they can easily mislead the reader or be improperly prepared. Research shows that readers' perceptions of the percentages represented by the pie slices are consistently inaccurate.[9] Consider the following suggestions when designing pie charts:

MANAGEMENT
Tip

- Show 100 percent of the subject being graphed.

- Always label the slices with "call-outs" and with the percentage or amount that is represented. This allows you to dispense with a legend.

- Put the largest slice at twelve o'clock and move clockwise in descending order.

- Use light colors for large slices, darker colors for smaller slices.

- In a pie chart of black and white slices, a single red one will command the most attention and be memorable. Use it to communicate your most important message.[10]

- Do not show evolution over time with pie charts as the only medium. Since pie charts always represent 100 percent, growth of the overall whole will not be recognized. If you must use a series of pie charts, complement them with an area chart.

As shown in Exhibit 20–9, pie charts portray frequency data in interesting ways. In addition, they can be stacked to show relationships between two sets of data.

Bar Charts   **Bar charts** can be very effective if properly constructed. Use the horizontal axis to represent time and the vertical axis to represent units or growth-related

EXHIBIT 20–9   **Examples of Area Charts: A Stratum Chart and Two Pie Charts**

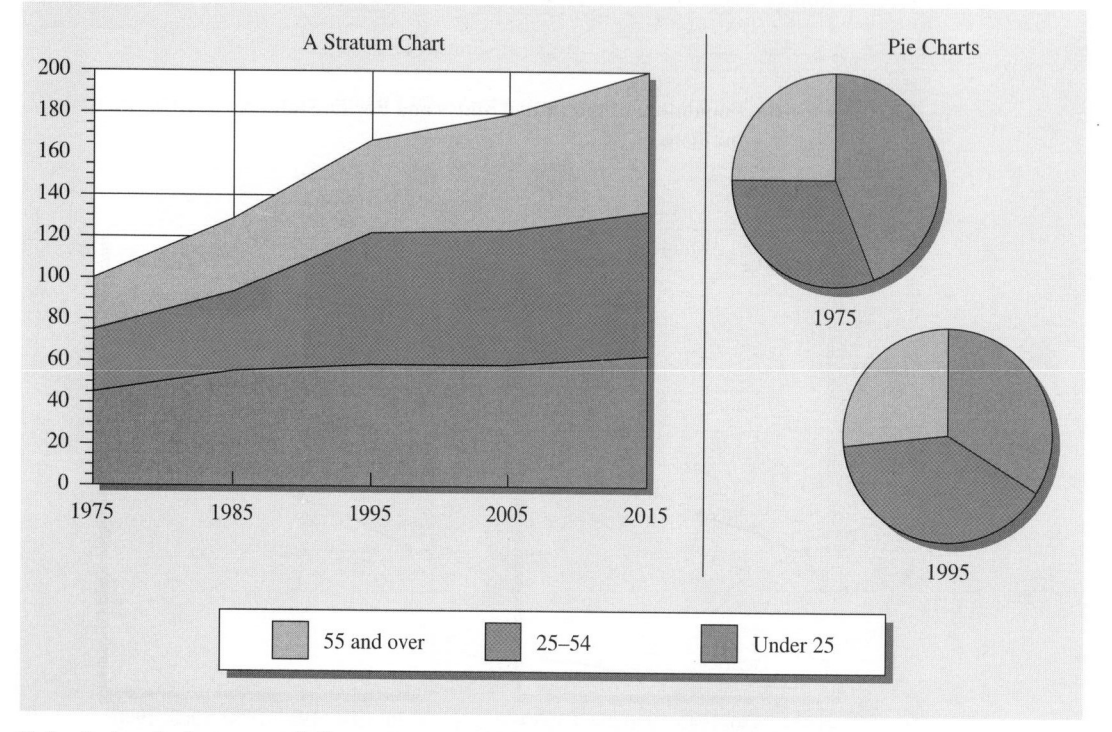

Notice the two pie charts seem to indicate a dramatic decrease in the "under 25" category. Now look at the stratum chart. The "under 25" category never decreased; it only changed relative to the entire population. It is important not to use pie charts alone in a time series, to avoid giving erroneous impressions.

variables. Vertical bars are generally used for time series and for quantitative classifications. Horizontal bars are less often used. If neither variable is time related, either format can be used. A computer-charting program easily generates charts. If you are preparing a bar chart by hand, leave space between the bars equal to at least half the width of the bar. An exception to this is the specialized chart—the histogram—where continuous data are grouped into intervals for a frequency distribution (see Chapter 16). A second exception is the multiple variable chart, where more than one bar is located at a particular time segment. In this case, the space between the groups of bars is at least half the width of the group. Bar charts come in a variety of patterns. In Chapter 16, Exhibit 16–3 shows a standard vertical bar graph. Variations are illustrated in Exhibit 20–6.

Pictographs and Geo-Graphics These graphics are used in popular magazines and newspapers because they are eye-catching and imaginative. *USA Today* and a host of imitators are often guilty of taking this to the extreme, creating graphs that are incomprehensible. A **pictograph** uses pictorial symbols (an oil drum for barrels of oil, a stick figure for numbers of employees, or a pine tree for amount of wood). The symbols represent data volume and are used instead of a bar in a bar-type chart. It is proper to stack same-size images to express more of a quantity and to show fractions of an image to show less. But altering the scale of the symbol produces problems. Since the pictures represent actual objects, doubling the size will increase the area of the symbol by four (and the volume by more). This misleads the reader into believing the increase is larger than it really is. The exception is a graphic that is easily substituted for a bar, such as the pencils in Exhibit 20–6.

The research presentation provides a final opportunity to imbue research findings with clarity and perhaps draw additional information from the data. When the data lend themselves to spatial display, software such as MapInfo can prove to be a useful presentation tool. www.mapinfo.com

As this Arc View map illustrates, public services are increasingly using geographic displays of data to assist in personnel and resource allocation.

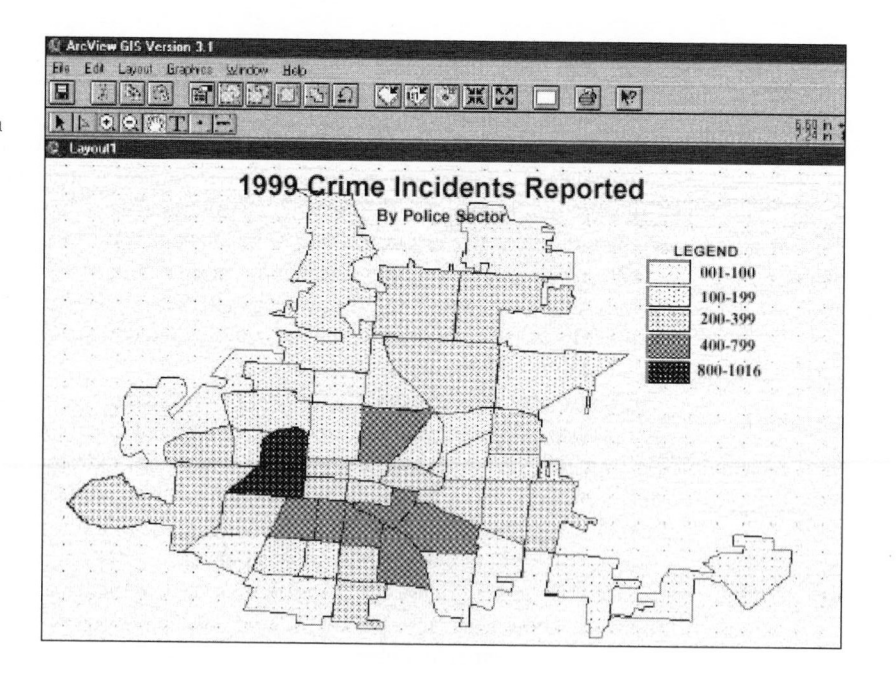

See the section on
Geographic Information
Systems in Chapter 16.

Geo-graphic charts use a portion of the world's map, in pictorial form, to show differences in regions. They can be used for product production, per capita rates, demographics, or any of a number of other geographically specific variables.

As we noted in Chapter 16, management applications for GIS mapping abound. Stacked data sets produce variables of interest that can be aligned on a common geographical referent. The resulting pictorial display allows the user to drill through the layers and visualize the relationships. With better Windows-based software and government agencies providing geo-codes and reference points, geographic spatial displays like the image below are becoming a more common form of graphic.

3-D Graphics   With current charting techniques, virtually all charts can now be made three dimensional. Although **3-D graphics** add interest, they can also obscure data. Care must be used in selecting 3-D chart candidates (see Exhibit 20–10). Pie and bar charts achieve dimensionality simply by adding depth to the graphics; this is not 3-D. A 3-D column chart allows you to compare three or more variables from the sample in one bar chart–type graph. If you want to display several quarters of sales results for Hertz, Avis, Budget, and National, you have 3-D data. But be careful about converting line charts to ribbon charts, and area charts to 3-D area charts.

Surface charts and 3-D scatter charts are helpful for displaying complex data patterns if the underlying distributions are multivariate. Otherwise, do not enter the third dimension unless your data are there.

Oral Presentations

Researchers often present their findings orally. These presentations, sometimes called **briefings,** have some unique characteristics that distinguish them from most other kinds of public speaking: Only a small group of people is involved; statistics normally constitute an important portion of the topic; the audience members are usually managers with

EXHIBIT 20–10   3-D Charts

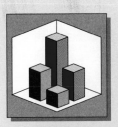  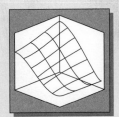 

3-D Column
A variation on column charts, they compare variables to each other or over time. Axes: X = categories, Y = series, Z = values. Other variations include 3-D area charts and connect-the-dots scatter charts.

3-D Ribbon   This example is a one-wall plot showing columns of data (series) as ribbons. One or more columns are used. Axes: X = categories, Y = series, Z = values.

3-D Wireframe
A variation of a contour or response surface; suitable for changes in time and multivariate data. Axes: X = categories, Y = series, Z = values.

3-D Surface Line
Handles three columns of data and plots XYZ coordinates to show a response surface. Helpful for multivariate applications.

an interest in the topic, but they want to hear only the critical elements; speaking time will often be as short as 20 minutes but may run longer than an hour; and the presentation is normally followed by questions and discussion.

Preparation

A successful briefing typically requires condensing a lengthy and complex body of information. Since speaking rates should not exceed 100 to 150 words per minute, a 20-minute presentation limits you to about 2,000 to 2,500 words. If you are to communicate effectively under such conditions, you must plan carefully. Begin by asking two questions. First, how long should you plan to talk? Usually there is an indication of the acceptable presentation length. It may be the custom in an organization to take a given allotted time for a briefing. If the time is severely limited, then the need for topical priorities is obvious. This leads to the second question: What are the purposes of the briefing? Is it to raise concern about problems that have been uncovered? Is it to add to the knowledge of audience members? Is it to give them conclusions and recommendations for their decision making? Questions such as these illustrate the general objectives of the report. After answering these questions, you should develop a detailed outline of what you are going to say. Such an outline should contain the following major parts.

1. **Opening.** A brief statement, probably not more than 10 percent of the allotted time, sets the stage for the body of the report. The opening should be direct, get attention, and introduce the nature of the discussion that follows. It should explain the nature of the project, how it came about, and what it attempted to do.

2. **Findings and conclusions.** The conclusions may be stated immediately after the opening remarks, with each conclusion followed by the findings that support it.

3. **Recommendations.** Where appropriate, these are stated in the third stage; each recommendation may be followed by references to the conclusions leading to it. Presented in this manner, they provide a natural climax to the report. At the end of the presentation, it may be appropriate to call for questions from the audience.

Early in the planning stage you need to make two further decisions. The first concerns the type of audiovisuals (AV) that will be used and the role they will play in the presentation. AV decisions are important enough that they are often made *before* the briefing outline and text are developed.

Presenting your research findings using PowerPoint™ or other presentation software requires preparation similar to presenting with nonelectronic visual aids. The researcher must still determine his style of presentation, the order of findings, and which findings will be presented graphically, in tabular format, or verbally. As most visual aids are prepared using computer software, the key hyperlink files are already available. It might seem as though the presenter could bypass the costly printing of visual aids, which can be a time-consuming task. However, the electronic presenter must have a contingency plan for a malfunctioning computer. Color transparencies are the low-tech backup but clearly don't allow the full range of possibilities that electronic hyperlinks afford. Having a second laptop and projection system, as well as multi-prong power cords and spare computer connection cords are the usual high-tech insurance plan. The same general rule applied to all presentations is critical for electronic ones—practice, practice, practice—but a caveat is added: Practice *with your equipment* so movement between files, and between hyperlinks and your PowerPoint™ control presentation seems effortless.

The second decision you must make as you plan for your presentation is what type it will be. Will it be memorized, read from your manuscript, or given extemporaneously? We rule out the impromptu briefing because impromptu speaking does not involve preparation. Your reputation and the research effort should not be jeopardized by "winging it."

Memorization is a risky and time-consuming course to follow. Any memory slip during the presentation can be a catastrophe, and the delivery sounds stilted and distant. Memorization virtually precludes establishing rapport with the audience and adapting to their reactions while you speak. It produces a self- or speaker-centered approach and is not recommended.

Reading a manuscript is also not advisable, even though many professors seem to reward students who do so (perhaps because they themselves get away with it at pro-

Today's formal research presentation often takes place in a decision-making environment where the researcher and the decision maker collaborate on problem solving. Interactive presentations are particularly well suited to the use of electronic presentation software, like PowerPoint™. Such software can incorporate hyperlinks to graphical verbal, tabular, or video displays of data, as well as to the actual written report. Software utilities, like the PowerPoint™ add-ons described in this Crystal Graphics ad, enhance the capability of presentation software. To learn how to set up a PowerPoint™ presentation with hyperlinks, visit our text website. www.crystalgraphics.com

fessional meetings). The delivery sounds dull and lifeless because most people are not trained to read aloud and therefore do it badly. They become focused on the manuscript to the exclusion of the audience. This head-down preoccupation with the text is clearly inappropriate for management presentations.

The **extemporaneous presentation** is audience centered and made from minimal notes or an outline. This mode permits the speaker to be natural, conversational, and flexible. Clearly, it is the best choice for an organizational setting. Preparation consists of writing a draft along with a complete sentence outline and converting the main points to notes. In this way, you can try lines of argument, experiment with various ways of expressing thoughts, and develop phraseology. Along the way, the main points are fixed sequentially in your mind, and supporting connections are made.

Audiences accept notes, and their presence does wonders in allaying speaker fears. Even if you never use them, they are there for psychological support. Many prefer to use 5-by-8-inch cards for their briefing notes because they hold more information and so require less shuffling than the smaller 3-by-5-inch size. Card contents vary widely, but here are some general guidelines for their design:

- Place title and preliminary remarks on the first card.

- Use each of the remaining cards to carry a major section of the presentation. The amount of detail depends on the need for precision and the speaker's desire for supporting information.

- Include key phrases, illustrations, statistics, dates, and pronunciation guides for difficult words. Include also quotations and ideas that bear repeating.

- Along the margin, place instructions and cues, such as SLOW, FAST, EMPHA-SIZE, TRANSPARENCY A, TURN CHART, and GO BACK TO CHART 3.

After the outline and the AV aids comes the final stage of preparation—the rehearsal. Rehearsal, a prerequisite to effective briefing, *is too often slighted,* especially by inexperienced speakers. Giving a briefing is an artistic performance, and nothing improves it more than for the speaker to demonstrate mastery of the art. First rehearsal efforts should concentrate on those parts of the presentation that are awkward or poorly developed. After the problem areas have been worked out, there should be at least a few full-scale practices under simulated presentation conditions. All parts should be timed and edited until the time target is met. A videotape recorder is an excellent diagnostic tool.

Delivery

While the content of a report is the chief concern, the speaker's delivery is also important. A polished presentation adds to the receptiveness of the audience, but there is some danger that the presentation may overpower the message. Fortunately, the typical research audience knows why it is assembled, has a high level of interest, and does not need to be entertained. Even so, the speaker faces a real challenge in communicating effectively. The delivery should be restrained. Demeanor, posture, dress, and total appearance should be appropriate for the occasion. Speed of speech, clarity of enunciation, pauses, and gestures all play their part. Voice pitch, tone quality, and inflections are proper subjects for concern. There is little time for anecdotes and other rapport-developing techniques, yet the speaker must get and hold audience attention.

Speaker Problems   Inexperienced speakers have many difficulties in making presentations. They often are nervous at the start of a presentation and may even find breathing difficult. This is natural and should not be of undue concern. It may help to take a deep breath or two, holding each for a brief time before exhaling as fully as possible. This can be done inconspicuously on the way to the podium.

Several characteristics of inexperienced speakers may be summarized as questions. Even if you are an accomplished speaker, it is helpful to review them as you watch a videotape of your presentation.

MANAGEMENT

1. **Vocal characteristics:**
   a. Do you speak so softly that someone cannot hear you well? It is helpful to have someone in the back of the room who can signal if your voice is not carrying far enough.
   b. Do you speak too rapidly? Remind yourself to slow down. Make deliberate pauses before sentences. Speak words with precision without exaggerating. However, some people talk too slowly, and this can make the audience restive.
   c. Do you vary volume, tone quality, and rate of speaking? Any of these can be used successfully to add interest to the message and engage audience attention. Speakers should not let their words trail off as they complete a sentence.
   d. Do you use overworked pet phrases, repeated "uhs," "you know," and "in other words"?

2. **Physical characteristics:**
   a. Do you rock back and forth or roll or twist from side to side or lean too much on the lectern?
   b. Do you hitch or tug on clothing, scratch, or fiddle with pocket change, keys, pencils, or other devices?
   c. Do you stare into space? Lack of eye contact is particularly bothersome to listeners and is common with inexperienced speakers. Many seem to choose a spot above the heads of the audience and continue to stare at this spot except when looking at notes. *Eye contact is important.* Audience members need to feel that

---

S N A P S H O T

Overcoming the Jitters

The fear of public speaking ranks up there with the fear of death and/or public nudity. Whether you are a seasoned pro or this is your first speech, stage fright, the illogical fear of facing an audience, can be a paralyzing emotion. How do you handle those times when your mind starts going blank and your stomach is turning? Patricia Fripp, an award-winning keynote speaker and speech coach, provides some answers. She suggests that you "need to anticipate your speech mentally, physically, and logistically." Mental preparation is key and should be a six-to-one ratio: Invest three hours of preparation for a 30-minute speech. There is no substitute for rehearsal. Spend some time memorizing your opening and closing—three or four sentences each. Although you may speak from notes, knowing your opening and closing helps your fluency, allowing you to make the vital connection in rapport with your audience when you are likely to be most nervous.

Logistically, know the room. Go there as early as possible to get comfortable in the environment. Practice using the microphone and check the equipment. A quick review of your visual aids is also helpful. Then, during the presentation, you can focus on your audience and not be concerned with the environment.

The physical part of overcoming nervousness is varied and may be constrained by your setting. In a small group setting, shake hands, exchange greetings, and make eye contact with everybody beforehand. In a larger meeting, at least connect with the people in the front row. Do so sincerely and they'll be cheering for your success. They are not waiting for you to fail—they are far too worried about themselves—and they are there to listen to you. If possible, avoid sitting while you're waiting to speak. Find a position in the room where you can stand occasionally. The rear of the room gives you access to the bathroom and drinking fountain.

If your anxiety level is still high, then you need an outlet for your energy. Comedians and actors find that doing light exercises in their dressing rooms or in another private area can relieve the excess energy. Fripp adds, "Find a private spot, and wave your hands in the air. Relax your jaw, and shake your head from side to side. Then shake your legs one at a time. Physically shake the tension out of your body." The object is to release enough nervous energy to calm your anxieties—without becoming so stress-free that you forget your purpose and audience.

www.fripp.com

---

you are looking at them. It may be helpful to pick out three people in the audience (left, right, and center) and practice looking at them successively as you talk.

    d. Do you misuse visuals by fumbling, putting them on in incorrect order or upside down? Do you turn your back to the audience to read from visuals?

Audiovisuals

Researchers can use a variety of AV media with good results. While there is need for computer-assisted media in many business applications, they will be mentioned only briefly. Our emphasis is on **visual aids** that are relatively simple and inexpensive to make.

1. **Chalkboards and whiteboards.** Chalkboards are flexible, inexpensive, and require little specific preparation. On the other hand, they are not novel and do not project a polished appearance. Whiteboards, both portable and installed, provide visual relief, particularly when color markers are used. Both varieties reduce speaking time while the speaker is writing. If you use either, write legibly or print, leave space between lines, and do not talk to the board with the audience to your back. If you are in an unfamiliar room, it is best to arrive prepared with erasable markers (or chalk) and erasure materials.

2. **Handout materials.** These are inexpensive but can have a professional look if done carefully. Handouts can include pictures and graphic materials that might be difficult to display otherwise. The disadvantages include the time needed to produce them and their distracting impact if not properly used. You may distribute them when the audience leaves, but a better use is to refer to them during your talk. If you use them this way, *do not hand them out until you are ready to refer to them.*

3. **Flip charts.** You can show color, pictures, and large letters with these. They are easy and inexpensive to make; they can focus listener attention on a specific idea. If not well made, they can be distracting. Unless they are large, they should be restricted to small groups and to types of material that can be summarized in a few words.

4. **Overhead transparencies.** These may be of different sizes, but the most common is about the same as an 8 1/2-by-11-inch page. They are easily made with color markers or with a copy machine. Computer graphics can be plotted or printed directly to transparencies for a more accurate and professional look. Multiple-color and single-color renditions are available. You can also show overlays and buildups. In using transparencies, be sure they are in correct order and right side up when you place them on the projector.

5. **Slides.** Most slides are 35mm, but larger sizes are sometimes used. They are relatively inexpensive and colorful and present a professional-looking image if done well. They are somewhat more difficult to make but can be prepared with a personal computer and slide-construction software.

6. **Computer-drawn visuals.** For transparencies and slides, the draw and paint programs for personal computers provide the presenter with limitless options for illustrating the message. Stored visuals can be teamed with a device for projecting the computer output to a screen, or the briefer can use the software to create the image at the moment a question is asked or a demonstration is appropriate. Be careful that the technology does not distract from the purpose of the message.

7. **Computer animation.** The development of larger and faster processors, memory chips, and disks has made it possible to store voice and image data in quantity in personal computers. Technology permits multimedia presentations using videotape, videodisc, and CD-ROM elements that are integrated for the ultimate in image reproduction. For proposals, large contracts, or other business applications, the preparation and expense may be justifiable.

The choice of visual aids is determined by your intended purpose, the size of the audience, meeting room conditions, time and budget constraints, and available equipment.

As technology advances, the Internet has become a medium for oral presentations and videoconferences. Like other presentations, you need to be cautious with equipment and look for software glitches. Have a backup copy of your presentation on your laptop or your company's server. Test your external mouse as well as the one that is connected to your computer. Be certain that your screensavers are disabled. And most important, be prepared to give your presentation even if the technology fails.

Visual aids serve the presenter of a research presentation in several ways. They make it possible to present materials that cannot otherwise be communicated effectively. Statistical relationships are difficult to describe verbally, but a picture or graph communicates well. How better to describe some object or material than to show it or picture it?

Visual aids help the speaker to clarify major points. With visual reinforcement of a verbal statement, the speaker can stress the importance of points. In addition, the use of two channels of communication (hearing and sight) enhances the probability that the listener will understand and remember the message.

The continuity and memorability of the speaker's message are also improved with visual aids. Verbal information is so transient that any slight lapse of listener attention results in losing the information thread. The failure to fully comprehend a given point cannot be remedied by going back to hear it again, for the speaker has gone on. With a visual aid, however, there is more opportunity to review this point, relate it to earlier comments by the speaker, and improve retention.

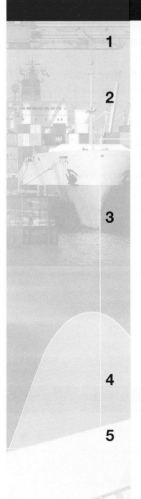

SUMMARY

1   A quality presentation of research findings can have an inordinate effect on a reader's or a listener's perceptions of a study's quality. Recognition of this fact should prompt a researcher to make a special effort to communicate skillfully and clearly.

2   Research reports contain findings, analysis, interpretations, conclusions, and sometimes recommendations. They may follow the short, informal format typical of memoranda and letters, or they may be longer and more complex. Long reports are of either a technical or a management type. In the former, the problem is presented and followed by the findings, conclusions, and recommendations. In the management report, the conclusions and recommendations precede the findings. The technical report is targeted at the technically trained reader; the management report is intended for the manager-client.

3   The writer of research reports should be guided by four questions:

- What is the purpose of this report?
- Who will read it?
- What are the circumstances and limitations under which it is written?
- How will the report be used?

Reports should be clearly organized, physically inviting, and easy to read. Writers can achieve these goals if they are careful with mechanical details, writing style, and comprehensibility.

4   There is a special challenge to presenting statistical data. While some of this data may be incorporated in the text, most statistics should be placed in tables, charts, or graphs. The choice of a table, chart, or graph depends on the specific data and presentation purpose.

5   Oral presentations of research findings are common and should be developed with concern for the communication problems that are unique to such settings. Briefings are usually conducted under time constraints; good briefings require careful organization and preparation. Visual aids are a particularly important aspect of briefings but are too often ignored or treated inadequately.

Whether written or oral, poor presentations do a grave injustice to what might otherwise be excellent research. Good presentations, on the other hand, add luster to both the research and the reputation of the researcher.

KEY TERMS

area charts 689

bar charts 690

briefings 692

executive summary 662

extemporaneous presentation 695

letter of transmittal 660

line graphs 688

management report 659

pace 671

pictographs (geo-graphics) 691

pie charts 690

readability indexes 671

sentence outline 666

technical report 659

3-D graphics 692

topic outline 666

visual aids 697

EXAMPLES

Company	Scenario	Page
Central City Bank[*]	A findings page in a commercial bank market study.	664
CrystalGraphics	Designing software (PowerPlugs) to enhance PowerPoint™ presentations.	695
Forbes 500	Text presentation of statistics.	685
Good Housekeeping Institute	Research center that conducts product performance tests for all products advertised or featured in articles in *Good Housekeeping* magazine.	666
"Good Housekeeping Institute Savvy Consumer"	New syndicated column for newspapers by King Features based on research results from experiments conducted by Good Housekeeping Institute.	666
MapInfo	Software useful for the spatial analysis and display of data.	691
McGraw-Hill	Website has tutorial for including hyperlinks within PowerPoint™ for research presentations.	695
Medical Radar International (MRI)	Swedish research company that publishes research on European doctors' use of pharmaceuticals.	659
MindWriter[*]	A final report, culminating from the book's vignettes, Close-Ups, and examples.	BRTL, 673
Shoe industry	A profile of industry production as an example of tabular presentation.	686
SPSS	Provided the software products—including *In2 data, Quantum,* and *SmartViewer*—used by MRI to conduct pharmaceutical research.	659
U.S. Department of Commerce	Population charts.	689
U.S. Government	GNP charts.	688

*Due to the confidential and proprietary nature of most research, the names of some companies have been changed.

DISCUSSION QUESTIONS

Terms in Review

1. Distinguish between the following:

    a. Speaker-centered presentation and extemporaneous presentation.

    b. Technical report and management report.

    c. Topic outline and sentence outline.

Making Research Decisions

2. What should you do about each of these?

    a. Putting information in a research report concerning the study's limitations.

    b. The size and complexity of tables in a research report.

    c. The physical presentation of a report.

    d. Pace in your writing.

3. What type of report would you suggest be written in each of the following cases?

    a. The president of the company has asked for a study of the company's pension plan and its comparison to the plans of other firms in the industry.

    b. You have been asked to write up a marketing experiment, which you recently completed, for submission to the *Journal of Marketing Research.*

    c. Your division manager has asked you to prepare a forecast of cash requirements for the division for the next three months.

    d. The National Institutes of Health has given you a grant to study the relationship between industrial accidents and departmental employee morale.

4. There are a number of graphic presentation forms. Which would you recommend to show each of the following? Why?

    a. A comparison of changes in average annual per capita income for the United States and Japan from 1990 to 2000.

    b. The percentage composition of average family expenditure patterns, by the major types of expenditures, for families whose heads are under age 35 compared with families whose heads are 55 or older.

    c. A comparison of the change between December 31, 2001, and December 31, 2000, in the value of the common stock of six major electronics firms.

From Concept to Practice

5. Outline a set of visual aids that you might use in an oral briefing on these topics:

    a. How to write a research report.

    b. The outlook for the economy over the next year.

    c. The major analytical article in the latest issue of *Business Week.*

6. Conduct a search of websites that provide Internet presentations. Select one and critique its content, visuals, and the presenter's skills.

7. Research reports often contain statistical materials of great importance that are presented poorly. Find examples of research reports, annual reports, or government reports that illustrate this point and devise ways to improve their presentation.

WWW Exercises

Visit our website for Internet exercises related to this chapter at
www.mhhe.com/business/cooper8

CASES[*]

INQUIRING MINDS WANT TO KNOW—NOW!

 PERFORMANCE EVALUATIONS

 KNSD SAN DIEGO

 THE BRAZING OPERATION

 MASTERING TEACHER LEADERSHIP

 VIOLENCE ON TV

 NCR: TEEING UP A NEW STRATEGIC DIRECTION

[*]All cases indicating a video icon are located on the Instructor's Videotape Supplement. All nonvideo cases are in the case section of the textbook. All cases indicating a CD icon offer a data set, which is located on the accompanying CD.

REFERENCE NOTES

1. Paul E. Resta, *The Research Report* (New York: American Book Company, 1972), p. 5.
2. John M. Penrose, Jr., Robert W. Rasberry, and Robert J. Myers, *Advanced Business Communication* (Boston: PWS-Kent Publishing, 1989), p. 185.
3. Ibid.
4. Most word processors contain dictionaries. All-purpose word processors such as MS Word, WordPerfect, WordPro, or Macintosh products contain a spelling checker, table and graphing generators, and a thesaurus. For style and grammar checkers, programs such as Grammatik, RightWriter, Spelling Coach, and Punctuation + Style are available. New programs are reviewed periodically in the business communication literature and in magazines devoted to personal computing.
5. Robert R. Rathbone, *Communicating Technical Information* (Reading, MA: Addison-Wesley Publishing Company, 1966), p. 64. Reprinted with permission.
6. Ibid., p. 72.
7. Penrose, Rasberry, and Myers, *Advanced Business Communication,* p. 89.
8. The material in this section draws on Stephen M. Kosslyn, *Elements of Graph Design* (San Francisco: W. H. Freeman, 1993); DeltaPoint, Inc., *DeltaGraph User's Guide 4.0* (Monterey, CA: DeltaPoint, Inc., 1996); Gene Zelazny, *Say It with Charts* (Homewood, IL: Business One Irwin, 1991); Jim Heid, "Graphs that Work," *MacWorld* (February 1994), pp. 155–56; and Penrose, Rasberry, and Myers, *Advanced Business Communication,* Chapter 3.
9. Marilyn Stoll, "Charts Other than Pie Are Appealing to the Eye," *PC Week,* March 25, 1986, pp. 138–39.
10. Stephen M. Kosslyn and Christopher Chabris, "The Mind Is Not a Camera, the Brain Is Not a VCR," *Aldus Magazine* (September/October 1993), p. 34.

REFERENCES FOR SNAPSHOTS AND CAPTIONS

Medical Radar International

"Medical Radar," SPSS, February 2002 (http://www.spss.com/spssatwork/template_view.cfm?Story_ID=24).

"Take Action with Organized, Interactive Analytic Information," SPSS, February, 2002 (http://www.spss.com/svws).

Good Housekeeping Institute

"Good Housekeeping Institute," *Good Housekeeping,* July 2000 (http://goodhousekeeping.women.com/gh/institute/ghinstr1.htm).

"About the Good Housekeeping Institute," *Good Housekeeping,* February 2002 (http://magazines.ivillage.com/goodhousekeeping/consumer/institute/articles/0,12873,284511_290570,00.html).

"The GH Institute Report," *Good Housekeeping,* February 2002 (http://magazines.ivillage.com/goodhousekeeping/consumer/institute/articles/0,12873,284511_290570-4,00.html).

Public Speaking Jitters

Patricia Fripp, CSP, CPAE. Award-winning keynote speaker and speech coach, author of *Get What You Want!* and past president of the National Speakers Association. PFripp@fripp.com, 1-800-634-3035 (http://www.fripp.com)

CLASSIC AND CONTEMPORARY READINGS

Campbell, Steve. *Statistics You Can't Trust.* Parker, CO: Think Twice Publishing, 2000. An enjoyable and entertaining approach to interpreting statistical charts and arguments.

Kosslyn, Stephen M. *Elements of Graph Design.* San Francisco: W. H. Freeman, 1993. Fundamentals of graph and chart construction.

Lesikar, Raymond V., Marie E. Flatley, and John D. Pettit. *Lesikar's Basic Business Communication.* 8th ed. Burr Ridge, IL: Irwin/McGraw-Hill, 1999. Practical guidance for writing and presenting reports.

Penrose, John M., Robert W. Rasberry, and Robert J. Myers. *Advanced Business Communication.* 3rd ed. Cincinnati, OH: South-Western Publishing, 1997. A presentation of all aspects of business communications from organization through final writing and oral presentation.

Strunk, William, Jr., and E. B. White. *The Elements of Style.* New York: Macmillan, 1959. A classic on the problems of writing style.

Tufte, Edward R. *The Visual Display of Quantitative Information.* New Haven, CT: Graphics Press, 1992. The book that started the revolution against gaudy infographics.

Tufte, Edward R. *Visual Explanations: Images and Quantities, Evidence and Narrative.* New Haven, CT: Graphics Press, 1997. Uses the principle of "the smallest effective difference" to display distinctions in data. Beautifully illustrated.

Cases

A GEM of a Study

What government policies and initiatives are most likely to generate high levels of entrepreneurial activity? Which are positively correlated with the economic well-being of a country as measured by growth in GDP and job formation? Project directors of the Global Entrepreneurship Monitor (GEM), who define entrepreneurship as "any attempt at new business or new venture creation, such as self-employment, a new business organization, or the expansion of an existing business, by an individual, a team of individuals, or an established business," suggest the following:

- Promoting entrepreneurship, especially outside the most active age group (25–44), with specific programs that support entrepreneurial activity.

EXHIBIT C-GEM 1–1 Conceptual Model: The Entrepreneurial Sector and Economic Growth

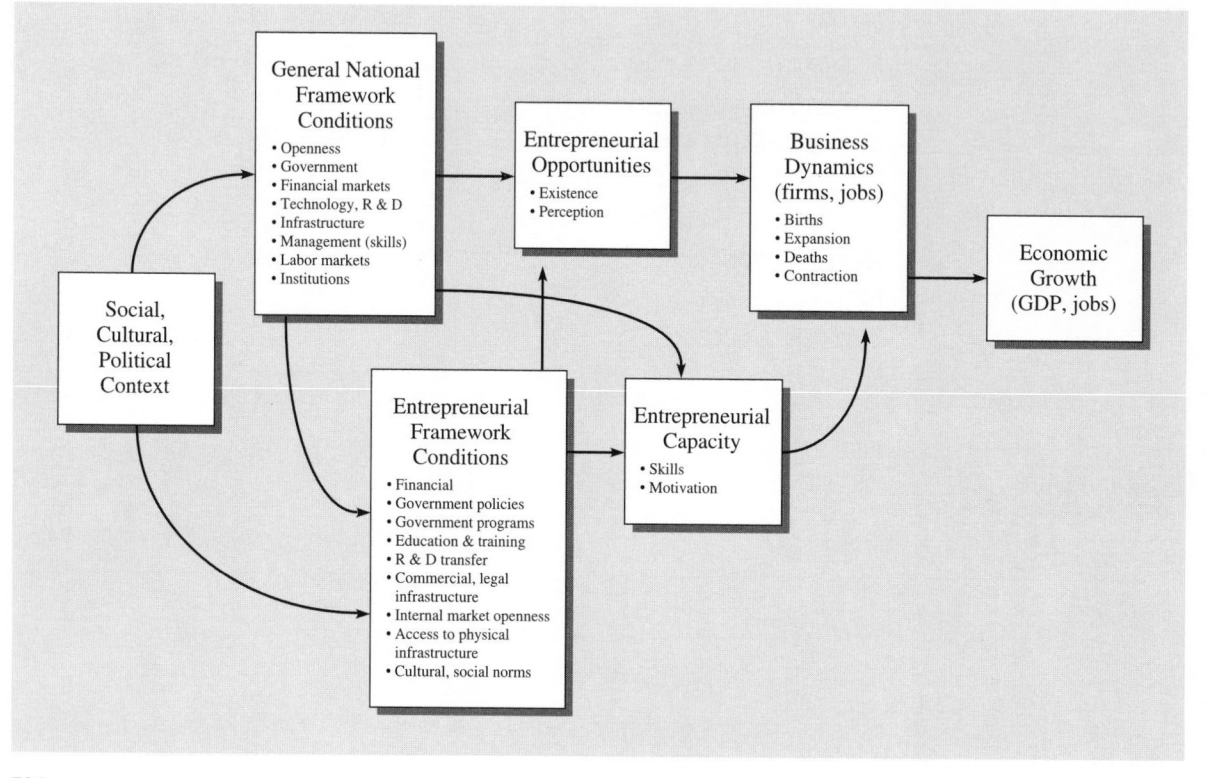

- Facilitating the availability of resources to women to participate in the entrepreneurial process.

- Committing to long-term, substantial postsecondary education, including training programs designed to develop skills required to start a business.

- Emphasis on developing an individual's capacity to recognize and pursue new opportunities.

- Developing the capacity of a society to accommodate the higher levels of income disparity associated with entrepreneurial activity.

- Creating a culture that validates and promotes entrepreneurship throughout society.

Researchers at the Kauffman Center for Entrepreneurial Leadership (Babson College) and the London Business School revealed these propositions based on a study designed to prove a causal relationship between factors that affect entrepreneurial opportunities and potential, to business dynamics and national economic growth and well-being. The research design compensated for lack of control of extraneous variables by using data from 10 nations "with diversity in framework conditions, entrepreneurial sectors, business dynamics, and economic growth." The longitudinal study proposed to prove or disprove a new conceptual model of cultural, economic, physical, and political factors to predict economic growth (Exhibit C-GEM 1–1).

EXHIBIT C-GEM 1–2 **Entrepreneurial Framework Conditions: Cross-National Comparisons of Key Informant Multi-Item Indexes**

	Culture	Equity	Debt	R&D	Education	Subcontractor	Legal, Banking
U.S.	0.8	1.23	0.44	0.21	−0.46	0.8	0.88
Canada	0.15	0.55	0	−0.12	−0.28	0.22	0.86
Israel	0.34	−0.06	−0.97	0.29	−0.26	0.04	0.67
U.K.	−0.07	0.17	−0.03	−0.02	−0.97	0.08	0.57
Germany	−0.2	−0.22	−0.21	0.03	−1.24	0.15	0.29
Denmark	−0.09	−0.3	−0.56	−0.12	−0.52	0.39	0.33
France	−0.92	−1.01	−0.81	−0.23	−1.21	−0.1	−0.49
Japan	−0.65	0.29	−0.52	−0.39	−1.06	−0.68	−0.61
Finland	−0.36	−0.94	−0.33	−0.1	−0.94	−0.22	1.03
Correlation to Start-Up Rate	0.87	0.79	0.58	0.69	0.65	0.71	0.55

Various data collection methods were employed, including:

- Current, nonstandardized data collected by each national research team.

- Two rounds of adult population surveys (1,000 randomly selected adults per country) to measure entrepreneurial activity and attitude, completed and coordinated by an international market survey firm by phone—or face-to-face in Japan. (Market Facts [Arlington, VA] did the first round of data collection in June 1998 [Canada, Finland, Germany, the United Kingdom, and the United States]. Audience Selection, Ltd. [London] conducted the second round in March 1999 from all 10 countries.)

- Hour-long personal interviews with 4 to 39 experts (key informants) in each country.

- Detailed 12-page questionnaire completed by each key informant.

The perception of opportunity (.79) and the two measures of entrepreneurial potential of the population—capacity (.64) and motivation (.93)—positively correlate with business start-up rates. And start-up rates positively correlate with growth in GDP (.60) and level of employment (.47).

While many cross-sectional measures still remain in this ongoing study, study directors claim, "The support for the conceptual model is encouraging, although clearly not conclusive. GEM provides a robust framework within which national governments can evolve a set of effective policies for enhancing entrepreneurship."

Questions

1. What are the independent and dependent variables in this study?

2. What are some of the intervening, extraneous, and moderating variables that the study attempted to control with its 10-nation design?

3. Can you do a causal study without controlling intervening, extraneous, and moderating variables?

4. What is the impact on study results of using national experts (key informants) to identify and weigh entrepreneurial framework conditions?

5. Can you do a causal study when much of the primary data collected is descriptive opinion and ordinal or interval data?

SOURCES

Global Entrepreneurship Assessment: National Entrepreneurship Assessment, UK, 1999 Executive Report. Center for Entrepreneurial Leadership of Ewing Marion Kauffman Foundation, 1999.

Reynolds, P., M. Hay, and M. Camp. Global Entrepreneurship Monitor: 1999 Executive Report. Kauffman Center for Entrepreneurial Leadership of Ewing Marion Kauffman Foundation, 1999.

Reynolds, P., J. Levie, and E. Autio. Global Entrepreneurship Monitor: 1999 Data Collection-Analysis Strategies Operations Manual. Babson College and the London Business School, 1999.

Reynolds, P., J. Levie, E. Autio, M. Hay, and B. Bygrave. Global Entrepreneurship Monitor: 1999 Research Report: Entrepreneurship and National Economic Well-Being. Babson College and the London Business School, 1999.

Zacharakis, A., P. Reynolds, and W. Bygrave. Global Entrepreneurship Assessment: National Entrepreneurship Assessment, United States of America, 1999 Executive Report. Center for Entrepreneurial Leadership of Ewing Marion Kauffman Foundation, 1999.

AgriComp

"How do I make sense of all this?" asked Jody, as he prepared to write his report to the dealer relations committee. He stared at the 292 responses to a survey of AgriComp's dealers as he began to ponder the problem. The question was whether to recommend a change to AgriComp's current procedures for settling warranty claim disputes with its dealers.

AgriComp sold computer systems to farmers, who used the systems for such purposes as crop rotation planning and spreadsheet analysis for financial planning. Many also used the systems to provide remote access to agriculture-oriented databases, market news, and even weather information. The equipment was assembled at company headquarters in southern Minnesota. The software was provided by subcontractors but was distributed under AgriComp's name. Both the hardware and software were sold through some 350 affiliated dealers nationwide, 292 of whom had responded to Jody's survey. It was relations with these dealers that concerned him.

The local dealers handled warranty service for AgriComp products. When hardware or software problems occurred, they arranged for appropriate repairs to be made locally and submitted vouchers to AgriComp headquarters in Minnesota. The headquarters staff reviewed the vouchers and issued reimbursement checks to the dealer. Occasionally claims were denied when the staff found that the particular repair was not covered by the company's warranty or the warranty had expired. In such cases, the dealer was more or less stuck for the cost of the repairs, and this had caused occasional hard feelings.

The company had an internal appeals process for dealers to follow to protest such denials but, at the last dealers' meeting, Jody had heard a lot of grumbling about that process. More than one dealer had suggested that it was useless, as appeals were always denied. For the dealers, the costs of repairs might correspond to the profits on many systems, so their concern was understandable.

Jody knew that clearer warranty instructions would help. Sometimes the dealers couldn't understand exactly what was or wasn't covered by warranty. In that kind of case, they often arranged for the repairs (to keep the customer happy) and took their chances on reimbursement. New documentation currently being developed would probably help with that part of the problem.

This case was inspired by an actual survey taken during 1993, but we have disguised the nature of the organization and its products, as well as the particular issue in the survey.

In a corridor conversation at the dealers' meeting, one dealer had suggested that perhaps in cases of dispute, an impartial mediator, external to the company, might be called in to settle the matter. In the annual survey of dealers, Jody had included a question about that proposal. As part of a one-page survey, dealers were asked to respond to the statement "The warranty appeals process should be replaced by a process using impartial mediators," on a scale of 1 to 5, where 1 indicated "Strongly agree," 3 indicated "Neither agree nor disagree," and 5 indicated "Strongly disagree." Each dealer was also asked to give the number of times in the last three years in which he or she had used the warranty appeals process. Answers to this question were 0, 1, 2, and "3 or more."

Part of the data from that survey is contained on the accompanying CD in the file AGRICOMP.

Jody was willing to consider changing the warranty appeals process along the lines suggested, if it was important to the dealers. It would cost the company some money, both for the external mediator and (perhaps) for increased costs from appeals the company lost, but keeping the dealers happy was obviously important.

Variable	Label
REP	The dealer's support for replacing the existing warranty appeals system with a mediator system (1 = "Strongly agree," 3 = "Neither agree nor disagree," and 5 = "Strongly disagree").
USE	The number of times the dealer used the appeals process (3 = 3 or more).

Question

1. Jody wonders just how important the process is to the dealers. Was there widespread discontent, or had he just heard from a few malcontents at the dealers' meeting?

Source: Used with permission of Peter G. Bryant and Marlene A. Smith, *Practical Data Analysis: Case Studies in Business Statistics,* Irwin, 1995.

AIDS Rates for Females

 Early reports of Pneumocystis carinii pneumonia, Kaposi's sarcoma, and other opportunistic infections in young homosexual men in Los Angeles, New York City, and San Francisco were filed in 1981. At that time, the Centers for Disease Control and Prevention (CDC) began surveillance for a newly recognized constellation of diseases, now called the acquired immunodeficiency syndrome (AIDS).

HIV, the etiologic agent of AIDS, has been identified and diagnostic tests for infection with this virus have been developed. Exact definitions of AIDS and diagnostic practices have changed over time. State and local health departments report cases of AIDS to the CDC, but they vary widely in the structure and organization of their surveillance systems and, therefore, in the completeness of their case reporting. Reporting delays vary widely, too, and have been as long as several years for some cases. Generally, between 50 percent and 60 percent of patients are reported to the CDC within three months of diagnosis, about 80 percent within one year, and about 90 percent within two years.

AIDS has become a major public health issue, and the expense of treating cases has led insurance companies to require screening in some cases before issuing life and health insurance policies. This in turn has led to concerns about privacy. AIDS is, thus, an economic and political issue for businesses and private citizens alike.

In the early years of the pandemic, AIDS was not generally considered a big issue for women, because the overwhelming majority of the cases reported were in homosexual males. Is that still the case?

The data on the accompanying CD show the number of new AIDS cases reported in various years for adult and adolescent females. From these data, prepare an appropriate chart or other summary that highlights the salient features of the data and makes evident any important trends.

Source: U.S. Department of Health and Human Services, Public Health Service, Centers for Disease Control, *AIDS Public Information Data Set,* July 1991. Used with permission of Peter G. Bryant and Marlene A. Smith, *Practical Data Analysis: Case Studies in Business Statistics,* Irwin, 1995.

BBQ Product Crosses Over the Lines of Varied Tastes

Rich Products Corp. is hoping its frozen barbecue will appeal to the wide tastes in its narrow market, but it realizes consumers will need a nudge in that direction.

Enter Ruby Taylene Dodge, waitress down at the Port-O-Rama and major figure in the company's marketing campaign for its new product, Rich's Southern Barbeque.

Barbecue is a regional delicacy; it varies in taste from county to county throughout the Southeast. According to Joe Tindall, the company's product development manager of new products, Rich Products (Buffalo, New York) had to develop a tangy product to appeal to varied tastes and had to persuade consumers they'd like it.

To cross over regional and local differences in the six-city market in the Southeast, Long, Haymes & Carr Advertising (LH&C), Winston-Salem, North Carolina, has launched a series of 30-second TV ads called "Please Don't Tell 'Em Ruby Sent You."

"The fictitious Ruby is supposed to give the product authenticity without trying to compete with barbecue restaurants or stands," said Don Van Erden, vice president/ management supervisor, LH&C.

"Our research told us that no one has more rapport and credibility with the barbecue-eating public than the real-life barbecue waitress," Van Erden said. "In Ruby, we have a vivid persona who's believable because she's based on real barbecue wait-resses we've observed."

Rich Products hopes Ruby will reach all consumers with her friendly Southern accent and down-home sincerity.

"I'm a loyal employee of the Port-O-Rama, but my real true love is Rich's Frozen Barbeque," Ruby says in one spot. In another she's wearing a disguise. "I can't just go to my grocer's freezer for Rich's Barbeque," she says. "I've got a career at the Port-O-Rama to consider."

She praises the product in all the spots but, fearful of losing her job, warns viewers, "Just please don't tell 'em Ruby sent you."

The microwavable barbecue entrees were test marketed last year in Nashville, Tennessee, Little Rock, Arkansas, and the Alabama cities of Birmingham, Huntsville, Montgomery, and Tuscaloosa. "That's the market now, but expansion into other areas is planned," Tindall said.

Questions

1. What measurement and scaling issues should be considered when developing a study to measure consumers' attitudes toward barbecue in general and, specifically, Rich's Southern Barbeque?

2. Assume Rich's wanted to test people's preference for its barbecue versus the other leading brands (of which there are five). What would you recommend to measure these preferences?

3. What measurement and scaling issues should be considered when developing a study to measure the effectiveness of "Ruby" as a character spokesperson for Rich's Southern Barbeque?

Source: "BBQ Product Crosses Over the Lines of Varied Tastes" (September 12, 1988, p. 24) used with permission of *Marketing News*. Case notes used with permission of William R. Dillon, Thomas J. Madden, and Neil H. Firtle, *Marketing Research in a Marketing Environment,* 3/e, 1994, Irwin. Used with permission of The McGraw-Hill Companies.

Calling Up Attendance: TeleCenter System Users Forum

Nashville-based TCS Management Group markets TeleCenter System, software used to forecast staffing needs for reservation centers, order centers, or customer service centers. Using TeleCenter System allows companies to have the correct number of people on duty at any given hour of the day or night, thereby optimizing the delivery of good service while holding costs as low as possible. TCS has an impressive list of customers, including American Express, British Airways, Sears, Amtrak, and Citicorp.

TCS was planning a special two-day educational event, Users Forum, for its 300-plus customers, but was unsure how many TeleCenter System users would attend. Scheduled at the Opryland Hotel, the forum would offer speakers, workshops, and presentations. While TCS would underwrite the costs associated with planning the meeting and preparing the presentations, customers would be responsible for paying a fee to attend, as well as their own hotel and travel expenses to Nashville. "Ten weeks before the forum, we weren't sure whether we would have 40 people or 140 people coming to Nashville," shared Jim Gordon, CEO of TCS.

While TCS had previously done most of its own customer satisfaction research, given the time frame of the need, it turned to Nashville-based Prince Marketing, who promised to design, conduct, and interpret survey results within 21 days.

Three objectives were set for the phone survey:

- Determine the likelihood of Users Forum attendance.

- Update the TCS software users database (for subsequent use in mailing quarterly newsletters, special announcements, and software updates).

- Measure the level of user satisfaction (with the company and its software generally, as well as regarding specific software features and issues).

Respondents were asked to rate on a 7-point scale the software's ease of use, the usefulness of software-generated reports, and satisfaction with service. They were also asked whether they would recommend the software and why/why not; whether they were aware of the Users Forum; whether their company planned to send a representative; and whether the customer needed or wanted more information on the Users Forum. Prince faxed the names and addresses of respondents indicating an interest in the Users Forum to TCS, which sent promotional materials immediately.

Prince surveyed 315 customers: 161 users and 154 managers. Prince predicted that 115 people would attend the forum. Actual Users Forum attendance was 139.

On customer service, 34 percent of respondents gave TCS a 7, the highest point on the rating scale. Yet respondents also offered that they wanted shorter response time and longer operating hours for telephone support staff, including Saturday access. TCS CEO Gordon said, "We have redeployed some of our people, expanded Saturday coverage, and instituted a beeper system to increase our responsiveness."

TCS received its lowest scores on ease of use, with 60 percent of respondents giving it a 5 or higher on the 7-point scale, while 16 percent refused to answer. The research confirmed anecdotal evidence and reinforced internal initiatives to improve ease of use.

Fully 84 percent said they would recommend the TCS system to colleagues, with 16 percent indicating they were too new to the software to form an opinion. TCS plans to use this endorsement to attract new users.

"The positive survey results created tremendous esprit de corps for the whole staff," claims Gordon. "We were able to identify these concerns ahead of our Users Forum and develop appropriate responses. All in all, the survey told us we're on the right track—and that alone justified our investment in the research."

Questions

1. Build the management-research question hierarchy.

2. Discuss the communication methodology chosen.

3. Develop the preliminary analysis plan.

4. How would you deal with the 16 percent of the sample who were new to the software?

5. Discuss the advantages and concerns of incorporating or closely linking marketing activities with research activities.

Source: http://www.quirks.com/CGI-BIN/SM40i.exe?docid=3000:58911&%70assArticleID=409. Used with permission of Pamela S. Schindler and Donald R. Cooper. © 2001.

Can This Study Be Saved?

"What's troubling me is that you can't just pick a new random sample just because somebody didn't like the results of the first survey. Please tell me more about what's been done." Your voice is clear and steady, trying to discover what actually happened and, hopefully, to identify some useful information without the additional expense of a new survey.

"It's not that we didn't like the results of the first survey," responded R. L. Steegmans, "it's that only 54 percent of the membership responded. We hadn't even looked at their planned spending when the decision (to sample again) was made. Since we had (naively) planned on receiving answers from nearly all of the 400 people initially selected, we chose 200 more at random and surveyed them also. That's the second sample." At this point, sensing that there's more to the story, you simply respond, "Uh huh . . ." Sure enough, more follows:

"Then E. S. Eldredge had this great idea of following up on those who didn't respond. We sent them another whole questionnaire, together with a crisp dollar and a letter telling them how important their responses are to the planning of the industry. Worked pretty well. Then, of course, we had to follow up the second sample as well." "Let me see if I understand," you reply. "You have two samples: one of 400 people and one of 200. For each, you have the initial responses and follow-up responses. Is that it?"

EXHIBIT C-CAN 1–1 Methodology Details

	Pilot Study	First Sample	Second Sample	Both Samples	All Combined
Initial Mailing					
Mailed	12	400	200	600	612
Responses	12	216	120	336	348
Average	$39,274.89	$3,949.40	$3,795.55	$3,894.45	$5,114.47
Standard deviation	$9,061.91	$849.26	$868.39	$858.02	$6,716.42
Follow-Up Mailing					
Mailed	0	184	80	264	264
Responses	0	64	18	82	82
Average		$1,238.34	$1,262.34	$1,243.60	$1,243.60
Standard deviation		$155.19	$156.59	$153.29	$153.29
Initial and Follow-Up					
Mailed	12	400	200	600	612
Responses	12	280	138	418	430
Average	$39,274.89	$3,329.73	$3,465.13	$3,374.43	$4,376.30
Standard deviation	$9,061.91	$1,364.45	$1,179.50	$1,306.42	$6,229.77

"Well, yes, but there was also the pilot study—12 people in offices downstairs and across the street. We'd kinda like to include them, average them, with the rest because we worked so hard on that at the start, and it seems a shame to throw them away. But all we really want to know is average spending to within about a hundred dollars."

At this point, you feel that you have enough of the background information to evaluate the situation and to either recommend an estimate or an additional survey. Exhibit C-CAN 1–1 offers additional details for the survey of the 8,391 overall membership in order to determine planned spending over the next quarter.

Questions

1. Was drawing a second sample a good idea? Explain.

2. Were the follow-up mailings a good idea? Explain.

3. Which of the results are useful? Are these data sufficient to solve the management dilemma or is further study needed?

Source: Adapted from "Can This Survey Be Saved?" Used with permission of Andrew F. Siegel, *Practical Business Statistics,* 4/e, (Irwin/McGraw-Hill, 2000), p. 298.

Healthy Lifestyles

The Centers for Disease Control and Prevention (CDC) in Atlanta, Georgia, is the government agency responsible for disease-related issues in the United States. The CDC coordinates efforts to counteract outbreaks of diseases and funds a variety of medical and health research studies. The CDC also serves as a central clearinghouse for health-related data.

The CDC conducts the annual Behavioral Risk Factor Surveillance Survey. The survey measures a whole series of lifestyle characteristics that relate to health and longevity, such as smoking and use of seat belts. The survey compiles data on a state-by-state basis. Not all states are surveyed.

The data set from the 1990 Behavioral Risk Factor Surveillance Survey is on the accompanying CD in the file named HEALTHY. All numbers are percentages, and asterisks indicate the missing data for that state.

Variable	Label
SMK	Current cigarette smokers.
WEI	Overweight (top 15 percent of population, according to the CDC height-weight formula).
SED	Sedentary lifestyle (less than three 20-minute exercise sessions a week).
ACT	No leisure time activity (off the job).
ALC	Binge drinking (five or more drinks on occasion, previous month).
DWI	Drinking and driving (after "too much" to drink, previous month).
SEA	Seat-belt use (occasionally or never).
STATE	U.S. state (alphanumeric).

Your task is to prepare a summary of these data. Your report is to be issued to major news organizations, such as the Associated Press, and will appear in major newspapers around the United States. For this reason, it would be inappropriate to use technical jargon in your report.

Your boss has suggested a few general ideas about what is likely to appeal to your target audience. As you study the data, you might find other things worth including.

Questions

1. Report any interesting (i.e., unexpected, humorous, or odd) differences between states.

2. Devise a weighted index of all seven lifestyle variables. The weighted index is to serve as an overall or composite measure of healthy lifestyles. Apply your weight to the states of Minnesota, Florida, and California as an example of what your weighted index shows.

3. Discuss any noteworthy limitations of the survey or data set.

Source: Used with permission of Peter G. Bryant and Marlene A. Smith, *Practical Data Analysis: Case Studies in Business Statistics,* Irwin, 1995.

HiTech Engineering

 HiTech Engineering, Inc. (HEI), a company located in Minnesota, designs and manufactures a variety of industrial products. HEI sells its products directly to existing customers and also uses authorized distributors around the globe to assist in sales and distribution. Although HEI has an edge on the market in terms of engineering and manufacturing expertise, it falls a bit short in knowing the best way to market and sell its latest industrial inventions and innovations.

HEI gets word to the market about a new product in various ways. For instance, sometimes it purchases magazine advertisements and sometimes it issues news releases. Because HEI produces industrial products and not consumer products, it never uses broadcast media such as television or radio, but concentrates on print media for the purpose of advertising.

HEI management would like to understand how effective each of the five basic types of advertising they've used has been.

1. **Magazines** (MAGS). Advertisements are placed in about 150 different industrial magazines and trade journals. These ads are designed by HEI's advertising department.

2. **Postcard decks** (POST). Publishers of various magazines and journals assemble postcard announcements of new products from a number of different companies. The postcard decks are then sent out to their list of subscribers. HEI must pay for the postcard deck service.

3. **Editorials** (EDIT). HEI's advertising department occasionally produces editorials for magazines or trade publications and hopes that the editorial will be published. In response to the editorial, readers will occasionally write back to HEI requesting more information. HEI's expenses for this type of marketing are employee salaries for writing the editorial and the cost of preparing a camera-ready version of the editorial.

4. **News releases** (NEWS). A news release is a one-paragraph description of a new product that typically appears in the back of a magazine. News releases will be published for free by magazines that are already carrying HEI advertisements as a courtesy to the client. Like requests for literature (below), interested readers send a postcard to the magazine, which is then forwarded to HEI. Costs incurred for this type of advertising are employee salaries for processing requests.

5. **Literature** (LIT). Readers of magazines or trade journals may make a request for literature or more information about HEI by circling a request number on a "bingo

card" and sending it back to the magazine or journal. Requests are then sent from the magazine or journal to HEI, which responds to the requests appropriately.

Requests for information by prospective customers are called "leads." By asking customers where they heard about the new product, the advertising group is able to compile information about the number of leads generated by each of these media types; they also know the expenses incurred in each media class. The data cover the last 17 months. These data have been assembled on the accompanying CD in the file named LEADATA.

Variable	Label
MONTH	Actual month of exposure (= 1 to 17).
RESPONSE	Actual number of responses.
SPEND	Dollar cost incurred in that month.
MAGS	Magazines used (1 = used, 0 = not used).
POST	Postcard decks used (1 = used, 0 = not used).
EDIT	Editorials used (1 = used, 0 = not used).
NEWS	News releases used (1 = used, 0 = not used).
LIT	Literature used (1 = used, 0 = not used).

Question

1. What is the most effective type of advertising outlet for HEI? Do you have any recommendations on the appropriate mix of the five different types of advertising?

Source: These data are real even though the name of the company and its location have been changed. Tessa E. Alexander and Edwin C. Peterson have granted permission to use these data, which they originally collected for the study. Used with permission of Peter G. Bryant and Marlene A. Smith, *Practical Data Analysis: Case Studies in Business Statistics,* Irwin, 1995.

Inquiring Minds Want to Know—NOW!

Penton Media, a publisher of such business magazines as *Industry Week, Machine Design,* and *Restaurant Hospitality,* was experiencing a decline in use of publication reader service cards. This postcard-sized device features a series of numbers, with one number assigned to each ad appearing in the publication. Readers circle the advertiser's number to request product or service information by mail. Cards are used to track reader inquiries stimulated by advertising within the magazine. "By 1998 there was a growing belief in many quarters that business publication advertising was generating fewer leads than in the past," shares Ken Long, director of Penton Research Services. "Knowing whether or not this is true is complicated by the fact that many companies don't track the source of their leads." This belief, however, could ultimately lead to lower advertising revenues if alternate methods of inquiry stimulation went untracked.

Penton started its research by comparing inquiry response options offered within September issues of 12 Penton magazines, including *Industry Week*. Ads were drawn from two years: 1992 (648 ads) and 1997 (690 ads). The average number of response options per ad was 3.3 in 1992, growing to 4.1 in 1997. More than half of 1997 ads offered toll-free telephone numbers and fax numbers. "Two inquiry methods that are commonplace today, sending e-mail and visiting an advertiser's Internet website, were virtually nonexistent in 1992," noted Long. Not a single 1992 ad invited readers to visit a website and just one ad listed an e-mail address. Website addresses were found in three of five (60.9 percent) 1997 ads, with e-mail addresses provided in 17.7 percent of ads. Today, many websites contain a "contact us" feature that generates an e-mail message of inquiry. In 1997, advertisers were including their postal mailing address only 55.5 percent of the time, compared with 69 percent in 1992 ads.

Penton pretested a reader-targeted mail questionnaire by phone with a small sample drawn from its database of 1.7 million domestic subscribers. A second pretest, by mail, involved 300 subscribers. Penton mailed the finalized study to 4,000 managers, executives, engineers, and purchasing agents selected from the U.S. Penton database. The survey sample was constructed using stratified disproportionate random sampling with subscribers considered as belonging to one of 42 cells (seven industry groups by six job titles). A total of 710 completed questionnaires were received, with 676 of the respondents indicating that they were purchase decision makers for their organization. Penton analyzed only the answers of these 676 buyers. Data were analyzed by weighting responses in each cell by their percentage makeup in the overall population. The overall margin of error for the survey was ± 4 percent at the 95 percent level of confidence. In-depth follow-up telephone interviews were conducted with 40 respondents, to gain a deeper understanding of their behavior and attitudes.

Almost every respondent (97.7 percent) had contacted at least one advertiser during the past year. Newer methods of making inquiries—Web visits, fax-on-demand, or e-mail—were used by half (49.1 percent) of the buyers surveyed. But a look ahead shows the true impact of information technology. Within the next five years, 73.7 percent expect to respond to more ads by sending e-mail to the company. In addition, 72.2 percent anticipate visiting an advertiser's website, and 60 percent expect to increase their use of fax-on-demand. Three out of five purchasing decision makers have access to the Internet, and 74.3 percent of those without Internet service expect to have it within the next five years. Seven of 10 (72.4 percent) respondents plan to use the Internet to research potential suppliers, products, or services during the next five years, compared to 33.1 pecent using it for that purpose during the past year.

Findings revealed that the need for fast response and the need for information on product availability and delivery are influenced by the following:

1. Time pressures created by downsizing of the work force and demands for greater productivity.

2. The fast pace of doing business.

3. Cost considerations.

Behavior varied depending on immediacy of purpose. When buyers have an immediate need for a product or service, telephone contact is the inquiry method of choice. Of the respondents, 79.5 percent reported that they had called a toll-free number in the past year for an immediate need, while 66.1 percent had called a local number, and 64.7 percent had called a long-distance number. When the need for a product or service is not immediate, buyers are more likely to use the mail. Among respondents, 71.4 percent reported they had mailed a reader service card in the past year for a nonimmediate need, and 69.3 percent had mailed a business-reply card to an advertiser.

"A new paradigm is emerging for industrial purchasing," concludes Long. "Buyers are working in real time. They want information more quickly and they want more information."

Questions

1. Build the management-research question hierarchy.

2. What ethical issues are relevant to this study?

3. Describe the sampling plan. Analyze its strengths and weaknesses.

4. Describe the research design. Analyze its strengths and weaknesses.

5. Critique the survey used for the study.

6. Prepare the survey for analysis. Set up the code sheet for this study. How will this study be set up to be tabulated by a statistical analysis program like SPSS?

7. Assume you are compiling your research report. How would you present the statistical information within this case to the *Industry Week* decision maker, the manager who must decide whether or not to continue to publish reader service cards?

8. Assume you are compiling your research report. What are the limitations of this study?

9. Assume you are the decision maker for *Industry Week*. Given the declining value of the reader response card to subscribers, originally designed as a value-enhancing service to *IW* readers and advertisers alike, what further research might be suggested by the findings of this study? Or do you have sufficient information to stop the use of reader response cards in *Industry Week*?

Source: Ken Long, Director of Penton Research Services, provided the data and the instrument in November 1999. Used with permission of Pamela S. Schindler and Donald R. Cooper, © 2001.

Cover Letter and Questionnaire for Mail Survey

Could we ask a favor of you?

We are conducting a nationwide survey of executives to help companies better understand and respond to your requests for information.

Your name has been selected as part of a relatively small sample, so

WIN A HAND-HELD COLOR TV!!

We will enter your name in a random drawing for a FREE Casio Portable Color Television when you complete and return this questionaire to us. This high resolution TV comes with an external power jack and earphones!

your reply is vital to the accuracy of the study findings. All individual responses will remain completely confidential, with answers combined and presented in statistical form only.

We would be grateful if you could take a few minutes to respond to this survey. A postage-paid envelope is enclosed for your convenience.

We look forward to your reply!

Cordially,

Director of Research

P.S. To ensure a correct entry in the random drawing for the hand-held color TV, please make any necessary changes to your mailing label.

PLEASE TURN PAGE . . .

Questionnaire for mail survey:

1. Are you involved in specifying, recommending, purchasing, or approving the purchase of any of the following for your organization? (Check *all* that apply.)

   ❏ Construction/renovation work

   ❏ Equipment/machinery

   ❏ Maintenance/repair/operating supplies

   ❏ Production material/components

   ❏ Services

   ❏ Other

   ❏ Not involved in purchasing decisions

2. During the **past year,** which of the following actions have you taken in response to an ad, to obtain information about potential suppliers/products/services for your organization? (Check *all* that apply.) Please check the box in the last column if you have not taken the indicated action in the past year.

	Action Taken During the Past Year		
	For an Immediate Product/Service	For a Nonimmediate Product/Service	Did Not Do in the Past Year
Faxed			
Business reply card to company	❏	❏	❏
Coupon from ad	❏	❏	❏
Letter to company	❏	❏	❏
Publication reader service card	❏	❏	❏
Mailed			
Business reply card to company	❏	❏	❏
Coupon from ad	❏	❏	❏
Letter to company	❏	❏	❏
Publication reader service card	❏	❏	❏
Sent e-mail to company	❏	❏	❏
Telephoned company			
Local number	❏	❏	❏
Nontoll-free (long distance) number	❏	❏	❏
Toll-free (800 or 888) number	❏	❏	❏
Used advertiser's fax-on-demand service	❏	❏	❏
Visited the company's Internet website	❏	❏	❏
Other	❏	❏	❏

3. What are the ***three*** most useful types of information an advertiser can provide when responding to your inquiry? (Please check only *three*.)

❏ Ability to customize products/services	❏ ISO/professional certification
❏ Availability/delivery	❏ List of sales/service locations
❏ Complete company catalog	❏ Price list
❏ Short-form (condensed) catalog	❏ Product specifications
❏ Company experience/expertise	❏ Quality/reliability
❏ Company financial strength/stability	❏ Savings in time/money
❏ Customer/client list	❏ Warranty/guarantee offered
❏ Customer service/technical support	❏ Other (please specify): _____

4. a. Please estimate the change over the ***past five years*** in your use of each of the following methods of obtaining information, in response to advertising, about potential suppliers/products/services for your organization. Check the box in the fourth column if you have not taken the indicated action in the past five years.

   b. Over the ***next five years***, do you expect your use of each method of obtaining information to increase, decrease, or stay about the same?

Method Used to Obtain Information	a. Change over the Past Five Years:				b. Expected Change over the Next Five Years:		
	Has Increased	Has Stayed the Same	Has Decreased	Haven't Done in Past 5 Years	Will Increase	Will Stay the Same	Will Decrease
Faxing							
Business reply card to company	❏	❏	❏	❏	❏	❏	❏
Coupon from ad	❏	❏	❏	❏	❏	❏	❏
Letter to company	❏	❏	❏	❏	❏	❏	❏
Publication reader service card	❏	❏	❏	❏	❏	❏	❏
Mailing							
Business reply card to company	❏	❏	❏	❏	❏	❏	❏
Coupon from ad	❏	❏	❏	❏	❏	❏	❏
Letter to company	❏	❏	❏	❏	❏	❏	❏
Publication reader service card	❏	❏	❏	❏	❏	❏	❏
Sending e-mail to company	❏	❏	❏	❏	❏	❏	❏

(continued)

Method Used to Obtain Information	a. Change over the Past Five Years:				b. Expected Change over the Next Five Years:		
	Has Increased	Has Stayed the Same	Has Decreased	Haven't Done in Past 5 Years	Will Increase	Will Stay the Same	Will Decrease
Telephoning company							
Local number	❐	❐	❐	❐	❐	❐	❐
Nontoll-free (long distance) number	❐	❐	❐	❐	❐	❐	❐
Toll-free (800 or 888) number	❐	❐	❐	❐	❐	❐	❐
Using advertiser's fax-on-demand service	❐	❐	❐	❐	❐	❐	❐
Visiting the company's Internet website	❐	❐	❐	❐	❐	❐	❐
Other	❐	❐	❐	❐	❐	❐	❐

5. a. Overall, which one method of obtaining information about potential suppliers/products/services for your organization do you most prefer to use? (Please check only *one*.)

Faxing:

❐ Business reply card to company

❐ Coupon from ad

❐ Letter to company

❐ Publication reader service card

Mailing:

❐ Business reply card to company

❐ Coupon from ad

❐ Letter to company

❐ Publication reader service card

❐ Sending e-mail to company

Telephoning the company:

❐ Local number

❐ Nontoll-free (long distance) number

❐ Toll-free (800 or 888) number

❐ Using company's fax-on-demand service

❐ Visiting the company's Internet website

❐ Other *(please specify:)* _____

b. Why do you prefer to use this method? _____

_____

6. a. Do you currently have access to the Internet? (Check *all* that apply.)

❐ Yes, at work   ❐ Yes, at home/away from home   ❐ No current Internet access

b. If you don't currently have Internet access, do you expect to have access in the future?

❐ Yes, within the next year   ❐ Yes, in 1–5 years   ❐ No, not within next 5 years

(continued)

7. a. If you currently have Internet access, in which of the following ways have you used the Internet in your job during the **past year?**

   b. If you currently have or plan to have Internet access, how do you expect to use the Internet in your job in the **next five years?**

	a. Use of the Internet During the *Past Year*	b. Expected Use of the Internet During the *Next Five* Years
Reading industry/professional newsgroup postings (e.g., bulletin boards)	❐	❐
Researching potential suppliers/products/ services for your organization	❐	❐
Obtaining technical information	❐	❐
Communicating by e-mail:		
With potential suppliers for your organization	❐	❐
With other buyers about potential suppliers/ products/services	❐	❐
Purchasing products or services for your organization	❐	❐
Other (*please specify*): _____	❐	❐
NO JOB-RELATED USE OF INTERNET	❐	❐

GENERAL INFORMATION

8. Are you male or female?   ❐ Male   ❐ Female

9. What is your age?   ❐ Under 30   ❐ 30–39   ❐ 40–49   ❐ 50 or older

10. How many years have you been with your current organization?   _____ years

11. How many years have you been involved in the purchasing process at your organization?   _____ years

Mastering Teacher Leadership

Ohio legislators recently implemented new standards for those wishing to teach within Ohio's public and private schools. Teachers certified to teach in Ohio in 2002 or later will need to complete a master's degree before obtaining their second licensure renewal. New teachers, therefore, will have a five- to seven-year window to complete the master's degree after their initial licensure to teach.

Historically, teachers have looked to graduate level courses to fulfill their professional development requirements. According to the newly passed Ohio Department of Education Teacher Certification Standards, for the first time all professional development activities must be tied to professional development plans customized by local school district goals. All such plans will be approved and monitored by Local Professional Development Committees. These LPDCs will look favorably on courses that fit local goals, which are increasingly motivated by student performance variances on standardized tests.

Wittenberg University is primarily a resident campus of 2,000 students affiliated with the Lutheran Church in America. Located in central Ohio, Wittenberg is a comprehensive liberal arts institution with professional programs in education, business management, pre-med, and pre-law. It has been training teachers for more than 150 years and has earned a reputation for producing exceptional teachers for K–12 programs. This high quality, as perceived by local teachers who supervise Wittenberg undergraduate field teaching experiences, is expected to be Wittenberg's greatest asset in pursuing the development of a master's program.

Wittenberg, historically, has not offered a graduate degree in education, but it has offered graduate degrees in its nationally recognized music program and, until the mid-1980s, in its theology program. Wittenberg sees the change in Ohio Teacher Certification Standards as an opportunity for its Center for Professional Development (WittCPD), a program of professional development courses designed to fulfill the continuing education requirements of teachers in the area.

Central Ohio is rich with high quality universities. Within a 30-minute drive of Wittenberg's campus, undergraduate teacher education programs can be found at Wright State University (WSU), the University of Dayton (UD), Urbana College, Cedarville College, Wilberforce University, and Central State University. WSU and UD currently offer Master of Arts degrees in teaching. WSU offers continuing education programs that fulfill professional development programs.

Increased turnover is also expected to be a motivating factor contributing to increased enrollment in university development programs. Ohio's schoolteacher turnover is expected to increase due to the aging of the teacher population, incentive buyout programs designed to encourage aging teachers to retire, and the need to hire experienced teachers in the hard-to-fill math and science areas. With an average 15 years teaching experience, Clark County schools have more than 900 certified staff and hire 50–60 new teachers each year. Springfield City schools have more than 800 certified staff and hired 119 teachers in 1997, 99 in 1998, and 118 in 1999.

The faculty of the education department, in concert with university administrators, conducted a brainstorming session in early fall 1998 to identify university resources that might contribute to a master's program in education. This was followed by a retreat with an Ohio Department of Education consultant, who reiterated the advantages of a liberal arts-based program in the ongoing preparation of K–12 teachers.

To further explore the opportunity for offering a Master of Arts degree in Classroom Leadership, WittCPD conducted three focus groups: two with Springfield City district teachers and one with local school superintendents. Both groups were positive about the likelihood of a program customized to the needs of the various local school districts. Additionally, they provided direction for the desired content and orientation of an effective program. Such a program would need to:

- Deal with the diverse cognitive and social needs of students.
- Emphasize technological literacy for both teachers and students.
- Emphasize both program and classroom assessment by providing a sound research foundation for both curriculum and instruction.
- Address classroom management issues of student social skills, moral education, and discipline.
- Provide a framework for teachers to learn to collaborate with other teachers and with community professionals.

In the spring of 1999, Education faculty associated with the WittCPD drafted a market survey and mailed it to 2,000 practicing teachers in a four-county area. Each of the 1,600 teachers in Clark County, Wittenberg's home county, received a questionnaire, with the remaining 400 surveys delivered to a systematic sample teaching in the outlying counties of Green, Montgomery, and Champaign. By September 1, 1999, 763 teachers had returned their surveys (31.8 percent response), of which 53.8 percent of respondents had completed or were enrolled in degree programs beyond the bachelor's level.

Out of 763 teachers, 21.2 percent said they definitely would enroll, with an additional 57.7 percent who might enroll, citing professional requirements, professional advancement, or keeping their certification as the three primary reasons for enrolling. Those who expressed a lack of interest in a Master of Arts program at Wittenberg claimed as three obstacles the anticipated high cost, their holding a current master's degree, or family responsibilities.

In order for the Wittenberg Board to approve the offering of the new degree program, the program needs to continue the liberal arts tradition and strengthen the undergraduate teacher education program, as high quality undergraduate education is seen as part of Wittenberg's primary mission. Additionally, new academic initiatives such as the one proposed are increasingly asked by the board to reach break-even within their first operating year.

Questions

1. Build the management-research question hierarchy for this opportunity.

2. Evaluate the appropriateness of the exploratory stage of the research design.

3. Evaluate the sampling strategy.

4. Evaluate the survey:
   a. In terms of structure, what is the quality of this instrument? What improvements would you make?
   b. In terms of measurement questions, are the chosen response strategies appropriate?
   c. Does this instrument meet the needs summarized in the investigative questions noted in your management-research question hierarchy (question 1 above)?

5. Prepare a preliminary analysis plan for this study. Which variables do you want frequencies on? Why? Which variables do you want to cross-tabulate? Why?

6. Analyze the data from this study on your CD (Excel 97 file format: Witt Masters CPD.xls). With respect to creating a Master of Arts in Classroom Leadership program, what recommendation is supported by your data analysis?

7. What role could GIS play in this analysis?

Source: Dr. Robert Welker, Director, Wittenberg Center for Professional Development, provided the data and survey instrument to the authors in November 1999. Used with permission of Pamela S. Schindler and Donald R. Cooper, © 2001.

Survey Cover Letter and Graduate Program Survey

February 22, 1999

Dear Colleague:

Wittenberg University is exploring the potential of a Master of Arts program in education. In order for us to understand the promise of such an effort, we are asking that you complete the following survey. Our purpose is twofold. We would like to understand your potential interest in a master's program at Wittenberg and in taking courses for graduate credit here. Second, we would like to use the information you provide to create a graduate program as receptive to the needs of practicing teachers as possible.

Please complete the attached survey form and return it in the postage-paid envelope provided by March 20, 1999. Thank you for completing this survey and thank you for your continued work with our community's young people.

Regards,

Robert Welker, Ph.D.

Director

Wittenberg Center for Professional Development

Graduate Survey Program

1. Counting this year, how many years have you taught?

   ❏ 0–5 years   ❏ 6–10 years   ❏ 11–15 years   ❏ 16–19 years   ❏ 20 or more years

2. Professional responsibility and subject field. Check all that apply.

Grade Level	**Subject Area**	
❏ Preschool to grade 3	❏ Art	❏ Music
❏ Grade 4 to grade 8	❏ Business/Economics	❏ PE/Health
❏ Grade 9 to 12	❏ 0–5 years	❏ Social studies
❏ Special education	❏ 0–5 years	❏ Science
❏ Administration	❏ 0–5 years	❏ Other _____
❏ Other: _____		

3. Highest level of education obtained. Please select one from the list below.

   ❏ Less than a B.A./B.S.   ❏ B.A./B.S.

   ❏ B.A./B.S. plus graduate work   ❏ Currently in M.A./M.S. program

   ❏ M.A./M.S.   ❏ Ph.D. or currently enrolled in Ph.D. program.

   ❏ M.A./M.S. plus additional graduate work

   If you are currently enrolled in a graduate program, which college or university are you attending?

   _____

4. Which of the following qualities are most important to you in a graduate program? (Please rank the top three qualities with "1" being of most importance, "2" being of next most importance, etc.)

   ____ Reputation   ____ Quality of instruction   ____ Class size

   ____ Schedule flexibility ____ Closeness to home   ____ Individual attention

   ____ Cost   ____ Other

(continued)

5. If costs were kept competitive, how likely would you be to apply to a master's degree program in education at Wittenberg?

❏ Definitely would apply   ❏ Might apply   ❏ Would not apply

6. If costs were kept competitive, how likely would you be to enroll in graduate courses at Wittenberg to enhance skills without pursuing a master's degree?

❏ Definitely would apply   ❏ Might apply   ❏ Would not apply

7. Please indicate the three most important reasons for your interest in graduate education at Wittenberg, with "1" being your most important reason, "2" your next most important reason, etc.

_____ Professional requirements   _____ Increased employability

_____ Professional advancement   _____ Additional money

_____ Personal satisfaction   _____ Keep certification

_____ Future requirement   _____ Upgrade certification

_____ Career change   _____ Improving skills

Other: _____

8. Please check the two most important reasons for your lack of interest in graduate education at Wittenberg.

_____ Cost   _____ Live too far away

_____ Family responsibilities   _____ Too near retirement

_____ Time to complete the degree   _____ Lack of information

_____ Professional commitments   _____ Already have a master's degree

_____ Enrolled in master's program

Other: _____

9. Please indicate from the list below which of the following might be anticipated as an obstacle to your enrolling in a master's level or graduate class at Wittenberg.

_____ Child/elder care   _____ Travel

_____ Financial need   _____ Employment schedule

_____ Family commitments

Other: _____

10. What professional development areas most interest you? Please rank the top three professional development areas that interest you, with "1" being your area of strongest interest, "2" being your area of next strongest interest, etc.

_____ Enhancing subject matter knowledge   _____ Teaching Arts

_____ Using technology in the classroom   _____ Teaching Social Studies

_____ Child development   _____ Teaching English/Language Arts

_____ Teaching reading/writing   _____ Teaching Math

_____ Specific learning disabilities   _____ Teaching Science

_____ Teacher leadership development   _____ Urban social backgrounds

_____ Developing social skills in students   _____ Moral and character development

Other: _____

(continued)

11. How far would you have to drive to attend WU?

    ❏ under 10 minutes   ❏ 10–20 minutes   ❏ 21–30 minutes

    ❏ 31–45 minutes   ❏ 46–60 minutes   ❏ more than 60 minutes

12. When during the year would you be able to take graduate courses? (Check all that apply.)

    ❏ Fall (Aug.–Dec.)   ❏ Spring (Jan.–April)   ❏ Summer (May–July)

13. Which day and time scheduling option below most appeals to you?

    ❏ Fall through spring: Day (8:00 AM–4:00 PM)

    ❏ Fall through spring: Late afternoon (4:00 PM–6:00 PM)

    ❏ Fall through spring: Evening (6:00 PM–10:00 PM)

    ❏ Fall through spring: Saturday

    ❏ Summer day (8:00 AM–4:00 PM)

    ❏ Summer evening: (6:00 PM–10:00 PM)

If you would like to receive more information about graduate progamming in education at WU, please add your name and mailing address below.

Name: _____

Address: _____

Thank you for your time and assistance. Please return the survey in the postage-paid envelope by March 20.

Match Wits with Jason on Sampling Theory

"Do you know if the post office accepts checks?" asks Audrey, the business manager at the Chevron station.

"Couldn't say," Jason replies.

"Because I am going to spend a fortune on stamps and I don't want to carry a lot of cash down there." She waved a thick folio of three-up mailing labels. "I've got to survey our customers. Our banker insists. You know that new loan officer? The MBA? The one named Jasmine, who calls herself 'Jazz'?" We asked her for $50,000 so we can open at 5 A.M. and stay open until midnight—we have to put up a fence and some shrubbery, so as not to disturb the apartments in back, and install two new bays—and she told us to survey our customers to find out if many of them are retirees who go to bed early and wake up late and wouldn't use our service. And find out when the others leave for work in the morning and come home at night."

"So you have to do a survey."

"Yes. Three or four questions, maybe—nothing complicated. Like the two I mentioned and 'How long have you been our customer?'"

"How many years have you been our customer," Jason murmured reflexively.

"Oh, yeah, right. More precise, isn't it?" Audrey said. "But the point is, do you know what it costs to write to 1,000 customers?"

He crunches the numbers in his head. Postage to send out the survey. Postage prepaid to have it mailed back. Paper and printing. One envelope outbound and one inbound. Stuffing the outbound and opening and coding the inbound. "Minimum of $1.50 a survey," he says, "if your kids do the stuffing and opening and encoding. Maybe more. You generate labels from your computer, so you don't pay for labels, which saves a mint, maybe 25 cents a name."

"Right. A \$1.50 times 1,000. Plus the kids' time, if I can pry them away from Little League, MTV, and personal calls."

"You don't need to survey 1,000 customers, you know."

"Whaaat?"

"Pick 100 at random from your computer list. You'll get a 10 percent margin of error and save \$1,350, plus the kids' time."

"That's hard to believe."

"But it's true," he said. "Look, why don't you take some of the money you save, and instead of just sampling 100 from your existing customer base, also do a separate survey of every 20th person from the Chamber of Commerce directory. You'll have one survey of customers and another of potential customers, and you'll still end up saving over \$1,000."

She thought for a moment. "The banker will never believe this," she objects.

"The next time I make a deposit, I'll explain it to her."

"You do that," she said, "and we'll wax your car every three months for the next two years."

Jason was excited by the idea of having his car washed and waxed at no charge. He knew he was trading consulting services cheaply for automotive services, but it felt free, so the next day when he went to the bank he approached the new bank officer—the new market development VP, actually—with carefully disguised excitement. This was going to be more fun than working for money.

Gosh, she was a tall woman. Jasmine Rogers. Thirty-five, he guessed, 6 feet 2 inches or even 6 feet 3. Hard to tell when she was sitting. She sat grandly behind a mahogany desk in a cubicle with three glass walls. But the back wall was covered—by sports memorabilia. A basketball shirt said, "Morgan State—African Tour, 1985," and there was another shirt that said, "Harvard B-School Intramurals." There were crossed field hockey sticks, too, and a boomerang and a picture of her holding the boomerang with small folks he supposed were Australian nationals casting admiring glances at this tall American woman.

She came out to greet him and propelled him—almost lifted him—to a seat in her cubicle.

"So, what's up, Jason? Are we taking good care of you? Do you need another dozen computers? What?"

"I want to talk to you about the survey you asked Audrey to make. She and Juan own the Chevron station . . ."

"Oh, sure. Audrey and Johnny. Good people . . . Say, if you are thinking of getting a BMW, I can give you a good rate on a loan."

"Well, I'm not in that bracket, Jazz . . . Look, you told Audrey to take a survey of her customers, and that's what I want to discuss."

"I didn't intend her to have to hire a high-powered business consultant."

"Well, actually, this is more or less a favor, you see . . ."

She chuckled. He thought she had a nice disposition for a banker. "A favor? By any means did she offer to wax your car about a million times for this favor? I had to turn down that particular offer, being her loan officer. Conflict of interest, you know. But if you want to help her, hey, I say that's great."

"Well, this is no big deal, Jazz. More or less a back-of-the-envelope computation, you see. Except I did it in my head, as there was no envelope handy."

"In your head? Impressive. I was on the math team in high school . . ."

"Here's the thing. Audrey was about to do a census of her customers . . ."

"A census? Surely not a survey of *all* her customers. I want just a sample. She must have misunderstood."

"Well, that's the thing . . . I mean, I believe that a sample of maybe 100 customers will do the trick."

"I took marketing research in B-school, Jason, and while I certainly don't want to break Audrey's back, a sample of 100 seems kind of . . . well, thin."

"Maybe I can convince you."

"Maybe." She steepled her fingers thoughtfully and smiled wickedly. "Are you a betting man, Jason?" She placed a tall glass tumbler holding several dozen drinking straws between them. "I am willing to bet you cannot convince me."

1. Well, we've set the stage for you. Now see if you can anticipate how Jason will convince Jazz to accept a small sample rather than the larger sized sample she obviously has in mind. Assume Jason wants to win this battle of wits. What would he argue?

[Instructor will provide additional material.]

"Let me jump ahead here, Jason, because lunch approaches rapidly. I am willing to settle for a 95 percent chance of correctly locating the population proportion of retirees within an interval . . ."

2. Assume Jason interrupts Jazz before she specifies her error interval. What will Jason come back with if he is mentally calculating sample size?

[Instructor will provide additional material.]

Jazz leaned forward and grasped Jason's left hand with her right hand, to prevent him from writing formulas in the air, and held up the index finger of her left hand for attention. "One second, Jason. I am willing to bet you this," she extracted one drinking straw from the glass, "this valuable drinking straw, that I can tell you the formula to use. We take .2 and multiply by .8, and divide by 100 (which is your proposed number of subjects), and take the square root, which is, um . . ."—she rolled her eyes to the ceiling—"which is .04. And we multiply by 2. So the 95 percent confidence interval extends between .20 plus and minus 0.08, from .12 to .28." She laughed merrily and moved the straw closer to her side of the desk. "Come on, Jason, play this game to win. I won't take it out on Audrey."

3. Is Jazz correct? Or has Jason won this point? What will Jason tell Jazz to do to improve her estimate?

[Instructor will provide additional material.]

4. Assume Jason lets Jazz keep the straw even though she could have done her calculation differently. What might be considered Jazz's error(s)?

[Instructor will provide additional material.]

"OK, I'll give that to you, Jason, a sample of 100 will give me all the precision I want for that question. But what about the next question, 'What time do you leave your home in the morning to go to work?'"

5. Jason's being put through his paces here. What should his answer be this time? Look at the nature of the second question to determine the correct formula to use.

[Instructor will provide additional material.]

She reached into the tumbler and withdrew another straw. "Wait just a second, Jason. I will bet you this straw that you don't know the standard error of the sample until after you have taken the sample."

6. This is Jason's last chance to impress Jazz . . . and win. What must he know, and where might he have gotten this information, for a quick answer to the standard error of the sample?

[Instructor will provide additional materials.]

7. So, what's Jason's final rebuttal?

"OK, Jason, you win. You have convinced me. If she can retrieve 100 surveys, I'll be satisfied. But I'll bet she will have to send out 200 surveys to get 100 replies."

Source: The authors adapted this case from their Chapter 9 Close-Up, *Business Research Methods,* 6th edition. Used with permission of Pamela S. Schindler and Donald R. Cooper, © 2001.

McDonald's Tests Catfish Sandwich

Nashville, Tennessee—McDonald's Corp. is trying to hook customers in southern test markets, including one in Kentucky, on a new catfish sandwich.

The chain is serving its newest sandwich in Bowling Green, Kentucky; Memphis, Chattanooga, and Jackson, Tennessee; Huntsville, Alabama; Jonesboro, Arkansas; and Columbus, Tupelo, Greenville, and Greenwood, Mississippi, said Jane Basten, a marketing specialist for McDonald's in Nashville.

The sandwich consists of a 2.3-ounce catfish patty, lettuce, and tangy sauce served on a homestyle bun.

The company will evaluate the sandwich based on sales and supply availability after a six-week ad campaign ends in mid-April.

"The advertising will be similar to what we're doing right now with the grilled steak sandwich," Basten said. "We will promote it to the fullest and see what happens."

The Catfish Institute, an industry promotion association based in Belzoni, Mississippi, is supplying the catfish.

Catfish Institute director Bill Allen said catfish farmers, processors, and marketers are "very excited about this prospect for our industry. This is super good news.

"But we don't want to get our hopes up too much and start thinking this is going to be our salvation, because we already have a viable industry."

Allen said that catfish firms that remember earlier tie-ups with major restaurant chains such as Church's Fried Chicken are cautiously optimistic about the McDonald's deal.

Questions

1. The management team for new product development was interested in assessing the relevancy of the chosen test markets to the three states designated for rollout if the test market was satisfactory (Tennessee, Alabama, and Georgia).
   a. What are your conclusions about the representativeness of the test cities to the designated rollout states?
   b. What secondary data should you present to support your conclusions? Where will you obtain this data?

Source: "McDonald's Tests Catfish Sandwich" (March 18, 1992, p. 10), used with permission of *Marketing News.* Case notes used with permission of William R. Dillon, Thomas J. Madden, and Neil H. Firtle, *Marketing Research in a Marketing Environment,* 3/e, 1994, Irwin. Used with permission of The McGraw-Hill Companies.

Medical Laboratories

Your hospital does medical tests on-site whenever possible but sends more complicated or technologically advanced tests to a commercial testing facility. About 70 percent of your lab tests are done at an outside medical laboratory.

You have been quite pleased with your outside medical lab, but it has just announced a 20 percent increase in its fees and claims that its lab is merely passing on increasingly higher costs of performing medical tests. It says that commercial medical laboratories across the country have had low profit margins for years because of the high costs of doing technologically sophisticated medical tests. A 20 percent increase would have serious consequences for your own profit margin and might require cutting down or eliminating other services within the hospital.

To study this problem, you have collected a random sample of 16 medical laboratories across the country. The laboratories chosen for study are indicated below. You have five years of data covering the years 1986–1990 for each of these 16 labs. The data file on the accompanying CD is named MEDLABS.

Questions

Use these data to undertake a study of the financial health of these laboratories. As your measure of financial health, you have chosen to use OPASSTS, net operating assets in millions of dollars.

1. Use an appropriate statistical method to characterize OPASSTS.

2. What factors influence OPASSTS? How?

3. Does your study shed any light on the claims made by your own medical laboratory?

4. Prepare a summary of these matters for presentation at a meeting next week.

Variable	Label	
FIRM	1 = Enzo Biochem Inc.	10 = Damon Corp.
	2 = Nichols Institute	11 = Damon Group Inc.
	3 = Princeton Diagnostic Labs	12 = Diagnostic Sciences Inc.
	4 = United Medical Corp.	13 = FCS Labs Inc.
	5 = Vivigen Inc.	14 = Keystone Medical Corp.
	6 = American Cytogenetics	15 = National Imaging Inc.
	7 = Bio Reference Labs Inc.	16 = Unilab Corp.
	8 = Compuchem Corp.	
	9 = Consolidated Imaging	
YEAR	Year, 19XX	
PPE	Property, plant, and equipment—Total (net), in millions of $	
ASSETS	Current assets—Total, in millions of $	
LIAB	Current liabilities—Total, in millions of $	
OPASSTS	Net operating assets—Total, in millions of $	

Source: These data come annually from Standard & Poor's COMPUSTAT® Databases, Standard & Poor's Compustat, a division of McGraw-Hill, Inc., New York, NY. Copyright © by McGraw-Hill, Inc. Used with permission of Peter G. Bryant and Marlene A. Smith, *Practical Data Analysis: Case Studies in Business Statistics,* Irwin, 1995.

NCR: Teeing Up a New Strategic Direction

NCR Country Club (NCRCC) started in 1954 as an employee benefit of the National Cash Register Co. but is now an open-membership club. This country club located in Kettering, Ohio (near Dayton), hosts two 18-hole golf courses. The NCR South course, a par 71 championship course of 6,824 yards of heavily wooded rolling countryside, the site of the 1996 PGA Championship, the 1986 U.S. Open, and the 1998 U.S. Mid-Amateur, is consistently ranked by *Golf Digest* as one of the top 100 courses in the United States. The prairie-links style of the North course, a 6,358-yard par 70 course, is considered challenging. In southwestern Ohio, the active golf season usually lasts from May through October. Within a 30-minute radius of NCRCC, the avid golfer will find eight other private golf and country clubs as well as 29 public golf clubs and courses.

In 1997, after the purchase of NCR Corporation by AT&T, AT&T provided a $4.0 million interest-free loan to raze the original clapboard-sided clubhouse and replace it with an all-brick colonial-style facility. Boasting both formal and informal, inside and outside eating facilities as well as banquet and party rooms, the members voted that the new clubhouse would be totally smoke-free. The rich cherrywood paneling and the hunter green and burgundy décor mellow the high-ceiling, interior spaces. Golf memberships are $20,000 with social (nongolf) memberships at $1,000 each. NCR employees did not and do not pay membership fees to join. Additionally, each member must spend $150 per quarter in dining receipts and pay $225 (golf) or $160 (social) in annual dues.

Needing to attract new members to support the renovated facility after AT&T divested itself of NCR and given the growing age of its members, NCRCC implemented an aggressive membership campaign in 1998. The goal was to bring golf memberships to 680 and attract as many social memberships as possible. After only moderate success, NCRCC commissioned McMahon Group to assist with strategic planning.

McMahon Group specializes in providing research and strategic consulting to golf clubs and full-service golfing facilities. "Golf club membership within the United States is perceived as a discretionary luxury of life. NCR faces a similar situation found elsewhere in clubs around the country—an older satisfied membership which sees no reason to change what they perceive to be a good thing," shared Frank Vain, president of McMahon Group. "With NCR, we faced another wrinkle. Because NCR was once corporately owned, NCR retirees and current employees saw membership as an entitlement, a right."

After McMahon's First Impressions visit (a free on-site assessment where a club specialist tours facilities, collects information on membership and operations, and discusses industry trends with strategic planning committees), NCRCC's board hired McMahon to provide direction and assistance to NCRCC's strategic planning committee. "Historically, NCRCC has a 7 percent penetration rate among NCR employees. NCR's employee pool was trending smaller, providing continuing downward pressure on NCRCC membership," explained Vain. "With membership segments of NCR retirees (1/3 of members) and current NCR employees (another 1/3 of members) getting less numerous each year, only the segment comprised of non-NCR affiliates provides an opportunity for growth. NCRCC needs to become a stand-alone club to survive."

McMahon Group conducted six focus groups at NCRCC on December 3–4, 1998, involving 43 members, seven nonmembers, and 12 employees. Especially among younger members (under 46) and nonmembers, a golf-only club was less attractive than the full service array that some other area country clubs offered. A consistent theme was that members did not feel they received the overall level of service at NCRCC that they expected from a fine private country club, whether it be in the dining operation or on the golf course. Staff members were frustrated that meeting the board's profit directive was often counterproductive to a high level of service. The NCRCC board directed McMahon Group to conduct a membership study to explore the feasibility of adding additional facilities, including swimming and fitness facilities to attract younger adults and families with children.

McMahon Group distributed mail surveys to 1,650 members and their spouses in January 1999 (see Exhibit C-NCR 1–2). A return rate of 57 percent and 48 percent, respectively, netted 886 usable surveys. Data were interpreted at ±3% (or ±0.1) at the 95 percent confidence level. Due to McMahon's extensive consulting and research experience with golf facilities nationwide, it was able to compare NCRCC's membership survey results with those of members of 80 other country clubs.

Overall, 72 percent of NCRCC members were either satisfied or very satisfied. This is slightly less than the 79 percent satisfaction level for other clubs. Only 12 percent are very satisfied, with other clubs averaging 21 percent. The group with the highest dissatisfaction rate (19 percent dissatisfied or very dissatisfied) was the key 55–64 age group, with the under 46 group generating 11 percent dissatisfaction. While members currently saw the club as an "Adult Golf and Dining Club" (63 percent), many believed its future would need to incorporate facilities for children, if the club were to remain competitive for new members. This was especially true for those members under age 46.

Most current members joined for golf (80 percent either important or very important) or dining (77 percent either important or very important). Most members were satisfied with golf (81 percent either satisfied [29 percent] or very satisfied [69 percent]). However, level of satisfaction was lower with the over 65 group when it came to course layout (58 percent very satisfied) and condition (77 percent very satisfied). Fewer members were satisfied with dining (49 percent either satisfied or very satisfied). However, even given some dissatisfaction, 61 percent felt their membership was a good value.

The 37th Hole, the casual dining facility, generated concerns about speed of service (27 percent either dissatisfied or very dissatisfied), professionalism of wait staff (19 percent either dissatisfied or very dissatisfied), and menu variety (36 percent either dissatisfied or very dissatisfied). The same concerns surfaced in the formal dining area, with menu variety and meal-to-meal consistency generating the highest dissatisfaction scores. It is very important for NCRCC to provide casual adult dining (95 percent either very important or important), but less so for casual family dining (78 percent), outdoor dining (69 percent), formal dining (44 percent), men's grill (37 percent), and women's grill (22 percent). Dining prices are seen as the same (65 percent lunch, 48 percent dinner) or higher (32 percent lunch, 47 percent dinner) than other clubs and restaurants frequented by members. Members overwhelmingly continue to endorse the no-smoking rule (97 percent formal dining, 94 percent 37th Hole, 83 percent bar/lounge).

"Members think of NCRCC as first a golf club, but the golf wasn't meeting expectations. Second, members see NCRCC as a dining club, but the members were dissatisfied with the casual dining product and service," shared Vain.

Survey results offered good and bad news. Additional facilities would not be attractions to most current members, but many members are interested in improving the current facilities. Fully 59 percent, however, were unwilling to pay higher dues (including 43 percent of under age 46) to obtain the changes they found attractive.

	% All Members	% Members under 46
Facility Additions		
Swimming pool	30	60
Tennis courts	22	36
Health and fitness center	30	49
Spa	30	58
Activities		
For adults	26	40
For families	23	53
For children	18	47
Current Facility Alterations		
Expanding bar/lounge	41% *Important or very important*	
Improving the driving range	36% *Important or very important*	
Improving short game practice area	40% *Important or very important*	

"New facilities were an attraction for the non-NCR affiliated segment," summarized Vain in discussing what McMahon Group shared with the strategic planning committee following the completion of the study. "New facilities, especially swimming, fitness, and outdoor dining, provide the best opportunity to broaden the attraction of the club."

Who Answered the Survey?

- 74% golf (single or family) and 24% social, with 2% corporate memberships.
- 65% are (23%) or had been (42%) employed at NCR.
- 55% male, 45% female.
- In each of four age groups:

Under 46	(19%)
46–55	(23%)
56–65	(26%)
66 or older	(33%)

- 74% lived within seven miles of NCRCC.
- 42% had been members for 20 or more years.
- 78% did not have children (under age 21) living at home.
- 41% belonged to a swimming/tennis club (15%) or fitness facility (26%).
- 81% reside in the Kettering-Dayton area year round.

Questions

1. Build the management-research question hierarchy, through the investigative questions stage. Then compare your list with the measurement questions asked.

2. Given the research question, how appropriate were the measurement questions?

3. Describe the sampling strategy. How appropriate were the various sampling design decisions?

4. What, if any, problems did you find with the questionnaire as a whole? Consider structure, directions, question order, question phrasing, appropriateness of response strategy chosen, etc.

5. If you were McMahon Group, how would you present the findings of your study to the NCRCC board? Explain the rationale for your chosen method.

6. Given the data presented in the case:

   a. What would you recommend to the board of NCRCC with respect to adding facilities like tennis courts, a swimming pool, a spa, a fitness center, and a year-round driving range?

   b. What would you recommend to the board of NCRCC with respect to adding or changing programming activities like social activities for adults, families with children, and children?

   c. What would you recommend with respect to changing current operations?

Source: Frank Vain, president, McMahon Group, provided the instrument and data with the permission of Larry Appleby, general manager, NCR Country Club in November 1999. Used with permission of Pamela S. Schindler and Donald R. Cooper, © 2000.

	Total %	Age Under 46 %	46-55 %	56-65 %	Over 65 %	Gender Male %	Female %	Member MBR %	Spouse %	Children? Yes %	No %	Member Tenure 1990-prior %	1991-1994 %	1995-now %	Membership Status NCR emp %	NCR Ret or RIFd %	Assoc. MBR %	Membership Class Family %	Single %	Other %	Mean
Swimming Pool																					
Very important	14	37	16	7	5	13	16	13	16	35	8	6	20	27	23	6	17	15	9	18	
Important	16	23	16	17	11	14	18	15	18	24	18	18	15	26	15	12	22	15	10	24	
Neutral	13	9	13	12	15	13	11	12	11	13	13	13	9	14	14	14	14	14	12	15	
Unimportant	11	7	11	12	13	12	11	13	10	8	12	11	7	8	10	12	17	11	12	15	
Very unimportant	46	25	43	53	56	48	44	49	43	23	53	58	42	24	55	61	28	49	57	31	
TOTAL Count	797	149	183	209	245	421	326	475	322	175	594	468	94	213	181	309	259	375	207	204	2.40
Tennis Courts																					
Very important	8	20	9	4	3	7	9	8	8	20	4	4	7	17	12	4	10	8	6	14	
Important	14	16	18	12	12	14	14	13	15	17	13	1	21	14	14	15	17	12	17	24	
Neutral	18	22	14	17	19	17	18	18	19	22	16	14	23	18	15	20	14	14	17	26	
Unimportant	13	14	13	14	12	12	15	12	14	12	13	13	12	13	12	24	15	15	15	11	
Very unimportant	47	28	46	53	55	49	45	49	44	29	53	58	41	26	54	41	28	50	45	13	
TOTAL Count	777	146	185	206	230	412	320	459	318	171	581	455	92	207	179	295	258	366	198	198	2.23
Health/Fitness																					
Very important	12	21	15	9	6	10	13	11	13	22	9	7	14	12	13	6	19	11	14	14	
Important	19	28	21	20	10	18	21	19	20	23	18	14	28	26	24	15	21	20	21	21	
Neutral	20	18	23	19	19	20	21	20	21	21	20	20	21	21	16	18	24	14	15	30	
Unimportant	14	13	13	11	21	16	13	16	14	14	15	17	13	11	14	18	9	17	17	15	
Very unimportant	34	22	28	41	43	37	32	35	29	20	39	43	26	20	33	42	28	45	21	21	
TOTAL Count	769	148	179	198	229	410	312	463	306	173	569	454	92	203	176	297	253	368	196	193	2.59
Enlarge Bar/Lounge																					
Very important	14	23	17	14	6	16	10	16	11	15	14	13	19	14	22	7	18	15	8	8	
Important	27	30	32	27	22	28	24	28	26	30	26	25	34	28	34	27	22	30	27	22	
Neutral	27	23	23	32	32	25	30	25	31	24	28	25	25	34	20	30	30	23	20	43	
Unimportant	19	19	20	18	21	19	22	18	20	22	19	21	15	17	14	21	20	20	22	16	
Very unimportant	13	4	8	14	19	11	15	12	13	9	14	16	7	6	7	16	10	13	14	13	
TOTAL Count	847	158	189	219	264	437	344	510	337	182	629	507	97	219	187	334	274	400	221	214	3.11
Improve Driving Range																					
Very important	14	20	18	15	5	18	9	15	11	21	12	11	24	17	22	8	19	15	19	5	
Important	22	33	24	23	13	23	20	24	19	25	21	19	22	28	27	16	25	29	19	10	
Neutral	40	30	34	42	51	36	46	38	45	32	42	42	40	34	34	49	36	34	38	58	
Unimportant	14	13	15	12	16	13	16	13	16	12	15	17	10	13	17	14	11	14	13	13	
Very unimportant	10	4	9	8	15	11	9	11	9	9	11	12	4	6	5	13	9	8	11	13	
TOTAL Count	815	155	191	212	240	432	314	501	314	178	629	490	92	209	186	316	264	395	220	183	3.15

	Very Important N	Important N	Neutral N	Unimportant N	Very Unimportant N	Mean
Short game practice area	13/17	27/31	38/35	14/12	8/4	3.21
Year-round driving range	11/22	28/35	29/24	15/12	17/8	3.00
Add spa	10/25	20/33	22/17	15/11	33/13	2.60

Percent of sample/percent of under 46

EXHIBIT C-NCR 1–2   NCR Country Club Membership Survey[*]

INSTRUCTIONS:

Please complete the questionnaire, answering all questions that pertain to your interests at the Club. If you do not participate in a particular Club activity and do not feel qualified to respond to the questions regarding that activity, please leave those questions blank or indicate "No Opinion" and move on to the next question. *Note:* Space is provided at the end of the questionnaire for your written comments and suggestions.

Completed questionnaires should be mailed in the enclosed postage-paid envelope by the date printed on the cover letter directly to McMahon Group at 884 Woods Mill Road, Suite 201, St. Louis, MO 63011.

IMPORTANT: Completely fill in the ovals that correspond to your answers for each question with either a pen or a pencil. The surveys will be electronically scanned. Please do not make extra marks on the questionnaire except in the space provided for written responses at the end of the survey.

> Fill in your answers like this   ●
>
> Not like   ☑   or   ⊗   or   ◎

1. Please indicate your "overall" satisfaction with NCR Country Club:

(5) Very Satisfied	(4) Satisfied	(3) Neutral	(2) Dissatisfied	(1) Very Dissatisfied
○	○	○	○	○

2. Which of the following best represents what you feel (1) is currently and (2) should be the primary purpose of NCR Country Club? (Please mark only one per column.)

	(1) *Currently*	(2) *Should be*
A *family* oriented, full service country club with activities for children.	○	○
An *adult* oriented, full service country club with *limited* activities for children.	○	○
A golf *and* dining club primarily for adults.	○	○
A golf club primarily for adults.	○	○

3. Using a scale from "5" (Very Important) to "1" (Very Unimportant), how important were each of the following to you in your decision to join NCR Country Club?

	(5) Very Important	(4) Important	(3) Neutral	(2) Unimportant	(1) Very Unimportant
To meet new friends	○	○	○	○	○
Club location					
—in relation to home	○	○	○	○	○
—in relation to work	○	○	○	○	○
Club social functions	○	○	○	○	○

(continued)

[*]This survey has been reformatted from its original design to fit the specifications of this text. Neither the questions nor the essence of the design has been modified.

	(5) Very Important	(4) Important	(3) Neutral	(2) Unimportant	(1) Very Unimportant
Friends were/are members	○	○	○	○	○
Parents were/are members	○	○	○	○	○
Exclusivity of club's members	○	○	○	○	○
Affiliation with NCR Corporation	○	○	○	○	○
Competitive initiation fee	○	○	○	○	○
Private parties/banquets	○	○	○	○	○
Reputation of club	○	○	○	○	○
Dining	○	○	○	○	○
Golf	○	○	○	○	○
Availability of 36 holes of golf	○	○	○	○	○
"Top 100" ranking of golf course	○	○	○	○	○

4. Please indicate your satisfaction with these characteristics of your Club's Board of Trustees, Committees, and Management:

	(5) Very Satisfied	(4) Satisfied	(3) Neutral	(2) Dissatisfied	(1) Very Dissatisfied
BOARD					
Communication with the membership	○	○	○	○	○
Degree to which board is representative of membership	○	○	○	○	○
COMMITTEES					
Effectiveness of Club committees	○	○	○	○	○
MANAGEMENT/STAFF					
Effectiveness of Club management	○	○	○	○	○
Responsiveness to member questions and suggestions	○	○	○	○	○
Overall level of service provided by Club's management & staff	○	○	○	○	○

5. Please indicate how important each of the following Club activities/services is to you and also how satisfied you are with each:

Rating scale: 5 = Very satisfied, 4 = Satistifed, 3 = Neutral, 2 = Dissatisfied, 1= Very dissatisfied, N.O. = No opinion

Rating scale: 5 = Very important, 4 = Important, 3 = Neutral, 2 = Unimportant, 1 = Very unimportant, N.O. = No opinion

	SATISFACTION						IMPORTANCE					
	5	4	3	2	1	N.O.	5	4	3	2	1	N.O.
Golf	○	○	○	○	○	○	○	○	○	○	○	○
Dining	○	○	○	○	○	○	○	○	○	○	○	○
Club social functions	○	○	○	○	○	○	○	○	○	○	○	○
Private parties	○	○	○	○	○	○	○	○	○	○	○	○
Children's activities	○	○	○	○	○	○	○	○	○	○	○	○
Family activities	○	○	○	○	○	○	○	○	○	○	○	○

6. Please respond to the following statement: "I receive good value for the cost of my membership at NCR Country Club."

(5) Strongly Agree	(4) Agree	(3) Neutral	(2) Disagree	(1) Strongly Disagree	No opinion
○	○	○	○	○	○

7. Please respond to the following statement: "There are a sufficient number of social activities at the club that appeal to my age and interest group."

(5) Strongly Agree	(4) Agree	(3) Neutral	(2) Disagree	(1) Strongly Disagree	No opinion
○	○	○	○	○	○

8. Do you have access to the Internet?

   ○ Yes   ○ No

   Are you aware the club has an Interent website?

   ○ Yes   ○ No

   Would you like e-mail notifications from the Club on a regular basis?

   ○ Yes   ○ No

9. Please indicate your satisfaction with the following aspects of the Club's newsletter, *The Mulligan,* and also Club communication in general.

Newsletter Content	(5) Very Satisfied	(4) Satisfied	(3) Neutral	(2) Dissatisfied	(1) Very Dissatisfied
Notification of upcoming events	○	○	○	○	○
Membership activities and stories	○	○	○	○	○
Club business (reports from board committees)	○	○	○	○	○
Newsletter appearance/format	○	○	○	○	○
Newsletter timeliness	○	○	○	○	○
Club communication in general	○	○	○	○	○

Section II. Golf

IF YOU ARE NOT FAMILIAR WITH THE GOLF FACILITIES AND OPERATIONS, PLEASE SKIP TO THE NEXT SECTION OF THE QUESTIONNAIRE.

10. Please indicate your satisfaction with these aspects of the SOUTH and NORTH golf courses:

Rating Scale: 5 = Very satisfied, 4 = Satisfied, 3 = Neutral, 2 = Dissatisfied, 1 = Very dissatisfied, N.O. = No opinion

	SOUTH COURSE						NORTH COURSE					
	5	4	3	2	1	N.O.	5	4	3	2	1	N.O.
Course layout	○	○	○	○	○	○	○	○	○	○	○	○
Overall course condition	○	○	○	○	○	○	○	○	○	○	○	○
Course landscaping (flowers and plantings)	○	○	○	○	○	○	○	○	○	○	○	○
Tee box condition	○	○	○	○	○	○	○	○	○	○	○	○
Condition of fairways	○	○	○	○	○	○	○	○	○	○	○	○
Condition of greens	○	○	○	○	○	○	○	○	○	○	○	○
Condition of bunkers	○	○	○	○	○	○	○	○	○	○	○	○

	SOUTH COURSE						NORTH COURSE					
	5	4	3	2	1	N.O.	5	4	3	2	1	N.O.
Irrigation	○	○	○	○	○	○	○	○	○	○	○	○
Drainage	○	○	○	○	○	○	○	○	○	○	○	○
Condition of cart paths	○	○	○	○	○	○	○	○	○	○	○	○
Course restrooms	○	○	○	○	○	○	○	○	○	○	○	○
Availability	○	○	○	○	○	○	○	○	○	○	○	○
Condition	○	○	○	○	○	○	○	○	○	○	○	○
Availability of drinking water	○	○	○	○	○	○	○	○	○	○	○	○
Beverage cart availability	○	○	○	○	○	○	○	○	○	○	○	○

11. Please indicate your satisfaction with these aspects of the golf operations at the Club:

(answer survey for question 11 on the following page)

	(5) Very Satisfied	(4) Satisfied	(3) Neutral	(2) Dissatisfied	(1) Very Dissatisfied	No Opinion
Golf Pro Shop						
Interior appearance	○	○	○	○	○	○
Pro Shop cleanliness	○	○	○	○	○	○
Merchandise selection	○	○	○	○	○	○
Pro Shop service	○	○	○	○	○	○
Pro Shop prices	○	○	○	○	○	○
Pro lessons	○	○	○	○	○	○
Bag drop service	○	○	○	○	○	○
Bag storage and club cleaning service	○	○	○	○	○	○
Cart service	○	○	○	○	○	○
Cart cleanliness	○	○	○	○	○	○
Practice range						
Condition	○	○	○	○	○	○
Size	○	○	○	○	○	○
Range ball condition	○	○	○	○	○	○
Speed of play	○	○	○	○	○	○
Tournaments						
Quality	○	○	○	○	○	○
Value for price	○	○	○	○	○	○
Format of tournaments	○	○	○	○	○	○
Adult golf programs (i.e., leagues)	○	○	○	○	○	○
Junior golf programs	○	○	○	○	○	○
Tee time reservation system	○	○	○	○	○	○
Halfway House						
Hours of operation	○	○	○	○	○	○
Service	○	○	○	○	○	○
Menu variety	○	○	○	○	○	○

12. How do you feel about the overall use of the golf course as it now exists at the club?

	(5) Excessive	(4) Somewhat Excessive	(3) Fine as Is	(2) Not Quite Dissatisfied	(1) Not Enough
Amount of time available for casual, open member play	○	○	○	○	○
Amount of time permitted for guest use	○	○	○	○	○
Amount of time available for junior play	○	○	○	○	○

(continued)

	(5) Excessive	(4) Somewhat Excessive	(3) Fine as Is	(2) Not Quite Dissatisfied	(1) Not Enough
Number of member-scheduled events/tournaments	○	○	○	○	○
Number of nonmember outings on Mondays	○	○	○	○	○
Number of nonmember outings on days other than Mondays	○	○	○	○	○

13. Please respond to the following statement: "If the Club had a caddy program I would support the program and use caddies on a regular basis when I play golf."

(5) Strongly Agree	(4) Agree	(3) Neutral	(2) Disagree	(1) Strongly Disagree	No opinion
○	○	○	○	○	○

14. Please indicate your satisfaction regarding these aspects of the dining in the 37th HOLE, the MEMBERS' DINING ROOM, and for PRIVATE PARTIES:

Rating scale: 5 = Very satisfied, 4 = Satisfied, 3 = Neutral, 2 = Dissatisfied, 1 = Very dissatisfied, N.O. = No opinion

	37th HOLE						MEMBERS' DINING ROOM						PRIVATE PARTIES					
	5	4	3	2	1	N.O.	5	4	3	2	1	N.O.	5	4	3	2	1	N.O.
Service:																		
Staff appearance	○	○	○	○	○	○	○	○	○	○	○	○	○	○	○	○	○	○
Speed of service	○	○	○	○	○	○	○	○	○	○	○	○	○	○	○	○	○	○
Friendliness of wait staff	○	○	○	○	○	○	○	○	○	○	○	○	○	○	○	○	○	○
Professionalism/ training of wait staff	○	○	○	○	○	○	○	○	○	○	○	○	○	○	○	○	○	○
Food:																		
Quality—Food well prepared	○	○	○	○	○	○	○	○	○	○	○	○	○	○	○	○	○	○
Food presentation (visually pleasing)	○	○	○	○	○	○	○	○	○	○	○	○	○	○	○	○	○	○
Meal-to-meal consistency	○	○	○	○	○	○	○	○	○	○	○	○	○	○	○	○	○	○
Menu variety	○	○	○	○	○	○	○	○	○	○	○	○	○	○	○	○	○	○

(continued)

	37th HOLE						MEMBERS' DINING ROOM						PRIVATE PARTIES					
	5	4	3	2	1	N.O.	5	4	3	2	1	N.O.	5	4	3	2	1	N.O.

Other:

Ambiance/décor of rooms	○	○	○	○	○	○	○	○	○	○	○	○	○	○	○	○	○	○
Wine list/selections	○	○	○	○	○	○	○	○	○	○	○	○	○	○	○	○	○	○
Value for the price	○	○	○	○	○	○	○	○	○	○	○	○	○	○	○	○	○	○
Party planning assistance	○	○	○	○	○	○	○	○	○	○	○	○	○	○	○	○	○	○
Party follow-up by staff	○	○	○	○	○	○	○	○	○	○	○	○	○	○	○	○	○	○

15. How important is it for the Club to provide each of the following dining styles?

	(5) Very Important	(4) Important	(3) Neutral	(2) Unimportant	(1) Very Unimportant
Casual adult dining	○	○	○	○	○
Casual family dining	○	○	○	○	○
Formal dining (coat & tie required)	○	○	○	○	○
Outdoor dining	○	○	○	○	○
Men's grill	○	○	○	○	○
Women's grill	○	○	○	○	○

16. How do the Club's prices compare to the prices charged for similar meals at other clubs and restaurants you visit regularly? Please compare similar dining experiences (i.e., dining in the 37th Hole should be compared to dining in a casual, grill-type restaurant and dining in the Members' Dining Room should be compared to a more upscale-type restaurant).

The Club's prices are . . .	(5) Much Lower	(4) Lower	(3) About the same	(2) Somewhat Higher	(1) Much Higher
Lunch	○	○	○	○	○
Dinner	○	○	○	○	○
Private parties	○	○	○	○	○
Social events	○	○	○	○	○
Wine	○	○	○	○	○
Cocktails	○	○	○	○	○

17. Please respond to the following statement: "The clubhouse should remain a totally nonsmoking facility."

(5) Strongly Agree	(4) Agree	(3) Neutral	(2) Disagree	(1) Strongly Disagree	No opinion
○	○	○	○	○	○

Section IV: The Future

18. Listed below are examples of new facilities or additional services the Club may consider adding in the future. Using a scale from "5" (Very important) to "1" (Very unimportant), please indicate how important you feel each item is to the future of the Club.

	(5) Very Important	(4) Important	(3) Neutral	(2) Unimportant	(1) Very Unimportant
Add a swimming pool	O	O	O	O	O
Add tennis courts	O	O	O	O	O
Add a health/fitness facility	O	O	O	O	O
Add paddle tennis courts	O	O	O	O	O
Add a bowling alley	O	O	O	O	O
Add spa facilities (sauna, steam room, Jacuzzi, etc.)	O	O	O	O	O
Provide more social activities	O	O	O	O	O
Provide more family activities	O	O	O	O	O
Provide more children's activities	O	O	O	O	O
Add a year-round driving range	O	O	O	O	O

19. Listed below are examples of improvements to the existing Club facilities that may be considered in the future. Using a scale from "5" (Very important) to "1" (Very unimportant), please indicate how important you feel each item is to the future of the Club.

	(5) Very Important	(4) Important	(3) Neutral	(2) Unimportant	(1) Very Unimportant
Enlarge the bar/lounge	O	O	O	O	O
Enlarge the banquet room to better accommodate large functions such as weddings	O	O	O	O	O
Provide better pedestrian access	O	O	O	O	O
Improve the golf driving range	O	O	O	O	O
Improve the golf short game practice area	O	O	O	O	O
Modify the North Course where possible to make it more challenging	O	O	O	O	O
Modify the South Course where possible to make it more challenging	O	O	O	O	O

20. *a.* Please respond to the following statement: "I would be willing to pay somewhat higher annual dues in order to make the Club more private and provide a higher level of service."

(5) Strongly Agree	(4) Agree	(3) Neutral	(2) Disagree	(1) Strongly disagree
○	○	○	○	○

b. How much of an annual dues increase would you be willing to pay to make the Club more private and provide a higher level of service? (Please mark only one.)

○ Nothing   ○ 20%

○ 5%   ○ 30%

○ 10%   ○ 40%

○ 15%   ○ 50% or more

21. At present, the Club allows nonmember outings on the golf course on Mondays as well as other days of the week. These outings generate substantial revenue for the Club, which helps to keep member dues lower than they would be without this revenue. However, these outings also reduce member access to the courses, add wear and tear to the courses, and limit the amount of time available for course maintenance.

Please respond to the following statements.

a. "The Club should eliminate outings on days of the week other than Mondays, and I would be willing to pay an additional $100 in annual dues for improved course access and to make up for this lost revenue."

(5) Strongly Agree	(4) Agree	(3) Neutral	(2) Disagree	(1) Strongly Disagree	No Opinion
○	○	○	○	○	○

b. The Club should eliminate half the outings on Mondays and all outings on days of the week other than Mondays and I would be willing to pay an additional $300 in annual dues for improved course access and to make up for this lost revenue."

(5) Strongly Agree	(4) Agree	(3) Neutral	(2) Disagree	(1) Strongly Disagree	No Opinion
○	○	○	○	○	○

c. The Club should eliminate all outings, both on Mondays and other days of the week, and I would be willing to pay an additional $500 in annual dues for improved course access and to make up for this lost revenue."

(5) Strongly Agree	(4) Agree	(3) Neutral	(2) Disagree	(1) Strongly Disagree	No Opinion
○	○	○	○	○	○

22. Please respond to the following statement: "One of the golf courses should always be open for member play on Mondays."

(5) Strongly Agree	(4) Agree	(3) Neutral	(2) Disagree	(1) Strongly Disagree	No Opinion
○	○	○	○	○	○

23. Some clubs include additional fees such as locker rental, bag storage, shoe-shine service, and driving range in the annual or monthly dues. At NCR Country Club, additional charges such as locker rental and shoe-shine service are optional services and fees and are billed as separate items.

Please respond to the following statement: "Over the next few years NCR Country Club should move in the direction of bundling all fees and charges (such as locker rental and shoe-shine service) into one dues amount to be paid annually."

(5) Strongly Agree	(4) Agree	(3) Neutral	(2) Disagree	(1) Strongly Disagree	No Opinion
○	○	○	○	○	○

Section V: About You

24. Your membership classification is (spouses of members—please mark the membership classification of your husband or wife):

    ○ Family, Golf   ○ Corporate   ○ Social

    ○ Single, Golf   ○ Nonresident

25. Which of the following best describes your membership status?

    ○ Current NCR employee   ○ Retired or RIF'd NCR employee   ○ Associate member

26. What is your gender?

    ○ Male   ○ Female

27. What is your age category?

    ○ Under 36   ○ 46–55   ○ 66–75

    ○ 36–45   ○ 56–65   ○ Over 75

28. How many miles is your home from the Club?

    ○ 0 to 3 miles   ○ 8 to 15 miles

    ○ 4 to 7 miles   ○ More than 15 miles

29. How many miles is your business from the Club?

    ○ 0 to 3 miles   ○ 8 to 15 miles

    ○ 4 to 7 miles   ○ More than 15 miles

30. When did you first become a member of NCR Country Club?

    ○ 1970 or before   ○ 1981–1985   ○ 1991–1994

    ○ 1971–1980   ○ 1986–1990   ○ 1995–present

31. Do you have any children age 21 or younger living in your home?

    ○ Yes   ○ No

32. What other types of clubs do you belong to in the Dayton area? (Please mark all that apply.)

    ○ Another Golf/Country Club   ○ City/Dining Club   ○ Fitness/Health Club

    ○ Swim/Tennis Club   ○ Fraternal Club   ○ None

33. How much of the year do you reside in the Dayton area?

    ○ Year round   ○ 6 to 8 months

    ○ 9 to 11 months   ○ Less than 6 months

Written Comments and Suggestions

Please provide any comments and suggestions you may have regarding the FUTURE DIRECTION OF THE CLUB:

If you could improve EXISTING OPERATIONS OR SERVICES at the Club, what would you improve?

What do you feel NCR Country Club needs to do to ATTRACT MORE MEMBERS?

The Board of Trustees thanks you for helping us in the evaluation of your Club. Please send the survey back to the McMahon Group in the enclosed envelope.

Very truly yours,

McMahon Group, Inc.

Overdue Bills

Your employer, Quick Stab Collection Agency (QSCA), is a bill-collecting agency in an eastern town. The company specializes in collecting small accounts. QSCA does not deal in large accounts and does not take on risky collections, such as those in which the debtor tends to be chronically late in payments or is known to be hostile.

To distinguish itself from competing collection agencies, the company wants to establish a reputation for collecting delinquent accounts fast. The marketing department has just suggested that QSCA adopt the slogan "Under 60 days or your money back!!!!!" At the last staff meeting in which this slogan was proposed, the marketing department was asked how it arrived at the number 60. You found the reply unsatisfactory at best: "Well, uh, 60 sounded like a nice round number."

Since you work as an accountant at QSCA, you look at account balances all of the time. In fact, you suspect that the number of days to collect the payment is related to the size of the bill. If this is the case, you may be able to estimate how quickly certain accounts are likely to be collected, which, in turn, may assist the marketing department in determining an appropriate level for the money-back guarantee.

To test this theory, you've taken a random sample of accounts closed out during the months of January through June. The data set includes the initial size of the account and the total number of days to collect payment in full. Because QSCA deals in both household and commercial accounts in about the same proportion, you've collected an equal number from both groups. The first 48 observations in the data set are residential accounts and the second 48 are commercial accounts.

The data are in the file named OVERDUE on the accompanying CD.

Variable	Label
LATE	Number of days payment is overdue.
BILL	Dollar amount of the overdue bill.

Questions

1. What must you do during data preparation to enable you to compare commercial and household accounts?

2. Is the "60-day" money-back guarantee supported?

Source: Used with permission of Peter G. Bryant and Marlene A. Smith, *Practical Data Analysis: Case Studies in Business Statistics,* Irwin, 1995.

Performance Evaluations

Ann, an independent contractor who specializes in human resources issues, has been asked by the XYZ company to undertake an independent study of its employee performance evaluation practices. XYZ, a nonprofit organization, is a professional review organization in the health care industry. Most of its revenue comes from government contracts for Medicare and Medicaid utilization reviews.

The employee performance appraisal involves a fairly complex mix of subjective and objective scoring. Each evaluator fills out a form that covers 11 categories of employee performance, such as adaptability, accountability, communication and decision-making skills, sensitivity to cost-effectiveness issues within the organization, attendance, and training and development of other employees.

Nonsupervisory personnel are evaluated on 8 of the 11 categories; supervisory and management employees are rated on all 11 categories. The same form is used for all employees, although the weight applied to each category varies with the employee's grade and responsibilities. Weights are assigned in such a way that any employee can receive a final score anywhere from 0 to 200. Higher scores mean better performance.

Each employee has an evaluation initiated on the 12-month anniversary of his or her hire date, so evaluations go on at XYZ throughout the year. Any employee who is a new hire, has been transferred between departments, has been promoted, or has been demoted is considered to be on probation. These employees are given three-month evaluations in addition to the annual evaluations.

Accurate performance appraisals are important. They provide feedback on an employee's contribution to the company, and the annual appraisal score is used to determine merit raises. When this appraisal system was introduced several years ago, evaluators attended extensive training sessions designed to ensure as much consistency and fairness as possible. In spite of this, employee complaints continue to surface. Ann's job is to uncover any nonwork-related biases in the evaluation process.

Concerns expressed by the employees at XYZ include the following.

- Evaluators are occasionally late with their evaluations. Rumors at the company suggest that the later the evaluation, the lower the score, as the manager may be attempting to postpone a controversial or hostile discussion with the employee about poor performance.

- There may be interdepartmental biases. Some managers may be attempting to raise their own department's status and salaries by artificially inflating the evaluation scores.

- Scores may be bumped up a few points to push a favored employee into the next higher raise category.

Variable	Label
SCORE	Evaluation score in points.
LAG	Difference between the due date of the evaluation by the manager and the day on which the results are discussed with the employee, in days.
EMP@EOY	Years with the company at the end of the year.
POS@EOY	Years in the current position at the end of the year.
TYPE	Type of evaluation (0 = 3 month evaluation, 1 = annual evaluation).
GRADE	Employee's grade scale: 1–7 are clerical or technical; 8–9 are skilled employees; 10–12 are supervisory; 13–17 are management.
DEPT	Employee's department number.
EDUC	Employee's education level: 12 is high school grad; 13 is one year training beyond high school (e.g., secretarial training); 14 is two years beyond high school (i.e., associate's degree, nursing diploma); 16 is bachelor's degree; 18 is master's degree; 20 is Ph.D.
EMP@EVAL	Years with the company at the time of the evaluation.
POS@EVAL	Years in the current position at the time of the evaluation.

- Three-month probationary evaluations are considered unnecessary by the employees, because three months is generally not enough time to adjust to a new position or reach the peak level of efficiency in a new job.

- There are rumors that the company is attempting to force early retirement by giving the long-time employees lower scores than others.

Ann has a sample of 144 employee evaluations conducted over the past calendar year; 10 variables were collected from each employee record as described below. The first 125 observations in the data set on the accompanying CD refer to employees who were still employed at XYZ at the end of the year; the remaining group left the company at some point during the year.

Question

1. What should Ann recommend?

Source: Used with permission of Peter G. Bryant and Marlene A. Smith, *Practical Data Analysis: Case Studies in Business Statistics,* Irwin, 1995.

Ramada Demonstrates Its *Personal Best*

In 1996 the latest D. K. Shifflet survey of customer satisfaction in the hospitality industry showed mid-tier hotels continuing their downward trend in perceived customer service, reflected by more and more respondents giving ratings on customer service in the 7 or lower range on Shifflet's 10-point scale. While Ramada's satisfaction rates held steady, "It was only a matter of time before we experienced the problem," says Tim Pigsley, director of operations for Ramada Franchise Systems (RFS). Shifflet research highlighted three critical areas for study that could influence customer satisfaction: hiring (finding the best people to deliver Ramada's brand of exceptional service), training (giving employees the tools to deliver exceptional service), and motivation (providing the impetus for Ramada employees to deliver exceptional service).

Unlike some of its competitors, RFS is a totally franchised system. In such an environment, not only must headquarters contend with the variable human factor of all service operations, but additionally, RFS must contend with differing "exceptional service" standards among owners of the nearly 900 Ramada properties. "Due to the franchised system of property management, we needed for each management team and each employee to be committed to the change—to buy in to any new program—whatever shape it would take," explains Pigsley.

Research

"We wanted to learn and borrow from the best so we started with Disney. In every study done, the Disney experience is the benchmark for exceptional customer service. And they have a reputation for hiring the best people." Next, RFS approached Southwest Airlines. "They have captured the essence of 'fun' when air travel is seen as a commodity, a hassle. People disembarking Southwest planes have smiles on their faces," shares Pigsley. Next Ramada's fact-finders approached Carlson Hospitality, owners of restaurant TGI Friday's. "We wanted to understand what Carlson did to generate their low employee turnover, and high employee loyalty and commitment."

Ramada's individual property owners do their own hiring. The process differs widely from property to property. Ramada called on research firm Predictive Index to identify characteristics that were indicative of self-motivated performers. Ramada also brought in American Hotel and Motel Educational Institute to learn what other companies were doing correctly to identify and hire the right people.

RFS also wanted direct, face-to-face employee input into the process of developing new programs in hiring, training, and motivation. "But this was a daunting prospect with more than 31,000 employees, many of whom spoke a language other than English," explains Pigsley. Twenty-four researchers spanned out to visit each of Ramada's 900 properties within a six-month period. "To bring about change in corporate culture and mindset would take more than employees checking off boxes on a piece of paper," claims Pigsley. So Ramada launched the research project more like the opening of a new hotel—a festive atmosphere, complete with food and comedic entertainment. Headquarters staff arrived at each property, usually spending the morning extracting issues and information from management. Then in an atmosphere evocative of a new hotel launch, employees were invited to share their ideas and concerns about the three initiatives. Employee suggestions and needs flowed as freely as the food and beverages. The information collection team recorded employee and management input on a detailed summary form generated for each property.

Research with employees revealed the current training approach was boring and ineffective. Most training involved videotapes, developed internally or purchased, with new hires or groups of employees watching the videos. RFS's benchmarking research with the hospitality industry's stellar examples of exceptional customer satisfaction, however, demonstrated that training incorporating high employee involvement generates more knowledgeable employees, one of the critical elements of customers' perceptions of higher quality customer service. And training approaches that involve "fun" are winners with all employees—no matter what position they fill—and are more likely to generate a positive employee attitude, a second critical element of exceptional customer service.

It was standard industry practice for employee motivation programs to develop around a limited number of big-ticket rewards. Employees indicated that they had a hard time maintaining enthusiasm for a program that took too much effort to achieve one or a limited number of rewards over a long time. RFS found that more numerous awards that directly affect their everyday lives motivate employees.

Before Ramada started on its program of change, it knew it would need to document the program's success. So it hired Unifocus to conduct in-depth guest surveys at every property as the *Personal Best* program rolled out. Additionally, it continues to subscribe to D. K. Shifflet's syndicated research on customer satisfaction.

Management Decisions

In hiring, Ramada property managers now screen prospective employees for characteristics revealed by Predictive Index. RFS scrapped its traditional training, replacing it with interactive, CD-based, multimedia training. Self-paced learning now drives the lighthearted, 24-component training sequence. Property managers, who often do not hire large numbers of employees at any one time, are pleased with the more flexible approach and employees find the process more interesting.

The newly devised motivation program focuses on rewarding employees, not only for exceptional performance reflected in customer letters and surveys, but also for supervisor and peer nominations, completion of training modules, and continued self-directed efforts for personal development by employees. "We had had grandiose ideas of awarding big-ticket items like airline tickets to the vacation of a lifetime, but after listening to employees, we substituted certificates for shoes at FootLocker, lunch at Macaroni Grill, and free tanks of gas. We literally have hundreds of reward partners in the *Personal Best* program," reveals Pigsley, "all related to the way our 31,000 employees spend their personal time."

By many standards the *Personal Best* initiative is a success.

- In the latest D. K. Shifflet service ratings, Ramada's scores in the 8–10 range (good to exceptional) were up 30.5 percent, and its scores in the 1–4 range (unacceptable to poor) were down 24 percent.

- Employees are cashing in exceptional service points for a growing number of rewards each year.

- *Personal Best* is no longer just a human resources program but an overall strategic planning initiative. Employees' stories of exceptional customer service are prominently reflected in Ramada's advertising, and RFS has committed $8 million over the past three years to sharing these stories.

"Ramada's *Personal Best* hospitality advertising campaign (winner of the travel industry's most prestigious advertising award: HSMAI's Best of Show) is a reflection of our commitment to the employee of Ramada franchises," says Steve Belmonte, president and CEO of RFS, Inc. One spot's closing line, "At Ramada, we throw ourselves into our work," sums up the effort that Ramada is placing on customer satisfaction—an effort that won it the 1999 American Express "Best Practice" award.

Questions

1. Build the management-research question hierarchy for Ramada.

2. Apply the research process model to the Ramada research initiative.
   a. Explain the role and process of exploration in Ramada's research.
   b. What role did secondary data play in the exploration phase of the research?
   c. What steps and phases in the process model can you match to the Ramada research?
   d. What research process decisions were made? (Remember to include research by outside suppliers.)
   e. What sampling methodology was used? Why was this appropriate for this study?
   f. Describe the research design and discuss its strengths and weaknesses.
   g. What role did property owners/managers play in the research design?
   h. Why did Ramada choose to conduct the research in a nontraditional, party-like atmosphere? What are some advantages and disadvantages of such an approach?

3. How are the research findings reflected in the ultimate management decisions?

Source: This case was developed from interviews with and material provided by Tim Pigsley, director of operations for Ramada Franchise Systems. Used with permission of Pamela S. Schindler and Donald R. Cooper, © 2001.

Retailers Unhappy with Displays from Manufacturers

Supermarket executives are unhappy with manufacturer-provided displays, according to a recently released study by the Howard Marlboro Group (HMG), New York.

Of the 129 members of HMG's Retail Advisory Board who were surveyed, 60 percent indicated they were at most marginally satisfied with their current racks.

Reasons for dissatisfaction included such things as the racks were ineffective for inventory control, they used space poorly, and they did not aid consumers in shopping, the study said. Retailers also noted many of the racks were unattractive and did not fit their store's décor.

Although supermarket executives were not enthused with most manufacturer-provided racks, they rated L'eggs displays the best, the study said. The retailers indicated the racks had a "consistent presentation and appearance," and that the company showed its support by regularly providing renewal parts for the displays, according to the survey.

HMG also questioned retailers on their use of interactive merchandising systems (IMS).

Forty-five percent of the retailers already use at least one IMS, and these displays are used in a variety of departments, the study said, including generic grocery, meat and seafood, spices, and electrical and hardware.

Seventy-seven percent of the retailers surveyed said IMS use will continue to increase, the report found, and 93 percent were interested in learning more about the systems.

Raid, the popular insecticide, has developed an Insect-A-Guide to help people learn about the pests they're trying to kill. The in-store display features various Raid products arranged under a color code to help consumers pick the right spray for the right bug. A flip chart gives information on the habits of insects and suggests ways to "knock 'em dead." The unit, designed by the Howard Marlboro Group, New York, can be arranged in three configurations to accommodate various store sizes.

Question

1. Design an experiment to test the new display for Raid. Be sure your design will test for both customer and retailer satisfaction with the display.

Source: "Retailers Unhappy with Displays from Manufacturers" (October 10, 1988, p. 21), used with permission of *Marketing News*. Case notes used with permission of William R. Dillon, Thomas J. Madden, and Neil H. Firtle, *Marketing Research in a Marketing Environment*, 3/e, 1994, Irwin. Used with permission of The McGraw-Hill Companies.

Rubbergate

Frank works as the statistician for a large lobbying group based in Washington, D.C. His job is to collect all sorts of data for his firm, prepare various reports and summary statistics, and serve as a spokesperson for the group whenever necessary.

The House banking scandal (dubbed by the media as "Rubbergate") has created quite a bit of talk within Frank's firm. The Rubbergate scandal has disillusioned a large number of U.S. voters, who believe that part of the current economic crisis is related to the lack of fiscal responsibility on the part of their chosen representatives. The CEO of Frank's firm suspects that the public outrage over bounced checks will cause a significant turnaround in upcoming elections. Needless to say, the firm does not wish to commit time or resources toward lobbying Congresspersons who will not likely be in office in the near future.

Frank has collected a random sample of 146 members of the 1992 House of Representatives, which may be found in the file named RUBBERG8 on the accompanying CD. Eight characteristics were collected about each representative.

Questions

Frank must prepare a report that characterizes the data set. In particular, what are Frank's responses to the following questions?

1. What is the general nature of the sample in terms of average and typical fluctuation around the average for the variables named SERVICE, AGE, VOTES, DISTRICT, and STATE?

2. How do these variables differ in a comparison of check-bouncers and check-nonbouncers?

3. How does party affiliation enter into the analysis?

Variable	Labels
CHECKS	Whether the representative wrote bad checks (1 = bad check; 0 = no bad checks).
PARTY	Political affiliation: 1 = Democrat; 0 = Republican (no independents are in the sample).
SERVICE	Total number of calendar years in service in the House of Representatives (service beginning in November or December is not counted as a year).
AGE	The representative's age in years.
VOTES	The percent return for the most recent election in which the representative participated.
DISTRICT	Population of representative's home district in thousands to the nearest thousand.
STATE	Population of the representative's home state.
BADCHKS	Number of bad checks written.

4. For those individuals who did write bad checks, summarize the total number of bad checks written in some appropriate fashion.

Source: This case is based on data provided to us by Chris A. Wilson. The data come from three sources: *Politics in America,* Congressional Quarterly, Inc., Washington, DC, 1991, pp. 9–12; *Vital Statistics on Congress 1991–1992,* Congressional Quarterly, Inc., Washington, DC, 1992, pp. 214–231; and *Rocky Mountain News,* "The House List," Friday, April 17, 1992, pp. A50–A51. Used with permission of Peter G. Bryant and Marlene A. Smith, *Practical Data Analysis: Case Studies in Business Statistics,* Irwin, 1995.

State Farm: Dangerous Intersections

State Farm Insurance has a rich history of proactive safety involvement in auto and appliance design to reduce injury and property loss. In June 2001, State Farm Insurance, Inc., released the second report in its Dangerous Intersection reporting series. State Farm modeled its program after an initiative by the Insurance Corporation of British Columbia, Canada (ICBC), and the American Automobile Association of Michigan (AAA) to help position the nation's largest auto insurer as the most safety-conscious insurer. ICBC had patterned its program on an earlier effort in Victoria, Australia. AAA, in turn, benchmarked its program on the ICBC program. AAA invited State Farm to help fund one of its intersection studies. State Farm saw this as an opportunity to expand its effort into a nationwide campaign in 1999. "The 2001 study is part of a larger effort focused on loss prevention and improving the safety of intersections around the U.S.A.," shared State Farm research engineer John Nepomuceno. State Farm has allocated significant resources as well as funds to the initiative. Since its inception, every city with an intersection on the overall list of dangerous intersections is eligible to apply for a $20,000 grant to defray the cost of a comprehensive traffic engineering study of the intersection. Additionally, each city named to the national top 10 dangerous intersection list is eligible for a grant of $100,000 per intersection to defray some of the cost of making improvements. All totaled, State Farm offered $4.44 million to the safety initiative in its first year.

Due to its large market share, State Farm is the only U.S. insurer in a position to mine its databases for the requisite information on accidents to come up with a viable U.S. list. But it found that although it had the interest to do so, its data warehouse did not have sufficient information to tally accident rates for intersections. To rectify this, in 1998 State Farm included a location field as part of the data that its claims adjusters regularly complete. This location information, in open-text format, indicates whether the accident took place in an intersection or as part of an incident related to an intersection accident, and identifies the intersection. Following the 1999 study, the fields for identifying intersections were further refined.

In the first study using 1998 data (reported in June 1999) as well as the 2001 study, State Farm looked at accidents involving only intersecting roads. They excluded any accident that occurred at the intersection of a road and a highway access or egress ramp. State Farm also looked only at accidents where the State Farm–insured driver was at fault.

Because of the study's focus on road safety engineering, the first study ignored accident severity and made no attempt to isolate demographic (age or gender of driver, driving record, etc.) or geographic (weather conditions, population of area, etc.) factors related to the accident. It also looked only at State Farm's own internal incident reports, not at any public records involving traffic patterns or volume or police incident reports. Based on industry market share information, State Farm was able to estimate the total number of crashes at a given intersection. "There was good reason to exclude police reports and traffic counts," explained Nepomuceno. "The reporting threshold for police filing reports on accidents differs widely from jurisdiction to jurisdiction. Some will only fill out reports when personal injury or criminal behavior is involved. Others will fill them out only when a vehicle is damaged to the degree that it needs to be towed from the scene. Still others fill out such reports on every incident. Traffic volume reports are often prepared infrequently and often by independent sources. Not only may the data quality be questionable, but the time period in which the data was collected may not match our 1998 incident reports in every city involved. Also, when traffic volumes are factored in, low volume roads with relatively few crashes are often deprioritized. Now that we're through with the 2001 study, we are asking ourselves if intersection volume should be factored in, and if so, how it can be included without significantly increasing our effort in data processing."

In the 1998 study, State Farm identified 172 dangerous intersections. The top 10 most dangerous intersections in the United States were released publicly (www.state-farm. com). Public affairs staff for each state could request that up to 10 intersections be identified for their state. "This was usually determined by the resources that our local public affairs staff were willing to put toward the program," shared Nepomuceno. "Each state had to recognize a top 10 national intersection, but they could request that no more be released or that up to 10 intersections within their state be released." As of August 2001, 97 cities (56.4 percent) had applied for State Farm grants.

"While some in the media claimed we had 'hit a home run' with the program, we quickly learned that there was a lot more at stake than we had anticipated in generating goodwill with transportation engineers," indicated Nepomuceno. "This is, after all, a traffic safety program and we would not achieve that goal without having the cooperation of the traffic and transportation engineering community. First, while initially they lauded us for the attention our listing brought to traffic concerns, we and they soon discovered that the spotlight generated demand for immediate solutions, solutions that they often didn't have budgets to implement. Also, from their perspective, not all accidents are the same; locations with accidents that result in injuries and death should be given more attention. Some jurisdictions were upset that we didn't consider intersection volume and we didn't include accident rate data.[1] The fact that the State Farm grants were intended to study the intersection more completely wasn't always seen as a solution to their immediate problems."

To include accident severity, State Farm needed a measurement system for classifying accidents. For the 2001 study, which used 1999 and 2000 accident data, State Farm calculated a median property damage accident payout (approximately $1,700). Incidents requiring payout of more than the median amount were classified as "high severity"; those requiring less, "low severity." Additionally, State Farm chose to classify each accident using a multipoint scale. Zero was assigned to "no property damage, no personal injury" incidents and a higher number was assigned to "High property damage, personal injury" incidents, with numbers in between assigned to levels of property damage and personal injury (see Exhibit C-SF 1–1). Accident scores were summed to create an aggregate danger index for each intersection. Each intersection was then weighted by dividing the danger index by State Farm's market share in the area. Of the 224 intersections identified, the top 10 were released to the national media. Each of those 224 is now eligible for the $20,000 grant to study the intersection to identify specific improvements; the top 10 are also eligible for $100,000 grants for improvements. In this second round, State Farm has committed $5.48 million to the safety program.

State Farm is making plans to track the success of the Dangerous Intersection program. Once cities notify them of the completion of an intersection's improvements, State Farm will start tracking accidents for that intersection for a period of one year. The first post-improvement evaluation study is expected in 2002. Additionally, State Farm is taking steps to learn from the characteristics of the dangerous intersections. Each grant application for an affected city's study of a dangerous intersection must include:

- Collection and analysis of police report data.
- An engineer's "geometric review"[2] of the intersection.
- A capacity profile of the intersection.
- A traffic conflict study.[3]
- A benefit-cost analysis.
- A schedule of improvements (short-term, intermediate-term, and long-term).[4]

State Farm plans to use the new data to identify patterns of problems. This may lead to a model of desired intersection traits against which improvement plans can be assessed, further increasing the effectiveness of the loss prevention program and making life a little easier for the transportation engineers with whom they must partner to achieve safety success.

EXHIBIT C-SF 1–1 Danger Codes

	No Personal Injury	With Personal Injury
No property damage	0	Y
Low property damage	1	$1 + Y$
High property damage	X	$X + Y$

Questions

1. Identify the various constructs and concepts involved in the study.

2. What hypothesis might drive the research of one of the cities on the top 10 dangerous intersection list?

3. Evaluate the methodology for State Farm's research.

4. If you were State Farm, how would you address the concerns of transportation engineers?

5. If you were State Farm, would you use traffic volume counts as part of the 2003 study? What concerns, other than those expressed by Nepomuceno, do you have?

Sources: This case is based on information provided by John Nepomuceno in interviews that took place on August 9, 2001, and September 13, 2001. Other sources include: "Miami Area Intersection Tops State Farm List of Most Dangerous in the United States," State Farm press release, June 27, 2001 (http://www.statefarm.com/media/release/danger00.htm); "Research" (http://www.statefarm.com/media/methods.htm); and "State Farm 1999 Dangerous Intersection National Status List" (http://www.statefarm.com/media/statustop.htm); and "State Farm's Dangerous Intersection Initiative," Institute of Transportation Engineers press release, June 27, 2001 (http://www.ite.org/press_release.htm).

NOTES

1. Accident rate is calculated by dividing the number of accidents in a given period by the total traffic volume over the same period.

2. The intersection geometry or physical layout of the intersection can play an important role in influencing driver behavior at intersections. For example, a curve on the approach to an intersection may impede the sight distance to a traffic signal, preventing drivers from stopping in time. Or, a driver approaching two signalized intersections very closely spaced may see the traffic signals at both intersections and become confused about which traffic signal to obey.

3. A traffic conflict study is an observation study of traffic conflicts that do not necessarily end in an accident but have the potential to do so. Recording and studying observations of dri-

ver behavior is expected to help traffic engineers understand the same problems that result in collisions. Some examples of conflicts are the sound of sharply applied breaks; sudden, unsignaled lane changes; or drivers hitting their horns.

4. Short-term improvements might include sign changes, changes in lane markings, or signal-timing changes. Most short-term improvements can be implemented in less than two years. Intermediate-term improvements might involve lane widening, the addition of turn lanes, etc., and be accomplished within 2–5 years. Examples of long-term improvements include grade separation of the intersecting roads and can take 5–10 years to implement.

Sturgel Division

"Now that I write it all down, I see we have changed a lot!" mused Martha as she put the finishing touches on her annual status report. "In fact," she went on, "the name Information Services indicates most of the changes. We used to be Information Systems."

Martha was Information Services (IS) manager for the Sturgel Division of a major manufacturing company. Sturgel developed and manufactured (mostly small) household appliances on a 230-acre site in the southeast part of the United States. While she had managed the IS department for only 15 months, Martha had been part of the department for nine years, all at the same location.

The late 1980s and early 1990s were a time of many changes for the information systems departments in most companies, including the Sturgel Division. Technological change drove most of the organizational change: The price performance of most computer equipment had improved by compound rates of perhaps 30 percent per year for several decades. This meant that many companies perceived that they no longer needed a "computer center." Individual users could simply do whatever they needed to do on a desktop computer in their own offices.

Martha made a rough list of the major influences she'd dealt with over the last few years, calling them "IS Transitions." They included:

- From running the computer to providing information services to the company.

- From "owning" the data to consulting with user departments about use of the company's information resources.

- From emphasizing mainframes to emphasizing terminals, personal computers, and telecommunications. Indeed, sometimes it seemed that the telephone, word processing, and clerical and library departments had all been combined.

- From developing the company's applications to advising users on how to develop their own applications.

Each transition had been difficult, for each required its own combination of hardware, software, data, procedures, and people, most of which were different at the end of the transition.

Currently, the Information Services department had four sections, each with a manager who reported to Martha:

1. **Systems operations.** The systems operations section ran two mainframe computers and one minicomputer that operated as a telecommunications "node" and link to other divisions and corporate headquarters. This section provided operator support for three shifts of operation, as well as systems maintenance, operating system updates, and so forth. The vendor of the mainframes handled hardware maintenance.

2. **Application development.** The application development section really should be renamed, Martha thought. Most of its activities involved database design and maintenance, though two small groups developed financially oriented applications and maintained several software packages aimed at serving the (fairly small) engineering staff at Sturgel.

3. **PC services.** The PC services section developed division standards for personal computers at Sturgel and consulted with users who wanted PCs of their own. The users purchased PCs out of their own budgets, but they were required to meet certain hardware and software standards as set by IS. This section also evaluated general-purpose software, such as word processing and spreadsheet packages, and recommended to users when they should switch to a new version or release. They also did a fair amount of "hand holding" for users who had difficulty in developing their own applications.

4. **Telecommunications.** The telecommunications section maintained the local area network at the Sturgel site as well as links to corporate headquarters and other company divisions. This section also advised users on such activities as links to legal databases and information retrieval services, though that activity, thought Martha, might really fit better in the application development section.

Martha felt good about the organization in general. While it had been a bit of a scramble to develop an organization that could deal with the fast pace of technological change in the computer field, she felt they had more or less done it. One part of it still made her nervous, though. The biggest theme in all the changes, from an IS perspective, was the change from computing and running computers to serving large numbers of people directly.

She felt they were providing good service, but she had no regular way of knowing how her users perceived it. She thought she should consider a regular survey of her users and their perceptions of service received from the IS department. That way, she figured, she would be in a position to have data to back up her informal sense, and she would (presumably) learn about changes in those perceptions (for better or for worse) more quickly.

Questions

1. Martha would like you to develop an appropriate research design.
   a. What kind of survey should Martha run, or should she?
   b. How should it be administered?
   c. What kinds of forms, questionnaires, or other survey approaches should be developed?

Source: Used with permission of Peter G. Bryant and Marlene A. Smith, *Practical Data Analysis: Case Studies in Business Statistics,* Irwin, 1995.

The Brazing Operation

In one of the phases in manufacturing a precision flow meter, a vacuum brazing process is used to attach hardware to the flow meter tube. The process consists of placing the "fixtured" assembly in a sealed vacuum furnace, pumping a hard vacuum on the furnace, slowly heating the assemblies to approximately 2050 degrees Fahrenheit, and then rapidly cooling them down to the ambient temperature.

The company wants the assembly to have a metallurgical structure that resists corrosion. One aspect of such a structure is a good grain size, a measure of the size of the actual crystals in the crystalline structure of the flow wall. The grain size is measured by a standard specification called the grain count, a numerical reading between 1 and 10. The larger the grain count, the finer the crystalline structure (and the more corrosion resistant).

The data on the CD in the file BRAZING were gathered from process control charts. The run numbers are not consecutive because a variety of operations, not just the brazing operation, are performed in the furnace.

Variable	Label
RUN	Run number.
TEMPAVE	Average maximum temperature (degrees Fahrenheit).
TIMEAVE	Average time at the temperature (minutes).
VACLEVEL	Vacuum level (in torr units, higher numbers indicate a poorer vacuum).
COOLRATE	Cooling rate, in degrees Fahrenheit per minute.
GRNCOUNT	Grain count, in standard units, computed from a sample of the resulting product.

Question

1. Based on the data, what recommendations do you make concerning the brazing process?

Source: David R. Berge provided the data on which this case is based and described the manufacturing situation. Used with permission of Peter G. Bryant and Marlene A. Smith, *Practical Data Analysis: Case Studies in Business Statistics,* Irwin, 1995.

The Catalyst for Women in Financial Services

In 1996 Pamela K. Martens, Judith P. Mione, Roberta O'Brien, and 22 others filed a class action suit in U.S. District Court, New York, against Smith Barney and former Garden City, New York, office manager Nicholas Cuneo, citing a rash of complaints. These included "intimidation, retaliation, and humiliation," as well as lack of fairness in pay, denial of promotion, demotion due to maternity leave, unfairness in distribution of accounts, sexual harassment, and discharge without cause. Initially Cuneo was discharged, but when the plaintiffs did not drop their suit, he was reinstated as a sales agent. In May of 1998, Judge Constance Baker-Motley approved a settlement, which had been accepted by 23 of the 25 plaintiffs.

As part of the settlement in *Martens, et. al. v. Smith Barney* (S.D.N.Y., 96 Civ 3779), Smith Barney was charged with paying for a study of the issues underlying the suit. The female judge ordered a research project done by "Catalyst or other similar firm," one which understood the issues under study. "Catalyst is a nonprofit research and advisory organization working to advance women in business," shared project director Paulette Gerkovich. "There are no other firms that do exactly what we do, so we were the clear choice."

Catalyst, a New York firm, was hired and directed the subsequent research project designed to accomplish five goals:

- To assess employees' perceptions of their work environments.

- To examine why employees seek careers in the financial services industry, why they stay, and why they might leave.

- To examine the connection between perceptions of the work environment and job satisfaction, job commitment, and employees' intent to stay with their firms.

- To determine what barriers women face in advancing within their firms.

- To assess how employees balance the demands of work and personal life.

"Our prior research with women's issues provided several tested measurement questions that were suitable to use in this study," explained Gerkovich. Catalyst also conducted nine focus groups—two all-men, six all-women, and one mixed-gender group—to add insight to developing other measurement questions and clarify numerous concepts and constructs. At no time during the research did the plaintiffs, defendant, or the court influence the process.

Catalyst mailed the survey to approximately 2,200 potential respondents, men and women employed in the financial services industry. A second mailing was sent to the whole sample frame to increase the participation rate. 838 (38 percent) members of the sample responded, 482 women (57.5 percent) and 356 men (42.5 percent).

"Our prior research led us to believe that a gender gap would exist between men and women on some fundamental issues. So men's opinions were sought to give the women's opinions a context," said Gerkovich.

To measure job satisfaction, Catalyst used a multiple-item evaluation including current position satisfaction, satisfaction with employer, work schedule control, career advancement opportunities, opportunities for networking and mentoring, and compensation fairness. Only on "opportunities to network with influential clients" and "compensation fairness" did men and women differ significantly ($p < .05$). Women's greater dissatisfaction with these two constructs did not, however, significantly affect their overwhelmingly positive satisfaction with their current position and their employer (77 percent and 74 percent, respectively).[1]

EXHIBIT C-CATALYST 1–1   Barriers to Advancement of Women at Current Firm, by Gender

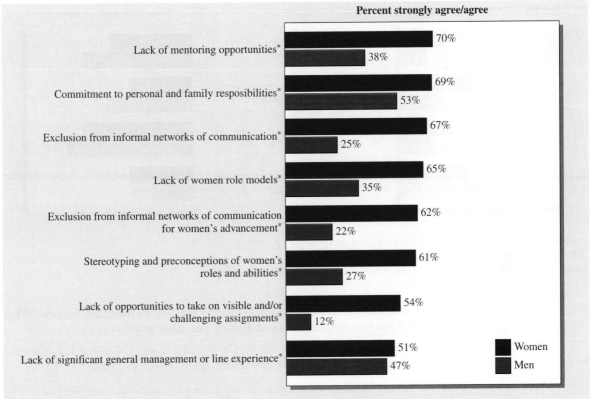

*Significant difference between women and men, $p < .05$.

"Because of our interest in advancing women in management, we were particularly interested in the factors that might lead a qualified woman to leave the profession," said Gerkovich. The executive summary of the findings noted: "Money appears to be a critical driver of intent to stay, both for men and women."

To assess barriers to advancement, Catalyst used a multiple-item 5-point scale exercise. As Exhibit C-Catalyst 1–1 shows, women's perceptions were significantly different compared to men's for almost all of these items.

As Exhibit C-Catalyst 1–2 shows, on four elements used to assess fairness (assignment of clients, opportunities for promotion, pay for performance, and rewards for performance), women again had significantly different perceptions compared to men ($p < .05$).

Court-ordered research, while not commonplace, has certainly become an accepted part of legal remedies. This study is now a benchmark measure for the financial services industry. While Smith Barney agreed to improve conditions as part of the settlement, the court did not mandate a follow-up study.

Questions

1. Discuss the potential conflicts between researcher (Catalyst) and research user (Smith Barney).

2. What constructs and concepts are inherent in this study?

3. What are the ethical considerations in this study?

4. Speculate on how the researchers created operational definitions for the constructs.

EXHIBIT C-CATALYST 1–2 Perceived Fairness of Reward Allocation, by Gender[**]

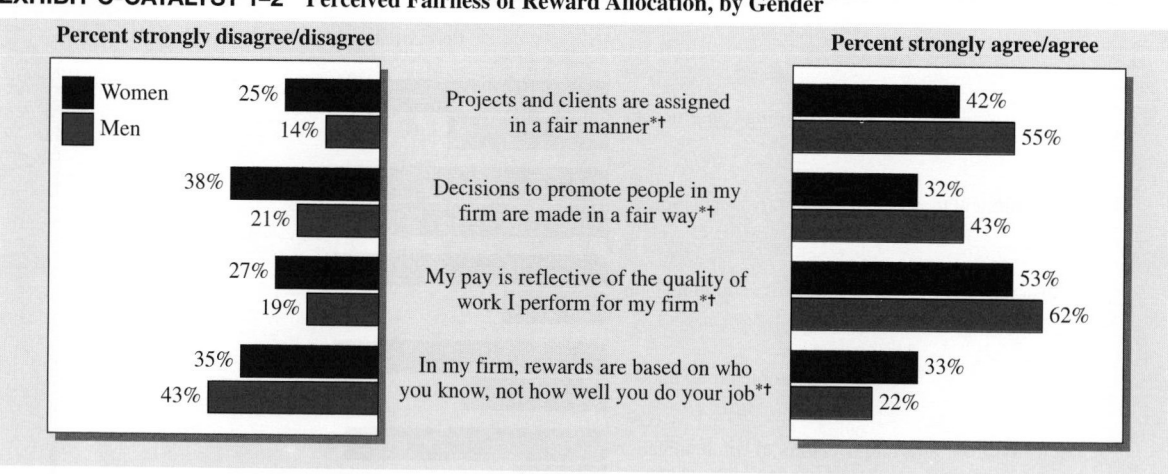

Percent strongly disagree/disagree | Percent strongly agree/agree

		Women	Men
	Projects and clients are assigned in a fair manner[*†]	25% (Women) / 14% (Men)	42% (Women) / 55% (Men)
	Decisions to promote people in my firm are made in a fair way[*†]	38% / 21%	32% / 43%
	My pay is reflective of the quality of work I perform for my firm[*†]	27% / 19%	53% / 62%
	In my firm, rewards are based on who you know, not how well you do your job[*†]	35% / 43%	33% / 22%

[*]Significant difference between women and men who strongly agree/agree, $p < .05$.
[**]Percent respondents choosing "neither agree nor disagree" not reported.
[†]Significant difference between women and men who strongly disagree/disagree, $p < .05$.

5. Assume that the limited findings presented here are all the study covered. What would you recommend that Smith Barney include in a follow-up study?

6. Evaluate the data displays in exhibit C-Catalyst 1–1 and C-Catalyst 1–2 as part of a research report. What recommendations, if any, would you make?

Sources: *Executive Summary, Women in Financial Services: The Word on the Street,* July 2001; and Interview with Paulette Gerkovich, project director, Catalyst, August 9, 2001.

NOTE

1. *Women in Financial Services: The Word on the Street,* Executive Summary, Catalyst, NewYork ©2001 (ISBN#0-89584-219-X), p. 4.

T-Shirt Designs

Julio has one semester left in his MBA program and is looking at paying back some hefty student loans. Even though he has had to borrow money to complete the program, he's decided it was a worthwhile investment. Nonetheless, Julio would like to repay some of his loans before graduating, if at all possible.

Julio has recently taken entrepreneurial and small-business classes and has decided to put some of this knowledge to work. He suspects that a number of his fellow students would be willing to shell out a few bucks for school memorabilia. Since summer is right around the corner, Julio is pretty sure that he can make some money by selling t-shirts to students on campus.

Informal conversations with people in the hallways have given him some ideas about popular t-shirt designs. Julio has narrowed down the possibilities to two. He's given sketches to a local t-shirt printing company, and they have made two prototype shirts. At this stage, Julio has no idea about the relative demand for the two t-shirt

T-Shirts Survey Questionnaire

I am trying to measure people's preferences for one of two different t-shirt designs. Please help me with my study by answering each of the following questions to the best of your ability. Do not put your name on this page because all responses should be anonymous.

1. My gender is

   1 = female

   0 = male

2. My current or most recent scholastic grade-point average on a 4-point scale is _____.

3. Circle the number that most accurately describes your attitude about the red and white t-shirts on the table.

   1 = I strongly prefer the red t-shirt to the white t-shirt.

   2 = I somewhat prefer the red t-shirt to the white t-shirt.

   3 = I like both equally, or am indifferent between the two.

   4 = I somewhat prefer the white t-shirt to the red t-shirt.

   5 = I strongly prefer the white t-shirt to the red t-shirt.

4. I am _____ years old.

5. My gross annual income for 1993 was $___. (If you were not gainfully employed, enter 0.)

6. I am (circle one)

   1 = left-handed

   2 = right-handed

   3 = ambidextrous (both left- and right-handed)

designs. If he's going to all the trouble and expense of having the shirts made up, it would be useful to know which of the two shirts is more popular.

The two shirts look something like this. The red shirt has a scoop neck and is made of 100 percent cotton. On the back of the shirt is a logo of the school. Under the logo are the words "PARTY TIME at PU UNIVERSITY!" Julio suspects that this shirt will mostly appeal to the party-goers.

The other shirt is more conservative. It is a white, button-placket, collared t-shirt made of 50 percent cotton and 50 percent synthetic materials. This shirt has a simple, and small, version of the school logo on the upper right-hand section of the front of the shirt.

Julio has decided to gauge the relative markets for his two t-shirts by running a quick survey. With permission from the student government, he has set up a table in the student union. The two prototype shirts are there for inspection, along with a survey designed to gauge people's reactions to the two shirts. He has a big sign over the table offering a free soft drink to all participants to induce people to stop by the table and participate in the survey. On the corner of his table is a big cardboard box with a slit in the top. Students are instructed to put their completed questionnaires in the box, thereby guaranteeing anonymity of the responses.

The data set is on the accompanying CD in the file named T-SHIRTS.

Variable	Label
GENDER	Female = 1, male = 2.
GPA	Current grade point average on the 4-point scale.
PREFER	Preference of red or white shirt (1, 2 = red; 3 = neutral; 4, 5 = white).
AGE	Age in years at the time of the survey.
INCOME	Gross annual income for 1993.
HANDED	Left-handed (= 1), right-handed (= 2), or ambidextrous (= 3).

Questions

1. Reconstruct the management-research question hierarchy.

2. Evaluate the sampling design.

3. How would you judge the quality of the survey instrument? Explain.

4. Interpret the data in reference to Julio's management dilemma.

5. Prepare a report about the preferences revealed.

Source: This case was based on a survey designed by M. A. Smith, who also wrote the survey questionnaire. Used with permission of Peter G. Bryant and Marlene A. Smith, *Practical Data Analysis: Case Studies in Business Statistics,* Irwin, 1995.

Violence on TV

As the general manager of KTDS, the NBC affiliate in Tidusville, Oklahoma, Chris has a range of responsibilities that include programming, personnel, advertising, and public relations. His least favorite activity is responding to customer complaints. Unfortunately, there's been an unusually large number of complaints in the past few months from viewers and advertisers alike.

Most of the recent comments are objections to the level of violence on KTDS programs. Chris is sensitive to this issue because he has observed a gradual increase in violence on TV over the past 20 years. Chris really prefers the old-time movies in which dirty deeds were neatly sanitized and violent crimes occurred behind the scenes. He is sympathetic to the recent callers.

Nonetheless, he's in a tight spot. Chris knows that small, vocal groups do not necessarily represent the population at large. People who feel strongly about an issue are likely to speak out, while those who are content tend to remain silent. While the recent callers have denounced the level of violence on KTDS shows, Chris knows he must understand and serve *all* of the KTDS viewers.

Chris has a suspicion about the source of the recent calls. Four months ago, a flamboyant politician announced his candidacy for mayor. This candidate has received a great deal of air time on the local news due, in part, to his impassioned outbursts. Some people love him, others despise him, but almost everyone tunes in to the evening news in hopes of catching the latest controversy. One continuing theme of his platform is violence in America in general and violence on KTDS in particular. Over the past four months, the candidate has suggested that those opposed to violence in the media "let their voices be heard." Chris suspects that this fellow has inspired a large portion of the recent complaints to KTDS.

Chris needs to sort all of this out. To understand the views of all KTDS patrons, he has commissioned you to undertake an opinion poll. A survey has been designed, and

94 telephone survey responses have been compiled. The results of the survey reside in the file named VIOLENCE on the accompanying CD and the actual survey included in this case. You'll need a copy of the survey to understand the numerical codings in the data set.

The survey design and data set compilation were undertaken by Ann Lee Bailey, an MBA student at the University of Colorado at Denver. The scenario has been altered to preserve the anonymity of the survey respondents.

The survey was done over a three-week period in October. Two hundred phone calls were made, and 106 people declined the invitation to participate in the survey. Of the 94 participating respondents, 2 were offended by the question of income and refused to answer that particular question. Nonresponses are indicated in the data set by an asterisk. A random selection of phone numbers from the Tidusville phone book was used to select the sample. Chris needs a report as soon as possible.

Violence on TV Survey

1. Gender   (0) male   (1) female

2. Age   (1) under 20   (2) 20–30   (3) 31–40   (4) 41–50   (5) over 50

3. Marital status   (0) married   (1) single or divorced

4. Do you have children at home?   (0) yes   (1) no

5. Household income

(1) under $20,000   (2) $20,000–$40,000   (3) $40,00–$60,000   (4) over $60,000

6. Education

(1) high school   (2) some college   (3) college graduate   (4) graduate school

7. How many hours per week do you watch TV?

(1) 0–7   (2) 8–14   (3) 15–21   (4) 22–28   (5) 29–35   (6) 36–42   (7) 43 or more

8. In your opinion, how violent are most TV programs?

(1) much too violent   (2) somewhat too violent   (3) violent
(4) a little violent   ,   (5) not very violent

Questions

1. What is Tidusville's perception of the level of violence on KTDS?

2. Does one's perception of violence on TV vary with gender, age, marital status, income, or education?

3. Do parents with children at home have a different tolerance for violence than those without children at home?

4. Do viewers who spend a lot of time watching TV become desensitized to violence?

Source: Used with permission of Peter G. Bryant and Marlene A. Smith, *Practical Data Analysis: Case Studies in Business Statistics,* Irwin, 1995.

Waste Paper[1]

Waste accompanies any production process. Waste may provide opportunity, as Harvey Mackay points out, but usually it's a problem.

In this case, the production process is a printing press that produces small books for a variety of customers. Data from 127 runs of this press, gathered over about a month, are provided on the accompanying CD in the file WASTEPAP.

An analyst expected the following variables to be important (at least potentially) in determining waste.

Variable	Label
OBS	The recorded observation or printing job.
NET	Number of books requested by the customer.
GROSS	Total number of books actually produced to satisfy the customer's request.
WASTE	The number of books wasted (WASTE = GROSS – NET).
PAGES	Total number of pages in the book (8, 16, 24, or 32); 8- or 16-page books can be handled with a single "web" of paper; 24- and 32-page books require two webs.
PAPER	Basis weight (in pounds) of the paper used.
COLORS	Number of colors printed (four is standard, but occasionally a single-color run is made and other variations occur, too).

In pricing its four-color services, the company assumes a certain amount of waste. Currently it assumes a common "waste factor" for each of the different sizes of books (8-page, 16-page, etc.). Price quotes for other than four-color books are handled separately, but the analyst wants to know whether the "waste factor" really should be the same for all sizes of four-color books.

Question

1. How would you advise the analyst?

Source: This case is based on a real situation, described to us by Don W. Hansen, VP Operations, American Web, Inc., who also provided the data. Used with permission of Peter G. Bryant and Marlene A. Smith, *Practical Data Analysis: Case Studies in Business Statistics* (Burr Ridge, IL: Irwin, 1995).

NOTE

1. See Harvey Mackay, "Why Waste Waste?" in *Beware the Naked Man Who Offers You His Shirt* (New York: William Morrow and Company, Inc., 1990), pp. 238–39.

Workload Ratings

Many organizations use opinion surveys as one part of their evaluation of managers or executives. The people being evaluated often wonder how fair these processes are. In particular, they wonder if they will somehow get lower ratings if they strictly enforce rules or set high standards for work.

In universities the same problem affects instructors, who complain about the student evaluations of the instructors and their courses. In particular, they complain that when instructors make students work hard, the students give them low ratings. Is this really true? (The students, in turn, often wonder if anyone ever looks at the evaluations they fill out, but that's another story.)

All of the fall 1987 students enrolled in classes offered by the University of Colorado at Denver College of Business and Administration evaluated each class using a standard form prescribed by the University's Board of Regents. Students responded to 12 questions, each of which was scored from 0 to 4 (0 = "F", 4 = "A"), and the class averages for the responses to each question were tabulated. These tabulations were provided to the instructor and given to deans, department chairs, and to the student government, which published them for general review.

For each of the 161 sections, the class averages for three of the questions are available in the file WORKLOAD on the accompanying CD. All of the numbers given are class averages for particular sections offered in fall 1987.

Variable	Label
CRSRTG	Rating for this course compared with your other university courses.
WORKLOAD	Rating for the work required for this course. (F = too little = 0, C = about right = 2, A = too much = 4).
INSTRTG	Rating for this instructor compared to your other university instructors (0 = failing, 4 = perfect).

Questions

1. Do WORKLOAD and INSTRTG appear to be related, based on these data?

2. Do they appear related if we adjust first for the effects of the course rating?

3. Do these data support the rumors about instructors being penalized for making students work hard?

Source: Used with permission of Peter G. Bryant and Marlene A. Smith, *Practical Data Analysis: Case Studies in Business Statistics* (Burr Ridge, IL: Irwin, 1995).

Xerox Abuses

Your firm is located in a 10-story building. Each floor has its own Xerox machine in a copy room. The firm owns these machines but must pay for paper, toner, and occasional maintenance. Each employee has a key that opens the copy room door on his or her floor only and does not have access to Xerox machines on other floors.

Because the Xerox machines are "free goods" right now, you suspect that the firm's Xerox costs could be cut pretty drastically. To test this theory, you have decided to perform an experiment. Each person on the 10th floor has been given a card that operates the 10th-floor machine. These employees have been told that their card will generate a daily accounting of their Xerox activity. Tenth-floor employees have also been told that they will not be *charged* for their use of the machine, but they certainly know that *someone* will have some sense of individual usage patterns.

To establish a basis of comparison, the group on the third floor has not been converted to the card system. The third-floor machine has an internal mechanism that totals the number of copies made each day, but you do not know *who* is doing *what,* and the third-floor employees have no reason to believe that they are being monitored. The 3rd and 10th floors have been chosen for this experiment because these two floors have had about the same usage rates in the past.

You have collected data from the two machines over the last 50 working days. The data are on the accompanying CD in the file named XEROX. This file has 50 observations and three variables:

Variable	Label
DAY	An indicator of the day data were extracted.
TENTH	The number of Xerox copies made on the 10th floor.
THIRD	The number of copies made on the 3rd floor.

Question

1. Use appropriate graphical or statistical techniques to determine whether the card accounting system will effectively lower inappropriate Xerox usage if implemented companywide.

Source: The scenario described in this case was related to the author by one of his students, who was employed at the firm when the Xerox machine experiment was undertaken. Used with permission of Peter G. Bryant and Marlene A. Smith, *Practical Data Analysis: Case Studies in Business Statistics* (Burr Ridge, IL: Irwin, 1995).

Appendixes

Core Business Reference Sources, Printed and Electronic[1]

101 Business Ratios: A Manager's Handbook of Definitions, Equations, and Computer Algorithms. How to Select, Compute, Present, and Understand Measures of Sales, Profit, Debt, Capital, Efficiency, Marketing, and Investment. (C. Sheldon Gates) McLane, 1993.

411 Stocks—http://www.411stocks.com/

A

ABI World—http://www.abiworld.org/

Accountants' Handbook. (Carmichael, D.R., Steven B. Lilien, and Martin Mellman, eds.) 6th ed. Wiley, 1996. 2v.

Accounting and Tax Index. UMI, quarterly and annual.

Accounting Desk Book: The Accountant's Everyday Instant Answer Book. (Tom Plank) 11th ed. Prentice-Hall, 2000.

Accounting Handbook. (Joel G. Siegel and Jai K. Shim, eds.) 3rd ed. Barron's, 2000.

Accounting Literature Index. (Jean Louise Heck et al., eds.) 4th ed. McGraw-Hill, 1996.

Accounting Research Directory: The Database of Accounting Literature. 3rd ed. Wiener, 1994.

Accounting websites (compiled by the American Accounting Association)—http://accounting. rutgers.edu/raw/aaa/links/accsites.htm

Ad*Access—http://scriptorium.lib.duke.edu/adaccess/

Advertising Age—http://www.adage.com/

Advertising Research Foundation—http://www.arfsite.org/

Advertising World (University of Texas)—http://advertising.utexas.edu/world/

AFL-CIO—http://www.aflcio.org/

AICPA Audit and Accounting Manual as of June 1, 1998. AICPA, annual.

AICPA Professional Standards as of June 1, 1997. 2v. AICPA, annual.

AICPA Technical Practice Aids as of June 1, 1996. AICPA, annual.

Almanac of Business and Industrial Ratios. Prentice-Hall, annual.

American Academy of Advertising—http://advertising.utexas.edu/aaa/

American Advertising Federation—http://www.aaf.org/

American Almanac of Jobs and Salaries. (John W. Wright) 2000–2001 ed. Avon Books, 2000.

American Arbitration Association—http://www.adr.org/

[1]Compiled by Judith L. Violette, MLS, Director of Library Services, Walter E. Helmke Library, Indiana University–Purdue University, Fort Wayne, IN.

American Association for Public Opinion Research—http://www.aapor.org/main.html

American Association of Individual Investors—http://www.aaii.com/

American Banker's Association—http://www.aba.com/default.htm

American Banker's Banking Factbook. American Banker, annual.

American Demographics—http://www.inside.com/default.asp?entity=AmericanDemo

American Enterprise Institute for Public Policy Research—http://www.aei.org/

American Finance Association —http://www.afajof.org/

American Institute of Certified Public Accountants—http://www.aicpa.org/

American League for Financial Institutions—http://www.alfi.org/

American Management Association—http://www.amanet.org/

American Marketing Association—http://www.MarketingPower.com/

American Public Health Association—http://www.apha.org/

American Salaries and Wages Survey: Statistical Data from More Than 300 Government Business News Sources. Gale, annual.

American Society for Public Administration—http://www.aspanet.org/

American Society for Training and Development—http://www.astd.org/

American Statistics Index. Congressional Information Service, monthly and annual.

American Stock Exchange—http://www.amex.com/

American Taxation Association—http://www.atasection.org/

Americans for Tax Reform—http://www.atr.org/

Americans with Disabilities Act Handbook. (Henry H. Perritt, Jr.) 3rd ed. Wiley, 1997.

AMEX Fact Book. American Stock Exchange, annual.

AMEX Glossary—http://www.amex.com/reference/glossary.stm

Annual Report Gallery, A–Z link—http://www.reportgallery.com/

Annual Reports Online—http://www.zpub.com/sf/arl/arl_www.html

Association of Consumer Research—http://www.acr_news.org/

AuditNet.org—http://www.auditnet.org/karlhome.htm

Ayer Glossary of Advertising and Related Terms. 2nd ed. Ayer, 1977.

B

Background Notes on Countries of the World—http://www.state.gov/www/background_notes/

Bank Administration Institute—http://www.bai.org/

Bank Marketing Association—http://www.aba.com/MarketingNetwork/default.htm

Barkley's Comprehensive Financial Glossary—http://www.oasismanagement.com/glossary/index.html

Barron's Finance and Investment Handbook. (John Downes and Jordan Elliot Goodman, eds.) 5th ed. Barrons, 1998.

Basic Business Library: Core Resources. (Bernard S. Schlessinger) 3rd ed. Oryx, 1995.

Basic Guide to Exporting. 1998 ed. U.S. Department of Commerce, 1998.

Biographical Dictionary of American Business Leaders. (John N. Ingham) Greenwood, 1983. 4v.

Biographical Dictionary of Management. (Morgan Nitzel, ed.) University of Chicago Press, 2001. 2v.

Blackwell Encyclopedia of Management. (Gary L. Cooper and Chris Argyris, eds.) Blackwell Business, 1997. 11v.

Bloomberg.com—http://www.bloomberg.com/

BNA's Human Resources Library. Bureau of National Affairs, update varies with format.

Book of the States. Council of State Governments, annual.

Brands and Their Companies. Gale, annual. 2v.

Business Advisor—http://www.business.gov/busadv/index.cfm

Business and Company Resource Center. Gale Group, updated daily.

Business Buzzwords: The Tough New Jargon of Modern Business. (Michael Johnson) Blackwell, 1990.

Business Information: How to Find It, How to Use It. (Michael R. Lavin) 3rd ed. Oryx, 2001.

Business Periodicals Database. H. W. Wilson, updating varies with version.

Business Plans Handbook: A Compilation of Actual Business Plans Developed by Small Businesses Throughout North America. (Erin Hoss, ed.) Gale, annual.

Business Source. EBSCOHost, updated daily.

Business Statistics of the United States. 7th ed. Bernan, 2002.

C

Cabell's Directory of Publishing Opportunities in Accounting, Economics, and Finance. 7th ed. Cabell, 1997. 2v.

CCH Internet Tax Research Network—*http://tax.cch.com/ipnetwork*

CDA/Wiesenberger Mutual Funds Update. CDA Investment Technologies, monthly.

Certified Financial Planner Board of Standards—http://www.cfp_board.org/

Chicago Mercantile Exchange—http://www.cme.com/

CIFAR's Global Company Handbook. Center for International Financial Analysis & Research, annual.

Citizens for a Sound Economy—http://www.cse.org/n_index.php

CNNfn—the financial network—http://www.cnnfn.com/

Codification of Statements on Auditing Standards, Numbers 1 to 87. AICPA, 1999.

Collective Bargaining Negotiations and Contracts. Bureau of National Affairs, looseleaf.

Commercial Atlas and Marketing Guide. Rand McNally, annual.

Companies and Their Brand Names. Gale, annual. 2v.

CompaniesOnline—http://www.companiesonline.com/

Complete Guide to Human Resources and the Law. (Dana Shilling) Prentice-Hall, 1998.

Conference Board—http://www.conference_board.org/

Consumer Connection—http://www.aba.com/consumer+connection/default.htm

Consumer Expenditure Survey. U.S. Bureau of Labor Statistics, annual. http://www.bls.gov/cex/

Corporate Information—http://www.corporateinformation.com/

Council of State Governments—http://www.statesnews.org/

Country Commercial Guides—http://www.state.gov/www/about_state/business/

CRB Commodity Year Book. Commodity Research Bureau, annual.

D

D&B Million Dollar Directory: America's Leading Public & Private Companies. Dun & Bradstreet, annual. 5v.

Daily Stock Price Record: American Stock Exchange. Standard & Poor's, quarterly.

Daily Stock Price Record: NASDAQ. Standard & Poor's, quarterly.

Daily Stock Price Record: New York Stock Exchange. Standard & Poor's, quarterly.

Data Sources for Business and Market Analysis. (John V. Ganly) 4th ed. Scarecrow, 1994.

Dictionary of Accounting Terms. (Joel G. Siegel and Jae K. Shim) 3rd ed. Barrons, 2000.

Dictionary of Arbitration and Its Terms: Labor, Commercial, International. (Katharine Seide, ed.) Oceana, 1970.

Dictionary of Business and Management. (Jerry M. Rosenberg) 3rd ed. Wiley, 1993.

Dictionary of Conflict Resolution. (Douglas H. Yarn, comp.) Jossey-Bass, 1999.

Dictionary of International Business Terms. (John J. Capela and Stephen W. Hartman) Barron's Educational Series, 1996.

Dictionary of Marketing and Advertising. (Jerry M. Rosenberg) Wiley, 1995.

Dictionary of Marketing Terms. (Peter D. Bennett, ed.) 2nd ed. NTC Business Books, 1995.

Direct Marketing Association—http://www.the_dma.org/

Direction of Trade Statistics Yearbook. International Monetary Fund, annual.

Directory of American Firms Operating in Foreign Countries. Uniworld Business Publications, annual. 3v.

Directory of Corporate Affiliations. National Register, annual. 5v.

Directory of Foreign Firms Operating in the United States. 9th ed. Uniworld Business Publications, 1998.

Directory of Marketing Information Companies Featuring the Best 100. American Demographics, annual.

Directory of Mutual Funds, Closed-End Funds, Unit Investment Trust Sponsors. Investment Company Institute, annual.

Dow Jones Averages, 1885–1995. (Phyllis Pierce, ed.) Irwin Professional Pubs., 1996.

Dun & Bradstreet/Gale Industry Reference Handbooks. Gale, 1998.

Dun & Bradstreet's Guide to Doing Business Around the World. (Terri Morrison et al.) Prentice-Hall, 2001.

E

E-Commerce: The Complete Reference Guide. (Arthur H. Bell) Greenwood/Oryx, 2001.

Ecommerce-guide.com—http://ecommerce.internet.com

Economic Indicators Handbook. 6th ed. Gale, 2002.

Economic Report of the President. Office of the President of the U.S., annual.

EDGAR Database of Corporate Information—http://www.sec.gov/edgarhp.htm

EEOC Compliance Manual. Bureau of National Affairs, looseleaf.

Elsevier's Dictionary of Financial Terms in English, German, Spanish, French, Italian, and Dutch. (Diana Phillips and Marie-Claude Bignaud, comp.) 2nd ed., rev. and enlarged Elsevier, 1997.

Elsevier's Banking Dictionary in Seven Languages. (Julio Ricci) 3rd ed. Elsevier, 1990.

Employee Benefit Plans: A Glossary of Terms. (Mary Jo Brzezinski, ed.) 8th ed. International Foundation of Employee Benefit Plans, 1993.

Employee Benefits Research Institute—http://www.ebri.org/

Encyclopedia of American Industries. (Scott Heil and Terrance W. Peck, eds.) 3rd. ed. Gale, 2001. 2v.

Encyclopedia of Associations. Gale Group, annual.

Encyclopedia of Banking and Finance. (Glenn G. Munn and Charles J. Woelfel) 9th ed. St. James Press, 1991.

Encyclopedia of Business Information Sources. 16th ed. Gale, 2000.

Encyclopedia of Business. (Jane A. Malonis, ed.) 2nd ed. Gale, 2000. 2v.

Encyclopedia of Consumer Brands. (Janice Jorgensen, ed.) St. James Press, 1994. 3v.

Encyclopedia of Emerging Industries. 4th ed. Gale, 2001.

Encyclopedia of Housing. (William van Vleit, ed.) Sage, 1998.

Encyclopedia of Major Marketing Campaigns. Gale, 2000.

Encyclopedia of Management. (Marilyn M. Helms, ed.) 4th ed. Gale, 1999.

Encyclopedia of Taxation and Tax Policy. (Joseph J. Cordes, Robert D. Ebel, and Jane G. Gravelles, eds.) Urban Institute Press, 1999.

Entreworld: Resources for Entrepreneurs—http://www.entreworld.org/

Eurojargon: A Dictionary of European Union Acronyms, Abbreviations, and Sobriquets. (Anne Ramsay, ed.) 6th ed. Dearborn, 2000.

Europa World Year Book. Europa Publications, annual.

Exporters' Encyclopedia. Dun & Bradstreet, annual.

F

F&S Index: United States. Information Access Co., monthly and quarterly with annual cumulation online.

Fed in Print—http://www.frbsf.org/publications/fedinprint/index.html

Federal Register—http://www.access.gpo.gov/su_docs/aces/aces140.html

Federal Tax Handbook. Research Institute of America, annual.

Federation of Tax Administrators—http://www.taxadmin.org/

FedStats—http://www.fedstats.gov/

Finance Literature Index. (Jean Louise Heck, ed.) 3rd ed. McGraw-Hill, 1992.

Financial Accounting Standards Board—http://www.rutgers.edu/Accounting/raw/fasb

Financial Accounting Standards Board. Current Text, Accounting Standards as of June 1, 2002. FASB, annual.

Financial Accounting Standards Board. Original Pronouncements. Accounting Standards as of June 1, 2002. Wiley, annual.

Financial History of the United States. (Jerry W. Markham, ed.) Sharpe, 2002. 3v.

Financial Planning Association—http://www.fpanet.org/

FINWeb—http://www.finweb.com/

FIS\online. Mergent FIS, updated weekly.

Forbes 200 Best Small Companies in America—http://www.forbes.com/200best/

Fortune 500—http://www.pathfinder.com/fortune/fortune500/

Free Management Library—http://www.mapnp.org/library

G

Geographic Reference Report. ERI Economic Research Institute, annual.

Global Edge (MSU-CIBER International Business Resources on the WWW)—http://globaledge.msu.edu/ibrd/ibrd.asp

Glossaries of Financial Terms (from the Federal Reserve Bank of Chicago)—http://www.chicagofed.org/publications/glossary/index.cfm

Government Accounting Standards Board—http://raw.rutgers.edu/raw/gasb/welcome.htm

GPO Access—http://www.access.gpo.gov/su_docs/

Green Box Resources—http://www.indiana.edu/~libgpd/guides/green/home.html

Guide to Country Information in International Governmental Organization Publications. American Library Association, Government Documents Round Table, 1996.

Guide to Labor-Oriented Internet Resources—http://www.lib.berkeley.edu/IIRL/iirlnet.html

Guide to Reference Books. (Robert Balay, ed.) 11th ed. American Library Assn., 1996.

H

Handbook of Common Stocks. Mergent FIS, quarterly.

Handbook of Interest and Annuity Tables. (Jack C. Estes) McGraw-Hill, 1976.

Handbook of Loan Payment Tables. (Jack C. Estes) McGraw-Hill, 1976.

Handbook of Mortgage-Backed Securities. (Frank J. Fabozzi, ed.) 5th ed. McGraw-Hill, 2001.

Handbook of NASDAQ Stocks. Mergent FIS, quarterly.

Handbook of Public Administration. (Jack Rabin, W. Bartley Hildreth, and Gerald J. Miller, eds.) Dekker, 1989.

Handbook of Public Relations. (Robert L. Heath and Gabriel Vasquez, eds.) Sage, 2001.

Handbook of State Government Administration. (John Gargan) Dekker, 2000.

Handbook of Strategic Public Relations & Integrated Communications. (Clarke L. Caywood, ed.) McGraw-Hill, 1997.

Handbook of U.S. Labor Statistics: Employment, Earnings, Prices, Productivity, and Other Labor Data. (Eva E. Jacobs, ed.) 5th ed. Bernan, 2001.

History of Accounting: An International Encyclopedia. (Michael Chatfield and Richard Vangermeersch, eds.) Garland, 1996.

Hoover's Handbook of World Business. Reference Press, annual.

Hoover's Online—http://www.hoovers.com/

Household Spending: Who Spends How Much on What. 4th ed. New Strategist Publications, 1997.

I

Inc. 500 Fastest Growing Companies in America—http://www.inc.com/500/home.html

Independent Community Bankers Association of America—http://www.ibaa.org/

Index to Accounting and Auditing Technical Pronouncements as of July 1, 1994. AICPA, annual.

Index to Current Urban Documents. Greenwood Press, monthly.

Industrial Relations Research Association—http://www.irra.uiuc.edu/

InfoNation—http://www.un.org/Pubs/CyberSchoolBus/infonation/e_infonation.htm

Internal Revenue Code (Title 26 of U.S. Code)—http://www.access.gpo.gov/congress/cong013.html

International Accounting and Auditing Standards as of October 1, 2001. AICPA, annual.

International Accounting Standards Committee—http://www.iasc.org.uk/

International Business Information: How to Find It, How to Use It. (Ruth A. Pagell and Michael Halperin) 2nd ed. Oryx, 1998.

International City/County Management Association—http://www.icma.org/

International Directory of Company Histories. (Thomas Derdak, ed.) St. James Press, 1988.

International Directory of Finance and Economics Professionals—http://welch.som.yale.edu/dir/

International Economics—http://www.mnsfld.edu/depts/lib/globecon.html

International Encyclopedia of Business and Management. 2nd ed. Thompson Learning, 2001.

International Encyclopedia of Public Policy and Administration. (Jay M. Shafritz, ed.) Westview, 1998. 4v.

International Financial Statistics Yearbook. International Monetary Fund, annual.

International Guide to Accounting Journals. (J. David Spiceland and Surendra P. Agrawal, eds.) 2nd ed. Wiener, 1993.

International Labour Organization—http://www.ilo.org/

International Marketing Data and Statistics. Euromonitor, 2001.

International Monetary Fund—http://www.imf.org/

International Trade Statistics Yearbook. United Nations, annual. 2v.

Internet Public Library Business Associations—http://www.ipl.org/cgi_bin/ref/aon.out.pl?id=bus0000

Internet Resources for International Economics & Business—http://www.ship.edu/~business/

Investment Company Institute ("the mutual fund connection")—http://www.ici.org/

IRS Bulletin—http://www.irs.ustreas.gov/prod/bus_info/bullet.html

IRS Tax Terms—http://www.irs.ustreas.gov/prod/taxi/taxterms.html

Irwin Investor's Handbook. Irwin Professional Publications, annual.

K

Kipplinger's Global Investor—http://www.global_investor.com/

Knowledge@Wharton—http://knowledge.wharton.upenn.edu/

L

Labor Arbitration Reports and Dispute Settlements. Bureau of National Affairs, looseleaf.

Labor Conflict in the United States: An Encyclopedia. (Ronald L. Filippelli, ed.) Garland, 1990.

Labor Research Association—http://www.lra_ny.com/

Lexis-Nexis Academic Universe. Lexis-Nexis, updated daily. http://web.lexis-nexis.com/universe/

M

Major U.S. Statistical Series. (Jean Stratford) American Library Association, 1992.

Mark Bernkopf's Central Banking Resource Center—http://www.patriot.net/users/bernkopf

Market Share Reporter, an Annual Compilation of Reported Market Share: Data on Companies, Products, and Services. Gale, annual.

Marketing Information: A Professional Reference Guide. (Hiram C. Barksdale and Jac L. Goldstucker, ed.) 3rd ed. Georgia State University Business Press, 1995.

Marketing Research Association—http://www.mra_net.org/

Marketing Virtual Library (Knowthis.com)—http://www.knowthis.com/

Marketing: The Encyclopedic Dictionary. (David Mercer, ed.) Blackwell Business, 1999.

Mergent Bond Record. Financial Information Services, monthly and annual.

Mergent Dividend Record. Mergent FIS, weekly and annual.

Mergent Unit Investment Trusts. Mergent FIS, annual.

Miller GAAP Guide: Restatement and Analysis of Current FASB Standards. (Jan R. Williams). CCH, annual.

Money—Past, Present & Future—http://www.ex.ac.uk/~RDavies/arian/money.html

Monthly Labor Review. U.S. Bureau of Labor Statistics, monthly.

Moody's Handbook of Dividend Achievers. Mergent FIS, annual.

More Words of Wall Street: 2000 More Investment Terms Defined. (Allan H. Pessin and Joseph A. Ross) Dow Jones-Irwin, 1986.

Mortgage Bankers Association of America—http://www.mbaa.org/

MSU-CIBER International Business Resources on the WWW—http://globaledge.msu.edu/ibrd/ibrd.asp

Multilingual Dictionary of Local Government and Business. (Clive Leo McNeir) Cassell, 1993. See also multilingual and bilingual dictionaries listed in the library's online catalog.

Municipal Year Book. International City/County Management Association, annual.

Mutual Fund Encyclopedia. (Gerald W. Perritt) 1993–1994 ed. Dearborn Financial Publishing, 1993.

Mutual Fund Fact Book—http://www.ici.org/facts_figures/factbook_toc.html

N

Nasdaq Stock Exchange—http://www.nasdaq.com

National Assembly of State Arts Agencies—http://www.nasaa_arts.org/

National Association of Counties—http://www.naco.org/

National Association of Credit Management—http://www.nacm.org/

National Association of Purchasing Management—http://www.icma.org/

National Association of Securities Dealers—http://www.nasd.com/

National Association of State Information Resource Executives—http://www.nasire.org/

National Association of Tax Practitioners—http://www.natptax.com/

National Center for State Courts—http://www.statesnews.org/

National Conference of State Legislatures—http://www.ncsl.org/

National Governors' Association—http://www.nga.org/

National Labor Relations Board Decisions and Orders. NLRB, irregular.

National League of Cities—http://www.nlc.org/

National Tax Association—http://ntanet.org

National Taxpayers Union—http://www.ntu.org/

Nelson's Directory of Investment Research: The Financial Professional's Guide to the Research Marketplace. Nelson Publications, annual.

New Palgrave Dictionary of Economics and the Law. (Peter Newman, ed.) Macmillan, 1998. 3v.

New Palgrave Dictionary of Money & Finance. (Peter Newman, Murray Milgate, and John Eatwell, eds.) Stockton, 1992. 3v.

New York Stock Exchange—http://www.nyse.com/

New York Stock Exchange Fact Book. New York Stock Exchange, annual.

New York Stock Exchange Glossary of Financial Terms—http://www.nyse.com/

North American Industry Classification System (NAICS). U.S. Office of Management and Budget, 1997.

NTC's Dictionary of Advertising. (Jack G. Wiechmann, ed.) 2nd ed. National Textbook Co., 1992.

O

Occupational Employment Statistics. U.S. Bureau of Labor Statistics website—http://stats.bls.gov/oes/

Occupational Outlook Handbook. U.S. Bureau of Labor Statistics, annual.

OTC Bulletin Board—http://www.otcbb.com/dynamic/

Other Markets Online (from NASDAQ)—*http://dynamic.international.nasdaq.com/asp/globalmarkets.asp?lang-eng*

Overseas Private Investment Corp.—http://www.opic.gov/

P

P.A.I.S. International. OCLC Public Affairs Information Service, updates vary with subscription.

Pacific Exchange—http://www.pacificex.com/

Portable MBA Desk Reference: An Essential Business Companion. (Paul A. Argenti) Wiley, 1994.

Principal International Businesses: The World Marketing Directory. Dun & Bradstreet. annual.

Public Relations Society of America—http://www.prsa.org/

Q

Quarterly Financial Report for Manufacturing, Mining, and Trade Corporations. U.S. Department of Commerce, quarterly.

R

Rand McNally Commercial Atlas and Marketing Guide. Rand McNally, annual.

Reference Book of Corporate Managements. Dun & Bradstreet, annual.

RIA OnPoint Federal Tax Service (available through Lexis-Nexis).

RMA Annual Statement Studies, Including Comparative Historical Data and Other Sources of Composite Financial Data. Robert Morris Associates, annual.

Robert Morris Associates, the Association of Lending and Credit Risk Professionals—http://www.rmahq.org/

Roberts' Dictionary of Industrial Relations. (Harold S. Roberts) 4th ed. Bureau of National Affairs, 1994.

Rutgers Accounting Web—http://accounting.rutgers.edu/raw/

Rutgers University Libraries: Research & Reference Gateway: Business—http://www.libraries.rutgers.edu/rul/rr_gateway/research_guides/busi/business.shtml

S

S&P Advantage. Standard & Poor's, updated daily.

Sales and Marketing Management —http://www.salesandmarketing.com/

Scout Report—*http://scout.cs.wisc.edu/*

Securities Industry Association—http://www.sia.com/

Sexual Harassment on the Job: What It Is and How to Stop It. (William Petrocelli and Barbara Kate Repa) 4th ed. Nolo Press, 1999.

Standard & Poor's Bond Guide. Standard & Poor's, monthly.

Standard & Poor's Corporate Descriptions. Standard & Poor's, semimonthly. 6v.

Standard & Poor's CreditWeek. Standard & Poor's, weekly.

Standard & Poor's Dividend Record. Standard & Poor's, quarterly.

Standard & Poor's Industry Surveys. Standard & Poor's, quarterly.

Standard & Poor's Outlook. Standard & Poor's, weekly.

Standard & Poor's Register of Corporations, Directors, and Executives. Standard & Poor's, annual.

Standard Directory of Advertisers. National Register, annual.

Standard Industrial Classification (SIC) Manual. U.S. Office of Management and Budget, 1987.

STAT-USA/Internet—http://www.stat_usa.gov/

Statesman's Year-Book: The Essential Political and Economic Guide to All the Countries of the World. St. Martin's Press, annual.

Statistical Abstract of the United States. U.S. Bureau of the Census, annual.

Statistical Abstract of the World. (Marlita A. Reddy, ed.) Gale, 1996.

Still More Words of Wall Street. (Allan H. Pessin and Joseph A. Ross) Dow Jones-Irwin, 1990.

SuperPages.com, the Yellow Pages on the Web—http://www.bigyellow.com/

Survey of Current Business. U.S. Bureau of Economic Analysis, monthly.

T

Tax Analysts: Tax Information Worldwide Online—http://www.tax.org/default.htm

Tax and Accounting Sites Directory—http://www.taxsites.com/

Tax Executives Institute—http://www.tei.org/

Tax Foundation—http://www.taxfoundation.org/

Taxpayer Information Publications—http://www.irs.ustreas.gov/prod/forms_pubs/pubs/index.htm

The 100 Best Stocks to Own in the World. (Gene Walden) 4th ed. Dearborn Financial.

The Ad Men and Women: A Biographical Dictionary of Advertising. (Edd Applegate, ed.) Greenwood, 1994.

The International Business Dictionary & Reference. (Lewis A. Presner) Wiley, 1991.

The New Illustrated Book of Development Definitions. (Harvey S. Moskowitz and Carl G. Lindbloom) Center for Urban Policy Research, 1993.

Thomas Register of American Manufacturers—http://www.thomasregister.com/index.html

Thomas: Legislative Information on the Internet —http://thomas.loc.gov/

Thomson/Polk Bank Directory. Thomson, semiannual.

Thorndike Encyclopedia of Banking and Finance Tables. (David Thorndike) 3rd ed. Warren, Gorham, & Lomont, 1983.

U

U.S. Bureau of the Census—http://www.census.gov/

U.S. Bureau of Labor Statistics—http://www.bls.gov/blshome.html

U.S. Chamber of Commerce—http://www.uschamber.org/

U.S. Conference of Mayors—http://www.usmayors.org/uscm/

U.S. Congress House Banking and Financial Services Committee—http://www.house.gov/banking/

U.S. Congress Joint Committee on Taxation—http://www.house.gov/jct/

U.S. Congress Senate Banking, Housing, and Urban Affairs Committee—http://www.senate.gov/~banking/

U.S. Customs Service—http://www.customs.ustreas.gov/

U.S. Department of Commerce—http://www.doc.gov/

U.S. Department of Commerce. Office of Trade & Economic Analysis—http://www.ita.doc.gov/tradestats/

U.S. Department of Labor—http://www.dol.gov/

U.S. Department of State, Bureau of Consular Affairs—http://travel.state.gov/

U.S. Department of the Treasury (includes the U.S. Comptroller of the Currency)—http://www.ustreas.gov/

U.S. Employment and Training Administration—http://www.doleta.gov/

U.S. Equal Employment Opportunity Commission—http://www.eeoc.gov/

U.S. Federal Deposit Insurance Corp.—http://www.fdic.gov/

U.S. Federal Reserve System—http://www.federalreserve.gov/

U.S. Internal Revenue Service—http://www.irs.gov/; http://www.irs.ustreas.gov/

U.S. International Information Program—http://usinfo.state.gov/homepage.htm

U.S. International Trade Administration—http://www.ita.doc.gov/

U.S. International Trade Commission—http://www.usitc.gov/

U.S. Justice Department, Tax Division—http://www.usdoj.gov/tax/

U.S. Master Tax Guide. CCH, annual.

U.S. Multi-State Tax Commission—http://www.mtc.gov/

U.S. National Credit Union Administration—http://www.ncua.gov/

U.S. National Labor Relations Board—http://www.nlrb.gov/

U.S. Securities and Exchange Commission—http://www.sec.gov/

U.S. Small Business Administration—http://www.sbaonline.sba.gov/

U.S. State & Local Gateway—http://www.statelocal.gov/

U.S. Tax Court—http://www.ustaxcourt.gov/

U.S. Tax Forms—http://www.irs.ustreas.gov/prod/forms_pubs/index.html

U.S. Trade Representative—http://www.ustr.gov/

U.S. Treasury OTS Glossary of Thrift Terms—http://www.ots.treas.gov/glossary.html

Understanding American Business Jargon: A Dictionary. (W. Davis Folsom) Greenwood, 1997.

Understanding the Census: A Guide for Marketers, Planners, Grant Writers, and Other Data Users. (Michael R. Lavin) Library Edition. Epoch Books, 1996.

Union Labor Report. Bureau of National Affairs, looseleaf.

University of Michigan Documents Center—http://www.lib.umich.edu/govdocs/index.html

V

Value Line Investment Survey. Value Line, weekly. http://www.valueline.com/

Virtual International Business and Economics Sources (VIBES)—http://libweb.uncc.edu/ref_bus/vibehome.htm

VNR Investor's Dictionary. (David M. Brownstone and Irene M. Franck) Van Nostrand Reinhold, 1981.

W

Wall Street Journal Index. Dow Jones, monthly. http://public.wsj.com/home.html

Wall Street Words: An Essential A to Z Guide for Today's Investor. (David L. Scott) Rev. ed. Houghton Mifflin, 1997.

Washington Post Business Glossary—http://www.washingtonpost.com/wpdyn/business/specials/glossary/index.html

WorkIndex—http://workindex.com/

World Directory of Marketing Information Sources. 3rd ed. Euromonitor, 2001.

World Fact Book—http://www.odci.gov/cia/publications/factbook/index.html

World Market Share Reporter: A Compilation of Reported World Market Share Data and Rankings on Companies, Products, and Services. (Marlita A. Reddy and Robert S. Lazich) Gale, annual.

World Trade Organization—http://www.wto.org/

World Trade Organization—http://www.wto.org/ABI/Inform. Proquest Information and Learning, updated daily.

Decision Theory Problem

The value of research information can be assessed by several means, one of which is decision theory. The example considered here concerns the case of a manager who is deciding on a change in production equipment. Research information will play a major role in this decision. The new equipment can be leased for five years and will replace several old machines that require constant attention to operate. The problem facing the manager is, "Shall I lease the new machines with the attendant efficiencies, reduced labor, and higher lease charges, or shall I continue to use the old equipment?"

The decision situation has been prompted by news that the firm might secure several large orders from companies that have not been previous customers. With added volume, departmental profit contributions will increase substantially with the new equipment. For this decision, the manager adopts the decision variable "average annual departmental profit contribution."[1] The decision rule is, "Choose that course of action that will provide the highest average annual contribution to departmental profits."

Exhibit B–1 indicates the results of the evaluation of the two available actions. Under the conditions cited, it is obvious that course A_1 is preferred.

Conditions of Certainty

Exhibit B–1 presents the case with the assumption that the anticipated new business will materialize. It therefore represents, in decision theory terminology, *decision making under conditions of certainty*. It is assumed the payoffs are certain to occur if the particular action is chosen and the probability of the additional business being secured is 1.0.[2] The decision to choose action A_1 is obvious under these conditions with the given payoff data and decision rule.

Conditions of Uncertainty

In a more realistic situation, the outcome is less than certain. The new business may not materialize, and then the department might be left with costly excess capacity. The union may resist introduction of the new equipment because it replaces workers. The new equipment may not perform as anticipated. For these or other reasons, the decision maker may be uncertain about the consequences (for instance, that course A_1 will result in a $20,000 contribution).

Suppose the manager considers these other possible outcomes and concludes the one serious uncertainty is that the new business may not be forthcoming. For purposes of simplicity, one of two conditions will exist in the future—either the new business will be secured as expected (O_1), or the new business will not materialize (O_2). In the first case, the expected payoffs would be the same as in Exhibit B–1; but if the new business is not secured, then the addition of the new equipment would give the department costly excess capacity, with fixed lease charges. The payoff table may now be revised as Exhibit B–2.

Under these conditions, the original decision rule does not apply. That rule said, "Choose that course of action that will provide the highest average annual contribution to departmental profits." Under the conditions in Exhibit B–2, action A_1 would be better if the new business were secured, but A_2 would be the better choice if the new business were not secured. If the decision

EXHIBIT B–1   Payoff Under Conditions of Certainty

Course of Action	Average Annual Departmental Profit Contribution
A_1—Lease new equipment	$20,000
A_2—Retain old equipment	12,000

EXHIBIT B–2   Payoff Under Conditions of Uncertainty

	Average Annual Departmental Profit Contribution		
Course of Action	New Business (O_1)	No New Business (O_2)	Expected Monetary Value
A_1—Lease new equipment	$20,000	$5,000	$14,000
A_2—Retain old equipment	12,000	9,000	10,800

can be delayed until the new order question is resolved, the dilemma is escapable. However, because of lead times, the equipment decision may need to be made first.

When faced with two or more possible outcomes for each alternative, the manager can adopt one of two approaches. First, the likelihood that the company will receive the new business cannot be judged. Even so, a rational decision can be made by adopting an appropriate decision rule. For example, "Choose that course of action for which the minimum payoff is the highest." This is known as the *maximum criterion* because it calls for maximizing the minimum payoff. In Exhibit B–2, the minimum payoff for alternative A_1 is shown as $5,000, and the minimum payoff for A_2 is $9,000. According to the *maximum rule,* the choice would be A_2 because it is the best of the worst outcomes. This decision is a "cut your losses" strategy.

The second approach is to use subjective judgment to estimate the probability that either O_1 or O_2 will occur.[3] When the assumption was decision under certainty, only one event was possible (had a probability of 1.0). Now, however, with experience and information from other sources, there is a less-than-certain chance of the new business materializing, and this doubt should be part of the decision.

One might estimate that there is a 0.6 chance the new business will be secured and a 0.4 chance it will not. With this or any other set of similar probabilities, an overall evaluation of the two courses of action is possible. One approach is to calculate an *expected monetary value (EMV)* for each alternative.[4]

The Decision Flow Diagram

The decision problem already has been summarized in a payoff table, but further illustration in the form of a decision flow diagram (or decision tree) may be helpful. The decision tree for the equipment problem is shown in Exhibit B–3. The diagram may be seen as a sequential decision flow. At the square node on the left, the manager must choose between A_1 and A_2. After one of these actions, a chance event will occur—either the new business will be received by the company (O_1), or it will not be received (O_2). At the right extremity of the branches are listed the conditional payoffs that will occur for each combination of decision and chance event. On each chance branch is placed the expected probability of that chance event occurring. Keep in mind that these are subjective probability estimates by the manager that express a degree of belief that such a chance event will occur.

EXHIBIT B–3 **Decision Tree for the Equipment Problem**

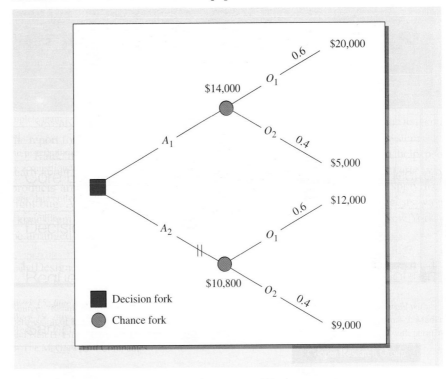

Having set up this series of relationships, one calculates back from right to left on the diagram by an *averaging out and folding back* process. At each decision juncture, the path that yields the best alternative for the decision rule is selected. Here the EMV for A_1 averages out to $14,000, while the EMV for A_2 is $10,800. The double slash line on the A_2 branch indicates it is the inferior alternative and should be dropped in favor of A_1.

The Contribution of Research

Now the contribution of research can be assessed. Recall that the value of research may be judged as "the difference between the results of decisions made with the information and the results of decisions that would be made without it." In this example, the research need is to decide whether the new business will be secured. This is the uncertainty that, if known, would make a perfect forecast possible. Just how much is a perfect forecast worth in this case?

Consider Exhibit B–3 once again. What would happen if the manager had information to accurately predict whether the new business orders would be secured? The choice would be A_1 if the research indicated the orders would be received, and A_2 if the research indicated the orders would not be received. However, at the decision point (before the research is undertaken), the best estimate is that there is a 0.6 chance that the research will indicate the O_1 condition and a 0.4 chance that the condition will be O_2. The decision flow implications of the use of research are illustrated in Exhibit B–4.

The decision sequence begins with the decision fork at the left. If the manager chooses to do research (R), the first chance fork is reached where one of two things will occur. Research indicates either that the orders will be received (R_1) or the orders will not be received (R_2). Before doing the research, the best estimate of the probability of R_1 taking place is the same as the estimate that O_1 will occur (0.6). Similarly, the best estimate that R_2 will occur is 0.4.

After the manager learns R_1 or R_2, there is a second decision fork: A_1 or A_2. After the A_1-A_2 decision, there is a second chance fork (O_1 or O_2) that indicates whether the orders were received.

EXHIBIT B–4   The Value of Perfect Information

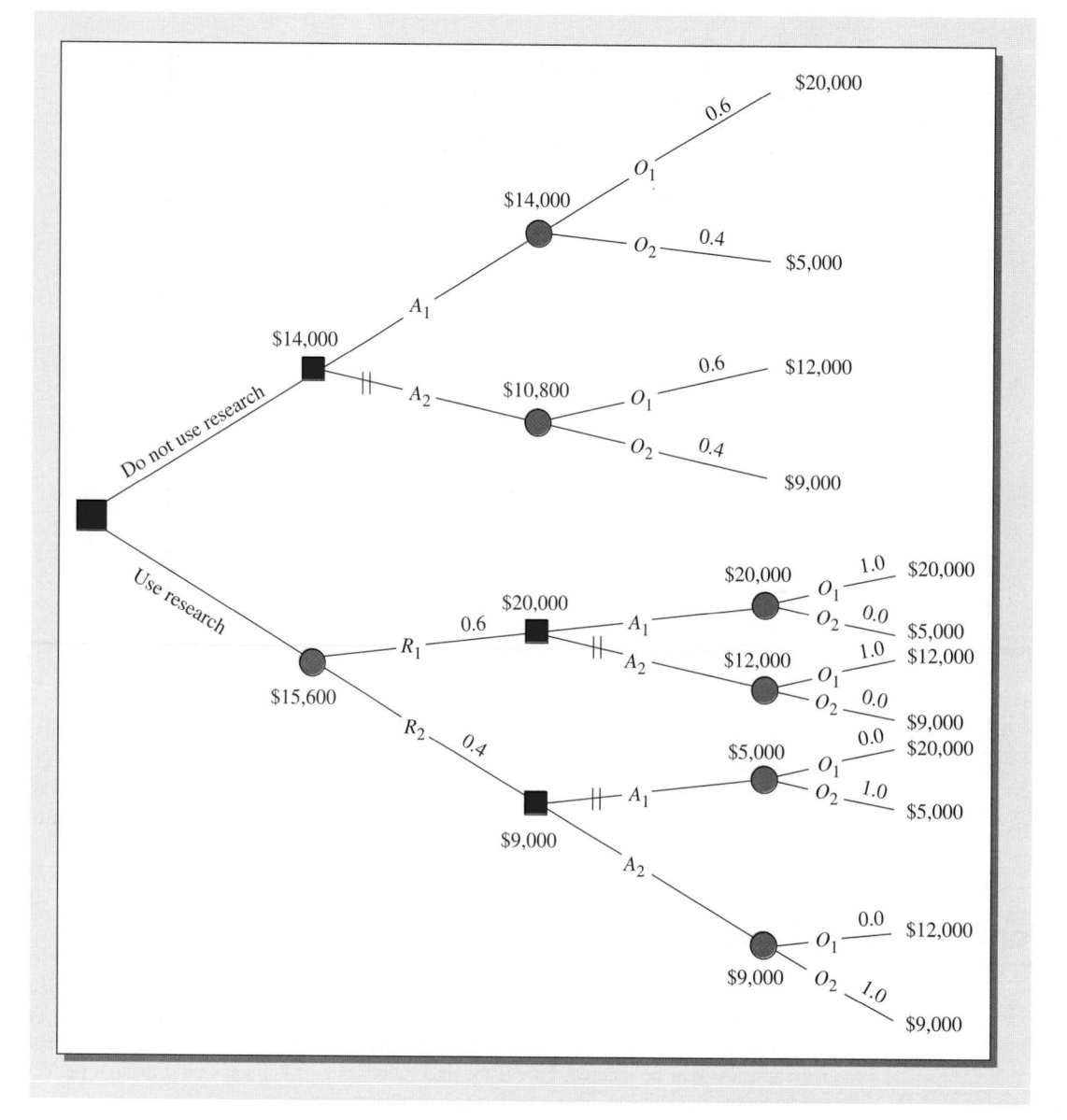

Note that the probabilities at O_1 and O_2 have now changed from 0.6 and 0.4, respectively, to 1.0 and 0.0, or to 0.0 and 1.0, depending on what was learned from the research. This change occurs because we have evaluated the effect of the research information on our original O_1 and O_2 probability estimates by calculating *posterior probabilities.* These are revisions of our prior probabilities that result from the assumed research findings. The posterior probabilities (for example, $P(O_1|R_i)$ and $P(O_2|R_i)$ are calculated by using Bayes's theorem.[5]

The manager is now ready to average out and fold back the analysis from right to left to evaluate the research alternative. Clearly, if R_1 is found, A_1 will be chosen with its EMV of $20,000 over the A_2 alternative of $12,000. If R_2 is reported, then A_2 is more attractive. However, before the research, the probabilities of R_1 and R_2 being secured must be incorporated by a second averaging out. The result is an EMV of $15,600 for the research alternative versus an EMV of $14,000 for the no-research path. The conclusion then is this: Research that would enable the manager to make a perfect forecast regarding the potential new orders would be worth up to

$1,600. If the research costs more than $1,600, decline to buy it because the net EMV of the research alternative would be less than the EMV of $14,000 of the no-research alternative.

Research Outcomes	States of Nature O_1	States of Nature O_2	Marginal Probabilities	Posterior Probabilities $P(O_1|R_i)$	Posterior Probabilities $P(O_2|R_i)$
R_1	0.6	0.0	0.6	1.0	0.0
R_2	0.0	0.4	0.4	0.0	1.0
Marginal probabilities	0.6	0.4			

Imperfect Information

The analysis up to this point assumes that research on decision options will give a perfect prediction of the future states of nature, O_1 and O_2. Perfect prediction seldom occurs in practice. Sometimes research reveals one condition when later evidence shows something else to be true. Thus, we need to consider that the research in the machinery decision will provide less-than-perfect information and is, therefore, worth less than the $1,600 calculated in Exhibit B–4.

Suppose the research in that example involves interviews with the customers' key personnel and some customers' executives. They might all answer our questions to the best of their ability but still predict imperfectly what will happen. Consequently, we might judge that the chances of their predictions being correct are no better than 3 to 1, or 0.75. If we accept that our research results may provide imperfect information in this manner, we need to factor this into our evaluation decision. We do this by averaging out and folding back again. The results are shown in Exhibit B–5. The revised EMV, given research judged to be 75 percent reliable, is $14,010. This

EXHIBIT B–5   **The Value of Imperfect Information**

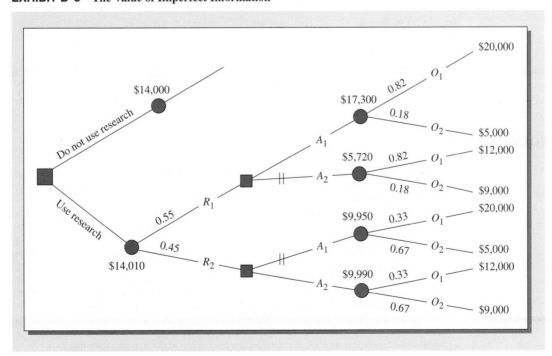

revised EMV is only $10 higher than the $14,000 EMV using no research and would seem to be hardly worth consideration.

Pragmatic Complications

This discussion, while simplified, contains the basic concepts for finding the value of research. Practical difficulties complicate the use of these concepts. First, the situation with two events and two alternatives is artificial. Problems with more choices and events are common, and the chief complication is the increased number of calculations.

Research Outcomes	States of Nature		Marginal Probabilities	Posterior Probabilities	
	O_1	O_2		$P(O_1|R_i)$	$P(O_2|R_i)$
R_1	0.45	0.10	0.55	0.82	0.18
R_2	0.15	0.30	0.45	0.33	0.67
Marginal probabilities	0.60	0.40			

A more serious problem is posed by the measurement of outcomes. We have assumed we could assess the various actions in terms of an unambiguous dollar value, but often we cannot. It is difficult to place a dollar value on outcomes related to morale or public image, for example.

An allied problem lies in the exclusive use of EMV as the criterion for decision making. This is correct in an actuarial sense and implies that each decision maker has a linear system of evaluation. In truth, we often use another evaluation system. The person who accepts EMV as a criterion sees that an even bet of $20 between two people on the toss of a fair coin is a fair bet. Many people, however, may not be willing to make such a bet because they fear the loss of $20 more than they value the gain of $20. They may need to be offered a chance, say, to win $20 but to lose only $10 before they would be willing to bet. These persons have a nonlinear decision scale. The "utility" concept is more relevant here.

The development of more precise methods of evaluating the contribution of research continues. In the meantime, continued emphasis on the improvement of our understanding of the researcher's task and the research process will make research more valuable when it is conducted.

Reference Notes

1. Recall that the decision variable is the unit of measurement used in the analysis. At this point, we need not be concerned with how this measure is calculated or whether it is the appropriate decision variable. Assume for purposes of this illustration that it is appropriate.
2. A probability is a measure between 1.0 and 0.0 that expresses the likelihood of an event occurring. For example, the probability of a "head" on a toss of a coin is 0.5. Under conditions of certainty, the forecasted outcome is assumed to have a probability of 1.0 even though we might agree that we normally cannot know the future with certainty. In most forecasting where a specific amount is named, there is an implicit assumption of certainty.
3. Concepts of probability enter into three types of situations. In the classical situation, each possible outcome has a known chance of occurrence. For example, a coin tossed in the air has a 0.5 chance of landing heads up; a spade card has a 0.25 chance of being drawn from a well-mixed deck.

   In the same type of situation, probabilities are thought of as "relative frequencies." Even if the probability is not known from the structure of the problem (as it is in the classical case), it can still be estimated if there is a body of empirical evidence. For example, experience may show that about 1 in 50 products produced is defective. From this statistic, one can estimate there is a 0.02 chance that any given product will be defective.

   If there is no direct empirical evidence, one can still assess probability on the basis of opinion, intuition, and/or general experience. In such cases, uncertainty is expressed as a subjectively felt "degree of confidence" or "degree of belief" that a given event will occur. The discussions in this appendix are cases in point. For more information on probability concepts, see any modern statistics text.

4. One calculates an EMV for an alternative by weighting each conditional value (for example, $20,000 and $5,000 for A_1) by the estimated probability of the occurrence of the associated event (0.6 probability of the $20,000 being made).

$$EMV = P_1(\$20,000) + P_2(\$5,000)$$

$$= 0.6(\$20,000) + 0.4(\$5,000)$$

$$= \$14,000$$

5. Bayes's theorem with two states of nature is

$$P(O_1|R_1) = \frac{P(R_1|O_1) \times P(O_1)}{P(R_i|O_1) + P(O_1) \times P(R_i|O_2) \times P(O_2)}$$

$$= \frac{1.0 \times 0.6}{(1.0 \times 0.6) + (0.0 \times 0.4)}$$

$$= 1.0$$

APPENDIX C

Request for Proposal (RFP): Assessment and Contents

Chapter 4 identified the request for proposal (RFP) as a means to formalize the process of documenting, justifying, and authorizing a procurement of research. RFPs provide the opportunity to evaluate different solutions and offer a mechanism to establish, monitor, and control the performance of the winning supplier of research services.

Summary of RFP Effectiveness

In the literature (the *ABI/Inform* database), over 100 journal articles discuss the role of RFPs, ranging from the reasons to use them to specific industry applications. The emerging consensus is that, except for government contracts and highly specialized industrial applications (e.g., engineering, manufacturing, construction, hospital systems), *traditional RFPs are not time and cost effective*. Commonly, the cost of preparing the RFP exceeds 15 percent of the final bid, the preparation can take as long as two years, and the document may run between several hundred and a thousand pages. An article in the *Journal of Business Communication* said this device has become virtually worthless for the procurement of services. Several modifications or alternatives to RFPs are currently being considered:

- Send shorter RFPs by investing time up-front to decide specific, desirable outcomes.
- Use site visits and demonstrations to be certain the suppliers' designs or systems can meet their claims.
- Automate the process to reduce time and cost of preparation (Strategic Systems Solutions International offers software called Product Analyzer to simplify objective supplier evaluation through various scoring algorithms).
- Replace the RFP with a request for application (RFA). The RFA would consist of the following:
  - An overview of the requesting firm's organizational structure.
  - Business objectives.
  - Basic operational procedures.
  - Problems that the supplier's bid should address.
- Replace the RFP with a request for recommendation (RFR). The RFR would contain a clear statement of the problem and be sent to a small number of credible suppliers. The suppliers' responses would
  - Be limited to a 10-page reply.
  - Contain ballpark prices for the information to be provided.
  - Include supplier recommendations with brief descriptions of solutions and support that can be offered.
  - Be due in three to four weeks (saving the cost of a consultant to prepare an RFP and leaving the firm with the flexibility to maintain control of the project's ultimate direction). Suppliers (usually no more than six) would be invited to visit the firm and make a two-

hour presentation. The firm's statement of work would then be refined and the supplier list narrowed.

- Similar to RFAs and RFRs, the request for information (RFI) is often the first step in overall RFP development. The RFI lets a supplier know you are gathering information but are not prepared to purchase a good or service. It provides the company with an opportunity to more carefully define its requirements and alerts suppliers to the opportunity to respond to its requirements. There are several advantages to RFIs. An RFI

  - Is an accepted method for determining if the techniques and methods are available, if cost estimates are reasonable, and if solutions exist.

  - Requires in-house people to agree on the requirements and set minimal expectations.

  - Eliminates supplier surprise, thereby helping suppliers to build a better response.

  - Requires a formal written response that may later be incorporated into the contract.

  - Provides a qualified list of suppliers and eliminates those who could not have responded to the RFP.

The Organization and Content of an RFP

The RFP process, properly modified, allows an organization to analyze its current operations, problems, and future challenges. Communications with potential suppliers can be clear and based on a mutual understanding of the problems being addressed and the proposed solutions. Proper planning and management commitment to the project are essential.

The first step in developing an RFP is to fully understand and define the problem being addressed. In a formal RFP process, an internal set of experts defines the problem. (One can hire an expert or a group of experts who specialize in the problem area to help in defining the problem and writing the RFP.) Once the problem is defined, the technical section of the RFP can be written.

Besides defining the technical requirements, critical components of the RFP include project management, pricing, and contract administration. These sections allow the supplier to understand and meet expectations of the management team for carrying out the contracted services. Also, a section on the proposal administration, including important dates, is included.

The components of an RFP are

- Proposal administration information.
- Summary statement of the problem.
- Technical section.
- Management section.
- Pricing section.
- Contracts and license section.

Proposal Administration

This section is an overview with important information on the administration of the proposal itself. It establishes the dates of the RFP process—when the RFP is released, the time when the RFP team is available for questions, the date the proposals are expected, and the dates of the evaluation and supplier selections. It includes all requirements for preparing the proposal and describes how the proposals will be evaluated. Contact names, addresses, and relevant telephone and fax information are listed.

Summary Statement of the Problem

This section can be an abstract of the technical section, or it can be included as the first page of the technical section.

Technical Section

Technical information needed for the supplier to create the proposal is presented in this section. It begins by describing the problems to be addressed and the technical detail of each requirement. It loosely describes the services to be performed and the equipment, software, and documentation required. This section should be neither too specific nor too general to allow the suppliers flexibility in design creativity but should restrict them to meeting the needs of the corporation. Typically, the following would be included:

- Problem statement.
- Description of functional requirements.
- Identification of constraints.

Management Section

Each project requires some level of management. The extent to which the corporation expects schedules, plans, and reports is included in this section. The management section should include requirements for implementation schedules, training and reporting schedules, and other documentation. If specific supplier qualifications are needed, they should be shown here. References from the supplier's customers should also be requested.

Pricing Section

To cost the proposal, all information needed by the supplier is contained in this section. By using a rigid format, proposals with different approaches can be compared on costs. The following list shows examples of items that should be included:

- Services.
- Data collection.
- Data analysis.
- Meetings with client.
- Travel.
- Respondent survey incentives.
- Mail and telephone costs.
- Design meetings.
- Facilities and equipment.
- Extensions to work agreements.
- Pilot tests.

- Report preparations.
- Computer models.
- Project management.
- Deliverables:
  - Training
  - Brochures/literature
  - Videotapes
  - Reports
- Questionnaire and reproduction costs.
- Manpower costs.

Contracts and License Section

This section includes the types of contracts the supplier is expected to sign and any nondisclosure agreements. The safeguarding of intellectual property and the use of copyright are discussed. Terms of payment and required benchmarks are set forth. Typically a sample purchase contract would be included.

Conclusion

A well-written RFP allows an organization to request state-of-the-art proposals for dealing with complex problems. When not done properly, the process will take longer, cost more, and not provide a complete long-term solution. Therefore, when an organization decides to put a project to bid using an RFP-type mechanism, it is essential that time and effort be invested at the beginning of the process. Modifications to traditional RFP methods would also be beneficial. Clear communications with suppliers through a coherent RFP will result in a well-managed project with long-term benefits.

Sample External Proposal: Seagate Technology

Contract research requires a more formal proposal, such as this one prepared by Cooper Research Group for Seagate Technology.

Visit our website to see the actual proposal: www.mhhe.com/business/cooper8.

Customer Satisfaction Measurement for Seagate Technology

Cooper Research Group

Table of Contents

- Background

- Objectives and Scope

- Design

- Timeline

- Team and Professional Fees

Cooper Research Group

Seagate seeks to develop and implement . . .

a successful improvement strategy obtained by a systematic understanding of their customers' satisfaction with their products and (sales & marketing) services

Through:

• an identification of aggregate and subgroup customer responses.

• an understanding of the elements necessary to create and execute a plan for enhanced customer perceptions.

• a program to achieve and sustain competitive advantage through successive identification and correction of customer issues.

Cooper Research Group

Table of Contents

• Background

• Objectives and Scope

• Design

• Timeline

• Team and Professional Fees

Cooper Research Group

Project Objectives

• to discover customers' perception of doing business with Seagate from a sales and marketing perspective

• to profile attributes and characteristics of customer satisfaction in order to develop a proactive plan for product/service enhancement and customer retention

• to assess how different customer segments perceive Seagate and provide information to decision makers assisting them in building effective action plans that leverage strengths and improve weaknesses

• to establish a research methodology that can be subsequently extended to other business functions and geographies (Europe and Asia-Pacific markets)

Cooper Research Group

To obtain accurate and actionable information

Team Objectives

Our primary concern is to meet Seagate's stated objectives to produce superior knowledge of customer expectations as measurable results leading corrective action and improved customer perceptions.

This task involves an application of marketing research and organizational development expertise. As outlined in this proposal, our goals are to use exploratory methods to thoroughly understand the customer sets, advanced statistical techniques to profile and confirm quantitative findings, and organizational change strategies to assist the Seagate team with the identification and implementation of action plans.

Cooper Research Group

Table of Contents

Cooper Research Group

Our approach includes thorough and collaborative planning, design, pilot testing and fieldwork, data analysis, and recommendations

Approach Summary

Step 1	Step 2	Step 3	Step 4	Step 5
Initiate Project/ Strategy Work Session	Study Design	Fieldwork	Data Analysis	Recommend

Step 1	Step 2	Step 3	Step 4	Step 5
• Identify team members • Announce project • Develop work plan • Create team understanding of the priorities • Understand linkages and logistics for Seagate and the vendor • Formulate action plans to address study objectives	• Conduct focus groups • Design sample from existing databases and supplemental sources • Collaboratively prepare interview schedule/ questionnaire • Design pretest • Prepare data analysis plan including database structure	• Develop questionnaire with Seagate • Create and reproduce questionnaire • Pretest the questionnaire • Conduct telephone interviews	• Assess instrument reliability and validity • Assess sample adequacy, error rates, outlier detection • Profile segments and key demographic variables • Evaluate statistical differences, attribute strengths & weaknesses • Identify key drivers of customer satisfaction	• Provide guidelines for Seagate's marketing strategy and resource allocation • Develop a results-oriented program leading to increased customer satisfaction • Present findings for implementation • Reassess implementation success

Communication with client, partner, vendors

Cooper Research Group

Sample Design

- design the sampling frame based on Seagate requirements; use the sampling frame for selection of focus group members and survey participants

- identify subpopulations and subsets (resellers, distributors/desktop HD, server systems/managers, directors) in the proportions specified by project director and the RFP)

- acquire sample from Seagate databases and from other agreed upon sources

- select focus group participants using quota-based techniques

- secure (probability-based) representative samples controlling for segment, geography, enterprise size, etc. (A conventional stratified probability sample may used.)

- draw the probability sample

Cooper Research Group

Focus Group Design

- Two sessions of focus groups:

  - Round 1, **Problem Definition:** Identify the attributes, factors, and characteristics that are important to various customers, the way these factors interact and how they relate to satisfaction and loyalty. Include utility of key processes (how much and at what cost). Use neural network analysis if possible. We recommend at least two groups for this round.

  - Round 2, **Test Improvement Plans:** A focus group to test solutions to issues arising from surveys. Taking key improvements to be planned: define packages; create trade-off analyses. We recommend three focus groups for this round, the last of which is for the Seagate (implementation) team.

- Round 3: We would recommend a follow-on survey rather than a third focus group given the importance of corrective action to Seagate's decision making. This survey would contact approximately 150 individuals and would include questions common to the first survey (for pre-post comparisons) and trade-off analyses. Advantages would include wider representation and much greater statistical rigor.

Cooper Research Group

Fieldwork Highlights

- develop questionnaire between Cooper Research and XLM based upon focus group results and Seagate knowledge

- create questionnaire and program in CATI

- pretest the questionnaire for appropriateness

- revise CATI programming as necessary

- brief interviewers

- execute survey

- provide action cards as required

- weekly updates from the field

- code open ends on an ongoing basis

- data compilation

- generate electronic data files

- tabulate data

Cooper Research Group

Data Collection

- data gathering (based in Canada for cost effectiveness)

- develop initial coding scheme; code open ends

- CATI programmed

- pretest

- revise questionnaire as needed

- interviewing through June and early July

- provide action cards as situation warrants

- coding and error checking

- high-level data to Seagate

- data cleaned and initial tables developed

- data file delivered

- data tables and final data sets delivered

Cooper Research Group

Data Analysis

- perform outlier detection (multivariate statistics are sensitive to the presence of outliers)

- split data and cross-replicate to assess the stability of solutions (a missing data contingency)

- evaluate results by segments and key demographics

- seek additional input from Seagate team members to gain insight into statistical results

- profile segments in terms of characteristics of interest to Seagate

- develop a profile of key drivers of customer satisfaction: describe strengths and weakness

- prepare report on implementation targets based on study findings

- begin transition to implementation-solution testing

- repeat analysis process for mini survey (assessment of the success of implemented solutions)

- revise data strategies for continuation of a results-oriented program leading to increased customer satisfaction.

Cooper Research Group

Table of Contents

- Background

- Objectives and Scope

- Design

- Timeline

- Team and Professional Fees

Cooper Research Group

Preliminary Project Schedule

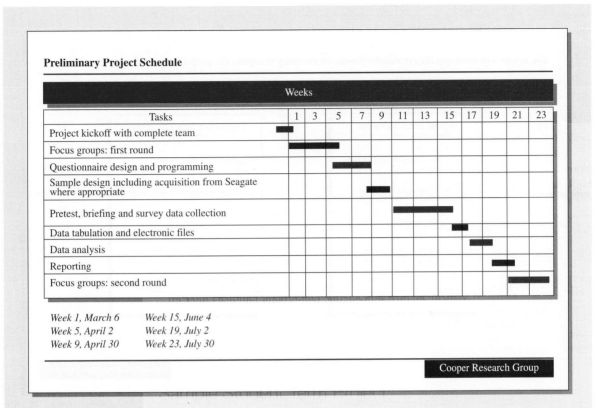

Weeks												
Tasks	1	3	5	7	9	11	13	15	17	19	21	23
Project kickoff with complete team	▬											
Focus groups: first round		▬▬										
Questionnaire design and programming			▬									
Sample design including acquisition from Seagate where appropriate				▬								
Pretest, briefing and survey data collection						▬▬						
Data tabulation and electronic files								▬				
Data analysis									▬			
Reporting										▬		
Focus groups: second round											▬▬	

Week 1, March 6   Week 15, June 4
Week 5, April 2   Week 19, July 2
Week 9, April 30   Week 23, July 30

Cooper Research Group

Table of Contents

• Background

• Objectives and Scope

• Design

• Timeline

• Team and Professional Fees

Cooper Research Group

The teams will have specific responsibilities to successfully complete the project

Team Representations

Client Team Members

- demonstrate leadership and support for project objectives

- provide knowledge of Seagate organization

- schedule participants for workshops and interviews

- collaborate on questionnaire design and segment profiling decisions

- provide adequate on-site facilities for focus group sessions

Consulting Team Members

- apply research methodology experience

- execute the activities outlined in the approach

- develop actionable recommendations

- communicate regularly with sponsors

- transfer knowledge of research concepts and techniques to client team

Cooper Research Group

Cooper Research Group: Overview

Cooper Research Group, Inc., is a customer satisfaction and market research consultancy based in Boca Raton, Florida. We help companies understand their customers' satisfaction with products and services, their marketplace, and their competitors. With a concentration on high tech, our services speed critical information for decisions made in dynamic and changing environments.

CRG specializes in quick turnaround, thoughtful client education, and leading-edge measurement and statistical analysis. With a small staff of highly trained experts, we are many times more responsive than full-service houses. By selecting our projects carefully, we can dedicate considerable energy to early completion. The reduced lag between data collection and reporting accelerates early warning of opportunities and obstacles.

Services

Our services include research design, data analysis and reporting, expert consultancy, vendor evaluation, and education. Advanced statistical techniques such as Conjoint Analysis, Factor Analysis, Discriminant Analysis, Cluster Analysis, Multiple Regression, and Structural Equation Modeling are regularly employed for our clients with complex marketplace questions.

We design questionnaires and sampling frames to best meet your needs and budget. Reliability and validity studies, both as an integral part of

our own designs and as specialized studies, are typically conducted. We use exploratory data analysis to give you the big picture and confirmatory analysis to zero-in on your strategic options.

Projects

During the last ten years, CRG has completed projects several hundred satisfaction, loyalty, and competitive brand analysis projects for major I/T providers, working in Europe, Latin America, and the U.S. markets. Among these was the development of IBM's customer satisfaction program for European Community countries. The scope of this program required coordination with many vendors throughout the continent.

We are currently involved in research on service satisfaction with the repair of mobile computers. Our closed-loop feedback system provides weekly reports to managers alerting them to actual problems while anticipating trends. We have also provided sophisticated customer satisfaction market modeling (LISREL) for all Latin American country/regional operations of a major I/T provider in a multi-year project. Other programs provide monthly measurements of satisfaction and repurchase intention. Our ongoing brand satisfaction research monitors progress in the market indexed to the Best of Class and targeted competitors.

Cooper Research Group

Strategic Partner: Overview

XLM Marketing Group (disguised for this example) is leading the way in developing successful, integrated Relationship Marketing applications that offer a unique breadth of abilities across an array of industries and disciplines.

Our professionals are strategic marketing experts backed by extensive marketing services, utilizing the latest technological advances in marketing. They can act locally or globally by tapping into a worldwide network to deliver a single service or to integrate a wide spectrum of marketing services for any business. At XLM, we use the strength of our experience, technology, research, and assessment tools to evaluate and design the right solutions to help you stay ahead of your competition.

Running ongoing relationship marketing programs for employees or channels takes a huge investment of time, capital, and technology. XLM offers solutions that simplify your research tasks, with a variety of cost-effective efficiencies built in.

XLM is wired for results today, with clients worldwide:

- Operating more than 180 support programs for Fortune 1000 clients.

- Employing full-time administrative pros worldwide.

- Developing customized solutions with minimal lead times.

We have the technology, systems, and resources to set up and manage the business processes that support your sales and marketing programs.

- Designing, testing and implementing customized research solutions.

- Providing complete coordination of survey data and processing support.

- Communicating program-specific feedback to clients.

- Converting survey data into meaningful marketing information.

Our leading-edge technology solutions can be matched to your individual requirements, with a process that's been fine-tuned and proven successful:

- Client-focused teams continuously manage, monitor, and measure results.

- Periodic benchmark measurements ensure the program is meeting your goals.

- XLM makes program adjustments as needed.

- Enhanced reporting helps you understand data that impacts your decisions.

Cooper Research Group

Relevant Industry Experience: XLM Marketing Group

The following is a list of studies XLM has conducted in the industry. Although the list is not exhaustive, it is provided as an example of the broad spectrum of studies conducted in this area.

Technology Industry:
Studies within the North American and European markets to measure customer satisfaction and corporate identity. Entailed a variety of methodological approaches including focus groups, depth interviews, and business to business interviews.

Pharmaceutical Industry:
A series of surveys have been conducted to determine competitive strengths, customer satisfaction, and segment awareness. Decisions concerning corporate direction are made based on the information gathered.

Telecommunications Industry:
Multiple surveys were conducted to understand both business-to-business customers and consumer customers. Linkages were created to a parallel employee survey to determine value chain impacts.

Retail Industry:
Store specific customer satisfaction linked to employee satisfaction and mystery shopping assessments to optimize service though optimal staffing and training.

Distribution of Consumer Products:
Value chain analysis of distribution, retail and consumer satisfaction of fast moving consumer goods. Information used to modify merchandising contracts, displays and value added information in the distribution chain.

Auto Parts Distribution Customer Satisfaction:
Customers satisfaction survey among customers for a major automotive parts organization.

Cooper Research Group

Project Costs

The cost for conducting the U.S. research is $142,500. Reimbursable expenses for travel and living away from home will be billed at cost. Project contingencies typically will not exceed 10% of proposed fees.

Estimates for your anticipated international projects are based on 150 completed surveys in Europe and 150 in Asia-Pacific. The estimate does not include focus groups or other exploratory analysis. The range for Europe: $35,000–$45,000. Asia-Pacific: $40,000–$55,000.

Our standard payment terms are 1/3 at the commencement of work, 1/3 at midpoint, and 1/3 upon project completion, subject to negotiation.

CRG and XLM will devote their best efforts to the work performed on this engagement. The findings, recommendations, and written materials we provide will represent our best professional judgment based on the information made available to us.

We require a one-week period from signature of the Document of Understanding to appropriately staff the engagement before beginning work. During this time we will be available to meet with you. Our timeline schedule and subsequent project execution is based on early notification by Seagate.

Cooper Research Group

Notes

1. It is the policy of Cooper Research Group to present proposals with the understanding that their contents are copyrighted and that the ideas, conceptual approaches, and techniques expressed in them are the intellectual property of the Cooper Research Group, Inc. Nothing contained in this document may be divulged to any third party without the prior written permission of Cooper Research Group, Inc.

2. The concept specifications and costs will remain valid for a two-month period from the date of this proposal.

3. Pricing does not include travel and accommodation costs related to client meetings or focus groups. The cost for facilities and other focus group-related costs (other than professional fees) are also not included in the project costs.

Cooper Research Group

Sample Student Term Project

Four members of a graduate research methods course formed a team to investigate career prospects in product management. Their stated research objectives were (1) to provide an inventory of major U.S. manufacturers that use the product management system, (2) to gather descriptive data on the nature and degree of product management, and (3) to collect information on how product managers are recruited, selected, and prepared for their responsibilities.

The research question was: "What is the role and scope of product management in U.S. manufacturing companies?" Since financial support from the student research fund was limited to *Fortune*'s top 1,000 manufacturing companies, the students further defined manufacturers according to this criterion. Their investigative questions were:

1. What is the incidence of use of the product manager system?
   a. To what degree is it presently in use?
   b. Has it been used in the past and discontinued?
   c. Was it considered and not adopted?
   d. What are future expectations regarding its use?

2. How are product managers recruited and selected?

3. What are the qualifications for employment as a product manager?

4. How does the product manager function in the company?

5. How can we classify the characteristics of individuals and companies to discern trends and differences?

The students selected a mail survey as their data collection method. Their initial plan was to use a screening or qualifying question to establish which companies use product management.

The team members developed the following procedure for constructing their questionnaire. Having agreed on the investigative questions, each member attempted to write measurement questions aimed at tapping the essence of each investigative question. Each measurement question was written on a 5-by-8-inch card to facilitate comparisons, revisions, additions, and deletions. At a meeting of the team, all questions were reviewed, duplicates were eliminated, and a general winnowing occurred. The remaining 31 questions were included in questionnaire draft 1, shown in Exhibit E–1. In this first draft, there was no effort to place questions in sequence or to present them graphically as they would eventually be seen by respondents.

After discussion, the team members concluded the questionnaire would probably need to be three pages long. In addition, the cover letter would require a page. They decided to use a printed cover letter and to incorporate it as the first page of the questionnaire. The combination would be printed on both sides of an 11-by-17-inch sheet of paper, folded in booklet form to 8 1/2-by-11 inches.

Each team member was assigned the task of translating draft 1 into draft 2. In the new draft, the questions were in planned sequence, had response formats chosen, and had graphic arrangements selected. Individual drafts were submitted to a subcommittee of the team who used them as the basis for developing questionnaire draft 2. This is shown in Exhibit E–2.

Draft 2 was reproduced and submitted to other members of the research class for critique. Comments and challenges were sought on (1) sources of confusion and vagueness; (2) question value (What useful information does the question provide? Not provide?); (3) appropriateness of the proposed response formats and suggestions for improvement; and (4) gaps in question coverage.

EXHIBIT E–1   Preliminary Questionnaire, Product Manager Study—Draft 1

1. What is your position in the company?

2. Is your company engaged primarily in industrial products, consumer products, or both?

3. Does your company use product managers?

4. How many product managers does the company have?

5. How many products are assigned to one PM?

6. Would you please give or include a job description of your company's PM position?

7. How many brands does your company have?

8. Approximately what percentage of your company's brands have product managers?

9. What percentage of sales volume do the brands in question 8 account for as a whole?

10. How long have product managers been used in your company?

11. Has a PM system been used and dropped in your company? If yes, why was it dropped?

12. Has a PM system ever been considered but never adopted in your company? If yes, why was it not adopted?

13. Are there any plans for the adoption of a PM system in the future?

14. What percentage of your product managers come *directly* from each of the following sources? Campuses, within the company, other companies, other (list).

15. If PMs come from within the company, what department or departments do they come from? Sales, marketing, production, advertising, other (list).

16. If PMs come from outside the company (other than campuses), what department or departments do they come from? Product manager, sales, marketing, production, advertising, other (list).

17. If PMs are recruited directly from campuses, what, if any, are typical degrees required?

18. Rank on a scale from 1 to 5 the relative importance of each of the following qualifications for a PM (1 denotes the greatest importance): Education, age, work experience, personality, creativity.

19. If PMs are recruited from within the company, what is the average age, length of work experience (with the company), and educational background?

20. If PMs are recruited from outside the company (not including campuses), what is the average age, length of work experience, and educational background?

21. What functions (advertising, pricing, etc.) does the PM actually perform in day-to-day activities, and what percentage of time is spent on each?

22. Of those functions listed in question 21, which, if any, does the PM have *final* authority over?

23. To whom does the PM report?

24. Does your company have a structured training program for product management? If yes, please explain.

25. On the basis of which of the following is the PM evaluated? Market share, ROI, sales volume, profits, other (list).

26. What were the objectives of the company in instituting the PM concept?

27. How successful has the PM concept been in fulfilling the objectives set for it?

28. What were the characteristics of the PM concept that contributed to the fulfillment of these objectives?

29. What elements, if any, of the PM system did not adequately contribute to the fulfillment of the objectives?

30. What specific actions, if any, have been taken to deal with the inadequacies listed in question 29?

31. If your company is currently planning any broad revisions in the present PM program, please describe.

EXHIBIT E–2   **Product Manager Questionnaire—Draft 2**

1. Does your company now use product managers? yes _____ no _____ (If no, please go to question 17).

2. Would you please send a copy of your job description?

3. How many product managers does your company have? _____

4. What percentage of your total sales is accounted for by product managers? _____ %

5. How long have product managers been used by your company? _____ years

6. What percentage of your personnel enters the product management program from the following sources?

   Campuses _____ %

   Within the company _____ %

   From elsewhere _____ %

7. If product managers come from within the company or elsewhere, what department(s) do they come from?

   Sales _____ %

   Marketing _____ %

   Production _____ %

   Advertising _____ %

   Other product management programs _____ %

   Advertising agencies _____ %

   Elsewhere _____ %

8. If product managers are recruited directly from campuses, please rank the following degrees from 1 to 6, with 1 being the most desirable, 2 the next most desirable, and so forth.

   BS   _____   areas   _____

   AB   _____   areas   _____

   BSBA (BBA)   _____   areas   _____

   MA   _____   areas   _____

   MBA   _____   areas   _____

   PhD   _____   areas   _____

9. Briefly state what you consider to be an appropriate profile of a product manager recruited directly from the campus.

   Age:

   Work experience (length and type):

   Personal traits (personality, creativity, aggressiveness, etc.):

   Education:

EXHIBIT E–2 (Continued)

10. What do you consider to be an appropriate profile for a product manager recruited from within or from another company?

    Age:

    Work experience (length and type):

    Personal traits (personality, creativity, aggressiveness, etc.):

    Education:

11. To whom does the product manager report? _____

12. What percentage of his or her time does the product manager spend in various functionary areas, such as production, advertising, pricing, etc.? Please list.

13. Please rank on a scale of 1 to 5 (1 is most important) the following criteria used in evaluating a product manager.

    _____ Market share

    _____ Return on investment

    _____ Sales volume

    _____ Profits

    _____ Other (please explain) _____

14. Does the company have a structured training program?

    yes _____ no _____ If yes, please describe. _____

15. What prompted your firm to initiate the product manager system?

16. Is your company currently planning any future revisions in the product manager system?

    yes _____ no _____ If yes, please explain. _____

17. Is your company primarily engaged in

    Industrial goods _____ %

    Food products _____ %

    Consumer package goods _____ %

    Consumer durable goods _____ %

    Automotive products _____ %

    Other (list)

    _____ _____ %

    _____ _____ %

18. What is your company's total sales volume? $ _____

    If you answered question 1 yes, you have completed the questionnaire. If your answer was no, please answer question 19. Thank you for your cooperation.

19. Please check which of the following best describes your company's use of product managers.

    _____ Have never considered product managers.

    _____ Have considered, but never adopted product management.

    _____ Have used previously and discontinued.

    _____ Presently considering adoption of the system in the future.

After this critique, a second subcommittee revised the questionnaire. This resulted in questionnaire draft 3 (not presented here). The draft was again reviewed by the full team, and modest changes were made to produce draft 4.

By this time, the team members were eager to test the questionnaire with respondents. Arrangements were made to have several local corporate executives complete the questionnaire. Team members picked up the completed questionnaires, interviewed the executives about their answers, and secured comments they had about the questions and the study. These experiences led to a revised draft 5. This was repeated twice more with other executives, finally ending with draft 7 shown here as Exhibit E–3. The limitations of time and money led the team to depend on local product managers for testing rather than on a full-scale dress rehearsal by mail. This decision limited the value of the pretesting but was accepted as a limitation of a student project.

The survey was sent to the top 1,000 manufacturing companies in the form described. Only one mailing was made because of time and money limitations. Usable returns numbered 492 at the cutoff point. Approximately 50 companies sent job descriptions of their product management positions.

EXHIBIT E–3   Product Manager Questionnaire—Final Draft

METRO UNIVERSITY
GRADUATE SCHOOL OF BUSINESS ADMINISTRATION
DES MOINES, IA 50301

Inside Address

Dear Sir:

We at the Metro University Business School are interested in learning more about the actual recruitment and use of product or brand managers. Our objective is to help expand the body of knowledge about this important area of marketing.

To do this, of course, means going to someone such as yourself who *knows*. Your help with the few questions on the attached pages will take only a few minutes and will make a real contribution to the accuracy and success of this study.

Your reply will be treated in strict confidence and will be available only to my research staff and me. Any publication will be only of statistical totals for groups of companies.

Your assistance will be greatly appreciated and will help us to know more about product management and to teach about it in a more relevant and effective manner.

Sincerely,

William Urbandale
Professor of Marketing

We define a *product manager* (also called a *brand manager*) as one who is responsible for the integration and planning of a broad range of marketing functions (pricing, distribution, and so forth) for a specific product, brand, or homogeneous group of products. The position usually has limited or no line authority, especially over the sales force.

1. Please indicate which of the following best describes your company/division's use of product managers.

_____ We are currently using product managers.

_____ We have previously used product managers, but discontinued.

_____ We have considered the system, but never implemented it.

_____ Presently considering adoption of the system in the future.

_____ We have never considered product managers.

If you are currently using product managers, please continue. If you are not currently using product managers, you have completed the questionnaire. Thank you for your cooperation.

EXHIBIT E–3   (continued)

(please check)

2. Will you be answering the following for: _____ your company

          _____ your division

3. How many product managers (include all levels such as group PM, PM, assoc. PM, and assistant PM) does your company/division employ? _____

4. How long have product managers been used by your company/division?   _____ years

5. What percentage of your company/division total sales are accounted for by products controlled by product managers?   _____ %

6. From the following, please indicate whether the position exists in your company/division. Then indicate the source from which the personnel at the various levels were obtained to fill that position. If you have a similar position but with a different name, please indicate that position in the blank.

	Do You Have?		**(please check) Major Sources Within Company**			
	Yes	**No**	**Campuses**	**Other PM Jobs**	**Other Jobs**	**Other Companies**
Group PMs	____	____	____	____	____	____
PMs	____	____	____	____	____	____
Assoc. PMs	____	____	____	____	____	____
Asst. PMs	____	____	____	____	____	____
Other (specify)	____	____	____	____	____	____

7. What is the typical age of your

    Group product managers   _____ years

    Product managers   _____ years

    Associate PMs   _____ years

    Assistant PMs   _____ years

8. Of the following personal traits, please indicate their degree of importance in the evaluation of a candidate for a product management position.

	(please check)			
	Not Important	**Desirable**	**Very Desirable**	**Essential**
Leadership	____	____	____	____
Creativity	____	____	____	____
Aggressiveness	____	____	____	____
Analytical ability	____	____	____	____
Communications skill	____	____	____	____
Ability to work with others	____	____	____	____
Other _____	____	____	____	____

EXHIBIT E–3   (continued)

9. If you recruit directly from campus, please indicate the importance of the following traits of a product manager candidate.

(please check)

	Not Important	Desirable	Very Desirable	Essential
Business experience	____	____	____	____
High grade-point avg.	____	____	____	____
Extracurricular activities	____	____	____	____
MBA	____	____	____	____
Master's, technical	____	____	____	____
Bachelor's, business	____	____	____	____
Other (specify) _____	____	____	____	____

10. If you recruit into your PM group from other jobs (either from within your company or from other companies), please indicate the importance of the following experiences.

(please check)

Experience	Not Important	Desirable	Very Desirable	Essential
Sales	____	____	____	____
Other product manager programs	____	____	____	____
Other marketing positions	____	____	____	____
Production	____	____	____	____
Ad agencies	____	____	____	____
Undergraduate degree	____	____	____	____
Graduate degree	____	____	____	____
Other (specify) _____	____	____	____	____

11. Please indicate the percentage of time a typical product manager spends in the following activities:

Advertising	_____ %
Pricing	_____
Distribution	_____
Packaging	_____
Product development	_____
Marketing research	_____
Production liaison	_____
Finance and budgeting	_____
Other (specify) _____	_____
Other (specify) _____	_____
Total	100%

EXHIBIT E–3   (continued)

12. Please indicate which of the following criteria are used in evaluating product managers in your company/division.

    a.   _____ Market share

        _____ Return on investment

        _____ Sales volume

        _____ Dollar profits

        _____ Other (please specify)

    b. Which one is most important? _____

13. Does your company/division have a structured training program for product managers?

    yes _____ no _____ (If yes, please describe.)

    _____

14. Is your company/division currently planning any revision in its product manager system?

    yes _____ no _____ (If yes, please describe.)

    _____

15. Judging from your company's experience, what do you feel is the major problem facing the product management system?

    _____

16. It would be most valuable to our studies if you could supply a sample job description of your product manager positions.
Are such available?

    ____ Yes, examples enclosed

    ____ Yes, examples sent under separate cover

    ____ Not available

Thank you for your assistance.

17. If you would like a summary of the results of this survey, please check here. ____

Thank you for your assistance.

Nonparametric Significance Tests

This appendix contains additional nonparametric tests of hypotheses to augment those described in Chapter 17 (see Exhibit 17–7).

One-Sample Case

Kolmogorov-Smirnov Test

This test is appropriate when the data are at least ordinal and the research situation calls for a comparison of an observed sample distribution with a theoretical distribution. Under these conditions, the Kolmogorov-Smirnov (KS) one-sample test is more powerful than the χ^2 test and can be used for small samples when the χ^2 test cannot. The KS is a test of goodness of fit in which we specify the *cumulative* frequency distribution that would occur under the theoretical distribution and compare that with the observed cumulative frequency distribution. The theoretical distribution represents our expectations under H_0. We determine the point of greatest divergence between the observed and theoretical distributions and identify this value as D (maximum deviation). From a table of critical values for D, we determine whether such a large divergence is likely on the basis of random sampling variations from the theoretical distribution. The value for D is calculated as follows:

$$D = \text{Maximum} \left| F_0(X) - F_T(X) \right|$$

in which

$F_0(X)$ = The observed cumulative frequency distribution of a random sample of n observations. Where X is any possible score, $F_0(X) = k/n$, where k = the number of observations equal to or less than X.

$F_T(X)$ = The theoretical frequency distribution under H_0.

We illustrate the KS test, with an analysis of the results of the dining club study, in terms of various class levels. Take an equal number of interviews from each class, but secure unequal numbers of people interested in joining. Assume class levels are ordinal measurements. The testing process is as follows (see accompanying table):

1. **Null hypothesis.** H_0: There is no difference among student classes as to their intention of joining the dining club.

   H_A: There is a difference among students in various classes as to their intention of joining the dining club.

2. **Statistical test.** Choose the KS one-sample test because the data are ordinal measures and we are interested in comparing an observed distribution with a theoretical one.

3. **Significance level.** $\alpha = .05$, $n = 60$.

4. **Calculated value.** $D = \text{Maximum} |F_0(X) - F_T(X)|$.

5. **Critical test value.** We enter the table of critical values of D in the KS one-sample test (see Appendix Exhibit G–5) and learn that with $\alpha = .05$ the critical value for D is

	Freshman	Sophomore	Junior	Senior	Graduate
Number in each class	5	9	11	16	19
$F_0(X)$	5/60	14/60	25/60	41/60	60/60
$F_T(X)$	12/60	24/60	36/60	48/60	60/60
$\lvert F_0(X) - F_T(X) \rvert$	7/60	10/60	11/60	7/60	0

$D = 11/60 = .183$;

$n = 60$

$$D = \frac{1.36}{\sqrt{60}} = .175$$

6. Interpret. The calculated value is greater than the critical value, indicating we should reject the null hypothesis.

Two-Samples Case

Sign Test

The sign test is used with matched pairs when the only information is the identification of the pair member that is larger or smaller or has more or less of some characteristic. Under H_0, one would expect the number of cases in which $X_A > X_B$ to equal the number of pairs in which $X_B > X_A$. All ties are dropped from the analysis, and n is adjusted to allow for these eliminated pairs. This test is based on the binomial expansion and has a good power efficiency for small samples.

Wilcoxon Matched-Pairs Test

When you can determine both *direction* and *magnitude* of difference between carefully matched pairs, use the Wilcoxon matched-pairs test. This test has excellent efficiency and can be more powerful than the *t*-test in cases where the latter is not particularly appropriate. The mechanics of calculation are also quite simple. Find the difference score (d_i) between each pair of values, and rank-order the differences from smallest to largest without regard to sign. The actual signs of each difference are then added to the rank values, and the test statistic T is calculated. T is the sum of the ranks with the less frequent sign. Typical of such research situations might be a study where husband and wife are matched, where twins are used, where a given subject is used in a before-after study, or where the outputs of two similar machines are compared.

Two types of ties may occur with this test. When two observations are equal, the d score becomes zero, and we drop this pair of observations from the calculation. When two or more pairs have the same d value, we average their rank positions. For example, if two pairs have a rank score of 1, we assign the rank of 1.5 to each and rank the next largest difference as third. When $n < 25$, use the table of critical values (see Appendix Exhibit G–4). When $n > 25$, the sampling distribution of T is approximately normal with

$$\text{Mean} = \mu_T = \frac{n(n + 1)}{4}$$

$$\text{Standard deviation} = \sigma_T \sqrt{\frac{n(n + 1)(2n + 1)}{24}}$$

The formula for the test is

$$z = \frac{T - \mu_T}{\sigma_T}$$

Suppose you conduct an experiment on the effect of brand name on quality perception. Ten subjects are recruited and asked to taste and compare two samples of a product, one identified as a well-known drink and the other as a new product being tested. In truth, however, the samples are identical. The subjects are then asked to rate the two samples on a set of scale items judged to be ordinal. Test these results for significance by the usual procedure.

1. **Null hypothesis.** H_0: There is no difference between the perceived qualities of the two samples.

        H_A: There is a difference in the perceived quality of the two samples.

2. **Statistical test.** The Wilcoxon matched-pairs test is used because the study is of related samples in which the differences can be ranked in magnitude.

3. **Significance level.** $\alpha = .05$, with $n = 10$ pairs of comparisons minus any pairs with a d of zero.

4. **Calculated value.** T equals the sum of the ranks with the less frequent sign. Assume we secure the following results:

Pair	Branded	Unbranded	d_i	Rank of d_i	Rank with Less Frequent Sign
1	52	48	4	4	
2	37	32	5	5.5*	
3	50	52	−2	−2	2
4	45	32	13	9	
5	56	59	−3	−3	3
6	51	50	1	1	
7	40	29	11	8	
8	59	54	5	5.5*	
9	38	38	0	*	
10	40	32	8	7	$T = 5$

*There are two types of tie situations. We drop out the pair with the type of tie shown by pair 9. Pairs 2 and 8 have a tie in rank of difference. In this case, we average the ranks and assign the average value to each.

5. **Critical test value.** Enter the table of critical values of T with $n = 9$ (see Appendix Exhibit G–4) and find that the critical value with $\alpha = .05$ is 6. Note that with this test, the calculated value must be smaller than the critical value to reject the null hypothesis.

6. **Interpret.** Since the calculated value is less than the critical value, reject the null hypothesis.

Kolmogorov-Smirnov Two-Samples Test

When a researcher has two independent samples of ordinal data, the Kolmogorov-Smirnov (KS) two-samples test is useful. Like the one-sample test, this two-samples test is concerned with the agreement between two cumulative distributions, but both represent sample values. If the two samples have been drawn from the same population, the cumulative distributions of the samples should be fairly close to each other, showing only random deviations from the population distribution. If the cumulative distributions show a large enough maximum deviation D, it is evidence for rejecting the H_0. To secure the maximum deviation, one should use as many intervals as are available so as not to obscure the maximum cumulative difference.

The two-samples KS formula is

$$D = \text{Maximum } |F_{N1}(X) - F_{N2}(X)| \quad \text{(two-tailed test)}$$

$$D = \text{Maximum } |F_{N1}(X) - F_{N2}(X)| \quad \text{(one-tailed test)}$$

D is calculated in the same manner as before, but the table for critical values for the numerator of D, K_D (two-samples case) is presented in Appendix Exhibit G–6 when $n_1 = n_2$ and is less than 40 observations. When n_1 and/or n_2 are larger than 40, D from Appendix Exhibit G–7 should be used. With this larger sample, it is not necessary that $n_1 = n_2$.

Here we use a different sample from the smoking-accident study. (To make $n_1 = n_2$, we increased the sample size of no accidents to 34. Nonsmokers with no accidents is 24.) Suppose the smoking classifications represent an ordinal scale, and you test these data with the KS two-samples test. Proceed as follows:

1. **Null hypothesis.** H_0: There is no difference in on-the-job accident occurrences between smokers and nonsmokers.

   H_A: The more a person smokes, the more likely that person is to have an on-the-job accident.

2. **Statistical test.** The KS two-samples test is used because it is assumed the data are ordinal.

3. **Significance level.** $\alpha = .05$. $n_1 = n_2 = 34$.

4. **Calculated value.** See the one-sample calculation (KS test) and compare with table below.

5. **Critical test value.** We enter Appendix Exhibit G–6 with $n = 34$ to find that $K_D = 11$ when $p = \leq .05$ for a one-tailed distribution.

	Heavy Smoker	Moderate Smoker	Nonsmoker
$F_{n1}(X)$	12/34	21/34	34/34
$F_{n2}(X)$	4/34	10/34	34/34
$d_i = K_{D/n}$	8/34	11/34	0

6. **Interpret.** Since the critical value equals the largest calculated value, we reject the null hypothesis.

Mann-Whitney *U* Test

This test is also used with two independent samples if the data are at least ordinal; it is an alternative to the *t*-test without the latter's limiting assumptions. When the larger of the two samples is 20 or less, there are special tables for interpreting U; when the larger sample exceeds 20, a normal curve approximation is used.

In calculating the U test, treat all observations in a combined fashion and rank them, algebraically, from smallest to largest. The largest negative score receives the lowest rank. In case of ties, assign the average rank as in other tests. With this test, you can also test samples that are unequal. After the ranking, the rank values for each sample are totaled. Compute the U statistic as follows:

$$U = n_1 n_2 + \frac{n_1(n_1 + 1)}{2} - R_1$$

or

$$U = n_1 n_2 + \frac{n_2(n_2 - 1)}{2} - R_2$$

in which

> n_1 = Number in sample 1
>
> n_2 = Number in sample 2
>
> R_1 = Sum of ranks in sample 1

With this equation, you can secure two U values, one using R_1 and the second using R_2. For testing purposes, use the smaller U.

An example may help to clarify the U statistic calculation procedure. Let's consider the sales training example with the t distribution discussion. Recall that salespeople with training method A averaged higher sales than salespeople with training method B. While these data are ratio measures, one still might not want to accept the other assumptions that underlie the t-test. What kind of a result could be secured with the U test? While the U test is designed for ordinal data, it can be used with interval and ratio measurements.

1. **Null hypothesis.** H_0: There is no difference in sales results produced by the two training methods.

   H_A: Training method A produces sales results superior to the results of method B.

2. **Statistical test.** The Mann-Whitney U test is chosen because the measurement is at least ordinal, and the assumptions under the parametric t-test are rejected.

3. **Significance level.** α = .05 (one-tailed test).

4. **Calculated value.**

Sales Per Week per Salesperson			
Training Method A	**Rank**	**Training Method B**	**Rank**
1,500	15	1,340	10
1,540	16	1,300	8.5
1,860	22	1,620	18
1,230	6	1,070	3
1,370	12	1,210	5
1,550	17	1,170	4
1,840	21	1,770	20
1,250	7	950	1
1,300	8.5	1,380	13
1,350	11	1,460	14
1,710	19	1,030	2
	$R_1 = 154.5$		$R_2 = 98.5$

$$U = (11)(11) + \frac{11(11+1)}{2} - 154.5 = 32.5 \qquad U = (11)(11) + \frac{11(11+1)}{2} - 98.5 = 88.5$$

5. **Critical test value.** Enter Appendix Exhibit G–8 with $n_1 = n_2 = 11$, and find a critical value of 34 for α = 0.5, one-tailed test. Note that with this test, the calculated value must be smaller than the critical value to reject the null hypothesis.

6. Interpret. Since the calculated value is smaller than the critical value ($34 > 32.5$), reject the null hypothesis and conclude that training method A is probably superior.

Thus, one would reject the null hypothesis at $\alpha = .05$ in a one-tailed test using either the t- or the U test. In this example, the U test has approximately the same power as the parametric test.

When $n > 20$ in one of the samples, the sampling distribution of U approaches the normal distribution with

$$\text{Mean} = \mu_U = \frac{n_1 n_2}{2}$$

$$\text{Standard deviation } \sigma_U = \sqrt{\frac{(n_1)(n_2)(n_1 + n_2 + 1)}{12}}$$

and

$$z = \frac{U - \mu_U}{\sigma_U}$$

Other Nonparametric Tests

Other tests are appropriate under certain conditions when testing two independent samples. When the measurement is only nominal, the Fisher exact probability test may be used. When the data are at least ordinal, use the median and Wald-Wolfowitz runs tests.

k-Samples Case

You can use tests more powerful than χ^2 with data that are at least ordinal in nature. One such test is an extension of the median test mentioned earlier. We illustrate here the application of a second ordinal measurement test known as the Kruskal-Wallis one-way analysis of variance.

Kruskal-Wallis Test

This is a generalized version of the Mann-Whitney test. With it we rank all scores in the entire pool of observations from smallest to largest. The rank sum of each sample is then calculated, with ties being distributed as in other examples. We then compute the value of H as follows:

$$H = \frac{12}{N(N + 1)} \sum_{j=1}^{k} \frac{T_j^2}{n_j} - 3(N + 1)$$

where

T_j = Sum of ranks in column j

n_j = Number of cases in jth sample

$N = \Sigma w_j$ = Total number of cases

k = Number of samples

When there are a number of ties, it is recommended that a correct factor (C) be calculated and used to correct the H value as follows:

$$C = 1 - \left\{ \frac{\sum_{i}^{G} (t_i^3 - t_i)}{N^3 - N} \right\}$$

where

G = Number of sets of tied observations

t_i = Number tied in any set i

$H' = H/C$

To secure the critical value for H', use the table for the distribution of χ^2 (see Appendix Exhibit G–3), and enter it with the value of H' and d.f. $= k - 1$.

To illustrate the application of this test, use the price discount experiment problem. The data and calculations are shown in Exhibit F–1 and indicate that, by the Kruskal-Wallis test, one again barely fails to reject the null hypothesis with $\alpha = .05$.

EXHIBIT F–1   Kruskal-Wallis One-Way Analysis of Variance (price differentials)

One Cent		Three Cents		Five Cents	
X_A	Rank	X_B	Rank	X_C	Rank
6	1	8	5	9	8.5
7	2.5	9	8.5	9	8.5
8	5	8	5	11	14
7	2.5	10	11.5	10	11.5
9	8.5	11	14	14	18
11	14	13	16.5	13	16.5
	$T_j = 33.5$		60.5		77.0

$$T = 33.5 + 60.5 + 77$$

$$= 171$$

$$H = \frac{12}{18(18+1)} \left[\frac{33.5^2 + 60.5^2 + 77^2}{6} \right] - 3(18+1)$$

$$= \frac{12}{342} \left[\frac{1{,}122.25 + 3{,}660.25 + 5{,}929}{6} \right] - 57$$

$$= 0.0351 \left[\frac{10{,}711.5}{6} \right] - 57$$

$$H = 5.66$$

$$C = 1 - \left(\frac{3[(2)^3 - 2] + 2[(3)^3 - 3] + 4[(4)^3 - 4]}{18^3 - 18} \right)$$

$$= 1 - \frac{18 + 48 + 60}{5814}$$

$$= .978$$

$$H' = \frac{H}{C} = \frac{5.66}{.978} = 5.79$$

$$d.f. = k - 1 = 2$$

$$p > .05$$

Selected Statistical Tables

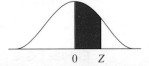

EXHIBIT G–1   Areas of the Standard Normal Distribution

z	0.00	0.01	0.02	0.03	0.04	0.05	0.06	0.07	0.08	0.09
					Second Decimal Place in z					
0.0	0.0000	0.0040	0.0080	0.0120	0.0160	0.0199	0.0239	0.0279	0.0319	0.0359
0.1	0.0398	0.0438	0.0478	0.0517	0.0557	0.0596	0.0636	0.0675	0.0714	0.0753
0.2	0.0793	0.0832	0.0871	0.0910	0.0948	0.0987	0.1026	0.1064	0.1103	0.1141
0.3	0.1179	0.1217	0.1255	0.1293	0.1331	0.1368	0.1406	0.1443	0.1480	0.1517
0.4	0.1554	0.1591	0.1628	0.1664	0.1700	0.1736	0.1772	0.1808	0.1844	0.1879
0.5	0.1915	0.1950	0.1985	0.2019	0.2054	0.2088	0.2123	0.2157	0.2190	0.2224
0.6	0.2257	0.2291	0.2324	0.2357	0.2389	0.2422	0.2454	0.2486	0.2517	0.2549
0.7	0.2580	0.2611	0.2642	0.2673	0.2704	0.2734	0.2764	0.2794	0.2823	0.2852
0.8	0.2881	0.2910	0.2939	0.2967	0.2995	0.3023	0.3051	0.3078	0.3106	0.3133
0.9	0.3159	0.3186	0.3212	0.3238	0.3264	0.3289	0.3315	0.3340	0.3365	0.3389
1.0	0.3413	0.3438	0.3461	0.3485	0.3508	0.3531	0.3554	0.3577	0.3599	0.3621
1.1	0.3643	0.3665	0.3686	0.3708	0.3729	0.3749	0.3770	0.3790	0.3810	0.3830
1.2	0.3849	0.3869	0.3888	0.3907	0.3925	0.3944	0.3962	0.3980	0.3997	0.4015
1.3	0.4032	0.4049	0.4066	0.4082	0.4099	0.4115	0.4131	0.4147	0.4162	0.4177
1.4	0.4192	0.4207	0.4222	0.4236	0.4251	0.4265	0.4279	0.4292	0.4306	0.4319
1.5	0.4332	0.4345	0.4357	0.4370	0.4382	0.4394	0.4406	0.4418	0.4429	0.4441
1.6	0.4452	0.4463	0.4474	0.4484	0.4495	0.4505	0.4515	0.4525	0.4535	0.4545
1.7	0.4554	0.4564	0.4573	0.4582	0.4591	0.4599	0.4608	0.4616	0.4625	0.4633
1.8	0.4641	0.4649	0.4656	0.4664	0.4671	0.4678	0.4686	0.4693	0.4699	0.4706
1.9	0.4713	0.4719	0.4726	0.4732	0.4738	0.4744	0.4750	0.4756	0.4761	0.4767
2.0	0.4772	0.4778	0.4783	0.4788	0.4793	0.4798	0.4803	0.4808	0.4812	0.4817
2.1	0.4821	0.4826	0.4830	0.4834	0.4838	0.4842	0.4846	0.4850	0.4854	0.4857
2.2	0.4861	0.4864	0.4868	0.4871	0.4875	0.4878	0.4881	0.4884	0.4887	0.4890
2.3	0.4893	0.4896	0.4898	0.4901	0.4904	0.4906	0.4909	0.4911	0.4913	0.4916
2.4	0.4918	0.4920	0.4922	0.4925	0.4927	0.4929	0.4931	0.4932	0.4934	0.4936
2.5	0.4938	0.4940	0.4941	0.4943	0.4945	0.4946	0.4948	0.4949	0.4951	0.4952
2.6	0.4953	0.4955	0.4956	0.4957	0.4959	0.4960	0.4961	0.4962	0.4963	0.4964
2.7	0.4965	0.4966	0.4967	0.4968	0.4969	0.4970	0.4971	0.4972	0.4973	0.4974
2.8	0.4974	0.4975	0.4976	0.4977	0.4977	0.4978	0.4979	0.4979	0.4980	0.4981
2.9	0.4981	0.4982	0.4982	0.4983	0.4984	0.4984	0.4985	0.4985	0.4986	0.4986
3.0	0.4987	0.4987	0.4987	0.4988	0.4988	0.4989	0.4989	0.4989	0.4990	0.4990
3.1	0.4990	0.4991	0.4991	0.4991	0.4992	0.4992	0.4992	0.4992	0.4993	0.4993
3.2	0.4993	0.4993	0.4994	0.4994	0.4994	0.4994	0.4994	0.4995	0.4995	0.4995
3.3	0.4995	0.4995	0.4995	0.4996	0.4996	0.4996	0.4996	0.4996	0.4996	0.4997
3.4	0.4997	0.4997	0.4997	0.4997	0.4997	0.4997	0.4997	0.4997	0.4997	0.4998
3.5	0.4998									
4.0	0.49997									
4.5	0.499997									
5.0	0.4999997									
6.0	0.499999999									

EXHIBIT G–2   Critical Values of *t* for Given Probability Levels

d.f.	Level of Significance for One-Tailed Test					
	.10	.05	.025	.01	.005	.0005
	Level of Significance for Two-Tailed Test					
	.20	.10	.05	.02	.01	.001
1	3.078	6.314	12.706	31.821	63.657	636.619
2	1.886	2.920	4.303	6.965	9.925	31.598
3	1.638	2.353	3.182	4.541	5.841	12.941
4	1.533	2.132	2.776	3.747	4.604	8.610
5	1.476	2.015	2.571	3.365	4.032	6.859
6	1.440	1.943	2.447	3.143	3.707	5.959
7	1.415	1.895	2.365	2.998	3.499	5.405
8	1.397	1.860	2.306	2.896	3.355	5.041
9	1.383	1.833	2.262	2.821	3.250	4.781
10	1.372	1.812	2.228	2.764	3.169	4.587
11	1.363	1.796	2.201	2.718	3.106	4.437
12	1.356	1.782	2.179	2.681	3.055	4.318
13	1.350	1.771	2.160	2.650	3.012	4.221
14	1.345	1.761	2.145	2.624	2.977	4.140
15	1.341	1.753	2.131	2.602	2.947	4.073
16	1.337	1.746	2.120	2.583	2.921	4.015
17	1.333	1.740	2.110	2.567	2.898	3.965
18	1.330	1.734	2.101	2.552	2.878	3.922
19	1.328	1.729	2.093	2.539	2.861	3.883
20	1.325	1.725	2.086	2.528	2.845	3.850
21	1.323	1.721	2.080	2.518	2.831	3.819
22	1.321	1.717	2.074	2.508	2.819	3.792
23	1.319	1.714	2.069	2.500	2.807	3.767
24	1.318	1.711	2.064	2.492	2.797	3.745
25	1.316	1.708	2.060	2.485	2.787	3.725
26	1.315	1.706	2.056	2.479	2.779	3.707
27	1.314	1.703	2.052	2.473	2.771	3.690
28	1.313	1.701	2.048	2.467	2.763	3.674
29	1.311	1.699	2.045	2.462	2.756	3.659
30	1.310	1.697	2.042	2.457	2.750	3.646
40	1.303	1.684	2.021	2.423	2.704	3.551
60	1.296	1.671	2.000	2.390	2.660	3.460
120	1.289	1.658	1.980	2.358	2.617	3.373
∞	1.282	1.645	1.960	2.326	2.576	3.291

SOURCE: Abridged from Table III of Fisher and Yates, *Statistical Tables for Biological, Agricultural, and Medical Research,* 6th ed., published by Oliver and Boyd Ltd., Edinburgh, 1963. By permission of the publishers.

EXHIBIT G–3   **Critical Values of the Chi-Square Distribution**

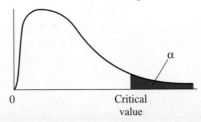

0   Critical
value

d.f.	Probability Under H_0 that $\chi^2 \geq$ Chi Square				
	.10	.05	.02	.01	.001
1	2.71	3.84	5.41	6.64	10.83
2	4.60	5.99	7.82	9.21	13.82
3	6.25	7.82	9.84	11.34	16.27
4	7.78	9.49	11.67	13.28	18.46
5	9.24	11.07	13.39	15.09	20.52
6	10.64	12.59	15.03	16.81	22.46
7	12.02	14.07	16.62	18.48	24.32
8	13.36	15.51	18.17	20.09	26.12
9	14.68	16.92	19.68	21.67	27.88
10	15.99	18.31	21.16	23.21	29.59
11	17.28	19.68	22.62	24.72	31.26
12	18.55	21.03	24.05	26.22	32.91
13	19.81	22.36	25.47	27.69	34.53
14	21.06	23.68	26.87	29.14	36.12
15	22.31	25.00	28.26	30.58	37.70
16	23.54	26.30	29.63	32.00	39.29
17	24.77	27.59	31.00	33.41	40.75
18	25.99	28.87	32.35	34.80	42.31
19	27.20	30.14	33.69	36.19	43.82
20	28.41	31.41	35.02	37.57	45.32
21	29.62	32.67	36.34	38.93	46.80
22	30.81	33.92	37.66	40.29	48.27
23	32.01	35.17	38.97	41.64	49.73
24	33.20	36.42	40.27	42.98	51.18
25	34.38	37.65	41.57	44.31	52.62
26	35.56	38.88	42.86	45.64	54.05
27	36.74	40.11	44.14	46.96	55.48
28	37.92	41.34	45.42	48.28	56.89
29	39.09	42.56	46.69	49.59	58.30
30	40.26	43.77	47.96	50.89	59.70

SOURCE: Abridged from Table IV of Fisher and Yates, *Statistical Tables for Biological, Agricultural, and Medical Research,* 6th ed., published by Oliver and Boyd Ltd., Edinburgh, 1963. By permission of the publishers.

EXHIBIT G–4   Critical Values of T in the Wilcoxon Matched-Pairs Test

n	Level of Significance for One-Tailed Test		
	.025	.01	.005
	Level of Significance for Two-Tailed Test		
	.05	.02	.01
6	0	–	–
7	2	0	–
8	4	2	0
9	6	3	2
10	8	5	3
11	11	7	5
12	14	10	7
13	17	13	10
14	21	16	13
15	25	20	16
16	30	24	20
17	35	28	23
18	40	33	28
19	46	38	32
20	52	43	38
21	59	49	43
22	66	56	49
23	73	62	55
24	81	69	61
25	89	77	68

SOURCE: Adapted from Table 1 of F. Wilcoxon, *Some Rapid Approximate Statistical Procedures* (New York: American Cyanamid Company, 1949), p. 13, with the kind permission of the publisher.

EXHIBIT G–5   Critical Values of D in the Kolmogorov-Smirnov One-Sample Test

Sample Size n	Level of Significance for $D = $ Maximum $|F_0(X) - S_N(X)|$				
	.20	.15	.10	.05	.01
1	.900	.925	.950	.975	.995
2	.684	.726	.776	.842	.929
3	.565	.597	.642	.708	.828
4	.494	.525	.564	.624	.733
5	.446	.474	.510	.565	.669
6	.410	.436	.470	.521	.618
7	.381	.405	.438	.486	.577
8	.358	.381	.411	.457	.543
9	.339	.360	.388	.432	.514
10	.322	.342	.368	.410	.490
11	.307	.326	.352	.391	.468
12	.295	.313	.338	.375	.450
13	.284	.302	.325	.361	.433
14	.274	.292	.314	.349	.418
15	.266	.283	.304	.338	.404
16	.258	.274	.295	.328	.392
17	.250	.266	.286	.318	.381
18	.244	.259	.278	.309	.371
19	.237	.252	.272	.301	.363
20	.231	.246	.264	.294	.356
25	.21	.22	.24	.27	.32
30	.19	.20	.22	.24	.29
35	.18	.19	.21	.23	.27
Over 35	$\dfrac{1.07}{\sqrt{N}}$	$\dfrac{1.14}{\sqrt{N}}$	$\dfrac{1.22}{\sqrt{N}}$	$\dfrac{1.36}{\sqrt{N}}$	$\dfrac{1.63}{\sqrt{N}}$

SOURCE: F. J. Massey, Jr., "The Kolmogorov-Smirnov Test for Goodness of Fit," *Journal of the American Statistical Association* 46, p. 70. Adapted with the kind permission of the publisher.

EXHIBIT G–6 Critical Values of K_D in the Kolmogorov-Smirnov Two-Samples Test (small samples)

n	One-Tailed Test[*]		Two-Tailed Test[†]	
	$\alpha = .05$	$\alpha = .01$	$\alpha = .05$	$\alpha = .01$
3	3	–	–	–
4	4	–	4	–
5	4	5	5	5
6	5	6	5	6
7	5	6	6	6
8	5	6	6	7
9	6	7	6	7
10	6	7	7	8
11	6	8	7	8
12	6	8	7	8
13	7	8	7	9
14	7	8	8	9
15	7	9	8	9
16	7	9	8	10
17	8	9	8	10
18	8	10	9	10
19	8	10	9	10
20	8	10	9	11
21	8	10	9	11
22	9	11	9	11
23	9	11	10	11
24	9	11	10	12
25	9	11	10	12
26	9	11	10	12
27	9	12	10	12
28	10	12	11	13
29	10	12	11	13
30	10	12	11	13
35	11	13	12	
40	11	14	13	

[*]SOURCE: Abridged from I. A. Goodman, "Kolmogorov-Smirnov Tests for Psychological Research," *Psychological Bulletin* 51 (1951), p. 167, copyright (1951) by the American Psychological Association. Reprinted by permission.

[†]SOURCE: Derived from Table 1 of F. J. Massey, Jr., "The Distribution of the Maximum Deviation Between Two Sample Cumulative Step Functions," *Annals of Mathematical Statistics* 23 (1951), pp. 126–27, with the kind permission of the publisher.

EXHIBIT G–7 Critical Values of D in the Kolmogorov-Smirnov Two-Samples Test for Large Samples (two-tailed)

Level of Significance	Value of D So Large as to Call for Rejection of H_0 at the Indicated Level of Significance, Where $D = $ Maximum $|S_{n1}(X) - S_2(X)|$
.10	$1.22 \sqrt{\dfrac{n_1 + n_2}{n_1 n_2}}$
.05	$1.36 \sqrt{\dfrac{n_1 + n_2}{n_1 n_2}}$
.025	$1.48 \sqrt{\dfrac{n_1 + n_2}{n_1 n_2}}$
.01	$1.63 \sqrt{\dfrac{n_1 + n_2}{n_1 n_2}}$
.005	$1.73 \sqrt{\dfrac{n_1 + n_2}{n_1 n_2}}$
.001	$1.95 \sqrt{\dfrac{n_1 + n_2}{n_1 n_2}}$

SOURCE: Adapted from N. Smirnov, "Table for Estimating the Goodness of Fit of Empirical Distribution," *Annals of Mathematical Statistics* 18 (1948), pp. 280–81, with the kind permission of the publisher.

EXHIBIT G–8   Partial Table of Critical Values of U in the Mann-Whitney Test

	Critical Values for One-Tailed Test at $\alpha = .025$ or a Two-Tailed Test at $\alpha = .05$											
$n_1 \backslash n_2$	9	10	11	12	13	14	15	16	17	18	19	20
1												
2	0	0	0	1	1	1	1	1	2	2	2	2
3	2	3	3	4	4	5	5	6	6	7	7	8
4	4	5	6	7	8	9	10	11	11	12	13	13
5	7	8	9	11	12	13	14	15	17	18	19	20
6	10	11	13	14	16	17	19	21	22	24	25	27
7	12	14	16	18	20	22	24	26	28	30	32	34
8	15	17	19	22	24	26	29	31	34	36	38	41
9	17	20	23	26	28	31	34	37	39	42	45	48
10	20	23	26	29	33	36	39	42	45	48	52	55
11	23	26	30	33	37	40	44	47	51	55	58	62
12	26	29	33	37	41	45	49	53	57	61	66	69
13	28	33	37	41	45	50	54	59	63	67	72	76
14	31	36	40	45	50	55	59	64	67	74	78	83
15	34	39	44	49	54	59	64	70	75	80	85	90
16	37	42	47	53	59	64	70	75	81	86	92	98
17	39	45	51	57	63	67	75	81	87	93	99	105
18	42	48	55	61	67	74	80	86	93	99	106	112
19	45	52	58	65	72	78	85	92	99	106	113	119
20	48	55	62	69	76	83	90	98	105	112	119	127

EXHIBIT G–8   Continued

$n_1 \backslash n_2$	9	10	11	12	13	14	15	16	17	18	19	20
1											0	0
2	1	1	1	2	2	2	3	3	3	4	4	4
3	3	4	5	5	6	7	7	8	9	9	10	11
4	6	7	8	9	10	11	12	14	15	16	17	18
5	9	11	12	13	15	16	18	19	20	22	23	25
6	12	14	16	17	19	21	23	25	26	28	30	32
7	15	17	19	21	24	26	28	30	33	35	37	39
8	18	20	23	26	28	31	33	36	39	41	44	47
9	21	24	27	30	33	36	39	42	45	48	51	54
10	24	27	31	34	37	41	44	48	51	55	58	62
11	27	31	34	38	42	46	50	54	57	61	65	69
12	30	34	38	42	47	51	55	60	64	68	72	77
13	33	37	42	47	51	56	61	65	70	75	80	84
14	36	41	46	51	56	61	66	71	77	82	87	92
15	39	44	50	55	61	66	72	77	83	88	94	100
16	42	48	54	60	65	71	77	83	89	95	101	107
17	45	51	57	64	70	77	83	89	96	102	109	115
18	48	55	61	68	75	82	88	95	102	109	116	123
19	51	58	65	72	80	87	94	101	109	116	123	130
20	54	62	69	77	84	92	100	107	115	123	130	138

Critical Values for One-Tailed Test at $\alpha = .05$ or a Two-Tailed Test at $\alpha = .10$

SOURCE: Abridged from D. Auble, "Extended Tables from the Mann-Whitney Statistic," *Bulletin of the Institute of Educational Research at Indiana University* 1, no. 2, reprinted with permission. For tables for other size samples consult this source.

EXHIBIT G-9 Critical Values of the F Distribution for $\alpha = .05$

Degrees of Freedom for Numerator

n_2	1	2	3	4	5	6	7	8	9	10	12	15	20	24	30	40	60	120	∞
1	161.4	199.5	215.7	224.6	230.2	234.0	236.8	238.9	240.5	241.9	243.9	245.9	248.0	249.1	250.1	251.1	252.2	253.3	243.3
2	18.51	19.00	19.16	19.25	19.30	19.33	19.35	19.37	19.38	19.40	19.41	19.43	19.45	19.45	19.46	19.47	19.48	19.49	19.50
3	10.13	9.55	9.28	9.12	9.01	8.94	8.89	8.85	8.81	8.79	8.74	8.70	8.66	8.64	8.62	8.59	8.57	8.55	8.53
4	7.71	6.94	6.59	6.39	6.26	6.16	6.09	6.04	6.00	5.96	5.91	5.86	5.80	5.77	5.75	5.72	5.69	5.66	5.63
5	6.61	5.79	5.41	5.19	5.05	4.95	4.88	4.82	4.77	4.74	4.68	4.62	4.56	4.53	4.50	4.46	4.43	4.40	4.36
6	5.99	5.14	4.76	4.53	4.39	4.28	4.21	4.15	4.10	4.06	4.00	3.94	3.87	3.84	3.81	3.77	3.74	3.70	3.67
7	5.59	4.74	4.35	4.12	3.97	3.87	3.79	3.73	3.68	3.64	3.57	3.51	3.44	3.41	3.38	3.34	3.30	3.27	3.23
8	5.32	4.46	4.07	3.84	3.69	3.58	3.50	3.44	3.39	3.35	3.28	3.22	3.15	3.12	3.08	3.04	3.01	2.97	2.93
9	5.12	4.26	3.86	3.63	3.48	3.37	3.29	3.23	3.18	3.14	3.07	3.01	2.94	2.90	2.86	2.83	2.79	2.75	2.71
10	4.96	4.10	3.71	3.48	3.33	3.22	3.14	3.07	3.02	2.98	2.91	2.85	2.77	2.74	2.70	2.66	2.62	2.58	2.54
11	4.84	3.98	3.59	3.36	3.20	3.09	3.01	2.95	2.90	2.85	2.79	2.72	2.65	2.61	2.57	2.53	2.49	2.45	2.40
12	4.75	3.89	3.49	3.26	3.11	3.00	2.91	2.85	2.80	2.75	2.69	2.62	2.54	2.51	2.47	2.43	2.38	2.34	2.30
13	4.67	3.81	3.41	3.18	3.03	2.92	2.83	2.77	2.71	2.67	2.60	2.53	2.46	2.42	2.38	2.34	2.30	2.25	2.21
14	4.60	3.74	3.34	3.11	2.96	2.85	2.76	2.70	2.65	2.60	2.53	2.46	2.39	2.35	2.31	2.27	2.22	2.18	2.13
15	4.54	3.68	3.29	3.06	2.90	2.79	2.71	2.64	2.59	2.54	2.48	2.40	2.33	2.29	2.25	2.20	2.16	2.11	2.07
16	4.49	3.63	3.24	3.01	2.85	2.74	2.66	2.59	2.54	2.49	2.42	2.35	2.28	2.24	2.19	2.15	2.11	2.06	2.01
17	4.45	3.59	3.20	2.96	2.81	2.70	2.61	2.55	2.49	2.45	2.38	2.31	2.23	2.19	2.15	2.10	2.06	2.01	1.96
18	4.41	3.55	3.16	2.93	2.77	2.66	2.58	2.51	2.46	2.41	2.34	2.27	2.19	2.15	2.11	2.06	2.02	1.97	1.92
19	4.38	3.52	3.13	2.90	2.74	2.63	2.54	2.48	2.42	2.38	2.31	2.23	2.16	2.11	2.07	2.03	1.98	1.93	1.88
20	4.35	3.49	3.10	2.87	2.71	2.60	2.51	2.45	2.39	2.35	2.28	2.20	2.12	2.08	2.04	1.99	1.95	1.90	1.84
21	4.32	3.47	3.07	2.84	2.68	2.57	2.49	2.42	2.37	2.32	2.25	2.18	2.10	2.05	2.01	1.96	1.92	1.87	1.81
22	4.30	3.44	3.05	2.82	2.66	2.55	2.46	2.40	2.34	2.30	2.23	2.15	2.07	2.03	1.98	1.94	1.89	1.84	1.78
23	4.28	3.42	3.03	2.80	2.64	2.53	2.44	2.37	2.32	2.27	2.20	2.13	2.05	2.01	1.96	1.91	1.86	1.81	1.76
24	4.26	3.40	3.01	2.78	2.62	2.51	2.42	2.36	2.30	2.25	2.18	2.11	2.03	1.98	1.94	1.89	1.84	1.79	1.73
25	4.24	3.39	2.99	2.76	2.60	2.49	2.40	2.34	2.28	2.24	2.16	2.09	2.01	1.96	1.92	1.87	1.82	1.77	1.71
26	4.23	3.37	2.98	2.74	2.59	2.47	2.39	2.32	2.27	2.22	2.15	2.07	1.99	1.95	1.90	1.85	1.80	1.75	1.69
27	4.21	3.35	2.96	2.73	2.57	2.46	2.37	2.31	2.25	2.20	2.13	2.06	1.97	1.93	1.88	1.84	1.79	1.73	1.67
28	4.20	3.34	2.95	2.71	2.56	2.45	2.36	2.29	2.24	2.19	2.12	2.04	1.96	1.91	1.87	1.82	1.77	1.71	1.65
29	4.18	3.33	2.93	2.70	2.55	2.43	2.35	2.28	2.22	2.18	2.10	2.03	1.94	1.90	1.85	1.81	1.75	1.70	1.64
30	4.17	3.32	2.92	2.69	2.53	2.42	2.33	2.27	2.21	2.16	2.09	2.01	1.93	1.89	1.84	1.79	1.74	1.68	1.62
40	4.08	3.23	2.84	2.61	2.45	2.34	2.25	2.18	2.12	2.08	2.00	1.92	1.84	1.79	1.74	1.69	1.64	1.58	1.51
60	4.00	3.15	2.76	2.53	2.37	2.25	2.17	2.10	2.04	1.99	1.92	1.84	1.75	1.70	1.65	1.59	1.53	1.47	1.39
120	3.92	3.07	2.68	2.45	2.29	2.17	2.09	2.02	1.96	1.91	1.83	1.75	1.66	1.61	1.55	1.50	1.43	1.35	1.25
∞	3.84	3.00	2.60	2.37	2.21	2.10	2.01	1.94	1.88	1.83	1.75	1.67	1.57	1.52	1.46	1.39	1.32	1.22	1.00

Degrees of Freedom for Denominator

SOURCE: Reprinted by permission from *Statistical Methods* by George W. Snedecor and William G. Cochran, 6th edition, © 1967 by Iowa State University Press, Ames, Iowa.

EXHIBIT G–10 Random Numbers

97446	30328	05262	77371	13523	62057	44349	85884	94555	23288
15453	75591	60540	77137	09485	27632	05477	99154	78720	10323
69995	77086	55217	53721	85713	27854	41981	88981	90041	20878
69726	58696	27272	38148	52521	73807	29685	49152	20309	58734
23604	31948	16926	26360	76957	99925	86045	11617	32777	38670
13640	17233	58650	47819	24935	28670	33415	77202	92492	40290
90779	09199	51169	94892	34271	22068	13923	53535	56358	50258
71068	19459	32339	10124	13012	79706	07611	52600	83088	26829
55019	79001	34442	16335	06428	52873	65316	01480	72204	39494
20879	50235	17389	25260	34039	99967	48044	05067	69284	53867
00380	11595	49372	95214	98529	46593	77046	27176	39668	20566
68142	40800	20527	79212	14166	84948	11748	69540	84288	37211
42667	89566	20440	57230	35356	01884	79921	94772	29882	24695
07756	78430	45576	86596	56720	65529	44211	18447	53921	92722
45221	31130	44312	63534	47741	02465	50629	94983	05984	88375
20140	77481	61686	82836	41058	41331	04290	61212	60294	95954
54922	25436	33804	51907	73223	66423	68706	36589	45267	35327
48340	30832	72209	07644	52747	40751	06808	85349	18005	52323
23603	84387	20416	88084	33103	41511	59391	71600	35091	52722
12548	01033	22974	59596	92087	02116	63524	00627	41778	24392
15251	87584	12942	03771	91413	75652	19468	83889	98531	91529
65548	59670	57355	18874	63601	55111	07278	32560	40028	36079
48488	76170	46282	76427	41693	04506	80979	26654	62159	83017
02862	15665	62159	15159	69576	20328	68873	28152	66087	39405
67929	06754	45842	66365	80848	15262	55144	37816	08421	30071
73237	07607	31615	04892	50989	87347	14393	21165	68169	70788
13788	20327	07960	95917	75112	01398	26381	41377	33549	19754
43877	66485	40825	45923	74410	69693	76959	70973	26343	63781
14047	08369	56414	78533	76378	44204	71493	68861	31042	81873
88383	46755	51342	13505	55324	52950	22244	28028	73486	98797
29567	16379	41994	65947	58926	50953	09388	00405	29874	44954
20508	60995	41539	26396	99825	25652	28089	57224	35222	58922
64178	76768	75747	32854	32893	61152	58565	33128	33354	16056
26373	51147	90362	93309	13175	66385	57822	31138	12893	68607
10083	47656	59241	73630	99200	94672	59785	95449	99279	25488
11683	14347	04369	98719	75005	43633	24125	30532	54830	95387
56548	76293	50904	88579	24621	94291	56881	35062	48765	22078
35292	47291	82610	27777	43965	31802	98444	88929	54383	93141
51329	87645	51623	08971	50704	82395	33916	95859	99788	97885
51860	19180	39324	68483	78650	74750	64893	58042	82878	20619
23886	01257	07945	71175	31243	87167	42829	44601	08769	26417
80028	82310	43989	09242	15056	48250	04529	96941	48190	69644
83946	46858	09164	18858	12672	55190	02820	45861	29104	75386
00000	41586	25972	25356	54260	95691	99431	89903	22306	43863
90615	12848	23376	29458	48239	37628	59265	50152	30340	40713
42003	10738	55835	48218	23204	19188	13556	06610	77667	88068
86135	26174	07834	17007	97938	96728	15689	77544	89186	41252
54436	10828	41212	19836	89476	53685	28085	22878	71868	35048
14545	72034	32131	38783	58588	47499	50945	97045	42357	53536
43925	49879	13339	78773	95626	67119	93023	96832	09757	98545

SOURCE: The Rand Corporation, *A Million Random Digits with 100,000 Normal Deviates* (Glencoe, IL: Free Press, 1955), p. 225.

Photo Credits

Examples Index

Company	Scenario	CH
ABC News	Commissioned TNS Intersearch to conduct numerous opinion polls following the September 11, 2001, attacks on the World Trade Center and the Pentagon.	7
Abiomed	Medical trial for the AbioCor implantable replacement heart system.	2
ACNielsen	Ad recall survey and purchasing behavior data drawn from its Household Scanner Panel™ served as the test and control groups for the Magazine Publishers of America study on ad effectiveness.	14
Advertising World (University of Texas)	Developing a portal to advertising websites of interest to students and practitioners.	10
Airsole*	Constructing agreement items for a scale.	9
Albany Outpatient Laser Clinic Inc.*	A preprocedure self-administered study of patients awaiting eye surgery on patient issues and attitudes.	11, 12
American Demographics	Used TNS Intersearch to measure attitudes toward copyright infringement for a special issue on privacy.	8, 12
American legal system	Correct and incorrect decisions about hypothesis testing are compared to the U.S. legal system's presumption of innocence until guilt is proven.	17
Army Reserve	Testing weaponry and ammunition.	2
ArtDecoAppliances*	A company choosing a location for a new manufacturing plant.	3
Association of American Publishers	A trade association that conducted research to develop an ad campaign that would encourage the reading of books.	3
Audience Selection, Ltd.	Conducted the second round of phone interviews in the Global Entrepreneurship Monitor (GEM) study.	6
AutoCorp*	An automotive manufacturer, about to do research on competitive issues, that finds a competitor's intelligence report.	5
Avionics Inc.*	An aviation firm conducting an employee survey.	5
Bank of America	Using data-mining software to pinpoint marketing programs that attract high-margin, low-risk customers.	10
BankChoice*	A bank experiencing eroding profits and lackluster growth using a descriptive study of account owners' activity to develop new strategies for targeting large, active accounts.	3, 6
Bayer Consumer Care	Used personal interviews, phone interviews, and syndicated data to reposition Aleve; resulting ad campaign increased market share by 1 percent, a major feat in the highly competitive analgesic category.	11
Bissell, Inc.	Small-budget ethnography study to guide the development of the Steam 'n Clean marketing plan.	4

*Due to the confidential and proprietary nature of most research, the names of some companies have been changed.

Company	Scenario	CH
BizRate	An independent company that uses purchaser panels (computer-delivered self-administered surveys) to evaluate e-business customer service.	11
Blue Cross Blue Shield	Using data mining to staff and train customer service call centers.	10
BMW	Using data mining to design improvements to the crashworthiness and safety of automobiles.	10
Booth Research Services	Digesting reams of data to assist research sponsors in making management decisions.	16
Brain Reserve	A trend-spotting organization that uses content analysis.	15
Bridgestone/Firestone	Studying secondary data to understand tire tread separation.	1
British Chemical[*]	A study of the value of job enrichment as a builder of job satisfaction.	14
Bulk container shipping	Implementing a smoke-free workplace policy by evaluating accidents and smoking.	17
Burke CSA	A research company using measurement scales to provide companies with customer feedback.	8
Business Week's "Executive Compensation Scoreboard"	Multidimensional scaling of 16 (fuel segment) 601–603 companies based on executive compensation and return on equity.	19
CadSoft[*]	Job description analysis for technical writers who document architectural software.	2
CalAudio[*]	Using MANOVA to assess the manufacturing quality of CD players.	19
Campbell Soup Company	Content analysis is used to structure the promotional message for V-8.	15
Catalyst, Inc.	The nonprofit research organization charged with executing the court-ordered multistage research study in the Smith Barney sexual harrassment case.	6
Census 2000	The largest survey in the United States provides data for a variety of purposes.	12
Centers for Disease Control	Using an ex post facto design to determine causation of inhalation anthrax contamination at the USPS.	6
Central City Bank[*]	A findings page in a commercial bank market study.	20
Charles Schwab	Describing the Internet's importance to investor research.	10
CHILDCO[*]	Company researching the acquisition of a toy manufacturer.	1
City Center for Performing Arts[*]	Preliminary data analysis described.	16
CityBus[*]	A city transit authority is determining how to best promote a new route structure to current and potential riders.	7
CLT Research Associates	Conducted more than 800 in-home personal interviews in the Aleve repositioning research.	11
CNN	With *USA Today*, commissioned opinion polling after the September 11, 2001, attacks on the World Trade Center and the Pentagon.	7
CNNfn	Design of a website for a special-interest audience.	10

Company	Scenario	CH
Coca-Cola FEMSA	Using data mining for inventory, production, and promotion management in Mexico, Argentina, and Latin America.	10
Colgate-Palmolive Co.	(1) Using data mining to improve forecasting, production, and customer order fulfillment.	10
	(2) Study of toothbrushing ergonomics revealed that some users change their grip more than 100 times during brushing and that thicker-handled brushes promote longer brushing.	17
ColorSplash*	A paint manufacturer studying inventory control options to improve profitability.	1
Compass Marketing Research	Providing a wide array of facilities capable of handling many research designs.	4
Containers, Inc.*	Implementing a smoke-free workplace policy by evaluating the relationship between accidents and smoking.	17, 18
Copper Industry Association*	A study of the outlook of the copper industry in the next 10 years.	6
CPG Industry	Testing the use of RFID technology for tracking exchanges, as well as product use, storage, and speed of comsumption.	13
Croyland Associates*	Secondary research to prepare for an interview with a potential research client.	10
CrystalGraphics	Designing software (PowerPlugs) to enhance PowerPoint™ presentations.	20
Cummins Engines	A manufacturer uses data mining and customer relationships to design signature 600 engines.	5
Dean Merrill*	(1) Testing the effectiveness of two sales training methods for account executive trainees.	17
	(2) A brokerage firm recruiting account executive trainees using discriminant analysis to predict whether future candidates will be successful account executives.	18, 19
Decisive Technology	Developed MarketView software that permits Hewlett-Packard to quickly and less expensively evaluate new products online.	15
Dow Chemical	Using data mining to increase sales call effectiveness.	10
Dynamic Logic	Research firm that studied ad effectiveness measures being used to evaluate Internet advertising.	8
Economic Development Council of Palm Beach*	Evaluating a proposal for a study designed to ascertain job creation practices among local companies.	4
EducTV*	An educational television consortium serving a poorly educated population attempting to assess programming needs.	3
EntryPoint	Formed an alliance with PWC to launch an e-business, TelecomInsider, which provides timely decision-making information to telecommunication managers.	19
Envirosell	A comparison of store traffic behavior in the United States, Great Britain, and Australia.	13
Ernst & Young	A conuslting services firm that does research for its clients and values the increased knowledge level of its employees.	1
Espace Van*	Measuring attendees' reactions at an auto show.	8
European MBA programs	Specialty programs in business administration reflect emerging market niches.	18
e-WEAR*	Controller of e-commerce division of large retail chain evaluates receivables.	17

Company	Scenario	CH
Greenfield Online	(1) A program—FieldSource—used to create a custom-selected opt-in panel used to provide quick, cost-effective samples; draws samples from 3 million participants from various demographic and lifestyle groups.	6
	(2) A provider of computer-delivered surveying for Hewlett-Packard's study of printer performance.	11
Hart/Teeter	Conducted opinion polling after the September 11, 2001, attacks on the World Trade Center and the Pentagon for NBC and *The Wall Street Journal*.	7
Henry J. Kaiser Family Foundation (KFF)	(1) Conducted a benchmark study on U.S. public and private school sex education among teens, their parents, teachers, and principals.	7
	(2) One-year tracking study to assess physicians' knowledge and attitudes regarding mifepristone (RU486).	9
Hewlett-Packard	(1) Used data mining to respond to the September 11, 2001, World Trade Center collapse.	10
	(2) Used Greenfield Online's *QuickTake* Web survey to shorten the turnaround time for data collection.	11
	(3) Used online software from Decisive Technology to provide quicker, less costly evaluation of new products.	15
Hill Top Research, Inc.	Human odor detectives employed to test the effectiveness of underarm deodorants.	14
IBM	Using its *GeneMine* technology to help biologists develop better cures and treatments for disease.	10
Inferential Focus	A trend-spotting organization uses content analysis.	15
Information Resources Inc. (IRI)	Syndicated research supplier to CPG manufacturers that was forced to redesigned its sampling and research design when Wal-Mart chose not to renegotiate its contract to supply point-of-sale data; introduced *InfoScan*® *Advantage*.	7
Informative, Inc.	A provider of real-time customer feedback to Nortel Networks through the deployment of an Internet survey.	12
Institute of Traffic Engineers (ITE)	Contracting information on State Farm's Dangerous Intersection Initiative.	2
Insurance Institute for Highway Safety	Conducted safety experiment involving frontal offset crash tests of competitive, full-sized trucks, including those manufactured by Ford, GM, DaimlerChrysler and Toyota.	16
Interactive Advertising Bureau	A trade association's research reveals what ad sellers are using to measure ad effectiveness.	8
John Deere and Company	A manufacturer of construction and agriculture equipment conducting both quantitative and qualitative studies to understand its environment.	6
Johns Hopkins Medical School	Failing to obtain consent during clinical trials of high-risk drug therapy research.	5
JRP Marketing Research Serivces, Inc	Using experience and satisfaction of prior clients to convince new prospects of their quality research.	1
K2Sports	A study reveals the effectiveness of a retailer sales associate training program for an in-line skates manufacturer.	17

Company	Scenario	CH
KeyDesign[*]	Managerial employees at a large industrial design firm are evaluated for coronary risk.	18
Knowledge Networks	A provider of probability-sampled Web-based surveys working with RTI International on Internet surveys.	12
KNSD	A San Diego TV station that undertook a segmentation study—KNowSanDiego—of its viewing audience.	12
Kraft Foods	(1) Research was used to develop of a new advertising strategy for Kraft Singles.	3
	(2) Used a two-stage design study to develop the sales stimulus ad campaign for Kool-Aid.	6
Kroger Co.	(1) Using its Kroger-Plus Shopper's Card program to track customer purchase behavior.	5
	(2) Pioneering use of bar code data in the grocery industry.	15
L&E Research	Recruits child participants for focus groups and other research studies.	6
LIMRA International	Conducted large scale telephone survey of 1,622 small businesses for the financial services industry.	16
Literary Digest	Published the 1936 presidential election poll that falsely predicted a Republican victory.	7
LiveWorld	Prepared a 10–15 minute computer-delivered packaging survey employing 75 images of bottle shapes and label designs as visualization techniques.	11
Magazine Publishers of America (MPA)	Conducted a study to prove the sales lift following magazine advertising using the purchasing behavior of a panel.	14
MapInfo	Software useful for the spatial analysis and display of data.	20
Maritz Marketing Research, Inc.	Conducts focus groups in specially designed facilities that permit observation by the research sponsor.	6
Market Facts, Inc.	(1) Conducted phone surveys to discover what would make moms buy the pricier Kraft Singles.	3
	(2) Conducted the first round of phone interviews in the Global Entrepreneurship Monitor.	6
MarketWatch.com	An ad seller trying to determine the best way to evaluate ad effectiveness.	8
Marriott International, Inc.	An international hotel chain seeking an understanding of how hotel guests interpret the term *concierge service*.	2
MasterCard	Detection of stolen credit cards based on data mining of credit card transactions.	10
McDonald's	Evaluating the effectiveness of a cashless payment system.	18
McGraw-Hill	Website has tutorial for including hyperlinks within PowerPoint™ research presentation.	20
McMahon Group	A research and golf course management specialist helps NCR Country Club design a new strategic vision.	19
Mediascope	Conducted a content analysis of the top 200 movies to determine level of substance abuse in movies targeting teens.	17
Medical Radar International (MRI)	Swedish research company that publishes research on European doctors' use of pharmaceuticals.	20
Meineke Discount Muffler Shops	Using data mining to plan more effective advertising, as well as select new locations.	10

Company	Scenario	CH
MonsterVideo*	A national video sales and rental chain collecting video viewing, rental, and purchase behavior through phone interviews.	5
Moskowitz Jacobs, Inc.	Conducted phone surveys to help Bayer identify emotional triggers for the new ad campaign repositioning Aleve.	11
Motion picture industry	Cluster analysis of films into homogeneous subgroups based on genre and country of origin.	19
Naisbitt Group	A trend-spotting organization uses content analysis.	15
NATA*	An aviation trade association study to examine radiation risks for flight crews and passengers.	1
National Institutes of Health	The funding agency with partial ethical oversight responsibility for Johns Hopkins' research on hexamethonium.	5
National Opinion Research Center	A source of questions for measuring U.S. trends.	12
NBC News	Commissioned Hart/Teeter to conduct opinion polls after the September 11, 2001, attacks on the World Trade Center and the Pentagon.	7
NCR Country Club	A prestigious country club transforms its facilities, image, and target members through research.	19
Neiman Marcus	Fractal-based transformations to discover likely customers for catalog merchandise.	10
Nortel Networks Corporation	A company with a portfolio of products, services, and solutions, working with Informative, Inc., to evaluate the quality of its website via an Internet survey.	12
NUCMED*	Physician specialists in nuclear medicine and imaging evaluating a health care cost containment plan.	1
Office of Industry Analysis*	A study to determine if executives would reveal what criteria they use when one raw material is substituted for another in manufacturing.	6
Office of National Drug Control Policy	Commissioned Mediascope to study substance abuse in movies targeting teens.	17
Palm Grove High School*	The 10-year reunion planning committee is planning to assess the success of its graduates via a questionnaire.	12
Pebble Beach Company	Research with employees to assess customer service.	4
Peter D. Hart Research Associates, AFL-CIO	A study to determine motivating factors for retaining and recruiting workers in a tight job market; further analysis regarding young workers' interest in unions.	8
PhaseOne Communications	Conducted content analysis of V-8 ads for Campbell Soup, resulting in a more effective promotional campaign.	15
Philips Electronics North America	Sponsoring a research study to encourage employees to increase their 401k savings rate.	14
Pocket-Phone*	A producer of portable, wallet-sized wireless telephones studying the data collected from a recent survey to assess the newest generation of phones.	3
Point of Purchase Advertising Institute	A trade association that determines the value of retail display materials.	13

Company	Scenario	CH
PricewaterhouseCoopers LLP	(1) Using data mining to plan on-location promotional store displays in German retailers for Gillette Co.	10
	(2) A widely respected consulting firm enters a strategic alliance with EntryPoint to provide instant information and website click-throughs.	19
Prince Corporation*	A study to discover the public's opinions about the company and the origin of any generally held adverse opinions.	8, 12
Princess Cruises (P&O Princess Cruises plc)	Quick turnaround for a customer satisfaction study using optical scanning for data entry.	15
Princeton Survey Research Associates	(1) The survey research organization commissioned by the Henry J. Kaiser Family Foundation for its study on sex education in America.	7
	(2) Conducted the phone survey of physicians in KFF's one-year tracking study of physicians' knowledge and attitudes regarding mifepristone (RU486)	9
Privacy Technologies	Introduced an electronic device that rejects in-coming calls from predictive dialers used by telephone researchers.	11
Procter & Gamble (P&G)	Returned confiscated marketing documents to Unilever after discovering that the information had been retrieved from trash receptacles by contract P&G competitive intelligence agents.	5
Progressive Insurance, Inc.	Tracking actual driver behavior with a "black box" device for cars.	13
ProSec Electronics*	An observational study to discover process or equipment errors contributing to defective merchandise.	13
Research House Inc.	A Canadian firm offering a variety of facilities for different types of studies.	14
Roper Starch Worldwide	A source of questions for measuring U.S. trends.	12
RTI International	(1) Annually fields 100,000 telephone interviews in its two state-of-the-art CATI facilities.	11
	(2) A research company with extensive CATI and CAPI capabilities working with Knowledge Networks on a Web-based panel.	12
Rubinstein Consulting	Used personal interviews to determine an alternative recruiting program for a harbormaster in Finland.	11
Sacramento FastShop	Unidimensional and historical query in data mining; finding and explaining combination purchases.	10
SalesPro*	(1) A national sales organization facing unexplained sales variations by territory.	3
	(2) A study to evaluate sales performance.	8
SAS	A statistical package for data entry and analysis.	15
Shoe Industry	A profile of industry production as an example of tabular presentation.	20
Smith Barney (Salomon Smith Barney)	The investment and financial services firm, ordered to do attitudinal research as part of the negotiated settlement of the sexual harassment suit brought by 25 current and former employees.	6

Company	Scenario	CH
TNS Intersearch	(1) Conducted opinion polling after the September 11, 2001, attacks on the World Trade Center and the Pentagon for ABC News and *The Washington Post*.	7
	(2) A study for *American Demographics* about adult attitudes related to copyright infringement included in its special issue on privacy.	8
	(3) Provider of *Express*, a weekly omnibus study used by American Demographics to measure attitudes about copyright issues.	12
TechByte*	A company interested in enhancing its position in a given technology that appears to hold potential for future growth.	3
Tennessee Valley Authority	Instrument development; reliability and validity emphasis.	8
The Wall Street Journal	With NBC News, commissioned Hart/Teeter to conduct opinion polling after the September 11, 2001, attacks on the World Trade Center and the Pentagon.	7
The Washington Post	Commissioned TNS Intersearch to conduct opinion polling following the September 11, 2001, attacks on the World Trade Center and the Pentagon.	7
Top Cannery*	An experiment to determine the ideal price difference between private and national brands.	14
Travel Industry Magazine*	Comparison of in-flight service differences among three carriers; seat selection and repeated measures of service are also examined.	17
TrolleyScan	Provider of RFID tags for the CPG industry, marking a new phase of direct observation for the future.	13
U.S. Census Bureau	(1) Substituting statistical sampling in the decennial census.	7
	(2) Designed confusing question regarding participants' employment.	12
U.S. Department of Commerce	(1) Complying with new European Union standards for data transmission.	5
	(2) Population charts.	20
U.S. Federal Emergency Management Agency (FEMA)	Using GIS to provide national-level support in responding to disasters.	16
U.S. Food and Drug Administration	Federal agency with oversight responsibility for John Hopkins' drug-performance testing for hexamethonium.	5
U.S. government	(1) Using data mining to detect tax fraud, eavesdrop on foreign communications, and process satellite imagery.	10
	(2) GNP charts.	20
U.S. Internal Revenue Service	Use of computerized number and character recognition to process 1040EZ forms.	15
U.S. Postal Service	Attempting to determine the source of workers' exposure to inhalation anthrax.	6
UCLA, U of PA, UC-Berkeley, Columbia, Harvard, Yale, and Northwestern Universities	Business schools with wine clubs.	18

Company	Scenario	CH
Unilever, Inc.	Negotiating a settlement for damage to its hair care business caused by the unethical intelligence-gathering behavior of a competitor.	5
University of Michigan	The source of lifestyle index questions used in MindWriter's CompleteCare study.	12
USA Today	Commissioned Gallup to conduct opinion polling after the September 11, 2001, attacks on the World Trade Center and the Pentagon.	7
Vanguard	Conducting a study to determine whether employees will save more in 401k savings if their savings increase comes from future raises rather than current earnings.	14
Video Software Dealers Association	Provided the database to determine the top 200 movies used for the Office of National Drug Control Policy's study of substance abuse in movies.	17
Viewpoints Consulting, Inc.	Used focus groups to identify that Aleve users represented a distinct segment of the pain-relief market.	11
Voter News Service (VNS)	The election polling consortium of ABC, NBC, CBA, CNN, FOX, and the Associated Press, responsible for the early mispredictions in the 2000 presidential election.	15
Wal-Mart Stores	(1) Maintaining a mamoth data warehouse to improve profitability.	1
	(2) Using data mining to design and modify store layouts to reduce shoplifting and theft.	10
WebVan	How an absence of research contributed to the failure of the venture.	1
White Ice Summer Festival Orchestra[*]	A study of conditions influencing rapid turnover of performers.	8
Wittenberg University Department of Education	Determining demand for a new program.	9
York College[*]	(1) A multiphase study by a university alumni association to evaluate a proposal to build a retirement community to serve alumni.	1, 2
	(2) A causal study to determine the power of emotional versus rational appeal on financial contributions to a new program.	6

Index